A MANUAL

OF

YACHT AND BOAT SAILING.

NINTH EDITION.

BY

DIXON KEMP,

ASSOCIATE OF THE INSTITUTE OF NAVAL ARCHITECTS.

AUTHOR OF

"Yacht Designing" and "Yacht Architecture."

REVISED AND PARTLY RE-WRITTEN BY

B. HECKSTALL SMITH,

ASSOCIATE OF THE INSTITUTE OF NAVAL ARCHITECTS.

THE LORDS COMMISSIONERS OF THE ADMIRALTY HAVE BEEN PLEASED TO DIRECT THAT THIS
BOOK SHOULD BE ISSUED TO SHIPS OF THE ROYAL NAVY.

LONDON:

HORACE COX,

"THE FIELD," OFFICE, BREAM'S BUILDINGS. E.C.

1900.

PREFACE TO THE NINTH EDITION.

THE first edition of "Yacht and Boat Sailing" was published in 1878, and, whilst the general plan of that edition has been maintained in successive issues, the matter relating to yachts and sailing boats has from time to time been considerably altered or exchanged for new subjects. The instruction as to rigging a yacht, seamanship, and the general handling of vessels under sail remains much the same as originally written, but where necessary each subject has been revised and made to accord with present practice. The chapters dealing with yacht racing have also been revised, and in many instances re-written; in short, the whole work has been brought up to date and made thoroughly representative of contemporary yachting in all its branches.

Many new designs have been introduced into this edition, and it was found necessary to exclude several which had formerly appeared; but the new designs are of a more interesting and useful type than those omitted. Amongst the designs now presented I am indebted to Mr. C. E. Nicholson (of Messrs. Camper and Nicholson) for the "Coquette" (0·5-rater), "Worry-Worry" (1-rater), and "Dacia" (5-rater); to Mr. C. P. Clayton for the 1-rater "Gaiety Girl"; to Mr. A. E. Payne for the "Lady Nan" (2·5-rater), "Papoose" (2·5-rater), "Maharanee" (1 rater), and "Baby" (0·5 rater); to Mr. A. Burgoine for the "Ruby," "Mona," and "Mirage"; to Capt. du Boulay for the Bembridge Rig; to Mr. C. Livingston for the Mersey Boat "Deva" and Windermere Yacht "Midge," &c.; to Mr. C. Friend for the Mersey

Boat " Venture "; to Mr. W. H. Willmer for the Mersey Boat "Zinnia ";
to Mr. G. L. Watson for the Royal Clyde Sailing Boats; to Mr. T. D.
Lingard for the Windermere Yachts "Rosita" and "Snipe," and the
Windermere "Una"; to Mr. A. F. Fynn for the Falmouth Quay Punt;
to Mr. R. Fry for the Dublin Bay Boats, &c.; to Mr. W. Fife, jun., for
the Clyde Boat "Hatasoo"; to Mr. J. M. Soper for "Flat Fish" (5-rater)
and mast fittings of a modern large racing yacht; to Mr. Linton Hope
for the single-handed cruiser "Dorothy" and the 1-rater "Sorceress,"
&c.; the late Captain Bayley for the "Scourge," and Mr. J. C. Enberg
for the single-handed cruiser "Ære Perennius"; to Mr. Harley Mead
for the cruiser "Marjorie"; and to Mr. S. Bond for the Mersey Canoe
Yawl, 1890.

DIXON KEMP.

The chapter dealing with the Rules of the Yacht Racing Association,
and the notable cases of protest that have occurred under them, has been
revised and brought up to date. The full text of the Y.R.A. Rules for
the year 1900 will also be found in the Appendix.

B. H. S.

May, 1900.

CONTENTS.

Chapter XI.

Chapter XII.

Chapter XIII.

Chapter XIV.

Chapter XV.

Chapter XVI.

Chapter XVII.

Chapter XVIII.

Chapter XIX.

Chapter XX.

Chapter XXI.

Chapter XXII.

Chapter XXIII.

Chapter XXIV.

Chapter XXV.

Chapter XXVI.

Chapter XXVII.

Appendix.

ERRATA.

———

Page 37. " Plate IV." should be " Plate V."

Page 49. " Plate VII." should be " Plate VI."

Page 257, line 21. " (*See* page 207) " should read " (*See* page 195)."

Page 258, line 18. " Rule 21 " should read " Rule 29."

Page 260, line 17. " (*See* page 229) " should read " (See page 188)."

Page 267, line 33. " Rule 24 " should read " Rule 33."

Page 385, line 12. " Plate LV." should be " Plate LVI."

Page 409. " Plate LXIX." should be " Plate LXX₃ "

Page 427. " Plate XCVIII." should be " Plate XCIX."

Page 429. " Plate XCIX." should be " Plate XCIXᴀ."

LIST OF PLATES.

YACHT AND BOAT SAILING.

CHAPTER I.

SELECTING A YACHT.

IN selecting a yacht, a man, as in making other purchases, will be guided by his tastes and his means. If he is really fond of the art of fore and aft sailing, and looks forward to a life on the sea with the professional keenness of a middy or apprentice, his desire will be to obtain a yacht which he can direct the handling of himself. If, on the other hand, the dawning yachtsman has boundless wealth, is a little of a sybarite, and determines to spend two or three months afloat because it is the fashion, he, too, will get a yacht to his taste; but she will probably be a large steamer, unless he has determined on racing, when a large cutter, yawl, or perhaps a schooner would be chosen.

The man who desires to eventually become a thorough yacht sailor should begin his apprenticeship on board a cutter, in the small classes. If she is, say, of 52ft. rating or 45ft. water-line length, he should make all the passages in her when shifting ports, and not bid farewell to her at one pier head, and welcome her arrival from another pier head at the next watering place on the coast; nor follow her nor precede her from port to port in a larger steam yacht. If a man goes about attended by the uncomfortable feeling that he shirks all the real daring and adventure of yacht cruising he is not likely to make a perfect yacht sailor, as sailing in ten or twenty matches during a summer can only give a very circumscribed idea of the sea and its charms, compared with the experiences of passage making; although a man may, it is true, become an adept in the highly diverting sport of yacht racing. But it is not only the 52ft. rating yacht which is large enough to convey the racing yachtsman from port to port; many owners of vessels of 42ft. rating, or even smaller, like Will Watch, "take the helm and to sea boldly steer"; and these are the men who get the most real enjoyment

B

out of their vessels, and are the best sailor-men, apart from the knowledge of racing. Of course, living in a yacht of 42ft. rating (say, 40ft. on L.W.L.) would be to many young yachtsmen utter misery, and disgust. The budding yachtsman has been in the habit, perhaps, of spending a couple of hours every morning over his toilet, surrounded by all the luxuries of the upholsterer's art—velvet-pile carpet, satin damasks, cheval glasses, water-colour drawings, Dresden china, aromatic baths, and a valet-de-chambre. The man who has been used to such luxuries as these must have the big schooner or yawl, or a huge steam yacht, as he will find no room for them inside the little craft. He would have to carry his clothes in a bag, or cram them into a locker 2ft. by 6in.; go on his marrowbones to shave; into the sea for his bath—it is only one step and overboard;—and if he is addicted to cosmétique, he will probably find a piece of "common yellow" a good substitute. The cuisine, of course, would not be such as would raise water bubbles in the mouth of a valetudinarian; the carnivorous propensity will mostly be gratified by steak which, when cut, will resemble the Mudhook Yacht Club burgee of *rouge et noir*; and savoury soups, luscious salmon, and piquant *entrées* will be luxuries only obtainable in "canister" form. With all these discomforts, the man who really works his 42ft. yacht in earnest will very rapidly become a sailor, and the little ship below will be as neat and cosy as a woman's boudoir; he will have a place for everything, down to a housewife; and at the end of one summer there will not be a part of the ship, from the breast-hook forward to the transom-frame aft, that he will not know the use of.

Of course, for real comfort at sea, the larger the yacht a man can afford to have the better; but it was never found advisable to go much beyond 300 tons,* as very large sailing vessels are more or less, according to size, unhandy in narrow channels and crowded roadsteads. A yacht exceeding 150 tons should be rigged as a schooner or ketch; and we are inclined to think, if her size reaches 300 tons, or say 120ft. in length on the load water-line, that she should be schooner rigged, and have three masts, with all fore-and-aft canvas. "Square rig forward" is generally recommended for a three-masted vessel, as square topsails may be of occasional use in backing and box-hauling, or in scudding in a heavy sea, when small trysails set on the lower masts might get becalmed whilst the vessel dropped between the crests of two seas; but the extra weight aloft, and the extra gear, are to some extent a set-off against these advantages.

A yacht from 150 to 80 tons downwards can also be schooner-rigged,

---

* When "tons" are quoted it means tons by Thames rule as given in Lloyd's Register. (See "Tonnage" in the Appendix.)

but many yachtsmen prefer the yawl rig for these and intermediate tonnages. The yawl will be the more weatherly craft, will reach as fast, and be faster down the wind. The actual weight of spars will be less for the sail area; there will be less gear; and there will be no mainmast obtruding in the main cabin, or in one of the berths abaft it. It is undeniable, however, that in heavy weather the schooner, appropriately canvased, is a very easy and handy vessel. In a "fresh gale" (see "Winds" in the Appendix) she would be under main trysail, reefed fore staysail and fourth jib (foresail stowed); a yawl under similar conditions would have main trysail, or double-reefed mainsail, reefed foresail, and fourth jib, with mizen stowed, and would be quite as handy, and would lie-to quite as quietly. As there will be no difference in the number of men required to work either rig, size for size, we are on the whole inclined to think that the yawl rig is to be preferred for yachts under 130 tons.

But the yawl must be snugly rigged, and not merely a large cutter with a mizen mast stepped over the archboard for the sake of a long main boom. This latter class of yawl has really a greater weight of spars in proportion to sail area than a cutter. The main boom is, in a yawl say of 100 tons, within 10ft. or 11ft. as long as the main boom of cutters of equal tonnage; the mast is as long, the bowsprit is nearly as long, the topmast is as long, the gaff is generally longer in proportion to length of boom; and the weight of the mizen mast, bumpkin, yard, boom, and rigging is generally about ten times the weight of the extra length and extra size of the cutter's boom. These are not the yawls which have an advantage over even large cutters for comfort. In short, the racing yawl of a few years ago had but little advantage in snugness over a cutter of equal size, and was as costly to equip and build as a cutter. However, in a cruiser above 100 tons two masts become a necessity in order to divide the sails, as they would be larger than the ordinary crew of a cruiser could well handle, and a yawl should be chosen up to 140 tons, and a schooner above that tonnage.

But the cruising yawl proper is a very snug vessel indeed, and has nearly all the good qualities of a cutter, and is really a more comfortable craft, and can be worked with fewer hands, which of course means with less cost. Her mizen mast will be stepped nearly close abaft the rudder head, instead of near the taffrail; her bowsprit will be shorter and lighter than the bowsprit of a similarly sized cutter (see page 4); her mast will be lighter than a cutter's; and so will her boom, gaff, and topmast be lighter. Her mizen mast will be so stepped that it will be safe in the most violent wind storm to put sail upon it; and this may be often of real advantage in clearing out from an anchorage in a hurry.

The advantage of the yawl mainly depends upon the reduction of weight of spars and gear, and the economy of labour in working sails which are more subdivided than those of a cutter.

We have calculated what the difference in the cubical contents of the spars of a cutter of about 90 tons would be if she were changed from cutter to yawl, her length of mainmast remaining the same. Difference in mast, 20 cubic feet; difference in bowsprit (3ft. shorter), 12 cubic feet; difference in main boom (12ft. shorter), 25 cubic feet; difference in main gaff, 4 cubic feet—making a total difference of 61 cubic feet, or one ton weight. The topmast would remain about the same. The bulk and weight of mizen spars would be as nearly as possible as follows: mast, 16 cubic feet; boom, 4 cubic feet; yard, 3 cubic feet; boomkin, 2 cubic feet; or a total of 25 cubic feet, making a net reduction of about 12cwt. The difference in the weight of rigging and blocks would be from 4cwt. to 5cwt., making a total reduction in the weight of spars and rigging of about 17cwt. The removal of this weight would bring about nearly 2in. difference in the vertical position of the centre of gravity of the yacht, and would be equal, so far as influencing her stiffness went, to the taking of 2 tons of lead from the top tier of ballast inside and putting it under the keel outside. The effect of the reduced spars on the momentum acquired during pitching will be mainly governed by the reduction made in the bowsprit; that is, by the influence that reduction has on the longitudinal radius of gyration. To reduce the momentum to its utmost limit, the bowsprit should be reefed close in, and mizen mast unstepped and stowed amidships.

It will be gathered that the advantages of a yawl are mainly dependent on the general weight of her spars and rigging being less than are the weight of the spars and rigging of a similarly sized cutter. Taking a cutter and merely reducing her boom in length, whilst all her other spars and her rigging and blocks remain unaltered, and incumbering her with a mizen, would be no advantage at all, either for racing or cruising; in fact, the mizen would far exceed in weight the trifling reduction that had been made in the main boom; hence many "converted cutters" were failures as yawls. Neither had a racing yawl, as sparred up to the prevailing main-boom rule, any advantage in point of weight of spars and rigging over the weight of spars and rigging of a similarly sized cutter, and it could not be expected that such a yawl would obtain any advantage beyond her rig allowance, in competitive sailing, so far as sailing by the wind goes. Down the wind and along the wind the inferiority would be less patent, and occasionally a heavily sparred yawl, with her rig allowance, would beat the cutter.

Allowing—as there is not the least doubt about the matter—that a

judiciously sparred racing or cruising yawl has less weight of spars than a
cutter of similar tonnage, we come to the consideration of the usefulness
of the mizen sail. About this matter opinions widely differ. For sailing
to windward, most sailors will agree that the mizen sail is not worth its
attendant weight of spars and rigging; but as to the extent it affects the
handiness of the craft there will be no such agreement. In 1875 the
Oimara was converted to a yawl for her winter cruise to the Mediterranean;
but, before she was clear of the Clyde, the mizen went by the board. She
proceeded without a mizen, and with her yawl boom sailed all over the
Mediterranean, and for two seasons, in a similar guise, cruised in British
waters. Her sailing master declared that he never felt the want of the
mizen in any weather that he encountered; and this is conceivable when we
consider that generally, in heavy weather, the first sail to stow on board a
yawl is the mizen. This brings us to consider whether, after all, the
advantages of the yawl are not entirely dependent upon her resemblance to
a very reduced cutter, with short boom and bowsprit; and whether the
advantages would not be increased by the absence of the mizen altogether?
The fact that the mizen can be stowed in bad weather, to avoid reefing the
mainsail, is hardly an argument in favour of having one; and, as what may
be termed its active advantages in affecting the handiness of a vessel are
not of much importance, we think that the "reduced cutter," as before
hinted, has all the advantages of a yawl without the incumbrance of a
mizen. Of course, a cutter with her main boom end inside her taffrail is not
a very sightly craft; but still, with the length of counter now given to
yachts, this must be put up with. With the short bowsprits now carried,
the symmetry and beauty of the cutter rig would not be outraged,
whilst the general weight of spars, rigging, and blocks could be very
much less than the weight of spars of a yawl with similar sail area.
However, in a fashionable cutter, where the tonnage approaches 100 tons,
the main boom becomes a very awkward stick to handle, and for cruising
there is not the least doubt that a yawl of 80 or 100 tons with a main
boom plumb with the rudder head is a much more comfortable craft to
work than a cutter of similar tonnage. We have evidence of the objection
taken to long booms in the case of the large pilot vessels and fishing
vessels, as whilst they are invariably cutter-rigged up to about 80 tons, we
find that the yawl, ketch, or schooner rig is preferred above that tonnage.

A modification of the ketch rig is much in use by coasters, and we
have often heard it recommended as superior to the yawl rig; but
with this we do not agree, as, owing to the narrowness of the mainsail,
there is no rig which, area for area, yields such a heeling moment as does
the ketch rig. The final conclusion which we arrive at is that, for the yawl
to possess any advantages over a snug cutter, she must be very judiciously

sparred, and it should be always recollected that the mere fact of carrying a mizen does not make a comfortable sea boat. The yawl's mast can be a trifle less in diameter than a cutter's (we are assuming that the sail area is to be nearly equal), the bowsprit can be very much less, the boom can be very much less, and so can the gaff; the standing and running rigging can be lighter, and so can be the blocks; but great care should be taken that the spars and rigging of the mizen do not exceed the total reduction that has been made in the weight of the main spars and rigging. The weight of mizenmast and rigging on the counter will not, it is true, punish a vessel like a heavy bowsprit outside the stem; but it must be remembered that almost the sole advantage of a yawl, so far as behaviour in a sea goes, depends upon her total weight of spars being less than would be the total weight of spars of a cutter with a similar sail area. The supposed requirements of a racing yawl are incompatible with the advantages generally claimed for the rig; it is, however, some satisfaction to know that the yawls which have hitherto been most successful are those which have been sparred and rigged with an intelligent appreciation of the conditions upon which those advantages depend. Apart from behaviour in a sea, the principal advantage of the yawl rig is that, even if her spars as a whole be equal in weight to those of a cutter of similar size, she can be handled with a smaller crew; but this advantage will not be very apparent until 70 or 80 tons are reached.

A snugly rigged cutter of 80 tons, of about $4\frac{1}{4}$ beams in length, can be as easily handled and as cheaply worked (six A.B.'s would be required for either) as a yawl of 80 tons, and a cutter should be preferred on account of her grand sailing qualities. The line is drawn at 80 tons for this reason: a gig's crew must be had out of either yawl or cutter, and if four hands be taken away in the gig, two will be left on board to work the yacht with captain and mate; and even a 60-tonner cannot very well do with less than six A.B.'s for the reason just given. But, whereas six men may work an 80-tonner, whether cutter or yawl, six would be insufficient for a 100-tons cutter, although they might be quite equal to a yawl of that tonnage; and moreover, if there was anything like a breeze, and four men had to leave the cutter in the gig, it would be hardly prudent to leave the sailing master and mate with two men only on board.

Of all the rigs which the ingenuity of man has devised, not one is equal to the cutter, whether for clawing to windward, reaching along the wind, or running down wind. A cutter with a true wind will beat as far to windward in a day as a yawl will in a day and a quarter; will walk off with a light air when the yawl will scarcely move; and in a breeze under topsail is even more comfortable and easy than the yawl. But the cutter must be snug; and not sparred like a racing vessel.

A common argument in favour of yawls as against cutters is this: a racing cutter of 80 tons is a more expensive vessel to work, is an awkward vessel to tackle in a sea, especially if the mainsail has to be got off and trysail set for lying to; a cutter will not lie to the wind under headsail, and this disability has been much aggravated by the modern fashion of cutting away the forefoot.

A yawl to be a successful racer against cutters must be ballasted and canvased pretty much as a cutter of equal size, and the expense of racing such a yawl will differ very little from that of racing a cutter; probably, tonnage for tonnage, the expense would be the same. There is as much difference between a cruising yawl and a racing yawl as there is between a cruising cutter and a racing cutter, and it is a great mistake to suppose that a racing yawl of say 80 tons includes the comforts of a good cruising cutter of equal size.

The ultimate conclusion is, that the particular rig will depend upon the size of the yacht, and for cruising the rig should be: cutter up to 80 tons; yawl from 80 to 140 tons; schooner above that tonnage.

We have hitherto almost entirely considered the selecting of a yacht from a cruising point of view; the racer must now be dealt with.

The rating rule,* adopted in 1887 by the Yacht Racing Association, greatly influenced the proportions of yachts, and the new proportion of beam to length being much the same as that which was the fashion

In 1899 Meteor was converted into a yawl, but as Britannia in that year was not sailing in her best form, and there was no other cutter of her own rating to test her speed, the value of her performances could not be gauged. The best judges considered that the yacht was very fast under yawl's canvas, and when the yawl's rig allowance is considered in conjunction with the scale of time allowance, given in the Appendix, it is probable that the yawl rig will again become popular for racing vessels of upwards of 90ft. linear rating.

Ailsa, or Britannia: such a yacht is generally ahead of the fleet—and the sympathies of the crowd invariably go with the leading craft; and if she wins (say from a yacht of 80ft. rating), she is almost certain to be three

* The rule introduced in 1887 to replace the old tonnage rule was sail area multiplied by length of load line, and divided by 6000. The quotient is the rating. A rule, which includes girth and breadth, came into operation in 1896.

or four miles ahead at the finish. This feature in itself is, no doubt, a most impressive one, both on the owner and on the spectator; and there can be no question about the *éclat* of winning with a large craft eclipsing the splendour of winning with a small one. This certainly is the vanity of the thing; but there are vanities in sport as there are in other occupations, and if it is a man's vanity not only to win prizes, but to revel in the glory of "coming in first" in the cutter class, then he must have a large vessel. If, on the other hand, the desire is simply to win, one way or another, the greatest number of prizes, irrespective of the value, then the wish may be gratified by owning a yacht not larger than a 20-rater; and there are indications that this will be a fashionable size for racing for some time to come.

For real sport, there is not much doubt that class racing, from 64ft. rating downwards, is to be preferred to racing large vessels: there is no time allowance; the exact merits of the vessels, and merits of their handling, are easily read; and, as a rule, the winning vessel can only arrive first at the goal by contesting every inch of water sailed through.

The old 20 tons class, afterwards the 20-rating class, and now the 52ft. class, has become a very numerous one, and in no class has competition been more keen than in this since the introduction of the new rating rule in 1887. The 42ft. rating class is not quite the success it at one time promised to be, and seemingly for the principal reason that the cost of one is so very near what a yacht of 52ft. rating costs, which has of course much superior accommodation. It is not likely that anyone would "yacht" in a 52ft. rating yacht, or in one of 42ft. rating, for the sake of the mere repute of owning a yacht; a man, to own, race, and live in one of these craft, must love the art of sailing, be enthusiastic in competition, and think of gaining the honours of the match by sheer hard sailing and correct judgment as to the tactics of a match. This also must be said of the 36ft., 30ft., 24ft., and 18ft. classes, and so long as these small classes exist, so long will there be evidence that love of the art of yacht sailing is one of the most striking characteristics of the British gentleman. Some men, of course, revel in the passive pleasure of sailing in a yacht, without knowing anything or caring anything about the mariners' art, just as some men will derive pleasure from riding on the back seat of a drag, and knowing and caring nothing about the tooling of the team in front of him. These are the gentlemen whose yachts we meet and hear of in all sorts of out-of-the-way ports; and as their long purses enable them to make "life on the ocean wave" very pleasant, be assured that they are agreeable men to cruise with.

CHAPTER II.

EXAMINATION OF THE YACHT.

HAVING decided upon the size of the yacht, the next step will be to find a suitable one of that size. If the intending purchaser advertises his wants, he is certain to have a great many vessels offered him, and all will be highly recommended by the agents of the vendors; each vessel will be the best sea boat of her tonnage, the staunchest built, the best found, and the handsomest; and, moreover, the present owner is almost certain to have recently spent hundreds or thousands of pounds upon her reconstruction or redecoration. The intending purchaser will be delighted; and, after having got through particulars of the yachts which have been offered for sale, something like bewilderment will naturally follow, and the task of making a final selection will be a little difficult. The best plan will be to begin with treating all the answers as mere information of vessels for sale. Find out when they were built, and by whom, and when last surveyed, from Lloyd's Yacht Register, and if the yachts which seem unobjectionable, so far as age is concerned, are suitable also in price, go to see them. Then, if one appears to be in every way a desirable craft, bid for her, " subject to the yacht being approved of by the intending purchaser after a survey and inspection of inventory, which must show her hull and equipment to be in a seaworthy and thoroughly satisfactory condition, retaining the right of rejecting the yacht if the survey is not to his satisfaction." It will always be necessary to have a vessel surveyed before completing a purchase, unless it is found by Lloyd's Register that the yacht is quite new, or has recently been surveyed by an experienced surveyor or builder. The fees for surveying will vary from five to twenty guineas, according to the size of the yacht and the extent of the survey, the fees being exclusive of travelling expenses.

In agreeing to purchase a yacht " subject to survey," the best plan is for the vendor and purchaser to agree upon a competent surveyor, as a rule a vendor prefers this plan to calling in a Lloyd's surveyor if the yacht is not already classed in Lloyd's " Yacht Register;"

on the other hand, the intending purchaser, for obvious reasons, prefers employing his own surveyor.

If the yacht as to her frame and planking is found to be unsound she can be rejected, as it might not suit the intending purchaser's purpose to wait whilst she is put into a sound condition or repaired. If it is a mere case of a few defects, or a rotten mast or other spar, the vendor usually agrees to supply and fit new spars, and generally to make good all small defects which may be discovered during the survey.

The hauling up or docking expenses and the cost of survey are borne by the intending purchaser, unless a special arrangement is made concerning them.

A man may perhaps desire to act as his own surveyor; if he does, he will act very unwisely, as it is only by long experience, and a perfect knowledge of the construction of vessels and of the decay and strains they are subject to, that a man can become competent for such surveys. Nevertheless, as the yachtsman who takes to the sport enthusiastically, and with a resolve to be "thorough," will necessarily want to know in a general kind of way the "marks" to distinguish a good vessel from a bad one, some instruction must be given him.

In the first place as to age. Speaking generally, a yacht should not be more than twenty years old; we do not mean that all yachts upwards of that age should be broken up or sold into the coasting, or fishing, or piloting trade; but that yachts so old as twenty years should be put through a very searching survey. Yachts seldom are broken up, and their fate is to lie year after year in mud docks for sale, and till they are far on the shady side of thirty. If money is no object, do not be tempted by cheapness into buying one of these; it would certainly end in mortification and disappointment. If the vessel were merely patched up, she would be a perpetual trouble and expense; and if repaired or renewed as she ought to be, a new vessel had much better be built, as it would be cheaper in the end.

Some old vessels are, however, desirable craft enough; their condition depends upon the way they have been used and "kept up," and upon the amount of repairs and "renewing" they have undergone. For instance, some vessels at the end of fifteen years are stripped, newly planked, and decked, and all doubtful timbers and beams replaced by new; such a craft would be good for another ten years without further outlay, and she might be bought with as much confidence as a perfectly new vessel. Or if the yacht was originally well built in the best manner by one of the best builders she may at the end of fifteen years require neither new plank nor new frames, but if she has seen much service she is almost certain to require new decks. The condition of a yacht at the end of fifteen years will very greatly depend upon the quality of the materials used in her construction, upon the sizes of the timbers and their disposition, and upon the thickness of the planking, and upon the strength of the fastenings. Some idea of what these should be can be gleaned from the tables in "Yacht Architecture" or Lloyd's "Yacht Register," compiled from the practice of the best builders of yachts. The timbers (called also frames, or floors, first, second, and third futtocks, where the lengths of the frames are in two, three, or more pieces) will be "double," that is, two timbers will be placed close together, or nearly close together, and act as one frame. Then there will be a space, and hence "timber and space" means the distance from the centre of one double frame to the centre of another. The spacing should not be greater than the limits given in the table, as if the frames are too wide apart the vessel will work and the caulking become loose, with the final result of troublesome leaks. Some builders do not place the timbers of a double frame quite close together, as some ventilation is considered a good thing; but greater strength is obtained if the timbers of each double frame are close together, and the general practice is to so place them close together.

Occasionally (though very rarely now, except in very small vessels) a single-framed vessel is to be met with—that is, instead of two timbers being worked close together to form one almost solid frame, one single timber forms each frame, placed at regular intervals. These vessels, unless the timbers are of superior size and placed very close together, should be regarded with great suspicion; the space from centre to centre of the timbers should be at least 35 per cent. less than in a double-framed vessel, and the sizes should be 15 per cent. greater; and if the timbers are too long to be all in one piece, the "shifts" or lengthening pieces of the timbers should be so arranged that two shifts never come on the same horizontal line in adjoining timbers, and the heads and heels should be dowelled, and thick strakes worked over them inside—through fastened. In almost all vessels the frames of the bow forward of the mast are single, and in some very old vessels these bow frames might be found to be of fir; these frames will require a great deal of inspection and pricking. Some 20-tonners which we have met with have had single frames 12in. from centre to centre in the middle of the vessel, these frames extending over a distance equal to half the length of the vessel; similar frames were used in the bow and stern, but the spacing was increased to 16in. There does not appear to be any objection to this plan, and it has a slight advantage in weight of timber. A favourite plan for small vessels, and one that answers very well, is to increase the spacing between the frames, and work a steamed timber of American elm between. This plan is also used in combination with a double skin.

With regard to materials, all the frames should be of oak and so should be the stem piece, stern post, upper portion of dead woods, knight heads, apron, beams, shelf clamp, bilge strakes, and keelson; the keel will generally be found to be either English or American elm. The garboard strakes are generally of American elm, and it is best that the planking above should be of American elm or oak to within a foot or so of the load water-line, and teak above to the covering board or deck edge. Very frequently, however, only the garboard strake is of American elm, and the remainder red pine or pitch pine, with a top strake of oak or teak. Again, sometimes the first four strakes above the garboard are of American elm, and the first four strakes below the deck of oak or teak, and the remainder pine; but pine between wind and water is liable to rapid decay; the teak should be carried two or three strakes below the water-line. Formerly oak plank was used at the bilge, with a wale or "bend" of oak above the water-line; and sometimes the plan was all oak from keel to plank sheer, but teak is now generally preferred, as it is so little influenced by heat or damp.

The floors and keel fastenings of yachts are now variously contrived. Twenty years ago a builder never thought of constructing a vessel without grown floors and a keelson; but, owing to the increasing sharpness in the bottoms of vessels, or increasing "dead rise," it became very difficult to find suitably grown floors. The result was that iron floors were cast, and these, whilst having an advantage in strength and durability, have the additional recommendation of forming excellent ballast. In some cases (almost always in vessels of 40 tons and under) grown floors, or floors of any kind, are dispensed with entirely; the heels of the first futtocks are brought down to the keel and connected by iron V knees, which are securely bolted in the throat through the keel or through a hogging piece and keel, and through the timber and plank.

If a yacht is met with that has these iron knee-floors, it should be ascertained if she has been ballasted with lead; if it turns out that her ballast has been lead, it will be necessary to have the iron knees very carefully examined, as lead very quickly destroys iron. It should also be ascertained whether or not the floor bolts and other fastenings are of iron; if they are, it is just possible that the lead ballast, or copper sheathing, may have eaten off their heads; and if the yacht has a lead keel bolted with iron (a not very likely thing in these days), the bolts may have decayed between the wood keel and lead.

If the yacht has been cemented between garboards and keel up to the level of the floors, some of the cement should be cut out to examine the plank, heels of floors, &c.

If the yacht be twelve or thirteen years old, it will be incumbent to examine her very thoroughly inside and out, unless it is satisfactorily shown that she has recently been so examined, and all necessary repairs made. To effectively examine a yacht the copper should be stripped off, and the planking scraped clean; if, however, the copper be good it will be a pretty fair evidence that the plank underneath is sound, as the copper in such a case is not likely to have been on more than three years; and, of course, the plank and caulking would have been thoroughly examined and made good when the vessel was re-coppered.

If it is stated that the vessel does not require re-coppering nor needs stripping, it will be well to be present when she is hauled up high and dry, or as the water is pumped out of the dry dock into which she has been placed, as the case may be; as, if there are wrinkles or folds in the copper, giving evidence of strains, it is quite possible, where the opportunity exists, that these "wrinkles" would be "dressed" out. The wrinkles will generally appear in a longitudinal direction, under the channels and under the bilge over the floor or futtock-heads, and often in the vicinity of plank butts. But if the vessel has been subject to very severe racking or twisting strains, or has bumped on a rock or on very hard ground, the wrinkles may run diagonally or in half circles across the copper; and the caulking or stopping may be found to be working out of the seams. Very long and deep yachts, which have not been properly strengthened longitudinally by internal bilge strakes and continuous diagonal braces across the back or inside of the frames, may be subject to great racking or twisting strains; if there be evidence of such strains, the yacht need not be condemned, but she will require strengthening, and should be put into a builder's hands. In a case where the copper shows unmistakable signs that the vessel works or strains, she should be thoroughly examined in the vicinity of the supposed strains, and be strengthened and fastened in the manner which a builder from his experience may consider necessary. If iron fastenings have been used in the vessel, it is very likely, unless the heads have been counter-sunk and well cemented, that iron rust stains will show on the copper; if such stains are met with, it will be best to have as much of the copper stripped off as the case requires, so that the fastenings may be driven out and new ones put in. The keel should be examined for rot, shakes and splits; and if the keel or false keel pieces be worn away from the through bolt fastenings, the bolts should be cut off and re-clinched, and if necessary new false keel pieces should be fitted.

The stern-post, rudder-post, rudder braces, or gudgeons and pintles must be examined, and if the rudder-post is twisted, or braces or pintles much worn, there will be work for the shipwright.

The chain plates and chain-plate bolts and the surrounding planking and its caulking should be closely examined for flaws and strains, and so also should the stem piece and bobstay shackle plates.

Signs of straining on deck will mostly be apparent in the seam of the covering board abreast of the runners, the mast, at the stem, knightheads, bowsprit bitts, and near the mast partners. If the seams are unusually wide here, as they frequently may be in a yacht which has been much pressed with canvas, "sailed hard" in heavy seas, or that has been weakly built, some strengthening will be required by more hanging knees under the beams, lodging knees, additional knees at the mast partners, diagonal straps across the frames, or it may be new beams, partners, and knees altogether. If the covering board shows signs of having opened badly in the seam, or lifted from the top strake, the beam ends and shelf or clamp will require very careful examination—the shelf and clamp especially at the scarphs and butts.

To examine the floors and frames of the vessel, the ballast should be removed, and some of the ceiling should be stripped off. Lloyd's surveyors, in examining an old yacht, cut out listings from the plank the whole length of the ship; and they also similarly cut listings from the ceiling inside, under the deck, and over the floor heads; planks are taken off, too, at different parts of the ship, equal in the whole to her length; and the beam ends and their fastenings are examined either by taking out the top strake under the covering board, or by boring under the covering boards. Fastenings, such as trenails and bolts, are driven out, to further test the condition of the frames and fastenings; and the condition of the oakum and caulking is ascertained by examination in several places besides at the listings. If the ship or yacht be completely ceiled up inside, it is obvious that the whole of the framing cannot be examined by such means; but generally a yacht is not so closely ceiled, and an application of a pricker to the frames will soon determine whether they are rotten or not.

There is scarcely any limit to the number of years frames of autumn-cut oak will last; but occasionally a sappy piece will find its way among the frames, and it may not last a year, or the frames may decay in consequence of leakage and defective ventilation; but from whatever cause rot may arise, any frame so affected should be removed. Heels and heads of floors and frame timbers are the most likely places to find rot; but of course it may occur in any part of a frame, and, if possible, every timber in a vessel should be thoroughly examined from heel to head.

Old decks are a great trouble to keep tight; and if there is any sign of " weeping " either under the deck at the seams, round the skylights, shelf, or mast, there will be sufficient evidence that caulking is necessary. New decks, however, frequently give trouble in this way if they have been carelessly caulked, or if the yacht has been weakly constructed, or if the caulking was done during wet weather and not under a shed. As the plank dries, it shrinks away from the caulking and paying, and leakage is the inevitable result; this condition can be somewhat ameliorated by wetting the deck two or three times a day, but wet decks are almost as bad as leaky ones, and re-caulking and hardening down and re-paying will be the best remedy. It is the fashion now to lay the deck planks very close together, in order that narrow seams may be obtained; narrow seams of course look very nice, but, as the seams are scarcely wide enough to receive the caulking iron, very little oakum or cotton is driven into them, and very little marine-glue run in; then, as the paying or putty stopping shrinks, leaks are the result.

The examination of an iron or steel yacht should be very carefully made by a competent person, and for this to be done she must be placed in a dry dock or on a patent slip. The cement over the floors and bottom plating inside should be carefully examined and sounded, to see if it is loose—that is, if it has come away from the iron. If the edges of the cracks are damp it will be pretty certain that there is a wasting by rust going on underneath, and the same if the cement has been worn or chipped. All rust and scale should be removed from the frames and plates inside and out, and if the rust appears to have eaten deeply into the plate, holes should be drilled in the latter to ascertain its thickness. If it is less than three-fourths the original thickness Lloyd's require the plate or other part of the structure to be renewed.

All the deck beams, stringers, keelson, tie plates, and pillars will require examination, as well as the butt straps and all the rivetting and caulking. Also the plating inside should be very carefully examined in the wake of the side port-lights, as, if they have been carelessly drained, there will be leakage and rust. The deck and wood fittings about the deck will also come in for survey. If the yacht has, however, been up for survey within two years—Lloyd's require a survey every four years —then it may be prudent to dispense with placing the yacht in dock, unless she has been ashore or has not been painted outside during the time.

In the case of a steam yacht the machinery will have to be examined, and this can only be properly done by an engineer of experience. The chief parts for examination will be the sea connections and pumps, to see that they are in good serviceable condition, and also that there is no leakage running down on the inside of the plates. The screw shaft should be disconnected and withdrawn, to be examined, and the stern bush examined as well, for wear, fractures, &c. Also the cylinders and slide valves, pistons and rods; but only the experienced eye of an engineer could tell if they are worn so as to require taking to the shop.

The boiler, if five or six years old, should be tested by drilling to ascertain the thickness of the plates, and by hydraulic pressure as well, if it has been much used, and the condition of the furnace crown should also be ascertained. The safety-valves must also undergo inspection; and if the surveyor is of opinion that the working pressure should be reduced, then they must be re-set accordingly. If the pressure is greatly reduced the slide valves may require readjusting to get the most possible out of the engines.

The spars of all yachts will require careful inspection, and if either has cracks running transversely or diagonally, it will be pretty sure evidence that it is sprung. The longitudinal cracks or fissures are not of much consequence unless they gape very much, run deep and show a crack across the grain between two shakes; sometimes, however, if the cracks have not been stopped with putty or marine glue, the wet might have got in and caused internal decay. The insertion of a knife into various parts of the crack will soon settle this matter. The mast should be carefully examined at the partners, and the masthead will require very careful examination under the eyes of the rigging, behind the bolsters, and under the yoke (which should be removed) for rot, and right away to the cap for wrings, which generally show themselves by a lot of little cracks. The main boom should be examined, and if sprung it is most likely to be near the outer end; the bowsprit at the gammon iron, or stem head, and at the outer end above and about the sheave hole.

The rigging, blocks, and sails will of course require an overhauling. The standing rigging is now generally made of galvanised steel wire; if it has seen much service, rust from the inner strands will show itself, and the "lay" of the strands will have been stretched nearly straight; also now and again a broken strand or wire may be come across. Hemp and manilla rope, if much worn, with a washed-out appearance, should be in certain places unlaid, or untwisted, and if stranded, with a dried up dull appearance of the yarns, the rope should be condemned. The shells of the block will require examination for splits, and the hook, eye, sheave, and pin for flaws of whatever description. The sails should be laid out and examined; if the stitching in the seams or roping be worn and ragged, if the canvas be black looking, very soft and thin, admitting a great deal of daylight through the woof, then the sails will be only fit for a fisherman or coaster. As a rule, for a cruising yacht, a suit of sails will last through four or five summer cruises; but three months' knocking about, winter cruising in the Mediterranean or elsewhere, will do as much harm as two summer cruises, and it will never be prudent to start on a long winter cruise with sails that have seen more than three seasons' wear. Of course sails may have been exceptionally well cared for—never rolled up wet or unfairly stretched—and the vessel may have been in the happy condition of never having been under way in much of a breeze. Then if they are six or seven years old, and an expert pronounces them fit for a winter's cruise, they can be depended upon; but to be caught in a breeze is bad enough, and it is a great deal worse if when so caught some of the spars, rigging, blocks, or sails give out. A mainsail is most likely to go at the clew or to split from foot to head, but occasionally they split right across from leech to luff. A jib will go all ways; its head will come off, tack or clew will come off, and sometimes they will split or burst out of the stay rope.

For racing, a mainsail is of little use after the first year, and even with the greatest possible care they will hardly do the second, as they get thin and soft and bunt away from the spars into bags with the least weight in the wind. The owners of some yachts have a new mainsail every season, or even two in a season; and this may be quite necessary if the yacht is sailed in as many as forty matches, and if the saii has been frequently reefed.

Lastly, the ground tackle or holding gear must be examined. The anchors and chains should be galvanised, and be of the weight and size set forth in the tables before referred to.

Occasionally a yacht is sold "in commission"; this means with crew actually on board and found in clothes according to yacht customs, and ready to proceed to sea at short notice; but the vendor may get into a difficulty if he does not make a special arrangement with the crew to transfer their services to a new owner.

It is evident that, if a man sells his yacht in commission, he cannot sell the services of his crew as well, and no law at present exists to compel them to re-ship under a new master. In the Royal Navy a ship is not in commission until the captain is on board and her pennant hoisted, although the crew may be appointed and the officers be on full pay. Yacht customs mostly come from those of the Royal Navy, and a yacht is not said to be in commission unless she has captain and crew on board, although her equipment may be all in place or, as the term goes, "fitted out." Still, selling a yacht in commission and then inducing the crew to aid the vendor in carrying out his contract, are very different matters.

c

CHAPTER III.
BUILDING A YACHT.

SOME men seem to have quite a passion for building yachts, whether for cruising or racing, and do not believe in the paraphrased adage that "fools build yachts for wise men to buy." So far as a racing yacht is concerned, it is quite natural that a man should wish her first success or fame to be identified with his name, and that he would not care to own a vessel which had already become famous under another man's flag. On the other hand, there are plenty of men who, directly they hear that a yacht is successful, and read of her marvellous exploits in the reports of matches, long to possess the wonderful craft. And so it happens that there is always something for the builder to do. The man who finds excitement in building is always certain to fancy that there is something even in his last success that can be improved upon; and he is glad to meet with the obliging purchaser who so covets the possession of the property he is anxious to discard.

The man who knows nothing whatever of yachts and yachting, in setting out to build, will perhaps be troubled to know which designer or builder to employ. But of this he may rest pretty well assured that, if he explains clearly what he requires, the designer, whoever he may be, will most probably suit him; and, so far as the builders go, there is little variation in the excellence of the work among the leaders of the trade; and the main thing to consider will be the price. The price, to some extent, will be governed by the materials used, and classing at Lloyd's will also affect the price. If the specification for the yacht is drawn by a competent yacht designer of experience, there will not be much object in employing Lloyd's to look after the construction, if the designer has to superintend the building. Still, some owners like to have the yacht classed at Lloyd's, because they fancy she will sell all the better for it; and if a yacht is to be classed she had better be built under Lloyd's special survey at the outset, or there will be a great deal of trouble about it afterwards; the owner, designer, and builder will be worried by innumerable suggestions as to what should be done, and a great many of these may be avoided if a sectional drawing of the proposed construction and the specification are submitted to Lloyd's Committee at the outset. And it will be better for the designer to do this before any estimates are obtained from the builders, as, if Lloyd's Committee should think proper to vary the construction or add to the specification in any way, the builder may require to revise his estimate or make out a bill for extras, either of which are always more or less annoying to the owner. Lloyd's surveyors do not pay much attention to the cabin fittings, spars, blocks, and rigging of a yacht, and so long as what the builder proposes to supply appears to be sufficiently strong they are satisfied; but there are a good many details to think of, to say nothing of the finish of the work, the more practised yacht designer will know how they should be done. In the end, it will be generally found that building according to Lloyd's tables is a safe thing to do, and that if building under Lloyd's survey does not always insure a perfectly sound vessel, it will be because their surveyors, like other human beings, are not infallible.

We were saying just now that the price would be, to a great extent, governed by the quality of the materials used. Thus, say a yacht is to be built under a roof up to the requirements of the 18 years' class, with oak frame, teak topsides, and all hard wood below, and copper and yellow metal fastenings, she will cost very nearly 10 per cent more than a 12 years' yacht, which has pitch pine plank, and perhaps similar shelf and beams. Then, again, builders, for precisely the same material and work, vary so in their prices (beyond the variations always found in tenders and traceable to errors in pricing the quantities). Still, as a rule, if money is no object it will be some advantage to employ the builder who has made the largest provision for profit; then, when it comes to the various items of the equipment enumerated in the specification, it will be found that they are more liberally supplied and of better quality and finish, and that generally there is better finish to the work. But, as said before, the practice of leading builders is pretty uniform in this respect, and variations of 5 per cent. in their estimates, or even as much as 10 per cent., will not much affect the ultimate result on the value of the vessel.

As a matter of fact, there is a great deal more variation in the quality of the materials used and workmanship among the cheap builders than among those who can command the highest prices; and yet there are some excellent cheap builders who have a good knowledge of what yacht work should be like. These by clever management of labour and saving in the purchase of material under the most favourable conditions, manage to build yachts at a low rate, which compare favourably with those which have cost perhaps 15 or 20 per cent. more by a fashionable builder.

c 2

In choosing a cheap builder, the owner, if he has no experience to guide him, will be governed by the advice of the yacht designer he employs, and there is not much doubt that in the end he will be satisfied.

Yachts, whether intended for racing, and even if for cruising, are now built with keels out of all proportion to the sizes of their other scantling: thus a racing yacht of 95ft. rating may have a keel sided (by "sided" is meant its transverse thickness) amidships 5ft. or even 6ft. This enormously broad keel of course tapers fore and aft, and has rounded ends and underside, and is only so broad amidships in order that a heavy weight of lead or iron might be carried underneath. A similar weight could only be carried on a smaller wood keel by greatly increasing the draught, and then the strength and thickness of the keel might be unequal to the weight of the lead and to the boring for the necessary bolts. Sometimes a lead keel, or keelson, is worked inside, fore and aft, between the heels of the floor timbers and on top of the keel proper.

Various plans have been used for strengthening and binding together the fabric of the hull; but the diagonal iron braces previously referred to are seldom used except in large yachts of great length. In yachts of eighty feet and over in length, two thick strakes of English oak or pitch pine are worked under the clamp, and run the whole length of the vessel, and are through-fastened with metal bolts. Two limber strakes are also worked over the heels of the first futtocks which join the heads of the floors, and are through-fastened. Similarly, in small vessels, two bilge strakes are worked along the curve of each bilge on each side and through-fastened. Limber strakes in a cruising vessel with a floor construction, where there is no keelson, greatly adds to the strength of the vessel; but in yachts of 70 tons and under it would scarcely be necessary to have thick strakes besides the bilge strakes. Outside, a wale or bend is worked and through-fastened; but where all the planking is of hard wood, the wales are dispensed with.

It must be understood, if the yacht about to be built is intended for racing rather than cruising, that it will be an advantage to reduce the scantling, and increase the spacing so far as may seem compatible with strength. The plank also (if the owner is not particular about obtaining a class in Lloyd's Register), from the bilge upwards, can be of red pine instead of teak or oak, and the deck beams can also be of red pine; the bulwarks of red pine, and the stanchions and rails reduced in size so far as may appear consistent with strength. There are racing vessels, of similar tonnage, with as much as three-fifths difference in the size and height of stanchions; and in a 200-ton vessel half a ton of top weight might very well be disposed of in this way. Of course it is only fair to say that some of the most successful large racing yachts, built between 1875 and 1883, such as Florinda, Samœna, or Marjorie (composite build, and classed 20 years), were built up to Lloyd's rules, of the best material, and full-sized scantling. However, although this may show that a vessel can be so built and succeed as a racer, it is at least an open question whether she would not have been a still greater success had her scantling been reduced. For small racing yachts Lloyd's rules are not applicable.

The metal fastenings of yachts form a subject about which there is a great deal of opposite opinion. The builder who constructs cheaply contends stoutly that there is nothing like iron fastenings, above water at any rate; on the other hand, the builder who always asks and gets a good price for his work recommends copper and yellow metal for all the fastenings. Others recommend iron or steel for dead-wood bolts, shelf bolts, and floor bolts, with Muntz' yellow metal for plank fastenings, except the butt bolts, which should be of copper. Others recommend Muntz' metal for all bolts, and a mixture of that metal and trenails for plank fastening. There is no doubt that iron has some advantages, so far at least as long dead-wood bolts are concerned. Iron can be driven very much tighter than copper-rod or yellow metal, and its strength is greater. We have seen iron bolts, that had been made hot and dipped in varnish or oil before they were driven, taken out of a vessel thirty years old, long before galvanised iron was heard of, as clean and bright—in fact, the varnish unperished—as they were at the moment of driving. On the other hand, if the iron were driven through badly caulked seams in the dead-wood, or through a shaky piece of timber, or be loosely driven, so that salt water might get to it, decay of the iron would be very rapid; hence preference must be given to copper or yellow metal. Galvanised iron is often used for shelf fastenings, and it is less objectionable there; but preference should be given to yellow metal for all dead woods, as it can be driven almost as tightly as iron, and, if of the best quality, will clench well. Inferior yellow metal is very brittle, and care must be taken to obtain metal of the very best quality.

Lloyd's give an additional year to all ships or yachts which are fastened from the keel upwards (to within one-fifth the depth of hold amidships from the deck) with yellow metal or copper bolts and dumps, or trenails; in such case the fastenings for the upper strakes of plank to the deck must be properly galvanised, it being also understood that the iron bolts for frames, beams, &c., are to be galvanised. And a further two years are granted if *no trenails* are used at all.* Whether

* Lloyd's also give an extra year if the vessel is built under a shed or roof.

trenails or bolts are used, one is to be put in each plank or strake at every timber; two-thirds of the trenails are required to be driven through. The butts of the plank and the bilge strakes and limber strake should be through-fastened with copper bolts, not yellow metal.

Trenails are scarcely adapted for vessels of less than 50 tons, on account of the small size of the timbers; and even in these they should be very sparingly used (and only in the bottom plank), as a 3in. timber must be very considerably weakened if it is bored with holes to receive 1in. trenails.

Metal bolts should in all cases be used for bolting on lead keels; iron keels can be bolted on with iron bolts, but if the vessel is coppered a 3in. strip of zinc should be put between the lower edge of the copper and the iron keel, and frequently renewed.

Some ten years ago it seemed likely that composite vessels would quite supersede those entirely of wood construction; but so far the composite plan, on account of its costliness, has not advanced very rapidly in favour, except for racing vessels, where it is preferred for lightness. The composite build also offers this advantage over the wood structure: so very much more room is obtainable inside on the same tonnage or displacement; and this is a consideration in these days of very narrow racing yachts. The great question was, ten years ago, could a composite vessel be so fastened as to be insured against the possibility of the fastenings giving out? We think the question has now, after nearly thirty years, been satisfactorily answered by such vessels as Selene (1865), Bella Donna and Nyanza (1867), Oimara (1867), Palatine (1870), Garrion (1871), Modwena (1872), Sunbeam (1874), Soprano (1877), Lancashire Witch (1878), May (1881), Marjorie (1883), Maid Marion *ex* Yarana (1888), Britannia (1893), Meteor (1896), Bona and Aurora (1897), and many others. None of these vessels have, so far as we know, ever shown the slightest signs of straining, nor have their fastenings decayed; although the American elm plank used as a bottom skin has shown in one or two cases rather extensive decay from the inside through the plank not being of the best quality; or, in other words, it was that known among builders as bog or marsh elm. Canadian rock elm is the name of the best quality. For a composite yacht it is best that all the planking (excepting the deck) should be of extra thickness to the extent of 10 per cent., and that the plank fastenings should be of yellow metal screw bolts, sunk in the plank, and so insulated that galvanic action could not be set up with the outside copper, the bolts, and the frames.

A great many experiments have from time to time been made with compositions for preventing the fouling of the bottom of ships; but up to the present time no specific has been discovered, and the opportunity for someone to realise a large fortune still exists. So far as yachts are concerned, they are generally sheathed with copper, which may last from seven to ten years; and, for these waters at least, the bottom can be kept clean enough by a couple of scrubbings throughout the season. Of course, for a racing yacht, the copper cannot very well be cleaned too often; and a month is quite long enough for the vessel to be without a scrub, although there are but few which get one so often. The Admiralty some time since made experiments with zinc as a sheathing for iron ships (the iron being first protected by a slight wood skin), but so far zinc does not appear to offer many advantages. Copper, on the other hand—if the ship be kept constantly moving, or moored, say, in a five-knot tide—will keep comparatively clean, on account of the extensive exfoliation which goes on of the oxychlorides and other soluble salts produced by the action of the salt water on the copper. Oxychlorides are similarly and much more rapidly formed on zinc, but are not so readily soluble; hence very little exfoliation takes place, and a corroded and rough surface is the result, the zinc being finally eaten through. Zinc, therefore, we may conclude, is unsuitable as a sheathing for yachts, especially as evidence exists that such sheathing ½in. thick has been eaten through in one year. An alloy of copper (2) and zinc (3), popularly known as Muntz' metal, is largely used as a sheathing for ships; but it is scarcely so good as copper for yachts, as, owing to its greater stiffness, it cannot be laid on so well, and is subject to a rough oxydization; hence it does not exfoliate to the extent copper does, and therefore fouls with weeds and barnacles more quickly; and that after being under the influence of salt water any considerable time —say three or four years—the metal becomes rotten; but this defect, it is said, can be remedied by an addition of a small quantity of tin to the alloy. For composite ships Muntz' metal sheathing has some advantage, as it sets up very little, if any, galvanic action with iron; but the risk of galvanic action from copper sheathing in a well-constructed composite ship is so remote that copper is to be preferred even for these, if the difference in cost is not a consideration.

For iron yachts copper sheathing is out of the question, and none of the compositions which contain copper should be put on without first coating the hull with a mixture of nine parts of coal tar and one part of quick lime, or coat with thick red lead paint. In the case of steel yachts the "scale" due to the manufacture requires removing before the yacht is coated (unless it has been done whilst building), and for this purpose, if time admits of it, the yacht may be left afloat (in fresh water if possible) for a few months without any coating on. In all cases all rust and scale should be carefully removed from the hull before any coating is put on. The coal tar mixture is put on to prevent corrosion and deleterious action of the anti-fouling composition. The action of the latter is either to kill animal or vegetable life, or prevent their formation by constant exfoliation. The coal tar prevents, as before said, corrosion of the iron or steel.

Of the many compositions in use, the best are J. W. Blake and Son's, High-street, Gosport; Jesty's, High-street, Gosport; Peacock's, Southampton; Day's, Salmon-lane, Limehouse; Rahtjen's, Suter, Hartman and Co., Billiter-street, London; Thrift's enamel anti-fouling, Towerbuildings, Water-street, Liverpool; Haley's, 131, Narrow-street, Limehouse; Denny's, and many others.

For small wooden racing yachts thin black varnish is commonly used; it fouls quickly, but, on the other hand, it presents a very smooth surface, and hauling up a small racing yacht for a scrub and recoating is not a very serious matter. Davis's anti-fouling varnish (to be obtained of the Varnish Paint Company, Spekeland-buildings, Liverpool) and the paint manufactured by the Liver Colour Company, Liverpool, are recommended for cruisers; but, of course, any of the compositions named will answer as well. In applying any of the compositions, the manufacturer's instructions should be followed. (See " Composition " in the Appendix.) The old-fashioned blackleading, and polishing with a brush, is still followed in America, where it is termed pot leading, and for getting a good surface for racing nothing is better, but it does not last clean any length of time, and soon wears or washes off.

One gallon of tar or paint will cover about 100 sq. ft. of surface first coat, and about three-quarters of a gallon will cover 100 sq. ft. of surface the second coat.

CHAPTER IV.

THE EQUIPMENT OF THE YACHT.

THE EQUIPMENT OF THE YACHT.

THE equipment of a yacht embraces generally everything that is used or required for working her. Usually it is understood to consist of the spars, standing and running rigging, sails, various tackles or purchases, anchors, chains, warps, boats, lights, &c. The diagram, Plate I., and the references, will assist the explanations that will follow of the various parts and uses of a vessel's outfit or equipment.

SAILS.

A. Mainsail.
a. Clew of mainsail, with shackle as traveller on the horse 13 (chain or wire rope outhaul and tackle shown underneath boom).
b. Main tack.
c. Throat.
d. Peak earing.
e. Head.
f. Foot and roach of sail.
g. Luff or weather leech.
h. Leech, or after leech.
i. First, second, third, and close reef cringles.
j. First, second, third, and close reef points.
k. First, second, third, and close reef cringles or luff cringles.

B. Foresail.
a. Luff.
b. Foot.
c. Leech.
d. Head.
e. Tack.

f. Reef points.
C. Jib.
a. Luff.
b. Foot.
c. Leech.
d. Head.
e. Tack.
D. Gaff Topsail.
a. Clew.
b. Tack.
c. Weather earing, or head earing.
d. Peak earing.
e. Head.
f. Foot.
g. Luff.
h. Leech.
E. Jib Topsail.
a. Luff.
b. Foot.
c. Leech.
d. Head.
e. Tack.

SPARS.

1. Mast.
2. Top Mast.
3. Bowsprit.
4. Boom.

5. Gaff.
6. * Topsail yard.
7. Spinnaker boom.
8. Hounds, bolster, and yoke.

* Balloon topsails, with a footyard or jackyard, are now again common in all racing yachts; they were for a while done away with, excepting in schooners and yawls, as the long yard greatly increased the weight aloft, without much increasing the size of topsail. The upper yard is now much shorter, and there is less of it on the fore side of the top mast.

SPARS—*continued.*

9. Cap.
10. Masthead.
11. Pole of topmast.
12. Truck.
13. Iron horse at boom end for mainsail outhaul to travel on.
14. Mast hoops.

RIGGING.

1. * Main rigging shrouds.
2. * Sheer pole, termed also sheer batten and sheer stretcher.
3. * Dead eyes and lanyards.
4. * Fore stay.
5. * Pendant
6. * Runner.
7. Runner tackle.
8. Fall of runner tackle.
9. * Topmast stay (the topmast back-stays are not shown). See Fig. 1.
10. * Topmast shifting backstay, or "preventer backstay."
11. Tackle of shifting backstay.
12. * Bobstay.
13. Bobstay tackle and fall.
14. Main halyards.
15. Peak halyards.
16. Main sheet.
17. Topping lifts.
18. Reef-earing or pendant.
19. Foresail halyards.
20. Foresail sheet rove through block on clew of sail.
21. Foresail tack.
22. Jib halyards.
23. Jib sheets fast to clew of sail.
24. Jib tack.
25. Jib traveller.
26. Jib outhaul.
27. Jib downhaul and foresail downhaul.
28. Topsail halyards.
29. Topsail upper halyards, or tripping halyards.
30. Topsail sheet, leading through block with pendant, fast round masthead.
31. Topsail tack.
32. Topsail tack tackle.
33. Topsail clew line.
34. Jib-topsail halyards.
35. Jib-topsail tack.
36. Jib-topsail sheet, fast to clew of sail.
37. Mainsail downhaul.
38. Spinnaker-boom; topping lift.
39. Spinnaker-boom; after guy.
40. Spinnaker-boom; hauling and standing parts of whip purchase of after guy.
41. Spinnaker-boom; fore guy.
42. Spinnaker outhaul, the hauling part on the under side of the boom.
43. Spinnaker outhaul, on the upper side of boom; this is the part made fast to spinnaker tack.

The parts of the rigging marked thus * are termed "standing rigging," and the other parts running rigging." Large racing cutters have a masthead shroud each side.

HULL.

1. Load water-line. (L.W.L.)
2. Keel.
3. Sternpost.
4. Rudder.
5. Deadwood.
6. Forefoot, termed also gripe.
7. Stem.
8. Freeboard.
9. Counter.
10. Archboard.
11. Taffrail.
12. Quarter timbers.
13. Covering board or plank sheer
14. Rail, or rough tree rail.
15. Channel.
16. Chain plates, or channel plates.
17. Bobstay shackle plates.

FIG. 1.

HULL.

1. Floor.
2. Frames or timbers.
3. Keel.
4. Garboard.
5. Bilge.
6. Deck.
7. Deck Beam.
8. Bulwark stanchions.
9. Channels and channel plates.

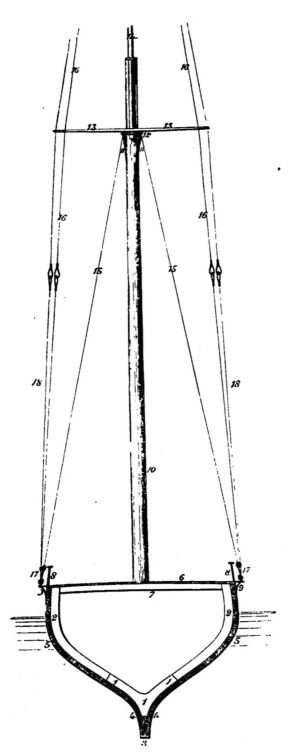

FIG. 1.

MAST AND RIGGING.

10. Mast.
11. Hounds.
12. Yoke or lower cap and bolster.
13. Crosstrees.
14. Topmast.

15. Main rigging or shrouds.
16. Topmast shrouds or backstays.
17. Backstay falls or tackles.
18. Legs of topmast backstays taken off when the topmast is housed.

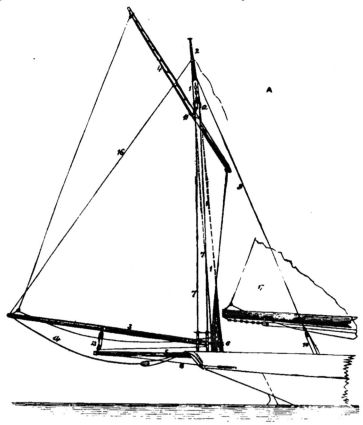

FIG. 2.

LUG MIZEN OF YAWL.

1. Mizen mast.
2. Pole of mizen mast.
3. Mizen boom.   [instead of a yard)
4. Mizen yard (a gaff is now generally used
5. Mizen bumpkin.
6. Spider band on mast.   [sheer pole.
7. Mizen shrouds set up with lanyards and
8. Mizen bumpkin guys or shrouds. A bumpkin bobstay set up to a bolt in the ridge of counter is usually fitted as well.
9. Mizen shifting stay, one on each side.
10. Tackle for mizen shifting stay.
11. Strop on mizen yard.
12. Iron Traveller on mizen mast, with chain

tye or halyard passing through sheave hole above. The tackle on the chain halyard is on the other side of the mast.
13. Mizen sheet leading in board.
14. Mizen outhaul and whip purchase slackened up. It is also sometimes arranged in this manner : the outhaul is put over the boom and by a running eye, then through a single block on the clew cringle through a sheave hole in the boom end, and then on board. In such case there is no whip purchase.
15. Mizen tack and tack tackle.
16. Mizen topping lift.
17. Mainboom and part of mainsail.

The rigging of a schooner, for any given hoist of one mast, is somewhat lighter than that of a cutter or yawl; but for the sail spread the total weight of rigging and spars is heavier, as there are two masts and two sets of rigging to deal with.

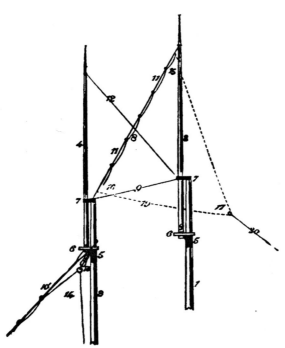

Fig. 3.

MASTS AND RIGGING OF SCHOONER.

1. Mainmast
2. Foremast.
3. Main topmast.
4. Fore topmast.
5. Hounds or cheeks of mast.
6. Lower cap on which crosstrees rest, fore side of topmast.
7. Cap.
8. Topmast fid.
9. Triatic stay.
10. Forestay.

11. Main-topmast stay.
12. Fore-topmast backstay.
13. Fore-staysail halyards.
14. Head of fore-staysail.
15. Head of main-topmast staysail.
16. Tack   ,,   ,,
17. Clew   ,,   ,,
18. Luff   ,,   ,,
19. Foot   ,,   ,,
20. Sheet   ,,   ,,
    leading to quarter rail.

The other parts of the rigging are identical with those of a cutter, except that the head gear is different in a schooner, which has a standing bowsprit and jib-boom. The latter rig has very much gone out of fashion of late years, and most yachtsmen and seamen prefer the cutter bowsprit, which can be reefed in more easily than the jib-boom in bad weather, and will then ease the vessel as much or more.

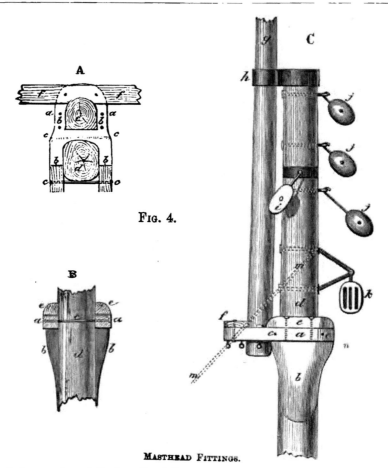

FIG. 4.

MASTHEAD FITTINGS.

Fig. A shows a view of the top side of the yoke or lower cap.

a is the yoke with an iron band round it.

b is a U-shaped iron plate, sometimes fitted over the yoke as shown, and is the strongest plan.

c c iron bolts.

d is the mast.

e is the topmast.

f the crosstrees fitted with screw bolts and nuts on the fore side of topmast as shown.

Fig. B is the yoke and mast viewed from aft.

a, the ends of the aft arms of yoke.

b, the cheeks, the upper part on which the bolsters rest being the hounds.

c, iron bolt at aft side of mast.

d, the mast.

e, bolsters on which the rigging rests.

Fig. C shows a broadside view of the yoke and masthead.

a, the yoke.

b, the cheeks.

c c, iron bolts.

d, the masthead.

h, iron cap.

i, jib halyard block (one on each side of mast, on iron band).

j j j, peak-halyard blocks.

k, throat-halyard block, and span bolt. This bolt should be long enough to keep the parts of the halyards clear of the yoke. Sometimes a single bolt is used with strong spur and plate below.

m, forestay. (*See* page 61).

n shows the position on the cheeks where the eye plates are bolted to take the blocks for the topping lift.

e, bolster resting on the yoke.

f, crosstrees.

g, topmast.

The sheave in the masthead for the heel rope of the topmast is not shown; the sheave is fitted diagonally, not in the fore and aft line.

See also Plate II.

In yachts above 20 tons the fittings on the mast below the hounds consist of two iron mast hoops. The upper one carries the winches for

FIG. 5.

heaving out topsail sheet, purchasing up, &c., and the lower one carries the main boom and sometimes the spinnaker boom as well.

The "Gipsy" winch, or Paget's, is usually fitted to a mast hoop of yachts of 20 tons and over, above the mast hoop for main boom. Fig. 5 shows the foreside of this winch mast hoop, with spinnaker boom goose-neck and belaying pins.

Fig. 6 shows the aft side of the mast and a different winch. Both views are taken from winches supplied by Messrs. Atkey and Son, of

FIG. 6.

Cowes. Fig. 7 shows the mechanism of a winch invented by the late Mr. Bentall, of Maldon. All the moving parts are inside. It was designed to

FIG. 7.

give two and a half times the purchase of the ordinary winch, but of course it is slow. The handle on the pinion A transmits motion to the idle pinion B, and so to C.

The main boom mast hoop and universal joint are illustrated on Plate III. The spinnaker boom, it will be seen, has also a universal joint to the gooseneck, but more generally a socket and jointed gooseneck, as shown in Figs. 5 and 8, are used. The plan shown in the plate was adopted in the Jullanar, and the plate was engraved from the original drawing for the same.

The mast hoop and boom end of small yachts is shown by Fig. 8. No belaying pins, it will be seen, are shown in this sketch of mast hoop, but it is usual to have them, or to fit dagger (†) belaying pins in the deck round the fore side of the mast. In this case the belaying pin racks are under the bulwarks as shown.

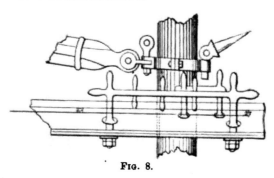

FIG. 8.

Generally, instead of the pin rack fitted in the deck round the mast, the boom or winch mast hoop forms a spider band. Fig. 5 shows the arrangement with spider band spinnaker boom gooseneck, and if there were no winches the main boom would be on the other side of the hoop shown in the figure.

Formerly wooden jaws, with tumbler, were usually fitted to gaffs, but iron jaws, leather bound, are now generally adopted, as shown by Fig. 9. The eye plate, A, on each side of the gaff has a bolt, and takes the nock or throat cringle of mainsail. The throat halyard band is represented by B. The inner side of the jaws, D, is covered with thick hide; sometimes, however, a sheepskin with the wool on is used. Frequently the jaws are secured to the gaff by several iron bands instead of bolts; the band B is not then used, but a bolt working in a slot, as shown in Plate IV. This plan was engraved from the drawing used in making the jaws for Jullanar's gaff, and has never received the attention it merited. The large bearing surface of the slipper renders any chafing of the mast impossible, and there is an entire absence of that annoying grating noise inseparable from the usual gaff jaws. A rope and ball parrel is shown in the plate, but we believe a steel band was substituted for this in Jullanar. Mr. R. Aldous, of Brightlingsea, has patented a modification of this plan, as shown by Fig. 10.

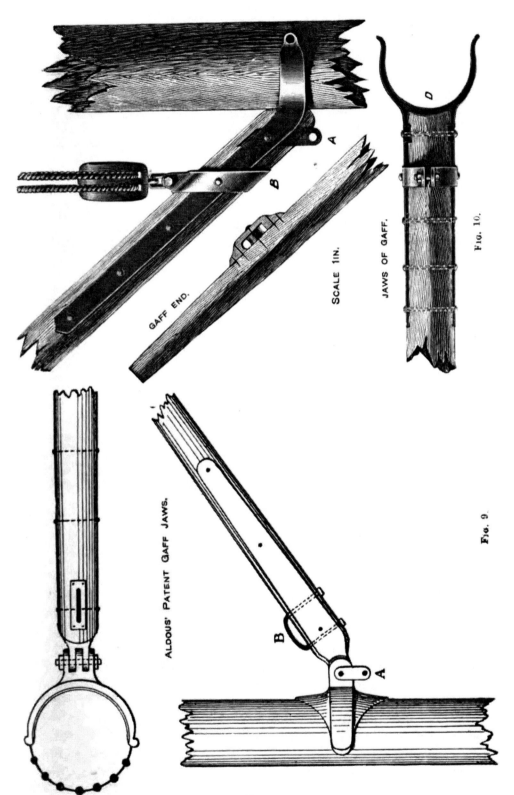

GAFF END.

SCALE 1IN.

JAWS OF GAFF.

Fig. 10.

ALDOUS' PATENT GAFF JAWS.

Fig. 9.

D

An efficient appliance for getting the anchor is a most necessary part of a yacht's outfit, and hitherto yachts under 20 tons have seldom had a compact modern capstan, but a time-honoured windlass of some pattern or other. However, Messrs. Pascal Atkey and Son, of Cowes, and Messrs. W. White and Sons, Vectis Works, Cowes, now make a capstan with a winch top for small yachts, which will take ¼in., ⁵⁄₁₆in., ⅜in.,

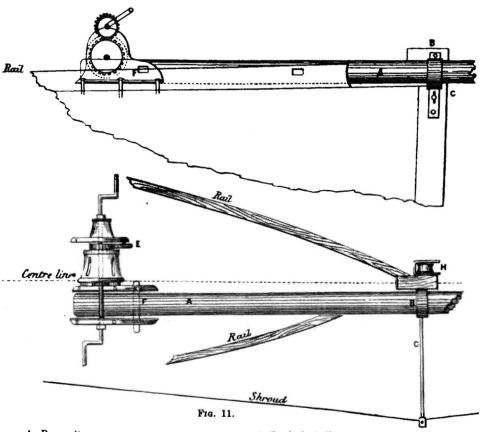

Fig. 11.

A. Bowsprit.	E. Pawl of windlass.
B. Span shackle.	F. Fid of bowsprit.
C. Whisker for bowsprit shroud.	H. Iron roller sheave for mooring chain.

and ⁷⁄₁₆in. chains. These are suitable for yachts down to 3 tons. The small sized capstans with winch tops are not fitted for "capstan bars," but in yachts of considerable size, say of 60 tons and upwards, where there is plenty of deck room, a capstan, which can be worked with bars as well as by the winch top, should always be had to use in the case of heavy heaving. There are various makers of these combination capstans.

Windlasses are of varied pattern, and one made by the Troon Yacht Building Company, Troon, N.B., has iron bitts and knees complete, and is worked by crank handles. This windlass is shown in Fig. 11, and has been fitted to yachts of 3 tons and upwards.

Messrs. W. White and Sons, Vectis Works, Cowes, Messrs. Atkey and Son, of West Cowes, Messrs. Blake, of Gosport, and Messrs. Watkins

Fig. 12.

and Co., Blackwall, make a ratchet windlass, with lever heaving handle, for small yachts, and these are as a rule preferred to those with crank handles. They are fitted with iron bitts, as shown, or wood bitts as required (*see* Fig. 12).

Anchors for Small Boats.

For light open boats which carry little or no ballast, and are not moored in a very strong current, the anchor should weigh 1lb. for every foot of length up to 20ft. For other boats anchors would be chosen according to the total weight of the boat, including her ballast and equipment, &c.; thus—for a boat of the weight of ½ ton, 20lb.; 1 ton, 25lb.; 1½ tons, 30lb.; 2 tons, 34lb.; 2½ tons, 38lb.; 3 tons, 42lb. This supposes the boat to be moored in not more than a two knot tide, or in a sheltered position. Anchors for small boats should be long in the shank, and of the old-fashioned pattern, especially if the scope of cable is short. The usual length of cable allowed is three times the depth of water at top of the flood. The size of link of chain would be about ¼in.

Fay and Co., of Northam, Southampton, make two folding anchors suitable for small yachts. One is the invention of Colonel Bucknill, R.E., and the other of Mr. Sinnette, N.A. (*See* "Anchor" and "Grapnel" in the Appendix.)

ANCHORS FOR SAILING YACHTS.

Thames Tonnage.	Number of Anchors.	1st Anchor. Weight.	1st Anchor. Test.	2nd Anchor. Weight.	2nd Anchor. Test.	3rd Anchor. Weight.	3rd Anchor. Test.	4th Anchor. Weight ex Stock.	4th Anchor. Test.
			Tons.		Tons.		Tons.	Cwts.	Tons.
3	2	With Stock 75lb.	—	With Stock 28lb.	—	—	—	—	—
5	2	Cwts. With Stock $\frac{3}{4}$	—	With Stock 40lb.	—	—	—	—	—
10	2	With Stock 1	—	Cwts. With Stock $\frac{1}{2}$	—	With Stock 20lb.	—	—	—
20	2	With Stock $1\frac{1}{4}$	—	With Stock $\frac{3}{4}$	—	With Stock 35lb.	—	—	—
30	2	Ex Stock $1\frac{1}{2}$	$3\frac{18}{20}$	With Stock 1	—	With Stock 50lb.	—	—	—
40	2	2	$4\frac{10}{20}$	With Stock $1\frac{1}{4}$	—	With Stock $\frac{1}{2}$cwt.	—	—	—
50	3	$2\frac{1}{2}$	5	Ex Stock $2\frac{1}{4}$	$4\frac{15}{20}$	With Stock $\frac{3}{4}$	—	—	—
60	3	3	$5\frac{10}{20}$	$2\frac{3}{4}$	$5\frac{5}{20}$	With Stock 1	—	—	—
75	3	$3\frac{3}{4}$	$6\frac{3}{20}$	$3\frac{1}{2}$	$5\frac{18}{20}$	With Stock $1\frac{1}{4}$	—	—	—
100	3	$4\frac{1}{2}$	$6\frac{17}{20}$	$4\frac{1}{4}$	$6\frac{18}{20}$	With Stock $1\frac{1}{2}$	—	—	—
125	3	5	$7\frac{7}{20}$	$4\frac{3}{4}$	$7\frac{3}{20}$	Ex Stock $1\frac{1}{2}$	$4\frac{4}{20}$	—	—
150	4	$5\frac{1}{2}$	$7\frac{18}{20}$	$5\frac{1}{4}$	$7\frac{11}{20}$	2	5	1	—
200	4	$6\frac{1}{4}$	$8\frac{10}{20}$	6	$8\frac{5}{20}$	$2\frac{1}{2}$	$5\frac{5}{20}$	1	—
250	4	7	$9\frac{5}{20}$	$6\frac{1}{2}$	$8\frac{15}{20}$	3	$5\frac{10}{20}$	$1\frac{1}{4}$	—
300	4	8	$10\frac{3}{20}$	$7\frac{1}{2}$	$9\frac{13}{20}$	$3\frac{1}{2}$	$5\frac{15}{20}$	2	$4\frac{10}{20}$

CHAINS FOR SAILING YACHTS.

Thames Tonnage.	Chain Cable. Minimum Size.	Chain Cable. Test.	Chain Cable. Breaking Test.	Chain Cable. Length.	Stream Chain. Length.	Stream Chain. Size.	Hawser. Length.	Hawser. Size.	Warp. Length.	Warp. Size.
	Ins.	Tons.	Tons.	Fathoms.	Fathoms.	Ins.	Fathoms.	Ins.	Fathoms.	Ins.
3	$\frac{5}{16}$	—	—	50	—	—	40	3	40	2
5	$\frac{6}{16}$	—	—	50	—	—	40	$3\frac{1}{2}$	40	$2\frac{1}{2}$
10	$\frac{7}{16}$	$3\frac{5}{10}$	$5\frac{1}{4}$	60	—	—	45	4	45	3
20	$\frac{8}{16}$	$4\frac{5}{10}$	$6\frac{3}{4}$	60	—	—	50	$4\frac{1}{2}$	45	3
30	$\frac{9}{16}$	$5\frac{5}{10}$	$8\frac{1}{4}$	60	—	—	60	$4\frac{1}{2}$	45	3
40	$\frac{10}{16}$	7	$10\frac{1}{2}$	75	—	—	60	5	50	3
50	$\frac{10}{16}$	7	$10\frac{1}{2}$	90	—	—	75	5	60	$3\frac{1}{2}$
60	$\frac{11}{16}$	$8\frac{5}{10}$	$12\frac{3}{4}$	105	—	—	75	$5\frac{1}{2}$	75	$3\frac{1}{2}$
75	$\frac{11}{16}$	$8\frac{5}{10}$	$12\frac{3}{4}$	120	—	—	75	$5\frac{1}{2}$	75	$3\frac{1}{2}$
100	$\frac{12}{16}$	$10\frac{1}{8}$	$15\frac{1}{8}$	135	—	—	75	6	90	$3\frac{1}{2}$
125	$\frac{12}{16}$	$10\frac{1}{8}$	$15\frac{1}{8}$	150	45	$\frac{8}{16}$	75	6	90	4
150	$\frac{13}{16}$	$11\frac{7}{8}$	$17\frac{8}{10}$	150	45	$\frac{8}{16}$	75	6	90	4
200	$\frac{14}{16}$	$13\frac{3}{4}$	$20\frac{5}{8}$	150	45	$\frac{9}{16}$	75	$6\frac{1}{2}$	90	4
250	$\frac{15}{16}$	$15\frac{8}{10}$	$23\frac{7}{10}$	165	45	$\frac{9}{16}$	75	$6\frac{1}{2}$	90	$4\frac{1}{2}$
300	1	18	27	165	45	$\frac{9}{16}$	75	7	90	$4\frac{1}{2}$

The weight of chain cable per fathom can be found by multiplying the square of the diameter (diameter^2) by 54.

Foredeck Fittings, Bowsprit and Rigging.—Plate IV. V.

A. The bowsprit.
B. Bitts, pin roller and fid.
B 2. Knees of bitts.
C. Compressor.
D. Chain pipe and compressor.
E. Bollard.
F. Gammon iron, also called span shackle.
G. Whiskers hinged or hooked to the stem.
H. Wire shrouds.
J. Tackle for setting up bowsprit shrouds; blocks are iron and one a fiddle.
K. Covering board.
L L. Cavels ; those next channels with pins.
M. Mast and mast bitts.
N. Fore hatch.
O. Eye bolt for gaff topsail tack.
P.   „   jib halyards.
Q.   „   topsail halyards.
R.   „   jib purchase.
S.   „   throat purchase.
T T. Channels and dead-eyes.

U U. Eye bolt for boom guy and fore guy.
V.   „   peak purchase.
W.   „   topmast backstays.
X X. Socket for davits.
Y. Cathead.
Z Z. Eye bolts for topping lifts.
a a.   „   fore sheet.
b. Sheave for fore tack.
c. Score for forestay.
d. Eye bolt for setting up forestay.
e. Carlines.
f. Bilge strakes.
g. Breast hook.
h. Hanging knees.
i. Shelf.
j. Clamp.
k. Mast step.
l. Bobstay plate.
m. Iron floors.
n. Hawse pipe.

Fittings on the After Deck.

At the after end of the vessel the principal fitting is the main sheet buffer. It consists of several thick indiarubber rings with thin brass rings between. The two patterns most approved of, and made by

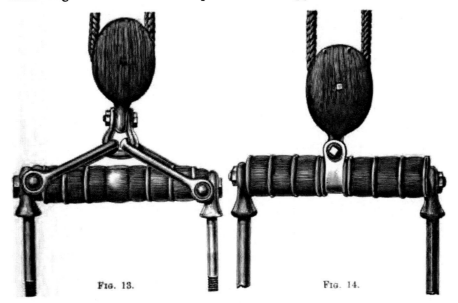

Fig. 13.   Fig. 14.

the inventors, are shown by Figs. 13 and 14. In the case of small yachts, an iron horse only is often used, with one of the indiarubber rings at either end to ease the shock when the boom goes over.

TABLE I.—BLOCKS FOR RACING YACHTS BY Y.R.A. RATING.

	Description of Blocks.	No. of Single Blocks.	No. of Double Blocks.	18ft. Rating.	24ft. Rating.	30ft. Rating.	36ft. Rating.	42ft. Rating.	52ft. Rating.	56ft. Rating.	64ft. Rating.	70ft. Rating.	80ft. Rating.	95ft. Rating.
				Inches.	Inches.	Inches.	Inches.	Inches.	Inches.	Inches.	Inches.	Inches.	Inches.	Inches.
Throat halyards.........	Shackle...........	—	2a	2	2¾	4½	5	5½	7	8	9	10	10½	11
Throat purchase.........	Shackle...........	1	1	2	2¾	3	3½	4	5	6	6½	7	7½	8
Peak halyards...........	Hook	5	—	—	—	4½	5	5½	7	8	8½	9½	10½	10½
Peak purchase	Shackle...........	1	1	—	—	3	3½	4	5	6	6½	7	7½	8
Fore halyards...........	Cliphook	2b	—	2	2½	3	3½	4	5	6	6½	7	7½	8
Jib halyards	Shackle...........	3b	—	—	—	4	4½	4½	6	7½	8½	9	9½	10
Jib purchase	Shackle...........	1	1	—	—	3	3½	4	5	6	6½	7	7½	8
Runner pendant..........	Lugs	2	—	2	2½	3	3½	4	5	6	6½	7	7½	8
Runner tackles	Hook & Fiddle...	2	2c	—	2½	3 & 7	3½ & 7½	4 & 7½	4½ & 8	5 & 9	5½ & 10	6 & 11	6½ & 12	7 & 13
Topping lift	Hook..............	2	—	2	2½	4	4½	5	5½	6	6½	7	7½	8
Topping lift purchase	Lugs	2	2	—	—	3	3½	4	5	5½	6	6½	7	7½
Main sheet	Lug and strop...	—	2d	2½	3	4½	5	5½	7	8½	9½	10½	11	12
Main sheet leads.........	Swivel	2	—	—	2½	3	3½	4	5	6	7	7½	8	8½
Topmast backstays ...	Shackle...........	4	4	—	—	3	3½	4	5	5½	6	6½	7	7½
Preventer backstays ...	Shackle...........	4	—	—	—	3	3½	4	5	5½	6	6½	7	7½
Topsail sheet	Shackle.......... .	1	—	—	—	3	3½	4	5	5½	6	6½	7	7½
Topsail halyards	Hook..............	1	—	—	—	3½	4	4½	5	5½	6	6½	7	7½
Fore sheet	Hook..............	2	—	2	2	3	3½	4	4½	5	5½	6	6½	7
Reef tackle	Hook & Fiddle...	1	1	2	2¾	3 & 7	3½ & 7½	4 & 7½	4½ & 8	5 & 9	5½ & 10	6 & 11	6½ & 12	7 & 13
Jib tack	Hook..............	1	1	2	2¾	3	3½	4	5	5½	6	6½	7	7
Main outhaul	Hook..............	1	1	2	2¾	3	3½	4	5	5½	6	6½	7	7
Trysail sheets...........	Hook..............	2	2	2	3	4	4½	5	6	7	7½	8	8½	9
Bobstay	Steel shackle ...	1	1	2	2¾	4	4½	5	5½	6	6½	7	7½	8
Bowsprit shrouds	Shackle & Fiddle	2	2	2	2¾	3 & 7	3½ & 7½	4 & 7½	4½ & 8	5 & 9	5½ & 10	6 & 11	6½ & 12	7 & 13
Sundry tackles	Rope strop	12	12	2	2¾	3	3½	4	5	5½	6	6½	7	7½
Gaff bulls' eyes	Iron bound	2	—	—		3	3	3½	4½	5	5½	6	6½	7
Jib sheet ditto	Iron bonnd	2	—	—	—	3	3	3	4	4½	5	5½	6	6½
Spinnaker halyards, spinnaker guys, and jib topsail halyards and down-hauls	Rope strop	7	—	2	2½	3	3	3½	4	4½	5	5½	6	6½

(a) In yachts of 42ft. rating and over where a throat purchase is used, the upper block has three sheaves, as there is no standing part to the halyards. The blocks, if of steel, are about 20 per cent. smaller in the shell, but the sheaves are full size. In yachts of 36ft. rating down to 24ft. rating the halyards are of flexible wire and the blocks of steel. (b) These are steel blocks. (c) The double block is fiddle-shaped. (d) The upper block has three sheaves, and wire rope stropped. The lower block has lugs.

TABLE II.—SIZES FOR STANDING AND RUNNING RIGGING FOR RACING YACHTS.

	Description.	18ft. Rating.	24ft. Rating.	30ft. Rating.	36ft. Rating.	42ft. Rating.	52ft. Rating.	56ft Rating.	64ft. Rating.	70ft. Rating.	80ft. Rating.	95ft. Rating.
		Circumference. Inches.	Circumference. Inches.	Circumference. Inches.	Circumference. Inches.	Circumference. Inches.	Circumference. Inches.	Circumference. Inches.	Circumference. Inches.	Circumference. Inches.	Circumference. Inches.	Circumference. Inches.
Shrouds *a*	Crucible steel	½	¾	1¼	1¼	1⅝	1½	1¾	2	2¼	2½	3
Runner pendants ..	Crucible steel	⅜	½	1⅛	1¼	1⅝	1½	1¾	2	2¼	2½	3
Forestay	Crucible steel	⅜	½	1⅛	1⅜	1⅛	1¾	1¾*c*	2*c*	2¼*c*	2½*c*	2¾*c*
Bowsprit shrouds	Crucible steel	½	¾	1⅛	1¼	1⅞	1⅝	1¾	2	2¾	2½	2¾
Bobstay pendant...	Crucible steel	½	¾	1¼	1⅜	1¾	2	2¼	2½	2¾	3	3¼
Topmast backstays	Crucible steel	—	—	⅝	¾	1	1⅛	1¼	1⅝	1½	1⅝	1¾
Preventer back-stays	Crucible steel	—	—	⅝	¾	⅞	1	1½	1⅝	1½	1⅝	1¾
Topmast stay	Crucible steel	—	—	¾	⅞	1	1⅛	1¼	1⅝	1½	1⅝	1¾
Topping lifts	Flexible steel	⅜	½	⅝	¾	⅞	1	1¼	1⅝	1½	1⅝	1¾
Jib halyards	Flexible steel	—	—	⅞	1	1⅛	1¼	1½	1¾	1⅞	2	2¼
Topsail halyards...	Flexible steel	—	—	⅞	1	1⅛	1¼	1½	1¾	1⅞	2	2¼
Runners	Flexible steel	—	—	⅞	1	1⅛	1¼	1½	1¾	1⅞	2	2¼
Bobstay tackle ...	Flexible steel	—	—	⅞	1	1¼	1½	1¾	2	2¼	2⅝	2½
Jib tack	Flexible steel	⅜	½	⅞	1	1¼	1½	1¾	2	2¼	2⅝	2½
Throat halyards ...	Hemp*b*.........	½	¾	1¼	1½	2	2½	2¾	3¼	3½	3¾	4
Peak halyards	Hemp	¾	¾	½	¾	2	2½	2½	3	3¼	3½	4
Fore halyards *b* ...	Hemp	¾	½	½	¾	1½	1¾	2¼	2½	2¾	3	3¼
Fore sheets	Hemp	¾	1	1	1¼	1½	2	2¼	2½	2¾	3	3¼
Jib sheets...........	Hemp	—	—	1	1½	1¾	2¼	2½	2¾	3	3¼	3½
Purchases	Hemp	¾	1	1	1	1¼	1½	1¾	2	2¼	2½	2¾
Spinnaker and jib topsail gear	Hemp	¾	1	1	1	1¼	1½	1¾	2	2¼	2½	2¾
Spinnaker guys ...	Hemp	¾	1	1¼	1¼	1½	1¾	2	2¼	2½	2¾	3
Main sheet	Manilla	¾	1	1½	1¾	2	2	2½	2¾	3	3¼	3¼
Runner tackles ...	Manilla	—	—	1½	1½	1¾	2	2¼	2½	2¾	3	3¼
Topsail sheet	Manilla	—	—	1½	1¾	1¾	2	2¼	2½	2¾	3	3¼
Topping lift tackles	Manilla	¾	1	1¼	1¼	1½	2	2¼	2½	2¾	3	3¼
Diameter of rigging screws	Gn. mtl. & steel	⅜	½	½	⅝	¾	⅞	1¼	1¼	1⅜	1 7/16	1½
Ditto topmast back-stays..............	Gn. mtl. & steel	—	—	5/16	⅜	½	⅝	¾	⅞	1	1 1/16	1⅛

(*a*) One on each side only in 18ft. rater and 24ft. rater; two 30ft. rater and 36ft. rater. (*b*) Flexible steel in 1 to 5-rating (see Plate V.). Hemp or manilla in 18ft. rating. Manilla can in all cases be substituted for hemp if preferred. In 36ft. raters a double whip of 2in. manilla and 1¾in. manilla purchase is used. In 2·5 rating, 1 rating, and 0·5 rating, single whip manilla and purchase. (*c*) Double forestay.

BLOCKS FOR YACHTS BY THAMES TONNAGE.

The sizes given for blocks in the following table are for cutters and yawls up to 100 tons Thames tonnage (*see* Table VII., on page 44). If the tonnage exceeds 100 tons, the sizes will increase in the ratio shown in the table.

TABLE III.—SIZES OF BLOCKS FOR YACHTS OF VARIOUS SIZES.

Name of Block.	Description. Number. Double.	Description. Number. Single.	Tons. Cut. 3. Yawl 5. Size.	Tons. Cut. 5. Yawl 7. Size.	Tons. Cut. 10. Yawl 14. Size.	Tons. Cut. 15. Yawl 20. Size.	Tons. Cut. 20. Yawl 30. Size.	Tons. Cut. 30. Yawl 40. Size.	Tons. Cut. 40. Yawl 60. Size.	Tons. Cut. 60. Yawl 80. Size.	Tons. Cut. 80. Ywl. 100 Size.	Tons. Cut. 100. Ywl. 130 Size.
			Ins.	Ins.	Ins.	Ins.	Ins.	Ins.	Ins.	Ins.	Ins.	Ins.
IRON STROP BLOCKS.												
Throat halyards *a*	2	—	4	4½	5	5½	6	7	8	9	9½	10
Peak halyards	—	5	4	4½	5	5½	6	7	8	9	9½	10
Main sheet	1	1	4½	4½	5	5½	6	7	8	9	9½	10
Main sheet lead	—	2	3	3	4	4½	5	5½	6	6½	7	7½
Jib halyards	—	3	4	4½	5	5½	6	7	8	9	9½	10
Fore halyards	—	2	3	3	4	4½	5	6	6½	7	7½	8
Bobstay (iron blocks)	1	1	4	4½	5	5½	6	7	8	9	9½	10
Bowsprit shrouds *b*	2	2	6 & 3	6 & 3	6½ & 4	7 & 4½	7½ & 5	8 & 5½	8½ & 6	9 & 6½	9½ & 7	10 & 7½
Pendant blocks	—	2	3½	3½	4	4½	5	5½	6	6½	7	7½
Runner tackle *b*	2	2	6 & 3	6 & 3	6½ & 4	7 & 4½	7½ & 5	8 & 5½	8½ & 5½	9 & 6	9½ & 6½	10 & 7
Main outhaul	—	1	3	3	3½	4	4½	5	5½	6	6½	7
Topsail sheet (cheek)	—	1	3	3	3½	4	4½	5	5½	6	6½	7
Topmast backstays *c*	4	4	3	3	3½	4	4½	5	5½	6	6½	7
Preventer backstays	2	2	3	3	3½	4	4½	5	5½	6	6½	7
Preventer backstay whips	—	2	3	3	3½	4	4½	5	5½	6	6½	7
Jib tack	—	1	3	3	3½	3½	4	4½	5	5½	6	6½
Jib purchase	1	1	3	3¼	3½	4	4½	5	5½	6	6½	7
Jib purchase runner	—	1	—	—	—	—	—	—	5	6	7	8
Main purchase	1	1	3	3¼	3½	4	4½	5	5½	6	6½	7
Peak purchase	1	1	3	3¼	3½	4	4½	5	5½	6	6½	7
Topping lifts	—	2	3	3¼	—	4	4½	5	5½	6	6½	7
Topping lift purchase *d*	4	—	3	3	3½	4	4½	5	5½	6	6½	7
Spinnaker topping lift *e*	2	—	3	3	3½	4	4½	5	5½	6	6½	7
ROPE STROP BLOCKS.												
Jib topsail halyards	—	2	3	3	3½	4	4½	5	5½	6	6½	7
Spinnaker halyards	—	1	3	3	3½	4	4½	5	5½	6	6½	7
Spinnaker guy whips	—	2	3	3	3	3½	4	4½	5	5½	6	6½
Trysail sheets	2	2	4	4½	5	5½	6	6½	7	7½	8	8½
Fore sheets	—	4	4	3½	4	5	5½	6	6½	7	7½	8
Reef-tackle (fiddle dbl.)	1	1	6 & 3	6 & 3¼	6½ & 4	7	7½	8	8½	9	9½	10
Boom guy	1	1	—	—	3	3½	4	4½	5½	6½	7	7½
Tack tackles	3	3	3	3	3½	4	4½	5	5½	6	6½	7
Burton	—	2	—	—	3	4	4½	5	5½	6	6½	7
Gaff topsail sheet whip	—	1	3	3	3½	4	4½	5	5½	6	6½	7
Downhauls (forward)	—	3	—	—	3	4	4½	5	5½	6	6½	7
Dead-eyes *f*	—	—	3¾	3¾	4	4¼	4½	5	5¾	6½	7½	8½

(*a*) If a throat purchase is used (as it generally is in racing yachts of 10 tons and over, the upper throat halyard block is a threefold, as one part of the halyards is required for the purchase, and another for the hauling part.

(*b*) The double blocks on the bowsprit shrouds and runner tackle are fiddles.

(*c*) A five-tonner has only four single blocks for backstays, two on each side.

(*d*) These would be single up to 20 tons.

(*e*) These would be single up to 10 tons.

(*f*) Some five-tonners have only two shrouds on each side; 10 tons and upwards three shrouds; above 60 tons four shrouds for racing.

The sizes of cordage are arranged suitably for Thames tonnage, but Table VII., page 44, should be consulted before deciding upon the cordage.

TABLE IV.—SIZES OF CORDAGE FOR CUTTER AND YAWL YACHTS OF VARIOUS SIZES BY THAMES TONNAGE.

NAME OF ROPE.	TONS. Cut. 3. Yawl 5.	TONS. Cut. 5. Yawl 7.	TONS. Cut. 10. Yawl 14.	TONS. Cut. 15. Yawl 20.	TONS. Cut. 20. Yawl 30.	TONS. Cut. 30. Yawl 40.	TONS. Cut. 40. Yawl 60.	TONS. Cut. 60. Yawl 80.	TONS. Cut. 80. Ywl. 100	TONS. Cut. 100. Ywl. 130
	Cf.	Cf.	Cf.	Cf.	Cf.	Cf.	Cf.	Cf.	Cf.	Cf.
	Ins.	Ins.	Ins.	Ins.	Ins.	Ins.	Ins.	Ins.	Ins.	Ins.
Throat halyards	1½	1¾	2	2¼	2½	2¾	3	3¼	3½	3¾
Peak halyards	1½	1¾	2	2¼	2½	2¾	3	3¼	3½	3¾
Main sheet (manilla)	1½	1½	1¾	2	2¼	2½	2¾	3	3¼	3½
Fore halyards	1	1¼	1½	1¾	1¾	2	2¼	2½	2¾	3
Bobstay tackle †	1½	1¾	2¼	2½	2¾	3	3¼	3½	3¾	4
Bowsprit shrouds tackle	1	1¼	1¼	1½	1¾	2	2¼	2½	2¾	3
Pendant	1½	1¾	2	2¼	2½	2¾	3	3¼	3½	3¾
Runner	1½	1¾	2	2½	2¾	3	3¼	3½	3¾	4
Runner tackle	1	1¼	1½	1¾	1¾	2	2¼	2½	2¾	3
Main outhaul	1	1	1¼	1½	1½	1¾	2	2¼	2½	2¾
Reef pendants	1¾	1¾	2	2¼	2½	2½	3	3¼	3½	3¾
Topsail sheet	1	1¼	1½	1¾	2	2¼	2½	2¾	3	3¼
Topmast backstay tackles	1	1¼	1¼	1½	1½	1¾	2	2½	2¾	3
Preventer backstay tackles	1	1¼	1¼	1½	1½	1¾	2	2½	2¾	3
Preventer backstay whips	1	—	1¼	1½	1½	1¾	2	2½	2¾	3
Jib tack	1¾	1¾	2	2¼	1¼ *w*	1½ *w*	1¾ *w*	2 *w*	2¼ *w*	2½ *w*
Jib halyards (chain)	3/16	3/16	3/16	¼	5/16	⅜	⅜	7/16	½	½
Jib halyards (manilla)	1¾	1¾	2	2¼	2½	2¾	3	3¼	3½	3¾
Jib sheets	1½	1½	1¾	2	2¼	2½	2¾	3	3¼	3½
Jib purchase	1	1¼	1¼	1½	1½	1¾	1¾	2	2¼	2½
Jib purchase runner	—	—	—	—	—	—	1½ *w*	1¾ *w*	2 *w*	2¼ *w*
Throat purchase	1	1¼	1¼	1½	1½	1¾	1¾	2	2¼	2½
Peak purchase	1	1¼	1¼	1½	1½	1¾	1¾	2	2¼	2½
Topping lifts	1½	1¾	2	2½	2¾	3	3¼	3½	3¾	4
Topping lift purchase	1	1¼	1¼	1½	1½	1¾	1¾	2	2¼	2½
Jib topsail halyards	1	1¼	1¼	1½	1½	1¾	1¾	2	2¼	2½
Spinnaker halyards	1	1¼	1¼	1½	1½	1¾	1¾	2	2¼	2¼
Spinnaker guy whips	1	1¼	1¼	1½	1¾	2	2½	2¾	2¾	2¾
Spinnaker topping lift	1	1¼	1¼	1½	1½	1¾	1¾	2	2¼	2½
Trysail sheets	1	1¼	1¼	1½	1¾	2	2¼	2¾	3	3¼
Fore sheets	1	1¼	1¼	1½	1¾	2	2¼	2¾	3	3¼
Reef tackle (fiddle)	1	1	1¼	1½	1½	1¾	1¾	2	2¼	2½
Boom guy	1	1	1¼	1½	1½	1¾	1¾	2	2¼	2½
Tack tackles	1	1	1¼	1½	1½	1½	1¾	1¾	2	2¼
Burton	—	—	—	1½	1½	1¾	1¾	2	2¼	2½
Gaff topsail sheet whip	1½	1¾	2	2¼	2½	2¾	3	3¼	3½	3¾
Downhauls, peak, fore sail, and jib	1	1	1	1	1¼	1½	1½	1¾	2	2
Lanyards	1	1	1¼	1½	1¾	2	2¼	2½	2¾	3
Topsail halyards	1¼	1¼	1½	1¾	1¾	2	2¼	2½	2¾	3
Topsail trip halyards	1	1	1¼	1½	1½	1¾	1¾	2	2¼	2½

(*w*) Flexible steel wire jib tack and jib purchase runner. Cf. Circumference.

In the case of jib halyards the size of the iron of the link is given.

† Or equivalent in flexible steel wire.

TABLE V.—CIRCUMFERENCE IN INCHES OF STEEL WIRE FOR STANDING RIGGING FOR CUTTERS AND YAWLS.

NAME.	TONS. Cut. 3 or 5 Yawl 7.	TONS. Cut. 10. Yawl 14.	TONS. Cut. 15. Yawl 20.	TONS. Cut. 20. Yawl 30.	TONS. Cut. 30. Yawl 40.	TONS. Cut. 40. Yawl 60.	TONS. Cut. 60. Yawl 80.	TONS. Cut. 80. Ywl. 100	TONS. Cut. 100. Ywl. 120	TONS. Cut. 120 Ywl 140
Shrouds	1¼	1⅜	1⅜	1¾	2¼	2⅜	3	3	3⅛	3⅝
Pendants	1¼	1⅜	1¾	2	2¼	2⅜	3¼	3⅛	3¾	4
Bowsprit shrouds	1¼	1⅜	1¾	2	2¼	2⅜	2¾	3	3¼	3⅛
Forestay	1⅜	1¾	2	2¼	2⅜	2¾	3¼	3⅜	3⅝	4
Bobstay pendant	1⅜	1¾	2	2¼	2⅜	2¾	3¼	3⅜	3¾	4
Topmast stay	⅞	⅞	1	1	1¼	1⅜	1¾	2	2¼	2⅜
Topmast backstay	¾	⅞	⅞	1	1¼	1⅜	1¾	2	2¼	2⅜
Preventer backstay ...	¾	⅞	1	1	1¼	1⅜	1¾	2	2¼	2⅜
No. of shrouds a side...	2	2	3	3	3	3	3	4	4	4
No. of backstays a side	1	1	2	2	2	2	2	2	2	2
Copper bobstay bar ...	⅝	¾	⅞	1	1¼	1⅝	1⅜	1¾	2	2¼

NOTE.—*Steel Wire.*—Although the matter is referred to farther on under the head of "Rigging," that in using steel wire of "equivalent strength" instead of iron, it would be always safe to choose a size next above that given in the table. For instance, the size of iron wire given for an 80 tons cutter's shroud is 3in., the equivalent strength for steel wire is 2¼in.; but it would be better to choose 2½in. if the yacht is sparred up to the extreme limit given in Table VII.

TABLE VI.—RELATIVE SIZE AND STRENGTH OF HEMP, IRON, AND STEEL ROPE.

Hemp Rope.		Iron Wire Rope.		Steel Wire Rope.		Equivalent Strength.	
Circumference.	Pounds weight per Fathom.	Circumference.	Pounds weight per Fathom.	Circumference.	Pounds weight per Fathom.	Working Load in Cwts.	Breaking strain in Tons.
2¾	2	1	1	...	...	6	2
...	...	1⅛	1½	1	1	9	3
3¾	4	1⅜	2	...	...	12	4
...	...	1½	2½	1½	1½	15	5
4½	5	1⅝	3	...	...	18	6
...	...	2	3½	1⅝	2	21	7
5½	7	2⅛	4	1¾	2½	24	8
...	...	2¼	4½	...	...	27	9
6	9	2⅜	5	1⅞	3	30	10
...	...	2½	5½	...	...	33	11
6½	10	2⅝	6	2	3½	36	12
...	...	2¾	6½	2⅛	4	39	13
7	12	2⅞	7	2¼	4½	42	14
...	...	3	7½	...	...	45	15
7½	14	3⅛	8	2⅜	5	48	16
...	...	3¼	8½	...	...	51	17
8	16	3⅜	9	2½	5½	54	18
...	...	3½	10	2⅝	6	60	20
8½	18	3⅝	11	2¾	6½	66	22
...	...	3¾	12	...	...	72	24
9½	22	3⅞	13	3¼	8	78	26
10	25	4	14	...	...	84	28
...	...	4¼	15	3⅜	9	90	30
11	30	4⅜	16	...	...	96	32
...	...	4½	18	3½	10	108	36
12	36	4⅝	20	3¾	12	120	40

THE SIZES OF RIGGING AND BLOCKS NOT UNIFORMLY GOVERNED BY TONNAGE.

It is obvious that the strength of the rope and size of the blocks must largely depend upon the size of the spars and area of sail; and as these vary very considerably as between racing and cruising yachts of equal tonnage, it would be impossible to fix on sizes which will be suitable for yachts of all tonnages without reference to the spars and area of sail they are to carry. Again, the "tonnages" for any given length of the modern racing yachts differ so considerably from the yachts of a decade ago (even among themselves according to their beam) that the tonnage test for any purpose of comparison may be very misleading. For instance, the Britannia cutter of 1893 is 88ft. on the water line and of 221 Thames tons, has a mainmast 64ft. deck to hounds, and her main halyard blocks are 13in. The racing cutter Genesta of 1885 is 81ft. on the water line and of 80 tons, and has a mast 52ft. deck to hounds, and a main boom 70ft. long. These are about the lengths of spars which a cruising cutter of 130 tons would carry, and are larger than provided for in the tables. Genesta's throat halyard blocks are 10½in., and peak 10in.; rope for throat halyards 4in., and peak 3¾in. These would be the sizes for 120 tons if a column for that tonnage had been provided in Tables III. and IV.

In all cases the rigging, &c., for racing yachts should be decided by Tables I. and II.; and for cruising yachts Table VII. should be consulted before fixing on sizes for the blocks and cordage.

TABLE VII.—DIMENSIONS OF SPARS TO WHICH THE BLOCKS AND CORDAGE GIVEN IN THE PRECEDING TABLES ARE SUITABLE.

NAME.	Tons. Cut. 3. Yawl 5.	Tons. Cut. 5. Yawl 7.	Tons. Cut. 10. Yawl 14.	Tons. Cut. 15. Yawl 20.	Tons. Cut. 20. Yawl 30.	Tons. Cut. 30. Yawl 40.	Tons. Cut. 40. Yawl 60.	Tons. Cut. 60. Yawl 80.	Tons. Cut. 80. Ywl 100	Tons. Cut. 100. Ywl 130
	Ft.	Ft.	Ft.	Ft.	Ft.	Ft.	Ft.	Ft.	Ft.	Ft.
Mast, deck to hounds...	21	23	27	30	34	37	40	44	47	50
Topmast, fid to hounds.	17	19	24	28	29	30	33	36	40	44
Main boom	27	29	33	38	43	47	51	55	61	68
Main gaff	18	20	22	25	28	30	33	36	40	45
Bowsprit outboard	16	17	18	21	24	25	27	30	32	34
Topsail yards {	27	30	35	36	37	38	39	41	43	46
{	18	20	21	22	23	24	25	26	28	30
Spinnaker boom	30	35	40	42	44	45	46	50	54	58

TABLE VIII.—SCHOONERS.

CIRCUMFERENCE IN INCHES OF STEEL WIRE FOR STANDING RIGGING.

R. Racer. C. Cruiser.	Tons. R. 20. C. 30.	Tons. R. 30. C. 40.	Tons. R. 40. C. 60.	Tons. R. 50. C. 75.	Tons. R. 75. C. 100.	Tons. R. 100. C. 140.	Tons. R. 125. C. 180.	Tons. R. 150. C. 220.	Tons. R. 175. C. 250.	Tons. R. 200. C. 275.
Shrouds	1¼	1½	1¾	2¼	2½	3	3	3¼	3½	4
Pendants	1¼	1½	2	2¼	2½	3¼	3½	3½	4	4¼
Bowsprit shrouds	1¼	1½	2	2¼	2½	2¾	3	3¼	3½	3¾
Forestay	1¾	2	2¼	2½	2¾	3¼	3½	3½	4	4¼
Bobstay pendant	1¾	2	2¼	2½	2¾	3¼	3½	3½	4	4¼
Topmast stay	¾	1	1	1¼	1½	1½	2	2¼	2¼	2¾
Topmast backstay	¾	¾	1	1¼	1½	1½	2	2¼	2¼	2½
Topmast preventer backstay	¾	1	1	1¼	1½	1½	2	2¼	2¼	2½
No. of shrouds a side	2	3	3	3	3	3	3	3	3	3
No. of backstays a side	1	2	2	2	2	2	2	2	2	2
Copper bobstay bar	¾	¾	1	1¼	1¼	1¼	1¼	2	2¼	2¼

TABLE IX.—SCHOONERS.

MAINMAST.

IRON STROP BLOCKS.

R. Racer. C. Cruiser. NAME OF BLOCK.	Number Double.	Number Single.	Tons R. 20. C. 20. Size.	Tons R. 30. C. 40. Size.	Tons R. 40. C. 60. Size.	Tons R. 50. C. 75. Size.	Tons R. 75. C. 100. Size.	Tons R. 100. C. 140. Size.	Tons R. 125. C. 180. Size.	Tons R. 150. C. 220. Size.	Tons R. 175. C. 250. Size.	Tons R. 200. C. 275. Size
			Ins.	Ins.	Ins.	Ins.	Ins.	Ins.	Ins.	Ins.	Ins.	Ins.
Throat halyards a	2	—	4½	5	6	7	8	9	9½	10	10½	11
Peak halyards	5	1	4½	5	6	7	8	9	9½	10	10½	11
Peak downhaul	—	1	3½	4	4	4½	4½	5	5	5	5	5
Main sheet	2	—	4½	5	6	7	8	9	9½	10	10½	11
Main sheet lead	—	2	4	4½	5	5½	6	6½	7	7½	8	8½
Pendant	—	2	4	4½	5	5½	6	6½	7	7½	8	8½
Runner tackle b	2	2	4	5 & 4½	6 & 5	7 & 5½	8 & 6	9 & 6½	9½ & 7	10 & 7½	10½ & 8	11 & 8½
Outhaul	—	1	3½	4	4½	5	5½	6	6½	7	7½	8
Topsail halyards	—	1	3½	4	4½	5	5½	6	6½	7	7½	8
Topsail sheet	—	1	3½	4	4½	5	5½	6	6½	7	7½	8
Topmast stay purchase	1	1	3½	4	4½	5	5½	6	6½	7	7½	8
Topmast backstays	4	4	3½	4	4½	5	5½	6	6½	7	7½	8
Preventer backstays	2	2	3½	4	4½	5	5½	6	6½	7	7½	8
Preventer backstay whips	—	2	3½	4	4½	5	5½	6	6½	7	7½	8
Throat purchase	1	1	3½	4	4½	5	5½	6	6½	7	7½	8
Peak purchase	1	1	3½	4	4½	5	5½	6	6½	7	7½	8
Topping lifts	—	4	3½	4	4½	5	5½	6	6½	7	7½	8
Topping lift purchase	2	2	3½	4	4½	5	5½	6	6½	7	7½	8
Spinnaker topping lift c	2	—	3½	4	4½	5	5½	6	6½	7	7½	8

ROPE STROP BLOCKS.

NAME OF BLOCK.	Number Double.	Number Single.	R. 20. C. 20.	R. 30. C. 40.	R. 40. C. 60.	R. 50. C. 75.	R. 75. C. 100.	R. 100. C. 140.	R. 125. C. 180.	R. 150. C. 220.	R. 175. C. 250.	R. 200. C. 275.
Reef tackle d	1	1	5½ & 3½	7 & 4	7½ & 4½	8 & 5	8½ & 5½	9 & 6	9½ & 6½	10 & 7	10½ & 7½	11 &
Tack tackles	3	3	3½	4	4½	5	5½	6	6½	7	7½	8
Spinnaker halyards	—	1	3½	4	4½	5	5½	6	6½	7	7½	8
Spinnaker guy whip	—	1	3	3	3½	4	4½	5	5½	6	6½	7
Topsail sheet whip	—	1	3½	4	4½	5	5½	6	6½	7	7½	8
Topmast staysail halyards	—	1	3	3½	4	5	5½	6	6½	7	7½	8
Topmast staysail tack	—	1	3	3½	4	5	5½	5	5½	6	6½	7
Topmast staysail sheet	—	1	3	3½	4	5	5½	6	6½	7	7½	8
Trysail sheets	2	2	5	5½	6	6½	7	7½	8	8½	9	9
Boom guy	1	1	3½	4	4½	5	5½	6	6½	7	7½	8
Dead-eyes e	—	12	3½	4	4½	5	5½	6	6½	7	7½	8

(a) The upper throat halyard block will be treble.
(b) Fiddle blocks.
(c) Single blocks under 75 tons.
(d) Fiddle blocks.
(e) Only two shrouds a-side under 40 tons.

Table X.—SCHOONERS.

FOREMAST.

IRON STROP BLOCKS.

R. Racer. C. Cruiser. / NAME OF BLOCK.	Description. Number. Double.	Description. Number. Single.	Tons R. 20. C. 30. Size.	Tons R. 30. C. 40. Size.	Tons R. 40. C. 60. Size.	Tons R. 50. C. 75. Size.	Tons R. 75. C. 100. Size.	Tons R. 100. C. 140. Size.	Tons R. 125. C. 180. Size.	Tons R. 150. C. 2[illegible]0. Size.	Tons R. 175. C. 250. Size.	Tons R. 200 C. 275. Size.
			Ins.	Ins.	Ins.	Ins.	Ins.	Ins.	Ins.	Ins.	Ins.	Ins.
Throat halyards	2	—	4½	5	6	7	8	9	9½	10	10½	11
Peak halyards	5	—	4½	5	6	7	8	9	9½	10	10½	11
Downhaul	—	1	3½	4	4½	5	5	5	5	5	5	5
Vang	—	1	3½	4	4½	5	5½	6	6½	7	7	7
Fore sheet..............	—	2	3½	4	4½	5	5½	6	6½	7	7½	8
Fore sheet purchases	2	2	3½	4	4½	5	5½	6	6½	7	7½	8
Pendant.................	—	1	4	4½	5	5½	6	6½	7	7½	8	8½
Runner tackle *a*	2	2	6½ & 3½	7 & 4	7½ & 4½	8 & 5	8½ & 5½	9 & 6	9½ & 6½	10 & 7	10½ & 7½	11 & 8
Topsail halyards	—	1	3½	4	4½	5	5½	6	6½	7	7½	8
Topsail sheets (cheek)	—	2	4	4½	5	5½	6	6½	7	7½	7½	8
Sheet lead..............	—	2	3½	4	4½	5	5½	6	6½	7	7½	8
Topmast backstays ...	4	4	3½	4	4½	5	5½	6	6½	7	7½	8
Preventer backstays ..	2	2	3½	4	4½	5	5½	6	6½	7	7½	8
Throat purchase	1	1	—	—	—	—	5½	6	6½	7	7½	8
Peak purchase	1	1	3½	4	4½	5	5½	6	6½	7	7½	8
Spinnaker topping lift	2	—	3½	4	4½	5	5½	6	6½	7	7½	8
Fore staysail sheets	—	2	3½	4	4½	5	5½	6	6½	7	7½	8
„ „ purchases	—	4	3½	4	4½	5	5½	6	6½	7	7½	8
Fore staysail halyards	—	2	3½	4	4½	5	5½	6	6½	7	7½	8
Downhaul	—	1	3½	4	4	5	5	5½	6	6½	7	7
Bobstay.................	1	1	4½	5	6	7	8	9	9½	10	10½	11
Bowsprit shrouds......	2	2	6½ & 3½	7 & 4	7½ & 4½	8 & 5	8½ & 5½	9 & 6	9½ & 6½	10 & 7	10½ & 7½	11 & 8
Jib halyards	—	8	3½	4	4½	5	5½	6	6½	7	7½	8
Jib tack................	—	1	3½	4	4½	5	5½	6	6½	7	7½	8
Jib purchase runner	—	1	—	—	—	5	5½	6	6½	7	7½	8
Jib purchase...........	1	1	3½	4	4½	5	5½	6	6½	7	7½	8
Dead-eyes..............	12	12	4	4½	5	5½	6	6½	7	7½	8	8½
			ROPE STROP BLOCKS.									
Spinnaker halyards...	—	1	3½	4	4½	5	5½	6	6½	7	7½	8
Spinnaker guy whip...	—	1	3	3	4	4½	5	5½	6	6½	7	7
Trysail sheets	2	2	5	5½	6	6½	7	7½	8	8½	9	9½
Jib topsail halyards...	—	1	3½	4	4½	5	5½	6	6½	7	7½	8
Fore staysail sheets ..	2	2	3½	4	4½	5	5½	6	6½	7	7½	8
Jib sheets..............	—	2	—	—	4½	5	5½	6	6½	7	7½	8
Burton	—	2	3	3½	4	4½	5	5½	5½	6	6½	7
Downhaul (forward)..	—	1	8	4	3½	4	5	5	5	5	5	5

(*a*) The double blocks are fiddles.

Table XI.—SCHOONERS.

SIZES OF CORDAGE.

R. Racers. C. Cruiser.	Tons. R. 20. C. 30.	Tons. R. 30. C. 40.	Tons. R. 40. C. 60.	Tons. R. 50. C. 75.	Tons. R. 75. C. 100.	Tons. R. 100. C. 140.	Tons. R. 125. C. 180.	Tons. R. 150. C. 220.	Tons. R. 175. C. 250.	Tons. R. 200. C. 275.
Name of Rope.	Cf.	Cf.	Cf.	Cf.	Cf.	Cf.	Cf.	Cf.	Cf.	Cf.
	Ins.	Ins.	Ins.	Ins.	Ins.	Ins.	Ins.	Ins.	Ins.	Ins.
Main and fore halyards	1¾	2	2½	2¾	3	3¼	3½	3¾	4	4¼
Fore staysail halyards..	1½	1⅛	1⅛	1¾	1¾	2	2¼	2½	2¾	3
Jib halyards *a*...........	1¾ (3/16)	2 (3/16)	2¼ (¼)	2½ (5/16)	2¾ (5/16)	3 (⅜)	3¼ (⅜)	3½ (⅜)	3¾	4
Topsail halyards.........	1¼	1⅛	1¾	1¾	2	2½	2¾	3	3¼	3½
Topsail trip halyards...	1	1	1¼	1⅛	1⅛	1¾	2	2¼	2½	2¾
Jib topsail halyards ...	1	1¼	1¼	1⅛	1¾	1¾	2	2¼	2½	2¾
Maintopmast staysail halyards	1	1¼	1¼	1⅛	1¾	1¾	2	2¼	2½	2¾
Spinnaker halyards and topping lift; also fore vang....................	1	1¼	1⅛	1⅛	1¾	1¾	2	2¼	2½	2¾
Main sheet	1⅛	1¾	2	2½	3	3¼	3½	3¾	4	4¼
Fore sheet	1¾	2	2½	2¾	3¼	3¾	4¼	4¾	5	5¼
Fore staysail sheets ...	1⅛	1¾	2	2½	3	3¼	3½	3¾	4	4¼
Jib sheets.................	2¼	2½	2¾	3	3¼	3½	3¾	4	4¼	4½
Topsail sheets...........	1⅛	1⅛	1¾	1¾	2	2¼	2½	2¾	3	3¼
Jib topsail sheets	1	1¼	1¼	1⅛	1⅞	1¾	2	2¼	2½	2¾
Maintopmast staysail sheets	1	1¼	1¼	1⅛	1¾	1¾	2	2¼	2½	2¾
Spinnaker sheets.........	1	1¼	1¼	1⅛	1¾	1¾	2	2¼	2½	2¾
Trysail sheets...........	1¾	1¾	2	2¼	2½	2¾	3	3¼	3½	3¾
Jib tack	2	2¼	1¼ *w*	1⅛ *w*	1¾ *w*	2 *w*	2¼	2½ *w*	2¾ *w*	3 *w*
Tack tackles	1¼	1¼	1⅛	1⅛	1¾	1⅞	2	2¼	2½	2¾
Main, fore, and jib purchases	1¼	1¼	1⅛	1⅛	1¾	1¾	2	2¼	2½	2¾
Downhauls	1	1¼	1¼	1⅛	1¾	1¾	2	2	2	2
Burton....................	1	1¼	1⅛	1¾	2	2¼	2½	2¾	3	3¼
Bowsprit shrouds tackle	1¼	1¼	1⅛	1⅛	1¾	1¾	2	2¼	2½	2¾
Fore sheet purchases...	1¼	1¼	1⅛	1⅛	1⅞	1¾	2	2¼	2½	2¾
Bobstay tackle	1⅛	1¾	2	2½	3	3½	3¾	4	4¼	4½
Runners (wire)	1¼	1⅛	1¾	1¾	2	2¼	2½	2¾	3	3¼
Runners (hemp or manilla)	2	2¼	2½	2¾	3	3¼	3½	3¾	4	4¼
Runner tackles	1¼	1¼	1⅛	1⅛	1¾	1¾	2	2¼	2½	2¾
Topping lifts	1¼	1¾	2	2½	3	3½	3¾	4	4¼	4½
Topping lift purchase...	1¼	1¼	1⅛	1⅛	1¾	1¾	2	2¼	2½	2¾
Reef pendants...........	1⅛	1¾	2	2½	3	3½	3¾	4	4¼	4½
Reef tackle	1¼	1¼	1⅛	1⅛	1¾	1¾	2	2¼	2½	2¾
Boom guy	1⅛	1¾	2	2½	3	3½	3¾	4	4¼	4½
Boom guy purchase ...	1¼	1¼	1⅛	1⅛	1¾	1⅞	2	2¼	2½	2¾
Lanyards.................	1¾	2	2¼	2½	2¾	3	3¼	3½	3¾	4

The remarks on page 43 apply equally to schooners, and the tables of blocks and cordage in Tables IX., X., XI., will be suitable for schooners rigged pretty much as those mentioned in Table XII. are.

(*a*) The small figures in brackets are the size of the links for chain halyards.

(*w*) Wire rope.

TABLE XII.—DIMENSIONS OF YACHTS AND SPARS.

Name, with dates when the spars were carried.	Rig.	Length of L.W.L.	Extreme Beam.	Extreme draught of water.	Length of Mainmast, Deck to Hounds.	Length of Bowsprit outside Stem Head.	Length of Main Boom, Mast to Pin of Out-haul.	Length of Main Gaff.	Length of Topmast Fid to Halyard Sheave.	Area of Mainsail.	Area of Head Sail, Y.R.A.	*Total Sail Area, Y.R.A.
		FT.	FT.	FT.	FT.	FT.	FT.	FT.	FT.	SQ. FT	SQ. FT	SQ. FT
Amphitrite (1890) ..	s	94·5	19·4	...	...	...	64·0	37·5	...	3158	2618	8297
Waterwitch (1887)...	s	95·7	19·3	12·2	58·0	33·0	62·0	36·0	37·0	2868	2649	8090
Egeria (1880)	s	93·7	19·2	12·5	58·0	32·0	66·0	38·5	35·0	3040	2600	8500
Pantomime (1876) ...	s	91·5	19·3	12·0	57·5	31·5	58·0	35·0	34·0	2622	2350	7870
Miranda (1879)	s	86·7	18·9	13·0	58·8	27·5	64·8	35·5	34·0	3075	2136	7700
Dracæna (1876) b ...	s	80·0	18·0	10·0	52·0	28·0	48·0	30·0	30·0	2040	2008	5920
Flying Cloud (1872)..	s	73·5	15·7	9·5	46·0	23·5	46·5	28·0	28·0	1690	1920	5500
Latona (1882)........	y	93·6	20·2	12·5	58·3	39·0	63·0	48·0	48·5	3390	3900	8880
Florinda (1878)	y	85·7	19·3	11·9	54·5	36·0	56·5	42·5	44·0	2923	3300	8280
Jullanar (1877)	y	99·0	16·9	13·8	53·0	24·5	56·5	42·0	38·5	2737	2900	7800
Constance (1885) b...	y	82·8	18·2	12·0	49·0	28·5	53·0	37·5	39·0	2330	2600	6190
Lethe (1890)	y	93·3	19·6	...	...	...	63·2	40·3	...	2936	3454	7958
Caroline (1878) b ...	y	75·0	16·1	11·5	43·5	31·0	50·7	37·0	35·0	1950	2340	5050
Foxglove (1890)......	y	61·1	13·9	...	37·8	23·0	43·2	30·5	34·5	1451	1592	3919
Oimara (1872)	c	95·0	19·9	13·0	64·0	46·0	72·0	49·0	49·5	3960	4500	9520
Thistle (1887)	c	86·4	22·2	...	...	35·0	81·4	51·5	...	4563	3770	9957
Britannia (1896)......	c	87·8	23·6	...	64·0	...	91·0	55·0	...	5165	3889	10057
Meteor (1896)	c	89·0	24·3	...	69·0	...	96·6	58·7	...	5910	4718	12327
Isolde (1896)	c	60·0	17·0	11·5	41·5	...	60·5	34·0	...	2110	1292	4006
Saint (1896)	c	46·9	12·2	...	33·2	...	51·5	28·1	...	1508	1026	2976
Satanita	c	98·1	24·7	16·3	62·0	...	89·3	54·0	...	4972	3802	10048
Vigilant (1895)	c	87·3	26·0	14·0	...	...	96·7	53·5	...	5695	4397	11588
Iverna (1890)	c	83·5	19·0	13·0	...	...	77·9	47·3	...	3856	3410	8458
Valkyrie (1890)	c	69·2	15·9	...	...	...	69·0	42·2	...	3047	2736	6707
Yarana (1890)	c	65·7	14·9	...	...	...	62·7	40·6	...	2624	2276	5651
Vanduara (1890) ...	c	81·3	16·2	12·4	48·5	31·0	68·3	43·3	42·7	3170	2930	7283
Genesta (1887)	c	81·0	15·0	13·0	52·0	35·0	70·0	46·0	47·5	3090	3360	7646
Marjorie (1884)	c	75·4	14·5	...	...	...	...	...	...	2964	2928	7022
Annasona (1883)......	c	64·3	11·9	10·7	41·0	31·0	55·0	37·0	38·0	2130	2104	4986
Creole (1890)	c	59·3	13·3	12·1	...	...	56·1	34·0	...	1881	1570	4008
Carina (1895)	c	60·8	15·8	12·8	...	...	60·0	35·3	...	2167	1306	3947
Vendetta (1894)	c	60·5	17·1	11·8	...	...	61·0	34·5	...	2151	1282	3963
Tara (1883).............	c	66·0	11·5	11·5	42·5	30·0	58·0	39·5	40·0	2270	2150	5280
Freda (20 tons) (1881)	c	49·0	9·8	9·5	34·5	24·0	43·0	28·0	30·0	1450	1480	3150
Vanessa (20 tons) ('78)	c	47·0	9·8	7·8	31·5	24·0	39·0	27·5	26·5	1150	1170	2720
Vreda (1889)	c	45·4	10·1	...	34·0	c 21·0	42·6	26·0	...	1230	1024	2641
Stephanie (1895) ...	c	46·7	12·3	10·9	33·0	10·0	49·0	28·8	23·4	1497	689	2565
Dragon III. (1894) ..	c	46·1	13·2	9·0	...	...	47·0	27·0	...	1354	874	2600
Audrey (1895)	c	44·03	13·16	9·0	...	...	48·5	27·0	...	1403	976	2740
Asphodel (1894)......	c	46·6	12·3	9·1	...	...	46·2	27·2	...	1352	876	2576
Luna (1894)	c	46·1	13·0	9·7	...	...	47·8	26·5	...	1348	916	2599
Ulerin (1884)	c	41·5	7·2	...	29·0	19·0	38·5	25·0	28·0	1040	1049	2492
Decima (1889)........	c	35·7	10·2	8·5	31·0	...	34·5	23·8	...	905	497	1679
Lilith (1894)	c	35·2	10·6	7·5	...	...	38·0	21·5	...	866	568	1695
Archee (1890)........	c	30·4	9·6	...	...	...	30·6	19·5	...	675	305	980
Flat Fish (1894) ...	L	32·0	10·0	7·5	...	...	31·8	32·4	...	687	232	919
Gareth (1894)........	L	28·9	6·9	6·7	...	...	24·9	24·5	...	442	97	538
Meneen (1894)	L	24·8	7·0	6·0	...	...	27·2	27·0	...	474	123	603
Humming Bird (1890)	L	25·9	7·3	5·7	25·5	7·0	23·5	34·2	...	432	135	567
Babe (1890)	L	26·8	6·8	5·9	...	...	23·6	22·8	...	418	135	553
Dolphin (1890)	L	25·7	7·4	5·8	...	...	23·5	23·5	...	428	152	580
Doris (1890)	c	33·62	5·73	6·3	21·5	...	35·0	21·3	...	782	686	1730
Currytush (1885).....	c	28·53	4·7	5·5	23·0	...	26·2	18·0	.	539	422	1047

* This includes topsails.   Several accurate sail plans will be found among the plates.

b Cruiser.   c From fore end of L.W.L. to cranse iron.

STANDING RIGGING.

MAIN RIGGING.

The usual plan of measuring off the rigging for a yacht is to make a spar plan to scale—that is, a plan showing a broadside view of the yacht with all her spars in their places, as shown by Plate I. and Fig. 1. The latter plan, Fig. 1, is necessary to obtain the correct lengths of the lower-mast shrouds and topmast backstays, as merely taking the length deck to hounds makes no allowance for the "spread" the rigging is to have. A further allowance must be made for the eyes of the rigging going one over the other, and this allowance will be equal to twice the diameter of a shroud. (*See* Plate VII.) For instance, the eye of the starboard fore shroud is put over the masthead first; then the port fore shroud, which follows, must be cut longer than the starboard rigging to the extent of twice the diameter of a shroud (twice the diameter is equal to two-thirds of the circumference, the circumference being three times the diameter). The second and third starboard shrouds form a pair, and the allowance will be four times the diameter; and so on. (The forestay goes over all, resting on the throat or peak halyard bolt.) (*See* page 30, Fig. 4, and Plate VII.) For the eye and splice an allowance equal to one and a half the circumference of the masthead must be made; for the dead-eye an allowance equal to one and a half the circumference of the same. The eye to go over the masthead should be one and a quarter the circumference of the mast at the hounds; the eye at the other end of the shroud should be one and one-eighth the circumference of the dead-eye, so that the latter could be removed if split or damaged, and replaced. The length for each shroud is measured from the top of the bolster to the dead-eyes; the drift or space between the upper and lower dead-eyes, or from the channel to the top of the upper dead-eye, will be about the height of the bulwark.

There are two plans for fitting the shrouds, one known as "single eye," and the other as "pairs." In the former plan each shroud has its own eye; but when shrouds are fitted in pairs the wire goes from one dead-eye up round the masthead, and down to the next dead-eye (on the same side). A wire seizing close up to the bolster, round both shrouds, forms the eye. This is the most generally used plan, and the only objection to it is that if the eye bursts a pair of shrouds are gone; and even if one shroud burst, the strain on the remaining one might prove too much for the seizing. This, however, can be said in favour of the "pair" plan, that there are just half the number of eyes to go over the masthead, and consequently there is a trifle less weight aloft and a neater-looking

E

masthead. If there are four shrouds a side two "pairs" are fitted; if three one "pair" and one "single."

Formerly, in the case of three shrouds a side, instead of one single eye and one "pair," two "pairs" were fitted, the aftermost shroud doing duty as a pendant; this plan has been abandoned, as the seizing so constantly burst in consequence of the great angle the pendant made with the shroud.

Recently mast head shrouds have come into use again for racing yachts, and the manner of fitting them and the crosstrees in a 20-rater is shown on Plate VII., which represents the mast head arrangements of the 52ft. rating yacht Stephanie.

There are three plans in use for covering the eyes of rigging: 1. Parcelling and serving with spun yarn; 2. Covering with canvas and painting it; 3. Covering with leather.

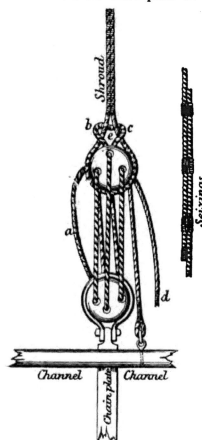

FIG. 15.

The first plan is cheapest, but will require renewing every year; the third is the most costly, and lasts the longest; whilst the second is most used, and perhaps looks the neatest. The eyes at the lower ends of the shrouds are generally served with spun yarn; but leather looks neater, and will not turn white, as spun yarn will, by the continual washing whilst dragging through the water; an occasional black painting will remove the washed-out appearance.

Lanyards are rove in this manner: A Matthew Walker, or wall knot, is made in one end of the lanyard; the other end is rove *out* through the foremost hole of the upper dead-eye; *in* through the corresponding hole of the lower dead-eye; out through the centre hole of the upper dead-eye, and so on, the hauling part coming in through the aftermost hole of the lower dead-eye and is then set up by a luff upon luff tackle. The hauling part (*a*, Fig. 15) is then secured to its next standing part by a racking; it is then carried up and *out* through the eye of the shroud at *e*; round the back part of the eye at *b*, and *in* through at *c*; a tackle is then put on the end, *d*, and when set up the part *d* is seized to a standing part of the lanyard. Sometimes the fall *d*, instead of being passed through the shroud eye at *e*, is secured by a couple of half-hitches round the shroud and seized as before described. Also, sometimes the fall of the lanyards is secured by a couple of simple turns and seized in the usual way round the eye of the shroud. The sheerpole passes across the eyes of the shrouds immediately over the dead eyes.

Wall knots and Matthew Walkers have, however, been known to draw, and now the general practice is to have a thimble eye spliced in one end of the lanyard, which eye is shackled to an eye bolt in the channel (see Fig. 15) rather ahead of the foremost chain plate; the other end of the lanyard is rove *out* through the foremost hole of the upper dead-eye (always commencing with the starboard fore shroud) *in* through the corresponding hole of the lower dead-eye, and so on; passing round the aft side of the mast, and ending with the port fore shroud : on the port side the lanyard is shackled to the channel under the after hole of the upper dead-eye. As this makes another part, extra setting up will be required, as most likely the lanyards will not render freely through the holes in the dead-eyes; sometimes three parts are set up first, then secured with a racking, and the tackles shifted to set up the remaining parts.

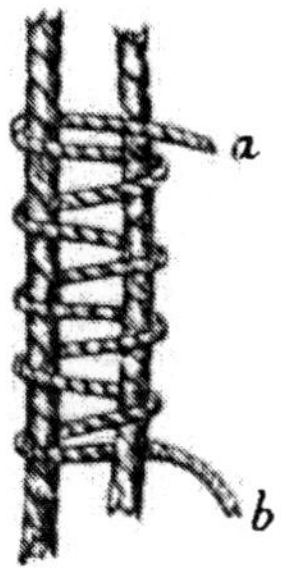

FIG. 16.

A racking is made as follows: a piece of rope, two or three feet long, is secured to one of the parts of the lanyard by a running eye at *a* (Fig. 16). The other end is then passed in and out as shown. They are then jammed up close together and hove up taut, and the part *b* properly secured.

Very great care must be taken in setting up rigging so that an equal strain is brought on all its parts.

Cutter or yawl yachts of from 3 to 15 tons usually have two shrouds a side; those from 20 to 75 tons three shrouds a side; and those above that tonnage four shrouds a side.

Racing yachts up to 52ft. rating have two shrouds a side; 60ft. rating up to 64ft. rating three; and above 64ft. rating four. It should, however, be remarked that some of the 52ft. rating yachts have three shrouds on each side.

Schooners usually have three shrouds on each side of main and fore mast. Schooners, however, like Guinevere, Boadicea, of from 250 to 400 tons, have been fitted with four shrouds on each side of main and fore mast, or sixteen shrouds in all.

For racing yachts rigging screws, as shown by Fig. 17, have

E 2

FIG. 17.

entirely superseded dead-eyes and lanyards, for the principal reason that they do not stretch and they are so much more easily set up. The cylinder nut is made of gun metal, Delta, or other suitable metal, and the rigging screws of steel. The eye of the shroud is spliced round a solid thimble, with hole through it for the bolt at A. In large yachts instead of a shackle to take the channel the lower screw is made with jaws like the one to take the eye of the shroud.*

Crucible steel wire rope is now universally used for racing yachts, because it does not stretch to the extent iron wire rope does. As a rule, in selecting steel wire, it would always be safest to choose the size next above that given in the table of iron and steel equivalent strengths. Iron wire varies greatly in its stretching qualities (see foot-note, page 53), and whilst some 3in. rope may stretch 18in. in lengths of 40ft. under a given pressure, other may not stretch half as much.

When wire rigging was first introduced, great objection was taken to it, on account of its rigidity; and it was declared that the stretching of the lanyards would not compensate for the stretching which was due to hemp shrouds. Various plans were suggested to supply the deficient stretching quality of wire rigging, such as spiral spring lanyards, and screw lanyards with india-rubber buffers. The fact is, however, that the stretching sought to be given to the wire rigging by such means is not required, and might end in the dismasting of the yacht. Mr. W. John, in his elaborate report to Lloyd's in 1877 on the dismasting of ships, shows the stretching qualities which wire rope has, and the general elasticity of wire shrouds and hemp lanyards combined. From his report we learn that the stretch wire rope is capable of before breaking is very considerable,

* White and Sons, Vectis Works, Cowes, and Messrs. Fay and Co., Northam, Southampton, make these rigging screws and fittings.

and that not half of that stretch and strength would be exhausted when the mast had arrived at its breaking point, due to its bending.*

The maximum recorded stretch before breaking varies from 2 to 7 per cent. of the length. The stretch, of course, is influenced largely by the core and lay of the rope, the actual wire stretching very little.

Hemp or Manilla rope is more or less elastic—that is, it will " take up again" after it has been stretched, but never quite so much as it may have been extended; and old rope has scarcely any elasticity at all.

Thus so far there is little danger that a yacht's spars will be lost in consequence of the wire rigging giving out from its actual bursting, and, as in ships, it is found that if a mast is so lost, it is generally through some defective ironwork or careless fitting of the rigging.

It has been contended that a yacht's main rigging should be stretchable, because, if she were sailing in squalls or under the influence of successive shocks of wind force, if the rigging did not give to some extent, it would

* Mr. W. John, in his report, gives the following formula for ascertaining in tons the breaking strain of wire rope. The square of the circumference of the rope in inches, multiplied by 1·034; that is to say, if the rope be 2in. in circumference, the breaking strength will be $2 \times 2 \times 1\cdot034 = 4\cdot13$ tons, or about 25 per cent. less than authorities on the subject have usually given. The size of steel wire of equivalent strength is generally given as 0·8 of the size of the charcoal iron wire rope; that is to say, if the iron be of 2in. circumference, the equivalent strength in steel would be thus found $2 \times \cdot8 = 1\cdot6$in. or 1⅝in. However, from experiments made by Mr. John, it would appear that the strength of the steel wire varies very considerably, and, whilst the ratio in some cases with soft steel was less than that given, in other cases with hard steel, the ratio of strength was greater.

The breaking strain in tons of single rope, such as the lanyards, was found to be equal to the square of the circumference in inches, multiplied by the fraction 0·2545.

The whole breaking strain in tons of the lanyards, rove in six parts, was found to be equal to the square of the circumference of a *single* part multiplied by the fraction ·843. The joint strength of the six parts is considerably less than six times the single part, and the disparity varied between 2·97 and 4·98; and it would appear that ill-made or defective dead eyes had a great deal to do with the apparent loss in strength.

The stretch of lanyards in six parts was found equal to the strain in tons multiplied by the distance from centre to centre of the dead eyes, and divided by six times the square of the circumference in inches of a single part of the lanyards. The stretch of wire rope varies greatly within the limits of proof, and the average was found to be equal to the length of the shroud multiplied by the strain in tons, and divided by the square of the circumference in inches and by a divisor ranging from 9 to 36. The mean divisor of the cases experimented with was 20.

Generally it is found that wire rope, when the strain is removed, does not "take up" all that it has been stretched, and ultimately the stretching quality of the wire will be lost without much loss in strength. The stretching quality of wire rope to some extent depends upon the core being of hemp, and to reduce the stretch it has been suggested that the core should be of wire. Wire rope stretches more rapidly as the strain increases, whereas hemp rope stretches less rapidly; but these peculiarities are mainly observable as the ropes approach the breaking point.

The weight of iron or steel wire rope per fathom can be found by dividing the square of the circumference (circumference ²) by 1·1; the weight of hemp rope by dividing the square of the circumference by 4. (See also Table VI., page 42.)

In selecting wire shrouds, pendants, or stays, care should be taken that slack laid rope with large core is not supplied; as it stretches very badly, "takes up" again very little, and "constant setting-up and never taut" will be the inevitable result. As a proof of what iron wire rope will stretch, it may be mentioned that the shrouds of the Constance yawl, in 1885, stretched until the dead-eyes came together, or about 18in., and then all the stretch was not out of it.

be like attempting to drive a railway train by a succession of blows from a sledge hammer. In stating the case thus ludicrously the fact is entirely overlooked that a vessel's heeling facility affords much greater relief to such shocks than could the yielding property of any rigging, unless indeed the latter were to be so stretchable as to be perfectly useless for stays. In fact, Mr. John clearly shows in his report that, so far as safety goes, the rigging cannot be set up too rigidly, and the less it stretches the better. Instead of elastic lanyards, long screw bars are now often used, and invariably for iron masts in the merchant navy.

In the case of narrow yachts built under the old tonnage rule, with great height of mast deck to hounds, the shrouds are of little use unless they are set up rigidly and spread by wide channels; so far as the requirements of match sailing go, there can be no doubt that the more rigid the rigging can be kept the better are the results. The old-fashioned theory is that the rigging should give readily, and that the masts should have plenty of play. This curious fallacy has been maintained by still more curious arguments and theories; and we have known some sailing masters slack up the rigging to give it the required play. It is obvious that the mast would yield under such circumstances, as the strain would not come upon the rigging until the mast had been very considerably bent—perhaps almost to the breaking point. We need not dwell upon the bad effects of slack rigging and a yielding mast further than to say, that anything which tends to render the application of the propelling force intermittent, or to absorb any portion of it and reduce its effect, must in some measure detrimentally influence the speed of a vessel; and if rigid rigging is necessary for the good performance of sailing ships, it is equally necessary for the attainment of the highest results in competitive yacht sailing.

TOPMAST RIGGING.

The topmast rigging will be cut (due allowance being made for the spread of the cross-trees), fitted, and served in the same manner as the main rigging, but with single eyes and not in "pairs," the eyes at the lower end of the shrouds will be turned in round galvanised iron thimbles, to take the hooks of the rigging screws (see Table II.) or setting-up tackles, or falls, as they are termed.

Each topmast backstay is usually in two parts, the lower part being the leg, which is in length equal to the housing length of the topmast. A thimble is eye-spliced into the upper and lower end of the leg, and a shackle joins it to the upper part.

Racing yachts above 52ft. rating usually have two topmast shrouds, or two backstays as they are more generally termed, on each side, and one "preventer" or shifting backstay each side. In yachts of above 64ft. rating the "preventer" is usually in two parts, the leg being of a length to suit the upper part of the backstays. In yachts of 52ft. rating and under one backstay and one preventer each side are generally considered sufficient; in these vessels a thumb cleat is usually fitted to the cross-trees, and when the yacht is at anchor the preventer is put in this and set up with its tackle, for the sake of tidiness. In large yachts a cleat or score is also provided on the cross-trees, for the preventers when not in use. A favourite plan, however, is to set up both preventers from their eye bolts aft on the counter; and the only objection to this plan is, that there is more gear for the yards or jibbooms of passing craft to pick up if they come dangerously near; on the other hand, so far as appearance goes, it makes a yacht look a little more rigged.

Schooners, in addition to topmast shrouds and preventers, have a main-topmast stay which leads from the shoulder of the main-topmast to the fore mast head (*see* Fig. 3); some cruising schooners further have a standing fore-topmast stay, which leads from the fore-topmast shoulder to the main mast head.

The shifting or "preventer" backstays will be measured for length from the shoulder of topmast to taffrail, and then deduct from this length about six or seven feet for the setting-up tackle. In large vessels this tackle always consists of two double blocks, the standing part being generally made fast to the upper block, and then the fall leads from the upper block; but sometimes the tackle is put the other way up, so that the fall leads from the lower block. The advantage of this plan is that several hands can get on the fall for a "drag;" the other plan, however, is more shipshape, and if the fall be put under the cavel round a belaying pin, with a couple of hands to "swig" and one to take up the slack, the tackle will always be set up taut enough. The tackles are hooked to the trysail sheet bolts on the quarter. In racing yachts, to avoid any possible mishap before the backstay can be properly set up, a tail block is seized to the lower end of the preventer just above the eye; a single rope is rove through this block, and one end of it is secured by a running eye to the cavel aft; a knot is made in the other end to prevent the rope unreeving. The rope is of sufficient length to admit of the preventer being carried into the main rigging without being unrove. When shifting the backstays, as in gybing, one hand takes hold of the hauling part of this "whip" to leeward, and hauls the backstay aft and gets it set up fairly taut, whilst another hand prepares the tackle for hooking on as the boom settles over. If backstays are properly worked in this way, a topmast should never be lost in gybing. Another plan is to have a tapering "fall" to the setting up tackle and overhaul the parts until the backstay can be stopped into the rigging. This, on the whole, is the simpler plan. The fall must, of course, be hauled on smartly in gybing so as to get the tackle set up in good time.

It may be a great advantage to be able to get the topmast quickly on deck, and in those of 20 tons and under the man-of-war plan of sending the rigging up on a funnel can be recommended for single-handed cruising or limited crew. A topmast on deck, instead of up and down the mast, is as good as a reef; and in small yachts under 20 tons, where the stick can be easily "man-handled," the funnel arrangements can be made use of. In the annexed diagram *a* is the topmast, and *b* the pole of the topmast; *s* topsail halyard sheave; *k* is the funnel; *m* and *m* are two catches rivetted to the funnel; the catches rest on the cap of the mast in a fore-and-aft direction when the topmast is lowered, and prevent the funnel going down through with the topmast. The funnel, it will be seen, is made to fit on the shoulder of the topmast, the lower part of the funnel being greater in diameter than the upper part. Fig. A shows the funnel viewed from above, *o* being the shoulder,

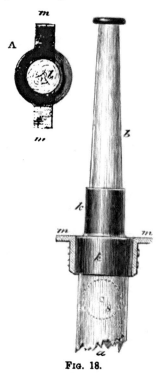

FIG. 18.

b the pole of topmast, and *m m* the catches. All the topmast rigging, including preventers, also spinnaker and jib topsail halyard blocks, are fitted on the funnel over the shoulder. A stout rope grommet should be fitted on the shoulder of the funnel as a bolster to prevent the rigging being cut. In lowering the topmast the halyards must be unrove from the sheave *s*; then, when unfidded, the topmast will come down; but the funnel, with the catches resting on the upper cap, will remain at the masthead—that is, the lower half of the funnel will be inside the cap, and the upper half above the cap. All the rigging, &c., of course remains on the funnel. To get the topmast up again, the pole will be shoved up through the funnel, and, when clear of the cap, a hand aloft will reeve the halyards through the sheave hole *s*. In lowering whilst racing, the flag would have to be taken off before bringing the pole through the funnel, as it might foul. So also if there are signal halyards or trip halyards, they must be unrove. Any good brazier would make the funnel, and rivet or weld the iron catches on. The funnel would, however, be better made of copper. Care should be taken that the lower part of the funnel is made as deep as the cap, and that it fits inside the cap easily, but not too loosely. The upper part of the funnel must be high enough to take all the eyes of the rigging and tails of blocks. The man-of-war funnels have no lower part, and the catches when the topmast is down have to be lashed to the cap; this of course takes up time. A topmast, with the funnel as described in a 5-tonner, can be got on deck in one minute, and be got up again in nearly as little time.

Mr. Thomas Butler, of Barrow-in-Furness, invented a topmast funnel, on the plan shown in the annexed diagram (Fig. 19), and used it in his 3-ton yacht (O.M.) for getting his topmast on deck without unrigging. The funnel (shown by A) is cast in brass, about $\frac{3}{8}$ inch thick. *a* is the pole of the topmast, which is fixed or jammed in the funnel, and does not come below *c*. *b* is the lower part of the topmast. *x* is a stud to insure the funnel getting on the right part of the topmast. *c* is a shoulder to strengthen the funnel, and rests on the masthead cap when the topmast is lowered. *d* is a hole in the funnel through which the halyard is rove. *g* is a part of the funnel bevelled away to prevent the halyard being cut. *f* is a rib, of which there are three. (As the funnel is necessarily larger at the bottom than at the top, the top part would fit loosely in the masthead cap; hence the ribs are made to taper to nothing at the bottom, and just fill out the cap when the funnel is lowered

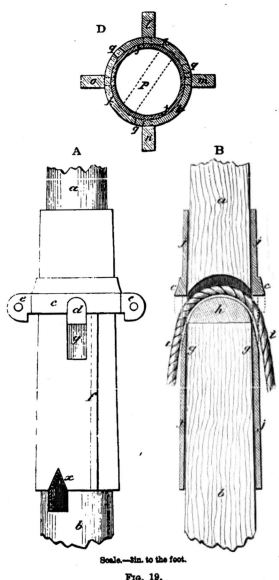

Scale.—3in. to the foot.

Fig. 19.

inside the cap.) *e e* are two eyes; of these there are four, two for shrouds, one for topmast forestay, and one for shifting backstay. They can either bo cast with the funnel or rivetted in afterwards. B is a section of the funnel, viewed nearly broadside on; *j j j j* shows the thickness of the brass, and *g* the bevellings; *i* the halyard; *h* is a piece of hard wood fitted on the upper end of the topmast, as shown, forming a dumb sheave. If a sheave were used, it would require a broad one with a good deep score in it. D is an end-on view of the funnel; *l* is the fore eye, looking in a fore-and-aft line corresponding with *n*; *o* and *m* are the two eyes for the shrouds; *q q q* are the ribs; *k k* are the shoulders; *p* is the opening for the halyard; *j* is the funnel. If other halyards are required, tail blocks can be made fast round the shoulders for them to run through.

The feature of this arrangement is that the topmast may be got on deck, or rather all that portion of it which is below the topsail-halyard sheave hole, leaving the pole and funnel, with the signal and topsail-halyards, and be sent up again without anyone going aloft to reeve the halyards or fid, as the heel rope can be trusted to keep the topmast up.

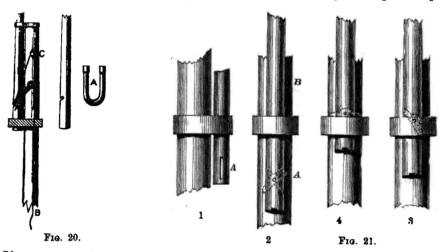

Fig. 20.   Fig. 21.

If necessary, in a squall, topsail and topmast could be lowered altogether by letting go the heel rope; this is of great consequence in small boats, as it enables a larger topsail to be used than a pole mast will admit of without the latter being too big for a sea way.

Various plans have been devised for fidding and unfidding topmasts. In Fig. 20, A is a pawl pivoted in slots which drops into a score in the topmast as the latter is got up. When the topmast has to be lowered, haul on the heel rope; and when the topmast is lifted sufficiently high, pull on the small rope B (which passes over the sheave C) until the pawl is clear of the score. The topmast can then be lowered.

Mr. Augustine L. Dunphy describes his self-acting fid as follows (Fig. 21):

"The iron fid works rather stiffly on a pin in the slot at heel of the topmast (see A, 1) ; a bolt, B (2), screwed into the masthead, completes the mechanical part of the arrangement.

"*To Fid the Topmast.*—The fid is placed in position, A (2), whilst the topmast is down, and then haul on the heel rope until the projecting part (A) strikes the bolt B (a score is cut in the cap to enable the fid to clear), and is pushed into a horizontal position when the heel rope is slacked, and the topmast will fall a few inches, fidded securely (*see* 4, Fig. 21).

"*To Unfid.*—Haul on the heel rope until the fid strikes the bolt B, thereby changing its position to that shown in (3), and the topmast is then free to come down.

"A little extra care is necessary in sending up the topmast, as, if driven up too high the fid is fidded and unfidded, when a hand must go aloft to right, or the topmast be lowered so as to place the fid in position again.

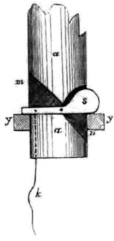

FIG. 22.

The most approved plan for a self-unfidding topmast is shown by Fig. 22. *a* is the topmast, *y* the yoke, *s* is an iron tumbler fid, pivoted by a bolt shown above *a*. *m* and *n* are slots cut in the topmast, *k* is a small line fastened to the fid, and passed up through a hole bored in the heel of the topmast. To unfid hoist on the heel rope until the tumbler falls into the slot *n*, then lower away. To fid, hoist by the heel rope until the slot *n* is above the yoke. Then pull on the line *k* until the fid is in the horizontal position shown in the drawing. We think this fid is to be preferred to either of the other two.

PENDANTS AND RUNNERS.

The pendants are made of wire rope, and are put over the masthead before the shrouds are. They are covered with canvas. The pendant is usually in length two-thirds the distance deck to hounds, but it should not be longer, otherwise the runner will not overhaul sufficiently without unhooking, which only ought to be necessary when the boom is eased off the quarter. The lower end of the pendant is shod, or, if not shod, an eye is turned in over an iron thimble. A single block is shackled to this end of the pendant, and through the block the runner is rove.

The runner is sometimes made of hemp or Manilla rope, but in large racing vessels it is more frequently made of flexible iron or steel wire rope. The runner in total length is generally three-fifths the distance deck to hounds. It should be made as long as possible, so that there may be plenty to overhaul when the boom is eased off.   It should not be necessary to unhook the runners and tackle every time the boom is eased. Each end of the runner has a thimble-eye splice, with a strong hook at the end of the standing part, which leads aft to be hooked to an eye bolt on the rail.*   The tackle is shackled to the eye at the other end of the runner, and usually consists of a fiddle block on top and single block below, but sometimes the upper block is a common " double."   The fall of the tackle always leads from the upper block.   With the wind much forward of the beam, very little strain comes on the runners; but they should be kept well set up, or otherwise the mast may go forward, and bring about a slack forestay, hollow luff to jib, and throw an undue strain on the aftermost shrouds.

Mr. C. P. Clayton has adapted the American plan for runners in yachts of 52ft. rating, and it has been introduced into yachts of 64ft. rating as well. In Fig. 23 the pendant block is about 21ft. abaft the mast and 3ft. 6in. above the deck; the bullseyes B and B 1 are about 1ft. 4in. apart.   They are bolted through the beams, work fore and aft, and swivel.   The tackle being

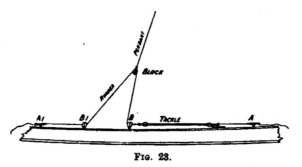

Fig. 23.

released at A, and a haul taken on the runner at A 1, the tackle block is drawn up to B.   The weight of the boom will then overhaul the runner through B 1 and the pendant block.   In setting up, the runner is hauled upon until hand taut, and the rest is done with the tackle.

FORESTAY.

The forestay goes on "over all;" but now the practice is to have the eye, or collar, large enough to go well up the masthead, above the yoke and over the throat-halyard-block bolt, or a hook bolt; in a racing yacht the latter is preferable, as the mainsail puts quite enough strain on the throat-halyard-block bolt.   The collar encircles topmast as well as the yoke.   The eye should be made so that the splice comes well under

---

* The runner should be always hooked so that the point of the hook comes uppermost; this will bring the strain fairly on the throat or bight of the hook; otherwise the hook may be straightened or broken.

the cross-trees, and should be long, so as not to bring strain on the splice. (*See* page 30.) The yoke gives the spread to the collar necessary to allow the topmast to go up and down without touching it. The collar should be leathered. The stay leads down to the fore side of the stemhead in a score (*see c*, Plate V.), where it is rove through a hole. The

FIG. 23A.

end A is then made into a bight round a heart block D, with seizings at intervals, as shown; it is then set up with a lanyard C (Fig. 23A) to the bitts B, with an iron bound heart E. In reeving the forestay through the stemhead it must not be forgotten that the iron hanks or rings for the foresail must go on it first.*

TRIATIC STAY.

Formerly, in schooners, a stay on each side led from the main mast head to the deck, forwards, and was set up by a tackle; in tacking or wearing, the lee tackle had to be set up and the weather tackle let go. This plan was very inconvenient in racing schooners, and, about the year 1858, the fashion became general to carry a stay from mast head to mast head, a larger forestay being introduced to bear the extra strain thrown upon it. The disadvantage of this plan is that it entails some trouble in tacking or gybing, as double fore-topsail sheets and tacks are required, and the fore topsail has to be clewed up every time the schooner is put on a different tack. To obviate this trouble, double triatics have been tried, the lee one being always eased up; but they were found to be a great nuisance, as there was still the difficulty of getting the clew over the main-topmast stay, and the danger of not getting the triatic set up before the vessel filled. On the whole, the single standing triatic gives the least trouble and is the safer.

There are two ways of fitting a triatic stay to the mastheads; the most approved plan is to have a thimble eye spliced into either end of the stay, and shackle it to an eye welded on the masthead caps. The other plan is to shoe the stay with lugs to fit an eye bolt on the masthead cap.

TOPPING LIFTS.

In vessels about 64ft. rating there is one Manilla topping lift a side, and the standing part is hooked to an eye in an iron band round the boom.

---

* In schooners, and in some cutters, when the bowsprit goes out over the stem, the forestay is set up to lugs on the span shackle by a screw bolt and nut, or lanyard.

The topping lift is then rove through a single block shackled to an eye plate on the cheeks of the mast. The hauling part of the topping lift has an eye, to which the purchase block is hooked or shackled; the purchase consists of a double and single block.

In vessels from 30 to 60-rating the topping lift is single, with the addition of a runner, the standing part of which and the purchase are shackled to eye bolts on the channel; but sometimes they are shackled to an eye bolt in the rail, or to the cavel abreast of the mast.

In vessels above 60-rating it is usual to have double topping lifts, with runner rove through a block on the end of the hauling part of the lift; a tackle is hooked to the runner; in such case the standing part of the lift is shackled to the block at the masthead, and leads thence through a block on the boom, and back through the block at the masthead.

Most large racing yachts have a single topping lift a side, made of flexible wire and covered with canvas. These, of course, have the runner and tackle. These topping lifts look neater than those of double (Manilla rope), and overhaul just as readily.

Very small craft have only a single topping lift, and of course, when under way, this one is always slack if to leeward so as not to girt the sail; the practice in larger craft is always to have the weather lift set up just hand taut and belayed.

BOWSPRIT SHROUDS.

Bowsprit shrouds are made of iron or steel wire rope, and have a thimble eye-splice in each end; one end is shackled to the iron cranse at the bowsprit end, the other to the setting-up tackle or to screws like the shroud screws (see Fig. 17). The tackle formerly was always outboard, hooked to an eye bolt on the top strake, or on the channel, where it not only dragged through the water and picked up weeds, but was not so readily got at when reefing the bowsprit. The tackle consists of an iron fiddle block and a single block, the latter being at the after end of the tackle. (*See* J, Plate V.) An eye bolt is usually put in the deck to take the tackle. This bolt should go through a beam, and have a plate and spur on deck; the strake of deck plank where the bolt is should be of hard wood, and the bolt should be a very strong one. Several vessels have lost their bowsprits through this bolt drawing, crushing through the plank, or breaking off short. In some yachts an iron clamp band is fitted, with an eye bolt in it, round one of the bulwark stanchions, for the shroud tackle block to be hooked to. Another fruitful cause of mishap to bowsprits has been the practice of having an iron shoe instead of a thimble eye-splice in the shroud for the shackle. Even when the shoe is a long one, it will occasionally strip in consequence of the wire parting where the rivets go through, and a shoe should never be trusted for any part of the wire standing rigging.

In the case of the rigging screws being used for the bowsprit shrouds bolts will require to be fitted at intervals equal to the distance between the fid holes for reefing the bowsprit. In most of the small racing yachts the bowsprit is, however, too short to require reefing.

BOBSTAY.

Various ingenious plans have been invented for bobstays, as no part of a yacht's gear so frequently gives out; but the most usual plan of making up a bobstay is as follows: a copper bar * shackled to the stem, and about as long as the bowsprit is high out of the water; then a wire pendant and tackle. The tackle has a single block next the pendant, and a double one at the bowsprit end, the fall leading inboard at the stem. The cordage selected for the tackle is usually bolt rope, and some racing yachts have flexible wire rope. A common practice in racing vessels is to have a " baby bobstay," or preventer, which is not set up quite so taut as the other; this preventer has no doubt saved some bowsprits, but, on the other hand, it has undoubtedly been the cause of many being carried away. Constantly setting up the jib, or the strain of the jib alone, or the strain of the bowsprit when set down to a crook, will soon cause the fall to stretch or " come up," and then an equal strain comes on both. But very frequently the preventer is set up a little tauter than the other; in such cases, if there be any weight in the wind, the preventer is almost certain to part, and the other if the jerk be very great, may go with it. If the main bobstay should go first, it would be hardly reasonable to expect the other and weaker one to stand; it may, it is true, just save the bowsprit, but the sailing master will have so little confidence in the preventer that he will order the jib sheets to be eased up, and will gill his vessel along, whilst the other bobstay is being patched up, if such a thing as patching be practicable. Another danger attending the practice of having two bobstays is that the main one is never quite so stout and strong as it otherwise would be; and, as it is almost certain that an unequal strain will come upon them, one only has practically always to do the work. Therefore by far the wiser plan is to have one stout and strong bobstay, equal in fact to the united strength of the two.

* The eyes in the bobstay bar must not be welded or braised. The ends of the bar should be heated and hammered back by striking the end of the bar on the anvil end on; when the end is driven up twice as thick as the other part of the bar, the hole can be drilled or punched—drilling is to be preferred.

RUNNING RIGGING.

Jib Traveller, Jib Tack, Jib Halyards, and Jib Sheets.

The Cowes plan for traveller is to have a short eye shackle (*b*) on the traveller to take the jib clew cringle, and shackle (*a*) for the tack, as shown in Fig. 24. The common plan is to have a hook for the clew

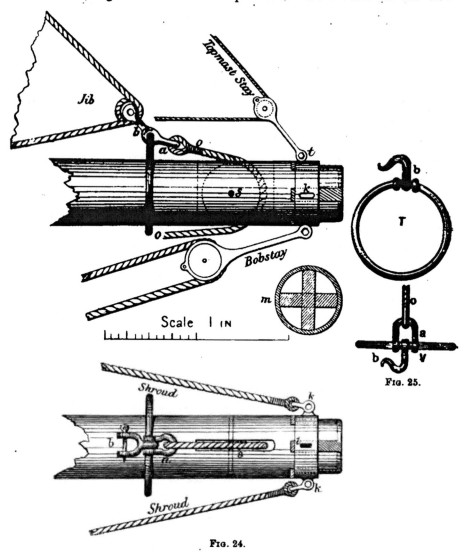

Fig. 25.

Fig. 24.

cringle of the jib, and a shackle for the outhaul or jib tack (*o*), as it is termed. (*See* T and V, Fig. 25.) The shackles and hook are fitted loose to the traveller, so as to turn easily; the end of the leather covering of the traveller prevents their slipping round. In some cases, in small vessels, where no shackle is used, the eye in the jib tack is seized to the ring. Again, in large vessels, another plan is to open the strands of the wire rope and make them into two parts. Two thimbles are put on the ring traveller, one on each side of the hook, and the two parts of the jib tack are eye-spliced round the thimble. The jib tack thus forms a sort of bridle.

The jib tack requires to be of great strength, and is made, according to the choice or judgment of the person who has the fitting out of the yacht, of rope, chain, or flexible wire rope. Rope does very well in small

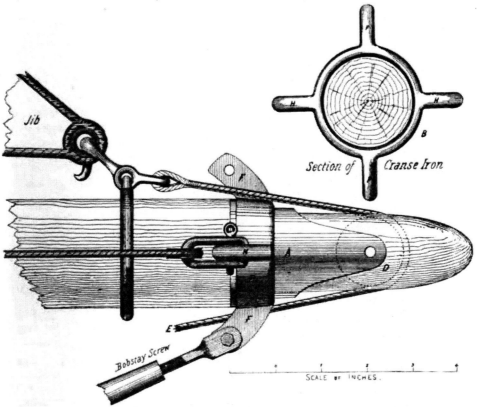

FIG. 26.

vessels, but flexible steel wire rope is to be preferred, and it is found to stand better than chain. The tack leads down through a sheave hole *s* at the bowsprit end; a block is shackled to the end of the tack through which the outhaul is rove. The standing part of the outhaul is put over one of the bitts with a running eye; the hauling part leads on board by the side of the bowsprit. A single rope inhaul is generally fast to the traveller.

The cranse iron, it will be seen, is fitted with four single lugs—eyes to take the shackles; *k k* for the shrouds and *t* for the topmast stay; and

F

the other for the bobstay.   Another form of cranse iron will be found illustrated farther on in the chapter on Clyde Lugsail Boats.

The score in the end of the bowsprit has necessarily to be very long, and frequently it is made wider than it need be; at any rate the sheave hole is a source of weakness, and generally if the end of the bowsprit comes off it is at the sheave hole, the enormous lateral strain brought on the part by the weather shroud causing the wood to give way.   To avoid such accidents we for some years advocated a plan for putting the sheave outside the cranse iron, and the plan is now generally adopted in small racing yachts.   A collar piece, *A*, Fig. 26, is fitted on the bowsprit end, and the cranse iron, *B*, goes on over that.   The score for the sheave, *D*, is cut a little out of the vertical so as to throw the outhaul, *E*, on opposite sides of the lugs, *F F*, to avoid straining or chafing.   The example given shows the bowsprit end fittings of a 36ft. rating yacht, drawn to one-quarter full size.

Jib halyards are, as a rule, made of chain, or for racing yachts of crucible steel wire rope, as either runs better than Manilla or hemp rope, and does not stretch, and the fall stows in a smaller compass when the jib is set; in fact, the fall is generally run through one of the chain pipes into the forecastle, where it helps a trifle as ballast.   In cruising yachts, where chain is not used, Manilla rope is employed.   The jib halyards are rove through an iron (single) block (which is hooked or shackled to the head cringle of the jib), and then each part leads through an iron (single) block on either side of the masthead (*see* Fig. 4).   The hauling part usually leads down the port side of the mast; the purchase is shackled to the part that leads through the block on the starboard side.   In vessels of 64ft. rating and over a flexible wire runner is invariably used in addition to the purchase; one end of the runner is shackled to an eye bolt on deck, and the other, after leading through a block on the end of the jib halyard, is shackled to the upper block of the purchase.   The purchase consists of a double and single block, or two double; in the former case the single block is below, with the standing part of the tackle fast to it; but where two double blocks are used, the standing part of the tackle is made fast to the upper block.   As a great deal of "beef" is required to properly set up a jib, it is usual to have a lead of some kind for the "fall"* of the purchase on deck, such as a snatch block.   It is, of course, necessary to have a "straight" luff to a jib, but very frequently the purchase is used a little too freely; the result is that the forestay is slackened, and perhaps a link gives way in the halyards; or the luff rope of the jib is stranded (generally near the head or tack, where it has been opened for the splice),

* The fall of a "tackle" is the part that is taken hold of to haul upon.

and sometimes the bobstay-fall is burst. These mishaps can be generally averted by "easing" the vessel whilst the jib is being set up, choosing the time whilst she is in stays or before the wind, and watching to stop purchasing when the forestay begins to slacken.

Jib sheets in vessels under 52ft. rating are usually single, but in vessels above that rating they are double. In the latter case there are two blocks, which are put on the clew cringle; a sheet is rove through each block, and the two parts through the jib sheet holes in the wash strake of the bulwarks; one part of the sheet is then made fast and the other hauled upon.

The foot of the jib should make about the same angle as the foot of the other sails when close-hauled, and in extremely narrow vessels it has been sometimes found necessary to have an outrigger with a block on it for the jib sheet to reeve through, but it was oftener found in small yachts than large.

FORE HALYARDS, FORE TACKS, AND FORE SHEETS.

The fore halyards are usually fitted as follows : The standing part is hooked or shackled to an eye bolt under the yoke on the port side, then through a single block hooked to the head of the sail, and up through another single block hung to an eye bolt under the yoke on the starboard side. The downhaul is bent to the head cringle or to the hook of the block. No purchase is necessary, as the sail is set on a stay; but in yachts above 10 tons the luff of the sail is brought taut by a tackle hooked to the tack; the tack leads through the stem head. The tackle consists of a single and double block, or two doubles according to the size of the yacht. In yachts of 64ft. rating and upwards the tack is usually made of flexible wire rope.

Fore sheets in yachts under 52ft. rating are usually made up of two single blocks. The standing part is made fast to the upper block (hooked and moused or shackled to the clew of the sail). In larger vessels a double, or single, or two double blocks are used, the hauling part or fall always leading from the upper block. In cutters or yawls of or above 80ft. rating, or in schooners of and above that rating, "runners" are used in addition to tackles. These are called the standing parts of the sheets : one end is hooked on the tackle by an eye; the other end is passed through a bullseye of lignum vitæ on the clew of the sail, and is then belayed to a cavel. The sail is then sheeted home with the tackle.

In the case of schooners a favourite plan for cruisers is to have a boom foresail with sheet rove similar to the main sheet, except that there are no quarter blocks. Occasionally a short horse is fitted in the deck

F 2

for the lower block to travel on, but more frequently a bolt only. When there is no boom the sail is termed a lug foresail, and the bolts for the standing parts of the fore sheets are usually put in so that the foot of the sail, when straightened flat in for close hauled work, makes an angle of from 13° to 15° with the middle line of the keel. As this usually brings the bolts a considerable distance inboard on the deck, it is usual to have them screwed into sockets so that they can be removed and the sockets plugged when the vessel is not under way; otherwise they may make awkward things to kick the toe against.

Main and Peak Halyards, Main Tack, Main Sheet, and Main Outhaul.

The main or throat halyards are generally rove through a treble block at the masthead, and a double block on the jaws of the gaff. The hauling part of the main halyards leads down the starboard side of the mast, and is belayed to the mast bitts. The main purchase is fast to the standing part, and usually consists of a couple of double blocks, and the lower one is generally hooked to an eye bolt in the deck on the starboard side. Formerly it was unusual to have a main purchase in anything under 30-rating, and when there was no purchase the upper main halyard block was double, and the lower a single. However, now a racing 20-rater has a main purchase, and most 10-raters have one. The principal object in having a main purchase in a small craft is that the mainsail can be set better, as in starting with "all canvas down" the last two or three pulls become very heavy, especially if the hands on the peak have been a little too quick; and a much tauter luff can be got by the purchase than by the main tack tackle. Of course the latter is dispensed with in small vessels where the purchase is used, and the tack made fast by a lacing round the goose-neck of the boom. By doing away with the tack tackle at least 6in. greater length of luff can be had in a 36ft. rating yacht, and this may be of some advantage. The sail cannot be triced up, of course, without casting off the main tack lacing; but some yacht sailers consider this an advantage, as no doubt sailing a vessel in a strong wind with the main tack triced up very badly stretches the sail, and looks very ugly.

The peak halyards in almost all vessels under 140 tons, O.M., are rove through two single blocks on the gaff and three on the masthead, as shown in Plate I. and Fig. 4. Some large cutters have three blocks on the gaff, and in such cases one of the blocks on the masthead (usually the middle one) is a double one. The standing part of the peak halyards to which the purchase is fast leads through the upper block and down on the port side.

The usual practice in racing vessels is to have a wire leather-

covered span (copper wire is best) with an iron-bound bullseye for each
block on the gaff to work upon, and this plan no doubt causes a more
equal distribution of the strain on the gaff. The binding of the bullseye
has an eye to take the hook of the block. In Fig. 27 *a* is a portion of
the gaff, *b* is the span; *c c* are the eyes of the span and thumb cleats
on the gaff to prevent the eyes slipping. *d* is the bullseye with one of
the peak halyard blocks hooked to it.

The main tack generally is a gun tackle purchase, but in vessels above
40 tons, or say 60-rating, a double and single or two double blocks are used.
In addition, some large cutters have a runner rove through the tack cringle,
one end being fast to the goose-neck of the boom, and the other to the
tackle. In laced mainsails the tack is secured by a lacing to the goose-neck.

The main boom is usually fitted to the spider hoop round the mast
by a universal joint usually termed the main boom goose-neck.

The main sheet should be made of left-handed, slack-laid, six-
stranded Manilla rope. The blocks required are a three-fold on the boom,

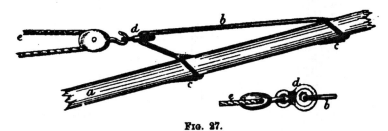

FIG. 27.

a two-fold on the buffer or horse, as the case may be, and a single block on
each quarter for the lead. Yachts of less than 52ft. rating have a double
block on the boom, and single on the buffer.

Many American yachts have a horse in length about one-third the
width of the counter for the main sheet block to travel on. For small
vessels, at any rate, this plan is a good one, as the boom can be kept down
so much better on a wind, as less sheet will be out than there would
be without the horse. A stout ring of indiarubber should be on either
end of the horse, to relieve the shock as the boom goes over.

In modern racing yachts the main boom end is fitted with a " slide "
in order to get the clew of the mainsail out to the extreme end of the boom,
which forms a base for the measurement of the area of the sail. In Fig. 28
is shown the fittings of a 52ft. rating for the mainsail outhaul, on a scale
one-quarter of the real size. *A* is the boom and *B* the " slide." *C* is the
traveller made with two lugs or ears, *D*; the clew cringle of the mainsail
is put between these ears and secured by a bolt and nut as shown. The
" slide " is made of gun metal.

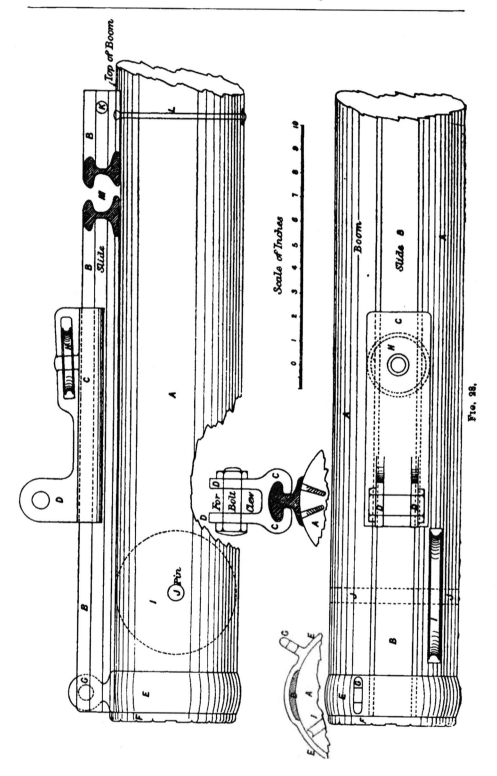

Fig. 28.

E is an iron hoop, and *F* is the usual turned end cover of the boom. *G* is an eye welded to the hoop, *E*, and the standing part of the outhaul is spliced or shackled to this. The outhaul then leads through the sheave, *H*, fitted in the traveller, *C*, and back over the sheave, *I*. This sheave, *I*, it will be seen, is out of the vertical—that is, on the top of the boom it is on the starboard side; underneath, it is in the centre line of the boom, so that the tackle which is on the outhaul has a fair lead on whichever side of the beam it is hauled upon. *J* is the pin of the sheave, *I*. *K* is a hole for lacing of mainsail. The slide for a 52ft. rating yacht is secured to the boom with 2¼in. screws and four through bolts, as shown by *L*. *M* shows sections of the slide *B*.

The mainsail outhaul is usually, in cruising yachts, made up of a horse on the boom, a shackle as traveller, a wire outhaul shackled to the traveller

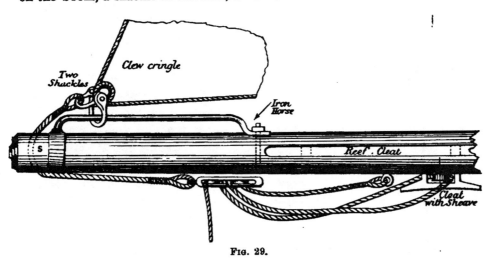

Fig. 29.

shackle, and rove through a sheave hole at the boom end, and a tackle. (*See* Fig. 29.) In small vessels the tackle consists of one block only; in large vessels of two single, or a fiddle and single, or two double blocks. There is a dummy sheave at *s*, and sometimes a whole sheave in large vessels.

The old-fashioned plan of outhaul, and one still very much in use in cruisers consists of an iron traveller, like the jib traveller (*see* Fig. 26), on the boom end, a chain or rope through a sheave hole and a tackle. This latter plan is perhaps the stronger of the two; but an objection to it is that the traveller very frequently gets jammed and the reef cleats have to be farther forward than desirable, to allow the traveller to work.

Sometimes, instead of a sheave hole, an iron block is fitted outside the extreme end of the boom.

Topsail Halyards, Sheets, and Tacks.

The topsail halyards in vessels under 52ft. rating consist of a single steel wire, hemp, or Manilla rope rove through a sheave hole under the eyes of the topmast rigging.

Yachts of 52ft. rating and over have a block which hooks to a strop or sling on the yard, or if the topsail be a jib-headed one, to the head cringle. The standing part of the halyard has a running eye, which is put over the topmast, and rests on the eyes of the rigging; the halyard is rove through the block (which has to be hooked to the yard), and through the sheave hole at the topmast head. It is best to have a couple of thumb cleats on the yard where it has to be slung; there is then no danger of the strop slipping, or of the yard being wrongly slung.

When the topsail yard is of great length an upper halyard is provided (called also sometimes a tripping line or trip halyard, because the rope is of use in tripping the yard in hoisting or lowering). This is simply a single rope bent to the upper part of the yard, and rove through a sheave hole in the pole, above the eyes of the topmast rigging. The upper halyards are mainly useful in hoisting and for lowering to get the yard peaked; however, for very long yards, if bent sufficiently near the upper end, they may in a small degree help to keep the peak of the sail from sagging to leeward, or prevent the yard bending.

The topsail sheet is always a single * Manilla rope, as tarred hemp rope would stain the mainsail in wet weather. It leads through a cheek block on the gaff end, then through a block on a pendant or whip. This pendant is shown in Plate I., and goes round the masthead with a running eye, or is shackled to an eye bolt in the masthead. Formerly the block was shackled to an

Fig. 30.

eye bolt under the jaws of the gaff, but by the modern arrangement as described the strain is taken off the jaws of the gaff and consequently off the main halyards. One plan of fitting this block and whip is shown in Fig. 30. The hauling part of the sheet is generally put round one of the winches on the mast to "sheet home" the topsail.

The topsail tack is usually a strong piece of Manilla with a thimble spliced in it, to which the tack tackle is hooked.

* Some large cutters have double topsail sheets rove in this way: one end of the sheet is made fast to the gaff end; the other end of the sheet is rove through a single block on the clew of the sail; then through the cheek block at the end of the gaff, through a block at the jaws of the gaff, and round the winch.

Jib-topsail halyards and main-topmast-staysail halyards are usually single ropes rove through a tail block on topmast head; but one or two large vessels have a lower block, with a spring hook, which is hooked to the head of the sail. In such cases, the standing part of the halyards is fitted on the topmast head with a running eye or bight.

Spinnaker Halyards, Outhaul, &c.

Spinnaker halyards are invariably single, and rove through a tail block at the topmast head.

The spinnaker boom is usually fitted with a movable goose-neck at its inner end. The goose-neck consists of a universal joint and round-neck pin, and sockets. (Square iron was formerly used for the neck, but there was always a difficulty in getting the neck shipped in the boom, and round iron was consequently introduced.) The pin is generally put into its socket on the mast, and then the boom end is brought to the neck.

At the outer end of the boom are a couple of good-sized thumb cleats, against which the running eye of the after and fore guy are put. The fore guy (when one is used) is a single rope; the after guy has a pendant or whip with a block at the end, through which a rope is rove. The standing part of this rope is made fast to a cavel-pin on the quarter, and so is the hauling part when belayed. The after guy thus forms a single whip-purchase (*see* Plate I.). The outhaul is rove through a tail block at the outer end of the spinnaker boom, and sometimes a snatch block is provided for a lead at the inner end on the mast. The topping lift consists of two single, a double and single, or two double blocks, according to the size of the yacht.

The upper block of the topping lift is a rope strop tail block, with a running eye to go round the masthead. The lower block is iron bound, and hooks to an eye strop on the boom.

In the early days of spinnakers a bobstay was used; but, if the boom is not allowed to lift, it will bend like a bow; in fact, the bobstay was found to be a fruitful cause of a boom breaking, if there was any wind at all, and so bobstays were discarded. The danger of a boom breaking through its buckling up can be greatly lessened by having one hand to attend to the topping lift; as the boom rears and bends haul on the lift, and the bend will practically be "lifted" out.

Small yachts seldom have a fore guy to spinnaker boom, but bend a rope to the tack of the sail (just as the outhaul is bent) leading to the bowsprit end; this rope serves as a fore guy, or brace, to haul the boom forward; and when the spinnaker requires to be shifted to the bowsprit, the boom outhaul is slackened up and the tack hauled out to bowsprit end.

Thus double outhauls are bent to the spinnaker tack cringle, and one rove through the sheave hole or block at the spinnaker boom end, and the other through a block at bowsprit end. But generally the large spinnaker (set as such) has too much hoist for the jib spinnaker, and a shift has to be made for the bowsprit spinnaker, which is hoisted by the jib topsail halyards if that sail be not already set; even in such case no fore guy is used in small vessels, but to ease the boom forward one hand slackens up the topping lift a little, and another the after guy, and, if there be any wind at all, the boom will readily go forward. In a 5-tonner the after guy is a single rope without purchase, and the topping lift is also a single rope, rove through a block under the lower cap.

A schooner has a main and fore spinnaker fitted in the manner just described, and the usual bowsprit spinnaker as well, which is usually hoisted by the jib-topsail halyards.

As spinnaker booms will not go under the forestay when the spinnaker has to be shifted, the boom must be unshipped. To shift the boom, the usual practice is to top it up, lift it away from the goose-neck, and then launch the inner end aft till the outer end will clear the forestay, or leech of foresail if that sail be set. If the boom is not over long, the inner end can be lowered down the fore hatch or over the side of the vessel until the other end will clear the forestay. Some large racing yachts have a well from deck to keel to lower the boom into to get it under the forestay, the well being sunk into the lead in the case of an iron or steel yacht (*see* also the chapter on Seamanship).

When spinnakers were first introduced no goose-neck was used, the heel of the boom being lashed against the mast or to the rigging. A practice then sometimes was to have a sheave hole at either end of the boom, with a rope three times the length of the boom rove through each sheave hole. One end of this rope served as the outhaul, the other for the lashing round the mast. To shift over, the boom was launched across the deck to the other rail, and what had been the inboard end became the outboard end. Of course the guys had to be shifted from one end to the other. As spinnaker booms are now of such enormous length, it would be almost impossible, and highly dangerous, to work them in this way, although it might do for a small yacht.

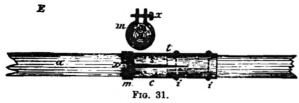

FIG. 31.

A plan for " telescoping " a spinnaker boom is shown by Fig. 31, *a* is the inner part of the boom; *c* is a brass cylinder with an angular slot in it at *s*. This cylinder is fixed tightly to the outer part of the boom by the screw bolts *i i*. The two parts of the boom meet inside the cylinder at the ticked line *t*. When the two parts of the boom are to be used together, the ring *m* is put on the cylinder. The inboard part of the boom is then put into the cylinder, and the whole is firmly screwed up by the thumb-screw *x*. Both parts of the boom have their ends "socketed" so as to take a goose-neck, and thus either part can be used alone.

ARRANGEMENT OF CABINS AND FITTINGS.

The fitting up of sailing yachts do not admit of much variety, as certain arrangements may be considered as arbitrary. For instance, there are so many reasons for berthing the crew forward that no one ever dreams of placing them elsewhere. Next it is so much more convenient to have the saloon (or main cabin, as it was formerly always termed) next the pantry and galley, that placing it farther aft has generally been regarded as a disadvantage. And then there is a good reason for placing the ladies' cabin aft because they are there less liable to interruption. Beyond that, the cabin is not often sub-divided, and whilst men object, as a rule, to be stowed away in the same cabin, women do not appear to object to it.

The common way of arranging a 200 tons schooner is shown on Plate VIII. In still larger vessels a "drawing room" is sometimes formed—abaft the dining room, or main cabin. The Lyra (364 tons), Boadicea (380 tons), and other large yachts have been so fitted. The Gwendolin (200 tons) was originally fitted in the same way, but it very much cramped the forecastle and the sleeping accommodation, and she was re-arranged below.

On Plate IX. a good plan of arranging the cabins below is shown, by having the companion placed farther aft. The yawl Constance is fitted in this way; and the advantage of having the greater portion of the passage in the centre of the vessel is that two very fine cabins can be obtained on both port and starboard side. It will be seen that on the starboard side of the Constance there is one long cabin, but this could easily be bulkheaded off so as to form two cabins if required. It may be mentioned that the Egeria schooner has one long cabin like this, but, the passage not being in the centre, the berths on the port side are narrow.

Another arrangement is to have the saloon aft next the ladies' cabin; the Pantomime, Gelert, and Harlequin were fitted in this way. The companion is then forward, with a passage down the centre to the saloon, with the sleeping berths on each side of the passage. The chief objection to this arrangement is the distance the saloon is away from the pantry and companion, and its interference somewhat with the privacy of the "ladies' cabin."

Yachts of 100 tons have not usually a cabin abaft the "owner's berth" on the starboard side, if there be also a cabin forward of the saloon on the starboard side; but the Vol-au-vent and some other yachts have had them; still, with less than 83ft. on the load line, the berths must be rather short or the forecastle very much curtailed.

Coming down to yachts of 60 and 40 tons, a common arrangement is that shown on Plate IX. of the Beluga cutter. We have seen this arrangement in vessels as small as 25 tons, but the cabins are necessarily very narrow, and require copious ventilation. A common plan in cruising 20-tonners is to have a sleeping cabin on the starboard side, forward of the saloon; a lavatory and stairs next abaft the saloon, and then the ladies' cabin; or a stair-ladder leads into the main cabin direct from the deck, with nothing but a sleeping cabin (or ladies' cabin, as it is always termed) abaft the main cabin. Often, too, there is no berth forward of the main cabin in yachts so small as 20 tons.

An admirable plan for a yacht which is likely to be used oftener by day than night, is that adopted in the Alpha Beta (Plate X.); it is a plan frequently met with in America, where the saloon is almost invariably entered from a cockpit aft. The Alpha Beta is 49ft. from stem to stern post on deck, with 11ft. 10in. beam, making 27 tons Thames measurement. With so much beam two very fine bed cabins can be had, as will be seen, and many will prefer this arrangement to an attempt to get the accommodation of a 40-tonner into a 25-tonner.

Ten-tonners boast of a "ladies' cabin," and beyond that some—the Saraband, for instance—have a lavatory and w.c. between it and the main cabin. In some respects a much better arrangement is one similar to that of the Alpha Beta's, and shown on Plate XI., which represents the cabin plan of the yacht Fee. This arrangement gives one good sleeping cabin and an airy and easily accessible saloon, with plenty of stowage room. The only objection is that the "steward," or, say, his "equivalent," has occasionally to pass through the sleeping cabin, but that is a very small matter, and in the early morning, when the owner and his friend are finishing off a night's sleep, the steward can always go over the deck to get to the saloon. The ordinary plan of arranging a 10-tonner is with the inevitable "ladies' cabin" aft. This plan is also shown on the same Plate.

In the case of fitting up a yacht like the Fee it would be well to have one of the folding washstands, as when folded up they are only about 8in. deep. (*See* Figs. 32 and 33.) The manufacturers are Messrs. J. Stone and Co., of Deptford, who make every variety of water-closet, pumps, cocks, &c., necessary for yachts.

In yachts of 5 tons and under, the "ladies' cabin" arrangement is not possible, and the sofas usually form the sleeping berths. A common

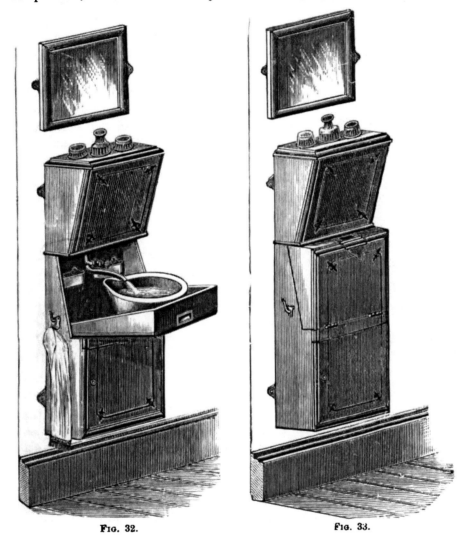

Fig. 32.   Fig. 33.

arrangement for a 5-tonner is that shown of Vril (Plate XII.); but some— as, for instance, like the old 5-tonner Freda—are decked in, back to the steering well, and have no raised deck on.

An old-fashioned 3-tonner, owing to the still narrower beam, is more difficult to arrange into cabins than one of the old narrow 5-tonners; and a great deal of experience and ingenuity is required to make anything like a decent living place below. Still it is done, and Spankadillo (Plate XIII.), built and fitted up by a very old hand, Capt. H. Bayly, in 1884, gives a good idea of what can be done on board so small and narrow a craft. There is one bulkhead just abaft the mast, which has a sliding door communicating with the forecastle. Right in the eyes of the forecastle is a large cupboard, fitted with shelves, where all loose things in the way of crockery, lamps, &c., are stowed, when not in use. There are two glass side lights (*a*) on each bow to light and help ventilate the forecastle.

On the port side is a long locker, which also forms a bunk, and on the starboard side a fold-up cot. The cooking stove (*s*) is a Rippingille (Fig. 34), and is fitted on double gimbals—a necessary arrangement for the oil cooking stove of a small yacht if an attempt is made to use the stove in very rough water. The stove cost 10*s*., and the gimbal frame would be made by any ironmonger at about the same cost. The

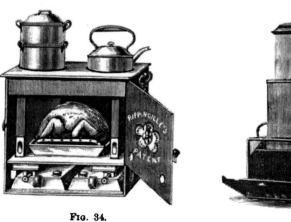

Fig. 34.   Fig. 35.

cistern oil chamber has two perforated partitions, arranged in the form of +, to prevent the oil slopping in case the yacht jumps about with unusual violence. A methylated spirit lamp, for boiling eggs and making hot water in a hurry, is also carried.

In the cabin there is a sofa on the starboard side 7ft. long. The locker space is divided into three lockers; the forward one is used for storing away tinned meats, soups, &c.; the middle one for bottles, and the aft one for clothes. The cushion is also in three pieces to suit each locker.

Over the sofa is the owner's sleeping cot, 2ft. wide, which turns up under the beams by day.

At the aft end of the sofa is the wash stand (with enamelled iron basin), door, &c., as shown in the drawing (Fig. 33). The mirror above the wash stand is not attached, and is an optional arrangement.

On the port side of the cabin is the table, which is attached to a shelf with a deep coaming. There are two hooks on the table which slip into eyes in the shelf. The legs of the table are hinged. It can be stowed as shown in the cross section, or unhooked and stowed elsewhere.

The shelf is used for stowing all sorts of things in constant use, such as pipes, tobacco, water bottle, whisky bottle, &c. The lamp is one of the usual pattern, on double gimbals, and can be unshipped to stand on the table if required. On each side of the lamp is a rack for tumblers. Over all a long rack for charts, &c.

In the wake of the table is another sleeping folding cot 1ft. 9in. wide.

The after end of the cabin, which is open right away to the counter, is kept for sails and gear on gratings, to keep them free of moisture from the plank. Hanging hooks for clothes of course can be placed wherever the owner fancies they will be the least in the way.

In yachts of the length of an old 3-tonner, but having from 8ft. to 10ft. beam, a good plan is to have a lavatory containing a w.c. forward on the starboard side.

There are a great variety of oil and spirit cooking stoves made, all more or less of the stowable order (one part in the other), and a good serviceable spirit stove (Fig. 35) is sold by Messrs. Pascal Atkey and Son, West Cowes. The "Stella" Company, of Oxford-street, make a spirit stove which is much in use; also the Albion Lamp Company, Birmingham; the "Victor," made by Wright and Butler, Charterhouse-street, London; and the "Rippingille" and "Boddington" stoves are all highly spoken of.

The "Cera Light Company," 70, York-street, Glasgow, has brought out a stove for burning their "Cera Wax." The great advantage of this wax is that it is carried solid, and only melts when the stove is in use; there is little smoke or smell from it, and no danger of explosion, &c.

Oil and spirit cooking stoves are continually being improved upon, as those who use them discover the advantages of some modified arrangement. We believe Mr. G. Wilson, of 23, Sherwood-street, Piccadilly, keeps himself informed of all the various stoves introduced, and would give any necessary information.

With regard to the relative merits of petroleum (Kerosine should be always used if procurable) and spirit stoves, there is no doubt that spirit is to be preferred on account of its cleanliness and the little trouble it gives. It is, however, dangerous on account of its high inflammability, and may be objected to on account of its costliness compared with Kerosine. The latter is simple enough to light, but the burners and surroundings must be kept scrupulously clean, and evenly trimmed, or there will be deficient heating and most unpleasant odours.

A cooking stove, useful for river work, or any kind of cruising where fuel can be obtained, is shown by Fig. 36. It boils, bakes, fries, or broils extremely well, and one apparatus of the pattern shown in our engraving will bake and boil enough for a party of six. When packed up it is contained in a space of 12in. by 9in. by 8in.; it consists of two cookers and an oven, baking dishes, frying-pan, gridiron, &c., and will cook for half a dozen people; it weighs about 10lb. A smaller apparatus cooks

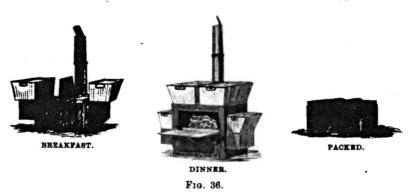

BREAKFAST.　　　DINNER.　　　PACKED.

Fig. 36.

for two to three people, and weighs 5lb. Any rubbish, such as brushwood, faggots, &c., generally obtainable on a river's bank, may be burnt. The makers are Messrs. Lineff and Jones, Engineers, 12, Buckingham-street, Adelphi.

Messrs. Pascal Atkey and Son make an admirable little cast iron stove suitable for cooking and warming, to burn coal, coke, &c. It can be recommended for the cabins of small yachts which may be used for winter work, wildfowling, &c.

The "Clyde Model Cooking Stove" is also well adapted for small yachts, and is made by Messrs. Ferguson, 34, Trongate-street, Glasgow.

CHAPTER V.

SEAMANSHIP.

SEAMANSHIP comprises the practice of the whole duties of a sailor, including all kinds of work upon rigging, making sail, taking in sail, steering, reefing, working the ship, marking and heaving the lead, and whatever else relates to the management of a ship. Before a man can be called a seaman, he must have practised all the duties enumerated, and be capable of performing them in a satisfactory manner without supervision; he is then called an able seaman, as distinct from an "ordinary seaman," who is a young sailor not yet versed in the practice of the seaman's art. A seaman, as generally understood, is one who is perfect in the art of square rig sailing, but there are "fore and aft rig" men as well, and the instruction given in this chapter will relate to the duties of the latter alone, as the square rig, so far as sailing yachts are concerned, has practically disappeared.

To BEND A MAINSAIL.—The throat cringle is first shackled to the eye bolt under the jaws of the gaff. The head of the sail is then stretched along the gaff, and the peak earing passed (*see* Fig. 37, page 82).

The earing is spliced in the cringle by a long eye splice. The splice is shown at *n*. The earing is passed through *d* round through the cringle *e*, through *d* again and through *e* again; then up over the gaff at *i* and *k*, down the other side and through *e* again, and so on up round the gaff four or five times; at the last instead of going up over the gaff again the earing is passed between the parts round the gaff, as shown at *f*, round all the parts that were passed through *d* as shown at *m*, and jammed by two half hitches *m* and *h*. The end *g* would then be seized to the part at *n*.

When the earing is first passed through *d* it is hauled upon to well stretch the head of the sail along the gaff unless the sail be a new one.

In the sketch the earing is not represented hardened up as it would have to be in practice. The cringle *e* would be jammed up

G

close to the gaff, and the half hitches hardened back to the cringle at *m.*
The earing is shown loosely passed for the sake of distinctness.

As a rule the cringle comes about under the cheek block *b,* but often
when the head of the sail becomes stretched the cringle comes outside
the cheek block *b.* The earing then has to be passed round the gaff
between *d* and the cheek block. This in some respects is an advantage,
as it prevents the topsail sheet chafing the lacing; on the other hand it
looks awkward, as the leach of the topsail is necessarily some distance
inside the leach of the mainsail; the leach of mainsail and topsail ought
to make an unbroken line. (*See* the Y.R.A. rules.)

It is usual to put a piece of canvas parcelling round the earing over
the parts where the topsail sheet chafes.

The earing being passed the head of the sail is laced to the gaff.
A half hitch is usually taken at each eyelet hole; the lacing then crosses
up over the gaff at right angles instead of diagonally, and holds the

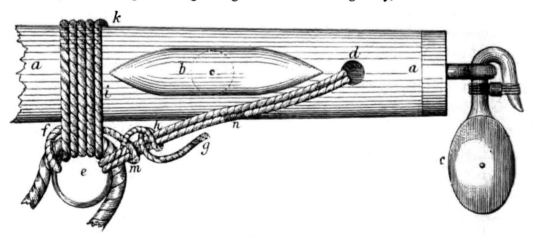

Fig. 37.

a a is the peak end of the gaff.
b is a cheek block for the topsail sheet.
c is a block for peak downhaul, and used
also as ensign or signal halyards. The
hook of the block, it will be seen, is
moused. The block is hooked to an

eye-bolt screwed into the end of the gaff.
The worm of the screw is, of course, a
deep cut one.
d is a hole in the gaff end through which the
earing is passed.
e is the peak cringle of the mainsail.

sail closer to the gaff. Sometimes the head of the sail is laced from
eye to eye with diagonal turns, and laced back again so that the lacing
crosses on the gaff thus—XX.

The luff of the sail is next seized to the mast hoops with spun yarn.
The clew is shackled to the traveller, and the sail is then bent.

In bending a new mainsail great care should be taken not to get
any strain on the head or foot at first. In first hoisting take the weight

of the boom with the topping lifts; set the throat up taut by the halyards, and then get the peak a little more than half up. Then set the luff taut with the tack-tackle, and afterwards set the peak up, but still leave the leech slack. If the weather is damp and any strain comes on the foot, ease the outhaul to let the traveller in. So also if the sail is set and it should rain, ease in the traveller. It is a good plan, especially if the sun is out, to hoist the sail up several days before getting under way, and as it blows about with head and foot slack, it will stretch fairly. If a chance occurs it is an excellent plan to run before a good strong wind for some hours, especially if the leech of the sail appears to be unduly slack. After a few days the head can be hauled out fairly taut on the gaff, and the foot on the boom; but the traveller should always be eased in for shrinking by rain or dew. Even for an old sail the traveller should be eased in a little if the sail gets wet, and if it appears necessary the tack or throat purchase should be eased as well for rain or dew. Nothing is so likely to spoil a new sail as attempting to make it sit flat by putting a great strain on the foot before the sail is stretched.

To Set the Mainsail.—Take the coats off. Hook on the peak halyards, and mouse the hooks. Overhaul the main sheet. Top* the boom up five or six feet clear of the crutch, taking care that the crutch is not lifted out of the sockets and dropped overboard; haul the main sheet taut, and belay. Cast off the tyers, leaving one as a " bunt gasket" amidships at present to keep the sail from blowing out. See that the purchases have been well overhauled (fleeted); and that the peak downhaul and the topsail sheet are rove. Man the peak halyards, cast off the bunt tyer, and hoist the gaff end between the topping lifts, guiding it with the peak line. When the gaff shows above the lifts, hoist away on the throat halyards, and let the sail go up with the gaff as nearly as possible at right angles to the mast. If the sail is peaked before the throat is up (*i.e.*, if the peak of the sail goes up faster than the throat), it will be hard work getting the throat up, if it can be got up at all without the purchase. Get the throat as high as possible with the halyards, and belay. Leave the peak for the present, and pull the sail out on the foot by the outhaul. Purchase up the throat as high as required, and set the peak up, using the peak purchase until the sail begins to girt in the throat; a few girts here will not matter, as the peak will be sure to settle down a good deal. Sometimes in small yachts, after the throat is set up hand-taut, the peak is got as high as

---

* It is a practice in racing vessels, if the wind be not very strong, to unhook from the boom what is to be the lee topping lift whilst hoisting, so that the mainsail will not girt across it, and cause a delay.

it can be without the purchase. The sail is then set up by the throat purchase, "peak and all" going up bodily.

When the foot of the sail is laced to the boom the tack is lashed down to the gooseneck, and the throat purchase brings the luff of the sail taut—like a bar of iron. When the sail is not laced, the tack-tackle is hooked on after the throat and peak are up, and the luff of the sail is brought taut by this tack-tackle. But the better plan for a racing yacht is to make the tack fast before hoisting by passing a lashing through the tack cringle and round the gooseneck of the boom; then pull the sail out on the boom; the throat purchase will now get the luff of the sail much tauter than the tack-tackle. We are speaking now of setting the sail to the best advantage; but it is possible the skipper may want the tack triced up, for which purpose the tricing line will be hooked on to one of the mast hoops near the throat, and to the tack cringle of the sail.

When the sail is set, coil away the halyards and purchase falls, and, if not previously done, make the tyers up in neat bunches, and fold the sail coats ready for stowing away in the sail room.

It is the practice to always have one reef earing rove, and if the weather looks at all threatening a second one should be rove. The first earing should be fast round the boom, then, if the outhaul should burst, or the clew of the sail tear out, the sail will not fly in along the boom nor get adrift. In anticipation of such accidents a common plan is to pass a tyer through the clew cringle and round the boom, three or four times.

If whilst sailing the peak should settle down so much as to require setting up, the best time to choose for doing so will be when the vessel is head to wind in stays. The weight of the boom should be taken by the weather topping lift before using the peak purchase.

To REEF A MAINSAIL.—Get the reef tackle on deck and bend it (*see* Fig. 40) to the reef earing (previously rove), and hook the fore block to the eye bolt or strop on the boom. Take the weight of the boom by the weather lift, and ease the main sheet, if required, to allow the boom being tossed up. Cast off the main tack, if the sail be not a laced one. Ease up the throat and peak purchases till the sail has settled down a reef, and if necessary ease up the halyards by the fall; no more of the peak than actually necessary should be settled down, as the peak will be the heavier work to get up again. Put plenty of strength on the reef tackle (ease the helm a little, so as to take the weight of the wind out of the sail) and harden the earing down on the boom until the last inch is got. Should the cringle not come right home pass a tyer two or three times through it and round the boom. This "preventer" lashing is commonly rove when match sailing with a reefed mainsail. Then roll the foot of the sail up tightly and neatly, and tie up the reef points (*see* Fig. 38); set up the throat by the purchase, and then the peak if necessary. Bowse the tack down. Ease up the topping lift and trim the sheet. A racking should now be put round the boom and earing, and the reef tackle cast off. Then make the earing fast by jamming turns round the boom (*see* Fig. 39). In Fig. 39 the turns and hitches are shewn loosely for the sake of

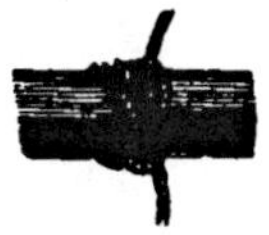

Fig. 38.

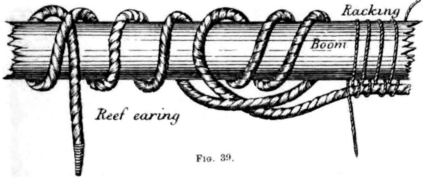

Fig. 39.

distinctness; to secure the earing all the turns and hitches are jammed up close together. The end of the racking is also secured before taking off the reef tackle. A couple of hitches round the earing will secure the end of the racking.

Reeve another earing and bend the tackle on to haul down the second reef if necessary. The reef tackle block next the earing has a thimble eye strop. The earing is bent to the eye by a sheet bend with a bight (*see* Fig. 40).

Fig. 40.

Never reef a new unstretched mainsail if it can be avoided, but stow it and set the trysail if necessary.

Having reefed the mainsail, prepare to shift jibs. The jibs generally carried with mainsail reefed or otherwise are as follows :

Mainsail and topsail … … … … …	No. 1 jib.
Whole mainsail and housed topmast … …	No. 2 jib.
Single-reefed mainsail … … … … …	No. 3 jib.
Double-reefed mainsail and reefed foresail*	No. 4 jib.
Three-reefed or closed reefed and double-reefed foresail* … … … … … …	No. 5 jib.
Trysail … .. … … … … … …	Storm jib.

The bowsprit should be reefed in as the jibs are shifted.

* Sometimes in match sailing, if there be much reaching and if the water is pretty smooth, No. 3 and even No. 2 jib is carried with double-reefed mainsail, and No. 3 or 4 jib with

To Shake a Reef out.—Set taut the weather topping lift to take the weight of the boom. Untie all the reef points, and be careful that not one is left tied, as the sail may be torn thereby. Ease up (handsomely) the tack-tackle and unhook it. Ease up the reef earing. The reef will now be fairly shaken out, and the mainsail can be set by the purchases, always recollecting to set the throat up first. Bowse down the tack, ease up the topping lift, and trim the sheet.

To Stow a Mainsail.—Put the tyers at proper intervals across the boom. Ship the crutch. Set taut the topping lifts. Overhaul throat and peak purchase. Lower the boom by the topping lifts into the crutch. Haul taut the main sheet and belay; cast off the falls of throat and peak halyards, and lower (by the throat the faster) and gather in the sail on deck. Belay the peak halyards so that the gaff end rests on (say) the port side of the boom. Pull the foot of the sail up on the top of the boom so that the roach just hangs over on one side, say the port side; next lay the leech of the sail along as far as it will go on the top of the foot. Then the whole of the bag of the sail will be on the starboard side. Take hold of this bag (outside) part and lift up and roll over, repeating the operation until the sail is rolled up in a snug bag. [The process of thus lifting the bag or bunt of the sail is termed " skinning " by sailors.] Then hoist the gaff up clear of the boom and lift the whole sail bodily up on the boom, over the foot of the sail. Throw the ends of the tyers up over the gaff, and thereby haul the sail snug up to the gaff; then take the ends of the tyers under the boom up over the gaff again, and tie. Unhook peak halyards and put on the mainsail covers. The peak halyard blocks can be then hooked on again, or hooked to a sling passing under main boom, and will thus keep the boom from sagging with its own weight. When the peak halyards are not so hooked on, an X crutch should support the boom amidships.

To Stow the Mainsail and Set the Trysail.—In heavy weather it is always better to set a trysail than a close-reefed mainsail, as the mast is thus relieved of the heavy strain of the main boom and gaff. Get the trysail gaff clear of the other spars on deck. Bring the trysail on deck, and the trysail sheets. Prepare to heave to under the two head sails by hauling the foresheet a little a-weather of the mast. Ship the boom crutch. Set the topping lifts taut. Overhaul the main and peak purchase. Settle the main boom down into the crutch. Haul the sheet taut and belay. Stow the mainsail and make it up on the boom. Put a lashing on the boom from each quarter, or secure

---

three reefs. A racing yacht usually carries a jib larger than No. 1, as a " reaching jib," because it is set when a long distance is to be done by reaching with the wind more or less free.

the boom down in the crutch by tackles on to each quarter. Take off main and peak halyards and hook the same to the trysail gaff. Unhook the topping lifts, and make them fast in main rigging. Ship the jaws of the trysail gaff to the mast, and make fast the parrel round the mast, the gaff end resting on the deck. Lace the trysail to the gaff. Bend the sheets and belay both hand taut. Hoist and toggle on the parrels, or strops, or lacing (as the case may be) on the luff of the sail round the mast, as the sail goes up.

If the yacht be yawl rigged, and the mizen has been stowed, it should be set before the mainsail is taken off, as the mizen will keep the yacht's head up to the sea. The storm mizen, of course, would be chosen for this purpose.

To Set a Stay-Foresail. (In a schooner this sail is termed the fore-staysail, and the foresail is the gaff sail set abaft the foremast; in cutters the foresail, although, as in a schooner, set on the forestay, is simply termed the foresail or staysail; the proper term is stay-foresail). —Take off the coat and hook on or bend the sheets, hauling in slack of port or starboard one (or both), and belay. See that the downhaul or block is bent to the head cringle, and hoist away.* When the sail is high enough, hook on the tack tackle and bowse down.

To Reef a Stay-Foresail.—Cast off the tack tackle and lower the sail; unhook the sheets; tightly and neatly roll up the foot of the sail and tie the reef points. Hook on the sheets to the reef cringle and belay; re-hoist the sail; hook the tack to the reef cringle and bowse down with the tackle.

To Shift a Stay-Foresail for a Ballooner.—Let go the halyards and haul down the foresail by the downhaul; unhook the halyards from the head cringle; hook them on to the balloon foresail with downhaul; and, as the sail is hoisted, toggle the luff on to the forestay, or hook on as the case may be; carry the lee sheet aft and belay (slack) as the crew start hoisting. When the head is chock-a-block bowse down the tack. Trim the sheet. On a wind the sheet is generally brought inside the main rigging, or between the main rigging and the topmast backstays. For reaching, the sheet is carried outside of all.

To Set a Jib.—Carry the sail forward tack first. Hook the tack cringle to the traveller; hook on the halyards and downhaul to leeward of the forestay and foresail; belay the sheets hand taut, or one a-weather, as required. Hoist away by the halyards until the sail is about half up; then haul the tack out by the traveller outhaul, hoist the sail and set

---

* The downhaul is sometimes kept rove through the hanks and leads through a block inside the stem head. In a racing yacht it is best to have the downhaul made fast to the halyard block and not rove through the hanks, because it is so frequently necessary to shift for a balloon foresail.

taut with the purchase. Trim the sheets. Always be careful that the jib sheets are rove through the right holes; nothing shows up the careless mate so much as the sheet for first jib rove through the holes for second jib, or the contrary.

In light winds it will be found less trouble to pull the jib out on the bowsprit before hoisting, and with a few stops uncut.

Generally in getting under way the jib is set up in stops, that is, before it is unrolled. The jib is hoisted up some distance, and then the tack is pulled out on the bowsprit, the sheets being loose, as otherwise the stops would be broken. Upon getting under way the stops are easily broken by hauling in the jib sheet.

When the second jib is set the bowsprit should be reefed, and double-reefed for third jib; otherwise the strain from the jib on the jib traveller may nip the bowsprit and cause it to break, as the traveller would come far inside the support of the bobstay.

Before purchasing up a jib the runner-tackles should be set taut, and swigged upon unless it is desired to "stay" the mast forward by the jib. If the runners are slack, the effect will be to pull the mast forward and slacken the forestay instead of to straighten the luff of the jib, thus a straight luff to the jib cannot be made until the runners and pendants are "bar taut." It is also of course necessary that the bobstay should be set well taut by its tackle.

To Shift a Jib.—Ease up the purchase handsomely, slack up the outhaul and pull in by the inhaul, and gather the sail in board by the sheet and foot; then pull the head of the sail down by the downhaul, gathering the sail in-board, and "muzzling" it as it comes on deck over the lee bow. The purchase should always be eased before the outhaul is let go, so that it may be overhauled ready for use again. If the outhaul or purchase is let go suddenly it may cause such a jerk that the bowsprit might be sprung or the bobstay burst.

If possible, the jib should be shifted when the vessel is before the wind; and often a sailing master will run his vessel off whilst the crew are getting the jib in, so that the sail is becalmed. Sometimes two or three or more hands go on the bowsprit, and gather the sail up as it comes down, but in bad weather the traveller is always let run up close to the stemhead.

If it is seen beforehand that one jib will have to be shifted for another, the tack of the jib which is to be first used is *lashed* to the bowsprit end; the other jib is run out by the traveller and stopped along the bowsprit. To shift, haul taut the weather sheet; one hand cut the lashing at the bowsprit end; as the jib flies aft haul in by the mainparts of the sheet, and pull down by the downhaul. Hook the halyards, down-haul, and sheets on the other jib and hoist away.

In light weather when a bowsprit spinnaker is carried, it is unusual to let the jib run in, but several of the hands stow and stop it along the bowsprit.

To SET A GAFF TOPSAIL.—Bend the sail to the yard; pass the weather earing first, and then haul the head taut along the yard by the peak earing (see how the peak earing of the gaff was passed, page 85). Tie the stops round the yard, or lace, as the case may be. Bend the sheet to the clew cringle (*see* Fig. 41). See that the sheet is inside the topping lift, and that it passes under the yard from the mast side before it is bent to the clew cringle. See that the clew line is fast to the clew cringle. Hook on the halyards and bend the trip halyards (*see* Fig. 42), and hoist the sail clear of the deck. Hook on the tack tackle. A mousing should be put on all hooks. (*See* "Knots and Splices" in the Appendix.)

To keep the sail from blowing away from the mast, it is usual to have a "lazy tack," which consists of a short line, one end of which is fast to the tack cringle of the sail; the other end is passed round that

FIG. 41.   FIG. 42.

part of the main or peak halyards which has been belayed to the mast bitts, and is then made fast to the tack cringle the same as the other end was; the line thus forms a kind of traveller, and the main or peak halyard serves as a jackstay.

A gaff topsail should be always sent up to windward, and if the halyard and sheet are to leeward they should be shifted over.

Hoist on the trip halyards until the peak is well up inside the topping lift (the peak will always be the aft end of the yard), then hoist away on all, hauling out the sheet as the sail goes up; otherwise, if the sail blows about, the sheet may get a turn round the gaff end. When the yard is so high that the point where the trip halyards are bent is level with the trip halyard sheave in the topmast, leave the trip halyards adrift, and all hands hoist by the other halyards. When the yard is chock-a-block, belay. Bowse down the tack to the last inch to take all the "render" out of the halyards, and belay. Set taut the trip halyards. Pass the lacing and haul taut round the masthead. Haul out the sheet until the sail sits as desired. *A topsail should never be sheeted until the*

tack has been bowsed down, so as to well peak the sail and take the
" render " out of the halyards. If during sailing it is found that the tack
requires bowsing down (which will have the effect of setting the peak
up), the sheet should be eased up first.

Before the topsail is sheeted, a look should always be given to the topmast stay (*see* " Bobstay "). The topmast should cant forwards a trifle, so as
to insure plenty of drift for the sheet, as it is unusual to "sheet home." Also
a look should be given to see if the peak requires purchasing up, as a topsail
will always require " sheeting " after the mainsail has been " peaked."

If the head of the sail be short, the trip halyards will not be used.

In the case of a jib-headed topsail, it will be hoisted as fast as
the masthead-man can lace it. The safest plan is to send the sail up
in stops, and make a traveller of the upper lacing round the standing
part of the throat or peak halyards. In rolling up a sail the luff rope must
be kept outside the roll, and not be rolled into the sail.

In running before the wind with the boom square off, if the topsail
tack is to windward of the gaff the sheet should be eased a little ; and, if
necessary to relieve the strain on the weather cloths, the lacing or tack
should be eased as well.

To TAKE IN A GAFF TOPSAIL.—One hand will go aloft to cast off the
lacing. When all is ready for lowering, cast off the halyards and trip
halyards from the belaying pins. Lower away with the halyards, but
keep the trip halyards hand taut, until the yard is " up and down "
the mast. Ease up the sheet, and lower away all. If there be much wind,
several hands must be put upon the tack at first to haul down as the
halyards are started, otherwise the bellying bunt of the sail is certain
to blow in between or over the parts of the peak halyards, and will
thus prevent the sail lowering. In such a case do not cast off the
" lazy tack " until the sail is on deck. The hand aloft will keep the
heel of the yard inside the topping lift as it passes down.

As the yard comes down between the topping lift and the mainsail,
haul forward by the tack (casting off lazy tack), so that the heel of the
yard (the lower end) goes forward.

When the sail is on deck, unbend the halyards and make the ends fast
to a belaying pin. Unbend the sheet, and make it fast round the boom.
Roll the sail up on the yard ; or unbend it, roll up, and stow below.

Formerly the practice was to lower the topsail to leeward of the
mainsail, as it was thought to come down more freely under the lee of
the lower sail ; but the difficulty is that the sail or yard is almost certain
to get foul of the topmast rigging or lee crosstrees, and the crew cannot
handle it so well from the lee scuppers. Very often in attempting to take

in a topsail to leeward it will take charge and blow out, whereas if it were to windward it would lie flat on the mainsail, and could not blow away. So now the practice is, if the tack be to leeward, for a hand to go aloft in the lee rigging or up the mast hoops and unhook the tack tackle, whilst another hand goes aloft on the weather side to the masthead, and lowers a line to him to bend to the tack. When the line is so bent, the hand at the masthead pulls the tack up over the peak halyards, so that the sail can be got down to windward. The heel of the yard is pushed to the weather side of the topmast whilst lowering.

To Set a Schooner's Fore Gaff Topsail.—The sail should be sent up stopped to the yard, with the clew and tack cringles showing clear. Bend on the halyards, and hoist to the masthead. The hand aloft will then bend on the lee sheet and lee tack to the cringles; then the weather sheet and tack will be bent, first passing them over the main-topmast stay. When this is done, hoist the sail chock-a-block, bowse down the lee tack, then heave the lee sheet taut by the winch.

To Work a Fore Gaff Topsail.—When the order comes "ready about," ease up the sheet and tack; clew the sail well up. The foremasthead man will clear the tack and sheet over the main-topmast stay, and must well overhaul the same. As the vessel comes head to wind, bowse down the tack as smartly as possible, at the same time haul out the sheet; but do not sheet home until the topsail is tacked, as it must always be recollected that a topsail cannot be peaked to sit properly if it is sheeted before the tack is down.

To Set a Jib Topsail.—Pass along the sail, head first, one hand going to bowsprit end with the head cringle in his hand. In large vessels this hand bestrides the bowsprit end outside the topmast stay, with his face towards the vessel; generally in such small vessels as five-tonners there is not such a "seat" at the extreme end, and the hand will sit on the bowsprit weather shrouds if the sail has to be hanked. Bend the sheets, and pass them outside of all. Haul in the lee sheet, and place one hand to attend to it, and ease up if necessary. Hook or toggle the hanks on to the topmast stay, cutting the stops and hoisting as the hanks are so hooked or toggled. When all the hanks are on, hoist to the required height, set the tack down, and trim the sheet.

A jib topsail in very small yachts is sometimes set flying, as the bowsprit end of such craft is not a pleasant place for a man of the customary weight of eleven stone. At the bowsprit end a tail block is fast; through this block a rope is rove, both ends being kept in-board. To set the sail, bend both ends of this rope to the tack cringle, and bend the halyards to the head cringle. Haul the sail out on the bowsprit by the *under* part of the outhaul, and hoist at the same time. The bight of the outhaul will therefore come in-board, and its *upper* part will serve as the inhaul when the sail has to be handed. The sail can be hoisted to any required height. One hand, of course, must go to the bowsprit end to pass the sheet round the jib.

If the halyards are to windward the sail can be hoisted to windward; if otherwise it will be hoisted to leeward of the foresail and jib.

In strong winds a jib topsail should never be hoisted so high as in light airs, as the higher it is the more strain it will bring on the topmast.

Also, in strong winds, one hand should always be stationed at the sheet to ease up during strong puffs. A good plan is to put a tail-tackle on the sheet. The sheet can then be eased or hauled in as required very readily by the tackle.

To Set a Schooner's Main Topmast Staysail.—See that the halyards are on the lee side of the main-topmast stay. Bend on the halyards, tack and sheet; see that the sheet has been passed outside the main rigging and main-topmast rigging. Hoist to foremast head in a bunch; then, as the hand aloft hooks the hanks on the main-topmast stay, the deck hands will hoist. When hoisted, set the tack taut, and belay. Trim the sheet. It is very usual for the sheet to lead to the boom end; it cannot very well be got too far aft.

To Set a Squaresail.—The yard has a strop and thimble eye seized in it at the centre of length of yard; on the fore side of the mast a wire jack stay or jumper reaches from masthead to deck, on which the thimble eye on the yard strop travels. The braces are rove through single blocks at each yard arm, and one end made fast to the cavel aft, the other part is for hauling. The fore braces are single ropes leading from each yard arm through single blocks at the bowsprit end. The lifts go from each yard arm through single blocks hooked to the upper cap at masthead, and lead to the deck. When at anchor the yard is generally lowered half-way down, and then pointed up and down the mast. It is more ship-shape, however, to lower the yard down to about level with the tier of mast hoops and square across, with all the braces and lifts set taut. The only objection to the latter plan is that it may be fouled by passing vessels.

To set the sail, reeve the earings through the block at each yard-arm, and through a block near the strop on the yard amidships; then hoist the yard up. Bend or hook one end of each earing to the corner head cringles of the sail, and hook the four halyards to the middle cringle; hitch the lizard to the cringle or hook of halyard block. (The lizard is a short piece of rope with an eye at one end; the eye travels on the jumper, and the tail is fast to the sail; thus the sail is kept from blowing away.) Bend on the tack and sheet; then hoist by the halyards, and afterwards pull out the weather earing; take in the slack of the lee earing. Get out the boom with fore and after guys on it, and the outhaul rove through the sheave hole at boom end; bend the outhaul to the tack cringle of the sail, and haul out.

To take in the sail, let go the weather and lee earing; then let go the sheet, and tack outhaul, and gather the sail aboard; then, when the sail is all in-board, let go the halyards and haul down with downhaul. As the sail is hoisted by the foresail halyards, the fore downhaul will be used as well.

Fig. 43.

To Set a Spinnaker.—The boom must be got ready first. Hook on (or bend if it is a tail block) the lower block of the topping lift to the boom. Bend the outhaul block at the spinnaker boom end; be careful that the part of the outhaul which has to be bent to the tack cringle is on the fore side of the spinnaker boom topping lift and over the fore guy; put on the after guy and fore guy.* Hoist the boom well above the rail, and launch forward until the gooseneck† can be shipped in the socket; hoist until the boom is "up and down" the mast, and high enough for the lower end to be shipped on the gooseneck. (It is usual to put the gooseneck in the socket on the mast first, and then bring the socket which is in the end of the boom to the shank—*see* Fig. 43—c is the boom and p the gooseneck, a the mast.) Lower the boom and haul aft, or "square the boom." If the boom be already shipped and "up and down the mast," one or two hands will take the guys and outhaul aloft and put over the end. The standing part of the after whip will be made fast to the weather quarter, and the hauling part rove through a sheave hole or turned round a pin. The hand aloft will cast off the boom lashing, and push it away clear of mast and crosstrees for lowering by topping lift.

See that the spinnaker halyards are clear on the fore side of the boom topping lift. Bend on the halyards and the outhaul to the sail (*see* Fig. 41). If the spinnaker is to answer the purpose of bowsprit spinnaker as well, another outhaul must be bent, leading through a block on bowsprit end. Generally the fore guy in such cases is made to do duty for this purpose; but if there be a fore guy beside the tack

* A fore guy is not always used in small yachts.

† Square goosenecks have gone out of fashion now, as it was difficult to get the socket fair for taking the gooseneck. With a round gooseneck and round socket this difficulty is avoided. If the boom should be shipped unfair, a marling spike in one of the holes in the boom will easily twist it round.

outhaul, care must be taken in bending the latter to see that it is *over* the fore guy, and not *under*. Bend on the sheet and belay on one of the cavel pins inside the lee rigging, with one hand to attend to it to ease up if necessary. Hoist away on the halyards, and when the sail is up chock-a-block put all hands on the outhaul, easing up the sheet all that is necessary, so as to make the sail lift in order that it may be boom-ended; drop the boom down and trim the sheet. In light winds, the sail is usually pulled out on the boom whilst it is being mast-headed. This is all very well if there be plenty of help at hand, and if there is not much wind; but generally, if the sail be hauled out on the boom first, it is found almost impossible to get the head up chock-a-block. If the sail cannot be boom ended, slacken up the sheet until the sail lifts, and haul it in again as the tack is brought to the boom end.

The American plan, and one sometimes adopted in this country, is to hoist the sail in stops, and it breaks out as the tack is hauled out to the boom end. If there be much weight in the wind, care must be taken, if the sail breaks out suddenly, that there is no great strain on the sheet, or something will be broken.

To prevent the sail going up full of turns, there is a swivel at the head, but this will not always prevent turns, as the swivel is likely to jam if any part of the sail fills; and a good plan is for a man to stand by the mast and run the luff of the sail through his hands as it goes up.

When sailing in a strong wind more or less quarterly, the boom will often rear on end in a troublesome manner, and sometimes fall forward with the sail round the topmast stay. To prevent this, "square" the boom a little and ease the sheet. Sometimes a spinnaker is reefed by tying a knot in the head; and sometimes the balloon foresail is set as a spinnaker.

To TAKE IN A SPINNAKER.—Top the boom up well clear of the rail, otherwise when the sail is taken off it the boom may drop into the water and be broken. Take hold of the foot of the sail, let go the outhaul, and haul the sail in smartly by foot and sheet; gather the sail in to the mast, well muzzling it, and then let go the halyards, and haul down.

The halyards should never be started until the sail has been hauled in-board from the boom; if the halyards are started first, and there be much wind, the sail is almost certain to blow away and then get into the water, and cause a great deal of trouble.

To SET A SPINNAKER ON THE BOWSPRIT.—Bend on the tack and halyards to leeward of jib and foresail; hoist and then pull out by the outhaul; pass the sheet outside of all and trim as required; belay to a cleat or pin aft; take in the jib, or let it run down by the head and stow and stop along the bowsprit.

To Take a Spinnaker in from the Bowsprit.—Pass the weather sheet round the fore stay to leeward and make fast to the bitts; let go the outhaul, and haul the sail in-board smartly by the weather sheet and by the foot over the lee bow. If there is only one sheet, bend a line to this sheet, with a running bight in it. Take this line forward, and haul the bight close up to the clew cringle of the sail, and haul inboard as the tack is eased up. In fresh winds the sail will have to be cut adrift. One hand will go out on the bowsprit and cut the tack (outhaul), which he will not allow to unreeve, and will bring the end in-board with him. As the sail flies aft, smartly haul it inboard by the line that has been bent round the sheet, and get hold of the foot as soon as possible; gather the sail together, so that it cannot blow out whilst the foot is being hauled inboard; when the foot is all inboard gather the sail together and lower by the halyards.

It should be clearly understood that the halyards must not be started until the foot is hauled in and the sail gathered together or "muzzled"; and, should the sail blow out, "spill" it by gathering the folds together, or it may take command and blow away, and perhaps at the same time pull someone overboard, or foul the lee crosstrees and be torn.

Racing yachts have special bowsprit spinnakers, and these are set much the same as a jib topsail, one or two hands laying out on the bowsprit and carrying the tack out; the sail is sometimes hanked to the topmast stay like a jib topsail.

To Shift a Spinnaker Boom.—Man the topping lift and hoist away. Slack up the fore guy, ease up the after guy as required, and do not let the boom swing forward as if it had to be got in on deck for stowing. When topped sufficiently carry the after guy and whip forward, passing it outside runners and rigging. Top the boom until it is lifted clear away from the gooseneck; lower by the topping lift, whilst three or four hands take it by the heel and carry it aft on the side of the mast it has to be next used. Lower sufficiently low and far enough aft to pass the upper end under the forestay, and clear of the foresheets and foresail, launch forward again and top up; ship the gooseneck as before, and shift the gear. Some large racing vessels have a well to take the heel of the boom (*see* page 74). Sometimes, where the forehatch is near the mast, as in small vessels, the heel of the boom is lowered into the forecastle; this, of course, is a simpler plan than launching the heel of the boom aft. If handled with care in smooth water, the heel of the boom can be lowered over the side.

Often, especially in small yachts which have spinnaker booms as long as the deck length is overall, the boom is topped a few feet and then let swing forward. It is then unshipped and launched aft on the opposite side of the mast until the fore end can be cleared of the forestay or foresail sheets; it is then launched forward again and re-shipped, on gooseneck.

To Set a Ringtail.—A hand must get on the main boom to fit on the ringtail boom iron, which is similar in form to the iron cap at the masthead. Bend the main peak downhaul to the boomkin (generally called ringtail boom), and hoist it to the main boom; steady it through the iron at the main boom end; cast off the peak downhaul; reeve an outhaul through the sheave hole in the end of the boomkin, and launch the spar the required distance out; then lash the heel to the main boom. In reeving the outhaul, care must be taken that the hauling part only is outside the topping lift. The head of the ringtail is bent to a yard, with three or four spare feet for the overlapping inner end. Bend the main peak downhaul to this yard for a halyard; bend both ends of the down-haul to the tack cringle (the clew cringle for the sheet will be in-board). Hoist the sail, then pull out to boomkin end by the under part of the downhaul, and sheet as required. To take this sail in, the first thing to do is to haul it in by the sheet and inhaul whilst the outhaul is slacked up. Lower by the halyards as fast as the sail is gathered in. The boomkin will be got on board by aid of the peak downhaul.

To Send up a Topmast.—Lash a tail block to the upper cap at masthead; through this reeve a rope and bring down to deck; reeve an end through the sheave hole in topmast, and make it fast some distance below the shoulder, stopping the end securely. (The heel of the topmast should be aft.) Hoist away; point the topmast through the lower cap; then make the heel rope fast to topmast, cast off the other rope, and hoist the topmast up through the upper cap by the heel rope. Put the eyes of the rigging over the pole, topmast stay over all; reeve the halyards, hitch on the tail blocks for jib-topsail and spinnaker halyards, and then send up the topmast by hauling on the heel rope and fid. Set up the backstays by the tackles and topmast stay.

The topmast will be sent down by reversing the order given above.

To House a Topmast.—Ease up the topmast stay and backstay falls. Hoist away on the heel rope until the topmast is sufficiently above the lower cap for the hand aloft to unfid. Settle down the topmast by easing up the heel rope. When lowered, so that the eyes of the rigging come close to the cap, belay the heel rope and lash the heel of topmast to the mast. Unshackle the legs of backstays and preventer backstays; hook the tackles on again, set hand taut and round in on the topmast stay.

If the vessel has much list, the topmast will not come down very readily, and the weather backstays should be kept taut, so as to keep the topmast in the line of the mast, and to prevent it breaking by sagging to leeward with its own weight. Also if there be much sea it may be found necessary to steady the topmast by the preventer and topmast stay. Generally the vessel should be eased up in the wind or hove to whilst a topmast is being housed if there be much wind and sea.

Plans for fidding and unfidding topmasts from the deck without going aloft are given on page 59, that shown by Fig. 22 being the plan most generally preferred.

To Reef a Bowsprit.—If the jib is set, ease up the sheets and belay them, well slack. Cast off the bobstay fall and the falls of the shrouds and topmast stay. Knock out the fid, and then launch the bowsprit in by the shroud tackles; fid and set up all the tackles.

To take a Reef out of the Bowsprit.—Overhaul all the tackles; launch the bowsprit out with heel rope and tackle, or by the rack-plate and wheel; fid and set the tackles taut again.

Bobstay.—In the days of long bowsprits, it was the fashion in setting up the bobstay tackle, in small racing yachts, before starting in a match, to set the bowsprit end down until it nearly touches the water. This was done in order to give more hoist and drift for the jib, as by frequent setting up the blocks would soon come "chock-a-block"; moreover, the bobstay fall is certain to "come up" or stretch a good deal, so much so that very frequently at the end of a match a bowsprit, instead of being bent downwards, is steeved in the air. The topmast stay should in such cases be looked to when heaving on the bobstay fall.

To get under Way riding Head to Wind and Tide, to run before the Wind.—Heave short; set up the bobstay; set the jib in stops; take the foresail coat off and hook on the halyards and sheets; top the boom and cast the gaskets off the mainsail. To cast to starboard, put the helm to port, heave the anchor up smartly; as the anchor is a-weigh break out the jib and set the foresail, keeping the port jib and foresheet taut. As her head goes off set the mainsail, steady the helm, and trim the sheets.

To get under Way riding Stem to Tide with Wind astern, to run before the Wind.—Heave short; loose the mainsail; set jib and foresail; break out the anchor, and when a-weigh set the mainsail.

To get under Way riding Head to Tide and Stern to Wind, to Beat to Windward.—Heave short; set the jib in stops, and hook on the fore sheets. To cast to port: put the helm to starboard, heave up the anchor; break out the jib, set the foresail (with starboard sheets hauled flat) and smartly set the mainsail. If the mainsail is set before the anchor is a-weigh, the peak should be dropped down.

To get under Way when riding Head to Wind and Tide by Casting to Starboard, to proceed on Port Tack Close-hauled.—Heave short;

H

set the jib in stops; hook on the fore sheets with the port one fast. Set the mainsail. Put the helm to port, and heave up the anchor. As the anchor is a-weigh break out the jib with port sheet hauled a-weather. Slack off the mainsheet. As the vessel's head pays off let draw the head sheets, haul in mainsheet and sail her.

To get under Way; riding Head to Wind and Tide, by Casting to Port to proceed on Port Tack.—Heave short; set the jib in stops; bend on the fore sheet, with starboard one fast. Set the mainsail. Put the helm to starboard; get the anchor; break out the jib, hauling starboard sheet in; ease off the main boom a little on the port quarter; keep the helm to starboard till the vessel's head wears off so as to bring the wind on the port quarter; the main boom will then gybe over; trim the sheets and sail the vessel. It may sometimes be advisable not to set up the peak of the mainsail until after the vessel has wore round. In the case of a yawl the mizen would be set to get under way with, and not the mainsail.

To get under Way and Leave an Anchorage to Run for it.—If possible choose slack-water time or when the tide is running to leeward. Set the trysail, reefed foresail and fourth jib. Watch for "smooths" to heave up the chain; but, if the sea is so bad that the vessel pitches head and shoulders under, so that there might be danger in pinning her down by heaving short, or if she sheers about so as to get the cable jammed hard athwart the stem, then unshackle the chain, make fast the buoy rope outside the hawse pipe, wait till the vessel sheers the way she is wanted to cast, then slip the chain and sail her.

If the vessel is wind rode, and on a lee shore, it will be prudent to claw out to sea for an offing. Set the storm canvas as if for a thrash to windward. Heave short, set the jib with the sheets slack, set the foresail, and if the vessel is to be cast on the port tack, haul in the port foresheet; put the helm to port; slack out a little mainsheet. As the vessel sheers to starboard break out the anchor or slip, and when she pays off enough so as to make sure of not flying to again, ease the fore sheet over, trim the main sheet and sail her. If the vessel does not gather way, but drives towards the shore, stand by to let go the anchor again: if one anchor has been slipped, the other should be ready on the bow. If there is not too much sea, the kedge with hawser bent to it should now be carried out in a boat; then as the anchor is hove short haul in on the hawser. When the anchor is off the ground haul the vessel ahead by the hawser, when the kedge is apeak, sheet the jib, and break out the kedge. When anchored on a lee shore a vessel should never wait till the wind and sea gets so bad that it is neither safe to remain nor to attempt to leave.

To Tack a Cutter.—When the order is given "ready about," the fore deck hands will go to their stations at fore sheets and jib sheets, and one of the after guard to the main sheet, seeing all are clear. The cry of "Lee O!" or "Helm's a-lee" will be the signal that the helm is about being put down, or is put down. As the vessel nears the wind the jib will begin to lift; then handsomely ease up the sheet and overhaul it. If the vessel is coming round smartly like a racing yacht, ease up the fore sheet or fore sheet purchase as well; the hand aft hauls in the main sheet if the breeze be very light and the vessel slow in coming up to the wind. When the vessel has passed the point "head to wind," begin to haul in the jib sheet, and get the sail sheeted and belayed before the vessel is full again and gathers way; handle the fore sheet in the same way, and overhaul the main sheet. Care must always be taken not to pull the jib sheet over the forestay, and get a strain on it before the vessel has passed the "head to wind" point, or is filling on the opposite tack to the one upon which she has been sailing; otherwise a back sail will be formed, and the vessel may fall off again. On the other hand the jib, when the time comes for working the sheets, must be sheeted with all despatch; as, if the vessel is allowed to fill before the jib sheets are in, it will be hardly possible to get them in properly without a tackle if there be a nice breeze. So with the fore sheet.

In tacking a vessel in a sea, the fore sheet should not as a rule be let go until it is seen whether the vessel is going to fill on the other tack or not, as the sail may be wanted to pay her head off: when the vessel fills, the fore sheets must be handled with smartness. If there is much sea, a "smooth" should be watched for, to tack in. Never, if it can be avoided, attempt to tack with a big comber rolling in on the weather bow, as a "miss-stays" may be the consequence, to say nothing of the water that might be thrown on deck.

The helmsman will soon find out how the vessel likes the helm put down for quick staying; but generally the vessel should be kept a good full before giving lee helm. Then at first ease the helm down gradually, so as to shoot a good distance, and make as big a circle as possible, but be very careful not to keep the vessel shooting till her way is stopped; as she comes near head to wind, put the helm right over to the rail, and keep it there till the vessel fills and gathers way on the other tack; keep the vessel a little off a good full till she is reaching along, and then bring her to the wind "full and bye."

To Tack a Yawl.—The only way in which tacking a yawl is different from tacking a cutter is that there is the mizen-stay to work. The stays lead forward from the mizen-mast head, and are set up by tackles; only the weather one is set up. The weather tackle is overhauled in tacking, and the lee set taut, and forms the weather one when the vessel has filled on the opposite tack. Generally a yawl does not stay so quickly as a cutter, and more frequently requires backing off by the foresail.

To Tack a Schooner.—Keep the vessel a good full. As the vessel comes head to wind ease up the jib sheet, but do not let it "fly"; overhaul the fore sheet purchase and fore-staysail purchase, and overhaul fore-topsail tack and sheet and clew up. When the vessel is head to wind cast off the standing part of fore sheet and fore-staysail sheet. As she passes the point "head to wind" haul in jib sheets and belay; haul in the standing part of the fore sheet and fore-staysail sheet and belay; then be smart with the purchases and get the foot of the foresail as straight as possible; fore-staysail sheet not quite so "straight," as there should be a little flow in the after leech, owing to the angle made by the luff of the sail, and if the foot be hauled "bar taut," the leech will generally be so too. Tack and sheet the foretopsail.

In hauling in the fore sheet all hands should be outside it, and not between the sheet and the rail. Care should also be taken that the fall of the purchase is clear and ready to lay hold of directly the standing part of the sheet is fast. One hand should be selected to stand by the fore sheet cavel, and he should belay. Directly the order "belay!" is given all hands should haul on the fall of the purchase; the belaying hand taking care that a turn of the standing part of the sheet is caught round the cavel. It is highly important that the fore sheet of a schooner should be well taut; as, if the foot be slack, the sail, not being set on a boom, is certain to bag more or less. And when sailing close-hauled and the wind frees a trifle, the fore sheet should always be the last one to be checked.

Stern Way in Tacking.—In square-rigged ships "stern way" is commonly the result of letting the head yards lie aback during tacking, but a fore-and-aft vessel, in tacking under ordinary conditions, should not be subject to stern way. However, sometimes, even in smooth water, if a vessel has been brought head to wind either too suddenly or too slowly, she may get stern way, or be placed in the situation known as "in irons," when she will neither fall off on one tack nor the other, after being brought head to wind. If the vessel has stern way, it must be recollected that the action of the rudder is different from what it is with head way; that is to say, if during stern way the helm be put to starboard, the action of the water on the rudder will force the stern to port and the bow to starboard; and if the helm be put to port, the stern will be forced to starboard and the bow to port. Under the influence of head way opposite results are obtained. The rudder has very reduced effect in turning a vessel one way or the other during stern way.

Let it be assumed that a vessel has been sailing on the port tack, and on the helm being put down that she failed to get farther than head to wind, or that she got in irons; the result would be that the wind would drive her astern—this would soon be discovered by looking at the water over the quarter or stern, as the "wake" will show in eddies along the side of the vessel. The helm would be to starboard, and would have to be shifted to port, and the starboard fore sheet and jib sheet hauled in, and the main boom eased off. The stern would gradually drive to starboard, and the bow, under the influence of head sails aback, would go off to port. The head sails being aback would of course increase the stern way, and directly the vessel's head was well off the wind, and the vessel insured against coming to again, the head sheets should be eased up and hauled in to leeward. She would require to fall off till the wind was brought nearly abeam before she gathered headway, and then the boom could be hauled aboard again.

Under the influence of stern way the pressure of water on the lee quarter can be made to help turn the vessel just the same as the pressure on the lee bow helps to press the bow towards the wind when a vessel moves ahead. Or suppose the vessel be head to wind, and has stern way on, and it is desired to cast her head to port, or fill her on the starboard tack; then if she be listed or heeled to port by all hands going on the port side or port quarter, the ardency of the pressure on the port quarter will press the stern to starboard, and necessarily the bow turns to port.

Thus, it will be frequently found, that the bow of a vessel, if she has sternway, and is heeled, will very rapidly fall off to leeward; even though the head sails are not aback, and the rudder, from the way it is turned, should prevent her doing so.

It should, therefore, be remembered, that when a vessel gets in irons, and is under the influence of stern way, that she should be, if possible, listed on the side it is sought to make the lee side. Easing the main boom off will allow the stern to come up against the wind more rapidly, and will help heel the vessel.

MISSING STAYS.—To get in irons or to get stern way on a vessel is not exactly missing stays, as to miss stays means to come up head to wind and then to fall off on the same tack again—in fact, to fail in going about. Generally a vessel has a tendency to miss stays through having too little after-canvas; that is to say, the centre of effort of the sails is too far ahead of the centre of lateral resistance, and consequently she may even carry her helm a-lee and have very little to work upon in tacking. The fault may be cured by reducing the head sail; by increasing the after sail; by shifting the mast aft without reducing the sail; by rounding up the fore foot and heel; or by rounding up the heel.

But a vessel may generally stay well enough, and only fail in going about through meeting a sea on her weather bow as she is brought to the wind; or through the wind following her round; or through the helm being put down too quickly or too slowly; or through the head sails being badly worked; or through her having insufficient way on when the attempt was made to tack. Whatever the cause, directly it is seen that the vessel is going to fall off on the same tack again after coming to, lose no time; haul the fore sheet, and jib sheet too, if necessary, up to windward, slack out the main sheet, and, if the vessel has stern way, bring the helm amidships. Directly she has fallen six or seven points off the wind, ease over the head sheets and trim them to leeward; and as she gathers headway haul in the main sheet, and sail the vessel a good full, and try again. At the next attempt, as the helm is put down, ease up the jib sheet smartly and haul in the main sheet, but let the fore sheet lie till the vessel falls off on the desired tack.

GYBING OR WEARING.—To gybe or wear is to keep the vessel off the wind by bringing the helm to windward until the wind comes astern and then on the opposite side to which it has been blowing. This manoeuvre has sometimes to be resorted to when a vessel miss-stays. Set taut the weather topping-lift. Ease off the main sheet until the boom is well off the lee quarter, and if there be much wind or sea, trice up the main tack and lower the peak; if a topsail is set it should be clewed up. Have as many hands as can be spared at the main sheet. Put the helm up. As the vessel's head goes off and brings the wind nearly astern, rally in the main sheet, and be careful that there is a smart hand stationed to take a turn with it. As the vessel comes nearly stern on to the wind, overhaul what has been the weather runner; catch a turn with the main sheet; and, as the boom goes over, meet her with the helm, so that she does not fly to, head to wind. Ease up the topping lift, and trim tacks and sheets.

If the vessel be already before the wind with the main boom square off, when it is necessary to gybe her, take the same precautions, if there be much wind, by tricing up the main tack, lowering peak, and clewing up topsail, not forgetting to set the weather topping-lift well taut, if it is not already taut, as it certainly should be. Luff a little, and get in some of the main sheet; when the boom is on the quarter (at about an angle of 45° with the keel), steady the helm and put up gradually, still getting in the main sheet. Hook on what has been the lee runner and set taut. Then, as the wind is brought astern, overhaul the weather runner, belay the main sheet, let the boom go over, and meet the vessel with the helm. Overhaul the lee-topping lift, and trim tacks and sheets.

These are the ordinary precautions taken in gybing in strong breezes whilst cruising; but in match sailing, unless something like a gale of wind be blowing, the main tack is not triced up, nor is the peak lowered, nor the topsail clewed up. There will, however, be the topmast preventer backstay to attend to. Station one man at the weather preventer to overhaul and unhook the tackle as the boom comes amidships. One hand to the fall of the whip of the lee preventer, who must haul the backstay aft as fast as the main boom is brought aboard; he must get the whip as taut as he can, and belay before the boom is gybed. The tackle (already hooked on the preventer) must be set smartly as the boom swings over. In large vessels two hands should be told off to the lee preventer to get it set up smartly.

In a schooner similar precautions will be taken, and there will be the fore-topmast preventer backstays to attend to, and the fore-topsail should be clewed up. The fore sheet can be left until after the main boom is over.

GYBING ALL STANDING.—In very light winds it is a common practice to "gybe all standing," that is without rounding in the main sheet; but care should always be taken to let go the topmast preventer backstay and the runner. To gybe all standing when there is much wind is a very dangerous operation, and special alertness should be shown to endeavour to "meet" the vessel with the helm, as she will most likely fly to, after the boom goes over. (See the article "Running before the Wind," and the chapter on "Yacht Racing.")

CLUB HAULING.—Club hauling may have to be resorted to in a narrow channel sometimes when there is neither room to stay nor wear. Get an anchor on the lee bow with a warp bent to it; lead the latter to the lee quarter. Have the cable ranged on deck unshackled; put the helm down, and keep shooting with the sails shivering. When way is stopped, let go the anchor; as she is brought head to wind let all the cable run out through the hawse pipe, and haul in on the spring. The anchor, of course, will be got in over the stern. Another better plan for a small vessel is to bend a warp to the kedge, and as the helm is put down drop the kedge over the stern, then hold on and haul in on the warp.

To HEAVE TO.—Haul the fore sheet up to windward, and the jib sheet until the clew just clears the forestay; ease the main sheet until the vessel lies quiet with her helm amidships, or a little to leeward. A vessel will lie like this very quiet, just forging ahead perhaps a knot an hour or so, and occasionally falling off, when she will take a great list as the wind comes abeam; directly, however, the after canvas is well filled she will spring to again, and if she is coming up with too much way on, so as to be likely to get head to wind, she must be checked by weather helm. To lie-to very dead so as to pick up a boat or speak another vessel, &c., it will be well to let the jib sheet fly and haul the fore sheet hard a-weather, with main sheet eased and helm a-lee.

In heaving to in heavy weather the mainsail is stowed and boom lashed, in the crutch, to each quarter. Instead of the mainsail a reefed trysail is set, or storm trysail, which is either jib-headed or has a very short gaff, and is hauled up close to the hounds in order that it should not get becalmed when the yacht is in the hollow of the sea. Bowsprit is run in until the outer end is within a few feet of the gammon iron, and storm jib set on it, with both sheets fast, and clew hauled up to windward of the forestay. Foresail stowed. Trysail sheet (a luff tackle) hauled aft. In the case of a schooner the storm jib can be tacked inside the forestay to the bitts, with clew just to windward of the foremast; main-trysail close reefed, or storm trysail, as the weather requires.

A yawl would be hove to just the same as a cutter, but if she were riding to a floating anchor a storm mizen might be set, but no other sail. As a rule the more sail a vessel will bear when she is hove to in bad weather the better, as the sail will tend to check the weather rolling; for this reason ships usually heave to under topsails, as the lower sail might be becalmed in the trough of the sea; for the same reason the trysail is cut narrow and high, and the same amount of canvas close to the deck would not be nearly so effective. Sail at the extreme ends of a vessel is never required, and a yawl hove to under storm jib and mizen would not lie nearly so quiet as she would if hove to under storm trysail and storm jib inside the forestay, as every time the headsail was becalmed she would be fetched to against the sea very hard by the mizen, or as the mizen was becalmed as she scended, she would fall off to a troublesome extent.

The helm can be left to take care of itself, or the tiller lines will be belayed on each side, slack, so as to allow a great deal of freedom for falling off with the sea. The general practice, however, is to have a hand to attend to the helm to humour the vessel as she falls off and bring her to again quietly up to the sea. A vessel will generally fall off as the crest of a wave comes in on the weather bow, and come to as the bow is in the hollow of a wave, or as the crest of a wave lifts the stern. Shallow vessels fall off much more freely than deep vessels, and come to with much more way on. The principal danger is that, if much way be gathered in coming to, a vessel should also meet with a big comber on the weather bow; to avoid this danger the man at the helm should meet the vessel as she runs off, and bring her to with the helm so that she fairly bows the sea, always being careful not to get her head to wind. At the same time, as before said, a vessel must be allowed to fall off freely with the sea, to the extent perhaps of three or four points, or until the wind was nearly abeam; but in bringing her to, her head should never be allowed to come within a couple of points of the wind.

To HEAVE TO AFTER RUNNING BEFORE A HEAVY SEA.—Give warning below that the vessel is about to be brought by the wind, and see that everything is well secured about the deck. Watch for a "smooth" (which is brought about by several large waves meeting, and being broken up and dispersed into several small ones). Put the helm down, rally in the main sheet smartly; meet the vessel with the weather helm before she gets head to wind. Trim the head sheets as necessary. If the vessel has been running with a great deal of canvas set, it must be reduced as the vessel is brought to the wind; and the throat of the mainsail should be lowered half down, and the tack triced up as the vessel comes to.

To HEAVE TO TO PICK UP A BOAT.—It will be supposed that the wind is blowing off shore, and that the yacht is in the offing waiting for the boat. As the boat gets off into deep water, the yacht will reach in past to leeward of her from fifty to one hundred yards clear; then put the helm down, and shoot up towards her, keeping the jib sheet and fore sheet fast so as to lie a-weather as she fills on the other tack; or the jib sheets can be slackened well up so that the jib can blow about. If well judged the boat will now be close under the lee side of the yacht, and a hand will be ready to throw a line into her as she comes alongside. If the wind is blowing on the shore similar tactics will be observed, but a greater sweep must be taken in coming to, and the main sheet must be well rounded in as the helm is eased down. Sometimes under such conditions the yacht will run in to windward of the boat and wear round, but generally it is safer to keep to leeward and bring the yacht to.

SQUALLS.—If a squall is long foreseen, the sailing master will of course have snugged down and got his vessel so as to meet it end on if possible; but if caught unawares lose no time in letting jib sheets fly, and haul down the foresail. Set the topping-lifts taut; let the throat run half down the mast, and trice up the main tack. Or let the peak drop down between the topping-lifts until the gaff is about square to or at right angles to the mast. Then haul up the main tack and the mainsail will be scandalised. If the sail be a laced one the throat must be let down instead of the peak, keeping the peak downhaul fast to the centre of the boom to leeward to prevent the sail blowing out. In short-handed vessels the throat is generally let down in preference to the peak, as the sail is then more easily managed, and it is easier to get the throat up again than the peak.

If the vessel has the wind abaft the beam when she is actually struck, put the helm up a little to keep her before the squall. If the squall strikes her before the beam, put the helm down. If the vessel gets struck or knocked down on her side before the sails can be lowered, and will not come to, cast off the jib sheets, pull the foresail down by the downhaul. Haul the main boom well aboard, cast off the throat halyards and the throat will fly down, then cast off the peak halyards and haul in on the peak downhaul. If the vessel does not right, get the kedge up if a bottom can be reached, bend the hawser to it and let go over the stern; then the vessel may wear round so that the wind will take her on the other side. If the ballast or anything else shifts to leeward, trim it back to windward. Close up the companion hatchways and skylights to keep the water out.

To Scandalise a Mainsail.—Set taut the topping lifts. Trice up the tack as high as possible, and lower down the peak between the lifts.

Sailing by the Wind.—Sailing a vessel successfully on a wind is quite an art, and no amount of tuition will make a man a good helmsman if he be not "to the manner born." However, there is scarcely a yacht sailor who does not think he can steer a boat on a wind better than any other man. Still the fact remains, that some men cannot sail a vessel on a wind, and no amount of instruction will teach them to know for themselves when a vessel's sails are full or when they are "starved of wind." Some vessels are so beautifully balanced—that is, the centre of effort of their sails and centre of lateral resistance so nicely adjust themselves—that in moderate breezes they will "sail themselves" if close hauled, and only require a little weather helm now and again as the wind heads them. Yet a bad helmsman will find more difficulty or do worse in steering one of these vessels than he would in steering a very hard-mouthed vessel—one that carries a lot of weather helm, for we never suppose that a yacht carries lee helm. The well-balanced vessel is what may be called sensitive to her helm, or "tender mouthed," and the least touch of her helm will bring her to, and the gentlest pull on the weather tiller lines will take her off; such a vessel steered by a man with a "coarse hand" will be always "off" or "near," and never really "full and bye;" one minute he will slam the helm down to bring her to the wind, and the next haul it savagely to windward to keep her off the wind; whereas, if the vessel had been left alone with a free tiller, or with only the very slightest strain on the weather tiller lines, she would keep herself full and at the same time eat to windward as she luffed to every free puff. A vessel which carries much weather helm does not require such delicate handling, and a man may tear away at the weather tiller lines until he is black in the face without doing much harm; he will be delighted to find he has something to "hold on by," and all the strength in his arms will no more than keep the vessel out of the wind. But, although a good helms-man cannot be made out of a naturally bad one, it does not follow that a few hints would not be of service to the inexperienced who may have the light hand, quick eye, and sensitive skin of a perfect timoneer.

In the first place the sails should be as nicely balanced as possible, so that in a topsail breeze, when the channels are barely awash, the weather tiller lines only require to be kept hand taut, with the rudder turned no more than six or seven degrees off the keel line. We are, of course, assuming that the sail plan has been so judiciously arranged that the effort of the sails when effectively trimmed, will be balanced by the lateral pressure on the hull. If the sails are so well balanced then the weather helm will about equal five or six degrees in a moderate breeze, and it should not much exceed this nor be much less; if it is much in excess the vessel will be what is called ardent, and her constant effort to fly to, will necessitate the helm being kept "right across her keel," which will very much interfere with her speed. On the other hand, if much less than six degrees of weather helm is carried in such a breeze the vessel will be what is called "slack," and will require constant doses of lee helm; the result will be that the vessel will crab to leeward, and in tacking will be so slow in coming to that she will probably lose all way ere she gets head to wind, and then will require helping round by the foresail.

If the vessel in a nice breeze does not seem to gripe as she ought—that is, does not make much effort to fly to, and so cause a good strain on the weather tiller lines to keep her off the wind—first see what the effect of drawing in the main sheet a trifle will do; if this only improves matters a trifle, and the boat seems dead in the water or does not pass through it with any life, go forward or to leeward, under the foot of the mainsail near the mast, and have a look at the jib sheets and foresheet. See that the jib sheets are not pinned in, and that they are rove through the right holes. If the first jib be set and the sheets rove through the second jib-holes, the foot will be drawn into a curve and the sail more or less in a bag; the effect will be to drag the vessel's head off the wind, and not assist in driving her ahead an inch. If the sheets be rightly rove, but hauled in too flat, the foot of the jib will be straight enough, and the sail generally be flat enough; but the effect will be that the sail, being trimmed too flat, will, as in the other case, press the vessel's head off the wind, and be of little service towards driving her ahead. It requires some experience of jibs and the way of trimming their sheets to know when they are trimmed so as to be most effective, and it would be difficult to frame advice on the point to meet all cases; but the leech should be straight, the foot gently curved or "flowing" with the sheet, and the luff should not lift—*i.e.*, shake into ripples. If the other sails are full and the luff lifts it will be a sign, as a rule, that the sail is not sheeted flat enough. On the other hand, the clew should be well off the lee rail, and the sheet and the foot should make a gentle flowing curve from bowsprit end to sheet hole; if the sheet and the foot, when the sails are full, make a "straight line," it will be a pretty sure sign that the sheet is too flat. It is a good plan to mark the jib sheets where they nip the sheet holes by a piece of yarn, for sailing by the wind; yet it is always to be remembered that a jib must be sheeted to suit the strength of the wind.

If the vessel carries an excessive amount of weather helm, more than previous experience of her sailing would lead one to expect, and does not pass through the water freely, it may be relieved by easing off the mainsheet a trifle, and flattening-in the jib sheets, but the main sheet must not be so much eased as to cause the weather cloths of the sail to lift, nor must the jib sheet be flattened-in so as to make the jib simply a pressing sail. In vessels which are broad across the deck at the bow like the modern "raters," the jib sheets can be much better trimmed, as there is less chance of getting the sheets too flat; hence, as a rule, second jibs are always made to stand better than first jibs, as they do not go out so far on the bowsprit, and the angle made by the sheet is therefore coarser. [In very narrow vessels outriggers were formerly sometimes used to lead the sheets through and get more spread.]

It can be supposed that the sails are all nicely trimmed, doing their work properly, and that the vessel carries just the right amount of weather helm, and will fly to directly the weather tiller lines are released. Under these conditions the tiller is handed over to the young helmsman, and we will first say a few words as to the position he should take. As a rule, the steersman stands near to, or sits on the weather rail, and this is undoubtedly the best position; he can then look into the jib and foresail, see when they are inclined to lift, and at the same time watch the luff of the mainsail and the vane or flag, which, if there be a topsail set, should flicker just on the weather side of the yard. But sometimes in light winds a man may sit on the lee rail and watch the head sails from under the lee of the mainsail, and this will be occasionally a capital position if a jib topsail be set. The weather tiller-line must, of course, be rove through the sheave in the weather rail, then, with the fall in his hand to leeward, the helmsman can keep his vessel off or bring her to at will. Of course, we do not mean that a man might always equally well sit down to leeward and steer, but there is no better place for seeing the sit of the sails, and an occasional visit to leeward will often prevent the necessity for shouting out "How are the head sheets?" which invariably produces a general scramble of the crew to the lee bow, and a meaningless chorus "All right, sir!" Some men we have seen get a deck cushion and sit down by the side of the tiller and hug it as if they had got hold of the neck of a favourite donkey. They may be very good helmsmen, but their hunched-up appearance, as they squat on their haunches cuddling the tiller, necessarily makes one form a very poor opinion, at least, of their "style," and frequently the man can be put down as more or less of a sloven.

It can be concluded that the best position for the helmsman when sailing on a wind is as near the weather rail as possible; he can then really see for himself what the head sails are doing, and the admonition " She's near for'ard " need never be heard.

The jib, when properly sheeted, is perhaps the best guide for the young helmsman, and if he steers by that alone, he ought always to be able to keep his vessel full and yet not allow her to get off the wind. With a nice topsail breeze—not strong enough to lay the vessel in to the deck—the luff of the jib will be just rippled, or the canvas into which the luff rope is stitched will more or less "bag," and will be in a constant state of quivering; but the luff of the sail must not be allowed to lift, *i.e.*, to go into large folds, as, if it does, it will be a sign that the vessel is too near. If you are keeping the vessel a good full there will be no ripples or wrinkles in the luff of the jib—unless the jib be a very old and badly-stretched one—and all the sails will be quiet.

In sailing by the luff of the mainsail, as some men do who cuddle the tiller, the young helmsman may be apt to get his vessel off the wind, as he will be constantly thinking she is "near," through the eddy wind out of the foresail making the luff of the mainsail lift into wrinkles. The luff of the mainsail is thus a not very trustworthy guide for the inexperienced helmsman; still, as a rule, when the luff of the mainsail lifts and the disturbance begins to travel aft across the belly of the sail in waves, it will be a pretty sure sign that the vessel is "starved of wind," and a little weather helm should be given her.

Sailing by the vane, whip, burgee, or racing flag, is sometimes said to be the easiest and at the same time the most trustworthy guide for close-hauled sailing; but a very little experience will soon prove the fallacy of this. If the vessel is moving along at a good pace, say five or six knots an hour, the flag will blow aft nearly in a line with the keel, and if there be a square-headed topsail set, the flag will flicker on the weather side of the yard. But in such light winds as we are now assuming to blow, there may be quite a different current of wind aloft. Thus we frequently hear the remark " She's near for'ard " responded to by the helmsman, " She's all full aloft—look at the flag,"—and probably the flag will be right across the vessel. Or the flag may blow out to windward of the topsail yard, or droop and cause the helmsman to think that he has got his vessel head to wind, and he will of course haul the tiller to windward. This, perhaps, will cause a shout of " Bring her to !" or " Let her luff, she's all off the wind," and an appeal to the vane or racing flag will only show what a misleading guide it is. In fact, trying to sail the vessel by a vane, or by the luff of a topsail, will be certain to cause " remarks " to be made forward, and as these remarks have always an irritating effect on the steersman, he had better sail on a wind by the head sails than by the flag, especially so as he will thereby be able to keep the lower sails doing their work, and it is the lower sails which must be mostly depended upon for getting through the water.

An old hand will sit down by the tiller and, perhaps, close his eyes, and still fairly sail a vessel on a wind, as long practice will tell him whether the sails are full or not by the feeling of the wind on his face. He will not deign to look at jib, mainsail, or flag, but will give the vessel lee or weather helm just as he feels the wind on his face comes freer or shorter. This really is a very good guide, and the steersman, when he gets thoroughly acquainted with the sailing of a vessel on a wind, will find a " chill " on his face a very trustworthy hint as to the doing of a paltry, shy, or baffling wind.

In sailing on a wind, keep an eye on the head sails, after sail, upper sail, and vane, and the other eye to windward, for nine times out of ten the direction of an impending puff can be seen as it travels towards the weather bow of the vessel, rippling the water in its course. If the dark ripples are seen coming broad on the bow, you will know that it will be a good luffing puff, and as it takes hold of the vessel, ease the weather tiller lines, and let her luff to it freely, but do not allow the jib to lift; then, if the puff is a mere " chill," out of a passing cloud, perhaps, and leaves the wind as before, do not wait till the puff has passed over before the helm is hauled a-weather again, or the vessel will be left nearly head to wind, and this would be a very lubberly proceeding; therefore, before the " free puff " has blown itself out, haul up the helm and get the vessel full and bye again.

If you see that the puff is a strong one, of the nature of a squall, do not get nervous and luff before it strikes the vessel, unless of course it is considered prudent to shoot up head to wind to meet it. If you begin luffing and lifting the sails before the squall strikes, you will deaden the way of the vessel, and then the squall will have much greater effect in heeling the vessel, and will perhaps take the topmast away—as a very frequent cause of topmasts being broken is by being caught in a puff when the vessel has no way, or but little way, on.

But puffs as frequently come ahead as they do broad on the bow, and the head puffs are the more difficult to deal with. Keep a good look-out for these "nose-enders," and if lucky enough to see one before it reaches the jib, keep the vessel off a little, and, if possible, prevent the sails lifting at all. These puffs will be most frequently met with when sailing along under high land or under trees; one minute a puff will come broad on the bow or on the beam and lay the vessel in to the skylights, and the next one will come right ahead and bring her upright as a monolith; and what with luffing to one puff and keeping away for another, the helmsman will have his vigilance very highly tested. He, of course, will not be able to keep the sails from lifting at all, as the puffs are more or less revolving, and Palinurus himself could not successfully dodge them; still, with care, a vessel should never be allowed to get head to wind so as to want backing off by hauling the fore sheet to windward and easing off the main boom—this would not be seamanlike, and would betoken great inattention.

In luffing to free puffs, or in keeping away for foul ones, do not "slam" the helm about; that is, do not shove it down as if you were trying to avoid striking something, or haul it up as if you were bearing away round a mark. In most cases easing the tiller lines will enable the vessel to luff all that is necessary, and when free puffs are prevalent a very light hand should be kept on the tiller lines, and the vessel will dance herself to windward and eat out on the weather of one whose tiller has been held in an iron grip, or with two or three turns round the tiller head, during all the puffs. Get all the luffing possible out of a vessel, and never miss the smallest chance of a gripe to windward, even to a quarter of a point of the compass; but do not put the helm down so coarsely that there is a danger of bringing the vessel nearly head to wind; if this is done the helm will have to be put hard up to get her off the wind again, and nothing so interferes with good performance on a wind as too much ruddering. A good helmsman must have a light hand and unceasing vigilance, as weatherliness is no small degree dependent on the helm. Therefore it cannot be too frequently repeated that the faintest semblance of a luffing puff must never be disregarded, and the vessel must at the same time be humoured so tenderly to it, that no one shall see what the helmsman is about unless by watching his movements very closely. On the other hand, in using weather helm in keeping off to avoid a foul puff, it will not do to be too slow with the helm, or the vessel will be stopped, and, without way on, it will be some trouble to get her full and going again. Therefore always haul the helm up as promptly as possible, but do not haul it savagely on to the weather rail as if you were going to sail "large" for the rest of the day. If a puff is not seen coming broad on to the bow, but more or less ahead, be careful that directly the jib shows the slightest sign of lifting to drag steadily on the weather tiller lines; if the puff is a very bad one, the helm must be smartly hauled aweather, but as a rule the foul puffs will not vary in direction more than a couple of points from the direction of the true wind, and they must be accorded with by as delicate a use of the helm as for "luffing puffs."

Thus the secret of close-hauled sailing consists in such a constant watching of the wind and such a use of the helm to meet its variations, that the vessel is always "full and bye," and never "near" and never "off" the wind. A man who can so sail a vessel is a perfect helmsman.

Speaking of professional skippers reminds us that many of the old-fashioned yacht "captains" had a funny habit of "sawing" the helm backwards and forwards; that is, they haul on the weather tiller lines and then ease them without apparent motive, generally accompanying the performance with a corresponding see-sawing motion of the body, by first resting on one foot and then on the other. Probably this peculiar habit was acquired on board fishing vessels in the winter, when the men might find sawing the helm and working their bodies about promote warmth. It certainly is no assistance to a vessel, and is very "bad form." Others have a worse habit than this, of taking a turn round the tiller head with the tiller lines, and never easing them for a free puff or hauling on them for a foul one.

Sailing a vessel in a strong wind, say with the scuppers full of water, will not be quite such a delicate operation; still, the wind will vary a great deal, and the very most must be made of the free puffs, and the effect of foul ones reduced as much as possible. The vessel will of course carry a great deal more weather helm, and when the sails are nicely trimmed the jib will be found the most reliable sail to steer by, as the luff of the mainsail will lift a great deal from the mere effect of the wind out of the foresail. Look out for the very hard puffs, and do not allow the vessel to needlessly bury herself; on the other hand, do not get frightened at a little water on deck, and throw the vessel in the wind. Sail her along heartily, even to the rail under, but never forget to ease the tiller lines for the smallest freeing of the wind; and for the very heavy puffs do not luff before they strike, but luff into them as they strike; the vessel will then not be knocked down so badly, and will walk off with increased speed by the aid of the puff.

It must not be supposed that it is a good thing for a vessel to be sailed with her rail under and the water nearly up to her skylights; but in sailing on a wind she should not be luffed up for the mere sake of getting her out of such a condition if it is only a passing puff that has laid her in; luffing, as a rule, in close-hauled sailing, in our heavily-ballasted yachts, is to take advantage of free puffs; but occasionally when the puff is very strong, and neither free nor foul, advantage may be taken of its strength to do a little luffing, and at the same time clear the lee deck of water; in such luffing the chief care of the helmsman will be not to get the vessel so near the wind as to much stop her way or to risk getting into irons.

Frequently in match sailing a vessel is found to be heading for her mark, and the hope of the helmsman will very properly be that she will fetch without making a tack; but he must not get anxious about it, and hug the wind; if he does the vessel's way will be deadened, she will make an unusual amount of leeway, and it will be a hundred to one against her fetching. He must sail her along boldly, not getting off the wind and courting another tack, but exercising all his care in keeping her an exact full; she will probably fetch, and if her head now and again falls to leeward of the mark, it will probably come to windward of it again: on no account get nervous and try to *steer* for the mark. If such an attempt is made, the mark will not be fetched, and the attempt will be quite contrary to the principle of the art of close-hauled sailing, which art cannot be regulated by "steering" for fixed marks. There is an old saying "keep a vessel full and she will eat herself to windward, but try to sail her in the wind's eye and she will crab to leeward." Occasionally a little "niggling," as it is called, may be indulged in if the mark is very near; but even then the vessel must not be sailed so fine as to cause the head sails to actually lift; and when within one hundred yards or so of the mark she should be ramped along a good full and shot up to windward of the mark with good way on, as if she be gilled up to the mark with little way on, and got met at the last moment by an unfriendly puff, a collision with the mark would be almost a matter of certainty. This, although a most humiliating spectacle, very often happens, as skippers will do almost anything to save a tack; but it is only the smartest of them that can judge when a tack can be profitably saved and when not. (*See* "Over-reaching.")

SAILING A VESSEL ON A WIND IN A HEAVY SEA.—It will require some nerve to sail a vessel successfully on a wind in a heavy sea. Often a haunting fear that the bowsprit will be carried away, or the deck swept by a green sea, makes a man have the vessel's sails constantly lifting; the result is that she tumbles about in the sea like a log, sags to leeward,

I

and gets the character of being a bad sea boat.   Do not fear the breaking of a bowsprit or a green sea on deck ; be not unmindful of either, but above all things keep the sails full; this is the secret of success in sailing on a wind in a sea.   Of course it is assumed that the vessel is properly canvassed, and the sheets eased a bit to what they would be in smooth water : if she has two reefs down in the mainsail, that the foresail is single reefed, third jib set, bowsprit reefed, topmast housed, and everything securely lashed on deck.   The vessel should be canvassed so that in the true strength of the wind the covering board would be well out of the water—a fourth of the height of freeboard.   It is of the first importance to remember that in a sea it will not do to sail a vessel rail under, as a weight of water on deck and the fact of the vessel being over on her side will greatly interfere with her good performance; therefore a vessel should be canvassed so that her rail will not go under, and in the squalls she must be eased judiciously with the helm, always remembering that although occasional easing may be prudent the chief aim must be to keep her full.   The main boom should be carried a couple of feet or so farther off than it is in smooth water, and the weather topping-lift should always carry the weight of the boom.   The fore sheet should also be eased, but the jib sheet should not be eased so much as to cause the jib to lift badly, as the jib will be wanted to keep the vessel out of the wind, especially after she has been eased into a sea.

As a rule the vessel will be found to pitch pretty regularly, and one sea being very much like another, the vessel will be sailed through all, hard and a good full.   Do not let her sails shake, as her way will be stopped ; she will then pound the sea and jump two or three times into the same hole.   Those on board will say " what a horrid bad sea boat she is, that she pitched two or three times to the once of any other vessel, and always had her deck full of water."   But keep a wary look-out for the big seas.   One will be seen rolling in on the weather bow, gradually gaining in height, and perhaps rising, pinnacle like, just at the point where the vessel will meet it.   This is the wave to be ready to meet ; it will rise higher and higher as it gets towards you, and will either curl over and break up by its own exhaustion, or from the fact of its meeting the vessel, and there will be in either case a ton or two of green water on deck.   Just before the big wave reaches the vessel there will be an unusual hollow or deep trough, and into this she will and must go ; before she can recover herself the big wave will roll over and fairly swallow her up; then there will be a smooth; a number of small waves will be formed; the vessel will give one or two deep dives—the result of her bow being thrown up by the big wave—and then be steadied for a minute or so in the smooth.

When a big sea like this is seen on the weather bow, the vessel's helm should be eased down a little just before the sea reaches her, so that she may take it more fairly stem on; but in luffing into the wave do it in good time, and directly she is fairly into it put up the helm again, and fill her sails before she has time to get head to wind. The object in easing the vessel is of course to ease the shock both by deadening her way and by presenting the stem to the sea instead of the bluff of the bow; therefore directly the sea and the vessel have met, the effect is over, and the sails of the vessel must be filled instantly; that is, she must be put off the wind again to a good full and bye.

The most tiresome of all seas to sail a vessel in are those which are met with on a weather-going tide in more or less shallow water, such as on the Brambles, at the mouth of Southampton Water, or on the Bar at the entrance to the Mersey, or at the Nore. Here the sea is furrow-like; that is, the troughs are long and deep, and the crests of the waves are a succession of sharp ridges instead of the long-backed waves met with in deep water. So long as a vessel keeps time with these waves, that is, so long as she only pitches once into each hollow, there will be a regular succession of pitching and scending; but if, through the wind heading her, or through careless steering, her way becomes deadened, and she pitches twice into the same hollow, or if she does so through meeting a trough of unusual breadth, there will be trouble on deck in the way of water, as the vessel will meet the wave crest just as she takes her second dive instead of when she scends from her first. There will be two or three very quick dives after this, and the helmsman must keep the vessel full; not shake her up because she is taking these unpleasant plunges, but keep her full in order to help her going through the sea, and to get her into the regular fall and rise of the waves again, or, as the sailors say, make her toe and heel to the tune.

It can be supposed that the vessel is sailing in a pretty regular sea, and that she rises, and at the same time cleaves through a wave as at A (Fig. 44). Whilst she is going up through the wave, or scending, she will show a tendency to come up to the wind, as her stern will be so little pressed by the water that it will go off to leeward. She will stop in suspense for a moment and then pass rapidly through the wave, and the next moment will be in the position B (Fig. 45), when her bow, being unsupported, it will fly off the wind. This latter tendency must be guarded against, as in another moment the vessel will be in the position C (Fig. 46), with water well nigh up to the bowsprit bitts. She will rise streaming with water at *d*, and take the position A again, and so on *ad nauseam*. Very frequently a vessel will shoot so far through a wave when in the position A, that she even gets farther through it than shown by B; this is what a vessel does that is sailed fast through a sea with a lot of canvas and with a tremendous momentum, due to the speed and weight of the

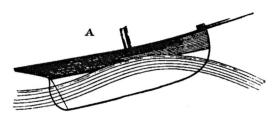

FIG. 44.

vessel and her manner of ballasting. Often two or three bigger waves than usual will come one after the other and then there will be a smooth as the waves break up. Frequently these bigger waves apparently follow each other, when in reality the vessel is only plunging from the effects of the

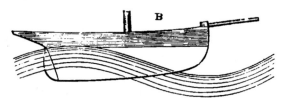

FIG. 45.

motion imparted to her by one big wave. At any rate when the vessel gets into the position B, she should be put as fairly into the sea ahead of her as possible. If there is no big sea ahead she will fall harmlessly enough into the trough and will hardly require easing.

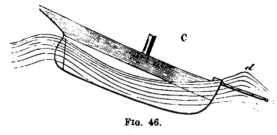

FIG. 46.

In sailing a vessel hard through a sea like this, the motion will necessarily be unpleasant, as, instead of rising leisurely as it were to the waves, and pitching gently, the vessel will more or less of her own momentum throw herself ahead; this will not only make the motion quick and unpleasant, but will put a great strain on the gear, but as it is more a question of getting through the sea than riding over it with comfort and with safety to the gear, the last words on this subject will be, keep a firm hold of the weather tiller lines.

SAILING OFF THE WIND.—Sailing off the wind means that the vessel is more away from the wind than the close-hauled point, and applies up to the time when the wind blows four points abaft the beam, when the wind would be quarterly. In sailing with the wind abeam, the head sheets must not be eased up too much, but a good strain must be kept on them, as the vessel is almost certain to gripe a great deal, and to show a tendency to fly to; of course, if the head sheets are eased up so that the sails are always lifting, this tendency will be much more urgent.

Neither must the main sheet be eased off too far; if it is, the weather cloths of the sail will "lift" and go into folds. If the fore part of the sail does so lift, the main sheet must be drawn in a little until the sail has the full weight of the wind, and falls "asleep." Frequently the luff of the sail may be quiet enough, but the topsail may lift, and that will be a sign that the main boom wants hauling aboard a little, so as to get the peak more inboard, and thus make the topsail stand better. But the mainsail must not be pinned for the mere object of making the topsail stand; if the luff of the latter be to windward of the topmast, the cause of its lifting may be the eddy wind round the topmast.

With the wind abeam the vessel will be three or four points free, and the helmsman will have to steer by compass or by keeping some object straight on for the bowsprit end. Every tendency the vessel shows to fly up in the wind must be promptly met by the helm; do not hold the helm as if the object was to keep it rigidly in one position, nor wait until the vessel's head has ranged up two or three points. Watch the compass card or the object you are steering for, and directly the vessel brings her head to windward give her a little weather helm and keep her straight if you can. If she shows a tendency to fall off, meet her promptly with a little lee helm, and always remember that the object is to make her keep a straight course, and to prevent her yawing either on or off the wind. It will not be a question of keeping the sails full and no more than full, but that of making the vessel go straight as an arrow for her object, always recollecting that if she yaws about that of itself will stop her way, and there will be also the retarding action of the rudder to bring her back on her course; therefore using a little helm promptly will prevent yawing, and the checking of the vessel's way from this cause will be reduced to a minimum.

But a vessel may gripe through the wind shifting more aft, or she may show a tendency to run off through the wind coming more ahead, therefore the vane must be watched, and the blowing of the wind on the face should also be regarded. In match sailing especially, slight alterations in the wind should be observed, and usually the main sheet in small vessels, and sometimes in large ones, is laid along the weather side of the deck in the hands of the crew, who slackened off or drew in the boom to suit every slight alteration in the wind. Of course this would only be done in very light winds, but all cases and alterations in the wind that make a palpable difference on the amount of weather helm carried, should be promptly provided for by trimming the sheets.

With a beam wind if there is much strength in it—so strong that a topsail lays her in to the deck edge—the vessel in the puffs will now and again shove her rail under, but she should never be permanently sailed with more than two or three planks of the deck awash. Sail should be shortened without hesitation if the reach is a long one, and if the wind seems bent on a good steady blow. But if it is a mere puff, or if the reach be a short one of a half mile or so, the vessel must be eased to get the water off deck, and ramped along again in the lulls. Some judgment must be exercised in so easing a vessel, as if her sails are made to lift very much her way will be stopped; on the other hand, if she has to sail with her lee deck full of water up to the rail, that will stop her way, and so the aim must be to stop her speed as little as possible from either cause, and as before said, if the reach be long and the wind a lasting one shorten sail.

Sailing off the Wind in a Heavy Sea.—In sailing along the wind in a sea—it would not be attempted if the sea were very heavy—the helmsman will find some difficulty in keeping his vessel from griping-to or running off, as the sea will carry her about a great deal. He should be well prepared to give her lee helm promptly if she shows a sign of running-off, and should either keep the lee tiller line in his hand, or the tiller itself, or should have someone to leeward of the tiller, the latter if the vessel be a big one, say of 70 tons, or upwards. If the vessel gripes-to, she must be given weather helm; but checking the tendency to "run off her helm" will require the most care, and lee helm should be given a vessel directly her head begins to fall off when sailing along the wind. With a heavy beam sea a sensation will be experienced of slipping down the side of the waves as the seas pass under her; but the great danger will be from a beam sea breaking aboard, and, as before said, if the sea is very heavy, she should be either put head to it or before it.

To Run before the Wind in a Heavy Sea.—Have the boom topped up, so that the boom end will clear the combers if possible during the lee roll. Bend the boom-guy by making fast with a clove-hitch the thimble end to the boom, about two-thirds of the length of the boom from the mast.

Take the guy forward, pass the bight round a cleat or snatch block, and bring the end back, and reeve through the thimble, and belay. Sometimes the guy is simply taken forward and belayed, or set up by a tackle.

If the sea is very heavy the mainsail should be stowed and trysail set. The squaresail, reefed, should be always set under such circumstances, but it is best to have the trysail as well, because if an accident happened to the squaresail, the vessel can be brought to wind and hove to under the trysail. The trysail should be sheeted pretty flat, as the sail will then tend to check the weather rolling and inclination to fall off. The foresail would be lowered, but a small jib should be always kept set.

Another reason for preferring a trysail to a close-reefed mainsail is that the head of the sail would be higher, and would keep the wind whilst in the trough of the sea, whereas a close-reefed mainsail might be becalmed. For the same reason, to avoid being becalmed, a reefed square sail should always be hauled close up to the hounds.

In running before a wind and sea great care must be taken that the vessel does not get by the lee; that is, that she does not run off so much as to bring the wind on the other quarter and gybe. The lazy guy would most likely prevent the boom coming over; if it did not, look out, and keep clear of the main sheet if you are near the counter; and lie down on deck, as, if the boom is brought up suddenly by the runner, it may break and sweep the deck.

Supposing the vessel gybes without any other accident, "meet" her promptly with lee helm, and do not let her fly to; then prepare to gybe the vessel back again if necessary; get in some of the main sheet; drop the throat or peak down; put the helm up and gybe her handsomely.

If when running under squaresail the vessel broaches to, that is, flies up into the wind and gets aback, brace the squaresail sharp up, and haul the weather jib sheet taut; keep the helm hard up until the vessel is before the wind again. If the vessel flies-to quite head to wind, the squaresail must be stowed and the foresail set, if necessary, to back her head off.

It is generally supposed that a large quantity of sail must be carried when running before a heavy sea, in order to keep ahead of the waves; or, in other words, to avoid being pooped. This is not exactly the case, as the speed of large waves is much too great for any vessel to run away from them; thus an Atlantic wave 200ft. in length (such as would be met with in a brisk gale) travels at the rate of twenty miles an hour, and no vessel could run at that speed. The height of such a wave might be about 35ft., but probably would be not more than 15ft. and the object of having much canvas set would be that a vessel might not get becalmed in the trough of the sea, and by suddenly losing her way cause an overtaking wave to be broken up; a quantity of water might then possibly fall on board. [It must always be understood that it is not the water which travels, but only the wave motion.] This would be termed "pooping," and to avoid such accidents square topsails have been much recommended for large cruising yachts, as, owing to their loftiness, they are unlikely to get becalmed in the trough of the sea. However, pooping more frequently happens from quite a different cause, in this way : as a wave advances it will sometimes grow in height and lose in length, and as a wave form cannot be sustained after a certain proportion of height to length has been reached, the crest of the wave becomes suddenly sharp and still higher, and ultimately curls over on the side it has been advancing. If this breaking up of a wave—which under such circumstances might rise to a height of 50ft.—should happen close to the stern of a vessel, she will be inevitably pooped ; that is to say, some of the water will fall on board, and the crew will have to hang on for their lives.

Large deep sea waves, when they approach shallowness, alter in form and lose their speed ; they become shorter and higher (deep-sea waves whose original height was 40ft. have been said to rise to 150ft. as they approach the coast), and then the crests, travelling faster than the troughs, topple over in broken masses. Hence waves in shallows or near the coast are more dangerous than deep-water waves.

CARRYING AWAY A BOWSPRIT.—If by the wind, directly the bowsprit is gone ease the main sheet and haul the fore sheet a-weather ; but if the vessel has been reaching well off the wind, she must be brought near the wind, and in either case hove to. If the bowsprit is carried away near the stem, in consequence of a shroud bursting, the outer end will fly aft. Lower the jib and unhook from the traveller. Put the bight of a rope under each end of the bowsprit, the end of the inner part of each rope being fast on the deck ; haul on the other part, and thus roll or parbuckle (*see* Fig. 47) the bowsprit up the side of the vessel to the deck. Then clear the gear. The bowsprit may be got out again properly

Fig. 47.

secured. If the end of the bowsprit breaks off outside the jibtack sheave hole, let the jib sheet fly ; or take the jib in altogether, as most likely a change will have to be made. Get the end of the bowsprit on deck, take the gear off, and re-fit it to the bowsprit end by lashings.

If the topmast should not be carried away by the loss of the bowsprit, try and save it. Let go the topsail sheet and halyards, and get the topsail down. Take the jib topsail halyards or spinnaker halyards forward, and set taut as a topmast stay, to steady the topmast.

CARRYING AWAY A BOWSPRIT SHROUD.—Let the jib sheet fly. Put the helm down and bring the vessel on the other tack immediately; if there is not sea room to keep the vessel on the other tack, let the jib run in and heave to. Then repair damage, or set up the shroud by tackles. (To put on tackles, *see* page 123.)

CARRYING AWAY A BOBSTAY.—Let the jib sheet fly and heave to if not match sailing. If it is the fall that has broken, the bobstay will have to be fished up and a new one rove. If the shackle on the stem or the bar is broken so that it cannot be repaired, and there is no second shackle or bar on board, the vessel must be sailed without a bobstay. Reef the bowsprit in, set a small jib, and do not sheet the jib too taut. In squalls, or when falling into a wave hollow, ease the vessel with the helm. Many fishing vessels, some of 80 tons, are never fitted with bobstays; but of course they have very short bowsprits.

If there is any sea, the vessel should not be sailed without a bobstay and with no jib set, as the bowsprit would under such conditions most likely be carried away. The stay rope of the jib will support the bowsprit, but the jib sheet should be well lightened up.

CARRYING AWAY A TOPMAST.—A topmast when broken invariably falls to leeward, and it would be very difficult to give directions for clearing the wreck away. It will hang by the topsail sheet from the gaff, by the tack over the peak halyards, by the backstay over the peak halyards, and by the topsail halyards if they were belayed to windward. In clearing the wreck and unreeving, be careful not to let anything go until it has been properly secured or lashed, so as not to tumble on deck.

CARRYING AWAY A MAST.—The best thing to do, if the weather is very heavy, is to unreeve tacks, lanyards, and backstay tackles, and ride to the wreck of spars, as they will make a capital floating anchor. When the weather moderates, the mast can be got alongside, the gear cleared, and the boom gaff and sail got on board. In a large vessel the mast will probably be too heavy to handle, and will have to be made fast astern. In a small yacht the mast may be rigged as a jury mast. Supposing the mast has been carried away five or six feet above the deck, put the heel of the mast against the stump on the aft side so that it cannot fetch away; take the lower main halyard block forward to stem head; put guys on the masthead, and lead one to each side of the yacht. Lift up by the masthead, and set taut by the main halyards, and when the latter have got sufficient purchase hoist the mast to a perpendicular, steadying by the guys. When upright lash the mast to the stump, seize bights in the shrouds to shorten them, and set up by the lanyards. If the mast be worked round to the fore side of the stump, the boom gooseneck can be shipped as before. Set the mainsail reefed or double reefed as required, or set the trysail.

If the mast be carried away close to the deck, unship the stump, and step a spare spar to lash the heel of the mast to. Or the broken mast could be stepped. In this case it would be better to improvise sheers by taking a couple of spars, such as topsail yard and trysail gaff; and, after lashing their ends together, rear them over the mast hole, one leg in either scupper. A tackle should be lashed to the apex of the sheers for hoisting the mast by. Keep the sheers in their place by guys leading forward and aft.

Sheers might be used for getting the mast and boom on deck, or for rearing the mast on end at first, by rigging them aft, when the heel of the mast is to be lashed on deck.

In case of a mast being carried away close under the hounds, preparations for getting the rigging and halyards aloft again can be made by throwing a line over the masthead, and hauling a tackle to pull a man aloft by. If the masthead is carried away, the main halyard block can be lashed above the rigging round the yoke. The peak hoisted by one of the topping-lifts, or by a couple of blocks of the peak halyards, one to be lashed to the masthead over the main halyard block.

When the masthead is badly sprung above the yoke, but is kept from falling by the topmast, let fly the jib sheets, heave the vessel to, and lower the mainsail as quickly as possible. Lower the topmast half-way down, and lash the heel to the mast. Unhook main and peak halyard blocks, and unreeve jib halyards. Then prepare for rehoisting mainsail as if the masthead had come down. (*See* previous paragraph.) The topmast will keep the mast head from falling.

CARRYING AWAY THE FORE STAY.—Ease up fore and jib sheets, slack out the main sheet, and run the vessel off the wind. Put a strop round the bowsprit close to the stem, and set the lee runner up to it. Then if the stay burst at the nip it may be secured by tackles and the runners released. If the stay cannot be secured by tackles, haul an end of the cable up to the masthead by the foresail halyards, and take a bight round the mast above the yoke. Set up the cable through the hawse pipe. Sometimes a jury fore stay is rigged out of one of the hawsers, passed under the bowsprit and round the masthead in two or more parts, according to the size and condition of the hawser.

CARRYING AWAY A RUNNER.—The greatest strain comes on the runners (by runners is meant the pendant runners and tackle), when the wind is a little abaft the beam; and if the weather one is carried away, the vessel should be instantly thrown head to wind, and put on the other tack until the runner is repaired. The vessel should be met by the helm when near head to wind, and not put on the other tack until the main sheet is hauled in. If there be not sea room to sail the vessel when on the other tack, heave to.

CARRYING AWAY A TRIATIC STAY.—If the triatic be carried away, and the mainmast does not go with it, put the helm up, slack out the main sheet, and run the vessel off the wind. Take the lee main runner forward, outside the main rigging, and set up to the fore-runner bolts. If there be a fresh breeze, stow the mainsail, and then repair the damage.

CARRYING AWAY A TOPMAST BACKSTAY.—Throw the vessel up in the wind, let fly the topsail sheet, jib topsail sheet or spinnaker sheet, and if the damage cannot be quickly made good take in the topsails.

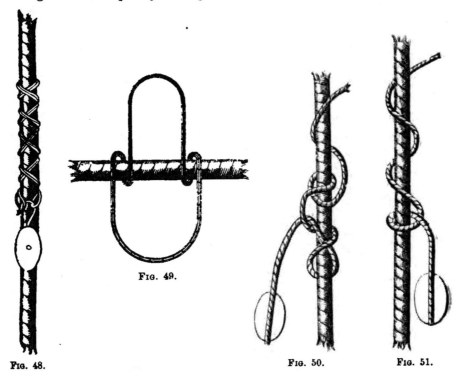

FIG. 49.

FIG. 48.

FIG. 50.

FIG. 51.

To Put a Strop on a Rope.—A strop is put on to a rope to hook a block or tackle to, as shown in Fig. 48, the whole of the strop being used up in the cross turn.

Another way of putting a strop on a block is shown in Fig. 49. The bights are passed through and through, round the rope until used up; the tackle is then hooked to the bights as in Fig. 48. A strop is usually put on a wire rope in this way, as it is less likely to slip. (*See* "Selvagee" in the Appendix.)

To Put a Tail Block on a Rope.—A tail block is put on to a rope by a rolling hitch, as shown in Fig. 50. The hitches are jammed up close together. If the block is to remain on the rope the end of the tail can be seized back to the rope if required. Often when in a hurry only one hitch is taken (Fig. 51), the tail being gripped round the rope with the hand. A tail tackle is put on to a rope in the same manner as a tail block.

TO ANCHOR WHEN ON A WIND WITH WEATHER-GOING TIDE.—Get the anchor ready on the bow, and some cable ranged on deck. Have the mainsail ready for lowering. When nearly abreast to leeward of the spot where the anchor is to be let go, lower the main sail and put down the helm; when head to wind bring the helm amidship, take in jib and foresail and shoot to the spot where the anchor is to be let go. Unless there is so little wind that the vessel will be wind rode when she is brought up, it is important that the mainsail should be stowed before she comes to anchor; otherwise as she swung round to before the wind with the tide, the consequences might be very awkward.

TO ANCHOR WHEN ON A WIND WITH LEE-GOING TIDE.—Have the anchor and cable ready. Have jib and foresail ready for lowering. When abreast to leeward of the spot where the anchor is to be let go take in jib and foresail, put the helm down and shoot up head to wind, and when way is deadened let go the anchor and stow the mainsail; or if plenty of hands are on deck, lower the mainsail as the vessel is brought to. The vessel will of course lie head to wind and tide.

TO ANCHOR WHEN RUNNING BEFORE THE WIND, BUT AGAINST THE TIDE. —Stow the mainsail, take in the jib, put the helm down, shoot head to wind, lower the foresail, and let go the anchor.

Or stow all the sails, and do not alter helm. When the tide has brought the vessel to a standstill, let go the anchor.

TO ANCHOR WHEN RUNNING BEFORE THE WIND, AND WITH THE TIDE.— Take in jib and foresail, haul in the main sheet, put down the helm, and when head to wind keep shooting till way is stopped; let go the anchor, and stow the mainsail.

If moorings have to be picked up, the same course will be followed; but judgment must be exercised, so that when the vessel shoots up to the watch buoy her way is almost or quite stopped.

ANCHORING IN AN OPEN ROADSTEAD.—In coasting it may be frequently convenient to bring up for the night under the land, but if the weather looks at all bad seaward, the precaution should be taken to unshackle the cable and bend the watch buoy on. Then if the sea did get up in a great hurry the cable could be slipped, and recovered on another occasion.

TO MOOR.—Veer out chain about double the length of cable it is intended to ride by; when the vessel has dropped astern and brought the cable taut, let go the second anchor; veer out chain, and heave in on the anchor first let go until an equal length of chain is out. If the yacht will not drive to a spot suitable for the second anchor, send out a kedge and warp in the boat; warp the yacht to the kedge, and let go the anchor. Or the second anchor and chain can be carried out in the required position in a boat. In such case, only as much chain as it is intended to ride by need be veered out to the first anchor.

The quantity of chain to ride by will greatly depend upon the nature of the bottom, the strength of the tide and wind or sea. Generally about three times the depth of water at the top of flood is sufficient for a smooth-water berth.

To UNMOOR.—Heave in on one anchor, and pay out chain on the other. Break the first anchor out of the ground, cat, and then get the other. In some cases the second anchor might be got by the boat under-running the chain.

SCOWING AN ANCHOR OR KEDGE.—When boats or yachts have to anchor on ground known or suspected to be foul, it will always be prudent to scow the anchor. Unbend the cable from the ring, and make the end fast round the crown, shank, and flukes with a clove hitch, and bring the end *a* (Fig. 52) back to *s*, and stop it round the cable with spun yarn

FIG. 52.

or hitches; take the cable back to the shackle and stop it as at *b*; when the cable is hauled upon by the part *o* the stop at *b* will break, and the fluke of the anchor can be readily lifted out of its bed. Sometimes, instead of scowing the anchor a trip line is bent to the crown and buoyed. (*See* "Anchor" in the Appendix.)

To PASS A SEIZING.—A way of securing a bight of a rope by a lashing so as to form an eye, or of securing any parts of ropes together. A seizing is thus passed: an eye is spliced in a piece of small cordage which is to form the seizing (Fig. 53), and the seizing is then passed through its eye and round the rope as shown; the end is brought down through the turns and through the eye splice (or not, as preferred). It is then brought over at *a* (Fig. 54), which is the back view of Fig. 53, round and over again at *b*; the end is then passed under *a* at *c* (by aid of a marling

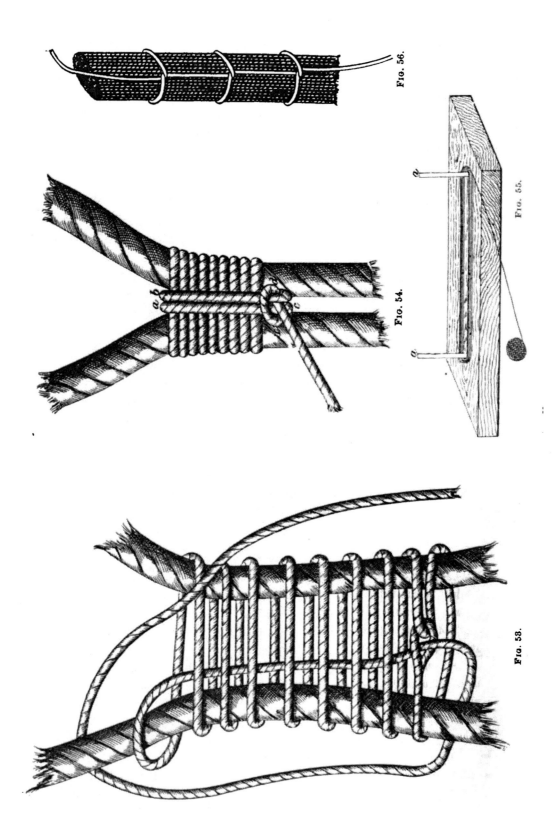

FIG. 56.

FIG. 55.

FIG. 54.

FIG. 58.

spike), out at *x*, and hitched under *b* at *d* as shown. Sometimes the cross turns are not taken, but the end of the seizing made fast to a part of the large rope; in such a case riding turns are usually taken; that is, the seizing is passed twice round—once over itself.

To MAKE A SELVAGEE STROP.—This is a strop made of spun yarn laid up in coils and marled; a board has two pegs, *a a* (Fig. 55), inserted at intervals suitable to the required length of the strop. Layers of spun yarn are put round these pegs, and when enough turns have been taken the marling is passed by single hitches as shown in Fig. 56.

CHAPTER VI.
MANAGEMENT OF OPEN BOATS.

QUALITIES OF OPEN BOATS AS TO STIFFNESS.—Small open boats must never be regarded as if they possessed the qualities of deep and heavily ballasted yachts. They should not be sailed "gunwale under" as a deep, keeled yacht is, and the puff or squall which a small yacht can be sailed through with impunity, will necessitate the open boat being thrown head to wind with head sheets eased up, or off the wind with aft sheets eased.

No system of ballasting will much increase the *range* of stability of a boat, although the initial stiffness may be increased—(by boat is meant something of the type of the Surbiton open gig or a yacht's gig)—and it must be clearly understood that it is not the initial stability, or the stiffness of the boat at small angles of heel, upon which her safety depends, but upon her range of stability; that is to say upon the amount of stability or power to recover herself she has, when heeled through successive angles until the gunwale might be pressed under water. After this point is reached stability vanishes very rapidly. For competitive sailing, a boat to succeed must resist being heeled at all very potently, that is, she must have great initial stability, so as to be able to carry a large area of canvas without heeling more than to a point midway between her water line and gunwale. This stiffness is more dependent upon breadth of beam than upon the weight of ballast carried low, and an inexperienced boat-sailer finding a boat very stiff at first might be tempted into pressing her beyond the danger point.

On the other hand, depth of hull of itself does not add to stability, but by ballasting it does, and, if accompanied by a high side out of water, lengthens out the range of that stability so that a boat made deep like a yacht may always have righting power at any possible angle of heel, providing she does not fill with water and sink. Thus safety does not so much depend upon the great stiffness which enables a boat to carry a large press of canvas without heeling to any considerable extent, as upon the range of her stiffness or the continuation of that stiffness, even up to the time when she might be blown over on her beam ends. Shallow open boats have a very low range of stability, and directly their gunwales are put under, they are likely to be blown over, fill, and sink, if ballasted. A high side out of water in a large way increases the range of stability, and the higher, in reason, a boat's side is out of the water the safer she will be. Thus if the two boats are the same in height to the gunwale, and one above that height is fitted with a 5in. wash strake, she will be a safer one to sail than the other.

Sailing an open boat with a quantity of lead or iron ballast on board is at all times a very risky proceeding, especially if a man is out alone and away from the track of passing vessels. If the boat fills she is bound to sink, and the safest plan is to carry water ballast in open boats.

Boats are most frequently capsized in disturbed water, and the cause is generally ascribed to a sudden squall, or to the fact that, the boat being unduly pressed, some of her loose ballast shifted to leeward ; or that she was sailed so long "gunwale under" that the weight of water taken in and resting in her lee bilge caused her to lose stability and so capsize. But a boat among waves might be, and no doubt frequently is, capsized without any accession of wind, or movement of the ballast.

It can be supposed that a boat is sailing with a beam wind, and with a beam sea, and that her inclination, due to the pressure of wind on her sail is 15°. If she got into the position shown in Fig. 57, she would practically be inclined to 30° and she would probably upset. Assuming that the boat had no sail set, she would not get into such a position, as she would accommodate herself to the wave surface and her mast would correspond to the perpendicular drawn to the wave surface (*see* Fig. 57). Even with sail set the boat would more or less so accommodate herself to the wave surface, minus her steady angle of heel ; but the increased pressure on the canvas, due to the righting moment of the boat, which would have to be overcome, would prevent her recovering herself entirely. That is, if the boat be heeled to 15° relative to the horizon, or to the normal surface of the water represented by the vertical line, and a wave came to leeward as shown, she would be in the position of a heel of 30° relative to the perpendicular to the wave surface ; but, inasmuch as the wind pressure is only capable of heeling her to 15° the boat would ultimately recover herself to that extent, and her mast would be represented by the vertical. However, long before a boat could so recover herself, she might be swamped or blown over.

With a beam sea a boat will roll a great deal, and this condition is a prolific source of accidents. If a boat is being sailed at a permanent angle of heel of 15°, and by the action of the wave she is made to roll

K

another 15°, she will frequently be in the position of being heeled to 30°; and if the extreme part of the roll should occur jointly with such a position as shown in Fig. 57, the boat would inevitably upset.

Next it can be supposed that the boat is being sailed at a permanent angle of heel of 15°, that she has an extreme roll of 15°, and that there came a sudden wind squall. Then if the extreme leeward roll, and the squall took place together when in the position shown by Fig. 57, she would blow over and nothing could save her. But she need not be in such a position as that depicted and yet be blown over; if the boat has a heel of 15°, and an extreme leeward roll of 15°, then if the extreme roll and a squall occurred together the boat would be upset, whatever her actual position among the waves, whether she was on the trough, on the side, or on the crest of a wave. Further it must be always understood that a force of wind which will, if applied steadily, heel a boat to 15°, will if applied suddenly heel her to double that inclination; thus it is not so much the force of the squall as the suddenness of its application wherein lies the danger.

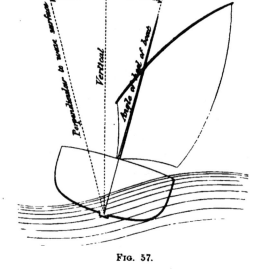

Fig. 57.

Sailing Amongst Waves.—When a boat is among waves (especially with a beam wind), ballast should not be trimmed to windward, nor should the passengers sit on the weather gunwales, as a boat after being in a position similar to that shown by Fig. 57 will take a very heavy weather roll, possibly fly up in the wind, be taken aback, and blown over.

The canvas that will permanently heel a boat to 15° may be carried safely enough in smooth water with a beam wind, but the case is altogether different among waves, and so much canvas should not then be carried, perhaps by one half. Many ships' boats and pleasure boats are annually lost through recklessness in carrying canvas in rough water; and, although a boat may go out among waves a dozen times without being subject to either of the coincident conditions described, yet may she the very next time; therefore immunity is not necessarily impunity. It will thus be seen that there is very considerable danger attendant upon sailing a boat among waves, a danger perhaps not always understood.

In sailing among waves the ballast (if any) should be well secured, the passengers should sit in the bottom of the boat, and the main sheet should be kept in the hand. If the sea is abeam the boat should be watched very closely, and if a bigger wave than usual rolls in on the weather beam, ease the sheet and run off the wind a little, the wave will then pass harmlessly under the boat. In sailing with a beam wind or sea an experienced sailor might ease the sheet and run the boat off in a squall; but it will be always better to luff up sharply, and if necessary ease the sheet too.

In sailing by the wind among waves the danger of being blown over will be considerably less, but nevertheless there is danger, and it must not be assumed that because an experienced and skilful boat sailer sails a mere cockle-shell safely about among waves, that anyone could do so without experience or skill. In boat sailing safety mainly depends upon knowing what is dangerous.

In sailing by the wind the main sheet might be belayed with a slippery hitch, with the fall close to the hand (resting over the knee is a good plan) and the fore sheet should lead aft. If there is much sea do not pin the main sheet in, but the fore sheet can be drawn fairly taut. Luff the boat fairly into the big seas that roll in on the bow, and fill her again promptly. The foresail will be found of great assistance in taking her head off again, and hence it should be sheeted pretty flat. In puffs and squalls the boat should be luffed up and the fore sheet eased if she does not spring to readily; never wait until the gunwale gets under, as when the gunwale goes under the boat soon loses way, and then the power of luffing will be gone, and the boat may perhaps fill and sink. If there is no boom to the mainsail, and the boat does not "come to" quickly and relieve herself of wind, let fly the main sheet and ease her that way; but recollect in all cases that whatever is done must be done promptly.

If the boat has a mizen the main sheet can be eased at the time of putting the helm down, as the mizen will bring the boat head to wind, but generally in luffing for hard squalls the main sheet need not be eased; but the fore sheet should be directly the squall is seen approaching, as that will allow the boat to fly to more readily when the squall strikes.

If the boat has only a mainsail and mizen, ease the main sheet in luffing if the squall be heavy, and leave the mizen to bring her to.

In luffing for squalls, should the boat get head to wind, haul the fore sheet a-weather, put the helm up, keep the main sheet eased off and press down what is to be the lee quarter (see foot-note in the Chapter on New Brighton Boats). If the boat has only one sail, haul the boom on what is to be the weather side and put the tiller on the opposite side; as the boat gets sternway on she will pay off, then right the helm, ease the boom over, and sail her. If the boat has a mizen as well as mainsail, the mizen sheet should be eased whilst the boom is held over. If an oar is handy, the boat can be helped off the wind by a "back-water" stroke or two off the lee quarter, or a forward stroke or two on the weather bow. But the boat sailer must not get nervous and throw his boat head to wind for every little catspaw or small sea; he must, whilst being careful that his boat is not capsized by a squall or filled by shipping water, sail her boldly but not recklessly, and keep her a "good full," or she will surely drive to leeward. It is particularly incumbent that a boat should be kept full when sailing among waves, hence the great necessity of her being appropriately canvased. However, if the boat is sailing across a weather-going tide she may be "squeezed" a little, but never allow the sails to lift.

Tacking.—Whilst tacking a small boat always remember that it is not the tiller of a big yacht that is grasped, and do not shove the helm down with all the force at hand; bring the boat head to wind with the tiller about half over, then put it hard up and ease again to amidships as the vessel gathers good way. With a big boom mainsail a small boat in smooth water will shoot head to wind and fill on the other tack in less time than it takes to write it, but in a sea she may require some help, and the moment for tacking should be when a "smooth" comes on the water. If there is an uncertainty about the boat coming round, do not let go the fore sheet until the boat's head is fairly off on the other tack. If the boat has no head sail, and there is a doubt of her staying, catch the boom amidships as she comes head to wind, and then shove it over to what is to be the weather side, and keep it to windward until she pays off. Never forget that a boat can always be helped round by an oar.

Above all things never attempt to tack with a big wave coming in on the weather bow.

Sailing along a Weather Shore with a Squally Wind.—In sailing along a weather shore with a squally wind, it is generally found safer with a *boom mainsail* to luff up in the wind and ease the fore sheet, if there be one, than to ease the main sheet and attempt to relieve the boat without much altering her course; however, if the weather shore be the bank of a river and close aboard, there will be the risk of going stem on into the bank; and this will be especially awkward if the boat has a long bowsprit. It is not pleasant to go into the bank of a river, but it would be preferable to capsizing. Still, in match sailing a great deal of valuable time might be lost by luffing up into a bank, and a boat can be relieved and kept going by judiciously easing the main sheet and running her off; but the sheet must be eased handsomely, and not in a half hearted manner. Never deliberate as to what shall be done—that is, whether the boat shall be luffed up at the risk of running into the bank, or whether the sheet shall be eased and the boat run off the wind. Always remember in the case of squalls that " he who hesitates is lost."

SAILING ALONG A LEE SHORE.—When sailing along a lee shore in squally weather (if it is a matter of choice, always work the weather shore), smartly luff up to the squalls in preference to easing the main sheet, and thus keep the boat going. If the squall be very heavy, and the boat will not come to, but is dragging through the water, the fore sheet should be let fly so as to bring the boat head to wind quickly. If the main sheet is eased off much the boat loses way, and then by help of her foresail may take off against her helm and shove her nose ashore. Generally the boat will "come to" quickly enough without the fore sheet. If a squall looks to have much weight in it, luff up in good time, and prepare to lower the mainsail, if necessary.

In lowering a sail in squalls, great care should be taken to spill the sail as it comes down, as, if it fills and blows out in bags, it may not only cause trouble in handing it, but upset the boat.

RUNNING BEFORE THE WIND AND SEA.—Running before a wind and sea in a small boat may to the inexperienced appear a very simple and safe operation; but, in reality, it is a very dangerous one, and many a small boat has been lost in attempting to "run away" from a sea. The two principal dangers will arise from getting by the lee and broaching to: the boat's head will be most likely to fall off to leeward, or rather her stern lift to windward, as a wave crest passes underneath her bottom from astern. But with equal peril she might have "broached to" as the wave crest lifted her bow; the boat's head will be turned towards the wind, and then, if she be not well managed, she will get broadside on to the waves, and the next roller will almost inevitably swamp her. If the rig be mizen, mainsail, and foresail, the mizen should be stowed before the boat is put before the wind; the lee foresheet should be belayed slack, and the weather one should be led aft. As the boat begins to fly to, haul the weather fore sheet in, and put the helm up; but very frequently the helm is not of much use if the boat is among breakers in shallow water, as she will be carried along on the back of a comber. Thus it very frequently happens that a boat that has successfully battled with the waves in the offing comes to grief as she gets among the surf to try and effect a landing or to run over a bar into harbour. In running over a surf an oar off the quarter will be found much more effective than the rudder to steer with, but the oar should always have a line fast on it, and it should be belayed to a cleat on the gunwale, in case it has to be left when the sail requires attention.

A small boat, if there is much wind, and especially if there be sea as well, should never be run dead before the wind with the sheet right out, but with the wind a little on the quarter; then gybe over, and run on the other tack, to make the destination. On the other hand, it is dangerous to get dead before the wind with the main sheet close in, as in yawing about the sail might be gybed with very awkward consequences.

In gybing a boom mainsail always haul the boom well aboard as the helm is put up, and take a turn, but hold the sheet in the hand. As the

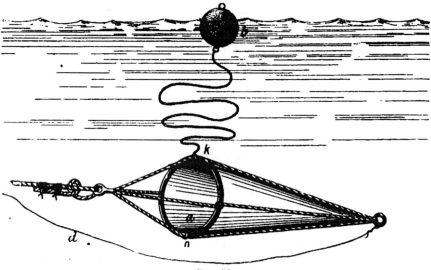

Fig. 58.

wind passes from dead astern and comes on the other quarter, taking the boom over, shift the helm promptly and prevent the vessel flying to. It is also well, even when the mainsail has no boom, to get the sheet well in before gybing if there is much wind.

HEAVING TO.—Circumstances may arise when it will be necessary to heave to. The best plan will be if the boat has a mizen to set it on the mainmast, or shift mizen-mast and all to the mainmast step, stowing the mainmast ; a small piece of the foresail might be shown with the fore leech just to windward of the mast. A boat will lie to pretty comfortably under a small head sail with sheet hauled up close to the mast. The helm will require unremitting attention. However, if an open boat has to be hove to on account of the sea and wind, the best plan will be to ride to a raft made of mainmast, oars, &c., lashed together. This will break the seas, and keep the boat head to the sea. For half decked boats a drogue is a good contrivance for keeping head to the sea. They are much used on the north-east coast. The drogue consists of a hinge-jointed galvanised iron ring about 2ft. in diameter. A conical canvas bag, made of No. 0 canvas, is sewn to this ring, and roped as shown in the sketch, Fig. 58. A bridle is fitted to the ring, to which the riding hawser is bent; *d* is a tripping line; *b* a cork buoy to prevent the drogue diving. When thrown overboard the mouth of the drogue, *a*, opens and fills. To get the drogue on board the tripping line *d* is hauled upon. When not in use the ring is folded together by the joints at *k* and *n*, and the bag snugly stowed round it.

When riding to a drogue a boat might keep a small mizen set; it would help keep her head to the sea, and make it easier work for the man who had charge of the helm. Of course only a reefed or small mizen would be set. When riding to a drogue, oil would be found of immense service in preventing the waves breaking. (*See* " Oil for Stilling Waves " in the Appendix).

REEFING.—In reefing, the tack and sheet should always be shifted to the reef cringles before the foot of the sail is rolled up and the points tied. Always roll up neatly and as tightly as possible, not only for the look of the thing, but because otherwise the points for the second or third reef may not be long enough in case they are required. In shaking out a reef always untie the points and loosen the foot before shifting the tack and sheet.

ROWING IN A SEA.—The principal thing to avoid in rowing in a sea is getting broadside on to the waves; it will be extremely difficult to work the oars in a beam sea, and if a boat gets into such a position she may roll over or be knocked over or be swamped. If possible, row head to the sea, and if the boat is carried too far to windward, take the opportunity of running her off whenever a smooth presents itself. In rowing before the sea the boat will most likely show a tendency to broach-to, and so get into the trough of the sea that way; this tendency must be instantly checked. In landing on a beach through a surf, it is frequently a good plan, if the boat is not sharp sterned, to row her in stern first or bow on to the following surf.

In boarding a vessel that is under way, always row up under her lee. In boarding a vessel at anchor, always bring the boat's head up to the tide, and take a good sweep in coming alongside. Give the order " In bow " when about thirty or fifty yards off, according to the tide, and " Oars " (the order for the men to toss their oars in), according to the speed of the boat, so that she may shoot alongside with her way nearly stopped. Avoid if possible going alongside a vessel stem on.

As a rule a boat should always be beached through surf with her sails stowed, as, if she got broadside on among the breakers with sail up a capsize would be inevitable. Upon nearing the beach on a flat shore recollect that here the wave water itself is moving, and will carry the boat along until it finally casts her up on the beach; as each wave overtakes the boat care must be taken by skilful use of an oar that it does not twist her round broadside on.

As the water at the stern may be moving faster than that at the bow, the tendency of the stern wave will be to turn the boat round if the wave does not take the boat fairly end on. This effect of the overtaking waves can be reduced by towing something astern—a spar broadside on, for instance, made fast to a bridle—and by approaching the shore stern first, so that the bow is presented to the overtaking waves.

If the beach is a steep one the best plan is to row in as hard as possible, choosing at last as an opportunity for beaching when a sea begins to break and pour in on the beach.

General Cautions for Sailing Boats.—Great care should always be taken when passing under the lee of a ship at anchor or other large object, if there is anything like a breeze, as when the boat draws clear she will have but little way on, and to be met then by the full blast of the breeze will cause her to heel dangerously; or, if she has to go under the lee of a passing or meeting vessel, she will equally get becalmed, though not for so long a time; she will, however, get the breeze again much more suddenly than if the passing ship had been at anchor, and may consequently be knocked down more. None of the crew of a boat should ever sit on the weather gunwale when approaching to pass under the lee of a ship, as the sudden loss of wind will bring the boat upright, and so much weight on one side may cause the crew to be pitched into the water, or possibly, if the boat got caught aback as she heeled to windward, she might capsize.

The first best thing to do is to give all large and lofty objects such a wide berth that the boat cannot be becalmed by them. If the boat is beating to windward, and would have to bear up very much to clear the ship at anchor, it would be better to make a board and weather the ship; this can also be done, if managed in good time, to weather a ship that is *meeting* the boat, *i.e.*, is running before the wind; but a boat should never be put across a vessel unless so far ahead as to render collision impossible. If in the attempt to weather a ship there seems a doubt about doing it, do not commence squeezing or nipping; ramp the boat along, and tack or bear up in good time and go under the ship's stern if both are beating, and under her lee if the ship is free.

If there be no choice, and the small boat has to pass under the lee of the ship, then have the main sheet cast off and held ready and clear to run out; if the boat has nearly lost her way before she gets the breeze again she will scarcely answer her helm to luff; and if she is knocked down to near the gunwale edge let the sheet fly without hesitation.

If the passing vessel be a steamer going at a great speed, she will leave a considerable wash, and small boats should avoid this, although it is the delight of some boat sailers to get into it and ship " green water," as they love to call it.

If the boat carries lee helm trim her by the head a little, or if the main sheet will admit of it harden it in and ease the fore sheet a trifle; at all events so manage that the boat carries enough weather helm to fly up in the wind when the tiller is let go. If a boat carries lee helm she may refuse to come head to wind, and under some circumstances this might be highly dangerous.

A man single handed should never attempt to row and sail a boat at the same time; if occupied with rowing he cannot attend to the helm and sheets, and the prudent course would be to lower the sail and propel the boat entirely by oars. In case the rig includes a mizen or foresail, one or both could be kept set, but the fore sheet should be so belayed that a slight pull on the fall will release it.

The crew of the boat should invariably sit on the bottom boards on the weather side, or, if there be much sea, in the fore and aft line over the keel. No one should be allowed to climb the mast if the boat is under way, as the weight aloft might capsize her. Nor should any of the crew stand on the thwarts so that they might get thrown down in the lee side of the boat when she lurched, or otherwise imperil her safety.

In cases where the main sheet leads through a block, through a bull's-eye, through a thimble, through a hole, or other similar arrangement, the boat sailer should ever and anon cast his eye on the fall of the sheet and see that there are no turns or kinks in it. If the fall be coiled up, see that the running part is uppermost and the end underneath. New rope and wet rope are specially liable to get foul turns in them. Never forget to see that nothing like a boat's stretcher, mop handle, thole pin, or bailer lies in the coil of a fall of a sheet, as in running out the sheet might get toggled thereby.

CHAPTER VII.

THE GENERAL MANAGEMENT OF A YACHT.

THE OWNER, MASTER, MATE, &c.

THERE is no code of regulations for the discipline of a yacht, but generally the customs of the Royal Navy and merchant service are observed. The master is not required by law to have a Board of Trade certificate of competency, and frequently he is only capable of making coasting passages. However, most masters of large vessels are skilful navigators, and could take a yacht to any part of the globe. The chief requisite in a master for a yacht, whose cruising does not extend beyond the English and Irish Channels, is that he should be a thorough master of fore-and-aft sailing, and that he should be clean and tidy in his habits, able to enforce cleanliness and tidiness in the crew, have perfect command over the crew, and carry out the owner's wishes cheerfully and respectfully. Most yacht masters rise from "before the mast" after they have served a season or two as mate or second mate, and generally they assume their new station with a full appreciation of its consequence—that is, they are alive to the serious responsibility of being in charge of a vessel—take her about with a caution and patience that are unceasing, and assume an appropriate dignity in their intercourse with the crew. Some men, however, appear to be quite incapable of feeling that dignity, and at one moment are too familiar with the crew, and the next squabbling with them. Such men should not have charge of a yacht, and if an owner wishes to cruise in comfort he will get a sailing master who, above all things, is "master of the crew," conducts himself as such, and is observed as such.

The master has sole control on board, subject of course to the wishes of the owner, who ought, however, never to have occasion to interfere with the discipline or working of the yacht. If the owner has any fault to find with the conduct, whatever its nature, of any member of the crew, he should make that complaint to the master; this will show the master that he is responsible for the discipline, good behaviour, and efficiency of the crew, and the crew will not have the opportunity of saying they do not know who is master, or that the owner is master, and that the titular master is only so in name.* But if the owner observes any misconduct or gross inefficiency on the part of any member of the crew, and the master apparently does not notice it, then the owner should bring the master's attention to it, and, if necessary, insist on the delinquent being discharged. This will really strengthen the position of the master, and inspire him with courage to take command of the crew, instead of being content with a kind of slovenly discipline.

In large yachts the owner should always keep up a kind of formality in sending a message through the steward or mate or other member of the crew to the sailing master, and address him as Mr. So-and-so, and not as Harry or Charley or Bill, as the case may be (many owners, however, prefer to address the master as Captain So-and-so). The owner in this way can do a great deal towards making the crew regard the master with respect; as, if it is seen that the owner treats the master with a flippant familiarity, the crew will do so too. In small yachts less formality is .observed, and the owner usually calls the master by his surname. The crew should always address the master as " Sir," and not in an offhand way, such as " All right, skipper," or " All ready, captain."

If the owner wishes any work done on board, or requires the gig or boat, he should tell the master of his wishes or send a proper message to him, and not issue direct orders to the crew; all such usurpations of the proper duties of the master are subversive of discipline, and should be carefully avoided. If the owner goes on shore and wishes the boat to return for him, he should give the orders to the master; but if he forgets to do this he should upon landing give the order to the coxswain, whose duty it will be to repeat the order; thus, if the owner says, " Come for me at half-past four," the coxswain will answer, " Half-past four, sir," to show that he understands the order; or in large yachts the owner would say, " Tell the captain to send the gig for me at half-past four."

The master should always ship the crew, and generally should be allowed to ship the mate as well.

The mate, like the master, should always be addressed as " Mr.," alike by the owner, master, and crew. When the master is on deck the mate's place is forward, and he superintends the setting and taking

---

* In some small vessels the owner is actually master, and then he deals with the crew as such. But if the owner is registered as master and takes charge of the yacht, it may in some cases affect liability for damage and policies of insurance. *See* " Insurance," in the Appendix.

in sails, and generally sees that the master's orders are efficiently carried out. He also takes charge of the yacht's spars and rigging, and with the assistance of the carpenter and boatswain sees that all necessary work is done upon it, and from time to time reports the condition of the rigging, spars, and sails, to the master.

When orders are given to get under way, the mate superintends all the necessary preparations for weighing the anchor and making sail; so also in bringing up, he prepares for taking in sail and letting go the anchor.

When the master is below, the mate goes aft and takes charge of the deck and issues orders as if he were the master; but, although it may be his watch on deck, he does not make any serious alteration in the vessel's course, or shorten, or set sail, or reef without informing the master of what he is about to do. Then if the master considers it necessary, he may go on deck himself, and perhaps summon his watch from below.

The boatswain takes charge of the sail room and ship's chandler's stores, sees that all the tackles, spare sails, &c., are properly stowed and in good order. With the mate he superintends the washing down, scrubbing, cleaning of brass work, and blacking down the yacht or rigging.

In a few instances a quartermaster is shipped, and his duties are to look after the signal flags, guns, the helm, time, the watches, and the stowage of heavy stores.

The carpenter notes the condition of the spars, decks, fittings, &c., sounds the pumps every morning or oftener if the condition of the hull requires it.

The coxswain of a boat has to see that she is kept clean and in readiness for use, rows the stroke oar if passengers are in her, and takes the yoke lines if the crew only are on board. The coxswain of the owner's gig has usually one shilling or so a week extra for taking charge of her, and he, as before said, is held responsible by the master for her condition and the condition of everything belonging to her.

The dinghy man (in a large yacht he has a mate) is at everyone's call on board, goes on shore on errands, rows the steward on shore, &c. He is generally given 1s. a week extra.

WATCHES, BELLS, THE HELM, THE CREW.

WATCHES.—The master is always in charge of the deck, excepting when long passages are being made; then watches are set. The master takes the starboard watch, and the mate the port watch. The second mate is in the master's watch, or, if no second mate, the boatswain.

The two mates generally tell the men off into their respective watches when they are shipped. If the yacht is short-handed in making a passage, the steward musters in the master's watch and the cook in the mate's. The watches are usually set at eight o'clock of the first night at sea, and the master takes the first watch; but on leaving a foreign port for home the mate takes the first watch. Following out the axiom that the "master takes the ship out, but the mate brings her home," the mate has thus charge of the navigation on the homeward voyage, if he is capable of the duty, the master superintending only.

When a yacht is in harbour, or when only sailing or steaming about in the daytime and bringing up at night, no watches are kept, and the whole crew, including master and mate are on deck. In yachts, say, of 150 tons and under, when sailing about for a few hours in the daytime the master takes sole charge of working the yacht and generally steers. He issues all orders, and the mate sees that they are carried out. Thus, in working to windward, if the yacht has to be tacked, the master says "Ready about!" or "Lee O!" The mate answers "All ready, sir." The master then puts down the helm, or orders it to be put down, saying "Helm's-a-lee!" the mate answers "Helm's-a-lee, sir!" and directs the crew to ease up the head sheets and haul them aft again as required. When the master hails with "Ready about," none of the crew should bawl out "All right, sir," or answer in any way whatsoever, but if the mate is not on deck, the second mate or boatswain should take his place, answer "All ready, sir," and see that the head sheets are worked properly. The master will see that the aft sheets are properly worked. With a good and attentive crew, the first hail of "Ready about," or even a sign, will send all the men to their stations, and the more quietly a yacht can be worked the better it will be for the nerves of the passengers.

In making long cruising passages watches are set, and the master and mate take alternate watches, as before stated. The twenty-four hours are divided into seven watches, thus—five of four hours duration, and two of two hours, the latter being called "dog watches" and always occurring between four and eight o'clock in the afternoon. The object of having dog watches is to obtain an uneven number, as otherwise the same men would always be on duty in particular watches. During the dog watches—from four o'clock to eight—a great deal of liberty is allowed the men, and the watch below as well as the one on deck do their own odd jobs, tell yarns, sing, and generally amuse themselves in such a way as is consistent with the good working of the yacht.

When going to sea the first (starboard) watch is set at eight p.m., and the master takes that watch. Eight bells are struck and the port watch retires below. At twelve o'clock (midnight) the port watch is called by the second mate or boatswain going to the fore hatch or scuttle, and hailing "Port watch ahoy!" or "Eight bells, sleepers!" The watch below should answer "Ay, ay!" turn out immediately, and be on deck in five minutes. Any lagging is regarded as very bad form, and a man is looked upon with contempt who does not turn up on the first summons. The watch lasts from twelve to four, and is termed the middle watch. At four a.m. the sleeping watch would be called in the same way, to come on deck and take the morning watch from four to eight, and so on for the forenoon watch, afternoon watch, the "dog watches," and first watch again. When in harbour, or at moorings, an "anchor watch" is kept by one man, or in some cases two men, whose spell is two hours, the port and starboard watch supplying the men on alternate nights. This watch looks out for any dangers that a yacht may be in, summonses the watch below if necessary, and strikes the bells.

BELLS.—As a rule, "Bells" are only struck on board yachts between eight in the evening and eight in the morning, but in large yachts they are regularly struck all through the twenty-four hours, whether the yacht is at sea or in harbour.

The bells are struck in this way: one stroke (or one bell) is half-past twelve; two strokes struck quickly (or two bells) one o'clock; two strokes struck quickly, followed by one (or three bells), half-past one; a double two (or four bells) two o'clock; a double two and one (or five bells) half-past two; a treble two (or six bells) three o'clock; a treble two and one (or seven bells) half-past three; four double strokes (or eight bells) four o'clock. Then commences one bell for half-past four, two bells for five o'clock, and so on, eight bells struck every four hours.

But during the dog watches after four bells have been struck for six o'clock, one bell is struck for half past six, two bells for seven o'clock, three bells for half-past seven, but eight bells again for eight o'clock.

HELM.—When watches are set it is usual for one of the crew to steer, and not the master or mate. Two men out of each watch are usually selected (generally among themselves) to steer, who are known to be good helmsmen. Each man is at the helm for two hours, and this is called a "trick." When the time has expired the other man goes aft as four bells are struck. If he does not go immediately he is reminded by the hail "Spell O!" The man who relieves should always, if the weather will permit, come aft along the lee side, and, crossing over the tiller, from the lee side to weather side, come behind the other helmsman, and take the lines out of his hand from abaft.

The man, as he gives up the helm, states the course as, say, E.S.E., or "Full and by," as the case may be. It is the duty of the new comer to repeat the course, to show that he understands it, and the officer in charge of the deck, should be near to hear that the course is correctly given. The relieved man retires behind the other one, crosses the tiller, and finds his way forward along the lee side of the yacht.

If the officer of the watch requires the course altered, he gives the course anew, as E. by S., or "keep her off," or "bring her to," or "no more away," or "no closer," &c., and it is the duty of the man at the helm to repeat the order audibly, to show that he understands it. In bad weather, it is usual to place a second hand at the helm, and then the man whose trick it is, stands to windward of the tiller, or wheel, with the weather tiller lines or spokes of the wheel in his hand, and the other to leeward with the lee tiller lines. The second hand assists in pushing the tiller to windward, or hauling it to leeward, as occasion requires. Frequently a young hand is given a spell at the helm in light winds, in order that he may gain a knowledge of steering.

THE CREW AT WORK.—When an order is given to any member of the crew by the master or the mate, such as "Ease the fore sheet," or "Take in the slack of that sheet," it is the duty of the man to audibly repeat the order to show that he understands it, as "Ease the fore sheet, sir," &c. While the crew are at work, or during the watches from 8 a.m. to 4 p.m., there should be nothing like "recreation" permitted on the fore deck or in the forecastle, but the men should go about their work quietly, never converse loudly, nor hail one another from one end of the vessel to the other. All orders should be obeyed instantly and cheerfully, with a ready response or a cheery "Ay, ay, sir!" Nothing could be worse than for the crew when an order is given to sit and stare, and then to leisurely proceed to do it with an air which plainly says, "I am doing it, but I don't like doing it." In most cases, in working the yacht the master should give the order to the mate, who will direct the particular man or men who are to carry out the order. As before said, the order should be obeyed with alacrity; if it is not, it will appear that the men do not know how to execute it, or that they are so stupid that they do not understand it, or that they are such bad sailors that they do not know that a seaman's first duty is ready obedience.

Whenever any member of the crew shows the least slackness in executing orders, or in any way neglects the ship's work, shows symptoms of insubordination, indulges in mutinous talk, gives insolent or even pert answers, he should be instantly warned by the master of the mistake he has made, and upon the second offence should be given his " discharge

ticket." If a seaman obeys all orders promptly and executes them conscientiously, he will be respected by the master and other officers; but
if he is doubtful in obedience and a sloven in his work, the master,
very properly, will have a contempt for him, and will take advantage
of the first opportunity for unshipping him.

AGREEMENTS, LIBERTY MEN, DISCIPLINE, &c.

In all cases a clear and distinct agreement should be signed by
the crew, even though they do not "sign articles" under a shipping
master; and this agreement should contain in detail such regulations
as are referred to in No. 7, sect. 149, of the Merchant Shipping Act,
1854, which says that regulations may be made with the crew "as to
conduct on board, and as to fines, or other punishments for misconduct
which have been sanctioned by the Board of Trade as regulations
proper to be adopted and which the parties agree to adopt." The
agreement should therefore clearly set forth the rules to be observed
on board as to wages, clothes, duties, general conduct, liberty, discipline, &c. (*see* the article "Seamen" in the Appendix). It will be
found to be a very difficult matter to make and enforce rules after
the crew has been shipped and berthed on board. The rules should
therefore be agreed to and signed at the time of shipping.

As a rule there is more difficulty in maintaining discipline on board
a yacht seldom under way than on board one which is constantly making
passages. A yacht is in such thorough order, that after she is washed
down, the brass work cleaned, and her sides "chamoied," there is nothing
left to do except perhaps row the owner on shore and bring him off again.
The men have nothing to do but eat and sleep, and as they cannot be
doing this all day, there comes a longing for going ashore. The master
has to be asked for "liberty," and if the man cannot claim it as a
right the master may refuse, and the man then most likely has a fit of
sulks, and takes the first opportunity of being insolent. This is frequently
the origin of squabbling on board; but, on the other hand, sometimes
the master allows too much liberty, and almost permits the crew to leave
and rejoin the vessel when they please in spite of a signed or understood agreement to the contrary. This is worse than no liberty at all,
and usually ends with the contented men who stay on board from week's
end to week's end abusing those who are everlastingly on shore, and
the result is a regular fo'c'sle row. The master in all cases should make
known the "custom of the ship" as to liberty as the men are shipped.
The usual plan is for the crew to have alternate afternoons and evenings

on shore, or " watch and watch," when lying in a harbour or safe roadstead; but when lying in an open roadstead the question of liberty should
be left entirely to the discretion of the master.

It is useless to tell an owner that he should not keep his yacht at
anchor for weeks at a stretch, but get underway every day; there may
be a variety of reasons why he does not want to get underway, except
for making passages, which perhaps is the only purpose for which he
requires the yacht. As a rule, the master will know the habits of
the owner, and only engage men whom he knows can stand a life of
comparative idleness and confinement.

Drink should be under very strict regulation. It is customary to
serve out grog, just one " glass," on Saturday nights to drink to " sweet-
hearts and wives," and as a rule owners allow the master to serve out a
glass on a dirty night at sea, or after a long dusting to windward, or after
heavy work—striking topmasts and reefing or setting trysail in heavy
weather; or when the whole ship's company have been kept up to
midnight or later; but the master should take every precaution to prevent
drunkenness among the crew, and should never overlook more than one
offence in a season. This rule should be observed with great strictness.

Smoking should be permitted on the fore deck for a half hour
after breakfast and dinner; also during the dog watches, and in the first
watch if the men so please; and the men are sometimes allowed a pipe
in the morning at eleven o'clock as " lunch." On board some yachts
indiscriminate smoking is permitted, but in those best regulated smoking
is only permitted at the times stated. Smoking should not be permitted below, and only on the fore deck—it should not be permitted
aft, unless the crew space is aft as it is in some steam yachts. Some
owners, however, permit the men to smoke below just whenever they
please; other owners permit it at any time except when meals are underway in the main cabin.

In the daytime the crew should always appear in the uniform of
the yacht; but at night when making passages they are allowed to wear
any old clothes they have on board; but when the forenoon watch comes
on deck at 8 A.M. to relieve the morning watch they should be in uniform.
If there is still work to do, such as cleaning out boats, or work upon
rigging, the watch would appear in their dongaree suits, or " jumpers "
if they have any, but the man who took the helm would be in his cloth
and serge uniform. In bad weather the men wear any old clothes under
their " oilys."

A great many complaints are made about yachts' crews, and some
very hard things have been said against them; no doubt some yacht

L

sailors are ill-behaved, sometimes indolent, sometimes intemperate and dirty in their habits, and frequently show a spirit of insubordination. Now, we are not inclined to wholly blame the crews for this; in the first place, they are almost entirely untutored in anything like discipline, or the discipline they are used to is of the most slipshod character; there is no restraint on their habits, and if they exhibit anything like insubordination, the master, perhaps as ignorant as they are, has no code or system to guide him in restraining it. Again, it must be understood that very much more is expected from a yacht sailor than from a seaman of the mercantile marine. He should be smartly built, be very active, be pleasant in his manners, and be as cleanly, as respectful, and as well conducted as a highly trained man-servant; at the same time he must be a seaman. Now all that is required of a merchant sailor is that he should be a thorough seaman, and should show no mutinous tendency; he may be as ill-shapen as Caliban, and as rough in his manner, and dirty in his person as a pitman, but no one will complain of this. He is kept in restraint by very severe laws, but the very nature of the characteristics expected in a yacht sailor forbids the application of the Merchant Shipping statutes to him in their integrity. A yacht sailor must be governed by quite a different hand, and in a large measure discipline and good behaviour on board must rest with the moral force of the master rather than with any restraints that could be employed under the Merchant Shipping Act. No Act of Parliament will make men clean in their persons, respectful in their manners, or shapely in their forms; and a master in seeking these characteristics in a crew can only employ the means adopted for such ends as in a household. He will take particular care, of course, that the men he engages are seamen; and he must exercise the same care in seeing that they are men who have the other qualifications for a yacht sailor.

We hear a great deal about men saying "this is not according to yacht rules," and "that is not yacht rules," but if the seamen venture to say this we immediately think that it is the master does not know what "yacht rules" and customs are. We have already shown that such rules as there are for working ship are in accordance with the custom of the Royal Navy and Merchant Service, and should be, and generally are, rigidly observed. The other rules for the good conduct and personal behaviour of the men must rest entirely with the master; if he has the moral force necessary to govern men he will have a happy and orderly yacht's crew; if he has not, and attempts to supply the deficiency by the application of statutes that were intended for quite a different condition of things he will always be master of a bad crew.

Masters as a rule have that necessary moral force, and the very fact that most of them rise from "before the mast" is evidence of this. And this brings us face to face with the fact that yacht sailors, taken as a whole, are well behaved, of good manners, amenable to discipline, and exceptionally expert in their vocation, and it can be said that most masters exhibit a wonderful tact in maintaining what is not so much discipline as a ready compliance and respectful demeanour in the crew. (*See* the article "Seaman" in the Appendix).

WAGES OF THE CREW—CLOTHES—GENERAL EXPENSES.

The expenses of yachting are largely governed by the number of hands employed, and the magnitude of this part of the necessary expenditure can be calculated from what follows. (For form of agreement between a sailing master and owner, *see* the article "Seaman" in the Appendix.)

It is usual to pay the master of a yacht by the year, and the wages vary according to the size of the yacht and the qualifications sought. Thus, the master of a 42ft. rating racing yacht may only have 50*l*. a year, whilst one in charge of a 100-tonner may have 100*l*., and one in charge of a 300-tonner 150*l*., and we have known instances of the master of a large steam yacht receiving as much as 400*l*. per annum. Again, if a master for a racing yacht is required, very nearly as much will have to be paid for one to take charge of a 65ft. rater as for one of 200 tons. The master is not always paid by the year, and for a cruising yacht the terms range from 1*l*. 15*s*. to 3*l*. a week whilst the yacht is in commission, and sometimes, for the sake of securing a master's services, 10*s*. per week whilst the yacht is laid up; when such is the rule the master does not always keep charge of the yacht whilst she is laid up, but the owner pays a trifling sum per week —ranging from 5*s*. to 10*s*.—to a shipkeeper who may be an agent who undertakes such work, or a yacht sailor; but it is better for the master to have charge if he lives near the place where the yacht is laid up. One argument in favour of paying greater wages while the yacht is in commission is this—the master, if paid alike all the year round, will be indifferent as to whether the yacht is in commission or not; if paid a larger sum whilst afloat he will be anxious to keep the yacht in commission, and therefore strive to make the life on board as agreeable as possible for the owner.

The remainder of the crew will be paid as follows—from the time they are engaged commencing to fit out the yacht until she is laid up :—

		£	s.	d.			£	s.	d.
Mate ....per week	to {	1	10	0	Cook.................(about) per week		1	15	0
		2	0	0	Seaman........................... „	to {	1	3	0
Boatswain .... „		1	8	0			1	6	0
Steward ....(about) „		1	15	0					

The seamen find their own provisions; but if a long voyage is contemplated they should either be victualled by the owner or he should ascertain that they lay in sufficient stores for the requirements of the voyage.

Often 1s. per week is kept back from the seamen's wages as conduct money, and if any seaman commits an offence during the week the 1s. is stopped; the fine, however, is seldom inflicted, as few masters have the courage to enforce it.

The coxswain of the gig is usually given 1s. per week more than the other men, and it will be his duty to keep the gig clean and fit for use. The "dinghy man," whose duty it is to row the steward ashore, &c., for marketing, and to fetch letters off, and generally to do the carrying to and fro, also has 1s. per week extra. He also has to keep the dinghy clean. In racing yachts the masthead men are sometimes paid 1s. per week extra.

The steward and cook sometimes have more than the wages stated, and sometimes less. In large yachts, where a second steward is carried, the wages given to a good steward are perhaps as much as 2l. The second steward's wages will vary from 1l. to 1l. 10s. according to whether he is a man or a boy, and to his efficiency.

We have known a professed cook to receive as much as 5l. per week, but generally a sufficiently good cook can be obtained for 1l. 10s. or 1l. 15s. It is a common practice in yachts of 70 tons and under to have steward and cook combined in one. In this case one of the fore deck hands acts as cook for the forecastle, and assists the steward at times at the caboose.

The outfit of clothes for the crew is rather an expensive item, as will be seen from the table which follows; but very frequently, especially in small yachts of 40 tons and under, only one suit and one cap or hat is given all round, with one pair of shoes. Thus the crew's outfit largely depends upon what the owner considers it necessary to give them.

It has been established over and over again in law courts, that the clothes are a livery and belong to the owner, but it is the custom to allow the men to take them away when the yacht is paid off. If a seaman is discharged for misconduct his clothes are retained; if he takes them away under such circumstances he can be sued for the value of them in the County Court. (*See* the article "Seaman" in the Appendix.)

The clothes given to the crews of the most liberally found yachts are usually as follows : *

MASTER.	£	s.	d.
2 blue cloth suits, or one cloth and one serge	8	8	0
1 cloth cap with peak and gold band	1	1	0
1 silk neckerchief	0	6	0
1 pair canvas shoes	0	7	6
1 pair leather shoes	0	15	0
	10	17	6

MATE.	£	s.	d.
1 blue cloth suit......	4	4	0
1 pair pilot trousers	1	1	0
1 frock......	0	10	6
1 cloth cap with peak	0	5	0
1 neckerchief	0	5	0
2 pairs of shoes	1	2	6
	7	8	0

BOATSWAIN.

Similar to Mate.

STEWARD.	£	s.	d.
1 blue cloth suit	4	4	0
1 serge suit	3	3	0
1 neckerchief	0	5	0
1 cloth cap with peak	0	5	0
2 pairs of shoes	1	2	6
	8	19	6

COOK.	£	s.	d.
1 blue cloth suit......	4	4	0
1 neckerchief	0	5	0
1 cloth cap	0	5	0
2 pairs shoes	1	2	6
2 white trousers......	0	15	0
2 white jackets	1	4	0
2 white caps	0	3	0
2 white aprons	0	5	0
	8	3	6

SEAMEN.	£	s.	d.
1 pair pilot trousers	1	1	0
2 pairs of white duck trousers	0	10	6
1 serge frock	0	10	0
2 white duck frocks	0	12	0
1 cloth cap	0	5	0
1 red cap	0	1	6
1 straw hat	0	4	0
1 hat or cap riband, including name of yacht	0	1	6
1 neckerchief	0	5	0
1 pair canvas shoes	0	7	6
1 pair leather shoes	0	10	0
Suit of waterproof " oiley's " including south-wester	1	0	0
	5	8	0

Sometimes in small yachts the master is given only one suit of blue cloth and a jersey.

If white duck suits are not given to the men, it is usual in large yachts to give them a dongaree suit (at about 10s. 6d. per suit) of blue linen to do their rough work in, an extra pair of pilot trousers, and a "jersey" besides the serge suit.

It would of course be impossible to estimate what the exact expenses of yachting would be apart from those enumerated, as so much depends upon the owner himself and how he likes the yacht "kept up." Also a great deal depends upon the sailing master, as no doubt the custom of ship chandlers to pay commissions greatly influences unscrupulous masters in "making bills." Roughly the expenses, inclusive of those incidental to the crew as already enumerated, can be set down at from 10l. to 12l. per ton, assuming the yacht to be five months in commission from the day she commenced to fit out to the day she laid up.

* The number of hands carried by yachts of different tonnages will be found set forth in a table in a succeeding chapter on Yacht Racing.

These expenses would be (applied to a yacht of 60 tons) made up as follows :

	£	s.	d.
Interest on £2000	100	0	0
Insurance	35	0	0
Annual depreciation	100	0	0
Repairs and renewal of hull, taking an annual average of 5 years	70	0	0
Renewal of sails and rigging, taking an annual average of 5 years	60	0	0
Ship chandlers' stores, oil, paint, varnish, brushes, charts, flags, coke, &c.	50	0	0
Hire of store	10	0	0
	425	0	0

The above expenses would not vary much whether the yacht were out four months or six months.

The crew expenses would be as follows :

	£	s.	d.
Sailing Master, per annum	70	0	0
Mate 20 weeks	35	0	0
Steward ditto	35	0	0
Four seamen ditto	100	0	0
Clothes	45	0	0
Dues, pilotage, and unforeseen expenses	40	0	0
	325	0	0
	425	0	0
Total	750	0	0

The master, mate, cook and steward, usually live at the expense of the owner in yachts of 100 tons and upwards, and a pint of ale or its equivalent being found. If a table is not kept for them they are sometimes paid board wages from 12s. to 14s. each per week. The matter of board wages is, however, entirely one of option, and often the master and steward of a 40-tonner might be found receiving them, whilst the master and steward of a 100-tonner find themselves in food. Also it is a matter of choice as to whether the mate and cook are paid board wages.

If board wages are not given, or if the owner does not provide for the master, mate, steward, and cook, they usually mess together and share the expense. In very small yachts one mess does for the whole crew.

One argument used against board wages is that, if they are given, the steward and cook will still generally so contrive that their mess is provided at the owner's expense. On the other hand, if the owner agrees to provide, the steward may cater extravagantly. This is very likely to be the case where the steward is not a yearly servant, as he very seldom is, although a few owners make it a point to engage a man who can act as butler in his shore establishment. Under any circumstances, the steward's book should be carefully gone into every week, and any extravagance instantly checked, as there is no reason why living on board a yacht should vary from living in a house.

When yacht is hired (the usual charge for which is from 30*s.* to 40*s.* per ton per month) the owner finds clothes and pays the crew, except occasionally the steward and cook; and the hirer sometimes pays half the laying up expenses, and generally the hirer pays the insurance; the latter will be about 7*s.* 6*d.* per cent. per month. These things are, however, all matters of agreement; and the hirer before entering upon any undertaking to pay so much per ton per month, or any gross sum irrespective of tonnage, should clearly understand all the conditions; also as to how payment is to be made. It is usual for the hirer to retain half of the money until the termination of the hire, and advance wages to the crew if required, and there may be other contingencies necessitating the hirer to disburse money on behalf of the owner.

The owner would have to see that the hirer covenants to make good all damage not covered by insurance, unless caused by the neglect or wilfulness of the owner's servants; also that the advances to the master for the wages of the crew do not exceed a certain weekly sum. Also that the hirer pay all pilotage, harbour dues, &c., and pay for all consumable stores, and finally re-deliver the yacht in a specified port on or before the day appointed for the termination of the hire. (*See* the article "Hiring a Yacht" in the Appendix.)

CHAPTER VIII.

THE RULES OF THE YACHT RACING ASSOCIATION.

It is the custom of all yacht clubs of importance in the British Isles to hold their regattas under the racing Rules of the Yacht Racing Association. These rules, which were instituted in 1875, have since been amended and altered, and in 1899 it was considered that they had become somewhat involved and that their sequence undoubtedly required re-arrangement.

The Council of the Yacht Racing Association accordingly revised and rewrote the rules, and in the year 1900 they came into force in the form set forth in the ensuing chapter. They are simpler and more explicit than the original rules, and have the advantage of embodying a number of previous decisions of the Council upon points of doubt that have from time to time cropped up.

The rules have been divided into four sections under the following headings: Part I., dealing with Management; Part II., Sailing; Part III., Protests; and Part IV., Measurement.

The first three parts, excepting where it is specially provided that a rule relates solely to races under Y.R.A. rating, are applicable to *all* kinds of matches alike, irrespective of any restriction as to measurement or class. The fourth part deals with the measurement of yachts according to the linear rating rule adopted by the Association in 1896.

PART I.—MANAGEMENT.

RULE 1.—GENERAL AUTHORITY OF SAILING COMMITTEE.

All races, and yachts sailing therein, shall be under the direction of the flag officers, sailing committee, or officers of the day of the club under whose auspices the races are being sailed, hereinafter referred to, together or separately, as the sailing committee. All matters shall be subject to their approval and control; and all doubts, questions, and disputes which may arise shall be subject to their decision. Their decisions shall be based upon these rules so far as they will apply, but as no rules can be devised capable of meeting every incident and accident of sailing, the sailing committee should keep in view the ordinary customs of the sea, and discourage all attempts to win a race by other means than fair sailing and superior speed and skill.

The first rule of the Yacht Racing Association deals with the general authority of the sailing committee of a yacht club giving a regatta under Y.R.A. rules. It provides that all races, and yachts sailing therein, shall be under the direction of the sailing committee, that all matters are to be subject to their approval and control, and all questions and disputes which may arise are to be subject to their decision. It should be borne in mind by the sailing committee that it is their duty to apply the rules as stringently as possible, but, at the same time, they should remember that the rules were founded upon the principle of "fair play" only, and were not intended to be penal in their operation. Exemplary penalties or decisions should be avoided, for, in the majority of cases, when breaches of the rules occur they are the result of accident, errors of judgment, or ignorance. Care, therefore, should be taken to consider the character of the breach and the manner of its occurrence. A yacht club should, as far as possible, refrain from inserting reserving clauses in the programme or sailing instructions to the effect that any particular rule may be dispensed with or waived, but should adhere to the Y.R.A. rules in their entirety. In some localities, owing to the peculiarities of the course, which may have to be selected through narrow channels or rivers, a modification of certain rules may be unavoidable, but no departure from the Y.R.A. rules should be countenanced merely on the score that individual members of the sailing committee disapprove of the sense of any particular rule.

RULE 2.—RECOGNISED YACHT CLUBS.

The term, a recognised yacht club, shall include every British yacht club holding an Admiralty Warrant; and also such other yacht and sailing clubs giving races under these rules as may be accepted as recognised yacht clubs by the Council.

The Council shall have the power of cancelling recognition of any club should they deem it expedient to do so.

A club wishing to be placed on the list of recognised yacht clubs should apply to the secretary of the Yacht Racing Association for recognition. The application should be accompanied by a list of members and book of rules, and should be supported by two members of the association. The Council will then consider the application, and if they are satisfied with the status of club, its recognition will be duly approved.

RULE 3.—OWNERSHIP OF YACHTS.

Every yacht entered for a race must be the *bonâ fide* property of the person or persons in whose name or names she is entered, who must be a member or members of a recognised yacht club.

A yacht let on hire may be raced provided—

- (*a*) That she is let for a period in excess of one month ;
- (*b*) That she is entered in the name of the owner, who is to be responsible in all contingencies, for all entries, racing expenses and damages ;
- (*c*) That the crew are to be considered the servants of the owner ;
- (*d*) That the hirer (who must be a member of a recognised Yacht Club) shall, as representative of the owner, comply with all the rules and regulations of the Y.R.A.

Formerly, hired yachts could not be raced under any circumstances, but the rule has now been amended, and stands in the form shown above, which permits of their being raced in the name of the actual owner or owners.

Rule 4.—EVERY YACHT TO HAVE A CERTIFICATE.

A valid Y.R.A. certificate shall be held by every yacht starting in a race under Y.R.A. rating, unless the owner or his representative signs and lodges with the sailing committee before the start, a statement in the following form, viz. :—

UNDERTAKING TO PRODUCE CERTIFICATE.

The Yacht   competes in the race of the   on the condition that a valid certificate is to be produced within one fortnight, and dated not more than one week after the race, that she is not to be altered between the race and the date of certificate, and that she competes in the race on the rating of that certificate.

Signed _____

Date _____

Every yacht starting in a race under Y.R.A. rating should hold a certificate of rating, but should it occur that an owner has been unable to get his yacht measured in time for the start, then he may still claim the right to sail his yacht in the race if he signs and lodges with the sailing committee before the start the foregoing form of undertaking.

For the purposes of this rule it should be remembered that a certificate of rating is considered to be held from the date the final measurement necessary for the completion of the certificate is taken.

Rule 5.—TIME ALLOWANCE.

In all Races under Y.R.A. rating, the time to be allowed on arrival for differences in rating shall be according to the annexed scales, in proportion to the length of the course as notified on the programme or instructions.

A case occurred in Dublin Bay where a race was advertised to be sailed with a "time allowance for a course of ten miles." Upon being measured by chart it was found that the distance was only nine miles, and the case was referred to the Y.R.A. The Council decided as follows :

If the race was sailed upon the understanding that the time allowance was to be in accordance with the scale for a ten miles course, no alteration should be made in the time allowance on the ground of the actual length of the course not being precisely accurate.

If a course is notified by the sailing committee to be of a certain distance, the time allowance must be in accordance with that distance, and a competitor has no right to appeal against the decision of a sailing committee on the ground that they have calculated the length of the course erroneously.

In August, 1877, a case was sent to the Council by the Corinthian Yacht Club as to measuring a course in a channel marked by buoys, the distance varying considerably if measured along the channel as against from buoy to buoy, &c. The council decided as follows :

The length of a course must always be measured along the low water deep ship-channel, and not from buoy to buoy or point to point.

Rule 6.—ENTRIES.

Entries shall be made with the secretary of the club in the following form at least forty-eight hours previous to noon of the day appointed for starting each race. In case of a Sunday intervening, twenty-four hours shall be added. Entries may be made by telegram, and it shall be deemed sufficient that the same shall have been despatched before noon of the day on which the entries close, subject to the provision as to Sundays, but such entries by telegram must be confirmed in the proper form, in course of post :

Form of entry to be signed by the owner or his representative :

Please enter the yacht   , owner   , for the   race at   , on the   . Her distinguishing flag is   ; her rig is   ; and her Y.R.A, rating* is   . And I agree to be bound by the racing rules of the Y.R.A.

Signed this   day of

* The rating may be omitted for races not under Y.R.A. rating.

In case the rating has from any reason been incorrectly stated in the form of entry, if the fact is notified to the sailing committee in writing before the entries close, the sailing committee shall regard only the yacht's correct rating at the time of starting; but otherwise the yacht cannot sail at a lower rating than that entered.

An owner cannot be too careful to enter his yacht correctly, and the actual rating should be stated in the form of entry, for instance—an owner should not enter his yacht in round figures as 65 if her rating is stated on the certificate to be 64·91. It may sometimes occur that at the time of entry the owner has not received his certificate of rating, and is therefore ignorant of his yacht's correct rating; in such a case he is, of course, unable to fill up the form accurately. The proper course to adopt is to notify the sailing committee of this fact in writing at the time of entry or before the entries close. Supposing an owner wishes to enter his yacht in a race for the 65ft. class, but for some reason he cannot state the yacht's rating accurately in the form. He should either leave the rating blank or fill it in, approximately, as 65, but in either case he should be careful to inform the sailing committee before entries close, that he has not stated the yacht's rating correctly in the entry form.

The sailing committee will then be able to notify on their programmes that the yacht's rating is " unknown " or is only " provisionally stated," thereby warning other competitors in the class that if she is found to be less than 65 they may be required to concede time allowance. If, however, a yacht is entered at 65 rating and *no intimation* is made to the sailing committee before the entries close that her rating has been incorrectly stated, the yacht cannot receive time allowance upon a lower rating than that at which she is entered, but must race as 65ft. rating, even though her actual rating at the time of starting is only 64·9.

In races not under Y.R.A. rating, the rating may be omitted from the entry form altogether. Some clubs giving handicap races, require the length and sail area of the yacht to be given, in accordance with Rule 69. Whenever this is the case, the actual measurements certified by the Y.R.A. should be supplied, and no others should be recognised or accepted.

Many a time an owner has been disappointed in sailing because his entry arrived too late, and he should recollect that by the Y.R.A. rules, a yacht must be entered for a match at *least* forty-eight hours before noon of the day appointed for starting the race. But a club may take as much *longer* time as they may consider necessary; therefore the dates for the closing of entries in accordance with Rule 6 should be inserted in a diary, the dates of closing the entries provided by the club should also be noted.

In 1896 the Castle Yacht Club referred a case to the Council as follows: The club allows entries to be made for the season but requires that such entries shall be made in accordance with the Y.R.A. entry form. An entry was received Aug. 4 from the master of the Audrey as follows: " Aug. 4, 1896. Sir,—Will you please enter Audrey, 20-rater, flag yellow and blue, for all coming races; owner, Lord Dunraven.—Signed Capt. Bevis."

It was contended that Audrey's entry was accepted because her name appeared in the programme. The committee replied that the name only appeared subject to the entry form being properly delivered. In the end the committee disqualified Audrey.

The council of the Y.R.A. upheld the decision of the committee.

Entries can be made by telegram, and the Council of the Y.R.A. decided in the Vanduara case that it must be considered a good entry if proof is given that the telegram was despatched or handed in at the telegraph office *before* noon of the day on which the entries closed. So also if it can be *proved* that a letter was posted in such time that the entry ought in the ordinary course to have arrived before noon of the day on which the entries close, the entry should be considered a good one. A plea of forgetfulness, or a general statement that somebody was "told to enter the yacht, and forgot to do it, or neglected doing it, or was given a letter to post and forgot to do so, or was told to despatch a telegram and forgot to do so," does not justify the acceptance of an entry after the stipulated time for closing. Telegrams should be confirmed by letter, accompanied with a proper entry form.

A club cannot accept post entries under Y.R.A. rules, but sometimes a yacht, which was not properly entered, is allowed to start upon the other competitors signing a paper that they do not object. If the other competitors did not do this, and if the post entry won and was given the prize, the club or regatta committee could be sued by the owner of the second vessel if he had not agreed to the post entry starting; and he could recover the amount of the prize.

On the other hand, in the Norman-Bloodhound case tried at Plymouth in 1877, the judge held that if a post entry started contrary to the rules, such post entry could not claim the prize, but only the value of the entrance fee and the attendant racing expenses. In this particular case the secretary was alleged to have accepted the entry on his own responsibility; and the judge ruled that this would not be binding on the committee, as they had not directed that such an entrance should be accepted, but he, the secretary, would have to refund the entrance fee and disburse the expenses; however, this was not actually done, as the evidence further disclosed the fact that the secretary received the entry only "subject to protest" from any of the other entries.

Post entries are condemned for two strong reasons; in the first place, they are disliked by the owners of the yachts that have already entered in good time; in the second place, they are disliked by clubs and regatta committees, because owners are induced to hang back until the last moment to see if the weather will suit their yachts, or to see if they can arrive in time to sail. The chance of swelling an entry by admitting a late comer, that had not deferred entering for any of the above reasons, is a very remote one, and post entries are now rarely heard of.

The terms of a match are often vague as to the limitation of the rating of the yachts for which the match is intended. Matches are frequently advertised for yachts under a certain rating, as, for instance, "Match for yachts under 10 rating," &c. This has often given rise to a yacht just under the rating claiming to sail. In 1880 the following case occurred: The Mabel of 9·71 tons was entered for a race at the Paignton Regatta advertised for yachts " under 10 tons." She was protested against, that as a fraction of a ton counted as a ton she was not under 10 tons. The case was referred to the council of the Y.R.A., who decided as follows:

" The Mabel by Y.R.A. rules is 10 tons, and ineligible for a race advertised for yachts under 10 tons."

RULE 7.—REFUSAL OF ENTRY.

A sailing committee may, if they consider it expedient, refuse any entry.

RULE 8.—OWNER TO ENTER ONE YACHT ONLY.

An owner may not enter more than one yacht in a race, nor the same yacht for two or more races advertised to be sailed on the same day and under the same club.

RULE 9.—POSTPONEMENT OF RACES.

The sailing committee shall have power to postpone any race, should unfavourable weather render such a course desirable. Letter N of the commercial code hoisted over the flag denoting the race shall be the signal that a race has been postponed.

No new entry shall be received under any circumstances whatever for a postponed race.

The sailing committee can only postpone a race on account of unfavourable weather, such as a calm, a fog, or a heavy wind which may be blowing in the *actual locality* of the regatta, so as to prevent the yachts getting round the course. Often, however, some yachts may be detained at a distant port by stress of weather, and for the sake of sport it might be desirable to postpone a race. In such a case it would be necessary for the committee to obtain the consent to the postponement of the owners present and ready to stay their yachts.

RULE 10.—SAILING OVER.

A yacht duly entered for a race shall be entitled to sail over the course (subject however to Rule 9), for not less than half the value of the first prize.

RULE 11.—RE-SAILED RACES.

A yacht which did not start or which has, in the opinion of the sailing committee, committed a breach of the rules in the original race, shall not be allowed to compete in a re-sailed race.

RULE 12.—SHORTENING COURSE.

The sailing committee may shorten the course during a race, and the flag denoting the race, hoisted under the white peter, or in case of fog or darkness two guns fired, shall be the signal that the race is to finish with the round about to be completed, or at such mark as the sailing committee may appoint, and the time allowance shall be reduced in proportion.

RULE 13.—REMOVAL OF FLAG VESSEL OR MARK.

Should any flag vessel or other mark be removed from its proper position, either by accident or design, the race shall be re-sailed, or not, at the discretion of the sailing committee.

The following case occurred at Southampton in 1877, and was adjudicated upon by the council of the Y.R.A. in August of the same year.

Four yachts started knowing that a buoy had been removed, the secretary of the club telling the owners "to do the best they could without it." One yacht turned at a spot where the buoy ought to have been, the other three went a mile farther on to a different buoy altogether. The first-mentioned yacht on passing the committee vessel was told she had done right and was to go on, whereupon the other yachts gave up and protested. The council decided that the race must be re-sailed round fixed marks.

RULE 14.—DECLARATION OF OBSERVANCE OF RULES.

The sailing committee shall award the prizes, subject to these rules, but before they do so, the owner, or his representative, shall sign a declaration that the yacht has strictly conformed to all the sailing regulations, as follows :

FORM OF DECLARATION.

"I   a member of the
Yacht Club, do hereby declare that I was on board and in charge of the yacht
                            while sailing in the race this day, and that all rules and regulations were obeyed during that race."

(Signed)_____

Date_____

RULE 15.—IF A YACHT BE DISQUALIFIED.

If any yacht be disqualified the next in order shall be awarded the prize.

PART II.—SAILING.

RULE 16.—DISTINGUISHING FLAG.

Every yacht must carry, at her main topmast head, a rectangular distinguishing flag, of a suitable size, which must not be hauled down unless she gives up the race. If the topmast be lowered on deck or carried away, the flag must be re-hoisted in a conspicuous place as soon as possible.

A yacht which is competing in a match is required to fly a distinguishing "rectangular flag of suitable size." Flags of "suitable size" for yachts of various tonnages will be found under "Flag" in the Appendix.

RULE 17.—FITTINGS AND BALLAST.

All yachts exceeding 36ft. rating must be fitted below deck with the ordinary fittings of a yacht, including the following:

In Yachts not Exceeding 42ft. Rating.

Two complete transverse bulkheads of wood of average thickness, at least ⅜in., the spaces between to be fitted to form a forecastle and also one or more cabins.

The cabin or cabins shall contain not less than two sofas upholstered and two sideboards or sideboard lockers and a table.

Water-tanks of not less than 15 gallons' capacity.

In Yachts Exceeding 42ft., and not Exceeding 52ft. Rating.

Three complete transverse bulkheads of wood of average thickness, at least ⅜in., the spaces between to be fitted to form a forecastle and also one or more cabins.

The cabin or cabins shall contain not less than two sofas upholstered, or two standing cabin bunks fitted complete, two sideboards or sideboard lockers, one swing table, one fixed lavatory.

Water-tanks of not less than 20 gallons' capacity.

One fixed under-water w.c., fitted complete with all pipes and connections.

In Yachts Exceeding 52ft. and not Exceeding 65ft. Rating.

Four bulkheads as described above, the spaces between to be fitted to form a forecastle, saloon, and one or more other cabins.

The saloon to contain not less than two sofas upholstered, one swing table, two sideboards or sideboard lockers.

The cabins to contain not less than three standing cabin bunks fixed complete and two fixed lavatories.

Water-tanks of not less than 40 gallons' capacity.

Two w.c.'s as described above.

In Yachts Exceeding 65ft. Rating.

Four bulkheads as described above, the spaces between as described for 65ft. rating.

Saloon and cabins as described for 65ft. rating, but cabins to contain not less than four standing cabin bunks.

Water-tanks of not less than 60 gallons' capacity.

Two w.c.'s as described above.

All yachts exceeding 42ft. rating shall have a fixed companion or ladder, and the forecastle furniture shall comprise cots or hammocks equal to the number of crew, and the usual lockers, seats, cooking apparatus, &c.

The following shall apply to all yachts starting in a race:—

During a race the platforms shall be kept down and bulkheads standing. and all the other fittings above specified retained on board except cots, cushions, and bedding ; no water may be started from or taken into the tanks ; no more than the usual anchors and chains may be carried ; no bags of shot may be on board ; all ballast must be properly stowed under the platforms or in lockers ; and no ballast or other dead weights may be used as shifting ballast or for altering the trim of a yacht.

No ballast shall be shipped, unshipped, or shifted, after 9 p.m. of the day previous to that on which the race is sailed.

RULE 18.—BOATS AND LIFEBUOYS.

Every yacht exceeding a rating of 50ft. and under a rating of 80ft. shall carry a boat on deck not less than 10ft. in length, and 4ft. 3in. beam ; and every yacht rated at 80ft. and over, one of not less than 12ft. in length, and 4ft. 3in. beam, ready for immediate use, with oars lashed therein.

Every yacht shall carry at least one lifebuoy on deck ready for use.

The Council have decided that a Berthon or James' folding boat complies with this rule if kept open and ready for immediate use.

RULE 19.—LIGHTS.

All yachts sailing in a race at night shall observe the Board of Trade Rules as to the carrying of lights.

This rule interpreted strictly would mean that the side lights are to be put in their places at sundown. Sailing masters exhibit an extraordinary aversion to exhibiting side lights in a match, for the reason, as they say, that it is not politic for any vessel to let another know what she is.

doing. This is a reason which will not hold water, and owners should insist upon lights being carried in their proper places. Of course if a match is within a half hour or so of being concluded at sundown, in "broad daylight," the rule would not be enforced, but where a case of "sailing at night" is involved, it would be inexcusable not to carry lights. It is sometimes supposed that it is sufficient to have the lights on deck ready to show, but, obviously, if all the yachts in a match did this the lights would be useless, as if the yachts could see each other so as to know when to show their lights, there would be no occasion for exhibiting them at all, and no need of the rule.

This is one of the rules which owners should see observed as a matter of honour, and no occasion for protest should ever occur under it. Also as a matter of protection of rights in case of damage by collision.

RULE 20.—CRUISING TRIM.

When yachts are ordered to sail in cruising trim, the following rules are to be strictly observed throughout the race :—

1. No doors, tables, cabin skylights, or other cabin or deck fittings (davits excepted), shall be removed from their places before or during the race.
2. No sails or other gear shall be put into the main cabin in yachts exceeding a rating of 73ft.
3. Anchors and chains suitable to the size of the yacht shall be carried, and yachts over 42ft. shall carry one at least on deck, with chain rove and shackled on ready for use.
4. Every yacht exceeding a rating of 50ft., and under a rating of 80ft., shall carry a boat on deck not less than 10ft. in length and 4ft. 3in. beam ; a yacht rated at 80ft. and over, her usual cutter and dinghy.
5. No extra paid hands, except a pilot, beyond the regular crew of the yacht, shall be allowed.

These conditions are always stringently enforced. Several cases—the Olga, schooner, in a match to Harwich in 1876; the Constance, yawl, at Ryde in 1885 ; and the Namara, yawl, at Cowes in 1898—have occurred of yachts being disqualified for not having the anchor on the bow, although it was clear it was an oversight in each case.

Several cases have also occurred of yachts being disqualified for having an extra hand or hands on board ; the American schooner, for instance, in a R.Y.S. match at Cowes, 1895. Substitutes have been allowed in the case of any of the crew being actually on shore ill.

RULE 21.—RESTRICTIONS AS TO CANVAS TO BE CARRIED—MANUAL POWER ONLY TO BE USED.

There shall be no restrictions as to sails, or the manner of setting and working them ; but manual power only may be used for hoisting and working them, or for working a centre-board or plate.

M

A yawl is not rated for a mizen staysail; neither is a schooner for main topmast staysail.

Water sails or "save alls," under booms, &c., are not allowed unless rated.

Special rules are frequently made for cruiser races in which balloon canvas is not allowed. In such cases the committee should clearly, not to say minutely, define all the sails, which are disallowed. It is not sufficient to say "balloon sails are not allowed," as no satisfactory definition of what a "balloon sail" is exists.

A question was referred by the Royal Western (of Scotland) Yacht Club as follows :

R.W.Y. Club v. Marguerite.

Marguerite, in a match in which balloon canvas was prohibited, carried what her owner contended was her working fore staysail, as she has no smaller, and she carried it in all weathers, and it is made of duck, has reef points and reef cringle, all this being admitted by the club. The owner also states that he has a much larger sail made of cotton, which is his balloon staysail, and contends that all the Royal Western matches are sailed under Y.R.A. rules, and these rules contain no definition or prohibition of balloon sails. The committee, on the other hand, contend that balloon sails were specially prohibited in the match in question, and that Marguerite's is a balloon fore staysail, inasmuch as the clew of it extends abaft the aftermost shroud of the main rigging.

The matter was considered by the Council, and the following decision was unanimously adopted :

"That from the information placed before the Council by both parties, the sail carried by Marguerite in the way described must be considered to be a working staysail."

The Royal Northern Yacht Club referred the following case to the Y.R.A. for decision :

Stranger v. Amphitrite, 1889.

The yacht Stranger competed in a match in which it was advertised that " spinnakers " would not be allowed. The Stranger, however, set a bowsprit spinnaker, once " flying " and once hanked to topmast stay, and was protested against. Her owner, however, contended that he had no intimation of a notice posted in the club on the evening previous to the match that bowsprit spinnakers would be also prohibited ; and as his sail was hanked to the topmast stay, it was not a spinnaker as ordinarily understood. The committee decided to disqualify the yacht, but, at the request of her owner, referred the case to the Y.R.A.

The Council now decided that the term " spinnakers " included all descriptions of the sail, and that the decision of the club must be upheld.

See " Balloon Canvas " in the Appendix.

RULE 22.—MEMBER ON BOARD.

Every yacht sailing in a race shall have on board a member of a recognised yacht club to be in charge of the yacht as owner or owner's representative.

It may sometimes occur that an owner is unable to be present in person on board his yacht during a race, and in such a case it is his duty to appoint, as his representative, a member of a recognised yacht club to sail on board and be in charge during the match. It is very important that the owner should take care to appoint as his deputy a gentleman with some knowledge of the Y.R.A. rules, because in event of the yacht being involved in a protest, or in case of the sailing master being guilty of a breach of the rules, the representative in charge will know the proper course to adopt, and, if necessary will be able to supply the sailing committee with a correct report of the occurrence and all the facts relating thereto. If the owner's representative happens to be a club member possessed of no knowledge of yacht racing or sailing, in fact, a mere passenger, all kinds of irregularities are apt to take place.

We remember a case at Ryde, in 1899, when a yacht A crossed the line too soon at the start, her recall number was hoisted by the sailing committee and a sound signal was made, but neither the owner's representative sailing on board nor the sailing master saw the number or heard the signal. The owner of one of the competing yachts B, with the sportsmanlike spirit customary amongst yachtsmen, hailed the representative on board A, informing him that he should go back and recross the line because his recall number was being exposed. A took no notice of the hail and proceeded to sail the course and engage in vexatious luffing matches with other yachts in the race, although manifestly disqualified. After the race the owner's representative on board A, said that he heard B's hail, but thought that the latter was merely "having a game with him." In this instance the owner's representative must have been, not only unacquainted with the customs of yacht racing, but, we think, a very poor sportsman, and his ignorance was, rightly, the source of much annoyance to other competitors.

RULE 23.—OWNER STEERING.

An owner shall not steer any other yacht than his own in a race wherein his own yacht competes.

In 1894 a case occurred where an owner steered a friend's yacht A instead of his own yacht B, and became involved in some vexatious luffing matches with a competitor C. It was alleged that C was thereby prevented from winning, and B proved the winner. There have never been any charges of malpractice in connection with this rule, but the incident quoted above was considered of sufficient significance to warrant the addition of a rule dealing with the subject.

M 2

RULE 24.—CREW AND FRIENDS IN YACHTS OF 42FT. AND UNDER.

In yachts of 42ft. rating and under the total number of persons on board during a race under Y.R.A. rating shall not exceed the number set forth in the following table :

	Persons.
Not exceeding 18ft. rating	2
Exceeding 18ft. and not exceeding 24ft. rating	3
Exceeding 24ft. and not exceeding 30ft. rating	5
Exceeding 30ft. and not exceeding 36ft. rating	7
Exceeding 36ft. and not exceeding 42ft. rating	9

If an owner of a yacht elects to have such yacht measured for rating length with a smaller number of persons on board than set forth in the foregoing table, such number shall be stated on the certificate of rating, and shall not be exceeded in any race sailed under that certificate.

RULE 25.—CREW AND FRIENDS IN YACHTS ABOVE 42FT.

In yachts above 42ft. rating there shall be no limit as to the number of paid hands, and no restrictions as to the number of friends or their working.

RULE 26.—INSTRUCTIONS FOR THE RACE.

Every yacht entered for a race shall, at the time of entry, or as soon after as possible, be supplied with written or printed instructions as to the course to be sailed, marks, &c. Nothing shall be considered as a mark in the course unless specially named as such in these instructions.

Each yacht shall be given a number with the sailing instructions for purposes of recall as specified in the succeeding rule.

Sailing committees should be very clear in the instructions they issue as to the manner of starting and the marks in the course, and in no case should verbal instructions be given, nor should verbal alterations be made to written instructions unless urgent necessity arises.

If a sailing committee, owing to some unforeseen circumstances, are obliged to issue verbal alterations to instructions, such verbal alterations should be clearly made known to the person in charge of *every* competing yacht in the race, otherwise a yacht which had not been made acquainted with the alterations, but had fulfilled the original instructions, could claim the prize, so also could the yacht that won the prize by fulfilling the altered instructions. As mistakes in giving verbal alterations to instructions are usually the result of a simple misunderstanding, the fairest way is to pronounce the race void, and order it to be re-sailed.

A secretary, acting under the direction of the committee or flag officers, can deliver verbal alterations or instructions; but such alterations or instructions would render a race void, or cause the yacht or yachts acting upon such verbal alterations or instructions to be disqualified under a protest, if it were proved that the secretary had acted without authority or direction from the flag officers or sailing committee.

The following case occurred in a regatta of the Lough Erne Yacht Club, and was decided by the Council on Dec. 10, 1879: Owing to some oversight, the instructions given to two yachts about to compete for a prize varied so much that one was directed to round a small island on port hand, and the other on the starboard. The committee gave the prize to the yacht which came in first, whereupon the other yacht claimed it, she having, as alleged, sailed a somewhat longer course, and at the same time fulfilled the conditions as handed to her owner before the start. The case was referred to the Council, who decided as follows:

The committee had rightly awarded the prize to the yacht which came in first, she having carried out the instructions.

The "other yacht" might have had a legal claim on the committee for a similar prize, but the Y.R.A. was only concerned with the actual prize put up for competition. In a case where the competitors did not object, the fairer course would be to have the match re-sailed; but a committee could not claim a right to have this done if the yacht which came in first or that saved her time objected, providing, of course, that she had carried out the instructions given her.

The following curious corollary to the foregoing case came before the Council on Aug. 14, 1886.

The case was referred by the sailing committee of the Orford Regatta, as follows:

The instructions given to the Amelia, as to the course, were—" To start from an imaginary line, drawn from committee vessel; round mark boat at Raydon Point Reach; thence round the Island (going down the Main and up the Gulls), twice round."

The instructions given to Keepsake were—" Start from an imaginary line drawn from committee boat, up round mark boat at Raydon Point; down round the Island twice, down the Main and up the Gulls."

The instructions given to Phya were—" Start from committee boat, up round mark boat at Raydon Point, down round the Island, leaving everything on starboard hand, twice round."

Phya did not start. The Amelia, after sailing round the Island, returned to the committee vessel and then went on the other round.

The Keepsake after rounding the Island once, proceeded to round it again, the Amelia being at the time ahead; but Keepsake arrived home first and claimed the prize. Amelia also claimed the prize.

The instructions given to the Amelia were an exact copy of those originally drawn up by the sailing committee. Those given to Keepsake and Phya were varied in copying.

The committee wished the competitors to sail the match over again, but this the owner of the Amelia declined to do.

The Council decided, in accordance with the decision given in 1879, " that if Keepsake came in first, and had carried out the instructions given to her owner, she must be awarded the prize."

In June, 1881, a case occurred in a Royal London Yacht Club match where, in a channel race, the buoys, &c., marking the channel were not specifically named, and at the end of the race it was contended that every mark was not intended to be cleared, and in support of this view it was stated that the committee had excepted some by name. The case was referred to the council, who decided as follows :

In a case where channel marks are named, all are included, unless any are specially excepted in the instructions.

The following case was referred for decision to the Y.R.A. by the Bournemouth Regatta Committee :

Melissa v. *Foxhound,* 1888.

In the first race Foxhound, Sibyl, and Melissa started, but when reaching the point where markboat No. 1 should have been, no mark was to be seen (the marksman having rowed ashore), so the two leading yachts, Foxhound and Sibyl, went straight on and rounded Christchurch Ledge Buoy. The Melissa did not follow this course, but turned where she thought the markboat should have been. As all three yachts came round committee vessel the first time (the committee not knowing but that all had gone round the Christchurch Ledge Buoy), told all three of the yachts to go the same course again. The Foxhound and Sibyl went the second round as they did the first, viz., round Christchurch Ledge Buoy, but the Melissa turned where she did before, the markboat No. 1, according to Melissa, now being in position; that is, where she thought No. 1 mark should be. The Melissa went the shorter course and came in first, claiming first prize; the Sibyl also claimed first prize, and the Foxhound claimed second prize. The Melissa had not paid her entrance fee, hence breaking Condition V. of the regatta committee. The Melissa, on passing committee vessel first round, did not protest according to the Y.R.A. rule. In the Sailing Conditions, No. 3, of the regatta committee, 10s. should be paid at the time of handing in written protest. Melissa eventually entered protest, but paid no fee.

The Council decided that Melissa was not entitled to a prize.

It is the *duty of the sailing committee* to supply competitors with " instructions as to the course to be sailed, marks, etc."

Some doubt has been expressed as to what the term " etc. " is intended to include. It has been held that it does not comprise *all* the conditions of the race, and it is therefore the *duty of the owner* to make himself acquainted with the conditions, and to ascertain from the club whether the race is to be sailed in cruising trim. The following case occurred in 1899 :

Hythe Yacht Club and the Osra.

This was a case in which the owner of Osra appealed against the decision of the committee disqualifying his yacht in the cruiser race, held off Hythe, in July, 1899.

The race was advertised by sending to all the Solent yacht clubs a printed bill giving the full conditions of the race, one of the conditions being that yachts were to sail in cruising trim, with certain exceptions as to limit of crew.

This bill was also sent to owners of boats which were thought likely to compete. Not knowing that Osra would be likely to enter, the bill was not sent her.

Shortly after the race was over, two of the competitors reported to the race officer that certain of the boats, including Osra, had not complied with the conditions by not having an anchor at the bows, with chain shackled on, according to the Y.R.A. rule as to cruising trim.

The race officer thereupon made enquiries, and, as a fact, could see for himself that Osra had no anchor at the bow.

This fact being indisputable, and having no connection with the sailing of the boat during the race, it was considered that it was the duty of the race officer, representing the sailing committee, to disqualify Osra under Rule 48, which was accordingly done.

The owner of Osra appealed against the decision of the sailing committee, stating his case as follows :

"I cannot but think that the committee of the Hythe Yacht Club were incorrect in their decision to disqualify Osra in the Cruiser Handicap on July 28th.

"I submit that in small cruiser racing it is very unusual to insist on the details of 'Y.R.A. cruising trim,' and that, therefore, when it is enforced it is obligatory on the sailing committee to issue individual instructions on the point to the competitors. This was not done. The conditions of the race were fully stated on a bill which I saw in a club, but, being in a hurry, I did not read the small print. Had a copy of this bill been given me after my entry was sent in, there would have been nothing to say when my boat was disqualified for not complying with the conditions.

"The only instructions, however, which I received gave details of the course, handicap, &c., but absolutely no mention of cruising trim, so that I never knew of this condition until after the race.

"I contend that I was not in the least bound to notice or receive any instruction from a club notice board ; and the condition being most unusual in the Solent, for boats of that size, the committee was not justified in disqualifying Osra for not complying with it.

"To turn to a totally different point, there is, I believe, a second reason why my boat should not have been disqualified.

"The fact of my not having carried an anchor on the bows was not the subject of any protest from a competitor, but was ' brought to the notice of the sailing committee ' by two competitors."

The sailing committee contended that, with reference to Osra's first ground of appeal, the card with handicap and course did not contain any of the conditions of the race, not even that it was held under Y.R.A. rules.

They also disagree with the contention that it is unusual in similar races to insist on the cruising trim of the Y.R.A.

On seeing, therefore, that there were no conditions of any sort stated on the card containing the course and handicap, the committee do not consider Osra was justified in assuming that the race was to be sailed without any conditions,

The owner of Osra admitted that he saw the printed bill containing full particulars, a copy of which was conspicuously displayed in the club house, but did not read the small print on the bill.

With reference to Osra's second ground of appeal, the committee were of opinion that the question of not carrying an anchor at the bow is clearly one on which a boat could be disqualified without protest.

The Council decided that the decision of the sailing committee should be upheld, and that Osra should be disqualified.

RULE 27.—THE START.

Fifteen minutes before the time of starting one of the following flags of the commercial code shall be hoisted as a preparatory flag for the yachts of each successive race to approach the starting line, viz. :

B of commercial code for the yachts of the 1st race.
C	,,	,,	,,	2nd ,,
D	,,	,,	,,	3rd ,,
F	,,	,,	,,	4th ,,

and so on.

Five minutes before the start the preparatory flag shall be lowered, a blue peter hoisted, and a gun fired, after which the yachts in the race shall be amenable to the rules. At the expiration of five minutes *exactly* the blue peter shall be hauled down and a second gun fired as a signal to start. Should a gun miss fire the blue peter shall be the signal.

. If any yacht, or any part of her hull, spars, or other equipment be on or across the starting line when the signal to start is made, her recall number shall be displayed as soon as possible, and a suitable sound signal also given to call the attention of the competitors to the fact that a recall number is being displayed. The yacht recalled must return and recross the line to the satisfaction of the committee, and the number must be kept displayed until she has done so; and a yacht so returning, or one working into position from the wrong side of the line after the signal to start has been made, must keep clear of all competing yachts.

The numbers should be in white on a black ground, and the figures not less than 2ft. 6in. in height.

In the foregoing rule it is enjoined that the signal flag (of the Merchant Shipping Code) denoting the race shall be hoisted a quarter of an hour before the signal to start is made. This is sometimes supposed to mean that there must be a separate quarter of an hour between each race; this, however, is not the case, and so long as the signal flag for a race is hoisted a quarter of an hour before the time appointed for the race to be started, the rule will have been complied with. This may be of great importance at some regattas where several matches are to be sailed. (*See* 13th clause appendix to Y.R.A. rules.)

The flag denoting the race *must* be hoisted for ten minutes before the time set down for the start, and then pulled down so that the blue peter may be hoisted for the remaining five minutes; but, as before said, there may be *any* interval between distinct matches which a committee may find convenient. For half hour and quarter of an hour intervals between the races the starts could be thus arranged :

Signal flag denoting race.	Time for hoisting signal flag.		Time of hauling down signal flag, hoisting blue peter, and firing preparatory gun.		Time of hauling down blue peter, and firing gun for the start.	
	H.	M.	H.	M.	H.	M.
B	9	45	9	55	10	0
C	10	0	10	10	10	15
D	10	15	10	25	10	30
F	10	30	10	40	10	45
G	10	45	10	55	11	0
H	11	30	11	40	11	45
J	12	0	12	10	12	15

THE STARTING LINE.

To assist sailing masters in judging whether their vessels are over the line or not, it is desirable that there should be two marks on one end of the line, so that by bringing them into one it can be seen exactly when a vessel reaches the line. There should be a flag boat to limit the length of line at the other end, otherwise the start might be of a very sprawling character.

Sometimes it is convenient to have two marks on shore which have to be brought into one to form the starting line. A church tower and tall chimney, a flagstaff, or any conspicuous objects on shore will answer the purpose (Fig. 59). These shore marks, if they stand out well, are to be preferred, as the look-out on board can judge by them better, and so can the committee. In case of the marks indicating the line being on shore,

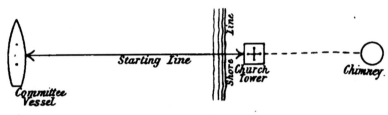

FIG. 59.

the committee vessel should be kept in the same line. The "flag boat," forming the outer boundary of the line (Fig. 60), to avoid complications, should be strictly in a line with the "mark vessel" and inner mark,

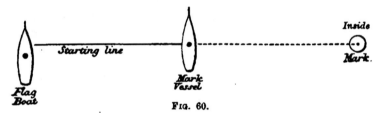

FIG. 60.

whether the latter be on shore or not. However, in case of the "flag-boat" not being exactly on the line, the start should be timed, or judged, irrespective of its position when the yachts brought the two marks, forming the line, into one.

LUFFING ON THE STARTING LINE.

It frequently happens that two yachts get into a luffing match after the first gun has been fired, and the question has often arisen as to whether an overtaken yacht has the right to luff the one overtaking her over the line. We take it that she would have the right; but if two yachts, say, are overlapping before the first gun, it would be rather straining the intention of the rule for the leeward yacht to luff the other over the line; however, the rules must be observed at all costs, no matter whether or not a yacht, by observing them, is herself forced over the line. (*See* "Luffing" and "Bearing Away.")

It is enjoined that if a yacht gets over the line too soon she must recross the line; the rule then goes on to say, "A yacht so returning, or one working into position from the wrong side of the line after the signal to start has been made, must keep clear of all competing yachts." The question is often asked how long "a yacht so returning or working into position from the wrong side of the line" would be required to keep clear of competing yachts which are crossing the line properly; or how far up above the line she would have to sail before the ordinary rules would affect her again? At first sight it would seem unreasonable that the time or distance should be indefinite; but we do not see how exceptions or qualifications could be safely introduced. If a yacht is on the wrong side of the line at gunfire, it is no great hardship that she should keep clear of all yachts which are going for the line from the right side; but, if a time limit or distance limit were introduced into the rule to govern this obligation, it would certainly lead to misunderstandings, and consequent collisions. So also might regulations which overrule the usual rule of the road; but the case of starting is an exceptional matter, and a yacht which has bungled the start should not be allowed to impede those which are about to cross the line properly. The only way to prevent this is by some such rule as the Y.R.A. has adopted; it is a single exception to the ordinary yacht racing rule of the road, and was made for a definite object, and is now well understood; that is to say, a case of non-observing it rarely occurs.

Case Referred by the Royal Dorset Yacht Club.

Castanet v. Reverie, August 20, 1892.

In consequence of a collision, at the start of the third race at the Royal Dorset Yacht Club Regatta, held at Weymouth on August 20th, between Reverie and Castanet, a protest was received from the owner of Castanet as follows :

Castanet being over the line at the start, the sailing committee were of opinion that, according to the paragraph in Rule 17 relating to yachts over the line at the start having to keep clear of all competing yachts. there was no penalty attaching to Reverie, although such action on her part would have led them to disqualify her had not Castanet crossed the line too soon.

However, the case being one which it is believed has never cropped up before, it was decided to ask, from the ruling body of the Y.R.A., for an authoritative decision on the point.

Two plans (Fig. 61) are subjoined giving positions of the yachts both at gunfire and at the time of collision. These plans have been examined and approved of as correct by all the members of the sailing committee.

The owner of Reverie contended that Castanet was over the line, and her number noisted before Reverie reached the committee vessel. It was therefore incumbent on her to get out of the way, however difficult it might be.

In reply to a query as to whether Castanet's helm had been altered with the object of luffing up under the committee vessel's stern and making a fresh start, the owner of Castanet answered :

"Castanet's helm was not altered for luffing under committee vessel's stern, as when Reverie struck us we had not seen the recall numbers."

The sailing committee of the Royal Dorset Yacht Club, without expressing any opinion as to whether Castanet furnishes an example, would ask the Council of the Y.R.A. to consider whether the sentence in Rule 27, "A yacht so returning or working into position from the wrong side of the line after the signal to start has been made, must keep clear of all competing yachts," applies to a yacht which has crossed the line too soon, but is proceeding on her course to the first mark boat when she is run into. Do they consider that such yacht can be said to be "returning" or "working into position

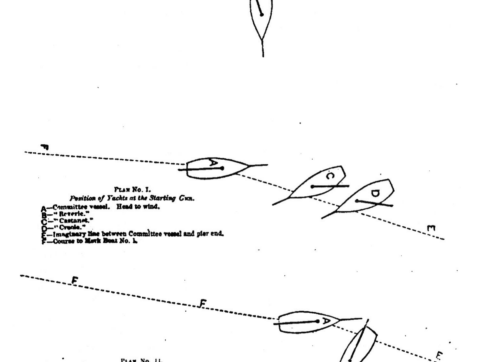

Plan No. I.
Position of Yachts at the Starting Gun.
A—Committee vessel. Head to wind.
B—" Reverie."
C—" Castanet."
D—" Creole."
E—Imaginary line between Committee vessel and pier end.
F—Course to Mark Boat No. 1.

Plan No. II.
Position of Yachts at the time of collision.
A—Committee vessel. Head to wind.
B—" Reverie."
C—" Castanet."
D—" Creole."
E—Imaginary line between Committee vessel and pier end
F—Course to Mark Boat No. 1.

Fig. 61.

from the wrong side of the line?" If they do not consider such yacht to be fulfilling either of the above conditions, but still consider her blameworthy, it is suggested that an alteration of the paragraph in question be made by substituting the word "on" for the line commencing "so returning," which would give the following amended reading: "A yacht on the wrong side of the line after the signal to start has been made must keep clear of all competing yachts." If, however, the Council should not deem such yacht, by a too hasty start, to have placed herself entirely outside the pale of their protection, they will doubtless see their way to safeguard her interests.

DECISION OF THE COUNCIL.

Although the recall numbers of Castanet and Creole were displayed, these yachts had not, under the circumstances, an opportunity of getting out of Reverie's way; and the latter was not justified in attempting to force a passage between them and the committee vessel, there not being room; Reverie must, therefore, be adjudged to blame for the collision. The sentence quoted from Rule 27 (a yacht so returning, &c.) does not apply to a yacht which has crossed the line too soon, but is proceeding on her course to the first mark.

The Council appear to have taken the view that Castanet was not returning to recross the line, in fact, according to the statement of Castanet, the recall had not been observed. The decision of the Council, therefore, only applies to a special case like that of Castanet, which, in spite of being over the line, was sailing on for the first mark.

It frequently happens that when a yacht has been recalled that those on board her have been positive that she was not over the line. There probably have been cases where committees have made mistakes, but this much is certain, that a committee must be the sole judge of when a yacht is over the line and has to be recalled.

GIVING ROOM AT THE START.

In 1896 the Royal Munster Yacht Club submitted the following case to the Council:

Two yachts are sailing up to the line, and B cannot weather the lee mark nor tack without fouling A. Can A force B to leeward of the mark, or can B make A give room?

The Council replied that B had no right to ask A for room, nor to tack so as to interfere with A. (*See* the first paragraph, Rule 32, as to a mark vessel.)

NOT AT THE RENDEZVOUS IN TIME.

A question has often arisen as to whether a yacht which is not at the rendezvous when the signal to start is made can subsequently start. A case occurred in the Thames in 1881 in a match started from Greenhithe to Ramsgate, Magnolia being in Long Reach when the other yachts started. Magnolia won the prize, but was protested against, on the ground that she was not really in the race, as she was not on the station at the time when the starting signals were made. The Council decided as follows:

"As Magnolia was properly entered, and crossed the line from the proper side after gunfire, she must be considered to have been in the race, although not on the station at the time fixed upon."

STARTING TO QUALIFY ANOTHER, AND LATE STARTING.

A straggling starter like this is sometimes put over the line to merely qualify a yacht when a club condition is made that "two are to start, or no race;" or when the second prize is to be withheld unless there are three or more starters, and such like conditions.

In 1893, the following case was referred by the Kirkcubbin Regatta Committee:

"Natica and Eurynome entered for race, Natica started but Eurynome remained at anchor until after the starting gun was fired, she then leisurely commenced lifting her anchor, and eight minutes after the starting gun moved off with only a trysail on, and towing a punt. She sailed a short distance and returned to her moorings. Natica got half the prize for a sail over, but Eurynome maintained that her start under Y.R.A. rules was a legitimate start and entitled Natica to claim the full money. Is that so?"

The owner of Eurynome stated:

"I sailed from Stranford to Kirkcubbin under trysail solely for the purpose of giving Natica a start and entitle her to the prize, the conditions being 'no race unless two yachts start,' which appears to be in contradiction of Rule 8 of the Y.R.A., under the rules of which the Regatta was held. I had a punt in tow, as I had some ladies on board, whom I intended to land at Kirkcubbin. When I reached Kirkcubbin I anchored on the right side of the line for starting, and as it was blowing and raining very hard I could not land the ladies, who were to take the punt with them. When the first gun went, I proceeded to weigh my anchor, and I crossed the line about three minutes after the second gun, and rounded the first mark-boat, and then returned to Kirkcubbin. I preferred to sail under trysail to putting three reefs in a new mainsail.

"I contend that neither starting late, nor towing a punt, nor sailing under trysail, prevented my start from being sufficient to entitle Natica to the prize."

The Council decided that the Eurynome made a legitimate start according to the rules.

Wrong Intervals Between the Guns.

Cases have occurred of a timekeeper giving the wrong time interval between the guns at a start. If the error is discovered at once the yachts should be recalled, or, at any rate, stopped as soon as possible. If, however, the start is a very level one, and no protest is made, the starters and the result need not be interfered with. If the start is a straggling one in consequence of the mistake in the gun, one of the competitors might protest and claim the prize if his yacht finished within the space of time the gun was too soon, and providing the yacht is clear of time of all other competitors. The rights, however, of a competitor in the case of mistakes made by committee are not at all clear. (*See* "Protests," farther on.)

Rule 28.—YACHTS MEETING.

When two yachts are approaching one another, so as to involve risk of collision, one of them shall keep out of the way of the other as follows, viz.:

A yacht which is running free shall keep out of the way of a yacht which is close-hauled.

A yacht which is close-hauled on the port tack shall keep out of the way of a yacht which is close-hauled on the starboard tack.

When both are running free with the wind on different sides, the yacht which has the wind on the port side shall keep out of the way of the other.

When both are running free with the wind on the same side, the yacht which is to windward shall keep out of the way of the yacht which is to leeward.

A yacht which has the wind aft shall keep out of the way of the other yacht.

a. CLOSE-HAULED AND SAILING FREE.

According to the Y.R.A. rule, a yacht which is sailing with the wind free must keep out of the way of one which is close-hauled, and there appears to be only one exception to this rule, which will be alluded to under the " Meeting end on " section. In match sailing yachts are likely to get into positions where one going free might foul one that is close-hauled under the following conditions:

1. In beating for a mark when a yacht which is close-hauled might meet one that has already rounded.

2. In running for a mark when the yacht which is before the wind might meet one that has rounded, and is now close-hauled.

In either case it is the duty of the yacht which has the wind free to give way to the yacht that is close-hauled. In most cases it will be safer for the yacht which is free to go under the stern of the other, as by crossing ahead she might compel the yacht that was close-hauled to bear up or luff, and if she did so, the yacht that had the wind free would be disqualified. (*See* the last paragraph of " Meeting end on " section.)

b. PORT AND STARBOARD TACK—CROSS TACKING.

One of the most frequent causes of protest arises out of the *b* section of the foregoing rule, which provides for keeping vessels clear of each other when crossing on opposite tacks. The Y.R.A. rule is simply that of the Board of Trade, which says that " a ship which is close-hauled on the port tack shall keep out of the way of the ship which is close-hauled on the starboard tack."

In the first place, it must be clearly understood that the rule was not intended to put any penalty or odium on a vessel for being on the port tack; the rule was solely intended to keep vessels clear of each other, and for this purpose it was necessary that the rule should say which of two positions should be the one which must *always* yield. It was decided that the port tack should be chosen, but there could be no particular reason for preferring the port tack to the starboard tack for the purpose. It undeniably gives an advantage to starboard tack, and often, so far as match sailing is concerned, a seemingly unfair one; and hence, perhaps, there is often some feeling imported into the situation when two yachts are crossing on opposite tacks.

A yacht on the port tack may be so far ahead of the one on the starboard tack as to be able to almost cross clear ahead of her, but not quite. If there is the least doubt about it, the yacht on the port tack must give way, however hard or apparently unfair it may seem for her to do so. If she does not so give way and fouls the other yacht, or if that other yacht has to bear away or luff to avoid a collision, the yacht on the port tack must be disqualified without hesitation.

But frequently the yacht on the port tack could have crossed clear ahead of the yacht on the starboard tack, providing the latter had not luffed at the last moment, and by so luffing succeeded in striking the lee quarter or boom end of the yacht on the port tack.

Apart from the obligation* of conforming to match sailing rules, if it were proved in court that no collision would have happened if the vessel on the starboard tack had not luffed, the decision would be that the vessel on the port tack should not be liable for any damage done to the other vessel : or that each vessel should pay her own damages. The Board of Trade rule is that, when one of two vessels has to keep out of the way, the other shall hold a steady course, and also that no vessel shall neglect any ordinary precaution in special cases. On the other hand, the decision of a sailing committee, in such a case as just quoted, would properly be that the vessel on the port tack was alone in fault. In competitive sailing, the temptation to make close shaves is very great, and any decision which would tend to encourage such practices should be avoided as the risks are so great.

By the Y.R.A. rule the yacht on the port tack is bound, to give way if a *risk* of collision is involved. It is usual for the vessel on tho starboard tack to "nip" a little when one on the port tack is coming towards her; and this tells the vessel on port tack that she must not expect her to give way. If, however, a vessel on the port tack is crossing just clear ahead of the other, and that other luffs and touches the quarter of the vessel on port tack, as before stated, the case is somewhat altered, and involves wilfulness on the part of the vessel on the starboard tack; but the answer manifestly is that the vessel on the port tack is not justified under the rule in placing herself in a position where the other can touch her, as the *risk of collision* is clearly involved. However, as the rule was not intended to give a special advantage to the vessel on starboard tack, she should not needlessly bully the unfortunate one on port tack by luffing for the *purpose of making a foul.*

---

* If two yachts agree to sail under and be bound by particular rules, such as those of the Y.R.A., and whilst sailing under them a collision or damage occurred, it would not be right to repudiate such a contract for the sake of appealing to another set of rules, such as sanctioned by an Order in Council under the Merchant Shipping Act, which might be different.

The right of luffing has been claimed for the starboard tack, because some old yacht-sailing rules enjoin that the vessel on the starboard tack should *never bear away*, but *luff* or *tack* if a collision is imminent; no such rule now exists, and the right of luffing is claimed by the yacht on the starboard tack on the ground that the vessel on port tack has under Y.R.A. rules unconditionally to get out of the way. Nevertheless, if a man luffed his yacht and wilfully struck another yacht on port tack, which would have gone clear but for the luffing, and loss of life or injury to person ensued, it would not avail him in a court to plead that the yacht on the port tack was bound to get out of the way whatever the yacht on starboard tack did. A sailing committee might, as before said, reasonably hold that view, but no court of law would. Frequently we hear an ignorant sailing master threaten to give another yacht (which is crossing him on port tack) the bowsprit or stem; it need scarcely be said if a collision did ensue that a court would properly take account of the threat, and in case of loss of life a more serious charge even than that of wilful injury would be made against the person responsible for the collision.

It has already been said that it is the practice to nip or luff the vessel on starboard tack a little when approaching one on the port tack, to show the latter that she must give way; and it is most important that the vessel on the starboard tack should never begin to *bear away* under such conditions unless she positively intends to go under the stern of the one on the port tack. By bearing away it will encourage the belief on board the vessel on the port tack that she is to pass ahead; then if the vessel on the starboard tack luffs, and says she will not allow this, it may be too late for the vessel on the port tack either to bear away or to go about to avoid the risk of collision. The safer thing for the yacht on port tack to do under such circumstances will be to luff or tack, as this will deaden her way. The vessel on the starboard tack should also luff up, and the two will probably come alongside. A protest will follow, and the vessel on the port tack will excuse herself by saying it would not have happened if the vessel on the starboard tack had not begun to bear away. This may be true, but inasmuch as it was the duty of the vessel on the port tack to keep clear, no matter what the vessel on the starboard tack might do, the former would be disqualified.

Further, the practice of bearing away by a yacht on the starboard tack when approaching one on port tack is a dangerous one, from the fact that, if the vessel on the port tack also bears away, a collision is almost inevitable, and under the aggravated conditions of accelerated speed. Beyond this, in the event of the vessel on the port tack not giving way, there is generally great difficulty in proving that it was necessary for the vessel on the starboard tack to bear away to clear her. Legal decisions could be quoted in which, in the case of collisions, the vessel on the starboard tack has been distinctly blamed for not having luffed, instead of having kept away; but the Board of Trade rule is absolutely silent on the point, and gives no instructions whatever to the vessel on the starboard tack further than enjoining that when one of two vessels has to keep out of the way, the other shall keep her course; the Y.R.A. rule is equally silent on the point, and it was found inconvenient to stipulate (on account of the " Luffing and Bearing Away" rule, and some of the rules as to rounding marks) that where one of two vessels has to keep out of the way the other shall keep her course.*

However, many cases do occur, when it would be much easier for the vessel on starboard tack to avoid one which has actually and improperly got across her on port tack, by using a little weather helm instead of lee helm; in fact, if the vessel on starboard tack is to strike the other on the starboard quarter (well aft), it is evident that the collision could be better avoided by the vessel on starboard tack bearing away than by luffing. Of course this assumes that the vessel on the port tack has fairly got across the other, and is thus unable to do anything herself to avoid the impending collision. It is quite natural that the masters of square-rigged ships should prefer bearing away to going about, on account of the ease of the one operation in comparison with the labour of the other; but if there is any law (beyond the seaman-like custom of the sea) which condemns them in penalties for the consequences of bearing away instead of tacking, the Board of Trade rule ought clearly to warn them of it. In the merchant navy the general practice is for the vessel on port tack to go about some time before she gets near the other; but in the case of yachts in competitive sailing the vessel on port tack invariably holds on to the last moment, and the vessel on starboard tack, knowing that the other, according to the rule, ought to give way, does the same. And the result is that the question generally amounts to this—What is best to do?—and not what the sailing rule says ought to be done. So far as we know, the rule that the vessel on starboard tack should luff, and not bear away, has never been general; and, although some clubs formerly went so far as to say what the vessel on the starboard tack was to do, we cannot call to mind any case where a

* For instance, the " luffing and bearing away" rule is contrary to the spirit of such a direction as this, but it has been argued that the overtaken vessel should neither be allowed to bear away nor luff to prevent another passing.

N

yacht has been mulcted in a penalty for bearing away instead of luffing. The clubs which had an instruction on the point before their adoption of Y.R.A. Rules were Royal Dart, Royal Victoria, Royal Cornwall, Royal Albert, Royal Welsh, Royal Cinque Ports ; all the others (including Royal Squadron and Royal Thames) were silent on the point, simply requiring the vessel on port tack to keep out of the way of the other. The Royal Victoria rule was the most explicit, and ran as follows : " Yachts on the port tack must give way to those on the starboard tack ; and wherever *a doubt exists* of the possibility of weathering the one on the starboard tack, the one on the port tack shall give way ; if the other keep her course and collision occurs, the yacht on port tack shall pay all damages and forfeit all claim to the prize. The yacht on the starboard tack shall never bear away ; but if she is obliged to luff or tack to avoid the other yacht, the yacht on the port tack (so obliging her to luff or tack) shall lose all claim to the prize."

We believe this rule was framed by the late Mr. G. Holland Ackers, who had a very strong opinion on the point, and published it as a kind of axiom in his Signal Book, &c. The effect of the rule would be, if stringently enforced, that no protest would stand if the vessel on starboard tack kept away instead of luffed. Would this check the dangerous practice of bearing away? We think not. We believe that the greatest safeguard will be in sailing committees and the Council of the Y.R.A. firmly administering the very letter of the rule, as it now exists, in all cases wherever a risk of collision has been proved through the vessel on the port tack not giving way. It is much too late to talk about disqualification and penalties after a collision has occurred.

A vessel on port tack approaching another on the opposite tack should never be "nipped" in the hope of weathering. It will not aid her if the other "nips" also, and a collision may be the result. A trusty hand should be placed in the lee quarter to watch the other vessel. Pilots, as a rule, cannot be trusted for this task ; they are unused to vessels of such speed, as yachts which, so to speak, slip from under their feet, and so their judgment is often entirely at fault. If the look-out in the lee quarter has the least doubt about weathering, and if you know he can be trusted, put the helm down at once so as to tack some distance clear ahead to leeward of the other vessel, and not have to hustle round close under her lee bow and get a tremendous smothering whilst in stays. If it is decided to bear away, begin in good time so that the vessel on the starboard tack may know what you are going to do. It should be always remembered that the whole onus of keeping clear rests with the vessel on the port tack.

As a rule, a sailing master, when he has stood on to the last moment on the port tack, will prefer bearing away to tacking, as less ground is lost, and the risk of getting a smothering is avoided.

In bearing away a hand should be always sent to the main sheet (whether it be the vessel on port or starboard tack), to slack out some if necessary, to enable the vessel to get off the wind more rapidly. (*See* also " Approaching a Shore Close-hauled.")

A yacht on the port tack can therefore be disqualified under the following conditions :

1. If she is struck by a yacht which is on the starboard tack, no matter how that striking was brought about.

2. If she herself strikes a yacht which is on the starboard tack.

3. If she causes a yacht which is on the starboard tack to luff or tack to avoid a collision.

4. If she causes a yacht on the starboard tack to bear away to avoid a collision.

The following case occurred in 1876, and illustrates an instance of disqualification for causing a yacht to bear away :

Egeria v. Olga.

The owner of the Egeria gave evidence that she was on starboard tack, and Olga on port, as they met in cross tacking. The helm of the Egeria had to be put hard up to the weather rail to get under Olga's stern and avoid striking that vessel. Even then Egeria was only just able to clear Olga. He and a friend assisted the sailing master in hauling the tiller to windward.

The owner of Olga stated that he was watching Egeria from under the boom as the two yachts approached for crossing, and to the best of his observation Egeria did not alter her course, but he could not see whether any movement in her tiller was made. He would not assert that it was not moved, but he could detect no alteration in the vessel's course. As they crossed, he heard some one hail—" You have made us bear up."

Several witnesses were called, on behalf of Olga, who declared that, so far as they could see, Egeria did not alter her course.

Another witness said he saw Egeria end on for Olga's beam, about two lengths off, when her sailing master began putting the helm *down*; but he looked under the boom and saw the position of the yachts, and steadied the helm. At that moment Olga passed ahead, and the next instant he could see two or three persons holding the helm *up* or to windward.

It will be gathered that the evidence was pretty conclusive that Egeria did bear up, and the only question was as to whether she was obliged to do so. The owner of the Egeria stated positively that after bearing up a considerable distance his vessel was only just able to clear Olga; on the other hand, on the part of Olga, it was declared that she cleared Egeria by a distance variously estimated at 100ft., 30 or 40 yards, and two lengths. It was quite useless to attempt to arrive at what would appear to be a just and positive conclusion from such conflicting evidence, and the Council appear to have based their decision upon the fact that a risk of collision was run, as, after disqualifying Olga, they made the following note :

" Any infringement of Rule 19 [this was the rule as to port and starboard tack in 1876] which may be brought under the notice of the Council, will invariably lead to the disqualification of the vessel on the port tack in all cases where the slightest risk of collision may be satisfactorily proved."

TACKING WHEN THERE IS NOT ROOM TO TACK.

We have often heard it contended that if two yachts are standing on port tack, as shown in the diagram (Fig. 62), A can go on starboard tack, although she has not room to do so without coming into collision with B, or force her to tack also. This is an entire mistake, as A has no such

FIG. 62.

right, although it might be greatly to her advantage to do so if B were overtaking her. (*See* Gem *v.* Maud case, also "Rounding Marks," "Obstructions to Sea-room," and the section "Luffing and Bearing Away.")

A protest was referred to the Y.R.A. by the Royal Southern Yacht Club as follows:

Vreda v. *Dragon,* 1889.

In a match on Southampton Water, Vreda tacked close under the lee bow of Dragon, and the bowsprit of the latter subsequently fouled the mainsheet block of Vreda; whereupon the owner of Vreda protested against the prize being awarded to Dragon. The club, however, decided that the Vreda was to blame for the foul, in consequence of the position in which she tacked. The Council having considered the statements of the parties concerned, decided that the decision of the club must be upheld.

In 1892 the Royal Torbay Yacht Club referred the following case to the Council:

Wild Rose v. *Doreen,* August 23, 1892.

Both yachts crossed the line on starboard tack, Doreen about a length ahead under the lee bow of Wild Rose. Doreen thinking Wild Rose was going round to port, put her helm down and got across Wild Rose, who held on to starboard tack. A foul ensued.

The decision of the Council was as follows:

"The Doreen was not justified in attempting to tack under the circumstances admitted by her owner, and thus place herself in a position where she brought about a foul with Wild Rose."

(*See* also the Gem v. Maud case, p. 195.)

Hove To on Port Tack.

Ordinarily, if a yacht is hove to on port tack and another yacht is approaching her, close-hauled on starboard tack, the one on port tack should in good time fill and get way on and tack or bear away so as to clear the other yacht. But if the yacht on port tack is disabled she could hardly be expected to do this, and the yacht on the starboard tack should keep clear; so also if the yacht on the starboard tack is free and the yacht on the port tack is hove to (whether disabled or not), the former should keep clear.

c. Meeting with the Wind Free and Close-hauled—Meeting End On.

In sailing with a beam wind, or if one yacht has the wind abaft the beam and another yacht has the wind on the bow, and they be going in opposite directions, they may meet each other end on so as to involve a risk of collision.

Formerly in such a case it was the duty of each yacht to put her helm to port; that is, the yacht on the port tack *bore away*, whilst the yacht on the starboard tack *luffed*.

The new rule which came into operation September, 1880, has been incorporated in the Y.R.A. rules, and enjoins that when yachts are sailing with the wind free on opposite tacks, the yacht with the wind on the port side must keep out of the way of the other.

The new rule is an improvement on the old "meeting end on" rule, as frequently two ships not actually meeting end on would port and risk a collision, when, by each holding on her course, they would have gone clear. Also frequently when meeting end on, one might be close-hauled and the other free; in such a case it was still the duty of both to port, but often the close-hauled ship contended that the one which was free ought alone to give way. By the new rule, in all cases of yachts meeting end on, or nearly end on, the yacht on port tack must keep out of the way of the yacht on starboard tack; and it is understood that the yacht on the starboard tack must keep her course, and not endeavour to prevent the yacht on port tack passing to windward.

In Fig. 63, let A be a yacht close-hauled, and B one with the wind on the quarter; it is quite plain if B attempted to pass to leeward that she might go ashore; B would therefore haul out and pass on the weather side of A, and A would get a momentary blanketing; also, if there were no shore, B could elect to pass on the weather side of A.

Her duty is to keep clear, and A would not be justified in frustrating her movements.

But the close-hauled vessel might be on the port tack (*see* C, Fig. 63).

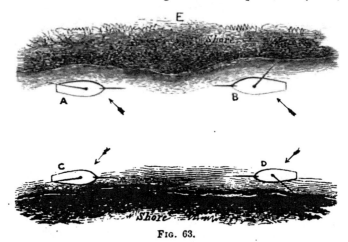

FIG. 63.

In such a case it would be the duty of D (although having the wind on the starboard side) to keep clear.

If sailing along a shore D would not risk getting aground, but would haul out and pass on the weather side of C.

GIVING ROOM WHEN MEETING.

In 1896 the following case was submitted to the Council of the Y.R.A.: Two yachts, A and B, were running before the wind, and met the yacht C, which was close-hauled. The yacht A could clear C astern to windward, but B could not, and would have to cross C's bows to leeward at the risk of being run down. B at last was luffed and fouled A; the latter protested.

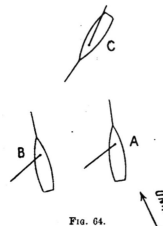

FIG. 64.

The Council decided that, under the circumstances, A should have given way to B, and allowed her to pass under the stern of C.

This decision was somewhat questioned at the time, and it was understood that the Council were not unanimous in giving it. It is, however, difficult to see what other decision could have been arrived at. In the first place, if C had been an obstruction, as ordinarily understood, A would have been bound to have given room, and it cannot be contended that A would in any way suffer from doing so. On the other hand, a view was taken that B could have kept away a little more and have safely crossed the bows of C; or have taken in spinnaker and hauled in main sheet to have stopped her way.

Such things might be done on a very still day, but the risk of failure would be very great in anything like a breeze. Beyond this, why should B be put to such a disadvantage by going out of her course or having her way stopped?

CROSSING WITH THE WIND FREE.

It may so happen that the two yachts may be free and be crossing on opposite tacks. Thus, say the wind is W., and one yacht is steering N.N.W., and the other S.S.W., each a point and a half free, they will be approaching each other at an angle of 134°. In such case it will be the duty of the yacht with the wind on the port side to keep clear of the other, as this would be a clear case of crossing on opposite tacks, and not of "meeting end on." This, however, is a situation not likely to occur in match sailing.

d. SAILING FREE WITH THE WIND ON THE SAME SIDE.

In sailing free, if two yachts have the wind on the same side, the one which is to windward must keep out of the way of the other. (This is explained under the head of "Luffing and Bearing Away.")

e. YACHT WITH THE WIND AFT.

This section requires no explanation.

RULE 29.—OVERTAKING YACHTS—LUFFING AND BEARING AWAY.

A yacht overtaking any other shall keep out of the way of the overtaken yacht; and a yacht may luff as she pleases to prevent another yacht passing to windward, but must never bear away out of her course to hinder the other passing to leeward—the lee side to be considered that on which the leading yacht of the two carries her main boom. The overtaking vessel, if to leeward, must not luff until she has drawn clear ahead of the yacht she has overtaken.

The Council of the Y.R.A. have decided that if a yacht allows another yacht to come up on her weather and to be actually in the act of passing clear ahead, the yacht to leeward may not deliberately luff for the mere purpose of causing a foul. If the overtaken yacht allowed the other to come up and be passing ahead (say) before she luffed, it is obvious that the weathermost yacht may be unable to luff also to keep clear ; in such a case a foul would be the deliberate act of the leeward yacht, and the foul could not be claimed.

The question has often arisen as to how long a yacht which is rightly luffing an overtaking yacht can continue to luff. The plain answer is, so long as she likes ; but it has been contended that this may mean that she may luff until she comes head to wind and fills on the other tack, compelling the other vessel to tack, and then gaining the weather position. It is quite clear that no such luffing as this was ever contemplated under the rule, and would not be allowed ; but luffing head to wind or nearly so is a frequent practice.

An *overtaking* yacht, if to leeward, is not allowed to luff so as to cause the yacht to windward to luff to avoid a collision until she (that is the *overtaking* yacht) has drawn clear ahead. Thus the *overtaking* yacht, under such circumstances, continues to be "overtaking" until she has drawn clear ahead.

It must be clearly understood that the foregoing relates to "yacht racing" alone. Yachts ordinarily are subject to the customary rule of the road, which enacts "that if two yachts are running free with the wind on the same side, the yacht which is to windward shall keep out of the way of the yacht which is to leeward ;" and "every vessel overtaking any other vessel shall keep out of the way of the last-mentioned vessel ;" and "when one of two ships are to keep out of the way the other shall keep her course." It is thus quite clear that by the ordinary rules of the sea a yacht that is being overtaken must neither luff nor bear away to prevent an overtaking vessel of whatever description passing her. (*See* "Head Reaching," farther on.)

By the rule of the road before referred to, a steam yacht must keep out of the way of all sailing vessels ; but there is one position in which the sailing vessel would have to keep clear of the steam yacht. It frequently happens that a sailing yacht is overtaking a steam yacht, and in all cases the overtaking vessel, whether she be under steam or sail, or both, must keep out of the way of the one she is overtaking. The popular opinion was, that in all possible directions of approach, the steam yacht must keep out of the way of the sailing yacht ; but by the new regulations which came into force September, 1880, there is, as shown, one direction of approach under which it is the duty of the sailing yacht to keep clear of the steam yacht. A vessel, it must be understood, is only considered as an overtaking one when she is steering in the direction of the one ahead or in the wake of the one ahead, and only in such case would the sailing vessel have to keep clear of the steamer she might be overtaking.

Several cases under this rule have been brought before the Council of the Y.R.A., and the right of the leading vessel to luff to prevent another passing to windward has been maintained. When the overtaking vessel has failed to luff also and keep clear, she has been held responsible for the foul. The following cases illustrate this :

Boadicea v. *Samœna*, August, 1881.

According to the evidence, Boadicea was overtaking Samœna, and the latter luffed, and either Boadicea did not see Samœna luff and did not herself luff at all, or, seeing her, did not luff sufficiently to keep clear. In the end, the jib boom of Boadicea went through the mainsail of Samœna, and considerable damage was done. The Council decided that Boadicea was in the wrong.

Katie v. *Buttercup*, Dec. 7, 1882.

The Buttercup was overtaking Katie, and the latter luffed; Buttercup also luffed, but a foul ensued. The Council, after hearing the evidence, decided as follows : "The luffing having commenced at a time when Katie had a right under Rule 29 to luff to prevent Buttercup passing to windward, the latter was bound to keep clear, and as a foul ensued Buttercup must be held to have been in fault."

Hinda v. *Vanessa*, August 14, 1886.

Case referred by the Bristol Channel Yacht Club : Hinda and Vanessa were running down to a mark, the wind being dead aft, and spinnakers were boomed out to starboard. Vanessa overtook and ran up on Hinda's starboard (weather) side, the overlap being a little more than the length of bowsprit, according to the owner of Hinda; and the bowsprit and half the length of hull, according to the owner of Vanessa. Hinda was luffed to prevent Vanessa passing to windward, and the latter luffed also and hauled main boom aboard. A foul, however, ensued, Hinda's spinnaker boom touching Vanessa's balloon foresail.

The question asked was—" Had the Vanessa ceased to be an overtaking vessel, under Rule 29, when Hinda's helm was ported for the purpose of luffing."

The Council decided that Vanessa had not ceased to be an overtaking yacht, and was bound to keep clear.

The Council has, however, been careful that no unfair advantage should be taken of the rule on the part of the overtaken vessel by wilfully or vexatiously bringing about a foul, as the following cases will show :

Senta v. *Rival*, March, 1881.

Rival, it was alleged, overtook and nearly passed clear ahead of Senta, when the latter luffed, and, with her bowsprit, struck the after cloths in Rival's mainsail. Senta claimed the foul; but, on the part of Rival, it was alleged that Senta luffed nearly head to wind for the sole purpose of causing a foul. The Council decided that from the position of the yachts, and from the spar and sail which came into contact when the foul took place, that the helm of the Senta could not have been altered to prevent Rival passing to windward, as allowed by Rule 29, but for the purpose of making a foul, and Senta must therefore be adjudged in the wrong.

Freda v. *Louise*, June, 1881.

Freda overtook Louise, and, after sundry luffing bouts, the two had borne up for their mark; Freda out on the weather bow of Louise, having so far got past her. They were sailing parallel courses when Louise was suddenly luffed, and Freda luffed also, but Louise's bowsprit struck the after leech of her mainsail. The owner of Louise claimed the foul under Rule 29, but admitted that his vessel was luffed for the purpose of causing the foul. The Council decided that a yacht could not claim a foul under the conditions disclosed by the evidence.

The following case was referred to the Y.R.A. by the Royal Southampton Yacht Club:

May v. *Mohawk*, 1888.

May and Mohawk were with other yachts in a race, and, whilst running from Lepe Buoy to the Calshot Spit Lightship, a foul ensued between the two named. Both yachts protested, and the officer of the day undertook that the case should not be decided without the owner of Mohawk having an opportunity to give evidence. However, some of the sailing committee had witnessed the occurrence from a steamer which accompanied the race, and, being unaware of the undertaking given to the owner of Mohawk by the officer of the day who was on board the station vessel, proceeded to adjudicate upon the case, and decided in favour of May. The prize was subsequently sent to the owner of that yacht.

The owner of Mohawk objected to this decision, and asked to have the case referred to the Y.R.A. To this the club assented, but the owner of May declined to take any part in the proceedings, on the grounds that the club referred the case without consulting his wishes, and because the matter had already been decided by the club committee and the prize paid over to him.

The statement of the members of the committee who saw the foul was as follows: The yachts rounded Lepe Buoy in the following order, May, Neptune, Mohawk, a short distance between each. Mohawk overhauled May, and passed her to windward. The Mohawk, when about two lengths ahead, and a little on May's starboard bow, took in her spinnaker in order to gybe over, then the May suddenly, and not before, became the overtaking vessel. The May, running as dead as possible, was then steering clear of Mohawk, and passing clear of her on her port side when the Mohawk gybed, but, finding she could not head the May, she had to gybe back again, and it was during this second gybe that the foul took place. These facts being confirmed by another member of the sailing committee, who was in his yacht and saw the foul, the sailing committee decided in favour of May, on the ground that it was an error of judgment on the part of Mohawk, she not having established a sufficient lead before attempting to cross May's bows, Rule 30 requiring that "no yacht shall be considered clear of another yacht unless so much ahead as to give a free choice to the other on which side she will pass." Rule 29 also bears on the case.

The owner of Mohawk stated she passed on May's weather. After this Mohawk obtained a lead of four or five lengths, and both had got so far to windward of their course that they could not run for the Spit Lightship, and both were by the lee in trying to do so. Mohawk was still four lengths ahead, when she took in her spinnaker preparatory to gybing. May kept hers on, and, blanketing Mohawk, came upon her very fast, Mohawk being at the time a little on May's starboard bow, or nearly dead ahead of her, both still by the lee. Eventually Mohawk's main boom came over to starboard quarter when the yacht was about two lengths ahead of May. She was immediately afterwards run into by May, whose bowsprit struck Mohawk's taffrail on the port side, and grazed along the rail until brought up by May's whisker getting hung up in the fair leader on Mohawk's port quarter. During the foul Mohawk's mainboom swung on board again and rested on May's headsail, but the boom was pushed back again to starboard quarter. Mohawk sprung to a little when she gybed, but she was not luffed.

The sailing master of Mohawk and the mate gave similar testimony, and declared that the fact of May running so dead after Mohawk brought the latter's boom over before they were quite ready for it, and when they were about a clear length ahead. The foul took place immediately afterwards. If May, when she began to overtake Mohawk, had got in her spinnaker and gybed she could have avoided the foul.

All the witnesses declared positively that Mohawk only gybed once, and that the foul took place immediately after that gybe.

It was stated that the club steamer was from a mile to a mile and a half away from the yachts at the time of the foul, and about abreast of them.

The Council having remarked on the unsatisfactory circumstance of being called upon to give a decision without any direct evidence from the May, unanimously resolved as follows : " That from the evidence before them the Council decide that the May was the overtaking yacht, and therefore alone to blame for the foul."

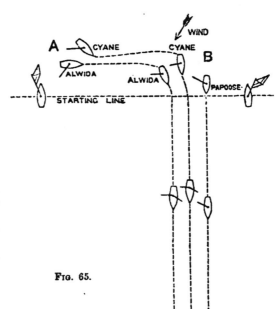

Fig. 65.

The following case was referred to the Council by the Aghada committee, 1884 :

The facts were as follows: After first gun, Alwida came under Cyane's lee while both were working into position, as shown in the diagram marked A.

At gunfire both put up their helms, and squared away for line, crossing some moments later (*see* B, Fig. 65).

Alwida slightly ahead, Cyane overlapping, they continued in the same position relatively to each other, towards next mark (both carrying spinnakers to port), when Alwida luffed Cyane and fouled her. Papoose, also in the race, was to windward of both boats at the time Alwida luffed (*see* C).

Alwida won the race, but protested against the awarding of a 2nd prize to Cyane, on the grounds that she refused to luff, and caused the foul.

The committee decided that Alwida was not luffed for the *bonâ fide* purpose of preventing Cyane's passing on her weather, but in order to cause a foul.

The case was subsequently referred to the Council of the Y.R.A., who decided as follows :

"Alwida under the circumstances had the right to luff as she did, and Cyane should have luffed to avoid her."

On Oct. 31, 1895, the Council decided in a case referred by the Fairlie (N.B.) committee, between Lufra and Rosetta, as follows :

(1) A yacht is not luffing within the meaning of the rule when passing from one tack to the other.
(2) A yacht in luffing under the rule cannot force another yacht to go about.

The following questions arising out of cases which had occurred under the luffing rule in 1894, were asked by the Royal Northern Yacht Club :

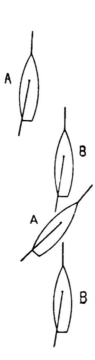

FIG. 66.

Question : (1) A. and B. are both reaching on starboard tack. B. is overtaking A., meaning to pass her to windward (Fig. 66).

    (1) When B.'s bowsprit overlaps A.'s counter by (say) 1 yard, A. luffs across B.'s bow, and a collision follows.

Answer : A. right.

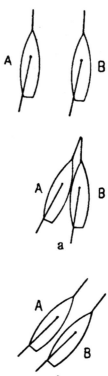

b

FIG. 67.

Question : (2) If B. draws right abeam with A., and the latter luffs (Fig. 67).

    a. B. refuses to luff, and strikes A.
    b. B. luffs all he can, but cannot avoid A., who continues to luff until the boats touch.

Answer : *a.* A. right.
            b. A. right.

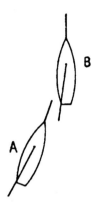

FIG. 68.

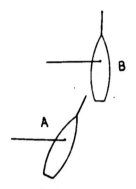

FIG. 69.

Question: (3) When B. has drawn nearly ahead of A., so that B.'s counter overlaps A.'s bowsprit, A. luffs sharply, and strikes B. (Fig. 68).

Answer: B. right.

Question: (4) If (1) is decided in favour of A.; and (2) and—or—(3) in favour of B.; then at what point does A. lose the right to luff?

Answer: When from the position of the yachts it is apparent that A. has luffed too late to prevent B. passing to windward, and a foul ensues, the act of A. could not be upheld.

FIG. 70.

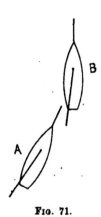

FIG. 71.

Question: (5) Further—If the boats are running dead before the wind (Fig. 69), would that make any difference in the decision?

Answer: If the yachts were dead before the wind, that would make no difference.

Question: (6) A. and B. are both close-hauled on starboard tack, and B. is astern, but a little to windward of A. But B. is sailing more water than A., and A. is lying a better wind than B. B. runs into A., striking the latter on the counter with her bowsprit (Fig. 70). Which is in the right?

Answer: A. right.

Question : (7) Assume that B. was first round the lee mark, and that A. has caught her to windward, does this fact make any difference ? (Figs. 71 and 72).

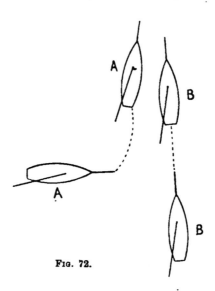

Fig. 72.

Answer : B. right, and A. would have to keep clear.
(In connection with the above, *see* "Head Reaching and Weathering " farther on.)

RULE 30.—ROUNDING MARKS.—GIVING ROOM.

When rounding any buoy or vessel used to mark out the course, if two yachts are not clear of each other at the time the leading yacht is close to, and actually rounding the mark, the outside yacht must give the other room to pass clear of it, whether it be the lee or weather yacht which is in danger of fouling the mark. No yacht shall be considered clear of another yacht, unless so much ahead as to give a free choice to the other on which side she will pass. An overtaking yacht shall not, however, be justified in attempting to establish an overlap, and thus force a passage between the leading yacht and the mark after the latter yacht has altered her helm for the purpose of rounding.

APPROACHING MARKS ON THE SAME TACK FOR ROUNDING.

By the Y.R.A. rule, yachts must give each other room at marks, but a yacht is not justified in attempting to establish an overlap at the last moment, when it may be impossible for the outside yacht to give room. A yacht in rounding a mark, whether she is hauling round or wearing round, always deadens her way more or less, and if a yacht is close astern so as to be only just clear, it is quite easy for her to make an overlap; but this is just what she is not allowed to do. The overtaking yacht must have, beyond all dispute, established an overlap before the other has altered her helm to round; this means before the other has altered her course and is actually rounding the mark. It frequently happens in light winds that a yacht gets jammed by the tide at a mark, and can only just hold her own abreast of it. A yacht that comes up astern can pass between such other yacht and the mark if there be room; but, if there be not room, she must pass outside.

The following case was adjudicated upon by the Council of the Y.R.A. in August, 1877:

Britannia v. Coralie, 1877.

Coralie and Britannia were reaching for a mark at Falmouth, two or three points free. According to the evidence of the owner of the Britannia, she caught Coralie when about twenty yards from the markboat, her bowsprit end being nearly up level with Coralie's runner. When at the mark, Coralie put down her helm and luffed across Britannia, the latter being unable to luff on account of being so close to the markboat, and could not bear away under Coralie's stern.

This was confirmed by the skipper of the Bloodhound, who was close astern of the two.

On the part of Coralie it was urged that her helm was not put down, and that only her main sheet was drawn in, and this brought her across Britannia, but the latter had plenty of room to bear up and go under Coralie's stern. Britannia struck Coralie just abaft the runner. Britannia caught Coralie whilst the latter was shifting her balloon foresail.

The Council, in coming to a judgment, considered it clearly made out that the collision took place at the markboat, and not after the markboat was rounded; also, that from the part where the Coralie was struck being so far forward it was equally clear an overlap was established at or before the time when the markboat was reached; and, finally, that the Coralie made no attempt by putting up her helm to give Britannia room. Coralie was therefore adjudged in the wrong.

Roberta v. Sweetheart, 1882.

In a case which occurred in the Tenby Regatta, 1882, the Roberta overtook Sweetheart before or at a mark, and a foul ensued. The case was referred to the Y.R.A. Council, but, as usual, the evidence was most conflicting.

On the part of Sweetheart it was alleged that her owner or the master told Roberta

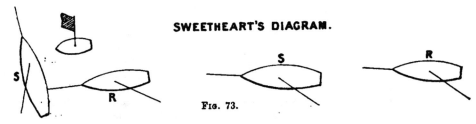

SWEETHEART'S DIAGRAM.

Fig. 73.

to keep away under Sweetheart's stern when room was asked for. At the same moment Sweetheart's helm was put down for rounding, and the collision occurred a moment afterwards when Sweetheart was half round the markboat.

On the part of Roberta it was alleged that she overtook and was overlapping Sweetheart some considerable distance away from the markboat, and requested room as she could not bear up across Sweetheart's stern without striking her.

From statements placed before the Council it appeared that Roberta's bowsprit first struck Sweetheart on the rail 23ft. abaft the mast. The representative of the Roberta said he felt no concussion aft, and Roberta's bowsprit was across Sweetheart's deck by the mast. He had no doubt, however, that the bobstay had scraped along the rail.

There was positive evidence, however, that Sweetheart was first struck 23ft. abaft the mast, which would be 10ft. or 11ft. ahead of the sternpost.

The diagrams, which are facsimiles of those put in (*see* Figs. 73 and 74), agree that Sweetheart was well round the mark when the collision occurred, and that Roberta had not apparently quite got into a position for rounding.

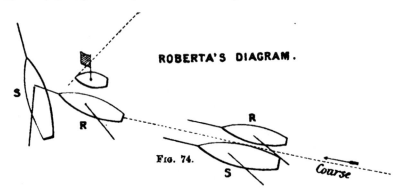

ROBERTA'S DIAGRAM.

FIG. 74.

The Council concluded that there must have been a mistake made as to the statement that Roberta was overlapping Sweetheart before the mark was reached, and decided that she (Roberta) was in the wrong.

GIVING ROOM AT MARKS AT THE START.

Miranda-Samœna Case.

At a start it frequently happens that yachts approach the line from different directions, and very nice steering and a great deal of " give and take " are necessary to keep them clear. A case occurred on Southampton Water, in August, 1881, in a regatta of the Royal Southern Yacht Club, and, although it did not come before the Council of the Y.R.A. so far as the prize was concerned, it did on a question of alleged foul sailing on the part of the master of Miranda, under Rule 49.

Before the start the Miranda and Samœna were reaching up Southampton Water on port tack ; both then stayed (Samœna first) to starboard tack and reached down towards the line formed by the schooner Star of the West and a flag boat (*See* the diagram, Fig. 75). The wind was abeam of whole sail strength. When both were sailing down for the line Samœna was ahead, and to windward, and was also to windward of the Star of the West ; Samœna had, therefore, to keep away to get to the line, and she bore away across the Miranda's bows, and hauled to under that vessel's lee bow near the Hornet. (*See* Fig. 75.) The two vessels were very near together as they crossed, and the Miranda was going the faster through the water. When, therefore, Samœna straightened for the line, the Miranda came on her weather quarter. Miranda, still going the faster through the water, overlapped Samœna as they approached the line ; and it was alleged that Samœna luffed across Miranda, and the latter to avoid a collision put down her helm also. Miranda was thus forced a little too far to windward to clear the Star of the West, the result being that Miranda's fore-starboard rigging caught the boom end of the Star of the West, and two or three gentlemen were thrown into the water, one having his arm broken.

On the part of Samœna, it was alleged that when about three-quarters of a length ahead, and a little on the weather bow, if anything, of Miranda, the latter was luffed across her stern, and then, going the faster, made an overlap after Samœna had altered her helm to pass close under the stern of the Star of the West, the contention being that

Miranda had no right to luff across Samœna's stern when so near the mark-boat, which both, to get all the advantage possible, were bound to shave, as it was on the weather end of the line.

It will be gathered from the foregoing that the evidence was very conflicting as to the nature of the luffing, and as to the overlap; but it was

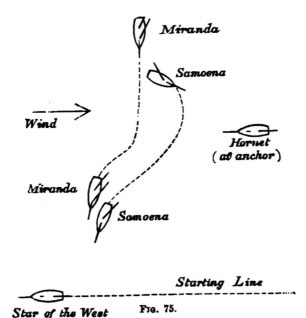

Fig. 75.

also very clear on three points: 1st, that the Samœna did cross Miranda as alleged in position A (Fig. 76); 2nd, that she immediately straightened

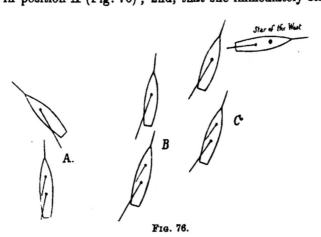

Fig. 76.

again to position B when 150 yards, or less, from the Star of the West, and, continuing to luff, Miranda luffed also; 3rd, that Miranda, sailing

o

the faster, had established an overlap upon reaching the Star of the West when they came in the position C. The diagram of these three positions (Fig. 76) was testified to by witnesses who were watching the two yachts from on board the Star of the West.

It can be taken for granted that, even if no actual overlap had been established before the Star of the West was reached, that, at any rate, Miranda had got so close up that she could not bear away across Samœna's stern without some risk of striking her, she going, be it remembered, the faster through the water.

The question of foul sailing thus turned upon the point whether Miranda was justified in luffing when Samœna luffed whilst in position B, the yachts being so close to the mark-boat. The sailing committee decided that she was not so justified, and withheld the prize from Miranda. The Council took a different view, and decided as follows as to the charge of foul sailing :

"The charge has not been made out, as the evidence shows that the Miranda must have been overlapping the Samœna before the mark vessel was reached."

Occasionally a case is complicated by a vessel overtaking and passing a vessel just before reaching a mark. Such a case occurred in the regatta of the Royal Dart Yacht Club in August, 1883, and ultimately came before the Council on Nov. 27 of the same year.

May v. Tara.

The Tara, 40 tons, had led May, 40 tons, over the greater part of the course, but approaching a mark under spinnakers to starboard, wind very light, May overtook and, as alleged, passed clear ahead of Tara. They had to get in spinnakers and gybe round the mark to leave it on the port hand, and after gybing, May, when abreast of the mark, luffed up across Tara to get on her course for the next mark ; and Tara, which was on May's weather quarter, having the inside berth, fouled her—Tara's bowsprit striking May's mast. On the part of Tara it was contended that May had not at any time a clear lead in the meaning of Rule 30—that is, Tara had not a choice as to whether she would cross May's stern and take an outside berth, or stick to the inside berth as they got near the mark.

The question really turned on a question of fact as to the position of the yachts at the time when May altered her helm to round, which can be taken in this case to be the time when she gybed.

On behalf of May, it was contended that she had this clear lead, and the committee of the club, who saw the occurrence, supported this contention, although they only had an end on view.

It should be stated that, when about a mile from the mark, the yachts were the best part of a quarter of a mile apart in a broadside direction, and Tara at that time, it was admitted, could have luffed out across the stern of May; but this would have thrown her considerably out of her course, as the two yachts were in reality converging towards the mark from different positions.

Ultimately the Council, after reviewing the very conflicting evidence, felt bound to give a decision in accordance with the independent testimony of the committee of the club as follows :

The sailing committee having testified that May had passed Tara and had a clear lead when she altered her helm to round the mark-boat, the May was not responsible for the foul.

REACHING A VESSEL ON BEYOND A MARK.

It frequently happens that when yachts are approaching a mark close-hauled (or free), that the leading yacht may be a little to leeward, as in Fig. 77. The yacht A cannot tack to round the

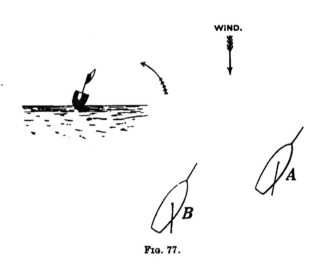

FIG. 77.

mark on port hand, because she could not clear B, and she must therefore wait until B chooses to tack.

It should be noted that it does not matter which tack the yachts are on; A has no right to tack until she can do so clear of B.

Often a yacht in the position of B proves very obstinate, and "reaches her antagonist along" until both have stood farther than is necessary, but B has a right to do this.

A case bearing on this happened on the East Coast, and the dispute was decided by the Y.R.A., in August, 1884. The case was as follows :

Gem v. Maud.

After passing a mark the Maud was reached off by the Gem, the latter being astern on Maud's weather quarter. Maud tacked but could not clear Gem, and a foul ensued.

The Council decided that Maud was not justified in tacking until she could do so without bringing about a collision, and must therefore be adjudged in the wrong.

(*See* also " Obstructions to Sea Room.")

In considering the undoubted right of a vessel in the position of B (Fig. 78) to reach A on out of the course, it must not be overlooked that under certain conditions it may not be right for B to hold on, as it would be contrary to the rules of fair play.

It can be supposed that two vessels are standing on a course for a buoy, and B, the one to windward, can weather an obstruction, such as a pier (*see* Fig. 78), and A, the one to leeward, cannot; but after the obstruction is weathered they can bear up two or three points for the buoy which

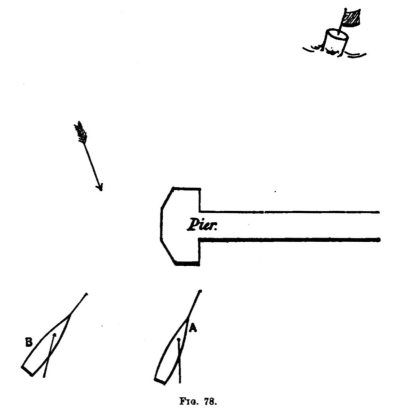

Fɪɢ. 78.

has to be rounded. A, the leeward yacht, hails B, the windward yacht, to go about, and the latter complies, and both come on the starboard tack, with A now on the weather quarter of B. (*See* Fig. 79.) It would be no more than fair if A tacked again directly she could weather the obstruction; but she might elect to reach B on, and we have heard it justly contended that, although as a general right A is allowed to do this, she ought not to be permitted to do it where she has gained the position solely by hailing the other vessel about under Rule 32. The remedy, of course, would be to give B the right to hail A to go round again directly she can weather the obstruction.

HAILING TO GO ABOUT AT MARKS.

If, instead of being at the pier, the yachts had been at the buoy,

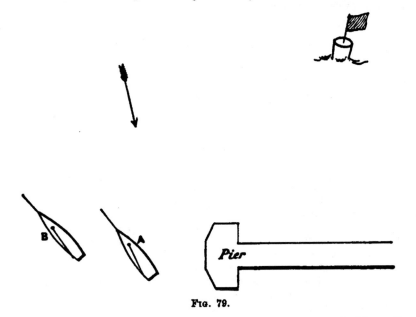

FIG. 79.

then A could not have hailed B to go about, as under Rule 32 marks are excepted.

APPROACHING A MARK ON OPPOSITE TACKS FOR ROUNDING.

It frequently happens that two yachts are approaching a mark on opposite tacks, and the one on the port tack may be able to weather the

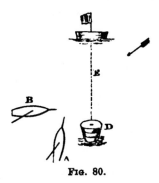

FIG. 80.

mark, whilst the one on the starboard tack cannot do so until she goes on the other tack. In Fig. 80, D will be the mark, A a vessel on the

starboard tack, and B the one on port tack. It would be the duty
of B to give way, even though it were at the finish of a race, and
that she was in a position to cross the line E; she would be clearly
ahead of A, but might not be able to quite weather her, and so would
have to give way. We recollect a case similar to the above happening
at Cowes between the Kriemhilda, 106 tons, and Arrow, 107 tons, in
1874, in a match of the Royal Albert Yacht Club; the Arrow was on
port tack and gave way, but the late Mr. Thomas Chamberlayne (a
yachtsman of great experience) said he never gave way more reluctantly
in his life; yet, as it was clearly his duty to do so, he ordered the
helm of the Arrow to be put down, and the Kriemhilda got round the
mark first.

Another case happened at Plymouth, in 1879, between the Formosa,
cutter, 102 tons, and Florinda, yawl, 135 tons :

> There was a very strong westerly wind, and Florinda was going for the Penlee mark
> on port tack, and Formosa on starboard. Florinda was expected to stay, but she did not,
> and if Formosa had held on she would have struck her about the main rigging. Formosa's
> helm was, however, hauled hard a-weather, and her head payed off almost sufficiently
> to clear Florinda, but not quite, and the mizen of the latter was knocked out. It was
> never for a moment contended that Formosa was in any way to blame for this collision,
> and we think she could not have been expected to do more than she did. If those on
> board Formosa had given way earlier—which she would scarcely have been justified in
> doing—it would only have encouraged those who always reluctantly give way when on
> port tack, because they know, if the vessels do not actually touch, how difficult it is for
> the yacht on starboard tack to prove her case.

A case occurred during the summer of 1890, which varied somewhat
from the foregoing as follows :

> The yacht A, on port tack, had come from the direction indicated by the arrow *d*, and
> the yacht on starboard tack from the direction indicated by *k* (*see* Fig. 81). A commences
> to bear up to round the buoy, and B, instead of bearing up to go under A's stern, luffs in
> between her and the buoy. A foul ensues, and A claims to be in the right, because she
> had altered her helm for the purpose of rounding, when B luffed between her and the
> buoy. But clearly A had no right to bear away whilst she was across B, and compel B
> to bear away also to go under her stern; and B could claim the right to luff, as the onus
> of getting out of the way does not rest with her; indeed, in many cases B could claim
> and prove that had she not luffed the consequences of the collision might have been much
> more disastrous. A, by bearing away to round the buoy when she was across B, increased
> the risks of collision, and it was her duty to have gone into the wind and have conceded
> the passage to B. Of course there is the contingency that if A tacked she might be
> reached on past the mark by B; but, although such a proceeding is permissible under the
> rules, it is usually considered rather bad form to exercise the privilege under con-
> ditions as just recited.

The foregoing cases are very clear, and there can be no doubt as to
what the vessel on the port tack should do; but the case would be more
difficult to deal with if the yachts were in the position with regard to a

mark shown in Figs. 82 and 83. Also if the vessel on port tack
is nearest the mark which has to be rounded, as at B (Fig. 83),
she must give way to a vessel on starboard tack in the position of
A when both are close-hauled approaching a mark, as D, to proceed

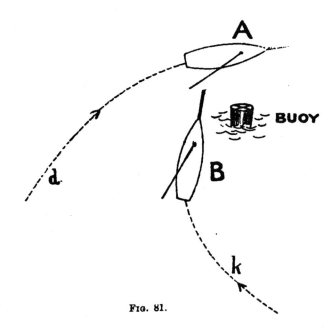

Fig. 81.

in the direction of (say) E. It is evident that B must get out of the
way by bearing up and passing under the stern of A, unless B is so
far ahead as to be able to stay round the mark clear of A. In such

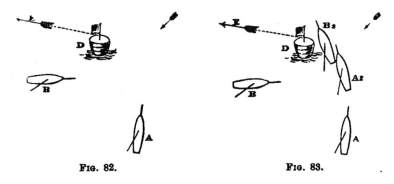

Fig. 82.   Fig. 83.

a case the following conditions must be considered: A is the yacht
on the starboard tack; B the yacht on the port tack; D a buoy which
the yachts have to round and proceed in the direction of the arrow
E. B goes into stays under the lee bow, but a little ahead of A, so that

when they arrive at the buoy they are in the position of A 2 and B 2 (Fig. 83), and a collision ensues. B will claim the foul, and argue that A should have given her room at the buoy; A will claim the foul, and say that B should not have gone into stays in a position where A could strike her. B in this case would be in the right, *provided always that the foul would not have occurred if A had not altered her helm by putting it up.* But B would not be justified in tacking in such a position if she thereby caused A to put her *helm down or luff* to avoid a collision; nor would she be justified in so tacking if a collision ensued, and A did not alter her course one way or the other. On the other hand, A would not be justified in putting her helm up, and so cause a collision or a fouling of the mark.

The following case occurred in the regatta of the Royal Yacht Squadron in 1885:

Galatea, Irex, and Tara were standing for the Yarmouth markboat on starboard tack, Galatea leading under the lee bow of Irex, a couple of cable lengths ahead, and

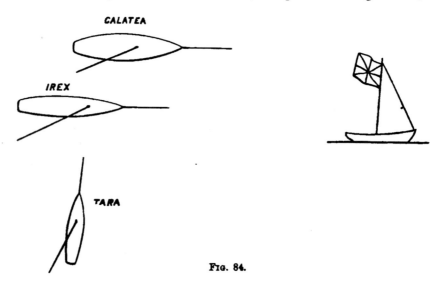

Fɪɢ. 84.

Tara as far off Irex, and up on her weather quarter. Galatea stayed to port tack to stand for the mark, and at once came across Irex, the mark now being about a couple of hundred yards ahead. It was plain from the first that Galatea could not clear Irex, and the latter hove round under Galatea's lee, and the pair came into the position on port tack shown in the diagram (Fig. 84); Irex would thus have cut her out at the mark; but here a fresh difficulty presented itself—there was still Tara on starboard tack to reckon with, and she refused to give way, going straight for Irex's rigging. The latter at last eased her helm, and Galatea, too, did the same, the pair going nearly up head to wind. It was too late, however, for them to clear Tara, and the latter had to hustle round to port tack to avoid striking Irex. Directly Tara had given way, Galatea and Irex filled on port tack again, smothering up Tara, and nearly jammed her on to the mark, and it looked as if Irex's mainsail did actually foul Tara. Luckily there was not much weight in the wind, or the result might have been very serious.

It is quite clear that Galatea brought about this embroglio through having forced Irex round to port tack (*see* " Tacking when there is not room to Tack ") ; and it would be a moot point whether Irex could also have been held to blame through being in a position which caused Tara to go about to avoid a collision.

RUNNING FOR A MARK ON THE SAME GYBE.

Three boats, A, B, and C, running dead before the wind (*see* Fig. 85) so close together that their booms were almost touching, B asked A for room round the mark, which is a quarter of a minute ahead. A gybed,

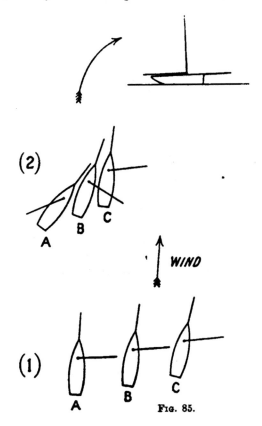

FIG. 85.

and ran into B, who could not gybe without sweeping A's deck with her boom and ram C, as the boats are so close. B eased off to starboard to mitigate the force of collision with A, and is forced into C, and squeezed between the two, A and C (*see* Fig. 85); the boats were absolutely abreast, and had been running so for some minutes before the collision ; A struck B on the rigging, and B struck C on the port quarter. The boats were going about five to six knots.

It was decided that A should not have gybed so as to interfere with B and C.

RUNNING FOR A MARK ON OPPOSITE GYBES.

The following case occurred at Plymouth in 1892. Two yachts, A and B, are running for a mark with main booms on opposite sides. They arrive near the mark, as shown in Fig. 86.

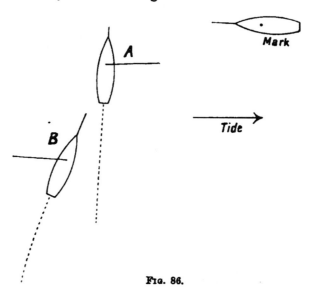

Fig. 86.

A, it will be seen, has to gybe to get round the mark, and B is preparing to cut in between her and the mark as the gybe takes place. The next position is shown by A, B, on the left of Fig. 87, A having run

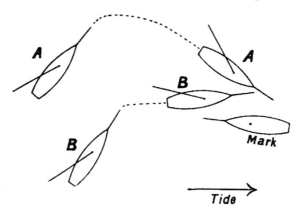

well on before letting her boom over, probably to make sure of not being carried on to the mark by the tide. The collision occurred as shown in the second position near the mark, Fig. 87.

It was held that A was bound to keep clear of B; and B knowing that A could not get round the mark without gybing, was justified in taking advantage of the room A had left. Supposing A had elected to run on, for, say another two lengths, it could not be maintained that B had not the right to cut in between A and the mark. A case like this, however, must be decided on its merits; and the points in the one illustrated are that A had left so much room as to justify B in choosing an inside berth, and that A should have been met with the helm after bearing up to get her boom over, and not have tried to shut out B.

FORCED ON TO A MARK BY A ROWING BOAT.

A case occurred on the Mersey in the autumn of 1891, which is not met by any of the sailing rules. A competitor was reaching for the winning mark and was forced on to it by a large four-oared rowing boat. The rowing boat was regarded as a vessel which had wrongfully forced the yacht on to the buoy. This was in accordance with the decision of the committee of the Royal Yacht Squadron in 1872, when the schooner Gwendolin, in order to avoid sailing over a yacht's gig, ran into and sunk the mark-boat. The committee held that under the circumstances she should not be disqualified for fouling and sinking the mark-boat.

RULE 31.—OBSTRUCTIONS TO SEA ROOM.

When passing a pier, shoal, rock, vessel, or other obstruction to sea room, should yachts not be clear of each other, the outside yacht or yachts must give room to the yacht in danger of fouling such obstruction, whether she be the weather or the leeward yacht; provided always that an overlap has been established before an obstruction is actually reached.

SAILING ALONG A WEATHER SHORE OR LEE SHORE—OVERTAKING.

In sailing along a weather shore always remember that, although a yacht may "luff as she pleases to prevent another yacht passing to windward," she may not shove the other yacht ashore or on to any obstruction; on the other hand, a yacht overtaking another yacht should not attempt to make an overlap just upon reaching an obstruction. This means that *the leading yacht can keep her luff up to the very moment that an obstruction is reached, even supposing that an overlap will occur simultaneously with reaching an obstruction. If the overtaking yacht goes ashore or in any way receives or inflicts damages under such circumstances, she is solely responsible.*

In all cases remember that the windward yacht can only demand room in case she would, by holding to her course, actually strike an obstruction or take the ground.

It frequently happens, when sailing along a shore, bank, &c., to shun a tide or otherwise, that an overtaken yacht allows one astern to come up on her weather, being fearful of getting into a luffing match when so near the ground; in such a case the overtaken yacht often warns the other that she is coming to windward at her own risk, and that no further room will be given her. Presently an arm or outward bend in the bank, or a shallow, warns the overtaken yacht to bear away a little, but she is careful to do so only just far enough to clear the ground herself, and leaves no room for the overtaking yacht on the ground that a warning was given the latter that she came to windward at her own risk. The warning, however, would be of no avail if the windward yacht got ashore or if a foul ensued, providing always that the overtaking yacht had established an overlap with her bowsprit or some part of her hull before reaching the obstruction.

In sailing along a lee shore, the weather yacht in all cases is bound to give the one to leeward room.

A yacht is not justified in making another yacht either bear away or luff to avoid striking an obstacle of any kind.

Several protests have been decided by the Y.R.A. under this rule, notably the Vanessa v. Enriqueta case, in 1879; and the Silver Star v. Tara case in November, 1883. In the "Silver Star v. Tara" case the decision rested on a question of facts, and, as usual, the evidence was most conflicting. This much, however, can be said, that the decision is not likely to encourage a yacht to try to get the inside berth in sailing along a weather shore.

The "Vanessa v. Enriqueta" case presented some peculiarities:

Vanessa v. *Enriqueta*, 1879.

After rounding the Nore, they were returning along the Jenkyn Sand, Vanessa leading by about ten lengths, both yachts being on port tack a point or so free. Vanessa took the ground, and Enriqueta did so also. She was the first to get off, and reached up close under Vanessa's lee just as the latter got off again. A foul ensued, Enriqueta's crosstrees getting hung up in the leech of Vanessa's mainsail.

The owner of Vanessa protested on the ground that Enriqueta, being the overtaking vessel, was bound to keep clear; and, moreover, Vanessa at the time of the foul being barely afloat, she herself was unable to do anything to avoid a collision. Enriqueta, on the other hand, had plenty of sea room to leeward, but instead of bearing away luffed into Vanessa.

The owner of the Enriqueta declared that at the time of the foul the yachts had got into deep water by bearing away. Enriqueta had been drawn-to again on her course, but Vanessa, in spite of a warning that there was plenty of water, continued to bear away, and thus caused the foul. After the foul Enriqueta passed Vanessa, and luffed across her, having plenty of water.

The owner of Enriqueta gave the positions of the yachts as follows (*See* Fig. 88): A shows Enriqueta ashore; B shows Vanessa ashore; E shows Enriqueta bearing away after she got afloat, and reaching up level with Vanessa just as the latter began to move ahead again; K M shows the yachts as they came into collision.

The Vanessa's pilot stated that at the time of the foul the Vanessa only had about 9ft. of water under her. The pilot of Enriqueta, on the other hand, declared that there were four and a half fathoms. Neither took a cast of the lead, and each spoke to having a perfect knowledge of the depth of water from fishing over the ground almost daily.

The Council came to the conclusion that the evidence of the pilots was quite worthless, but that, judging from the admission made by the owner of the Enriqueta of the easy manner he reached past to leeward of Vanessa when in the position K M, they were inclined to think that the owner of Vanessa was correct in saying that she was barely afloat at the time when she was bearing away, and through which it was alleged by the owner of the Enriqueta that the foul occurred; and that they were not in such deep water as represented by Enriqueta's pilot, and as indicated in the diagram.

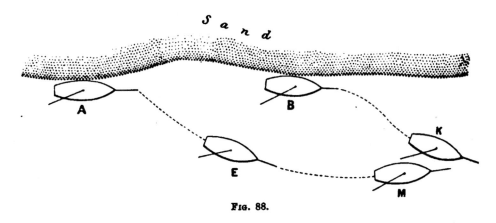

FIG. 88.

Whether or not Enriqueta did or did not luff into Vanessa it would be impossible to say on the evidence, but a foul occurred, and the sole question was " had Vanessa the right to bear away and ask for room?" At the time when Enriqueta luffed clear across Vanessa they were no doubt in deeper water, but that must clearly have been a minute or two after the foul took place.

In the end the Council adjudged Enriqueta to be in the wrong for not giving room when Vanessa was bearing away to get clear of the sand.

Lil v. *Verena*, August 14, 1886.

Case referred by the Royal Southampton Yacht Club: Both vessels had rounded a markboat and were reaching up the Southampton Water, south shore. Lil was the weathermost vessel and had overlapped Verena, while the latter was luffing to prevent Lil passing to windward. Verena continued to luff, and her owner considered that he was justified in so doing, under Rule 31. Lil at last hailed for room, but Verena took no notice of the hail, and at last drove Lil on shore. The owner of Verena admits that Lil had established an overlap some time previously to her going on shore, her bowsprit-end being level with Verena's rigging.

The Council decided that under Rule 30 Verena was bound to give room, as the overlap was established before the obstruction was reached.

A case where another kind of obstruction was involved occurred at Falmouth in 1882, and was adjudicated upon by the Council as follows :

Volante v. Chough.

The Volante, yawl, 7 tons, and Chough, cutter, 23 tons (with others), started in a yacht match, Volante leading with main boom on port side ; Chough started from the opposite end of the line, and with boom on starboard side was overtaking Volante, as shown in the diagram, the wind being dead aft, Chough perhaps running a little by the lee (*See* Fig. 89).

Two schooners, A B, were at anchor in the course, and Volante had a small sailing boat on her lee bow and Cockatoo (in the match) on her lee quarter.

Chough caught Volante and put her bowsprit over Volante's quarter, between the mizenmast and rigging. Chough starboarded her helm (she could not port to any extent without gybing), and took the mizenmast out of Volante. The latter was turned round by the Chough, and she struck the schooner B with her bowsprit and carried it away.

On the part of Chough, it was stated that she could not keep away and go the other side of the schooner B, because she would have struck some moorings near the schooner.

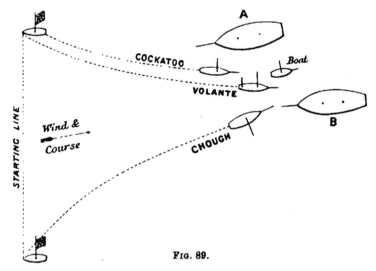

FIG. 89.

It was contended that Volante had room, and should have starboarded her helm, instead of which she ported.

The owner of Volante submitted that he did not port, and could not have done so, as his yacht would have struck the schooner B, as she subsequently did when whisked round by Chough. If he had put his helm to starboard, he would have struck the accompanying sailing boat, which was under his lee bow.

The Council does not appear to have attempted to reconcile the conflicting evidence, but decided that, as " Chough was in the position of an overtaking vessel, she was bound to have kept clear, and must be held responsible for the collision."

It frequently happens that a yacht overtakes a number of other yachts, and finds it difficult to make a passage between them on account of one forming an obstruction to windward. The following case was referred to the council of the Y.R.A. by the Solent Yacht Club in November, 1890 :

Humming Bird v. Dolphin.

Troublesome, Dolphin, Mliss, Humming Bird, and Cock-a-Whoop, were started in a race, the Humming Bird being a few lengths astern of Troublesome and Dolphin. They

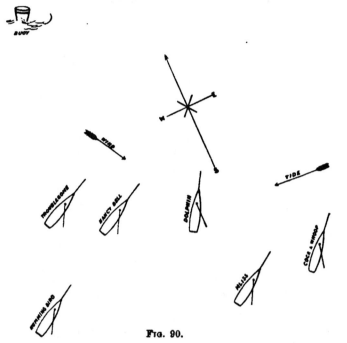

Fig. 90.

overtook the Nancy Bell, as shown by Fig. 90, as they neared the Warden Ledge Buoy, all reaching broad to avoid being set the wrong side of the buoy by the tide.

Dolphin was luffed in the hope of drawing across Nancy Bell's bow, but failed, and dropped back again to the position shown in Fig. 91, where she was overtaken and fouled

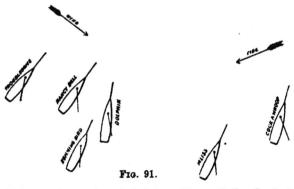

Fig. 91.

by Humming Bird; the latter then luffed into Nancy Bell, who in turn luffed into Troublesome.

On behalf of the Humming Bird it was alleged that she, as overtaking vessel, had elected to go to leeward of Troublesome and Nancy Bell, but as there was ample room between Nancy Bell and Dolphin she sought a passage there. It was further alleged that she would have kept clear of both had not Dolphin luffed across her bows and brought about the foul. It was further contended that, supposing there was not room for Humming Bird, Dolphin was in a position to bear away and give room, and ought to have done so, as she was overlapped by Humming Bird before the obstruction to windward (Nancy Bell) was reached.

On the part of Dolphin the luffing was denied, and witnesses were called to prove that Dolphin did not luff; also, that as she and Nancy Bell were not more than a length apart (in a broadside direction), there was not room for Humming Bird between them; and they had been in such position some time before Humming Bird overtook them; and, moreover, as Humming Bird was the overtaking vessel, she was bound to keep clear of the others, and could have gone to leeward of them. It was further claimed by Dolphin that the nature of the collision showed that she was not luffed, Humming Bird's starboard channel striking her twice; first on the port quarter, 3ft. abaft the rudder post, and then 4ft. ahead of it, a hole being knocked in Dolphin's side at the latter point.

In the foregoing case Nancy Bell would be regarded as an "obstruction" under Rule 31; and under that rule the question would have to be considered whether Dolphin had the right to luff and shut out Humming Bird, or whether she was bound to bear away and give room. Dolphin, it was alleged, had been sailing for some time under the lee of Nancy Bell, and whilst Humming Bird was a length or two off—astern of Nancy Bell and Troublesome. Dolphin had therefore arrived at the "obstruction" (Nancy Bell) before Humming Bird made the overlap which resulted in the foul, and it is clear she could not, under such circumstances, claim room under the provisions of Rule 31 so far as causing Dolphin to bear away is concerned. It also seems clear that Dolphin would have had the right to luff and shut out Humming Bird before the latter made an overlap. In short, a yacht sailing in between two other yachts which are in positions resembling those occupied by Nancy Bell and Dolphin does so at her own risk, and if Dolphin had kept away to give room she would have had a grievance against Humming Bird.

The Council of the Y.R.A. appear to have taken this view of the case, as their decision was as follows: "The Humming Bird was to blame for the collisions, and the Dolphin did not contribute thereto."

(*See* also "Hailing to go about approaching marks.")

A case, which was dealt with by the Council in 1899, has relation to this rule as follows:

Eelin v. Astrild, New Thames Yacht Club, June, 1899.

The yachts were running up the river Thames, with main booms to starboard, along the Essex shore, having rounded the Mouse lightship (*see* Fig. 92). Wind, light; tide, ebb. Astrild was leading, and Eelin overtaking her to leeward. Eelin ran up under Astrild's lee, and when they gradually came into the shallows along the edge of the sand, Eelin had established an overlap. Presently Eelin hailed for water, but Astrild did not respond to her hail and held her course, and a foul occurred, as shown in the diagram. Astrild contended that she had a right to hold her course on the pretext that the shore was an "obstruction" within the meaning of the rule, and Eelin had forced a passage between her and it, because Astrild had *reached*

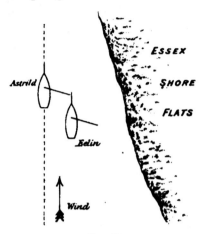

FIG. 92.

the obstruction before Eelin obtained her overlap. Eelin contended that Astrild was bound to give her room when she hailed for water, and that as Astrild did not give her room she had no alternative but to foul her.

The Council decided that Eelin was in the right, and disqualified Astrild.

RULE 32.—CLOSE-HAULED APPROACHING A SHORE.—REQUIRING A YACHT TO TACK WHEN APPROACHING A SHORE OR OTHER OBSTRUCTION CLOSE-HAULED.

If two yachts are standing towards a shore or shoal, or towards any buoy, boat, or vessel, and the yacht to leeward is likely to run aground, or foul of such buoy, boat, or vessel (a mark vessel excepted), and is not able to tack without coming into collision with the yacht to windward, the latter shall at once tack, on being hailed to do so by the owner of the leeward yacht, or the person acting as the owner's representative, who shall be bound to see that the leeward yacht tacks at the same time.

When two vessels are standing on the same tack for the shore, a shoal, or other obstruction, and the leeward yacht cannot tack without coming in contact with the windward one, she may hail the windward yacht to go about, but she must herself at the same time tack; but if the obstruction is a *mark* in the course, such as a buoy or vessel, &c., which has to be rounded, the leeward yacht cannot so hail the windward one to go about and give her room to tack. If the leeward yacht requires to tack to weather the mark she should ease her helm, and wait till the other one has drawn clear.

When one of two yachts has to tack, the common practice is for the windward one to wait until the other has actually put her helm down before she does so herself; if this is not done she will probably find that

P

the yacht which was to leeward of her has shot up on her weather quarter—some distance astern perhaps, but still on her weather quarter—instead of under her lee beam or lee quarter. This will be annoying, but naturally it is the thing that the vessel which was to leeward will endeavour to effect; and if previous to tacking her position was under the lee bow of the other, she is almost certain to effect her object whatever the other might do.

The rule clearly says that the windward vessel shall tack directly she is hailed to do so (it being assumed that the vessel to leeward is in actual danger of running aground if she holds on any longer), and that the leeward vessel must at the same time tack ; but what the sailing master of the lee-ward vessel generally does is to gently ease the helm down, and sail his vessel to the last moment, so as to bring her round well on the weather quarter of the other. This is not always achieved, for the reason, as before said, that the windward vessel waits until the other is fairly tacking, or else, in staying, sails round in the same way that the leeward vessel does.

If the yachts are abeam and very close together—say not more than a length apart—the windward yacht should put her helm down directly she is hailed. If she waits until the other is putting her helm down, and then eases her own helm, the bowsprit of the leeward yacht may strike the counter of the other, as the bow of the one will be swinging round against the stern of the other. Therefore, in such a case the windward yacht should be very prompt in putting her helm down, and if the other fails to put hers down at the same time she can be protested against.

The leeward vessel is the judge of her own peril, but this does not justify her in needlessly putting another vessel about, and in all cases actual peril of striking the ground or other obstruction must exist.

Some pilots and sailing masters will venture much closer in shore than others, and give way reluctantly, or not at all, when hailed ; but, if there be reasonable grounds for believing a yacht to be in danger, the weather-most one is bound to tack when hailed ; she could, however, protest if wrongfully put about by the leewardmost yacht tacking when the latter was not in immediate danger of going aground or striking an obstruction. This rule must be interpreted by the ordinary customs dictated by prudence, and such careful navigation as yacht racing admits of.

The following are decisions of the Council of the Y.R.A. on the point :

Silver Star v. Tara, 1883.

Tara and Silver Star were reaching across the Thames on starboard tack (Silver Star on weather quarter of Tara), and they fetched to within some two hundred yards of th West Blyth Buoy. Tara hailed Silver Star three or four times to go about, and the latter did not comply. Tara's helm was eventually put down, and she struck Silver Star when head to wind or filling on port tack. Silver Star alleged that there was no reason for Tara hailing, as, after the collision, they stood on for two hundred or three hundred yards, and still found 3½ fathoms by the lead, when she stayed. To this Tara replied that this might be so, as both yachts when hung up drifted up with the tide into deeper water. It was also averred on the part of Silver Star that Tara could have avoided the collision by keeping her helm hard up after filling on port tack, and so pass under Silver Star's stern; instead of which she put her helm down. Tara's crew, however, adhered to their statements that Tara was in stays or filling when the yachts struck, and further averred that if Silver Star had gone about when hailed the last time or when Tara's helm was put down, that the collision would have been avoided, whereas nothing was done on board Silver Star to avert a collision.

The helmsman and owner of Silver Star declared that the reason they did not go about when hailed was because the pilot informed them there was plenty of water—over 4 fathoms by the lead. Tara's pilot, on the other hand, declared there was not more than 2½ fathoms, and, being a fisherman, he knew the ground well; Tara was inside of a straight line from the buoy to the beacon on the point.

The Council decided that Silver Star, when hailed, should have gone about, and, if the owner considered that he had been hailed without reason, he could have protested; and with regard to Tara they arrived at the following decision :

" The Council is unanimously of opinion that the Tara was justified in tacking as she did, and consequently decide that she ought not to be disqualified."

If, when a vessel has just tacked for water, she meets another vessel standing in on starboard tack, she should promptly hail that vessel to go about; but if she herself has gathered way on the port tack, and is reaching along, the one on starboard tack can force her round again; and it is no excuse for non-compliance if the vessel on the port tack says, " We have just tacked for water." If she has room to tack again without getting aground, she must do so, and then immediately afterwards can, if necessary, hail the vessel on her weather to tack, to enable her to avoid striking the ground. As a rule, it is a dangerous experiment for a vessel that has just stayed to attempt to clear another by putting her helm up, as she may have little or no way on; the safer plan is to put her helm down.

In December, 1879, a question was asked by a yacht club as follows :

In the event of a yacht on the port tack having only just gone about for water, and meeting a yacht on the starboard tack immediately afterwards, is the yacht on the port tack bound to give way ?

The Council of the Y.R.A. decided as follows :

PORT AND STARBOARD TACKS.

In all cases the yacht on the port tack should give way, if she has room to do so, by bearing up clear astern of the vessel on the starboard tack or by going about if she has room to stay clear of the ground. If she apparently has room and does not give way, the yacht on the starboard tack should endeavour to avoid striking her and protest. The onus of proving that the yacht on the port tack had not room to give way would then be thrown on that vessel

Bedouin v. *Halcyone*, 1885.

Bedouin and Halcyone, in Belfast Lough, were working along a shore with a smart breeze; both were on starboard tack, with Halcyone (H) under the lee bow of the other (B, as shown in Fig. 93), from thirty to forty yards off. Halcyone, when as close in shore as she

FIG. 93.

dared go (*see* Fig. 94) tacked, and hailed Bedouin to do so also; this the latter declined to do, as there was room for Halcyone to go under her stern or to tack again. In the end they got into the position shown in Fig. 95, and Bedouin had to go about, and

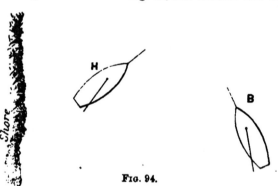

FIG. 94.

Halcyone had to shoot up in the wind to avoid a collision. Bedouin protested against Halcyone that the latter, being on port tack, caused her to go about to avoid a collision. It was stated that when the yachts met (as in Fig. 95) and Bedouin had to go about, that

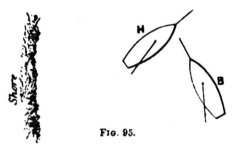

FIG. 95.

if Halcyone had tacked again they could have kept reaching a considerable distance on starboard tack without danger of getting ashore.

The Council decided that, according to the evidence placed before them—1st, that the

Halcyone had no right to hail Bedouin to go about; 2nd, that she should have tacked again to avoid Bedouin; or, 3rd, that she could have gone under Bedouin's stern. The Council therefore adjudged Halcyone to be in the wrong.

The following protest was referred by the Royal Forth Yacht Club, and decided Aug. 17, 1889, by the Council of the Y.R.A:

Georgie v. *Enriqueta*, 1889.

It appears from the evidence that the yachts were close-hauled on the starboard tack, Enriqueta leading under the lee bow of the other. Enriqueta stayed to port tack, and Georgie was crossing her bows, when she was struck in the lee runner by Enriqueta's bowsprit end.

It was contended on behalf of the Enriqueta that at the time she struck Georgie she had just stayed for water, and had not gathered way, and the sailing master averred that she was only three lengths from the shore at the time. He also declared that when remonstrated with for going so close in shore, he replied he did so in order to give Georgie room to round the markboat, which was (according to the owner of the Enriqueta) 100 yards distant. The staysail sheet was not home, and the helm was still a-weather.

On the part of Georgie, her sailing master said at the time of collision they were about fifty yards from the markboat, and they, after losing the bowsprit, stood on another 100 yards before staying to port tack.

Mr. G. R. Rimer, who represented the owner of Georgie, stated that when Enriqueta stayed to port tack she was 300 yards from the markboat. The collision occurred after this, when the yachts were about seventy-five yards from the markboat. He heard shouts from Enriqueta just before the collision, but could not distinguish what was said. He heard one of Georgie's crew say, "Keep her sailing, we are on the right tack." After the collision the Georgie stood on in shore, and, after seeing her man who was knocked overboard safe on board Enriqueta, they put about to port tack. At the time of the collision Enriqueta had very little way on, but she would have had way enough had she not been kept hanging in the wind.

The owner of the Georgie made the following statement: "The Enriqueta had stayed, and the sole cause of the collision was that in place of bearing away, as she ought, she was kept shivering in the wind attempting to weather the Georgie, apparently. Had the Georgie bore away or luffed at the last moment, I do not think the collision could have been averted, and disastrous results might have followed, for which Georgie, had she disregarded the rule of the road, would have been solely to blame. The sole cause of the collision is very clear, and that is the Enriqueta being kept hanging in the wind, in place of in time bearing away and allowing Georgie to pass ahead as it was her bounden duty to do."

There were other witnesses on both sides.

The sailing committee found as follows: "1. That at the time of the collision the Georgie was on starboard tack. 2. That at the time of the collision the Enriqueta was on port tack. 3. That the Enriqueta had stayed a considerable time before the collision, and that she was not in stays at the time of collision. 4. They find that either yacht could have avoided the collision, and decide that both yachts be disqualified." The committee supported their decision as follows:

"ENRIQUETA.—The main point which the committee had to consider in respect to this vessel was the assertion by Mr. Robertson, owner of the Enriqueta, in his protest that, at the time the collision occurred, his yacht was hanging in stays, and they found that the allegation was not supported by evidence. The witnesses for Enriqueta all state that at the time of the collision the yacht was in stays and had not gathered way, but this statement conflicts with their own evidence as to the respective points at which the vessel stayed and the collision occurred. The pilot, lately a petty officer in the navy, and presumably a man accustomed to judge distance at sea, states that the point of staying was about three cables' lengths (600 yards) distant from the markboat, and the master confirms this by stating that he was only 150ft. from the shore; while Mr. Robertson states that the collision occurred 100 yards from the markboat, and Georgie's crew and the markboat men state the point at from forty to seventy yards. Taking, therefore, Mr. Robertson's extreme distance (100 yards) as correct, the Enriqueta must have travelled 500 yards to reach the spot where the collision occurred, and the committee considered this fact incompatible with the allegation that she was hanging in stays. Again, the evidence of Georgie's crew and the markboat men is unanimous as to the fact that she (Georgie) stood on her course forty to 100 yards after the collision, which she could not have done had the collision occurred at Enriqueta's staying point, viz., 150ft. from the shore.

" GEORGIE.—The committee found this vessel in fault in so far that the steersman, seeing a collision imminent, made no endeavour to avoid it, but deliberately courted it. They hold that, life and property being at peril through collision, it was his duty to luff, or even to have put about, in order to avert the mishap, and in accordance with the general rule of the Board of Trade that at all cost collisions must be avoided when possible, and then protested against Enriqueta for having forced him to do so. It is proved by the evidence of the master of Enriqueta, Mr. Rimer, member on board Georgie, and a paid hand on board Georgie, that the steersman's attention was directed to the imminence of the collision before it occurred by the calling of one of his crew, ' Keep her sailing, we're on the right tack,' and that there was actual danger to life is proved by the fact that Georgie lost a man overboard, who was picked up by Enriqueta."

The owner of the Georgie was not satisfied with this decision, and the club referred the case to the Y.R.A. The Council decided as follows :

"The facts are in accordance with the foregoing statement of the committee, and they rightly disqualified Enriqueta, she being alone to blame for the collision; the Georgie would not therefore be disqualified also."

It was contended on the part of Enriqueta that she had only just stayed close in shore—that she was, in fact, hanging in stays without way on, and could do nothing to avoid Georgie. The evidence, however, showed that she must have sailed 200 or 300 yards after she stayed, and that she consequently could have stayed again, or, with proper management, have kept away, and gone under the stern of Georgie. The committee, therefore, very properly disqualified Enriqueta, but, in addition, found Georgie in fault also, because she did not adopt means to avoid a collision, which those on board must have seen was imminent. The committee accordingly disqualified Georgie also; but their decision appears to have been based more upon the international " Steering and Sailing Rules " than upon yacht racing rules.

Undoubtedly, a vessel would not be justified in standing on so long as Georgie did under ordinary circumstances, as she would be bound to do her best to avoid a collision, and, on the facts, a Board of Trade inquiry would probably have resulted in much the same decision as the committee of the Royal Forth Yacht Club gave. The Council of the Yacht Racing Association had, however, to consider the inducements to run risks in match sailing, and found Enriqueta solely to blame for the collision. Any yachtsman accustomed to racing would hold that Georgie, under the conditions, was justified in crossing ahead of the other, and those on board had a perfect right to assume that the Enriqueta would do the right thing, and either go about, luff up, or bear away. Georgie, when she got so far across the bows of the other yacht, could do nothing to avoid the collision; and, unless she could by the rules be proved to be wrong in so getting across the other yacht's bow when one had just tacked for water, we cannot see how she could be found in fault.

HAILING A VESSEL TO GO ABOUT AT A MARK VESSEL.

Irex v. *Jane Elizabeth*, 1890.

The Irex, pilot cutter, was standing for a mark under the lee bow of the Jane Elizabeth in much about the same positions shown in Fig. 75, page 193, substituting a mark vessel for the pier. The Irex hailed the Jane Elizabeth to go about, as she, the Irex, could not weather the mark. The Jane Elizabeth did not go about, and a foul ensued. The Irex protested, and claimed that Jane Elizabeth ought to be disqualified for not going about when hailed.

The case was referred to the Council of the Y.R.A., who decided that the Irex had no right, under Rule 32, to hail the other to go about, and must therefore, be held to blame for the collision.

RULE 33.—FOULING OR IMPROPERLY ROUNDING MARKS.

A yacht must go fairly round the course, rounding the series of marks as specified in the instructions; and, in order to round each mark, the yacht's track from the preceding to the following mark must enclose it on the required side. A yacht which, in rounding a mark, fouls it, or causes the mark vessel to shift her position to avoid a foul, shall be disqualified, unless on her protest it is established that she was wrongfully compelled to do so by another yacht, in which case such other yacht shall be disqualified. The yacht which fouled the mark must immediately either abandon the race or hoist a protest flag.

In 1897 the following case occurred:

A is a markboat, attached by rope from her bowsprit end to a buoy (Fig. 96)—the buoy was 10ft. from the bowsprit end. A yacht fouled the buoy, and the sailing committee disqualified her. The owner of the yacht objected, on the ground that the buoy was not part of the mark vessel; but the committee were no doubt right.

Several cases have occurred of boats—especially centre-boards—fouling the cables of markboats, but, as far as we know, no case has been brought before the Y.R.A.

If the buoy were regarded as an obstruction and not as part of the mark vessel, a yacht which could not clear it could hail another yacht to windward to tack to give her room, and this certainly would be in conflict with Rule 32.

At the Campbelltown Regatta, July 17, 1895, the following case occurred: Ailsa was passing a markboat in a light wind, and was driving on to it; the crew of the markboat took hold of her bowsprit shrouds, and shoved her clear, Ailsa not touching the markboat. On behalf of

Ailsa it was contended that she would have gone clear of the markboat without any aid from her crew. It was also stated that the men in the markboat were ignorant of yacht racing rules, and gave it as their opinion that Ailsa would have gone clear even if they had not touched her. Britannia protested, and the case was referred to the Y.R.A. Council, who decided as follows: "The touching of the Ailsa by the men in the markboat did not, under the circumstances as set forth in the case presented to the Council, disqualify her.

This decision cannot be regarded as wholly satisfactory, as it conveys an intimation that under different circumstances the act of men in a markboat touching a competing yacht would constitute a foul, and it is difficult to understand how distinctions are to be drawn, and for the Council of the

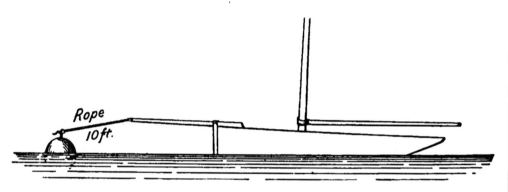

FIG. 96.

Y.R.A. to say to-day that if markboat men touch a yacht it is not a foul, and to-morrow that it is a foul. An absolute ruling on such a point is required.

Some years ago, in a match for small yachts, a guest on board one of the competitors, on passing the committee vessel in a light wind, put his leg over the rail, and touched her with his foot. The owner of the yacht at once regarded this as a foul, and gave up, and no doubt he was right.

Certainly if men in a markboat shove off a yacht it is equivalent to her veering out chain to avoid a foul.

FOULING A MARKBOAT'S CABLE.

If a markboat in a tide way or strong wind straightens her mooring chain or rope, and a yacht's keel fouled it and brought about a collision with the markboat, the yacht would be held to blame for not taking more room, and would consequently be disqualified.

By the Y.R.A. rules if a markboat shifts her position the race shall be re-sailed again if a committee chooses to so order it; and if a yacht causes a markboat to shift her position, by veering out chain for instance, a yacht can be disqualified. In light weather, when yachts have been driving with the tide, chain has frequently been veered out by the man in the markboat to enable a yacht to clear without fouling; but if a yacht is drifting helplessly on to a mark she must let go her anchor. It has been objected that the man in the markboat might get frightened and veer out chain when the yacht did not require it to be veered out to enable her to avoid fouling; but a man is hardly likely to get frightened when a yacht is slowly driving in a calm, and if there was any breeze at all he would have no time at the last moment to give chain to his vessel. Generally a yacht goes "straight for" the markboat, and clears it by an alteration of the helm at the last moment. If, under such circumstances, a man in a markboat got scared, and imagined that he could avoid an impending danger by veering out chain, it would show very great folly, as if the markboat was to be struck it could not be avoided by veering out chain at the last moment.

CIRCUMNAVIGATING MARKS.

Formerly a good deal of discussion arose upon what should be considered a proper rounding within the meaning of the rules, and not a few

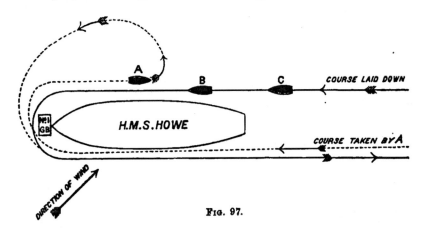

Fig. 97.

"hard cases" were set forth which were regarded as too difficult to prove to the satisfaction of a sailing committee.

But now that the wording of the rule has been revised we do not think that any misunderstanding will be likely to occur in the future.

It is clearly enjoined that in order to round each mark that the yacht's track from the preceding to the following mark must enclose it on the required side.

A case was submitted by the Queenstown Regatta in 1897 :

Three yachts, A, B and C, started in a race for yachts not exceeding 36ft. linear rating. In the course laid down it was stated that the yachts on the first round should "leave No. 1 Government Buoy on the port hand." Now yacht A left the buoy—to which H.M.S. Howe was moored—on the starboard hand (*see* Fig. 97), and when exactly amidships of the Howe discovered her error by observing yacht B sailing a course under the lee of the Howe for the purpose of leaving the buoy on the port hand. A accordingly gybed, making a loop, as shown in the dotted line on the diagram, before going round the buoy from the port side.

The disputed question was : Did yacht A leave No. 1 Government Buoy on the port hand as required in course as laid down ?

The majority of the sailing Committee of the Q. P. Regatta were of opinion that A did not leave the mark on the port hand.

The Council decided that this view was correct, namely, that yacht A did not leave the mark on the port hand.

Note.—The name of H.M.S. Howe was not mentioned in the sailing instructions.

Rule 34.—FOULING COMPETING YACHTS.

If a yacht, in consequence of her neglect of any of these rules, shall foul another yacht, or compel other yachts to foul, she shall be disqualified, and shall pay all damages as provided by Rule 41.

Rule 35.—RUNNING ASHORE.

A yacht running on shore, or foul of a buoy, vessel, or other obstruction, may use her own anchors, boats, warps, &c., to haul off, but may not receive any assistance except from the crew of the vessel fouled. Any anchor, boat, or warp used must be taken on board again before she continues the race.

In August, 1880, the Council decided, in spite of Rule 37, on a case of "poling" to get afloat after taking the ground as follows :

"A pole or spar can be used for the purpose of getting afloat after running aground."

Rule 36.—ANCHORING DURING A RACE.

A yacht may anchor during a race, but must weigh her anchor again, and not slip. No yacht shall during a race make fast to any buoy, stage, pier, or other object, or send an anchor out in a boat, except for the purpose of Rule 35.

Yachts may anchor during a race, but must weigh again, and not slip. Several instances have occurred where a yacht, when kedging in a tideway on foul ground, has been unable to get the kedge on board again. In such a case the crew would heave on the warp until it burst ; but if the yacht had let go her bower and chain this could not be done, and the yacht would be compelled to slip and buoy the chain.

No adjudication has been made by the Council that exactly bears upon these cases, but the common sense view would appear to indicate that if a yacht burst her warp in endeavouring to recover her kedge, she should not be disqualified on the grounds of slipping; and, from the same point of view, neither should a yacht be disqualified if after making every endeavour to weigh her bower, she failed and slipped. Yet when we consider how many cases would occur of bursting warps and leaving the anchor behind, in order to be away sharp, there is not much doubt that the rule must be rigidly adhered to. We recollect that the late Mr. R. Y. Richardson once retired from a race in Coryphée, at Dover, after failing to get her kedge through bursting a warp.

Cases have occurred in calms where kedging has been resorted to as a means of propulsion. The kedge has been dropped over at the

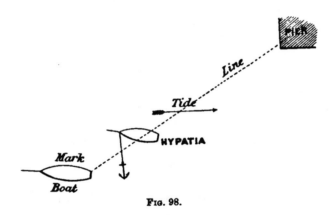

FIG. 98.

bow, and the crew walked aft with the warp, hauled the kedge up over the stern, and let it go again over the bow; or the kedge has been let go over the stern, and recovered at the bow. To get round a mark against a tide such kedging might be successfully practised, but under the rule "that no mode of propulsion except sails shall be allowed," it is clearly forbidden.

The following cases have been decided by the Council of the Y.R.A. :

Katie v. Hypatia, 1883.

The Hypatia, yawl, was finishing a race in a calm with the tide running at an angle with the line to be crossed. Hypatia had to let go her kedge when close to the line in order to prevent her driving away. (*See* Fig. 98.)

She was then sheered across the line, and the committee fired the gun in ignorance that the yacht's kedge was on the ground. The Council decided that Hypatia, not having weighed her anchor, in accordance with Rule 35, before she crossed the line, had not, therefore, completed the race when the gun was fired, and the prize must be awarded to the first vessel within her time which crossed the line, in accordance with the rules.

WARPING AND HOLDING ON TO MOORINGS AFTER THE FIRST GUN.

In 1897 the following case occurred in a match sailed in a regatta of the Royal Mersey Yacht Club: Owing to a strong wind a boat held on to her moorings half a minute after the first gun had been fired; another boat for two and a half minutes. Both slipped, and the case was referred to the Council, who decided that the boats must be disqualified.

Warping: Fair Geraldine v. *Satellite,* 1884.

It having been proved to the satisfaction of the committee that the Satellite held on to and used for the purpose of canting a warp fast to a mooring buoy after the firing of the first gun, the Council decides that the committee were correct in disqualifying her.

RULE 37.—MEANS OF PROPULSION.

No towing, sweeping, poling, or pushing, or any mode of propulsion except sails, shall be allowed, except for the purpose set forth in Rule 35.

PROPULSION BY SCULLING.

The practice of sculling small boats by moving the rudder backwards and forwards (*see* " Sculling " in the Appendix) is common in calms, and considerable progress can be made by this means. The question has been raised on several occasions as to the permissibility of such sculling during a match, and two or three protests have arisen out of the practice. It is very useful to scull even large yachts occasionally when they will not come round in light winds, and no one could contend that this was not a legitimate use to make of the rudder—it would be simply " steering; " but as no means of propulsion but sails are permissible, sculling, if used as a means of propulsion, is not allowed. The Council, in March, 1879, decided that sculling with the rudder is only permissible for actual steering as follows:

" Sculling with the rudder to propel a boat or yacht is not allowed under Rule 37, but sculling with the rudder to legitimately alter a vessel's course could not be considered an infringement of the rule."

In 1889 the Eastern Sailing Club, Granton, stated a similar case, in which it was alleged that a competitor in a match had used the rudder as a means of propulsion by sculling with it. The owner of the yacht protested against declared that the rudder was only moved to keep the yacht straight in a tideway during a calm. The secretary was directed to reply that sculling with the rudder is not allowed, but that moving the rudder as stated to legitimately alter a vessel's course could not be considered an infringement of the rule.

USING AN OAR.

In 1897 the Council of the Y.R.A. decided that a boat could not use an oar to assist her in going from one tack to another.

PROPULSION BY KEDGING.

In 1891 the Island Sailing Club referred the following case to the Y.R.A. :

The committee, acting under the latter part of Rule 48 (disqualifying without protest), disqualified the yacht Minnow in a race sailed under Yacht Racing Association Rules, on September 23rd, on the statement of her owner, that he had, during a calm, propelled the Minnow by means of kedging, thus infringing Rule 37.

The owner contended that the use he made of his anchor was legitimate, and such use is not excepted in Rule 36, which allows a yacht to anchor, and that as the anchor was both let go and weighed at the stem head, he had a right to use any impetus or way thus given to the boat to his advantage, there being no record of a protest against any yacht for so doing. Also that it is undoubtedly a custom among racing yachts to use their anchors in this way, and as it was only done at intervals of about ten minutes, and the boat's ordinary anchor and warp used, the rules had not been infringed. That Rule 37 does not refer specifically to this method of propulsion as an exception, and that if the Council consider that it should not be allowed, a new rule is necessary to provide against it, and the committee had no power to disqualify under the existing rules.

The Council of the Y.R.A. decided that the decision of the committee disqualifying Minnow was correct.

RULE 38.—SOUNDING.

No other means of sounding than the lead and line shall be allowed.

In the Y.R.A. rules it is enjoined that no instrument other than the lead and line shall be used for sounding. This rule was adopted many years ago by the Thames clubs to stop the practice of shoving a boat along by a pole, yard, or sweep under the pretence of sounding with the same; and, moreover, a very heavy weight or "sinker" might be used as a sort of kedge to drag the yacht through the water in a calm under the plea of sounding; and so the "hand lead" is always understood to be meant.

RULE 39.—MAN OVERBOARD.

In case of a man falling overboard from any yacht, all other yachts in a position to do so shall use their utmost endeavour to render assistance; and if it should appear that any yacht so assisting was thereby prevented from winning a prize, the committee shall have power to order it to be resailed between any yacht or yachts so prevented and the actual winners. A yacht shall be disqualified from winning a prize in a race or a resailed race if, when in a position to render assistance, she shall have neglected to do so.

Rule 40.—FINISHING A RACE.

A yacht shall be timed for completing a race as soon as any part of the hull or spars be on or across the finishing line, but continues amenable to the rules so long as any part of the hull or spars remain on the line.

Formerly a yacht was considered to have completed the race as soon as any part of her hull or spars was on or across the finishing line, and therefore could not be held responsible for any collision that occurred after she had crossed the line, or, indeed, whilst she was on it. A yacht might win a race by crossing the line with her bowsprit end and foul the mark a second later.

In 1892 the Medway Yacht Club referred a case to the Council as follows: Can a yacht be disqualified for fouling a markboat after the winning gun has been fired for her, her spinnaker boom having fouled the flagstaff of the committee vessel after the gun was fired? The Council decided that, as far as the yacht mentioned was concerned, the race terminated for her when the gun was fired, and she could not be disqualified for anything she did afterwards.

Under the present rule, introduced in 1900, this decision has been reversed, and a yacht is now amenable to the rules until she has either drawn clear ahead over the line or dropped back astern equally clear of it.

Finishing Line.

Sailing committees should remember, when drawing up the sailing instructions, that whilst it is most necessary to mark the starting line by means of two marks at one end of the line, so that by bringing them into one the sailing master of a competing yacht can see exactly when his vessel reaches the line (see Rule 27), it is not necessary, nor is it desirable, that this plan should be adopted at the finish of a race.

The set of the tide will often influence the position of the marks and break up the line, in fact a line of marks accurately placed at 10.30 a.m., the hour of the start, may prove no line at all by 3.0 p.m., when the tide has turned and the yachts are about to finish.

Sailing instructions should therefore direct the yachts to finish *between* an outer mark A and an inner mark B, or *between* a certain part of a pier and a committee vessel, as the case may be. If this is done all difficulty about the boundary buoy drifting here and there owing to wind and tide will be avoided.

Of course the "flag boat" and mark vessel must form "marks in the course," and must be cleared on the right side at the start and finish;

otherwise at the finish a helmsman might be tempted to shoot up round the flag boat and get the gun when the yacht could not clear it, and, in fact, actually foul the mark after gun-fire. To obviate this, a yacht at the finish should clear the marks fairly in passing them, and then keep clear of all other competing yachts.

It is of great importance that a yacht should, after finishing a contest, be most careful to keep clear of all other yachts that have not completed the course, even to the extent of giving way to one sailing free on port tack if she herself is close-hauled on starboard tack.

Part III.—PROTESTS, &c.

Rule 41.—PENALTIES FOR INFRINGING RULES.

Any yacht disobeying or infringing any of these rules, which shall apply to all yachts, whether sailing in the same or different races, shall be disqualified from receiving any prize she would otherwise have won, and her owner shall be liable for all damages arising therefrom, not exceeding in amount and subject to the same limitations as provided by the Merchant Shipping Act of 1894. A breach of these rules shall be considered "improper navigation" within the meaning and for the purposes of that Act.

Until 1895, the first paragraph of this rule ended with " all damages." In the Valkyrie *v.* Satanita Collision Case (where Valkyrie was sunk) the judge held that " all damages meant " such damages as are by law recoverable under the Merchant Shipping Act, which limits the amount recoverable to 8*l.* per ton on the registered tonnage of the offending vessel. The Y.R.A. upon this added the words in italics to the rule, " *all* damages arising therefrom *which are by law recoverable.*" The case was taken to the Court of Appeal, where the Master of the Rolls held that the Valkyrie and Satanita had contracted themselves out of the provision referred to of the Merchant Shipping Act, by agreeing to sail under Y.R.A. rules, and that " all damages " in Rule 41, meant absolutely the amount in money value of all damage.

The case was subsequently taken to the House of Lords, and the decision of the Master of the Rolls was reversed. The rule was then altered as it now is.

Rule 42.—PROTESTS.

A protest on the score of a breach of the rules occurring during a race must be signified by showing a flag conspicuously in the main rigging of the protesting yacht on first passing the sailing committee.

All protests must be made in writing, and signed by the owner or his representative, and lodged with the sailing committee with such fee, if any, as may have been prescribed, within two hours of the arrival of the protesting yacht, unless such arrival shall be after 9 o'clock p.m. and before 8 o'clock a.m., in which case the time shall be extended to noon on that day.

A protest made in writing shall not be withdrawn.

A protest should not be dismissed for the mere reason that it has had no effect on the issue of a race, although in certain instances that feature could be properly considered; still, in the majority of cases, it is impossible to say how far a breach of the rules has influenced a result, even though it be such a trifling matter as carrying an anchor on the bow in a "cruising trim race" or "side lights in a race at night." It is not a sufficient excuse to say that such breaches of a rule were the result of an error of judgment, carelessness, forgetfulness, or ignorance; no such pleas are admissible; nor should it be overlooked that a rule may be designedly and persistently broken. On the other hand, a rule might be broken through an entirely accidental cause; such, for instance, as a delay in the delivery of an entry, through neglect of the post office, or the dragging of moorings; such breaches might reasonably be overlooked, if satisfactorily accounted for; but if a yacht crosses a line too soon through an error of judgment, or touches a mark through an error of judgment, or in a cruising-trim race fails to start with an anchor on the bow, and fails to carry one all through the race, or be holding on to moorings after the first gun, or carries an extra hand, such errors of judgment or persistent breaches of rules could only be regarded adversely.

Rule 43.—SAILING COMMITTEE'S DECISION.

Before deciding a protest a sailing committee shall give notice to the party protested against, and shall hear such evidence and make such inquiries as they may consider necessary.

Rule 44.—APPEALS TO COUNCIL.

A protest which has been decided by a sailing committee shall be referred to the Council of the Y.R.A.

  (a) If the sailing committee, at their own instance, should think proper to so refer it.

  (b) If either of the parties interested make application for such reference, on a question of interpretation of these rules, within one week of the sailing committee's decision.

In the latter case (b) such reference must be accompanied by a deposit of 5l. in the case of yachts exceeding 36ft. rating, and of 3l. for yachts not exceeding 36ft. rating, payable by the party appealing, to be forfeited to the funds of the Yacht Racing Association in the event of the appeal not being sustained.

Rule 45.—PARTICULARS TO BE FURNISHED BY SAILING COMMITTEES.

The reference to the Council must be accompanied by the following particulars, as far as the same are applicable:

1. A copy of the protest and all other written statements that may have been put in by the parties.

2. A plan showing—

    (*a*) The course ;

    (*b*) The direction and force of the wind ;

    (*c*) The set of the tide ;

    (*d*) The positions and tracks of the competing yachts involved in the protest.

3. A copy of the advertised conditions of the race and the sailing instructions furnished to the yachts.

4. The observations of the sailing committee thereon, with their decision.

RULE 46.—EXPENSES OF RE-MEASUREMENT INCURRED BY PROTEST.

In the event of a protest involving the re-measurement of a yacht, the fees and expenses of such re-measurement shall be paid by the unsuccessful party to the protest.

RULE 47.—PERSONS INTERESTED NOT TO TAKE PART IN DECISIONS.

No member of the sailing committee or Council shall take part in the discussion or decision upon any disputed question in which he is an interested party.

RULE 48.—DISQUALIFICATION WITHOUT PROTEST.

Should it come to the knowledge of a sailing committee, or should they have reasonable grounds for supposing, that a competitor in a race has in any way infringed these rules, they shall act on their own initiative as if a protest had been made.

The rule enjoining that a sailing committee shall disqualify a yacht without protest, should it come to their knowledge that a breach of the rules has been committed, has never been quite understood. Some committees interpret it to mean that it gives them the power, but that they may please themselves about exercising it. We think that this interpretation—at any rate, so far as the letter of the rule goes—is incorrect. The rule, as we understand it, leaves no choice whatever, and a sailing committee, whether it is agreeable to them or not, must disqualify any yacht, if they have positive evidence that she has committed a breach of the rules. There were several reasons why this imperative rule was made, but it should be clearly understood that not one of them was intended to relieve competitors from the responsibility of protesting. One of the principal reasons was, however, to prevent collusion between competitors, who had severally committed breaches of the rules, not to protest. To strengthen the hands of sailing committees who might suspect collusion, the Y.R.A. made an addition to the protest rule, that a protest made in writing shall not be withdrawn. This gives a committee the power to inquire into a case which owners might wish to withdraw from, even though they had deliberately placed the cause of complaint in writing,

Q

and lodged it with the sailing committee. We have often heard a question asked, what is the nature of the information a committee must have to warrant them concluding it "has come to their knowledge that a breach of the rules has been committed?" If they saw a thing with their own eyes of course that would be direct knowledge, and there is no doubt what their action should be. Also if they placed a man in each of the markboats—as was formerly sometimes done—to report on cases of fouling, it could be said that such reports conveyed direct knowledge; in fact, the object of placing the men would be to obtain knowledge for the committee to act upon. But supposing a competitor came on shore, and stated to the committee that he had seen a yacht on port tack put one on starboard tack about, could it be said it had come to the knowledge of the committee that a breach of the rules had been committed? We think not, because all cases which arise under the port and starboard tack rule require sifting, and unless a committee had seen the case themselves, and were thus in a position to almost positively judge who was to blame, we do not think it could be affirmed it had "come to their knowledge that a breach of the rules had been committed." Beyond this, it must not be overlooked that if the owner of the yacht on starboard tack knew that his vessel had been improperly put about, it would be his duty to protest, and not leave the matter to the casual intervention of another competitor or informer. So also in tacking for water the vessel on starboard tack might be in fault, and similarly it would be the duty of the owner of the vessel on port tack to protest. Of course, there might be cases where a committee would be justified in acting (when no protest has been lodged) on second-hand knowledge, and opening an inquiry into an alleged breach of the rules. For instance, it might not have come to the knowledge of the owner most concerned that a breach of the rules had occurred until after the time for handing in a protest had passed, and then, if the alleged breach is clear and well defined, and the facts undisputed, we think a committee would be bound to disqualify a yacht, although no protest had been made. In fact, a yacht has been disqualified, without any protest being lodged, on information such as we have just described. The entry might be bad or the rating wrong; in short, a number of cases might arise under the rules in which a committee would be bound to disqualify a yacht, although no protest had been lodged.

Supposing a committee are witnesses, say, of a port and starboard tack case (*vide* the Bembridge Sailing Club or May-Mohawk cases), or a case of bearing down at the start, and are reasonably certain that one, or it may be both yachts are in fault, their duty is to proceed to institute an inquiry exactly as if a protest had been made. Clearly it would not be just for a committee to disqualify a yacht without giving an owner an opportunity of having his version of the matter considered; but if they disqualified her off-hand that is what they would be doing. On the other hand, if they had made up their mind to disqualify the yacht, the owner might be aggrieved if an intimation were not at once made to him (if practicable) of the intention. He could then please himself about continuing the race, according as he considered whether he had or had not sound and good reasons to urge why his yacht should not be disqualified. Under any circumstances a committee should not do anything tantamount to ordering a yacht out of a race, but they should investigate the case at the conclusion of the race. At the same time, if a yacht owner has committed a breach of the rules, and knows or feels that he has no answer to the case—as, for instance, fouling a markboat by misadventure or faulty steering—he ought to do the "happy despatch" himself, and retire from the contest, and not by continuing in it possibly interfere with some other vessel's chance of winning.

The following interesting case was submitted to the Council by the Bembridge Sailing Club in 1899 :

A and B are two boats in a sailing race; after a luffing match they foul each other, and A calls out to B to give up the race and go home, as he is in the wrong; B replies that the foul was A's fault, and goes on racing.

These two boats afterwards, in the same race, are cross-tacking, and A, on the port tack, refuses to make room for B, who is on the starboard tack, and a foul ensues; the sailing committee witness this last foul, and investigate the matter after the conclusion of the race; they are then informed about the first foul, and they go into it and decide that B must be disqualified for it.

A justifies his not giving way to B at the second foul on the ground that he considered B to be out of the race owing to the first foul, and therefore ignored him altogether. The question now is whether A ought to be disqualified for the second foul, or whether the fact that B's being disqualified for the first foul justified A in breaking the rule of the road ?

Neither A nor B flew a protest flag, nor did they protest against each other, but all the foregoing facts came out on the sailing committee's investigation of the second foul, as this latter one came to their knowledge through being seen when occurring.

The Council decided that both A and B should be disqualified.

Under Rule 48, "Disqualification without protest."

The secretary of the Y.R.A. was directed to explain that if any yacht competing in a race infringes a sailing rule she should retire from the race at once ; but if the owner or other person in charge is guilty of such unsportsmanlike conduct as to continue racing, other competitors are bound to treat the yacht as a competitor, and observe the sailing rules accordingly.

PROTESTING AGAINST THE ACTS OF A COMMITTEE.

A sailing committee is practically all powerful, and it is a difficult matter to successfully question any of their acts without resorting to the Law Courts.

For instance, on the Clyde in 1894, there was an error in timing at the start, and one of the competitors demanded that the race should be re-sailed; but there is absolutely nothing in the Y.R.A. rules which directly indicates what shall be done in the case of an error in timing, whether at the start or the finish. The protest rule only says what shall be done in case the owner of a yacht has infringed one of the sailing rules. This rule, apparently, does not contemplate any protest against an *ultra vires* act of the sailing committee; neither is there in the rules any right given to an owner to demand a race to be re-sailed; but by Rule 39 (man overboard) and Rule 13 (removal of markboat), a sailing committee can do as it pleases in ordering a race to be re-sailed. The matter is left absolutely, in these cases, to the discretion of the sailing committees. Also, under the general spirit of Rule 1 as to the management of races, "all doubts, questions, and disputes" shall be subject to the decision of the sailing committee.

RULE 49.—PENALTIES FOR FLAGRANT BREACH OF RULES.

Should a flagrant breach or infringement of any of these rules be proved against the owner of a yacht, or against the owner's representative, or amateur helmsman, such owner, his representative, or amateur helmsman may be disqualified by the Council, for any time the Council may think fit, from steering or sailing in charge of a yacht in any race held under the rules of the Yacht Racing Association; and should a flagrant breach of these rules be proved against any sailing master, he may be disqualified by the Council, for such time as the Council may think fit, from steering or acting as sailing master of a yacht in any race held under the rules of the Yacht Racing Association.

We are glad to say that we do not know of a single instance having been recorded of a sailing master being suspended by the Council of the Yacht Racing Association under this rule, though there was a case during the season of 1899, when a severe censure was administered to a yacht master for foul sailing. There is no sport purer than yacht racing, and, we may add with some pride, that British seafaring men and yacht hands take a delight in sailing a race, and winning one, "fair and square." In nearly every instance in which a breach of the racing rules occurs it is through ignorance of their meaning and intent, and not on account of malevolent design.

THE RESPONSIBILITY OF PILOTS.

In February, 1877, the Council was requested to recommend that pilots should also be liable to be disqualified for flagrant breaches of the rules, but the following reply was made:

The Council is of opinion that it would be unwise to hold pilots responsible for the acts of a yacht during a match. The duty of a pilot is to keep a yacht clear of the ground, and to see that she is not placed at a disadvantage on account of the tide; but the actual directions for the handling, the manœuvring, and the sailing generally of a yacht must be held to rest solely with the sailing master. If an attempt were made to render a pilot responsible under the sailing rules for the acts of a yacht during a match, it would tend to relieve the sailing master of the sense of responsibility he must necessarily be made to feel.

PART IV.—MEASUREMENT.

RULE 50.—INTRODUCTORY.

The measurements of hull and spars shall be taken by the official measurer of the Y.R.A. in accordance with the following rules. The sail area may be computed from measurements supplied by the sailmaker, checked by the aforesaid spar measurements, but if sailmakers' measurements cannot be obtained, or in case of dispute, the sail area shall be ascertained by the official measurer in the manner hereinafter directed.

RULE 51.—RATING RULE.

The Y.R.A. rating shall be ascertained by the following formula:

$$\frac{L + B + 0.75\,G + 0.5\,\sqrt{SA}}{2} = \text{Rating.}$$

where L=length in feet, B=beam in feet, G=girth in feet, and SA=sail area in square feet, measured as hereinafter specified. In the rating, figures in the second place of decimals below 0.05 shall be disregarded, and those of 0.05 and upwards shall count as 0.1.

EXAMPLE OF WORKING THE RULE.

	Then the sum will be:
L.W.L. = 45·6ft.	
Beam = 13·0.	L ... ... 45·60
Girth = 23·4.	B ... ... 13·00
Sail area = 2600.	·75 G ... 17·55
The girth multiplied by ·75 is 17·55.	·5√SA ... 25·50
The square root of the sail area 2600 is 51,	2)101·65
which multiplied by ·5 equals 25·5	50·87 = 50·9 linear rating.

In the rating measurements and calculations, figures beyond the second place of decimals shall be disregarded.

RULE 52.—LENGTH.

The length shall be the fore and aft distance between the outer edges of the official length marks (*see* Rule 56). To this must be added the fore and aft distance of any projection beyond the plumb of these marks, of any part of the hull below them; also the fore and aft distances, beyond the actual water-line endings, to the fair lines, bridging any notches or hollows that there may be in the profile of stem, stern-post, or ridge of counter, within 6in. of the water level.

RULE 53.—BEAM.

The beam shall be taken from outside to outside of the planking, at the breadest place, including wales, doubling planks, and mouldings of any kind.

RULE 54.—GIRTH.

The girth shall be measured along the actual outline of the vertical cross section from L.W.L. to L.W.L. under the keel at a station 0·6 of the distance between the outer edges of the length marks from the fore-end (*see* Figs. 1 to 4). To this must be added twice the

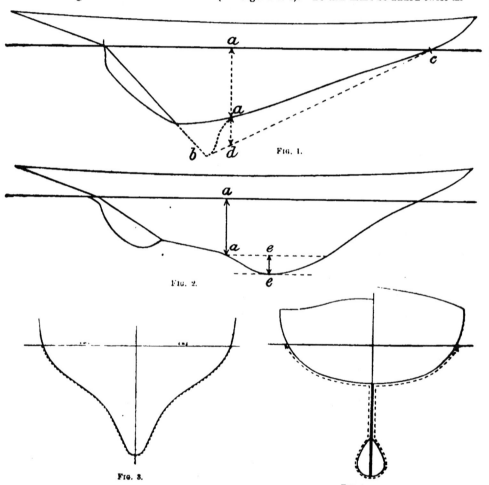

FIG. 1.

FIG. 2.

FIG. 3.

FIG. 4.

excess of draught at any point forward of that station, over the draught at that station (*see e e*, Fig. 2). For the purposes of these measurements any hollow in the fore and aft under-water profile must be treated as if filled up straight (as, *e.g.*, by the line *c d* in Fig. 1).

Rule 55.—CENTRE-BOARDS.

Movable keels of any kind are to be treated as fixed keels, and measured in the position which will give them the maximum measurement.

Rule 56.—OWNERS TO MARK LENGTH AND GIRTH.

Owners must affix the official length marks at the bow and stern, on both sides of the yacht, in such manner as the Council may direct, so that, when lying in smooth water in her usual racing trim, with crew on board, at or about the mid-overall length, she shall not be immersed beyond the plumb of the outer edges of the marks. Owners must affix the official girth marks on both sides, as follows, viz.: One under the rail or covering board, one not less than 2in. or more than 6in. above the water-line, and another on the side of the keel; these three marks to be in the same transverse plane, which must be perpendicular to the water-line, and at the distance 0·6 from the fore edges of the bow marks (*see* Figs. 1 and 2).

The distances between the water-line and the middle marks are to be measured on both sides when the yacht is lying in smooth water, trimmed as above specified, and deducted from the girth as obtained from mark to mark.

Rule 57.—SAIL AREA. MEASUREMENT OF SAILS.

The secretary shall supply sailmakers, upon request, with diagrams in accordance with the subjoined sketch (*see* Fig. 99), and the measurements shall be taken as follows:

MAINSAIL.

A.—Measured from the top of the boom (under the pin for outhaul shackle on traveller, or clew slide, when hauled chock out) to the gaff under the pin of the sheave of the topsail sheet, provided the peak cringle of the mainsail does not extend beyond the pin; in the case of the yacht having no topsail, or of the peak cringle extending beyond the pin of the topsail sheet sheave, then the measurement to be taken to the peak lacing hole.

B.—Perpendicular to A, measured to under side of gaff close in to the mast.

C.—Measured from top of boom over the pin of the sheave or outhaul or end of clew slide to under side of gaff close in to the mast.

D.—Perpendicular to C, measured in to the mast, in a line with the top of the boom, or to tack cringle of mainsail, if below top of boom.

YARD TOPSAIL.

E.—Measured from upper side of gaff close in to the mast to pin of sheave for topsail sheet, or to lacing hole in jackyard.

F.—Perpendicular to E, measured to lacing hole in yard.

G.—From lacing hole to lacing hole in yard.

H.—Perpendicular to G, measured to pin of sheave for topsail sheet in gaff; or to lacing hole in jackyard.

JIB HEADER.

K.—Measured from top of gaff close in to mast to pin of halyard sheave in topmast.

L.—Perpendicular to K, measured to pin of topsail sheet sheave in gaff; or to lacing hole in jackyard.

LUGSAIL.

To be measured as mainsail except as follows :

A.—Upper end measured to peak lacing hole in yard.

B and **C.**—Forward end measured to lower lacing hole in yard.

D.—Lower end measured to tack cringle of mainsail, if below top of boom, or forward of mast.

HEAD SAILS.

I.—The perpendicular I to be measured from the deck at the foreside of the mast to where the line of the luff of the foremost head sail or spinnaker halyard, as the case may be, when extended, cuts such perpendicular. In the case of a schooner the per-

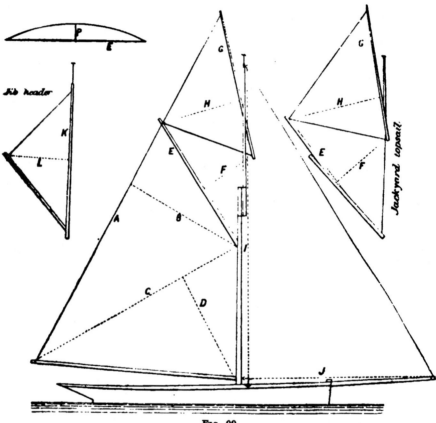

FIG. 99.

pendicular I shall be measured upon the foremast, unless she has a main spinnaker, the height of which exceeds the perpendicular upon the foremast, in which case the excess shall be added to the perpendicular I.

J.—The base J to be measured from the foreside of the mast to where the line of the luff of the foremost head sail when extended cuts the bowsprit, other spar, hull, &c., as the case may be. In all cases, if the distance from the centre fore and aft line of the end of the spinnaker boom exceeds the distance from the foreside of the mast to the outer bowsprit end (where cut by the line of the luff of the foremost head sail), the excess shall be added to the base of the fore triangle. In the case of a schooner, the base J shall be measured from the foremast, but if the main or longest spinnaker boom exceeds the before-mentioned distance the excess shall be added to the base J.

In the case of a yacht having no head sail, but carrying a spinnaker, the area for head sail shall be computed from the length of spinnaker boom, and the height from deck to where the line of the halyard of the spinnaker when extended cuts the mast.

A spinnaker may have a head-stick or board not longer than one-twentieth the length of the spinnaker boom, but not a foot yard, or more than one sheet, or any other contrivance for extending the sail to other than a triangular shape.

In the case of a yacht carrying a squaresail, or square topsail, or raffee (together or separately), the actual area of the same shall be computed; and if such area exceed the area of the fore triangle, the excess shall be used in the total area for determining the rating.

FORESAIL OF SCHOONERS.

To be measured as mainsail, except that the lower end of A is to be taken at foreside of mainmast, in a line with main boom goose-neck.

RULE 58.—DIRECTIONS FOR MEASURING SAILS.

The measurer shall himself take measurements I and J for fore triangle, G and E for yard topsail, and the length of spinnaker boom. If the other measurements are supplied by the sailmaker, the measurer shall check them himself by measuring the following :—

Boom : From lower end of A to lower end of D.
Gaff, or lug yard : From upper end of A to forward end of B.
Jackyard topsail : Sheet to outer lacing hole.

In cases where it is necessary for the official measurer to measure the sails, he shall do so in the following manner :—Take the length of boom from mast to pin of sheave for outhaul, and length of gaff from mast to pin of topsail sheet sheave or lacing hole as the case may require; then hoist the sail with the tack fast, and set the peak and luff up taut, and let go the topping lifts so that the weight of the boom comes on the leach of the sail. With a line and tape measure the leach and luff and the diagonal C. For the head sail measure the height I, and the distance J, as provided for in the section dealing with head sail. For topsail the sail should be hoisted and marked in a line with the gaff; then lowered and the other dimensions taken. From the measurements so taken a sail plan should be made and the other above-specified measurements obtained therefrom.

RULE 59.—CALCULATION OF SAIL AREAS

MAINSAIL.

Multiply A by B and C by D, and add the two products together and divide by 2.

YARD TOPSAIL.

Multiply E by F and G by H, and add the two products together and divide by 2.

JIB HEADER.

Multiply K by L and divide the product by 2.

HEAD SAILS.

Multiply I by J and divide by 2.

Lug Sails and Head Sails.

No deduction is to be made from head sail area on the score of any portion of the lug sail area ahead of the mast.

Sails Bounded by Curved Edges.

Any increase in the area of sails due to curved edges, extended by battens or otherwise beyond the line between the points for measurement, shall be computed as follows: Multiply the base E by two-thirds of the perpendicular P. (*See* Fig. 100.)

LUG SAIL.

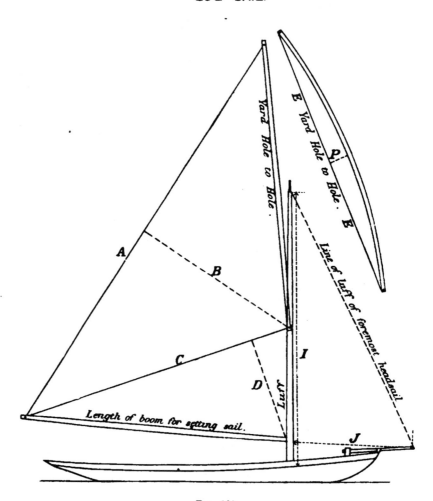

Fig. 100.

Rule 60.—CERTIFICATE OF RATING.

As soon as a yacht has been measured, the official measurer shall forward the measurements, with the sailmaker's diagram, to the secretary of the Yacht Racing Association, who shall thereupon issue a certificate of rating, which shall be in force from the date of the completion of the measurement. If from any peculiarity in the build of the yacht, or other cause, the measurer shall be of opinion that the rule will not rate the yacht fairly, or that in any respect she does not comply with the requirements of these rules, he shall report the circumstances to the Council, who, after due inquiry, shall award such certificate of rating as they may consider equitable, and the measurement shall be deemed incomplete until this has been done.

RULE 61.—ERRORS IN CERTIFICATE.

Should the certificate under which a yacht has sailed in any race or races, be proved to have been incorrect for any reason, the Council may, after inquiry, correct such certificate as they may deem proper, and may revise the claim of the yacht to the prizes which she may have been awarded in such race or races.

RULE 62.—CERTIFICATE NOT TO BE GRANTED TO YACHTS UNDER 15cwt. IN WEIGHT.

No certificate of rating shall be granted to any yacht weighing less than 15cwt. in racing trim without crew.

RULE 63.—OBLIGATIONS OF OWNER RESPECTING CERTIFICATE.

The certificate of rating shall cease to be valid under any of the following contingencies :—

(a) If any dimension measured for rating is found to exceed the measurement stated on the certificate.

(b) If one or both of the length marks fall within the length immersed when the yacht is lying in smooth water in measurement trim.

(c) If any alteration is made so as to increase the beam or girth, or the length of any spar or spars, or the sail area, as respectively measured for rating.

(d) If any length or girth mark is moved from its position.

(e) If the weight is reduced below 15cwt., without crew.

(f) At the expiration of two years from the date of the latest certificate for which all the measurements were taken.

In such case the owner or his representative shall forthwith notify in writing the invalidity of the certificate to the secretary of the Y.R.A. A fresh certificate will afterwards be issued, to date from the completion of such re-measurement as may be requisite.

It is especially incumbent on the owner, or his representative, to ascertain from time to time, by inspection of the length marks, whether the immersion of the yacht has from any cause whatever become such as to render the certificate invalid.

RULE 64.—PENALTY FOR INFRINGEMENT OF PROVISIONS RELATING TO CERTIFICATE.

If an infringement of any of the foregoing provisions in respect of the validity of the certificate of a yacht should in the opinion of the Council be proved against any yacht, such yacht shall be liable to be disqualified by the Council from starting in any race sailed under Y.R.A. rules for the remainder of the current year, or such period as the Council may direct, reckoning from the date at which her certificate is proved to have become invalid.

RULE 65.—INSPECTION TO BE PERMITTED BY OWNER.

Every owner sailing under Y.R.A. rules shall permit all reasonable inspection by or on behalf of the Council, and shall afford all reasonable facility to carry out such inspection in regard to measurements, marks, and such other matters as fall within the scope of an official measurer's duty.

Rule 66.—FEES FOR MEASUREMENT

The owner of a yacht shall pay all fees and expenses for measuring such yacht to the measurer previous to the yacht being measured. A yacht shall not be measured until all arrears of subscriptions and fees due from the owner to the Yacht Racing Association have been paid.

Rule 67.—RE-MEASUREMENT BY ORDER OF COUNCIL.

Where a re-measurement is made by the authority of the Council, the expenses and fees of such re-measurement shall be paid by the Y.R.A. if the certificate is upheld.

Rule 68.—PUBLICATION OF CERTIFICATES.

The principal particulars of measurements, with the dates of the certificates, shall be published periodically.

Rule 69.—PARTIAL MEASUREMENT.

For the information of handicappers, or for other purposes, an owner, on payment of the specified fees, may have his yacht measured for length and sail area only, and receive a certified statement of such measurements from the secretary of the Y.R.A.

Instructions for the Measurers issued by Direction of the Council.

Official measurers shall take the measurements of yachts in the manner hereinafter described.

All measurements should be taken and recorded in the measurement book twice, and a third time if there is any material disagreement.

A steel tape or rods must in all cases be used for taking the measurements.

Immediately the measurements to be taken are complete, the measurer shall forward particulars of the same, together with the sailmaker's diagram if required, to the secretary in accordance with Rule 60.

The measurer shall not measure for the Yacht Racing Association a yacht or boat which he has designed or built, or which any firm he is interested in has designed or built; nor shall he measure any yacht in which he is interested as owner or otherwise.

Before measurement the yacht must have on her length and girth marks, and before testing the marks and measurements the measurer must ascertain from the owner or his representative that the yacht is in her correct racing trim.

All fittings specified in Rule 17, sails, spars, gear, &c., as usually carried by the yacht when racing, must be on board, and also the usual racing crew when the measurements for the length or girth are being taken or checked.

The measurer may allow sails, spinnaker gear, tackles, &c., to be put amidships whilst the measurements and marks for the length and the girth are being tested.

The measurements to be taken are the length, beam, and girth, and the lengths of the spars, or dimensions of sails, in accordance with the Yacht Racing Association rules for the rating of yachts.

Length.—The length (L) for use in the formula shall be obtained by measuring the length over-all on deck, and deducting from this length the distances in to the bow and stern marks as fixed by the owner, from perpendiculars let fall from the bow and taffrail, as shown in the diagrams. These perpendiculars, if measured when the yacht is afloat, are to be obtained by a hand lead sunk two or three fathoms deep, so as to ensure a steady line to measure from. The distances in from the line are to be taken by a rod placed parallel to the water surface, as shown in the diagrams.

After the over-all length has been taken, the measurer must see that the crew are placed at and about the mid over-all length. (See Rules 24 and 25.) He must then ascertain that the yacht is not immersed at the load water-line beyond the length represented by the owner's marks at the bow and stern.

If a yacht is measured in a tide way, the measurer must view and verify the marks in smooth and during slack water; and the overhangs must be measured in smooth and during slack water.

If the measurement for length is obtained when the yacht is ashore, the position of the bow and stern marks must be afterwards verified or checked when the yacht is afloat in racing trim, in smooth water, and before the particulars of the measurements are sent to the secretary.

The over-all measurement must be taken parallel to the L.W.L. above the deck, starting from any convenient point forward on the rail, knee, &c., ahead of the fore end of the load water-line.

When the length over-all is taken with rods, a line should be stretched taut from the point forward to the taffrail to facilitate the accurate shifting of the rods.

BEAM.—The beam may be measured when the yacht is afloat or ashore. The beam shall be taken by means of a straight edge and plumb line.

GIRTH.—The girth is to be taken from disc to disc (a a') at right angles to the load water-line under the keel, following the curve of the cross section as shown in Figs. 1, 2, 3, and 4, and must necessarily be measured when the yacht is on the stocks or laid ashore.

The measurer must take the distance between the disc nearest above the L.W.L. and the covering board or plank sheer on each side of the vessel, and record it in the particulars of measurements furnished to the secretary.

When the yacht is afloat for the other measurements, the measurer shall accurately measure the distance between the girth disc nearest above the L.W.L. and the actual water-line level. This measurement shall be made on each side of the vessel, and shall be recorded in the particulars of measurements furnished to the secretary.

The measurements must be taken when the yacht is afloat in smooth water, in racing trim and crew on board stationed amidship in accordance with the rule, and deducted from the girth as taken from disc (a) to disc (a)

In the case of a yacht being fitted with a centre board or lifting keel, the owner shall either block up the yacht so as to show the board or lifting keel lowered to its full extent, or shall furnish the measurer with a true drawing to scale of such centre board or lifting keel lowered to its full extent.

SPARS AND SAILS.—In measuring the main boom length from the mast to the pin of out-haul shackle, the measurer should see that the traveller, whether on a slide or round the boom, is chock out. For this purpose the clew of mainsail should be unshackled, and the traveller hauled out to the farthest point to which it can be taken.

The measurer should ascertain for himself the point on the bowsprit or cranse iron to which the base measurement for fore triangle must be taken.

In measuring the height for fore triangle, a piece of white linen should be attached to the ring of the tape, and the tape can be then hoisted by the signal halyards.

Before measuring a jackyard, the sail should be bent to it, or the foot laid parallel to the yard and fairly stretched; and, as a check, besides measuring the distance from the sheet to the outer lacing hole, the number of cloths from sheet to clew should be counted.

TRIM AND LENGTH MARKS.—The measurer must take and record in the Measurement Book such notes of the yacht's trim and length marks, by measuring the height above water at the taffrail and stem, or by such other means, as will enable him at any subsequent date easily to ascertain if the immersion at the water line or the marks at the bow and stern have been altered since measurement.

BALLAST.—If a yacht has movable ballast on board, the measurer must note its position.

WEIGHT.—When measuring any yacht under 36ft. rating. the measurer must inform the owner or his representative that before the certificate can be issued, a declaration must be forwarded to the secretary of the Y.R.A.. signed by the owner or builder, declaring that the weight of the yacht, when in measurement trim. but without crew on board, exceeds 15cwt. Should a protest be lodged against any yacht on the alleged ground that she is less than 15cwt. in weight, the parties concerned must make arrangements for the yacht to be weighed. and must refer such arrangements to the measurer of the district for his approval. The measurer must attend the weighing, and see that it is performed to his satisfaction; and either immediately before or after the weighing he must see the yacht floated with crew on board, and satisfy himself that she floats fairly to her marks as when measured, and with this object he must measure the height of the girth marks above the water line, and compare the measurements with the figures on the certificate.

The measurer's fee for attendance at weighing, and all other expenses incidental to such weighing, must be paid by the unsuccessful parties to the protest.

N.B.—In the event of any difficulty arising under the fifth paragraph of these Instructions, or otherwise, as to the measuring of any particular yacht. the secretary shall make arrangements for the measuring of the yacht.

The Y.R.A. measurer takes the dimensions of all the spars as a check upon the measurements supplied by the sailmakers; not that the latter are doubted, but it was a common practice for spar makers to send the sailmaker "short measure" and then make the spars longer to allow for the anticipated stretching of the sails; this, of course, only applies to the days before sail area measurement. The sailmakers are now given the exact dimensions of the spars, and they supply the other measurements of leach, luff, diagonal C and the perpendiculars B and D as they will be when the sail is fully stretched.

The Y.R.A. manner of taking length of water line is as follows: The length is first taken "over all" by a couple of rods or a steel tape. [A linen tape is not allowed to be used, as it stretches so considerably; that is, from 1ft. to 1ft. 6in. in 100ft. when the tape is only apparently fairly straightened over the distance to be measured.] If there be much difference between the heights at the bow and stern the "over all" must be taken on a level line and plumbed down to the taffrail, otherwise the length over all will make the length of water line longer than it actually is. The overhang forward and aft is then taken, and subtracted from the length over all. The overhang is thus taken (*see* Fig. 101): A plumb line is dropped over the taffrail at the centre, and a rod is then floated into the edge of the Y.R.A. mark on the stern post at the load line. The length of the load line is taken to be at the edge of the groove for the rule joint in the stern post, as indicated by the arrow, and not to the

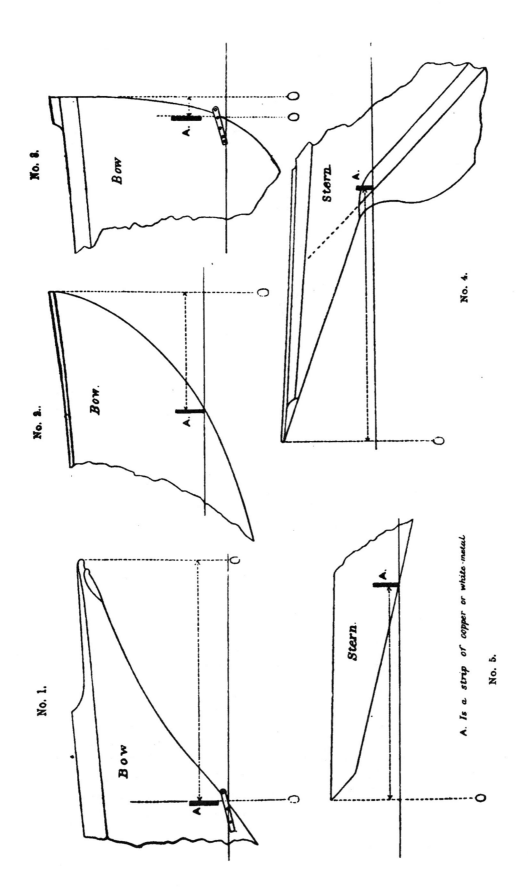

No. 3.

Bow

No. 2.

Bow.

No. 1.

Bow

Stern.

No. 4.

Stern.

A. Is a strip of copper or white-metal

No. 5.

hollow of the groove (*see* Fig. 101). In case of an immersed counter the marks are placed and measured to as shown on page 239.

In July, 1879, the Assegai (10 tons) was brought out with notches cut in her stem and stern post at the L.W.L., as shown by Fig. 102. It

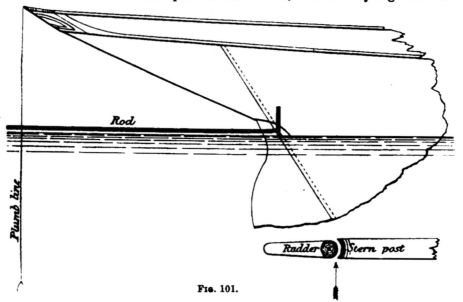

Fig. 101.

will be seen that the yacht has an immersed counter, and the notch was cut at A, close down to the water line. There was a similar notch forward. B is the rudder post and D the stern post.

This case was brought before the Council, and they decided that such notches as A could not be allowed for in measurement of length.

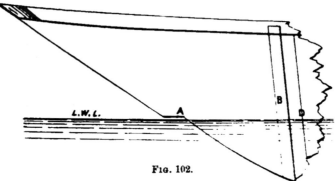

Fig. 102.

In 1882, Bonina (a length class boat) appeared with a notch cut out of the edge of the groove in the sternpost at the water-line. The Council of the Y.R.A. decided that it could not be allowed for, and, to meet such cases as the two mentioned, framed that part of the rule which disallows notches or hollows in the counter or stem if they are within 6in. of the water level.

In April, 1900, a case was submitted to the Council of the Y.R.A. of a very similar nature to the Bonina case of 1882. Two yachts of the 18ft. restricted linear rating class at Burnham-on-Crouch, My Lady Dainty and Nanki Poo, were built with a reverse curve in the profile of the stem within

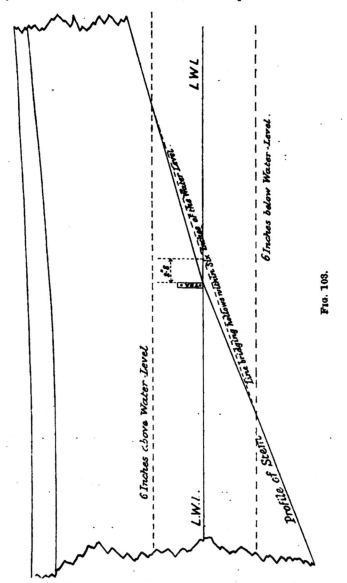

FIG. 103.

6in. of the water level. (See Fig. 103.) The introduction of a sudden hollow in the longitudinal vertical section was obviously for the purpose of shortening the L.W.L. as measured for rating, and, in point of fact, was nothing more than an attempt to revert to the old system of

R

tonnage cheating of twenty years ago, under a more ingenious disguise. The council rightly decided that the fore and aft distance beyond the actual water-line ending, about 2·8in. in My Lady Dainty and 2·74in. in Nanki Poo, to a fair line bridging the hollow should be added to the rating length in accordance with the Y.R.A. rule for the measurement of length. (See Rule 52.)

Small yachts having balance rudders are, of course, built without any stern post at all, and the longitudinal vertical section of the counter often forms a fair curve down to the keel. (See Fig. 104.) In such case the hollow within 6in. of the water level above and below, being a continuation of a fair line, could not be regarded as an infringement of the rule. Before the rules were re-drafted the wording of the clause ran thus: " Pieces of any form cut out of the stem, stern post,

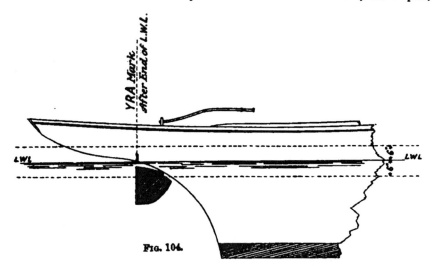

Fig. 104.

or fair line of the ridge of the counter, with the intention of shortening the length, shall not be allowed for in measurement of length, if at or immediately below the marks for the length, nor above if within 6in. of the water level." On reference to the existing Rule 52 it will be seen that it is not enjoined that the hollows or notches shall be filled up straight, but that the bridging should be measured to the *fair lines*; in practice this means that the measurer should not place a straight-edge on the stem or stern of the vessel, but should bend a batten to the fair line of the longitudinal vertical section. In the plan of the 18-footer (Fig. 104) the after-end of the L.W.L. terminates at the Y.R.A. mark, and her length, according to Rule 52, should be measured to this point, no addition being necessary on the score of any hollow in the profile or ridge of counter.

A curious point in measurement arose in 1894 out of a yacht built on the Clyde of the " fish torpedo type." She has circular sections aft, as

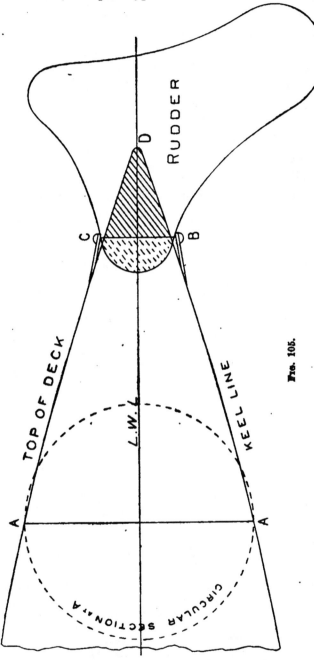

Fig. 105.

shown in the diagram at A A, Fig. 105, and is 26ft. on the L.W.L. Of course, if the longitudinal vertical section had been carried out to the point D, the fixing of a rudder would have entailed the employment of long struts and stays. The owner got over the difficulty by making the tapered end of the boat work in a hollow as shown at B C. Two lugs are here fixed to the top side and under side of the boat, through which a bolt passes, as well as through the pear-shaped bulb on the rudder. The bulb is about 8in. through at B C, and about 1ft. 4in. long. The point raised was whether the boat should be measured for rating length to abreast of the bolt through B C or to the end of the bulb at D. It is obvious that with a construction something like this a boat could be built in two halves and claim to be measured for one half only. The matter was referred to the Council of the Y.R.A., who decided that as the bulb portion of the rudder is solid (it is of mahogany), it adds nothing to the buoyancy or power of the boat, and is not to be measured in the rating length, but if hollow, it would be measured. This decision is, no doubt, ingenious; but, at the same time, we must remember that the specific gravity of some kinds of mahogany are not nearly so great as that of water, and also that the specific gravity of cork is not so great as that of mahogany. It is possible to conceive that a very large bulb—say 4ft. or 5ft. long—could be made solid of cork, and veneered over with mahogany to fashion off the water line of a racing craft; and what would be the ruling then?

As might be expected, attempts "to cheat the length" were made by "placing the crew," in one or two cases, whilst small yachts or boats were being measured; accordingly the Y.R.A. passed a rule that the crew must be on board and amidships whilst the marks for rating length and girth are tested.

APPENDIX TO Y.R.A. RULES.

The Yacht Racing Association further recommend for the consideration of sailing committees :—

1. MIXED RIG RACES.—That yachts of different rigs should, whenever practicable, be kept separate.

ALLOWANCE TO SCHOONERS AND YAWLS.—The rating of schooners and yawls to be reckoned for time allowance as follows, viz., schooners at 0·85, and yawls at 0·92 of their actual rating; provided that in case of a yawl, her mainsail does not exceed 0·37 of her total sail area, and that her mizen is not less than 0·06 of her total sail area. In the case of a pole-masted yawl, her mainsail shall not exceed 0·46 of her total sail area, and her mizen shall not be less than 0·075 of her total sail area. In schooners the foreside of the mainmast shall at the deck be not farther forward than the middle of the rating length.

KETCHES AND LUGGERS.—Ketches and luggers shall be reckoned for time allowance at 0·85 of their rating; provided that in a ketch the distance between the masts does not exceed half the rating length of the yacht, and that the smaller sail is carried aft.

LUGGERS.—In the case of a lugger, to be entitled to the rig allowance, the yacht must have two or more masts, and the after, or the middle mast, at the deck must not be forward of the middle of the rating length, and in the case of a two masted lugger if the area of the after lug be less than half the area of the main lug, she will be rated as a yawl.

FRACTIONS TO BE USED IN REDUCING THE RATING.—In calculating the deduction for difference of rig, the rating by certificate to the exact fraction must be used. The time allowances to be calculated from each yacht's reduced rating; but schooners, ketches, luggers, and yawls shall not be allowed to qualify to enter by their reduced rating in a class race.

2. TIME TO BE CALCULATED ON REDUCED RATING ALL THROUGH.—In races for mixed rigs, the time allowances between yachts of the same rig must be calculated on each yacht's reduced rating.

3. FLYING STARTS.—That flying starts should be adopted when practicable, but no time should be allowed for delay in starting.

4. MOORED STARTS.—That if the start is to be made from anchors or moorings, lots shall be drawn for stations, and springs shall be allowed on the same bridle or anchor chain or warp as the bowfasts, but are not to be carried to a buoy, pier, other vessel, or fixed object. If any yacht lets go or parts her bridle before the signal to start, or if she drags any moorings or anchor to which she is made fast for the purpose of starting, she shall be liable to be disqualified, unless such parting or dragging be explained to the satisfaction of the committee, or unless she has returned, after the signal to start, within the line of starting buoys so as not to obtain any advantage by the accident.

In a race starting from moorings, no paid hand may join or leave the yacht after the first gun.

5. That as weatherliness is a quality which it is especially desirable to test in yacht racing, the courses should wherever possible be so laid out as to include a large proportion of windward work.

6. NO LIMIT TO RACE.—That any limit to the time for concluding a race should be avoided as far as possible.

7. CLASSIFICATION BY RATING.—That the classification of yachts should, when practicable, be as follows:

For yachts whose rating, by Rule 3, does not exceed 18ft.
Above 18ft. and not exceeding .... 24ft.
     ,, 24ft.   ,,   ,, ... 30ft.
     ,, 30ft.   ,,   ,, ... 36ft.
     ,, 36ft.   ,,   ,, ... 42ft.
     ,, 42ft.   ,,   ,, ... 52ft.
     ,, 52ft.   ,,   ,, ... 65ft.
     ,, 79ft.

8. That whenever practicable a clause should be inserted in the programme providing that there shall be no time allowance in races for the classes not exceeding 65ft.

9. Yachts which have been raced previously to 1896, and which are over the new classes of linear rating (corresponding with the classes they competed in under the old rating rule), shall be allowed to compete in such new classes by allowing time on the

excess rating, providing no alteration has been made in their hulls and no increase made in their load water-line length as defined by the Y.R.A. marks, and no increase made in their sail area since 1895.

10. LENGTH OF COURSES SHOULD BE EXACT.—That as distance is an important element in the calculation of time allowance, the marks and flag boats should be placed so as to mark as accurately as possible the length of the course, for which time is allowed.

11. ROUNDING MARKS IN HEAVY WEATHER.—That in heavy weather it should be arranged, if practicable, for yachts to stay instead of gybe round marks.

12. ROOM AT STARTING.—That sailing committees should be particularly careful to provide ample room between the points marking the starting line.

13. TIME TO ELAPSE BETWEEN RACES.—That when in the opinion of the sailing committee it is not desirable to observe the period of fifteen minutes provided for in Rule 27, the time may be shortened to ten or five minutes as may be desirable, but the time to elapse shall always be distinctly stated on the instructions for the race.

CHAPTER IX.

YACHT RACING: HANDLING A YACHT IN A MATCH.

ONE of the principal causes of success in yacht racing is that of being "always ready;" ready with the entry, ready with the vessel whether she requires copper scrubbed or trim altered, ready with the sails and gear, ready with the instructions, ready in getting into a berth, ready to start, ready for every shift of canvas, ready for every evolution in sailing, and ready to receive the first gun at the finish. Therefore, always be ready and never be above being prepared. The experienced racing man knows that if he is prepared with his spinnaker, and another man is not, after bearing up round a mark, that an enormous advantage will be gained. Or in hauling round a mark if he has got everything in time made snug, and sheets laid along and manned ready for rallying aft, and another man has to luff round with everything adrift on deck, and the boom off the quarter, his vessel will get a quarter of a mile out on the weather of the sloven before the latter has got his boom aboard or jib sheets in. If proper preparation is made for every shift of canvas or manœuvre in sailing, the vessel will be worked as if all the gear and sails were parts of machinery, but if no preparations are made, everything will be in confusion on board; there will be shouting and bawling and running about, sails sent up head downwards, sheets and halyards bent on foul, or fouled among the numberless coils of ropes on deck, the crew will be distracted, the sailing master hoarse and furious, and the owner mortified to see such an utter want of discipline and system on board his vessel. On the other hand, if everything is ready beforehand, the crew will understand exactly what they have to do, each man will fulfil his task with a cool head and ready hand, the sailing master will be tranquil and manage the vessel cleverly, and the owner will be delighted, and think that half the pleasure of match sailing is in seeing a good crew, who know their work, set about it in a seamanlike and systematic manner. There must be no shirking; whatever a man is set to do, he must do thoroughly, and with a will; if he does not do this he should be unshipped without compunction, as one lazy, slovenly, or half-hearted hand on board will spoil three good ones.

Various things have to be done on board a yacht when sailing a match, at one and the same time, and it will be patent that it is desirable that each thing should be done by the same hands each time, if possible. Nothing· looks worse on board a racing yacht if when such a simple order as "check the fore sheet a trifle," a half a dozen men or so jump up and rush into the lee bow, when one of the crew could have quietly executed the order. On the other hand it shows a worse spirit if the men ┃begin talking among themselves as to who shall go to do it; but if one hand is told off as the fore sheet man, he will know that he has to check the sheet, and if the sheet has to be got in instead of eased, the mate will send another hand or more to help. For the more important stations men always are told off; thus one hand is always selected for masthead-man, bowsprit end-man, &c.; and so far as the number of the crew will admit, there should be a just and effective division of labour.

CREWS.

Under the Y.R.A. rules, in the classes of 42ft. rating and under, there is a limit to the number of hands a yacht may carry in a match, but in the classes above 42ft. there is no restriction, and this plan is found to work best, as no sailing master will carry more hands than are absolutely necessary, and if crews were limited, sails must be limited also, or a yacht would be frequently short handed. The only argument used in favour of limiting hands, in all classes, is that a man who has a large income and a disposition to spend it, would, by carrying a great number of hands, get an advantage over a man with less money or differently disposed about spending it. The plain answer to this is that no sailing master ever dreams of carrying more than the number of hands considered necessary for properly working the ship, and every yacht should be allowed to carry that number.

For match sailing, the table on next page will be found to accord pretty regularly with present practice. The numbers include master, mate, and boatswain, but not pilot, cook, or steward.

It is usual, however, for cook and steward to muster on deck during a race and assist in hauling, &c., and if they do so they justly claim "racing money" the same as received by seamen.

Rating of Yacht	Ordinary Crew* of Racing Yacht.	Extra Hands.	Total Racing Crew.*
18ft.	1	1	2
24ft.	2	1	3
30ft.	2	3	5
36ft.	2	5	7
42ft.	3	6	9
52ft.	5	6	11
64ft.	7	5	12
70ft.	10	5	15
85ft.	14	8	22
100ft.	16	12	28

* Cook and steward not included; nor sailing master in yachts above 20 rating.

The number of the ordinary standing crew given for a racing yacht is in excess of what a cruising yacht would carry, but as the spars, sails, and gear of a racing yacht are so much heavier, the crews must be heavier also.

For racing it will not matter what the rig is, whether cutter, schooner, or yawl, the same number of hands will be required. In a cutter, the sails, spars, and gear are heavier to handle than in a schooner, or yawl of similar tonnage, on the other hand, the number of sails and the extra gear of a schooner or yawl require more hands.

A sailing master will generally endeavour to make up a racing crew from men who have been in a racing yacht before; this of course cannot always be done, and it follows that somebody must ship the green hands. However, excepting the circumstance that a hand who has been in a racing yacht is already "proved and rated," there is no disadvantage in having one or two green hands, as a couple of matches will make them perfect, if they have been trained as good yacht sailors in other respects. The most approved plan is to have the same crew season after season, as the men by constantly working together become much more expert in handling the yacht.

Men widely differ in their smartness and in their habits; and a man may be tolerated in a racing yacht in spite of his moral delinquencies and faults of temper, because he is a very smart seaman, but a sloven should be given a very wide berth, as he will not only be offensive to the rest of the crew, but in all probability not a good seaman. As a rule, the smartest men (*i.e.*, the cleverest and most active) are the most cleanly in their habits, the most prompt in doing their work, and in obeying orders, and the most satisfied, not to say proud, of their lot.

A sloven quarrels with the catering, with the work he has to do, with the liberty he gets, and with the places he visits. Such a man should find no berth in a racing yacht, and if a sailing master unfortunately ships such a creature, he should unship him when he is found out.

Sometimes what is known as a "sea lawyer" is met with; a man who is always standing on his rights, and is ever on the look out to see that another member of the crew is not requested to do something which he is not compelled to do by Act of Parliament. He is generally brimful of "instances," which as a rule are about as *àpropos* as a fiddle at a funeral, and perpetually debating whether he is obliged to do what he is told or not. The "sea lawyer" will upset and make dissatisfied any crew, and should be cut adrift on the first opportunity.

It is frequently said that the men who come from this place, or that place, are better or smarter than others; but this is entirely a mistake. Good Cowes men are as good as good Southampton men; good Colne men are as good as either; and so are good Scotchmen; and as there is no difference in the degrees of worth of the men, so is there no difference in the degrees of their badness. At Cowes, or Southampton, if a man is shipped who has never been in a yacht before, the probability is, that he will be no seaman at all—a sort of half waterman and half labourer. If a man who has never been in a yacht is shipped from the Colne, the probability is that he will be a thorough seaman as represented by a smacksman, and will be good at hauling, good at belaying, good at reefing, and good and trustworthy in bad weather, and respectful in his manner. He will also very rapidly accommodate himself to yacht customs, and earn and deserve the respect of owner and sailing master by his smart seamanship.

THE COST OF YACHT RACING.

The cost of yacht racing is a very important item, and, of course, so far as crew expenses go, will depend upon the number of matches sailed. The other expenses, which relate to the hull, sails, spars, and rigging, can be put down at from 50 per cent. to 60 per cent. greater than those for the cruising yacht. The crew expenses will also be a heavy item, as the number will not only be greater, but there will be the extra money, and food and drink or "grub money" on racing days. Formerly, the invariable practice was to give the men meat, bread, and beer (or, on wet cold days, rum), on the days when matches were sailed; no doubt this practice is in much favour among the crews, as frequently enough food is left to supply the mess another day. However, a fashion has been introduced of paying the men half-a-crown each on racing days, and making them find themselves. This greatly simplifies the accounts, and prevents the owner's good nature or inexhaustible means being imposed upon.

The expenses of a 20-rater will serve to show the nature and extent of the cost of yacht racing. It will be assumed that she commences to fit out on the 1st of May, and is laid up on the 30th of September, therefore that she is in commission twenty-two weeks, and sails thirty matches.

Expenses of a Twenty-Rater.	£	s.	d.
Sailing master (per annum)	50	0	0
Four seamen, twenty-two weeks, at 27s.	119	16	0
Clothes for master and men	30	0	0
Six extra men for thirty matches, 10s. each	90	0	0
Food and drink money for thirty matches with paid crew at 3s. per head *	45	0	0
Winning money to master and men for (say) thirty matches, at 1l. first prize, 10s. second prize, 5s. third prize	80	0	0
Captain for thirty starts, at 1l. each	30	0	0
Pilot for the thirty matches sailed, at 2l. a match	60	0	0
Entrance fees	20	0	0
New sails	75	0	0
Fitting out expenses and new gear, &c.	40	0	0
Ship Chandler	10	0	0
Store	10	0	0
Hauling up and launching	15	0	0
Travelling expenses of crew	10	0	0
Washing, coal, oil, candles, leathers, &c.	10	0	0
Insurance for four months	15	0	0
	£709	16	0

As a set off to these expenses, there will be, of course, the prizes, which would probably amount to 200l. But even deducting this, it will be seen that racing a 20-rater is a very expensive amusement.

Of course, these expenses could be very greatly reduced. In the first place, no more than twenty matches need be sailed; next, amateur crews might be more often made use of; losing money need not be paid; a pilot need not be had so often if the owner or his master, or one of the owner's friends is well acquainted with the waters in which the matches are sailed; and a new mainsail need only be had every other year. However, if forty matches were sailed in one season, a new mainsail would be a necessity.

The expenses of a 52ft. rating yacht will not greatly exceed that of a 42ft., and the general cost of keeping one, irrespective of racing, will not be much in excess of the smaller vessel. But in a 20-rater, although two hands might very well manage her, the sailing master takes the form of a regular "skipper." In a 10 or 15-rater, the master works just as the man does; turns out at six o'clock to scrub down, takes

* Until the year 1880 the invariable practice was to find the men in food, beer, and grog, and many years' experience proved that the liberality of the owner was almost systematically abused; consequently the practice of giving "grub money" was introduced, and has been found to work well.

his turn with the other hand at every kind of work and liberty. In a 20-rater, the skipper does not show on deck until after breakfast, and his greatest exertion is usually steering the vessel and talking to the owner, the same as it is on board other large yachts.

RACING MONEY.

With regard to one branch of the expenses enumerated, that of "racing money," or the extra money given to crews on racing days, long formed a vexed question, but now practically a uniform system prevails. Formerly it was 1*l*.* all round and 5*l*. for the skipper, and giving the men 10*s*. for racing and losing.

The general practice now is to give 1*l*. for a first prize, 10*s*. for a second, and 5*s*. for third. Nothing for losing; but in a 52ft. yacht or 42ft. a skipper gets 1*l*. for each start.

The sailing master is also rewarded by a percentage on the nominal amount won; a "crack skipper" will expect 10 per cent. on the total year's winnings, but it is unusual to pay more than 5 per cent.

It has been argued that if racing money is given at all, the 1*l*. for winning and nothing for losing system does not seem just. A vessel cannot win by the exertion of the crew alone, and if she could, it may be taken for granted that the crews would exert themselves to the utmost without the stimulus of extra pay. A yacht's success depends upon her excellence as compared with the excellence of other vessels, upon her canvas, upon her sailing master and crew, and upon the varying fortune of wind. It therefore does not seem just that if a crew exert themselves to the utmost and lose, that they should have nothing, whereas if they had won, a douceur of 1*l*. to each man would have been given. It may be argued that many owners would not race if they had to pay 10*s*. losing money, because they know their vessels are not so good as some others, and therefore that their chances of winning are more remote. This it has been said may justify the owner in not racing, but it is hardly fair to the crew if he does race. If the 1*l*. winning money is fairly earned, the 10*s*. losing money is equally well earned, and the difference of 10*s*. between the two douceurs is quite sufficient to maintain the desire to win. But there is still another very strong argument to be advanced on behalf of the 10*s*. losing money plan. The extra men get 10*s*. for coming on board to race, and if these men are given 10*s*., besides

---

* It was quite common until about the year 1870 for the owner of a yacht, such as belonged to the Royal Yacht Squadron, to present the crew with 2*l*. each after winning a prize; but then that prize would most likely be the only one of the season, and won in the only match the yacht sailed.

their ordinary day's pay, to come out of a strange vessel, it certainly is no more than just that the regular crew of the yacht should have 10s. besides their day's pay as well. The extra men have comparatively little work to do beyond the pulling and hauling during the race, but the regular crew of the yacht have most likely a hard day's work before the race, and a harder one after the race. It is not the fact that the work is no harder on board a racing yacht than on board a cruiser; in reality there is no comparing the two, and the life on board a cruiser is ease, luxury, and indolence, compared with the worry, discomfort, and work on board a racing yacht.

THE START.

It will be assumed that the race is for 52ft. rating yachts; and, as the method of starting and general conduct of a race is the same for yachts of all sizes, a yacht of this rating will answer the purpose of illustration as well as one of larger size. If the start is from moorings, go up to the buoy to pick it up just as you would to pick up any other buoy. (*See* " Seamanship.") If the yacht is before the wind, lower all sail and go up to the buoy with way so much deadened that the yacht scarcely moves, due allowance of course always being made for tide, whether foul or fair; in beating up to the buoy, the yacht must be rounded to and made shoot head to wind up to the buoy. Get hold of the buoy and hawser and haul about ten or twelve fathoms on board; then bend on the quarter spring to the hawser, veer out the hawser again and belay the spring with some slack aft. In starting from anchors, if the chain has to be slipped, the spring will be bent to the chain as it would be to the hawser. If the anchor has to be weighed, no spring will be bent on. If a yacht starts from her own anchor and slips and the anchor has to be got by a boat, it is best to bend a trip line to the crown of the anchor with a buoy. Also if the anchor has to be weighed in a 5-tonner, it will be found best to put a trip line on the anchor and pull it up over the bow regardless of the cable, which can be got in at leisure.

Too much of the hawser should not be hauled in, as the yacht may drag, and this would render her liable to disqualification; neither should the rudder be put hard across, as that will cause the yacht to sheer and bring the stream of the tide on one bow, or on the broadside, and the force of the stream acting on such a surface may cause the yacht to drag, and this would render her liable to disqualification.

Sometimes when starting from moorings or anchors, permission is given to set after canvas prior to the gun for the start being fired; but if the yacht is riding head to the tide with the wind blowing astern, she could not keep at her moorings with mainsail set. In such cases the sail will not be hoisted till the last two or three minutes. But everything must be got ready long before the five-minutes gun.

The breeze we will assume to be of whole-sail strength, that is that the best topsail, can be just carried on a wind, and that the first part of the course is to windward. See that the topsail is bent to the yard, and that the halyards are properly bent. Haul No. 1 jib in stops out by the traveller, hook on the halyards, and let it lie on the bowsprit; get the mainsail (with boom well topped) and the foresail ready for hoisting. If the jib topsail will be wanted, hank it on to the topmast stay, stow it on the bowsprit end, and bend the sheets. See that the sheets are clear for hauling in aft.

See that everything is stowed below that will not be required on deck, and also see that everything that is on deck and not in immediate use is securely lashed. Have an axe ready to cut the quarter spring in case it jammed.

At the five-minutes gun place the crew at their stations.

The helmsman of the day then takes the helm; with him aft will be the pilot, who will also look after the quarter spring and attend to the main sheet; the mate will cast off the bow fast or hawser forward, clear the jib halyards for hoisting, and with another hand hoist the jib and take in the lee jib sheet or weather sheet if required for paying off; one hand will hoist the foresail and attend to the lee fore sheet if necessary; three hands will man the peak halyards, and two the throat alternately, the jib and foresail men tailing on directly they have pulled these sails up. This will be work for nine hands; if the pilot is not allowed to work, a peak-halyard hand will go aft and cast off the spring and jump forward directly it is done.

As the time approaches for the firing of the gun to start, try to realise that everything must be done at once. If the yachts are lying head to wind and tide, and have to fill on starboard tack, the helmsman in the last fifteen seconds will put his helm to starboard, so as to make sure of the wind catching the yacht on the starboard bow. As the gun fires the mate will throw overboard the bow fast, and the quarter spring will be hung on to until the yacht is fairly filled on the right tack, when it will be thrown overboard by the pilot; all hands will hoist away. The pilot will overhaul some of the main sheet and drag it in again directly the yacht begins to move through the water, and the helmsman will gradually bring her to the wind. Get all the sails set and properly purchased as quickly as possible is advice that cannot too often be repeated, and when they are so set coil up all ropes, &c., and " clear the decks."

If the yachts are to proceed against wind and tide, and to fill on starboard tack (*i.e.*, cast to port), the helm will be put to starboard just before the start, in order to sheer the yacht's head to port or off the wind (in reality the stern will come more to windward than the bow will go off to leeward). Great exertion must be made to get the mainsail up quickly if it is not already set.

In starting to run with the tide and wind, hold on the quarter spring until the vessel is fairly swung round before the wind. If to run before the wind against the tide no quarter spring will be required, although one is generally bent on. In all cases get the canvas set as quickly as possible, and directly the hands who are hoisting the head sails have got them up hand taut, they should jump on to the main and peak halyards; the purchasing will be done after the sails are fairly hoisted all round.

In starting every caution must be exercised to avoid fouling other yachts; but frequently a foul cannot very well be avoided if a yacht has no way on, and is simply moving with the tide; but if the vessel has gathered way she is under control, and no foul should take place.

STARTING UNDER-WAY.

In an under-way start great care must be exercised that *no part* of a yacht (her bowsprit, boom, and sails included) is on the line before the signal to start. (In case of a calm a yacht is not allowed to have her anchor out over the line to haul across with when the first gun has been fired; nor may she warp, nor hang on to moorings, nor be in tow after the first gun.)

The strength of the tide and the wind should be so well judged that the yacht can, with full way on, go over the line at the very moment the blue peter is lowered and the gun fired. In all cases the master should strive for a weather berth, especially so if the start is for a thrash to windward. If the yacht is a little too early she must be stopped: yaw her about; haul the foresail up to windward; haul the main boom in; or if the vessel is by the wind it can be run well off her quarter—this only if there be plenty of help to get it in again. In extreme cases the yacht can be put about, but she should not wear unless there be a lot of time, as it will take her right away to leeward.

If the wind is steady and it is a reach to the line, it is a good plan to sail up above the line and back again, taking the time each way and noting the difference. Then when the first gun is fired, a good idea can be formed of how far to get away from the line and return so as to reach it just as the starting gun is fired.

If the yacht is on the wrong side of the line when the gun fires she must be careful to keep clear of all yachts which are crossing or have crossed the line properly. ·(*See* the Royal Dorset case, page 170.) However, there is a special rule that yachts coming into position from the wrong side of the line after the signal to start must keep clear of yachts which are starting or have started properly.

Whether the start be from moorings or under-way the master should, to the best of his judgment, get the exact canvas up at first that can be carried; and if it is a case of reefing, always remember that it is a great deal easier to let out a reef than take one in.

After a start and run down wind, a reef may be required when the yachts draw on the wind; in such cases the practice is to start with a reefed mainsail and jib-headed topsail over it. Before hauling by the wind the topmast is housed.

OVERTAKING : LUFFING AND BEARING AWAY.

If, when before the wind, a yacht is ahead, and you cannot pass her, run dead in her wake or a little to windward of her wake, if the breeze is quartering, so as to cover her; you may do her a little harm in this way and prevent her getting away farther. If you are overtaking a vessel and desire to pass her, give her a wide berth either to windward or to leeward; to leeward for choice, as, if the vessels are dead before the wind, your antagonist cannot bear away after you to do any harm; if you try to pass to windward, a senseless luffing match will most likely be the result.

If a vessel is coming up fast astern and threatening your weather quarter, and you make up your mind that she shall not pass to windward, do not wait until her bowsprit is over your quarter before you luff, but take a wipe out across her when she is fifty yards off or so. If she is the more weatherly vessel, and faster withal, and once gets a weather quarter overlap, she cannot be stopped by luffing. If you luff in time she will know what you mean to do, will probably be unable to get on your weather at all, and more probably will not try it. If she bears up to attempt to go through your lee, do not follow her off; if you do, it will probably end, after frequent backing and filling, in her ultimately getting her bowsprit over your weather quarter, and a long luffing match will ensue, followed up perhaps by a protest for bearing away.

When one of two yachts which are close together succeeds in going through the lee of the other yacht, the latter, if possible, should cover the yacht which has just passed her. If the wind is very light, she may succeed in holding her. But the yacht which has just passed through the lee of the other should luff out to a clear berth, and she may thus be able to rid herself of the intended covering. If there be an obstruction to sea room she will be unable to luff out clear perhaps, and may very likely try to get a clear wind by running off to leeward; but here she will find that the sternmost yacht can follow her, and generally running off the wind in such a case is of no avail. It must be understood that the prohibition contained in the Y.R.A. rule on "luffing or bearing away" is not involved here, as it is presumed that one yacht has passed clean through the lee of the other, and if she drops back again that other yacht which was passed becomes in the position of an *overtaking yacht.* An *overtaking yacht* is not precluded from bearing away provided she does not cause the yacht overtaken to bear away also to avoid collision, and this she would not do by bearing away into her wake; but an *overtaken yacht* is forbidden to bear away to hinder another passing to leeward; that is, a yacht that is *overtaken* by another yacht must concede an unmolested passage to leeward.

HEAD-REACHING TO WINDWARD.

If two yachts are standing by the wind in close company on the same tack, and the weathermost yacht head-reaches so much as to get into the other's wind, the latter may require to tack; but she must not do so until she can clear the stern of the weathermost yacht, as fouling in attempting to stay under such conditions would be cause for disqualification. (*See* page 207, and the section "Weather Bowing," page 262).

HEAD-REACHING TO LEEWARD: TACKING.

If, when two yachts are beating to windward, and standing in close company on the same tack, the yacht to leeward head-reaches and requires to tack across the other's bow, she must not do so until she can tack without interfering with the windward yacht whether she is going to either starboard or port tack.

HEAD-REACHING AND WEATHERING.

It is assumed that the yachts in the match are close-hauled standing on starboard tack on their first board in the beat for No. 1 markboat; jibs have been purchased up till the luff is as straight as the forestay, peak purchased up, main tack bowsed down (if the mainsail be a loose footed one), topsail tack hauled down and clew sheeted,* and

---

* A gaff topsail is seldom "sheeted home" in a racing yacht; there is usually a foot or so drift of sheet between the gaff and clew cringle to insure being able to sheet the sail flat. When the cringle is "home" the foot of the sail will very likely not be stretched, and will belly away from the gaff; it will then be time to think about getting a pull on the topmast stay; or topsail halyards, if the topsail has settled down, as it frequently will, especially if the halyards be new. A gaff topsail will usually require "sheeting" after the main peak has been purchased up.

sails trimmed to the exact inch of sheet. With water just squeezing through the lee scuppers, there is plenty of weather helm to play upon in luffing to the " free puffs."

The yachts have started abreast of each other, but one of them a hundred yards or so to leeward. The one in the lee berth holds much the better wind, and is gradually eating up to the other and head-reaching too. At last she is close up under the lee bow of the craft to windward, and in another half-minute her weather quarter-rail will strike the bowsprit or lee bow of the other; which has to give way ?

To begin with, we must clearly understand what is taking place. Close-hauled means sailing so close to the wind as a vessel can be sailed with a view of economising distance or time, or both, in reaching a particular object. The vessel which is " weathering," and at the same time head-reaching, can be taken as a standard for one condition of being close-hauled. It is thus quite clear that the vessel to windward does not fulfil that particular standard, and is in the condition—an uncontrollable one it can be admitted—of bearing away on the other. This, under Rule 21 of the Y.R.A. (the Luffing and Bearing Away rule), a yacht is not allowed to do, and she must luff up to enable the other to clear her. However, the general practice in such a case is for the leeward yacht to be given weather helm to keep clear of the one to windward ; then when she has drawn clear ahead the weather tiller lines can be eased, and she will literally fly out across the bow of the other. This, on the whole, is the better course ; and further, it is the course which must be followed if the leeward yacht head-reaches from a position astern, as by the Luffing and Bearing Away rule "an overtaking vessel, if to leeward, must not luff, so as to interfere with the yacht she has overtaken, until she has drawn clear ahead."

It may possibly be argued that the leeward yacht is not luffing, that she is (for her) only a bare close-hauled, and that it is the windward yacht that is bearing away. Such a dispute can only be settled in one way: the leeward yacht was in the position of the overtaking vessel, and should have kept clear of the yacht to windward. Therefore in all cases if the leeward yacht is head-reaching, and at the same time weathering, we think it is good policy for her to keep clear of the yacht she is likely to foul to windward. It will not do for the yacht to defer using a little weather helm until her weather quarter is so close under the bow of the yacht to windward that the fact of putting her helm up would have the effect of swinging her quarter on the bow of the other. The Y.R.A. decided cases according to this interpretation of the rules in 1895.

In connection with this head-reaching and weathering, the following case often occurs. We will suppose that two yachts have to fetch by two or more boards from the buoy, A., to some other mark. The boat, B., is the more weatherly of the two, but D., astern, got some free puffs and crossed ahead of B. at E., and tacked to port on the weather quarter of D. The leading boat, when the crossing took place at E. (Fig. 106), was undoubtedly D.; but B., being the more weatherly, and D. the faster, the pair rapidly converged, and the question as to which was the overtaking boat, and which had to give way arose. B., owing to her superior weatherliness, was the overtaking boat, and this would have been surely

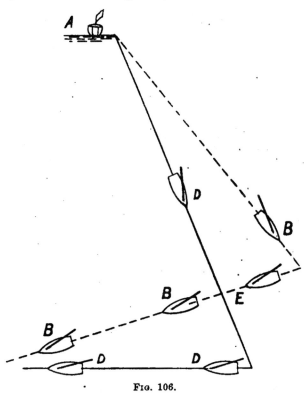

FIG. 106.

proved had the yachts been cross-tacking instead of working board and board. In deciding such a case, it should be considered that, if D. tacked, as shown, on the weather quarter of B., or on her weather beam or bow, B. would clearly come under the category of an overtaking vessel; and B. would be the yacht which had to give way.

The American yacht clubs have a converging rule, as follows :

When two yachts, both close hauled on the same tack, are converging, by reason of the leeward yacht holding a better wind, and neither can claim the rights of a yacht being overtaken, then the yacht to leeward shall keep clear.

s 2

If a yacht hangs under the lee bow of the one to windward, the latter would frequently do well to tack, as it is almost as bad to have a yacht close under the lee bow as on the weather bow.

HEAD-REACHING AND SAGGING TO LEEWARD.

But it may happen that the yacht which is to windward is head-reaching, although not holding so good a wind as the other; in such a case the yachts may converge, and the lee quarter of the windward yacht may be likely to foul the weather bow or bowsprit of the leeward yacht. In this case it will be the duty of the windward yacht to keep clear of the one to leeward, as she is in the condition of a yacht bearing away, and is the overtaking yacht and must keep clear of the other; and moreover, by the rule before referred to, a yacht in the position of the one to leeward, that is being overtaken, may luff as she pleases to prevent another passing to windward; and further, when two yachts have the wind on the same side, and if no question of overtaking is involved, the yacht which is to windward must keep clear of the other. The decision of the Y.R.A. on this point (see page 229) was in accordance with this exposition of the rules.

If the windward yacht has deferred luffing, or shaking up if necessary, until such time as the bowsprit end of the other is close to her lee quarter, it will be too late to luff, and a little weather helm will probably take the yachts clear. The leeward yacht will be pretty certain to have been well blanketed by the one to windward; her way will therefore be stopped, and the other, under the influence of her weather helm, will lift her stern to windward and forge clear.

If the yachts are not too close when the blanketing takes place, it is the practice for the helmsman of the leeward yacht to put the helm down as the sails begin to shake, and make a shoot to windward clear of the wash of the other; but care must be taken not to keep the vessel shooting so long as to lose her way, as she might get in irons.

When the leeward yacht is passed like this, it will be a good time to choose for getting a pull on any of the purchases that may require it.

The following case occurred in 1893 :

Three yachts cross the line at gunfire abreast, close-hauled; A. was about two lengths to windward of B., and B. about the same distance from C.

B., though travelling equally fast, is gradually sagging on to C.'s weather quarter. After travelling some time, it becomes evident that B. will have to luff or tack to prevent B. and C. soaking together. Meanwhile A. has maintained her position abreast of the other two; but, due either to making leeway or being sailed somewhat harder, has diminished the distance between herself and B.—say to one length. Can B. call upon A. to luff or tack ? If she can and A. should refuse, would A. be disqualified ?

The ruling was, that " A., the windward yacht, must keep clear, so B. could luff A. to avoid C." In this case the ultimate result would probably be that B. would fall astern of the other two.

SOAKING TOGETHER.

When two yachts are reaching along in close company, great care should be taken if sailing at a high rate of speed that they do not soak together. If the large hollow wave on the weather of the leeward yacht and the almost equally large wave under the lee of the windward yacht merge into one, the pair are bound to come together. A case like this occurred with the Kriemhilda and Fiona in the year 1873, and a similar case with Irex and Marjorie in 1886; both cases happened inside the Isle of Wight, off Osborne.

OVER-REACHING.

In beating to windward for a mark great care must be taken not to over-reach; that is, not to stand on so long as to be able to more than fetch a mark when the yacht is put about. In most cases a cutter yacht will fetch a mark (if not more than half a mile distant) on the next tack if the mark is brought to bear abeam—*i.e.*, at right angles to the keel, or eight compass-points from the direction of the vessel's head. This is supposing that there is no tide. If the tide be going to windward, so much need not be allowed; if the tide be going to leeward, more than eight points must be allowed. The helmsman, by watching his vessel and objects on shore or around on previous tacks, will be able to judge how much should be allowed for tide; and he should always remember that it is better to err by allowing too much than too little, providing of course that the vessel does not over-reach so much as to lose her position in the match.

Frequently when working across a lee-going tide it appears, when the yacht is put on her last board for the mark, that too much has been allowed for tide; this may or may not be the case, but great judgment should be exercised in ramping along, as not to fetch after over-reaching would be an error fatal to the reputation of a sailing master.

When working by long boards and a vessel tacks for her mark, say a mile off, and can just lie for it, she should be sailed along a good full and bye, and not be nipped or squeezed; if in the end she does not fetch, it cannot be helped, but it is certain that she will not have lost so much ground by having to tack again as she would by sailing out a long board with her sails lifting.

WEATHER BOWING.—BEARING AWAY.

A favourite pastime of a sailing master is to "weather bow" another vessel in working board and board to windward, or otherwise in cross tacking, that is in tacking to place his own vessel in such a position on the bow of the other that she immediately intercepts the wind of that other vessel, and causes her head sails to lift. If the vessels are pretty evenly matched, the leading one will be able to put the other under her lee quarter every time they tack. The one to leeward may ramp off, but she will never get clear unless she is a very much faster vessel. The object of the leeward yacht will be to get into cross tacking, and this her adversary will try to prevent, and tack as frequently as she does. This diversion may possibly be a bad thing for both, so far as the prize goes, if there are other yachts in the match, as their frequent tacking cannot be otherwise than a gain to the yachts which are working by longer boards.

If the leeward yacht finds that the one to windward will not permit her to get into cross tacking, she will probably, as aforesaid, ramp off and endeavour to get through the lee of the weather yacht. For the leeward yacht to do this successfully, that is, to be able to reach far enough ahead to tack across and weather the other one, she must be the faster vessel, or otherwise she will still find the other on her weather bow every time they tack. As the lee yacht is ramped off, the weather one is commonly sailed hard too, or what is known as a "good full." But the helmsman must be very careful with his weather helm, as the windward yacht is supposed to keep her luff, and is not allowed to bear away so as to prevent the other yacht passing to leeward; thus, the windward yacht should be kept no more than a "good full and bye" whilst another yacht is under her lee.

In speaking of "bearing away" it must not be assumed that the yachts get very much off the wind; if they did—say three or four points—the effect would be that the leeward yacht would come out clear ahead of the other. This is not the kind of "bearing away" which is practised. Strictly speaking the "bearing away" is simply sailing "ramping full," with a heavy hand on the weather tiller lines. It would be difficult to disqualify a yacht for this under the "bearing away" rule; but, nevertheless, if one yacht is sailing hard, when close hauled, to endeavour to get through the lee of the windward yacht, it would be most unfair for the other to ramp off after her.

A common practice to escape the vigilance of the "weather-bowing" craft is to make a feint at tacking, or, as it is sometimes called, to make a "false tack." The master sings out "ready about!" loud enough to be heard perhaps on board the windward yacht, and the crew go to their stations as if about to tack. The master eases the helm down, but is careful that the yacht does not get head to wind; he keeps her shooting, and one hand hauls the fore sheet up, and perhaps takes in the slack of the weather jib sheet. The master of the windward vessel thinks it is a real tack, and puts his vessel about; the other thereupon reverses his helm and fills off on the same tack again. This trick does not always succeed, but it does sometimes. In practising this subterfuge great care must be taken by the leeward yacht that she is not so close to the windward yacht as to bring about a collision by putting her helm down. If a collision ensued the leeward yacht would be held to blame.

In standing across another yacht with the intention of tacking, to give her a weather bower, great judgment must be exercised or the yacht may escape the intended blanketing. If the yacht *crosses* close ahead she must *tack* close ahead (a little to windward), and even then she may just miss getting on the weather bow of the other. The latter will know this, and instantly commence to ramp along and clear her wind; perhaps the next time she stays, if to starboard tack, she may be able to put about the one which offered her the weather bower.

If a yacht in standing across another is some three or four hundred yards to windward, and desires to weather bow her, the master must be careful not to stand too far, as if he does he will find himself on the weather beam of the other instead of weather bow when he stays. If the yacht crosses say ten lengths ahead, she should be tacked after she has passed clear three lengths; or, say when the other is seven lengths off her lee quarter. She will then be, allowing for the time or distance lost in tacking, exactly in her rival's wind.

A yacht that is head-reaching to windward of another yacht is frequently sailed hard so as to pass close on the weather of the other, as the "shake up" is effective in proportion to the closeness of the yachts to each other. This process of "killing" an antagonist was formerly very much practised; very few sailing masters now, however, ramp off after a vessel they are already beating by head-reaching. This insidious manner of giving a vessel weather helm is not perhaps "bearing away to hinder a yacht passing to leeward," as forbidden by the Y.R.A. rule; nor yet the bearing away which was sensibly forbidden by the old rule, which said, "a yacht may not bear away out of her course so as to cause another yacht to bear away to avoid a collision." It is a kind of jockeying which every helmsman very soon becomes acquainted with.

A great deal of time would be wasted by a sailing master attempting, by "weather bowing," to stop every vessel which came in his way, big or small; this would be very foolish. The first aim should be to get all the speed and advantage possible out of a vessel; secondly, if you come across a vessel that appears to have as good or better a chance of winning than yourself, endeavour to stop her by legitimate means, but do not needlessly waste time with a vessel that has little or no chance of winning; thirdly, if you are beating a vessel that, next to yourself, has the best chance of winning, by keeping with her, do not leave her; fourthly, if, when sticking to a vessel you are being beaten by her to windward, part company and try your fortune on a different cast, and get into cross tacking if you can.

BEFORE THE WIND UNDER SPINNAKER.

The crew ought to be able to rig and to have all the spinnaker gear ready in five minutes; thus in ordinary weather about that time should be allowed for getting the boom out and spinnaker halyards and outhaul bent, and shifting backstay aft, before bearing up round a mark. If it is to be a dead run, take care that the boom is on the right side, so that the vessel can be run for the next mark without gybing; allow for the tide, if any, scan the wind, and determine which side the spinnaker boom shall be on. If after bearing up it is found that a mistake has been made, and that the vessel will not run for the mark in consequence of the main boom being on the wrong quarter, do not try to make her and run by the lee. When running by the lee the mainsail will be doing little or no good, and, further, the main boom may come over suddenly and pull down the topmast by striking the preventer, or break itself on the runner. Haul up to windward a little, and fill the mainsail; but if it involves hauling up more than a point, and the "run" be a long one, gybe over at once and run straight for the mark.*

If the boom has to go square off, ease up the topsail sheet a little if the topsail tack is to windward of the gaff, and ease the topsail lacing and tack too, if it strains badly across the peak-halyard blocks. If the peak of the mainsail falls aboard, ease the peak purchase a trifle, but not until after the topsail sheet has been eased, as the sudden strain thrown on the after leech and sheet of the topsail might cause something to burst. Take in the slack of the weather topping-lift before easing up the peak purchase, or the boom may come down on the rail.

* If the run be 12 miles, and the vessel haul up a point and run, say, on port tack for half the distance, and then gybe over and run on the other tack, she will increase her distance to 12¼ miles.

The weather topping lift should always carry the weight of the boom in running or reaching with the boom broad off. In a sea the boom should be topped up three or four feet, so as not to strike more than the mere top of the combers.

Be careful, if there be much weight in the wind, not to ease the boom off so far as to allow the gaff to press heavily on the lee rigging, as the jaws of the gaff might thereby be broken.

In strong winds the small spinnaker only should be boomed out. and if the boom rears on end, the tendency can be checked by giving sheet as the boom commences to rear; also by pressing the boom down, but the boom should not be stopped down with a rope, as it is certain to break. Frequently when the topmast is housed the second spinnaker is boomed out with a Spanish reef in the head; *i.e.*, the head of the sail made into a bight, and the halyards bent to it; or sometimes the head of the sail is tied up in a knot.

In heavy weather it will not be prudent to run with the boom square off, nor to run dead before the wind; keep a little to windward of the course, and then gybe over and run for the mark on the other tack.

With the weight of the boom and spinnaker boom shifted forward the vessel will go down by the head, and if she does not like the trim the crew should be placed abaft the tiller lines or on the quarter deck.

If the run be a dead one, the helmsman will have two objects in view: 1. To run straight for the mark, or at least try to make the mark without having to gybe. 2. In endeavouring to carry out the first object the second aim will be to be careful that the mainsail is not gybed through getting by the lee. To accomplish these ends an average course will have to be made by running off when the wind will permit, and drawing to again as the wind shows a tendency to draw on the lee quarter.

GYBING ALL STANDING.

The helmsman has already been warned against running the risk of "gybing all standing" when before the wind, if by the lee, or caught by the lee, or through carelessness. Most serious consequences might ensue, and if the main boom once begins to get steam on in coming over, nothing will stop it until brought up by the preventer backstay, or what was the lee runner. It would be useless putting the helm down, but after the accident every care should be taken to steady the vessel.

Many accidents have happened through getting by the lee and gybing all standing, and the consequences may be fatal, especially if the mainsail is not laced to the boom. In the year 1871, during the regatta of the

Royal Harwich Yacht Club, the Volante "gybed all standing," and the boom broke against the runner. The aft end flew to windward and pinned a man on the rail, clean through his chest, killing him instantly.

ROUNDING MARKS.

In running for a mark to haul round, it is generally prudent (if not hauling against a foul tide) to keep well to leeward of the mark, and haul up gradually to it, so that by the time the mark is reached all the sheets are flattened in; in fact, the vessel should be almost "brought to" by the mere hauling aft the sheets, and with as little helm as possible. If the yacht has to be "brought to" against the tide, only a short sweep should be made in rounding; but the sheets must be got aft smartly, so that when the vessel is actually rounding the mark they are properly trimmed. This is particularly necessary if the yacht has to be brought by the wind, as, otherwise, when the helm is put down she will not come to quickly, and a yacht that may be astern could, by a better hauling of her sheets, come up and cut her out.

If the mark has to be gybed round and the wind is light, the yacht should be run dead for the mark, and should gybe close at the mark, always allowing for tide. The boom can be handled easily, and the shorter the circle the vessel can be turned in, the better. But if there is a strong wind, and an attempt is made to make a short turn by wearing close round the mark, it will probably end in disappointment or disaster. Instead of attempting a short turn, the vessel should haul up to windward of her course a little, and gybe over when one hundred yards or so from the mark; there will then be time to trim the sheets properly, and the vessel will not overshoot the mark nor lose any ground. When a vessel is judiciously rounding a mark like this, she may find one ahead that has attempted to make a short turn of it by gybing at the mark, more or less "all standing." This vessel, before she can be met with her helm, will probably fly to; so look out and go under her stern, if there is room to do so without striking her, and then through her lee. If an attempt is made to keep on her weather, a luffing match will be the result; or perhaps a disastrous collision, as your vessel that gybed first will have great way on, whilst the other, gybing and then flying to, would have almost stopped dead. If a collision under such circumstances did occur, the overtaking yacht would be held to blame, as, although it might have been a lubberly thing to have allowed the leading vessel to fly across the one that was coming up astern, still the latter, being the overtaking yacht, would have to keep clear. Therefore keep a sharp look-out, and, as before said, if there be room, go under the other vessel's stern, and you certainly will be able to get through her lee. If there be not room to so go under her stern, be ready to give lee helm if necessary to clear her to windward, and you probably will succeed in passing her.

In gybing always be smart with the topmast shifting backstays and the runners; get them hauled taut before the boom actually goes over, and let go the weather backstay and runner as the boom comes amidships.

If, when sailing pretty nearly close-hauled, the mark has to be rounded short by wearing or gybing, so as to return on a parallel course, the rounding will be an awkward one. If there is much wind it will be prudent to keep well to windward of the mark. Begin to bear up when a hundred yards or so away from it, easing the main sheet a little, and mizen sheet if it is a yawl, but not touching the head sheets; then as the yacht is nearly close to the mark hard up; as the vessel wears round to nearly before the wind, steady the helm and let the boom go over as easily as possible. Be careful not to ease too much main sheet; steady the helm directly it is seen that the vessel has had enough to bring the boom over. The object will be to turn the vessel slowly at first, making a long sweep; then quickly, and then slowly again at the last. In bearing up round a mark in this way care must be taken that neither the boom nor any of the lee rigging touches the markboat; and if the markboat is flying a large flag, be careful not to touch it, as although merely touching such a flag might not be held to be a foul, still there would be the risk of the flag getting hung up in some of the yacht's gear, and this would be considered a foul; and, moreover, in such a case the mark boat itself might be dragged alongside.

In rounding markboats in a strong wind or tide way care should be taken to take plenty of room, so that the keel does not foul the mooring chain of the markboat, if it be stretched out taut and straight. If the chain were touched it would probably bring the markboat alongside, and such a foul would involve disqualification under Rule 24, which enjoins that a yacht must not foul a mark, nor cause one to shift its position.

SETTING UP THE SAILS.

As a hauling mark is approached always get the sails well set for coming on the wind. Anything that requires setting up should be attended to before the mark is reached. If a jib requires shifting, do not forget that it can be done more easily whilst before the wind than on the wind. Very frequently a vessel is run off the wind on purpose to get in the jib; but this can only be done at a great loss of distance.

Sails will require frequent "setting" during a match, and a sharp look round must be taken constantly, especially when coming to wind from sailing off the wind. Before getting a pull on the topsail tack do not forget to ease the sheet first; and also see if the topmast requires staying forward. In setting up the peak of a mainsail always take the weight of the boom with the topping lift. In setting up a jib always see that the runners are taut.

RUNNING ASHORE.

In sailing along a weather shore, if the yacht drags the ground, promptly ease off the boom and put the helm up, and send all hands forward. The boom is run off to give the vessel greater list, so as to lighten her draught, and also to prevent her coming to, and so forge further aground. The object of sending the men forward is, that by tripping the vessel by the head, the draught is lessened. If the vessel drags whilst running along a lee shore, haul the boom in and put the helm down.

If other efforts fail run a kedge out broad on the weather bow, or aft a little over the weather quarter.

CHAPTER X.

CENTRE-BOARD BOATS.

THE centre-board, it appears, was invented, or rather adapted, from some
form of lee-board by Captain Schank, of the British Navy, some time prior to
1771. We have not come across any contemporary record of the invention,
but in Charnock's "History of Marine Architecture," published in 1802, the

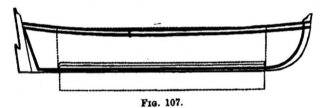

FIG. 107.

fact is alluded to, together with a description of a boat with a sliding
keel built by Captain Schank at Boston, Massachusetts, in 1771, for Earl
Percy (afterwards Duke of Northumberland). The engraving (Fig. 107)
represents this boat, and, so far as we know, is the oldest authentic

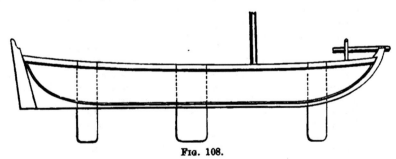

FIG. 108.

record of the sliding keel. At about the same time Captain Schank was
very strongly urging the English Government to cease building deep ships,
and to build shallow ones, fitted with one or more sliding keels. The
Admiralty were not, however, to be persuaded into such a startling revolu-

tion in naval architecture; still they so far humoured Captain Schank, that in 1789 a boat was built and fitted at Deptford Dockyard with three boards, according to the plan shown in the engraving (Fig. 108).* The use of the three boards was as follows : In tacking, or laying to, the centre-board and after board were raised; in wearing the centre-board and fore-board were raised; also in scudding the centre-board and fore-board were raised; going over shallows the three boards were raised. On a wind the three boards were lowered, each to such depth as seemed best to balance the sails. The report of the trials made with this boat seem to have very favourably impressed the Admiralty, and Captain Schank was instructed to design a cutter of 60ft. length and 20ft. beam, with three sliding keels. She had a midship section something like a barge, and a draught of water of 6ft. 6in., and was named the "Trial." In an elaborate report she was claimed to be a good sea boat, and very handy; but two other vessels with centre-boards, named the Lady Nelson and Cynthia, were less favourably reported upon, and the Admiralty, we believe, built no more centre-board ships. So far as we were concerned, the sliding keel was lost sight of until the visit of the America in 1851 drew attention

* In 1889 a gentleman, who resides in Formosa, sent me a model of a surf sailing-boat used by the natives of that island at Tai-Wan-Foo. The boat is called Tek-pai and Chu-pai (the latter Mandarin), "Tek" or "Chu" meaning bamboo, and "pai" platform or tray. The boat consists of a number of bamboos lashed together as a raft, and curved somewhat like a butcher's tray. It has three movable centre-boards (like those shown in Fig. 108), which are pushed down between the bamboos, and shifted about as the sailing or management of the boat requires. A tub in which the passengers sit, is lashed just abaft the mast. The mat is used as a weather screen to keep off spray. There is no doubt that this method of using the centre-board was that which gave Capt. Schank the idea of utilising it for deep bodied vessels, as recorded in Charnock's "History of Marine Architecture." The *European Magazine* for 1792, in discussing Capt. Schank's "invention" of the three sliding keels, as fitted to H.M.S. Trial, Lady Nelson, &c., says : "If the discovery of the sliding keels is great, the public are indebted for it to the Indians of South America, whose balsas, described in Ulloa's voyage (A.D. 1735), have these sliding keels; and from these the idea has been taken and very ingeniously improved upon." But these sliding keels of the Indians were seen by Pizarro two centuries earlier (A.D. 1535) In Prescott's "History of the Conquest of Peru," we read : "As he (Pizarro) drew near, he found it was a large vessel, or rather raft, called balsas, consisting of a number of huge timbers of a light porous wood, tightly lashed together, with a frail flooring of reeds raised on them by way of deck. Two masts or sturdy poles erected in the middle of the vessel sustained a large square sail of cotton; while a rude kind of rudder, and a movable keel made of plank and inserted between the logs, enabled the mariner to give a direction to the floating fabric, which held on its course without the aid of oar or paddle." Whether a Chinese raft got blown to Peru, or whether a Peruvian log-raft got blown to China, and so communicated the idea, cannot now be determined, but there is no doubt that the British have no more claim to the actual invention of the sliding keel or centre board than any of the United States citizens have. Capt. Schank, it is evident, as remarked in the *European Magazine*, merely adapted the South American sliding keels to the hulls of deep sea-going vessels; whilst Capt. Shuldham, of the English Navy, further improved on the adaption in 1809 by pivoting the board at one corner, and it was for the first time then termed a revolving keel. It is also worthy of note that Evelyn in his diary (November, 1622) records that Sir William Petty invented a "vertical keel hung on hinges for the improvement of the sailing of ships."

to it. Not that the America had a centre-board, but other American yachts had, and Englishmen about this time became much interested about Transatlantic naval architecture.

The "centre-board" of America was, however, the "revolving keel" invented by Capt. Shuldham (also of the British Navy), and, instead of being dropped equally fore and aft, was pivoted at the fore-end, as shown in the sketch below.

Capt. Shuldham devised his pivoted board plate whilst a prisoner of war at Verdun, in 1809, and made a model of a boat with the plate fitted. The plate was of lead, and, so far as shape goes, there it differs little from

Fig. 109.

the triangular plates of the present day. The model made by Capt. Shuldham at Verdun was deposited in the museum at Ipswich about the year 1820, and is still there. On Plate XIV. is an outline sketch of the model.

The small centre-board American sloop Truant was brought over here in 1853, and, although only 20ft. on the water line and 1ft. 2in. draught, beat all the crack 7-tonners in the Prince of Wales' Yacht Club a quarter of an hour in a thrash from Blackwall to Northfleet in a nice breeze, and was very roundly abused for her success. All sorts of stories were current about her shifting ballast, and that her crew had their pockets filled with lead shot ! After this success Truant went to the Mersey and Lake

Windermere, but what ultimately became of her we do not know.   Her rig
was as shown in the accompanying drawing (Fig. 110), and is the same as

Fig. 110.

the fashionable sloop of the present day, excepting that the foresail or jib is
laced to a foot yard, and tacked at about one-fifth its length from the outer
end of the yard on a bumpkin.

The Una was the next importation to this country from America, and,
although generally resembling the Truant in hull, differed in sail plan, as
the mast was stepped farther forward, and she had no headsail whatever.

The double centre-board was much advocated in America in 1871, but
we believe that no large yacht was built on the plan.   However, in 1876
the idea occurred to Mr. W. Jeans, of Christchurch, to have a small craft

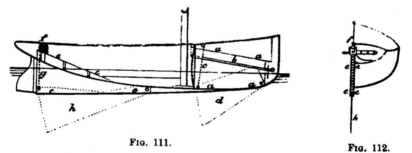

Fig. 111.   Fig. 112.

provided with two boards, and he published the following description of the
boat and drawing (*see* Figs. 111 and 112):

The letters *a a a a*, show the fore trunk; *b*, lever; *c*, chain; *d*, keel; *e*,
aft trunk; *f*, wheel; *s*, chain; *h*, aft keel.

The fore keel has its trunk in the cuddy. The trunk of the aft keel is the dead wood in the run of the boat. The keel is lifted by a small wheel and winch, the wheel being large enough to take up the chain in one turn without overlapping, a dog catching it at any required depth. Since the date given two centre plates have often been fitted to sailing canoes.

The advantages of the two boards would be similar to those claimed by Capt. Schank for his three boards, as follows: The keels take up no room in the body of the boat; they can be regulated to carry any kind of helm. By lifting up the fore keel in wearing the boat is much sooner round. If there is a doubt of her not coming about in a seaway, wind up the aft keel, when she will immediately shoot into the wind, dropping the board again as soon as she fills on the other tack.

Perhaps the two boards may be found useful under exceptional circumstances, but the single centre-board is much to be preferred. A boat fitted with a single board will be more sensitive to slight alterations of her helm, and generally will be more agreeable to sail on a wind; and, although she may be knocked off occasionally by combers on the bow, yet will she spring to more readily than if she had such an unusual amount of gripe as a board under the fore foot would give. The strongest reason for having two boards would be in the case of a shallow vessel which had to keep the sea, and might have to scud in very disturbed water and generally to encounter heavy weather. However, a yacht of the deep type, with fixed keel, would be better adapted for such work.

As a rule the centre of area of the board should be in the same vertical line as the centre of effort of the sails, unless the centre of lateral resistance shows a very great departure from the centre of effort, when the board may be used to adjust the centres.

There is no doubt that where a boat has to be of shallow draught, so that an effective area for lateral resistance cannot be obtained by a fixed keel, a centre-board or shifting keel of some form or other is a most valuable contrivance; and in the case where there is no restriction on beam, as, for instance, in the " Y.R.A. classes," the centre-board might be of value. Since 1888 the contrivance has been permitted by the Y.R.A., but the draught of water has not been much reduced when a small centre plate has been fitted and worked through the lead keel, and not showing above the cabin floor. The gain in weatherliness to these deep keel boats has not been apparent; and if there was any gain at all it was only whilst working against a foul tide.

T

It has been found that a board with a long leading edge of the dagger type is more effective than a short edge and great surface. (*See* the Sorceress centre plate 1-rater; also "Yacht Architecture," page 76.)

A belief sometimes exists that a centre-board adds to the stability of a boat: so it does if made of iron or other metal, just the same as an iron or other metal keel would; but if the material be wood not heavier than water, the tendency of the board would be to upset the boat, as the wood would strive to come to the surface, or, in other words, to float: thus, the larger a wood board were made, and the deeper it were lowered, the more urgent would be its tendency to assist in upsetting a boat. A board, however, causes the process of heeling to be a little more slowly performed,

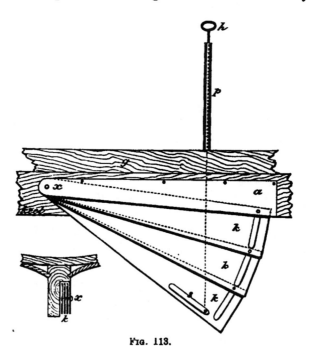

Fig. 113.

as the board has to be moved through water, and the resistance to the board being so moved is of the same nature as the resistance of the water to any plane moved in it. Thus, when a boat is once permanently heeled, or has settled down on "her bearings," as it is termed, the board will be of no more use for stability, as its tendency will be to float or come to the surface. If the boat is struck by a squall which only lasts, say, four or five seconds, the board may possibly prevent an upset that otherwise would take place; but if the squall continues, and is of a strength to upset the boat without the board, the boat will be assuredly upset with the board, only it may take two or three seconds longer to do so.

Numerous contrivances have been suggested to obviate the inside housing of the board and one practical plan proposed consisted of a single plate of iron pivoted at the fore end, and stowed, when hauled up, on one side of the keel. An extension of this plan by adding to the plates and forming them into a kind of fan has been adopted both in this country and in America. The plan will be found illustrated by Fig. 113. The leaves of the fan are pivoted to the side of the keel at *x*. The keel

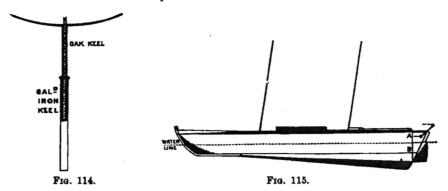

Fig. 114.   Fig. 115.

is cut away, and a plate, *a*, bolted over the chamber, so as to form a kind of box or case to take all the leaves when the fan is shut. See the small sketch. The leaves *k*, *k*, *k*, are connected at their after ends by studs and slots. The fan is closed by a bar, working in a pipe *p*, as shown. The bar is attached to the lower leaf by a stud, which works in a fore and aft slot, *s*. The lifting bar should be jointed, so that when the fan is closed, the handle part, *h*, will fold down by the side of the pipe. The slots should be cut wide enough to insure the studs working

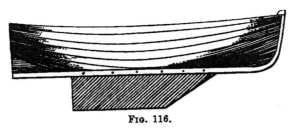

Fig. 116.

easily in them. The heads of the studs should be thin, and the edges nicely bevelled off. The number of leaves could be of course increased, but two would in most cases be probably found sufficient and less liable to get locked or jammed.

In 1870 a boat was built by Messenger, and called Wideawake, with a kind of shoe keel. The boat or rather canoe was 15ft. 10in. long, and 3ft. 2in. beam, depth, gunwale to keel, 1ft. 4in. She had an oak keel increasing in depth from 2in. forward, to 6in. aft. To this keel was fitted a hollow galvanised keel—a kind of case, in fact, to take the oak keel—12ft. long, made of ½in. iron (*see* Fig. 114). The keel was pivoted forward 4ft. from the stem plumb to load line. Care was taken to make the iron case fit the oak keel. The case was raised by a wire fastened to the stern end of the case, and passing through a tube as shown by A B, Fig. 115. The wire passed over a pulley on deck and was secured at mainmast. The keel weighed 28lb.

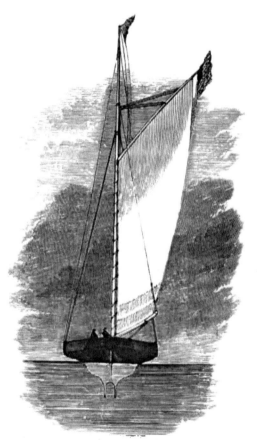

Fig. 117.

A better plan than the shoe keel was fitted in 1874 in a small boat, Robin Hood, by Searle, for Sir W. B. Forwood. She had an oak keel 5in. deep, in the under side of which a slot 9ft. long and 3in. deep was cut; into this slot a galvanised iron plate ½in. thick, 9ft. long, and 3in. deep was fitted. It was raised and lowered by a rod at each end, working in upright lead pipes. (For other plans for centre-boards see the articles "Centre-board" and "Lee-board" in the Appendix.)

Occasionally a boat is met with which has a fixed centre-plate or fin of iron (*see* Fig. 116). The plate is let into a slot in the wood keel, and held in position by screwed bolts with nuts counter sunk. Fin keels and fin bulb keels are now often fitted in this way in the smaller classes ; in 1885 the author pointed out in this work that there is no reason why the usual piece of wood false keel should be fitted at the fore end and aft end of any yacht ; and without it a considerable saving would be made in immersed surface. Four or five years later the fin keel became common in the classes of 5-rating and under.

Among the many curious contrivances to prevent leeway, one exhibited at the Exhibition of 1851 is as strange as any. The designer's idea appears to have been, that to obtain the greatest advantage in the way of stability, a yacht should be very broad and big above water, and very narrow and small under it (*see* Fig. 117) ; and that to get a large amount of lateral resistance, two keels should be had instead of one shaped longitudinally as shown by Fig. 118.

So far as the question of stability is concerned, we need scarcely say

FIG. 118.

more than that it would be much increased if the greatest beam were put on the water line ; but as the idea of parallel keels is continually cropping up, it may be well to point out that they cannot be of any advantage. In the first place, there is an extra surface for friction provided by the doubling of the keels, and as surface friction enters so largely into the aggregate resistance of a vessel double keels should be condemned for this reason alone. Secondly, the actual increase in the lateral resistance would be only a very small percentage of the added surface, as the water would practically be locked up between the two keels, and so really out of the four sides of the keels, only one side (the leeward one of the leeward keel) would meet with lateral resistance.

Among many other contrivances, the time-honoured lee-board may be mentioned, and the "horizontal keel," swinging keel, &c., descriptions of which will be found in the Appendix.

CHAPTER XI.

CENTRE-BOARD BOATS FOR ROWING AND SAILING.

ALTHOUGH it may be difficult to say what is a boat and what is a yacht, when we are speaking of small craft, yet we think a great deal of this difficulty will be removed if we define a boat to mean a vessel which is not wholly decked, and that can be rowed. In selecting one of these craft that is either open or partly open, the main guide, of course, will be the locality. Thus, if the boat is for Brighton, one of the shallow centre-board beach boats used thereat will be the most suitable, inasmuch as they can be readily "beached" or hauled out of water, it being necessary that they should be so hauled up, as there is no sheltered or safe anchorage at Brighton. For the Thames above bridge, where the winds are light and baffling, a very light centre-board gig is the most useful, as it sails well in light winds, and is easily rowed in calms. On the Mersey, where the boats can lie afloat, and where generally there is more wind and sea than any ordinary boat could well tackle, a heavier and deep keel sailing boat is in use. At the same time, a keel boat quite as light as the Surbiton boats has been introduced on the Mersey; but, in order that they may safely encounter the rough water, are nearly wholly decked in. On the south coast all sorts of sailing boats are to be met with, from the old-fashioned skiff and wherry to very many versions of the Itchen boat.

The boat most generally in request on the Thames is the one for "rowing and sailing," or centre-board gig. This boat, for the man who likes the exercise of rowing and the pleasure of dodging a wind between the banks of a river, is admirably contrived. But he who has one need be content to limit his cruises to the water upon which she was intended to sail, until he has become a perfect master of the art of boat sailing. He should not be tempted into "cruises" down the river to Sea Reach, to Sheerness, Leigh, or Shoeburyness, as he may be "caught" in a nor'-wester; and then, if he has only been used to open-boat sailing in smooth water, and to very little of that, it may go hard with him. He will find it

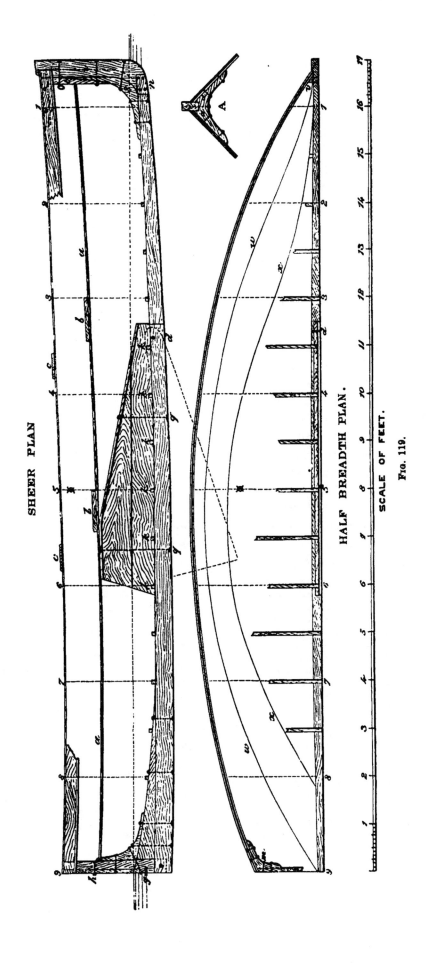

SHEER PLAN

HALF BREADTH PLAN.

SCALE OF FEET.

Fig. 119.

impossible, even supposing he can reef down and so far handle his craft as to tack her, to get to windward against a lee tide and yeasty sea; and the probability is that, even if the tide be a weather-going one, the sea will be so bad that she will be blown farther to leeward every tack than the tide will carry her to windward. Under these conditions there will be no alternative but to "up helm" and run for it; and, as it may be no more practicable to get into Sheerness than up Sea Reach, the situation of the "outward bound" boat sailer would be decidedly unenviable. Why not put her head to the sea and row her? she is a boat for rowing and sailing. Well, a man cannot row a boat head to sea and wind with much success, and the need of doing so would be a rather severe argument against the sailing qualities of the boat. Then rig and throw overboard a floating anchor, ride to that, and wait till the turn of the tide. Very capital advice, and an old hand might do it, but not a frightened novice. The broad truth is, that a light centre-board gig, easy to row, and not an indifferent performer under canvas in smooth water, is not fit for open water where there might be a real sea—as different to the "magnificent furrows" of up-river as a chalk-pit is to a fox-hole; and even in the hands of a skilled boat sailer, such as a coast waterman, they would be out of place in Sea Reach under canvas.

The annexed diagrams (Figs. 119 and 120) show a design by the author of this work for a centre-board gig which has been largely built from for river, lake, and coast work. The boats proved to be fast sailers, and very light to row. The drawing is made to half-inch scale; but, as it is rather small to work from, the table which follows can be referred to in laying off.*

* Full instructions for laying off will be found in "Yacht Architecture," but a brief outline of what has to be done can be given here. In the first place, the stem, keel, dead-wood, and sternpost should be laid off full size; if a floor cannot be obtained long enough to lay the keel off in one piece, it can be divided in two or three pieces; or a floor can be improvised by placing a sufficient number of deals or planks together, both for the keel and body plan. When the floor is prepared, strike in the load water-line with a chalk line or straight edge; then, at right angles on either side of this line, set off by aid of an L square all the sections 1, 2, 3, 4, &c. On each section mark off the distance from the load water-line to the top of the keel; and from the top of the keel to its under side. Place a batten (made of inch fir or American elm) over these marks or "spots," as they are called, and chalk in the shape of the keel. The batten can be kept in its place by a nail on either side of each spot. (Of course if the keel has no curve it can be laid off by a simple straight edge or chalk line.) The rounding up of the fore-foot can be obtained by putting in a couple of lines between No. 1 station and the fore-side of the stem, at right angles to the load water-line, and transferring the distances measured on these lines from the sheer plan to the floor. A mould out of a piece of half-inch fir can be made from the drawing on the floor, including stem, dead wood, and sternpost; but if the keel is to be cut out of a piece of American elm ten or twelve inches deep, then it can be laid off on the timber, striking the load water-line (or a line parallel to it) and sections as described. The remaining portion of the timber can be sawn into floors, &c. The body plan will be laid off by simply transferring the drawing from the paper to the floor. First, the load water-line w will be put in; then the middle vertical line o, and the perpendiculars p p; the base line m will follow;

The references to the body plan (Fig. 120) are as under: *w* is the load water-line (L.W.L.); *a a* 1 and *a a* 2; *b b* 1 and *b b* 2; *c c* 1 and *c c* 2 are "diagonals;" *o* is the middle vertical line, from which all distances are measured; *p p* are perpendiculars denoting the extreme breadth; *m m* is a kind of base line 10in. below the load water-line, and parallel thereto; *z* is a water-line.

The numerals 1, 2, 3, 4, &c., denote the respective sections or timbers, and their stations in the sheer plan and half-breadth plan. No. 9 is the "transom," and of course will be a solid piece of wood, and not a "frame."

LAYING OFF TABLE (FIGS. 116 AND 117).

Nos. of Sections.	1		2		3		4		5		6		7		8		9	
Sheer Plan and Half-breadth Plan.	ft.	in.	ft.	in.	ft.	in.	ft.	in.	ft.	in.	ft.	in.	ft.	in.	ft.	in.	ft.	in.
Heights above L.W.L. to top of gunwale	1	10¾	1	9¼	1	8¼	1	7¾	1	6¼	1	5¾	1	5¾	1	6	1	6½
Depths below load water-line to top of keel	0	2	0	3⅜	0	4¼	0	5	0	5¾	0	5¾	0	5½	0	5¼*	0	5
Depth of keel	0	3	0	3¼	0	3½	0	3¾	0	4	0	4	0	4	0	4	0	4
Half breadths at gunwale	0	7	1	6½	2	2	2	7	2	9	2	8½	2	6	2	1	1	5½
Half breadths at L.W.L.	0	2¾	0	11¾	1	8½	2	3	2	5½	2	5¼	2	0½	1	3½	0	1¼
Body Plan.																		
Diagonal *a*	0	3¾	0	10¼	1	2¼	1	4½	1	6½	1	6¼	1	4¼	0	11¼	0	3
" *b*	0	6½	1	6	2	1½	2	5½	2	7¾	2	7¼	2	4¼	1	10¾	1	0¼
" *c*	0	9	1	11	2	7½	3	0½	3	2¾	3	2¼	2	11½	2	6	1	9

and then the diagonals *a*, *b*, *c*. The distances given for No. 1 section will be taken from the table and set off on the diagonals *a*, *b*, *c*, each distance to be marked by a "spot" or small cross on the diagonal; the *height* of the section from the load water-line to the gunwale, and the *depth* from the load water-line to the top of the keel, will be taken from the table or from the sheer plan; the *half breadth* of the section at the gunwale, and at the load water-line, will be taken from the table or from the half-breadth plan. All the "spots" having been put on the diagonals, and on the water-line, and at the point representing the gunwale height and half breadth, a batten will be placed over the "spots," and its shape chalked in. The batten should be about 6ft. long, ¾in. deep, and from ⅛in. to $\frac{3}{16}$in. thick. The batten will be kept to the "spots" by nails on either side of the batten, not through it. If the curve be unfair, the nails must be slightly shifted until the curve shows fair. If great accuracy is needed, the diagonals can be laid off in long lines to represent a half-breadth plan to further fair the design; this, however, will be scarcely necessary. Moulds will be made to represent each half section; but the midship mould and two others, Nos. 3 and 7, should be a whole one. The moulds can be made from rough ⅝in. deal. A piece 2in. wide will represent the middle line *o*, and the curved parts will be nailed together as required, and fitted with saw, plane, or spokeshave to the lines on the floor. The load water-line must be carefully marked on each mould, both on the perpendicular (*o*) and on the curve. Having got the building blocks in readiness, set up a line by the aid of a spirit level, at a convenient height above them, to represent the load water-line—a straight edge would do. Put the keel on the blocks, and wedge it up until into its proper position with the load water-line. Then, having got the stem and sternpost into position, fix the representative load water-line to them inside, from the aft side of stem to fore side of stern post. A chalk line should be struck up the centre of both stem and sternpost. The transom and the "full" moulds will then be adjusted and fixed at their proper stations by ribbands. Presuming the rabbets to have been cut, the planking can be proceeded with, and the floors and timbers fastened in as the planking proceeds. The ribbands will be removed as the planking requires.

* Depth to top of dead wood, 3¾in.

The distance *a* (Fig. 120), above the load water-line, *w*, is 3½in. measured on the vertical line *o*. The distances *a* 1 and *a* 2 from the vertical line *o*, measured along the horizontal line *m*, are 2ft. 3½in.

The distance *b*, above the load water-line (*w*), is 1ft.; *b* cuts the perpendicular *p* at *b* 1 and *b* 2, 2in. below the load water-line *w*.

The distance *c*, above the load water-line *w*, is 2ft. 2in.; and *c* cuts the perpendicular *p* at *c* 1 and *c* 2, 3¾in. above the load water-line *w*.

x is a water-line struck 3in. below *w*, but will be of no assistance in laying off, as it does not intersect the frames sufficiently at right angles.

All the half-breadths, and the distances measured from the middle vertical line *o* along the diagonals to the various sections (as given in the

BODY PLAN.   OF FIG. 119.

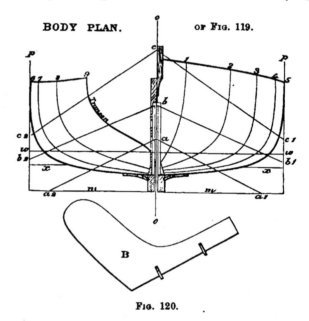

FIG. 120.

tables), are *without* the plank; so in laying off *no allowance* will have to be made for the thickness of the plank.

The length of the boat is 17ft., and the breadth 5ft. 6in., and the extreme breadth, with the plank on, 5ft. 7½in. Weight of displacement of boat to L.W.L. about 12cwt.

The sections 1, 2, 3, 4, &c., are 2ft. apart, and No. 1 is 1ft. from the fore side of the stem at the L.W.L.

The frames actually will only be 1ft. apart; but every other one is left out in the Body Plan.

The scantling of the boat will be as follows: Keel, sided (thick) amidships 4½in., tapering gradually to 2½in. forward, and 3½in. aft. The moulded depth of the keel will be found in the table.

Stem, 2¼in. sided; 4½in. moulded (*i.e.*, its fore and aft thickness) at head, and 5½in. at knee scarph.

Sternpost, 3in. sided and moulded at heel; 2in. moulded at head.

Floors, ¾in. sided and 2in. moulded (deep) at heels, the moulding gradually tapering to ¾in. at heads. The floors will be joggled to sink ¼in. across the keel. Timbers at the sides of and above the floors, ¾in. square.

Plank, ¼in. thick. Gunwales, 1in. thick, 1¼in. deep.

Stringers (lettered *a* in the Sheer Plan) 1in. square, fastened through timber and plank. Seats and rowlocks as at *b b c c*.

The centre-board or plate will be 5ft. 4in. long, pinned or pivotted in the keel below the garboard strakes, as shown in the Sheer Plan and Half-breadth Plan (Fig. 119) at *d*, 5ft. 9in. from fore side of the stem at L.W.L. The slot in the keel to admit the plate will be 5ft. 7in. long by ⅜in. in width. The floors where this slot comes will have to be cut through. The heels of these floors will be fitted with ½in. jogs, and let in to the under side of the centre-plate case, as shown at *k k k k k k* in the Sheer Plan. One 4in. copper nail through each heel (outside the centre-plate case) will be sufficient to fasten these floors to the keel. (The case must be very carefully fitted to the shape of the keel, and luted with white lead or strip of canvas saturated in thick varnish.) The centre-plate case will be fastened through the keel by long galvanised iron (¼in.) bolts, from three to four bolts being on each side, and one not more than 6in. from each end. The bolts will have heads and be rivetted up on the under side on rings. The case will be made of inch pine, and the ends will be rabbeted into the sides and through fastened; the plate of ⅜in. iron. *

Sometimes the case has been made of galvanised iron, and fitted into the slot. With such cases it will be best to fit a keelson over the heels of the floor, as at *k k*, &c., on either side of the case. These keelsons would require to be about 3in. deep and 2in. broad, with one fastening between each pair of floors. However, as a rule, no such keelson is fitted, a couple of screws or nails in each heel of the floor being considered sufficient. The case would be prevented dropping through the slot in the keel by two small iron knees on either side, riveted to the case and fastened to the keelson.

The following plan has been adopted in fitting a galvanised iron

---

* If the sides of the case have to be in two pieces, put the broader piece obtainable for the lower portion, and the narrower at the upper side. The wood should be free of shakes and knots. In boring the planks through from edge to edge with a long gimlet or augur like that used by bellhangers, place the plank in a horizontal position. A straight edge should be laid on the plank occasionally, to test the directness of the gimlet by bringing the straight edge over it, and observing whether the stem of the gimlet is parallel with the straight edge.

centre-board case. *a* (*see* sketch A, Fig. 121) is the iron case, passing through a slot in the keel and flanged up underneath as at *c*. Over these flanges, *c*, an iron keel-band is fitted, as at *s* in Fig. A; and *s* in Fig. B shows the under side of this keel-band. There are bolts through the keel-band, the flanges, and the wood keel, the bolts being set up on the top of the keel with washer and nut, as at *o o*. (The keel-band and flanges are

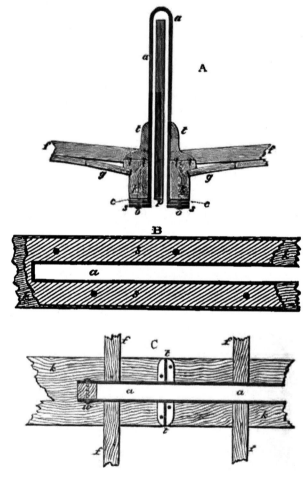

Fig. 121.

shown a little apart for the sake of distinctness; of course, in setting up the bolts all would be drawn close together.) Two small T angle-iron knees are fitted each side of the case (*a*), riveted through the case and screwed down to the keel *k*, as at *t t*, with coach screws. The ends of the angle irons are rounded off as shown. Without these knees the case is likely to get wrenched on one side or the other unless well secured to a thwart. To prevent leakage, a piece of canvas doubled, and well luted with Stockholm tar or varnish, should be laid in the angle of the flanges of the case before screwing it up with the keel-band. The latter can be made of ½in., 1in., or even thicker iron, as it will serve as outside ballast.

Fig. C shows a view of the case and its fittings, looking down from the inside of the boat; *a* is the inside of the case; *k* the keel; *t* the iron knees; *f f* two floors. *w* is a piece of wood forming one end of the case, and through-bolted or screwed up, as shown, with luted canvas between.

The dead wood, knee, and sternpost aft will be through-fastened, as shown in the Sheer Plan; and the sternpost should be tenoned into the keel. At the fore end the keel and stem will be box-scarphed into each other, and through-bolted, as at *n*. The apron (*s* in the Sheer Plan) will be bolted through keel and stem. The stemson *t* is a kind of filling-up piece, and serves as knightheads for additional plank fastenings forward. The upper through bolt in the stemson should have a mooring or towing ring through it, as shown.

The gunwale (or inwale, equivalent to the clamp or shelf in a yacht) rests on the timber heads, and will be secured to the stem forward by a " breasthook," as shown by *a*, diagram A (*see* Sheer Plan, Fig. 119). This breasthook will have one fastening through the stem, and two through each gunwale and top strake, as shown. The gunwale and top strake will be through-fastened between each pair of timbers, and secured to the transom by the knee, as shown at *m* in the Half-breadth Plan. A fastening will also be put through the gunwale and strake into the transom.

The floors should reach from the keel to three or four inches above the load water-line; and the timbers from the gunwale down the sides of the floors to within eight or nine inches of the keel.

The transom will be 1½in. thick, fitted at the back of the sternpost, as shown in the Sheer Plan.

The rudder will be shaped as shown by the diagram B (under the Body Plan, Fig. 120). Pintles will be dispensed with, and instead gudgeons and braces used, through which a brass rod will pass. This arrangement is necessary, as the rudder will hang considerably below the keel. If the braces are fitted over the gudgeons on the sternpost and a transom at *g h* (Sheer Plan), the rudder will lift on the rod if the boat drags on the ground, and will not unship.

The rabbet in the stem will be cut at about 2in. from the inner edges of the stem piece as shown by the ticked line *v* in the Sheer Plan. The rabbet in the keel (being a continuation of the rabbet in the stem) should be cut not less than about one inch from the upper edge, and not less than one inch deep, so as to take a good fastening through the garboards (*see* Fig. 122). The rabbet in the dead woods should be at least one inch from their upper edges.

Sometimes the upper part of the keel (A, Fig. 122) is a separate piece of timber: it is then termed a hogging piece.

The boat will take about 4cwt. of ballast with three hands on board; this ballast should either be in the form of shot bags, or flat bricks of lead cast to rest on the top of the floors, but sunk between them. These bricks would be under the platform or bottom board, which should be securely fastened, but at the same time be readily movable. If there is no objection to a cast-iron platform, the "bottom boards" can be dispensed with, and a thin iron slab cast to fit over the floors on either side of the centre plate. For such a boat as the design given the slabs would be 6ft. long by 1ft. 6in. broad, and 1½in. thick near the keel and ½in. nearest the bilge. They

Fig. 122.

would be cast with grooves to fit the floors, and the grooves would gradually deepen from nothing at the bilge to ½in. depth at the keel side. In the stern the usual bottom board or "stern sheet" would be fitted; and forward either a board or a grating would be similarly fitted.

Of course, no plan of lead or iron ballasting will make such a shallow boat as the centre-board gig stiff or uncapsizable, in the ordinary meaning of the terms, and the large sails (plans of which will be given hereafter) should not be set unless two or three hands are on board to sit to windward.

The plate or board is smaller in area than was usual at the time (1878) of making the design; but experience has proved it to be ample, and its proportion is now usually adopted.

THE OCEANA ROWING AND SAILING BOAT.

The design shown on Plate XV. was made by the author in 1886, and the Oceana was built from it by Mr. Turk, of Kingston-on-Thames. The boat was rather heavily built of all teak, but she proved a fast sailer and easy to row. She carried about 4 cwt. of ballast inside, and had none on her keel. She was yawl rigged, with balance lugs. The foreside mainmast is 3ft. from foreside of stem at gunwale, and a suitable height would be 18ft. gunwale to hounds (*see* Sail Plan of Ruby, further on); main boom 13ft., yard 11ft. 6in. The mizen mast is stepped 2ft. inside of stern-post, and with mizen boom 7ft. and yard 6ft. 6in.; bowsprit outboard 6ft.

A table of offsets has not been given for this boat, as the scale of the drawing is sufficiently large to take measurements from.

The Oceana, like the boat depicted by Fig. 119, was designed with a view of making the rowing qualities of first consideration, but they also showed excellent capacity for sailing.

CENTRE-BOARD BOAT FOR SAILING AND ROWING.

A centre-board boat, somewhat deeper, with more rise of floor, also with less length to beam, than the one of 17ft. length, shown by the design, Fig. 119, may perhaps be a handier boat in rough or narrow water where frequent tacking is inevitable, and at the same time be

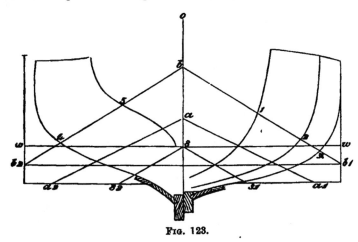

Fig. 123.

very little more laboursome to row. The lines for such a boat as given on Plate XVI., with body plan represented by Fig. 123, was designed and published by the author in 1878, and has been frequently built from since that date, one notable example being the 15ft. Mistletoe, built in 1893 by Sir George Greaves, and successfully raced by him on the Welsh coast up to the present date, 1895.

In order that the drawing may be utilised for boats of varying sizes, tables have been compiled to different scales, so that a boat of 10ft., 12ft.. 14ft., or 15ft., can be built therefrom.

The displacement (or weight of water which the boat displaces when immersed to the load line, or, in other words, the weight of the boat, including everything she carries) of each boat, as given, is not mathematically correct, and need not be so considered; it is only given as a guide for the builder in ballasting, and it may be necessary or convenient to sail the boat lighter or deeper.*

With regard to ballast, it will be found in practice that every passenger on board who sits to windward is of more value than an equal weight of ballast in the bottom of the boat would be; but as a rule, for good performance, two passengers besides the helmsman will be considered sufficient for a 12ft. boat. When sailing in smooth water, shifting the ballast to windward can be largely indulged in if a practised hand besides the helmsman is on board to look after it; but in a sea the ballast should be well secured in the bottom of the boat, and not shifted to windward.

The dimensions of the sails given are for cruising, and are not so large as those of the gigs raced at Surbiton; the difference is about equal to one-seventh the linear dimensions—that is to say, the sail of the 14ft. boat, or any of the other boats given, would be one-seventh longer in the foot, one-seventh longer in the head, one-seventh longer on the luff, and one-seventh longer on the leech for a racing outfit.

In setting the sail, attention should be paid to the position of the slings on the yard, and it may be found possible to improve the "sit" of the sail by a variation from the positions given in the tables.

In all cases where measurements are given they must be adhered to, as the drawings are too small to work from. The process of "fairing" the waterlines or moulds will be performed on the "give and take" plan, the battens being let out and taken in from the various "spots."

In the case of each boat the measurements are without the plank.

BOAT OF 10FT.—PLATE XVI.

	No. 1 Section.		No. 2 Section.		No. 3 Section.		No. 4 Section.		No. 5 Section. Transom.	
	ft.	in.	ft.	in.	ft.	in.	ft.	in.	ft.	in.
Height above L.W.L. to gunwale	1	2⅛	1	1	1	0	1	0	1	1
Depths below L.W.L. to top of keel	0	4	0	5⅛	0	6	0	6⅛	0	7
Half-breadths at gunwale	1	0	1	7⅛	1	10⅛	1	9	1	0
Half-breadths at L.W.L.	0	7¼	1	4	1	8	1	4¼	0	1
Half-breadths *s* diagonal	0	5	0	8¼	1	9¾	0	8	0	1
Half-breadths on *a* diagonal	0	8¼	1	2⅛	1	4¾	1	1⅛	0	4
Half-breadths on *b* diagonal	1	0¼	1	7⅛	1	10¾	1	8	0	10¼

* The displacement of these boats can thus be found approximately: multiply the length on the load line by the beam on the load line, and the depth amidships to the rabbet of the keel; next multiply the product by the co-efficient 0·4, and the product will be the displacement of the boat in cubic feet nearly. The co-efficient will of course vary according to the sharpness or fulness of the boat. The co-efficient for yachts varies from ·3 to ·4; the common co-efficient being ·32. There are 35 cubic feet of salt water in 1 ton. (*See* "Displacement per inch of Immersion" in the Appendix.)

Distance No. 1 section is from fore side of stem			1ft. 7in.
„ No. 2 „	No. 1 section		1ft. 7in.
„ No. 3 „	No. 2 „		2ft. 2in.
„ No. 4 „	No. 3 „		2ft. 4in.
„ No. 5 . „ (transom)	No. 4 „		2ft. 4in.

The water lines are 2½in. apart.

Diagonal *a* is struck 4in. above L.W.L., and *a* 1 and *a* 2 are 1ft. 7in. from the middle vertical line *o*. Diagonal *b* is 11in. above L.W.L. The diagonal *s* at *s* 1 and *s* 2 is 9½in. from the vertical line *o*. Plank ⅜in. mahogany.

Length, 10ft.
Breadth, 3ft. 9in.
Pin of centre plate from fore side of stem, 3ft. 3in.
Length of plate on top edge, 3ft. 6in.
Length of plate on under edge, 3ft. 10in.
Greatest breadth of plate, 1ft. 2in.
Least breadth of plate, 4½in.
Thickness of plate, ⅜in.
Weight of plate, 40lb.
Weight of displacement of boat when equipped and immersed to L.W.L., 3¾cwt.
Weight per inch of immersion at L.W.L., 1cwt.

BALANCE LUG SAIL.

Mast, thwart to sheave hole	10ft. 0in.
Luff of sail	4ft. 0in.
Leech	13ft. 3in.
Foot	10ft. 0in.
Head	10ft. 3in.
Tack to peak earing	14ft. 6in.
Clew to weather earing	10ft. 0in.
Area of sail	80 square ft.

BOAT OF 12FT.—PLATE XVI.

	No. 1 Section.		No. 2 Section.		No. 3 Section.		No. 4 Section.		No. 5. Section.	
	ft.	in.	ft.	in.	ft.	in.	ft.	in.	ft.	in.
Heights above L.W.L. to top of gunwale	1	5½	1	3¼	1	2¼	1	2¼	1	3½
Depths below L.W.L. to top of keel	0	4¾	0	6	0	7	0	7½	0	8
Half-breadths at gunwale	1	2½	2	0	2	3¼	2	1¾	1	3
Half-breadths at L.W.L.	0	8¾	1	7	2	0	1	7¼	0	1¼
Half-breadths *s* diagonal	0	6	0	10	0	11½	0	9½	0	1¼
Half-breadths on diagonal *a*	0	10	1	5¼	1	8	1	4½	0	4¼
Half-breadths on diagonal *b*	1	2½	1	11¼	2	8¾	2	0	1	0½

No. 1 section is 2ft. from the fore side of stem.
No. 2 section is 2ft. from No. 1.
No. 3 section is 2ft. 6in. from No. 2.
No. 4 section is 2ft. 9in. from No. 3.
No. 5 (transom) is 2ft. 9in. from No. 4.

The water lines are 3in. apart.

Diagonal *s* at *s* 1 and *s* 2 is 11½in. from the middle line *o*.

Height of diagonal *a* above load line, 4½in.; *a* 1 and *a* 2 are from the middle line *o*, 1ft. 11in.

Height of diagonal *b* on middle line *o* of Body Plan above L.W.L., 1ft. 1½in., and at *b* 1 and *b* 2 is 3in. below L.W.L.

Length from fore side of stem to aft side of transom, 12ft.

Greatest breadth moulded (*i.e.*, without plank), 4ft. 7in.

Aft side of mast from fore side of stem, 3ft.

Weight of displacement of boat when immersed to load line, 6½cwt.; weight per inch of immersion, 1¼cwt.

Pin of centre plate from perpendicular at fore side of stem, 3ft. 11in.

Length of plate on its under edge, 4ft. 8in.

Length on its upper edge, 4ft. 3in.

Greatest breadth of plate, 1ft. 4in.

Least breadth, 5½in.

Thickness, ⅜in.

Weight of plate, 50lb.

Siding (thickness) of keel amidships, 4in.; ditto at stem, 2in; ditto at sternpost, 2½in. Moulded depth of keel, 3½in. Plank ⅜in. mahogany.

BALANCE LUG SAIL.

Mast, thwart to sheave hole	10ft. 0in.
Luff of sail	5ft. 6in.
Leech	16ft. 0in.
Foot	12ft. 0in.
Head..	12ft. 3in.
Tack to peak earing	17ft. 6in.
Clew to weather earing	12ft. 0in.
Area	105 square ft.

Halyards bent to yard, 5ft. from lower end.

Tack, 1ft. 6in. from fore end of boom.

BOAT OF 14FT.—PLATE XVI.

	No. 1 Section.	No. 2 Section.	No. 3 Section.	No. 4 Section.	No. 5 Section.
	ft. in.	ft. in.	ft. in.	ft. in.	ft. in.
Heights above L.W.L. to top of gunwale	1 8¼	1 6	1 5	1 5	1 6
Depths below L.W.L. to top of keel	0 5¾	0 7	0 8	0 8¼	0 9¼
Half-breadths at gunwale	1 5½	2 4	2 8	2 6	1 5¼
Half-breadths at L.W.L.	0 10¾	1 10¾	2 4¼	1 10¼	0 1¼
Half-breadths *s* diagonal	0 6¼	1 0	1 1¼	0 11	0 1¼
Half-breadths on diagonal *a*	1 0	1 8¼	1 11¾	1 7¼	0 5¼
Half-breadths on diagonal *b*	1 5¼	2 3¼	2 8¼	2 4¼	1 3

No. 1 section is 2ft. 4in. from the fore side of stem.

No. 2 section is 2ft. 4in. from No. 1 section.

No. 3 section is 2ft. 10in. from No. 2 section.

No. 4 section is 3ft. 3in. from No. 3 section.

No. 5 section (transom) is 3ft. 3in. from No. 4 section.

The water lines are 3½in. apart.

Diagonal *a* above L.W.L., 5½in.; *a* 1 and *a* 2 from middle line *o* (*see* Body Plan, **Fig. 112**), 2ft. 3in.; diagonal *b* above load line, 1ft. 4in., and at *b* 1 and *b* 2 is 3½in. below the L.W.L.; diagonal *s* at *s* 1 and *s* 2 is 1ft. 1½in. from the middle line *o*.

Length from fore side of stem to aft side of transom, 14ft.

Greatest breadth moulded (*i.e.*, without the plank), 5ft. 4in.

Aft side of mast from fore side of stem, 3ft. 6in.

Weight of displacement of boat when equipped and immersed to load line, 9½cwt.

Weight per inch of immersion at load line, 1¼cwt.

Pin of centre plate from perpendicular at fore side of stem, 4ft. 6in.

Length of plate on its under edge, 5ft. 5in.

Length on its upper edge, 5ft.
Greatest breadth of plate, 1ft. 6in.
Least breadth, 6in.
Thickness of plate, ⅜in.
Weight of plate, 110lb.
Siding (thickness) of keel amidships, 4in.; ditto at stem, 2½in.; ditto at sternpost, 3in. Moulded depth (*i.e.*, depth from top to under side), 4in. Plank ⅜in. mahogany.

BALANCE LUG SAIL.

Foot	14ft. 0in.
Head, measured along the ticked line (*a*)	14ft. 3in.
Leech	19ft. 9in.
Luff	6ft. 0in.
Tack to peak earing	21ft. 0in.
Clew to weather earing	14ft. 8in.
Area	155 square ft.

Yard is slung 6ft. from lower end. Tack is bent 1ft. 9in. from fore end of boom.

BOAT OF 15FT.—PLATE XVI.

	No. 1 Section.	No. 2 Section.	No. 3 Section.	No. 4 Section.	No. 5 Section.
	ft. in.	ft. in.	ft. in.	ft. in.	ft. in.
Heights above L.W.L. to top of gunwale	1 10	1 7½	1 6	1 6	1 7½
Depths below L.W.L. to top of keel	0 6¼	0 7¾	0 8¾	0 9⅜	0 10
Half-breadths at gunwale	1 6¾	2 6	2 10	2 8	1 7
Half-breadths at L.W.L.	0 11	2 0¾	2 6½	2 0½	0 1½
Half-breadths *s* diagonal	0 7	1 0½	1 2¾	0 11½	0 1½
Half-breadths on diagonal *a*	1 1	1 10	2 1	1 9	0 5½
Half-breadths on diagonal *b*	1 6½	2 6	2 10½	2 6½	1 4

No. 1 section is 2ft. 6in. from the fore side of stem.
No. 2 section is 2ft. 6in. from No. 1 section.
No. 3 section is 3ft. 1½in. from No. 2 section.
No. 4 section is 3ft. 5¼in. from No. 3 section.
No. 5 section (transom) is 3ft. 5¼in. from No. 4 section.
The water lines are 3¾in. apart.

Diagonal *a* above L.W.L., 6¼in.; *a* 1 and *a* 2 from middle line *o* (*see* Body Plan, Fig. 112), 2ft. 4½in.; diagonal *b* above load line, 1ft. 5in., and at *b* 1 and *b* 2 is 3¾in. below the L.W.L.; diagonal *s* at *s* 1 and *s* 2 is 1ft. 2½in. from the middle line *o*.
Length from fore side of stem to aft side of transom, 15ft.
Greatest breadth moulded (*i.e.*, without the plank), 5ft. 8in.
Aft side of mast from fore side of stem, 3ft. 9in.
Weight of displacement of boat when equipped and immersed to load line, 12½cwt.
Weight per inch of immersion at load line, 2cwt.
Pin of centre plate from perpendicular at fore side of stem, 4ft. 9in.
Length of plate on its under edge, 5ft. 10in.
Length on its upper edge, 5ft. 4in.
Greatest breadth of plate, 1ft. 9in.
Least breadth, 6in.
Thickness of plate, ⅜in.
Weight of plate, 130lb.
Siding (thickness) of keel amidships, 4½in.; ditto at stem, 2¾in.; ditto at sternpost, 3in. Moulded depth (*i.e.*, depth from top to under side), 4in. Plank ⅜in. mahogany.

BALANCE LUG SAIL.

Foot	14ft. 0in.
Head, measured along the ticked line (a)	15ft. 3in.
Leech	20ft. 0in.
Luff	7ft. 0in.
Tack to peak earing	21ft. 6in.
Clew to weather earing	15ft. 6in.
Area	168 square ft.

Yard is slung 6ft. 3in. from lower end. Tack is bent 2ft. from fore end of boom.

The 10ft. boat would weigh, inclusive of centre-plate and case, sails, and spars, about 2cwt. Thus it would take ½cwt. of ballast and one person of 8st. (1cwt.) to bring her down to the intended load line; but she might with advantage carry one more passenger or 1cwt. more ballast. Every additional cwt. would sink her an inch deeper. For light rowing the plate, ballast, and sails could be removed.

The 12ft. boat, fully equipped, would weigh about 3½cwt., and should have at least 3cwt. of ballast, or one person and 2cwt. of ballast, besides the helmsman, for sailing with the large balance lug sail. Burgoine's price would range from 30 to 40 guineas.

The 14ft. boat would weigh about 4½cwt., and would require from 3cwt. to 4cwt. of ballast, according to the number of passengers on board.

The 15ft. boat would weigh about 5cwt., and would require 5cwt. or 6cwt. of ballast, according to the number of passengers on board.

THE CENTRE-BOARD GIG RUBY.

One of the most successful of the Surbiton centre-board gigs is the Ruby (*see* Plate XVII. and Fig. 124), built by Burgoine, of Kingston-on-Thames, in 1876, for Mr. E. Allen. This craft has won over one hundred prizes, and is undoubtedly the best of the fleet. The boat was awarded a silver medal at the Inventions Exhibition, and her model (half full dimensions, or on a scale of 6in. to the foot) has been placed, at the request of the Commissioners, in South Kensington Museum. Although she has less proportional beam for her length, she much resembles* the design given on Plate XVI., and in all respects is representative of the popular boat for "rowing and sailing."

The iron keel is about 4in. thick, and weighs 3½cwt., and she has 3cwt. of iron ballast inside. Weight of centre plate ½cwt.

---

* For instance, if the table for the 14ft. boat, page 290, be taken, and the spacing increased between the sections so as to make 17ft. 10in., a boat almost identical with Ruby would be produced. The spacings would be increased to (1 and 2) 2ft. 10in., (2 and 3) 3ft. 5¼in., (3, 4, and 5) 3ft. 11¾in. = 17ft. 10in.

Burgoine's price for a similar boat of pine, with mahogany fittings, iron ballast, calico sails, is 75*l.*; all mahogany, lead ballast, cotton canvas sails, 95*l.*

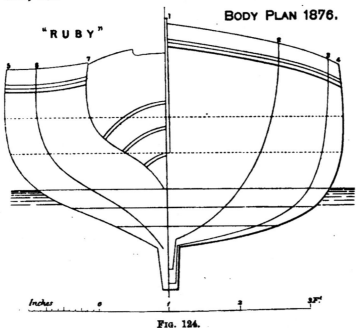

"RUBY"   BODY PLAN 1876.

FIG. 124.

DIMENSIONS OF "RUBY" 1876.

Length over all	18ft.	Leech of mainsail ...	25ft. 9in.
Length on L.W.L. ...	17ft. 8½in.	Foot of mainsail	16ft. 6in.
Beam extreme	5ft. 2in.	Head of mainsail......	17ft.
Draught of water extreme...............	1ft. 5in.	Tack to peak	27ft. 3in.
		Clew to throat.........	18ft. 4in.
Displacement	·85ton (17cwt.)	Area of mainsail	236 sq. ft.
Centre of buoyancy aft centre of length	0·4ft.	Area of jib	42 sq. ft.
Luff of mainsail	10ft. 9in.	Length of spinnaker. boom	18ft.

TABLE OF OFFSETS OF "RUBY."—PLATE XVII. (FIG. 124).

Numbers of Sections	1	2	3	4	5	6	7
	ft. in.	ft. in.	ft. in.	ft. in.	ft. in.	ft. in.	ft. in.
Heights above L.W.L. to top of gunwale	2 4	2 0	1 9½	1 8½	1 8	1 8½	1 8¼
Depths to rabbet in keel.............................	—	0 8	0 9	0 9½	0 10	1 5	—
Draught of water....................................	—	1 1½	1 4	1 5	1 5	1 4½	1 4
Half-breadths at gunwale	—	1 7	2 4	2 6	2 3	1 9½	1 1
,, 1ft. above L.W.L.	—	1 6½	2 3½	2 7	2 3	1 9½	1 3
,, 6in. above L.W.L.	—	1 4	2 2½	2 6	2 2	1 8	0 6
,, on L.W.L.	—	1 0½	2 0½	2 3½	1 9½	1 0	0 1½
,, on W.L. 2	—	0 9	1 9½	2 1½	1 3½	0 6½	0 1½
,, on W.L. 3	—	0 5½	1 4	1 6½	0 9	0 3½	0 1

No. 2 section is 3ft. 7in. from the fore side of the stem perpendicular. Nos. 2, 3, 4, and 5 are 3ft. 7in. apart; 5, 6, and 7 are 1ft. 9½in. apart. The water-lines are 3in. apart. The overhang aft at transom 3in.; at stem ½in. Half-breadths include plank.

THE RUBY AS ALTERED 1888.

In 1888 Mr. A. Burgoine adapted the Ruby to the "Mystery" form of afterbody (*see* Plate XVIII.). She, however, still retained a deep keel, although it had to be taken out and altered aft, and the iron keel re-cast. The mid-section and sections in the forebody remain unaltered, and the alterations to the afterbody were not very considerable. Plate XVIII. shows the alterations made to the afterbody and the counter which was added. The mast was shifted to 5ft. 9in. from the foreside of the stem head, and the bowsprit shortened 2ft. 6in. The alterations proved to be a great success, but she was defeated by the Mystery in an unexpected manner in the match for the Thames Sailing Club Challenge Cup in May, 1888.

THE RUBY AS ALTERED 1891.

In 1891 Ruby was further altered by being lengthened at the bow and given an overhanging stem, and a sort of "fin" lead keel, besides the centre plate. She was opened well back abaft the midship frame and her beam increased 1 inch. She is now 19ft. on the water-line, 5ft. 3in. beam, and 28ft. over all. When she first appeared in 1876 her sail area was 150 sq. ft. This year it is quite 350 sq. ft. Her sail plan is shown farther on, such as she raced with until 1888. The present sail plan is similar, but greater in area. She has already justified the latest improvements by competing with success. (*See* Plate XIX.)

THE MYSTERY.

In 1882 Mr. John Messer, of Reading, had the Mystery (Plate XX. and Fig. 125) built from his own design, somewhat on the lines of a coble without dead wood aft. He gave her a very flaring bow, and fitted her for coast cruising. She proved to be well adapted for the purpose, and, being decked in forward, she was successfully taken round the east coast, rarely stopping for weather, as she is exceedingly dry in a head sea. In 1885, when put into a match of the Upper Thames Sailing Club, she had a very easy victory, and subsequently won the Thames Sailing Club Challenge Cup, beating Ruby six minutes after two hours and a quarter hard sailing in a hard wind. Her "turn about" capabilities were found a great advantage in narrow water, and the fashion of cutting away the dead wood aft became general. There is a joint in the upper part of the iron rudder, so that it doubled up when touching the ground, or could be doubled up at will for beaching. The rudder works in an oak trunk 4in. by 4in., bored out to take the rudder post, which consists of 1⅜in. galvanised iron pipe. The trunk has an internal brass ferrule at each end, the bottom one being flanged to prevent leakage. The rudder consists of two parts hinged together. On Plate XX. the rudder is shown by A, in use with the drop piece. The rudder is made of ½in. galvanised iron plate (*see* B and C). A strengthening piece *a* under the hollow iron rudder post is riveted on. The long bolt *b* works in this hollow post (*see* B). To get the parts of the rudder together a list is given to the boat, and the bolt is then screwed in. The collar *c* (in A) prevents the rudder dropping, and is made uneven on the underside to counteract the tendency of the rudder to fall on either side, owing to the post tumbling in. *k* is the key. The figures D show different horizontal views of the rudder. *d* is the rudder post with bolt in the centre, *a* the strengthening pieces, and *h* the hinges.

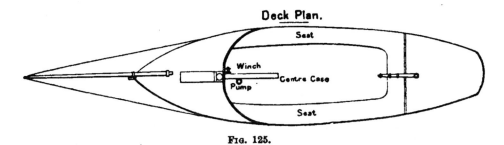

Deck Plan.

Fig. 125.

The Mystery has usually 4½cwt. shot in square, flat, stout, well painted canvas bags, a board top, and rope handle (Fig. 126). The canvas nailed to the edges of the board, as shown. She has no outside ballast, the inside ballast being increased as required for match sailing. Her working jib has a boom,

Fig. 126.

but is not laced, and works itself in stays without any attention. The balloon jib overlaps the mainsail, and has to be pulled clear of the yard by a light brail when going about. The brail is fast to the leech of jib, and leads through cringles down the luff of the jib, along the fore deck, into the body of the boat; but little difficulty is thus experienced in tacking. The main boom telescopes into a copper tube 3in. diameter, and revolves round the mast. (*See* Fig. 127).

The boom being thus secured, the yard and sail when lowered drops between the topping lifts without falling on the fore deck as usual. In reefing, the pin or stop is removed, and the boom runs into the pipe; a

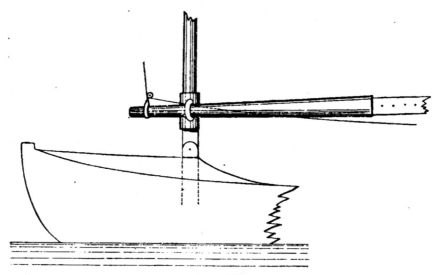

FIG. 127.

rope strop on the reef cringle of the after leach of the sail is then put over the boom end and the boom shoved out as required, and stopped.

The owner adapted the "Bembridge rig," as a shorter mast could be used.

DIMENSIONS OF THE MYSTERY.

Length over all	20ft. 10in.
Length on water line	16ft. 6in.
Beam extreme	5ft. 8in.
Displacement	0·87 ton.
Weight of centre plate	1cwt.
Weight of rudder	1cwt.
Weight of ballast	4½cwt.
Mast, deck to hounds	20ft. 9in.
Main boom extreme	18ft. 7in.
Main yard	18ft.
Foot of mainsail	18ft.
Head of mainsail	17ft. 4in.
Luff of mainsail	10ft. 6in.
Leach of mainsail	26ft. 6in.
Clew to weather earing	20ft. 6in.
Tack to peak earing	26ft. 8in.
Area of mainsail	272 sq. ft.
Slings of yard from lower end	8ft.

(The sail plan of Mystery will be found farther on, Plate XXIV.)

THE ZYTHUM.

A larger kind of open sailing boat, well adapted for sea work, was designed in 1880 by Mr. R. C. Carline, of Lincoln, and built for him by Patrick of that town. (*See* Plate XXI.)

The centre-board is so arranged that it is not in the way, as the box stands up only 1in. above the floor boards, except the aft end thereof, and the greater portion of it is under and abuts up to the aft thwart. Only 9in. of it projects on the fore side of the thwart, so as to enable a folding rod to work the board up and down. By the side of this raised part is fixed a square wooden force pump, which discharges the bilge water into the centre-board box. The chambers are 3in. square, and the exposed side of the pump can be readily taken off if required. It works easily, and gets rid of the water most rapidly—a very desirable thing in an open boat. The ballast consists of a lead and iron keel weighing 5cwt., with about 1cwt. of iron inside.

The main and mizen sails are batten lugs, with very high peaks, and it will be observed that the yards are slung so that the masts cut the yards nearly in the middle. This prevents the sail sagging to leeward, and the yard and boom can be kept very nearly at the same angle. Mr. Carline says he found that a boat can carry a greater area of canvas with battens than without. This is a common experience.

The boat carries her canvas well, and for racing is under-canvassed. She is a capital sea boat, handy and fast, although her centre of buoyancy is rather farther aft than is usual.

Length over all	20ft.
Length on load-line	19ft. 6in.
Beam	5ft. 9in.
Draught-water	2ft.
Displacement	1·4 ton.
C. B. aft centre of length	1·2 ft.
Mast, gunwale to truck	22ft. 6in.
Yard, extreme	20ft. 6in.
Main boom, extreme	14ft. 6in.
Mizen mast, gunwale to truck	14ft. 6in.
Yard, extreme	10ft. 0in.
Mizen boom, extreme	8ft. 3in.
Luff of mainsail	8ft. 6in.
Luff of mizen	6ft. 3in.
Bowsprit, outboard	6ft. 9in.
Foreside of mast from fore side to stem	5ft. 9in.
Area mainsail	230 sq. ft.
Area mizen	75 sq. ft.
Area jib	70 sq. ft.
Total area	375 sq. ft.

Centre-board boats are peculiarly adapted for shifting-ballast, as the centre-plate case makes a kind of fore-and-aft bulkhead which will always prevent the ballast sliding to leeward. Still, sliding is not the only danger accompanying the practice of shifting ballast. If a man is single-handed, he might be unable in an emergency to trim his shot bags or other dead weight in time, or his mate may be unable to do so, and it cannot be too often impressed upon the young boat sailer that he must well look after loose ballast in the bottom of a boat (secure it if possible), and never be tempted into carrying a lot of sail on the strength of the ballast being shifted to windward.

DECKS FOR BOATS.

The question of decking is one which will naturally arise in selecting a boat. No doubt a locker of some sort, to stow cushions, gear, and sails in, is a desideratum in a boat; but a deck forward and aft, with waterways amidships, as shown in a sketch given farther on, must increase the weight,

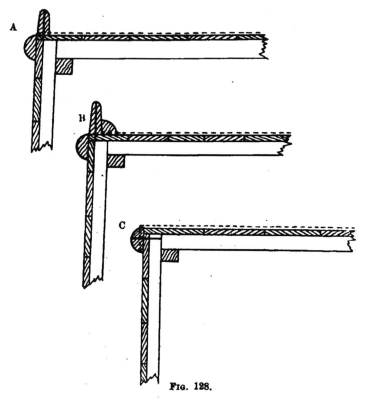

Fig. 128.

and for up-river sailing are quite unnecessary. However, if the boat-sailer is equal to the " stress and the strain of the wind and the reeling main," and can confidently knock about in Sea Reach, he will find the decks and waterways a great comfort. They will keep out all the water likely to lop on board, and nothing worse than spray need ever get into the well amidships.

A boat built from the design (page 277) has been partly decked and successfully raced at such places as Deal and Ramsgate, and the Mystery and Ruby have made trips round the coast; and, whilst they behaved just as they ought in a breeze with some sea, they were not too heavy to row if occasion arose.

A thick heavy caulked deck would of course not suit these light boats, and it is usual to cover them in with ½in. match board and then canvas it. The canvas duck is cut the shape of the deck to be covered. The deck is then coated with thick paint and the canvas stretched over it, as shown by the dotted line in Fig. 128. The rail A is then fastened on. In case it is an old boat, and it would be inconvenient to remove the rail A, a fillet B can be worked over the edges of the canvas (Fig. 128).

If there is no rail, the edge of the canvas is carried over the side to top strake and secured by the rubbing piece C.

COWES WATERMAN'S SKIFF.

The boats used by the Cowes and Ryde waterman are considered excellent of their kind, and as about as safe as an open boat can be made. In form they are not unlike the rowing and sailing boat shown on Plate XVI., and also they much resemble a yacht's dinghy or cutter. They are, however, flatter in the floor than either of these boats, and broader in the stern. The latter quality is given them because, as a rule, the greater portion of their passengers have to be seated in the stern. On Plate XXII. one of these boats is shown of the size usually in use among watermen—that is 15ft. long by 4ft. 9in. in beam. The position for a centre-board is shown in the plate.

These boats sail very well with a sprit sail rig, and usually have a mizen and foresail, the latter having its tack laced to the stem head. A far better rig, however, would be a standing lug or balance lug sail, with or without battens. The dimensions for such a sail would be

Foot	13ft. 6in.
Head	12ft. 10in.
Leech	18ft. 3in.
Luff	6ft. 6in.
Tack to peak-earing	19ft. 0in.
Clew to weather-earing	14ft. 0in.
Main boom tacked from fore end	1ft. 9in.
Yard slung from lower end	4ft. 6in.
Area of mainsail	134 sq. ft.
Area of foresail	30 sq. ft.
Mast gunwale to sheave	12ft. 9in.
Mast stepped from stem head	3ft. 6in.
Bowsprit outboard	3ft. 9in.
Foot of foresail	5ft. 6in.

With such sails the boat, if built of the usual strength, would take about 5 cwt. of ballast. (*See* Plate XXVI.)

The position for fitting a centre plate is shown.

YACHT'S CUTTER.

An ordinary yacht's cutter, such as a yacht of 156 tons would carry, is shown on Plate XXIII. She is 22ft. long, by 5ft. 4in. broad, and 2ft. 2in. deep, measured at the gunwale height to rabbet of keel. It has been a favourite practice to race these cutters, and an Association was formed to regulate the competitions. Its rules were as follows:

Objects.—The association is formed for owners to race their *bonâ fide* yachts' gigs, cutters, and dinghies, under a uniform code of rules.

Boats.—Every boat competing in a match must be clincher built, and not have any outside ballast, and the draught, with all ballast on board, shall not exceed ⅞in. to a foot of length on the L.W.L. in boats exceeding 16ft. Boats 16ft. and under allowed a maximum draught of 12in. The overall length of boats under 20ft. L.W.L. shall not exceed the L.W.L. by more than 6in., and the overall length of boats of 20ft. and upwards on L.W.L. shall not exceed the L.W.L. by more than 9in., any excess of overall length to be added to the L.W.L. length for measurement.

Centre-boards or Plates.—In boats under 20ft. L.W.L., the weight of centre-board or centre-plate not to exceed 1cwt., and in boats of 20ft. L.W.L. and over, 1½cwt.

Rating.—By Y.R.A. rule of length and sail area, with the exception that actual head-sail and spinnaker be measured as follows: If head-sail or spinnaker or both be carried, the actual area of same shall be taken, the area of the larger sail only being measured. The spinnaker-boom must not exceed the length of the foot of the spinnaker.

Time Allowance.—Y.R.A. scale; but no rig allowances.

Classes.—15ft. on L.W.L. and under = ½ rating; over 15ft. and not exceeding 20ft. on L.W.L. = 1 rating; exceeding 20ft. on L.W.L. = 1½ rating.

Crews.—Boats under 20ft., total number three; 20ft. and over, four, including helmsmen in both cases.

Helmsmen.—Helmsmen must be amateurs, who are members of any Royal or recognised yacht club.

According to these regulations the sail area allowed for different lengths would be as follows:

½-RATERS.		1-RATERS.		1½-RATERS.	
10ft. on water line...	300 sq. ft.	16ft. on water line...	375 sq. ft.	21ft. on water line...	428 sq. ft.
11ft. „ „ ...	272 „	17ft. „ „ ...	352 „	22ft. „ „ ...	409 „
12ft. „ „ ...	250 „	18ft. „ „ ...	333 „	23ft. „ „ ...	391 „
13ft. „ „ ...	230 „	19ft. „ „ ...	315 „	24ft. „ „ ...	375 „
14ft. „ „ ...	214 „	20ft. „ „ ...	300 „	25ft. „ „ ...	360 „
15ft. „ „ ...	200 „				

It must not be assumed that the possible area for the given length and rating will always be adopted; but we believe the 18ft. and 20ft. cutters, when racing have the full allowance.

The sail plans of these boats are usually of the standing or balance lug type, a specimen of which will be found on Plate XXVI. in the next chapter on sails for centre-board boats. The mainsail is usually ·8 of the total sail area allowed. For a 20ft. boat the following would be suitable dimensions :

Mainsail, luff	7ft. 9in.
Mainsail, leach	25ft. 9in.
Mainsail, foot	18ft. 0in.
Mainsail, head	18ft. 0in.
Mainsail, tack to peak-earing	25ft. 0in.
Mainsail, clew to weather-earing...............................	19ft. 6in.
Boom, tacked to mast from fore end	1ft. 4in.
Area of mainsail	240 sq. ft.
Area headsail	60 sq. ft.
Total area	300 sq. ft.
Mast, gunwale to sheave pin	16ft. 6in.
Mast, stepped aft foreside of stem	4ft. 0in.
Bowsprit outboard...	4ft. 0in.

To carry these large sails the boats were heavily ballasted with lead, a 15ft. cutter having about 8 cwt. on board, and a 20ft. cutter 15 cwt., and sometimes more. To render them safer, and to keep them drier when hard pressed, they were fitted with movable wash strakes above the gunwale of from 4in. to 6in. deep. However, open boats with such sail spreads as quoted, and heavily ballasted, cannot in any way be described as "safe," and require very skilful management even by experienced boat sailers. No person who is not most completely versed in open boat sailing should be in charge of such ballasted boats as these, and the whole crew should also be experts and able to swim. Even then it would be only common prudence for the whole crew to wear life belts.

CHAPTER XII.

SAILS FOR CENTRE-BOARD BOATS.

OPINIONS are very much divided as to the best kind of rig for a centre-board gig; but the standing lug or the balance lug in some form or other appears to be most generally in favour. It has been contended that a boat rigged with a single balance lug is likely to miss stays, and this is perhaps true in what is termed a "lop;" but a boat with one large sail in the hands of a clever boat-sailer, need never miss stays in smooth water at least, unless the wind headed the boat round, and then of course she would miss stays, whatever her rig. It is an advantage to have the sail all in one piece for going to windward—tacking out of the question—and for a single hand it is of course convenient to have no head sails to work. No description of boat will stay quicker or with more certainty than the American cat-boat, or Una, and, if not brought head to wind by too free a use of the rudder, they lose very little way in tacking.

On the other hand, a boat with one sail may fail to go about in a disturbed sea, or in light baffling winds, and may get in irons; whereas if she had a foresail the operation of tacking, without getting stern way on, might have been successfully performed by keeping the head sheets a-weather. A clever boat-sailer will always work his head sheets without inconvenience even in a lop, as he will see his craft safely filling on the opposite tack before he attempts to "let draw," and, as the head sheets will lead aft, he need not move from his seat. The argument *pro* and *con.* the foresail can, therefore, be summed up thus: In light winds it is an advantage to have the sail all in one piece, especially for beating, and the trouble of working the head sheets does not exist; but in strong winds and rough water there will be more security in a smaller mainsail, with the addition of a headsail; and, although there will be the trouble of working the head sheets, there need be no difficulty about it even for one hand. Concluding that it is "safest to be safe," it will be best to be provided with a foresail for sailing in rough water.

Another very strong argument in favour of the foresail or jib in addition to the balance lug is this: if there be much wind, the boat when sailing "along," or off the wind, will exhibit a very great tendency to come to against her helm, that is, she will require a great deal of weather helm to keep her out of the wind; this tendency will be greatly relieved by the jib. Again, if there be any sea, the boat will have to be constantly "chucked" up in the wind to avoid a comber that may be coming in on the weather bow, for it will not do to sail open boats very hard in rough water; yet must they be kept full, and to avoid getting into irons after luffing to a comber, or to meet a heavy puff, a foresail will be found very useful. The foresail can either be set on a bowsprit, like the Ruby's (Plate XXIV.), or on a bumpkin like Mystery's, as shown on the same Plate.

Many experienced boat-sailers recommend a mizen instead of a foresail, and they argue that a mizen can be made as great a help to a boat's staying as a foresail. There is not much doubt that a mizen is a powerful lever to assist in throwing a vessel's head to wind; but it is of no use for paying a boat's head off, if she gets in irons. However, as shown in Mr. Baden Powell's sketch, if the tiller is carried aft (say 2ft.) of the rudder, to act as a mizen bumpkin, then each time the tiller is put down, or to leeward, the mizen will be brought to windward and may help in pushing the stern round. This may be so, and, if the boat kept moving through the water, she would no doubt ultimately describe an arc of a quadrant through the wind acting on the mizen; but when a boat is in irons she does not move through the water— at least not ahead, although she may get stern way on. Now if the mizen is kept across the boat whilst she is in irons, it will, if it has any effect at all, drive her astern as well as tend to push the stern on one side. As the latter motion will be counteracted by the direction the rudder is necessarily turned (presuming that the boat is making stern way), we doubt if the mizen can be manœuvred so as to be of much service in the case of a boat that has no head sail getting into irons. In fact, the proper thing to do, if a boat in a "lop," when under main and mizen sail, did get into irons, would be to let the mizen sheet go, and reverse the helm, and then haul the mainboom over to the side which is to be the weather one when she has filled; then, with stern way on, the boat's head will be boxed off, and she may be helped by a timely kick from a cross sea. Thus far the conclusion is forced upon us that, if two sails are decided upon, the foresail and mainsail have a slight advantage over the mizen and mainsail.

There may possibly be some advantage in open water in the main and mizen rig, if warning of a "kick-up" has not been taken advantage of to reef. Going into the eyes of an open boat to reef her foresail in a "lop" is by no means a pleasant or safe operation to perform, and indeed it should not be attempted unless a counterbalancing weight is put in the stern; the boat will then plunge violently, but there will be less danger of her being swamped. Now, with the main and mizen rig there will be no foresail to reef, and as the mainsail will be all in board, reefing when *in extremis* will be a comparatively easy operation. Again, if the mainsail has to be lowered in a hurry, the mizen will bring the boat to the wind, instead of taking her off as a foresail might. But the danger as last indicated can easily be avoided by letting go the head sheets before lowering the mainsail. Then the foresail might be found of service for scudding before a strong wind at sea. On the other hand, the mizen might be of use in rowing, in keeping the boat's head to the wind at sea. However, as snugging down should be never deferred, with a rising storm, until the sea got up so as to make reefing a foresail a matter of danger, we still cast in favour of the sloop or main and foresail rig for small open boats.

The question here naturally arises, if the mizen is of use as well as the foresail, why not have both? We certainly do not see why both should not be had; and, if the wind is so strong as to necessitate the mainsail being stowed, the boat will be fairly handy and manageable under mizen and foresail, although the canvas would scarcely be large enough to get her to windward with the wind dead on end or against a foul tide.

The fashion of lacing the sail to the boom of small boats is now general whatever the rig, and no doubt the plan has many advantages —the principal of which are that the foot can be kept straighter, and thereby the sail generally flatter, and in easing the sheet little or much the sail does not go into a bag; on the other hand without the boom, if the boat be struck by a squall, the wind will be spilled from the sail directly the sheet is loose; but the case is different with a boom sail; and if the squall be heavy it will be necessary to luff the boat up in good time and then ease the sheet, and prepare to lower the sail in case the squall should not abate.

To the question of how much sail it is prudent to give an open boat, the answer very much depends upon the requirements and capabilities of the boat-sailer. Sail areas* of open boats, we find, vary very considerably —from 1 to 3 times the product of the length multiplied by the breadth. Thus we find some cruising gigs, 17ft. long by 5ft. 6in. in beam (equal to 93·5 square feet), with about 90 square feet of canvas in their sails; a boat like the Ruby has a sail area (small jib and mainsail) equal to the

---

* The area of a lug sail will be found in the manner prescribed for an ordinary mainsail by yacht racing rules.

product of her length and breadth multiplied by 3 (L × B × 3). Other boats, only 14ft. by 5ft. 3in. (L × B equal to 73 square feet) which are raced, have single-sail areas of 180 square feet, or 2·4 times the area of that found by multiplying the breadth into the length. The latter proportion will only be safe in the hands of an expert, and the novice should begin with very small sails, or, in other words, the sail area should not exceed the length of the boat multiplied by her breadth.*

Sometimes in the sloop rig the jib or foresail, instead of being tacked outboard to a bumpkin, is laced at its foot to a boom; the sail is then "tacked" by this boom to the stem head, so much sail being forward of the stem as the space between the mast and the stem requires. A pair of sheets are required as usual, and the *weather* one should always take the weight of the sail; the lee one is consequently slack, but only so slack that when the boat is put about it takes the strain as the weather sheet. Thus the sheets need no trimming in tacking. The objection to this "revolving jib" is that it cannot be readily "spilled," as after the sheet is gone the sail will sometimes be balanced by the wind; hence the sail may not only be an inconvenient one, but a dangerous one. This objection can be somewhat removed by having the tack fast some distance ahead of the centre of length of the boom.

The "balance lug," Fig. 129—which is an adaptation of the Chinese lug, and was introduced at Surbiton by Mr. Burgoine (boat builder, of Kingston-on-Thames), about the year 1870—is a sail so arranged that it requires no dipping in going about; that is, it lies on the mast on one tack, and from the mast on the other. In this respect it resembles the "standing lug" of fishing craft and the lug sails now commonly used in small racing yachts; but the Surbiton lug has a large piece forward of the mast to "balance" the after part of the sail; hence the term balance lug. But in reality if a sail has a yard or gaff and boom "balancing" the sail is nothing more than an arrangement to admit of the mast being stepped farther aft than it otherwise could be.

The boom and yard are generally of about the same length, and the length of the mast is in a measure governed by the amount of peak, or round given to the head of the sail. If the yard is slung in its amidships, the sail should have great peak, and it will stand or sit better than if the sail be cut flat-headed. If the yard be slung nearer its lower end than amidships, the

* The most successful gigs that compete in the matches of the many sailing clubs of the upper Thames have enormous sail areas, often in one piece as a balance lug. These sail areas frequently equal three times the area, found by multiplying the length of the boat by the beam; and the boats, being dexterously handled, carry the sail well, and appear wonderfully handy. Of course it would be madness for a mere tyro to think of handling such a sail, even with plenty of live ballast on board.

sail, if not cut with a high peak, is apt to sag to leeward; and the same
might happen if the sail be very flat-headed and slung, say, one-third of
the length of yard from the lower end or heel of yard. A good place for

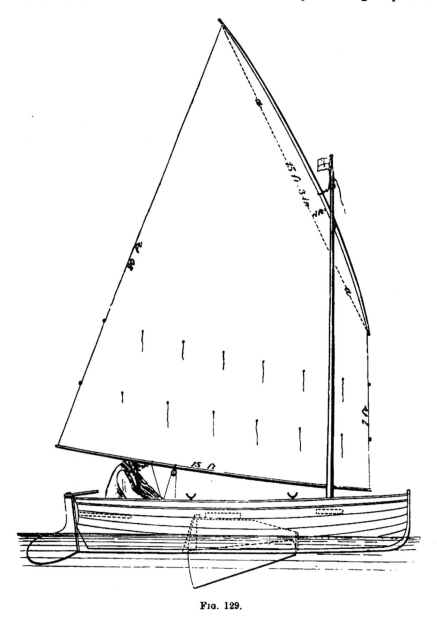

Fig. 129.

the slings of a well peaked and round headed sail will be about one-tenth
the length of yard from its amidships. (The head and foot of the sails
are always laced to yard and boom.)

The Surbiton boats originally had the yard slung at about two-fifths its length from the lower end, but a squarer sail and a better standing one can be obtained by slinging the sail nearer amidships (as shown in Plate XXIV. representing the Ruby and Mystery) and giving as much round to the head as shown in the drawing; the luff will be shorter than is generally given, but this probably will be found an advantage.

About one-seventh of the foot of the sail should be forward of the mast, and in slinging the yard and in bending the tack to the boom care must be taken that this proportion is not much exceeded. If too great a proportion of the sail is put forward of the mast it will not " balance," and in luffing to squalls, especially with the boom off the quarter, it will be found that, although the boat may come to a little, the sail will not spill. This peculiarity may be attended by some danger in the case of squalls or in clearing an obstacle, and may be accounted for by the fact that the ardency of the wind pressure on the fore part of the sail will be so great that it will more than balance the pressure on the greater area of the after-part, which, ordinarily, with the aid of the rudder, should bring the boat head to wind speedily.

No rig is handier for tacking in smooth water than the balance lug, and should a boat so rigged by any mischance show a tendency to miss stays or get in irons, her head can easily be paid off by holding the foot of the sail over to the side which is to be the weather one. This, of course, will stop the boat, and press her bodily to leeward or force her astern, and the sail should never be kept a-weather a moment longer than is necessary. Should the boat not gather way again quickly after the boom has been put over on the lee quarter again, the main sheet must be eased a trifle.

The sail is usually hoisted by a single halyard; to one end of this halyard a block is spliced; the other end is rove through a sheave hole in the mast head and bent to the yard; through the block a rope is rove, the standing part of which is made fast to the mast thwart and the hauling part through a block at the mast step. This forms a whip purchase, but if the sail be a large one a gun tackle purchase is used. The halyard is bent or hooked to a thimble-eye strop on the yard. The sail can be kept to the mast by a parrel thus contrived : a grommet strop, with thimble-eye seized in it, will be put on the yard about 6in. above the slings; another similar strop will be put on the yard at about 2ft. 6in. (for a 14ft. boat) below the slings; a line must be spliced to the lower thimble, and rove through the upper one round the aft side of the mast, back through the lower thimble. Thumb cleats must be put on the yard to prevent the strops slipping. When the sail is set, the line must be hauled as taut as it can be got and belayed.

x 2

But a neater plan than this is the mast iron, as shown in the diagram; the halyard is fast to an eye in the iron, and the latter is hooked to the thimble-eye strop on the yard. The disadvantage of the iron traveller is that the tack and sheet of the sail must be let go when the sail has to be lowered, or otherwise the sail will not lower. As the sail comes down the fore-end of the boom must be carried forward.

If an iron mast traveller be used the yard will be slung as shown in Fig. 129; if a parrel be used instead of the iron, the yard will be slung a little lower down, as the strop will be hauled close up to the sheave hole; consequently the sheave hole will be a little lower down, and the mast may be a trifle shorter (*see* "Mast Travellers" at the end of the chapter).

A downhaul should always be bent to the yard.

The tack will be bent to the boom abreast of the mast and lead through a block, either on mast thwart, or deck, as may seem most handy. The Surbiton plan for the tack is thus worked : a thimble is stropped to the boom abreast of the mast, and to the thimble 5ft. or 6ft. of line is spliced; the line is passed once round the mast, back through the thimble, then through a galvanised iron eye-bolt screwed into the mast some convenient distance below, and belayed to a cleat on the mast. For a 15ft. or larger boat a gun tackle purchase forms the tack. In setting the sail the luff can be got taut by swigging on this tack after hauling on the whip purchase of the halyards.

If topping lifts are used (they may be handy whilst reefing, or to brail the sail up), one part will be made fast to the masthead and lead across the sail, and through a thimble made fast under the boom by a seizing (or it can pass through the thimble in the strop of the main-sheet block) and up the other side of the sail, through a block at the masthead and the "fall" down by the side of the mast.

A wire forestay is generally set up to the stem head, and it is better that a gun-tackle purchase, or double-block purchase should be used for the setting up instead of a lanyard, as the mast (sails and all) can be lowered by it for passing under bridges, &c. The mast should be stepped in a tabernacle, which tabernacle will be open on the aft side and fitted in the aft side of the mast thwart. The forestay will go over the masthead by an eye; a thimble eye will be at the other end of the stay to take the lanyard or hook of the setting up tackle. In boats of 14ft. and under there will be a single wire shroud each side of the mast fitted the same as the forestay, but set up by lanyards to the eyes of neat chain plates fitted to the gunwale. Sometimes, however, the lanyard is rove through a thimble seized to the thwart or to a timber, or through a thole hole in a rowlock.

The main sheet is arranged thus ; standing part fast to the boom, then through a single block under one gunwale, then through a block stropped to boom and belayed under the other gunwale ; for the 10ft. boat, thimbles might be used instead of the blocks.

In the 10ft., 12ft., and 14ft. boat, the " Una " plan of main sheet may be suitable. An end of the sheet is fast to one quarter ; the other passes through a block on the boom, and through another block on the opposite quarter. For sailing on a wind it may be found that with the blocks on the gunwales the boom cannot be hauled in flat enough ; so, unless the blocks are on the transom at the extreme stern, the blocks should be fitted inside the gunwale. Another plan is to have the standing part of the sheet fast to the extreme end of the boom ; other end through a double block with traveller on a horse ; then through a single block on boom back through the double block, and belay by hitching the hauling part round the parts of the sheet above the double block.

Some of the Surbiton boats have the mainsheet thus fitted : A single block on main boom and one on a horse, also one on the deck a little ahead of the horse. The sheet is fast to the block on the boom, then leads through the block on the horse, back through the block on the boom, through the block on deck, and belay.

It will be seen that Ruby is fitted with bowsprit and foresail, and by an ingenious arrangement patented by Mr. Burgoine the foresail can be taken off or shifted or set without one of the crew going farther forward than the mast. Fig. 130 shows this arrangement in detail.

It is no doubt desirable that the sheaves C should be of good size, say 2¼in., with a deep score, and fit closely (and yet work freely) in the shackle. The inner edges of the shackle on the traveller should be rounded off to admit of the outhaul running freely.

The traveller is on the bowsprit as usual, but the tack of the foresail is attached to the traveller and outhaul by a running eye, or bight, and shackle, as shown by Fig. 130. In getting in the jib by hauling on the foot (which serves as an inhaul) the traveller runs up to the stem head, and by continuing to haul on the foot the rope H is further overhauled, and so the sail is hauled in close to the mast, and then lowered.

The sail plan of Ruby would do very well for the 17ft. boat given on page 311 ; but the sail would have to be cut down about 7ft. in leech, and 4ft. 6in. in luff.

Another form of the lug known as the " standing lug " or settee sail has been referred to, and is shown in Plate XXV., adapted from the lugs used in the boats belonging to the New Brighton Sailing Club on the Mersey. (A detailed description of the New Brighton rig will be given further on.)

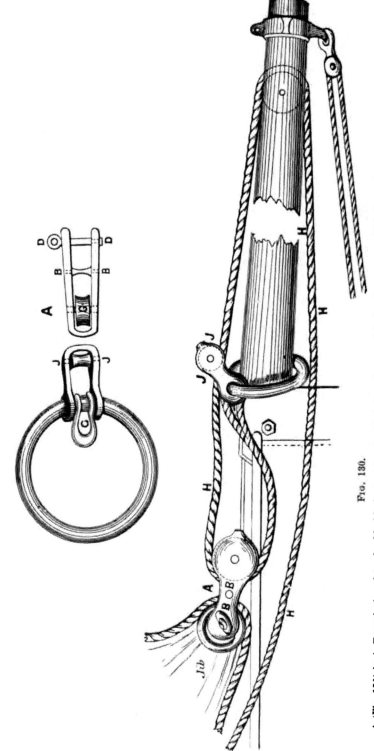

Fig. 180.

A (Fig. 180) is A. Burgoine's safety shackle block, to take the jib tack cringle.

B B is a safety pin or bar, riveted so as to prevent the sides of the shackle collapsing. It is also useful in preventing the shackle dropping off the outhaul when the cringle pin D is removed.

C is the sheave over which the outhaul runs.

The traveller has a shackle welded on it with a sheave J J. In this shackle is also a smaller shackle G, into which the outhaul H is eye-spliced.

It will be seen that the tack of the sail is close to the mast, and very little canvas is consequently forward of the mast. The dimensions and areas of the sails shown on Plate XXV., and adapted for a 17ft. boat, are as follows :—

MAINSAIL.

	ft.	in.		ft.	in.
Head (measured along the yard)	15	0	Luff	3	3
Leech..	18	0	Tack to peak earing	17	0
Foot	11	9	Clew to weather earing	13	0

This sail is drawn with 1ft. 4in. round to the head.

FORESAIL.

	ft.	in.			ft.	in.			ft.	in
Leech	8	6	Foot		6	6	Luff		10	9

MIZEN.

	ft.	in.		ft.	in.
Head	9	0	Luff	2	6
Leech	9	6	Tack to peak earing	10	6
Foot	6	6	Clew to weather earing	7	0

AREAS.

	sq. ft.
Mainsail	119
Foresail	27
Mizen	38
Total	184

Area of reduced mainsail for single-hand sailing, 85 sq. ft. (4ft. 6in. to be taken off yard).

The sail area shown in the drawing is a large one, but with three or four hands sitting to windward the boat would carry it well enough in moderate breezes and smooth water. For ordinary single-handed sailing it would be prudent to have a smaller mainsail, reduced as shown by the ticked line *a*; the sling would then come at *c*. The foresail should also be 2ft. shorter in hoist, and 6in. less on the foot; the mizen would be shortened 2ft. on the head.

The boat could be sailed with mainsail alone without shifting the mast, but she would probably be handier if the mast in such a case were shifted 1ft. farther forward. For turning her into the sloop rig, the mizen would be unshipped, the mainmast shifted 3ft. farther aft, and the foresail tacked to the stem instead of to the boomkin.

For a tyro who knows little or nothing of sailing, the 10ft. centre-board dinghy, rigged with a single balance lug, is a suitable craft for schooling, and, if he is fortunate enough to be located near a place where there is some shallow water, he may find out all about sailing without the assistance of a coach.

Sails suitable for a Cowes 15ft. skiff or a 20ft. cutter (not a racing suit) are shewn on Plate XXVI.

For centre board boats of the Una type various rigs are used, and on the Seine the French have brought into use an adaptation of the "sliding gunter rig." The drawing on Plate XXVII. illustrates this rig.

The rig, it will be seen, although of the sloop character, differs from the sloop in detail. The mainsail is a kind of sliding gunter, and the arrangements for hoisting and setting it are as follows. The mast is stepped on deck and pivoted in a tabernacle, by which it can be readily lowered

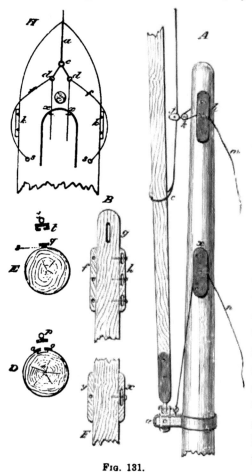

Fig. 131.

for passing underneath bridges, warps, &c. *a* shows the heel of the yard (*see* Plate XXVII. and A, Fig. 131). On this yard is a wire rope span from *c* to *a* (*see* large sketch), which passes through a block at *k*. The details of the arrangement will be more clearly understood by studying the smaller diagrams (Fig. 131). In A, *a* is an iron hoop traveller on the mast. Into the arms of this traveller the heel of the yard is inserted, and is so hinged as to form what is known as a universal joint. The hoisting halyard *n* is made fast to an eye in this traveller and passes through a cheek block on the mast at *x*. Sometimes a block is on the traveller, then (*see* F) one end of the halyard is put through the cleat on the mast as shown at *y*, and then has a knot tied in it to prevent it unreeving. The other end is passed through the block on the traveller, and then through the cheek block at *x*. If the sail is a very large one a whip purchase is also used. A block is seized to the halyard *n*, and through this block a rope is passed, one end of it being fast on deck.

In Fig. A, *c* represents an eye splice in the lower end of the wire rope span kept from slipping by a thumb cleat. This span passes through an iron block *j*. To this iron block a small wood block *k* is seized, and through the latter the halyard *m* is rove. The halyard *m*, in the first place, is rove through a cleat on the mast (*see* Fig. B) *f*; then through the block *k*, and over the sheave in the cheek block *h* (Fig. B). The halyard at *f* is stopped by a wall knot. In the diagram A, *m* is the hauling part or fall of the halyard. In the smaller sized vessels the block *k* is not used. One end of the halyard is seized to the iron or brass block *j*, and then passes over the sheave at *k*.

In Fig. B, the upper sheave above *h* is used for the foresail halyards; one end of the halyard is stopped by a wall knot after being rove through the hole above *f*; the other end is then passed through a block hooked to the head of the foresail, and then over the sheave above *h*.

The sheave *below h* is used for topping-lifts; one end of the topping-lift is stopped at the hole *below f*; the other is passed through a thimble seized on the under side of the main boom and is then carried up over the sheave below *h*. The large sheave hole at *g*, Fig. B, is used for spinnaker or square sail halyards. Mast hoops are not often seen. The sail is kept into the mast thus: Diagram D is a section of the mast; *o o* are two brass plates screwed to the lips of a channel cut on the aft side of the mast. *p* is a traveller about two inches deep which works in the channel formed by *o o*; the traveller has an eye to which one of the eyelet holes or cringles in the luff of the mainsail is seized. Generally as many of these travellers are used as there would be hoops if hoops were used.

Another arrangement is shown by E: *g* is a ⊤-shaped bar of iron screwed to mast (or sometimes instead of a ⊤-iron a plate of simple bar-iron is screwed over a fillet of wood, as shown by *s*, for lightness); *t* is the small traveller about two inches square which is shipped over *g*; *i* is the eye for seizing the luff cringles of the mainsail *x*.

If either of these travellers is used, the iron mast-traveller for the yard is dispensed with. A traveller (made with a socket to take a gooseneck on end of the yard) is inserted in the channel *o o* (*see* D) or over the guide *q* (*see* E).

One end of the main sheet is fast to the boom end; it from there leads through a double block on deck, through a single block on the boom, back through the double block on deck again, then through another single block on the boom and belay.

The bobstay is made of wire rope; one end has an eye in it, and this eye encircles the bowsprit at *v* (*see* large sketch); it then passes through a block on the stem at the water-line, through another block on the bowsprit end; a tackle is hooked to this end of the bobstay (at bowsprit end) to set it up.

The foresheets are very well arranged for handiness. In diagram H,
a represents the line of the foot of the foresail, *c* being the cringle in
the clew of the foresail.   To this cringle two short pieces of rope are
spliced with thimble eye at *d d* as well.   The foresheet is fast on the
deck to an eyebolt at *s*; it then passes outside the channels *k* through
the thimble *d* and through the coamings of the well at *x* and is then

FIG. 132.

belayed. It will be observed that in the diagram the foresail is represented
hauled amidships.

A very similarly worked mainsail is used in America for the "cat
boats" of Rhode Island. An illustration of this rig as given me
by Mr. R. B. Forbes, of Milton, Mass., is shown by Figs. 132 and 133,
a is a boom laced to the sail and used for reefing. *r* is a tackle for hauling

the reef down. The halyard *c* comes down to and belays to a cleat on the heel of the yard at *d*, close to the traveller *t*. By simply slacking the halyard *e*, and hauling on *r* the sail is reefed (*see* Fig. 133).

CHINESE OR BATTENED LUG SAILS.

The Chinese plan of battening a sail has been very much recommended, and there is not much doubt that battens will keep a thin calico

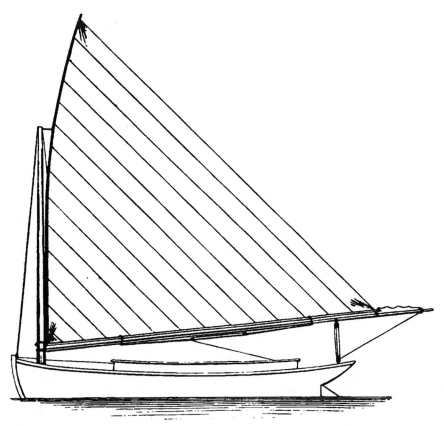

FIG. 133.

duck sail from going into a bag; the only objection to them of any importance is that they so much increase the weight of the sail. For a sail of the proportions given in Plate XXVIII., the battens are 1ft. 6in. distant at the luff of the sail, and 2ft. at the after leech.

The sketch shown on Plate XXVIII. (scale ½in. equal to 1ft.), made by Mr. W. Baden Powell, shews the arrangement of battens. Mr. Powell thus describes the gear and fitting of the sail:

"*Rig.*—Mainsail of the largest size the boat will carry in a steady moderate breeze, placed forward so that its centre of effort comes ahead of the centre of lateral resistance of the boat ; mizen of the same cut as main, but of such size and so placed as to bring the centre of effort of the whole sail plan aft of the centre of lateral resistance.

"*Fitting.*—The mainsail is fitted with a yard, a boom, and three or four battens ; the sail is laced to yard and boom ; the battens put into pockets formed by sewing a 'reef band' across the sail to take the batten. The battens are made of pine, and taper at the ends. They are about 1⅜in. deep, by 1in. thick in the middle. The reef earings reeve through thimbles on the boom.

"*Halyards.*—Toggle on the single part to a becket or strop on the yard. The battens and the yard are kept in to mast by toggle and becket parrels·

"*Tack* is a single rope, leading from the well to a block on deck at side of mast ; it then toggles to a becket on boom, about one-eighth the boom's length from fore-end.

"The mast fitted on a 'tabernacle'* and pinned above deck, is a *sine quâ non*, whether the boat be used for river or sea work ; bridges and tow ropes come against your mast in river work—ships' warps in harbours ; and, when at anchor fishing, &c., unshipping the mast will permit the boat to ride easy.

"A topping-lift is fitted, standing part fast to masthead, then down one side of sail, to reeve through sheet block strop thimble ; then up on other side of sail to and through a block at masthead, and down to the deck. Being through sheet block strop, which toggles on to boom, this topping-lift remains with sheet on mast when sail is taken off and stowed away, and is thus ready for a change of sails.

"A kind of gathering line, or sail keeper, is fitted to hold the sail up clear of the deck at the mast when it is lowered down, thus : one end fast at masthead, then down the side of sail on which the mast is not, and round under boom, and up, making it fast round the mast about 1ft. above the boom : thus, when going to set up sail, you place forward end of boom, yard, and batten all in a bunch, between the mast and gathering lines, then the after ends through between the two parts of the topping-lift ; toggle the sheet, tack, and halyard on, and the sail is ready to set ; the

---

* A tabernacle is a perpendicular square trunk, usually open on the aft side, made to take the lower part of the mast ; if the mast is stepped on deck (as those of the river barges are) the heel of the mast will be pivoted on a bolt passing athwartships through the sides of the tabernacle above the deck, as shown in Plate XXVIII. Brass or iron plates should be fitted to the tabernacle where the bolt passes through, and there should be an iron band or ring on the heel of the mast. In an open boat the mast can be pivoted near the bottom of the tabernacle on a bolt through the tabernacle (athwartship) ; on the heel of the mast are two scores 1¼in. deep cut in it to fit the bolt.

batten parrels can be toggled at any time afterwards, as they only effect a good ' sit ' to the sail.

" The tiller should be formed as if double, *i.e.*, one part leading aft, and used as mizen boomkin, and the other on fore side of rudder with a ∪ bend in it, to allow it to clear mizenmast. Thus fitted when working ship, on putting the helm down the mizen is brought to windward, and helps bring the boat to ; or when the helm is put up, mizen helps the boat off.

" A battened sail can easily be reefed ' in stays,' *i.e.*, while going about, without even checking the boat's way, for the battens do not require the reef points to be tied, except for neatness, unless it is a very deep reef.

" A boat thus rigged can be hove-to in bad weather at sea, or, when waiting for tide into harbour, thus : take the mainsail off the mast, bunch

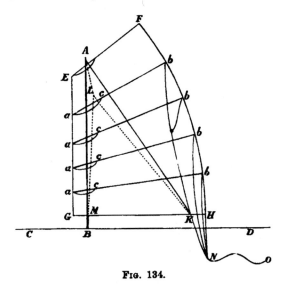

Fɪɢ. 134.

" AB, mast ; EF, head of sail ; EG, luff of sail ; *ab*, battens ; CD, line of gunwale ; GH, foot of sail ; FH, leech of sail ; *ac*, loops or parrels ; AK, brail leading through eye at K, the position of the brail on starboard side of sail being shown by dotted lines KL, AL, and LM ; the letters *b*N denote sheets hanging loose (over the sail instead of abaft it, as they would be when hauled in for sailing), leading into a single one, NO."

yard and boom together, and span it with a rope : to the centre of the span fasten your boat's hawser, let the sail and battens hang loose, heave it overboard, and pay out the hawser ; lower the mainmast, and haul mizen sheet fore and aft. Thus she will ride head to wind, and the sail will break much of the sea. The storm main lug may then be got ready, in case you have to cut and run."

In gaff sails made of stout canvas, where the peak halyards assist in keeping the sail flat, or in any sail that is well cut and can be kept flat, the advantage of battens will not be great.

In China, where battens are almost invariably used, the shape and "rig" of the lug much varies; but all are provided with a brail, which resembles in its uses a topping-lift.

To each batten is fastened a loop or parrel, made of rattan or rope. The shape and position of these loops are indicated in Fig. 134. There is no tack proper, but the lower batten is made fast to the mast at the point where they intersect. The luff projects about one-seventh of the breadth of the sail forward of the mast. The sheets generally lead from several of the lower battens, one from each, and are united into one sheet in such a way that the pull is everywhere equal. The brail or topping-lift is fitted

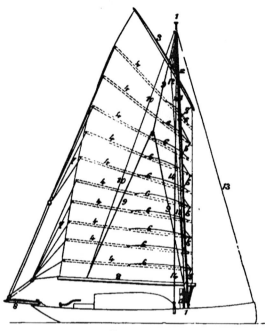

Fig. 135.

in a very simple and efficient manner. A line leads from the masthead down the inside of the sail (*i.e.*, the side on which the battens are), through an eye 1ft. or 2ft. from the after end of the lower batten, up again on the outside of the sail through another eye rove in the end of a short pendant from the masthead, and down again to the point where the lower batten and mast intersect, where it is made fast ready for use. The sail thus hangs in the bight of the brail as in a sling.

At Shanghae the completely battened lug sail is in much favour, as illustrated by Fig. 134.

Battens are shown by 4 (Fig. 135) on plan. The bridles lead into two bowlines (7), and the bowlines again into one part, the latter leading to a double block on the bumpkin (8), so that hauling on this single part brings an equal strain on each bowline-bridle. To keep the sail into the mast a lacing (5 in the drawing) rove through parrels which extend from the luff of the sail to well into its belly; these parrels are distinguished by 6 on the sail plan. Beyond this, a hauling parrel is used to keep the yard into the mast, marked 12. The standing part is made fast to the yard, passing round the mast, then through a block on the yard, the hauling part leading to the deck. The topping-lift shown by No. 9 explains itself, the line denoted by figures 10 being the topping-lift on the port side. The topping-lift passes through a single block at the masthead. The other figures indicate as follows : 1, the mast; 2, the boom; 3, the yard; 11, main halyards; 13, forestay; 14, shroud.

MOUNT'S BAY AND FALMOUTH LUG SAILS.

The Mount's Bay craft have foresail and mizen (Fig. 136). The mizen-mast has more hoist than is necessary for setting the ordinary mizen, so that the second foresail may be set in its place in light weather. A

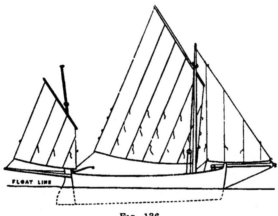

FLOAT LINE

Fig. 136.

longer outrigger than that shown would be then required. The Falmouth boats have no foresail, and the mast is stepped farther forward. The omission of a jib in the Falmouth boats is for the convenience of dispensing with a bowsprit whilst running alongside shipping. Fig. 137 is a sketch of the Falmouth waterman's rig. It is in use for boats from 14ft. long up to substantial little craft of 18ft. These boats go out in all kinds of weather, and, although the mast being so far forward might tend to increase their pitching, it could not make any considerable difference to their fore and aft motion, as the mast after all is very light and the bowsprit is dispensed with. There should be a horse of galvanised iron across the stern for the main sheet, with a single and double block, the double block grommeted to a thimble traversing on the horse. A

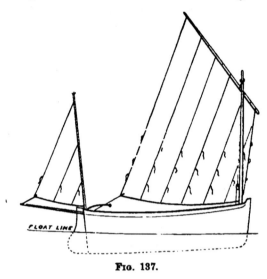

FLOAT LINE

Fig. 137.

collar should be welded on the horse at each elbow, to prevent the traveller getting round the bends, and so getting jammed.

SPRIT SAILS.

Sprit sails formerly were in high favour, but since 1860 they have gradually fallen into disuse. It is still a favourite rig, however, among watermen about the Solent, and they probably adhere to it because there is so little gear. The old Ryde wherries, celebrated for their fine weatherly qualities, were sprit-rigged, but of late years they have generally adopted the gaff instead of the sprit. The advantages of the sprit over a gaff for setting a sail in a small boat cannot be denied, as by crossing the sail diagonally it takes up all the slack canvas in the middle of the sail, even if it be an old sail. Also, by taking down the sprit, a nice snug three cornered sail can be had. On the other hand, a sprit is an awkward spar to handle, and it need be much longer and heavier than a gaff to set similar sails.

In small boats the luff of the sail is usually laced to the mast through eyelet holes about 2ft. apart; the throat is secured to an iron traveller, or sometimes to a grommet strop. In large sails galvanised iron rings or mast hoops are used. The tack is lashed to a small eyebolt screwed into the mast. The sail is hoisted by a single halyard and belayed to the gunwale to serve as a shroud. The foresail is also belayed by a single halyard, and belayed to the opposite gunwale. The sprit is supported on the mast by a strop called a snotter; this strop is a piece of rope with an eye spliced in each end; it is put round the mast, and one end rove through

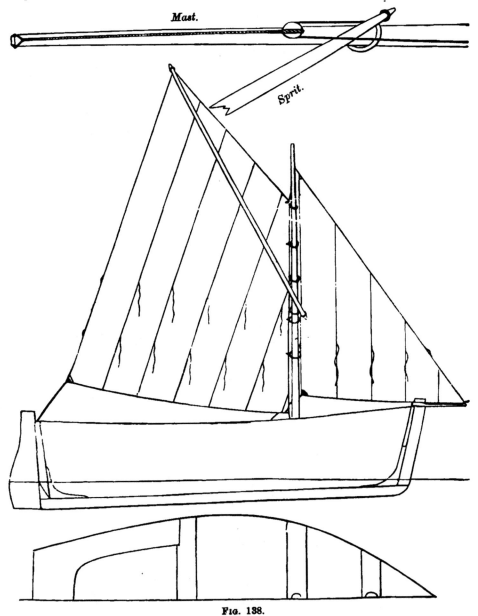

FIG. 138.

an eye; the heel of the sprit is put in the other eye. After the sail is hauled up on the mast the upper end of the sprit is put into the eye or cringle on the peak of the sail, and then shoved up and the heel slipped

Y

into the snotter.   The sail is then peaked by pushing the snotter and heel of sprit as high as required; the sail is then sheeted.   If the sail

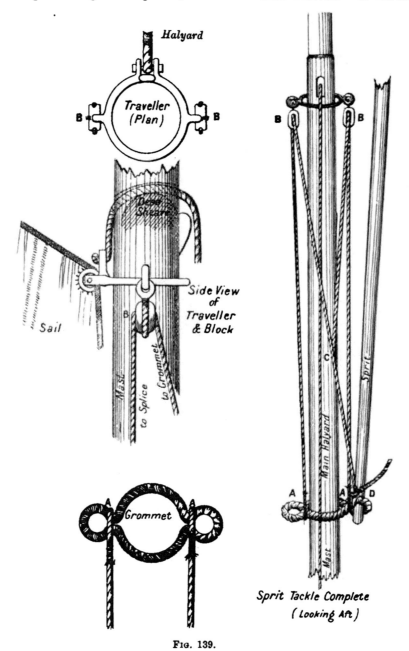

Fig. 139.

is large and the sprit heavy, a traveller and whip purchase are used for the sprit.   (*See* Fig. 139.)

A pendant with a running eye in it is fitted over the masthead; at the lower end of this pendant is a block, through which the hauling part is rove, one end being fast to the thwart. Sometimes a gun-tackle purchase is used instead of the whip purchase. Either is to be preferred to the snotter alone, as without any other support the snotter will be continually working down. If the heel of the sprit got jumped out of the snotter it might go through the bottom of the boat; this accident has often happened. The waterman's remedy against working down is wetting the mast, but the single whip purchase is to be preferred, and is necessary for large sails.

Mr. A. Strange has adopted the following plan for hoisting the sprit. (*See* Fig. 139.) There is a traveller on the mast, with halyard as shown. A dumb cleat on the mast keeps the hauling part of the halyard clear of the traveller. On the traveller are two blocks, B B. A grommet has two eyes seized in it, and again two eyes in the halyards, A A, are spliced round the eyes in the grommet. The sprit halyards are spliced at C; and the fall leading from C is belayed round the heel of the sprit at D. Lowering the sail or sprit is therefore one operation.

THE SLIDING GUNTER.

The sliding gunter, it has been claimed, has all the advantages of the lug sail; has lighter spars compared with sail area, and is less dangerous.

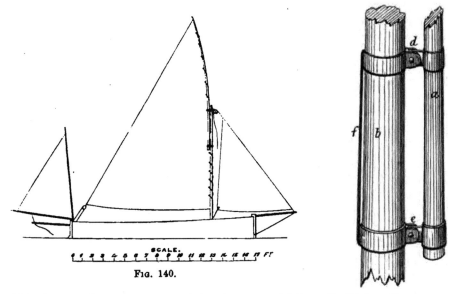

Fig. 140.

This is true of the old-fashioned dipping lug, which no doubt is a dangerous sail, but the gunter cannot compete with the balance lug, for effectiveness.

The mast, it will be seen by Fig. 140, is in two pieces, the upper part

Y 2

sliding on the aft side of the lower by two irons.   When hoisted the lower part of the luff of the sail is laced to the mast.   The irons should be of brass or of galvanised iron, covered with leather, and they should be kept well soaped or greased.   The irons are fitted to the hoisting part of the mast, *a* (usually termed the topmast or yard), and should fit the lower mast, *b*, very loosely, as a common peculiarity of the iron is to jam either in hoisting or lowering—mostly during the latter operation—especially if the boat be heeled.   The irons can be in two parts, *d* being freed when the sail has to be stowed, and then lowers on the hinge *e*.   A connecting rod is shown by *f*, which is also the fore side of the lower mast.   The yard is hoisted by a single halyard rove through a sheave-hole at the lower mast-head.   The halyard is fast to the heel of the yard, and a score is cut out for it on the fore-side of the yard ; it leaves the yard at the upper iron.   The gunter rig is sometimes applied to long boats with three masts, a stay foresail being invariably used.   The sketch given shows a sail fit for a 17ft. boat, and has foresail and Mudian mizen.

LOWESTOFT LATEEN SAIL.

Although the lateen rig is met with all over the world, it has not been much adopted on the English coast owing probably to the length and

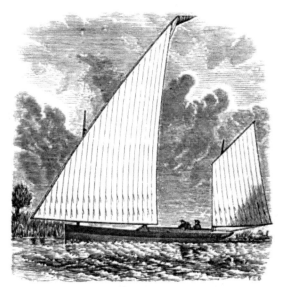

FIG. 141.

weight of the yard required, and the awkwardness of the reefing arrangements.   Sometimes the sail is reefed along the foot, as shown in the engraving of an old Lowestoft lateen (*see* Fig. 141), and sometimes along both foot and head yard. In the sketch given, the sail is shown with very great peak, but the sails are sometimes planned with the yard more across the mast, and with a longer boom. A lug mizen is generally a part of the rig. The boom is kept to the mast by an iron traveller or ring.

The settee sail is an adaptation of the lateen; the yard does not reach quite down to the tack, so that a short up-and-down luff is obtained to the extent of two or three reefs.

MAST TRAVELLERS.

A good mast traveller for small boats is a thing very much in request, not only for facility in hoisting, but above all for lowering without jamming.

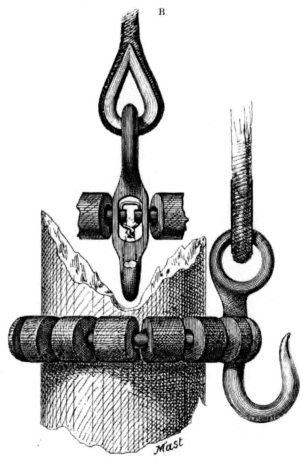

Fig. 142.

Such a traveller has been patented by Mr. R. D. Ferguson (of Messrs. Ferguson and Co., sailmakers, Roslin-street, Greenock). From Fig. 142 it will be seen that it somewhat resembles an ordinary parrel, but instead of a rope being rove through the reels, the latter are put on a stout steel wire, which will keep in shape (see A.). The ends of this wire are perforated, and, as will be seen in Fig. 142, meet in a slot in the hook ; they are then connected by small steel wire as shown, or by split pins. Further, it should be said, if a particularly neat appearance should be required, the connection could be made by a right and left screw nut ; or the holes in the hook could be tapped so as to form right and left screw nuts, providing it was not required to take the traveller off the mast. We have had no actual experience of this traveller, but we consider that it will do what Mr. Ferguson claims for it—run freely either in hoisting or lowering. Beyond

Fig. 143.

that, it admits of the yard or throat cringle of a boat's sail being hoisted close up to the sheave in the mast, and will hold the sail close in to the mast. It should be said that the ring can be hinged at the part opposite to the hook, and it can then be put on the mast without the mast being lowered.

It should be noted that a sail, the yard of which is kept to the mast by a traveller, is likely to jam under the following conditions, depending on the shape of the sail and the position of the slings :

1. If the length from clew to tack, added to the length of the yard from slings to throat, is greater than the length of the diagonal from clew to throat, then the yard will jam as soon as the diagonal becomes tight.

In this case the jamming may be prevented by letting go the outhaul before lowering, thereby reducing the distance from clew to tack to any desired extent.

2. If the luff of the sail is shorter than the part of the yard from slings to throat, the yard will not lower right down without unhooking the tack; but this should never be the case in a properly shaped sail, and in fact very seldom is.

To avoid the yard jamming Mr. W. W. Lloyd, of Castletownsend, Co. Cork, used a span on the yard, as shewn by Fig. 143, and he thus described it:

"A strong wire span, A, is spliced at both ends round the yard. The upper eye to be a couple of inches above the usual spot for slinging the yard, the lower eye a couple of inches below the spot on the yard that would come abreast of the mast when the yard is down.

"This span is put on as taut as can be got, and a seizing put round yard and wire just where the splice comes at both ends, the seizing put on somewhat slack, and finished off with enough turns under the wire to make it stand well clear of the yard; the object of the seizing is to prevent the traveller hook jamming.

"In hoisting, as the yard goes up the traveller hook, B, slips along the wire into its proper place at the upper end, and in lowering as soon as the yard comes to the sticking point the wire slips along the hook, and down it comes.

"The objection to any plan that entails extra length of halyard is, that if fitted with whip or gun-tackle purchase there is not enough drift between the blocks.

"A neater plan than the wire span would be a galvanised iron horse."

See also the Mersey Sailing Boats.

CHAPTER XIII.

SMALL CENTRE-BOARD YACHTS.

UNA BOATS.

THOSE wonderful little crafts called "Una" boats were introduced to us in 1853, in this way: the late Marquis of Conyngham (then Earl Mount-Charles), was in America in 1852, and in the boat building yard of Robert Fish (now well known as a yacht designer), saw and purchased the boat since celebrated as the "Una." He sent her to London by steamer, whence she was transported by rail to Southampton, and then towed to Cowes, having meanwhile spent a summer on the Serpentine, but without exciting the interest she did at Cowes. In fact, the Cowes people almost regarded the Una as a little too marvellous to be real. To see the Una dodging about on a wind and off a wind, round the stern of this craft, across the bows of that one, and generally weaving about between boats where there did not look room enough for an eel to wriggle, astonished the Cowes people, who had never seen anything more handy under canvas than a waterman's skiff with three sails, or an Itchen boat with two, or more unhandy than a boat with one sail—the dipping lug; but the Una with her one sail showed such speed, and was so handy, that in less than a year there was a whole fleet of Unas at Cowes, and about the Solent. The genus was named Una after Lord Conyngham's importation, and to this day no class of boat is a greater favourite for smooth-water sailing.

In America, the Una or "cat-rig" as it is termed, is very popular and at Newport, Rhode Island, where the rig is mostly seen, the boats enjoy a great reputation for handiness, weatherliness, and speed. There is no doubt that the one sail plan is the best for weatherly qualities and for handiness, if there be no sea, and if it is all turning to windward. In a sea, however, the heavy mast, stepped so far forward, makes the boats plunge dangerously, and the boats themselves are so shallow that they are not very well adapted for smashing through a head sea. Off a wind they are extremely wild, and show a very great tendency to broach to.

This tendency of coming to against the helm is common to all shallow boats when they are sailed off the wind; and if the rudder of a boat has to be kept right across her to check the tendency, speed is of course very much retarded. The rudder should be long—a fifth of the length of the boat—with a large piece out of water so that the stern wave may be made use of to assist in turning the boat (*see* the Plate of the "Parole"). In strong winds the boom should be well topped up when carried off the quarter, and if the boat gripes so badly that the helm will not take her off, the main sheet must be played upon. The first symptom of griping should be intercepted by the helm. As a rule it is found that lifting the centre board greatly relieves the weather helm; and as the board is not wanted off a wind to increase the lateral resistance, it is always better to haul it up; the boat will often steer all the better for it, and there will be less surface for friction.

Some boat sailers have used a small jib on a short bowsprit when sailing off a wind; but of course this destroys the "Una" or one sail rig. The bowsprit would run out through an iron fitted to the stem head, and the heel could be lashed to the mast if no bitts were fitted, as there need not be. A shroud would be required each side, and a bobstay, but if the bowsprit were a mere bumpkin only three or four feet long, no shrouds would be required.

A few years ago a boat built on the model of the Una, had her mast shifted to 5ft. abaft the stem and a foresail added and mainsail reduced; she was found very easy on her helm when sailing off the wind, as might be expected; but on a wind she would not lie so close, and quite proved the inferiority of the two sails, so far as sailing to windward in smooth water went. The advantages of the one sail are almost wholly confined to sailing to windward in smooth water, and, as putting small boats to windward under such conditions is the principal charm of sailing them at all, the Una rig will retain its popularity.

Una boats, of course, are prone to capsize, and a person might be tempted into pressing them, because of the enormous stiffness they show up to the time that their gunwale or deck becomes level with the water. However, with skilful management "Unas" are safe enough, and on the whole are not so dangerous as an open boat of similar length. They should always be luffed to squalls before their cockpit coamings have a chance of being immersed, and a foot or two of main sheet (which should be held in the hand) given them if they cannot be relieved sufficiently without their being brought head to wind—a course never desirable if it can be avoided, as the boats soon lose steerage way. It is never advisable to let the main sheet go altogether with a boom sail, as it is with one without a boom, as the sail will not spill, and the boom may get in the water, which would be awkward, to say the least, if the boat got stern way on.

The " Una's " stores, copied from an inventory of the same, made when she was packed off by rail to Southampton, were as under: "One mast, one boom, one gaff, one pair of oars, one sail, one sail cover, one hatch cover, one rudder and tiller, four blocks, one main halyard, two bell-metal rowing-pins, four pigs of lead ballast." All that need be added to this list is a " baler," and it would do for a Una of the present day.

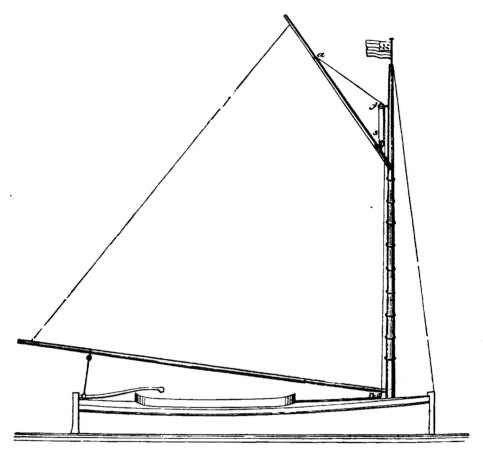

SAIL PLAN 'UNA' BOAT ⅜ INCII SCALE.

FIG. 144.

The rig, it will be seen upon reference to the sail plan, Fig. 144, is simple in the extreme, and even the famed balance lug cannot beat it in this respect. The sail is hoisted by a single halyard. The standing part is made fast on the gaff at *a*, then leads through a double block at *j* on the mast, through a single block *s* on the jaws of the gaff, up through *j* again, and down to the deck where the fall leads through a block *n* by the side of the mast, and belayed on the aft end of centre-board case. The fall can then be taken aft to the hand of the helmsman, who, in case of need, can drop the sail between topping-lifts (not shown in the drawing) without leaving the tiller. The Una had no stay at all, but the Cowes fashion now is to have a forestay, which prevents the mast going aft when sailing on a wind; and a slightly lighter mast can be carried if a forestay is used. All Una boats should have topping-lifts, as it is necessary to top the boom when sailing off the wind in strong breezes, and a lift is handy in setting, stowing, or reefing the sail.

The main sheet is made fast to an eye bolt on one quarter, close to the intersection of gunwale and transom; it then leads through a block on the boom, and through a block on the other quarter, the fall coming into the well or cockpit to belay. This plan of fitting the main sheet is still known as the "Una," just as the plan of working the halyards all in one is.

Practically, the Cowes Una boat of the present time differs very little from the original. The floor, it will be found, upon reference to the diagrams and tables, is a trifle flatter than the Una's; the quarters are lifted a little, as will be seen upon comparing the transoms; and there is more freeboard—the latter being a very desirable addition. The load water-line of the two crafts are almost identical, as will be found by comparing the half-breadths for the same. The centre-boards are of about equal area, the only alterations being that the modern plan is to pivot the board in the keel below the garboard, whilst formerly they were pivoted in the case inside the boat. The Cowes Una has a trifle less draught forward than the original, and the stem piece does not tumble aft; but, in other respects, there is not much difference in the two sheer plans, always of course remembering the increase in the free-board. The draught of water of the Cowes Una forward appears to be excessive, and off a wind at least she would be lightened by the head to the extent of three or four inches.

The design for a Cowes Una (Plate XXIX.) has been made so that it is adapted for either a real "Una" of 15ft. 6in. in length, or one of greater size 21ft. in length. The sail plan of the Cowes boat is a smaller one than the Una had, but it will be found large enough for ordinary sailing. The sail, of course, will be laced to the boom, and a topping-lift would be found of service to keep the boom up when the peak is lowered, or when running off the wind.

The original Una is still in existence on the estate of Lord de Ros, in Ireland, the late Marquis of Conyngham having presented her to that nobleman in 1873.

DIMENSIONS, &c.

	Una.		15ft. 6in.		21ft.	
	ft.	in.	ft.	in.	ft.	in.
Length, extreme	16	0	15	6	21	0
Beam, extreme	6	6	6	6	8	8
Keel sided amidships	0	7	0	4½	0	6
Keel sided fore end	0	2	0	2	0	2½
Keel sided aft end	0	2	0	2	0	2½
Moulding (depth) of keel	0	2¾	0	4	0	5
Floors sided	0	¾	0	1	0	1½
Floors moulded	0	1¼	0	1½	0	2
Timbers sided	0	¾	0	1	0	1½
Thickness of plank	0	⅝	0	½	0	¾
Thickness of top strake	0	¾	0	¾	0	1
Mast, deck to hounds	16	0	14	0	18	6
Boom	18	0	15	6	21	0
Gaff	9	3	7	6	10	0
Luff of mainsail	12	0	9	9	13	0
Foot of mainsail	17	6	15	6	20	8
Head of mainsail	9	0	7	0	9	6
Leech of mainsail	19	0	17	8	23	6
Tack to peak earing of mainsail	20	0	16	0	21	0
Clew to throat earing	19	0	17	0	22	9
Centre of mast from the fore side of stem at L.W.L.	2	0	2	0	2	6
Diameter of mast at deck	0	4½	0	4½	0	5
Diameter of mast at hounds	0	2¾	0	2½	0	2½
Weight of displacement of boat to L.W.L. (approximate)	13 cwt.		14 cwt.		1·4 ton.	

LAYING-OFF TABLE, COWES UNA AND UNA 1852, ¼IN. SCALE.

	1		2		3		4		5		6		7		8	
	ft.	in.	ft.	in.	ft.	in.	ft.	in.	ft.	in.	ft.	in.	ft.	in.	ft.	in.
Heights to top of timbers above L.W.L.	1	6½	1	3½	1	1½	1	0	0	11½	0	11	0	11½	1	1
Una of 1852 ,, ,,	0	11	0	9½	0	8½	0	8	0	8	0	8¾	0	9	1	0
Depths below L.W.L. to rabbet	0	6½	—		—		—		0	9	0	8½	0	6½	—	
Una of 1852 ,, ,,	0	7½	—		—		—		0	8¼	0	8	0	6½	—	
Half-breadths on deck	0	8¾	1	9	2	5½	2	11	3	2¼	3	1½	2	10	2	1¼
Una of 1852 ,,	0	7½	1	7	2	4	2	11	3	2¼	3	1	2	9¾	2	3
Half-breadths on L.W.L.	0	4¾	1	2	1	11¼	2	5¾	2	9¼	2	8	1	11¾	—	
Una of 1852 ,,	0	4	1	1	1	10¾	2	6	2	9¾	2	8½	2	1	—	
Half-breadths on diagonal *k*	0	7½	1	6¼	2	2¼	2	8¼	2	11¼	2	10¼	2	5	1	4½
Una of 1852 ,,	0	7	1	5¼	2	2	2	8½	2	11¼	2	10½	2	5½	1	6¼
Half-breadths on diagonal *m*	0	6	1	2	1	8	2	0	2	2½	2	1	0	9	0	5½
Una of 1852 ,,	0	5½	1	1½	1	8½	2	1½	2	3¼	2	1	1	7	0	6
Half-breadths on diagonal *x*	0	3½	0	7½	0	10½	1	0½	1	2	1	1	0	9	—	
Una of 1852 ,,	0	3¼	0	8	0	1	1	2¾	1	3	1	0½	0	7½	—	

All the half-breadths are without the plank.

In the body plan of the Cowes Una the midship section is shown on both sides of the middle line, *o*, between Nos. 4 and 6 sections. The station for the midship section is shown at No. 5 in the sheer plan.

No. 1 section is 1ft. 3in. from the fore side of the stem; all the other sections are 2ft. apart, but No. 8 (transom) is 2ft. 3in. from No. 7 station.

In the case of the Una of 1852, No. 8 (transom) is 2ft. 9in. from No. 7 station.

Diagonal *k* is struck 10¾in. above the L.W.L., and at *k* 1 and *k* 2 cuts the side perpendiculars *p p* 1½in. below the L.W.L.

Diagonal *m* is struck 4½in. above the L.W.L., and at *m* 1 and *m* 2 is 3ft. out from the middle vertical line *o*.

Diagonal *x* is struck 1¾in. below the L.W.L., and at *x* 1 and *x* 2 is 1ft. 6in. out from the middle vertical line *o*.

The base line *a a* is 9in. below the L.W.L., and parallel thereto.

LAYING-OFF TABLE FOR 21FT. "UNA" BOAT, ¾IN. SCALE.

	ft. in.	ft. in.	ft. in.	ft. in.	ft. in.	ft. in.	ft. in.	ft. in.
Heights above L.W.L. to top of timbers	2 0¼	1 8¼	1 6	1 4	1 3	1 3	1 3¼	1 5¼
Depths below L.W.L. to rabbet	0 8¼	—	—	—	1 0	0 11¼	0 8¼	—
Half-breadths on deck	0 11¾	2 4	3 3¼	3 11	4 3	4 2	3 9¼	2 10
Half-breadths on L.W.L.	0 6¼	1 7	2 6¼	3 4	3 8	3 6¼	2 7¼	—
Half-breadths on diagonal k	0 10¼	2 0¼	2 11¼	3 7¼	3 11¼	3 10	3 3	1 8¼
Half-breadths on diagonal m	0 8	1 6¼	2 3	2 8	2 11¼	2 9¼	2 1¼	0 7¼
Half-breadths on diagonal z	0 4¼	0 10	1 2¼	1 4¾	1 7	1 5¼	1 0	—

All the half-breadths are without the plank. No. 1 section is 1ft. 10in. from the fore side of the stem; all the other sections are 2ft. 8in. apart, but No. 8 (transom) is 3ft. 2in. from No. 7 station. Diagonal k is struck 1ft. 2½in. above the L.W.L., and at k 1 and k 2 cuts the side perpendiculars p p 2 inches below the L.W.L. Diagonal m is struck 6in. above the L.W.L., and at m 1 and m 2 is 4ft. out from the middle vertical line o. Diagonal z is struck 2½in. below the L.W.L. and at z 1 and z 2 is 2ft. out from the middle vertical line o. The base line a a is 1ft. below the L.W.L., and parallel thereto.

On Plate XXX. are the lines of the large Una boat Mocking Bird, built by Messrs. Stockham and Pickett, of West Quay, Southampton, for Mr. Prescott Westcar, from a design by the author in 1882. A lead keel as shown was, however, fitted instead of the centre-board, but the limited draught which had to be observed did not admit of the keel being deep enough for good weatherly qualities.

The Mocking Bird sailed a match against the American cat boat Gleam in a strong wind, and beat her by twelve and a half minutes; but it was about two-thirds reaching, and by the wind the Gleam showed herself to be the more weatherly craft; the case, however, might have been different had Mocking Bird been fitted with a centre-board. The Gleam usually had several hundredweight of shifting ballast, or a crew of a dozen to sit to windward in strong winds; otherwise she could not carry her large sail. The lines of Gleam are given on Plate XXXI.

The following table gives the dimensions, &c., of the two boats:

	GLEAM.	MOCKING BIRD.
Length on load-water line	25ft. 2½in.	30ft.
Breadth, extreme	11ft. 1in.	10ft. 6in.
Draught of water	2ft. 3½in.	4ft.
Length of centre-board	8ft.	none
Board pinned from stem	11ft.	—
Displacement	3·5 tons.	7 tons
Lead on keel	2½ cwt. iron.	2 tons
Lead inside	16 cwt.	2 tons
Mast deck to hounds	27ft. 6in.	28ft.
Boom, mast to pin of sheave	35ft. 4in.	36ft.
Gaff, mast to lacing hole	19ft.	18ft. 6in.
Luff of mainsail	23ft. 6in.	22ft. 9in.
Mast from fore-side of stem	1ft. 7½in.	2ft. 2in.
Area of sail	760 sq. ft.	760 sq. ft.
Y.R.A. tons	8·6	10

THE CENTRE-BOARD SLOOP PAROLE.

The light draught beamy centre-board boat is in high repute in America, and the sloop rig is quite as much the fashion as the cat rig. The "jib and mainsail boats," as they are characteristically termed, for speed in light winds and smooth water are probably unsurpassed, and the handling of them is followed with keen enjoyment by a large number of boat sailers on the American seaboard. Their length on water-line varies from 24ft. to 28ft., and their breadth from 10ft. to 11ft. 6in.

The drawing on Plate XXXII. shows the lines of Parole, one of the fastest boats yet built by Mr. Jacob Schmidt, of Tompkinsville, Staten Island, New York. He also built other successful boats, amongst which were Dare Devil, Pluck and Luck, Susie S., &c.; and he is one of the best open boat sailers in New York Bay.

The drawing is to ½in. scale, and the water-lines are 4in. apart. The scantling of the timbers of American elm would be 1½in. moulded by 2in. sided, and be spaced 1ft. apart. The plank would be ¾in. thick; stem and stern post 2¾in. sided. The centre-board appears to be unnecessarily large, and might very well be less in depth.

The sail plan shows the racing outfit. The main sheet is led through two blocks on outriggers extending some distance over the stern (an invention of Mr. Schmidt), and through a block travelling on a horse. The inner block on the boom is a snatch block, and only used when the boat is close-hauled.

The mast is 10in. diameter at the deck, and 5½in. at the truck. The mast is stayed on each side by one shroud with a "spreader" (a kind of crosstree, a view of which is given at *a*) about half-way up; *b* is the shroud. There is also a "spreader" for the bowsprit shrouds, or whiskers, as we should term them.

In racing, a crew of seventeen is sometimes carried, although it is difficult to see what good so many men can be on board a boat except to sit to windward and shift ballast.

The ballast of Parole consists of seventy-seven sand bags, the average weight of each being 45lb., or about 1½ ton in the aggregate.

TABLE OF DIMENSIONS, &c., OF PAROLE.

Length on load water-line	27ft.
Breadth, extreme	11ft. 3in.
Breadth on load water-line	10ft.
Draught of water	1ft. 8in.
Draught with board down	7ft. 3in.

TABLE OF DIMENSIONS, &c., OF PAROLE (*continued*).

Displacement	4·1 tons.
Centre of buoyancy abaft centre of length of L.W.L.	1·1ft.
Centre of buoyancy below L.W.L.	0·6ft.
Centre of lateral resistance abaft centre of length of L.W.L. (with board down or up), inclusive of rudder	2·3ft.
Centre of effort of sails (mainsail and jib) abaft centre of lateral resistance	0·4ft.
Area of immersed board	25 sq. ft.
Area of mainsail	1056 sq. ft.
Area of jib	484 sq. ft.
Total area of sails	1540 sq. ft.
Luff of mainsail	30ft.
Leech of mainsail	48ft.
Foot of mainsail	38ft. 6in.
Tack to peak earing	46ft. 6in.
Clew to throat	46ft. 6in.
Luff of jib	46ft.
Leech of jib	35ft.
Foot of jib	27ft. 6in.
Mast, deck to upper cap	38ft. 3in.
Fore side of mast from fore side of stem	8ft. 2in.
Bowsprit, outboard	22ft. 1in.

The water-lines 1, 2, 3, &c., are 4in. apart. The other measurements can be taken from the drawing, Plate XXXII.

THE SORCERESS.

The shallow saucer form of body so strikingly exemplified in the Una type of craft has been imitated in this country a great many times, but in no case more successfully than by Mr. Linton-Hope with his well-known 1-rater Sorceress, which has sailed most successfully on the Thames during the season 1894. She was designed by her owner for the Royal Corinthian and Junior Thames Yacht Club's circular courses at Erith and Greenhithe, with the idea that an extreme type of skimmer would be more likely to prove successful on the average than an ordinary ballasted centre-board or bulb fin boat. As both these courses are in fairly smooth water except with certain winds, and also because the races are usually sailed late in the afternoon (which, as a rule, means that the wind dies away towards the end of the race), this idea proved correct, and she won every race sailed on these waters. (Plate XXXIII.)

She also did very well in the London Sailing Club races at Hammersmith, winning every race she started in there except one, and then only lost first prize through starting very late, being over the line at gunfire. Out of fifteen races sailed under Y.R.A. rules she won fourteen first prizes and one second prize, also the Muriel Challenge Cup (£50) of the Royal Corinthian Y.C., which she holds for the year.

Though built for light winds and smooth water, Sorceress has proved herself to be a good performer in a hard breeze and short sea, such as one only gets in the Thames.

No doubt a great deal of her success and weatherliness is due to the form of her centre-plate and to her upright position when sailing, which gives her the greatest possible lateral resistance for the area of the plate (as explained in "Yacht Architecture.") Her upright position when usually sailing also prevents alteration of the form of her immersed body to any great extent, as would be the case if she heeled to anything like the degree the bulb fin and other boats do. This her designer considers important, as, when upright, her underwater body is exactly of the wave form, as will be seen from the curve of areas of sections shown below the half-breadth plan.

Having a watertight bulkhead at each end of the cockpit, she is quite unsinkable, and shows about half her normal freeboard when the cockpit is full and the crew on board, so that she is not so dangerous in the event of a capsize as she is supposed to be, and so far has shown no signs of doing anything of the sort.

She is very lightly built of Oregon cedar, and has all bamboo spars and steel running gear, the main halyards being on a winch of rather novel design, which, besides hoisting the sail, entirely does away with the nuisance of a lot of tangled wire in the bottom of the boat. The roller foresail and spinnaker combined is very handy, and is almost essential in a boat which turns so quickly as to throw her crew off their legs occasionally.

THE MIRAGE.

The Mirage, a centre-board boat of 1-rating, built by Mr. A. Burgoine, of Kingston-on-Thames, in 1891, for Mr. H. Wolton. She commenced her racing career in June, and won twenty-four prizes out of thirty starts; but this performance was beaten in 1892, when she took thirty-one prizes for thirty-two starts; 1893 her record was twenty-two prizes for twenty-four starts, and up to May, 1894, she had taken fourteen prizes in fifteen starts. She was then sold to Mr. Howey to sail in the River Deben Club on the east coast, and has followed up her successful career.

She has a lead keel (3 cwt.) and yellow metal plate (11½ cwt.), but having 1ft. 9in. draught she hangs to wind very well with the plate housed. The plate drops 2ft. 6in.

She is riband carvel built of ½in. red cedar. Her counter is decked in, and forward she is also decked, as shown in the plans (Plate XXXIV.), on the riband carvel plan. She is fitted with watertight bulkheads, giving sufficient buoyancy to float the boat, her ballast, and equipment.

THE MONA.

The Mona (Plate XXXV.) was designed to compete in the Upper Thames 0·85 class, and to be eligible to compete for the Queen's Cup at the Bourne End meeting. She is built of ⅜in. mahogany. Her lead keel weighs only ¾ cwt., and her metal plate 3 cwt.

THE CHALLENGE, 1-RATER.

Challenge (Plate XXXVI.), was designed by Mr. Walter Stewart in the autumn of 1892, and built for him by H. Smith, of Medley, Oxford, in the spring of the following year. Her marked success as a racer is undoubtedly due to a very large extent to the really excellent way in which the builder performed his share of the work in carrying out the design and saving unnecessary weight of structure. It is perhaps true to say that the Challenge, when first designed, was the most advanced specimen of the length cheater amongst craft produced on this side of the Atlantic. The designer frankly admits that, but for the extraordinary success of Herreshoff's Gloriana (vague reports of whose form were circulated in this country in 1892) the Challenge's bow would have been differently modelled; her stern, however, is practically the same as that of more than one of the 1-raters which he designed before the Gloriana was thought of.

The *raison d'être* of the Challenge's existence was a condition inserted in the regulations governing the race for the Queen's cup, presented by her Majesty for competition amongst boats belonging to Upper Thames Clubs. This condition was to the effect that no boat under 0·8-rating should be eligible to sail for the cup in question.

The Oxford University Sailing Club possessing at that time no boat of the specified size, it was decided to build two 1-raters to attempt to win the race. The Challenge was one of these two craft, but, although she finished two seconds ahead of the winning boat, the latter took the cup on time allowance. The rest of the fleet were a long distance astern. Since this race Challenge has started in thirty-five races, winning twenty-nine first, four second, and two third prizes. Of these races twelve were sailed in 1893 against the crack racing craft of the Norfolk Broads, twelve against the Oxford 0·5-rater canoe yawls (against which at one time it was thought that a 1-rater had not a fair chance of saving her

z

time), and three against boats of the Upper Thames and London Sailing Clubs. The remaining eight races were sailed in 1895 in matches of the Upper Thames, Thames Valley, and Thamesis Clubs, and the result shows that Challenge is a faster boat than when she was first launched in the spring of 1893; for she was then beaten in several successive races by Mirage, which craft, however, she in 1895 vanquished the five occasions of meeting her.

Her handiness is in a large measure due to the easy form of her ends, the concentration of weights amidships, and the nice adjustment of her centres of propulsion and resistance.

Challenge's best point of sailing is to windward, and it is in hard breezes, when the ratio of area of hull exposed to area of canvas which can be carried is largest, that her superiority is most marked. A more or less successful attempt to disguise the absence of sheer has been made by sheering the rubbing wale more than the deck. Up as far as the wale the hull is black leaded, above it is painted vermilion, and the line where the black cuts the vermilion is the line which catches the eye. There are many features about the rigging which distinguish the boat from the rest of the Upper Thames fleet, but, with the exception of the main and jib sheet, all the running, as well as the standing rigging, is of flexible steel wire. Jib and main halyards lead direct on to drums controlled by a winch handle which can be geared into whichever drum it is desired to work.

The main halyard, instead of leading through the usual sheave or block at the masthead, reeves over a special sheave fitted in a metal casing, which rotates on a vertical spindle, whereby the nipping of the wire is entirely avoided, owing to the fact that the sheave, instead of being always in a fore and aft line, is free to swing on the spindle which fits into a bushed hole in the top of the mast, thus allowing the whole block to swing as the sail gybes.

THE HOLLY.

This centre-board 1-rater was built by the Teignmouth Ship and Yacht Building Company for Sir George Greaves, from a design by the author. She was intended for sailing in the 1-rating matches of the South Wales Branch of the Minima Yacht Club, and was most successful in all kinds of weather. It will be seen that she is more of the cruiser type than the fashionable racer, and proved a fast, dry, and comfortable sea boat. She has the full sail area for an 18ft. 1-rater of the ordinary standing lug type, and carried it well. (Plate XXXVII.)

Length over all	19·4ft.
Length on L.W.L., with crew on board	17·8ft.
Breadth extreme..	6·6ft.
Draught of water without centre-board	2·3ft.
Displacement with crew on board	1·7 ton.
Ballast on keel	15cwt.
Ballast inside	3cwt.
Area mainsail	237 sq. ft.
Area foresail (Y.R.A. headsail)	88 sq. ft.
Total sail area	325 sq. ft.

This sort of craft could be easily turned into a single handed cruiser of the type illustrated further on.

RAGAMUFFIN III. (Now LA FRIVOLINE).

This centre-board 1-rater (Plate XXXVIII.) was built by Mr. H. C. Smith, of 78, Kingston-road, Oxford, and was successfully sailed on the Solent by Mr. Welch Thornton, under the usual lug rig. She is now the property of Mr. T. J. Bennett, of the Oxford University Sailing Club. For sailing in the matches of this club a gaff mainsail is considered more suitable, and under such a sail she was raced during the season 1895. Her total Y.R.A. sail area is 187 square feet.

BRIGHTON BEACH BOATS.

The Brighton beach boats, although very shallow, enjoy a very high repute on the South Coast, and no doubt they are very capable little vessels, and well adapted for the work they are put to. As there is no sheltered anchorage at Brighton, the boats are hauled up on the beach; and a more or less flat floor is necessary for this operation, in order that the boats may be floated as far up on the beach as possible. The boats are fitted with stout bilge keels three or four inches deep, on one of which a boat rests as she is hauled up. Ways are laid down for hauling the boats up and launching them off by a capstan, an anchor being laid out in the sea ahead. The latest boats are built with much more rise of floor than formerly, and their sailing qualities have been improved thereby.

There are many advantages justly claimed for the Brighton beach boats. They can be run over a sandbank in a foot or two of water to the "smooth on the other side;" whilst the deep boat, of equal length perhaps, must remain pile driving outside in the lop. They can be allowed to take the ground without fear of their being bilged or filling; and, if necessary, they can be run ashore to effect a landing. The counter has a long fore and aft slot or trunk in it, to admit of the rudder being lifted out when the boat is beached stern first.

z 2

Mr. Thomas Stow, of Shoreham, and Mr. Hutchinson, of Worthing, have built many successful beach boats, and the design, Plate XXXIX., was made by Mr. Thomas Stow.

The usual rig is that known as the cutter, and the boats, it will be seen, have large head sails, and in match sailing they are not spared so far as canvas goes.

The boats are decked-in up to the mast, and the counter is also decked, whilst a water-way is built round the midship sides of the boat about 1ft. wide, with 5in. coamings. The centre plates were formerly much larger than that shown in the design; but, with so much keel under the boat, very little plate is necessary, and, indeed, the boat would hang to windward very well without any plate down at all.

The general floor construction of the boats is shown by Fig. D, representing a floor section at No. 6. The floor is jogged to the keel as shown, and shaped to the mould at each section; the floor is then taken out and jogged and bevelled to receive the plank, as the boats are generally clench built. Where they are carvel built the construction is shown by Fig. A, representing the midship section; in either case the heels of the floors are cut through to admit the centre plate. As a rule the heels of the floor timbers are cut off a trifle short, so that they do not go right through the case, as shown in A. The heels of the floor timbers are, in fact, tenoned into the centre-board case. The construction at No. 7 station is shown by Fig. B, where considerable depth has to be given to the throat of the floor. Sometimes the floors aft and forward are steamed and bent into their stations, being afterwards removed to be jogged (as shown by Fig. C, representing No. 2 station forward) if the boat is clench built.

As already explained, the counter is generally fitted with a kind of long fore-and-aft rudder trunk or slot, enough to allow the rudder to be lifted up through the counter before beaching stern first.

The centre-board case is generally of wood with a knee, as shown by *a*, Fig. A, to keep it in its place, and to generally strengthen the floor of the boat.

Greatest length from fore side of stem plumb at L.W.L. to aft side of stern post on deck	21ft.
Greatest beam moulded	6ft. 10½in.
Greatest beam extreme	7ft.
Weight of hull (exclusive of iron plate, iron keel, and ballast, spars, sails, and crew)	14cwt.
Iron keel	4cwt.
Centre plate	1½cwt.
Ballast inside	5½cwt.
Spars, sails, and gear	7cwt.
Crew	8cwt.
Total weight of displacement to L.W.L.	2tons.

Moulding (depth) of wood keel from top to under side, 5in.
Siding (breadth) of wood keel 4in. amidships, tapering to 2½in. forward and 3in. aft.
Siding of stern post, 3in.
Siding of stem, 2½in.
Siding of floors, 1¾in
Siding of timbers, 1½in.
Distance floors are apart from centre to centre, 10in.
Thickness of plank, ½in. (Clench work.)
Length of iron keel, 12ft.; depth, 4in., tapered in breadth fore and aft to shape of wood keel.

Spars.	ft.	in.
Mast, deck to hounds	19	0
Boom, extreme	20	0
Gaff, extreme	16	0
Topmast, heel to hounds	16	0
Topsail yard	18	0
Bowsprit, outside stem	16	0
Mast stepped from the fore side of stem	8	0
Luff of mainsail	16	0
Head of mainsail	15	6
Foot of mainsail	19	3
Leech of mainsail	28	0
Tack to peak earing	30	3
Clew to throat	24	9
Foot of foresail	8	0
Luff of foresail	18	0
Leech of foresail	17	0
Foot of jib	16	0
Luff of jib	26	0
Leech of jib	16	0
Luff of jib topsail	24	0
Foot of jib topsail	12	0
Leech of jib topsail	15	0

LAYING-OFF TABLE.—Plate XXXIX.

No. of Section	1	2	3	4	5	6	7		9	10	11
Sheer Plan.	ft. in.	ft. in.	ft. in.	ft. in.	ft. in.	ft. in.	ft. in.	ft. in.	ft. in.	ft. in.	ft. in.
Heights above L.W.L. to deck*	2 9½	2 6	2 3¼	2 1½	2 0	1 10½	1 9	1 9½	1 10	1 11	2 0
Depths to upper edge of rabbet	—	1 2†	1 3½	1 4½	1 5	1 6	1 7†	1 8†	—	—	—
Depths to top of wood keel	—	1 0	—	—	—	—	—	1 7½	—	—	—
Half-breadth Plan.											
Half-breadths on deck	0 10	1 11½	2 8	3 1	3 4	3 3½	3 2	3 0	2 10	2 7	2 3½
Half-breadths on L.W.L.	0 5	1 3¾	2 3	3 0	3 3	3 2¼	2 9½	1 11	0 9	—	—
Body Plan.											
Diagonal *a*	0 9¾	1 11	2 8¾	3 3½	3 5¾	3 5¼	3 3½	3 1½	2 10	2 5	2 0½
Diagonal *b*	0 9½	1 10	2 8½	3 4	3 6¾	3 6	3 3½	2 11½	2 5½	1 10	1 0
Diagonal *c*	0 8½	1 8	2 6	3 1¾	3 4¼	3 3½	3 0	2 5¼	1 9½	1 0½	—
Diagonal *d*	0 6½	1 5	2 1¾	2 7½	2 9¾	2 8	2 4	1 8½	1 0	—	—
Diagonal *e*	0 4¾	0 11½	1 3½	1 6½	1 7½	1 7	1 4	0 10	0 3	—	—

* The deck is flush with the gunwale.

† The heels of the floors at Nos. 2, 7, and 8 stations are not joggled as those at Nos. 6, 5, 4, and 3 are (see diagram B). The ticked line in the drawing represents the lower edge of the rabbet 2¾in. from the top of keel.

No. 1 station is 1ft. 6in. from the fore side of the stem. Nos. 1, 2, 3, 4, 5, 6, 7, and 8 stations are 2ft. 6in. apart. No. 9 station is 1ft. 9in. from No. 8. No. 10 is 2ft. from No. 9, No. 11 is 1ft. 6in. from No. 10.

a diagonal is struck on the middle vertical line *o* (see body plan) 2ft. 2in. above the load water-line; it cuts the side perpendiculars *pp* at *a* 1 and *a* 2 at 1ft. 3in. above the load water-line.

b diagonal cuts *o* 1ft. 8in. above L.W.L.; cuts *p* 4in. above L.W.L.

c diagonal cuts *o* 1ft. 1½in. above L.W.L.; cuts *p* 4in. *below* L.W.L.

d diagonal cuts *o* 6½in. above L.W.L.; cuts *p* 1ft. 1½in. *below* L.W.L.

e diagonal cuts *o* 1in. *below* L.W.L.; and at *a* 1 and *a* 2 is 1ft. 3in. below L.W.L., and 1ft. 4½in. out from *o*.

All the half-breadths given are *without* the plank.

THE POLLYWOG.

The Pollywog is a 3-ton centre-board cutter, built for sailing in Milford Haven, the lower half of which, ten miles in length, varies from one and a half to three miles in breadth; and the upper portion, navigable for a further distance of thirteen miles, averages half a mile in width. There are also numerous creeks, locally called "pills," having a narrow deep-water entrance, but inside expanding to from two to four square miles in area, the greater portion of which is dry at half tide (Plate XL.).

The object aimed at was a boat light, handy and quick in stays for the quiet upper waters of the Haven, having sufficient weight and power to face the rougher and heavier seas of the lower portion, with light enough draught for the "pills," large enough to accommodate half a dozen people for an afternoon's sail, and small enough to be worked single-handed; to be, above all, safe, comfortable, and fast. This is the result: As regards speed, nothing of her size in the district has nearly equalled her. She is very dry, and a good sea boat in spite of her heavy spars, and is exceedingly quick in stays; she has frequently been worked single-handed by her owner in a strong breeze and a heavy sea, and has always behaved very well.

There are several peculiarities in her construction worth noticing.

The centre-board, weighing 1½cwt., is pivoted in the usual manner in the keel, and has the usual rope at the after end to pull it up with; but, as 170lb. is rather a heavy weight for one man to lift in a hurry, another cord is shackled to the centre-board a few inches in advance of the former one; it leads over a sheave at the top of the centre-board case and down the fore end, where it divides; *i.e.*, another cord is spliced in. These lead through two pulleys at the foot of the mast, and back, one on each side of the case under the platform; an end of each is fastened to an indiarubber spring, somewhat similar to a large chest expander, but with a thimble at each end, and requiring a weight of about 60lb. to stretch it 3ft. The other end of the spring is hooked to a floor right aft. When the centre-board is hauled up, the springs are relaxed, but upon its being lowered they are in tension and supporting about 120lb. of its weight, leaving only some 40lb. to be lifted by hand; if therefore the boat runs over a rock or bank, the board rises almost as easily as a wooden one would do. The springs are 1¼in. diameter, 4ft. long, weigh about 2lb. each, and were obtained from R. Middleton, Chester-street, Birkenhead, the price being 9s. per pound.

The centre-board case was made of 1in. American yellow pine, and thus fitted (*see* Fig. 145): A rabbet 1in. deep was cut in the keel to

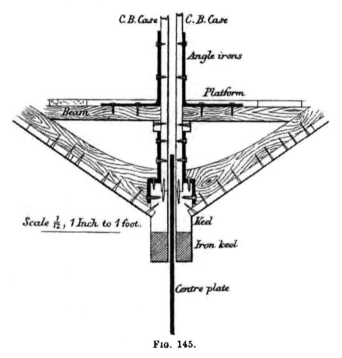

Fig. 145.

exactly take the case, three oak dowels being fitted on each side; the case was well luted with white-lead putty, and driven home; three iron supports on each side were screwed both to the case and to the keel; there has been no leakage from this joint since the boat was launched.

The Pollywog is half-decked, with waterways; and two bulkheads, one aft of the mast, the other about 2ft. forward of the sternpost; these are entered by close-fitting hatches; she is therefore practically a life-boat. A 3¼in. pump with ball valves, and discharging on both sides, will rapidly clear her of any water that may find its way in.

The spinnaker boom is in two pieces, with a simple socket joint (similar to a tent pole); the two ends, which are alike, have each a hole through which a piece of small line is passed, and, knotted or spliced, forms a loop. The spinnaker halyard is an endless rope leading from the masthead down each side of the forestay, with a piece about 3ft. long spliced in. The spinnaker itself has the sheet spliced into the claw cringle; the luff rope has a loop at the upper end, and is left about 4ft. long at the tack. The sail is thus set: The sheet first made fast to the bitts, the free part of the halyard bent to the head of the sail, the tack passed through the loop at the end of the boom (end immaterial),

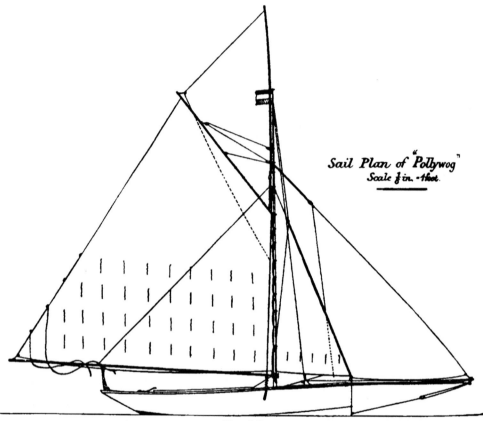

Sail Plan of "Pollywog"
Scale ⅜ in. = 1 foot.

FIG. 146.

and bent to it with a clove or other hitch, a guy passed outside the shroud and bent to the same end of the boom. The sail is then hoisted, and as it goes up the boom is fitted together and launched forward; the loop on the inner end dropped over any pin on the spider hoop, and then squared by the guy. In gybing, the inner end is lifted off the pin and launched aft, the guy being let go and passed round the mast and outside the shrouds to the other quarter; the sail is then lowered and run up the other side, without casting off, tack, sheet, or halyard;

as soon as the mainsail has swung over, the spinnaker boom is launched forward as before and squared by the guy.

The topsail is on the American plan, the yard being up and down the mast, and projecting about 5ft. above it. (*See* Fig. 146.)

The dinghy is 7ft. 6in. long over all, 3ft. 8in. beam, and 2ft. 2in. deep; weighs 90lb. with bottom boards, &c., but without oars or rowlocks, and has carried two ladies and three gentlemen at a time to the yacht, with about 5in. of freeboard. Its keel, gunwale, timbers, thwarts, garboards, and bilge strake are American elm, stern and stem oak, planking yellow pine. It tows well, and can be lifted easily by one man into the Pollywog, where it fits comfortably into the well.

The yacht was designed and built by Lieut.-Col. Barrington Baker during his leisure hours of the winter of 1880-81, with the occasional help of a man for rivetting, planking, &c.; the item of wages therefore

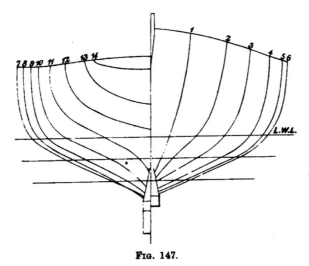

FIG. 147.

only came to 7*l.*; but, if built entirely by paid labour the wages would probably come to 35*l.*, more or less, according to the locality, and the skill of the men employed. The cheapest plan would be to employ one man, and get help as required for setting up in frame, clenching, &c.

The Pollywog has on several occasions sailed at a very high rate of speed for a boat of her length. In July, 1881, the distance between Dale Point and Pembroke Dock, nine statute miles, was covered in one hour and twenty-five minutes, being at the rate of 6·29 statute miles, or 5·46 knots, per hour. The wind was of lower sail strength abeam, and water smooth; but the boat was twice almost becalmed for a few minutes when passing under the headlands of South Hook and Weare. The tide was a very slack neap, but what little there was was against the boat.

The party on board consisted of five ladies and two gentlemen, who were all up to windward. Her best recorded speed, however, was on her return from Saundersfoot Regatta, near Tenby, in September, 1881, when she ran under all sail and spinnaker (with a gybe half way) from the Monkstone (3.33 P.M.) to Giltar Head, 3½ statute miles ; then hauling up with the wind just forward the beam to St. Govan's Head, 10 statute miles (5.30 P.M.) ; good steady breeze and nearly smooth water, slack neap tide, favourable first hour, then against her ; the total distance to St. Govan's being 13¼ statute miles in one hour and fifty-seven minutes, being at the rate of 6·92 miles, or 6·01 knots, per hour. From St. Govan's Head to Linney Head, six statute miles, almost close-hauled under all plain sail (topsail doused), tide *nil*, being in the slack water, took exactly fifty-nine minutes, being at the rate of 5·28 knots per hour.

These headlands are very well marked, and were passed within from ten to twenty fathoms, and the time carefully taken. The distances are from point to point, but the boat actually sailed a little more on account of other headlands projecting slightly.

DIMENSIONS, &c., OF POLLYWOG.—PLATE XL. AND FIG. 147.

Length on L.W.L., 18ft.
Length over all, 21ft. 6in.
Beam, extreme, 6ft. 8in.
Draught of water aft, 2ft. 3in.
Draught, including board, 4ft. 10in.
Displacement, 1 ton 15cwt.
Ballast on keel, 4½cwt.
Centre-plate, 1½cwt.
Ballast inside, 16cwt.
Total ballast, 22cwt.
Keel (American elm), sided amidship, 5in.
Keel, moulded, 6in.
Stem and sternpost (oak), sided, 3½in.
Worked timbers, sided, 1¼in., spaced 18in.
Bent timbers (American elm), ½in., moulded,
  by 1¼in., sided, between each pair of worked.

Plank (yellow pine), ½in.
Rail (American elm), ½in. by 2in.
Seats, &c., teak.
Sections are without plank and 18in. apart.
Mast, deck to hounds, 17ft.
Mast, deck to truck, 25ft.
Mast, diameter at deck, 4½in.
Boom, 23ft.
Diameter at sheet, 3¾in.
Gaff, 13ft.
Diameter, 2¼in.
Bowsprit, outboard, 11ft. 6in.
Bowsprit, diameter at gammon iron, 3¾in.
Spinnaker boom, 23ft.
Centre-board, ¾in. boiler plate.
Area of board immersed, about 12 square feet.

The sail plan is shown on page 344 (Fig. 146), and it will be seen that it is a very liberal one. However, the remarkably good performances of Pollywog shows that the plan was made with great judgment. The rather long boom and short gaff are " features " which tend to make the sail stand well to windward. The areas of the sails are as follows :

Area of mainsail	284 sq. ft.
Area of foresail	40 sq. ft.
Area of jib	84 sq. ft.
Area of topsail	50 sq. ft.
Total area of sails	458 sq. ft.
Area of spinnaker	250 sq. ft.

LIST OF BLOCKS, CORDAGE, &c., OF POLLYWOG.

—	Blocks.		Cordage.		Remarks.
	Number.	Size.	Fathoms.	Size.	
		in.		Cir. in.	
Main halyard	2	4	9	1¼	
Peak halyard	3	4	15	1¼	
Jib halyard	2	4	10	1¼	
Fore halyard	1	3	6	1	
Topsail halyard	—	—	9	¾	1 thimble instead of block.
Spinnaker halyard	—	—	10	¾	1 thimble instead of block.
Main sheet	{ 1 3	{ 4 3½	} 18	1¼	double block.
Jib sheet	—	—	7	1	
Fore sheet	—	—	5	1	leads through eye-bolts on deck.
Topsail sheet	—	—	10	¾	thimbles instead of blocks.
Topping-lifts (each)	1	3	6½	1	
Bobstay purchase	2	3	6	1¼	iron blocks.
Spinnaker guy	—	—	5	¾	
Reef pendants and outhauls	—	—	20	1¼	
Warp	—	—	25	2	
Wire shrouds, one on each side	—	—	12	1	
Wire bowsprit shrouds	—	—	3	¾	

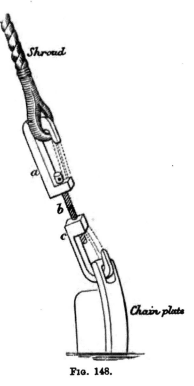

To obviate the stretching of lanyards, Colonel Baker invented the plan shown on Fig. 148. The hooks, *a c*, are of ⅜in. by 1in. galvanised iron, and the screw, *b*, $\frac{7}{16}$in. There is a hole in the head of the pin. The nut is formed by *c*; the dotted lines show how the hooks could be strengthened by making them into links. The rigging screws illustrated on page 52 would, however, be usually preferred.

The cost of materials only:

Timber	£10	0	0
Copper nails, &c.	3	0	0
Ironwork (galvanised)	7	0	0
Centre-plate	2	0	0
Iron keel	2	0	0
Ballast	2	0	0
Indiarubber springs	2	0	0
Spars	2	10	0
Cordage	1	0	0
Wire rigging	0	10	0
Sails	15	0	0
Blocks	1	10	0
Pump	2	0	0
Anchor and chain	3	10	0
Cork cushions	1	0	0
Warp	1	0	0
Painting and extras	4	0	0
Total	£60	0	0

Shroud

Chain plate

FIG. 148.

THE SINGLE-HANDED CENTRE-BOARD CRUISER HAZE, BALANCE LUGGER.

THE Haze was built during the winter of 1886-7 for Mr. Linton Hope from his own design (*see* Plate XLI.) Like other boats of this class she has a broad keel, it being 18in. across amidships. The object of this is to get the floor and lead low, and to get the largest displacement with a draught of 2ft. 6in., and a sharp rise of floor, also to give her great strength to knock about on the ground. She has a sliding hatch over the cockpit made to push forward on to a movable piece of the booby hatch, which then lifts up, and the two pieces can be stowed away below. To prevent leakage round the joint between the movable and fixed pieces of the booby hatch, there is a water course in the carlines, which carries off any water that may come through the joint. She has 4ft. head room, and four persons can sleep on the folding berths.

TABLE OF OFF-SETS.—PLATE XLI. AND FIG. 149.

No. of section	Stem.	1	2	3	4	5	Transome.
	ft.	ft. in.	ft. in.	ft. in.	ft. in.	ft. in.	ft. in.
Height above L.W.L. to covering board	3	2 6	2 3	2 0	1 11	1 11	2 2
Depth below L.W.L. to rabbet	—	1 8	1 11	2 0	2 0	1 9	—
Half breadth on deck	—	2 6	3 6	3 10½	3 8	3 0	2 1
Half breadth on 1st W.L.	—	2 2	3 3	3 9	3 6	2 7	0 1
Half breadth on L.W.L.	—	1 9	3 0	3 6	3 1	1 11	
Half breadth on 3rd W.L.	—	1 3	2 6	3 0	2 8	1 8	—
Half breadth on 4th W.L.	—	0 9	1 11	2 4	0 2	0 10	—
Half breadth on 5th W.L.	—	0 5	1 3	1 8	1 3	0 5	—

1st buttock line, 1ft. 9in. from centre.　　　2nd buttock line, 3ft. 6in. from centre.

The following are the sizes of the spars, &c., of the Haze, as shown in the accompanying sail plan (Plate XLI.):

SPARS.

Mainmast, deck to sheave	20ft.
Main yard	22ft.
Main boom	20ft.
Three oval pine battens	{ 19ft. 6in. / 18ft. / 16ft. 6in.
Mizen mast, deck to sheave	12ft.
Mizen yard	14ft.
Mizen boom	9ft.
Mizen jackyard	10ft.
Mizen bumkin, outside stern	4ft.
Fore bumkin, outside stem	3ft. 3in.
Jibboom, outside stem	14ft.

SAILS.

Mainsail (three battens), duck	270 sq. ft.
Jackyard mizen, calico	104 sq. ft.
Jib, for reaching, calico	100 sq. ft.
Storm mizen, duck	50 sq. ft.
Storm staysail (set when the main lug is stowed), duck ...	60 sq. ft.

It will be seen, on referring to the sail plan, that the centre of effort is considerably forward of the centre of lateral resistance; but the jib is not used except for reaching, as she is very light on the helm without it, though she will carry a jib going to windward.

The rigging is arranged as follows: Mainmast, one pair of shrouds each side, and runner tackles, forestay and tackle to set it up, all about

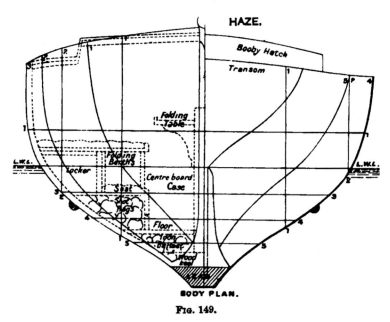

HAZE.

BODY PLAN.

FIG. 149.

1¼in. wire rope; mizen mast, one pair of shrouds a side, about ⅜in. wire rope. The after-mizen shroud each side is set up to a small iron outrigger; mizen bumkin, one shroud a side (set up to the same outriggers as the after-shroud), and bobstay, about ⅜in. wire rope. This gear is necessary to the mizen bumkin, as the jackyard mizen puts a great strain on it in gybing. The jibboom has a light bobstay rove through a single block at the crantz iron, and hooked to the same eye as the standing bobstay, and a light pair of shrouds; it is unrigged very quickly, and is seldom in use. The bobstay to the fore bumkin is a galvanised iron rod, ½in. thick, and the jibboom runs out through a cap at the end, in the same way as a schooner's jibboom.

The fore halyards consist of a 2in. Manilla tye, running over a large sheave in the masthead, and a tackle (two single 4½in. blocks). The sail is hoisted by this, and then set up by a tack tackle (two double and one single 3in. blocks). The main sheet has a double block on the boom, a single block travelling on a horse, and a leading block on one quarter, the standing part being fast on the opposite quarter. The main topping lift is double, leading through an iron double block at the masthead, and then spliced, so that the sail falls between the two ports when lowered. There is also a line from the masthead to just below the boom, to confine the sail in the same way. The jib and mizen are set in the usual way.

Mr. Linton Hope says he tried her in all weathers, and found it the handiest rig he ever had for cruising, though she has not nearly enough canvas for light winds, as she will carry a whole mainsail and jackyard mizen when the other boats of her size have a reef down.

LOUGH ERNE YACHTS—THE WITCH.

The shallowness of the upper waters of Lough Erne, and the turbulence of the lower, have necessitated a kind of compromise between the shallow American centre-boarder and the deeper-bodied English yacht. A large fleet of various sizes from 18ft. to nearly 40ft. in length—some thirty or forty in all—of these centre-board yachts are on the Lough, and most of them were designed and built by their owners. The Witch (Plate XLII.) was designed and built by Colonel Edward Saunderson, M.P., in 1878, and is a very capable boat, both on the smooth and narrow water of the Upper Lake, and in strong breezes on the rougher water of the Lower Lake.

Sometimes whilst sailing in shallow water the after end only of the dipper is raised; and at all times with the fore end below the keel the lateral resistance is found to be very effective.

Colonel Saunderson altered the Witch in 1880 by filling out the bow and rounding up the fore foot; these alterations are shown on the drawing. The alterations were pronounced improvements. During the winter of 1882 Colonel Saunderson further altered the Witch by giving her an over-hanging swan stem, and she now is as pourtrayed on Plate XLII.

The centre-plate or "dipper" is made of $\frac{3}{8}$in. boiler plate. A slot is cut inside the case at the fore end $1\frac{1}{4}$in. deep, and 2in. wide, the lips of which are protected by iron plates. A short iron bolt or stud projects on either side of the plate, and travels in the slot. The board can be raised bodily by two winches; but it is usual only to raise the after end.

The Witch has oak frames spaced as shown, with ½in. wrought iron floor-knees. Between each pair of frames is a steamed timber of American elm.

TABLE OF OFFSETS FOR WITCH (Plate XLII.).

No. of Section	1		2		4		6		8		10		12		14		16		17	
	ft.	in.	ft.	in.	ft.	in.	ft.	in.	ft.	in.	ft.	in.	ft.	in.	ft.	in.	ft.	in.	ft.	in.
Heights above L.W.L. to top of covering board	3	9	3	5	3	0	2	7½	2	4	2	2	2	0	2	1	2	3	2	5
Half-breadths on deck	1	11	3	1	4	6	5	6	6	1	6	2½	6	0	5	6	4	6	3	10
Half-breadths on W.L. 1	1	2	2	4½	4	2	5	5½	6	1	6	3	6	0½	5	6	4	6	3	7½
Half-breadths on W.L. 2	0	8	1	9½	3	8	5	2	6	0½	6	3	6	0	5	4½	3	5	—	
Half-breadths on L.W.L.	0	2½	1	2½	3	0	4	8½	5	10½	6	2	5	10½	4	5½	0	3	—	
Half-breadths on W.L. 3	—		0	10	2	5½	4	1½	5	5	5	10	5	2	2	10½	0	3	—	
Half-breadths on W.L. 4	—		0	4½	1	7	3	1½	4	5½	4	7½	3	8	1	2½	0	3	—	
Half-breadths on W.L. 5	—		—		0	5½	1	2	1	11	2	2½	1	4	0	4½	0	3	—	
Half-breadths on keel	—		—		0	4	0	5	0	6	0	6	0	6	0	4	0	3	—	
Depths below L.W.L. to underside of false keel and lead keel	—		2	1	3	3	3	11	4	3¼	4	6	4	5	4	2	3	9	—	
Depths to underside of main wood keel	—		—		2	4	2	9	3	1	3	4	3	6½	3	8	—		—	

No. 1 station is 6in. from the fore side of stem at the L.W.L. No. 2 is 3ft. 2in. from No. 1. The other stations to No. 9 are 2ft. 6in. apart. Nos. 9, 10, and 11 are 2ft. 4in. apart; and from No. 11 to No. 15 2ft. 6in. apart. No. 16 is 2ft. 10in. from No. 15, and No. 17 is 3ft. from No. 16.

W.L. 1 and W.L. 2 are 1ft. apart.; W.L. 2 and L.W.L. 10½in. apart; L.W.L. and W.L. 3 are 7in. apart; W.L. 3 and W.L. 4 8in.; and W.L. 4 and W. L. 5 1ft.

All the half-breadths include the plank.

DIMENSIONS, &c., OF WITCH.

Length on load-line	38ft. 9in.
Beam, extreme	12ft. 6in.
Draught of water extreme	4ft. 6in.
Displacement	15·8 tons.
Lead on keel	5 tons.
Lead inside	2 tons 9 cwt
Iron centre-plate	11 cwt.
Iron floors	3 cwt.
Mast, deck to hounds	33ft. 6in.
Masthead	6ft.
Main boom	43ft. 6in.
Main gaff	27ft. 6in.
Bowsprit outside stem	19ft. 6in.
Topmast fid to shoulder	24ft.
Topsail yards (extreme)	36ft and 22ft.
Fore side of mast from foreside of stem at L.W.L.	15ft. 3in.
Head of mainsail	26ft. 9in.
Foot of mainsail	42ft.
Leech of mainsail	53ft. 6in.
Luff of mainsail	29ft.
Clew to throat	47ft.
Foot of foresail	20ft. 6in.
Foot of big jib	30ft. 6in.
Area of mainsail	1200 sq. ft.
,, jib	500 sq. ft.
,, foresail	300 sq. ft.
Total area of lower sail	2000 sq. ft.

BEMBRIDGE BOAT FOR ROWING AND SAILING, SELF-RIGHTING UNSINKABLE.

The following is a description written by Captain Ernest Du Boulay of a 17ft. centre-board boat for rowing and sailing, and which is also a self-righting lifeboat. She was built by him in 1887, and was well tested in different weathers. (*See* Fig. 150.)

The boat is a model of the Mersey sailing canoe, 17ft. long, 4ft. 9in. beam, and 2ft. depth, and is one of the two original boats built at Bembridge, for the use of the members of the Bembridge Sailing Club. Planking, ⅜in. yellow pine, garboards and top strake elm, timbers American elm

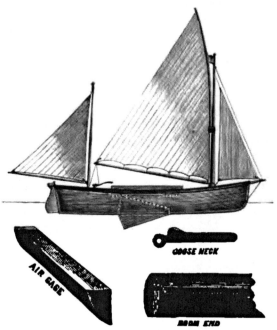

Fig. 150.

spaced 10in. apart, deck of ¼in. matchboarding, covered over all with one piece of unbleached calico from stem to sternpost.

The centre-board is made of ⅜in. boiler plate, galvanised, and weighs 80lb.; it works in a case made of two pieces of sheet iron, as described in page 284. Nothing could look neater than this case, which is only 1in. wide, and does not come above the level of the thwarts.

The board is raised or lowered its depth of 15in. by a flexible wire-rope running over a sheave in the after upper corner of the case, worked by a small tackle under the after thwart. By this means no water can possibly splash into the boat from the case. A hand pump discharges the bilge-water into this case.

A water-tight bulkhead cuts off the after 3ft. of the boat; this is made of a sheet of the thickest Willesden paper, clamped by battens and screws against the fore side of an extra stout timber cut to fit the planking, and bedded in red lead. The paper is protected from injury by a guard board. The buoyancy of the fore part of the boat is obtained by an air case each side under the fore thwart, and reaching up to within 2ft. 8in. of the stem, so as not to interfere in any way with the stowing of the oars, spars, and gear forward. These cases are made of Willesden paper, tacked, and then glued round a light wood skeleton frame, built up to fit close against the planking. They are lashed in their places, and a guard-board protects the inner sides and tops from injury, the outer sides being protected by fitting close against the timbers all along. This boat has been filled and capsized several times, but she cannot fail to right herself, and her buoyancy is such that when full of water she floated her ballast, centre-board, &c. (weighing some 420lb.), with her owner and another person (22 stone total) standing dry footed, one on the fore deck and one on the after deck. She was kept thus for forty-five minutes, before pumping her out.

246lb. of cast lead stow under the floor on each side of the centre-board case, making, with the latter, a total weight of 400lb.

The rig consists of staysail, mainsail, and mizen, made of duck and ochred. The staysail is hoisted and lowered by the same rope; pulling one way it is a halyard, and the other way a down-haul, when a turn round a pin with the slack stows the sail snug, supposing it is not practicable to get up right forward and unhank it.

The mainsail is cut on the Monte Video plan (*see* Plate XXV.), the yard is a male bamboo, fished with an elm batten; the boom is a hollow bamboo, and revolves to reef the sail; the sheet hooks on to a swivel fitted at the after end, whilst the forward end ships on to a gooseneck on the mast; a small hump on the gooseneck fits into a recess in the boom end, and prevents it from revolving.

In reefing, therefore, it is only necessary to slacken the halyard a little (this leads aft close to the seat), the boom is then unshipped along its gooseneck an inch and a half, when it can easily revolve, and the sail is then rolled up or unrolled; the boom is then pressed home again, the bump on the gooseneck fits into its recess, and a pull on the halyard jams the boom, so that it cannot become unshipped. This form of sail seems to me to be peculiarly adapted for small boats, as it sits wonderfully flat without the excessive strain on the halyards necessary with a lug. The mizen is a jib-header, with a boom at the foot: the step of the mast is round instead

A A

of square, so that to reef it is only necessary to turn the mast round in its step and roll up the sail; the outhaul leads through a sheave in the boom end, and is rolled round the mast the opposite way to the sail, so that if

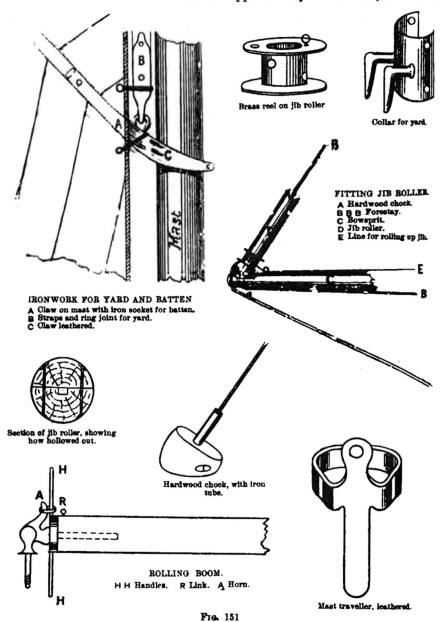

Brass reel on jib roller

Collar for yard.

IRONWORK FOR YARD AND BATTEN
A Claw on mast with iron socket for batten.
B Straps and ring joint for yard.
C Claw leathered.

FITTING JIB ROLLER.
A Hardwood chock.
B B B Forestay.
C Bowsprit.
D Jib roller.
E Line for rolling up jib.

Section of jib roller, showing how hollowed out.

Hardwood chock, with iron tube.

ROLLING BOOM.
H H Handles. R Link. A Horn.

Mast traveller, leathered.

Fig. 151

6in. of canvas be rolled up on the mast exactly 6in. of outhaul are slacked up, and *vice versâ*. Besides, leading as they do, one balances the other, and the mast has no tendency to revolve itself, though it can easily be made to do so with one hand. The tiller works the rudder, as usual in these boats, with two yokes, but an improvement is added in the form of a mahogany boss containing a nut, which screws down on the spindle on which the tiller works, so that half a turn will lock the tiller in any position it is placed in. This is particularly useful for tacking, wearing, mackerel or pollack fishing, and reefing.

With the above tiller and reefing gear the boat has been repeatedly put about and a reef taken in the mainsail and mizen before she filled on the opposite tack. As everything leads aft, a waterproof apron buttons over the well for bad weather. At moorings it completely covers in the latter, and when under way the portion unbuttoned comes up under one's chin, making a very snug boat of her. In calm weather she is easily sculled along, and she can be shoved over the sand in 9in. of water. A locker is fitted aft, between the backboard, which is hinged, and the watertight bulk-head. It has a perforated zinc bottom, so that everything inside is perfectly ventilated, and instead of things getting mildewed they actually dry if put away wet.

Mr. Damp, the boatbuilder of Bembridge, Isle of Wight, can build these boats for 35*l.* complete.

Plate XLIII., and Fig. 151, represent the improved Bembridge rig for larger boats, which has been fairly tested in all sorts of weather in boats up to 4 tons, and has proved thoroughly serviceable and trustworthy. It is particularly adapted for single-handed racing and cruising, as both the sails are reefed by rolling, which can be done in a very few seconds. The mainsail has only one halyard, though in shape and size it represents a gaff mainsail and topsail, which require five or six ropes to set them. It requires only a short mast for its area, and, when the mainsheet is in, it sits very flat indeed; the latter works on a swivel at the boom end down to an outrigger horse abaft the transom, made of galvanised iron gas pipe for lightness; with a counter this outrigger is not required. The luff of the *topsail* portion is seized to an upright pine yard of oval section, the lower end of which finishes with an iron eye and straps; this eye works on another eye clenched on to the claw which embraces the mast; this claw is forged with a hollow socket at the other end, which is driven tightly on to the lower end of the *batten* (made of a male bamboo); this batten lies in a pocket in the sail, and is hidden; its upper end projects some few inches, so as to haul the sail out by as it grows slack. The main halyard consists of a tie of flexible wire rope working over a sheave in the mast just under the hounds—one end is spliced into the traveller on the mast, and the other into a double block for the purchase.

A A 2

In order to keep the yard vertical and close into the mast on the yard, and at about two-fifths of its length from the lower end, is fixed an iron collar, which has two hooks sticking out of it downwards like walrus teeth. These hooks drop into two corrugations made in the mast traveller, and thus make a strong close connection, which can be hooked and unhooked in an instant when required.

In boats of over half-rating, as the yard is rather heavy to handle, an extra or trip halyard is used. This is bent to the upper end of the yard, so that the first pull on it brings the yard upright and close above the traveller. The two hooks are then dropped into their places in the traveller, and the sail is set by the main halyard. The trip is not touched again until it is required to stow the sail, when, after it has been lowered as far down the mast as it will run, a sudden jerk on the trip unhooks the yard, which is then gently lowered down on to the boom.

For reefing these larger boats, the gear shown in Fig. 151 is used. The boom is free to revolve on the iron pin hinged to the ordinary goose-neck. Two handles (H H) give the necessary purchase for reefing the sail, after the main halyard has been slacked up slowly, and a loose link, or grummet (R) drops over the highest handle, locking it to a horn (A) welded on to the iron pin. When, therefore, the halyard is again set up, this link prevents the boom from revolving. By removing this link, moreover, the boom can be easily unshipped off the iron pin, so that the whole mainsail can be easily stowed, when setting a trysail for instance.

The jib is cut full size and with a low foot like a balloon foresail; instead of a luff rope, a small wire cord runs through the selvedge, the jib is seized taut on to the jib roller by sail twine at each end and at intervals. This jib roller is made of yellow pine, and has a hole right through it for the forestay to lead through.

As this hole cannot well be bored, the spar is sawn down into two unequal parts, and a groove ploughed out in the larger portion, as shown in the diagram, the smaller portion is then put back, with a layer of varnish or waterproof glue between, and fastened with copper nails at intervals. The seizings of the jib also assist these fastenings. On the lower end of the roller is driven a small brass reel. A piece of hard wood of the right bevel is screwed on to the top of the bowsprit, with a hole through it in which a piece of galvanised iron gas pipe, just large enough to embrace the stay forestay, is firmly driven, this hole is continued right down through the bowsprit, and is rounded off so that the forestay can lead fairly, and without any sharp nip, down through the jib roller, and pipe in the hard wood block, right through the bowsprit and back underneath it to the stem head where it is set up.

One end of a small Manilla line is secured through a hole in the upper flange of the brass reel, the other end is then wound round the reel the requisite number of turns, and it then goes through a fair lead on the bowsprit and into the boat, where it belays on a rocking cleat.

It will now be seen by the sketch that a pull on this line, with the jib sheet slackened, will instantly reduce the jib, first of all to an ordinary jib for working to windward, and then further to any smaller size required, at the same time raising its foot (which is very requisite in rough water). A pull on the jib sheet, when the line is slackened, as instantly gives the boat her full jib for a run or reach.

The advantages of setting one's jib instantly when getting under way, and particularly of rolling it up completely just before picking up moorings, so as to have a clear fore deck, and no chance of one's hat being knocked off, to say the least, can only be appreciated by those who have tried it.

The jib roller being hollow and made of yellow pine only weighs a few pounds, and even should it be broken by fouling anything, this would not interfere either with the forestay or the working of the boat; neither is it so conspicuous as might be imagined, as a roller $1\frac{1}{4}$in. diameter is quite sufficient for a half-rater.

All these sails and spars, and ironwork, can be supplied by Mr. Woodnutt, sailmaker, at Bembridge, Isle of Wight.

CHAPTER XIV.
MERSEY SAILING BOATS.

THE Mersey Sailing boats, or what are known as the New Brighton Sailing Club boats, have undergone considerable alteration since 1880.

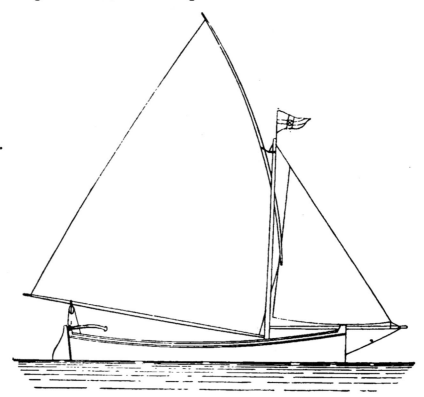

FIG. 152.

Originally the boats were allowed to be "50ft." club measurement,* with a counter. In 1881 the Y.R.A. tonnage rule was adopted, and

* The measurement rule of the New Brighton Sailing Club was as follows : " Take the extreme length from fore part of stem to after part of sternpost; girth at greatest circumference, by passing a line from gunwale under the boat's bottom, and back to the same point on the same

decks allowed. Since then the club has reverted to their girth rule of measurement, and allowed neither counter nor deck, and the boats must now be clincher built.

An open centre-board boat class was introduced by the New Brighton Sailing Club on the Mersey in 1888. One of the most successful all-round boats was the Venture (Plate XLIV.), designed and built by Mr. C. Friend, Tower Chambers, Liverpool, for Messrs. Dulley and Birkbeck, for the 40ft. class by the club rule of measurement (*see* foot-note, page 358). Venture had about 2 cwt. of ballast (including ½ cwt. in her centre plate).

The Deva was designed by Mr. Charles Livingston for Mr. T. G. Thompson, who sailed her with great success.

The rig is the standing lug, which for some years has been fashionable on the Mersey, and is illustrated by Fig. 152. There is 1ft. round to the head, and the foot is sometimes laced to the boom. The mast traveller is arranged as follows : An eye is welded on the traveller, *a,* the halyard, *e,* is rove through the sheave hole in the mast, and then through the hook, *d,* and the eye in the traveller, *a.* A knot, *c,* is then made in the end of the halyard. *b* is an eye strop on the yard. The part of the halyard between *e* and *c* is usually covered with leather (*see* Fig. 153). This arrangement has been adopted to facilitate the lowering of the sail. If the traveller jams, the sails will still lower by the halyard running through the eye of the hook.

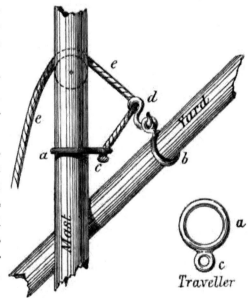

FIG. 153.

The spinnakers of these boats are worked without a topping lift or outhaul. The after guy is spliced to the tack cringle of the sail, to which is also spliced a rope eye. After the sail is hoisted this eye is slipped over the end of the boom, and is kept from running in by two thumb cleats. The after guy is passed aft, and the boom shoved out forward

gunwale. The total size of the boat is obtained by multiplying the girth by 1ft. 7in. (1·58ft.), and adding the product to the extreme length. The boats to be raced in one class, and the maximum size of the racing boats to be 40ft. club measurement."

and then squared aft. The heel of the boom has a hole burned in it, through which a rope is rove for securing the heel to chain plate, rigging, or mast.

	Venture.	Deva.	Zinnia.
Length over all	18ft.	18ft.	18ft.
Length on water-line	17ft. 11in.	17ft. 10in.	17ft. 9in.
Beam, extreme	5ft. 8in.	5ft. 8in.	6ft.
Draught of water aft	10in.	10in.	1ft.
Draught with centre-board down	2ft. 10in.	2ft. 9in.	2ft. 8in.
Length of centre-board	4ft. 10in.	4ft. 9in.	5ft.
Breadth of centre-board	1ft. 5in.	1ft. 5in.	1ft. 10½in.
Centre-board pivoted from fore side of stem	6ft. 4in.	6ft. 2in.	6ft. 3in.
Displacement	·65 ton.	·63 ton.	0·6 ton.
Fore side mast from fore side stem	4ft. 6in.	5ft. 6in.	5ft.
Mast, gunwale to halyard sheave	12ft. 9in.	12ft.	—
Bowsprit outboard	5ft. 6in.	5ft. 6in.	—
Main boom, extreme	13ft. 9in.	13ft. 6in.	—
Main yard, extreme	21ft. 6in.	21ft. 4in.	—
Luff of mainsail	4ft.	4ft.	—
Leech	23ft.	23ft.	—
Tack to peak earing	22ft. 6in.	22ft. 6in.	—
Clew to weather earing	14ft. 6in.	14ft. 6in.	—
Area of mainsail	160 sq. ft.	160 sq. ft.	—
Area of foresail	40 sq. ft.	40 sq. ft.	—
Area spinnaker	80 sq. ft.	80 sq. ft.	—
Total sail area	280 sq. ft.	280 sq. ft.	280 sq. ft.

These boats can be built (exclusive of the cost of the design) for 40*l*. The boats are given two coats of paint inside and out, and they have the following equipment for the sum named: Two yards; two booms; one bowsprit and spinnaker boom; two ash oars, 12ft.; one boat hook; two rowlocks; one anchor; one warp, 1¾in. and 12 fathoms long. Sails, by John Fraser, of Birkenhead, of 15in. cloths, consisting of two mainsails, three jibs, and one spinnaker. Wire shrouds, halyards, sheets, tacks, blocks, ironwork, lifebelts, &c., complete.

TABLE OF OFFSETS FOR "ZINNIA."—PLATE XLVI.

No. of Section	1		2		3		4		5		6		7		8	
	ft.	in.	ft.	in.	ft.	in.	ft.	in.	ft.	in.	ft.	in.	ft.	in.	ft.	in.
Heights above L.W.L. to top of gunwale	2	0	1	8¼	1	5½	1	3½	1	1½	1	1½	1	2¾	0	11
Depth from L.W.L. to rabbet of keel	0	6	0	7½	0	8	0	8½	0	9	0	9½	0	8	0	3
Half-breadths at gunwale	0	5	1	4½	2	1½	2	8½	3	0	3	0	2	8¾	2	2¼
Half-breadths 6in. above L.W.L.	0	3¾	1	1¾	1	11½	2	7½	3	0	2	11½	2	5½	1	5½
Half-breadths on L.W.L.	0	2¾	0	9¾	1	6¼	2	3	2	7¼	2	5½	1	9	0	7¼
Half-breadths on No. 2 W.L.	0	2½	0	8¼	1	3½	1	11½	2	3	2	0	1	3½	0	3
Half-breadths on No. 3 W.L.	0	2	0	6½	1	0	1	6	1	9¼	1	5½	0	9¼	0	1¼
Half-breadths on No. 4 W.L.	0	1½	0	4¼	0	8	1	0	1	1½	0	11	0	5	0	1¼
Half-breadths on No. 5 W.L.	0	1	0	1¼	0	1½	0	5	0	6	0	4¾	0	1	0	1¼

The sections are 2ft. 3in. apart, and No. 1 section is 11½in. from the fore side of stem.

The water-lines are 2in. apart.

Clincher built, ⅜in. larch plank; bent timbers, 1⅛in. by ⅝in., and tapered to heads; gunwale 1in. by 1¾in.; rising, 1¾in. by ½in.; keel, 6in. by 2in.; centre-board case, ¾in. pine; iron centre-plate, ¼in.; weight, 50lb.

Venture won the Champion Cup of the Mersey for 1895, and it became the property of her owner. She is better than Deva in light winds, but the latter is the faster when it comes to a case of the crew hanging out to windward. Zinnia is a good all-round boat, and can still occasionally win prizes against the later boats in almost any kind of weather.

The lug sails on the Mersey are cut with great roundness to the head (about 1ft.) ; it is recommended as an expedient for making a sail sit flat. Yards are made straight, but bend to shape of sail when set.

The yard is 3in. in diameter at the centre, and tapers well towards the ends. The yard should be made longer than at first required, as the head of the sail frequently requires pulling out.

The tack of the sail is set down by a gun-tackle purchase, or double purchase, leading from an eye-bolt on the keelson of the boat.

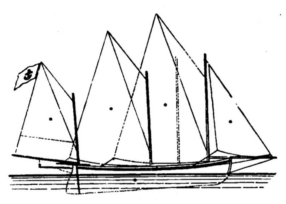

Fig. 154.

Unless the luff of the sail is kept taut, the peak drops and lets the boom down ; the peak should therefore be kept well set up, and a taut luff will generally succeed in doing this. The tack, the tack cringle, and luff rope of the sail must be strong, to stand the strain put upon it. The head of the sail must be tightly laced, and the lacing holes are best sewn, instead of " eyeleted."

The boom is sometimes fitted to the mast by a goose-neck, made to ship and collar, nut, or pin; but when laced mainsails came into use a bolt was fitted through the boom by the mast, with a hook on top for the tack cringle of the sail and an eye below for the tack tackle, the boom in this case having jaws. This plan has been retained by most of the boats, though laced sails have given way to loose-footed ones.

The clew of the sail must be free whilst the tack is bowsed down. The clew is sometimes hauled out on the boom by a traveller similar to a bowsprit traveller, but more generally the boom is fitted with a horse and hook same as a cutter's. The sheet is a gun tackle purchase.

In tacking, the heel of the yard is pulled the other side of the mast by a short line fast to the heel of the yard. The reef bands are 2ft. apart.

The tack and clew of a mizen are made fast to its boom by lashings.

The bowsprit is shipped through an iron hoop on the stem, and the heel fitted into a socket in the mooring bitt, ahead of the mast ; the bobstay is of wire, a single length of just sufficient length to shackle to plate on stemhead when bowsprit is bent down a bit.

The sprit rig as formerly in use on the Mersey is represented by Fig. 154. This is the rig of the gig used by the " speculation " men which hover about the mouth of the Mersey, except that they carry no jib. A very snug rig was made by stepping the mainmast in the thwart where shown by the dotted line ; jib tacked to stem head and mizen reefed.

If a sprit sail boat shows signs of missing stays, a hand going into the bows tends to bring her head to wind (this being a recognised dodge with Liverpool speculating gigmen).*

THE MANAGEMENT OF MERSEY OPEN SAILING BOATS.

In the case of a working mizen being carried it is found that hauling in the last inch of the jigger sheet, just as the helm is put down, is advisable in racing, as it helps make a boat come to quickly ; and then easing it off and not taking it in again until the boat is well under way, allows her to start again quickly.

The lug yard requires a little handling : the easiest and best way

---

* The practice of going into the lee bow of a boat as the helm is put down is a very old one ; by immersing the bow to leeward, the pressure is said to be increased and the boat's head forced to the wind. On the other hand, by collecting the crew on the weather bow as the helm is *put up* the boat will wear, or bear up faster. The author of an article on seamanship in the *Encyclopœdia Britannica*, in allusion to this subject, says " A practice of seamen in small wherries or skiffs, in putting about, is to place themselves to leeward of the mast. They even find they can aid the quick turning motion of these light boats by the way in which they rest on their two feet, sometimes leaning on one foot and sometimes on the other. And we have often seen this evolution (tacking) very sensibly accelerated in a ship-of-war by the crew running suddenly to the lee bow as the helm was put down. And we have heard it asserted by very expert seamen, that after all attempts to wear ship (after lying to in a storm) have failed, they have succeeded by the crew collecting themselves near the weather foreshrouds the moment the helm was put up." The man who goes into the lee bow to help bring the boat head to wind should not remain there, but move aft to the quarter on the opposite side ; this will assist the boat's head in falling off. The real reason why going into the bow will make a boat stay or wear quicker is, that by causing a greater immersion forward and lighter aft, the centre of gravity of a boat is shifted forward, thus bringing about a longer lever for the rudder to act upon. (*See* also " Sternway " in the chapter on " Seamanship.")

to get it over is by fixing a couple of light ropes, about a fathom long, to the foot of the yard, the ends being allowed to drop down at each side of the boom, and by hauling in the weather one, just before the boat comes upright in stays, the yard bends slightly, and passes round the left side of the mast, and flies into its position to leeward, ready for the next tack, this can be done by one hand without jerking the boat unnecessarily, for the most essential element for speed in these as in all other light boats is to get the crew to keep quiet, and if necessary to lay well up to windward, often to the extent of getting one leg and part of the body over the weather side—as the spare spars and sails are lashed up to the sides of the boats, they assist the crew in keeping this position.

Most careful handling of the helm is necessary in rough water, as a very slight touch will often keep a sea out. It is generally found that the light displacement boats are the liveliest, and driest, in rough weather; and those that take a large quantity of ballast have a high freeboard to keep them dry. A full section forward prevents a boat dipping and taking in volumes of water over the bows, but it is decidedly detrimental to speed in lumpy water, as it hammers on the top of the seas, and so stops the boat's way; a long floor with hollow sections near the keel under the mast seems to answer best.

In setting the spinnaker, the guy is passed outside the rigging; the halyards and sail are on the fore side of the mast shrouds and hoisted chock-a-block, being passed through the space between the mast and the rigging the sheet is secured to the bowsprit, or lee gunwale; the guy is bent to a small rope cringle in the tack of the sail; the cringle is of sufficient size to take the spritted point of the spinnaker boom, which is then pushed forward, and the heel of the boom goes into a snotter on the rigging. It is drawn aft by the guy, and trimmed to the wind.

Some of the boats use a boom with jaws, which fit on to the rigging. In taking the spinnaker off the guy is hauled aft until the boom is fore and aft, when the halyards are let go and the sail falls into the boat. This proves to be a quicker way of getting the sail off than taking it in forward in the ordinary manner.

CHAPTER XV.

CLYDE SAILING BOATS.

OPEN boat sailing has long been very popular on the Clyde, and this is hardly to be wondered at, as the Firth offers special opportunities for such a pastime. Snug anchorages, fairly smooth water, little or no run of tide, and the facilities given by the railway and steamboat companies for readily getting from the city to the coast, induce most young men who are in the least degree nautically inclined to keep a boat of some sort; and during the summer months, in the bright northern evenings, from every coast village may be seen a fleet of little vessels flitting along the shore in the smooth water, and lying over to the land wind, which, in good weather, rises as the sun sets. Many of these boats are racing craft, and as each principal watering place has its club, there is no lack of sport on the Saturday afternoons, there being always one, and sometimes two or three matches for the little ships. The class of boat has been gradually improved, and while in 1875 they were simply ordinary fishing skiffs, ballasted with stone or sand bags, these gave place to such powerful craft as shown in the drawing, with lead keels, spinnakers, and all the modern racing outfit.

The boats are divided for racing purposes into three classes, 17ft., 19ft., and 22ft. The drawing shows a 19ft. boat on a scale of $\frac{1}{4}$in.$=1$ft., but tables of offsets and proportional scales are given, so that it can be used for all three sizes; there are also a few 15ft. boats, but the principal racing is among the larger ones. Prior to 1878 the only dimension taken into account was length, that being measured over all, but as this was thought likely to produce a fleet of "Popophgas," the ordinary Y.R.A. rule was adopted by the Royal Western and Royal Rothesay Clubs, the classes being fixed at $1\frac{1}{2}$, $2\frac{1}{2}$, and $3\frac{1}{2}$ tons, so as not to unclass existing boats. As far as possible time allowances are discouraged, and no *new* boats are given time, but those built prior to 1878 get time from their

larger rivals according to the following scale, which has worked fairly well
in practice:

For 17ft. boats, 12 seconds per ¼ ton per knot.
For 19ft. boats, 10   „   „   „
For 22ft. boats, 8   „   „   „

Excepting one or two of the earlier boats, all are built with square
sterns, the increased power got by this form apparently making up for the
unavoidable drag aft, while the over-all measurement, which prevails in
most of the clubs, precludes a counter. It is questionable, however,
whether a short neat counter could not be made " to pay," at least in
heavy weather, and when the boats are necessarily travelling at a high
speed; though at small inclinations, and speeds up to three or four miles
an hour, this form of after end leaves the water smoothly enough, the
stern board being then fairly out of water.

The first boats did not displace much more than half a ton, and
carried about 6 cwt. of ballast (all inside), but the modern boats are
deeper, and some of them displace as much as 4 tons and carry 2½ tons
of ballast, the sail spreads being in proportion.

The boats were generally entirely open, but the Largs and Western
Clubs allow a deck, while one or two clubs even now permit the boat
to be covered from the mast forward, the space below forming what is
called " the den," where provisions, &c., may be kept dry, and where
the luxurious owner and friends sleep when away on a cruise, covering
the other four feet of their bodies with a tarpaulin.

There being no inducement, under the measurement rule, to cut
down free board, they are given plenty of it, some as much as 24in.
the average, as may be seen from the table, being about 22in. for a 19ft.
boat, which is not found too much for the heavy sea which a sou'-wester
tumbles up between Cumbrae and Porten Cross. Even with this a quantity
of water gets aboard, and employs any spare hand baling besides the man
at the pump. All the best boats are fitted with large pumps, 2½in. and
3in. in the barrel; they are generally on the aft thwart with discharge to
both sides, or through the bottom. An ingenious, albeit expensive, kind
of pump has been adopted in one or two instances; this is shown in the
mid section and general plan (Fig. 156, and Plate XLVII.)—the barrel is
pivoted at the foot so as to cant over to either side of the boat, the pumper
being thus able to sit up in the weather bilge while at work. The
discharge of this pump was through the lower part of the stern board,
possibly after the idea of Ruthven's jet propeller.

Another pump, made, and we believe patented, by Messrs M'Conechy
and Co., Glasgow, attains a like object in a simpler way. It is a lever
pump, and by a very simple but effective arrangement, the lever can be

shifted to either side, thus securing all the advantages of the other, and being much more easily worked.

The general construction and arrangement of these boats is shown in the drawings (Plate XLVII.), and the scantlings are in pretty close accordance with the following tables, but some of the fittings, being, as far as we know, peculiar to these boats, deserve particular mention, such as the ballast shelf, main-sheet horse, &c. These are illustrated in the cuts, and their uses further explained by the text.

In the larger boats, and where there is an extra heavy lead keel, a keelson may be advantageously adopted.

The weight of a 17ft. boat built to these scantlings would be about 5cwt., hull, spars, sails, &c., complete, of a 19ft. boat 7cwt. to 8cwt., while a 22ft. boat would weigh 15cwt. to 18cwt. The displacements, if built to this drawing, being 22cwt., 31½cwt., and 49cwt., would leave 17cwt., 23cwt., and 31cwt. for ballast and crew. Of this ballast, one-fourth might advantageously be put on the keel, but, unless lead were used, this amount could not be got in the space at disposal.

TABLE OF SCANTLINGS AND DIMENSIONS OF SPARS.

Length of boat	17ft. boat	19ft. boat	22ft. boat
Beam, extreme	5ft. 4½in.	6ft.	7ft.
Depth from top of gunwale to top of keel amidships	3ft. 0½in.	3ft. 4in.	3ft. 11½in.
Keel, of American elm, sided	2in.	2¼in.	2½in.
Keel, of American elm, moulded	6in.	7in.	8in.
Apron, of American elm	3¼in. × ⅞in.	3½in. × 1in.	4in. × 1¼in.
Frames, all bent, sided	1in.	1⅛in.	1¼in.
Frames, all bent, moulded	¾in.	⅞in.	1⅛in.
Frames, spaced centre to centre	8in.	9in.	9½in.
Floors, of oak (in every alternate frame space), sided	1½in.	1¾in.	2¼in.
Floors, moulded at throat	3in.	3½in.	4½in.
Stem, of oak, sided	1¾in.	2in.	2¼in.
Stem, of oak, moulded (about)	6in.	7in.	8in.
Sternpost, of oak, sided	2in.	2¼in.	2½in.
Sternpost, of oak, moulded at keel	7in.	8in.	9in.
Sternboard, of oak, thick	1in.	1⅛in.	1¼in.
Gunwale, American elm	1¾in. × 1¼in.	2in. × 1½in.	2¼in. × 1¾in.
Planking, garboard strake, elm	6in. × 7/16in.	6in. × ½in.	6in. × ⅝in.
Planking, thence to sheer strake, yellow pine	5in. × 7/16in.	5in. × ½in.	5½in. × ⅝in.
Planking, sheer strake, mahogany	5½in. × ½in.	5½in × ½in.	6in. × ⅝in.
Thwarts	7in. × 1in.	7in. × 1⅛in.	7in. × 1¼in.
Thwarts, mast thwarts	7in. × 1⅜in.	7in. × 1½in.	7in. × 1¾in
Wirings, elm	3in. × ⅞in.	3½in. × 1in.	3½in. × 1⅛in.
Mast beam, double-kneed, with lodging knee to wiring	2in.	2¼in.	2½in.
Mast, deck to hounds	18ft.	19ft. 6in.	20ft.
Mast, hounds to truck	—	—	9ft.
Mast, diameter at deck	3¾in.	4in.	4¾in.
Yard or gaff, length extreme	18ft.	20ft.	14ft.
Yard or gaff, diameter at slings	2⅜in.	2⅞in.	2½in.
Cruising yard or gaff, length extreme	15ft.	17ft.	—
Cruising yard or gaff, diameter at slings	2½in.	2¾in.	—
Boom, length extreme	16ft.	18ft.	18ft.
Boom, diameter at sheet	2½in.	2¾in.	2¾in.
Bowsprit, outboard	5ft.	5ft. 6in.	10ft.
Bowsprit, diameter at gammoning iron	2in.	2¼in.	2¾in.
Spinnaker or shadow sail boom, length extreme	16ft. 6in.	18ft. 6in.	21ft.

The usual rig for boats 19ft. and under is a single standing lug, as shown in the plan (Plate XLVIII.), but for cruising, and for racing in some of the clubs, a standing lug, with boom on foot, and short bowsprit with jib, are used; these are shown in the plan by dotted lines. For the single lug the mast is stepped about one-seventh of the boat's length from the stem, for the lug and jib, about 18in. further aft. Most of the boats are fitted for both rigs, and, farther, have several mast steps, so that the rake of the mast may be altered. One of the mast beams is

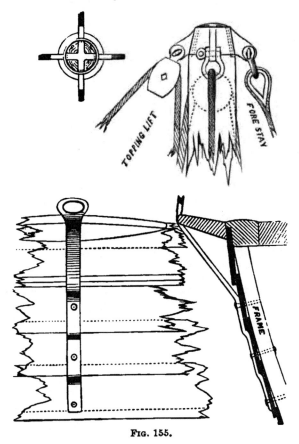

FIG. 155.

generally bolted to the gunwale, this being strengthened at the part by a heavy clamp piece running two to three feet fore and aft. The mast is further supported by a wire shroud on each side, and a forestay (1¼ steel). These are shackled to the cranse at the masthead, made as shown in Fig. 155, and have a large thimble spliced in at the other end to take the lanyard. Many of the boats are fitted with "channels," to give more spread to the rigging, the mast being so far forward, so lofty, and the boats so fine in the nose, that without these the shrouds would give little support; they are of the "skeleton" kind, being made as shown in the sketch. The lengths and diameters of mast and spars are given in the table. A traveller works on the mast, and in construction is identical with that of the New Brighton boats described at page 359, the hook being welded solid on the ring, and hooking into a selvagee strop on the yard, the halyard (2in. tarred hemp) being spliced into its eye. But into the other end of the halyard a double block is spliced; and a fall rove through this, and a single block at the foot, forms a luff tackle purchase for hoisting. The single thick rope is cut a foot or eighteen inches short, so that the yard has to be lifted up and hooked on; this of course is necessary, that the sail may be hoisted "chock-a-block." In the later boats a wire tie of ⅜in. or ½in. flexible steel wire rope is universally adopted. The tack is simply slipped on to a hook in the mast beam, the tackle on the halyards bringing the necessary strain on the luff to peak the sail. The main-sheet is a gun-tackle purchase, the upper block shackling on to the clew of the sail, while the lower has a thimble spliced on to its tail, which works on the horse across the stern, as shown in the sketch (Fig. 156). When the boom lugsail is in use, the same sheet is simply shackled into a strop on the boom, thus doing for both. It is evident that by carrying the horse back, say a couple of feet (which might easily enough be done), all the advantages of a boom sail could be retained; there is, therefore, a rule which enacts that "if a horse is used it must be at right angles to the keel."

The spars and sails carried by these boats are enormous; one 19ft. boat, indeed, having a mast 21ft., deck to hounds, or 18in. longer than the five-tonner Diamond. She, however, was exceptionally heavily sparred, the general proportions being :

	Luff.	Head.	Foot.	Leech.
	ft. in.	ft. in.	ft. in.	ft. in.
19ft. boats	12 6	16 0	14 6	25 6
17ft. boats	12 0	14 6	13 6	23 0

With such canvas aloft, the latest improvements in ballasting must be adopted, and the new boats are all fitted with metal keels, 3 cwt. to 5 cwt. in weight. In one or two, all the internal ballast is also lead; but, whether lead or iron, it is neatly cast in blocks, weighing about a hundredweight, which fit close down to the skin, but hang entirely on the keel and floor timbers. As shifting ballast is allowed in the Largs Club, most boats, whether belonging to this club or not, are fitted with a shelf for stowing weather ballast in each bilge, as shown in the arrangement plan and midship section (Plate XXXVII. and Fig. 156). This shelf also makes a capital seat for the crew, where they are well up to windward and also in shelter. The celebrated Largs

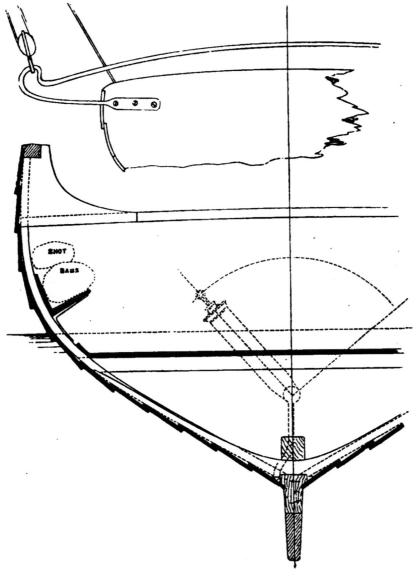

Fig. 156.

boat **Neva** (possibly borrowing the idea from the China clippers, which when racing, hung water-butts over the weather side) used to get her ballast still farther to windward, by slinging pretty nearly all of it

B B

(some 6cwt.) right outside. The Royal Western Yacht Club (of Scotland), however, has most stringent rules against shifting ballast, and rigidly enforces these rules, also limiting the crew to three in the 17ft. and 19ft. boats, and four in the 22ft. boats, so as to prevent, as far as may be, "live ballast."

These boats go out in pretty well any weather, the sail reefing down very snug, and when not recklessly driven they are most seaworthy little craft. Accidents of any kind are therefore rare, and we cannot call to mind a fatal one, owing doubtless to the excellent rule enforced in all the clubs, that "every boat shall carry life-saving apparatus sufficient to float every person on board." The modern boats seldom or never miss stays, but in the event of their doing so, it is admissible to use an oar to put them round, "but the strokes are to be backward, and in no case to be ahead," a very necessary clause, as before its introduction, a morbid horror of missing stays prevailed, especially in calm weather. At one time in running, the Western Club did not permit extra sails, and did not even allow "booming out," but the Western now follow the rule of the other clubs and allow spinnakers, or more generally "shadow sails." The shadow sail is generally an old lug sail hoisted opposite the other, and the boom shipped into a snotter on fore side of mast.

The 22ft. boats are invariably rigged as cutters, with mainsail, foresail, and jib, and small topsail on the pole mast. They carry also the usual balloon canvas for running to leeward, and occasionally indulge even in jib topsails. In the following table we give particulars of the best boats in this class, the "Thisbe," built by McLaren, of Kilcreggan, and owned by Mr. Allan Macintyre, and the "Ayrshire Lass," built by Fife for Mr. Thomas Reid, of Paisley. It is by the courtesy of these gentlemen we are able to give the following particulars. Alongside are given those of a 22ft. boat built to our drawing.

Name	THISBE.	AYRSHIRE LASS.	DESIGN.
Length, extreme	21ft. 11in.	22ft.	22ft.
Breadth, extreme	6ft. 11in.	7ft.	7ft.
Draught of water aft	3ft. 8in.	3ft. 6in.	3ft. 2in.
Draught of water forward	2ft.	2ft. 6in.	1ft. 9in.
Displacement (about)	3·15 tons	2·4 tons	2·45 tons.
Ballast (total)	2 tons 5cwt.	1 ton 10cwt.	1 ton 11cwt
Ballast lead inside	1 ton 9cwt.	1 ton 4cwt.	18cwt.
Ballast iron inside	—	10cwt.	—
Ballast on keel	16cwt.	6cwt.	13cwt.
Mast, deck to hounds	20ft. 6in.	19ft.	20ft.
Boom, extreme	18ft.	19ft.	18ft.
Gaff, extreme	14ft.	15ft.	14ft.
Bowsprit, outside	10ft.	12ft.	10ft.
Area of plain sail	513 sq. ft.	520 sq. ft.	500 sq. feet.

The Clyde boats are invariably clencher built (*see* Fig. 156). In building to our drawings it would be necessary to fasten a "roof tree" or stout batten to the top of stem and stern post; then make half moulds for, say, 2, 4, 6, and 8 sections, pivoting these on their centre lines to the batten and keel so as to swing round and do for both sides. She may be planked to these moulds, the frames then bent in, and last of all the floors, as if the floors are put on before planking it is unlikely that the bottom will be kept as fair. The sections, as shown in Fig. 157, can be drawn down full size from the table of offsets on the next page.

In all cases the water-lines are named from the load, or first water-line *downwards*. The diagonals are also named in like manner,

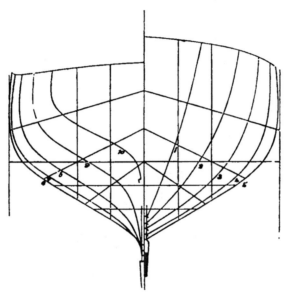

Fig. 157.

the *top* one being *first* diagonal, and so on. The gunwale heights and breadths explain themselves. The dimensions given are in all cases *moulded*, that is, to the inside of the plank. If it is desired to make calculations of any elements of these boats, once and a half the thickness of plank must be drawn on.

The stations (*see* Plate XLVII.) are spaced exactly $\frac{1}{10}$th of the extreme length apart, and are at right angles to the water line. The shape of stern-board is shown in projection on the body-plan; in laying it down for building, the rake of post would have to be allowed for to get the *actual* shape.

B B 2

TABLE OF OFFSETS FOR A 17FT. BOAT.

No. of Section	1		2		3		4		5		6		7		8		9		10	
	ft.	in.	ft.	in.	ft.	in.	ft.	in.	ft.	in.	ft.	in.	ft.	in.	ft.	in.	ft.	in.	ft.	in.
Heights above L.W.L. to top of gunwale	2	2⅞	2	1⅝	1	11¾	1	10⅛	1	9⅛	1	8⅛	1	7⅞	1	7⅞	1	8	1	8⅝
Depths below L.W.L. to rabbet	1	0	1	1⅝	1	2⅞	1	4	1	5¼	1	6⅝	1	7⅛	1	8⅛	1	8⅞	—	
Half-breadths at gunwale	1	1¼	1	9⅜	2	2⅛	2	4⅜	2	6	2	6⅛	2	5⅞	2	4⅛	2	1⅛	1	9
Half-breadths at L.W.L.	0	5⅛	1	0⅜	1	6⅞	2	0 1/16	2	8	2	3⅛	2	2⅞	1	10	1	0⅞	0	1⅞
Half-breadths, No. 2 W.L.	0	3½	0	8⅛	1	1⅞	1	6 1/16	1	8½	1	8⅜	1	6⅛	1	0⅛	0	5⅛	0	0⅞
Half-breadths, No. 3 W.L.	0	1	0	3⅝	0	7 1/16	0	10	0	11¾	0	11⅛	0	8⅞	0	5⅛	0	2	0	0⅝
Half-breadths on 1st diagonal	0	10½	1	6⅞	2	0⅞	2	5	2	7¾	2	8¼	2	7¾	2	5⅝	2	1⅛	1	7⅞
Half-breadths on 2nd diagonal	0	8	1	2⅞	1	8⅛	1	11⅞	2	2	2	2⅛	2	0¾	1	9⅜	1	3⅛	0	7⅛
Half-breadths on 3rd diagonal	0	5⅜	0	10 1/16	1	1⅜	1	3⅛	1	4¾	1	4⅜	1	3⅛	1	0⅞	0	7⅛	0	1⅞

The stations are spaced 1·7ft. apart (1ft. 8⅜in.), No. 1 station being the same distance from fore-side stem.

The water-lines are a bare 5⅜in. apart; the more exact way to lay them off will be to measure 16in. below the load line, and divide it into three equal parts.

The side lines are parallel to the centre line, and 2ft. 7½in. out.

The first diagonal cuts the centre line 1ft. 3½in. above the load line, and cuts the side line 7in. above the load line.

The second diagonal cuts the centre line 7½in. above the load line, and the side line 7½in below it.

The third diagonal cuts the centre line *at* the load line, and cuts the third water line 1ft. 3½in. out.

TABLE OF OFFSETS FOR A 19FT. BOAT.

No. of Section	1		2		3		4		5		6		7		8		9		10	
	ft.	in.	ft.	in.	ft.	in.	ft.	in.	ft.	in.	ft.	in.	ft.	in.	ft.	in.	ft.	in.	ft.	in.
Heights above L.W.L. to top of gunwale	2	6	2	4½	2	2⅜	2	1⅛	1	11⅞	1	10⅞	1	10½	1	10⅛	1	10⅛	1	11⅛
Depths below L.W.L. to rabbet	1	1⅛	1	3¼	1	4⅜	1	6	1	7⅜	1	8⅝	1	10¼	1	11⅜	1	11⅛	—	
Half-breadths at gunwale	1	2⅞	2	0	2	5¼	2	8¼	2	9⅜	2	10	2	9½	2	7⅛	2	4½	2	0
Half-breadths at L.W.L.	0	6⅛	1	1⅞	1	9	2	3	2	6⅜	2	7⅜	2	5⅞	2	0¾	1	2⅜	0	1⅞
Half-breadths, No. 2 W.L.	0	3⅜	0	9⅛	1	3⅜	1	8⅞	1	11⅛	1	11¼	1	8⅜	1	2¼	0	5⅝	0	0¾
Half-breadths, No. 3 W.L.	0	1⅛	0	4	0	7⅜	0	11¼	1	1⅛	1	1	0	10 1/16	0	6	0	2 1/16	0	0⅜
Half-breadths on 1st diagonal	0	11⅛	1	9	2	3¼	2	8⅜	2	11⅜	3	0⅛	2	11⅛	2	9	2	4⅛	1	9⅜
Half-breadths on 2nd diagonal	0	8⅞	1	4⅛	1	10¾	2	2⅞	2	4⅞	2	5⅛	2	3⅜	2	0	1	5⅜	0	8⅛
Half-breadths on 3rd diagonal	0	6 1/16	0	11⅛	1	3⅜	1	5⅞	1	6⅜	1	6⅞	1	5¼	1	2½	0	8⅜	0	2

The stations are spaced 1·9ft. apart (1ft. 10⅞in.), No. 1 station being the same distance from fore-side stem.

The water-lines are spaced exactly 6in. apart.

The side lines are parallel to the centre line, and 2ft. 11in. out.

The first diagonal cuts the centre line 18in. above the load line, and cuts the side line 8in. above load line.

The second diagonal cuts the centre line 8½in. above the load line, and the side line 8½in. below it.

The third diagonal cuts the centre line *at* the load line, and cuts the third water-line 1ft. 5½in. out.

TABLE OF OFFSETS FOR A 22FT. BOAT.

No. of Section	1	2	3	4	5	6	7	8	9	10
	ft. in.	ft. in.	ft. in.	ft. in.	ft. in.	ft. in.	ft. in.	ft. in.	ft. in.	ft. in.
Heights above L.W.L. to top of gunwale	2 10¼	2 8½	2 6¼	2 5	2 3¾	2 2¼	2 1½	2 1½	2 1¼	2 2¼
Depths below L.W.L. to rabbet	1 3¼	1 5¼	1 7¼	1 8¼	1 10½	2 0	2 1¼	2 3¼	2 3¼	—
Half-breadths at gunwale	1 5	2 3½	2 9¼	3 1¼	3 2¼	3 3¼	3 3¼	3 0¼	2 8¼	2 3¼
Half-breadths at L.W.L.	0 7¼	1 3¼	2 0¼	2 7¼	2 11¹⁄₁₆	3 0¹⁄₁₆	2 10½	2 4½	1 4½	0 2¼
Half-breadths at 2nd W.L.	0 4¾	0 11½	1 5¼	1 11½	2 2¼	2 2¼	1 11¾	1 4½	0 6¼	0 1
Half-breadths at 3rd W.L.	0 1¾	0 4¾	0 9¼	1 0¼	1 3¼	1 2¼	0 11½	0 7½	0 2¼	0 0¼
Half-breadths on 1st diagonal	1 1½	2 0½	2 8¼	3 1¼	3 4¼	3 5¼	3 5	3 2¼	2 9¼	2 1¼
Half-breadths on 2nd diagonal	0 10¼	1 7¼	2 2¼	2 7¼	2 9¼	2 10	2 8	2 3¼	1 8¼	0 10¼
Half-breadths on 3rd diagonal	0 7¼	1 1	1 5¼	1 8¼	1 10	1 10	1 8	1 4¼	0 10¼	0 2¼

The stations are spaced 2·2ft. apart (2ft. 2⅜in.), No. 1 station being the same distance from fore-side stem.

The water lines are spaced exactly 7in. apart.

The side lines are parallel to the centre line, and 3ft. 4¼in. out.

The first diagonal cuts the centre line 1ft. 8¼in. above the load line, and cuts the side line 9in. above load line.

The second diagonal cuts the centre line 9¼in. above the load line, and the side line 10¼in. below it.

The third diagonal cuts the centre line *at* the load line, and cuts the third water line 1ft. 8¼in. out.

As to cost, a modern racing 19ft. boat is a pretty expensive toy. About the most successful builder of them, Walter Paton, of Millport, N.B., charges 22s. to 23s. per foot, and other builders are pretty much the same; the items, therefore, would sum up about as follows:

	£	s.	d.
Hull and spars, 19ft., at 23s. per foot	21	17	0
Plain pump, and other fittings not supplied by builder	3	10	0
Lead keel, 6cwt., at 23s. per cwt.	6	18	0
Internal ballast, 10cwt., at 22s. 6d. per cwt.	11	5	0
Shot in bags, 4cwt., at 32s. per cwt.	6	8	0
Blocks, running and standing rigging	8	0	0
Sails	15	0	0
Three life belts, at 15s.	2	5	0
Total for boat complete and ready for racing	£75	3	0

If internal ballast is of iron, deduct 8l. 10s.

Iron masts were successfully introduced in 1881 in several of the boats, they being found as light as, and much stiffer than, the wooden ones. They were made of boiler tube, about 4in. diameter, and ⅛th to ¼in. thick, tapered at top by slipping a small piece inside, and then a smaller, somewhat after the fashion of the Chinese bamboo fishing rods. They have, however, been discarded, and although bamboos and hollow wooden spars have also been tried, the old fashioned solid stick has after all been found most reliable; and this it can be said is the common experience all round the coast.

Lead and everything else being now much cheaper, 5*l.* might be deducted from the cost as just given of a 19ft. boat of the old type. The cost of a 2½-tonner (corresponding to the old 19ft. class), with all lead ballast, racing sails, and gear would not fall far short of 150*l.*

In 1879 nearly all the clubs adopted the Y.R.A. rule of measurement, with the effect that a number of miniature yachts which in no way possess any special features as to hull, sails, or ballasting, appeared. They are simply models of big yachts; in one or two instances, indeed, they were built direct off the lines of five or ten tonners, the scale being altered to suit. Three-and-a-half, two-and-a-half, and one-and-a-half ton yachts have therefore been competing in the old 15ft., 19ft., and 22ft. classes, the new boats being one-third to one-half longer, and having half as much displacement again as their rivals, while they have the further advantage of carrying a large proportion of the ballast outside, the result being that the old type of boat is likely to be improved off the face of the water. One or two of the builders, however, stuck pretty closely to the old type of boat, simply adding a counter; the present build may be somewhat deeper than the vessel shown in the plate, but if a counter be drawn on (the buttock lines will give a reliable guide as to its outline) she will very fairly represent them.

After a few races it became perfectly evident the old class of boats had no chance with the model yachts, and the leading clubs arranged for separate matches for the yachts and open boats. This is found to work well where club funds admit of it. A new 15ft. class was started in 1884, and to encourage the building of such boats it was determined that no outside ballast should be allowed, and that they should be driven by only one sail, it being anticipated that these restrictions would reduce the cost. But lead was found to be as dear carried inside as out, and the "one sail" was made as big as two, the result being that the cost of such a boat, say 15 × 5 × 5ft. deep was about 50*l.* But few new boats have been built in the other classes, and these fifteen-footers probably represent the latest ideas in lug sail boats: they are simply a development of the boat shown in the drawing, but deeper drawn, with more displacement, more ballast, and more sail. The particulars of one of the most successful of them—the Mascotte, belonging to Mr. Dickie—may be interesting :—

Length, extreme	15ft.
Length on L. W. L.	15ft.
Breadth, extreme	5ft.
Draught of water, extreme	3ft.
Weight of ballast	21cwt.
Mast, gunwale to cranse	18ft.
Area of sail	190 sq. ft.

For a couple of years after 1884 there were few or no new lug-sail boats built, and though this form of racing was by no means extinct, and races were given for these little craft by all the clubs, there was not the same keen interest taken in it as heretofore. 1886 and 1887 each saw a new 15-footer which spread-eagled the existing boats, but showed no remarkable novelty in form, being very similar to the Mascotte, previously described, but deeper drawn and carvel built, and with all the lead outside.

The Clyde Canoe Club had, however, been meditating a change in its constitution, the members concluding that with increasing years, and waist-coats, their craft might be increased also, and in the fall of 1885 it was decided that three lug-sail boats should be built for the use of the members of the club.

The Royal Clyde Yacht Club also built three 19ft. boats, all six being identical in form, construction, ballasting, and sail area (*see* Plate XLIX.) On summer evenings, and especially on Saturday afternoons, members about the club caring to sail, chose three crews, generally by ballot, and some most enjoyable races have resulted, as, the boats being alike, winning depends solely on the smartness and good judgment of the crew. These boats are fine powerful vessels, and wonderfully fast considering the small sail area and mode of ballasting; they are extremely moderate in cost, and would suit admirably for many other harbours about the coast, such as Plymouth, Falmouth, Harwich, Cork.

DIMENSIONS, &c. (PLATE XLIX.).

Length, extreme	19ft. 2¼in.
Length on L.W.L.	18ft. 1¾in.
Breadth, extreme	6ft. 0¾in.
Depth, top of gunwale to rabbet	3ft. 10in.
Depth, top of gunwale to under side of metal keel	4ft. 8¼in.
Draught, extreme	2ft. 9in.
Freeboard, minimum	2ft.
Weight of iron keel	7cwt. 0qr. 11lb.
Weight of cast ballast	4cwt. 1qr. 16lb.
Weight of old furnace bars, about	10cwt.
Build, clincher.	
Rig, lug sail and jib.	
Mast, gunwale to pin of sheave	16ft. 8in.
Mast, centre to fore side stem at gunwale	5ft. 1in.
Yard, hole to hole	15ft. 9in.
Boom, mast to pin	18ft.
Bowsprit, outboard to outside of cranse	5ft.

The boats were built by McAllister, of Dumbarton, from designs presented to the club by Mr. G. L. Watson, the total cost for each boat, including sails, gear, anchor and chain, being 32*l*.

Early in 1888 a conference of yachtsmen interested in small boat sailing was held in Glasgow, members of the various Clyde clubs being invited to send delegates. Among other rules, the following for regulating the building were agreed on :—

" III.—Length Class—17ft. on L.W.L., and not exceeding 19ft. over all. Sail area limited to 530 sq. ft. No time allowance. Mainsail or lug sail not to exceed ·75 of total sail area.

" IV.—15ft. C.B. class—Boats not to exceed 15ft. over all; sternposts in a straight line; beam not to exceed 5ft. 6in.; keel not less than 2in. deep; depth of boat at one-third from aft not to exceed 2ft. 6in. Depth at any other part not to exceed 3ft. outside measurement. No decks allowed. Gunwale not to exceed 3in. broad. Weight of centre plate limited to 60lb., and metal band on keel not to exceed ¼in. thick; no other outside ballast allowed; boats all to be clinker built, and sail area not to exceed 150 sq. ft."

The rules definitely fixed, and with the understanding that they should remain unaltered for a term of years, a number of new boats were at once laid down in the 19-foot and 15-foot centre-board class. The new 19-footers, three of which were built from Fife's designs and two from Watson's, are fine powerful boats, all of them carvel built and half decked. All have the full allowance of sail—530 sq. ft.—thus bringing them to 1·5 rating, but we question if they would not have been just as well with a trifle less, say 480 to 500 sq. ft. The other particulars are as follows :—

Length, extreme	19ft.
Length on L.W.L.	17ft.
Breadth, extreme	6ft.
Depth, extreme	6ft. 8in.
Draught, extreme	5ft.
Freeboard, minimum	22in.
Ballast on keel	1 ton 15 cwt.
Ballast inside, about	4 cwt.
Area lug sail (part behind mast only)	397 sq. ft.
Area head sail (by Y.R.A. rule)	132 sq. ft.

The 15-foot centre-boarders are simply broad dinghies with a centre plate in them, not unlike the Kingstown Water Wags.

In 1890, the Royal Clyde Yacht Club, to accommodate those younger members wishing to make a more protracted cruise than was possible in the 19-footers built two 23-foot cutter rigged boats (*see* Plate L.). These were also from Mr. G. L. Watson's designs, and have proved most comfortable and able craft, and quite large enough for young fellows enjoying a week's holiday on board, as, with the help of their partial deck, and spreading a tent over the cockpit, two or three can sleep on board comfortably. These boats are the property of the club, but any member or members have the right of hiring them, and they form admirable training ships for the younger yachtsmen. The particulars of these boats are as follows (Plate L.) :

Length, extreme	23ft.
Length on L.W.L...	22ft.
Breadth, extreme	7ft. 1in.
Depth, extreme	6ft. 3in.
Draught, extreme	4ft. 6in.
Freeboard, minimum	2ft. 3in.
Weight of iron keel	2¼ tons.
Build, carvel, half-decked.	
Rig, cutter.	
Mast, deck to hounds	19ft.
Pole, hounds to hounds	7ft. 6in.
Mast, centre to fore side of stem at gunwale	8ft.
Boom, extreme	20ft. 6in.
Gaff, throat bolt to pin of sheave	14ft.
Bowsprit, outboard to inside of cranse	9ft.
Cost, 98*l*.	

Among the 19-foot craft no particular novelties have appeared, although several new boats have been built since 1888, any developments taking the direction of increased depth and breadth, the displacement remaining about the same.

In 1890, a 2¼-rating class was fairly established by the building of two 2¼ raters. These were simply model yachts, rigged with lugsail and very small staysail, the rig found most successful in the Solent 2¼. In anything of a breeze they simply lost the old boats against which they were pitted, though, on one or two occasions, the tables were turned in light breezes. In 1891 the class was fully developed, as Fife built five identical craft for local amateurs, and Watson two. These boats, however, presented no very special features, as they differ but slightly in design from the larger creations by these gentlemen.

CLYDE RESTRICTED CLASS, 1893.

During 1890 some capital sport had been enjoyed between the two 23ft. Royal Clyde Club boats Mayflower and Thistle, and a third boat, on the same lines, owned by Mr. Robert Wylie, and called after the American champion, Volunteer. But in 1890 a boat of the same length, but lead ballasted, and with much larger sail plan, was built, in the Erica, by Mr. Fife. Erica knocked the older boats out, and in turn was, in 1891, knocked out by the Verve, which Mr. Wylie had built for him by Watson, to replace the Volunteer.

By 1892 the 23-footers had crystalised into a class, and in November of that year a meeting was held in Glasgow, at which the Royal Northern,

Clyde, Western, Largs, Corinthian, Mudhook, and West of Scotland Yacht Clubs were represented.

The resolutions adopted at the meeting resulted in the following conditions, and came into force 1893 :—

I. In the 23ft. L.W.L. Class : (1) Over-all measurement restricted to 30ft.; (2) total sail area limited to 750 sq. ft., whereof the mainsail or lugsail not to exceed ·80; (3) centre-boards or plates, fin and bulb keels excluded; (4) these conditions to remain in force for five years.

II. In the 17ft. L.W.L. Class : (1) Over-all measurement restricted to 19ft. as formerly; (2) total sail area limited to 470 sq. ft., whereof the mainsail or lugsail not to exceed ·75; (3 and 4) same conditions as for 23ft. class.

N.B.—The hulls and sails are to be measured in terms of the Y.R.A. rules in force in 1893, and a certificate by a Y.R.A. measurer produced. The certificate will specify the length over-all and on load water line, the total sail area, and the proportion thereof in the mainsail or lugsail.

Three new boats were built for the 23ft. class by Mr. W. Fife, jun., and as many by Mr. G. L. Watson. Mr. Watson's Vida and Fife's Thaber getting the bulk of the prizes. All these were fine, wholesome vessels. Could beat the 2·5 raters turning to windward in pretty well all weathers, though failing a little reaching and running. They were fine sea boats, and, above all, were admirably fitted for young fellows of moderate means, as a couple of them could live on board with the greatest comfort, there being also a cot for the man forward. There was just head room under the skylight for dressing, while a fairly roomy cockpit made them most useful boats for day sailing.

Vida (the lines of which are given on Plate LI.) is a fair representative of these boats. In 1895 were added two boats—Klysma, by Mr. Fife, and Vida II., by Mr. Watson. Both these have more beam and less displacement than former productions, and are nothing like so comfortable for cruising, while it is doubtful if they are appreciably faster than Thaber or Vida.

Vida's (Plate LI.) record is : 1893—starts, 29; first prizes, 19; second prizes, 7; third, 1; total, 27. 1894—starts, 30; first prizes, 18; second, 6; total, 24. 1895—3 first prizes for 5 starts up to June 1st.

The smaller class of 17-19 footers has been but slightly augmented. The very great success of Mr. Fife's Hatasoo, built in 1894, having somewhat paralysed enterprise in this direction. Hatasoo is the most extreme boat of the class, being of great breadth and very small displacement. She has shown herself a good all-round boat in every weather, but her greatest successes have been made in light airs.

For 1895 yet another restricted class was instituted at Helensburgh for sailing in the Clyde weekly regattas. (Plate LII.)

The design to which all the boats are built was prepared by Mr. Linton Hope, of Greenhithe, and the following are the chief dimensions: Length over all, 18ft.; length on waterline, 16ft.; beam, 7ft.; draught of hull, 10in.; draught with plate, 6ft.; sail area, actual, 275 sq. ft.; sail area, per Y.R.A., 261 sq. ft.; rating, 0·7; displacement, 1818lb., or 0·81 tons. No ballast to be carried, and the crew is limited to three for racing. The boats are fitted with dagger centre-boards of the Sorceress type, but broader. They are decked, all but a roomy cockpit, at the fore and after end of which are watertight bulkheads which will give a certain amount of safety in a case of a not improbable capsize. From these particulars it will be seen that they are much more powerful boats than the Dublin Mermaids. Mr. Allister, Dumbarton, built the whole fleet. The cost of each for hull and spars was 33*l*.

CHAPTER XVI.

KINGSTOWN BOATS.

KINGSTOWN, in addition to being an important yachting centre, giving racing for all classes from the largest to the 0·5-rater, has evolved the above unique class, at first purely local, but now known all round the globe.

This class is the germ of the one model class, and has well carried out its initial objects, viz., restrictions on the advantage of a long purse; preservation of the selling value of the boat and combination of a serviceable and racing boat.

The Water Wags Association was started in 1887, and its origin was to provide several residents at Shankill, Co. Dublin, a portion of the coast where there is a shingly beach open to the surf of the Irish Channel, and where the boats have to be beached and carried up often by only two men, and where ballast is consequently inadmissible, with a light, strong, safe boat that would sail well to windward without ballast, and without a keel—rather a difficult problem to solve, but one that has been proved an accomplished fact. The design (Plate LIII.) of a boat 13ft. long by 4ft. 10in. beam, sharp at both ends, but rounder in the stern than the bow, with a flat floor, high sides, and a good sheer, was selected, to which was added a small centre-board to give the necessary grip when afloat; and, in order to enable the fleet to have close races in the class, to preserve the healthy lines, and to save the expense of outbuilding, it was agreed that all the boats should be built on the same model, and the canvas was limited to a maximum of 75 sq. ft. fore and aft, and 60ft. in a spinnaker. There was no restriction as to how it should be applied, but all the boats put it in one very pretty standing lug (Plate LIV.), designed by Messrs. Lapthorn and Ratseys, with the mast stepped 18in. from the bow, so that all the boats are practically identical. Although these boats were originally designed for beach boats, and are best adapted for that purpose, they have been principally used in Kingstown Harbour, where they make an exceedingly handy boat to sail in and out through the large fleet of vessels usually anchored there, as they spin round in their own length, never miss stays, and make little or no leeway. They have ventured on several occasions across Dublin Bay, and even as far as Malahide and Wicklow, and have been out in very rough water, and surprised their skippers at their good behaviour. As a proof of their stability it may be mentioned that with two persons sitting to windward eight or nine of them have been dismasted without capsizing. But with seventy-five square feet of sail, and no ballast, any 13-foot punt is liable to heel over in a puff till the water comes in, and the water wag is no exception to this. So the main sheet is never belayed, and the man at the tiller should always keep his weather eye on the look out to luff or ease the sheet if the squall looks stronger than the canvas set can bear. A standing lug is found much safer in this respect than a balance lug, because the wind can be completely spilled out of it, and there is no portion forward of the mast to retard her head flying up in the wind. All persons who use these very lively little boats should know the rudiments of open boat sailing, so clearly laid down in Chapter VI. of this book. When these boats do go over they do not go to the bottom as a boat with ballast will do, but will even support their crew if they do not try to climb up on them.

As to their cost. There are now a fleet of between forty and fifty in and around Kingstown. Of these, Robert McAlister, of Dumbarton, built most, and he turns them out from 15l. to 20l., according to finish. Doyle of Kingstown, and Atkinson of Bullock, Co. Dublin, and Holloway of Dublin, built several, and they charge about the same, and Fife of Fairlie built the remainder, but he charges 25l., as he says such small boats are not in his line, and it would not pay him to give his attention to them for less. Many of the boats intended only for racing are now built of cedar, and are beautifully turned out as regards fittings and finish, and cost fancy sums over 25l. Lapthorn and Ratsey furnish a cotton sail for 2l. 10s., and a silk one for 2l. 15s., and anyone will make the spinnaker for a few shillings. The silk sails are best for very fine weather, but the cotton stand flattest in a breeze. The best way to set the sail is by a single halyard running through a single sheave at the mast head, and a tack tackle for getting taut the luff, and so peaking the yard. (If the clew is attached to the boom before the sail is peaked, its weight should be relieved by the hand while the tack tackle is being hauled on.) A single main sheet, passing round a single peg or snatch block on the lee counter, and then to the hand, is the best, the sheet being passed over while in stays. With the single halyard, the sail will run down the moment it is let go, and no traveller is needed for the full sail as the yard will be chock-a-block, but for a reefed sail, it is well to have a mast-hoop on the mast that will hook or can be lashed to the yard when needed.

These boats give plenty of sport to men of limited incomes in races among themselves, as the old boats are well in it with the new, the original lines being strictly preserved.

As rowing boats they carry seven well, and can be rowed by either one or two persons, and they make a very handy dinghy for a yacht, as they are well adapted for exploring harbours and creeks, or for fishing, or rowing large parties on shore, and altogether they have proved themselves a favourite, and are now to be found in Argentine, Australian, and Chinese waters, besides in many other ports.

The draught of water, with centre-board up, is about 9in., varying according to the number of crew. The centre-board drops about 16in.

The following are the principal limitations of the water wags, but any person wishing to race should get the full limitations from the Hon. Sec. before he builds.

Length over all, 13ft.; beam, 4ft. 10in.; lines, those of the club model.

Centre-board to be of iron or steel. Length shall not exceed 4ft. When hauled up flush with top of casing, no portion shall project below keel. Immersed surface below keel shall not exceed $2\frac{1}{4}$ sq. ft. Thickness at any point shall not exceed $\frac{1}{4}$in., or less than $\frac{3}{16}$.

Keel outside garboard strake, inclusive of thickness of keelband, if any, shall not exceed in depth $1\frac{1}{2}$in., or 3in. in width. Keelband of iron, brass, or copper, not to exceed in thickness $\frac{1}{4}$in., or less than $\frac{3}{16}$.

Stem and stern post—moulded depth of, to be clear of hoods by not less than 2in.

Mast not to exceed over all 13ft., measured from top of keel to truck.

Fore and aft sails not to exceed 75 sq. ft. in area.

Spinnaker not to exceed 60, or less than 50 sq. ft. in area, and is only to be used before the wind, and in no case as a jib.

Boats not to carry more than three, or less than two persons during a match, all of whom shall be amateurs, and all matches shall be steered by a member or a lady.

Each boat shall carry a pair of oars not less than 8ft. long, with spurs or rowlocks for same; also one solid cork ring-shaped life buoy, not less than 22in. in external diameter, or two life cushions, with loop lines, of the same floating capacity.

Object of the Water Wag Association.—The promotion of amateur seamanship and racing in safe and useful boats, which are similar, and where the contest shall be one of skill.—Hon. Sec.: J. B. Stephens, Esq., No. 8, Clarinda Park, E., Kingstown.

The following particulars refer to the plates :

No. 1 section is 2ft. 1½in. from the fore side of stem.

No. 2 section is 4ft. 3in. from the fore side of stem.

No. 3 section is 7ft. from the fore side of stem.

No. 4 section is 10ft. from the fore side of stem.

The water lines are 4½in. apart.

Plank ⅜in. on bottom, ₁⁵₆in. top sides. Rabbet on stem and stern set 2in. back. Timbers ⅜in. by ⅝in.; spaced 5½in. apart centre to centre.

Centre of mast thwart 1ft. 6in. from stem; second thwart, 4ft. 3in.; third thwart, 7ft. 6in. Thwarts 7in. wide. Stern seat 1ft. wide, and fore edge 11ft. from stem. Side seats 6in. wide from stern to third thwart.

DUBLIN BAY SAILING CLUB.

This club, which has its head quarters at Bullock, Kingstown, Co. Dublin, was established during the year 1884, with the object of encouraging open boat sailing. At the time of its inauguration, it was intended to have only one class of boats, limited in length to 21ft. over all. Owing to the addition of a very fast and improved class of boats, it was found necessary to form a class, to which the old boats were relegated ; a further addition was made in 1888, of a third-class, to be 13ft. over all, and in this class centre-boards were optional. At a general meeting held in October, 1890, it was decided to introduce a new 18-foot centre-board boat, and the club boats are now classed as follows :—Class A.: All fixed keel open boats, not exceeding 21ft. over all ; no deck or counter allowed, unlimited sail area, and to be ballasted so that with crew and gear on board the draught will not exceed a tenth of length over all. Class B. or Mermaid class : Centre-boarders of 18ft. over all and of 6ft. beam, with sail area limited to 180 sq. ft., divided as follows : 153 sq. ft. in mainsail, and 27 sq. ft. in jib, with a mast-head spinnaker not to exceed 80 sq. ft., the centre-boat to be of metal ⅜ in. thick, with a superficial exposed area not to exceed 5 sq. ft., steel band to be ⅜ in. thick ; anchor not to exceed 22lb., the only ballast allowed to be water not exceeding 22 gallons in wooden tanks.

Since the former edition of this book was issued this club has made a most radical change in its constitution. Heretofore it existed for the encouragement of open boat sailing ; and, having very fully fulfilled that condition, it was decided, after very careful consideration by the committee of the club, to advise that the word "open" be eliminated from the rules, so as to enlarge the club's usefulness. This, however, was not so easily accomplished, as a number of the members felt that to make so decided a change would be injurious to the club. The committee, however, were determined that the club should not come to a standstill, and after the subject had been very fully considered by several general meetings, it was not until the meeting held March 21st, 1893, that the recommendation of the committee was carried.

As a result it was agreed to admit a Class of Boat, subject to limitations, the following being the most important, viz. :

(*a*) Length, 20ft. over all.

(*b*) Not to exceed one rating, Y.R.A. Rules.

(*c*) Minimum of ballast on keel, 10 cub. ft.

(*d*) Draught with crew not to exceed 3ft. 6in.

(*e*) Area of main sail not to exceed 80 per cent. of total sail area, &c.

It was, however, found that the restrictions were not of such a nature as would encourage members to build under them. It was therefore agreed, at a general meeting held on November 10th, 1893, to limit the restrictions on the A Class as follows :

A CLASS.

The A Class to comprise all boats that have raced in the old A Class, together with other boats, under the following restrictions :—

(*a*) Not to exceed one ton rating, in accordance with Yacht Racing Association Rules.

(*b*) Boats of one ton rating to carry as a minimum of ballast 5 cwt., which may be of lead. Smaller boats in same proportion.

(*c*) Boats to be decked, the area of cockpit not to exceed area of deck.

At a General Meeting, held on 9th April, 1895, it was agreed to admit half-raters, and for that purpose the following rule for the B Class was approved :—

The B Class shall consist of Boats not exceeding 0·5 rating, together with Mermaids, which shall be sailed strictly in accordance with their rating under Y.R.A. Rules, provided they are not altered so as to exceed 0·7 rating.

Thus the club consists of three classes, A and C restricted, B unrestricted, but all sailed under the rules of the Y.R.A. and in strict accordance with their rating.

The racing in Dublin Bay has been most successful, as already the A Class is represented by thirteen 1-raters (seven of which joined the fleet this year) and three of the old Class boats; the B Class has four Mermaids and ten Boats under 0·5 rating ; while the Wags now muster thirty Boats.

Races are sailed on all the Saturdays of May, June, July, and August, when, in addition to the ordinary club prizes, special ones are offered for competition, and at the close of the season prizes are given for helmsmen, crews, and most successful boats.

The roll of members is now close on 300. The club is governed by a committee of eleven, which includes Commodore, Hon. Treasurer, and Hon. Secretary.

On Plate LV., the drawing of a boat for this class, designed by Mr. R. Fry, Commodore, and built by Atkinson, boat builder, Bullock, Kingstown. The lug-sails are supplied by Lapthorn and Ratseys, Gosport, and are similar in shape to those shown on Plate LIV.

Class C.: Boats similar to those sailing in Water-wags Club. Plate LV. represents another Mermaid, designed by Mr. C. Livingston, of Liverpool.

The Hon. Sec. of the club is Mr. P. J. O'Connor-Glynn, 14, Braffni-terrace, Sandycove, Co. Dublin.

The C Class Boats, which shall be known by the distinctive name "Wags," to be centre-boarders not exceeding 0·4 rating, 13ft. over all, and 4ft. 10in. beam, to be built according to drawings marked A (deposited with the Hon. Secretary, December, 1892), and in accordance with the following limitations :

The moulds shown on the drawing shall be set up vertical and level along the keel, or inbreast, and the Boat between the fore and aft moulds shall not be rockered. No additional mould shall be used, save one, which may be placed not more than 12in. from the outside of sternpost, and which shall not touch more than the gunwale, and three upper lands of the planking.

Boats shall be built with not less than ten, or more than eleven planks on each side, and no plank shall exceed five inches in width outside measurement. The garboard and next four planks shall not be less than $\frac{3}{8}$in. thick, and the remaining planks not less than $\frac{5}{16}$in. thick. All planks shall be laid in clincher fashion, viz., the planks shall overlap, the outside lands being at least two thirds the thickness of the plank itself (except within 12in. of the bow and stern) but an arris, not exceeding $\frac{1}{8}$in. may be taken off the outside edge of the land. All nails shall be rooved.

The keel outside the garboards, inclusive of thickness of keelband, shall not exceed $1\frac{1}{4}$in. in depth, and 3in. in width, and after the 1st January, 1896, shall not be less than 1in. in depth between the moulds. Every boat shall carry a keelband, which shall be made of iron, brass, gunmetal, or copper, and every keelband which, after 1st June, 1894, shall be put upon a boat, shall not be more than $\frac{1}{4}$in., or less than $\frac{3}{16}$in. thick, and shall not be less than 1in. wide between the moulds.

o o

No balanced rudder shall be allowed. The rudder shall be made of wood, and shall not exceed 2ft. in length, and 6in. in depth below the level of keelband and sternpost.

Timbers shall not be less than $\frac{5}{8}$in. by $\frac{3}{4}$, spaced not more than $5\frac{1}{2}$in. apart, centre to centre.

Beam stringer shall not be less than $\frac{7}{8}$in. by $\frac{1}{2}$in.

Gunwales shall not be less than $1\frac{1}{8}$in. wide, and $1\frac{1}{4}$in. deep. Width to be measured from outside of shearstrake.

The position for the centre-board is optional.

The centre of the mast shall not be placed further aft than 21in. from outside of stem. Each boat shall have, in addition to the mast-thwart, two other thwarts, one near each end of the centre-board casing, and not less than $7\frac{1}{4}$in. by $\frac{3}{4}$in., permanently fixed with double knees, and not more than 8in. below the gunwale, also a thwart, or seat support of at least 2in. sectional area, permanently fixed, with the front face not less than 18in. from the after edge of sternpost.

Battens shall not be used in sails, except in the leach of the lug, and in that case they shall not exceed 2ft. in length.

The spinnaker boom must be stepped on the mast, and shall not be attached to any part of the boat forward of the mast.

The spinnaker guy shall not be *led* to anything outside the gunwale; it may, however, be held out by the crew without appliances.

The spinnaker sheet shall not be *led* to anything more than 2in. to leeward of the centre line of the boat, or abaft the mid-length of the boat; it may, however, be held in any position *by hand*.

The word "led" as here used refers to the direction in which the rope is brought direct from the boom or sail.

Each boat shall carry, when racing, all her platforms, floorings, and thwarts all fixed in their proper positions, a pair of oars not less than 8ft. long, with spurs or rowlocks for same. No ballast allowed.

No alteration or addition to any boat or to any part of her, or to her gear shall be made, except in accordance with the above limitations and whenever an alteration or addition of any kind is made, notice of same must be given to the Hon. Secretary, so that the Committee may, if necessary, re-examine the boat.

SUTTON YACHT AND BOAT CLUB.

The Sutton Yacht and Boat Club was started in September, 1894—just ten years after the start made by the Dublin Bay Sailing Club. There is not much water at the point of Kosh, where the Club-house is situated—

only about 3ft. at low water—but quite suitable for the class of boats used by the members, which are 18ft. about, open boats. Half-raters, with drop keel, C.B., and wags restricted by the same rules that govern the Wag Club at Kingstown. Most charts are not correct in giving the channel up to the Club-house; it is far more north, it having moved northerly within the last ten years. However, the Club have got down good buoys to mark its course. C.B. boats are most suitable for both Howth and Sutton, as in the harbour of Howth there are only a few boats drawing say 6ft. of water that can find a berth in which they float at all stages of the tide. It is to be hoped that something will be done soon to remedy this defect, as all of us can remember the strides made in this enjoyable pastime at Howth. Ten years ago it was such a busy port for herring fishing that yachts, to say the least of it, could not come into the harbour, it was so crowded with the fishing craft; but now the tables have turned, and there are only a few fishing boats (long line cod fishing), and the harbour is full of all kinds of pleasure craft from, say, 10 or 12 tons down to the Linton Hope, 0·5-raters, and Wags. A great advantage which Sutton has is that the channel runs up a long way inland, and affords a splendid place for rowing, on which the Club has also provided accommodation for the members by the erection of a long boat-house and convenient slipway.

CHAPTER XVII.

ITCHEN BOATS.

THE boats of the Itchen Ferry fisherman have a very high reputation in the Solent, and no doubt they are equal in model to any fishing craft on the coast. For more than a century match sailing amongst them has been an annual occurrence, and probably the contests on these occasions, combined with the true racing spirit which animates all the Itchen-Ferry-men, have tended to produce and maintain a model adapted for speed; and the nature of the work the boats are put to has happily prevented their sterling qualities as hard weather craft being in any way sacrificed to the exigencies of competitive sailing. The standard of value for competitive sailing among these boats has always been simple length, and as a consequence there has been no inducement to cut down the beam, which remains about one-third the length, more or less, according to the fancy of the designer; and although of late years gentlemen fond of racing small craft have built boats on the Itchen model, to compete under the "length rule," they did not become less broad in the beam, but deeper, and of greater displacement. The designs shown on Plates LVII., LVIII., and LIX. represent the fishing boats, and the racing craft, such as they were until 1878, when heavy lead keels and overhanging stems and counters were introduced, as shown by Plate LX. The overhang forward, shown on this plate, was not, however, introduced until 1882, when the Bonina and Keepsake were built.

The design of the Gipsy, shown on Plate LVII., represents one of the old-fashioned craft, and was made by W. Shergold, a well-known draughts-man of Southampton, to compete in the 27ft. class in 1877.

A boat was built from the design for Mr. A. F. Fynne in 1885, the builder being Trethowan, of Falmouth. She was decked over with a cockpit aft, and yawl rigged. She proved a very fast and an exceptionally good sea boat. Mr. Fynne named her Daphne; but, upon his selling her to Capt. T. V. Phillips, R.A., her name was changed to Gipsy. She is well known on the west coast.

A scale has been made to suit this drawing for a 30ft. 4in. boat.

The 25ft. (Plate LVIII.) boat was designed by W. Shergold for Mr. Fay, who successfully raced her under the name of Salus; she was subsequently re-named Israfel, and then Wild Rose. Under the latter name she was raced very successfully in the 25ft. class up to 1879.

The 21ft. (Plate LIX.) design represents that of the Centipede, the most successful fishing boat, so far as speed goes, ever turned out by the late Mr. D. Hatcher. In the drawing, the design is represented as for a boat of 22ft. 8in. length, but all the sections are exactly as they were in the 21ft. boat, the *spacing* between the sections only having been increased, so as to bring the length up to that necessary to make 5 tons with the same 8ft. beam. The water lines, with the extra spacing as shown, look very much better than they did in the 21ft. design, and no doubt a boat of the extra length would be a faster and still more capable craft.

The Centipede, we might say, had very much less weight in her iron keel than given in the table, and the siding of her wood keel was less: the siding of the keel has been increased solely with the object of getting more lead underneath it; but it by no means represents what a 21ft. racing boat of the present day has.

The Itchen fishing boats are always carvel built, and are usually decked forward, with a stern sheet aft, and are open amidships with a water way and coaming round. The floor construction is variously contrived, but the most approved plans are those shown in the designs for the 30ft. and 23ft. boat respectively (Plates LVII., LVIII., and LIX.). Sometimes a hogging piece, or keelson, of wood, iron, or lead, was worked upon top, the main keel of about half the siding of the latter, so as to form a stepping rabbet for the heels of the frames. A sectional view of this construction is shown at midship section, Plate LVII. The heels of the timbers rest on the top of the main keel, and are spiked to the keelson. The whole is secured by iron floor knees, bolted through frame and plank. Aft a stepping line to take the heels of the timbers has to be cut in the dead wood. The spaces between the plank floor and keelson are filled with concrete made with cement and boiler punchings, or cement and lead shot. This is smoothed off level with the top of keelson.

In the 21ft. design (Plate LVIII.), no keelson is worked. A stepping line is set off on the keel and dead woods, as shown by *s*. At each station for a frame, a joggle is cut in the keel and dead wood, *b b*, for the heel of the frame to be step-butted in, as at *a, a, a*. A sectional view of this fitting is shown by A. The heels of the frames are bolted through the keel, and the whole is secured by iron floor knees. This plan is to be preferred, unless the keelson is of metal, on account of it having an advantage for ballasting. Any spaces left between the sides of the keel and the plank should be filled with concrete, made as before described. The rabbet (r) will be cut as shown, and the garboard strake should be fastened with as long spikes as practicable.

All the Itchen fishing boats have what are known as " raking midship sections; " that is, the broadest width of each succeeding water line is progressively farther forward, from the load water-line downwards. This peculiarity is most apparent in the Centipede. It will be seen that her greatest beam on the L.W.L. is very far aft of the greatest breadth of the lower water line.

With regard to the great proportion of beam to length there is no evidence that the proportion will grow less, in spite of the introduction of the heavy lead keels in many fishing boats. The fishermen patronise beam, without any apprehensions, and one of the most successful boats in their class has 9ft. breadth to 21ft. length.*

Until 1876 an Itchen boat was never seen with a counter, the Rayonette being one of the first to have one in that year; now counters have become common, but, as the regular Itchen boats are square sterned, we have so represented them in the preceding designs. A counter of course gives them a more finished appearance, and helps hold the boats a little if much pressed on a broad reach. They, however, make very little back water wash off the lee quarter, as the transom is so high set. If a counter were given to the preceding designs, the buttock lines would be dropped a little at the transom, according to the length of overhang. The transom would have to be a little wider, too, as otherwise the counter would be very narrow at the arch board.

---

* There is not much doubt that a heavy lead keel (and a little less beam if thought desirable) is safer than so very much beam and very little outside weight. The fishing boats formerly had very little siding to their keels, and the weight of iron that could be got underneath was consequently very small. It is generally thought, however, among the fishermen, that a foot or so extra beam will more than compensate for the absence of a ton or so weight on the keel. There is a very great mistake about this, and the beamiest of the Itchen boats, as they are necessarily the shallowest, and have, moreover, little or no weight outside and loose ballast inside, are by far the most unsafe, as, although very stiff at first, they lose their righting power as they get near their beam ends. In 1880 one of the beamiest of the Itchen boats (19ft. by 9ft.) was capsized in a squall through the loose ballast shifting, and a beamy Itchen boat with no great weight on her keel requires as much looking after in a squall as a Una. The value of a heavy keel is now, however, so much recognised that some of the fishing boats recently built have a trifle less beam and lead keel. Lead is chosen in preference to iron because there is less trouble with the fastenings, and it does not " waste " so much.

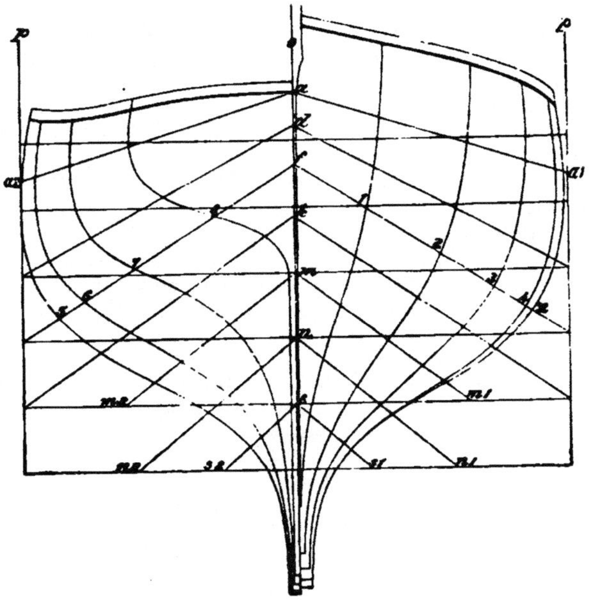

FIG. 158.

DIMENSIONS.

Length over all	27ft.	Main boom	17ft.
Length on L.W.L.	26ft. 9in.	Gaff	15ft. 8in.
Beam extreme	8ft. 6in.	Luff of mainsail	17ft. 6in.
Draught of water extreme	5ft.	Luff of mizen	14ft.
Displacement	7 tons.	Foot of mizen	8ft. 6in.
C.B. aft centre of length	·7ft.	Area of mainsail	306 sq. ft.
Iron on keel	1·5 tons.	Area of foresail	100 sq. ft.
Iron moulded inside, 3·3 tons; lead	0·7 tons.	Area of mizen	64 sq. ft.
Total ballast	5·5 tons.	Total area	470 sq. ft.
Mast deck to hounds	21ft.		

TABLE OF OFFSETS (27FT. ITCHEN BOAT GIPSY, PLATE LVII. and FIG. 158).

No. of section	1	2	3	4	⊗	5	6	7	8
	ft. in.	ft. in.	ft. in.	ft. in.	ft. in.	ft. in.	ft. in.	ft. in.	ft. in.
Heights to covering-board above L.W.L.	3 5	3 0½	2 8¾	2 6	2 5¼	2 4¾	2 4	2 4½	2 6
Depths below L.W.L. to stepping line	2 1	3 0	3 2	3 2	3 2	3 2	3 0	2 3	—
Depths below stepping line to under side of wood keel	3 7	—	—	—	—	—	—	—	3 10
Half-breadths at gunwale	1 3	2 7	3 6	4 0	4 0½	4 0	3 10	3 4	2 5
Half-breadths 2ft. above L.W.L.	1 2	2 6¼	3 5¾	4 0¼	4 1	4 0½	3 10½	3 4½	2 5¼
Half-breadths 1ft. above L.W.L.	1 0	2 4⅜	3 4¾	4 0¼	4 1½	4 1½	3 10½	3 2½	1 6¾
Half-breadths on L.W.L.	0 9	2 0	3 1¼	3 10	4 0	4 0	3 6	2 3¼	0 2
Half-breadths on No. 2 W.L.	0 4¾	1 3½	2 4	3 0¾	3 2¾	3 2¼	2 4½	0 9½	—
Half-breadths on No. 3 W.L.	0 1½	0 6½	1 1	1 5½	1 5¾	1 4½	0 9	0 3	—
Half-breadths on No. 4 W.L.	—	0 2	0 3¾	0 4½	0 4½	0 4½	0 2¾	—	—
Half-breadths, Diagonal *a*	1 3	2 7½	3 7½	4 2½	4 3½	4 3½	4 1	3 6	2 6
Half-breadths, Diagonal *d*	1 3	2 7¾	3 8½	4 4½	4 6¾	4 6½	4 1¾	3 4¾	2 2½
Half-breadths, Diagonal *f*	1 2¼	2 6	3 6½	4 1½	4 3	4 3	3 9¼	2 10½	1 4½
Half-breadths, Diagonal *k*	0 11¾	2 1¼	2 11½	3 5½	3 6½	3 6	3 0	2 0	0 5½
Half-breadths, Diagonal *m*	0 9	1 7½	2 3½	2 8	2 8¾	2 7½	2 2	1 3½	0 1½
Half-breadths, Diagonal *n*	0 4¾	1 0	1 5¾	1 8¾	1 9	1 8	1 3	0 7½	—
Half-breadths, Diagonal *s*	0 1½	0 6	0 9¾	0 11	0 11¼	0 10¾	0 7½	0 3¼	—

No. 1 section is 2ft. 8in. from the extreme fore side of stem. All the other stations are 3ft. 6in. apart, but the aft side of transom is only 3ft. 4in. from No. 7 section. The midship section is midway between No. 4 and No. 5 sections.

The water-lines are 1ft. apart.

Diagonal *a* is struck 2ft. 8½in. above the L.W.L., and at *a* 1 and *a* 2 cuts the perpendiculars *p p* 1ft. 5½in. above the L.W.L.

Diagonal *d* is struck 2ft. 2½in. above the L.W.L.

Diagonal *f* is struck 1ft. 7½in. above the L.W.L.

Diagonal *k* is struck 9in. above the L.W.L.

Diagonal *m*, at *m* 1 and *m* 2, is 2ft. 7in. from the middle vertical line *o*.

Diagonal *n*, at *n* 1 and *n* 2, is 2ft. 6in. from the middle vertical line *o*.

Diagonal *s*, at *s* 1 and *s* 2, is 1ft. 1in. from the middle vertical line *o*.

All the half-breadths are *without* the plank, but the drawing represents the boat with the plank on.

The iron keel will be 21ft. long, 8in. deep at its fore end, 1ft. 1in. at the midship section, 1ft. at No. 7 section, and 9in. at its after end; breadth, 6in. amidships, 3½in. forward, 4in. aft on its upper side; breadth on its under side, 3½in. all through.

LAYING-OFF TABLE FOR 30FT. 4IN. BOAT (SEE PLATE LVII. AND FIG. 158).

No. of Section	1		2		8		4		·		5		6		7		8	
	ft.	in.	ft.	in.	ft.	in.	ft.	in.	ft.	in.	ft.	in.	ft.	in.	ft.	in.	ft.	in.
Heights above L.W.L. to top timbers	3	10	3	5	3	1	2	10	2	9	2	9	2	8	2	8½	2	9½
Depths below L.W.L. to stepping line	2	3	3	4	3	7	3	7	3	7	3	7	3	4	2	6	—	
Depths below L.W.L. to underside of keel	4	0	—		—		—		—		—		—		—		4	3
Half-breadths at gunwale	1	5	2	11	3	11	4	5½	4	6½	4	6	4	3	3	9	2	9½
Half-breadths on L.W.L.	0	10¼	2	2½	3	5¾	4	3	4	5¾	4	5¼	—		—		—	
Half-breadths on diagonal *a*	1	4½	2	11½	4	0½	4	8	4	9¾	4	9½	4	7	3	11½	2	10¾
Half-breadths on diagonal *d*	1	4½	2	11½	4	1½	4	10¾	5	0¾	5	0½	4	8	3	9¾	2	5
Half-breadths on diagonal *f*	1	3½	2	9½	3	11	4	7	4	9	4	8¾	4	2	3	1½	1	6
Half-breadths on diagonal *k*	1	1	2	4	3	4¼	3	10¾	4	0	3	11¼	3	4½	2	3¼	6	0
Half-breadths on diagonal *m*	0	10	1	9½	2	6¾	2	11½	3	0	2	11	2	4¾	1	4¾	0	1¾
Half-breadths on diagonal *n*	0	5	1	1½	1	9	1	11¼	1	11½	1	10½	1	5	0	8½	0	1¾
Half-breadths on diagonal *s*	0	1½	0	6½	0	11¼	1	0½	1	0½	1	0	0	8	0	3	0	1¾

No. 1 section is 3ft. from the extreme fore side of stem. All the other sections are 3ft. 11in. apart, but the aft side of the transom is only 3ft. 10in. abaft No. 7 section. The midship section is midway between No. 4 and No. 5 section. The water lines are 1ft. 1½in. apart.

Diagonal *a* is struck 3ft. above the L.W.L., and at *a* 1 and *a* 2 cuts the perpendiculars *p p* 1ft. 8in. above the L.W.L.

Diagonal *d* is struck 2ft. 6in. above the L.W.L.

Diagonal *f* is struck 1ft. 10in. above the L.W.L.

Diagonal *k* is struck 11½in. above the L.W.L.

Diagonal *m*, at *m* 1 and *m* 2, is 2ft. 11in. from the middle vertical line *o*.

Diagonal *n*, at *n* 1 and *n* 2, is 2ft. 9in. from the middle vertical line *o*.

Diagonal *s*, at *s* 1 and *s* 2, is 1ft. 2in. from the middle vertical line *o*.

All the half-breadths are *without* the plank; but in the drawing the boat is represented with the plank on.

The lead keel will be 23ft. 6in. long, 9in. deep at its fore end, 1ft. 3in. amidships, and 11in. aft.

The breadth of the keel on the top at its fore end will be 4in.; amidships, 7in.; aft, 4in. uniform breadth of the under side, 3in.

LAYING-OFF TABLE FOR 25FT. BOAT (SEE PLATE LVIII.).

No. of Section	1		2		3		4		5		6		7		Trm.	
	ft.	in.	ft.	in.	ft.	in.	ft.	in.	ft.	in.	ft.	in.	ft.	in.	ft.	in.
Heights to top of timbers above L.W.L.	3	2	2	10	2	7½	2	5¼	2	4¼	2	4½	2	5½	2	7
Depths below L.W.L. to rabbet line...	1	6	2	9	3	1	3	2½	3	2	2	10	1	8	—	
Half-breadths at gunwale	1	3½	2	11	3	9	4	0¾	4	0¼	3	8½	3	0	2	5
Half-breadths on L.W.L.	0	6	1	11	3	3	4	0	3	11	2	10½	0	9¼	0	1¼
Half-breadths on diagonal *k*	1	2½	2	10½	3	11½	4	6	4	5½	3	11¾	3	1	2	6
Half-breadths on diagonal *m*...........	1	0½	2	7½	3	8	4	4½	4	3	3	6	2	4½	1	9
Half-breadths on diagonal *n*	0	8¼	1	11	2	10	3	3½	3	0	2	2¾	1	1	0	5½
Half-breadths on diagonal *z*	0	1¾	0	10	1	3½	1	6½	1	3¼	0	8	0	1¼	0	1

No. 1 section is 2ft. from the extreme fore side of stem; all the other sections are 3ft. 6in apart, but the transom is (at the deck) 2ft. from No. 7 section.

The water-lines are 1ft. apart.

Diagonal *k* is struck 2ft. 6in. above the L.W.L., and at *k* 1 and *k* 2 cuts the side perpendiculars *p p* 11½in. above the L.W.L.

Diagonal *m* is struck 1ft. 9in. above the L.W.L., and at *m* 1 and *m* 2 cuts the side perpendiculars *p p* 6½in. below the L.W.L.

Diagonal *n* is struck 7½in. above the L.W.L, and at *n* 1 and *n* 2 cuts the side perpendiculars *p p* at 2ft. below the L.W.L.

Diagonal *z* is struck 1ft. below the L.W.L., and at *z* 1 and *z* 2 is 3ft. 4in. from the middle vertical line of the body plan.

All the half-breadths are *without* the plank just as the others are, in readiness for setting off in the mould loft; but the design is shown with the plank on. The design also shows a keel of only 3in. siding amidships, instead of the thickness we have given in the table.

LAYING-OFF TABLE FOR 22FT. 8IN. BOAT (SEE PLATE LIX.).

No. of Section	1		2		3		4		5		6		7		8		9		10		Trm.	
	ft.	in.	ft.	in.	ft.	in.	ft.	in.	ft.	in.	ft.	in.	ft.	in.	ft.	in.	ft.	in.	ft.	in.	ft.	in.
Heights to top of timbers above L.W.L.	2	6¾	2	5	2	3	2	1¼	2	0½	1	11½	1	11	1	11¼	1	11¾	2	0½	2	1
Depths below L.W.L. to stepping line (*s*)...........	1	8	2	0½	2	1¼	2	2	2	3	2	3¼	2	3	2	1	1	8	0	6¾	—	½
Half-breadths at gunwale ...	1	6¾	2	6½	3	2½	3	6¾	3	8½	3	9	3	8¼	3	5¾	3	2	2	9	2	5
Half-breadths on L.W.L. ...	0	8¾	1	8	2	6¾	3	3¼	3	8	3	9	3	6¾	3	0¼	1	8¾	0	3½	0	1
Half-breadths on 2nd W.L...	0	3¼	0	9	1	4¼	1	10	2	1½	2	0	1	5¼	0	8¾	0	3	0	1	—	
Half-breadths on diagonal *i*.	1	7½	2	7½	3	4¼	3	10½	4	2	4	2½	4	1	3	10	3	5½	2	10½	2	7½
Half-breadths on diagonal *k*.	1	5½	2	5	3	2	3	9¼	4	1¼	4	2	4	0¼	3	8	3	1½	2	3¾	1	10
Half-breadths on diagonal *m*	1	2¼	2	0½	2	8¾	3	2½	3	6¼	3	6¾	3	4¼	2	11	2	2½	1	3	0	10½
Half-breadths on diagonal *n*.	0	9	1	4¾	1	11	2	3	2	4½	2	4	2	1½	1	8½	1	1	0	4	0	1
Half-breadths on diagonal *z*.	0	2½	0	6¼	0	10	1	0½	1	1¼	1	0½	0	9¾	0	6½	0	3¼	—		—	

No. 1 section is 2ft. 4in. from the extreme fore side of the stem. All the other sections are 2ft. 2in. apart, but the aft side of transom is only 10in. from No. 10 section.

The water-lines are 1ft. apart.

Diagonal *i* is struck 2ft. 5in. above the L.W.L., and at *i* 1 and *i* 2 cuts the perpendiculars *p p* 10in. above the L.W.L.

Diagonal *k* is struck 1ft. 10in. above the L.W.L.

Diagonal *m* is struck 1ft. 1½in. above the L.W.L.

Diagonal *n* is struck 3in. above the L.W.L., and at *n* 1 and *n* 2 is 2ft. 10in. from the middle vertical line *o*, and 1ft. 7in. below the L.W.L.

Diagonal *e* is struck at the 2nd water-line, and at *e* 1 and *e* 2 is 1ft. 3in. out from the middle vertical line *o*, and 1ft. 9½in. below the L.W.L.

The side perpendiculars *p p* are 3ft. 11in. out from the middle vertical line.

All the half-breadths are *without* the plank, and the boat is represented in the drawing *without* the plank.

Depth of lead keel at its fore end, 7in.; at its amidships, 8½in.; at its aft end, 5½in.

Width (siding) of lead keel at its fore end, 2¾in.; at its amidships, 5½in.; at its aft end, 4in

Length of lead keel, 14ft.

N.B.—In all cases in laying off the boats the table of offsets should be relied on rather than measurements taken from the Plates; and care should be taken to note if the plank is included in the measurements or not.

21FT. BOAT.

For the 21ft. boat the same laying-off tables will be used, the sections being identical with those of the 22ft. 8in. boat. The spacing between the sections is, however, less.

No. 1 section is 2ft. 2in. from the extreme fore side of the stem; all the other sections are 2ft. apart, but the transom is only 10in. abaft No. 10 section.

DIMENSIONS, &c.

Length, fore side of stem to aft side transom on deck	30ft. 4in.	27ft.	25ft.	22ft. 8in.	21ft.
Breadth (moulded)	9ft. 4in.	8ft. 4in.	8ft. 7in.	7ft. 10in.	7ft. 10in.
Breadth with plank on	9ft. 6in.	8ft. 6in.	8ft. 9in.	8ft.	8ft.
Draught of water, extreme	5ft. 4in.	4ft. 10in.	4ft. 1in.	3ft. 4½in.	3ft. 4½in.
Displacement	9 tons	6·5 tons	5·8 tons	3·8 tons	3·5 tons
Displacement per inch of immersion at L.W.L.	9cwt.	7cwt.	6cwt.	5½cwt.	4¾cwt.
Weight of ballast inside	3½ tons	2½ tons	2 tons	1½ tons	1¼ ton
Weight of lead keel	2 tons 8cwt.	1 ton 16cwt.	1½ tons	1 ton	18cwt.
Tonnage Y.R.A.	9 83/94	7 10/94	6 57/94	4 83/94	4 10/94

SCANTLINGS.

	30ft.	27ft.	25ft.	23ft.	21ft.
Siding of stem	3½in.	3in.	3in.	2¾in.	2¾in.
Siding of sternpost	4in.	3¾in	3½in.	3½in.	3in.
Siding of keel amidships	7in.	6in.	6in.	5½in.	5in.
Siding of keel fore end	3½in.	3in.	3in.	2¾in.	2½in.
Siding of keel aft end	4in.	3¼in.	3½in.	3½in.	3in.
Moulding (depth) of keel	7in.	6½in.	6in.	5½in.	5in.
Siding of timbers	2in.	2in.	1¾in.	1½in.	1½in.
Space centre to centre	1ft. 11in.	1ft. 9in.	1ft. 9in.	1ft. 1in.	1ft.
Thickness of plank*	1in.	1in.	1in.	¾in.*	¾in.*
Thickness of garboard strake	1¼in.	1¼in.	1¼in	1in.	1in.
Thickness of top strake	1¼in.	1¼in.	1¼in.	1in.	1in.
Thickness of clamp	1½in.	1½in.	1½in.	1½in.	1½in.
Thickness of transom	2½in.	2¼in.	2in.	2in.	2in.
Breadth of rudder	3ft.	2ft. 9in.	2ft. 6in.	2ft. 3in.	2ft.

* An inch strake as a wale should be worked above the water-line at the broadest part of the boat; this will make the boat the required width.

SPARS AND SAILS.

	30ft.		27ft.		25ft.		23ft.		21ft.	
	ft.	in.	ft.	in.	ft.	in.	ft.	in.	ft.	in.
Centre of mast from fore side of stem on deck ...	11	6	10	9	9	9	8	8	8	2
Length of mast, deck to hounds	25	0	22	6	21	6	19	6	18	9
Length of mainboom extreme	27	6	26	0	24	4	21	9	19	3
Length of main gaff extreme	20	6	18	6	17	9	16	3	14	3
Length of bumpkin outside...........................	2	6	2	4	2	0	1	9	1	3
Length of bowsprit outside	16	0	14	6	12	6	12	0	11	6
Length of topmast fid to sheave	20	6	19	6	18	0	17	0	16	0
Length of topsail yard	24	0	23	0	21	0	20	0	18	0
Length of topsail yard	18	0	17	0	16	0	15	0	14	0
Length of spinnaker boom*	27	6	25	0	23	0	21	0	19	0
Luff of mainsail..	23	0	20	0	19	3	17	9	16	6
Leech of mainsail	38	0	34	0	33	0	30	0	27	6
Foot of mainsail	27	0	25	9	24	0	21	4	18	10
Head of mainsail	20	2	19	0	17	6	15	8	14	0
Tack to peak earing...................................	40	0	36	0	34	6	31	6	28	6
Clew to weather earing (throat)	33	6	31	0	28	6	26	6	23	9
Area of mainsail	634 sq. ft.		544 sq. ft.		480 sq. ft.		410 sq. ft.		318 sq. ft.	
Area of foresail	153 sq. ft.		142 sq. ft.		120 sq. ft.		100 sq. ft.		80 sq. ft.	
Area of jib†	200 sq. ft.		175 sq. ft.		154 sq. ft.		138 sq. ft.		120 sq. ft.	
Area of topsail	204 sq. ft.		180 sq. ft.		165 sq. ft.		142 sq. ft.		120 sq. ft.	
Total area	1181 sq. ft.		1041 sq. ft.		919 sq. ft.		790 sq. ft.		630 sq. ft.	

* As they only have one spinnaker, it has to be set on the bowsprit occasionally; hence the length of the spinnaker boom is usually about the length from the mast to the bowsprit end.

† With a reef down the boats are frequently sailed without a jib, the bowsprit being run in and stowed.

Bonina and Keepsake were the first two of the length class type of yacht which was fashionable from 1882 to 1887. The Bonina was built from a design by the author by Watkins and Co., of Blackwall, for Mr. Arthur O. Bayly, in 1882. She in under water body plan much resembles the old Itchen type, with the usual rake to the midship section. She had a displacement of 13·2 tons, and a lead keel of 7·5 tons, the sail spread being 1746 sq. ft. by Y.R.A. rule.

The Keepsake was built by Messrs. A. Payne and Sons, in 1882, from a design by Mr. C. P. Clayton, and is of 13·7 tons displacement, and has 7·8 tons of lead on her keel.

It being evident that both Bonina and Keepsake were very much under-canvassed for their stability, the sail plan was increased in later boats to 2200 sq. ft., and a 21ft. boat had 1340 sq. ft.

The Minima (Plate LX.), represents what the 21ft. Itchen class came to. She was designed by Mr. Arthur Payne for Mr. St. Julien Arabin, in 1886, and proved the most successful of the class, especially to windward.

These new-fashioned Itchen boats were the natural outcome of a length on water-line measurement, there being no restriction on overhang of hull either forward or aft, and no restriction in sail area. The result was a rather expensive type of boat, with excessive overhang, and enormous sail spread. By the rating adopted in 1887 $\left(\frac{\text{Length} \times \text{sail area}}{6000}\right)$ the 30-footers, 25-footers, and 21-footers became obsolete, as a boat longer on the water-line, with less sail spread for any given rating was more than a match for any length class boat.

THE RIG OF ITCHEN BOATS.

In rig the Itchen boats have undergone very marked changes. Up to 1850 the common rig was foresail with tack fast to stem head, and sheet working on a horse; mainsail without boom, with sheet working on a horse, and occasionally a mizen was added. The mast was long, and the gaff short, and the rig was generally commended because all the sail was in board. However, it would seem that the boats were lacking in head canvas, as "bumpkins" and bowsprits were introduced in 1851, and boom mainsails in 1856.

The introduction of the boom mainsail soon caused an increase of canvas, with a long piece of the boom over the stern. Specimens of the rig in fashion in 1878, and that of the 1882-87 rig are shown on Plate LXI.

The dimensions for the sails given in the table on page 395 are intended for a racing outfit for the boats described. For a "fisherman's" outfit the mast would be reduced in length about one-ninth, and the boom and gaff about one-seventh.

All the Itchen pleasure boats formerly had the bumpkin, which is a small iron bar (see A, Plate LXI.) fitted to the stem head as shown at d; the bumpkin has an iron stay (s) welded to it, and bolted to the stem at k. The forestay is set up to the bumpkin by a lanyard, as shown at m. The boats have two shrouds a-side, a pendant and runner, topping lift, topmasts, backstays, preventers, and all the rest of the usual yacht gear, including, of course, purchases.

ITCHEN SAILING PUNTS.

Until 1877 the boats of this class sailing in the local match for punts 13ft. long were little better than ordinary rowing skiffs rigged with a foresail on a short bumpkin, and a sprit mainsail without a boom. In 1879 lead keels were added (see Plate LXII.) and the sail plan much enlarged.

They originally carried sprit mainsails, as shown in Fig. 159; but the latest fashion is shown by Fig. 161, on page 398, the sail plan of Vril.

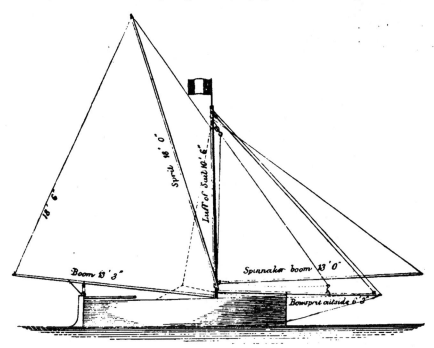

FIG. 159.

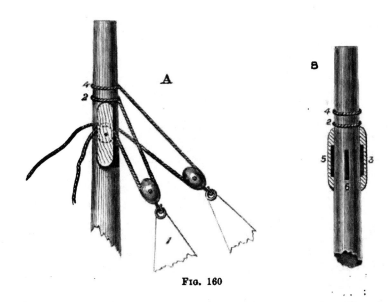

FIG. 160

The punts are mostly owned by fishermen, yacht sailors, and yacht masters; and in some the lead keels (also the pieces of false wood keel fore and abaft this lead) are put on with nuts and screws, and can easily be taken off, leaving the boat a serviceable punt (*see* Plate LXII.)

In the sprit rig the halyards are worked as shown by Fig. 160. In A, the head of the foresail is shown by 1; the standing part of the halyard is put over the mast at 2. The hauling part is rove through a cheek block; see 3 on B, which is the mast head viewed from astern.

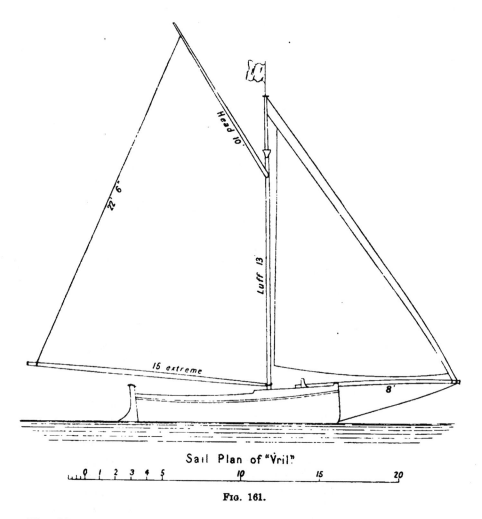

Sail Plan of "Vril."

Fig. 161.

The jib, or spinnaker halyards are similarly fitted; the standing part is at 4 in A, the hauling part is rove through 5 in B. The main halyard is fast to a mast traveller and then passes over a sheave in the mast at 6 in B.

The lead keel soon developed into a fixture with a moulded garboard like the larger boats. The last built and most successful of all was the

Vril (Plate LXIII.), designed by Mr. Arthur Payne in 1880. The design, of course, is far away ahead of the original Itchen punt, and the truth of this was very apparent, especially to windward, Vril on that point of sailing probably eclipsing anything before achieved by a 13ft. boat. She has a lead keel of 13cwt., and a sail area of 276 sq. ft., 190 of which was in the mainsail.

TABLE OF OFFSETS OF ITCHEN PUNT "VRIL."—PLATE LXIII.

No. of Section	2	4	6	8	9	10	Transom.
	ft. in.	ft. in.	ft. in.	ft. in.	ft. in.	ft. in.	ft. in.
Half-breadths at gunwale	1 8⅛	2 2⅛	2 7	2 5⅛	2 2⅛	1 10⅛	1 7½
Half-breadths at L.W.L.	0 11⅛	1 11⅛	2 5¼	2 1⅛	1 6¾	0 8	0 3⅛
Half-breadths at No. 2 W.L.	0 7¾	1 6	1 10⅛	1 3⅛	0 8	0 2	0 1¼
Half-breadths at No. 3 W.L.	0 4	0 8¾	0 1⅛	0 5⅛	0 2	0 1	0 1
Half-breadths on diagonal A	1 4¾	2 5⅛	2 11	2 8⅛	2 4¾	1 11⅛	1 8
Half-breadths on diagonal B	1 1⅛	1 10⅛	2 1¾	1 9¼	1 5¼	0 11⅛	0 7⅛

The sections are 1ft. 3in. apart. No. 1 section is 1ft. from the fore side of the stem.
The water lines are 6in. apart.
Diagonal A is struck from 1ft. 8¾in. above the L.W.L., and cuts the L.W.L. 2ft. 9in. out.
Diagonal B is struck 7¾in. above the L.W.L., and cuts No. 3 W.L. 2ft. 2⅛in. out.

CHAPTER XVIII.

FALMOUTH QUAY PUNTS.

THESE boats bear some resemblance to those of Itchen Ferry and the Clyde, and are wonderfully handy and seaworthy. Boys—some as young as ten years—constantly knock them about the harbour single-handed, whilst it is the event of every day and night for a man to go "seeking" in them alone, in all weathers, to the Lizard and even beyond, getting away as far as forty miles from harbour, and they remain at sea sometimes for a day or two. These boats have no hollow in the entrance, and vary in size from 20ft. to 30ft. over all, and from 7ft. to 10ft. beam, drawing from 3ft. to 6ft. of water; they are decked in to about two-fifths of their length from the stem; they have waterways 1ft. wide, and coamings, and all have square sterns—no counters. Freeboard, 2ft. 6in. to 3ft. The rig is uniform also (see Fig. 162), viz., gaff mainsail with boom, jib-headed mizen, and foresail set on a short iron bumpkin—simplicity itself —and, with patent blocks everywhere, and small ropes, everything is well within the strength of an ordinary man.

The forestay wire; bobstay chain or wire; one shroud a side wire; Manilla pendant and runners; mizen shrouds wire. Single blocks for foresail halyards and down-haul and peak halyards; throat halyards and main sheet, double and single blocks working on a horse; mizen sheet single block; fore sheet one block and belayed aft with half turn under a pin in the only thwart astern. The main boom is seldom fitted with reef cleats, but when reefing the sail is lashed down by a lacing through the cringle and round the boom.

The cost of one of these boats, as used by the local men, is about 30s. per foot; but if fitted up, rigged, and canvassed in yacht-like form the cost would be as much as 250l., more or less, according to the size, material, work, and finish.

The boat depicted on Plate LXIV. was built by Thomas, of Falmouth, and is one of the best boats about the port. These punts have scrap iron for ballast, and stow it all amidships to keep the ends light.

A jib and bowsprit are sometimes used in summer; then also a square-headed mizen is sometimes carried; but the working boats never have a topsail, because it would be in the way in going alongside shipping.

Fig. 162.

The forestay is set up to an iron bumpkin, which has a chain bobstay. A span-shackle is generally fitted on the bumpkin for a bowsprit.

DIMENSIONS.

Length over all	26ft. 4in.
Length on water-line	25ft. 9in.
Beam, extreme	8ft.
Draught of water	5ft. 3in.
Area of mid-section	15·3 sq. ft.
Displacement	6·8 tons
Mast, deck to hounds	20ft. 6in.
Main boom	16ft.
Main gaff	15ft.
Luff of mizen	13ft.
Foot of mizen	8ft.
Foreside of mast to foreside of stem head	8ft. 3in.

CHAPTER XIX.

THAMES DABCHICKS AND BAWLEY BOATS.

THAMES DABCHICKS.

THE " one class, one design " racing boat was introduced on the Thames in 1895. The design (Plate LXV.) of Mr. Linton Hope was adopted, and the little craft in many ways are similar to the Clyde unballasted class, by the same designer. They were built by Messrs. Forrestt and Sons, of Norway Yard, Limehouse, and are 20ft. over all, 15ft. water-line, 6ft. beam, sail area 200 sq. ft., 0·5-rating. They are ribbon carvel, built of cedar, and the total cost, including sails (of stout Union silk), running and standing rigging, oars, crutches, boathook, anchor, and cable, 50l. They competed mostly in the matches of the Royal Corinthian Yacht Club at Erith, and, like all unballasted boats, require careful handling under sail, although their non-sinking is pretty well assured.

BEMBRIDGE REDWING CLASS.

THE design for the one-design Redwings class produced a very large fleet. The class is named Redwing because the sails are of a red colour. They are made of dyed cotton yarns, and the sail-cloth can be obtained of Messrs. Ratsey and Lapthorn, Cowes. The boats are all built from the one design, and finished in the same way. They are 22ft. 1in. over all, and 16ft. on the water line, 5ft. 5in. beam, with a draught of water of 2ft. 11in., and a displacement of 1·05 tons. The ballast consists of a 10cwt. iron keel. The captain and honorary secretary of the class is Mr. Blair Cochrane, St. John's Park, Ryde, I. of W. He will be pleased to give information to anyone who desires to join the class. The design was prepared by Mr. C. E. Nicholson. (*See* Plate LXVI.)

EXTRACT FROM RULES.

Sail area is limited to 200 sq. ft., actual measurement of sails only. No spinnakers are allowed in class racing as separate sails, but jibs may be boomed out.

Each owner will be provided with a sheer plan of the boat, with the C.L.R. marked.

There shall be no limit to the number of persons on board, but no paid hands are allowed in class racing.

Each boat shall carry when racing an anchor weighing 20lb., and not less than 20 fathoms of 2in. grass rope cable, and sufficient life-saving apparatus for her crew.

SPECIFICATION FOR BOATS.

Planking, yellow pine, ½in. full when finished.

Keel, English elm, 4in. thick, about 8in. wide.

Stem, English oak, 4½in. moulded, 3in. sided.

Stern timber, English oak, 3in. moulded, 4in. sided.

Bent timbers, American elm, ⅞in. moulded, ⅞in. sided.

Clamp yellow pine, 3½in. moulded, 1½in. sided.

Beams, white pine, 2½in. moulded, 1½in. sided.

Cockpit carlines, 2½in. moulded, 2in. sided.

Coamings, English elm, 4in. above deck, fitted with outside capping.

Stern finishing, chock pitch pine. Covering boards, teak, ½in. thick. Deck, white pine, ½in. thick, painted, and covered with unbleached calico painted two coats.

Six wrought iron galvanised floors.

Twelve oak beam knees, mast partner 3ft. long, and all timbers in this length to be 1in. by 1½in., to take chainplates where required. One knee to be fitted where required for chainplates.

Rudder, English elm, blade with wrought-iron straps and stem working in iron tube. Galvanised iron tiller fitted to head of rudder stem, with nut and screw.

Cast-iron keel, 10cwt., fitted with 1in. and ¾in. through bolts, with nuts inside. Top sides and inside to be painted three coats, and bottom black varnished. All fastenings of copper.

White pine platform to be fitted where required.

Eyebolts each end of keel for hoisting out.

Boats to be delivered afloat in Portsmouth Harbour.

Length over all, 22ft. 1in.; length L.W.L., 16ft.; beam, 5ft. 5in.; draught, 2ft. 11in. Price, £45.

THAMES BAWLEY BOATS.

THE Thames bawley boats in some respects resemble the old-fashioned Itchen boats, but they are heavier, and have not quite such deep keels as the Southampton craft have—a feature which enables them to work over the flats on and about the Thames.

They are exceedingly handy little vessels, and may be seen in great numbers in the mouth of the Thames and Medway, and more especially in Sea Reach. For knocking about in all weathers in these waters, it would, perhaps, be impossible to find a better type of boat.

During the last fifteen years the bawley has grown considerably in size, and varied somewhat in build, the fishermen having to go farther afield and carry heavier nets and gear. The size of the boats ten or twelve years ago was about 22ft. by 8ft., with a draught of about 3ft.: they were clinker built, of oak, very strongly put together, and were fitted with fish wells. The more modern boats, however, are carvel built, and " dry bottomed," as it is termed, that is without wells, the altered conditions of the fishing rendering them unnecessary.

Recognising the good all-round qualities of the bawley, yachtsmen have occasionally bought them, and with slight alterations converted them into homely, but comfortable and serviceable cruisers, and the way in which they soak to windward in a strong wind and kick-up down Sea Reach is remarkable.

The lines given are those of a 32ft. bawley, built not long since by Mr. Douglas Stone, of Erith, and designed by him to give as much speed as could be obtained with the carrying capacity and light draught required

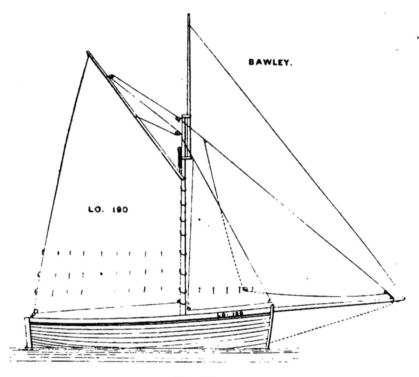

Fig. 163

by her owner. This boat has turned out very speedy, and is probably the fastest bawley of her length in the river.

It will be seen by the accompanying lines on Plate LXVII., and sketch of the sails Fig. 163, that the beam of the bawley is very great compared with the length, while the draught is very easy. Another peculiar feature is the low freeboard aft, and the high sheer forward, which enables them to make light work of the nasty short sea in the Hope when a 10-ton yacht would be head and shoulders into it. The Mayflower, it should be said, has been given a little more freeboard amidships than usual; this has been found to be a great advantage in a sea, and no disadvantage for working the nets, &c. As a matter of fact, the men generally trim them more by the stern than is shown on the accompanying sheer plan of the May-flower.

There is another class of bawley hailing from Harwich and Maldon of about the same proportion of length and beam, but with rather more draught of water.

The mainsail of the bawley is without a boom, and the sheet travels on a horse about a foot or so inboard, the lower block having an iron belaying pin through it to make the mainsheet fast. Brails are fitted, and help to make the sail a very handy one, often saving a heavy gybe, &c.

The mast is put well forward in order to get a good breadth of mainsail, and as a consequence the foresail is rather small. The bowsprit is usually of moderate length, without shrouds; and it is only off the wind that a large jib is carried. On a wind a very small jib is set, and it seems to be ample for the boat. A fleet of these boats cross-tacking in Lower Hope or Sea Reach in the grey dawn has a most weird effect, as they slip through the water so noiselessly, and look like shadows with their tanned sails.

Mr Stone estimates the cost of a boat similar to the design at about 140*l.*; and when one considers the accommodation and pleasure which can be got out of a craft of this size it is hardly to be wondered that there are so many inquiries respecting the Thames bawley.

DIMENSIONS, &c., OF A BAWLEY BOAT.

Length, fore side of stem to aft side transom on deck	32ft.
Breadth	11ft. 4in.
Draught of water, extreme	4ft.
Displacement	13·3 tons.
C.B. aft centre of length	0·6ft.
Weight of ballast	6 tons.
Centre of mast from fore side of stem on deck	11ft. 6in.
Length of mast, deck to hounds	20ft.
Foot of mainsail	19ft.
Length of gaff, extreme	20ft.
Length of bowsprit outside stem	17ft. 6in.
Length of topmast fid to sheave	18ft.
Leech of mainsail	32ft. 6in.
Tack to peak earing	32ft. 6in.
Clew to weather earing (throat)	25ft. 6in.
Area of mainsail	394 sq. ft.
Area of foresail	100 sq. ft.
Area of jib	180 sq. ft.
Total area	674 sq. ft.

TABLE OF OFFSETS OF THE "MAYFLOWER," BAWLEY BOAT (PLATE LXVII.).

No. of Section	1	2	3	4	5	6
	ft. in.	ft. in.	ft. in.	ft. in.	ft. in.	ft. in.
Heights above L.W.L. to deck	3 0	2 7	2 4	2 3	2 3½	2 5
Depths below L.W.L. to rabbet of keel	2 11	3 1	—	—	3 2	—
Depths below L.W.L. to underside of keel	3 6	—	—	—	—	4 0
Half-breadths on deck	3 0	5 0	5 8	5 5	4 5	2 11
Half-breadths on L.W.L.	2 2	4 5	5 6	5 5½	4 1½	0 1¾
Half-breadths on W.L. 2	1 6	3 9	5 2	4 10	2 10	0 1¾
Half-breadths on W.L. 3	0 11	2 4	3 4	3 0½	1 5	0 1¾
Half-breadths on Diagonal *a*	3 0	5 2½	6 1	5 9½	4 10	3 3
Half-breadths on Diagonal *b*	2 8½	4 11	6 0	5 9	4 7	2 8
Half-breadths on Diagonal *c*	2 3½	4 2½	5 2½	5 0	3 9½	1 6½
Half-breadths on Diagonal *d*	1 10	3 0	3 4	3 3	2 5	0 2

No. 1 section is 4ft. 1in. from the fore side of the stem at the L.W.L., and 4ft. 5in. from the perpendicular. The other sections are 5ft. 3in. apart; and No. 6 is 6ft. 7in. from the aft perpendicular.

The water-lines are 1ft. apart.

CHAPTER XX.

LAKE WINDERMERE YACHTS.

THE Windermere yachts were formerly distinguished for their long immersed counters. This fashion of immersing the counter, it appears, originated in 1872 out of an intended evasion of the rule of measurement, which at that time was simple length between stem and sternpost on deck. The Windermere Club, with a view of checking the advantages gained by immersion of counter, supplemented the rule by a condition that the counters abaft the sternpost should not exceed 6ft. 6in. in length.

We imagine that the advantages of getting an excess of length by immersing the counter were discovered in this way: The Windermere craft were more or less full in the bow, and consequently bored by the head, and, with a deep fore foot, carried a very great deal of weather helm. Hence they were being continually trimmed by the stern, and always with some advantage; and thus it was realised that an immersed counter is an advantage if length cannot be obtained in any other way without paying a penalty for it.

In the autumn of 1881 the Windermere Club adopted the water-line as the basis of measurement, but in 1883-4 the club made another rule limiting the length, draught of water, and spars.

The Windermere yachts, owing to their under water depth, heavy lead keels, and amount of dead wood, have been distinguished for their good weatherly qualities, and they are as safe as could be built for sailing on the deep waters of a lake, as they are really uncapsizable, just as modern yachts are; and if wholly decked in, or having a very wide waterway and high coamings, are practically unsinkable. The "Una boats" which have come into fashion on the Lake are made quite unsinkable by having water-tight bulkheads forward and aft. In the case of the sudden squalls met with on the lake the boat should be luffed into it directly the first breath of a squall is felt; but in a match the boats are always sailed through them by easing the helm a trifle, and if the squall be very black and heavy, the jib sheet is eased so as to luff quickly; but the main sheet is never in such cases started.

The sails of the yachts are made of duck, and usually by local sail-makers. The sloop rig, it has been proved by experience, is much the best for going to windward on the smooth water of the lake, and no difficulty is ever experienced in handling it.

The general rig and sail plan is shown by Plate LXVIII. The bowsprit goes over the stem and fore deck, the heel usually passing through the

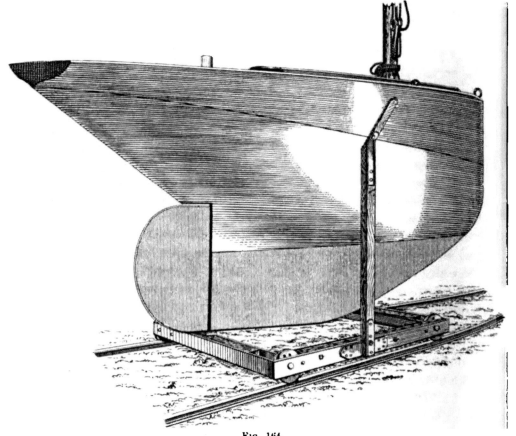

Fig. 164.

coaming round the waterways and jamming against the mast. Iron rods are used for bowsprit shrouds and bobstay, set up with screws. There are two jib halyard blocks, the upper being a double, and the jib is set taut by means of a tackle.

The hulls are painted and pumice-stoned outside, and finished as smooth as a carriage, and the portion below the water-line is then black leaded and polished with a brush, very great attention being paid to the condition of smoothness of the bottom. (*See* the article on " Black leading " in the Appendix.)

Ways are laid for hauling up, as shown in Fig. 164.

During the last few years the form of the boats have very much altered ; the deep fore foot and full bow having disappeared, and the boats built under the club rules do not now much differ from the boats built under Y.R.A. rules, with the exception that plumb stems are compulsory.

In 1897 the club adopted some new regulations for governing the size of the yachts and their spars which compete in the club matches. The following are the measurements :—

(*a*) Length of yacht on load water line shall not exceed 22ft., and the total length from fore side of stem to extreme end of counter shall not exceed 32ft., and no part of stem below water or stern post below water shall project beyond the 22ft. gauge. The overhang forward shall not exceed 4ft., the angle of this overhang shall not be less than 23° with the water line, the contour of the curve of the stem at and about the water line shall be a fair curve. The counter, or so much thereof as shall extend aft of the load water line of the yacht, shall not intersect a triangle or the produced perpendicular thereof described as follows : Base, 6ft. on load water line produced ; and perpendicular, 1ft. 4in. from water. Marks, in the form of horizontal plates, shall be placed on the yacht at the fore and aft extremities of her load water line, and the under side of such marks shall always be visible when the yacht is on her load water line. A yacht shall be considered to be on her load water line when she lies adrift from moorings, in smooth water, without crew, with all sails set, and racing gear on board. (*See* under the counter, Plate LXIX., for the gauge for the counter).

(*b*) No yacht, when on her load water line, shall have less than 2ft. 6in. freeboard at the stem, and the deck of the yacht shall be carried aft from that point in a fair or reasonable line or sheer.

(*c*) Beam (extreme outside measurement) shall not be less than 6ft. 6in., without beading or moulding.

(*d*) The draught of water shall not exceed 5ft. 6in. when the yacht is on her load water line.

(*e*) The length of the mast from deck to truck, or end of pole, shall not exceed 26ft. 8in. ; the bowsprit, from fore side of mast to extreme end, shall not exceed 15ft. in length ; the boom from aft side of mast to the end shall not exceed 22ft. in length ; and the gaff (measured parallel to the boom) shall (*see* Plates LXVIII. and LXIX.) not exceed 16ft. 6in. in length ; if an outhaul is used, the boom shall be measured from aft side of the mast to the aft side of sheave hole, and the foot of the mainsail shall not extend outboard of the sheave hole ; the topsail yard shall not exceed 18ft. in length.

(*f*) The hoist of mainsail, from thimble to thimble, shall not exceed 16ft.

(*g*) From deck to pin of jib halyard sheave or pin of block, when hanging parallel to mast, shall not exceed 23ft. 9in., and block (if used) shall be attached to a point as low as possible on mast to permit of hanging as aforesaid.

(*h*) The mast, from deck to pin of topsail sheave, shall not exceed 25ft. 9in.

(*i*) No yacht shall have less than 32cwt. of ballast, and no ballast shall be carried inside of yacht.

(*j*) All yachts are to be constructed with natural frames, spaced not more than 2ft. 3in. apart, with steamed timbers between, with single pine, larch, oak, pitchpine, American elm, English elm, baywood, or teak planking and decks. Iron floors are allowed, but no iron or steel frames.

(*k*) In case of bulb keels the keel above the bulb, either of lead or wood, shall not be less than 6in. in thickness anywhere in the thickest part, and the bulb shall not project fore and aft beyond the wood keel, and in neither the wood or lead keel shall there be a return curve. The rudder to be affixed to the stern post in the usual manner.

The foregoing rules to remain in force until 1902.

Fore and aft sails, namely, mainsail, jib, and topsail only, and no square sails, or other sails set as square sails, are to be used, and no footsticks or jack yards shall be allowed to the gaff topsails, and no booming out of the sails shall be permitted.

No yachts which are fitted to shift keels or otherwise alter their forms, and no yachts constructed with steel keels or plates fitted with lead in bulk, cigar, or other shapes attached to such plates are allowed.

It is advisable, before building any yacht that may materially deviate in form of construction to existing yachts, to ascertain the views of the sailing committee as to whether such yacht complies with the rules of the club, as no yachts are allowed which, in the opinion of the committee, may have been built, altered, or rigged to evade any of the club rules, or which they may consider not to be a properly constructed sailing vessel.

It will be apparent from the foregoing that very strict rules as to the form, construction, and dimensions of the Windermere yachts are insisted upon, and consequently comparatively little scope is left for the yacht designer to exercise his ingenuity. The rules, however, have since 1880 been found to work admirably, and the sailing committee of the club will not countenance any departure from the letter, or from the spirit of the established rules, and no yachts are allowed to race which, in the opinion of the committee, may have been built, altered, or rigged to evade the club rules, or which they may consider not to be a properly constructed sailing vessel.

In the winter of 1889-90 a new boat was built for Mr. T. D. Lingard by John Shaw, who also designed her. She is known as Rosita, and has been fairly successful as a racer on the lake. (*See* Plate LXVIII.)

The lines of another successful Windermere yacht, the Midge, are shown on Plate LXIX. She was designed by Mr. C. Livingston, of Liverpool, and built for Mr. A. D. Hannay, 1890, by Messrs. Holmes and Son.

A number of yachts have been built since the Rosita and the Midge of designs as various as the strictness of the rules permitted, but it is doubtful whether any very decided improvement has been made, though some of the newer yachts have had very considerable success, notably the Ruby, designed by the owner, Mr. A. R. Sladen, and built by G. Brockbank, of Bowness; and the Snipe, owned by Mr. Edmund Potter, designed by Mr. G. L. Watson, and built by G. Brockbank. The lines of the last named yacht will be found on Plate LXX.

TABLE OF DIMENSIONS AND ELEMENTS.

	Rosita.	Midge.	Una.
Length on L.W.L., including rudder post	19ft. 10in.	20ft. 0in.	16ft. 1in.
Beam, extreme	7ft. 0in.	7ft. 0in.	5ft. 9in.
Draught of water	4ft. 10in.	5ft. 0in.	2ft. 10in.
Area or mid-section	9·5 sq. ft.	9·8 sq. ft.	5·3 sq. ft.
Displacement	3 tons.	3 tons.	1·4 tons.
Centre of buoyancy aft centre of length	0·6ft.	0·46ft.	0·9ft.
C.E. ahead of C.L.R.	0·2ft.	0·3ft.	—
Lead on keel	1·92 ton.	1·95 ton.	0·7 ton.
Lead inside	0·05 ton.	—	—
Area of mainsail	342 sq. ft.	—	197 sq. ft.
Area of headsail Y.E.A.	225 sq. ft.	—	—
Area of topsail	130 sq. ft.	—	—
Total sail area	697 sq. ft.	695 sq. ft.	197 sq. ft.

The scantling of Rosita is as follows : Oak frames 2in. moulded by 1½in. sided ; American elm timbers 1in. by ⅞in ; beams 2½in. by 1½in.; thickness of planks ⅝in. ; stem is 14in. moulded by 3½in. sided ; stern post 9in. by 3in.; elm keel 6in. by 7in. ; planking of yellow pine.

In 1887 Mr. Thomas Dewhurst Lingard, owner of the Janira, and later of the Rosita, started a Una rig class of 16ft. on the water line, lead keels, &c., but no centre-board. (*See* Plate LXXI.) She was designed and built by John Shaw for Mr. Walter Whitehead.

One of the latest and most successful boats is shown on Plate LXXII. She was designed by Messrs. Shepherd, of Bowness, but the design was modified by Mr. C. P. Clayton. She was built for Mr. Walter Whitehead.

These boats are decked in forward and aft with a practically water-tight bulkhead 7ft. from the stem, and another aft 6ft. from the taffrail. They have waterways and coamings round the cockpit. The lead keels render them practically uncapsizable, and the water-tight bulkheads unsinkable. There are water-tight doors cut in the bulkheads, so as to render the spaces useful for stowage, &c.

The boats are very handy, and are comparatively safe, as they need be for deep water like Windermere. They carry no spinnakers, and the large mainsail of 197 sq. ft. drives them along very fast off the wind, and carries them to windward well.

DIMENSIONS OF SPARS AND SAILS.

Mast deck to halyard bolt	14ft.	Head of mainsail	9ft. 3in.
Boom	17ft. 6in.	Luff of mainsail	11ft. 8in·
Gaff	9ft. 6in.	Leach of mainsail	21ft.
Foreside of mast from stem	2ft. 3in	Clew to throat	20ft.
Foot of mainsail	17ft. 3in.	Tack to peak earing	20ft.

There is a forestay, and on each side of the mast a shroud, the eye of shrouds going over the mast, and resting on the main halyard bolt. The shrouds are set up on the gunwale 1ft. abaft the mast.

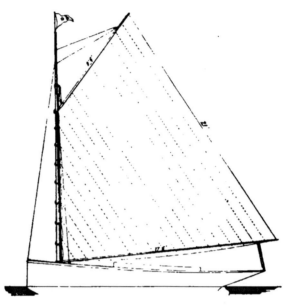

Fig. 165.

The peak halyard is fast to the mast 3ft. above the halyard bolt, and then leads to a block about 1ft. 6in. from gaff end, back through a cheek block on the pole midway between the standing part and the main halyard bolt.

CHAPTER XXI.

SMALL YACHTS AND BOATS OF ·Y.R.A. RATING.

THERE is not the smallest doubt that the action of the Y.R.A. in adopting the "length and sail area" rule for the rating of yachts in 1887 had a more wide-spread effect in promoting competition among small yachts and boats than it had on competitions between large yachts. Since 1876 the art or science of yacht and boat designing, and sailing has aroused unusual interest, and the knowledge of the subject has undergone a very extraordinary development. All the mysteries that surrounded "lines," and "centres," and the shibboleth of technical terms, have been swept away, and the average boat sailer of the present day knows a great deal more about the principles which underlie the science of naval architecture than the average builder did in the sixties.

In consequence of the practical study of yacht and boat designing being made subjects of so much interest the production of boats or yachts of small size for racing was much increased; still, this production was seriously hindered by the old tonnage rule, used for the rating of yachts which admitted of an endless drawing out of length of hull and increase of sail spread for any given tonnage. The "length and sail area rule" stopped this by introducing the condition, that if for any given rating a boat's length is increased her sail spread will have to be reduced.

This condition has given extraordinary impetus to the development of boat building and boat sailing, and, besides all round the coast, every available watercourse or lake has now its boat-sailing club. The boats vary in form and length, as might be expected, the most notable features being that for sailing in salt water—the length of hull is greater and the sail spread smaller than they are for river or lake sailing. The 2·5-raters, 1-raters, and 0·5-raters are the most popular sizes, and their varying length of hull and sail spread for coast or river work are given in the following table:

	COAST.			RIVER.		
	L. W. L. Length.	Sail Spread.	$\frac{L}{\sqrt{L}}$	L. W. L. Length.	Sail Spread.	$\frac{L}{\sqrt{L}}$
2·5 Rating	26ft.	576 sq. ft.	1·084	21ft.	714 sq. ft.	0·788
1·0 Rating	20ft.	300 sq. ft.	1·155	17ft.	353 sq. ft.	0·904
0·5 Rating	16ft.	187 sq. ft.	1·170	14ft.	214 sq. ft.	0·957
0·25 Rating	14ft.	107 sq. ft.	1·354	11·5	130 sq. ft.	1·009

The development under the length and sail area rating was in the direction of small displacement, and, to make up for the deficiency of weight, great beam was resorted to and the fin bulb keel. These features were objected to by many on account of the want of depth of hold or standing and living room on board, although the objection can scarcely apply to boats of 20ft. length which are built solely for racing. The Dacia (Plate LXXIII.), 5-rater, represents what the rule had produced in 1892, when she was designed by Mr. C. E. Nicholson and built by Messrs. Camper and Nicholson for Mr. H. R. Langrishe (afterwards sold to the Earl of Dudley). The Dacia was a very successful craft, and during the seasons 1892-3 she held her own against all comers, but in 1894 she was defeated by the broader and shallower boats, such as Flatfish (Plate LXXIV., designed by Mr. J. M. Soper for Mrs. G. A. Schenley).

This development went through all the classes, and Lady Nan, designed by Mr. A. E. Payne (Plate LXXV.) represents what the 2·5-raters were like in 1888 (the second year of the rule), Papoose (Plate LXXIV.), also designed by Mr. A. E. Payne, in 1892, and Virginia (Plate LXXV.) in 1895.

Papoose, was a most successful racing craft in the hands of Mr. Paul Ralli, who sailed her himself in all her matches whilst he owned her (1892-3). He also sailed her from the Solent to Plymouth in very coarse weather, and spoke most highly of her good qualities in a seaway. The lines of Papoose also represent those of two other successful 2·5-raters, Cockatoo and Yvery, these two, with slight variations, having been built from the same drawings.

Maharanee, 1-rating (Plate LXXIX.), was designed by Mr. A. E. Payne, and sailed a most successful career. Another 1-rater, Icipici, was built from her lines, and beat all comers at the Pola Regattas.

A centre-plate type of 1-rater is well represented by Gaiety Girl

(Plate LXXX.), designed by Mr. C. P. Clayton in 1894, whilst more extreme types of centre-board 1-raters will be found farther back in the chapter on small centre-board yachts, page 321.

The 0·5-raters are represented by Coquette (Plate LXXXI.), designed in 1891 by Mr. C. E. Nicholson, and by the later style Baby (Plate LXXXII.), designed in 1894 by Mr. A. E. Payne.

It is generally expected that the rating rule which came into operation in 1896 will modify these types by decreasing breadth and draught of water, and, at the same time, induce more depth of under water body and larger sail spreads.

A sail plan for a 2·5-rater is given on Plate LXXXIII., and in shape would be the same for a 1-rater or 0·5-rater.

CHAPTER XXII
SINGLE-HANDED CRUISERS.

SINGLE-HANDED CRUISING.

A GOOD deal has been written about single-handed cruising, and the best books on the subject are no doubt those written by Mr. MacMullen (" Down Channel " and accounts of the various cruises in " Orion," not excepting his famous sail round Great Britain and Ireland in the Jubilee Race, 1887); also the books written by Mr. John Macgregor (especially his " Voyage Alone in the Yawl Rob Roy "). These books can be obtained of George Wilson, Yacht Agent, Sherwood-street, Piccadilly-circus, Regent-street, London.

In selecting a boat or yacht for single-handed cruising, it must be realised that there is no special vessel adapted for this kind of thing which can claim to be better than another; the fact is, anything will serve as a single-hander up to say 7 tons, and Mr. MacMullen made a successful but laborious essay at single-handed sailing in the Orion, 19 tons.

It must be remembered that it is not so much the size of the boat as the size of the sails which is of importance in single-handed sailing; and large sails must, as a matter of course, never be indulged in. The gear, too, should be as simple as possible; the ropes must not be too small, and the blocks should be large. This will save labour, and cause everything to run freely whether in hoisting or lowering. The sizes of the ropes, &c., of vessels like that shown on Plate LXXXV. should not be smaller than those for a 5 rater given in the Table, page 40. A great deal has already been said about the handiness of the various rigs in the earlier portions of this work, and nothing more need be said about it here, beyond referring to the sail plan (Plate LXXXV.) of the boat designed for Mr. Percy Aylmer by the author. Of course it is incumbent that all the sheets should lead aft and belay, and for jib traveller nothing could possibly be better than Burgoine's patent, shown on page 310.

The design made for Mr. Aylmer has a raised deck 9in. high, and would be fitted below something like Spankadillo (Plate XIII., page 78).

For sailing in inland waters and on some coasts a smaller draught of water than 4ft. is necessary, and Cigarette (Plate LXXXVI.) is a type for this purpose, but it should be said she always sailed with a paid hand on board besides her owner. She was built for sailing on the Norfolk Broads, where in many places a draught of water of more than 3ft. is not practicable. The design was made for the late Sir George Prescott, Bart., and was built in 1886 by Stephen Field, of Thorpe, Norwich. In 1888 another boat, named Düne, was built by Stow and Son, of Shoreham, from the lines of Cigarette, and she is fitted with a centre-plate. It is pivoted 11ft. from stem, is 8ft. long, and drops 2ft. below keel at after end. Both proved fast and powerful boats.

	AYLMER.	CIGARETTE.	VIVID.
Length over all	27ft. 3in.	31ft. 6in.	29ft.
Length on deck stem to sternpost	23ft. 4in.	26ft. 4in.	—
Length on load water-line	22ft.	25ft. 6in.	20ft. 2in.
Beam extreme	6ft. 6in.	7ft. 8in.	6ft. 4½in.
Extreme draught of water	3ft. 10in.	2ft. 10in.	3ft. 11in.
Displacement	4·5 tons.	4·5 tons.	4·15 tons.
C.B. abaft centre of L.W.L.	0·68ft.	0·85ft.	—
Area midship section	12·5 sq. ft.	—	11·2 sq. ft.
Area vertical longitudinal section	73 sq. ft.	—	—
C.L.R. abaft centre of length	1ft.	—	—
C.E. sail ahead ditto	1·5ft.	1·3ft.	—
Weight of lead keel	1·8 tons.	2 tons.	2·3 tons
Mast deck to hounds	19ft. 9in.	21ft.	18ft.
Pole	8ft. 3in.	8ft. 9in.	9ft. 6in.
Main boom	16ft. 9in.	24ft.	19ft. 6in.
Main gaff	13ft. 6in.	16ft. 6in.	13ft. 6in.
Bowsprit outboard	9ft. 6in.	11ft. 3in.	10ft. 6in.
Bumpkin	2ft.	—	—
Topsail yard	16ft.	—	19ft. 9in.
Spinnaker boom	14ft.	—	—
Foreside mast to fore end L.W.L.	7ft. 9in.	9ft. 6in.	8ft.
Mizen mast deck to hounds	11ft.	—	—
Mizen boom	7ft. 9in.	—	—
Mizen yard	7ft.	—	—
Area mainsail	264 sq. ft.	430 sq. ft.	309 sq. ft.
Area foresail	72 sq. ft.	—	77 sq. ft.
Area jib	60 sq. ft.	220 sq. ft.	100 sq. ft.
Area mizen	54 sq. ft.	—	—
Total area lower sail	450 sq. ft.	650 sq. ft.	486 sq. ft.

THE VIVID, SINGLE-HANDER (PLATE LXXXVII.)

The Vivid is a cruising pole-masted cutter, designed by Mr. G. L. Watson for Mr. Butler, of Dalton-in-Furness, in 1886. She is 20ft. on the water line, and of a type suited to all weathers and waters, taking the ground, if necessary, in tidal waters. She is a handy craft, and will work to windward under head sail alone. She is unique as regards internal room, there being no timbers, but only floors to the height of the seats, and the head room being 4ft. between top of floor and under side of deck, on a draught of water of 4ft., with a lot of storage room under the floor between the angle-iron floors. She has one bulkhead, with two doors

E E

between cabin and cockpit, with one movable hatch over cabin, quite water-tight, and adjoining cockpit, so that when it is off there is ample room to move in, and it can be set on the cabin seats, forming a floor continuous and level with the cockpit floor. There are lockers under the seats, with two small sideboards at the after end of the cabin, and a pantry on each side of the mast. Earth closet forward, sail stowage in front of that and the counter is divided longitudinally into two lockers. Careful provision has been made for the stowage of " grounding legs," compass, lamps, candlesticks, glasses, &c., that they may not tumble about in a sea way. The floor is 1ft. 11in. wide; the skylight hatch is 5in. high, 3ft. wide, and 6ft. long, shaped to the vessel (oval); the 5in. coaming running right round the cockpit. She has a beautiful clipper stem, 3ft. over the water line and 6ft. counter, giving great deck room and lifting power in a sea. The bulwarks are 6in. high forward, tapering gradually aft. Her keel is 24in. by 5in., tapering to form of vessel; outside skin, $\frac{7}{16}$in. teak; inside, $\frac{3}{8}$in. cedar. She was cut away at the ends very considerably, to keep the skin resistance at a minimum, as she has a small sail area. The mast is 18ft. from deck to hounds; boom, 19ft. 6in.; gaff, 13ft. 6in.; bowsprit, over water line, 10ft. 6in. She has 2 tons 4¾ cwt. of lead ballast on her keel, which puts her down to 3ft. 11in., or 2in. below the designed water line. She has 1ft. 10in. freeboard, which has proven ample. This extra freeboard gives both power and head room, which amply balances any loss thereby going to windward. Her beam is 6ft. 4½in., and is only about 2in. less inside. The head sheets are belayed on cleats on a movable rail across the cabin doors, but there would have been no harm if it was a fixture. As the boat is so quick in stays, the usual places on the side of the cockpit coaming are often found unhandy. The head sheets are worked through eye-bolts well in on the deck, about a foot from the bulwarks, just as in a 5 beam boat. The rigging is all set up with screws. She was well built by the Barrow Shipbuilding Co., all the wood being cut and fitted like cabinet work, and the iron work all dressed up with a file after galvanising. All her fastenings are copper and yellow metal; rudder-fastenings, rigging, screws, and keel fastenings, being gun metal. She is lined with $\frac{3}{16}$in. cedar battens, open work; sideboards, doors, coamings, and hatches, teak; all the rest cedar. Her floors are of galvanised angle iron, and double knees of the same, alternating with hard wood fillings, tapering off to nothing at the top of seats. The keel side bolts go through the double knees in the thickening at the neck; the middle bolts through buttons edged on the angle iron flanges. The main sheet has a double fall, and there is a jib purchase. She has a working and balloon topsail, and a small spinnaker. The gunwale construction is shown on Plate LXXXVIII. The general arrangement and sail plan, Plate LXXXIX.

TABLE OF OFFSETS—VIVID (PLATE LXXXVII.)

Sections	B	0	1	2	3	4	5	6	7	8	9	10	11	Taffrail.
	ft. in.	ft. in.	ft. in.	ft. in.	ft. in.	ft. in.	ft. in.	ft. in.	ft. in.	ft. in.	ft. in.	ft. in.	ft. in.	ft. in.
Heights above L.W.L. to rail	3 1¾	2 11¼	2 9	2 7½	2 5½	2 4	2 2¾	2 1½	2 0¾	2 0¼	2 0½	2 1¼	2 2½	2 4½
Half-breadths on deck	0 7	1 5	2 0	2 6	2 10	3 0	3 1¼	3 1¾	3 1	2 11½	2 9	2 5¼	2 1½	1 8¾
Half-breadths on B horizontal	—	0 2½	1 0¾	1 9½	2 4¾	2 9¾	3 0¼	3 1	3 0	2 10	2 6½	1 11½	—	—
Half-breadths on L.W.L.	—	—	0 7½	1 4	2 0	2 6¼	2 10	2 11	2 9½	2 5	1 7	—	—	—
Half-breadths on No. 2 W.L.	—	—	0 5¾	1 2	1 10	2 4¼	2 8¼	2 9	2 7	2 1	1 0	—	—	—
Half-breadths on No. 3 W.L.	—	—	0 4	0 11¾	1 7½	2 2	2 6	2 6½	2 4	1 7½	0 6½	—	—	—
Half-breadths on No. 4 W.L.	—	—	0 2¾	0 9½	1 4¾	1 11	2 2½	2 3	1 11	1 2	0 3¾	—	—	—
Half-breadths on No. 5 W.L.	—	—	0 1¼	0 7	1 2	1 7½	1 10½	1 10¼	1 6	0 9½	0 2	—	—	—
Half-breadths on No. 6 W.L.	—	—	—	0 5	0 11	1 4	1 6½	1 6	1 1½	0 6¾	0 1	—	—	—
Half-breadths on No. 7 W.L.	—	—	—	0 3	0 8	1 0½	1 2¾	1 1¾	0 10	0 4½	—	—	—	—
Half-breadths on No. 8 W.L.	—	—	—	0 1½	0 5¾	0 9½	0 11¼	0 10¼	0 6½	0 3	—	—	—	—
Half-breadths on No. 9 W.L.	—	—	—	—	0 4	0 7	0 8½	0 8	0 5½	0 2	—	—	—	—
Half-breadths on No. 10 W.L.	—	—	—	—	—	0 5¼	0 6¾	0 6	0 4	0 1½	—	—	—	—

No. 1 section is 2ft. from the fore end of the L.W.L.

The other sections are 2ft. apart. B horizontal line is 1ft. above L.W.L.

The water lines are 4in. apart.

The half-breadths do not include the thickness of the plank.

THE SINGLE HANDED CRUISER GODIVA.

The single handed Godiva, Plate XC., was built for Mr. J. M.
Hamilton, jun., Stepney, Hull, in 1890, by J. W. Hodgson, of Hull. She
proved a very handy and comfortable little ship, and has also been fairly
successful in racing against boats of her class. She has cruised on the
Zuider Zee, Friesland Meres, &c., but principally in the neighbourhood
of the Humber, and has been used for wildfowl shooting during the
winter.

To provide for occasionally being shipped by steamer, a portion only of
the ballast is on the keel in the form of a half-ton iron shoe, the remainder,
about one ton, lead and iron, is inside, and therefore easily removed
when required. The mast is fitted to lower after the style of the Norfolk
Broad yachts, but is not provided with counterpoise weights, as it is
seldom necessary to lower it in home waters. The decks are laid double;
first, wide ½in. planks, covered with calico and plenty of paint, over which
the narrow planks, also ½in. thick, are secured and lightly caulked. By
adopting the above method, a perfectly watertight deck is produced,
capable of standing any amount of sun and weather—an important matter
in a small cruiser. There is room for two to sleep in the cabin, or one in
the forecastle, which is curtained off at the mast. During the winter a
small coal stove is used below, placed to starboard of the mast, the flue
pipe leading out through the fore hatch. As tanned sails are then used, it
does not matter about smoke.

The canvas used for the mainsail is rather heavier than is generally
made up for sails of Godiva's size; but with it she stands up to a breeze
better than with the first mainsail made for her of lighter canvas, and it has
the advantage of not bagging or stretching out of shape. The cloths are
14in. wide, seams overlap 1in., at foot 3in., and at head 2½in.; round on
foot 15in. There are three jibs; the working one is a size different to
the one shown in the sail plan, Plate XC.

MATERIALS USED IN CONSTRUCTION.

Keel. oak, 6½in. Stem and sternposts, rudder, coamings, housetop, &c., oak. Frames, oak,
1½in. by 1½in., and 3¼in. at throat, 20in. centre to centre, with two American elm ribs between
each. Planking, ½in., bottom redwood, top-sides oak, varnished. Covering board, oak. Deck,
1in. thick, redwood, double. Rail, American elm. Counter, bulkhead, and door, cabin doors,
&c., oak and mahogany. Keel, stem and sternpost bolts, galvanised iron, screwed and set up
with nuts inside. All iron work galvanised, copper fastened.

DIMENSIONS.

Length over all	23ft.
Ditto on L.W.L.	19ft.
Beam	6ft. 5in.
Draught, with all gear and two men on board	3ft. 3in.
Mast, goose-neck to cranse iron	17ft.
Ditto, pole	5ft.
Boom	16ft. 6in.
Gaff	14ft.
Bowsprit outboard	10ft.

MAINSAIL.

Head...	13ft. 8in.
Luff	13ft.
Foot (new, unstretched)	15ft.
Ditto (stretched)	15ft. 6in.
Leech	25ft.

FORESAIL.

Luff	17ft. 2ft.
Foot	9ft. 9in.
Leech...	15ft.

4in. blocks for main and peak halyards and main sheet. Halyards and sheets of 1¼in. Manilla rope.

THE SCOURGE—CRUISER-RACER OF 1-RATING
(PLATE XCI.)

Of the many amateur designers, Capt. H. E. Bayly, of Exmouth, has perhaps won most distinction, and has practised the craft now nearly forty years. He began with the 15-tonner Ethel in 1856, which had a lead keel of 1¾ tons—a really wonderful thing in those days—and since then has turned out fifty-two designs. In these he has, of course, suited all the moods of fashion that could be traced from the beamy craft of 1856; the plank on edge of 1886, and the broad, shallow, pram bowed bulb keeler of 1894. Noted among the racers which he designed and built was the famous 15-tonner Buccaneer of 1865; the successful Buccaneer (19 tons) of 1879; the extreme 3-tonner Spankadillo of 1882, and then, after 1887, such well-known names in the rating classes of 2·5 and under as Scaramouch, Jack o' Lantern, Picaroon, Thelma, and Soprano, besides many cruisers, from the 50-ton Frog to the 20-ton Murre. His latest contribution to specimens of marine architecture is the 1-rater Scourge, which has been designed for single handed cruising and handicap racing. The rig is main and mizen sail of the fashionable leg of mutton lug type; the yard points in a line with the mast, and its heel is "jawed" to the mast; the boom is goose-necked to the mast. The leach of the mainsail has a round of about 1ft., which is steadied by battens. The mizen is a simple 'Mudian. The lead keel is "bulbed," and weighs about 14cwt.; through the bulb a good-sized centre-plate is fitted, and there will be a small centre-plate under the fore-foot about 1·5 sq. ft. The boat was built by Mr. Hodge, of Dartmouth, and is quite a stylish looking craft.

DIMENSIONS—SCOURGE.

Length over all	25ft.
Length on L.W.L.	20ft.
Breadth	7ft.
Draught of water	2ft. 6in.
Displacement	1·9-ton.
Centre of buoyancy aft centre of length of L.W.L.	0·55-ton.
Central lateral resistance ditto	1·4ft.
Centre lateral resistance, including centre plate	1·1ft.
Centre of effort of sails abaft C.L.R., plate down	0·15ft.
Centre of effort of sails (mizen excluded) ahead ditto	1·6ft.
Weight of lead keel	13½cwt.

SPARS AND SAILS, CRUISING.

Mainmast, deck to pin of halyard sheave	17ft. 3in.
Mainmast boom	20ft. 6in.
Mainmast yard hole to hole	17ft. 6in.
Luff of mainsail	8ft.
Leach of mainsail	31ft. 6in.
Clew to throat earing	21ft. 4in.
Mizen mast, deck to pin of halyard sheave	11ft. 6in.
Mizen boom	6ft. 9in.
Area of mainsail	260 sq. ft.
Area of mizen	36 sq. ft.
Total sail area	296 sq. ft.

THE SINGLE-HANDED CRUISER "ÆRE PERENNIUS."

In the spring of 1895 the London Sailing Club had a competition for single-handed cruisers, which the club thus defined: "By the term single-handed cruiser is meant a craft not exceeding 30ft. overall, capable of being navigated single-handed in open waters, such as the lower reaches of the Thames, and providing cabin accommodation for her crew." The first prize was taken by Mr. J. C. Enberg, of Norrökping, Sweden. The design is an exceedingly good one, and the arrangement under deck excellent. All the falls of halyards, sheets, &c., lead to the cockpit aft, and the anchor chain is brought under deck to a ratchet winch in the cockpit, so that under ordinary conditions the latter craft could be got under way from the cockpit. This vessel is sloop rigged. See Plates XCII. and XCIII.

The ballast would be from 40 to 50 per cent. of the displacement (4·4 tons), according to the sizes of scantling used in the construction of the boat. She has an alternative yawl rig, as shown on Plate XCII.

TABLE OF OFFSETS.—ÆRE PERENNIUS PLATE (XCII).

Sections.	1	2	3	4	5	6	7	8	9	10	11	12	13	14	15	16	17	18	19	20	21
	ft. in.	ft. in.	ft. in.	ft. in.	ft. in.	ft. in.	ft. in.	ft. in.	ft. in.	ft. in.	ft. in.	ft. in.	ft. in.	ft. in.	ft. in.	ft. in.	ft. in.	ft. in.	ft. in.	ft. in.	ft. in.
Above L.W.L. Deck	0 6¾	1 0⅞	1 5½	1 10¼	2 2¼	2 6¼	2 9	2 11⅛	3 1	3 2⅞	3 3¼	3 3⅞	3 3	3 2¼	3 0¾	2 11	2 8⅜	2 5⅞	2 2½	1 10⅜	1 6½
„ No. 2	0 2⅜	0 8¼	1 2⅞	1 7¾	2 0⅜	2 5⅛	2 8⅛	2 11⅞	3 1⅛	3 2¾	3 3½	3 3¾	3 3¼	3 2⅛	3 1	2 11	2 8	2 4½	1 11¼	1 2½	—
„ No. 3	0 0¾	0 6	0 11⅜	1 5¼	1 10⅛	2 3⅛	2 7	2 10	3 0⅛	3 2	3 3	3 3⅛	3 2⅜	3 1⅜	2 11⅜	2 8¾	2 4¼	1 9¾	0 10¾	—	—
L.W.L.	—	0 3⅛	0 8⅜	1 1⅜	1 7	1 11¾	2 4¼	2 7⅜	2 10¼	3 0	3 1	3 1	3 0¼	2 10⅜	2 7¼	2 2	1 6⅞	0 8	—	—	—
W.L. No. 3	—	—	0 5	0 9⅜	1 2½	1 7⅛	1 11½	2 3	2 5⅞	2 7½	2 8½	2 8⅛	2 6⅜	2 3⅛	1 9⅜	1 2½	0 6¾	—	—	—	—
„ No. 5	—	—	0 1⅞	0 5¾	0 9¾	1 1⅛	1 5¼	1 8½	1 10⅜	2 0¼	2 0⅞	1 11⅜	1 8⅛	1 4¼	0 11	0 6¼	0 2¼	—	—	—	—
„ No. 7	—	—	—	0 2⅜	0 5⅜	0 8¼	0 11	1 1¼	1 2¾	1 3½	1 2⅜	1 1½	0 11⅜	0 8¼	0 5¼	0 3	—	—	—	—	—
„ No. 9	—	—	—	—	0 2	0 4¼	0 6⅛	0 7⅛	0 8½	0 8¾	0 8⅞	0 7⅜	0 6	0 4⅜	0 2¾	0 1⅜	—	—	—	—	—
„ No. 11	—	—	—	—	—	—	0 3	0 4¼	0 4¾	0 5	0 5	0 4½	0 3⅜	0 2⅜	1 0¾	—	—	—	—	—	—
Sheer at deck	2 10	2 8½	2 7¼	2 6	2 4⅜	2 3½	2 2½	2 1½	2 0¾	2 0	1 11⅞	1 10¾	1 10¼	1 10	1 9⅞	1 10	1 10⅛	1 10¼	1 10⅞	1 11¾	2 1
Profile above L.W.L.	0 6⅞	—	—	—	—	—	—	—	—	—	—	—	—	—	—	—	—	—	0 2½	0 9¾	1 5
„ below L.W.L.	—	0 8¾	1 7¾	2 3⅜	2 10½	3 3½	3 7¼	3 10¼	4 0¾	4 2	4 2¾	4 3	4 3	4 2½	4 2	4 0	2 1	0 4½	—		—

The Sections are spaced 16in., and the Waterlines 8in. apart.

THE SINGLE-HANDED CRUISER DOROTHY.

The design of the single-hander Dorothy (Plate XCIV.) was also in the London Sailing Club competition, and had the highest certificate of merit awarded. She was designed and built by Mr. Linton Hope, Greenhithe, Kent, in 1894, for Mr. E. Gould, and is wonderfully well thought out. She proved a staunch, fast, and good sea boat, and has done quite a record amount of cruising about the estuary of the Thames in all kinds of weather. Full particulars of the design and internal arrangements will be found on Plate XCIV.

THE SINGLE-HANDER RHEOLA.

The Rheola (Plate XCV.) was designed and built by J. Edward Vaughan, Esq., in 1889, and she was by him planned with a full knowledge of what is required in this style of craft. Mr. Vaughan's description of this well-arranged little craft will be found on Plate XCV.

MISSIONARY CRUISER FOR NEW GUINEA.

Plate XCVI. is that of a small cruising yawl designed for Missionary work at New Guinea, where she was built in 1898.

THE FAST CRUISER MARJORIE.

The Marjorie is a cruiser of a larger type. She was built by Messrs. Sibbick, of Cowes, for Mr. Averay Jones, from a design by Mr. Harley Mead. See Plate XCVII.

CHAPTER XXIII.

TYPES OF SAILING VESSELS.

PENZANCE LUGGER.

PENZANCE LUGGERS enjoy a very considerable reputation for seaworthiness, and vary in length from 40ft. to 52ft. length of keel, and have a beam of usually about 0·3 of the length on deck. The displacement of the fore-body and the displacement of the after-body are nearly equal, the comparative fulness of the buttock lines is compensated for by the fineness of the horizontal or water lines, as shown in the Half Breadth Plan. It is said that the Penzance luggers are wonderfully dry in a head sea, but particularly lively. They have long easy lines; no weight in the ends; no heavy bowsprit, or boom, or rigging; and not a large weight of ballast to carry. The mast, it is true, is stepped rather far forward, but the absence of a bowsprit compensates for this. A smaller class of lugger, built on the same lines, but about 30ft. on the keel, for the pilchard fishing, are open in the middle, and only decked fore and aft. One of these boats went to Australia in 1848 with five hands for the "diggings." She called off the Cape and took the mails to Melbourne, actually beating the regular packet, although she had to make a raft or floating anchor of her spars to ride to during a heavy gale.

The design we give (Plate XCIX.) is that of the Colleen Bawn, built at Penzance, by Mr. J. R. Wills, and she was considered one of the fastest luggers built in the west.

The rig it will be seen, upon reference to Fig. 168 (page 428), consists of two lug sails, usually made of cotton and tanned with oak bark and catechu. The fore lug has to be dipped in tacking, but the mizen is a working one and requires no dipping, the tack being made fast at the mast. There is no rigging to either mast, beyond a burton to the fore-mast and a stay to the mizen. The burton is brought to windward of the mast, and so is the tye-tackle.

The sails are seldom reefed, and they are made with only one reef band. When it is necessary to shorten sail, the mizen is shifted forward and a smaller mizen set; and this shifting goes on until the small "watch" mizen (used when riding to the nets with foremast unshipped) is reached. The boats are usually provided with the large fore lug, and three mizens besides the watch mizen. They cannot very well be hove to, and have to be kept "trying" by the wind or scudding before it; however, it must be a heavy gale that causes them to "up-helm," and then no craft of similar size afloat can excel them in running for the land.

The sail is hoisted by a chain halyard called a tye and a tackle or purchase, consisting of two double blocks, the fall leading from the lower block. The sheave hole at the masthead for the tye has only a "dead sheave," that is, a half sheave fitted in the hole. The mast traveller is two half hoops jointed together by eyes, and they are said never to jam (see "Traveller" in the Appendix). The tack of the fore lug is hooked to the short bumpkin outside the stem head, but when the other mizen-lugs are shifted forward the tack is hooked to the stem head. The fore sheet tackle is hooked to an outrigger outside on the wales just abreast of the mizen mast.

The mizen stay tackle is hooked to a ring bolt in the centre of the deck. The mizen chain sheet is fast to the underside of the traveller on the bumpkin; then (see Fig. 166) rove up through a sheave hole at

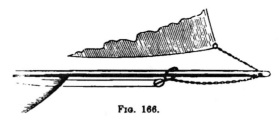

Fɪɢ. 166.

the end of the bumpkin and hooked to the mizen clew. A block is hooked to the traveller, through which the outhaul is rove, one end being made fast on board. There are no stays to the bumpkin.

In tacking, the fore sheet is unhooked from the sail as the helm is put down; as the boat comes head to wind, the halyards are eased up and the after-leach of the sail hauled down upon until the after-end of the yard or peak can be shifted round by the fore-side of the mast; the tack is never started. The sail is gathered in by the foot and leech, and passed round the fore-side of the mast. By not letting go the tack the fore-part of the sail acts as a jib, and assists in paying the boat's head off. If the boat does not pay off readily, the foreyard is kept into the mast so that only the fore-part of the sail can fill, and the mizen sheet is let fly.

The boats are usually manned by six men and a boy, who are employed as follows: Two at the capstan getting in the net; one forward to cast off the stops of the shoot rope; two at the net-room hatchway to shake out the fish, and stow the net; one at the helm, and the boy to coil away the shoot rope.

It will be noticed upon reference to the Body Plan and Sheer Plan that the top of the keel, and *not* the load water-line, is the base line from which all heights are measured. All the sections shown in the Sheer Plan are therefore perpendicular to the base line or keel, and not to the load water-line. The curved lines shown in the Body Plan are water-lines; they are set off in this way: in the Sheer Plan (Plate XCVIII.) at No. 3 section, measure the distance from *h* to *i*; set off this distance on the middle line (*o*) of the Body Plan as at *j*, measured from the base line; then draw the ticked line *t* at right angles to *o*, and where this line cuts No. 3 section at *v* will be the spot for the water-line on that section. The points in the other sections will be similarly found, and, when complete, a line drawn through the spots will represent the water-line, and will be more or less curved.

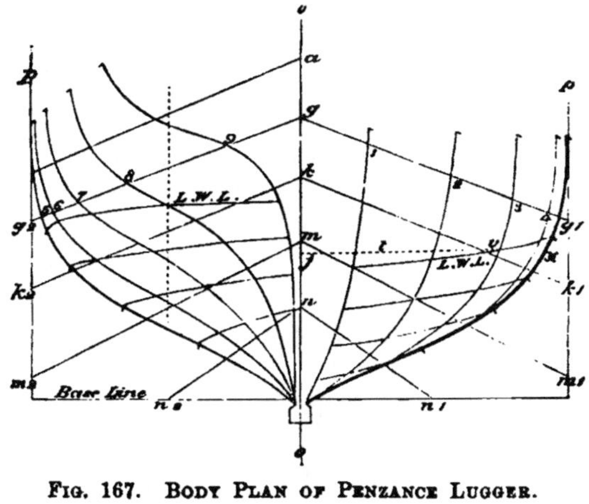

FIG. 167. BODY PLAN OF PENZANCE LUGGER.

No. of Section	1		2		3		4		ж		5		6		7		8		9	
SHEER PLAN.	ft.	in.	ft.	in.	ft.	in.	ft.	in.	ft.	in.	ft.	in.	ft.	in.	ft.	in.	ft.	in.	ft.	in.
Heights from top of keel to covering board	7	0	6	11	6	10	6	10	6	0	6	11	7	1	7	5	7	10	8	6
Depths from L.W.L. to top of keel	3	5		—		—		—		—		—		—		—		—	5	4
BODY PLAN.																				
Half-breadths at deck	1	9½	4	2½	6	0	7	0	7	3	7	3½	7	3	6	11	6	4½	5	6
Half-breadths, *a* diagonal		—		—		—		—		—	7	10½	7	9	7	4½	6	4	4	4
Half-breadths, *g* diagonal	1	9½	4	3½	6	2½	7	3½	7	6½	7	7¼	7	4	6	6¼	4	11½	2	2
Half-breadths, *k* diagonal	1	7¼	4	1	5	9¼	6	7½	6	9½	6	9¼	6	1	4	10	3	2	0	9
Half-breadths, *m* diagonal	1	5	3	5½	4	7½	5	1	5	0½	4	9¾	4	0¼	2	11½	1	8¾	0	4½
Half-breadths, *n* diagonal	1	0	2	3	2	9	2	10	2	8¼	2	6	2	0	1	4¾	0	9½	0	3

All the half-breadths are without the plank, which is 1¼in. thick.

No. 1 section is 3ft. 8in. from the fore perpendicular P. The other sections are 5ft. 8in. apart, and No. 9 section is 2ft. from the aft perpendicular P 2.

All the half-breadths given are without the plank.

The water-lines shown in the Half-breadth Plan are 1ft. apart in the Body Plan.

Diagonal *a* is struck 9ft. above the base line, and cuts the perpendicular *p* 6ft. above the base line.

Diagonal *g* is struck 7ft. 4in. above the base line, and cuts *p p* at *g* 1 and *g* 2 at 4ft. 9in. above the base line.

Diagonal *k* is struck 5ft. 11in. above the base line, and cuts *p p* at *k* 1 and *k* 2 at 2ft. 11in. above the base line.

Diagonal *m* is struck 4ft. 2in. above the base line, and cuts *p p* at *m* 1 and *m* 2 at 6in. above the base line.

Diagonal *n* is struck 2ft. 5in. above the base line, and at *n* 1 and *n* 2 is 3ft. 8in. out from the middle vertical line *o*.

The midship section is midway between No. 4 and No. 5 sections.

The fore bulkhead A, forming the warp room (see Sheer Plan), is 13ft. 9in. abaft the fore perpendicular. The bulkhead B is 6ft. from A, C 6ft. from B, D 7ft. from C ; E is the companion entrance to the cabin.

Siding of keel, stem and sternpost, 6¼in.; moulding (depth) of keel, 9in.; siding of frames, 4in. room and space, 1ft. 5in. In the drawing only every fourth frame or section is shown.

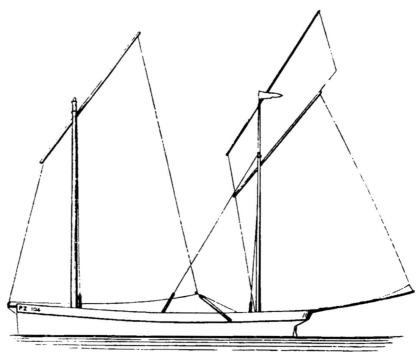

PENZANCE LUGGER.

FIG. 168.

	ft.	in.		ft.	in.
Length on deck, stem to sternpost	51	0	C. B. abaft centre L.W.L.	0	4
Length on keel	48	0	Displacement	36 tons	
Rake of sternpost	1	4	Displacement per inch at load line	1 ton 2cwt.	
Breadth, extreme, with plank on	14	10	Tonnage, B.M.	41 tons	
Draught of water	6	0	Ballast	14 tons	
Mid-section ahead of centre to L.W.L.	1	8			

	ft.	in.		ft.	in.
Fore mast, deck to sheave............	37	6	Foot of fore lugsail	34	0
Mizen mast, deck to sheave	29	0	Head of fore lugsail	28	0
Mizen pole to halyard sheave	8	6	Clew to weather earing of fore lugsail	36	0
Mizen bumpkin, outside	20	0	Luff of mizen lugsail..................	20	0
Fore tack bumpkin, outside	1	3	Leech of mizen lugsail	41	0
Foremast, diameter at deck	0	11	Foot of mizen lugsail.................	29	0
Foremast, diameter at sheave	0	6½	Head of mizen lugsail	24	0
Mizenmast, diameter at deck	0	10½	Clew to weather earing of mizen lug-		
Mizenmast, diameter at sheave ...	0	6½	sail	36	0
Luff of fore lugsail	26	0	Area, fore lugsail	980	sq. ft.
Leech of fore lugsail	46	0	Area, mizen lugsail....................	730	sq. ft.

THE YARMOUTH YAWL.

These craft, once famous on the East Coast, are not so numerous as they were a few years since; and the large class of 60ft. over all, which carried three lugs, have gone out of use, steam tugs doing most of the work. Lowestoft and Caister, however, still maintain their companies in good numbers, and have several fast yawls, the beachmen also working the life boats. The general run of the boats now in use is from 45ft. to 50ft., varying in beam and depth. The beam of this boat is 10ft., and depth 5ft. at stem and stern post to rabbet of keel. What was termed the main lug has quite gone out of use, and now two large sails are found more effective on most points of sailing. The two sails are also much handier to work with the smaller class of boats. The yawls used for racing are handsome models, with fine lines. The midship section varies, some having an easy rise, whilst others are rather flat, to suit the shore they are launched from and the purpose they are used for. The smaller class now in use also row well, having twelve or fourteen oars to assist the sails in light winds, &c. For launching skidds or rollers are used, and the boat is started clear of the beach by a long spar called a set; in bad weather a haul-off warp is used. The lines on Plate XCIX. are those of a 50ft. boat, by Hastings, of Yarmouth, which has won several prizes at regattas. The fore lug has a very long yard, which has to be shifted every time the boat goes about. The mizenmast has three burtons or shrouds, one on each side of mast, the other shifted on either side as required. The fore burtons are always to windward, and the halyards also help to keep the mast up. The boats, being very lightly built, wring very much in a sea way. A storm foremast and storm foresail is used in bad weather. The storm foresail hooks inside the stem, and the reefed mizen is tacked to the mast. The ballast consists of iron pigs and sand bags, and runs from 1½ to 2¼ tons, to suit the weather.

Plate C. represents a design for a Yarmouth yawl made by

Mr. G. L. Watson in 1894. She was tried against the local craft and proved a fast boat.

The crew are from eight to sixteen men. The gear comprises an anchor and warp, and spare gear is always on board. A large yawl can be launched in about ten minutes. They, as might be expected, are very fast off the wind, but their small draught of water does not admit of good weatherly qualities.

THE COBLE.

No boat is more distinctive in type than the coble of the north-east coast. Their high, sharp bow and long, flat floor adapt them for rough water and for beaching stern foremost through surf. Their speed and performance in a sea, as compared with the speed and performance of a yacht of similar length, are, however, no doubt somewhat exaggerated.

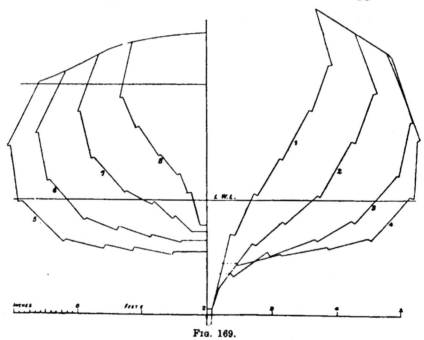

Fig. 169.

The boats are measured for length from the heel of the sternpost to the scarph of the stem or fore foot, and this length is called the "ram," which is about two-thirds of the over all length. The length of the "ram" varies from 15ft. to 40ft., and tapers at the fore end and aft end to suit the siding of fore keel and sternpost; the extreme breadth is about one-fourth the length over all.

In the drawings, Figs. 169 and 170, the sections are put in at right angles to the ram, and not to the L.W.L. The actual shape of the

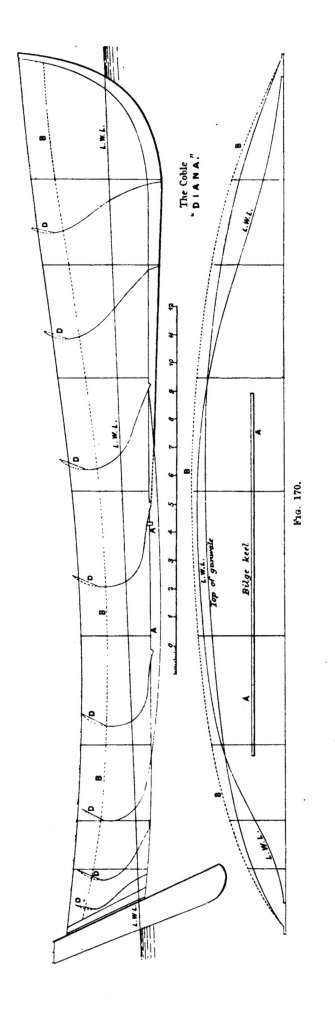

The Coble "DIANA."

Fig. 170.

sections when built is better shown by the body plan (Fig. 169). In the sections on the sheer plan D D D A show the actual shape of the gunwale strake above the line B B. The place for the side keels A A, or bilge keels, is shown in the half-breadth plan. The ends of the plank are not rabbetted into the stem, but finished flush. A false stem is then put on over the inner stem and ends of plank.

In coble building no moulds* are used beyond a piece of wood about a foot long, forming a very acute angle to see if the planks are set right. The boats are built by the eye, and long experience is necessary to turn out a fast boat. Larch is used almost universally, and the boats are clinker built, with sawn timbers. The gunwale or inwire is worked outside the top strake, instead of inside, as in most boats, and the pins for belaying the halyards project from the underside of it. The bight of the halyard or stay is put round this pin and set light, and the fall is jammed between the gunwale and the standing part of the rope, so that one pull will release it. There are no cleats or belaying pins in the boat, and no place to make the mainsheet fast, which is not a bad plan as regards safety in any open boat.

The boats are either round or square sterned. The former is coming more into use for pilots and for fishermen, especially when they have not to beach the boats. The square-sterned boats are faster on a wind; and the Whitburn Club allows 18in. in length to a round-sterned boat in racing; the round sterned boats are the safest. A flat floored boat is considered best in strong winds; a round bottom in light winds; a rising floor gives easy lines and speed; a flat floor gives stability. The pilots, who frequently tow at sea long distances astern of screw steamers, prefer the round sterned boat. The coble is towed stern first, with rudder unshipped. A pilot coble will draw 2ft. and 2ft. 6in. forward, and practically nothing aft. Cobles in a breeze, if with the wind abeam, are rowed stern first, because the high bow acts as a sail, and if rowed bow first they would make little headway.

Sailing to windward in a breeze, a square-sterned coble will carry more sail than she can run with. A round-sterned boat will run and go to windward under the same quantity of sail. Owing to the tumble home in the top sides, the water is thrown off at the shoulder and midships. The gunwale often seems actually below the water level without shipping any water.

The boats carry two masts (*see* Fig. 171), a long mast for fine weather, and a short mast, which sets the double-reefed lug, and is used as a bowsprit where a jib is set in fine weather. The mizen is little use on a wind, except to balance the jib, and it is the first sail stowed if wind

* The noted " Regina," a ribbon-carvel coble, was built from moulds, and is faster than any clincher boat of her size.

increases. Standing lugs and split lugs have been tried, but, according to the local authorities, always without success, for speed. A centre-board also was tried and condemned, the belief being that the lateral resistance the boats have is sufficient without it.

There are two steps at least for the mast, and the mast has considerable play fore and aft when the clamp is on, and by means of a wedge before and one behind the mast, the mast is raked to the exact pitch required—as much as 10ft. in a heavy sea.

The boat is not luffed up in squalls, but is sailed by the sheet; and, as there is no boom, the wind is easily spilled out of the sail. Working

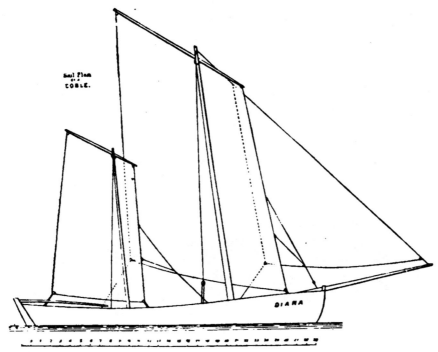

Fig. 171.

the main sheet so as to avoid shipping lee water, and to keep the boat going her best, requires nerve and skill. When sailing against a very heavy sea in a breeze the sheet is eased, as the men believe the boat will go so fast through the sea that she may split a plank as the lee bow falls upon the sea. The pressure of the water makes the tiller vibrate very much, and if sailing fast the whole boat and mast quivers and hums. The sail is generally lowered to tack, sometimes it is dipped, as in the Penzance boats. At some places it is not dipped in moderate weather, and the tack is hauled from lee to weather side, and the yard and sail are to windward of the mast.

F F

The good points of these boats are, they are easily beached, light to row; and they will work under canvas to windward as long as they can show sail. The bad points are, the dipping lug is a dangerous sail, and the square-sterned coble is apt to broach to in running before a very heavy sea, on the long rudder may break or be unshipped by a sea. A fisherman's boat of 30ft. by 7ft. would cost, say 25*l.*, and a pleasure or racing boat about 40*l.*

The Yorkshire cobles are generally round-sterned, and have very hollow bows at the load line, and a great deal of shoulder above. The Durham and Northumbrian boats are fuller at the load line. Builders of these boats are Mr. Cambridge, of Filey; Mr. Hopwood, of Flamborough; and Mr. Trotter, of South Shields. The Filey boats are noted for good qualities under canvas.

At Whitburn there is a squadron of "private" cobles, of which Sir Hedworth Williamson, Bart., is commodore. The Lalage (Fig. 172), one of the most noted of this fleet, and winner of four silver cups, is square sterned; she is now named Próserpine. Her dimensions are as under:

	ft.	in.		ft.	in.
Length over all	31	8	Mizen mast	20	6
Beam	21	8	Head of main lug	15	6
Breadth extreme	7	0	Foot of main lug	16	6
Side	2	5	Luff of main lug	21	6
Mast	30	5	Leach of main lug	23	0

FIG. 172.

The lug mizen is, mast for mast, of proportionate dimensions. The jib is about 10ft. on the foot. The foot of the lug sails shews some round mainly towards the clew. Standing lugs would probably be found much handier for ordinary work, as the constant dipping in beating to windward would be avoided.

The coble Regina (Figs. 173 and 174) was built in 1887, by James Aitkin, Sunderland, for Mr. Salmon, of Cleadon Park, but is now owned by the Rev. R. C. Nelson and Mr. L. C. Ridley. She is what is technically called "ribbon carvel," built from the design of Mr. William Gardner, of New York. She was considered to be the finest piece of boat workmanship ever turned out on the Wear. She was designed with special regard to

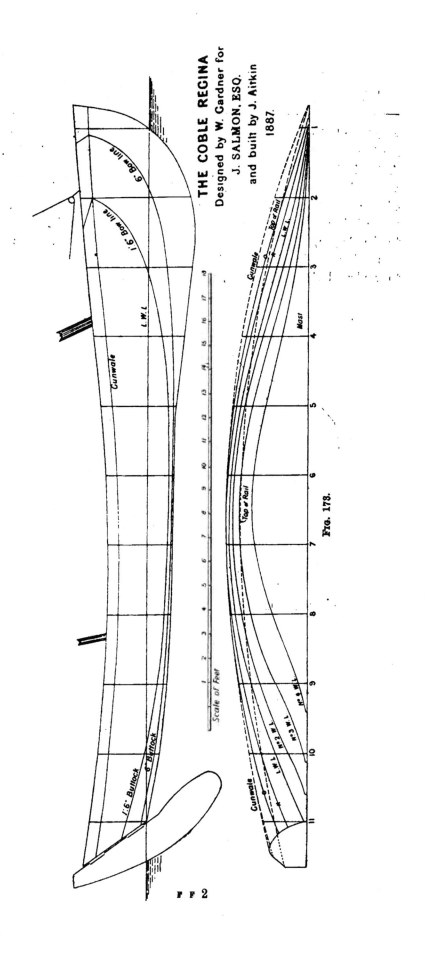

THE COBLE REGINA
Designed by W. Gardner for
J. SALMON, ESQ.
and built by J. Aitkin
1887.

FIG. 178.

Scale of Feet

F F 2

speed, and she was much admired during construction. She has several marked features, and is a departure from the ordinary type of coble. The first reliable opportunity of trying her against a boat of acknowledged speed occurred on the 2nd of June, 1887; this was the Proserpine, the winner of four cup races. The wind was of fair strength from the N.N.E., the water being comparatively smooth. The result was entirely favourable to the Regina, although she carried a smaller area of sail. This verdict was subsequently amply confirmed in club matches. She went clean to windward of the whole fleet, and outsailed them as well.

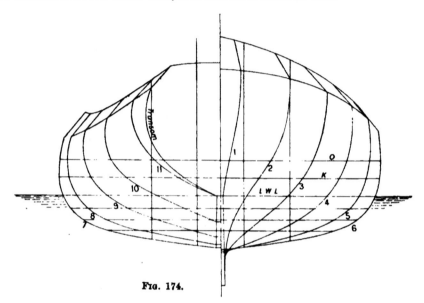

Fig. 174.

REGINA.

Length over all	31ft. 9in.
Length on water-line	29ft.
Breadth, extreme	7ft.
Displacement	2·6 tons.
Mast	27ft.
Mizen mast	18ft.
Bowsprit outboard	15ft.
Head of main lug	17ft.
Foot of main lug	19ft. 9in.
Luff of main lug	23ft. 6in.
Leech of main lug	26ft.
Clew to weather earing	23ft. 6in.
Tack to peak earing	36ft. 6in.
Head of mizen	11ft. 9in.
Foot of mizen	12ft. 3in.
Luff of mizen	15ft.
Leech of mizen	16ft. 3in.
Clew to weather earing	15ft. 9in.
Tack to peak earing	23ft.
Area of main lug	414
Area of mizen lug	180
Area of jib	130
Total	724

TABLE OF OFFSETS OF THE COBLE REGINA.

Nos. of sections	1	2	3	4	5	6	7	8	9	10	11
	ft. in.	ft. in.	ft. in.	ft. in.	ft. in.	ft. in.	ft. in.	ft. in.	ft. in.	ft. in.	ft. in.
Heights above L.W.L. to gunwale	2 7½	2 5	2 2	1 10¼	1 6½	1 4	1 2½	1 2¾	1 4½	1 7½	1 11½
Depths below L.W.L. to underside of ram or keel	0 0	1 9⅝	1 10½	1 6½	1 2½	1 1½	1 1	1 0	0 10¼	0 6½	0 0
Half-breadths at gunwale	0 5¼	1 6	2 3¼	2 10¼	3 3	3 5¾	3 6	3 3¾	2 11½	2 5½	1 10½
Half-breadths on *o*, 9in. above L.W.L.	0 2	1 1¼	2 0	2 8¼	3 2¼	3 5¼	3 6	3 3¾	2 11½	2 3¾	1 5
Half-breadths on *k*, 4½in. above L.W.L.	0 0¾	0 10¼	1 9	2 6⅝	3 1¾	3 5½	3 6	3 3¼	2 9½	2 0	0 11
Half-breadths on L.W.L.	0 0⅝	0 7½	1 5¼	2 3⅝	2 11¾	3 4½	3 4⅝	3 1½	2 5¼	1 4⅝	—
Half-breadths on No. 2 W.L.	—	0 5¼	1 1¾	2 0	2 9⅝	3 2½	3 2⅞	2 10½	2 0½	0 9½	—
Half-breadths on No. 3 W.L.	—	0 8⅝	0 10¼	1 7¾	2 5¼	2 11½	2 11¾	2 5¾	1 4¾	0 2	—
Half-breadths on No. 4 W.L.	—	0 2½	0 6½	1 1¾	1 10¼	2 4⅝	2 4¼	1 7	0 5½	—	—
Depths to 1ft. 6in. buttock	—	—	0 1*	0 7	0 10½	0 11	0 10¾	0 9½	0 5⅝	0 0½*	0 7½*
Depth to 6in. buttock	—	0 2	0 9½	1 0⅝	1 1	1 0⅝	1 0½	0 11	0 8⅝	0 4	0 9⅝

* Above L.W.L.

The sections are 2ft. 10⅝in. apart. The lines above the L.W.L. are 4in. apart. The water lines below the L.W.L. are 3in. apart. The buttock lines are respectively 1ft. 6in. and 6in. out from the middle line.

HUMBER "GOLDDUSTERS."

A "Goldduster" is 18ft. in length by 6ft. 6in. beam. It is a class of boat used by the Humber watermen for boarding ships coming into the

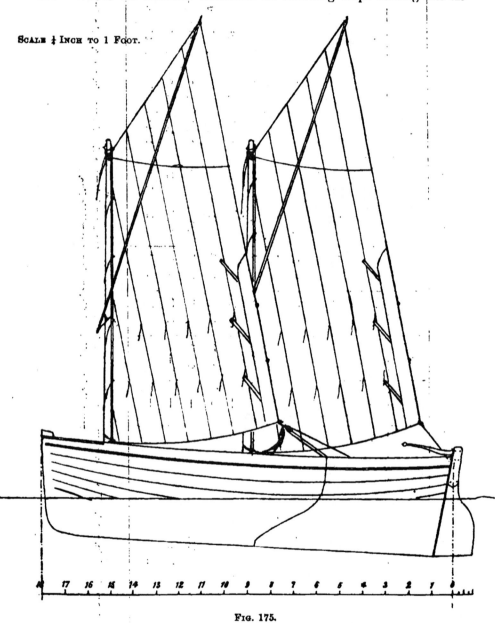

SCALE ¼ INCH TO 1 FOOT.

FIG. 175.

river, and taking the ropes ashore when going into dock, &c. They are ordinary clincher built of ½in. oak or larch for planks, with steamed

American elm ribs about six inches apart. In form they are much like the Clyde lugsail boat (*see* page 364). The ballast is usually of iron, carried inside. The masts are about 2ft. shorter than the boat, so as to stow well inside when down. Both foresail and mainsail are fitted with a brail at mastheads, so as to take in sail at once when hanging on to a steamer or vessel under way. They are very handy boats to manage, and will stay under the foresail alone. The main sheet is a short single rope, belayed to a pin, which is fixed through the transom knee on either side. The fore sheet is double, as shown in plan, so that it can be worked from aft.

There is also a larger class of the same type of boat used at Grimsby, about 22ft. by 7ft., only instead of sprit sails, two standing lugs are used.

THE GALWAY HOOKER AND POOKHAUN.

The Galway hookers (Plate CI.), average from 11 to 16 tons, and are noted on the west coast of Ireland for their weatherly qualities. They are short, broad boats, with very hollow bows; they are exceedingly lively in a seaway, but seldom ship a sea; perfectly safe in every way except running when deep, when they have sometimes been pooped, owing to their lean hollow runs.

Speaking of these hookers, Commander Horner, R.N., says "they are very bluff above and hollow beneath, and I often tried to persuade them to alter, and at last, after seven years, found one man, Gill, of Arran, who promised to do so, and who a year after sent me word that his new boat, launched just in time for a regatta, couldn't be looked at—beating everything."

The sails were made of a coarse stuff called "band linen," saturated with a mixture of tar and butter, which never thoroughly dried.

The main sheet is belayed by a single nipping hitch round the timber-head on the quarter, taut down, keeping the mainsail very flat.

They carry a strong weather helm, and are quick in stays.

The Galway pookhaun (Fig. 176) is a smaller boat than the hooker, and used for both rowing and sailing; but it is built with the same ideas, of great tumble-home of topside to keep the gunwale out of the water when heeling over, and very raking sternpost, for quickness in stays. The sail of the pookhaun is single, cut as a triangle, with a yard on part of fore side, to set as a lug; and when working to windward the fore end of the yard is dipped abaft the mast, and she is brought round very cleverly—often, when blowing fresh, the man at the tack taking a flying swing round the mast with it. They

sail exceedingly well, and are very graceful and picturesque boats
under sail.

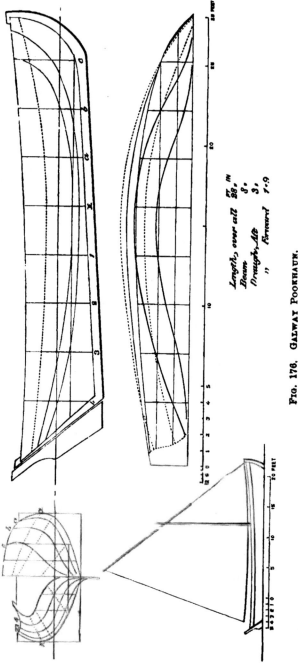

Length, over all   28, ⁿ
Beam   8,
Draught, Aft   3,
  ,,   Forward   1·9

FIG. 176. GALWAY POOKHAUN.

The mainsail in the hooker is laced to the mast, the lacing going
through the cringle and back again, round before the mast; the sail

coming down with the greatest ease when head to wind. The ballast is of stone, built into the bottom of the hooker and making a fire hearth, with a deck above as far aft as the mast.

BELFAST AND GROOMSPORT YAWLS.

This type of whale boat is said to have been imported from Norway, and even the Galway hooker and pookhaun exhibit evidence of Norwegian origin. The Belfast yawls vary in length from 20ft. to 30ft. The larger

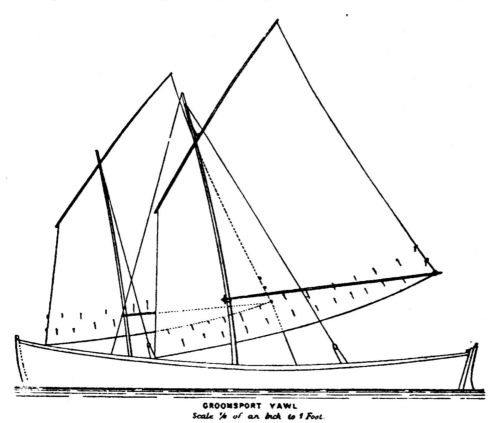

GROOMSPORT YAWL
Scale ⅛ of an inch to 1 Foot.

FIG. 177.

craft above 20ft. keel have two masts, the shorter one being stepped forward. The masts are stepped in the keelson; the main fits into a half circle cut out of the after side of the thwart, and is kept in position without any mast clamp. The foremast is put through a hole in the thwart, and has no forestay. (*See* Fig. 177.)

The tacks of the sail are hooked to a hook on the gunwales, about

5ft. forward of the mast. There are two hooks on each bow, the after one being used when before the wind. The halyard consists of a tye and single whip purchase. The standing part of the purchase is fast to cleats below the gunwale, fitted on the stringers, and the fall is also so belayed. There is no traveller, and the tye runs over a half sheave at the mast head. This fitting is in great repute among the Belfast men, as there is little chance of the yard jamming in hoisting or lowering.

The main sheet is a single rope rove through a bull's-eye on a swivel on the sternpost. The sail is extended by a boom, the latter having a pin at the outer end, which is put into the clew cringle of the sail. The other end is lashed to the mast. A bowline is sometimes used as represented in the cut (Fig. 178). This bowline is set up to the towing bollard or " Samson," with which these boats are always fitted. The sail is cut so high in the clew because it should not get into the water during rolling. In squalls the sheet or halyard is let go. In running, if the

Fig. 178.

bows dive, the halyard is eased a little. For reefing the fore lug is set on the mainmast. The boat is steered by a yoke and long lines, all the crew sitting amidships. Stones are used as ballast. If a boat has only one sail, the mast is stepped amidships (*see* Fig. 178).

The rig is a very rude one, and it could not be expected that such craft would do much to windward where short tacking would of necessity be frequent. Yet with the crew of five, and ballast of about two cwt. consisting of perhaps only the stones used for the fishing lines, they slip along very fast and the crew shift the lugs with great expedition. The Groomsport yawls enjoy a great repute on the coast about Belfast for speed and weatherliness.

EAST COAST SCOTCH FISHING BOAT.

Most people interested in boats who have visited any of the Scotch ports from Berwick to the Shetland Isles are familiar with the deck plans and general arrangements and rig of this class of fishing boat, all bearing the same family likeness, although varying in size. The nature of the work to which these boats are put during their voyages round the Scotch coast calls for many compromises; they must be of light draught to enable them to enter small tidal harbours, they must be easily rowed, and their stability and sail-carrying power must be above reproach. They enjoy a great reputation as dry and able sea boats, although their motions in the particular sea which brings out the peculiar lively qualities of the boat can

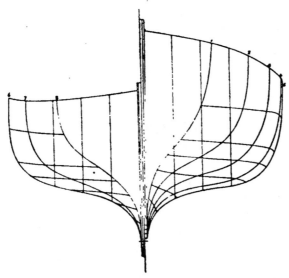

FIG. 179.—MIDSHIP SECTION OF EAST COAST SCOTCH FISHING BOAT.

only be compared to a bucking horse. Many a poor fellow has paid the penalty due to this quality in the stormy North Sea, their usual scene of operations. The building of boats of this model is almost entirely confined to the east coast of Scotland. They have not suffered in any way from the delicate attentions of the naval architect, the boat of the present day being the result of trial and error during many generations of their fearless and hard-working owners, the descendants of the Vikings who settled on the east coast of Scotland. Anyone taking the trouble to compare Scotch and Norwegian boats of this type will be surprised to find so many points in common.

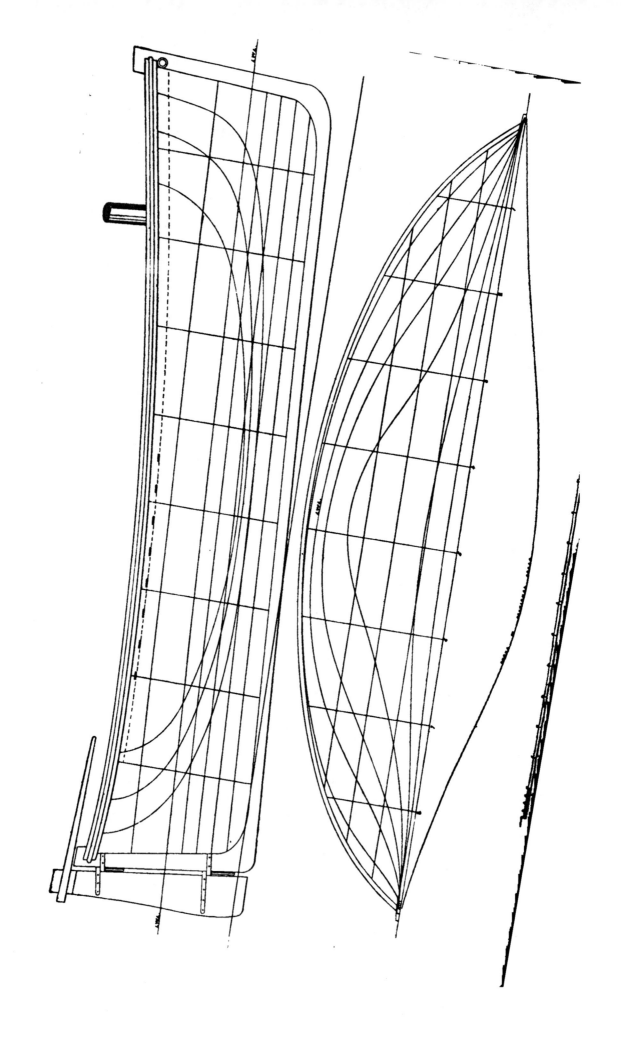

The enormous beam and hardness of bilge at once strike a stranger accustomed to the easy sections of such boats as the Penzance lugger. One of the reasons for this peculiarity is due to the fact that, when caught on a bar, which is very rare, the whole or a portion of the stone ballast has to be thrown overboard, and still leave a boat capable of carrying some sail, which would not be the case with a boat of the Penzance type. The ballast carried in proportion to the displacement is small, as the boats are very strongly built, the timbers of this boat being 2¼in. sided, and spaced 14in., planking 1in. Local peculiarities are to be noted in the boats of each port and builder; but, speaking generally, they are much the same in hull, making allowance for difference in size, with the exception of the Zulu boat, so called from making her appearance in the year of the Zulu war; a boat of the latter type, 40ft. to 45ft. long, would have a rake of sternpost of 10ft. It is not easy to find out whether this is an improvement or the reverse, as those who own them say they are handier, whereas the owners of the older type say the Zulu does not steer so well in a seaway. Be this as it may, the rake of sternpost eases the buttock lines, and generally gives the Zulu boat a more taking after-body than her older sisters. Unlike the Penzance fisherman, the Scotchman does not as a rule indulge in the luxury of a number of lugs of various sizes; with the exception of a large jib, used for reaching and running, he has only the main lug and a mizen in the larger boats. The former may have as many as ten rows of reef points. At sea the tack of the lug is made fast by a chain and hook through a hole in the stem; when tacking the lug has to be dipped and passed round the mast. When working in narrow waters, where they have to go about frequently, the tack is made fast to the foot of the mast; then dipping is unnecessary.

TABLE OF DIMENSIONS.

Length over all	26ft. 4½in.
„ on L.W.L.	25ft. 10in.
Beam over gunwale	10ft. 4in.
Draught of water	3ft.
Displacement	4·82 tons.
Centre of buoyancy from fore side of stem at L.W.L.	13·08ft.
Centre of lateral resistance from fore side of stem at L.W.L.	13·59ft.
Centre of gravity of L.W.L. plane from fore side of stem at L.W.I.	13·11ft.
Metacentre above centre of buoyancy	4·54ft.
Co-efficient of displacement	0·242
„ „ L.W.L. plane	0·623
„ „ midship section	0·439

NORWEGIAN PILOT BOATS.

The lines of a Norwegian pilot boat on page 447, Fig. 182, were drawn by Mr. Colin Archer, of Laurvig, Norway. It is not often that prettier or cleaner water lines will be met with; and if the flare of the bow were reduced, the fore-foot rounded up a little, a lead keel added, and a suitable sail plan, we think that a very fast and weatherly yacht could be built from the lines. Mr. Archer thus describes the boats:

"I doubt if English boats of the same size are as handy with a small crew in all kinds of weather. A pilot and his 'boy' (technically so called—he may be an 'old boy') will go to sea in one of these boats and stay there (perhaps for a week) till he finds a vessel. When this

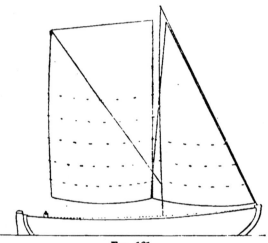

Fig. 181.

happens, perhaps somewhere between the Naze and the Skaw, the boat goes close alongside, the pilot jumps on board, and the 'boy' is left to bring the boat home the best way he can. The sail is a sprit (*see* Fig. 181), and, notwithstanding the formidable dimensions, one man is supposed to be equal to all contingencies.

Whole length of mast about	33ft.
Diameter at deck	11in.
Diameter at top	4¼in.

"There are no shrouds—only the forestay. They balance on a wind with the foresail and mainsail, but generally carry a jib or two for sailing free, and often a jib-headed topsail hoisted on a long pole."

The mackerel fishing-boat is the same model; they carry about 600 fathoms of nets, three to four hands. These boats will live a long time in a seaway and keep pretty dry (they are decked); but their great "forte" is their extreme quickness in answering their helm, a necessary quality when ships have to be boarded from them in a gale of wind; and they will work to windward through surprisingly narrow places, and at a good rate too. These boats are all oak except the

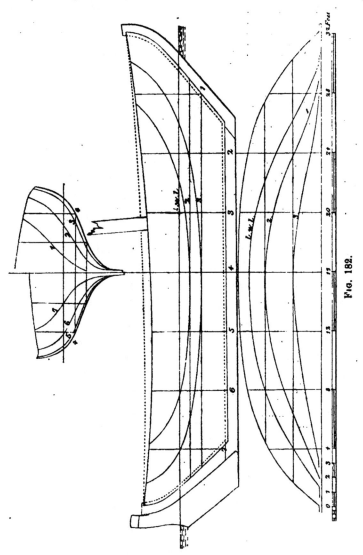

Fig. 182.

timbers—thirteen to fourteen strakes 1¼in. boards—clinker-built, with juniper treenails with heads, placed about 4½in. apart. They look clumsy, chiefly from their upper works spreading so much. If this feature— which, however, gives them an enormous reserve of buoyancy—were altered, they might be made to look well enough, though peculiar. The boats carry about one-third to one-fourth of their total weight in ballast, generally consisting of iron ore, which is plentiful in the neighbourhood of Laurvig.

Length extreme	33ft.	C.B. aft, centre of L.W.L.	5ft.
Length on L.W.L.	30·2ft.	Mid-section forward of centre of	
Breadth extreme	11·6ft.	L.W.L.	0·4ft.
Breadth on L.W.L.	10·0ft.	Area of mainsail	500 sq. ft.
Draught of water	4·2ft.	Luff of mainsail	24ft.
Displacement	7·5 tons.	Leech of mainsail	22ft.
Area midship section	15 sq. ft.	Head of mainsail	14ft.
Area load water-plane	198 sq. ft.	Foot of mainsail	14ft.

BERMUDIAN YACHTS.

Bermudian boats are short, broad, handy vessels, and one remarkable quality of these boats is their power of shooting in stays which enables them to work through a channel so narrow that she could not possibly have beaten through it. The mast (*see* Fig. 184) is stepped forward, and rakes aft. There is one small shroud on each side. The mainsail is laced to the mast, and when once thus laced they cannot reef; if a boat starts for a race with a whole sail, she must carry it. The Bermudian favourite point of sailing is to windward.

There is a peculiar plan in these boats for making the mainsail sit flat. The main boom, instead of being fitted with jaws in the usual manner, has an eye-hole in the foremost end of it, which runs from 3ft. to 4ft. the fore side of mast; the after end of the boom is secured to the clew of the sail, and the boom is then boused taut aft with a small tackle taken from the eye-bolt to a strop round the mast; this produces a wonderfully flat sail. The lines and sail plan given are the most modern.

The solid lines show the ordinary rig; the dotted lines the racing rig. Diameter of mast at partners 10¼in.; of racing mast, 11½in.

Length on water line	34ft.	Draught of water aft	5ft 10in.
Breadth extreme	11ft. 2½in.	Draught when racing	6ft. 6in.

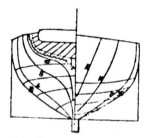

FIG. 183:—BODY PLAN OF "DIAMOND."

The drawings made by Mr. Wm. Prattent, of Devonport, and shown by Figs. 183, 184, and 185, are of the Diamond, which was one of the fastest of the Bermudian boats.

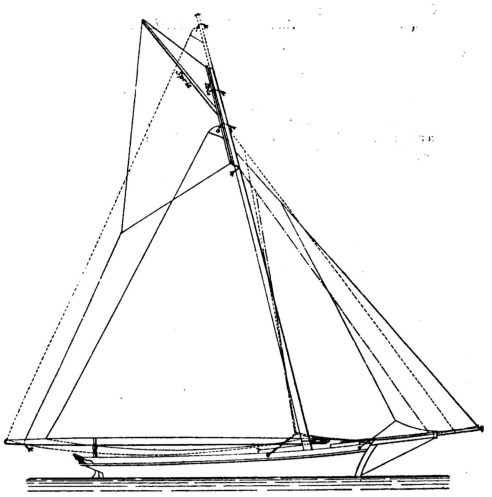

FIG. 184. SAIL PLAN OF "DIAMOND."

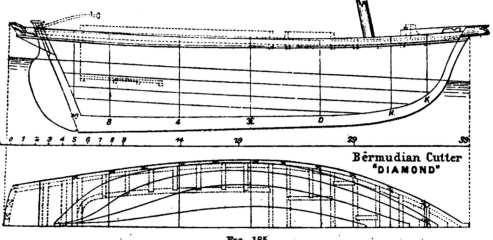

Bermudian Cutter
"DIAMOND"

FIG. 185.

G G

BOMBAY YACHTS.

The Bombay yachts are very peculiar in model, and some are even more exaggerated than those depicted on this page. The peculiarity of the boat is that she has a cambered keel, thus making the greatest

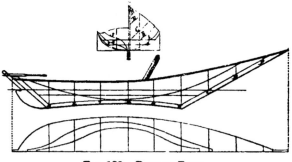

Fig. 186.—Bombay Boat.

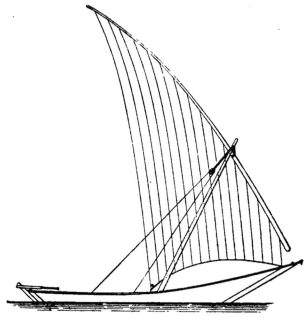

Fig. 187.—Sail Plan of Bombay Boat.

draught aft, and a deep gripe forward to hold them to windward (*see* Fig. 186); the mast rakes forward (*see* Fig. 187). Instead of tacking as other yachts, they are obliged to wear; they thus require a lot of sea room to work in. The sail is reefed on the yard.

At the South Kensington Museum there is a large model of a Bombay boat, with a keel much more cambered than shown above, and with even more overhang forward.

SYDNEY BOATS.

Sydney Harbour is one of the finest places for yachting in the world. There is a coastline of several hundred miles, formed into all manner of delightful little nooks and inlets, each of which has its beautiful sandy beach and deep, clear, blue, or green water overshadowed by big bluffs and overhanging gum-trees. Within an hour's sailing from Sydney itself, there are places which are absolutely as primæval as when Captain Cook discovered Port Jackson in 1787. From October to March, the north-easter comes in, steady, and of fair club-topsail strength. The Harbour is nowhere more than three miles wide, and the water is always smooth and never really cold.

The yachts at Sydney have no difference from those in the old country, except as concerns one or two minor points; but the sailing boats, from various causes, have developed into a distinct type. Firstly, the water is smooth and warm, and the breezes steady; secondly, the universal system of measurement is length over all, overhang fore and aft being therefore penalised. The consequence is that a boat has been evolved which has great beam, little depth, immense sails and large centre-board. Great numbers as crews are carried, the whole of whom sit up to windward, holding on to life-lines, and hang flat out over the water on the gunwale sills.

The boats are divided into length-classes, beginning at 8ft., and progressing by two feet on to 24ft., which is the largest class that can be conveniently managed, for a reason that will soon be apparent. Below 14ft. all the boats are built with ribands, a form of riband carvel building, except that the ribands are so broad as to almost touch one another, and instead of the outside planking there is painted canvas. This makes a very strong and light little craft, and as it is easily constructed the Sydney boys often spend their winter evenings in building "canvassers." A few dimensions of such a boat are as follows:—

Length over all	8ft.
Beam	3ft. 6in.
Depth	1ft. 10in.
Main-boom	13ft.
Bumpkin (bowsprit)	6ft. outboard
Gaff	8ft.
Hoist of mainsail	7ft. 6in.

The centre-board—locally termed the "gin"—is about 4ft. by 3ft.

G G 2

It is a funny sight to see these mites of dingheys, each "manned" by three or four boys, flying along under their astonishing press of sail. Their speed and weatherliness in light weather are extraordinary. The Sydney people aver that their canvas dingheys are the best school for yachtsmen that one could well have.

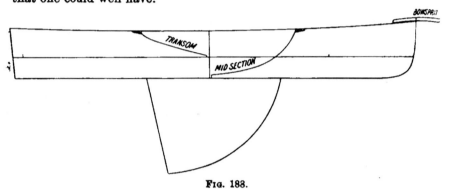

FIG. 188.

The 24-footers are somewhat different in proportions, but present the same main principles. The dimensions of the illustration, Fig. 188, are as follows :—

Length over all	24ft.
Beam (exclusive of moulding)	10ft.
Depth	2ft. 9in.
Centre-board length	8ft.
„ depth	5ft. 6in.
Main-boom	34ft. 6in.
Gaff	26ft.
Hoist of mainsail	25ft. 6in.
Bumpkin outboard	17ft.

The mainboom projects about 17ft. 6in. over the "tuck," as the square transom is called, and in order to keep it properly down, a stern outrigger some 12ft. long is necessary, as is seen in the American design for Parole, a somewhat similar boat. The centre-board is made of thin boiler-plate, galvanised. The pivoted gin is quite given up in Sydney in favour of the more effective "drop gin," and the centre-board shown has three handles. When it is completely up it projects about three feet or so above the box, and of course has to be lowered for a gybe. The difficulty of handling the great drop gin is certainly one of the defects of these boats. It takes five or six men to get it up smartly when rounding a windward mark for a broad reach or run home.

The free-board of the boat drawn, when she has her full crew of sixteen hands on board, will not be more than 18in. at the outside, and so very little heel is allowed. However, they habitually sail their boats with the lee gunwale two or three inches under water, and so a very powerful pump has to be carried, as the boats are usually completely open. This pump, in anything like a breeze, has to be kept working the whole time, at any rate on the wind, and it is very good exercise for the pumper.

The skipper knows to a fraction of an inch exactly how far his boat can heel before a luff becomes necessary, and to one unaccustomed to the conditions it is most exciting work watching the lee gunwale ploughing through it, while a great volume of water is pouring into the boat. However, length for length there are no boats afloat which will hold these Sydney "flat-irons" in a light day. Off the wind they tend to bury, and their great beam will prevent great speed; but on the wind in smooth water they have never been beaten by any boat which has been brought to race them. The great area of lateral resistance, the small displacement, and the very powerful sail plan are all in favour of weatherly qualities of no mean order.

In running and reaching kites of every description are carried— squaresails, raffees, jackyard topsails, jib topsails, water-sails, and gigantic ballooners. Of course, capsizes, especially in gybing, are very frequent. A 34-foot boom comes over with considerable momentum; and the writer has seen four 24-footers go "into the ditch" one after the other in gybing round a particularly bad headland.

These boats always have a broad moulding, as shown in Fig. 188, upon which the crews sit. A novelty was in surrounding the gunwale with a hollow box-moulding several inches in width. The special object of the idea described was to give increased buoyancy when lee-gunwale under, and to give greater floating power in case of a capsize.

The objections to these skimming-dishes are numerous. In a seaway they pound frightfully, and a Clyde 23ft. boat would do what she liked with them in a thrash to windward under such conditions. The huge crews necessary are a great objection. It is difficult to get a dozen or fifteen crews, of as many men each, every Saturday afternoon; and the Sydney man has such an innate objection to dead ballast, that no bulb keel idea seems to have ever caught on to take the place of some of the hands.

In races the handicap time allowances are generally given at the start, and it is very exciting for the little boats to watch the big fellows creeping gradually up from astern near the finish, when she may be becalmed and let the little ones run right up on to her, thus saving their time when all seemed hopeless. But under the Sydney system the boats at the end of a race are generally packed together within a few hundred yards, and bad luck to one will affect all equally.   Probably this system will never become popular here.

THE AMERICAN SHARPIE.

The existence of the sharpie can be traced back to 1835 on the Connecticut coast.   They are supposed to owe their origin to the oyster men, who originally pursued their calling in log canoes; but, large trees failing, they resorted to a flat bottomed boat something like the Wexford flat bottomed boat.   The floor of a sharpie is usually rockered or rounded up at both ends (*see* Fig. 189); but Mr. Thomas Clapham, a well-known builder of these boats at Rosslyn, Long Island, U.S., has introduced a form of the "skip jack" which he terms the "Nonpariel" (*see* Fig. 190), the bow

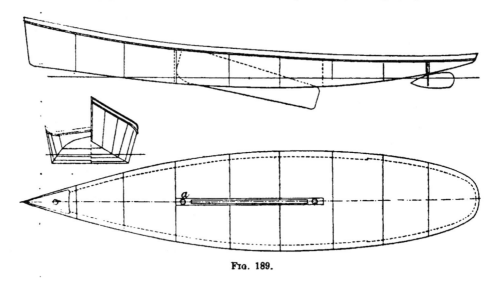

Fig. 189.

end being immersed.   The bow end was immersed in the Nonpariel with a view of obviating the "spanking," or hammering, of the flat floor when the boats are driven in lumpy water; but this was of no avail of course when the bow was lifted out of water.

The sharpie varies in her proportions of beam to length from four to five, but the craft of about five beams to length are said to make the greatest speed.   As a rule, the fore end and aft end of the boat are decked, and in the larger craft a cabin is built.   A sharpie 20ft. by 5ft. beam on deck would be 4ft. 3in. broad at the bottom, and 1ft. 8in. deep from gunwale to bottom amidships.

The foremast is usually about six times the beam in height, and mainmast shorter, or about five and a half times the beam,   The masts are very slight and tapering, bending like a bamboo yard. The sails are leg-of-mutton shaped, extended by a kind of horizontal sprit (*d*, Fig. 191), a tackle being on the mast for purchasing out the sprit. *b* and *c* are

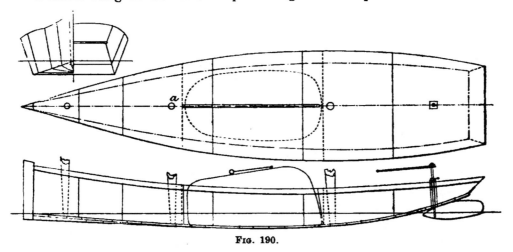

Fig. 190.

brails used for reefing the sail, reef points are also sewn on the reef bands as shown.

The centre-board is large, and so is the rudder. The latter is usually of the balance type, one-third being in front of the rudder

Fig. 191.

post. An iron pipe is fitted into the stern end to act as sternpost; through this the rudder post is carried, and secured by a collar. The ballast, if any is carried, usually consists of sand bags.

In Fig. 190 *a* shows where the mast would be stepped if rigged as an ordinary sloop.

With skilful management these boats can be sailed in lumpy water; but they heel very freely, and great dexterity and quickness are necessary in sailing them in a breeze. Off the wind it is said that a 40ft. sharpie will travel 12, or 14 knots an hour, and with everything flattened in and board down will lie to the wind like a centre-board sloop.

THE AMERICAN SNEAK BOAT.

The home of the sneak boat, or sneak box, or devil's coffin, as the contrivance is indifferently termed, is Barnegat Bay, a piece of water some forty miles long and six miles wide on the coast of New Jersey. It is separated from the Atlantic by a narrow strip of sand, and is thus cut off from anything like ocean waves. Large numbers of the sneak boats are to be seen in the bay, the usual size being 12ft. long by 4ft. breadth.

The keels are of oak 4in. wide and $\frac{3}{4}$in. deep; plank $\frac{1}{2}$in. thick. The keel has a crook or bend forward to suit the shape of the boat. The hood ends of the planks are fitted along the gunwale instead of in the stem, the bottom plank or garboard running along the keel and up round each side of the stem.

A square well is covered with a hatch with lock to stow guns, &c., as the boats are largely used for wildfowl shooting. No thwarts are used, a moveable box forming a seat for rowing. When duck shooting the crew sit or lie on the floor boards, the deck being covered with sedge.

The rowlocks are fitted in wooden brackets, which fold down to the deck. A strip of oak on each side aft serves as a washboard, and also as a rack for holding the decoys.

The most peculiar feature of the boats is the dagger centre-board, which lifts out of the case entirely, as a sword from its sheath. As a protection against rough water an apron is tacked to the deck forward of the well, and set up to a peak by a short spar as shown in Fig. 192.

With their flat bottoms the boats will float in very little water, and can be dragged with ease over mud or marsh. The rig is a small spritsail, and either an oar or a rudder is used for steering; the boats are taken out in all kinds of weather, and may be seen flying about the bay when larger craft are at anchor; but of course, as in all such boats, skill and experience in their management alone make them safe.

The "sneak box" appears to be an adaptation of the old Irish canoe as found at Kilkee on the West coast. These canoes developed into a

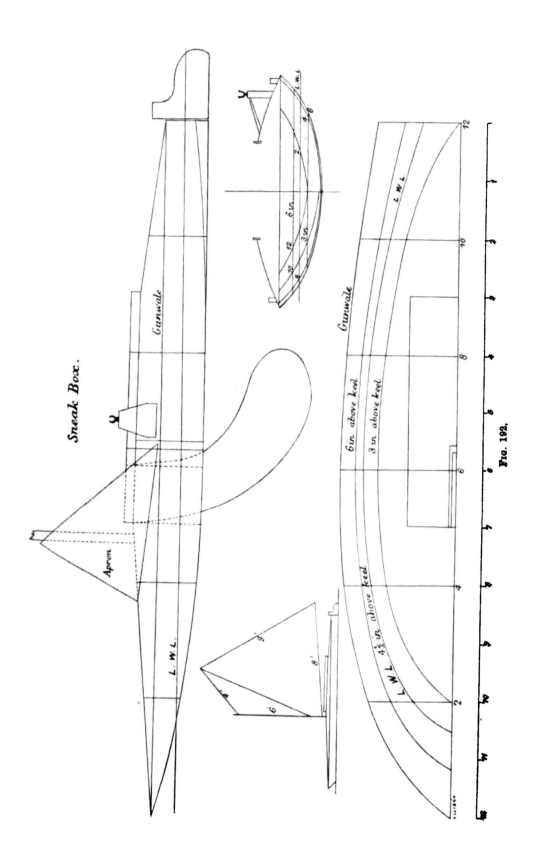

Sneak Box.

Gunwale

Apron

L.W.L.

Gunwale

6 in. above keel

3 in. above keel

L.W.L. 4½ in. above keel

FIG. 192.

rowing boat, and are illustrated (Fig. 193) and described by the late Commander Horner, R.N.

" I recommend any one, wishing for a new sensation, to take a pull in one after a gale. They never ship a drop of water, and literally dance

Fig. 193.

over the tops of the waves. A six-oared one, such as I went in once from Arran to Galway, would I think be very useful in going over surf." The lower sketch represents a similar boat, the caïque of the Bosphorus.

CHAPTER XXIV.

DOUBLE BOATS.

DOUBLE boats, in some form or the other, are met with all over the world, and the principle is adopted with the main object of acquiring great stability. But, although double boats may have in this way great stability, it must not be supposed that they are uncapsizable. They could be capsized by carrying a heavy press of canvas, or they might be thrown over by a sea, just as a lifeboat is sometimes.

In 1873, the late Mr. H. Melling, of Liverpool, had what he termed a safety yacht constructed on the double hull principle, as shown on the following page (Fig. 194), mainly with the object of using her on the shoal water in the estuary of the Dee and Mersey.

The boards were introduced for the uses as set forth on page 269, and claimed for them by the inventor, Capt. Schank. Her pontoons are 30ft. long, and 2ft. 6in. in diameter, representing enormous floating power.

In the spring of 1868 Mr. John Mackenzie, of Belfast, constructed a double boat (Fig. 195) without dropping keels. The boats were of equal size, each 21ft. keel, 3ft. beam, and 3ft. deep. Each boat is divided by bulkheads into four compartments, two of these being 6ft. 6in. long, so as to be used for sleeping purposes. A keel is fixed to each boat, 15in. deep at the heel, diminishing forward to 6in. Bolted to the keel by strong iron knees are stanchions which rise through the deck, on which the rail is fixed; to these stanchions the cross-beams connecting the boats are fixed, the timbers or ribs also rising through the deck for a similar purpose, where the cross-beams are placed. The skin is 1in. thick, being in one board on either side of the keel; the sides are in two, each 18in. deep, the seams being covered by a continuous strip of wood. The boats are connected by five trussed beams, the one at which the mast is stepped being double trussed. A platform rests on these beams, a space of 3in. being left at either side to allow air compressed by a cross-sea to escape from underneath; from the mast forward this platform is formed of open-work. Immediately under the platform is a chest, 2ft. broad and 6in. deep,

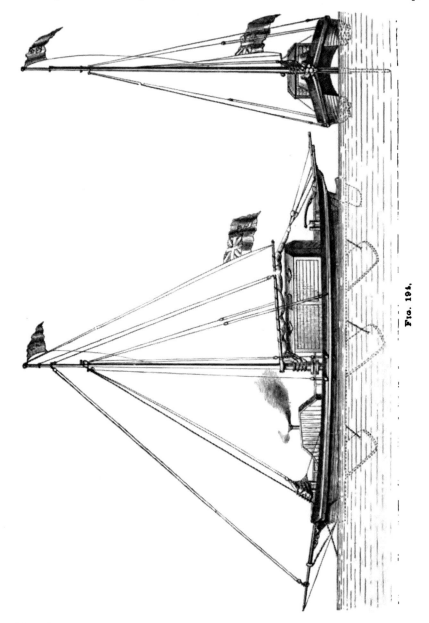

Fig. 194.

capable of carrying 6cwt. of water to serve as ballast in heavy weather. It is provided with brass valves in bottom, which in light weather or in case of accident can be opened, and the water discharged in a few minutes;

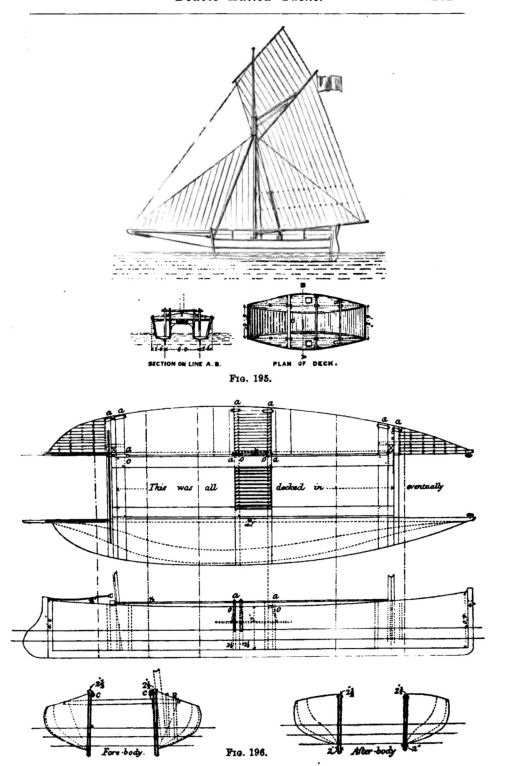

SECTION ON LINE A. B.   PLAN OF DECK.

FIG. 195.

This was all   decked in   eventually

Fore-body.   FIG. 196.   After-body.

when the box is emptied, by closing the valves a third chamber or boat is formed, capable of carrying 7cwt. or 8cwt., in case the other two got waterlogged. This extra weight is required to enable the boat to beat up in a strong sea. A helm is attached to each boat, and these, being coupled together by a connecting rod, are worked by a tiller in the centre, so that both are moved in the same direction.

We have seen double boats which were constructed out of two halves ; that is, an ordinary 5-tonner, say, was cut in halves in a fore and aft vertical direction through keel and deck, and then set apart 6ft. or 7ft., and connected by beams. Of course the inner sides of the halves were covered over with plank, and made a perfectly flat surface.

FIG. 197.

The late Colonel Conway Gordon built such a boat at Madras, which he sent to England and sailed about Southsea. Her construction is shown in Fig. 196. The late Colonel Conway Gordon built several similar boats in England, and made unsuccessful attempts to race them against 5-raters on the Solent.

In America a double boat was introduced in 1876 called a Catamaran. The boats were designed by Mr. N. G. Herreshoff. The catamaran has two faults, namely, it is slow in stays, and is prone to 'pitch pole,' or blow over endwise. (Plate CII. and Fig. 197.)

The Feejee boat and the majority of catamarans possess this objection —in rough water the separate motions of the hulls will ultimately wrench them from the deck, unless the connections are excessively heavy. Mr. Herreshoff's plan is to make the motion of the hulls independent of each other.

The Amaryllis, Arion, Teaser, John Gilpin, and Tarantella, the catamarans which Mr. Herreshoff has built thus far, are substantially alike, differing only in details and size.

When the stern of the weather boat lifts, it is customary for one of the crew to sit on it, as shown in Fig. 197.

The Tarantella and Duplex have been imported into this country.

As the reader could gain no clearer idea of the peculiarities of these boats than by reading Mr. Herreshoff's patent specifications, we subjoin an extract therefrom, to be read in connection with the accompanying illustrations of the John Gilpin (Plate CII.).

"'A A are respectively the port and starboard hulls, each complete in itself, and constructed with a centre-board case, centre-board, O, rudder, &c. There should be a tight deck on each, with provisions for pumping. In large vessels the space below deck in each hull may be utilised.

"'Points near the bow of each hull are connected by slightly curved beams, D, trussed with rods, *b*, and united to the hulls at each end by universal joints, C C. A similar trussed beam is similarly joined to each hull near the stern. The hulls may pitch independently of each other, and the universal joints, C, will impose no restraint on the movement. A straight timber, M, extends longitudinally along the centre, just below the transverse pieces, B, and secured to each. Two straight sticks, D, extend across at a higher elevation, about midway between stem and stern. An upright, or nearly upright link, E, bears on each hull a little one side of the centre line, with a universal joint free to work in all directions. The upper end of each link, E, is similarly jointed to the under side of the cross-piece, D. G″ is a car of light, oval form, G being a deck, and G″ the standing room, with a suitable raised rim or bulwark, adapted to accommodate persons, stores, &c. The car is secured to both the transverse beams, D, and the longitudinal piece, M. It is furthermore secured to the mast, H, which it aids to support, and by which it is in turn supported. The weight of any load upon the car, G″, is transmitted to the hulls, A, through the medium, mainly, of the cross beams, D, and upright links, E, which bear amidships, and partly through the other cross-pieces, B, which bear near the ends, respectively.

"'Stiff diagonal braces, D′, connect the ends of the beams, D, with the bowsprit, which latter is also firmly connected to the mast.

"'A short upright, M', is fixed to the forward end of the piece, M, and aids to support the bowsprit, I. It also receives a bob-stay, m, which extends from the forward end of the bowsprit under the piece, M', to the foot of the mast, H. Another fore-and-aft stay, m', extends from the foot of the mast to the after end of the timber, M. Two other stays, h h, connect the foot of the mast with each end of the cross-beams, D, and still another, h', with the top of the upright, M'. A pair of stays, d d, connect the ends of the cross beams, D, with the front end of the timber, M, and another pair, d' d', connect the same ends with a point near the after end of the same beam, M. All these may be steel wire, galvanised, tinned, or otherwise protected from oxidation. The whole produces a light framework, supporting the deck and its load, and also the mast and bowsprit, upon the hulls, with freedom for the latter to both pitch and roll.

"'An elastic restraint upon the rolling is imposed through the medium of arms, A¹ A¹, of ash, or other strong and elastic material, extending from each hull toward the other, and terminating near, but not touching the central timber, M. These arms, A¹, may be connected to the boat, through the medium of bolts, with indiarubber washers, or the like, to increase the elasticity.

"'Their inner extremities are connected by links, A³, with an inner piece, G', of ash, or other elastic material, held a little below the deck, G. When in either a ground swell or choppy sea, one or both the hulls seek to roll, the motion is arrested simply by this train of elastic connections. The result is a limited freedom of the rolling, the pieces, A¹ and G', yielding upward and downward to accommodate the motion, and promptly bringing each hull to an even keel so soon as the disturbing strain is diminished.

"'The helm, J¹, is applied, not on either of the rudder-heads, but on a shaft, J, in the central part of the structure, and further forward than the rudders. On the lower end of this shaft are arms, J², extending obliquely backward. To the end of each a rod, K, is jointed, which connects to an arm on the rudder on the opposite side—that is to say, the rod K from the port arm, J², extends to the starboard rudder, and the rod K from the starboard arm, J², extends to the port rudder.

"'In turning a double boat, one hull necessarily makes a shorter turn, or describes a curve of less radius than the other. This requires that the rudders of the two boats should be turned to unequal extents, the boat which is the inside one, or nearest the centre of the curvature, having its rudder turned to the greatest angle. Such motion is obtained through my arrangement.

" ' If the compound vessel is to be turned to port, the helm is put starboard in the usual manner; turning the arms, J^2 J^2, to the same extent, but by reason of their oblique position and their being centred considerably in advance of the rudder-posts, the port rudder is turned through a greater arc than the other. When on the other hand the vessel is to be turned to starboard, the helm, J^1, is put to port, as usual, and the rudder on the starboard boat, which is then on a similar circle, turns through the greatest arc.

" ' Each side, and below the bowsprit, are longitudinal pieces, L, of hard wood, which, in addition to their obvious service as supports for men handling the jib, contribute somewhat to the strengthening of the framework.'

" In the John Gilpin, the space between the deck, G, is divided into two parts, the after one containing the elastic beam, G', and the forward being used as a locker. The elastic arms, A^1, are strengthened by the diagonal arms, A^2. Also the inner or free ends of the elastic arms, A^1, connected with the mast by links, P, shewn in the sectional view. The sheet is run along the longitudinal timber, M, thence through the floor of the standing room, G".

" The dimensions of the John Gilpin are as follows : Length of hull, over all, about 32ft.; width of each hull, on deck, 28in.; depth of each hull at ends, 2ft. 5in.; draft of hulls, with load, 1ft. at each end, and probably about 21in. amidships; distance of hulls apart from centre to centre, 16ft.; mast is stepped 12ft. 10in. from extreme bows. The car is 14ft. 10in. long; length of bowsprit, 22ft. 8in.; length of boom, 31ft. 4in.; length of gaff, 17ft.; luff of mainsail, 20ft.; mainsail and jib are of the usual shape. The upright links, E, are 16ft. 6in. from extreme bows, and the centre boards, O, are immediately abaft, with wells 2ft. long on deck. The boats draw 4ft. with centre boards down. The rudders are about 2ft. long. In every part lightness and strength seem combined. The mast is very light, being about $5\frac{1}{4}$in. in diameter at H, and tapered to the foot. The shrouds are each three loose wires of the usual telegraph size. The iron work is galvanised throughout. Weight of boat, completely equipped, about 3300lb. (1·47 ton). It will carry seven or eight passengers, but the best speed is with the fewest on board. The cost was $1000."

The Tarantella, subsequently built, is 15in. longer, and is said to have been timed to make 14 knots an hour, with the wind free, and the maximum speed to windward, Mr. Herreshoff states, is $6\frac{1}{4}$ miles per hour; he does not, however, state whether this is speed through the water or distance made good to windward. The boat makes very little lee way in smooth water, but a rough sea lifts her bodily to leeward. She answers her helm very readily, but does not come about as quickly as a single-hulled boat. The stern of the weather boat will rise about eighteen inches out of the water, with the bow submerged, in strong winds. Her motions are easier than any other boat of the same size, but when driven very hard in rough water she is very wet."

CHAPTER XXV.

STEAM YACHTING.

THE introduction of steam into the pleasure navy was for a great many years retarded by two principal influences. In the first place, steam was considered, by the Royal Yacht Squadron, inimical to yachting, and it was not admitted to be yachting at all; in the second place, the old-fashioned jet condensing engines, with low pressure steam, were so extravagant in burning coal, that motives of economy prevented many who had no prejudice about the matter to adhere to sail. However, with the introduction of the compound surface condensing engine working at high steam pressures, the objection to steam on account of its extravagance was removed, and the many advantages the steam yacht has over the sailing yacht have proved too much for mere prejudice.

The principal advantage of a steam yacht over a sailing yacht is, leaving cost out of the question, that she can make passages or traverse the sea in the weather that is the most agreeable; that is, in calms and smooth water, when the sailing vessel would be lying helpless, and those on board half suffocated with the heat and stagnant air. In a calm twenty-four hours a steam yacht of moderate I.H.P. can reel off 240 miles, or, say, go from the Thames to Weymouth, whilst the sailing yacht would be waiting for a breeze, and perhaps when that breeze came there would be more than a comfortable amount of it for the passengers on board, and perhaps retard the speed of the yacht should there be much sea. Of course, as a sport or pastime, steaming can bear no comparison to sailing, and, as a recreation, the advantage is greatly on the side of the yacht with sails. It is true there are auxiliary steam yachts—yachts fully rigged for sailing and with steam power up to 10 knots an hour—but, whilst they have in a modified degree the advantages of both steam and sail, they are very costly to work.

In building a steam yacht, the aid of a person well acquainted with their construction and fitting with engines and their behaviour at sea

H H 2

should be sought; and in buying a second-hand vessel a competent surveyor should be employed to examine her. As a rule, iron or steel steam yachts are built up to Lloyd's highest class, but it is not always, even in such cases, that the work is of uniform excellence. Mild steel has since 1885 entirely superseded iron in yacht building, and is much to be preferred.

The first cost of a steel steam yacht, tonnage for tonnage, is not greater than that of a wood sailing yacht, unless the engines are unusually costly— the price for boiler and machinery over 100 I.H.P. varies from 6*l.* to 8*l.* per I.H.P.; but the accommodation of the steam yacht will of course be much inferior on account of the space taken up in the best part of the vessel by the boiler and engine; so, in considering the cost, it will be just to compare two vessels of about equal accommodation.

A steam yacht 56ft. on the load line, with 10ft. beam and 6ft. draught of water, would have accommodation about equal to that of a cruising sailing yacht 46ft. load line, 10ft. beam and 7ft. 6in. draught of water. The probable cost of the steam yacht, assuming her to be fitted with surface condensing engines of two or three cylinders by a good builder, would be from 1200*l.* to 1600*l.*, according to the character of the build, machinery, and fitting up. The sailing cruising yacht of 46ft. water line would cost from 1000*l.* to 1200*l.*

The expenses of working the steam yacht would be as follows:

Coals for 3000 miles steaming	£25	0	0
Engine room stores	8	0	0
Ship chandlers' stores	8	0	0
Repairs and renewals	40	0	0
Master, 16 weeks at 50s.	40	0	0
Engineer, 16 weeks at 50s.	40	0	0
One seaman at 25s., for 16 weeks	20	0	0
One seaman, to act also as an occasional stoker, at 26s.	20	16	0
Clothes for master	10	0	0
Clothes for engineer	10	0	0
Clothes for seamen	8	0	0
Board wages for master and engineer, 12s. each*	19	4	0
* Very rarely given in this sized yacht.	£249	0	0

To this might be added 75*l.* for interest on first cost, and 100*l.* for annual depreciation. Insurance 18*l.*

The wages for master are put high, as it is assumed he would not be a yearly servant; however, frequently a master of a small steam yacht is given no more than 40*s.* per week under a weekly engagement, and usually has no board wages.

A fireman or stoker of experience might be obtained for 2*l.*, or even 35*s.*, a week, who would be able to drive the engines; but in the end it would be found more economical to obtain the services of a skilled engineer even at a cost of 2*l*. 10*s*. per week, with a seaman-stoker in addition. There is no rule about boarding engineers, and frequently board wages are not paid if a good weekly wage is paid; but it is the same thing in the end whether the wages are divided under two heads or not.

If night passages have to be made, a good fireman, capable of driving the engines, would have to be shipped in addition to the engineer.

Expenses for working a 20-ton cruising sailing yacht:

Ship chandlers' stores	£10	0	0
Repairs and renewals	40	0	0
Master, at 40*s*. per week	32	0	0
Seaman, as mate, at 27*s*. per week	21	12	0
Seaman, at 25*s*. per week	20	0	0
Clothes for master	10	0	0
Clothes for seamen	8	0	0
	£141	12	0

Interest on capital, 50*l*.; annual depreciation, 50*l*.; insurance, 12*l*.

In making passages of more than twelve hours' duration, only one hand at a time would go below for a watch, unless the owner could take a watch on deck, which would be in the mate's watch.

It will be noted that in making these estimates stewards and cooks have not been included.

A well-built steam yacht of 100 tons would cost, when fully equipped, about 4500*l*., and have the accommodation of a cruiser of 60 tons, and the expenses of working her would be:

Engine room stores	£25	0	0
Coal for 5000 miles steaming	70	0	0
Ship chandlers' stores	15	0	0
Repairs and renewals	120	0	0
Master, 16 weeks at 50*s*. per week	40	0	0
Engineer, 16 weeks at 50*s*. per week	40	0	0
Stoker—engine driver, 16 weeks at 35*s*. per week	28	0	0
Mate, 16 weeks at 30*s*. per week	24	0	0
Three seamen, at 25*s*. per week each	60	0	0
Clothes for master	10	0	0
Clothes for engineer	10	0	0
Clothes for stoker and seamen	20	0	0
Board wages for master and engineer (optional)	16	0	0
	£478	0	0

Interest on capital, 225*l*.; annual depreciation, 300*l*.; insurance, 50*l*.

The stoker should be capable of taking charge of the engines during a watch, and two of the seamen should be able and willing to stoke if required. The stoker would only take charge when making long passages, when he would have one seaman in his watch; if merely cruising about for a few hours in the day, the stoker would be in the engine-room with the engineer.

The cost of a well built and fully equipped sailing yacht of 60 tons would be about 2400*l.*, and the expenses of working her as follows :

Repairs and renewal of hull, taking an annual average of 5 years ...	£70	0	0
Renewal of sails and rigging, taking an annual average of 5 years...	60	0	0
Ship chandlers' stores, oil, paint, varnish, brushes, charts, flags, coke, &c.	50	0	0
Hire of store	10	0	0
Sailing master, at 50*s.* per week	40	0	0
Mate, 16 weeks at 30*s.* per week	24	0	0
Four seamen 25*s.* a week each	80	0	0
Clothes	45	0	0
Board wages for master	8	0	0
	£387	0	0

Interest on capital, 120*l.*; annual depreciation, 60*l.*; insurance, 30*l.*

A 300-ton steam yacht of moderate engine power (12 knots an hour) would cost about 12,000*l.*, and afford the accommodation of a 200-ton sailing yacht, and the working expenses would be :

Engine room stores	£50	0	0
Coal for 5000 miles steaming	140	0	0
Ship chandlers' stores	20	0	0
Repairs and renewals	300	0	0
Master, at 3*l.* per week	48	0	0
Engineer, at 3*l.* per week	48	0	0
Mate, at 2*l.* 10*s.* per week	40	0	0
Second engineer, at 2*l.* per week	32	0	0
Three stokers, at 28*s.* per week	67	4	0
Boatswain, at 30*s.* per week	24	0	0
Carpenter, at 30*s.* per week	24	0	0
Three A.B.'s, at 28*s.* per week	67	4	0
Three A.B.'s, at 25*s.* per week	60	0	0
Clothes for master and mate	20	0	0
Clothes for engineers	20	0	0
Clothes for boatswain, seamen, and stokers	50	0	0
Board wages for officers optional	35	0	0
	£1045	8	0

Interest on first cost, 625*l.*; annual depreciation, 800*l.*; insurance, 125*l.*

The cost of a 200-ton cruising yacht, well built and equipped, would be about 7000*l.*, and the working expenses as follows :

Repairs and renewals	£300	0	0
Ship chandlers' and other stores	80	0	0
Master, at 3*l.* per week	48	0	0
Mate, at 2*l.* per week	32	0	0
Boatswain, at 30*s.* per week	24	0	0
Carpenter, at 30*s.* per week	24	0	0
Three A.B.'s, at 28*s.* per week	67	4	0
Six A.B.'s, at 25*s.* per week	120	0	0
Clothes for master and mate	20	0	0
Clothes for crew	50	0	0
Board wages	16	0	0
	£781	4	0

Interest on first cost, 350*l.*; annual depreciation, 450*l.*; insurance, 80*l.*

The accommodation steam yachts of different sizes will afford will be best seen from drawings, and on Plate CIII. will be found represented the cabin plans of two steam yachts—the Primrose (85 tons), Celia (25 tons), and on Plate CIV. the cabin plan of the Amazon (100 tons) ; Plates CV. and CVI., a light draught steam yacht of 90 tons named Linotte; Plate CVII., a more modern type of steam yacht named Speedy (140 tons), built in 1895 ; Plate CVIII. represents the Marcella, originally Queen Marfisa (160 tons), built 1887 ; and Plates CIX. and CX., the Maid of Honour (184 tons).

On Plate CXI. are the cabin plans of the steam yacht Oriental (232 tons), built by Mr. John Inglis, of Point House, Glasgow.

Plate CXII., represents the steam yacht Fauvette (420 tons), built and engined for high speed (15·6 knots an hour).

The Capercailzie (529 tons), shown on Plate CXIII., was built by Messrs. Barclay and Curle for Lord Inverclyde, and is a good example of a full power steam yacht, with great engine room space.

The auxiliary steam yacht Soprano, first known as Marchesa (377 tons), shown on Plate CXIV., is an auxiliary screw sailing yacht.

By the side of the Marchesa the cabin plan of a smaller steel auxiliary steam yacht is shown, designed by the author, intended to have power sufficient to drive her about 10 knots only, so as to get the maximum accommodation by a curtailment of the boiler and engine room space, with steam of 180lb. pressure. If much greater speed were required, the machinery compartment would require to be shifted aft, as the increased weight forward could not very well be provided for, and give a satisfactory vessel. All these things require to be very nicely adjusted, and one of the most difficult matters in designing an auxiliary steam yacht is placing the machinery and coal bunkers. Of course, if the machinery is in the middle of the yacht, as is the case of the Soprano, the difficulty for the naval architect is somewhat lessened; but it will be seen that in such a case either the saloon or some of the sleeping accommodation ought to be forward of the engine room; otherwise the room for owner and guests below will be very limited for the size of the yacht.

In apportioning power to an auxiliary steam yacht, it is important that the coal consumption should be considered, as putting in enough power to obtain another knot an hour speed may entail a serious increase in the daily consumption ; and this would necessitate either an increase in the size of the bunkers if long voyages had to be made, or frequent coaling for coast work if the bunkers were of small capacity. The Oriental at full speed and 330 I.H.P. made 11·4 knots, and her coal capacity is 33 tons; assume that she had to steam 3500 miles, with no possibility of coaling on the passage, if she started at full speed, and maintained it by keeping up 330 I.H.P., she would exhaust her coal in 105 hours (4 days 9 hours), or when she had only steamed 1200 miles; but if she started at eight knots, on 82 I.H.P., she would be able to steam the whole distance, 3500 miles, with the 33 tons of coal; but the time consumed would be 438 hours (18 days 6 hours), instead of 307 (12 days 19 hours) if she could have maintained full speed the whole distance; but to have kept up the speed of 11·4 knots for the shorter time she would require 97 tons of coal.

In the voyage of the Soprano (Marchesa) to South America the Marquis of Ailsa very carefully tested the coal consumption when the yacht was under steam, and found it to result as follows, the bunker capacity being 80 tons:

Coal burnt per 24 hours.	Speed per hour.	Coal would last	Total miles steamed.	Coal per mile.
3 tons	8 knots	26 days 14 hours	5104	35lb.
4 tons	8¼ knots	20 days	4200	43lb.
5 tons	9¼ knots	16 days	3552	51lb.

Thus, by burning 3 tons of coal per day instead of 5 tons, the Marchesa could steam 1552 miles farther, and would be only ten and a half days longer over the greater distance. It will thus be seen that great knowledge and judgment are necessary in designing and providing an auxiliary yacht with steam power. But it is no less important in a full power steamer, as, although the alteration of trim due to coal consumption may not be such a serious matter for her; yet it may happen to be of the greatest importance that the economical speed should be known, if the yacht is short of coal and far from a coaling station. It may be thought that the proper course would be to drive the yacht as fast as possible and reach the coaling place in the shortest time; but this may only result in the yacht being unable to reach her port at all, as can be seen by the particulars already given of the Oriental.

The Capercailzie is an example of a very fast steam yacht, her full power speed being 13.02 knots, and her bunker capacity 100 tons; and, with the daily consumption set forth in the tables, she would steam at the following rate and distances:

Coal burnt per 24 hours.	Speed per hour.	Coal would last.	Total miles steamed.	Coal per mile.
3 tons	8 knots	33 days 6 hours	6394	35lb.
4¼ tons	10 knots	22 days 2 hours	5328	42lb.
10 tons	13 knots	10 days 7 hours	3235	70lb.

This simply means that such a yacht (leaving stress of weather out of the question) could, at 8 knots an hour, steam to New York and back on 100 tons of coal; but if the attempt were made to reach there in about ten days, her coal would only last the outward voyage.

In making voyages to distant places it would also be right to consider the money cost, as coal on the Atlantic or Pacific sea-board, or even at some Mediterranean ports, cannot be procured for less than about three times the cost per ton in England.

The coal consumption per mile for yachts of varying sizes will be found to be approximately as set forth in the following table:

Tonnage of Yacht.	Speed.	Coal consumption per mile steamed.
50 tons.	8 knots.	15lb.
100 tons.	9 knots.	20lb.
150 tons.	10 knots.	30lb.
200 tons.	10¼ knots.	35lb.
300 tons.	11 knots.	40lb.
400 tons.	14 knots.	115lb.

The coal consumption given is for good modern triple compound engines, working at a boiler pressure of from 160lb. to 180lb. the square inch. The consumption of coal for engines ranges from 2lb. per I.H.P. per hour, with machinery developing 50 I.H.P., to 1¾lb. per I.H.P. per hour, with machinery of 300 I.H.P., and 1¼lb. per hour for 1200 I.H.P.

The advantage of an auxiliary steam yacht may be very considerable in extended voyages where the trade winds can be made use of, and even in head winds if she be a fairly weatherly vessel.

Some idea of what can be accomplished by an auxiliary steam yacht under her sails alone can be gathered from the following facts: The Lancashire Witch, entirely under canvas, did the distance (4458 miles) from the Falkland Islands to Natal in twenty-three days, the biggest run per twenty-four hours being 295 miles; and she did the distance from Yokohama (4400 miles), also in twenty-three days, her biggest run being again 295 miles in twenty-four hours; and she did the whole distance from Tahiti to Liverpool (11,030 miles) in seventy-nine days, having covered, owing to head winds, 12,230 miles. The Sunbeam, in her voyage round the world, covered 35,450 miles, and out of this distance 20,400 miles were done under canvas, without steam; she also, like Lancashire Witch, did many good runs under canvas, having on one occasion logged 299 miles. The Sunbeam's best day's steaming was 230 miles, and Lancashire Witch's 216.

The first cost of a 300-ton auxiliary steam yacht would exceed that of the cost of a full steam yacht, as, although the engines might not cost quite so much, the heavy spars, rigging, and sails would cost probably ten times as much as those in the plainly rigged steamer.

The 300-ton auxiliary would be shorter and broader, but in reality the accommodation would be superior, as the engine-room would be proportionately shorter, and the extra breadth would add to the size of the cabins.

The cost of working a 300-ton auxiliary steam yacht, so far as engine-room wages go, would be about the same as the full steam yacht; but there would be six additional seamen to provide for, amounting to 150*l.* for a season. There would be also wear and tear of sails; but, as the engine and boiler would probably be used less in proportion, a fair set-off would be arrived at. However, there is no doubt that for home cruising, or even for cruising to the Mediterranean or Baltic, the full power steam yacht will prove the more economical and most satisfactory.

But a still more important matter to consider is the fact that as an auxiliary steam yacht has generally more beam to length and a great deal more under-water depth of body than the full steam yacht, she is as a consequence a better and steadier sea boat, and on that account can be preferred.

In making a long voyage great care should be taken in selecting an engineer; a thoroughly experienced working man should be obtained— one who not only knows how to drive an engine, but who is also capable of readjusting any of its parts and effecting slight repairs. The second engineer should also be what is known as a "donkey man." As much as 4*l.* a week and board wages have been paid to an engineer for long voyages, and 3*l.* to second engineer.

A certificated "second engineer" is frequently engaged to take charge of a yacht's engines, and, if a steady, sober man can be found, a certificated "second engineer" will be a most valuable one to employ. These second engineers have often been "donkey men," that is, men who, having acquired a fair education, have risen from firemen or stokers. However, the Board of Trade second-class engineer must have served some time in the shop. The qualifications are as follows: "The candidate must be twenty-one years of age, and have served an apprenticeship to an engineer, and prove that during the period of his apprenticeship he has been employed in the making and repairing of engines; or if he has not served an apprenticeship, three years' employment in a factory or workshop where engines are made or repaired will suffice; but in either case he must also have served one year at sea in the engine-room. If he has not been apprenticed to an engineer, nor worked in a factory for the stipulated time, four years' service at sea in the engine-room will qualify him. However or wherever he may have been employed, he must be able to give a description of boilers and the method of staying them, together with the use and management of the different valves, cocks, pipes, and connections. He must know how to correct defects from accident and decay, and to repair them, and to understand the use of the barometer, thermometer, hydrometer, and salinometer. He must state, when asked, the causes, effects, and remedies for incrustation; and his educational attainments must be ample enough to pass in the first five rules of arithmetic and decimals, besides which he will be questioned as to the construction and fixing of paddle and screw engines."

In selecting a "second engineer" to put in charge of a yacht's engines, one who is fresh from the factory or with only one year's sea service should be avoided; the "donkey man," who has worked up to his certificate at sea, on the other hand, will be a thoroughly reliable engineer to engage.

In engaging an engineer the owner should make it clearly understood to him that he will be under the authority and direction of the master. This understanding is absolutely necessary.

The actual wages paid on board some steam yachts when in commission will be found set forth in the table. The Soprano (*née* Marchesa) is an auxiliary steam yacht. The others are full-power steamers.

Crew.	Capercailzie, 529 tons.	Fair Geraldine, 300 tons.	Marchesa, 408 tons.	Eothen, 345 tons.	Bulldog, 60 tons.	Northern Light, 75 tons.	Cella, 25 tons.
	£ s.	£ s.	£ s.	£ s.	£ s.	£ s.	£ s.
Master	2 18	3 0	3 0	3 10	2 0	2 0	2 0
Mate	1 15	1 15	1 10	2 14	—	1 15	—
Second Mate	—	—	—	2 0	—	—	—
Boatswain	—	1 10	1 8	1 10	—	—	—
Coxswain	1 7	1 7	1 7	1 8	—	—	—
Carpenter	—	1 8	1 7	1 10	—	—	—
Seamen {	7 at 26s. 9 2	5 at 26s. 6 10	10 at 25s. 12 10	7 at 26s. 9 2	3 at 25s. 3 15	2 at 26s. 2 12	1 at 25s. 1 5
Boy	0 16	—	—	—	—	0 16	—
Engineer	2 10	3 0	4 0	3 0	3 0	2 10	2 10
Second Engineer	2 0	2 0	3 0	2 10	—	—	—
Fireman	1 9	1 10	1 10	1 7	1 10	1 8	—
Second Fireman	1 7	1 10	1 10	1 7	—	—	—
Third Fireman	—	—	1 10	1 7	—	—	—
Steward	1 15	2 0	1 10	2 0	1 15	1 15	1 10
Second Steward	0 15	1 10	1 8	1 10	—	—	—
Cook	1 10	1 10	1 15	2 0	—	—	—
Cook's Mate	—	1 5	1 0	1 8	—	—	—
Total per week	27 4	29 15	38 5	38 3	12 5	12 16	7 5

With regard to the wages paid on board these steam yachts, there is some variation so far as the engineers and other officers are concerned, but the wages to the seamen are about the same in each case; and it should be noted that the Soprano and Eothen carried three firemen because of the long passages they made. In addition to the high wages paid to engineers in the Soprano, they, with the master, stewards, and cooks, were paid board wages of 12*s*. per week each, and the master and engineer of Bulldog also received board wages. In Eothen and Fair Geraldine the master, stewards, and cook only were paid board wages. No board wages were paid on board Capercailzie, Northern Light, or Celia, the whole crew finding themselves. The firemen in both Bulldog and Northern Light were capable of taking charge of the engines when necessary, and, in the case of the former, two of the seamen were always on deck when making night passages. The Northern Light, it will be observed, carried two seamen and a mate; but this is accounted for by the fact that her owner acted as master, and took his watch in turn, so that in reality nothing should have been put down in the table for master.

The owner of a steam yacht who desires to become acquainted with the working of his engines should obtain the following books: "Yacht Architecture" (2*l*. 2*s*.), Horace Cox, Bream's Buildings, London, E.C.; "The Safe Use of Steam" (price 6*d*.), Crosby Lockwood and Co., 7, Stationers' Hall-court; Donaldson's "Practical Guide to Marine Steam Machinery" (5*s*.), Norie and Wilson, Minories, E.C.; Goodeve's Text-Book of the Steam Engine" (6*s*.), Crosby Lockwood and Co.; "The Marine Steam Engine, for the Use of the Officers of Her Majesty's Navy," by Richard Sennett, published by Longman, Paternoster-row, 1882; and a "Manual of Marine Engineering," by A. E. Seaton, revised 1890, by Griffin and Co., Exeter-street, Strand; the latter book is the most practical of those enumerated.

CHAPTER XXVI.

ICE YACHTS.

———

ATTRACTIVE pastimes like yacht and boat sailing ought to sink into insignificance compared with the fascinations of ice yachting, if speed alone be the cause of excitement. It is, however, difficult for a Briton to realise the extraordinary enthusiasm ice-boat racing or sailing give rise to in Canada, the United States, and some parts of Europe. The mere idea of being conveyed through the air in a boat at a rate equal to the speed of the fastest express train repels rather than fascinates; however, those who have experienced the extraordinary velocity of an ice yacht say that when the first dread of the lightning-like flight is overcome, longing for the fast travelling of an ice yacht supervenes.

Ice yachting in England has been attempted on many occasions, and in Folkard's "Sailing Boat" are numerous plans for making such contrivances; however, none of these agree with the American method of making ice yachts, but, as the Americans have had more experience of ice-yacht sailing than any other people in the world, we may take it for granted that their plan is in every way better adapted than any other for the attainment of high speed and safety. A winter seldom occurs in America when ice-boat sailing is not possible; and on the River Hudson and on the smaller lakes of Canada the sport is as much a winter amusement as cat-boat sailing is at the sea-side resorts during the summer months. In the British Isles we do not often get a long enough duration of frost to render ice yachting possible; but ice yachts have been constructed and sailed, and the frequent inquiry for information concerning them would lead one to think that, with suitable opportunities, ice yacht sailing would become as popular here as it is in North America; and, as the yachts are very simple and inexpensive to construct, there is no reason why the amusement should not be taken up by anyone who is acquainted with

boat sailing or boat steering. The engraving, Fig. 198, which we give
of the American ice yacht, Haze (owned by Mr. Aaron Innes, of Poughkeepsie, U.S.), is, we presume, a fair example of Transatlantic ice yachts,
although they are not all exactly alike in every detail. The different
parts of the yacht and the mode of construction can be readily understood
from the engraving, and all we need do is to describe these parts, and

FIG. 198. THE AMERICAN ICE YACHT "HAZE."

give the sizes of the material, such as used in the construction of the
Haze.*

The keel, or centre timber, is 24ft. 6in. long, 3in. wide, and 9in. deep
(an ordinary "deal"). The side frames are 2½in. thick and 4in. deep.

At the mast a timber, 1ft. wide, by 3in. thick and 7ft. 6in. long, is
fitted on top across the side frames. Underneath the mast timber is the

* The engraving is copied from the *Scientific American.*

"runner" plank, of 1ft. width, 8in. depth, and about 16ft. long, the side frames, mast plank, and "runner" plank being all bolted together. Sometimes the side framing is continued forward of the mast timber round to the bowsprit, and thus makes the construction look more boat-like.

The after part of the frame is bottom-planked with inch boards to form the deck.

The "runners" are three in number, one fixed to either end of the runner plank (which crosses the keel at right angles), and the third is fitted aft to the keel timber and rudder post, and is used as a rudder, the pintles being "upside down." This rudder-runner is usually somewhat smaller than the other two, and is fitted with a tiller for steering.

The runners are securely fitted, in a line parallel with the keel, to the ends of the transverse runner plank. They are 6in. deep, 2in. thick, and 2ft. 6in. or 3ft. long. Each runner is shod with steel, and rounded up at the fore end. The shoe is solid, and is 1⅜in. deep. One inch of this depth is ground to an angle of 90° **V**; the remaining ⅜in. forms the upper part of the shoe, and is square with the top, which is 2in. wide. The steel is "tapped" on the upper side about an inch deep. Into these taps ⅜in. bolts are screwed, and are long enough to pass through the runner and runner plank; their heads are then secured with counter-sunk nuts before the runner is fitted to the "runner plank."*

As a rule, nothing but the two sails are carried, and the ice yachts of Toronto have but one lateen sail. These lateen sails are similar to the sail shown by Fig. 199. The dimensions of the spars of the Haze are as follows:

Mast, step to cap	20ft.
Mast, diameter at heel	5in.
Mast, diameter at cap	3¼in.
Bowsprit, beyond mast	16ft. 6in.
Bowsprit, depth at mast	6in.
Bowsprit, depth at outer end	3in.
Bowsprit, width†	3¼in.

* In the Naval Museum, South Kensington, there is the model of a Finland ice boat. The runners of this boat are large skates, 7in. or 8in. deep, about 2ft. long, and about 1in. thick. They are very much rounded up at the fore end, like a Dutch skate. They are fastened by transverse bolts to the sides of pieces of timber of the same length as the skates. The cross timber, or "runner plank," is sunk into the top of the pieces of timber to which the two side skates are bolted. The after centre skate (there are three skates in all, including the rudder skate) is of similar pattern, and is fixed as a rudder. The keel of this boat is 24ft. The breadth across the runners is 12ft. The Finland model is also said to represent a "Canadian" ice boat. It is of the ⊥ form, with timbers fitted to it in an X form for strength. An ice boat constructed in 1878 for Lake Windermere had the "skates" pivoted to the runners, so as to have a fore and aft motion. The idea was to ease jolting in coming upon irregularities in the ice, but it is difficult to understand that the jolting could be relieved by such a method.

† The bowsprit is fitted to the keel by a clamp iron ⅜in. by ¼in., and by a through-bolt abaft the iron. The bowsprit can be a mere continuation of the keel timber.

	ft.	in.
Jibboom, length (when one is fitted)	15	3
Jibboom, diameter at centre	0	2½
Jibboom, diameter at ends	0	2
Mainboom, length	29	4
Mainboom, diameter at centre	0	4½
Mainboom, diameter at ends	0	2⅞
Gaff, length	8	9
Gaff, diameter	0	2
Mainsail, luff	14	6
Mainsail, foot	28	0
Mainsail, head	8	0
Foresail, leech	15	0
Foresail, luff	22	0
Foresail, foot	14	6

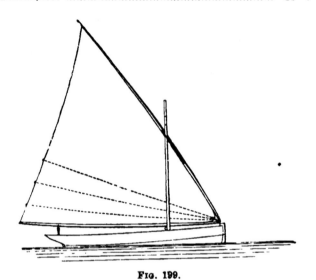

FIG. 199.

The ice boats are usually of about the dimensions given; but one, the Icicle, owned by Mr. J. A. Roosevelt, has a framework 32ft. long, is 26ft. between the runners, and the runners are 7ft. 6in. These appear to be extreme dimensions.

Another very successful ice yacht was the Jack Frost, designed and built by Mr. Archibald Rogers, and here represented by Figs. 200, 201, 202.

The favourite points of sailing are with the wind a point or so before the beam, right abeam, or a point abaft the beam. With such a wind, a straight course over perfectly smooth ice, free from hummocks and cracks, and with half a gale of wind, it is claimed that these yachts can and do travel at the rate of sixty or more miles an hour. Every winter we see numerous records of such time made, and they are apparently well authenticated; at any rate, it seems incredible that, year after year, American gentlemen should enter into a conspiracy to deliberately publish false times.

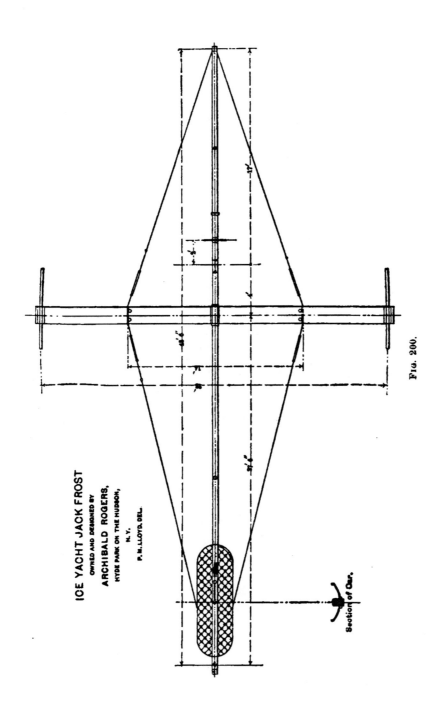

ICE YACHT JACK FROST
OWNED AND DESIGNED BY
ARCHIBALD ROGERS,
HYDE PARK ON THE HUDSON,
N.Y.
P. M. LLOYD, DEL.

Section of Oar.

FIG. 200.

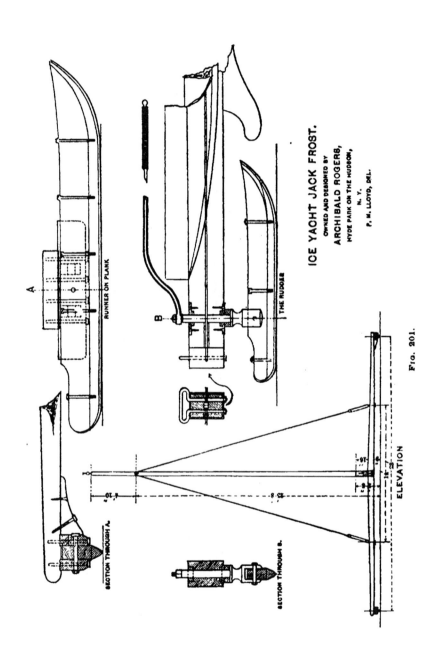

ICE YACHT JACK FROST.

OWNED AND DESIGNED BY

ARCHIBALD ROGERS,

HYDE PARK ON THE HUDSON,

N. Y.

P. M. LLOYD, DEL.

THE RUDDER

RUNNER ON PLANK

SECTION THROUGH A.

SECTION THROUGH B.

ELEVATION

Fig. 201.

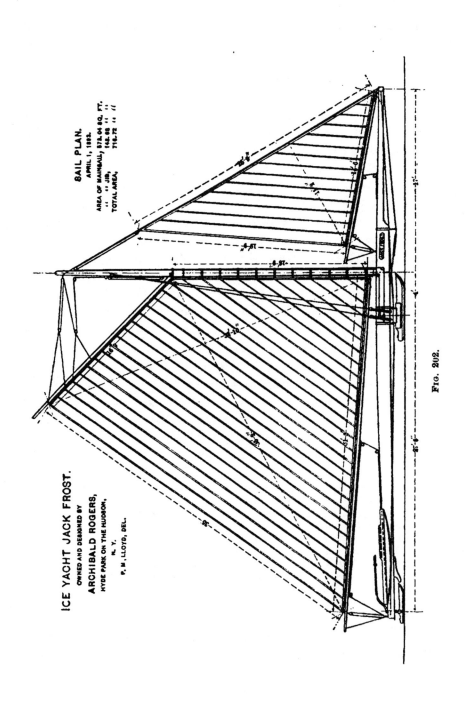

FIG. 202.

ICE YACHT JACK FROST.

OWNED AND DESIGNED BY

ARCHIBALD ROGERS,

HYDE PARK ON THE HUDSON,
N. Y.

P. M. LLOYD, DEL.

SAIL PLAN.

APRIL 1, 1882.

AREA OF MAINSAIL, 573.04 SQ. FT.
" " JIB, 142.68 " "
TOTAL AREA, 716.72 " "

There is not the shadow of a reason for believing that the time given for making a mile (a statute mile is here understood) is persistently exaggerated.*

An elucidation of the phenomenon of a vessel sailing faster than the wind has frequently been attempted; but, up to the time when this chapter was written in 1879, with no clear conception of the mechanical principles involved. In the first place, it must be distinctly understood that a boat's speed before a wind which blows with a constant velocity cannot equal the speed of the wind; under different conditions it is conceivable, and in accordance with mechanical principles, that the speed of a boat may equal, and greatly exceed, that of the wind. If the boat were before a wind which is travelling at the rate of 30 sea miles an hour, the direct impulse of the wind on the sails, if *fixtures,* would be equal to 6lb. per square foot. But the sails are not fixtures, and move before, or away from, the wind with the boat; the pressure is thereby gradually diminished until it is balanced by the resistance met with by the boat on the ice. As the resistance of an ice boat is very small, a high speed—nearly equal to that of the wind—is reached before the resistance and the wind pressure become uniform. Thus, say the velocity of the wind were 30 miles an hour, and the speed of the boat 20 miles an hour, the resultant pressure of the wind would be only of that due to a wind speed of 10 miles, or about ⅔lb. per square foot. But if the wind makes a more or less acute angle with the line of advance, the conditions are entirely altered; the pressure of the wind does not diminish with the advance of the boat, and its effective impulse is determinable on mechanical principles, which will admit as possible a speed of the boat much greater than the actual speed of the

* The following extract from a letter, copied from the *Spirit of the Times,* March 1, 1879, whilst it gives a denial to the fictitious speed attributed to some ice yachts, confirms the report of the amazing velocity an ice yacht is capable of: "As to the speed of ice yachts much has been said, and a great deal has been said devoid of truth. A wind on the beam—what we call three-quarters free—is the wind for speed, and there are times that a yacht attains a speed of sixty-five to seventy miles per hour (in fact, there is no limit to their speed, conditions of ice and wind favourable); but the yacht is not able to maintain this high speed long, as the helmsman is continually obliged to deviate from a straight course, on account of hummocks, cracks, or rough ice; beyond this the course of a yacht is always zigzag instead of straight. I have often, in company with Commodore Grinnell, of the N.H.I.B. Club, raced with the express trains on the Hudson River Railroad. We would beat down on a train with a good west wind, and often run side and side with the train over a mile; then the wind would lighten up, and the train would draw ahead. At other times we would pass a train like a rocket, and run a mile and a half ahead, when we would be compelled to tack across the river and get away again. Meantime the train would crawl up, only to be beaten again for a mile or two. The fastest time between Poughkeepsie and New Hamburgh that I know of was made this winter. The distance is nine and three-quarter miles, and the run was made by the yacht Zephyr. of the N.H.I.B.C., in ten minutes. The Phantom made the same run, some years ago, in twelve minutes. The yacht Whiz was reported, and has a record of the same course of nine and three-quarter miles in seven minutes. This is another mistake as she never made the time, but it went the round of the papers all the same."

wind. However, it is practically impossible that any water-borne boat propelled by sails could ever be made to exceed the speed of the wind which impelled it, on account of the enormous growth of the resistance due to wave-making; but "ice yachts" may be regarded as having almost no head-resistance; the slightest force will give them motion, and keep them moving. The only friction is from the lee runner, as when sailing the weather runner seldom touches the ice, and the lee runner, cutting into the ice, prevents excessive leeway.

To illustrate the principles involved, it will be assumed as a fact

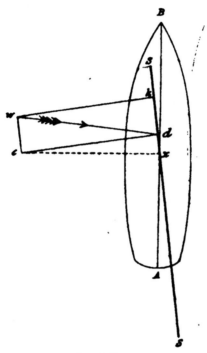

FIG. 203.

that ice boats in America have been timed to sail at the rate of one mile in a minute by the aid of a force due to a velocity of thirty sea miles an hour of the wind. Such a wind force is termed a "fresh gale" by sailors, and a ship would be under reefed topsails, reefed courses, or possibly fore and mizen topsails furled. In Fig. 203 we will suppose A B to be an ice boat fixed so that it cannot move. The line *w d* represents on a scale the direction and force or speed of the wind equal to 30 miles an hour. The line *s s* represents the balance lug sail of an ice yacht. It is obvious that the wind, blowing on the sail from the direction shown, would tend to drive the boat in the direction of its own motion. But the force *w d* is made up of two components—one, *c d*, is acting at right angles to the sail, and the other, *d k*, acting along the plane of the sail without any potent effect. The component *c d* can be further regarded as a force made up of three other components—one, *c z*, acting at right angles to the keel of the vessel, and tending to drive her to leeward;

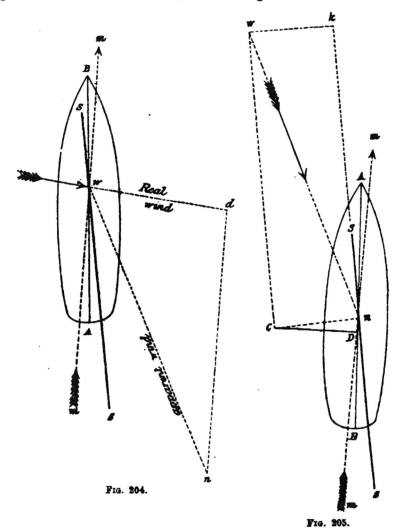

Fig. 204.

Fig. 205.

another, *z d*, acts in a line with the vessel's keel, and tending to drive her ahead. The third force is resolved vertically in a downward direction, and need not be considered.

Hitherto we have only dealt with the "real wind," and we have now to consider what takes place when a boat, under the influence of *z d*, gathers way, or commences to move in a direction to meet the wind at

a more or less acute angle. In Fig. 204 A B is the boat set in motion*
by the component of the wind *x d*, and is proceeding in the direction
of the arrow *m m*; the difference between the arrow and the keel line
represents the angle of leeway, or amount of leeway made. The dotted
line *w d* represents the direction and velocity of the real wind, as in
Fig. 203; but the wind *apparently* will now be blowing more ahead, and
it is the *apparent wind* with which we have to deal. The apparent wind
is thus determined : On a line parallel to *m m* set off a distance (see *d n*,
Fig. 204) by scale (same as the wind scale) to represent an opposing motion
equal to the speed of the boat (assumed in this case to be sixty miles an
hour, or double the velocity of the wind). Join *n w*, and the dotted line *n w*
will represent the force and direction of the *apparent wind*.

This apparent wind must now be regarded as the propelling force,
and not the real wind as shown in Fig. 203. In Fig. 205 let the dotted
line *w n* represent the direction and force of the *apparent* wind; by a
parallelogram of forces the line of force *w n* has two components, one
acting in the direction *w c*, or *k n*, and the other in the direction *c n*.
The component *c n* is farther resolved into three components, as before
shown by Fig. 203, represented by *c* D and D *n* in Fig. 205, and another
acting vertically, not shown. It is the component D *n* which impels the
boat forward. It will be seen that the force D *n* is very small, or only
about one-seventh of the force *c* D, which is striving to drive the boat to
leeward; but the resistance to leeway is very great, whilst the resistance
to headway is very small. Consequently the boat moves a scarcely
perceptible distance in a broadside direction, but gathers speed in the
direction of her keel, or rather in the direction of the line *m m*, which
includes the broadside motion or leeway. The boat continues to gather
way or increase in speed from the rest position shown in Fig. 203 until
the resistance she meets with, from friction of the skates on the ice and
resistance to the rigging, &c., equals the force shown by D *n*. The speed
of the boat then remains uniform so long as the wind is constant.

If the speed could be increased, by diminishing the resistance, beyond
sixty miles an hour, *with the same wind force*, the apparent wind would
draw more ahead, and then obviously the effective impulse, D *n*, would
be further diminished, until the apparent wind were brought right ahead,
when D *n* would disappear altogether; the sails would " lift," and a fresh
start would have to be made.

From what has been said it will be concluded that on any point
of sailing between a quarterly wind and a wind on the bow, if any great

* The sail is represented as hauled flat in. In practice the sail would be well off at the
moment of starting, and would be gradually hauled aboard as the speed increased and the
apparent wind drew more ahead.

speed is realised, the boom must be hauled close aboard, the exact angle with the keel being determined by the speed of the boat or by the direction of the apparent wind, and not by the direction of the real wind. When a point dead to leeward has to be made, it is thought that the point is reached more quickly by hauling up to 45° from the course, and then, when half-way, gybing or tacking, and making for the point to be reached, thus traversing a right angle.

The subject of the speed of ice yachts is frequently cropping up, and the mechanical principles involved in propelling them at speeds greater than the velocity of the wind we have just explained. The subject is, however, of ever recurring interest, and the paper read in 1893 at the Marine Engineering and Naval Architecture Congress in the United States, by Mr. Archibald Rogers, imparted new interest to ice yacht sailing. The scientific exposition of the phenomenon of sailing faster than the wind (or the propelling force) is travelling was supplied by Mr. Nathaniel Herreshoff, the well-known Rhode Island engineer, the general result of the investigation being as follows : " The closest the boat will sail to the real wind is 30°, or 2⅔ points. The best course, or the one which will take the boat farthest to windward, is 60°, or 5⅓ points from the wind, when the advance to windward would be at the rate of half the velocity of the real wind. . . . The greatest speed of the boat is attained when 120°, or 10⅔ points from the wind, then her speed is twice that of the real wind." In connection with this matter, Mr. Archibald Rogers says : " One point must always be borne in mind, and that is that an ice yacht is always sailed with her sails trimmed flat in, whether in beating to windward or driving off the wind." The fact is, the wind which has to be dealt with in propulsion by sails is, as we have already explained, the "apparent wind," which always appears to blow more or less ahead, according to the speed of the vessel propelled, excepting when sailing dead before the wind. Mr. Rogers gives records of speeds made on various courses, from which it appears that his own ice yacht Jack Frost has made the best recorded speed by sailing round a square course of twenty miles at the rate of one mile in 1min. 34sec., or 39·4 miles an hour. The quickest time on a measured mile, recorded under the most favourable conditions for speed, is 59sec., or at the rate of 61 miles an hour. Mr. Rogers, however, states that in sailing up and down the Hudson between known points, passages have been made at the rate of 80 miles an hour. He qualifies this statement as follows : " That this great speed is probable or possible is not to be doubted, but it occurs very seldom on the Hudson, as the danger of colliding with the rocky shores makes each helmsman keep his slippery charge under control."

RACES FOR THE ICE-YACHT CHALLENGE PENNANT OF AMERICA.

Name of Winning Yacht.	Club.	Date.	Distance between Buoys in Miles.	Number of Times Sailed Over.	Total Length of Course in Miles.	Calculated Distance Sailed in Miles.	Time.			Apparent Time per Mile.	Calculated Actual Time per Mile.
							h.	m.	s.	m. s.	m. s.
Phantom	New Hamburg vs. Poughkeepsie	March 5, 1881	....	....	20	....	0	57	14	2 51	—
Avalanche or Robert Scott	Poughkeepsie vs. New Hamburg	February 6, 1883	10	Once	20	31.38	0	57	0	2 51	1 49
Jack Frost	Poughkeepsie vs. North Shrewsbury	February 23, 1883	2½	Five	25	39.20	1	14	35	2 59	1 54
Haze	Poughkeepsie vs. North Shrewsbury	February 9, 1884	6 66/100	Three	20	31.38	1	5	30	3 16	2 5
Haze	Poughkeepsie vs. New Hamburg	February 14, 1885	2	Five	20	31.38	1	1	15	3 3	1 57
Northern Light	Poughkeepsie vs. North Shrewsbury	February 18, 1885	2½	Four	20	31.38	1	8	42	3 26	2 11
Jack Frost	Hudson River vs. Poughkeepsie	February 14, 1887	2	Four	16	25.10	0	43	40	2 43	1 40
Icicle	Hudson River vs. North Shrewsbury	March 8, 1888	2	Three	12	18.83	0	36	59	3 4	1 57
Icicle	Hudson River vs. North Shrewsbury	February 25, 1889	2	Four	16	25.10	0	51	41	3 13	2 3
Icicle	Hudson River vs. North Shrewsbury	February 5, 1892	1 48/100	Five	14 10/16	22.92	0	46	19	3 9	2 1
Jack Frost	Hudson River vs. Orange Lake	February 9, 1893	2	Five	20	31.38	0	49	30	2 28	1 34

Sailing for a point dead to windward is not such rapid work, and we believe ice yachts do not make a course nearer than 3½ points of the real wind, and their speed over the ice is not one-half of what it is with a beam wind, but still it is believed to equal the speed of the wind—but this is very doubtful.

The usual mode of coming to rest from a high speed is by running off to dead before the wind, and then luffing to sharply until head to wind. The boat is "anchored" by turning the "rudder runner" right across the keel.

The ice yachts just described would be much too heavy for sailing on the thin ice of our lakes, and Mr. Herbert Crossley for Windermere built one of very slight construction, as shown in Fig. 206.

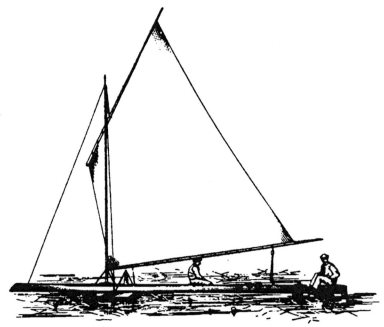

FIG. 206.

The fore-and-aft frames are made of yellow pine, 34ft. long, 9in. deep, and 1in. thick. These are spaced 1ft. 3in. apart (inside measurement) with a bottom plank of equal thickness; thus the structure forms an open box. Besides the bottom plank the fore-and-aft frames are connected forward by a cross piece of pine 9in. by 1in., in which is an eye-bolt for the forestay.

Aft is a similar cross piece 9in. broad fixed 2ft. 6in. from the end, and forms a seat for the steersman.

The foreside of the runner frame is 10ft. 6in. from the fore end of the frames, and is also of 1in. pine, 3ft. broad and 12ft. across from runner to runner. The runner frame is secured by screw bolts and nuts to the bottom plank, and also by 1in. iron stays, screwed up by a nut on an iron stanchion of 1in. iron. The stanchion is fitted with a shoulder at its lower end, and is screwed up with a nut underneath the bottom of the box and the runner frame. Two other stays of ½in. iron connect the head of the stanchion with the top edge of the fore-and-aft frames. This construction will be seen in Fig. 207.

The runners are 4ft. 3in. long and 3in. deep, also of 1in. pine, securely attached to the runner frames. On the lower edge is the steel skate, ¼in. thick and 2in. or 3in. deep. The lower edge is bevelled to make a sharp edge of about 45°. The flat side of the sharp edge is outside. These skates are rounded up at the ends like an ordinary skate. They are screwed to the side of the runner, or they can be let into a channel ploughed out of the underside of the wood runner and then be secured by screws.

The after runners are glass bullseyes, as shown by *b* in Fig. 208,

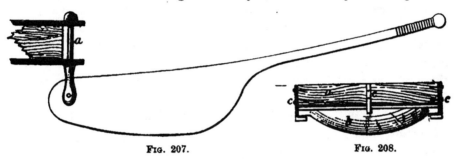

FIG. 207.   FIG. 208.

about 8in. in diameter. The bullseyes were cast with shoulders as shown, and secured to a wood circular chock by clamps, *c c c*, Fig. 208. The wood is 2½in. thick, and between it and the glass is a sort of buffer made of ½in. felt; india rubber will not do, as it gets hard or freezes. The bullseye is 1¾in. thick, ½in. of the thickness forming the shoulder for the clips *c c c* to take hold of. Through the centre of the wood a bolt with a broad head is passed (the head is sunk into the wood) and screwed up by a nut through the bottom plank on the under-side of the fore-and-aft frame. These glass runners are fitted nearly as far aft as the seat of the steersman.

The bullseyes were introduced to admit of the boat being readily swung round under the influence of the rudder.

Fig. 207 shows the rudder, 1ft. 3in. long, 4in. deep, with a handle 1ft. 9in. long. The rudder is of iron with under edge of steel ground to 9° thus, $\vee$. The under edge of the rudder has a longer bearing than shown in Fig. 207, or is deeper under the bolt *a*. The bolt *a* passes through two iron plates which are secured to a cross piece of 2in. deal, worked above the bottom board. It will be seen that the rudder is capable of an up-and-down motion as well as lateral. The bolt *a* is 2ft. 9in. from the fore edge of the seat of the steersman. To allow of the lateral motion of the rudder, a large dove-tailed slot $>$ is cut out of the bottom board, 1ft. 9in. long, and 1ft. across at the after end. The bolt *a* comes at the pointed end of the slot. A circular piece is cut out of the side of each fore-and-aft frame to allow the handle of the rudder to be put well over. The rudder, of course, is not intended to be used as a runner, as it is in the American ice yachts, but is used to assist in stopping the yacht by pressing it into the ice.

Six inches forward of the fore edge of the steersman's seat a cross piece is fitted, projecting on each side to form a place for the feet. Of course, this cross piece is fitted to the underside of the frame.

The mast is stepped in a chock on the bottom plank, 10ft. from the fore end of the frame, and is secured by three iron stays attached to an iron band round the mast 2ft. above the bottom plank. One stay forward, and one on each side leading a little aft. Besides these stays the mast has a shroud on each side, set up by a lanyard to the runner frame and a forestay.

Mast from the bottom plank to shoulder 22ft., luff of mainsail 11ft. 6in., leech 29ft. 6in., foot 20ft., head 17ft. 3in., tack to peak earing 26ft. 3in., clew to weather earing 25ft., slings 6ft. 3in. from weather earing.

The boom works on the mast by a gooseneck fitted into a socket on the iron band which goes round the mast for the lower stays before referred to.

The sail, it will be seen, is a standing lug.

During the severe winter of 1890-91 an ice boat was made by "Belooch" for use on the Ruislip reservoir, near London. He thus described it: The drawings (Plate CXV.) give all the necessary details for building a boat which will pack in a small space, and can be put together easily in half an hour by two men. The greatest length when in pieces is 12ft. 2in. The greatest breadth is in the runner plank, viz., 1ft. 6in, with blocks attached. These blocks should never be removed when once accurately fitted, as it is of vital importance that the runners should be always parallel. The actual irons are easily removable for portage by drawing the pins on which they rock. A canvas laced to the frame battens forms a most luxurious lounge for the crew and passengers. For clamping all the parts together, eye bolts are the handiest form. These should screw into plates fixed on the lower surface of the runner plank. In the stern the eyes should be on opposite sides, for the purpose of attaching the sheet. The use of eye bolts obviates carrying any wrenches or other tools. All planks and battens throughout should be of best yellow pine. Runner blocks and stern piece of oak, or other hard wood. The whole to be carefully varnished, as snow water is most penetrating.

The rudder-post should be covered with brass tubing, as it is likely to get fixed in a frost if the wood has become wet. The tiller must be kept high, to clear the reclining crew, and be about 5ft. long.

The best runners are wrought iron, shod with steel. They should be pivotted on a stout pin, slightly in advance of their centre, so as to trail on the ice, thus correcting any small deviation from their true course. A right angle bevel offers the least resistance, combined with sufficient grip to prevent leeway. When putting the runners away they should be carefully coated with Aspinall or other paint, as rust will considerably

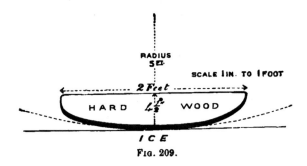

Fig. 209.

retard the boat's progress. A good makeshift runner can be made of flat 3in. by 1in. bar iron, the surface next the ice being honed up. The curve of a Canadian canoe bow is a very good one to imitate in the fore part of runner. Lighter runners with more curve than those shown on Plate CXV. are better for light boats.

This pattern is of hard wood, shod with square section 1 bar iron or steel, 2ft. long, by 4½in. at greatest depth, 1¼in. thick. Curve of iron on the ice a radius of 5ft.

An ice boat of the above description has been running on Ruislip reservoir, near Pinner, for the last four winters, and has certainly attained a speed of over twenty miles an hour at times when there was no snow on the ice. Let the novice beware of getting any part of his person in front of the runner plank, as a sudden puff of wind would be likely to break both his legs at once. Extra passengers can get a very comfortable seat on the runner plank, with their feet towards the stern. The skipper must never let go the tiller, for should the rudder scoot sideways, something will break.

FIG. 210.

FIG. 211.

To stop, run the boat into the wind, and put the helm hard over; she will not restart with the runner across.

Extreme length	18ft.
Extreme breadth	9ft.
Runner plank	9ft. × 8in. × 3in
Thwart	7ft. × 8in. × 1½in.
Mast hole	3in.
Side battens	12ft. 2in. × 3in. × 2in.
Middle battens	12ft. × 3in. × 2in.
Space between middle battens	3in.
Stern, front width	1ft. 4in.
,, back width	11in.
,, side	9in.
,, depth	6in.
,, gap for battens	3in. × 2in.
Rudder skate, length	2ft.
,, ,, height	6in.
,, ,, width	2in.
Rudder block, length	1ft. 6in.
,, ,, height	6½in.
,, ,, width	6in.
,, ,, gap for skate	2in. × 3in.
Shoulder on rudder block, on which stern rests	height, 1½in.
Runners—skate, length	3ft.
,, ,, height	6in.
,, ,, width	2in.
,, block, length	1ft. 6in.
,, ,, height	6½in.
,, ,, width	6in.
,, gap for skate	2in. × 3in.
A standing lug sail.	
Luff	9ft. 3in.
Leach	30ft.
Foot	19ft.
Head	18ft.
Tack to peak earing	26ft. 6in.
Clew to weather earing	21ft.

Yard to be slung 9ft. from the weather earing.
A small jib could also be carried.

Figs. 210 and 211 show two views of the ice boat under sail.

CHAPTER XXVII.

CANOEING.

BRITISH canoeing includes many forms of canoes, but what is known as "canoe yawls" is the only form we shall deal with.

Plate CXVI. represents a canoe yawl, built for Mr. W. Baden Powell by Turk, of Kingston-on-Thames, who has had great experience in canoe building. The timbers are 1ft. apart; the keel in the wake of the centre-board slot is sided at rabbet line 2½in., and is 2in. at lower edge; the sliding forward and aft of this should not be less than 1½in.

For hard work teak is recommended for the keel; but red pine is quite strong enough for all ordinary work.

A combination of mahogany and cedar, well seasoned, forms a strong and light planking; the three lower strakes mahogany (the garboard very wide), and the three upper strakes of cedar, ranging from about a quarter to three-eighths of an inch in thickness.

Various modes of planking have been tried with the object of obtaining a smooth outer surface, and a light but strong skin; of these the most successful are the "clincher," the "ribband carvel," and the "double skin." The "double skin" plan is as follows: When the stem and stern posts have been set up and fastened off, and the building moulds carefully and strongly fixed in position, and firmly battened round at their heads by a kind of temporary gunwale, and the centre-board case or cases fitted and fixed, this framework is turned upside down, and again fixed in position. Thin, well-steamed planks of cedar, about "wager boat" thickness, are tacked in position edge to edge, over the moulds, as if for carvel-planking; over this is then laid, plank by plank, a somewhat thicker skin of steamed cedar, the edges of which come over the centres of the planks of the inner skin. The two skins are then fastened off as if one, along the rabbet line, with brass screws; the edges of the outer skin are then pierced along and copper nailed as in ordinary building. The craft is then turned up and the nails are clenched off on the inside. It will also be found necessary on some strakes to nail along the inner skin edges also. In such case the holes will be bored from inside and nails driven from outside. Very few timbers will be needed, and the double skin will be found to possess great strength. A good coat of varnish or strips of varnished calico between the skins would no doubt add greatly to the strength and watertightness of the structure.

In the ribband-carvel build (see Fig. 212), the planks of, say ⅛in. to ⅜in. stuff, are tacked on to the building moulds edge to edge. Ribbands of clean-grained oak, about 1¼in. wide and ¼in. or ⅜in. thick, are laid along on the inside of the joints of the plank between the timbers which are placed in the vertical positions shown in the sheer plan; the edges of the planks are then pierced and nailed through the ribbands, and clenched on the inside, or they may be screwed into the ribbands. A stronger plan is to work a ¼in. ribband in whole lengths, cutting out

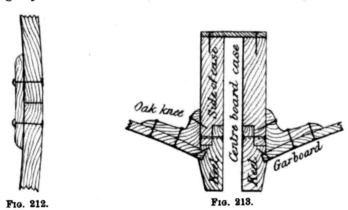

FIG. 212.   FIG. 213.

notches in the backs of the timbers and moulds to take each ribband. In all cases a strip of varnished linen should be laid over the joints of the plank before the batten is fitted, and the linen should be continuous from end to end. The timbers are about ⅜in. sided by ¼in. moulded. No doubt this mode, and that of the double skin, give a very fine outer surface; but the number of nails required is nearly double that employed in a clincher-built boat, and with neat workmanship a clincher boat can be built with next to no "lands" showing on the outside, and yet be of sufficient strength.

The garboard plank will be 6in. or 8in. wide at the broadest part, and the other planks will be as broad as the shape of the canoe will admit of being worked, and will of course vary in breadth and shape.

The construction of the section at slot in the keel and centreboard case is shown by Fig. 213.

K K

A convenient mode of "laying off" a canoe for building will be obtained by referring to "Boat Building" in the Appendix.

Three square feet area of centre-board has in practice been found amply sufficient.

For pumping and baling on rivers or small lakes a sponge and a baler will be ample; but for sea or large lake cruising it is a necessity to have an effective pump.

A class of boat has been in favour on the Mersey for some years, which is well adapted for "paddling and sailing" in the open sea. Plate CXVII. represents one of the earliest of these canoes, built for Mr. C. Arthur Inman in 1877. Although these Mersey sailing boats are termed "canoes" and "canoe yawls," they are as much "sailing boats" as the Surbiton gigs are. It is true that they have grown out of the

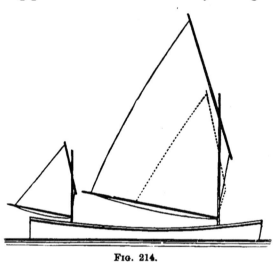

Fig. 214.

Rob Roy canoe; but a vessel 20ft. long, 5ft. 6in. broad, and 2ft. 6in. deep, which carries "passengers," 8cwt. or 9cwt. of ballast, has a large sail area, and is, moreover, rowed and not "paddled," is better described by the word "boat" than "canoe."

The boats originally were only about 17ft. long, with a breadth of 4ft. 6in. and varying depth; but the type has been so much approved of that a length of 20ft. has been reached, with 10cwt. of lead and a centre-plate 4ft. by 2ft. They are decked all over, excepting the well, which has a coaming all round, and is usually of the form shown in the drawing. The well is carried so far forward to enable the crew to reach the mast, or anything forward of it, without getting on the deck. The canoes are clench built, of white or yellow pine, usually ⅜in. thickness when worked up. The stem and sternpost are alike, 1¼in sided, with 2¼in.

outside rabbet, and about 3in. inside, enough to take the plank fastenings and serve as apron.

The steering arrangement is very capitally contrived with yokes coupled by rods or chains as a tiller, as shown. Strengthening pieces (running fore and aft) are worked above and below the deck, through which a bolt with collar passes, and is secured with nut and washer underneath. On the upper part of the bolt, above the collar, the yoke and tiller (all in one) are shipped on the bolt, and kept from unshipping by a pin. In case the tiller and yoke be of wood, a brass socket is fitted in the hole to prevent the collar of the boat wearing away the wood.

In the 17ft. boats about 1cwt. of ballast is carried, in flat lead or iron bricks. These boats carry three passengers; two sitting aft on the stern sheets, and one on the fore seat.

The rig (*see* Fig. 214) originally consisted of main and mizen; and in strong winds, with small mainsail and small storm mizen, they sail fast, and are dry. As they are decked in, these little boats may be seen out in all weathers, and are considered as dry and safe as the New Brighton boats; but, of course, could not compete with them.

In form the boats are comparatively full forward, and have a long clean after-body; compared with the usual run of sailing boats, they are longer in proportion to their breadth, but if cut off at No. 7 section they would not much differ from the ordinary sailing boat.

The fixed keel is usually considered sufficient, in the way of dead wood, to check lee-way; but of course when a centre-board has been fitted it has been found to greatly improve the weatherly qualities of the canoe.

The main and mizen rig is found to answer well, and the boats stay well under it in smooth water. In rough water, like all boats, they require to be handled with care in tacking; and if a boat seems likely to miss stays, the helmsman helps her round with a stroke of an oar. However, generally they are backed round by hauling the foot of the mainsail to windward if they hang in stays; but the oar, if used, has this advantage— it keeps the boat going.

	ft.	in.		ft.	in.
Mainsail, foot	10	0	Small mainsail, tack to peak earing	9	0
Mainsail, head	10	0	Small mainsail, clew to weather		
Mainsail, luff	5	0	earing	7	0
Mainsail, leech	14	6	Mizen, foot	4	6
Mainsail, tack to peak earing	14	8	Mizen, head	2	6
Mainsail, clew to weather earing	10	9	Mizen, luff	2	4
Small mainsail, foot	6	6	Mizen, leech	6	0
Small mainsail, head	7	6	Mizen, tack to peak earing	5	9
Small mainsail, luff	2	6	Mizen, clew to weather earing	4	9

It will be seen that the sails are not laced. The boom is fitted with goose-neck or jaws to the mast, and the tack is bowsed down by a rope which leads through a block on the aft side of mast on the deck.

On Plate CXVIII. are the lines of one of the larger canoes, named Vital Spark, which proved in every way a satisfactory craft.

She is 18ft. long by 5ft. beam, and her extreme draft is 2ft. 2in.; she is carvel built of ⅝in. planking, which is well seasoned, and carefully selected yellow pine; her timbers are of oak, ⅜in., and are spaced 6in. apart. The top strake is of teak, as also the deck, which is in three pieces of ⅜in., and is supported by thick beams of white pine. The coaming round the cockpit is of American elm, ½in.; the stem, sternpost, and all knees and breasthook are of oak; the bulkheads are placed 5ft. from either end, and are made of teak, ¼in.; they are watertight as possible; lockers

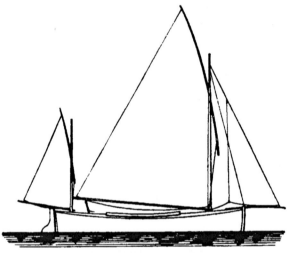

Fig. 215.

run fore and aft perpendicular with the coaming, they are also of teak and are very neatly fitted; when not in use air bags or zinc cases can be put in them, making the craft as safe as a lifeboat; the floor boards are of pine, ½in., and are laid on beams of oak, 1in., sided and moulded; the keel is of American elm, 3½in. in the middle, tapering to 1¼in.; it is rockered 8in., and has 4½ cwt. of lead on it; the remainder of the ballast, 4½ cwt., is cast to fit under the platform.

The sail plan includes headsail, as shown by Fig. 215 has an area of 178 square feet, and is convenient for cruising, but for racing it would be about 300 square feet.

Another Mersey canoe is shown on Plate CXIX. She was built in 1890 for Mr. W. B. Jameson, and proved a successful craft. She, like the other, is carvel built; plank, ¾in.; timbers, 1in. × ⅝in; spaced 7½in. Ballast, 6 cwt.

Area of mainsail, 251 sq. ft.; headsail, 49 sq. ft. Total sail area, 300 sq. ft.

The builder of the Mersey canoes is Mr. Samuel Bond, Mersey-street, Birkenhead. Sailmaker, Mr. J. E. Jarvis, 8, Tabley-street, Liverpool.

A good material for the sails would be "⅞ Bleached Linen Drill," made by Messrs. Foster Connor and Son, Linen Hall, Belfast. This material has been used for the lugs of centre-board gigs with excellent results.

Mr. Samuel Bond will give particulars as to cost, &c., of the tent.

The Humber yawl canoes bear a remarkable family likeness to the large Mersey canoe with the addition of a centre-plate, as represented by the Viking (Plate CXX.) (designed by her owner, Mr. John M. Hamilton). She somewhat differs in her under-water form from the general type met with on the Mersey.

	Viking.	Vital Spark.
Length over all	18ft.	18ft.
Length on water line	17ft. 7in.	17ft. 9in.
Beam, extreme	5ft.	5ft.
Draught of water, extreme	2ft. 5in.	2ft. 2in.
Area of mid-section	6 sq. ft.	5·6 sq. ft.
Displacement (1 ton 14cwt.) (1 ton 13cwt.)	1·7 ton.	1·65 ton.
Centre of buoyancy after centre of length of L.W.L.	0·9ft.	0·25ft.
Weight of iron keel	4¾cwt.	4½cwt.
Weight of inside ballast	7cwt.	4½cwt.
Weight of centre-plate	1½cwt.	—
Area of centre-plate exposed	5 sq. ft.	—
Area of mainsail	103 sq. ft.	—
Area of mizen	33 sq. ft.	—
Area of jib	24 sq. ft.	—
Total area	160 sq. ft.	178 sq. ft.

TABLE OF OFFSETS—VIKING.

Nos. of Sections.	1	2	3	4	5	6	7	8
	ft. in.	ft. in.	ft. in.	ft. in.	ft. in.	ft. in.	ft. in.	ft. in.
Height L.W.L. to top of gunwale	2 0	1 9	1 6¼	1 4½	1 3	1 2	1 2	1 3
Depths L.W.L. to underside keel	1 6	1 10	2 0½	2 1½	2 2½	2 3	2 4	2 5
Half breadths at gunwale	1 0	1 8	2 1	2 3¾	2 4½	2 3½	2 1	1 6¼
Half breadths at L.W.L.	0 7½	1 4	1 10½	2 2¼	2 4	2 3	2 0	1 4½
Half breadths W.L. 2	0 5	1 0	1 6½	1 11¼	2 2	2 1½	1 9	1 0¼
Half breadths W.L. 3	0 2	0 7	1 0	1 4¼	1 7½	1 7	1 3½	0 7¾
Half breadths W.L. 4	—	0 2¾	0 5½	0 8	0 10	0 10	0 8	0 3¾

The sections are 2ft. apart, and No. 1 is 2ft. from fore side of the stem at the gunwale. The water lines are 6in. apart.

The scantlings of the Viking are as follows:

Keel of American helm, sided, 6in., and moulded 4in.

Sternpost, 2¾in. sided and 4½in. moulded ; stem, 2½in. sided and 5in. moulded, bevelled to a ⅞in. edge, with galvanised iron band over it.

Bent timbers of American elm, sided 1⅛in. and moulded 1in.

Floors of oak, 2in. by 2in., and 3½in. deep in the throats.   There are three of these floor timbers.   One at the fore end of the centre-board case runs up to within 1ft. 3in. of the gunwale; the next is at the after end of the case, and rises to the level of the floor of cockpit; the third is midway between the aft end of centre-board case and the stern post, with 18in. arms.

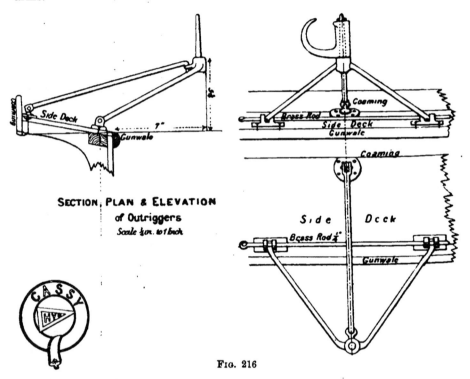

SECTION, PLAN & ELEVATION
of Outriggers
Scale ½in. to 1 foot

FIG. 216

The ribbands are of American elm, and 1½in. by 1in., and are notched to go over the bent timbers, as shown in the sketch, and the floor timbers are in turn notched to take the ribbands.

The plank is of larch, ½in. thick; deck plank, ½in. thick, and hatch, ⅜in., with battens underneath; hatch coaming, ¼in. thick; waterways, ⅝in. thick. The centre-board case is of 1¼in. pitch pine, and fastened with long through bolts to keel, set up with screw nuts on top of the case, the middle oak floor being cut through in the throat to admit the case and board.   Also on this floor timber there is a cross beam to the case, which also serves for the floor of the well.   The centre plate is of ½in. iron, galvanised.

The cruising rig is shown by the plan now published, but for racing a large balance lug of 180 sq. ft. is used. In the sail plan the hatch is shown raised, as used when more head room is required than it affords when close down on the coamings.

The yawl was built by Mr. J. A. Akester, boat builder, Hornsea, and a similar boat would cost from 55*l*. to 60*l*.

Mr. G. F. Holmes, of Hornsea, near Hull, designed and built the Cassy for sailing on the Humber, &c., 1883 (*see* Plate CXXI.) She proved to be a very capable little craft, both for rowing and sailing, and beaching. The position of the well is farther aft than usual, but experience proved that it is in the right place for rowing or sailing.

For sailing with the cruising sail Mr. Holmes seldom uses any ballast, the centre-board (70lb.) being sufficient; but, with the racing sail, he generally has a hundredweight of gravel or sand in bags.

The forward seat can be put either about 6in. above the bottom of the boat for sailing, or about 2in. below gunwale for rowing. The after seat is well down in the boat.

The connection between rudder and deck-yoke is made by a piece of brass rod, $\frac{1}{4}$in. thick, bent into square hooks at the ends.

Mr. Holmes says his outriggers (*see* Fig. 216) are firm when in use, and answer better than any other which he has used. By withdrawing the brass rod they may easily be taken off altogether, leaving no hole in the deck. The stay rod is pivotted through a brass plate close to the coaming, and when not in use may be hooked into a screw eye on the coaming. A good knee should be fitted under the side deck where the strain of the stay rod comes. The outriggers are made of $\frac{3}{8}$in. wrought iron.

The leading measurements are as follows :—

Length extreme	14ft.	Area racing mainsail	120 sq. ft.
Beam extreme	3ft. 4in.	Area cruising	70 sq. ft.
Centre-board case, mahogany	$\frac{3}{8}$in.	Area mizen	about 15 sq. ft.
Sculls	8ft. long.		

TABLE OF OFFSETS OF CASSY.—Plate CXXI.

	0	1	2	3	4	5	6	7	8	9	10	11	12	13	14
		in.	in.	in.	in.	in.	in.	in.	in.	in.	in.	in.	in.	in.	in.
Half breadths gunwale	—	6$\frac{3}{4}$	11$\frac{3}{4}$	15	17$\frac{1}{4}$	18$\frac{3}{4}$	19$\frac{1}{4}$	19$\frac{3}{4}$	19$\frac{1}{4}$	19	18$\frac{1}{4}$	17	14$\frac{1}{4}$	9$\frac{1}{4}$	—
12in. level line	—	4	8$\frac{1}{4}$	13$\frac{1}{4}$	16$\frac{1}{4}$	18	19	19$\frac{1}{4}$	19$\frac{1}{4}$	18$\frac{3}{4}$	18	16$\frac{1}{4}$	13$\frac{1}{4}$	8	—
6in. „ „	—	$\frac{3}{4}$	3$\frac{1}{4}$	7$\frac{1}{4}$	12	15$\frac{3}{4}$	17$\frac{1}{4}$	18	17$\frac{3}{4}$	17	15$\frac{1}{4}$	13	9$\frac{1}{4}$	4	—
3in. „ „	—	—	—	—	6	11	13$\frac{3}{4}$	15	14$\frac{3}{4}$	13$\frac{1}{4}$	11$\frac{1}{4}$	7$\frac{3}{4}$	3$\frac{1}{4}$	$\frac{1}{4}$	—
Heights above level ⎰ line of gunwale... ⎱	25$\frac{1}{4}$	22$\frac{1}{4}$	20$\frac{1}{4}$	18$\frac{3}{4}$	17$\frac{1}{4}$	16$\frac{1}{4}$	16$\frac{1}{4}$	15$\frac{3}{4}$	15$\frac{3}{4}$	15$\frac{3}{4}$	16	16$\frac{1}{4}$	17$\frac{1}{4}$	19$\frac{1}{4}$	21$\frac{1}{4}$
Underside rabbet	—	5$\frac{3}{4}$	4	3$\frac{1}{4}$	2$\frac{1}{4}$	1$\frac{3}{4}$	1$\frac{1}{4}$	1	1	1$\frac{1}{4}$	1$\frac{1}{4}$	1$\frac{3}{4}$	2$\frac{1}{4}$	3	—

In 1889 Mr. Holmes built the Ethel (Plate CXXII.), and he spoke most highly of her for speed, handiness, and seaworthiness. The cost of the boat complete was about 25*l.*

TABLE OF DIMENSIONS, &c.

	Cassy.	Ethel
Length	14ft.	13ft.
Beam	3ft. 4in.	4ft. 6in.
Height bow	2ft. 1½in.	2ft. 2in.
„ midships	1ft. 4in.	1ft. 6in.
„ stern	1ft. 9in.	1ft. 11in.
From bow to mast	3ft.	3ft.
„ fore end centre-plate	4ft.	3ft. 3in.
„ aft end centre-plate	7ft.	7ft. 6in.
„ aft end well	11ft. 6in.	11ft. 2in.
Weight centre-plate	70lb.	22lb.
„ ballast	None.	114lb.
Area of mainsail	85 sq ft.	87 sq. ft.
„ mizen	19 sq. ft.	19½ sq. ft.
Total sail area	104 sq. ft.	106½ sq. ft.

APPENDIX.

DICTIONARY OF GENERAL INFORMATION.

A.

A.B.—Able seaman, must be able to hand, reef, and steer by compass, splice, knot, turn in rigging, &c. An able-bodied seaman is distinguished from a boy or ordinary seaman.

Aback.—A sail is said to be aback when the wind strikes it from ahead and tends to force a vessel astern; generally applied to square-rigged ships. In a fore-and-aft vessel the sails would be said to be aback if their clews were hauled to windward, or if the vessel came up head to wind, and went off on the opposite tack without the head sheets being handed over; or if the wind headed the vessel and struck her from the opposite side to that which it had been blowing so as to cause the sails to lift. (See also "All Aback For'ard!" and "By the Lee.")

Abaft.—A relative term used to denote the situation of an object or point that is astern of another, and begins from the stem head, or from the fore part of any spar or other object; generally the term means towards the stern, or in the direction of the stern.

Abandon.—To leave a ship and take to the boats.

Abeam.—At right angles to a vessel's broadside or keel; opposite to the vessel's centre of length; abreast of.

Aboard.—Inside a ship or on the deck of a ship. "Come aboard, sir," is a sailor's way of reporting himself on board after leave of absence. To run or fall aboard a vessel is for one vessel to come into collision with another. A sail is said to fall aboard when, from the lightness of the wind or other causes, it ceases to blow out. To haul the boom aboard is to haul the boom in by the main-sheet from off the lee quarter.

About.—Having tacked. "She's about;" she is going to tack or has tacked. "Ready about" is the signal given for the men to prepare to tack the ship. "About ship" or "'Bout ship!" is the order given to tack, that is to put the vessel on the opposite tack to the one she is on when the order is given to tack. To go about is to tack.

Abreast.—Synonymous with "Abeam." Side by side. *To Breast.*—To come abreast.

Accommodation.—The cabins of a vessel.

Accommodation Ladder.—A side ladder, with platform, for boarding vessels. In the case of yachts, they are usually made to fold up on the bulwarks when the yacht is under way.

Acker.—A tide coming on the top of another tide.

Ackers' Scale.—A graduated time allowance on a tonnage incidence computed by the late Mr. G. Holland Ackers in 1850, now superseded by another scale.

A Cock Bill or Cock Bill.—An anchor hanging from the cat head ready to let go. The situation of yards when one arm is topped up as a sign of mourning.

Across Tide.—Crossing the stream of the tide so that it comes broadside on. If a vessel in beating to windward crosses a tide fairly at right angles on one tack, she will stem it on the next, or have it stern on, according to whether the tide be lee-going or weather-going. (See "Weather-tide.")

Admeasurement.—An old-fashioned expression for the builder's tonnage of a ship calculated by length and breadth, and abbreviated O.M. (old measurement) and B.M. (Builder's Measurement), which see.

Admiral.—The highest rank in the Navy. Formerly there were admirals of the red, white, and blue, with the intermediate ranks of vice and rear of the red, white, and blue. When the white ensign was taken exclusively for the Royal Navy in 1857, the red, white, and blue divisions were done away with. Admirals now fly a St. George's Jack, which is a white square flag with red St. George cross in it at the main, fore or mizen, according to their rank. A vice-admiral has a red ball in the upper (hoist) canton of the flag; a rear-admiral two balls.

Admiral of the Fleet.—An honorary distinction bestowed on admirals for long service, &c. If an admiral of the fleet has a command, he hoists the "union" at the main.

Admiralty Flag.—A red flag with yellow fouled anchor (horizontal) in it, flown by the Sovereign and Lords of the Admiralty.

Admiralty Warrants.—Warrants granted to clubs and the members thereof, granting permission to fly the white ensign, or the blue ensign, or the red ensign with device on it. The Admiralty

Admiralty Warrants—continued.

warrant will only be granted to yachts which are registered according to the provisions of the Merchant Shipping Act. The warrant itself, as delivered by the Admiralty to a club, is as follows:

"Whereas we deem it expedient that the members of the Royal . . . Yacht Club, being natural born or naturalised British Subjects, should be permitted to wear on board their respective vessels the blue ensign of Her Majesty's fleet, with the distinctive marks of the club, viz., a crown in the centre of the union, on the following conditions :

"We do therefore, by virtue of the power and authority vested in us, under the provisions of the 105th Section of the Merchant Shipping Act, 1854, hereby warrant and authorise the blue ensign of Her Majesty's fleet, with the distinctive marks of the Royal . . . . . Yacht Club thereon, as aforesaid, to be worn on board the respective vessels belonging to the Royal . . . . . Yacht Club, and to members of such yacht club, being natural born or naturalised British subjects, accordingly, subject to the following conditions :

"1. Every vessel belonging to the Royal . . . . . Yacht Club in order to be eligible to wear the ensign authorised by this warrant, shall have been registered as a British vessel in accordance with the Merchant Shipping Act, 1854.

"2. The ensign shall not, without our authority in writing, be worn on board any vessel belonging to the Royal . . . . . Yacht Club, while such vessel is lent, on hire or otherwise, to any person not being a member of the club, or who, being a member of the club, is not a natural born or naturalised British subject."

Thus a warrant is only granted to the owner of a registered yacht; the owners of yachts of 15 tons and under (which are not required by law to be registered) cannot legally hold a warrant to fly the white or blue ensign, or red ensign with device, unless such yachts are duly registered.

The hirer of a yacht cannot hold a warrant to fly such ensigns; but in case the hirer and the owner are members of the same club, and the owner holds a warrant, then the hirer, after obtaining special permission in writing from the Admiralty to exercise the privileges granted under the warrant, can fly the white or blue ensign as the case may be. The plain red ensign denoting the nationality of the yacht can be, and should be, flown in case the yacht has no warrant. These regulations, besides accompanying each club warrant, have over and over again been sent to the yacht clubs in circular form. Some clubs—the Royal Yacht Squadron and Royal Victoria, for instance—have in their rules a notice that a yacht, if lent, or let on hire, cannot fly the ensign and badge of the club unless the person to whom the yacht is lent

or hired is at the time a member of the club. This, however, is not in accordance with the Admiralty regulation, which, under date Nov. 2, 1880, was as follows: "Warrants to fly the ensigns of Her Majesty's fleet are only granted to owners of yachts belonging to a club holding a warrant from the Admiralty, and never to individuals hiring yachts." This in turn is modified by the regulation already referred to as follows : "If a member of a yacht club, having an Admiralty warrant to fly a special ensign, lets his yacht to another member of the same club, the member hiring the yacht cannot fly the club ensign without the special authority of the Admiralty in writing."

Under the "Queen's Regulations" (not Merchant Shipping Acts) a yacht can use the blue ensign if she is commanded by an officer of the naval reserve, and if ten of the crew are naval reserve men; but the Admiralty must be applied to for a warrant before flying the ensign.

In other cases the warrant to fly the blue ensign can only be obtained by a member of a yacht club which has an Admiralty warrant, and the application must be made through the club secretary.

When a yacht changes hands the warrant must be returned through the club secretary to the Admiralty ; and if an owner lets a yacht on hire he must return the warrant.

The Admiralty warrant is not granted to foreigners who may be members of British yacht clubs unless they have been naturalised, and can thus legally hold a British Register. A foreigner obtaining a British Register by making a false representation is liable to have the vessel made forfeit to the Crown (see "Ensign" and "Yacht").

The privilege bestowed by the document known as an Admiralty warrant is thus clearly set forth, and is nothing more or less than a permission to fly one of the ensigns used by Her Majesty's fleet. The red ensign, it can be stated, may, under the Merchant Shipping Act of 1854, be flown on board any vessel without permission of the Admiralty, unless a device be put on it ; in the latter case a warrant must be obtained from the Admiralty for permission to use the device.

Thus it will be seen that an Admiralty warrant confers only a single privilege, but the Government allows yacht owners who hold an Admiralty warrant to avail themselves of certain conditional exemptions from Excise and other dues. These exemptions are not important, and are briefly these : Members of yacht clubs (possessing the warrant) may remove their own furniture or property from place to place in the United Kingdom in their yachts (providing the furniture is for their own use) without taking out a coasting licence ; members may deposit wines or spirits, &c., as sea stock in the Customs warehouses, on arrival from foreign ports, free of duty (but not of warehousing dues), and re-ship such wines, spirits, &c., for another voyage ; members may enter Government harbours without paying dues, and may make fast and lie to any Government mooring buoys, when such are not required by any of H.M.'s ships.

[Exemptions from harbour dues can only be claimed in Government harbours, such as Portland, Plymouth, Kingstown, or Holyhead new harbour; and it is doubtful if the Admiralty can give exemption from all dues for such natural harbours as Portsmouth, Plymouth, Falmouth, Milford, Cork, or Dartmouth if the local harbour board think proper to impose dues; indeed, at some of these places dues are exacted. For instance, a yacht using the Catwater at Plymouth has to pay some trifling tonnage due, and we have even heard of yachts being asked for the "Tinker" buoy dues at Plymouth. However, these impositions are exceptional, and beyond the home harbours yachts, by special request, are privileged to enter all similar foreign harbours free of dues; but this exemption, whether at home or abroad, does not apply to private harbours or dock basins, such as Ramsgate, Torquay, Dover, Havre, Boulogne, Ostend, and such places. For using such ports or docks the dues or tolls must be paid, and they are fixed at a much higher rate per ton than the harbour or town dues levied at some ports.]

A yacht need not have her name painted on her stern; the master or mate need not have Board of Trade certificates, even for foreign cruising; men or boys can be shipped or unshipped, or agreements can be made with seamen without reference to the Registrar-General of Seamen; crew space is under no limitations, and official logs need not be kept (see the article "Seamen" further on); but any yacht taking on board a passenger at a foreign port, or leaving one at a foreign port, is liable to dues as a packet boat. It will thus be seen that a yacht owner has the privilege of considerable freedom in his avocation of pleasure, but before he can obtain the warrant which confers these privileges his yacht must, as before stated, be registered in accordance with the provisions of the Merchant Shipping Act, and it is compulsory that every yacht of and above fifteen tons internal capacity shall be registered. Yachts smaller than fifteen tons requiring to fly the blue, or white, or club red ensign must also be registered (see the article "Registry").

The following are the latest (1890) regulations as to yachts which may have taken in excisable goods at foreign ports: "The Commissioners of Customs inform you that new regulations have been issued with respect to surplus stores of yachts laid up, &c., and that in future, when yachts are laid up, or when, for other reasons, they are not about to cruise outside home waters, their stores which are liable to duty should, as a general rule, be deposited in the Queen's warehouse, unless satisfactory proof is produced that such stores have been shipped from a duty paid stock.

"As an alternative course, however, bond may be accepted, with one surety, from the owner of the stores, in the penalty of the duty

payable thereon, and in that event the stores may remain on board under seal for future use, or until the duty chargeable upon them be paid. Rent will be charged for the stores deposited in the Queen's warehouse under these regulations."

Exciseable goods are only allowed to be taken on board free of duty upon the yacht clearing for some foreign port; and, if a yacht owner purchases wines, spirits, or other excisable goods at a foreign port, he may deposit the same in a British Customs warehouse free of duty, and take the same on board again on his clearing for another foreign voyage, and paying the warehousing charge. Nothing is said about a yacht being allowed in a general sort of way to buy goods out of bond free of duty; but a great deal of laxity no doubt prevails in the matter, as it is a very easy thing for a yacht to be cleared for a foreign port without the owner having any intention of proceeding to the place mentioned in the clearance. A curious incident occurred in connection with this matter in 1864. A yacht cleared for a certain foreign port, and took on board wines and spirits from a Customs warehouse free of duty, the master giving the usual bond of 100*l.* that the same should not be landed or used out of the yacht. The yacht did not go foreign, and consequently did not call at the place mentioned in the clearance, and upon her return to the port of departure in Ireland the Customs officers paid her a visit. All the wines and spirits had been consumed, but, as the yacht had not been to the place mentioned in her original clearance, the officers proceeded to estreat the bond; however, on a declaration being made that none of the stores had been taken out of the yacht, and, in fact, were consumed on board, the bond was not estreated, and only double duty imposed on the total quantity of excisable goods which had been taken on board the yacht. The owner declared that this exaction by the Customs officers was owing to his not having "tipped" them when they paid a visit to his yacht. Be that as it may, there is little doubt that the officers were not exceeding their duty, although they must have been aware that many yachts when they take wines and spirits on board in the summer months from bond clear for a foreign port merely to comply with one part of the regulation, whilst no intention exists of paying anything more than a flying visit to the port. However, since the abatement of the duties on foreign wines and spirits, and tea, the practice of buying stores out of bond has practically ceased.

A yacht, on returning from a foreign port, should bring up at a Boarding Station, even though she has no wine, spirits, or other excisable articles on board. If she has only duty-paid stock on board the owner should have the invoices of the same ready to show the Boarding Officer, or the whole stock might be sealed up.

Adrift.—Floating with the tide. Generally driving about without control. Also a vessel is

Adrift—continued.
said to be adrift when she breaks away from her moorings, warps, &c. The term is also applied to loose spars rolling about the deck; sheets or ropes which are not belayed, &c.

Afloat.—The state of being waterborne after being aground. To be on board ship.

Afore.—The contrary of abaft. Towards the forward end of anything.

Aft.—An abbreviation of abaft, generally applied to the stern. To go aft is to walk towards the stern; to launch aft is to move a spar or anything else towards the stern. To haul aft the sheets is to bring the clew of the sail more aboard by hauling on the sheets.

After.—The state of being aft, as after-sail, after-leech, after-side, &c.

After Body.—The part of a vessel abaft her midship section.

After End.—The stern end of a vessel or anything else, or the end of anything nearest the stern of a vessel.

After-Guard.—Men stationed aft to work sheets, &c. In racing yachts, if there be any amateurs on board, they are generally made use of as an after-guard. In merchant ships the ordinary seamen or landsmen enjoy the distinction. (See "Waisters.")

After-most.—A thing or point situated the most aft of all.

Afternoon Watch.—The watch between noon and four o'clock.

After Part.—The stern extremities of a vessel or anything else.

After Peak.—The hold of a vessel near the run. A small cuddy or locker made in the run of a boat aft.

After Rake.—Contrary to fore rake. The rake or overhang the stern post has abaft the heel of the keel. To incline sternwards.

Aftward.—Towards the stern; contrary to forward.

Against the Sun.—An expression used to show how a rope is coiled: from right to left is against the sun, from left to right is with the sun. The wind is said to blow against the sun when it comes from the westward, and to back when it changes from west to east by the south.

Agreement with Crew.—A form of agreement provided by the Board of Trade for yacht sailors to "sign articles" on. The agreement forms can be obtained of Messrs. Eyre and Spottiswoode, Queen's Printers, London, E.C. (See "Seaman.")

Agreement.—The document executed, when a vessel is built, by the builder and the person for whom the vessel is being built. The following is a form of agreement which has been used:

[The specification relates to a wood yacht of about 25 tons.]

An Agreement between Messrs. , of , yacht builders, hereinafter called the builder, of the one part, and of , Esquire, hereinafter called the owner, of the other part.

The builders shall build and equip a yacht according to the specification and drawings marked A, B, C, and signed by the parties hereto. The yacht shall be built and completed in all particulars according to the requirements of the said specification, and the whole of the workmanship and material shall be such as shall be required by Lloyd's Rules, and such as will entitle the yacht to be classed at Lloyd's as a yacht A 1 for a term of years. The whole of the work shall be executed under the special survey of Lloyd's surveyor, and to the satisfaction of Lloyd's committee; and also to the satisfaction of , marine architect, hereafter called the architect. The yacht shall be delivered to the owner complete as aforesaid, safely moored in . In consideration of these premises, the builder shall be entitled to be paid by the owner as follows:— pounds on the signing of this agreement; a further sum of pounds when the said yacht shall be in frame, and the architect shall have given a certificate in writing under his hand that the yacht is in frame, and all the work up to that stage has been done to the satisfaction of Lloyd's surveyor and to the satisfaction of the architect; a further sum of pounds when the yacht shall be completely timbered and planked, and the deck laid, the coamings fixed, and the architect shall have given a certificate in writing under his hand that the yacht is completely timbered and planked, and the deck laid, and the coamings fixed, and that all the work up to that stage has been done to the satisfaction of Lloyd's surveyor and to the satisfaction of the architect.

When the vessel shall have been duly launched and classed at Lloyd's and when the said architect shall have given a certificate under his hand that the vessel has been completed in all respects to his satisfaction, according to the said plans and specification, and the vessel has been delivered afloat, and complete in all respects for sea, and moored in safety in , the owner shall pay to the builder the further sum of pounds.

The yacht from and after the payment of the said sum of pounds, to be paid on the signing of this agreement, shall be, and continue to be, the property of the owner; and all the materials intended for, or appropriated to the said yacht, shall be deemed to be the property of the owner.

If at any time the builder shall become bankrupt, or enter into any arrangement with his creditors under the Bankruptcy Acts, or shall fail or be unable to complete the said vessel in accordance with this agreement, or shall in the opinion of the architect be guilty of any unreasonable delay in the execution of the work agreed to be done, then it shall be lawful for the owner to enter upon the

Agreement—continued.

builder's yard and take possession of the said yacht, and to cause the work included in this agreement to be completed by any person or persons whom he shall see fit. All damage that shall happen to the said yacht agreed to be built as aforesaid, or to the materials intended to be used in her construction, by fire or otherwise, previous to her being delivered to the owner complete as aforesaid, shall be forthwith made good by and at the expense of the builder.

The architect and the owner shall at all times be permitted to have access to the said yacht during the progress of the works.

The builder shall deliver the said yacht complete for sea, according to the said plans and specification, afloat at and classed at Lloyd's as aforesaid, on or before the first day of , one thousand eight hundred and ninety, and in default he shall pay for each and every day after the said first day of during which the said yacht remains undelivered or unclassed as aforesaid, the sum of pounds a day as and for liquidated damages ; and the said sum of pounds a day may be deducted by the owner from any money payable, or to become payable, by him to the builder.

The builder shall not be entitled to make any claim or demand upon the owner for work done upon the said yacht, or in connection with the building or equipment thereof, or for any alterations or extras beyond the remuneration hereinbefore mentioned, except in respect of work for which written certificates, describing the work as extra work, shall be given under the hand of the architect and countersigned by the owner.

No work done on the said yacht without a written order signed by the architect, and countersigned by the owner, shall be deemed to be extra work. The builder shall not be entitled to an extension of the said time by reason of any extra work or alteration being ordered unless a written order for such extra work be signed by the architect and countersigned by the owner, and unless the architect shall think fit at the time such written order is given by written certificate under his hand to extend the time fixed for completion, and then the time shall be extended only so far as the architect by the said certificate shall determine.

Any dispute arising between the builder and the owner respecting anything contained in this agreement, or in the specification and plans above referred to, or in any way relating to the building, equipping, or delivery of the yacht, shall be referred to the said architect, whose decision shall be final, or, him failing, to some other arbitrator to be agreed upon between the parties, or to be nominated, in case of difference, by the registrar of the Admiralty Division. The costs of any such reference to be in the discretion of the arbitrator. This agreement may be made a rule of the High Court of Justice if the court shall so think fit.

Specification for a yacht of about 25 tons :

DESIGN AND DIMENSIONS : The yacht to be built according to drawings and plans furnished by , and to be of the following dimensions :—The length on deck from the fore side of the stem to the aft side of the stern post to be 50ft. ; and the length between perpendiculars, measured along the rabbet of the keel from the after side of the stern post, to a perpendicular dropped from the fore side of the stem at the deck to be 46ft. ; and the breadth, from outside to outside of the planking in the broadest part of the yacht, to be 11ft.

KEEL : The keel to be of sound English or American elm, 12in. sided, and not less than 10in. deep, to taper fore and aft to stem and stern post. If the keel be in two pieces, the scarph to be not less than 6ft. long, butted and bolted with $\frac{1}{2}$in. metal bolts, six in number. A solid [lead, iron] keel to be cast and fitted, bolted with yellow metal, underneath the main keel, as shown in plan ; the builder to make the moulds for the keel and find metal and bolts.

STEM : To be a sound piece of English oak, with a grown crook, 5in. sided and 14in. moulded, properly butted and scarphed into keel, and bolted with $\frac{1}{2}$in. copper bolts.

STERN POST : The stern post to be of English oak, 7in., sided at top, and 9in. moulded.

KNIGHTHEADS AND APRON : The knightheads and apron to be of English oak.

DEADWOODS : The upper deadwoods of English oak, and of sufficient depth to receive the heels of the timbers, and to be bolted with $\frac{1}{2}$in. yellow metal bolts.

FUTTOCKS AND TIMBERS : The futtocks and timbers to be of English oak, with room and space centre to centre of 18in., and to be 4in. sided and 4in. moulded, the top timbers to be 3$\frac{1}{2}$in. sided and 2$\frac{3}{4}$in. moulded. The heels of first futtocks butted or joggled into the keel, through-fastened, and to be secured with wrought-iron knee floors, through-bolted to keel and futtocks with $\frac{1}{2}$in. metal bolts. The double timbers to be bolted together with $\frac{1}{2}$in. square iron, galvanised, and the heels and heads to fit closely and neatly, and to be dowelled.

GARBOARDS : The garboard strakes to be of sound American rock elm, not less than 9in. wide and 2in. thick.

PLANKING : To be of teak from the covering-board to 2ft. below the load water-line, and the remainder of the planks to be of pitch pine, the whole to be wrought in parallel strakes 2in. thick, and not more than 5in. deep (the sheer strake to be 7in. wide), and in long lengths to have a $\frac{1}{2}$in. copper bolt clinched through every other frame, and to have a cast metal 4$\frac{1}{2}$in. dump in the remaining timbers. The butts of the planks to be well fitted and caulked, and to have not less than 5ft. shift unless a whole strake intervenes between two butts, and each butt to have $\frac{1}{2}$in. wrought copper bolt through the centre of the plank, and the timber next thereto. All fastenings to be counter sunk or punched home $\frac{1}{2}$in. deep to receive putty stops.

Agreement—continued.

SHELF: The shelf to be of English oak, of 15in. sectional area, as shown in the drawing C, of the midship section, through-fastened to top or second strake with ½in. metal bolts at every timber, and to have a strong galvanised iron breast-hook forward, and galvanised iron knees aft. The clamp to be 2½in. thick.

BILGE STRAKES: A pair of bilge strakes of English oak each 6in. by 2in., running fore and aft to be worked on each side, and to be through-fastened with ½in. copper bolts, and to have a galvanised iron breast-hook forward, and to be bolted into transom frame with metal bolts aft.

DECK BEAMS: The deck beams to be of English oak, 4in. sided and 4in. moulded, and to have about 4in. rise at centre; to have galvanised iron knees where required, carefully fitted, dovetailed and bolted to the shelf with ½in. metal bolts; the bitt and mast beams, and the other beams, to have a galvanised iron hanging knee at each end, with three ½in. metal bolts through each arm, and two other galvanised iron knees to be on each side. English oak lodging knees to be fitted between the beams in wake of the mast, and where required.

COVERING BOARD: The covering board to be of teak, 7½in. wide and 2in. thick, properly secured to top strake and beams and filling pieces between the beams, and to project about ½in. outside of the plank.

DECK PLANK: The deck plank to be of picked, well-seasoned Quebec yellow pine, free from knots, shakes, and other defects, in long lengths, tapered as required; no slab cuts to be used; and no feather edges to be left at endings of planks, forward or aft, the ends to butt ½in. into covering board; the plank to be 2in. thick, and not more than 3in. wide, and to be nailed diagonally, with yellow metal nails at the sides.

STANCHIONS AND BULWARKS: The bulwark stanchions to be of oak, 3in. moulded and 3½in. sided at deck. The bulwark skirting to be of teak.

RAIL: The top rail to be of American elm, 3½in. by 2in., free of defects, and fitted fair.

RUDDER: The main piece of rudder to be of one solid piece of English oak, and to have a carefully fitted water-tight rudder trunk; to have strong copper braces, fitted with a rule joint, sunk into stern post; also a strong brass or gun metal bearing at heel, to have an iron strap round the rudder head, and the rudder head to fit, and work in a metal collar, sunk into the deck with chock of teak; to have a neat brass cap, with name of yacht engraved thereon; to have two neat carved oak or mahogany tillers, with brass fittings.

CAULKING: The outside planking to be thoroughly and carefully caulked, and the seams carefully payed and puttied, and the deck to be very neatly and carefully caulked with cotton and payed with marine glue, the whole of the seams of hull and deck planking to be made tight; the outside planking to be painted with three coats of paint; two coats of composition to be laid on the bottom, and at the end of the season, or when required by the owner, the hull to be sheathed with copper sheets carefully laid on, 18oz. below the water-line and 20oz. at and above the water-line.

BALLAST: The builder to supply and carefully stow a sufficient quantity of pig-iron ballast (besides metal keel) to put the yacht to the designed load-line; none of the ballast to rest on the plank, but iron bearers to be supplied to take it between the frames; the ballast to be painted with one coat of red lead paint. The builder to supply lead ballast if so required by the owner, allowing for the difference between the prices of pig-iron ballast and lead.

BITTS: The bowsprit bitts to be of sound English oak fitted and fastened in the usual way, mast bitts of teak to be fitted on the fore-side and aft-side of mast, with usual cross pieces, with pins.

PUMP: A properly-constructed lead pump to be fitted, 4in. in diameter, with lead tail pipe, and rose at bottom, and the discharge pipe to lead on deck or overboard, as may be directed.

WATER-CLOSET: To have a patent water-closet of the most approved construction, with mahogany seat and fittings complete.

DECK FITTINGS: All the usual hawse pipes and chain pipes to be properly and carefully fitted; to have iron roller in sheave fitted for hawse pipe to take chain cable; channels and chain plates, bolts, and dead eyes as required; bowsprit gammon iron at stem to be covered with leather, and all necessary belaying pin racks, cleats, cavels, sheaves, fair leaders, eye bolts, and other usual deck fittings to be found and fitted as required.

BOBSTAY SHACKLE AND BAR: To have strong bobstay gun metal shackle cast to fit the stem, and to let in flush with the wood so far as may be prudent, and riveted through, the bobstay bar to be of copper.

DAVITS: To have boat's davits fitted to ship on one side, also one small anchor davit to ship on either bow.

RIDGE ROPE STANCHIONS: To have six brass stanchions for ridge ropes on either side of the same, to be hand-burnished in the best manner and fitted into square sockets in rail and lower part of bulwarks stanchions.

METAL WARPING CLEATS: To have two well-burnished brass warping cleats on taffrail, and two galvanised iron cleats on bow.

POOP: A laid deck poop, or if required, a neat elm grating fore side of mizen, with teak frame extending from taffrail to mizen mast.

HATCHES: The companion to be of teak fitted with brass slides as required, and to shut in with shifting panel or doors at after side, and secured with brass hasp and padlock. The fore hatch to be of teak, to be very carefully fitted as required by owner. The sail room hatch to be of teak of convenient diameter, to be securely fitted with coamings on deck, and fastened with brass lock on the

Agreement—continued.

aft side, and brass hasp and padlock on the fore side.

SKYLIGHTS : The main cabin and other skylights to be of teak, fitted on teak coamings, and made to ship and unship in the usual way, and to have proper brass fastenings inside, and to be thoroughly water-tight in every way, and the glass panes to be protected by neat brass guards or by galvanised iron or teak bars, as required by the owners. A curtain sliding on brass rods to be fitted to the skylight in the main and after cabins. Skylight coatings to be provided.

COMPANION STAIRS : The companion stairs to be of teak and fitted as required.

CEILING : The yacht to be ceiled throughout, down to the ballast line, with 1in. pine, carefully planned and fitted on the timbers ; below ballast line to be coated with red lead or varnish.

PLATFORM : The platform and platform beams to be of fir, and securely fitted as required ; the floor to be secured to beams with brass screws.

MAIN CABIN : The main cabin to be fitted according to the plans supplied by owner, with hard wood (mahogany and maple, or teak or pitch pine, or wainscot oak, &c., as may be directed) panelled bulkheads, doors, shelves, cupboards, lockers, drawers, racks, sofas to form also bed berths, with lee boards. One cupboard or sideboard to be fitted at the after end or both ends of each sofa, and shelf with small open rail extending the whole length of the cabin to be fitted above each sofa. A small bookcase to be fitted against one of the bulkheads. All locks, bolts, hinges, hasps, or other fastenings, and all keys in the main cabin, and in every other part of the vessel to be made of brass.

STOVE : An approved stove to be fitted in forward bulkhead of the main cabin, with fender and irons complete ; brass screw coamings for funnel, and length of copper chimney to lead clear of rail.

FORECASTLE : The forecastle to be bulkheaded, as required, and fitted with lockers, shelves, cupboards, locks, door, rack, table, seats with lockers underneath, and to have the usual lockers, and the lockers for chain and coke, closely ceiled to prevent dirt or dust from the same getting into the hold ; also similar lockers to be fitted below the pantry, and fore state room floor. To have a neat iron ladder from floor to deck, fitted to ship and unship ; a portable commode to be fitted, if required, in the forecastle, and one in after cabin.

SHEET LEAD COVERINGS : The floor underneath the cooking stove, and all the wood work near the stove, to be neatly covered with sheet lead, nailed with copper tacks.

WATER TANKS : Properly constructed galvanised iron water tanks of 30 cubic feet capacity, with manhole, to be provided, and fitted below the floor with pump and supply pipe attached, with brass deck plate, and screw cover for the same.

COOKING STOVE : A patent cooking apparatus to be supplied complete, the owner to select or approve of the stove, length of copper piping to funnel sufficient to lead clear of rail.

HAMMOCKS : Four hammocks or cots, with bedding complete, to be found.

MOPS, BROOMS, &c. : All the usual mops, brooms, brushes, buckets, squeegee, and other forecastle articles to be supplied.

DECK GEAR : All the usual deck appliances to be supplied, including iron main boom crutch, spar chocks, boat skids, boatswain's stool, gangway ladder, gangway stanchions and cotton ropes, meat safe, belaying pins, two indiarubber mats, ensign staff, four canvas-covered cork fenders for deck and gangway, two life buoys, two canvas buckets, one patent log, four cork deck cushions, foghorn, speaking trumpet, boat hook, anchor buoy, two snatch blocks, water *funnel*, spreaders for rigging, &c.

PANTRY : The pantry to be fitted up as required, with dresser, shelves, liquor holes, racks, hooks, drawers, lockers, &c., and mahogany door opening into main cabin.

FORE STATE ROOM : The fore state room to be fitted with bed berth of mahogany, with drawers underneath, mahogany washstand, and a folding mahogany slab to form a writing table ; cupboard, underneath shelves, racks, &c., mahogany door, &c. The space on port side of companion way to be fitted with seats or lockers, as required.

LADIES' CABIN : The ladies' after cabin to be fitted with polished wood panels, same as main cabin, with mahogany bed berths and washstands, cupboards and drawers, as required, and the sofas to be fitted with lockers underneath, and the doors to be fitted as required.

LAVATORY : The lavatory to be fitted with patent washstand, with tap and water ; a tank for water supply, and a patent water closet of the best construction, to be fitted with mahogany seat, the lavatory to be bulkheaded, as required.

SPARS : To be supplied with a complete set of spars, as required for a yawl of 25 tons, the whole to be carefully made, and all the ironwork to be of the finest quality, and galvanised, the dimensions of the spars to be according to plans supplied by the owner, and lettered D.

MAINMAST : The mainmast to be a picked spar, as free from knots as may be, of Oregon or Baltic red pine, fitted complete in every respect as required.

MAST STEP : The mast to be stepped into a solid iron mast step to be furnished by the builder.

WINCH : A gypsy winch to be fitted on the mast.

HOOPS : The usual mast hoops properly riveted to be fitted to mast.

CROSSTREES : The crosstrees to be carefully fitted as required.

BOWSPRIT : The bowsprit to have a galvanised iron rack plate on the upper side from the

Agreement—continued.

heel to the stem, and a stout galvanised iron pinion where fitted to the bitts, with handle for the same, and a lignum-vitæ roller between the bitts with a score round the centre to allow for the passage of the rack plate ; also a plain stout lignum-vitæ roller between the bitts on the under side of the heel of the bowsprit. A small, square, iron fid as required, sheave at outer end, traveller leather covered.

WHISKERS : Galvanised iron whiskers, fitted with preventer rods and all the other usual fittings for the bowsprit as required, to be carefully fitted.

MAIN-BOOM : The main-boom to be fitted to mast with iron band and universal joint, and all other fittings, including reef cleats, to be neatly fitted as required.

GAFF : The gaff to be fitted with strong iron jaws, and the other fittings as required.

TRYSAIL GAFF : The trysail gaff to be similarly fitted so that the jaws may be used with either gaff.

TOPMAST : The topmast to be fitted with galvanised iron self-acting fid and a brass-bound sheave in heel for mast rope ; all the other fittings to be carefully made as required.

TOPSAIL YARD : The topsail yard to be supplied of such dimensions as may be required.

SQUARESAIL YARD OR SPINNAKER BOOM : A square-sail yard or spinnaker boom to be fitted in the usual way as required.

MIZEN-MAST : The mizen-mast, boom, boomkin, yard, &c., to be fitted as required, and the mast to be stepped securely.

RIGGING AND BLOCKS : The standing and running rigging of wire, hemp, and manilla of suitable sizes, to be most carefully fitted, and the patent blocks for the same to be all of the best make, the whole standing and running rigging, blocks, tackle, &c., to be fitted complete in every detail. The main and gaff halyards to be of the best Russian hemp, the jib halyards of chain.

SAILS : A complete suit of sails fit for a yawl of 25 tons, to be found by the builder, and made by   , and to consist of mainsail, two mizens, foresail, four jibs, two topsails, squaresail or spinnaker, trysail, and a complete set of sail covers, properly painted, to be supplied, and bags for the smaller sails.

ANCHORS : One   anchor of 1½ cwt., one other anchor of 1½ cwt., and one kedge anchor, to be supplied.

CHAIN CABLE : Ninety fathoms of 9-16 chain cable, galvanised, to be supplied.

HAWSERS : Two hawsers of 60 fathoms each, suitable for the yacht, to be supplied.

WINDLASS : An improved ratchet windlass with double lever to be fitted, or a winch top capstan.

PAINTING : The outside of the vessel to be made as smooth as possible, and to have the usual number of coats of the best oil paint. A gilt strake.

VARNISH : Bulwarks and all woodwork fittings on deck to have three coats of the best varnish.

INSIDE PAINT : The underside of the deck, and such other parts of the vessel as may require it, to have three coats of paint—two of the best zinc white.

UPHOLSTERY : The upholstery work to be complete, and to consist of Brussels carpet for the main cabin, ladies' cabin, and state room, hard-seasoned oilcloth for the lavatory.

SOFAS : The sofa mattresses, backs, and pillows to be of hair, and covered with woollen tapestry, Utrecht velvet, or leather, as required.

CABIN TABLES, CHAIRS, &c. : A mahogany swing table to be fitted in main cabin, with cloth cover complete, also three folding chairs, an approved swing lamp, and the stove before mentioned.

STATE ROOM BEDS : The berths in the state room and ladies' cabin to be fitted with hair mattresses, down feather bolsters and pillows of the best quality, and three blankets of the finest quality to be supplied for each bed.

TOILET CHINA : The usual toilet china to be supplied to each berth, but to be selected by owner.

LAMPS : A suitable bronze swing lamp to be supplied to each berth.

STATE ROOM SOFAS : The sofas or seats in the after state room or ladies' cabin to be fitted with hair mattresses covered in tapestry, cretonne, rep, or Utrecht velvet, as the owner may decide.

BOATS : A suitable gig, to be supplied with oars, brass rowlocks and yoke, mahogany back board, and elm grating, and boat hooks, complete in every respect ; also a dinghey, with brass rowlocks and oars.

BINNACLE : A binnacle of brass or teak, with brass lamp and fittings, and approved compass.

SIDE LAMPS, &c. : Side lamps (diopteric) to be supplied, together with screens and galvanised iron stanchions, made to fit into the rail or into stanchions fixed on the rail. The lower part of the stanchions to be made to fit into the covering board, or into fastenings on the lower part of the bulwark stanchions. The side light screen to be made with brass hinges, so as to fall flat when out of use. An anchor lamp (diopteric) to be supplied. A rack to be fitted in the forecastle to receive the screens and lamps.

LEAD LINE : A hand lead and properly marked line to be supplied.

BELL : A ship's bell of the size required by the Board of Trade to be supplied, and to be fitted on deck if required.

FINALLY : The whole of the workmanship and materials to be of the very best quality ; and notwithstanding any omission from this specification, the builder is at his own expense to complete the vessel in every detail, in what is understood as hull, masts, spars, ironwork, and deck and cabin fittings as usual in first-class yachts, with all joiner's, cabinet maker's, painter's and plumber's, and upholsterer's work appertaining thereto.

Aground.—A vessel is said to be aground when her keel or bottom rests on the ground.

Ahead.—Forward; in advance of.

Ahoy.—An interjection used to attract attention in hailing a vessel, as "Cetonia Ahoy!"

A-Hull.—A ship under bare poles, with her helm lashed a-lee. An abandoned ship.

Air-Tight Cases for Small Boats.— By air-tight cases are meant cases that will keep out water. The most general form of case is made of zinc, copper, or Muntz metal. Macintosh bags have been used; they are put inside wood lockers, and then inflated, the object of inflation being of course to fill the lockers, and thus practically making the lockers impervious to the influx of water. As any kind of bag is liable to be punctured or otherwise damaged, metal cases are to be preferred—they should be fitted inside wood lockers. To render a boat unsubmergeable she must be provided with cases which will displace a quantity of water equal to the weight of the material used in the construction of the boat or which may be on board and will not float. Usually an ordinary fir planked boat will not sink if filled with water, the gunwale just showing above the surface; if, however, she has ballast on board or other weight, she would sink. Also the spare buoyancy would not generally be sufficient to support her crew.

A ton of salt water is equal to 35 cubic feet of the same: now suppose a boat 16ft. long and 6ft. broad weighed 15cwt. (¾ton) with all passengers, gear, air-tight cases. &c., on board, then she would require air-tight cases equal in bulk to 26¼ cubic feet, as there are 26¼ cubic feet of water to ¾ton weight. But it may be taken that the wood material used in the construction of the boat, the spars, and wood cases, would be self-supporting. Say that these weighed 5cwt., then 10cwt. (½ ton) would remain to be supported; ½ a ton is equal to 17½ cubic feet. A locker 6ft. long, 2ft. broad, and 1ft. 6in. deep would contain 18 cubic feet, and so would support the boat with her passengers on board, or prevent her sinking if filled to the gunwale with water. Of course it would be rather awkward to have such a large locker as this in so small a boat, and the air-tight spaces are usually contrived by having a number of lockers, some under the thwarts, in the bow end and stern end of the boat, and sometimes above the thwarts under the gunwales.

Some boats are made unsubmergeable by a cork belting fixed outside below the gunwale. One ton of cork is equal to 150 cubic feet of the same, and will support 3¼ tons in water. Thus, roughly, cork will support three times its own weight in water. Supposing it is sought to support a boat equal to 10cwt., as stated above; then a belting of cork will have to be used equal to 17½ cubic feet, plus a quantity equal to the weight of the bulk of the cork. Say the boat is 16ft. long, and the measurement round the gunwales will be 32ft. A tube 32ft. long to contain 17½ cubic feet

would require to be 10¼ inches in diameter. [The contents of a tube are found by multiplying its length by the area of one end. This area is found by taking the square of the diameter and multiplying it by ·78 (see "Areas of Circles").] The 17½ cubic feet of cork would weigh (17·5 × 15) 262½lb. equal to 4 cubic feet of salt water, and so an addition would have to be made to the tubing to that extent. Thus, in round numbers, 22 cubic feet of cork would be required to support 10cwt. net. A tube 32ft. long and 11in. in diameter would contain 22·0 cubic feet. The tubes that contain the cork are usually made of canvas and painted. The weight of the

FIG. 217.

canvas tube would have to be added to the general weight to be supported. Solid cork should be used, and not cork shavings, for filling the tubes; cork shavings get more or less saturated, and lose their buoyancy, and generally have less buoyancy than solid cork, in consequence of the multitude of spaces between the shavings which would admit water.

The accompanying sketch (Fig. 217) shows a small boat with a cork belting round under her gunwales. (See "Cork Concrete.")

A-Lee.—To leeward. The helm is a-lee when it is put down to leeward. Hard a-lee means that the helm must be put as far to leeward as it can be got. (See "Helm's a-lee.")

All.—A prefix put to many words to show that the whole is included, as "all aback," meaning all the sails are aback; "all-a-taunto," meaning that the ship is fully rigged and fitted out, with everything in its place; "all hands," the whole ship's company; "all standing," with everything in its place—nothing being shifted, &c.

All Aback For'ard.—A cry raised when a vessel is sailed so near to wind that the head sails lift or shake.

Alley.—The channel made in the after part of a steamship for the propeller shaft is termed the shaft alley. (See "Lane.")

Aloft.—Up the mast; overhead. "Aloft there! is a manner of hailing seamen who may be aloft on the mast, tops, yards, &c.

Along the Wind.—Sailing along the wind means to sail with the wind from a point to four points free, or with the wind abeam.

Along the Land.—To lay along the land is when a vessel can hug or keep close to the land without tacking.

Along Shore.—Close to the shore, by the shore, or on the shore.

Alongside.—By the side of the ship. "The gig is alongside, sir," is a common way of informing the owner, master, or other officers that the boat is manned and by the gangway, in readiness to take people off; also said when a boat

A sort of grapnel has been in use many years by fishermen for small boats (Fig. 218). E is the shank, D the usual ring. working in an eye (not shown in the engraving), B the bottom pair of claws, A the top pair of claws. The bottom pair of claws are welded on to the handle, but the top pair slide up and down, and it is usual to make the part under the ring D square so that the grapnel can be converted into an anchor by fixing the part A under the ring D by aid of a small key. A small portion of the bottom of the handle, shown by the shaded lines, is wrought square, and through the centre of the top pair of claws is a square hole, as at F. The sketch represents the

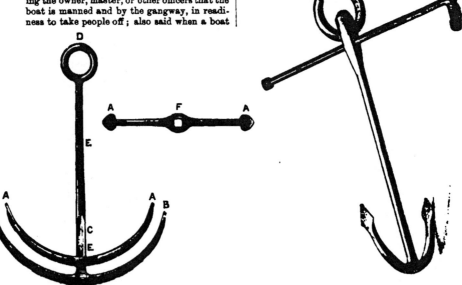

FIG. 218.   FIG. 219.

is brought to the gangway so that passengers can embark.

Amateur.—See "Corinthian."

Amidships.—The middle part of a ship. The middle part of anything. To put the helm amidships is to bring it in a line with the keel. Generally the word has reference to the middle fore-and-aft line of the ship, and to a middle athwartship part of a ship.

Anchor for Small Boats.—For small open boats the anchor should weigh 1lb. for every foot of length up to 20ft. For other boats anchors would be chosen according to the total weight of the boat, including her ballast and equipment, &c.; thus—½ton, 20lb.; 1ton, 25lb.; 1½tons, 30lb.; 2tons, 34lb.; 2½tons, 38lb.; 3tons, 42lb. The size of link of chain would be about ½in. Anchors for small boats should be long in the shank, and of the old-fashioned pattern.

gripper lying flat, and in its present position it is, of course, useless as a holdfast: it lies snug. Before heaving it overboard, take hold of the top pair of claws and slide them up the handle, till you get to the round part when turn them round, and drop them down upon the lower pair of claws on another square. You have now a most effective four-clawed gripper, which will hold like a bulldog. These grippers are made at the reasonable price of 6d. per lb., big or little, galvanised. About 1lb. per foot of length would be the weight for an ordinary boat. They are made by Messrs. Blake and Sons, Gosport, or obtainable from most of the ship chandlers or yacht fitters.

Anchor.—The old Admiralty dimensions for an anchor of 112lb. weight was 5ft. 8in. shank, with 1ft. 10in. arms, the flukes or palms of which were 9in., and the spread 3ft. 3in. No doubt such an anchor as this would hold like grim death. It is the weight of a 10-tonner's anchor, but such a thing on the bow of a 10-tonner would be, to say the least, rather in the way. Thomas and Nicholson's anchors are the best current examples of a good holder on the old-fashioned principle, and a hundredweight anchor of their pattern is, we believe, only 4ft. 6in. in length of shank, with 3ft. spread of arms. The length of shank must exist to get the holding power, and the arms ought not to be shorter than ·4 of the shank, nor make a less angle than 50° with the shank.

Anchor (Barlow).—Mr. G. T. Barlow, of Lytham, says he wanted a stocking anchor which could be instantly made serviceable, as he generally found at some critical moment the fastening arrangement was defective either through breakage or loss of locking,

and coinciding with the window (W) made in the top of shank. The parts (S S S) of shank are humped to a double thickness, thus providing three bearing surfaces for the crown. An iron hook (H) passes through the window (W), and secures the crown to the shank, the hook itself being clamped to the shank by the sliding ring (R). Thus there are no screws, pins, &c., to get out of order, and should the anchor drag, the tendency is to tighten the ring (R) on its seating.

For harbour work, a single arm, with hole for buoy line, can be supplied, but this is a spare part, and is not essential.

Messrs. Fay and Co., of Southampton, make anchors of this pattern to order, up to weights of 1cwt., which will hold a yacht of 20 or 25 tons, and can be stowed in quite a small bundle.

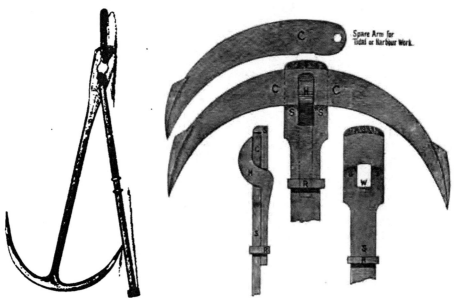

Spare Arm for Tidal or Harbour Work.

FIG. 220.   FIG. 221.

parts, and then turned his attention to stockless anchors, but found he could not place full reliance on these. He then made a stocking anchor, which proved efficient. The stock is fastening by half turning the anchor ring. To stow the anchor, half turn the ring, and lay the stock alongside the shank; then half turn the ring and the stock is fast without any lashing (Figs. 219 and 220).

Anchor (Bucknill's).—Col. Bucknill, R.E., invented the following anchor for small yachts in 1890. A sample, with a span of 22in. from fluke to fluke, and weighing only 39lb., has been tried on a 10-tonner, and has given great satisfaction (Fig. 221).

The drawing almost explains itself: The crown (C) of the anchor is made with a small indentation midway between the two arms,

The drawing represents a 40lb. anchor, suitable for an 8 or a 10-tonner.

Anchor (D. Cole's, Southampton).—This is an anchor something like the "old bay." It has a very long shank and sharp clean flukes. The crown is fitted to the shank and kept in its place by a pin. The advantage of this anchor is its great holding power, and the quickness with which it gets a hold even in hard ground. In letting go very little chain is required to bring a vessel up, but if the vessel has much way on a good scope should be given, as the anchor is a dangerous one to snub. The parts of the anchor are very light, and it is claimed that the weight required is 25 per cent. less than the weight of other anchors.

Anchor (Gales' Improved Trotman).—This

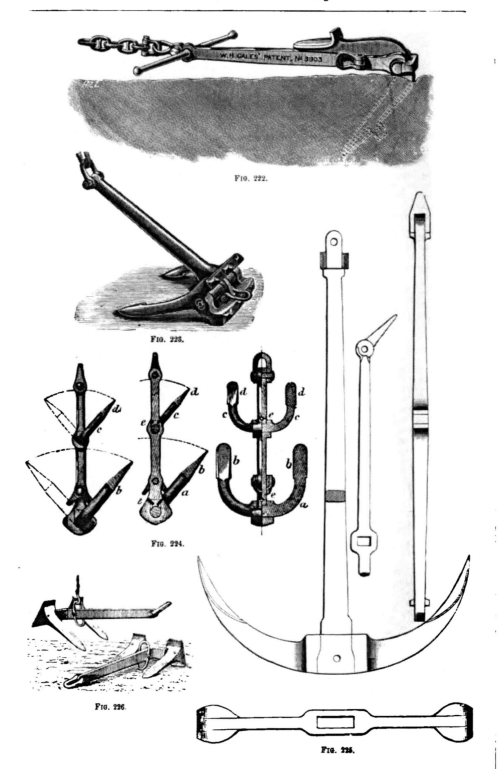

Fig. 222.

Fig. 223.

Fig. 224.

Fig. 226.

Fig. 225.

anchor was shown at the Inventions Exhibition, 1890, and the following is the inventor's description of it: "This invention (see Fig. 222) is an improvement upon the class of anchors known as 'Porter's,' 'Trotman's,' and others. In common with those referred to, the shank is so formed and proportioned as to receive at its crown the arms and flukes. Either arm or fluke is so arranged to work from a central point or pivot at the extremity of the shank, that upon its being 'canted,' instead of taking the pressure or bearing from the pivot, the entire bearing is given as parallel with and on to the shank, thereby giving additional holding power and strength, and materially helping to relieve the ordinary undue strain upon the fluke and bolt connection. The improved anchor will be found very compact and snug, when berthed, and for yachts, torpedo, and other craft of that class would be found very efficient in shallow water, and specially adapted for vessels of a larger class." Address 56, High-street, Poplar, E.

Anchor (Hall's Stockless). — This appears to be an adaptation of Wasteneys Smith's anchor. The flukes of the anchor are fixed at an angle of 54° with the shank, and, being part of the head, are at liberty to move freely on the trunnion of the shank. The whole of the holding strains are entirely contained in these two main pieces, without the intervention of bolts, cotters, pins, or keys. The shank of this anchor, being stockless, can be readily drawn into the hawse pipe and snugly stowed alongside the ship, where it is always ready for use without any catting or lifting on deck (see Fig. 223). The inventor is Mr. J. F. Hall, general manager to Messrs. Wm. Jessop and Sons Limited, of Sheffield.

Anchor (Liardet's).—The peculiarity of this anchor (Fig. 224) is that the stock is provided with flukes the same as the arms. The arms and stock are so fitted that they can move within a range of 45°. When stowed, the arms and stock lie in a line with the shank. There is a shackle for the cable and another near the crown for a buoy rope. The arms are shown by *a a* and the flukes by *b b* (Fig. 224). The arms and flukes of the stock are similarly shown. The manner of securing the arms to the shank is shown at *e*. We are informed that the P. and O. Company and some other companies are using the anchor. The manufacturers are Messrs. Parkes and Ross, of Tipton (Staffordshire) and Liverpool.

Anchor (Moore's).—The portable anchor (Fig. 225), invented by Mr. Louis Moore, has no fastenings except the chain shackle. It is easily taken to pieces, and stows snugly. The shank passes through the crown of the anchor like the handle of a pickaxe, and the stock passes over the end of the shank; no keys, bolts, &c., are required. The stock has loose pawls, as shown by the views. The

anchor is manufactured by Messrs. Mobbs, Vulcan Works, Northampton.

Anchor (Sinnette's).—Mr. Sinnette's anchors are of excellent proportions, and the arms are of the length and angle most suitable for holding. The spread of the arms is much the same as Thomas and Nicholson's; but being hinged, the spread, when the bills touch

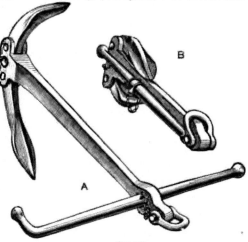

FIG. 227.

the shank for stowing, is only 1ft. in a hundredweight anchor. The usual objection to hinged anchors is that the crowns are weakened; but the long record of service of Trotman's and Porter's has shown that the objection is not a serious one. With regard to Sinnette's, the crown joint is so exception-

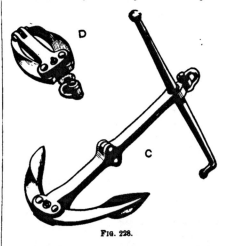

FIG. 228.

ally strong that the objection may be said not to exist at all.

A (Fig. 227) shows the anchor as prepared for use; by removing a centre tapered bolt the arms can be closed, as shown in B; the bolt is then replaced to lock the arms in the position shown, so there is no chance of fingers being injured through the arms opening and shutting. Thomas and Nicholson's anchor has also a tapered pin and tapered hole to receive it; this plan is found to answer much better than the parallel pin, which will always jam more or less, and require something to hammer it out with. The stock is also unpinned, and stows alongside the shank as shown.

In another form of this anchor the arms are not locked when in use, but only for stowing. The arms have back flukes, and the upper arm falls on to the shank when the lower one is in the ground. It thus becomes a non-fouling anchor with all the advantages of a Trotman in that respect, but with more compactness for stowing.

C (Fig. 228) shows yet another form of the anchor, the shank being jointed as well as the arms, the whole being made immensely strong.

D shows this anchor stowed. For facility in shifting about through hatchways or doors, nothing could beat this anchor in compactness, and it ought to be a great favourite among owners of small yachts.

The agents for the anchors are Messrs. Fay and Co., High-street, Southampton.

Anchor (Smith's Stockless).—This curious anchor is recommended by the patentees for the following reasons: It takes immediate hold; cannot foul; requires no stock; can be 20 per cent. lighter than other anchors; always cants properly; great strength; easily worked; lies flat on deck; stows in small space; easily tripped. The anchor is shown in the cut, Fig. 226.

The sizes recommended for yachts are, for

Sailing Yachts.		Steam Yachts.	
250 tons	6½ cwt.	250 tons,	4½ cwt.
200 "	5½ "	200 "	4 "
150 "	4½ "	150 "	3½ "
125 "	3½ "	100 "	2½ "
100 "	3 "	75 "	2 "
75 "	2½ "	50 "	1½ "
50 "	2 "	25 "	1 "
40 "	1¾ "	12 "	¾ "
30 "	1½ "		
20 "	1 "		
10 "	¾ "		
5 "	½ "		

The anchors are made by Mr. Wasteneys Smith, 58, Sandhill, Newcastle-on-Tyne.

Anchor.—Thomas and Nicholson's Patent (Camper and Nicholson, Gosport).—The patentees claim it to be by far the strongest disconnecting anchor ever yet introduced; and with the long but proportionate shank and the convex and elongated palms to have the very maximum of holding power, and may consequently be used considerably lighter than any other anchors.

The two taper bolts at the crown enables any person to disconnect or connect the anchor with the greatest despatch and certainty; as a taper bolt never requires any driving or drifting, inevitable at times with parallel bolts. The anchors are made in all sizes from 6lb. to 27lb. (*See* Plate CXXIII.)

Anchor, Mushroom.—This is a kind of moorings or anchor shaped like a mushroom, which, like a sucker, holds on to the mud or sand.

Anchor Shackle.—A shackle which connects the chain with the anchor.

Anchor, Tripping an.—If an anchor is let go on very firm holding-ground, or on ground where the anchor is likely to get foul, a tripping line is made fast to the crown of the anchor; to the other end of the line a buoy is made fast, and when the anchor is "wanted" it can be broken out of the ground by hauling on the tripping line if it cannot be got by hauling on the cable.

Another plan is to "scow" the anchor by bending the end of the cable to the crown instead of to the ring or shackle. The cable is then "stopped" to the ring by a yarn. When the cable is hauled upon the stop breaks, and, of course, the cable being fast to the crown, the anchor is readily broken out of the ground. A boat should not be left moored with her anchor "scowed," as, if any unusual strain came upon the cable, the stop would break, and the boat would probably go adrift. The trip line should be used in such cases. (See "Scowing.")

Anchor Watch.—A watch kept constantly on deck when a ship is at anchor, to be ready to veer out or take in chain, or to slip, make sail, give warning to the hands below, &c., if the vessel be in danger of collision or other mishaps. One hand may keep an anchor watch, and call up the officers and crew if necessary.

Anchor, Winch for Raising a Boat's.—Very neat and small capstans or windlasses are now made for almost any sized boat that has a deck forward, but these are not readily fitted to an open boat, and fishermen have a very simple contrivance to obtain the necessary power. Get a short piece of hard wood about 4in. in diameter, and of a length equal to the width

Fig. 229.

of the boat at the gunwale, where it is to be fitted to serve as the barrel of a winch (termed a "wink" by the fishermen). In either end drive an iron pin to form an axle, and to keep the wood from opening fit an iron band on either end (all the iron should be galvanised). On each gunwale fit an iron plate—a round hole in one plate and a hole and slot (opening aft) in the other. A hole must be bored through the wood to receive a short bar of tough wood or iron three or four feet long, to serve as a lever, or three or four pegs can be inserted, as is shown in the sketch (Fig. 229). The end of the cable will be fast to the wink, and as the latter is hove round the cable will be wound up. If there be two hands in the boat the cable need not be fast to the wink, but one hand can heave whilst the other holds on to the cable and coils away. A ratchet and pawl are sometimes fitted to the wink. Messrs. Pascal Atkey and Son, Cowes, manufacture a suitable ratchet windlass and also a capstan for small yachts.

Answer.—To repeat an order after an officer; thus, if the order be to the helmsman, "No more away," he will repeat, "No more away, sir;" or to the jib-sheetman, "Check the jib-sheet," he will answer, "Check the jib-sheet, sir." Thus the crew should always "answer" every order to show that they comprehend.

Answer Her Helm.—A vessel is said to answer her helm when she moves quickly in obedience to a movement of the rudder. Long, deep vessels, and full quartered vessels which have not a long clean run to the rudder, are slow to answer their helm. A vessel cannot "answer her helm" if she has not way on through the water, hence "steerage way."

A 1.—The highest class obtainable at Lloyd's. Formerly (from about 1760) all new ships were classed "A" with a term of years according to their port of building; after this term expired the ship was degraded to the E or I class, and so frequently it happened that a bad ship got a long term and a good one a short term; and perhaps the short-termed ship when repaired for the class E was better than the long-termed one was when first built. Such an absurd way of classing formed no useful guide for underwriters or insurance brokers, and in 1824 the present well-known committee of "Lloyd's Register" was established, by which ships are classed and given a term, according as they are built, in compliance with certain rules. A 1 is the highest class. "A" denotes that the hull is built of good materials, in accordance with certain rules, "1" is the symbol that the rigging and general equipment of the ship are in every way perfect. The number of years assigned to a ship as her term depends upon the quality of the materials used and the mode of construction, and may vary from eight to eighteen years. A well-built ship upon being restored may be retained in the A class. "A in red" are ships that have passed their term, or ships that were not classed when built. Class Æ applies to ships fit only for short voyages. Class E and I are similar to Æ, but denote that the ships are not fit to carry perishable goods on any voyage. It is seldom that any number is assigned but 1, and generally the classes will be found distinguished by A 1 15 years, A 1 (in red) 7 years, Æ 1; the classes Æ, E and I, are subject to annual inspection (see Lloyd's Yacht Register).

In the case of iron or steel ships, A means that the yacht is entitled to a character, but subject to periodical survey. The numeral 100, 90, &c., before A means that the vessel has been built up to Lloyd's rules and requirements, 100 A being the higher class. The letters M. C. in red denote that the boiler and machinery are certificated. See "Lloyd's."

A-Peek or Peak.—An anchor is said to be a-peak when the cable has been so much hove in as to form a line with the forestay; "hove short" so that the vessel is over her anchor. Yards are a-peak when topped by opposite lifts. See *A Cock Bill.*

Apostles.—Seaman's slang for knightheads, bollards, &c., for belaying warps to. They formerly had carved heads to represent the upper part of the human body.

Apron.—A piece of timber fitted at the fore end of the keel at its intersection with the stem and up the stem.

Arch Board.—The formation of the counter across its extreme aft end, being a continuation of the covering board, and covers the heads of the counter frames.

Ardent.—A vessel is said to be ardent when she gripes or shows a tendency to come to against a weather helm.

Areas of Circles.—The area of a circle is found by multiplying the square of the diameter by the fraction 0·7854. The areas of small circles in decimals of a foot are given in the following table:

Diameter in inches.	Equivalent diameter in decimals of a linear foot of 12 inches.	Area of circle in decimals of a square foot.	Circumference of the circle in inches.
1⅕	0·1	0·0078	3·92
2⅖	0·2	0·0314	7·46
3⅗	0·3	0·0706	11·38
4⅘	0·4	0·1256	14·92
6	0·5	0·1963	18·84
7⅕	0·6	0·2827	22·27
8⅖	0·7	0·3848	26·31
9⅗	0·8	0·5026	30·23
10⅘	0·9	0·6362	33·77
12	1·0	0·7840	37·69

The contents of a tube or cylinder can be found by the above table.

Thus, say a tube 30ft. long be 3⅗in. (equal to 0·3 of a foot) in diameter, then the area of one end of the tube will be ·0706 sq. ft. The contents of the tube will be found by multiplying its length by the fraction ·0706 ($30 \times ·0706 = 2·118$ cubic feet). If the tube were 6in. in diameter, then its contents would be $30 \times 0·1963 = 5·889$ cubic feet.

Arms.—The extremities of anything, as yard arms.

Ashore.—A vessel is said to be ashore when she is aground. To go ashore is to leave the ship for the land.

A-stay.—Synonymous with a-peak.

Astern.—Towards the stern. To move astern; to launch astern; to drop astern. An object or vessel which is abaft another vessel or object. Sailors never use the word "behind" to represent the position of being astern.

Astrolabe.—An ancient instrument for measuring the altitude of the sun, superseded by the quadrant and sextant.

A-taunto.—With all the masts on end, and rigging completely fitted. (See "All-a-taunto.")

Athwart.—Transversely, at right angles to fore and aft; across the keel. Athwart-ship is thus across the ship from one side to the other. Athwart hawse is when one vessel gets across the stem of another.

A-trip.—When the anchor is broken out of the ground or is a-weigh. A topmast is said to be a-trip when it has been launched and un-fidded.

Avast.—Stop, cease, hold, discontinue. As avast heaving (stop heaving), avast hauling (stop hauling), &c.

Awash.—Level with the surface of the water.

Away.—A general order to go, as "away aloft," for men to go into the rigging; "away aft," for the men to move aft, &c. "Gigs away there," or "cutters away there," or "dinghys away there," is the common way of giving the order to get the boats ready and manned. "Away with it," to run away with the fall of a tackle when hauling upon it. "Away she goes," said of a vessel when first she moves in launching. "Away to leeward," "away to windward," "away on the port bow," &c.

A-Weather.—The situation of the helm when it is hauled to windward. To haul a sail a-weather is to haul the sheet in to windward instead of to leeward, to form a back sail, to box a vessel's head off the wind or put stern way on her. Generally to windward.

A-Weigh.—Said of the anchor when it is a-trip or broken out of the ground. The anchor is weighed when hove up to the hawse pipe.

Axioms for Yachtsmen (by an American).—Don't stand up in a boat; don't sit on the rail of a boat; don't let your garments trail overboard; don't step into a boat except in her middle; don't stand up in a boat before you are along-side; don't pull under the bows of a ship—it looks green, and the consequences might be fatal; don't forget to "in fenders" every time you shove off; don't forget that a loaded boat keeps headway longer than a light one; don't make fast with a hitch that will jam; don't lower away with the plug out; keep the plug on hand by a small lanyard to it, so that it cannot be "led astray" and have to be hunted up when needed. Do.—Do hoist your flags chock up—nothing betokens the lands-man more than slovenly colours; do haul taut all your gear; do see that no "Irish pennants" are flying adrift aloft; do have a long scope out in a gale; do see that your crew keeps in its place and does not boss the quarter deck; do keep your men tidy and looking sailor-like; do keep to leeward of competing yachts when you are not in the match yourself.

Aye Aye, Sir.—The response made by seamen when an order or direction is given them, to show that they understand and will obey.

B.

Back.—To back a sail, is to haul the sheet to windward.

Back and fill.—To luff up in the wind, and then fill off again. Often a vessel is worked up a narrow channel with a weather tide by backing and filling: that is, the helm is put down slowly, and the vessel kept moving until she is nearly head to wind; the helm is then put smartly up, and the vessel filled again. Care must be always taken to fill before the vessel loses way. Figuratively, to back and fill is to blow hot and cold, or assent and dissent, or to go backwards and forwards with opinions.

Backing.—Timber fitted at the back of other timbers.

Backstays.—The stays that support the topmast with a beam or stern wind. The topmast shrouds or rigging. (See "Shifting Backstay, and Preventer.")

Backwater.—The water thrown back when waves strike a wall or other solid object. The water that appears to follow under the stern of a ship. To back water is to move the oars of a boat, so that the boat moves astern instead of ahead.

Baffling Wind.—A wind that is continually shifting its direction, so that it is difficult to keep the sails full or steady; more frequently used when the vessel is close or nearly close hauled.

Bag.—Sails are said to bag when they do not sit flatly.

Bagpipe.—To bring the sheet of an after-sail, such as the mizen, forward to the weather rigging, so that the sail forms a bag, or back sail: when head to wind useful to put stern way on a vessel.

Balance Lug.—A lug sail with a boom and yard. About one-sixth of the sail is on the fore side of the mast, and thus "balances" on the mast, requiring no dipping when going about; apparently adapted from the Chinese lug sail.

Balance Reef.—In gaff sails a band with reef points or eyelet holes for lacing, sewn from the throat to the clew. The reef is taken in by lowering the jaws down to the boom and lacing the sail along the reef band to the boom. Sometimes the gaff end is lowered down to the boom end; in which case the reef band is laced along the gaff.

Bale.—To throw water out of a vessel or boat by buckets or balers.

Baler or Bailer.—A small basin-like vessel, used for throwing water out of a boat.

Balk.—A hewn tree; a piece of timber for masts, &c.

Ballast.—Dead weight carried to assist the stability of a vessel. A ship is said to be in ballast when she has no merchandise on board, but only sand, gravel, mud, or rubbish as ballast. A yacht in marine parlance is always "in ballast."

Ballast, To Keep Clean or Sweeten.—The ballast of an old vessel should be removed every other season, scrubbed, and whitewashed with hot lime, or coated with black varnish, paraffin, or red lead. The hold of the yacht should at the same time be thoroughly cleansed and black varnished, distempered, or red leaded, or coated with one of the patent paints. A mixture of two-thirds Stockholm tar and one-third coal tar boiled together will make a good composition for the ballast and the inside of a vessel below the floor. Some vessels are now regularly hauled up every year, and of course their ballast is taken out and stored. The ballast of a new vessel generally requires cleansing when she is laid up, as the soakings from the oak frames make a very unpleasant odour. (See "Distemper," "Laying up," and "Limber Boards").

Ballast Bearers.—(See " Bearers.")

Ballast, Run, into a Vessel.—Before the days of heavy lead keels, several racing yachts had ballast run into them, but the plan was not approved of owing to the great labour of cutting the lead out again in case of alterations becoming necessary ; and moreover with a little trouble ballast can be moulded to fit into every cavity, however small, between the floors and keel. Before the lead is run into a vessel the timbers and plank should be cemented or smeared with wet clay ; the vessel should be caulked before the lead is run in. In iron vessels the ballast is run in to a hollow keel which is formed for the purpose.

Ballast, To Shift from Inside to the Keel.—The quantity of ballast that can be removed from inside the hull whilst the same stability is maintained by placing a certain amount of metal on the keel, can be ascertained as follows : before the vessel is hauled up to have the metal keel fixed, perform the following experiment : take a quantity of ballast (say 10cwt. for a 20 tonner) from the hull and place it on one side of the deck ; mark on the vessel's side the line to which she is heeled ; after the metal keel has been fixed and the vessel launched, put exactly the same weight of ballast (taken from the hull) as before on the side of the deck in exactly the same place ; then remove ballast from the inside until the vessel heels to the line she did before the metal keel was fixed. This experiment should always be made before sailing a vessel to a lighter load-line after fixing a metal keel or adding to one. The experiment should be performed in perfectly smooth water. (The result can be arrived at by calculation, as explained in " Yacht Architecture," but the process requires too many figures to introduce here.)

Ballast, Shifting.—To put ballast (usually duck shot in bags) in the weather side of a vessel during sailing. This practice for many years has been strictly forbidden in yacht racing, and if a man were known to practise it he would be shunned as a thoroughly unsportsmanlike person.

Balloon Sails. — Balloon canvas is a term applied to sails of large dimensions, made of light canvas, and generally only used in yacht matches. A balloon jib fills up the whole space from the bowsprit end, masthead, and mast at deck ; a balloon foresail is hanked to the forestay, but the clew extends some distance abaft the mast ; the foot of a balloon topsail extends beyond the gaff on a jack yard ; a balloon maintopmast staysail has an up and down weather leech extending below the lower corner of the sail, which is hanked to the maintopmast stay. A jib topsail was sometimes termed a balloon sail, but now it is generally considered a " working sail." Balloon jibs have gone out of fashion, as " bowsprit spinnakers " are now universally used, and are more easily handled. Schooners seldom now have a jack yard for fore topsail.

Balloon Topsail.—This is usually understood to be a topsail with a foot or jack yard to extend the foot beyond the gaff. Formerly, the foot yard was short and the head yard was of great length—as long as could be stowed on the deck of a yacht—and the sail, very heavy to hoist, was quite unfit for close-hauled work. As the hoisting of these heavy yards was an operation of so much labour, they fell into disuse for some years —between 1873 and 1883—but recently the sail has been re-introduced with a comparatively short head yard and longer foot yard. The sail has consequently nearly as much area as the old-fashioned " balloon topsail," and the combined weight of head yard and foot yard is about half that of the old yard ; beyond this, as the sail is well peaked, it sits and stands well on a wind in moderate breezes.

Bamboo Spars.—In small boats these are often used on account of their lightness. They vary much in strength, and should be from 10 to 20 per cent. greater diameter than solid wood spars.

Bare Poles.—With no sail set. With all the sails furled or stowed at sea for scudding before a heavy gale, or sometimes for lying to.

Bargee.—A seaman employed on board a barge.

Bar Harbour.—A harbour that has a bank or bar of sand or gravel at its mouth, so that it can only be entered at certain hours of the tide.

Bark.—A general term for a vessel.

Barque.—A ship without yards on her mizen mast.

Barquentine.—A vessel square rigged on her foremast, and fore-and-aft rigged on her two other masts.

Barra Boats.—Vessels of the Western Isles of Scotland, with almost perfect V section.

Barrel or Drum.—The part of a capstan, windlass, or winch round which the cable or rope is wound whilst heaving. Sometimes termed the drum.

Base Line.—In naval architecture a level line near the keel, from which all heights are measured perpendicularly to it. Generally in yacht designs the load water-line, as shown in a Sheer Plan, is made the base line, and all depths and heights are measured perpendicularly or at right angles to it.

Batten.—A long piece of wood used to lash to yards or booms to strengthen them. Thin pieces of hard wood fitted to spars to prevent their being chafed or cut. Thin splines of wood used by draughtsmen to make curved lines. A general term for a thin strip of wood. Battens fitted to sails.

Batten Down.—Putting tarpaulins over hatches or skylights, and securing them by iron bars or wood battens.

Beach.—A Shore. To beach is to lay ashore, or strand.

Beach Boats.—Flat floored boats that can be readily beached.

Beacon.—A stake, boom, or post put on a sandbank or shoal as a warning for vessels.

Beacon Buoy.—A buoy with a kind of cross upon top of it.

Beadon's Safety Reel.—Used for belaying the main sheet. This was a contrivance invented in 1833 described in "Folkard's Sailing Boat." This reel is said to have been contrived without cogs or catches, and released the main sheet upon the boat being heeled to a certain angle (See "Cruickshank's Patent Cleats" and main sheet slip.)

Beam.—A timber that crosses a vessel transversely to support the deck. The breadth of a vessel. "Before the beam" is forward of the middle part of a ship. The wind is said to be before the beam when the ship makes a less angle than 90° with the wind. A beam wind is a wind that blows at right angles to a vessel's keel. "Abaft the beam" is towards the stern.

Beam and Length.—The proportion a vessel's beam bears to her length. A quarter of a century ago it was considered that this proportion had a great deal to do with speed. hence many builders set great store on the particular amount of beam to length they gave a vessel. In sailing yachts it is found that for cruising a good proportion is from four to four and three-quarter beams to length. The comparatively deep and long-bodied vessels make the best sea boats. They are of a good weight, length, and depth, the conditions which tend to lessen the influence of the waves on their motions, and they are easier with a beam sea.

Beam Ends.—A vessel is said to be on her beam ends when she is hove down on her side by the wind or other force, so that the ends of her deck beams are on the water, or her deck beams perpendicular to the water. However, in sea parlance, a ship is said to be on her beam ends when knocked down to a squall to say 45°, so that when a ship is described as being on her "beam ends" the meaning need not be taken literally.

Beam Trawl.—A trawl whose mouth is extended by a long spar or beam.

Bear, To.—The direction an object takes from a ship expressed in compass points or by points in the vessel; as in reference to another vessel she bears S.E. or W.S.W., &c., or on the port bow, or weather bow, port beam or weather beam, port quarter or weather quarter, &c.; or two points on the weather bow or port bow, &c.

Bear a Hand There!—An admonition to hurry.

Bear Away, or Bear Up.—To put the helm to windward and keep the vessel more off the wind. Generally used in close-hauled sailing when a vessel begins to alter her course by sailing off the wind. (See "Wear.")

Bearers.—Irons fitted in between the frames of a yacht for ballast to be stowed on, so that it does not rest on the plank; also the beams which carry the cabin floor or platform of a yacht, termed platform bearers.

Bearings.—The direction between one object and another; generally the direction of an object on land to a ship.—The widest part of a vessel which may either be above or below water. A vessel is said to be on her bearings when she is heeled over, so that her greatest breadth is in the water.

Bearings by Compass.—An object is said to bear so many points on the port or starboard bow, or port or starboard quarter, or port or starboard beam as the case may be; or an object may be said to bear E.N.E. or E. or W., &c., from the point of observation. The usual plan of taking a bearing is to stand directly over the binnacle, and notice which point on the compass card directly points to the object. A more accurate way of taking bearings may be followed thus : on each quarter-rail abreast of the binnacle, have a half compass plate of brass fixed, or mark off compass points on the rail, and let two opposite points (say north and south) be in direct line or parallel with the keel. A pointer or hand, eight or nine inches long, must be fitted to the plate, to ship and unship on a pivot; move the pointer until it points directly to the object, then read off the number of points it is from the direction of the ship's head. Next observe the direction of the ship's head by the binnacle compass; if the ship's head points N., and the pointer showed the object to be, say, four points away westerly from the direction of the ship's head, then the object will bear N.W., and so on. If very great accuracy be required, and if the ship be yawing about, one hand should watch the binnacle compass, whilst another makes the observations with the pointer.

An object is said to bear "on the bow" if its direction in relation to the ship does not make a greater angle with the keel of the vessel than 45°. If the direction of the object makes a greater angle than that it would be said to bear "before the beam;" next on the beam, then abaft the beam, on the quarter, right astern.

Beat.—To beat to windward is to make way against the wind by a zigzag course, and frequent tacking. (See "Plying" "Thrashing" and "Turning to Windward.")

Beating to Windward.—(See "Beat.")

Becalm.—To deprive a vessel of wind, as by one vessel passing to windward of another.

Becalmed.—In a calm; without wind.

Becket.—A piece of rope used to confine or secure spars, ropes, or tackles. Generally an eye is at one end; sometimes an eye at either end; or a knot at one end and an eye at the other.

Beef.—Manual strength; generally the weight of the men hauling on a rope. "More beef here" is a request for help when hauling. Probably the term originated with the casks of beef used for food on shipboard.

Before the Beam.—Towards the bow or stem of a vessel.

Before the Mast.—A term used to describe the station of seamen as distinguished from officers. Thus a man before the mast means a common sailor, and not an officer. The term owes its origin to the fact that the seamen were berthed in the forecastle, which is usually "before the mast."

Before the Wind.—Running with the wind astern.

Behaviour.—The performance of a ship in a seaway or under canvas is generally termed by sailors her "behaviour."

Belay That.—An order given whilst men are hauling on a rope, &c., to cease hauling and make fast to the last inch they have got in. Also slang for cease talking or fooling.

Belay, To.—To make fast a rope or fall of a tackle. In hauling upon a rope the signal to cease is usually, "Belay!" or "Belay there!" Belay that, or "Avast hauling! Belay!"

To belay the mainsheet in small boats where the sheet travels on a horse through a block. The block will travel on the horse by a thimble

FIG. 230.

eye strop; the sheet will be spliced to the clew cringle in the sail and rove through the block. Bring the fall of the sheet down to the pin under the stern seat, round which pin take a single turn: then take a bight and jam it between the sheet and the seat, and a slight pull will release the sheet. The sheet can be

belayed in the same fashion by a turn taken under a thole pin in the gunwale; or a bight of the fall can be taken and made fast round the sheet above the block by a slippery hitch. A plan for belaying a single sheet is shown in the accompanying sketch (Fig. 230). A through pin is fitted into the transom as shown. The fall of the sheet is brought round the pin outside the transom, then round the pin inside the transom, and a bight jammed in between the transom and sheet.

Belaying Pins.—Pins in racks, in cavels, spider hoops, &c., to make fast ropes to.

Belaying the Binnacle.—A slang term applied to the acts of a greenhorn or sham sailor who uses unseamanlike terms, or misapplies well known terms, or makes unseamanlike or impracticable suggestions.

Bell Buoy.—A buoy with an iron cage upon top of it, with a bell which is struck by a hammer or hammers moved by the heave of the sea.

Bells.—The manner of keeping time on board ship by striking a bell every half hour. Thus one bell is a half hour, as half-past twelve; two bells one o'clock; three bells half-past one, and so on until eight bells are struck, which would be four o'clock. One bell would then be begun again and proceed up to eight o'clock. Thus eight bells are struck every four hours, the duration of a watch.

Below.—A general term for the under-deck space. To go below is to descend from the deck to the cabin, or to under the deck. A seaman always goes "below," and never "downstairs." It is considered very green and landsman-like to hear a person on board a vessel speak of going "downstairs" for below, or upstairs for "on deck."

Below! or Below There!—A mode of hailing or attracting the attention of the crew below by those on deck.

B.M.—Abbreviation for builders' measurement or tonnage, the formula for which is $\frac{(L - \frac{3}{5}B) \times B \times \frac{1}{2}B}{94}$. The length is taken from the after side of the sternpost in a line with the rabbet of the keel to a perpendicular dropped from the fore side of the stem on deck. This is "length between perpendiculars." O.M. is sometimes used, that being an abbreviation for "Old Measurement," which is the same as B.M.

Bend.—To fasten a rope to another; to fasten a rope to a spar; to bend a sail to a yard, &c. A knot, a mode of fastening a rope to a spar, &c.

Bends.—The wales of a ship. Stout planks on the side of a ship.

Beneaped.—Aground for want of water, owing to neap tides. The rise and fall of neap tides during quarter moons are less than during the full and change; consequently, if a vessel got ashore during a high water spring tide she might have to remain all through the neap period.

Bermudian Rig.—The mast of a Bermuda rigged boat is very long, and is placed far into the bow, which is usually very bluff. The mast rakes aft, and the sail set upon it is of the well-known sliding gunter shape. The objection to the rig is the long heavy mast placed in the eyes of the boat, and although the sail stands well when hauled in on a wind, yet off the wind it causes some trouble, as it is almost impossible — except in very strong breezes —to keep the sail from falling on board.

Berth.—A place to sleep in ; a cabin. Employment.

Berthed.—The situation of a ship when anchored.

Berthon's Logs, or Speed Indicators.—A log invented by the Rev. E. Berthon. A tube passes through the keel, and the water rises in this tube in proportion to the speed of the vessel through the water. A simple mechanical contrivance of weight, line, and pulley serves to indicate the speed on a dial.

Bevel.—In shipbuilding, the departure from the square a timber is made to take to suit the inclination of a plank. An oblique edge of a piece of timber or plank.

Bevelling Board.—A piece of wood used by ship builders on which the angle of the bevels for timbers are marked in lines.

Bibs.—Pieces of timbers fastened to the hounds of ships' masts to support the trestle trees.

Bight.—A loop or part of a rope doubled so as to form a loop, thus ∩.—The deepest part of a bay.

Bilge.—The round in a vessel's timbers where they begin to approach a vertical direction.

Bilged.—A vessel is said to be bilged when her framing is broken in, or damaged along her bilge by grounding, or falling down when shored up by the side of a wharf.

Bilge Keels.—Pieces of timber (sometimes termed rolling chocks) fitted longitudinally on a vessel's bottom, so that she may take the ground readily and not damage her bottom. Bilge keels, however, now fulfil different offices and are fitted to large ships to assist in checking their rolling. The Brighton beach boats are fitted with bilge keels, and it has been argued that they prevent a boat making lee way; of course only the lee bilge keel can so operate to any useful extent, and the effectiveness of this one would be interfered with by the disturbed state of the water near it. Bilge keels, if very deep, would affect very greatly a boat's handiness in tacking; also the lee one would assist in heeling the boat to an extent dependent upon the force of the lee way, and the area of the bilge keel; on the other hand, bilge keels will tend to check the sudden heeling of a boat, for the same reason that they cause the process of rolling to be more slowly performed, because they have to move a body of water. In steel and iron built steam yachts, bulb iron bilge plates are often fitted and check the rolling.

Bilge Kelsons.—Stout pieces of timber fitted inside a vessel in a fore-and-aft direction along the bilge to strengthen her.

Bilge Strakes.—Thick plank worked longitudinally in the ceiling of a vessel inside along the bilge, or over the heads and heels of the frames, to strengthen her—used instead of bilge kelsons, and through fastened.

Bilge Water.—The water inside a vessel, which in flat-floored crafts may rest in the bilge.

Bill.—A point of land ; also the extreme points of the flukes of an anchor.

Bill Boards.—Pieces of wood fitted to the bow of a vessel to protect the plank from the fluke of the anchor.

Bill of Health.—A document wherein it is certified that the condition of the crew is healthy or otherwise. Hence a clean bill of health means that all the crew are free from disorders, and a foul bill of health the contrary.

Bill of Lading.—A document setting forth the cargo of a ship, certified by the master.

Bill of Sale.—A document by which a vessel is transferred from one owner to another. A "Bill of Sale" must be produced before a register can be transferred. Forms of Bill of Sale can be procured from Waterlow and Sons, printers and stationers, City, London.

There are several points to which attention should be given before concluding a purchase. Wages form a prior claim on every vessel. It is therefore essentially necessary that a purchaser should satisfy himself that no claims of this description exist; or he may find, after he has completed his purchase, that he has some further large amount to pay before he can call the ship his own. In 1890 a case occurred in which the mortgagee of a large steam yacht, after taking possession, had to defend an action in the Admiralty Court, brought by the late master for wages and necessary payments, and eventually had to pay a large sum to settle these claims. It should also be seen, before a purchase is completed, that possession of the yacht can be given, and that she is in the hands of no shipbuilder who has a lien upon her and a right to detain her for work done. With regard to yachts, of course claims for salvage seldom arise; but it is just as well to remember that, if they do exist, they form a claim against the vessel.

As to the sale of yachts, very little need be said, but there are one or two simple rules which it is absolutely necessary to follow. A vendor should never, under any circumstances, give up possession of his vessel until he has the purchase-money in hand. A breach of this rule has not infrequently produced rather serious consequences. In 1890 an owner sold his vessel to an apparently rich man, and very weakly gave him possession. He had to sue for the purchase-money, and to get the sheriff to seize and sell the yacht again, at a considerable reduction in price, before he was paid. Fortunately for him, he did get his money eventually, although the purchaser became bankrupt within a few months after the transaction.

It is necessary to be very guarded in dealing with foreigners. A case occurred, some few years since, in which an American gentleman bought a schooner yacht, and was given possession before payment of the purchase-money. The purchaser thereupon proceeded to get under way for America, and neglected to pay for the ship. The owners pursued him in a tug and brought him back to Cowes; thus securing the vessel, but not the money.

Another rule which should be observed is never to send a vessel out of the country to a foreign purchaser until payment has been made in England. An owner may find it a very difficult matter to enforce payment in a foreign court. The purchaser may raise difficulties and objections to the yacht after she has got abroad, and the owner may have to bring his yacht home again, with the expenses of his crew and his outfit to pay.

Another point with regard to which vendors require to be careful is the commission payable on a sale. Few sales are effected nowadays without the intervention of an agent, and it is an ordinary practice to put a yacht into the hands of several agents for sale. A purchaser frequently writes round to every well-known agent for a yacht likely to suit him, and perhaps he gets particulars of the same vessel from three or four different agents. It is often very difficult to say which of them first introduces the vessel to him, and who is entitled to receive the commission on the sale. It is not an uncommon occurrence for two or three claims to be made for commission on the same vessel; and it is very needful for the owner, before he completes his contract, to satisfy himself on this point, and to make sure that he will not be called upon to pay more than one commission on the sale of his yacht.

Billy Buoy.—A bluff bowed vessel, common in the north, rigged with one mast, and usually with a square topsail.

Binnacle.—A case wherein the compass is contained. (See "Compass" and "Fluid Compass.")

Bird's Nest.—See "Crow's Nest."

Birlin.—A rowing and sailing boat of the Hebrides.

Bitter End.—The end of a cable left abaft the bitts after the turns have been taken. Sometimes the anchor is shackled to the "bitter end" when the used end has become much worn. The extreme end of a rope.

Bitts.—Stout pieces of timber fitted in the deck to receive the bowsprit; also stout pieces of timber fitted in the deck by the side of the mast, to which the halyards are usually belayed.

Black Book.—A book kept at the Admiralty, or said to be, wherein is recorded the offences of seamen. Several yacht clubs have kept "black books," but they have been of little use, as owners showed a disinclination to insist that no man should be engaged in his yacht who was on the "black book."

Black Leading a Boat's Bottom.—It was formerly a common practice to black lead the bottom of boats, especially for match sailing, and the custom is still much followed. There were several methods of getting the lead on, and the following is as good as any: First scrape the bottom clean of old paint, tar, &c., and stop open seams, nail holes, shakes, &c. Then put on a thin coat of coal tar, reduced by turpentine or naphtha until quite liquid. When dry and hard put on another coat, and if the boat is a large one this second coat should be put on by "instalments." When nearly dry, but yet sticky, put on the black lead, which must be mixed with water (and well stirred), and make a solution about as thick as paint. To get the mixture on a dabber must be used; a sponge tied up in a soft piece of cotton cloth is the best thing for the purpose. Care must be taken not to attempt to put on the black lead in the sun, or the tar will come through. On the other hand, if the tar is hard the black lead will not "take hold." When the whole is thoroughly dry and hard, polish up with the ordinary brushes used by housemaids for grates.

Mayflower, Puritan, and Galatea had blacklead mixed with copal varnish put on their hulls. The same was sand-papered and brushed smooth with hard shoe brushes, taking care to have a good smooth body of paint underneath. Galatea was also coated with blacklead on gold size, the blacklead being put on dry and brushed afterwards. This is the best method. Blacklead acts on steel. After being in the water three or four months rust will show in beads.

A blackleaded bottom will last clean for match sailing about five weeks.

Black Paint.—A good mixture for the outside of a boat is thus made: to 6lb. of best black paint add half pint of good varnish and ⅓lb. of blue paint.

Or, black 9lb.; raw linseed oil 1 quart; boiled linseed oil 1 quart; dryers ⅓lb.

For an iron yacht: 1cwt. of Astbury's oxide of paint; 6 gallons of boiled linseed oil; 1 gallon of turpentine; 3 gallons of varnish; 21lb. dryers. (Messrs Astbury's, King-street, Manchester.)

Blacking Down.—Painting or tarring the rigging, or sides of a ship.

Black Jack.—The black flag hoisted by pirates.

Fig. 231.

Blackwall Hitch.—A hitch used to jam the bight of a rope to a hook, &c. (Fig. 231.)

Blade.—The flat part of an oar or screw propeller.

Bleaching.—An American plan for bleaching sails is as follows :—Scrub with soap and fresh water on both sides, rinse well, then sprinkle with the following solution : slacked lime, 2 bushels ; draw off lime water and mix with 120 gallons water and ¼lb. blue vitriol. This also preserves the sails. (See " Mildew.")

Blind Harbour.—A harbour whose entrance cannot readily be made out from a distance.

Blisters.—Unsightly blisters on paint are generally caused by putting new paint upon the top of old, or using very thick paint. The old paint should be burnt or scraped off.

Block.—A pulley. A single block has one sheave ; double, two ; three-fold or treble, three ; and so on. (See " Fiddle block " and " Sister Block.")

Block and Block.—Chock-a-block. When the blocks of a tackle are hauled close together. A vessel is said to take her main sheet block and block, when the boom is hauled so much aboard that the two blocks come close or nearly close together.

Blow, A.—A gale of wind.

Blue Jackets.—Sailors.

Blue Peter.—A blue flag with a white square in the centre ; hoisted at the fore truck as a signal that the vessel is about to go to sea. Sometimes for brevity called Peter.

Blue Water.—The open sea or ocean.

Bluff.—A wall-like headland.

Bluff-bowed.—Very full bowed, thus ⊐.

Board.—In beating to windward a board is the time a vessel is on one tack and the distance she makes on that tack. Thus it may be a long board or a short board. Working to windward by a long board and a short board is when a vessel can more nearly lie her course on one tack than on another. Thus, suppose the wind be S.W., and the vessel's course from headland to headland S.S.W., and the vessel can lie four points from the wind ; then on the starboard tack the vessel will head S., or two points off her course ; on the port tack she will lie W., or six points off her course. The long board will be the one on the starboard tack. A vessel is said to make a good board when the wind frees her on one tack ; a bad board when it heads her. A stern board is to get stern way on whilst tacking.—To board a ship is to enter upon her deck, generally supposed to mean without invitation.

" By the board." To fall close by the deck. A mast is said to go by the board when it breaks by the deck and falls overboard.

Board and Board.—Vessels are said to work board and board when they keep in company and tack simultaneously.

Boat Builders' Union.—An association of boat builders, founded 1821, and called the " Sons of Sincerity Society of Ship-Boat Builders." Their place of meeting is the " City Arms," near Stepney Station, London. If any person desired to obtain a boat builder to assist in building a boat it could be done through this union.

Boat Building.—In the first place lay off the sections, keel and sternpost, and stem. If the keel has a straight edge, top and bottom, it will not require to be laid off. When the sections are laid off, proceed to make moulds to fit the curves ; these moulds will be made of ¼ inch, ⅜ inch, or 1 inch deal or elm, according to the size of the boat ; any odd pieces of stuff will do, and there can be as many joints in a mould as may be found convenient : (See Fig. 232.) The cross piece A should be stout enough to keep the mould rigid. The diagonal braces D need not be used if the mould can be made rigid without them ; in such case the joints in the mould should be secured by a doubling piece. The bar W.L.

MOULD

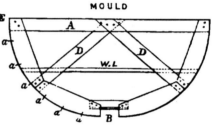

Fig. 232.

represents the load-water-line. B is the part that fits on the keel and represents the " joggle " in the floor-timber. The cross piece here should be securely attached and fixed so that the joggle is of the proper depth. A nail on each side of the mould, or a couple of pieces of wood nailed to the keel, will keep the mould in position on the keel.

The outer edges of the mould must be planed up to fit the curve of the section as drawn on the mould loft. When floors or timbers have to be sawn out, and not steamed, the mould is laid over the timber and its shape marked on it by pencil or chalk.

The stem and sternpost are tenoned into mortices in the keel ; but if the keel be not thick enough to take a tenon, the keel and stem, and keel and sternpost are box-scarphed together by halves : that is, half the thickness of each is cut away.

In all the drawings of small boats given in the body of the book, the load-water-line is made the base-line, and therefore everything must be plumb to that.

Having got the stem, sternpost, and keel shaped and put together, proceed to fix them to the stocks. [A deal firmly fixed edgeways at a convenient distance from the floor—high enough to enable the builder to drive the nails up through the bottom of the boat—will make the stocks.] A straight edge or line must be fitted from stem to stern-post to represent the load-water-line as shown on the Sheer Plan.

Also a stout bar of wood must be nailed to stem-head and stern-post-head, above the one marking the L.W.L., to firmly connect the two; this bar will be found useful for nailing the mould stays to.

In fixing the keel stem and sternpost frame on the stocks it must be wedged up forward until the line or straight edge representing the load-water-line is perfectly level or horizontal. A spirit level or plumb level can be used for this adjustment.

Fit the dead wood knee aft, and the stem knee or apron forward. Bore the holes for the through bolts with a long auger or gimlet. The heads of the bolts will be inside, and clenched outside over a ring.

Next the transom must be cut out from a mould and let into the sternpost and through bolted. The edges of the transom will require to be bevelled to suit the fore-and-aft curve of the boat.

When the keel, stem and sternpost are on the stocks and in position (the stem and sternpost must be plumbed to see that they neither cant to port nor starboard), they must be secured by stays; the stays will be bars of wood and reach from the stemhead and head of sternpost to the floor or ceiling of the building-shed, and they must be securely nailed. The keel can be kept in its position by similar stays; or if the keel be quite straight on its underside it can be kept in its position by thumb cleats nailed to the deal forming the stocks.

The lower edge and upper edge of the rabbet in the keel, stem, and stern dead woods must be next set off, and cut out with a chisel. The aft dead wood will probably require some adzing away back to the rabbet.

The moulds must be next put into their proper places. Care must be taken that they are "square" to the keel (*i.e.*, cross it at right-angles) that they are plumb (perpendicular) to the load-water-line, and that the bar W L (Fig. 232) is at the level of the line stretched between stem and stern-post to represent the load-water-line. The moulds must be kept in position by wood stays and ribbands formed by battens of fir. These ribbands can be let in flush with the outside edges of the moulds. They need not then be removed until the whole of the planking is complete and the timbers steamed in. This will be a great advantage for carvel build.

If the boat is to have a counter, the rudder trunk will be constructed as it is in yachts. In order to allow plenty of room in the trunk, pieces of wood an inch or so thick are fitted to the sides of the sternpost before the sides of the trunk are fixed on. The trunk in a fore-and-aft direction is also made about twice as deep as the diameter of the rudder post. Plank will vary according to the size of the boat and curve of the bilge, and in the widest part may be from 4 to 5 inches. Measure the half-girth of the midship mould (Fig. 232) from B to E by passing a tape or line round the outside curved edge. Divide this length into a

number of equal intervals to represent the breadth of the strakes as *a a*, &c. (see Fig. 232). Allowance must be made for about ⅛in. overlap of each plank which forms the lands. Count the number of intervals or strakes of plank, and set off the same number in equal intervals on the rabbet of the stem (see *x x*, Fig. 233) and on the transom. These intervals will be much closer together than on the

STEM

FIG. 233.

moulds, and will therefore show that the plank must taper towards the ends. The same number of intervals can also be set off on the intermediate moulds.

The garboard strake will be first fitted. This will be a strake quite straight on its upper edge before it is bent round the moulds from stem to stern post. The under edge will be cut to fit the rabbet in keel, and stem, and dead wood aft. When this plank has been fitted into the garboard and nailed at intervals of two or three inches to the keel, the next plank must be fitted. Take the board (out of which the plank is to be sawn) and hold it along as closely as possible outside the upper edge of the garboard strake. Mark a line along it to correspond with the top edge of the garboard. Remove the board and it will be found that the line is more or less curved. Saw down this curved line. Then fit the board to the garboard again, making it overlap (by its curved edge) the garboard by about ¼ of an inch. Now mark by spots on the upper edge of the board the next interval, representing the breadth of the plank (see *a a*, Fig. 232) for each mould, including stem and dead wood or transom aft. Remove the board and run a line in through

PLANK

FIG. 234.

the spots representing the intersections *a a* on with the moulds; this will show the shape, or the curve of the upper edge, and the curve of the lower edge of the next strake. The plank may possibly be shaped like the sketch (Fig. 233), but the greatest curvature will be found as the bilge is reached. It is not absolutely necessary that the plank should accord with the spots *a a* at every mould, as the intervals are more as a guide to get the curve of the strake than to show the shape of the curve arbitrarily.

Boat Building—continued.

When the strake has been cut out it will be planed and then fitted to overlap the garboard; whilst it is being nailed it will be held in position by a number of clamps (at intervals of two or three feet.)

The clamps are made of two pieces of hard wood loosely connected by a screw bolt (see Fig. 235) and has a wedge. The bolt must be allowed plenty of play, so that when the

PLANK

Fig. 235.

clamp grips the strakes it can be wedged up tightly as shewn.

The plank will be nailed together at intervals of 3 inches. The nails will be of copper, and will be rooved and clinched inside. At the stem and transom, the upper part of each strake is thinned away in order that the hood ends may fit into the rabbet flush.

To get the strakes round the bilge in a fair curve the upper outer edge of each strake is bevelled off, and sometimes the inner lower edge of the overlapping strake is also bevelled. The plank can be steamed if necessary.

Holes should be bored for the copper nails by a sharp bradawl a little smaller than the nails. The roove having been put over the nail, the latter will be cut off by a pair of nippers, leaving about ¹⁄₁₆ of an inch projecting above the roove. A "holder on" will be held to the head of the nail outside the boat, and the nail will then be clinched down over the roove inside the boat.

The boat being now planked up to the top strake, the floors and timbers must be put in. If the boat is a large one, such as the Brighton Beach boats (not the New Brighton boats, which are carvel built), the floors will be sawn out of timber of a suitable size and joggled (see Fig. 236) to fit in the

Fig. 236.

lands of the plank; but joggles are objectionable as they weaken the floors. The floors should extend across the keel and into the turn of the bilge; they will be fastened through the keel with a Muntz-metal, or copper, or galvanised iron bolt, and, if thought necessary, clenched with ring. A copper nail will be driven through the plank (where two strakes overlap), and be clenched on the top of the floor; frequently rooves are not used for these fastenings. A fastening is put through every overlap.

The timbers should be sawn out of a straight-grained piece of American elm, but sometimes English oak or ash is used; oak

is generally preferred for the floors, and American elm for the timbers.

The timbers, having been sawn out, must be planed up, and will then require steaming to get them into their places. The timbers should extend from one gunwale across the keel to the other gunwale, but frequently, where stout floors are inserted, the timbers are not worked across the keel, and do not reach within 6in. of the keel; in such cases the timbers are in "halves."

A steam chest or kiln will have to be constructed (see Fig. 237). In length it should be a foot or so longer than the longest timber, and be a foot deep and a foot broad. It should be made of 1¼in. deal. The end, *a*, is a door. Inside on the bottom should be nailed three or four cross pieces of wood, 2in. deep, for the timbers to rest upon, forming a kind of rack.

Steam can be generated in a common three-legged pot set up on bricks (see *k*). The pot should contain three or four gallons of water. The cover will be made of wood, cemented round with clay or mortar. *n* is a steampipe (made of inch deal, inside size 3½in. by 3½in.); *p* is a plug for the water supply. The door, *a*, should fit inside the steam chest, and fillets

STEAM KILN

Fig. 237.

of inch deal must be nailed inside for the door to rest against. Before putting the door in its place, clay or mortar should be smeared round the fillets to keep the door from leaking. The door need not be hinged, but can be kept in its place by a cross-bar of wood working through two staples driven into the ends of the chest. We have seen an excellent boiler extemporised by rivetting together the rims of two iron "coppers," thus (Fig. 238): A steampipe, *p*, is rivetted on the top of the upper part.

The timbers will require steaming three or four hours before they are sufficiently pliable. They must be taken from the steam chest and fitted into the boat one by one; the first fastening to put in will be the one through or in the keel (a Muntz-metal dump is best for this). Press with the foot or hands the timber into the bilge, and put a fastening through it here (from the outside). The stations for the timbers should be previously marked across each plank strake, and the holes through the overlaps should be bored before putting the timber in.

If the timber has to be joggled to receive the inside edges of each strake (see Fig. 236), the fastenings must not be clinched, as the timber will have to be removed for the joggles to be cut. The timbers, however, should not be removed until they are perfectly cool and rigid; they should be allowed to stay in the boat a day and night before removing. (If strength rather than neatness be required, the timbers should not be joggled.)

The gunwale must now be fitted (this is more properly termed the "in-wale," as it is the piece of timber which is fitted *inside* the top strake; it answers the purpose of the "clamp" used in larger boats). Having decided upon the size of the wale—its depth and thickness—it must be fitted. In the first

FURNACE.

FIG. 238.

place, the timber heads are cut down inside the top strake to the depth of the wale [one plan is not to cut the timbers so low as this by half an inch, and make joggles in the wale to receive the head of each timber; when this is done, however, the wale or clamp should be somewhat stouter, as it will be weakened by the joggles]. Usually the wale is flush with the top strake; but a better plan is to cut a rabbet in the wale to fit over the top strake. A nail is put through the top strake and wale (from the outside), and rooved; or clinched without a roove, inside. A nail is put through about every 4, 5, or 6 inches. Forward, the wale top strake, stem, and apron are kept together by a breast-hook or >-shaped knee. Aft, the wale and top strake are secured to the transom by a knee. The thwarts will rest on the stringers, which are fastened through timbers and plank. The thwarts are secured by knees. The knee is fastened through and out the wale and top strake, and with a long fastening through the overlap of strakes, and clenched with ring on the knee; there will also be fastenings through the thwart and knee.

In buying copper nails care must be taken that "land nails" are obtained for the plank fastenings, and "timber nails" for the timber fastenings. The rooves must match the nails. A rooving iron (which is simply a kind of punch with a hole in its end) will be required to drive the rooves on whilst a hammer is held to the head of the nail. The sizes of the plank nails will depend upon the double thickness of the plank; about one-sixth of the double thickness should be added to the length of the nails for rooving and clenching.

If the boat is to be decked, a clamp or kind of shelf must be fitted to the timbers, and thoroughly fastened at each timber. The clamp will be fitted low enough for the beams to come flush with the top strake. The beams will be arched as required, and fastened through the shelf. The top strake should be of sufficient thickness to take the fastenings of the covering board. The covering board should be of hard wood, such as oak, and must be cut to fit the curve of the deck, as shown in the Half-breadth Plan.

The deck plank will be nailed to the beams by galvanised nails; not *through* the plank from the top downwards, but diagonally through the side edges of the plank into the beams.

The under edges of the plank will meet closely on the beams; but the upper edges will "gape," according to the rounding up of the beams as shown, in an exaggerated way, by *a a*, Fig. 239; this is for the caulking.

FIG. 239.

An eighth of an inch will give a wide enough seam. The oakum or cotton thread (a couple of threads will be enough for inch plank) must be driven in tightly by the caulking iron or chisel, and then payed with marine glue or stopped with putty (see articles on these subjects). Generally the arch of the beams will give the seam opening enough, as at *a a*; but, where it will not, the plank should be bevelled to the extent of a shaving. The seam round the covering board should be caulked and payed with extra care.

A hanging knee should be fitted on each side under the beam abreast of the mast or rigging. If the boat is wholly decked, three pairs of such hanging knees should be fitted.

If the boat is half-deck, waterways should be fitted. Short beams will be worked for these, and their inner ends will be butted into a fore-and-aft beam termed a carline, which fore-and-aft piece will in turn be butted into the full beams at either end. Two or three pairs of hanging knees (made of oak) will support the waterways.

Chain-plates for the rigging will be fitted as shown by the Clyde boat (see Plate XLVII.)

M M

Boat Chocks or Skids.—Pieces of wood with a score in them to take the keel of boats when they are lifted in upon deck.

Boats' Etiquette.—If the person in charge of a yacht's boat desires to salute a passing boat containing an admiral, captain, commodore, or other person of consequence, he directs the crew to lie on their oars as the boat passes, and to raise their hats or caps. The owner on leaving his yacht with a party is the last in the boat and the first out; and on leaving the shore is last to get into the boat and the first to board the yacht. This is the custom in the Royal Navy (the senior officer taking the place of the owner), in order that the admiral, captain, or other person might not be kept waiting alongside, which might be an unpleasant situation in bad weather. Thus the saying " the captain is the last in the first out of a boat." (See " Salutes" and " Ensign."

Boat Hook.—A wood pole with a metal hook and prong at one end; sometimes with two hooks. A yacht's gig has two boat hooks—one for the use of the bowman, another for the stroke; by these means a boat is held alongside the steps of a jetty or by the gangway of a vessel, &c.

Boat Keeper.—The man left in charge of a boat when the other part of her crew go on shore.

Boat's Crew.—Men told off to always man a particular boat, such as the gig, cutter, or dinghy of a yacht.

Boatswain.—An officer who takes charge of a yacht's gear, and it is his duty to superintend all work done upon the spars, rigging, or sails. He also takes charge of all spare gear and sails, and sees that everything on deck and above deck is neat, clean, and ship-shape. He must in every sense of the word be a thorough seaman, and must know how all work upon rigging and sails should be done. As he has constantly to handle the sails and rigging, he necessarily has a knowledge of their condition, and it is his duty to report all defects in the same.

Boatswain's Call.—A whistle consisting of a hollow ball and a tube leading to a hole in it. By varying the sounds the men are " piped " to their work just the same as soldiers are ordered by the sound of a bugle. The pipe is seldom met with in English yachts, not even in those of large size, and the boatswain has little to do with giving orders.

Bobstay.—The bowsprit stay.

Body.—Part of a vessel's hull, as fore-body, middle-body, and after-body. A vessel is said to be long-bodied when the tapering of the fore-and-aft lines are very gradual; short-bodied when the fore-and-aft lines taper very suddenly; a long-body thus means a great parallel length of middle-body. (See " Straight of Breadth.")

Body Plan.—A plan which contains the cross sections of a vessel. The midship section or largest section is generally shown on the right-hand side of the middle line of the body plan; sometimes on both sides.

Bollard.—A stout timber to fasten ropes and warps to.

Bollard Timbers.—The bollard timbers of a vessel are the same as the knightheads; originally the knightheads were carved figures of knights (fitted near the foremast to receive the windlass), hence the name knightheads. (See " Knightheads.")

Bollock Blocks.—Two blocks in the middle of a topsail yard of square rigged vessel, used in hoisting.

Bolsters.—Pieces of hard wood bolted to the yoke or lower cap on the mast for the rigging to rest upon. They are sometimes covered with leather or sheepskin with the hair on, or raw hide, to prevent the rigging chafing. (See " Rigging Plans.")

Bolt.—A fastening of metal. An eye bolt is a bolt with an eye in it used to hook blocks, &c., to. A ring bolt is a bolt with an eye and a ring in the eye. An ear bolt or lug bolt is a bolt with a kind of slot in it to receive the part of another bolt, a pin keeping the two together and forming a kind of joint. Bay bolts are bolts with jagged edges to prevent their drawing. A bolt applies to a roll of canvas.

Bolt Rope.—The rope sewn round the edges of sails. It is made of the very best Riga Rhine hemp, dressed with Stockholm tar. A fore-and-aft sail is roped on port side, a square-sail on aft side. There is the weather (luff) rope, leech rope, foot rope, and head rope.

Booby Hatch.—A hatch on coamings used to give greater height in the cabin of small yachts, and which can be removed.

Boom.—A spar used to extend the foot of sails. To top the boom is to make sail and away. To boom off is to shove off a wharf, bank, &c., by the aid of spars. Stakes of wood used to denote a channel through shoal water are termed booms.

Boom Irons.—Iron bands on booms, with eyes, to which blocks or ropes may be hitched.

Boomkin.—A short boom of great strength, usually written " bumpkin."

Bonnet.—An addition to a sail by lacing a short piece to its foot; common in America, not often seen in British yachts.

Bore.—A sudden tide wave, which rolls along rapidly at certain times on some rivers, and makes a great noise.

Boreas.—The north wind. An old sailor's saying is, " as cold as Boreas with an iceberg in each pocket." Popularly the god that rules the wind, as Æolus is supposed to do.

Bore Away.—Did bear away. Said of a vessel that alters her course in a leewardly direction, as " she bore away."

Bore by the Head.—A vessel is said to bore by the head when she, whilst passing through the water, is depressed by the head.

Boring.—Forcing a vessel through loose ice in the Arctic Seas.

Boss.—A slang American term for sailing master, or chief in command, or the manager or master of any business or show.

Both Sheets Aft.—When a square-rigged ship has the wind dead aft, so that the sheets lead aft alike, with the yards square.

Bottom.—Usually understood as the part of a vessel below the water line or bilge.

Bottomry.—The hull or bottom of a ship pledged as security for a loan. If the ship be lost the money is lost unless the lender has covered himself by other means.

Bound.—Encased with metal bands. Also referring to the destination of a vessel.

Wind-bound means that a vessel is in a port or at an anchorage because the wind is unfavourable for her to proceed. Formerly square-rigged ships were everlastingly wind-bound, *i.e.*, waiting in port because the wind was adverse ; now they go out and look for a fair wind, and generally can sail so well on a wind that waiting for a fair wind would be considered an unpardonable piece of folly.

Bow.—The fore part of a vessel ; forward of the greatest transverse section. In taking bearings an object is said to be on the bow if its direction does not make more than an angle of 45° with the line of the keel.

Bower Anchor.—The anchor in constant use.

Bow Fast.—A warp for holding the vessel by the bow.

Bowing the Sea.—Meeting the sea bow on or end on, or nearly end on, as in close-hauled sailing. When the sea runs true with the wind

Bowline Haul.—The foremost man in hauling on a bowline sings out, " One ! two !! three !!! haul !!!! " the weight of all the men being thrown on the rope when the " haul " is shouted out. This chant is sometimes varied, thus :

> Heave on the bowlin'
> When the ship's a rollin'—
> One ! two !! three !!! haul !!!!

The origin of this probably is from the fact that when the ship takes her weather roll the sails lift and so some of the bowlines become slack and can be got in.

Bowline knot.—Formed thus : (Fig. 240.)

Bowlines.—Ropes made fast to cringles in the weather leech of squaresails, to pull them taut and steady when sailing on a wind. The bowlines usually lead into a bridle. Sailing on a bowline means sailing on a wind when the bowlines would be hauled taut ; hence the phrase " sailing on a taut bowline." Sailing on an easy bowline means sailing with the sails well full, and the bowlines eased up a little, so that the vessel is not quite " on a wind " or close hauled.

FIG. 240.

Bow-lines.—Continuation of buttock lines, showing the outline of vertical fore-and-aft sections in the fore-body. (See " Buttock-lines.")

Bowse.—Hauling with a will upon a rope.

Bowsprit.—A spar projecting from the bow of a vessel. A running bowsprit is one that can easily be reefed in like a cutter's. Sometimes when a bowsprit is reefed in by the fids it is wrongly said to be housed ; a bowsprit is housed when run close in to the cranse iron. A standing bowsprit is one fitted in a bed and generally prolonged by a jibboom.

Bowsprit Bitts.—Timbers fitted into carlines on the deck to take the bowsprit.

Bowsprit Cranse.—The iron cap at the bowsprit end, to which the gear is hooked ; in the case of the vessel having a jibboom the cap is a double one to take the jibboom.

Bowsprit Shrouds.—The horizontal stays of bow-sprits.

Boxhauling.—In tacking a ship to make her turn on her heel by hauling the head sheets a-weather, and getting stern-way on. Practised by square-rigged ships, sometimes, in working narrow channels.

Boxing off.—Assisting to pay a vessel's head off the wind by hauling the head sheets a-weather.

Box Scarph.—A method of joining two pieces of timber by letting each into the other one-half its own thickness ; sometimes termed a butt scarph.

Box the Compass.—To call over all the points of a compass in regular order. To understand the compass points and subdivisions. (See " Compass.")

Braces. — Copper, gunmetal, or brass straps fitted round the main piece of rudder or rudder-post and fastened to the sternpost.
Strengthening pieces of iron or wood to bind together weak places in a vessel.
Ropes used in working the yards of a ship.

Braced Sharp Up.—Said of a square-rigged ship when the weather braces are slacked up and the lee ones hauled in taut so as to trim the sails as close to wind as possible.

Brace-up and Haul aft ! — The order to trim sails after a vessel has been hove to with sails slack.

Brails.—Ropes fast to the leeches of fore-and-aft sails and leading through blocks on the mast hoops ; used to haul or truss the sail up to the mast instead of lowering it and stowing it.

Breach.—A breaking in of the sea. A clean breach is when a wave boards a vessel in solid form, and sometimes makes a clean sweep of the deck, taking crew, boats, and everything else overboard. To make a clean breach over a vessel is when the sea enters one side and pours out the other.

Break Aboard.—When the crest of a wave falls aboard on the deck of a vessel.

Breakers.—Casks for containing water. Also the disturbed water over reefs, rocks, shoals, &c.

Breakers Ahead !—The cry when breakers are sighted close ahead.

Break Off.—In close-hauled sailing, when the wind comes more from ahead so as to cause the vessel's head to break to leeward of the course she had been sailing. Not to be confused with "fall off," which means that the vessel's head goes off farther away from the wind.

Break tacks.—When a vessel goes from one tack to the other.

Breaming.—Cleaning off a ship's bottom by burning the excrescences thereon. Sometimes when a vessel is not coppered small worms will eat into the plank. It is usual then to scrape her bottom, coal tar her, and then bream her off by fire in basket breaming irons.

Breast Fast.—A warp fastened to a vessel amidships to hold her.

Breasthook.—A strong >-shaped wood knee used forward to bind the stem, shelf, and frame of a vessel together. Breasthooks are also used in other parts of a vessel. They are now usually made of wrought iron.

Breeze.—Small coke fuel, to be bought cheap at gasworks.

Breeze, A.—In sailor's parlance, a strong blow of wind; but generally a wind of no particular strength, as light breeze, gentle breeze, moderate breeze, strong breeze, &c. (See "Wind.")

Breeze of Wind.—A strong wind.

Breeze-up.—The wind is said to "breeze-up" when it increases fast in strength from a light wind.

Breezy Side.—The windward side of an object.

Bridles.—The parts of moorings to hold on by; many ropes gathered into one.

Brig.—A two-masted vessel, square-rigged on both masts.

Brigantine.—A two-masted vessel, differing from a brig by being only square-rigged forward. In the Cotton MSS. is preserved, under date Sept. 18 (13 Henry VIII.), an account of Ships of the King's Majesty between Gravesend and Erith. "The Great Henry" is among the number, and "Brygandyn, clerk of the ship, doth say that before the said ship be laid in the dock that her masts be taken down and bestowed in the great storehouse at Erith," &c. It is supposed by Charnock (Charnock, vol. ii. p. 106–117) that Brygandyn invented the brigantine rig. In the Harl. MSS. Edward VI. occurs the following: "The two gallies and brigandyne must be yearly repaired."

Bring To, or Bring Her To.—To luff or to come close to wind. To anchor. (See "Come To.")

Bring to Wind.—To luff a vessel close to the wind after she has been sailing off the wind.

Bring Up.—To come to anchor.

Bring Up all Standing.—To come to anchor, or to a stop suddenly without notice, or without any sail being lowered. To anchor without lowering sail.

Bristol Fashion.—In the best manner possible, Bristol shipbuilding and seamen formerly having a great reputation for excellence.

Broach To.—To come to against the wind and helm.

Broad Pennant.—The swallow-tail flag of a commodore. (See "Burgee.")

Broadside On.—When a vessel moves sideways, or when she is approached by an object at right angles to her broadside.

Broken Water.—When waves lose their form by breaking over reefs, rocks, or shallows, or by meeting waves from another direction, termed a cross sea.

Broom at the Masthead.—A signal that a boat or vessel is for sale. The origin of the custom appears to be unknown; but it is ingeniously argued that brooms were hoisted as a signal that a man wanted to make a clean sweep of his vessel; or the custom may have arisen from the common practice of selling brooms in the streets.

Brought To.—After a vessel has been sailing off a wind when she is brought to wind, or close to wind. Anchored.

Brought Up.—At anchor.

Brought Up with a Round Turn.—Figuratively, suddenly stopped; as for instance, when a rope is being payed out rapidly, if a turn or bight catches round some object and checks the paying out of the rope.

Bucklers.—Blocks of wood used to stop the hawse pipes.

Builder's Certificate.—A document given by the builder of a vessel to the owner when she is handed over, setting forth the builder's name, the name of the ship, place of building, manner of building, rig, dimensions, tonnage, N.M., and concluding with the following declaration: —" This is to certify that [I or we] have built at ————, in the county of ————, in the year ——, the vessel ————. The measurement, tonnage, and description of which are given above.

As witness my hand, this   day of ————.
                                        Signed,

This document must be produced when application is made for registration.

Builder's Measurement.—See "B. M." and "Tonnage."

Bulkheads.—The athwartship partitions which separate a vessel into compartments, cabins, &c. Fore and aft partitions are also termed bulkheads.

Bull's Eye.—A block without a sheave, and with one hole in it. They are usually iron bound.

Bulwark.—The side of a vessel above the deck.

Bumboat.—A boat used by shore people to carry provisions on sale to ships.

Bumpkin.—See "Boomkin."

Bunk.—A bed or place to sleep in in a cabin.

Bunt.—The middle part of a sail. To gather up the bunt is take hold of the middle part of a sail and gather it up.

Bunting.—Woollen stuff of which flags are made.

Bunter.—A kind of tackle.

Bunt Lines.—Ropes attached to sails to haul them up by.

Buoy.—A floating mark.

Buoyancy.—The quality of floating or being supported or borne up by a fluid. A vessel is buoyant in proportion as she is bulk for bulk lighter than the fluid she is supported in.

Burden or Burthen.—Supposed to mean the quantity in tons of dead weight that a vessel will carry. The quantity would be the difference between the weight or displacement of the ship when light and the weight or displacement of the ship when she was laden as deeply as prudent.

Burgee.—A triangular or square flag flown at the truck as a kind of pennant. A commodore's pennant is a "swallow-tail" burgee. A vice-commodore's burgee has one white ball in the upper corner or canton of the hoist; a rear-commodore's, two balls placed horizontally.

Burgee, Etiquette of.—It is considered etiquette, if a yacht is on a station where there is a club established, and her owner is a member of the club, that the flag of that particular club should be hoisted as the yacht arrives on the station, although the owner may be the commodore, or vice, or rear-commodore of another club. Frequently, however, in such a case the burgee is merely run up on arrival and then lowered and the commodore's pennant re-hoisted. But if the yacht has two or more masts, a flag-officer can fly his pennant at the main, and another club burgee at the mizen or fore. If several yachts are lying at an anchorage where there is no club, the yachts will fly the burgee of the senior flag-officer present; but if there be two flag-officers of equal rank present, then the flag of the one whose club is senior by virtue of the date of its Admiralty warrant will be flown. In the Royal Navy, if two or three ships are cruising in company, the title of commodore is given by courtesy to the senior captain present; but the rank does not seem very well defined, as, although an "appointed" commodore is said to rank next to a rear-admiral, yet he cannot fly his broad pennant in the presence of a "superior captain" without permission. In the case of the Yacht Navy, the senior officer would mean the one of highest rank; and where, in the case of clubs, the rank of the flag-officers is equal, seniority depends upon the date of the Admiralty warrant of the club which conferred the rank, and not upon the length of service of the officer; but a vice-commodore of a senior club does not take precedence of a commodore of a junior club. By the same rule, when several yachts are present belonging to clubs that have no Admiralty warrants, the date of the establishment of the several clubs would decide the seniority of flag-officers of equal rank, but clubs with Admiralty warrants always rank before those without. (See "Saluting," "Recognised Clubs," "Royal Clubs," "Admiralty Warrants," and "Ensigns.")

When the Royal Yacht Squadron was first established, members flew private signal flags, containing their crest or other device, and the fashion has, during the last few years, been much revived. Owners of yachts with more than one mast fly such a flag at the fore when the owner is on board, club burgee always at the main. If a yacht has only one mast the flag can be flown from the cross trees. During meals American yachtsmen sometimes hoist a "dinner napkin," *i.e.*, a square white flag at the fore or from the cross trees.

The Cambria in the Atlantic race flew her racing flag at the main, and the Royal Harwich Yacht Club burgee at the fore. See "Yacht Etiquette" farther on.

When a yacht wins a club prize, it is etiquette to hoist the winning flag under the burgee of the club giving the prize if the owner is a member; he should also do the same when going on to another port if a winning flag is hoisted. The rule cannot, however, be observed if there be several prizes and different clubs involved.

Burton.—A tackle composed of two single blocks; a double Spanish burton consists of two single and one double block.

Butcher's Cleaver Plate.—This plate was devised to get a greater area of board immersed without increasing its extreme dimensions, and

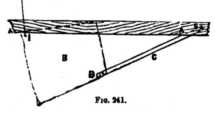

Fig. 241.

thereby increasing the surface for friction. The plate had an iron bar, C, two or three feet long riveted thereon; and pivoted by the bar

A is a portion of the keel.

B is the plate.

C is an iron bar riveted to the plate at D, and pivoted in the keel at E, and lifted by a jointed bar bolted at I.

The effective lateral resistance for any given plane would be considerably increased if one edge of the plane made a large angle with the direction of its motion; and for this reason a square plate is not so effective as a triangular one.

Butt.—The joining or meeting of two pieces of wood end-ways. Butt and butt means that two planks meet end to end, but do not overlap.

Butt End.—The biggest end of a spar.

Buttock.—The after-part of a vessel from her run upwards.

Buttock Lines.—Planes in a fore-and-aft direction, showing the outline of vertical fore-and-aft sections in the after-body.

By and Large.—Backing and filling, which see. (See also "Large.")

By the Head.—When the vessel is trimmed or

depressed by the head so that her proper line of flotation is departed from.

By the Lee.—To bring a vessel by the lee is when nearly before the wind she falls off so much as to bring the wind on the other quarter ; or the wind may shift from one quarter of the vessel to the other without the vessel altering her course ("See Lee").

By the Stern.—The contrary to being down by the head.

By the Wind.—Close hauled ; hauled by the wind.

By the Board.—Going or falling overboard.

C.

Cable.—A rope or chain by which a vessel is held at anchor. The length for a cable, according to the Admiralty, is 120 fathoms. The length of a cable for a yacht varies from 60 fathoms for a 10-tonner to 140 for a 300-tonner. A yacht of 60 tons should, however, have at least 100 fathoms.

Cable's Length.—A measure of one-tenth of a sea mile, 608 feet, or 101 fathoms, or 203 yards.

Caboose.—The cooking room or kitchen of a merchantman. Also the "galley fire" or cooking stove of a yacht or other vessel.

Cage Buoy.—A buoy with an iron framework upon the top. Formerly "cages" were put on poles in intricate channels, and for two hours about the time of high water at night fires were lighted in them.

Call.—See "Boatswain."

Callipers.—An instrument consisting of a "straight edge" beam with two legs, used for measuring the breadth of yachts, packages of merchandise, &c. Metal bow-legged compasses called callipers are used for measuring the diameter of spars.

Calm.—Stillness of the air. Stillness or smoothness of the sea. An unrippled sea. Dead calm, stark calm, flat calm, clock calm ; glass calm, glass smooth sea ; &c.

Cambered.—When the keel of a vessel has its ends lower than its middle, thus ⌒. Opposed to rockered.

Canoe.—A kind of boat used in many parts of the world and distinct from row boats, as they are propelled by paddles which are dipped in the water on alternate sides. There are paddles of one blade and two blades. Some canoes carry many occupants, some only one ; in the latter case the canoe is usually decked. They are variously built and usually sharp ended.

Canoe Hatch.—The double lines *c* are carlines, supposed to be seen through the hatch which is screwed to the two *dotted* ones (Fig. 242) ; the ends of the latter are made to slide in a groove in the coamings. The middle carline is fastened to the deck and prevents the latter sliding too far, and stops the water

getting into the well should any find its way under the hatch carline. A channel should be made round the rim of the well so that the person sitting therein could fit an apron

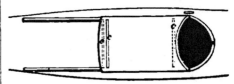

FIG. 242.

or waterproof into it after the fashion of the Esquimaux.

A preferable plan is to have the hatch and the frame on which it slides separate, so that it will fit over the rabbets round the coamings ; then if the canoe upsets, the hatch will float off and free the canoeist.

Mr. Rede Turner recommends the following plan for fastening down a canoe hatch :

A is a metal plate, screwed to hatch or door, and projecting somewhat beyond the edge of

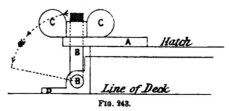

FIG. 243.

hatch, and in the projecting edge of it has a slot cut. (*See* Figs. 243, 244, 245, 246).

B is a screw at one end, and on this end works a butterfly nut (C) (Figs. 243, 244, 245) the other has two short arms at right angle to the upper part (*see* Figs. 243, 244, 245) which

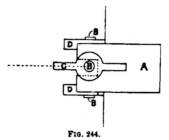

FIG. 244.

short arms are hinged at D (Fig. 244), and B moves freely when the butterfly nut C is unscrewed.

To open a hatch which has been fitted with this arrangement, the two butterfly nuts C must be unscrewed, and B allowed to fall down out of the way, and the hatch can then be lifted off. To fasten the hatch down B must be turned up, and the butterfly nut C screws down tight.

N.B. There should be two or more of this

arrangement on hatch, according to the size, viz., one on each side.

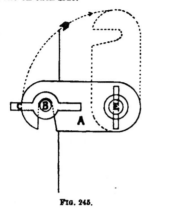

FIG. 245.

Fig. 245 is the same plan, except that B is fixed upright, and the plate A is centred on E,

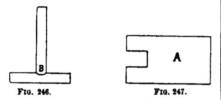

FIG. 246.   FIG. 247.

and works horizontally. (*See* dotted lines of Fig. 245.)

Cant Frames.—The frame in the bow and quarter of a vessel that are not square to the keel.

Canvas.—The weight of canvas used by Messrs. Lapthorn and Ratsey for yachts' sails is as follows :

No. of canvas.	Width of canvas in inches.	Weight of 60 yards in lbs.	Weight in lbs. per sq. foot when made up.	Size of yacht in tons.
0	18	61	0·270*	100 and upwards
1	18	57·5	0·255	40 to 60
2	18	54	0·240	20
3	18	50·5	0·225	15
4	18	47	0·210	10
5	18	43·5	0·195	7
6	18	40	0·182	5
7	18	35·8	0·165	3
1	12	40	0·265	40 to 60
2	12	37·2	0·250	20
3	12	34·4	0·235	15
4	12	31·6	0·220	10

* This includes the seams and tablings, but not roping, cringles, reef points, or lacings.

Canvas Back.—A term applied to boats covered with canvas to keep out the seas ; also applied to yacht sailors who are fond of a salting.

Canvas-back Duck.—A wild duck common in America, and highly esteemed for the table.

Canvas Boats.—These are boats made of canvas and used by the Galway fishermen, par-

ticularly at Dingle. The ribs of the boats are made of wood hoop, such as may be got off casks ; outside the ribs battens are nailed in a fore-and-aft direction ; a keel to which the ribs are also nailed is rounded up at the ends to form stem and stern post. The canvas is about two feet wide, and runs fore-and-aft. There is an inwale and gunwale as usual at the top of the ribs, the canvas going between the two. These boats are usually 20ft. by 4ft. They are very light, one man carrying them easily. They are manned by a crew of four, each man using a pair of oars. A lug sail is carried off the wind. These boats get through a great deal of rough water by aid of the eight oars they are propelled by.

The following directions for making canvas boats have been carefully compiled :—

For the keel get a piece of larch 15ft. long, 2½in. wide, and 2in. deep ; the stem and stern posts, with rake according to fancy, may be mortised into the keel ; these pieces must be bevelled off from the width of the keel, so as to have a cutwater of about half an inch, which will be sharp enough. Next get three good heavy blocks of wood, and lay them four feet apart in the place where you are going to build your boat ; then take the keel with the stem and stern posts already in, and fix it perfectly true on the said blocks, using a spirit level for the purpose. The easiest temporary way of fastening the keel down is to nail short pieces of wood firmly to the blocks, just wide enough apart for the keel to jam between them, and drive a small nail through these pieces into the keel on each side ; this will keep all firm, and prevent the keel from moving or twisting as you proceed with other work ; it is an important point, and must not be omitted. This done, the next thing is to get a good stout spar, about 2in. or 3in. square, and longer than the boat ; tack this on the top of the stem and stern posts ; as it is necessary that this fore-and-aft piece should be stayed stiffly in its position, this can easily be done by tacking some rough pieces to it here and there, and nailing the other ends to the rafters of your shed. The uses of this spar are many and obvious. You will thus get your stem and stern posts true, and it will be useful afterwards to keep the moulds in their places, and for shoring out the timbers and ribbands or battens so as to keep them shapely to the eye as the work proceeds. Your next business is to make what shipwrights call "the moulds," which is to give the shape, beam, and depth. To make the moulds, first strike it out full size with a piece of chalk on the floor of some room. For a boat 15ft. in length, the width ought to be at least 4ft., the depth not less than 2ft. Do not let the curve of the sides be too sharp, but give her a good round side and a flattish bottom. Having made your moulds to the exact shape of the pattern chalked on the floor, nail a thin strip of wood across the upper (gunwale) ends, which will keep them stiff and true ; next take the moulds and nail them on the

Canvas Boats—continued.

keel in their proper places, fastening it above to the fore-and-aft piece. The moulds being now firmly fixed in their places, you may proceed to what in other boats would be called the planking. Saw out some thin strips of larch, about 20ft. long, 1in. wide, and a quarter of an inch thick. Six of these on each side would be sufficient. Having chamfered off a little from one of the ends to make it fit the stem of the boat, fasten it with two small copper nails; carry the ribband in your hand, and humour it gently round the moulds tacking it slightly there, and bring it on to the sternpost. You will probably find your piece too long; mark the required length, cut, and nail it in its place. In laying on these ribbands you must begin at the bottom of the boat, and work up. Having fixed your ribband both sides, get two long pieces the same width, only double the thickness, for gunwales, and fix them; fit a breast hook stem and stern, and rivet the gunwales securely to them. Saw out a lot of thin stuff for ribs, half an inch wide, and about the eighth of an inch thick; they will bend easily, and will not require steaming. Put these on about six inches apart, and rivet them to the battens. Next put in your thwarts, fixing them well down in the bottom of the boat, which will make her safer, the weight being near the keel. Get some copper, galvanised iron, or oak knees, with one leg long enough to reach from the gunwale down to the seat; rivet this well to the battens and gunwale, and nail the other part on the seat; there should be four to each thwart, as they help to strengthen the boat immensely. You may now take your boat off the stocks, and she will be ready for the next operation. Get some good new sail canvas, not too stout, and cover one side at a time; tack the edge of the canvas all along the bottom of the keel and pull it to the shape of the boat, tacking it neatly to the sides of the stem and stern posts. Where you find it does not sit well, you may sometimes avoid cutting by folding the spare stuff, and, with a sailor's needle and palm, sew it to the main body of the canvas. Do this on a warm day, as the canvas will then be quite supple, and more easy to handle. Nail a strip of wood half an inch thick on the bottom of the keel to keep all snug, and as an extra security drive a row of tacks through the canvas on each side of the keel. You must be careful to nail over the canvas some narrow strips of wood, as "bilge pieces," where you see she would take the ground when lying on her side, otherwise the pulling and dragging over the sand in launching, &c., would quickly wear the canvas through. With care, and with an extra coat of paint now and then, a boat of this sort will last nine or ten years.

The following suggestions will be found effective to prevent the puckering of the canvas skin of the proposed boat. A framework of 4ft. beam will require about three breadths of canvas on each side, and waste should be avoided by preparing paper patterns by which to cut out the canvas. To do this cut some old newspapers to the width of the canvas, and paste sufficient pieces together end to end to give the required length of the boat. Turn the frame of the boat upside down, and stay it in a horizontal position and upright. Lay the edge of the paper on the flat keel along the middle, place weights upon it and measure off the distances from the middle line across the paper on the ribs, so as to keep the breadths horizontal from the middle to the stern and bow of the boat. Towards the bow and stern the breadths will be of course materially reduced. Remove the paper on to the floor, and draw a line from point to point marked on the paper at the crossings of the timbers. From this pattern you can easily cut out the two canvas strakes, one for each side of the boat against the keel, which are called the garboards. Replace the pattern; but, before doing so, mark the lower edge for the second breadth of paper, and, setting off the distances along the ribs to the width of the first pattern, you will be able to mark it out and cut it as the previous one. A double seam will be better than a single, as it will give great additional strength to the canvas, and the width of an inch and an eighth should be allowed for it. The lower edge of the third breadth can now be marked and cut out by the upper edge of the second, and if found to reach the gunwale, the top edge may be left uncut until the canvas is drawn over the framework. In applying the canvas to the keel, put plenty of thick paint on the inside to half the breadth of the keel, and nail the selvedge with copper tacks along the middle line; then screw on with brass screws, at 6-inch intervals, a piece of elm plank ⅜ths of an inch thick, and exactly the same width and length as the keel. Between the 6-inch intervals drive copper tacks. A small strip of copper at the fore foot and heel will prevent this shoeing, as it is called, from catching in anything. To make a good finish at stem and stern, cut out the thickness of the stem and sternpost to the eighth of an inch from top to bottom, as in an ordinary boat, which will form a groove or rabbet, and when you come to this part fold the end of the canvas back. This will give additional strength for the nails, and at the same time make a very snug finish.

A diagonal-framed canvas boat built in 1844 was in use for thirty years. The canvas was stout, and it was very thickly painted when dry, and not wetted, as is frequently the case, to prevent the absorption of paint. The boat was built on three moulds, the transom or stern board (for she is not canoe-formed at the stern) being one mould, the midship mould the second, and a third equi-distant between it and the bow. An inner keel or kelson having been connected with the stem and sternposts by mortices, this kelson was let into the moulds its own thickness, 1in., and secured. The moulds were steadied in their positions by the gunwales, of

½in. by 2in. yellow pine, nailed to the stern and transom board. The frame of yellow pine, ₁⁷₆in. by ½in., was then nailed on diagonally, leaving openings of 2½in. wide where crossing each other. The canvas, put on lengthways, was cut so as to run along the framework parallel with the kelson on each side; and the seams were sewn double, as sails are ordinarily made by sailmakers. There is one bottom and two side breadths, and, therefore, no join along the kelson. The canvas turns in over the gunwale, and is secured by a strip of the same wood. The framework is nailed with copper tacks. The canvas, being so well supported, is perfectly rigid, and the boat appears likely to last a number of years. See " Collapsible Boats."

Canvas Coracle.—Such a boat (Fig. 248) was built by Capt. J. Richards, R.N., in 1878, for the river Avon, 12ft. long, 3ft. wide, and 15in. in depth. She has a frame of American elm, fastened with rove and clench copper nails and wire; her floor is nearly flat, formed of ⅜in. white pine wood, lined inside with sheets of cork to fill up the spaces between the timbers,

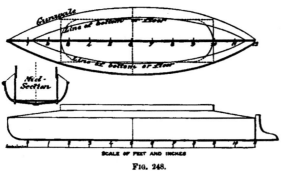

FIG. 248.

and form a level and solid platform within. Above the floor and outside the timbers (which are 6in. apart, and twenty-three in number), instead of the planking of an ordinary boat, there are stout fore-and-aft stringers of American elm three inches apart, outside all of which is stretched the thick No. 1 canvas skin of the outer boat. The principal materials required are keel of 1in. square ash; gunwale, 1in. square ash; cross-pieces of gunwales, 1in. square ash; keel chafing pieces, ¾in. by ½in. ash; fore-and-aft stringers, ½in. by ½in.; bilge stringers, ½in. by ½in.; twenty-three timbers, ⅜in. square.

Within this structure and securely attached to it, although quite distinct from it, there is an inner canvas boat, 8ft. long and 2ft. wide (having a separate gunwale), in which the crew sit on the floor.

The deck space between the gunwale and coaming is entirely covered in by canvas, supported on a strong framework of wood and cane; and, being under ordinary circumstances quite secure from wet, was intended by Capt. Richards for the stowage of bedding, clothes, and provisions of the crew.

The gunwale and the coaming are strongly braced together, and the ends of the gunwale are additionally secured to the stem and sternpost by strong iron plates, with eye-bolts above, in which are rove stout ropes, to moor the boat with when afloat, or suspend her to trees like a hammock whenever her crew may desire to sleep in that position.

The coracle is fitted with a couple of small light wheels and iron axle (weighing only about 12lb., and movable at pleasure in about a couple of minutes), which when attached to her keel afford her the locomotive advantages of a porter's truck.

The twelve-foot coracle weighs about 90lb. and draws three inches water when light; but, with her crew of two men and her gear on board, she drew five inches forward and seven aft. An inch of this, however, is due to her false keel, which, with bilge pieces, give ample lateral resistance when under sail in a seaway.

The entire structure was well saturated with boiled linseed oil, and then painted.

The inner boat can be disengaged at the gunwale, and removed altogether in about four minutes.

One of the principal advantages claimed for this "double-shell boat" consists in the fact that the outer boat may be stove in without rendering her unserviceable or wetting her crew; and so long as the outer boat is intact, a sea may be accidentally shipped in the inner boat without dangerously affecting the stability of the vessel; and should both the outer and inner boats be swamped with water, the cork floor and cushions will, neverless, still afford her the properties of a life buoy sufficient for her crew. (See "Coracle Life boat.")

The builders of these boats are Messrs. Hill, Canon's Marsh, Bristol. Price 6l. 10s. Carriage by rail 1d. per mile.

Cap.—A figure of 8 iron band fitted to the masthead, bowsprit end, for jib-boom, &c. Sometimes the yoke is termed the lower cap.

Capful of Wind.—A puff of wind soon passing away.

Capstan.—A mechanical contrivance for raising the anchor, said to have been introduced in Queen Elizabeth's reign. Sir Walter Raleigh says : "The shape of our ships have been greatly bettered of late. We have contrived the striking of the topmast, added the chain pump, devised studding sails, top gallant sails, sprit sails, and top-sails. We have also lengthened our cables, and contrived weighing of the anchor by the capstan." Capstans very compact in form are now made for yachts instead of the cumbrous windlass. The capstans most generally in use on board yachts are those manufactured by Cantelo,

Southampton; W. White and Sons, Vectis Works, Cowes; Atkey, Cowes; Harfield and Co., Mansion House Buildings, E.C.; Blake and Sons, Gosport; and Simpson and Strickland, Dartmouth. The Cantelo, White, and Atkey capstan have winch heads, so that they can be used without capstan bars.

A form of capstan made of aluminium was invented by Lieut. Oliver, R.N., and used by him in his 1-rater Querida during 1893. Its form is shown by the accompanying engraving (Fig. 249).

It was specially made for hoisting lugsails in small raters with single wire halyards, thus doing away with whips and purchases. One similar in size, but of gunmetal and weighing over 30lb., was first used. The method adopted is as follows: The capstan is secured in any convenient position in bottom of yacht, the wire halyards is lead through deck, and a leading block secured to mast step. To hoist sail, the halyard is manned and sail hoisted; it is then taken round the capstan (about four turns), and the end belayed round both arms of lever; the capstan is now hove upon, and the sail sweated up, after which it will be found unnecessary to be constantly pulling on halyards, as in

FIG. 249.

the case where purchases are in use, and which are always giving up. The capstan barrel, spindle, and bed of aluminium, the lever being made of aluminium bronze, the whole weighing only 10lb., and has been tested to 600lb., with the weight and power acting in the same direction.

The dimensions are: Height, extreme 6½in.; diameter of bed, 7½in.; barrel, 5in.; length of lever from centre of capstan to extreme end, 1ft. 7in. Price, 4l. 10s. Sole makers, Bickle and Co., Engineers, Great Western Docks, Plymouth.

Capstan Bar.—Bars of wood by which the capstan is turned, and so made to wind up the anchor or raise any weight.

Capstan for a Trawl.—A capstan for a trawl for a yacht of twenty or more tons is made at the Mount's Bay Foundry, Cornwall.

Card.—The dial of a compass upon which the points are marked.

Cardinal Points.—The compass points, E., W., N., and S.

Careen.—To heel, to list, to lean over.

Carlines.—Pieces of timber fitted between the deck beams in a fore-and-aft direction.

Carry Away.—The breakage of a spar, rope, &c.

Carry Canvas.—A vessel is said to carry her canvas well if she does not heel much in strong breezes.

Carvel Built.—Built with the plank flush edge to edge, and the seams caulked and payed.

Cast.—Said of a ship when she fills on one tack or the other after being head to wind. Used generally in getting under way, as cast to port, &c. The word is variously used, as to cast anchor, to cast off a rope.

Catamaran.—A small raft common in the East Indies. A double boat in use in America.

Cat Block.—The block used in catting the anchor.

Cat Boat.—A boat with one sail, like a Una boat.

Catch a Turn.—To take a turn quickly with a rope round a belaying pin, or bitt, or carel.

Cathead.—Timber or iron projection from the bow of a vessel by which the anchor is hoisted up to the rail, after it has been weighed to the hawse pipe.

Catspaws.—In calms, when the water is rippled here and there with passing airs of wind, it is said to be scratched by catspaws. A "catspaw" is also a bight double in a rope.

Caulking.—Driving oakum into the seams of a vessel. (See "Marine Glue.")

Caulking Iron.—A kind of blunt chisel used for driving oakum into the seams.

Caustic Soda.—A mixture of three-parts of soda to two of unslacked lime. The soda is boiled in the water, and then the lime added. The mixture should be applied hot, and be of the consistency of thick whitewash. In applying it great care should be exercised so as not to allow it to touch the hands. A brush of vegetable fibre should be used, as the composition will destroy hair. Caustic soda is used for cleaning off old paint or varnish; the mixture should be put on nine or ten hours before it is scraped off if a very clean job is desired. If it is a deck that has to be cleaned it is desirable to damp it with fresh water before an application of the mixture; hence it is a good plan to apply it on a dewy morning. Mahogany should be scraped, and not cleaned with caustic soda. A mixture of two parts soda and one part soap, simmered together and applied hot, is sometimes used.

Carson's "Detergent" (La Belle Sauvage-yard, London), is an excellent substitute for caustic soda, but care should be taken in using it for decks, as it injuriously affects marine glue. (See also " Sooji Mooji.")

Cavel (sometimes spelt "kavel" or "kevel")." —Stout pieces of timber fixed horizontally to the stanchions on bitts for belaying ropes to.

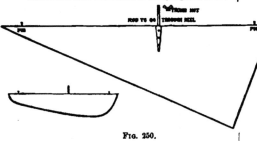

FIG. 250.

Ceiling.—The inside planking of a vessel.

Centre-board (a Temporary).—Make a board of the shape of either of those in the sketch (Fig. 250) about one-third of the length of the boat. Three bolts will be on the upper edge of the board; the centre bolt will have a thread longer than the other two, and protrude through the keel. When the board is fitted under the keel, it will be held tight to the keel by a thumb nut on the centre bolt. To unship the board when afloat unscrew the thumb nut, push the board down, and it will float up alongside. A cork will be put into the bolt hole. Of course the board cannot be shifted when the boat is afloat. It would be unsafe to sail about in shallow water with such a contrivance; nor should the boat under any circumstances be allowed to take the ground with the board fixed.

Another form of temporary board (Fig. 251) has been fitted to an ordinary boat, 18ft. long.

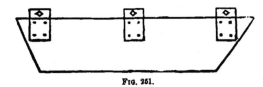

FIG. 251.

It consists of a board, to which are affixed iron clamps on either side, which admit of the main keel being inserted between them; through these are passed bolts with nuts, which firmly hold the two keels together.

The dimensions of a board for an 18ft. boat are 6ft. long, 1ft. 10in. deep, and 1½in. thick. The board is to be about 1ft. 6in. shorter on its under side than on its top side, the fore end sloping aft, and the aft end sloping forward; but the slope at the fore end is nearly double that at the aft end.

Place the centre of the board a trifle in advance of the centre of the main keel; it can be fixed in five minutes when the boat is in the davits; only one word of caution is necessary, that is, not to tow her with the keel on behind the yacht when sailing, or

in all probability she will take a sheer out and capsize.

This plan was introduced by Mr. G. H. Harrison, of the Siesta schooner; but it is not quite so good as the American plan below, because it cannot be unfitted or released whilst the boat is afloat; and, moreover, a triangular shape is to be preferred.

Centre-board (deflecting). — All boards of a fixed pattern are more or less in the way, and "the American Goodrich deflecting centre-board" (Fig. 252) was invented to do away with all inboard casing

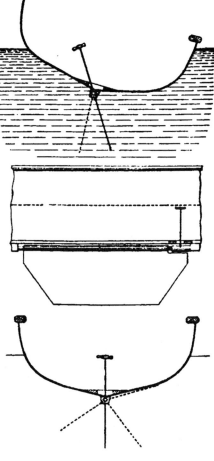

FIG. 252.

and make a board of less draught accomplish as much as a deep one could.

The "board" consists of a thin sheet stiff metal, swung to the keel by a long hinge, and can be rotated at will by applying force to a lever at the after end. The metal blade is 30in. long and 9in. deep for canoes, and 36in. long with 10in. depth adapted for row-boats and general use. The end of the shaft ships into a small lug socket on the keel. It is held in place by turning up a screw in the back of the after box, driving the forward end home into the lug. To remove or unship, it is only necessary to back out the screw, draw back the board until the shaft drops out of the forward lug, then pull forward until clear of the box also. To control the angular position of the blade, a lever is introduced inside the canoe. The top of the after box has an opening with a forked slide slipping over the slot. This slide is pushed clear, the lever then slipped into the middle hole of three in the shaft end. If the board is to be kept plumb, draw to the forked slide, so that the prongs grasp and hold the lever up and down. Leakage is prevented by having the shaft closely fit in the box. When so nipped, the blade is vertical, the same as is the case with

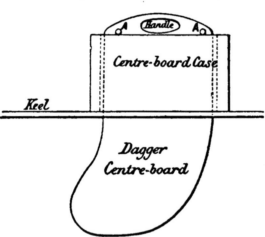

A.A...*Stops to prevent the plate dropping too far.*

FIG. 253.

an ordinary centre-board, and in this condition the canoe is prepared to sail in light airs, or before the wind, as it is impossible to trice up the blade. Being small, very thin, and with sides as smooth as you wish to finish them, no appreciable resistance will be experienced.

When heeling to a press of sail, or in beating up against the wind, the angle of the blade may be changed quickly to suit the demands of each tack. This is effected by shoving back the forked slide, and then pushing the lever up to windward, retaining it there by a small hook and eye supplied for the purpose. When going about, throw off the hook while in wind, push lever over to opposite side, and hook again. Until well settled down to the work, it is best to keep the lever approximately as desired by bearing against it with the knee or the foot. Should half the angle be sufficient, the lever may be allowed to come back till it takes against the outer

edge of the little sliding cap. When the board is to be got rid of temporarily for paddling or to clear a shoal, it is turned clear up under the bottom, as shown by the dotted line in one of the cuts, by taking hold with the lever in one of the outer holes of the three in the shaft. (See also " Butcher's Cleaver " and " Lee Board " Clip.)

Centre-plate (Dagger).—This portable plate (see Fig. 253) is in much use in America for very small shallow boats and canoes.

Centre-plate (Shot Ballasted).—No practice in the history of yacht racing has been more the subject of controversy or more condemned than the " shot bag " or shifting ballast; but " shot " it seems can be now utilised, under Y.R.A. rules, as shifting ballast if used in a particular form of keel or centre-plate. Such a keel is herewith illustrated. Mr. F. W. Brewster, of West Cliff Gardens, Bournemouth is the inventor. To the centre-plate is attached an elbowed cylinder, which is half filled with No. 4 shot. When the plate is lowered the shot descends into what is then the lower part of the cylinder, as shown, and returns to the long arm when the plate is housed. The arrangements are clearly shown in the engraving, and it is claimed by the inventor that the plate and cylinder afford great efficiency as a ballast contrivance with small resistance. The aperture in the keel, through which the end of the cylinder passes, is closed with weighted lids when the plate is lowered.

Centre-plates (the strains and stresses of).—Fig. 254 shows a boat heeled by a force represented by the arrow A, and this force also drives the vessel to leeward in the direction of the arrow. The motion in this direction is resisted, more or less, by the pressure of water on the hull and on the board B. This pressure is represented by the arrows CC. If, now, for the board we substitute a heavy metal plate, it is obvious that the weight of this D plate will act in the direction of the arrow E (Fig. 254).

The stress of the plate D acts in an exactly opposite direction to the board B. But, supposing the weight D exactly balanced the pressure CC on B, the board would have no straining effect whatever, but would rest free in its case as represented by F (Fig. 254).

This condition of equilibrium is only likely to endure momentarily, but the illustrations show how a heavy board may tend to reduce the strains on the keel and case. Of course the worst strains occur when a vessel is rolling in a seaway, whether she be before the wind or on a wind; and often it has been found dangerous to keep a board lowered when the vessel is hove-to, owing to the pressure set up by CC, which is much greater when a vessel is hove-to than it is when she is making high speed through the water; and also owing to the rolling which is always more or less apparent in disturbed water.

In connection with this matter, in "Yacht Architecture," we find the following:

"At the time the inquiry was held into the loss of the Captain someone raised the ques-

creasing the "amount of work to be done" in heeling; in other words, they would increase the dynamical stability. However, as further pointed out at the inquiry, the lee bilge keel will have a tendency, when the vessel is sailing with a steady wind pressure, to cause an increase of heel beyond that due to the actual pressure on the sails. A vessel,

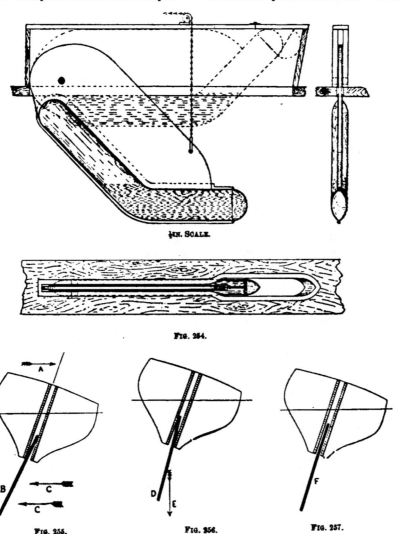

¼IN. SCALE.

Fig. 254.

Fig. 255.　　　Fig. 256.　　　Fig. 257.

tion as to whether keels and bilge keels would add to stiffness under canvas; it was properly pointed out at this inquiry that, so far as keels or bilge keels of wood are concerned, they tend to decrease statical stability, but on account of the resistance they offer to motion in the water they would check the sudden inclination of the vessel due to a sudden application of wind force by in-

when sailing with the wind abeam or forward of the beam, makes more or less leeway, or moves in a sideways direction; thus, an ardent pressure would be brought upon the upper side of the lee bilge keel, and this pressure would assist in a small degree in heeling the vessel."

It is quite a common belief that a centreboard, irrespective of its weight, somehow increases stiffness; but such is not the case. It is also sometimes thought that a metal centre-plate will enable a broad, shallow boat to carry as much canvas as can be got on her. This is a very great mistake, and we know from two or three examples that the effect of a centre-plate weighing nearly half a ton on a 25ft. boat, with a 11ft. beam, and about 1ft. 9in. draught amidships, is extremely small on the stability; and a "sandbagger," if fitted with a metal centre-plate, could not in consequence dispense with her sand bags stowed well in the weather bilge, any more than the cat boat tribe could dispense with their heavy crew up to windward.

Chain Locker.—The compartment in the hold of a vessel wherein the mooring chain is stowed.

Chain Pipe.—Iron pipe on the deck through which the cables pass into the lockers.

Chain Plates.—Iron braces on the side of a ship to which long linked chains are attached with the dead eyes for the lanyards of the rigging above.

Challenge Cups.—Cups which when won subject the yacht to be challenged to race for it again. Unless there is any stipulation to the contrary, a yacht can be altered during the period she holds the cup and still be eligible to defend it.

Channel Deep.—Said of a yacht when she is heeled over until her lee channels are under water.

Channel Plates.—Braces secured to the sides of vessels and extended by pieces of timber termed channels. The lower dead eyes are bolted to the channel plates.

Channels.—Strong pieces of timber fixed on the side of a ship inside the chain plates to give greater spread to the rigging.

During the existence of the old tonnage rule up to 1887 the channels of yachts were much increased in width in order to give the necessary spread to the rigging in consequence of the narrowness of the hull compared with the height of the mast. But even with this extra spread it was found difficult to keep the mast in its place; and in fact it could not have been done, but for the steel wire rope shrouds. These were set up bar taut and the drift of lanyard between the dead eyes was very short compared with what it once was.

Check, To.—To check a sheet is to ease it a little. To check a vessel's way as by a warp, or by backing a sail. To check a tide is to keep a vessel from her course, in order to allow for the influence or drift of a tide. A vessel is said to check the tide when it throws her to windward. To check a vessel with the helm is to prevent her altering her course. (See "To Meet.")

Cheek Blocks.—A sheave fitted on a spar inside a sort of cleat, as the cheek block for topsail sheet on the end of a gaff.

Cheeks of the Mast.—The hounds.

Cheering.—The loud, deep, and sonorous "hip, hip, hurrahs!" which the crew of a van-quished yacht greet the victrix with. A custom much honoured. The crew of the vanquished yacht line the bulwarks and give three consecutive "hip, hip, hurrahs!" the winning crew then does the same; the vanquished crew then give a single "hip, hip. hurrah!" to "come up with," or finish off, (See "Man Ship.")

Chill.—In very light winds, if a cloud passes overhead and a puff comes out of it, it is called a chill—probably on account of its coldness.

Chime or Chine.—The part of a waterway on the deck of a ship which joins the spirketting. The bilge joint of a barge is also termed a chime or chine.

Chinese Lug.—A lug sail with battens.

Chips.—A nickname for a ship's carpenter.

Chock.—A block or wedge of wood.

Chock a Block.—Said of two blocks when, in hoisting or hauling, the two blocks of a tackle are brought close together. Generally when two things are brought so close together that they cannot be got closer.

Chock Full.—Full to the brim. Frequently used in close-hauled sailing to let the helmsman know that the sails are full enough, and he need use no more weather helm. (See "Ramping Full.")

Chock Home.—Close up.

Choppy Sea.—A short, steep sea, which makes a vessel continuously pitch and 'scend.

Chuck.—To throw.

Chuckle-headed.—Full or bluff in the bow; thickheaded.

Chuck to Windward.—A weather-going tide is said to chuck a vessel to windward, and the contrary a lee-going tide.

Circumference of a Circle.—The diameter multiplied by 3·14159; in algebra denoted by the Greek letter π or perimeter.

Clamp.—A thick strake of wood worked inside a vessel under the shelf.

Clamps.—A kind of wedge vice, used in boat-building to hold the plank together. (See "Boat Building.") Various contrivances of wood or metal used in fitting up a vessel or in fixing parts in her construction.

Clap on Canvas.—To put on more canvas. "Clap on here" is a request frequently made to idlers to assist in hauling on a rope.

Claw.—To hang well to windward, as to "claw off a lee shore."

Claw to Windward.—To beat to windward under difficulties. To claw off a lee shore is to beat off and avoid getting stranded.

Clean Full.—Barely close-hauled; when all the sails are full.

Clear for Going About.—A question often asked when work is being done on deck, and the vessel has to be put about: "Are ye all clear there for going about?"

Cleats.—Pieces of wood with one or more arms fastened to spars, &c., for belaying to, or to prevent ropes slipping, &c. (See "Thumb Cleats" and "Cruickshanks' Patent Safety Cleats.")

Clench Work (spelt also "clencher," "clincher," and sometimes "clinker.")—In boat building when the edges of the plank overlap, forming lands.

Clew.—The lower corners of a square sail; in fore-and-aft sails only the lower after corner is called the clew.

Clew Lines.—Clew garnets. Ropes used for hauling up the clews of sails.

Clew Up.—To haul up a sail by the clew lines for furling, &c. Also used as a slang term for shut up or cease.

Clinch.—To fasten a rope by a half hitch, and seize the end back to the other part; a method adopted with very large ropes or hawsers after they have to be bent to rings, &c., in a hurry. To clinch is also to beat the end of a bolt or rivet until it forms a head; or to turn the end of a nail in so that it will not draw.

Clincher Work.—See "Clench."

Clinker.—The hard cinder which forms on furnace bars. Sometimes wrongly used for clincher work in boat building. (See "Clench Work.")

Clinometer.—An instrument for measuring the angle of inclination or the extent of heel a ship has under canvas or whilst rolling.

Clip for Chain of Centre-Board.—Captain E. du Boulay, of the Bembridge Sailing Club, recommends a clip made of galvanised iron as shown in Fig. 258, and fastened just behind the sheave over which the chain works. One

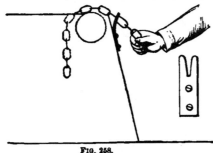

FIG. 258.

of the crew who has hold of the chain can, lowering his hand, drop the chain into the clip and jam it, but by keeping the chain level he can raise or lower his board freely.

Clip Hook.—A double hook (hinged to the eye) whose parts overlap when attached to a ring,

FIG. 259.

&c. A hook not much in favour, as it so frequently breaks or gets half detached.

Clipper.—A fine ship; first applied to the sharp-bowed ships that sailed out of Baltimore, U.S.

Clipper Stem or Bow.—An overhanging stem or prow.

Clock Calm.—So calm and still that the ticking of a clock could be heard.

Close Aboard.—Near to, as the land is said to be close aboard when a vessel has approached it very closely.

Close-hauled.—With all the sheets trimmed flat aft, and every rope that helps extend the sails hauled taut. Hauled as close to the wind as the sails will admit without shaking their luffs. When a square-rigged ship is close-hauled she is about from five to six points off the wind. A fore-and-aft schooner, with everything nicely trimmed for racing, will lie within four and a half points of the wind; a cutter within four and a quarter points. This, of course, supposes the water to be smooth and the wind of what is known as "whole sail strength." In rough water a vessel cannot be sailed so close; in the Atlantic race between the Cambria and Dauntless, the former, although she had head winds for a large part of the time, for two reasons was never hauled up closer than six points: generally there was too much sea to admit of it without being half hove to, and in such long passages it was thought better to sail her along hard on the chance of the wind freeing; or if it headed her she could have been put on the other tack. (See "Wind.")

Close Reefed.—When the last reef is taken in, generally the fourth reef; but some modern schooners with laced mainsails have only three reef bands, and it is thought that when the fourth reef is wanted that it is time to set the trysail.

Close to Wind.—Close hauled. As close to the wind as the sails will bear without lifting.

Clothes.—The outfit given to a yacht's crew by the owner, consisting of trousers, frocks, caps, shoes, and neckerchief. When the yacht is paid off the men take the clothes with them, but if a man is discharged for misconduct, he is made to leave his clothes behind. Under any circumstances the men have no legal right to the clothes if the owner chose to retain them, as it is only a kind of livery.

Clothes Lines.—A sail is said to be across a clothes lines when it is girted by a rope. Lines used on board men-of-war for drying the sailors' clothes on washing days.

Cloth in the Wind, A.—When the foremost cloth or luff of a sail is shaking through the vessel being brought too near the wind. A man is said to be three cloths in the wind when intoxicated.

Clove Hitch.—See "Scowing an Anchor."

Coal, Consumption of.—With engines of the old type a steamer consumed from 4lb. to 6lb. of coal per indicated horse-power per hour. With modern two-cylinder compound engines the consumption is about 2lb. per horse-power per hour; and with three-cylinder engines and 180lb. boiler pressure about 1½lb.

Coal, stowage of.—It is usual to allow 40 cubic

feet per ton for the stowage of coal in bunkers.

Coal Tar.—See " Varnish."

Coamings.—A raised frame fitted to and above the deck for the hatches, skylights, &c., to rest upon. Sometimes wrongly spelt combings.

Coats.—Painted canvas used to cover sails when they are stowed.

Coated.—Sails stowed and covered up by the coats.

Coble.—A boat common on the Yorkshire coast.

Fig. 260.

Said to run over a sea very dry. The peculiar deep rudder makes them steer well in a sea.

Cock Bill.—See " A Cock Bill."

Cockpit.—In a man-of-war, part of the ship below water where the middies were berthed, and where the wounded were attended in time of action. A kind of well in the deck aft, common in American yachts and in some small yachts in this country.

Coil.—Ropes packed up in rings one over the other. To coil away.

Collapsible Boats.—The first canvas collapsible boats were invented by the Rev. E. Berthon in 1851. They are made upon longitudinal frames with a double skin of stout canvas. When collapsed the gunwales fold outwards, back flat on the keel. (See Fig. 261.) A 7ft. dinghy which might suit a 5-ton yacht, will have 3ft. beam, and when folded

Fig. 261.

only require space of 7ft. × 2ft. × 6in. The weight of such a boat is about 40lb.

A small boat 10ft. long weighs, with all the gear, about 80lb. A yacht's gig 26ft. long, 5cwt. The price of a boat 10ft. long is 14 guineas. The preceding sketch shows the

boats open and collapsed. (See Waterproofing.) The boats are used for small yachts which cruise from port to port, as they are easily stowed and row fairly well.

A more modern canvas collapsible boat is known as the " James," and made by Captain James, Hyde Park Court, London.

Collar.—An eye or bight of a shroud, stay or rope to go over the masthead as the collar of the forestay. Also a rim on a bolt.

Collier.—A vessel employed to carry coal.

Collision.—When one vessel comes into contact with another.

Colours.—Flags denoting nationality, ownership, or other identity.

Comb.—The crest part of a wave.

Comber.—A big surf-like wave.

Combings.—See " Coamings."

Come no Nearer.—An order to the helmsman not to bring the vessel nearer the wind.

Come on Board, Sir.—A seaman's laconic speech when he reports his arrival on board to an officer in charge after leave.

Come To.—To fly up in the wind; to come nearer or closer to the wind; to luff. Generally used when a vessel comes nearer the wind after having falling off the wind.

Come Up.—Generally to slacken up. Whilst hauling on the fall of a tackle and the order comes, " Avast hauling there," the hand that has to belay sings out, " Come up behind;" all hands instantly release the fall, so that the one who has to belay may catch the turn round the belaying pin or cavel without " losing any." (See " Hold on the Fore Side " and " Belay.") In slang an admonition to cease fooling.

Come Up, To.—A vessel is said to come up when the wind frees her so that she can head nearer her course, or look, or point her course. In beating, a helmsman in reporting the progress made by the vessel may say, " She has come up two points this tack, sir," according to the extent of the wind freeing; if the wind came more ahead, he might say she has broken off or fallen off two points, &c.

Come up With.—To overtake; also to finish off, as to " come up with a round turn," meaning as the crew left off hauling one had to take a sudden turn of the rope round the cavel, &c., to belay.

Commodore.—An officer appointed to take the command of a squadron of ships. His rank, whilst he holds the appointment, comes next to the captain of the fleet in the Navy list; neither does the Commodore hold precedence of a captain who is his senior, and would cease to hold the advantages of his office should a senior arrive within the limits of his station.

A rank conferred by clubs upon members; and there are Commodores, Vice-Commodores, and Rear-Commodores. Their duties are to see that the laws of the club, especially those that apply to matters afloat, are properly carried out. Commodores fly the broad pennant or swallow-tail burgee. (See "Burgee.")

Companion.—The structure with sliding roof which forms the entrance from the deck to the cabins below.

Compass Bowl.—The bowl within the binnacle containing the compass.

Compass Card.—A circle divided into 32 parts, called points; and each part is again divided into 4 parts, and the whole is divided into 360 degrees.

Courses.	Degrees. ° ′ ″	Points.	Back Bearings.
N.	0 0 0	0 point	S.
N. ¼ E.	2 48 45	¼ „	S. ¼ W.
N. ½ E.	5 37 30	½ „	S. ½ W.
N. ¾ E.	8 26 15	¾ „	S. ¾ W.
N. by E.	11 15 0	1 point	S. by W.
N. by E. ¼ E.	14 3 45	¼ „	S. by W. ¼ W.
N. by E. ½ E.	16 52 30	½ „	S. by W. ½ W.
N. by E. ¾ E.	19 41 15	¾ „	S. by W. ¾ W.
N.N.E.	22 30 0	2 points	S.S.W.
N.E. by N. ¾ N.*	25 18 45	¼ „	S.W. by S. ¾ S.
N.E. by N. ½ N.	28 7 30	½ „	S.W. by S. ½ S.
N.E. by N. ¼ N.	30 56 15	¾ „	S.W. by S. ¼ S.
N.E. by N.	33 45 0	3 points	S.W. by S.
N.E. ¾ N.	36 33 45	¼ „	S.W. ¾ S.
N.E. ½ N.	39 22 30	½ „	S.W. ½ S.
N.E. ¼ N.	42 11 15	¾ „	S.W. ¼ S.
N.E.	45 0 0	4 points	S.W.
N.E. ¼ E.	47 48 45	¼ „	S.W. ¼ W.
N.E. ½ E.	50 37 30	½ „	S.W. ½ W.
N.E. ¾ E.	53 26 15	¾ „	S.W. ¾ W.
N.E. by E.	56 15 0	5 points	S.W. by W.
N.E. by E. ¼ E.	59 3 45	¼ „	S.W. by W. ¼ W.
N.E. by E. ½ E.	61 52 30	½ „	S.W. by W. ½ W.
N.E. by E. ¾ E.	64 41 15	¾ „	S.W. by W. ¾ W.
E.N.E.	67 30 0	6 points	W.S.W.
E. by N. ¾ N.	70 18 45	¼ „	W. by S. ¾ S.
E. by N. ½ N.	73 7 30	½ „	W. by S. ½ S.
E. by N. ¼ N.	75 56 15	¾ „	W. by S. ¼ S.
E. by N.	78 45 0	7 points	W. by S.
E. ¾ N.	81 33 45	¼ „	W. ¾ S.
E. ½ N.	84 22 30	½ „	W. ½ S.
E. ¼ N.	87 11 15	¾ „	W. ¼ S.
E.	90 0 0	8 points	W.
E. ¼ S., and so on.	92 48 45	¼ „	W. ¼ N.

* It is customary in the Royal Navy to call this N.N.E. ¼ E.; N.N.E. ½ E.; N.N.E. ¾ E., then N.E. by N. Either way is correct. Sometimes also E. by N. ¾ N. is called E.N.E. ¼ E.: or N.E. by E. ¾ E. is called for shortness E.N.E. ¼ N. The table, however, gives the more correct way. In calling off the points avoid such "lubberisms" as N.E. by E. ¾ N. for N.E. ¼ E., or S. by W. ¾ S. for S. ¼ W., &c.

It is commonly believed that the mariner's compass was introduced into Europe in the fifteenth century, but it seems to have been well known in a primitive form in the twelfth and thirteenth centuries. In one of the popular songs written in the time of King John, it is related that the sailors who went on long voyages to Friesland and the East, knew their way by observing the polar star, but, when the sky was covered with clouds, and they could no longer see the stars of heaven, they had a contrivance which consisted of a needle of iron put through a piece of cork so that one end remained out. This they rubbed with the loadstone, and then placed it in a vessel of water, and the needle pointed without error to the polar star. This formed a primitive but fairly perfect mariner's compass. If an ordinary needle be rubbed on a magnet and gently dropped into a glass of water it will float and point to the north. (See "Fluid Compass.")

Compass Point.—The 32nd part of 360 degrees, or practically 11¼ degrees.

Complement.—The full number; the whole ship's crew.

Composition for a Boat's Bottom.—Day's composition is said to prevent the growth of weeds, barnacles, &c. The boat should have a coat of common varnish first, and the composition should be applied before the varnish is quite dry. Only a part of the boat should be varnished at a time, or the varnish will dry before the composition can be put on. One gallon carefully put on will cover about 400 square feet or the immersed surface of a 10-tonner. The composition should be kept well stirred whilst being used, as the ingredients are heavy, and soon settle to the bottom. Day's address is Limehouse, London.

Peacock's composition has been used on iron ships with good effect. The composition can be obtained of Messrs. Peacock and Buchanan, Southampton. This composition should be applied in the same manner as Jesty's. Two, three, or four coats of black varnish, or coal tar, should be first put on. The plates of an iron yacht should be thoroughly cleaned of rust, &c., before applying the varnish. (See "Coal Tar or Black Varnish.")

The Protector Fluid Company, 8, Leadenhall-street, E.C., have a poisonous composition, said to very effectually prevent the growth of barnacles.

Jesty's composition is in great request for coating the bottoms of iron and wooden ships. Before applying it give the vessels one or two coats of coal tar thinned with turpentine; when this has dried on apply a couple of coats of the composition; a priming of black varnish made by Mr. Jesty is sometimes used instead of coal tar. The composition should not be put on over paint. It must be kept well stirred in the pot whilst it is being applied, as some of its ingredients are very heavy. The Jesty manufactory is at Gosport, Hants.

Blake and Son, of Gosport, manufacture a composition which is in much request.

Compressor.—A contrivance to prevent the chain cable being veered too quickly, or to stop its veering altogether.

Conduct Money.—Money kept back from a seaman's wages, but given up in whole at the end of an engagement if the seaman's conduct has been good; generally the amount kept back is 2s. per week, and a fine to that amount is levied for an offence.

Conning.—Directing a steersman in the use or management of the helm. Telling him how to steer.

Contrary Wind.—A wind that blows adversely down a vessel's course.

Copper Bottomed.—The bottom of a ship sheathed with copper. According to Charnock (Vol. III., page 201), copper sheathing was first introduced in the Navy as a remedy against the attacks of worms in 1758. (See "Sheathing.")

Copper Fastened.—Fastened with copper bolts and nails.

Coracle.—A small boat used by the ancient Britons. (See "Canvas Boats.")

Cordage.—A general term used to denote the rope used in the rigging of a ship.

Corinthian.—A term in yacht parlance synonymous with amateur. The term Corinthian half a century ago was commonly applied to the aristocratic patrons of sports, some of which, such as pugilism, are not now the fashion. The name was adopted in consequence of the similarity between the fashionable young men of Corinth who emulated the feats of athletes, &c., and their modern prototypes.

The qualifications of a "Corinthian" sailor are variously defined. The Royal Alfred Yacht Club formerly enjoined that in all matches the amateur element shall consist of "members of the club, their sons, or members of a royal, foreign, or recognised yacht club, or naval officers."

This club in 1895 adopted the following qualification:

"A person shall not be considered an amateur who is, or has been, employed for pay in any capacity on board a yacht or other vessel, commissioned officers of the Royal Navy, Royal Marines, and Royal Naval Reserve excepted; also officers of the Mercantile Marine if they have never served for pay on board a yacht and are members of a recognised yacht club, but not anyone who is by trade or employment for wages a mechanic, artisan, labourer, or servant."

Anyone who is not, at the time being, working at a trade, or who is not an artisan, mechanic, labourer or menial, is generally regarded as a qualified amateur. A ship's carpenter is reckoned as a paid hand. Sometimes a steward and cook are not; but they are not allowed to work in such cases if retained on board.

Some clubs in Corinthian matches do not allow any paid hand to be on board; others only allow yachts of 15 tons and under one paid hand, who is not permitted to touch the tiller. A later and more suitable plan is to have paid hands in the proportion set forth in the table, farther back. In all Corinthian matches an amateur must steer.

Corinthian Rule of Measurement.—A tonnage measurement adopted by the Corinthian Yacht Club. It is simply the shipbuilder's rule for roughly estimating the register tonnage of a vessel, thus $\frac{L \times B \times D}{200}$, where L length, B breadth, and D depth, amidships from deck to underside of keel. This rule was also adopted by the New Thames Yacht Club in 1875, but after a trial of two years it was abandoned, as the general opinion appeared to be that the rule would have an injurious influence on the form of yachts.

Cork Concrete.—A mixture of cork and marine glue used to fill the ends of boats, &c., to make them unsinkable. Some such composition is made by the "Unsinkable Boat Company," Wharf Road, North Greenwich. See "Airtight Cases."

Corky.—Light, buoyant, easily set in motion by the waves; floating with a high side out of the water, &c.

Cornette.—A swallow-tailed flag.

Cot.—(See "Wexford Flat-bottomed Boats.")

Cot.—The framework hinged to the lining of a yacht in the forecastle to form the bed when hammocks are not slung.

Counter.—The projecting part of a vessel abaft the sternpost.

Course.—Direction; the direction in which a vessel moves; the direction from one point to another point which a vessel has to reach. The distance yachts have to sail in a match at a regatta.

Courses.—The lower squaresails of a ship.

Covering Board.—The outside deck plank fitted over the timber heads. See "Plank sheer."

Coxswain.—The man who steers and has charge of a boat and her crew. Pronounced "cox'n."

Crabbing.—When a vessel tumbles down under a heavy press of canvas, or when she sags to leeward badly.

Cracking on.—Carrying a large quantity of sail.

Cracks in a Mast or other Spars, To Stop.—When the spar is quite dry run in marine glue; when the glue is hard, scrape out some of it, and stop with putty, coloured to imitate the colour of the wood.

Craft.—A vessel; also used in the plural, thus a number of craft, or a lot of craft, means a number of vessels.

Crank.—Not stiff under canvas; a boat that can be heeled or listed very easily; generally a dangerous boat.

Cranse.—An iron hoop band, with eyes fitted to bowsprit ends or the ends of other spars.

Creek.—An inlet of the sea.

Crests.—The top edges of waves.

Crew.—A ship's complement, and including every man employed on board in any capacity whatsoever, distinct from passengers.

Crimps.—Agents for engaging seaman: a vocation not in good repute.

Cringle.—A metal thimble worked into the corners and leeches of sails.

Cripple, A.—A vessel that does not carry her canvas stiffly.

Cross Chocks.—Pieces of wood used for filling in between lower futtocks where their heels do not meet on the top of the keel.

Cross-jack.—Cross-jack-yard is the lowest yard on the mizen mast. Pronounced "cro'jack."

Cross Sea.—Waves that come from divers directions, usually caused by sudden shifts of wind when it is blowing heavily.

Cross-trees.—The spreaders for topmast shrouds.

Crow-foot.—A number of lines attached to one line, and spreading out something like a bird's claw.

Crown of an Anchor.—The part of an anchor where the arms are joined to the shank.

Crow's Nest.—A place of shelter at the top-gallant mast-head for a look out man, used by whalers in Northern latitudes.

Cruickshank's Safety Cleats.—This is a contrivance for jamming the mainsheet without any turns or bights, so that when a certain pressure is put on the sail the sheet unreeves. The cleat was invented with a view of preventing boats being capsized when struck by sudden squalls. The objection to such cleats is that they may possibly foul, and moreover the pressure which if applied steadily would just cause the sheet to unreeve, might if applied suddenly capsize the boat long before the sheet would run through the jammers. With a "breeze of wind" there is generally some sea, and then it is not so frequently a sudden accession of wind or squall that causes the boat to capsize as her position among the waves. If she gets so placed as to lurch or roll to leeward from the effect of a wave crest passing underneath her, she may upset without any increase in the pressure of wind; that is to say, if her safe angle of heel under canvas is 20 degrees, and she be permanently heeled by the wind pressure to that angle, then, if the action of the waves caused her to heel further—say 10 degrees—she would capsize unless skilfully handled by the steersman. As there need be no increase of wind pressure to bring about such a catastrophe, the "safety cleat" would be of no avail under such circumstances. In smooth water it would never be prudent or safe to wait for a squall to strike a boat, as, if the squall were heavy enough to cause the boat to heel to the capsizing point, the safety cleat could not relieve the sheet fast enough to prevent such heeling. The squall must be "met," the boat thrown head to wind, and the sheet released, before the squall strikes. Sometimes in small boats, with the wind abeam or abaft the beam, it may be more prudent to run them off the wind; but scarcely in any case, either in a sea or in smooth water, could the safety cleat save a boat from being capsized if the helmsman or crew carelessly handled her when she is in danger of such a catastrophe. Mr. Cruickshank's cleat is provided with a releasing line, which is to be held in the hand, and if the break does not allow the sheet to be released fast enough, the line is to be pulled. Manifestly it would be safer and give less trouble to hold the sheet itself in the hand. (See "Beadon's Safety Reel.")

Crutch.—An iron support for a boom when the sail is stowed something in this form Y; the upright part fits into a socket on the taffrail. Crutches are sometimes made of two cross pieces of wood, thus X; in schooners the crutch for the fore boom is generally so formed; also a similar crutch is used to put the tiller in when the vessel is moored to keep it from flying about, and when by lashing the tiller lines across the vessel to either rail the passage fore and aft would be inconveniently obstructed. An X crutch is used to support the middle of the boom when the sail is stowed and not slung by the peak halyards. A crutch is also the metal fork used instead of tholes in a row boat.

Cubic Measure of Water.—One gallon contains 277·274 cubic inches, or 0·16 of a cubic foot. One cubic foot contains 1728 cubic inches, or 6·233 gallons. One ton of salt water contains 35 cubic feet. One ton of fresh water contains 35·9 cubic feet. A ton weight is equal to 2240lb. See "Decimal Equivalents." (See "Water.")

Cuddy.—A small cabin, a deck house, the space under the half deck of a boat.

Cunt-lins.—The space between four casks when they are stowed bilge to bilge.

Current.—The moving of the water in certain directions. To ascertain the rate or direction of a current when not at anchor or when becalmed, in a fog, or out of sight of fixed objects, see "Drifting."

Cutter.—A boat heavier than a gig, and used in bad weather when the lighter boat might get swamped.

Cutter.—A vessel with one mast rigged with mainsail, foresail, jib, and topsail, as shown in the accompanying sketch, and known as the "national rig." The bowsprit usually goes out on one side of the stem through an iron ring termed a spanshackle or gammon iron, but sometimes it goes out over the stem head, especially if there is a knee head. The bowsprit is fitted to run in and out between bitts, and hence is termed a "running bowsprit" in contradistinction to a standing or fixed bowsprit such as schooners have with jib boom. A cutter's sails are termed "fore-and-aft" sails, because they are always tacked and

FIG. 262.

sheeted in a fore-and-aft direction by the same corners in contradistinction to sails which are tacked and sheeted from alternate as squaresails are. (Fig. 262.)

Formerly cutters carried a large square sail and square topsail or raffee; but these are now almost obsolete excepting in revenue cruisers, having been superseded by the spinnaker and jib topsail. The latter is hanked to the topmast stay, and so also is the bowsprit spinnaker sometimes. A sloop as now understood differs from a cutter in only having one head-sail, properly termed a foresail.

D.

Dagger Centre-plate.—(See " Centre-plate.")

Dagger knee.—A piece of timber crossing the frames diagonally.

Dandy.—A cutter rigged vessel with lug mizen aft set on a jigger-mast.

Darning the Water.—When a vessel keeps sailing backwards and forwards, as before a bar harbour or pier, waiting for water or orders, &c.

Davit Guys.—The stays or ropes used to keep the davits steady.

Davits.—Strong iron stanchions with arms used for hoisting boats, &c.

Dead Calm.—Without a breath of wind.

Deaden-her-way.—To stop a vessel's way by backing and filling, or by hauling a sail aback, or by yawing her about with the helm, &c.

Dead Eye.—A circular block, with three holes in it (crow-foot fashion) without sheaves, used to reeve the lanyards through for setting up the rigging.

Dead Flat.—The midship section. The term is applied to the middle flat of a ship, where she gets no broader and no narrower; that is, where the cross sections for some distance amidships are of the same size and form: thus the side will present a " dead flat " for some distance. (See " Straight of breadth.")

Dead Lights.—Strong shutters made to fit the outside of cabin windows—closed in bad weather. In yachts small circular lights are generally fitted with iron shutters inside or outside.

Dead on end.—Said of the wind, when it blows straight down the course a vessel wishes to make. (See " Nose-ender," " Muzzler.")

Dead Reckoning.—The calculation of a ship's position by the log, the courses she has made, lee way, set of currents, &c., without an observation.

Dead Rise.—The approach the floor timbers of a vessel makes to a vertical. In the case of ships, the frames in the after body are called the dead-risings, because they only rise from the keel at a sharp angle, all the middle frames starting out nearly horizontally from the keel. A yacht is said to have considerable dead rise on a very rising floor, when she is more or less of the V form, but really vessels of the T form have the greatest dead rise, as the heels of the floors forming the framing to take the garboards do rise nearly vertically.

Dead water.—The water in a vessel's wake, close to her sternpost, that follows the ship.

Dead weight.—Concentrated weight in a vessel's bottom, such as a heavy cargo of ore or ballast.

Dead wood.—The solid wood worked on top of the keel forward and aft.

Decimal Equivalents—

	OF A FOOT.				OF A TON.			
In.	—	⅛	¼	⅜	Cwt.	Ton.	Cwt.	Ton.
0	·000	·021	·042	·062	1	·05	11	·55
1	·083	·104	·125	·146	2	·10	12	·60
2	·167	·187	·208	·229	3	·15	13	·65
3	·250	·271	·292	·312	4	·20	14	·70
4	·333	·354	·375	·396	5	·25	15	·75
5	·417	·437	·458	·479	6	·30	16	·80
6	·500	·521	·544	·562	7	·35	17	·85
7	·583	·604	·625	·646	8	·40	18	·90
8	·667	·687	·708	·729	9	·45	19	·95
9	·750	·771	·792	·812	10	·50	20	1·00
10	·833	·854	·875	·896				
11	·916	·937	·958	·979				
12	1·000	1·021	1·042	1·062				

Deck.—The platforms supported on the beams of ships. The old three deckers had upper deck, main deck, middle deck, lower deck, and orlop deck, no guns being carried on the latter. Below the orlop deck were the hold platforms, or decks. Yachts usually are said to have only one deck, *i.e.* the upper deck open to the sky; some large yachts, however, have a lower deck, laid and caulked. Smaller yachts have platform beams upon which the platform rests. The platform is the cabin floor.

Deck Caulking and Stopping.—(See " Marine Glue.")

Deck, to Whiten.—Make a mixture of 1lb. oxalic acid to 1 gallon of water. Damp the deck with this and wash off.

Deep sea lead (pronounced "dipsey lead").—A lead of 28lb. weight attached to a line of 200 fathoms. Now, automatically recording machines are generally used for deep sea soundings. (See " Lead.")

Delivery.—The quarter wash of a vessel. A yacht is said to have a good delivery if on passing through the water no large waves are raised at and about the quarters; she is then said to leave the water clean, to have a clean wake, clean delivery, or to run the water very clean aft; to have a sweet run, &c.

Demurrage.—Compensation paid to the owner of a ship when she has been detained longer than reasonable by a freighter or other person at a port.

Depth, moulded.—The terms used in ship and yacht building and relating to the depth of vessels are numerous and occasionally confusing. For instance, there is draught of water aft and draught of water forward, extreme draught and mean draught. In a merchant ship, draught aft and extreme draught would most likely be the same, but in many yachts, the extreme draught is amidships, or nearly so, and the draught at the sternpost is frequently less than the extreme draught. The draught forward in most sailing yachts would be a purely fanciful quantity, on account of there being no straight length of keel forward of amidships to measure the draught from. Beyond this, formerly depth or depth of immersion was used to denote draught; and then there was moulded depth, that is the depth from the lead line to the rabbet of the keel; after this came depth of hold, which in a man of war meant depth from the lower deck, or orlop deck, to the ceiling above the kelsons, and in a merchant or carrying ship, or yacht, the depth from the upper deck.

The term "moulded depth" is now never applied to the depth of immersion, and when the term is used it is always understood to mean the depth as defined by Lloyd's, as follows: "The moulded depth of an iron or steel vessel is the perpendicular depth taken from the top of the upper deck beam at the side at the middle of the length of the vessel to the top of the keel, and the bottom of the frame at the middle line, except in spar and awning deck vessels, in which the depth is measured from the top of the main deck beam. In wooden and composite vessels the moulded depth is taken to be the perpendicular depth from the top of the upper deck beam at the side of the vessel amidships to the lower edge of the rabbet of the keel. The form of the lower part of the midship section of many wooden and composite vessels being of a hollow character, the moulded depth in such cases should be measured from the point where the line of the flat of the bottom, if continued, would cut the keel." It will be seen that, even with this excellent definition of moulded depth, it may mean a great many things in the case of yachts with very hollow floors and great dead rise, or in the case of yachts with box keels the same as Vanduara, Galatea, and Wendur have. However, there is one definite point to start from in all cases, and that is the "top of the upper deck beam at the side."

Depth of a Yacht, to measure.—Very frequently it is necessary to know accurately the ex-

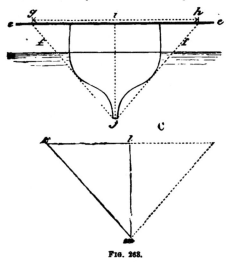

FIG. 263.

ternal depth of a yacht from rail to keel, or her draught; from load line to keel. The following simple plan is a ready means

of obtaining such depth and draught: To obtain the depth take a straight-edged bar of wood (see *e e*, Fig. 263) which will be placed across the rail, at right angles to the keel. A small chain, *f f*, will be passed under the bottom of the yacht, and one end will be made fast on the bar at *g*, so that the chain just touches the bilge; the chain will be drawn tight, and the other end made fast to bar at *h*. The distance *g h* must be accurately measured on the bar, as also, when removed, must the length of the chain which passed from *g* under the yacht to *h*. (To obtain the points for the measurement of the chain, it would be found convenient to fasten a small piece of cord or yarn at the points *g* and *h*, immediately under the bar, before the chain is cast off.)

Having obtained these measurements, it will be an easy matter to find the depth *i j*. The distance *g h* can be laid off to scale, divided in the centre by a perpendicular, *i j*: *half* the length of the chain will then be laid off from *g* and *h* to intersect the perpendicular, as at *j*; the distance from *i* to *j* on the bar, measured by the scale, will be the depth required.

The draught of water of the yacht will of course be found by subtracting her height out of water, from load line to rail, at the points where the depth was taken.

If no scale be at hand, the depth can readily be found by calculation. Take half the length *g h*, which call *k l* (Fig. 263), and half the length of the chain, which call *k m*; subtract *l* from *k m*; multiply the remainder by the sum of *k m* and *k l* added together; the square root of the product will be the required depth. Expressed in algebraic language:

$$\sqrt{(k m + k l) \times (k m - k l)}$$

Say *k m* is 10ft., added to *k l* 7ft., make 17ft.; next 7 subtracted from 10 leave 3, and 3 multiplied by 17 make 51. The square root of 51 is 7·1, which would be the required depth.

The mean draught would be found by taking the actual draught at several (say 4) equidistant intervals, commencing at the heel of the sternpost and ending at the stem; add these draughts together, and divide the sum by the number of measurements taken, including those at stem and sternpost. If the fore foot is very much rounded away, the measurement at the stem will be 0, but in counting the number of measurements, that for the stem must be included.

The Barrow Corinthian Yacht Club formerly included mean depth in their tonnage rule, and adopted, on the suggestion of Mr. R. S. White, the following plan for obtaining depth at any point without calculation. (See Fig. 264.)

A is the keel batten, graduated from centre, in feet and tenths, with slots marked C, at each end, to slide the side or depth battens to the exact beam of yacht.

BB. Side or depth battens, graduated at upper part in feet and tenths from top of keel batten, and secured to keel batten with thumb-screws marked D.

The manner of working is as follows: Having obtained exact beam of yacht, set the depth battens BB at this distance apart on keel batten A, by means of thumb-screws D tightly screwed up. Dip the keel batten under keel until opposite marks on gunwale, where depth is required to be taken; then bring it close up to keel, and take readings off depth battens BB, until they correspond

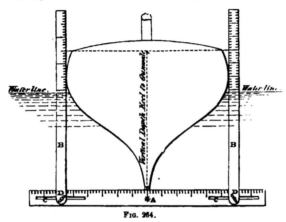

Fig. 264.

on each side—this being depth of yacht, keel to gunwale, in vertical line, as shown in sketch.

If the measurements have to be taken in a tideway, the batten A must be kept close up to keel to prevent its driving aft.

Depth of Hold.—In a single-deck vessel, the height between the kelson and deck.

Derelict.—A vessel abandoned at sea. It is said that an owner's rights are not also abandoned if any live animal be left and found on board.

Derrick.—A kind of crane.

Deviation.—A movement of the compass needle due to local attraction, principally met with in iron or composite ships, and distinct from variation.

Dhow.—A large Arab vessel, usually lateen rigged.

Diagonal Braces.—Strengthening straps of iron that cross the frames of a vessel diagonally.

Diagonal Lines.—Lines which cross the sections of a vessel shown in the body plan, in a diagonal direction with the middle vertical line.

Diameter of Circle.—Circumference multiplied by 0·31831.

Diminishing Strakes.—The strakes immediately above and below wales being the thickness of the wale on one edge, and diminishing to the thickness of the plank on the other.

Dinghy.—A small boat of Bombay, with a settee sail. Also a small skiff, or punt, carried by yachts. (See "Portable Dinghy.")

Dinghy-man.—The man who has charge of the dinghy of a yacht, whose duty it is to go on shore on errands, &c.

Dip.—The inclination the compass needle makes towards the earth in high latitudes.

Dip the Ensign, To.—To lower the ensign as a salute, or token of respect. (See "Dipping the Ensign.")

Dipping Lug Sail.—A sail hoisted by a halyard and mast hoop traveller. The sail is set to leeward of the mast, and the tack is usually fast to the stem or on the weather bow. In tacking or gybing the sail has to be lowered and the yard shifted to the other side of the mast. A plan has been proposed to perform this dipping by the aid of a topping and tripping line instead of by lowering the sail (see the sketch, Fig. 265); but the balance lug, which requires no dipping whatsoever in tacking, is to be preferred to the best dipping arrangement. (See "Penzance Luggers" and "Split Lug.")

Dipping the Ensign and Burgee.—The ensign is lowered or dipped as a means of saluting a commodore, &c., or member of a club. The junior member should be the first to dip. Sometimes, if no ensign is flying, the burgee is dipped; but this strictly is contrary to the etiquette of the Royal Navy. It is usual to "dip" on passing a man-of-war or royal yacht. A royal yacht never answers the salute by dipping her ensign. Strictly it is etiquette for the blue ensign to dip to the white; and red to the blue or white.

A club burgee being a personal flag is usually lowered half mast high in the case of death as well as the ensign. (See "Ensign," "Etiquette," "Saluting," &c.)

Discharge Ticket.—A formal document given to seamen when they are discharged.

Dismantled.—Unrigged: without sails or spars.

Dismasted.—When a vessel loses her mast by violence, or accident.

Displacement.—The quantity or weight of water a vessel displaces, which, in weight, is always equal to the total of her own weight, with everything on board.

Displacement per inch of immersion.—It is often necessary to know how much weight would have to be put into a yacht to sink her an inch or more deeper in the water or lighten her to a similar extent. Roughly, this can be ascertained by the following rule:— Multiply the length on the load line by the breadth on the load line and divide the product by 600. ($\frac{L \times B}{600}$.) The quotient will be the weight in tons or fractions of a ton. This rule would not hold good if the yacht were lightened more than three or four inches or deepened to that extent. The rule is based on the assumption that the area of the load line is ·7 of the circumscribing parallelogram. That is to say, the length and breadth multiplied together and again multiplied by ·7 will (approximately) give the area of load line. Divide this product by 12, and the area is reduced to cubic feet, and divide again by 35 and the answer will be given in tons or fractions of a ton. By this rough rule the displacement per inch at any part of the hull of the vessel (if the measurements are taken at the part) can be found approximately $\left(\frac{L \times B \times 7}{12 \times 35}\right) = \left(\frac{L \times B}{600}\right)$.

Distemper.—Red or white lead powder mixed in strong glue size and applied hot. Sometimes the part to be covered is first coated with lime whitewash. A yellow distemper for funnels is thus made: 6lb. glue made into size, and whilst hot added to ½ cwt. yellow ochre, ½ cwt. whiting, reduced to proper consistency by warm water.

Divisions.—The portions of a fleet; as the starboard, port, and centre divisions, the admiral in command always occupying the centre division. Prior to 1856, there were red, white and blue divisions, but now, as only the white or St. George's ensign is recognised, the divisions by colour have been done away with. (See "Admiral.")

Dock.—A basin into which a ship is floated and the gates closed upon her; the water is then pumped out and the ship left dry, supported on a framework and by shores. These are called dry docks.—A general name for a place to receive ships for repair or cleaning. A ship is said to dock herself when placed in a soft tidal bed of mud she buries herself in it more or less.

Dockyards.—Places where ships are built; usually, however, confined to government yards.

Dog Shores.—Pieces of timber used in launching ships.

Dog Vane.—A light vane made of bunting or feathers, to show the direction of the wind, and sometimes put on the weather rail.

Dog Watches.—The divided watch between four and eight in the evening; thus the first dog watch is from four to six, and the second from six to eight. (See "Watches.")

Doldrums.—The state of being becalmed. Parts of the ocean where calms are prevalent.

Dolphins.—Stout timbers or stone pillars placed on wharfs to make fast warps to.

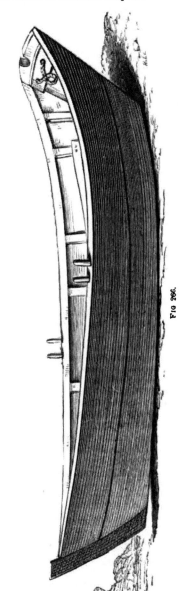

FIG 266.

Dolphin Striker.—The perpendicular spar under the bowsprit end by which more spread is given to the stay of the jib-boom.

Dory.—A flat-bottomed deep boat much used by American fishing schooners. (See Fig. 266.)

The dory is an awkward-looking flat bottomed boat, and some of the schooners carry as many as a dozen of them. They are of the proportions of an English dinghy, and of different sizes, so that several stow one within the other. They are of light construction, and are easily lifted by a rope becket at bow and stern. The sternmost becket is shown in the engraving, also the score for sculling the boat.

Double-banked.—When men sit on the same thwart to row oars from different sides of a boat. Double-banked frigates were two deckers, with the upper deck ports disguised.

Double Block.—A block with two sheaves.

Double Dutch.—A confused way of speaking. (See "Preventive Man.")

Double Gimbals.—See "Gimbals."

Doubling Plank.—To put one thickness of plank over the other.

Douse or Dowse.—To lower away suddenly, to take in a sail suddenly. "Dowse the glim;" to put out a light.

Dove-tail Plates.—Plates in form like a dove's tail.

Dowell.—A hard wood or metal pin used for connecting timber or the edges of plank.

Downhaul.—A rope used for hauling sails down.

Down Helm.—An order to put the helm to leeward and cause the vessel to luff.

Down Oars.—The order given for the crew of a boat to let fall their oars after having them on end in the boat. (See "Let Fall" and "Give Way.")

Down Wind.—Sailing in the direction of or with the wind; before the wind; with the wind astern.

Down Wind, Down Sea.—The sea will subside when the wind does; or the sea will go down when the wind is blowing the same direction as a tidal current, &c.

Drag.—The increased draught of water aft compared with the draught forward.

Drag, To.—To scrape the bottom; to search the bottom with grapnels.

Draught of Water.—The depth of a vessel to the extreme underside of the keel measured from the load water line.

Draw.—A sail is said to draw when it is filled by the wind. To let draw is to ease up the weather sheet of a sail after it has been hauled to windward, and trim the lee sheet aft.

Draw Her to.—In sailing large to bring a vessel closer to wind.

Dress.—To dress ship is to hoist flags from deck to truck; or from bowsprit end to truck and taffrail. Sometimes referred to as dressed "rainbow fashion."

To dress copper is to lay or smooth down wrinkles by going over it with a flat piece of hard wood and a hammer.

Drift.—To float about with the tide or current.

Drift.—The distance between two blocks of a tackle; or the two parts of one thing.

Drifting.—In a calm, in the case of being out of sight of land, or in a dense fog, and out of soundings, if it is desired to know the direction of the current or tide, drop a bucket or pig of ballast or anchor overboard, with as much line out as possible. Then throw some light substance on the water, like a piece of paper, &c., and watch the direction it drifts.

Drive.—To move to leeward by the force of the wind, or drive without control.

Dry-rot.—The decay timber is subject to, often through imperfect ventilation.

Duck.—Light canvas of which boat sails and balloon sails are made. To duck is to dive under water.

Ducks.—A sailor's white suit of duck.

Duff.—A sailor's facetious way of pronouncing dough, hence plum duff for plum pudding. Duff is sometimes applied to "soft tack" or fresh bread as distinct from biscuits.

Dumb Cleat.—A thumb cleat.

Dump.—A nail used in fastening plank to the timbers, as distinguished from a through-bolt.

Dungaree or Dongaree.—A blue linen or cotton cloth in use in India, now much used for the rough or working suits given to yacht sailors.

Dunnage.—Loose material such as cork, bamboo, shavings, ferns, coir, &c., used to jam in between a heavy cargo such as casks, iron, &c.

Dynamometer.—An instrument to measure forces.

E.

Earings.—Ropes used to fasten the corners of the heads of sails to the yards, by the cringles. The upper corners of sails are frequently termed earings. (See "Reef Earings.")

Ears of a Bolt.—The lugs or upper projections of a bolt with a score in it, into which another part is fitted and held by a through pin so as to form a joint like that of a gooseneck.

Ease Away.—The order to slacken a rope, &c.; to ease off a sheet, to ease up a sheet, are synonymous terms, and mean to slacken. (See "Check.")

Ease the Helm.—The order given when sailing against a head sea to ease the weather helm, and by luffing meet the sea bow on, and at the same time deaden the ship's way so that the sea and ship meet less violently. Generally to put the helm amidship, or more amidship after it has been put to port or starboard.

Eating a Vessel out of the Wind.—When two vessels are sailing in company, and if one soaks or settles out to windward of the other she is said to eat her out of the wind. In reality, to make less leeway.

Eating to Windward.—A vessel is said to eat to windward when she, apparently, soaks out to windward of her wake.

Ebb.—The receding of the tide.

Eddy.—Water or currents of air apparently moving in circles.

Edge Away.—To gradually keep a vessel more off a wind after sailing close hauled.

Edge Down on a Vessel.—To bear away towards a vessel to leeward, so as to approach her in an oblique direction.

End for End.—To shift a spar, rope, &c., by reversing the direction of the ends.

End On.—Said of vessel when she has an object bearing in a line with the keel, directly ahead of the bow. On approaching a mark or buoy it is said to be end on if it is directly ahead of the vessel, the bowsprit will then point to the object, hence it is sometimes said that an object is "right on for the bowsprit end."

Ensign.—A flag flown as a distinguishing mark of nationality. The red ensign, with "Union Jack" in the upper corner of the hoist, is the English national flag, and flown by merchantmen by law; but the ensign of the Royal Navy is white with red St. George's cross in it besides the Jack in the corner: this is called "St. George's ensign." Prior to 1856 the red (highest in rank) white and blue ensigns were used in the Royal Navy, and there were Admirals of the Red, Admirals of the White, and Admirals of the Blue; and there were Vice and Rear Admirals of the red, white, and blue. A fleet was divided into red, white, and blue divisions, according to the rank of the Admirals who commanded. In 1855 the red ensign was allotted to the British Mercantile Marine, the blue ensign to the Royal Naval Reserve, and the white ensign to the Royal Navy. However, the white and blue ensigns had always been reserved for the exclusive use of H.M.'s navy, and other vessels could not use either without an Admiralty warrant.

In the Royal Navy it was etiquette, when an Admiral was on board his ship, to fly the white ensign from the main truck, Vice-Admiral from the fore truck, and Rear-Admiral mizen truck. Admirals now fly St. George's Jack (which see) from the main, fore, or mizen, according to rank. A Union Jack is carried at the stem head or bowsprit end (all ships of the Royal Navy now so carry a Jack). When a council of war is being held on board a flag-ship, the white ensign is displayed in the main, fore, or mizen shrouds, according to the rank of the Admiral. If there is to be an execution after a Court Martial, the white ensign is hoisted on the main, fore, or mizen yard arm. Ships of the Royal Navy at the approach of Royalty, or whilst saluting, "dress" ship, by hoisting St. George's ensign at the fore, main, and mizen trucks.

By the Merchant Shipping (Colours) Act, 1889, it is enjoined that "a ship belonging to any subject of Her Majesty shall, on a signal being made to her by one of Her Majesty's ships, and on entering or leaving any foreign port, and, if of 50 tons gross tonnage or upwards, shall also, on entering or leaving any British port, hoist the proper national colours, or, in default, incur a penalty not exceeding 100l." The term "proper national colours" for all ships is defined as the red ensign, "except in the case of Her Majesty's ships or boats, or in the case of any other ship or boat for the time being allowed to wear any other national colours in pursuance of a warrant from Her Majesty or from the Admiralty." Thus, if a yacht is allowed to fly the blue or white ensign as a proper national colour, her owner may incur a penalty every time he enters or leaves a British port without flying such blue or white ensign.

If an ensign other than the red be flown by any vessel without a warrant from the Admiralty, a penalty of 500l. may be inflicted, and any Custom House or Consular officer or officer in the Royal Navy on full pay may board the vessel and seize the flag. Although the red ensign has been assigned to the mercantile marine, no device can be put in it other than the Jack without the permission of the Admiralty.

The jurisdiction of the Admiralty only extends to flags flown afloat, and any ensign or flag can be hoisted on flagstaffs on shore.

When a warrant is granted to a club to fly the white, blue, or the red ensign with a device, this warrant does not of itself entitle a member of the club to fly either ensign on board his yacht; before he can legally do so he must also obtain a warrant from the Admiralty through the club secretary. A warrant must be obtained for each club he belongs to, if he desires to fly the flags of the clubs. When the yacht is disposed of, the warrants must be returned through the club secretary to the Admiralty, and if the owner obtains a new yacht he must get fresh warrants.

Prior to 1858 the Royal Western Yacht Club of Ireland flew the white ensign with a wreath of shamrock in it. In 1847, the privilege of flying the white ensign was accorded to the Royal St. George's Yacht Club, Kingstown, but was afterwards rescinded upon a representation by the Royal Yacht Squadron that that club by its warrant of 1829—(prior to 1829, the R.Y.S. flew the red ensign)—had the exclusive privilege of flying the white ensign. In 1853 an application was made in Parliament to know if the R.Y.S. had that exclusive privilege. The first Lord of the Admiralty said it had not, inasmuch as the privilege had also been extended to the Royal Western of Ireland in 1832, and was still enjoyed by that club. (But it does not appear that the Royal Western ever applied for a separate warrant for a yacht to fly the white ensign.) In 1858 the Royal St. George's Yacht Club (also the Holyhead) again applied for permission to fly the white ensign; the permission was not granted, and the Admiralty informed the Royal Western that they were no longer to use it; on making search at the Admiralty, it was found that in 1842 a decision was come to that no warrant should be issued to fly the white ensign to any club besides the Royal Yacht Squadron; and the clubs affected by the decision were informed of it accordingly, but the Royal Western of Ireland was not interfered with, because up to that time no application for separate warrants from the club for yachts to fly the ensign had been received; and further, in 1853, the Royal Western obtained permission to continue to use the ensign.

The decision made in 1842 was at the instance of Lord Yarborough (commodore of the R.Y.S.). He then set no special value on the white ensign except that he wished it to be confined to the yachts of the R.Y.S. to distinguish them from the yachts of other clubs. Accordingly copies of the Admiralty minute were sent to the clubs using the white ensign (Royal Thames, Royal Southern, Royal Western of England, Royal Eastern, Holyhead, Wharncliffe, and Gibraltar), but, oddly enough, for the reason already stated, the Royal Western of Ireland, by an oversight, was omitted, and that club continued to use the ensign until the mistake was recognised by the Admiralty in 1857-8. At that date the white ensign was adopted as the sole flag of the Royal Navy, and naturally the Admiralty were obliged to be more particular in granting warrants for flying it than they were in 1842; however, the Royal Yacht Squadron, which had always been under the special patronage of the Royal family, was considered worthy of the privilege. The privilege to fly it is cherished and coveted, and other distinguished yachting nations like Austria-Hungary, Italy, Spain, Denmark, Portugal, Sweden, Norway, and France have each given one yacht club the privilege of flying the naval flag of the country. A notable exception is Germany, although the Emperor is Commodore of the German Imperial Yacht Club. In America, as in France, the naval colours are the same as those of the mercantile marine, and a special ensign has been accorded to yacht clubs—all using the same and enjoying the same privileges. In Russia this has also been done, the yacht club ensign being something like our white, but with blue instead of red cross. Our Admiralty refuse to allow any imitation ensigns, and this is quite right. Some years ago the Royal Cork Yacht Club applied for permission to use a green ensign, on the plea that the red, white, and blue were already appropriated by other clubs. The Admiralty replied they might (at that time) choose which of the three national ensigns they pleased, but the creation of a new colour could not be sanctioned. (See "Admiralty Warrants," "Royal and Recognised Clubs," "Burgee," "Dipping the Ensign," &c.)

Ensign for Hired Transports.—The blue ensign with Admiralty anchor (yellow) in the fly.

Ensign, Hoisting of.—Ensigns and burgees are hoisted every morning at eight o'clock (9 a.m. from September 30 to March 31), and hauled down at sunset. It is a slovenly habit to hoist and haul down colours at irregular hours. At sea it is only usual to hoist colours when passing another vessel.

Ensign of the Colonies.—The blue ensign with arms or badge of colony in it.

Ensign of the Customs.—The blue ensign.

Ensign of Naval Reserve.—The blue ensign.

Entrance.—The fore part of a vessel, the bow. A good entrance into the water means a long well-formed bow.

Entrance Money.—The money demanded by clubs from yacht owners, who enter their vessels for match sailing at regattas.

Entry.—The record that a yacht is engaged for a particular match.

Equipment.—The complete outfit of a vessel including everything used in her handling, working, and accommodation. The inventory comprises the equipment.

Esnecca.—A kind of yacht of the twelfth century. According to Diez, "Dictionary of the Romance Languages," the word is old French, esneque or esneche, "a sharp prowed ship."

Etiquette.—See "Saluting," "Ensign," "Boats," "Burgee," "Commodore," "Admiralty Warrants," &c.

Even Keel.—Said of a vessel when she is not heeled either to port or starboard, also when her keel is horizontal, that is when she is so trimmed that her draught forward is the same as aft.

Every Stitch of Canvas Set.—When all available canvas that will draw is set.

Extreme Breadth.—The greatest breadth of a vessel from the outside of the plank on one side to the outside of the plank on the other side, wales and doubling planks being included and measured in the breadth.

Eye Bolt.—See "Bolts."

Eyelet Holes.—Small holes worked in sails for lacings, &c., to be rove through.

Eyes of Her.—The extreme fore end of the ship near the hawse pipes, which are the "eyes of her."

Eyes of the Rigging.—The loops spliced into the ends of shrouds to go over the mast, and dead eyes.

Eye Splice.—The end of a rope turned in so as to form an eye.

F.

Fag End.—When there is "nothing left of the rope but the end." The frayed-out end of a rope.

Fairing a Drawing.—A process by which the intersections of curved lines with other lines in the body plan, half-breadth plan, and sheer plan are made to correspond. A fair curve is a curved line which has no abrupt or unfair inflexions in it.

Fair Lead.—When the fall of a rope leads fairly, without obstruction, from the sheave hole. Also a "lead" made for a rope through a sheave hole or through any other hole.

Fair Leads.—Holes in plank, &c., for ropes to lead through, so that they lead fairly and are not nipped or formed into a bight.

Fairway.—The ship's course in a channel. The navigable channel of a harbour as distinct from an anchorage in a harbour. A harbour master's duty is to see that the fairway is kept clear, and that no vessels improperly anchor in it. A fair way is generally buoyed

Fair Wind.—A wind by which a vessel can proceed on her course without tacking; it may range from close-hauled point to dead aft.

Fake, A.—One of the rings formed in coiling a rope. The folds of a cable when ranged on deck in long close loops. To fake is to arrange in folds.

Fall.—The loose end of the rope of a tackle, the hauling part of a tackle; also applied generally to the tackle of the bobstay and the topmast backstays.

Fall Aboard.—One ship sailing or driving into another. A sail is said to fall aboard when the wind is so light that it will not stay blown out.

Fall Astern.—To drop astern. When two vessels are sailing together, if one fails to keep company with the other by not sailing so fast.

Fall Off.—To drop away from the wind; when a vessel is hove to she is said to fall off if her head falls to leeward, in opposition to coming to; also when a vessel yaws to windward of her course and then falls off to her course or to leeward of it. Not used in the sense of breaking off, which means when the wind comes more ahead and causes an alteration in the direction of a vessel's head to leeward of a course she had previously been sailing.

Fall To.—To join in hauling, to commence work.

Falling Tide.—The ebbing tide.

False Keel.—A piece of timber fitted under the main keel to deepen it or protect it when taking the ground.

False Tack.—A trick sometimes practised in yacht racing when two vessels are working close hauled together, and one has been "weather bowing" the other every time they went about. To be rid of this attention the crew of the vessel under the lee quarter of the other makes a sudden move as if about to tack; the helm is put down and the vessel shot up in the wind; the other vessel does the same and probably goes on the opposite tack; if she does so the former vessel fills off on her original tack, and the two part company. To shoot up in the wind and fill off on the same tack again.

Fashion Timbers.—The timbers which form the shape or fashion of the stern.

Fast.—Made fast by belaying. (See "Breast Fast," "Bow Fast," "Quarter Fast.")

Fastenings.—The bolts, nails, &c., by which the framing and planking of a vessel are held together.

Fathom.—A sea measure of six feet. To fathom a thing is to arrive at the bottom of it, to understand it.

Fay, To.—To join pieces of timber together very closely. Plank is said to fay the timbers when it fits closely to it.

Feather Edge.—When a plank or timber tapers to a very thin edge, "tapering to nothing."

Feathering.—Turning an oar over on its blade as it comes out of the water.

Feeling her Way.—Proceeding by sounding with the hand lead.

Feel the Helm.—In close hauled sailing when a vessel begins to gripe or carry weather helm. Also, generally, when a vessel begins to gather head way, so that she can be steered, or "feel her helm."

Feint.—To pretend to tack. (See "False Tack.")

Fender.—A sort of buffer made of rope, wood, matting, cork, or other material to hang over the side of a vessel when she is about to come into contact with another vessel or object.

Fend Off.—To ward off the effects of a collision by placing a fender between the vessel and the object which is going to be struck.

Fetch Away.—To slip or move without intention. To fetch sternway or headway is when a vessel begins to move ahead or astern.

Fetch.—In close hauled sailing when a vessel arrives at or to windward of any point or object, as "she will fetch that buoy in two more boards," or "she will fetch the mark this tack," &c.

Fid.—A square iron pin used to keep topmasts and bowsprits in their places.

Fidded.—When the fid has secured the topmast or bowsprit in its proper place.

Fiddle Block—A long fiddle-shaped block with one sheave above another. (See "Sister Block" and "Long Tackle Block.")

Fiddle Head.—The curved part of the knee at the upper fore part of the stem in schooners, turned upwards aft like the curly part of a fiddle head. A scroll head turns downwards.

Fill, To.—When a vessel has been sailed so close to wind that the sails have shaken, and the helm being put up the sails are "filled" with wind. In getting underway after being hove to a vessel is said to fill, or to have been "filled upon."

Fillings or Filling Timbers.—Pieces of wood or timbers used to fill various spaces that may occur in ship building.

Fine.—To sail a vessel "fine" is to keep her so close to the wind that her sails are on the point of shaking; considered sometimes good sailing if done with great watchfulness. Too fine means too near the wind.

Fire Escape.—A term applied to chaplains by sailors. (See "Sky Pilot.")

Fish, To.—To strengthen or repair a damaged spar by lashing a batten or another spar to it.

Fisherman's Bend.—See "Knots."

Fisherman's Walk.—When there is very little deck room, "Three steps and overboard."

Fishing Tackle.—The lines, hooks, sinkers, &c., used by fishermen. Messrs. Hearder and Son, of 195, Union-street, Plymouth, publish a book giving a full description of all the lines, nets, &c., necessary for a yacht, with instructions for using the same. The book can be had on application to Messrs. Hearder.

Fitting Out.—Getting a ship's rigging, sails, &c. into place after she has been dismantled.

Fitted Out.—When a vessel is "all-a-taunto," which see. A vessel ready to proceed to sea.

Flag Officer.—An Admiral, Vice-Admiral, or Rear-Admiral; also the Commodore, Vice-Commodore, or Rear-Commodore of a club.

Flags.—Pieces of bunting of various forms, colours, and devices, such as ensigns, jacks, burgees, &c.

Flags, the size of.—The size of the racing flags usually carried is as under :

Tons.	ft. in.	ft. in.	Tons.	ft. in.	ft. in
5	1 6	by 1 0	60	3 0	by 2 3
10	1 9	by 1 2	100	3 6	by 2 9
20	2 3	by 1 9	150	4 0	by 3 3
40	2 9	by 2 0	200	4 6	by 3 9

and above 200 tons the same.

The burgee of a yacht 45ft. long over all would be 2ft. 6in. in the fly, and ½in. for every foot of length of the yacht up to 130ft. over all. The ensign would be 6ft. for a 45ft. yacht, and 1in. for every additional foot of length of the yacht up to 130ft. over all.

Flare.—To project outwards, contrary to tumbling home.

Flat Aback.—In square rigged ships when all the yards are trimmed across the ship, with the wind ahead so as to produce sternway.

Flat Aft.—When sheets are trimmed in as close as the vessel will bear for close hauled sailing.

Flat Floored.—When the bottom timbers or floors of a vessel project from the keel in a more or less horizontal direction.

Flatten in Sheets.—To haul in the sheets.

Fleet, To.—To overhaul a tackle or separate the blocks after they have been hauled close together.

Floating Anchor.—Although floating anchors are continually referred to in old writings as a means whereby many ships have been enabled to ride out very heavy gales in comparative ease, we seldom hear of their being used now. No doubt many a ship has been lost through getting broadside on to the sea, whereas they might have kept bowing the sea by such a simple contrivance as a floating anchor.

However, masters, it would seem, prefer to heave-to, as they like to keep their vessels under command. In a very heavy sea and gale a floating anchor may be of very great service, and no doubt if a vessel can be kept bow to the sea, she will feel the violence of it in a much less degree than she would if hove-to when she might be continually flying to against the sea after falling off.

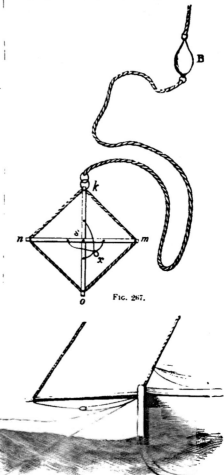

Fig. 267.

Fig. 268.

Many plans for floating anchors have been used, the simplest being thus made; three spars, in length about two-thirds the beam of the vessel, were lashed together by their ends in the form of a triangle; over this triangle a jib made of stout canvas was lashed. Then to each corner of the triangle a rope was made fast; the ends of these ropes were then bent to a hawser, and thus formed a kind of bridle. A weight was attached to one corner of the triangle to keep it in a vertical position; veer out the hawser and ride to 30, 50, or 70 fathoms, according to the sea.

But the old plan, given in "Falconer's Marine Dictionary" (date 1789), is the most approved (see the diagram, Figs. 267, 268); *k, m, n, o,* are the ends of two iron bars formed into a cross, and connected by a stout bolt, nut, and pin at their intersections *s.* At each end of the bars is a hole through which a strong rope is rove, hauled taut, and well secured. Thus a square is formed, and over the square a piece of stout canvas is laced to the roping. Four stout ropes are made fast to the iron bars, and make a sort of bridle or crow foot, the other ends being bent to a ring *s.* The ends should be well seized or "clinched." The hawser is bent to this ring to ride by. To prevent the anchor sinking, a buoy, B, is made fast attached to one corner with 6 or 7 fathoms of drift; this buoy will also prevent the anchor "diving" (as it would, like a kite flies into the air) when a strain is brought upon it. The buoy rope *p* should lead on board; *h* is the hawser to which the vessel is riding, A is the anchor, and B the buoy.

To get the anchor on board haul in on the line *p;* this will bring the anchor edgeways, and it can then be readily hauled in.

(See also "Oil at Sea.")

Floating Dock.—Upon lakes, where there are no tides, and no convenience for hauling a yacht up, a floating dock may be of service to get at a yacht's bottom. The dock would be rectangular in form, of which |___| might be a transverse section, and its size would depend upon the weight of the yacht that had to be docked. The weight of the yacht can roughly be arrived at thus: length on load line, multiplied by beam on load line, multiplied by draught of water to rabbet of keel; the product in turn being multiplied by the fraction 0·3. The decimal ·3 is used, as that fairly allows for the quantity cut away from the cube in modelling. Say the yacht is 40ft. long, 8ft. broad, and 6ft. deep to the rabbet in the keel, then $40 \times 8 \times 6$, equal to 1920 cubic feet. 1920 multiplied by 0·3 is equal to 576 cubic feet. There are 35 cubic feet of salt water to one ton, and 576 divided by 35 is equal to 16·4 tons. (There are 36 cubic feet of fresh water to one ton.) A dock 50ft. long, 16ft. broad, and immersed 2ft., would (omitting of course the reduction by the factor ·3, as the dock would be a cube) be equal to 45 tons; the weight of the dock made of 4-inch deal, would be, if the sides were 10ft. deep, about 20 tons; this would leave a margin of 25 tons for floating at 2ft. draught. A false bottom and sides 2ft. deep would have to be made in the dock; also a door at one end hinged from its lower edge, level with the top of the false bottom, and rabbeted at the sides. To get the yacht in the dock lower the door and fill the false bottom and sides with water until the dock sank low enough to be hauled under the keel of the yacht; then close the valve which lets the water in, shut the door and pump the water out of the false bottom and sides (a hose for the pump should be used in case the dock sank). The yacht should be shored up from the sides of the dock before she took any list. With caution such a contrivance could be used for floating a deep draught yacht over shallows from one lake to another, or through canals; in such cases, if the draught of water for going over the shallows were not limited to 2ft., it would be well to keep the false bottom full or partially full of water.

Flood Tide.—The rising tide, contrary to ebb.

Floors.—The bottom timbers of a vessel.

Flotsam.—The cargo of a wreck that may be floating about or liberated from the wreck.

Flowing sheet.—In sailing free, when the sheets are eased up or slackened off.

Flowing tide.—The rising tide, the flood tide.

Fluid compass.—A compass card in a basin of fluid, usually spirit, used in rough weather because the card should not jump about. In a small yacht a good and steady compass is an essential part of the outfit, and if there be any sea on the usual compass card and bowl are perfectly useless to steer by. The fluid compass then becomes necessary, and frequently a "life boat" compass, which costs about 5*l.*, is used. A more yacht-like looking liquid compass, however, is one sold by most

FIG. 269.

yacht fitters, like G. Wilson, Glasshouse-street, London; Fay and Co. of Southampton, price 6*l.* 6*s.*, shown by Fig. 269. The extreme height is only 1ft. 2in., and the card remains steady under the most trying circumstances of pitching and rolling. Spirit is usually used in the compass bowl in the proportion of one-fourth to three-fourths water; or glycerine in the same proportion; or distilled water can be used alone. A grain of thymol is said to prevent the spirit, &c., turning brown. (See "Binnacle and Compass.")

Flukes.—(Pronounced "flues" by seamen). The barb-shaped extremities of the arms of an anchor.

Flush deck.—When the deck has no raised or sunken part.

Fly.—The part of a flag which blows out; the opposite side to the hoist; the halyards are bent to the hoist.

Flying jib.—A jib set in vessels on the flying jib-boom. There is then the jib, the outer jib and flying jib, or inner jib, jib and flying jib; probably called flying jib because unlike the others it is not set on a stay. A yacht's jib topsail is sometimes termed a "flying jib," but, being set on a stay, this is incorrect.

Flying light.—Said of a vessel when she has been lightened in ballast so as to float with her proper load-line out of water.

Flying start.—In match sailing a start made underway. (See "Yacht Racing Rules.")

Flying to.—When a vessel in sailing free, luffs suddenly, or comes to suddenly; also after tacking, if a vessel's head is kept much off the wind, and the helm be put amidships, the vessel will fly to, *i.e.* fly to the wind quickly. A vessel that carries a hard weather helm will fly to directly the tiller is released.

Fly up in the Wind.—When a vessel is allowed to come head to wind suddenly.

Foot.—The lower edge of a sail. (See "Forefoot.")

Fore.—Front; contrary of aft; the forward part.

Fore-and-aft.—Running from forward aft, in a line with the keel.

Fore-and-aft rig.—Like a cutter or schooner; without yards, with all the sails tacked and sheeted in a line with the keel.

Fore-body.—The fore part of a ship which is forward of the greatest transverse section.

Forecastle.—The space under deck before the mast allotted to the seamen.

Fore Deck.—The deck before the mast.

Fore Foot.—The foremost part of the keel at its intersection with the stem under water.

Fore Guy.—The stay of a squaresail boom or spinnaker boom which leads forward.

Foremast.—The mast which occupies the most forward position in a vessel.

Fore Peak.—The forecastle, a space decked over forward in a small boat to stow gear in.

Fore-rake.—The rake the stem has forward beyond a perpendicular dropped to the fore end of the keel.

Fore-reach.—When one vessel reaches past or sails past another; generally applied in close-hauled sailing. Thus it is frequently said that one vessel "fore-reaches but does not hold so good a wind as the other;" meaning that she passes through the water faster but does not or cannot keep so close to the wind. A vessel is said to fore-reach or head-reach fast that is noted for great speed when sailing by the wind. (See "Head Reach.")

Foresail.—In square rigged ships the large lower-sail set on the foremast; in cutters the tri-angular sail or jib foresail set on the fore-stay; in fore-and-aft schooners the gaff sail set abaft the foremast.

Fore-staysail.—The jib foresail set on the fore-stay of schooners; properly "stay-foresail."

Foresheet.—The sheet of the foresail.

Foresheet horse.—An iron bar for the foresheet to work upon.

Fore-topman. — In a schooner yacht a man stationed aloft to work the fore-topsail tack and sheet in going about.

Fore-topmast.—The topmast over the foremast.

Foreyard.—The yard on the foremast for setting the foresail in square-rigged ships.

Forge ahead.—When a vessel that is hove to gathers way; generally when a vessel moves past another.

Foul.—Entangled, not clear. To touch another yacht.

Foul anchor.—When an anchor gets a turn of the cable round its arms or stock; when imbedded among rocks, &c., so that it cannot be readily recovered. Also a pictorial anchor with a cable round the shank, &c.

Foul berth.—When two vessels which are anchored or moored have not room to swing without fouling each other. If a vessel is properly moored and another fouls her berth she is held liable for any damage which may ensue.

Foul bottom.—A rocky bottom; also the bottom of a ship when it is covered with weeds &c

Foul hawse.—When moored if the cables get crossed by the vessel swinging with the tide. (See "Hawse.")

Frames.—The timbers or ribs of a vessel.

Frapping.—A rope put round the parts of a tackle or other ropes which are some distance apart, to draw them together and increase their tension or prevent them overhauling. Frequently a frapping is put on the parts of the head sheets, especially on the jib topsail sheet, to draw them down to the rail, and thus bring a strain on the leech and foot.

Frapping a ship.—Passing a chain cable or hawser round the hull of a ship to keep her from falling to pieces when she is straining in a heavy sea. Formerly common with timber ships.

Free.—Not close hauled. When a vessel is sailing with a point or two to come and go upon. The wind is said to free a vessel when it enables her to check sheets so as to be no longer close hauled. Also when it enables a vessel that is close hauled to lie nearer her course, as "the wind frees her."

Freeboard.—The side of a vessel which is above water.

French Nautical Terms—

Keel	Quille.
Stem	Étrave.
Sternpost	Etambot.
Rudder	Gouvernail.
Bulwarks	Pavois.

SPARS.	ESPARS.
Mainmast	Grand mât.
Topmast	Mât de flèche.
Bowsprit	Beaupré.
Mizen mast	Mât de tapecul.
Main boom	Bôme ou guy.

Gaff peak	Corne ou pic.
Main yard	Vergue de tapecul.
Bumpkin	Bout dehors de tapecul.
Topsail yard	Vergue de flèche.
Spinnaker boom	Tangon de spinnaker ou de vent-arrière.

STANDING RIGGING. — MANŒUVRES DORMANTES.

Forestay	Grand étai.
Topmast stay	Etai de mât de flèche.
Shrouds	Haubans.
Topmast shrouds	Galhaubans.
Runner tackle	Bastaque.
Bobstay	Sous-barbe.
Backstay	Pataras ou galhaubans volants.

RUNNING RIGGING. — MANŒUVRES COURANTES.

Boom topping lifts	Balancines.
Sheets	Ecoutes.
Main or throat halyards	Drisse de mât.
Peak halyards	Drisse de pic.
Spinnaker boom brace	Bras du tangon.
Spinnaker boom guy	Retenue du tangon.
Spinnaker boom topping lifts	Balancine du tangon.
Davits	Pistoleta.

SAILS. — VOILES.

Mainsail	Grand voile.
Gaff topsail	Flèche.
Jib topsail or flying jib	Clin-Foc.
Jib	Foc.
Foresail	Trinquette.
Mizen	Tapecul.

MAINSAIL. — GRAND VOILE.

Mainmast	Mât.
Gaff	Corne.
Boom	Bôme ou guy.
Luff or weather leach	Guindant.
Head	Têtière.
Leach or after leach	Chute arrière.
Foot or roach of sail	Bordant.
Tack	Point d'amure.
Clew or clue	Point d'écoute.
Throat	Empointure du mât.
Peak earing	Empointure du pic.
First, second, third, and close reef cringles	Cosses d'empointures des 1er, 2e, 3e, 4e ris.
Reef knittles or points	Hanets ou garcettes de ris.

GAFF TOPSAIL. — FLECHE POINTU.

Leach	Chute.
Halyards	Drisse.
Gaff topsail boom	Balestron.
Clew	Point d'écoute.
Tack	Point d'amure.
Truss	Collier de racage.
Weather leach	Guindant.
Yard	Vergue.
Backstay	Etai de flèche.
Foot	Bordant.

SQUARE TOPSAIL. — FLECHE CARRE.

Yard and head	Vergue de flèche et ralingue de têtière.
Leach	Chute arrière.
Luff	Chute avant.
Foot	Bordant.
Tack	Point d'amure.
Clew	Point d'écoute.
Head	Point de drisse.
Tack pendant	Pantoire d'amure.
Sheet pendant	Pantoire d'écoute.
Clew-line	Cargue.
Traveller	Rocambeau.
Bowline bridle	Patte de bouline.
Bowline	Bouline.

HULL. — COQUE D'UN BATEAU.

Keel	Quille.
Keelson	Carlingue.
Stem	Etrave.
Forefoot	Brion.
Sternpost	Etambot.
Arch board	Barre d'hourdi.
Long stern timbers	{ Allonges de voûte. „ de tableau.
Rudder	Gouvernail.
„ Afterpiece	Safran du gouvernail.
„ Spindle	Mèche du gouvernail.
„ Helm	Barre du gouvernail.

Helm-port	Trou de jaumière.
Beam	Barrots ou baux.
Deck	Pont.
Bitts	Bittes.
Windlass	Guindeau.
Partners	Etambrai.
Strep	Emplanture.
Frame—	
„ Floor timbers	Varangue des membres.
„ Timbers	Genou des membres.
„ Futtock	Allonge des membres.
Stanchions	Jambette.
Rail	Lisse.
Knees	Courbe.
Gunwale	Plat-bord.
Scuppers	Dalots.
Planking	Bordages.
Wales or bends	Préceinte ou carreau.
Channel	Porte-hauban.
Chain plates	Cadène de hauban.
Garboard strake	Gabord.
Rabbet	Rablure.
Inboard plank	Vaigrage.
Clamp	Bauquière.
Bulwarks	Pavois.
Flooring	Plancher.
Bending strake	Hiloire.
Skylight	Claire-voie.

JIBS. — FOCS.

Jib	Foc.
Foresail	Trinquette.
Flying jib or topsail jib	Foc volant ou foc en l'air.
Spinnaker	Spinnaker.
Halyards	Drisses.
Head	Points de drisse.
Clew or clue	Points d'écoute.
Tack	Points d'amure.
Sheet pennant and blocks	Pantoire et poulies d'écoute.
Jib purchase	Etarque de foc.
Flying jib tack	Amure de foc volant.
Sheets	Ecoutes.
Main stay and hanks	Grand étai, servant de draille, et bagues.
Topmast stay	Etai du mât de flèche.
Foresail bowline	Bouline de trinquette.
Inhaul of the traveller	Hâle-à-bord.
Foresail downhaul	Hâle—bas de trinquette.
Bobstay and tackle	Sous-barbe et son palan.
Bowsprit shrouds	Haubans de beaupré.
Foresail tack tackle	Palan d'amure de trinquette.

MAINMAST. — BAS-MAT.

Iron cap	Blin.
Top rope sheave	Clan de guinderesse.
Eye-bolt	Pitons de poulies (pic).
Jib halyard clamp	Latte de drisse de foc.
Gallows bitt	Potence.
Yoke	Chouque.
Crosstrees	Bare de hune.
Tressle trees	Elongis.
Cheeks	Jottereaux.
Topping lift clamp	Galoche de balancine.
Spider hoop	Cercle du mât.
Mast coat	Braie.
Masthead	Ton.

BOOM. — BOME OU GUI.

Boom	Bôme.
Boom iron	Ferrure.
Main tack	Amure de grand'-voile.
Main tack cleat	Taquet d'amure de grand voile.
Reef tackle cleat	Taquets d'Itagues de ris.
Main sheet strop	Estrope de grande écoute ou d'écoute de guy.
Topping lift strop	Estrope de balancines.
Reef earing bee blocks	Violons de ris.
Clew traveller on the boom	Rocambeau d'écoute.
Main sheet clamp	Clan d'écoute de grand'-voile.

TOPMAST. — MAT DE FLECHE.

Heel	Caisse.
Fid	Clef.
Top rope sheave	Clan de guinderesse.
Traveller	Rocambeau.
Halyard sheaves	Clans de drisses.

French Nautical Terms—continued.

Top rigging	Capelages.
Pole	Fusée.
Truck	Pomme.

BOWSPRIT.	BOUT DEHORS OU BEAUPRÉ.
Bowsprit heel	Talon.
Fidd	Clef.
Traveller	Rocambeau
Ironwork	Frette.
Jib tack	Clan d'amure de foc.

GAFF OR PEAK.	CORNE OU PIC.
Throat	Mâchoire.
Truss	Collier de racage.
Sheet sheave	Clan d'écoute de flèche.
Peak halyard strop	Estropes de drisse de pic.

MISCELLANEOUS.	
Fore part of ship	Avant d'un vaisseau.
Aft part of ship	Arrière d'un vaisseau.
Go ahead	Aller en avant; or, de l'avant.
Forward	de l'avant.
Aft	de l'arrière.
Fore and aft	De l'avant à l'arrière
Athwart	Par le travers.
Starboard	Tribord.
Port	Bâbord.
Below	En bas.
Aloft	En haut.
Avast	Tenez bon.
Crew	Equipage.
Boatswain	Maître d'equipage.
Sailmaker	Voilier.
Carpenter	Charpentier.
Steward or purser	Commis aux vivres.
Cook	Cuisinier.
Seaman	Matelot.
Boy	Mousse.
Belay!	Amarrez!
Let go!	Larguez!
Hoist away!	Hissez! or arborez.
Lower away!	Amenez!
Haul!	Halez!
Handsomely	Doucement
Hold on	Tenez.
Heave away	Vires.
Slack	Lâchez.
Bear a hand	Vite un homme.
To run foul	S'aborder.
Foul rope	Cordage engagé, embrouillé.
Foul ground	} Mauvais fond
Foul bottom	
Foul water	Eau salie.
Foul wind	Vent contraire.
Let go	} Files.
Ease off	
Weather gage	Dessus le vent.
Windward	Au vent.
Leeward	Sous le vent.
Catch hold	Attrappes.
Look out	Être en Vigie.
All right	Tout droit.
Ready about	Pare à virer.
Hard up the helm!	La barre au vent.
Down with the helm	Barre dessous.
Ease the helm	Mollis la barre.
Steady the helm!	Comme cela gouverne là
Let go the anchor	Mouillez l'ancre.
Pay out the cable	Filez de la chaine.
Right the helm	Dressez la barre.

Fresh Breeze.—(See "Wind.")

Freshen.—To alter the strain upon a rope.

Freshen Hawse.—To veer out or heave cable, so that a different part will take the chafe of the hawse pipe.

Freshen the Nip.—To shift a rope, &c., so that its nip, or short turn, or bight, may come in another part. In slang, to quench a desire for drink.

Full.—When all the sails are filled with the wind and quite steady.

Full Aft.—When a vessel is said not to taper sufficiently aft.

Full and Bye.—Sailing by the wind or close hauled, yet at the same time keeping all the sails full so that they do not shake through being too close to wind. Generally a vessel does better to windward when kept a "good full and bye" than when nipped or starved of wind.

Full and Change.—(See "High Water.")

Full bowed.—The same as bluff bowed.

Funeral Salute.—(See "Salutes.")

Furl.—To roll a sail up on a yard, &c.

Futtocks.—The timbers which abut above the floors called first, second, and third futtocks. This should properly be written foothooks.

G.

Gaff.—The yard to which the head of a fore-and-aft sail is bent. (See "Jaws.")

Gaff Topsail.—The topsail set over a gaff sail, such as the topsail set over a cutter's mainsail. Sometimes the sail has a head yard, and sometimes not. But it was originally set with a gaff and jaw on the head, hence the term gaff topsail.

Galley.—A long narrow rowing boat propelled by six or eight oars. A boat a little longer and heavier than a yacht's gig.

Galley or Galley Fire.—The caboose, or kitchen of a vessel.

Gallows.—Frames of oak erected above the deck in ships to carry spare spars on or the spanker boom instead of a crutch.

Gammoning.—The lashings which secure the bowsprit to the stem piece, and are passed backward and forwards in the form of an X, over the bowsprit. Now, generally chain is used. In yachts, an iron band or hoop, called the gammon iron or span-shackle, is fitted to the stem, through which the bowsprit passes.

Gammon Iron.—An iron hoop fitted to the side of the stem, or on top of the stem, as a span-shackle, to receive and hold the bowsprit.

Gangway.—The opening in the bulwarks, or side, through which persons enter or leave a vessel. Used generally as a passage, or thoroughfare of any kind. "Don't block the gangway," is a common admonition to thoughtless people who stand about in passages or thoroughfares, to the impediment of passers.

Gangway Ladder.—The steps hung from the gangway outside the vessel. Sometimes there is also a board, or kind of platform, called the "Gangway Board." (See "Accommodation Ladder.")

Gant-line.—A whip purchase; a single block with a rope rove through it. A Gant-line is used to hoist the rigging to the masthead on beginning to fit out.

Garboard.—The strake of plank next above the keel into which it is rabbeted and bolted.

Garland.—A strop put round spars when they are hoisted on board.

Garnet.—A kind of tackle used for hoisting things out of the hold of vessels; also used for clueing up squaresails.

Gaskets.—Pieces of rope, sometimes plaited, by which sails when furled are kept to the yards. The pieces of rope by which sails are secured when furled, such as the tyers of the mainsail, by which that sail when rolled up on the boom, is secured. (See "Tyers.")

Gather Way.—When a vessel begins to move through the water, under the influence of the wind on her sails, or under the influence of steam. (See "Steerage Way.")

Gawlor or Gawler.—An open boat which can either be rowed or sailed, common to Portsmouth watermen. They are very skilfully handled by the watermen, and go backwards and forwards to Spithead and elsewhere in all kinds of weather, and seldom meet with mishaps. They are sharp sterned, like the bow, and are rigged with sprit, main, and mizen, and jib-foresail. They have no boom to the mainsail.

Get a Pull.—To haul on a sheet or tack or fall of a tackle.

Getting Soundings Aboard.—Running aground.

Gig.—A long boat of four or six oars kept for the owner of a yacht. In gig races a boat should not be considered a gig if she has less than 1ft. of breadth for every 7ft. of length, and ½in. depth amidships for every foot of length. At the regatta held at Itchen-ferry by yacht-masters a "gig must not exceed 28ft. in length, and be in the proportions of 28ft. long, 4ft. broad, and 1ft. 8in. deep." A boat could be shorter if these proportions were maintained.

Gilling.—To gill a vessel along is to sail her very near the wind, so that very little of the weight of the wind is felt on the sails which are kept lifting, and only bare steerage way kept on the vessel. A vessel is generally "gilled" (pronounced "jilled") through heavy squalls or very broken water.

Gimbals.—The cross axles by which compasses, lamps, &c., are swung on board ship. Generally called "double gimbals." In Fig. 270 *a a* are the axles of the outer ring R, and *s s* of the inner ring M.

Girth,—The measurement round the skin or plank of a vessel; or a "string" measurement from deck or L.W.L. under the keel only.

Fig. 270.

Girt.—To moor a vessel so that she cannot swing by tide or wind. To draw a sail into puckers; to divide the belly of a sail into bags as by a rope.

Girt-line.—(See "Gant-line.")

Give Her.—A general prefix to an order, as "Give her sheet;" "Give her the jib-headed topsail;" "Give her chain," &c.

Give her the weight of it.—An admonition to a helmsman to sail a vessel a good heavy full when close-hauled.

Give Way.—The order to a boat's crew to commence rowing or to pull with more force or more quickly.

Giving the Keel.—Heeling over suddenly and bringing the keel near the surface; vessels that are not very stiff under canvas are said to "give the keel."

Glass.—The term by which a sailor knows the barometer. Also a telescope, and the sand glass used to denote half-hours on board ship, or the half-minute or quarter-minute glass used when heaving the log.

Glass Calm.—When it is so calm that the sea looks like a sheet of glass. (See "Clock Calm.")

Glue for Paper.—For joining paper, cardboard, or model work, or similar articles, a good glue can be made thus: dissolve 2oz. of the best transparent glue in ½pt. of strong cider vinegar. Let it simmer slowly by placing the dish containing it in a dish of boiling water. When it has become liquid, add 1oz. of highest proof alcohol, and keep it tightly corked. If cold, heat in hot water when needed for use.

Go About.—To tack.

Go Ahead!—The order to the engineer of a steam vessel. Also "Go astern;" "Easy ahead;" "Easy astern;" "Stop her!"

Go Down.—To sink. To go down below.

Going Large.—The same as sailing with the wind free. (See "Large.")

Going Through Her Lee.—When one vessel overtakes and passes another vessel to leeward; considered to be a very smart thing for a vessel to do if they are close together and of equal size.

Good Conduct Money.—A douceur of one shilling or more a week given to men at the end of a season for good behaviour, and withheld for the week in which any offence or offences were committed. (See "Conduct Money.")

Good Full.—Same as "Clean Full," or little fuller than "Full and By."

Gooseneck.—An iron jointed bolt used to fix the end of booms to the mast, &c. (See p. 32.)

Goose Wing, To.—A schooner "goose wings" when dead before the wind by booming out the gaff foresail on the opposite side to the mainsail. An uncertain operation, and a practice not now in much use, as the introduction of spinnakers has made it unnecessary. (See "Wing and Wing.")

Goose Wings.—The lower part or clews of sails when the upper part is furled or brailed up; used for scudding in heavy weather.

Graduated Sail.—A sail whose cloths taper towards the head from the foot upwards; so that a whole cloth forms the luff as well as the leech. Manufactured by Gordon, of Southampton, and Summers and Hewitt, of Cowes.

Granny Knot.—An insecure knot which a seaman never ties, but which a landsman is sometimes seen to do when trying his hand at reef knots. (See "Knots.")

Grapnel.—A grapling iron with four claws used to moor small boats by or to drag the bed of the sea.

Gratings.—Open woodwork put in the bottom of boats, in gangways, &c.

Graving.—Cleaning a vessel's bottom.

Graving Dock.—A dock which can be emptied of water by opening the gates as the tide falls, and its return prevented as the tide rises by closing the gates. Used for clearing the bottoms of vessels, repairing the same, &c.

Gravity.—Weight. The centre of gravity is the common centre of a weight or weights.

Great Guns.—A heavy wind is said to " blow great guns."

Green Hand.—A landsman shipped on board a vessel, and who has yet to learn his duties.

Green Horn.—A conceited simpleton, incapable of learning the duties of a seaman.

Green Sea.—The unbroken mass of water that will sometimes break on board a vessel as distinct from the mere buckets full of water or spray that may fly over her. Such bodies of water always have a green appearance, while smaller quantities look grey, hence we suppose the term.

Gridiron.—A large cross framing over which a vessel is placed at high water in order that her bottom may be examined as the tide falls.

Grin.—A vessel is said to grin when she dives head and shoulders into a sea and comes up streaming with water.

Gripe.—The forepart of the dead wood of a vessel ; the fore foot.

Gripe, To.—A vessel is said to gripe when she has a tendency to fly up in the wind, and requires weather helm to check or " pay off " the tendency. (See " Weather helm.")

Grommet or Grummet.—A ring formed of a single strand of rope laid over three times. Used for strops, &c. (Fig. 271.)

Fig. 271.

Grounding.—The act of getting aground or taking the ground as the tide falls.

Ground Sea, Ground Swell.—The swell that may be seen along shore sometimes, whilst in the offing the sea is calm.

Ground Tackle.—The moorings, anchors, chains, &c., used in securing a vessel.

Ground Ways.—The blocks on which a vessel is supported whilst she is being built.

Gudgeons.—Metal eye bolts fitted to the stern post to receive the pintles of the rudder. (See " Braces.")

Gunter Rig.—A rig for boats much recommended some years ago. A sliding gunter rig with battens has been in use since 1876, as shown in Figs. 272 and 273. A is the mast ; B, topmast or yard ; C and D, irons with a sheave at C ; E, connecting rod ; F, halyard fast to B, and rove through a sheave in the masthead ; G, a

socket and pivot for the heel of the yard to allow the peak of the sail to be lowered.

FIG. 272.

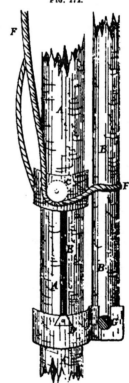

FIG. 273.

Gunwale.—In small boats the timber which fits over the timber heads, and is fastened to the top strake. (See " Inwale.")

Gunwale Under.—Heeling until the lee gunwale is in the water.

Guy.—A rope used to steady or support a spar.

Gybing (also spelt jibing and jib-bing).—To keep a vessel so much off the wind that at last it blows on the opposite quarter and causes the sails to shift over. The opposite of tacking, which is to come to the wind until it blows on the opposite bow of the vessel to the one on which it has been blowing.

Gyvers.—Tackles.

H.

Hail.—To speak to a ship at sea by signals or otherwise. To attract the attention of a ship by singing out "Ship ahoy!" or "Neptune ahoy." To "hail from" a locality is to belong to a particular place by birthright.

Half-breadth Plan. — A drawing showing the horizontal sections or water-lines of a vessel by halves.

ments of a vessel. An admonition to the crew to be smart in working the sheets in tacking or gybing. Also a steamboat master is said to "handle" his vessel in bringing her alongside a wharf, pier, &c.

Hand over Fist.—(See "Hand over Hand.")

Hand over Hand.—Hauling on a rope by one hand at a time and passing one hand rapidly over the other to haul. A very rapid way of hauling, hence anything done rapidly is said to be done "hand over hand."

Handing a Sail.—To hand a sail is to stow it or take it in.

Hand Sail.—(See "Sailing on Skates.")

Handsomely.—Steadily; with care. Not too fast nor yet too slow, but with great care; cleverly. As "Lower away handsomely." In easing up a sheet, if the man is likely to let it fly, the master or mate will sing out, "Handsomely there!" meaning that the man is to ease up the sheet carefully, not letting too much run out, nor yet letting it come up with

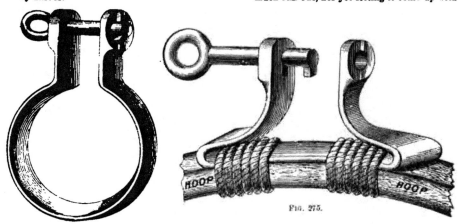

FIG. 274.

FIG. 275.

Half-breadths.—The width of horizontal sections at particular points; also half-breadths on diagonal lines.

Half-mast High.—Hoisting a burgee or ensign only halfway up as a mark of respect to a person who has recently died.

Halyards or Haulyards, or Halliards.—Ropes for hauling up sails, yards, &c., by.

Hammock.—A canvas bed swung to the deck beams.

Hand.—To hand a sail is to stow, furl, or take in; hence a sail is said to be "handed" when either of these operations has been performed.

Hand.—A man. A member of a ship's crew.

Hand Lead.—(See "Lead.")

Hand Masts.—Certain spars of Riga fir the girth of which is expressed in hands of 4in. Thus a mast which was 6½ hands, or 6½ "4in.," in circumference would be 26in. in girth, or about 8¼in. in diameter. (The circumference is the diameter multiplied by 3·1416.)

Handle Her.—The act of controlling the move-

a jerk, nor yet allowing it to run away with him.

Handspike.—A bar of wood, used as a lever.

Hand Taut.—As tight or taut as a rope can be got by the hand without swigging upon it.

Handy.—A vessel is said to be handy when she answers her helm quickly, and will turn in a small circle, or go from one tack to the other quickly.

Handy Billy.—A watch tackle kept on deck for general use to get a pull on whatever is required, such as sheets, tacks, or halyards.

Hang.—To lean towards. To hang to windward is to make but little leeway. "Hang on here!" an order for men to assist in hauling.

Hanging Compass.—A compass suspended under the beams with the face of the card downwards; termed also a "Tell-tale Compass."

Hanging Knee.—Knees that help keep the beams and frame together; one arm is bolted to the under side of a beam, the other to the frame.

Hank for Hank.—Slang for "tack for tack."

Hanks.—Rings or hooks made of rope, wood, or iron for fastening the luff of sails to stays. Iron rings are usually used for the stay foresail; iron spring hooks for the balloon foresail and jib topsail.

Various ingenious contrivances have been invented for securing sails to stays, &c., and Ramsay's patent keys are much used. Mr. Delap has adapted these for yacht purposes, and the first shown (Fig. 274) is for the fore staysail, the circular part travelling on the stay. Fig. 275 is for mast hoop attachments. The luff of the sail would be passed into the jaws, and then the key pushed through an eyelet hole and turned. Fig. 276 is a sheet shackle to supersede the usual toggle. The form of the head of the key precludes the possibility of its fouling any gear.

Mr. J. W. Collins, writing on the rig of fishing boats, says that a method adopted by the American fishermen for bending and unbending their riding sails would, doubtless, be well suited for the fore-and-aft-rigged English drift net boats. The "riding sail" referred to is a small three-cornered sail, which is bent to the mainmast when a schooner is riding at anchor, to keep her steady and head to the wind. The sail is set temporarily, and it is therefore desirable that

FIG. 276.

the arrangements may be such that it can be bent or unbent with as little delay as possible. For this purpose ordinary mast hoops are used; but about one-quarter of their length (where they are joined together) is sawed out, leaving square ends, to each of which is fastened an iron hook.

Fig. 277 shows how the hoops are fitted, and Fig. 278 shows how the thimble toggles are attached to the luff of the sail at regular intervals. The thimbles are slipped over the hooks on the ends of the hoops. The sail can be bent almost as fast as it can be hoisted.

Harbour Master.—An officer whose duty it is to see that vessels are properly berthed and moored in harbours. His authority cannot be disputed with impunity, as, in nine cases out of ten, if a dispute with a harbour master gets into court the decision will be for the harbour master.

Harbour Watch.—The watch kept on board a vessel at night when she is riding to an anchor in harbour; the anchor watch.

Hard.—A landing place usually made of gravel, piles, &c., across mud, as the "Common

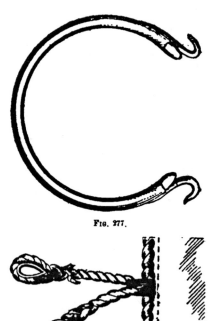

FIG. 277.

FIG. 278.

Hard," Portsea, where the small boats land and take in passengers.

Hard Down.—The order to put the helm hard-a-lee. Also the tiller may be put hard-a-port; hard-a-starboard; hard-a-weather; hard up.

Hard Up.—The tiller as far to windward as it can be got for bearing away.

Hard In.—Sheets are said to be hard in when a vessel is close-hauled.

Harpings.—Pieces of timber or battens that are fitted around the frames of a vessel in an unbroken line to keep the frames in their places before the plank is put on.

Harpoon.—A weapon like a spear with a flat, barbed, sharp head; the other end has a socket into which the wooden part is fitted, the whole making a long spear. The line is attached to the iron and the wooden part of the shank. The coil of rope is 130 fathoms.

Harpooner.—The bowman of a whale boat, who throws the harpoon.

Harpoon-log. — This is generally known as "Walker's" log, and is different from Massey's, inasmuch as the blades which give the rotation are attached to the part which holds the wheel work. In Massey's log the rotation is attached to the part containing the works by a piece of cord a yard or so long; the cord of course revolves with the spinning of the fly, and imparts motion to the wheel work.

Harpoon Sounding Machine.—A contrivance on the principle of the patent log such as Walker's, used for taking deep soundings. As the machine sinks the fly or fan blades rotate, and register by the aid of wheel work the distance sunk.

Hatches or *Hatchways.*—Openings in the deck. In a yacht there is usually the fore hatch used by the crew, and the sail room hatch aft. Generally the coverings for hatchways are termed hatches, but strictly this is inaccurate, and the correct term would be hatch covers.

Hatchway Coamings.—The raised frame above the deck upon which the hatches or hatch covers rest.

Haul.—To pull on a rope.

Haul the Boom Aboard!—An order to get the main boom hauled in on the quarter for close-hauled sailing.

Haul Aft the Sheets.—The order to haul in the sheets for close-hauled sailing.

Haul Her Wind.—To become close-hauled after sailing free. Generally to sail closer to the wind when sailing free. Haul to the wind. Haul on the wind.

Hauling up a Yacht.—Mr. J. C. Wilcocks gives the following directions for hauling up a small yacht: The yacht should first be lightened of all movable weights, such as ballast and spars and general outfit. This having been done, four 2½in. or 3in. deal planks must be provided, with four rollers 5ft. or 6ft. long and 3½in. diameter. The yacht should then be cradled with a very stout rope or reliable piece of chain, which should be lowered so far as the rabbet of the garboard strake, and be supported at that level by small lines under the quarters and at the bow above the forefoot, where the ends should be firmly secured with a lashing. A crab winch with a large double and single block is commonly used for heaving up, which must be firmly fixed by driving posts into the ground. As it is an inland lake, the first part of the business is the most difficult, for as the water will not leave the boat to allow adjustment of the preliminaries, the boat must be made to leave the water; and to do this, the deals, which

will do the duty of ways, must be got under her by loading the ends at the under sides. Two of the rollers should be made of sinking wood, and the yacht having been laid on her side, she should be hauled in until aground, and being still water-borne, the first roller can then be introduced under her, and shortly a second and third, when she can be hauled out of the water as the rollers travel on the deals. Four men should turn the winch handles, and not less than two must attend the rollers to watch and keep them square on the ways, which is done by striking the ends of them with a maul or small sledge hammer when they commence getting out of square. If the yacht is to be continually kept on this inland lake, it might be worth while to have an iron carriage made for her, consisting of an oblong frame of the length of a third of her load water-line, with 6in. iron wheels, with edges or rims. Edge rails for this can be nailed to the four deal ways, and a stout oak or elm plank could be bolted to the framework of the carriage. This plank should be, say, a foot wide and 2½in. thick, and about 6in. longer each side than the extreme breadth of the vessel, which should be provided with legs cut with tenons or having bolts to go through holes or sockets in this plank. The legs should be secured to the vessel's sides with through bolts, with either lever or butterfly nuts on the inside, screwing on against a metal plate. When this little temporary railway is once obtained, hauling the yacht up will be a very simple matter, and she may remain on one deal's length of it as long as required. There should be a hole in the forefoot, and also at the same level close to the sternpost, by which the yacht can be lashed square on the carriage, as soon as she is far enough out of the water; and when in the desired position she can be shored up by four shores, one under each quarter, and others under each bow, and a portion of ballast might be put on board, unless she has already sufficient lead or iron on her keel to steady her against violent gusts of wind, which have very great power on the side of any craft in an exposed position, and against which provision must be made. If such a carriage as above described is made, the rails will, of course, be carefully adjusted to the correct width, so that the wheels will travel easily on them, and about a foot from each end of the deal ways an iron plate should be screwed with socket holes to receive a clamp or sleeper bar, the ends turned down to form tenons to go into these socket plates, which will keep the rails and deals square with each other. By shifting the after pair of rails as required, it is evident that the yacht may be removed any reasonable distance on flat or nearly flat ground, with facility. Quite large fishing boats, and recently a barge, have been built, loaded on a low wheeled trolley, drawn over two hundred yards each, and launched sideways over the quay into the Great Western Floating Dock at Plymouth.

Haul Round a Mark, Point, &c.—When a vessel in sailing free has to come closer to the wind as her course alters round a point, buoy, &c. By hauling in the sheets the vessel will sometimes luff sufficiently without any help from the helm.

Haul Up.—To hoist a sail. A vessel is said to "haul up" when she comes, or is brought nearer the wind or nearer her course if she has been sailing to leeward of it. Haul up a point, haul up to windward of that buoy, &c.

Hawse Pipe.—The pipes in the hawseholes in the bow through which the cables pass.

Richard Falconer, in his Dictionary published at the end of the last century says, there are some terms in the sea language which have also immediate relation to the hawses, as :

"A bold hawse," signifies the holes are high above the water. [This would be equivalent to saying that the ship was high at the bows.]

"Veer out more cable" is the order when a part of the cable which lies in the hawse is fretted or chafed, and by veering out more cable another part rests in the hawse.

"Fresh the hawse" is an order to lay new pieces upon the cable in the hawses to preserve it from fretting. [The above two terms are applied to hemp cables.]

"Burning in the hawses" is when the cables endure a violent stress.

"Clearing the hawses" is the act of disentangling two cables that come through different hawses.

"To ride hawse full" is when in stress of weather a ship falls with her head deep in the sea, so that the water runs in at the hawses.

"Athwart hawse" is when anything crosses the hawse of a ship close ahead, or actually under and touching the bows; as "she fell athwart our hawse, and her side was stove in."

"Cross hawse," when the cables out of different holes cross on the stem as an X. Distinct from "clear hawse," which is when each cable leads direct to the anchor from its hawse hole.

"Foul hawse," when the cables are crossed in any way by the ship swinging round.

Hawse Bags.—Canvas bags filled with oakum, used in a heavy sea to stop the hawse holes, and prevent the admission of water. Wooden hawse plugs are generally used in a yacht.

Hawse Timbers.—The large timbers in the bow of ships in which the hawseholes are cut.

Hawser.—A large rope laid up with the sun or right-handed.

Head.—The fore part of a vessel. The upper part of a sail. "By the head" means pressed or trimmed down by the head, in contradistinction of "by the stern." To head is to pass ahead of another vessel.

Head Earings.—The earings of the upper part of a squaresail, &c.

Heading.—The direction of a vessel's head when sailing. Generally used when sailing close hauled, as "she headed S.E. on port tack, and N.E. on starboard tack." In such cases it is never said she "steered S.E.," &c., as practically the vessel is not steered, but her course alters with the wind. A vessel "steers" such and such a course when she is sailing large.

Headland.—A high cliff or point.

Headmost.—The first in order.

Head Reach.—In sailing by the wind when a vessel passes another either to windward or to leeward. A vessel is said to "head-reach" when she is hove to, but forges ahead a knot or two an hour. (See "Fore-reach.")

Head Rope.—The rope to which the head of a sail is sewn.

Head Sails.—A general name for all sails set forward of the foremost mast.

Head Sea.—The sea met when sailing close-hauled. In the case of a steamship she may meet the sea stem on.

Head Sheets.—The sheets of the head sails.

Head to Wind.—When a vessel is so situated that the wind blows no more on one bow than the other; when her head is directly pointed to the wind.

Head Way.—When a vessel moves ahead through the water.

Head Wind.—A wind that blows directly down the course a vessel is desired to sail. A foul wind. To be headed by the wind is when the wind shifts so that a vessel cannot lie her course, or puts her head off to leeward of the course she had been heading.

Heart.—A sort of dead-eye made of lignum vitæ with one large hole in it to pass a lanyard through turn after turn instead of through three holes, as in an ordinary dead-eye. They are something like a heart in shape, and the lower one is iron bound; the stay goes round the upper one either by a spliced eye or an eye seizing.

Heart Thimble.—A thimble shaped like a heart put in the eye splices of ropes. These are usually made solid for racing yachts.

Heave.—To bring a strain or drag upon a capstan bar, purchase, &c. To throw, as "heave overboard."

Heave About.—To go into stays to tack.

Heave Ahead.—To draw a vessel ahead by heaving on her cable, warp, &c.

Heave and Pawl.—In heaving on the windlass or capstan to give a sort of jerking heave, so that the pawl may be put in, and so prevent "coming up," or the cable flying out again. Also, in heaving on the mast winches "heave and pawl" is generally used in the sense of "belay;" that is stop heaving at the next fall of the pawl.

Heave-and-Weigh.—The last heave of the capstan that breaks the anchor out.

Heave Down.—To careen a vessel by putting tackles on her mastheads from a hulk or wharf, and heeling her so as to get at her side which was under water for repairs, &c. A vessel is said to be hove down by a squall when she does not right immediately.

Heave in Stays.—The same as heave about.

Heave Short.—To heave on the cable until the vessel is over the anchor, or the cable taut in a line with the forestay, so that with another heave, or by the action of the sails, the anchor will be broken out of the ground.

Heave and Rally.—An order to encourage the men to heave with energy when there is a difficulty in breaking the anchor out of the ground.

Heave and Stand to your Bars!—An order given after heaving until the vessel is over the anchor to give another heave as the bow descends with the sea and then stand fast, as in all probability the next time she scends, or lifts, her head with the sea she will break the anchor out of the ground.

Heave and Sight.—A call given after the anchor is off the ground, and when it is known to be near the surface on account of the muddy condition of the water it is making in consequence of the mud on the flukes. Literally it means one more heave and you will see the anchor above water.

Heave To.—To so trim a vessel's sails aback that she does not move ahead. The same as "lie to" or "lay to" as sailors call it. If the gale be a fair one the ship usually scuds before it; if a foul one she heaves to.

Heave the Lead.—The order to cast the lead for sounding.

Heave the Log.—The order to throw the log ship overboard to test the rate of sailing.

Heel.—The lower after end of anything, as heel of the keel, heel of the mast (the fore part of the lower end of a mast is called the toe), heel of a yard, heel of the bowsprit. The amount of list a vessel has.

Heeler.—A heavy puff that makes a boat heel.

Heel Rope.—The rope by which a running bowsprit is launched out.

Heel, To.—To incline, to careen, to list over, to depart from the upright.

Height.—A distance measured in a vertical direction, as height of freeboard, &c.

Helm.—The apparatus for steering a vessel, usually applied only to the tiller. The word is derived from Saxon *helma* or *healma*, a rudder; German *helm*, a handle and a rudder.

Helm's A-lee.—The usual call made in tacking or in going about, as a signal for the crew to work the sheets, &c. The helm is a-lee when the tiller is "put down" or to leeward. (See "Lee Helm" and "Weather Helm.")

Helm Port.—The rudder trunk in the counter.

Helm, to Port the.—To put the helm or tiller to the port side, and thereby bring the vessel's head round to starboard. If a wheel is used besides a tiller the action of turning the wheel to port brings the vessel's head round to port, as the tiller is moved by the chains to starboard. Thus with a wheel, when the order is given to port the wheel is turned to starboard.

The rule observed in French war ships and merchant ships, since 1876, is this : The order to "port" means to turn the vessel's head to port; and the order to "starboard" to turn the vessel's head to starboard.

Helm, to Put Down the.—To put the tiller to leeward, and thereby bring the vessel to the wind, or luff; the contrary action to putting up the helm.

Helm, to Put Up the.—To bring the tiller to windward, so that the rudder is turned to leeward, and consequently the head of the vessel goes off to leeward or "off the wind."

Helm, to Starboard the.—To put the tiller the way opposite to port.

Helm, to Steady the.—To bring the helm or tiller amidships after it has been moved to port or starboard, as the case may be.

Helmsman.—The man who steers a vessel. If a man can sail a vessel well on a wind he is generally termed a good "helmsman," and not steersman.

Hermaphrodite Brig.—A two-masted vessel, square-rigged forward, and fore-and-aft canvas only on mainmast.

High and Dry.—The situation of a vessel that is ashore when the ebb tide leaves her dry.

High Water: Full and Change.—On all coast charts the time of high water at the full moon and new moon is set down, the time of high water at the full moon and new moon always occurring at the same hour throughout the year; therefore, if the time of high water at full and change (new moon) is known, and the age of the moon, the time of high water for any particular day can be roughly calculated, about twenty-five minutes being allowed for each tide.

Hipping.—To make a vessel broader on the beam about the water-line. It is an American term, and became generally known in England in connection with the celebrated American yacht Sappho. After her defeat by the English yacht Cambria, in the match round the Isle of Wight in 1868, she was taken to New York and hipped; that is, her planking was stripped off amidships, and each frame backed with timber, so that the vessel might be made to have more beam about the water-line. The backing is "faired" to the frames and then planked over. Sometimes, if it is not sought to give the vessel more than five or six inches more beam, the hipping is accomplished by a doubling of plank; in such cases a rabbet is cut for the edges of the new plank in the old plank; the seam is then caulked and payed. If the new planks were worked to a feather edge water would get underneath, and it might soon bring about decay.

Hire of a Yacht.—The hire of yachts varies from 30*s.* per ton per month to 40*s.* per ton. Usually the owner pays all wages, including those of the steward and cook, unless the hirer specially desires to engage his own cook and steward; also often provides for the mess of the master and mate. The crew always provision themselves; the owner clothes the crew. The hirer pays insurance. The exact details of hiring are usually a matter of special arrangement. Sometimes at the end of a season, if a yacht is already fitted out, she may be hired for a less price per month. When a yacht is wanted on hire, the best plan is to advertise.

For a form of agreement, which can, of course, be varied, see the section which follows.

Hiring a Yacht (Agreement for).—Memorandum of Agreement made and entered into between , owner of the yacht , of or about tons y.m., and hereinafter termed the owner, on the one part, and hereinafter termed the hirer, on the other part, whereby the said owner agrees to let and the said hirer agrees to hire the said yacht for the period of calendar months from the day of to the day of for the sum of as rent to be paid in the manner following, that is to say, the sum of on the signing of this agreement, receipt of which sum is hereby acknowledged, and the balance at the expiration of the said term of hire, less any sum or sums advanced to the captain on account of current wages for himself and crew, which said advances the owner hereby authorises to be made and the hirer agrees to make if required, but not to exceed the total sum of during the aforesaid period.

The owner agrees to provide an efficient crew to manage and navigate the said yacht, consisting of master, mate, , and to clothe them and pay them their wages, but the hirer agrees to find his own steward and to pay him his wages. The owner agrees to leave such glass, crockery, and such linen as the yacht is provided with for the hirer's use, but the hirer agrees to find his own plate and cutlery.

The hirer agrees to pay for any damages or losses in or about the said yacht which shall not be recoverable under the clauses of the policy of insurance, which shall include the twenty pounds damage clause and the usual collision clause.

The hirer agrees to take over the said yacht at the port of on the said day of , she being in all respects ready for sea, and to redeliver her at the expiration of the said term of at the port of in the like good order as that in which he received her, reasonable wear and tear only excepted, provided always that in the event of the said yacht meeting with any accident to her hull or machinery whereby the hirer is deprived of her use for a period of not less than forty-eight hours, or if the hirer is deprived of the use of the yacht through any strike, mutiny, or disaffection on the part of the crew, such accident, strike, mutiny, or disaffection not being brought about by any act or order of

the hirer, the owner agrees to allow an extension of the said term for the like number of days the hirer has been deprived of the use of the said yacht from the causes named, but in the event of the hirer not requiring the use of the yacht for such extended period after the said day of , then a pro rata return of rent shall be allowed to him by the owner for such number of days as the hirer may have been deprived of the use of the yacht from the causes named.

It is further agreed that the hirer shall have the option of extending the said term of hire and to pay for the same at the rate of , providing he gives the owner weeks' notice of his intention of so extending the time; and, in all cases of such extension, the conditions named herein shall remain in force, and the owner shall not be bound to extend the time beyond the fortnight named unless he mutually agrees with the hirer so to do.

The hirer agrees to pay all harbour and dock dues, and for bills of health and all custom-house charges and pilotage, and to find and pay for all consumable stores, such as water, coal, oil, cotton waste, and the like, and generally to defray all current expenses in working the yacht during the period of hiring.

Signed,

Witness,

Hitch.—A mode of fastening a rope. There are many kinds of "hitches," such as Blackwall hitch, timber hitch, clove hitch, rolling hitch, &c. A hitch is also a short tack or board made in close-hauled sailing.

Hogged.—The situation of a vessel when she rises higher in the middle part than at the ends; the opposite of sagged.

Hogging Piece.—A piece of timber worked upon top of the keel to prevent its hogging or rising in the middle.

Hoist.—The length of the luff of a fore-and-aft sail, or the space it requires for hoisting. The hoist of a flag is the edge to which the roping is stitched.

Hoist, To.—To raise anything by halyards or tackles, &c.

Hoisting the Pennant.—A commodore is said to hoist his pennant when he goes on board the first time, as his pennant is then hoisted.

Hold.—The interior of a ship; generally understood to mean the space in which cargo, &c., is stowed away.

Hold-a-good-wind.—To sail close to the wind.

Hold her Head Up.—A vessel is said to "hold her head up" well that does not show a tendency to fall off.

Holding On.—To continue sailing without altering a course or shifting sail.

Holding On to the Land.—To keep the land aboard in sailing; not departing from the land.

Holding Water.—Resting with the blades of the oars in water to check a boat's way or stop her.

Hold On.—The order given after hauling on a rope not to slack any up, as "Hold on all that."

Hold On the Fore Side.—If, when hauling on the fall of a tackle, some of the hands have hold of it on the tackle side of the belaying pin, the hand that has to belay sings out, "Hold on the fore side" to those in front of him, and "Come up behind" to those behind. The hands on the fore side thus hold the fall and keep it from running through the blocks whilst it is being belayed. (See "Come Up.")

Hollow Lines.—The horizontal lines of a vessel that have inflections.

Hollow Sea.—When the waves have a short, steep, and deep trough.

Home.—Any operation that is completely performed, as "sheeted home" when the clew of a sail is hauled out to the last inch, &c. An anchor is said to come home when it breaks out of the ground.

Hood.—A covering for skylights, sails, &c.

Hood Ends.—The ends of the plank which are fitted into the rabbet of the stem or stern post; termed also the hooded ends, meaning probably that they are "housed" or covered in by the rabbet.

Hooker.—A small coasting craft.

Hoop.—(See "Mast Hoop" and "Spider Hoop.")

Horizontal Lines.—The curved lines on the Half-breadth Plan which show the water sections, the plane of each section being parallel to the horizon.

Horizontal Keel.—A plate of iron fitted to the underside of a boat's keel, a fore-and-aft view showing thus $\perp$. The plate should be made of iron plate of from $\frac{1}{4}$in. to $\frac{3}{8}$in. in thickness. For a boat 12ft. long the plate should be 8in. wide at the middle (so as to project about 3in. on either side of the keel), and 8ft. long, tapering each end to the width of the wood keel, to the underside of which it is screwed. The wood keel should extend at least 3in. below the garboards to render the plate effective. It is necessary that the plate should be kept horizontal, or in other words, in the same plane as the horizon; inasmuch as if the keel dips forward or aft the tendency of the plate will be to draw the boat either by the head or stern. A horizontal keel will increase a boat's weatherliness, but not to the extent of a centre board. The deeper the wood keel of the boat is the more effective the horizontal plate will be, as it will clear the eddy water along the garboards, and prevent the possibility of the bilge of the boat as she heels over being lower than the keel. However, if a very deep keel is necessary to make the horizontal plate effective, it may be as well to have another inch or so, and dispense with the plate altogether. The plan does not appear to have met with much favour.

Horns.—The projections which form the jaws of gaffs or booms. The outer ends of the crosstrees are sometimes termed horns.

Horn Timbers.—Timbers which help support the counter.

Horse.—A bar of iron or wood, or a rope for some part of a vessel's rigging to travel upon.

Hounds.—The projections on a mast which support the lower cap, cross trees, and rigging.

House.—To lower a topmast down within the cap. A snug house is when very little of the topmast shows above the upper cap. Sometimes in a racing yacht a topmast is fitted with one reef to shorten it about 3 feet, the same as a bowsprit. This plan has been adopted to be able to set a very large balloon topsail, but has very little to recommend it.

Housing of a Mast.—The part under the deck.

Hove Down.—Said of a vessel that is very much careened or heeled by the wind or other cause.

Hove her Keel Out.—Said of a vessel that heels over, so as to show her keel. (Generally used only as a figure of speech.)

Hove in Sight.—To come into view; said of a sail that appears above the horizon or round a headland; also of the anchor when it comes above water.

Hove in Stays.—Said of a vessel when she tacks, often meaning that a vessel tacks suddenly.

Hove Short.—When the cable is hove in so that there is but little more length out than the depth of water.

Hove-to.—The condition of a vessel with her head sails aback, so as to deprive her of way. Vessels hove-to on port tack should fill or get way on, if approached by a vessel on the starboard tack; but if the vessel on port tack can, by hailing or otherwise, make the other vessel understand the situation, the latter should give way; this is the custom of the sea, but there is no statutory regulations concerning the point.

Hoy.—A small vessel. Also an abbreviation of "Ahoy."

Hug the Land.—To sail along as close to a weather shore as possible.

Hug the Wind.—To keep very close, or too close to the wind.

Hulk.—A vessel whose seagoing days are over, but is still useful as a store ship, &c.

Hull.—The ship, as distinct from her masts and rigging.

Hull, To.—To strike the hull with shot, &c.

Hull Down.—On the sea when only a vessel's spars appear above the horizon.

Hull-to, or A-hull.—With all sails furled and the helm lashed to leeward, leaving the waves to do their worst.

I.

Ice Yachts.—A description of the ice yachts is given in the body of the book.

Immersed. —Under water. The opposite of emersed, which means taken out of water. The "wedge of immersion" is the part of a vessel put into the water when she heels over. The wedge of emersion is the part taken out of the water. Sometimes termed the "in" and "out" wedges.

In. —The prefix to a curt order to take in a sail, as "In spinnaker," "In squaresail," or "In boats," &c.

In and Out Bolts. —Bolts that pass through the skin and frame of a vessel through and through.

In Board. —Inside a vessel's bulwarks, being the opposite to outboard.

In Bow. —In rowing, the order to the bow man to throw up his oar and be ready with the boat hook, to help bring the boat alongside.

Inclination. —Heeling from an upright position. Synonymous with careening and listing.

Inner Jib. —The jib next the forestay sail in schooners where two jibs are carried.

Inner Post. —A piece of timber sometimes worked inside the sternpost.

In Haul. —A rope used to haul sails on board, as the inhaul of a jib or spinnaker.

In Irons. —A vessel is said to be in irons when she is brought head to wind, and, having lost her way, will not fall off on one tack or the other.

Insurance. —Yachts are generally insured against fire, but probably not more than half are insured against the risks of the sea when in commission. The rates vary from 5s. to 10s. 6d. per cent. per month on the amount insured, according to the nature of the voyage, the condition of the yacht, and the time of year. Also if the owner desires a £20 damage clause in the policy a higher rate must be paid, so also if the yacht is insured against the risks of yacht racing.

Compared with ordinary shipping insurances, the risks on yachts are very light. They are, almost without exception, well found, sufficiently manned, and perfectly seaworthy; and, as a rule, they avoid bad weather as much as possible. Except in rare cases, a yachting skipper is not compelled to drive on in the face of heavy weather. He is not generally tied to time in making a passage, and his owner does not look askance at him if he lies in harbour a few days waiting until an improvement takes place in the weather.

As a general rule, serious casualties to yachts are not frequent, and total losses are, fortunately, rare. Of course, with the largely increased number of yachts afloat, they do now and then happen, and the wreck of the Nyanza, of the Clarissa, and the Caterina, and the sad accident by which Lord Cantelupe lost his life, are instances in point. But still it must be admitted that these cases are exceptional, and, compared with ordinary shipping misfortunes, very uncommon.

It is a very common idea that it would be possible to insure yachts at a lower rate than they are at present insured, with profit to the underwriters, and the system of mutual insurance has more than once been hinted at. However, in these days of competition, it may be safely assumed that the present rates are not too remunerative. There can be no doubt whatever that of late years owners have become more awake to the effect of their policies, and are more prone than formerly to make a claim when any mishap occurs. Serious casualties are, fortunately, rare; but it will be readily understood that when a yacht does meet with even a slight accident the cost of repairs can hardly be compared with that arising from a similar mishap to a merchant vessel. A yacht owner is not content with mere patchwork repairs, he wants, and he is entitled to have, his vessel made as good as she was before the damage was sustained. If he has a small piece knocked out of his rail he probably wants it replaced, and if a plank or two be badly chafed he wants them taken out and new ones put in, instead of being simply planed down, or having the damage passed over altogether, as it would likely be in a trading vessel. Then it must be borne in mind that all yachting work is of a far more expensive and highly finished kind than ordinary ships' work. These facts must be remembered by the owner in estimating what is a fair premium on his policy.

Possibly underwriters do not, in considering the premiums, sufficiently distinguish between really first class yachts and those which are becoming the worse for wear. To a vessel in first rate condition a stranding, unless in a very exposed position, often means no damage at all, whilst to an old vessel it very probably means recaulking and new copper. Once insured, an owner may feel satisfied that any claim which he may send in will be fairly and even liberally dealt with. The form of policy which is adopted is certainly a rather antiquated kind of document, and to the uninitiated appears hardly suited to meet the requirements of yacht owners. It seems, however, to be well understood between underwriters and owners what the intention is, and the latter will find but little difficulty in obtaining payment for any fair claim which they may present.

The requirements of a yacht owner with regard to a policy are well understood, and any Lloyd's agent or respectable broker will see that it is put into proper form. It is usual and right to have a twenty-pound clause inserted, as the three per cent. clause is hardly suitable to meet the class of accidents to which yachts are liable. It is, of course, not essential that every policy should contain a collision or running-down clause, otherwise an owner may be called upon to pay some heavy sum for damage caused to another vessel, and by this clause the underwriters undertake to pay three-fourths of any sum which the assured may become liable to in the case of a collision.

Time policies are usually adopted by yacht owners, and are no doubt most convenient for them. It is, however, very necessary, in the case of an extended voyage, for the owner to leave instructions with his agent or broker to renew the policy in case the voyage is not completed at the time anticipated. An owner must bear in mind that, if he wishes to recover the full amount of his loss, he must insure his vessel up to her full value; and if, as he sometimes does, he declares her value, he must insure on that amount. In case an accident occurs, there are various steps necessary for him to take. The master must make a deposition before the Receiver of Wreck, and note a protest before a notary. If the damage is considerable, it is advisable for him, and for some of the crew, to extend the protest before a notary; or, if the accident happens abroad, before a British Consul. Such protests must give a full account of the manner in which the damage sustained occurred, and must clearly show that it arose from the perils insured against. It is also advisable to give notice to the nearest Lloyd's agent, and to call in Lloyd's surveyor to examine and report on the damage sustained, as his report will always be respected by underwriters, and as considerably less difficulty will arise in obtaining payment of a claim based on the report of a Lloyd's surveyor than on the report of any casual surveyor who may be consulted. An owner must always bear in mind, when any accident occurs, even although he be fully insured, that it is his duty to do everything which lies in his power to save loss to his underwriters, and in case of a collision, if he be not in fault, he must do all he can to enable his underwriters to obtain payment from the colliding vessel. A question often arises where a vessel is very seriously damaged, either stranded or sunk by a collision, whether or not she is to be considered as a total loss. It must be borne in mind by owners that if the vessel is not actually gone, underwriters always have the right to repair her at their own expense and hand her back to the owner if they think fit to do so.

Losses are of two kinds, either a total loss or a constructive total loss. In the latter case, if the owner has reasonable grounds for supposing that the repairs of the vessel will amount to more than her full value, he must send a notice of abandonment to the underwriters, which they must accept or decline within a reasonable time. If they accept it, they must of course pay on a total loss—they having the benefit of any salvage which may be made. If they decline to accept it, they must be prepared to bear the expense of restoring the vessel to her former condition. An owner must always remember that, though insured, it is his duty to act in every case as though he were uninsured, and when he presents his claim, he must be in a position to prove that he has used every reasonable exertion to prevent loss to his underwriters.

The following risks are not covered under an ordinary marine insurance policy, i.e., sums which an owner *may become liable for* in respect of:

1. One-fourth of the damage inflicted on another vessel by collision.
2. Injury to docks, wharves, piers, jetties, banks, buoys, etc., or the removal of any wreck or obstruction.
3. Loss of life or personal injury on board or near his vessel and life salvage (if not recoverable under the ordinary policy).
4. Law costs in defending any action in respect of a claim under paragraphs 2 and 3, provided such defence be made with underwriters' consent.
5. Costs or expenses properly incurred by an owner in connection with Board of Trade enquiries and coroner's inquests.

These liabilities can be insured against, but it is a condition of the insurance that the vessel shall also be insured under an ordinary policy containing the usual collision clause, and that the value insured shall be not less than the value insured under such ordinary policy.

The following rates were current in 1894, viz.: One month or under, 1s. 6d. per cent.; two months, 2s. 6d. per cent.; three months, 3s. 4d. per cent.; any period over three months, 1s. per cent. per month.

Some very grave questions may arise if an owner acts as his own sailing master, and manages or controls his yacht when underway.

In about 1625, limitation of the liability of shipowners came in as to British ships on the ground of public policy and as necessary for the encouragement of shipping, but not in any marked or effectual way until about 1734, and in the reign of George III. an Act was passed, "that it was expedient to encourage the owning of British ships," and for such end limited the owners' liability in collision to the value of ship and freight. In 17 and 18 Victoria, 104, the same limit was carried on as to damages recoverable in respect of loss of life or injury, and placed the value at £15 per ton of the wrong-doing ship. Difficulties were found in working these enactments, and in the result the Act (25 and 26 Victoria, c. 63, s. 54) was passed, and is continued by the Act of last year, placing the limit at £15 where there was loss of life, and at £8 per ton otherwise. There is, of course, no longer in these days the same ground for passing Acts of Parliament as in 1625, but the present state of shipping, the risks of the seas, and questions of freight earning and of insurance have not caused the Legislature to, as yet, find fault with the statutory limitation of liability.

The Act which gives the limitation of liability does so upon a term which is extremely hard upon yacht owners and upon the large class of coaster owners who command their own vessels, and it is a subject which demands serious consideration and amendment by the Legislature. The objectionable term is in section 54: "The owners of any ship, whether British or foreign, shall not in cases where all or any of the following events *occur without their actual fault or privity, that is*

Insurance—continued.

to say . . ." &c. So that the benefit of limitation given by the Act to the owner who remains ashore, or who is too ignorant of seamanship to be found in "fault or privy to" the collision, is denied to the expert owner who takes charge of his own craft, even though he be a Board of Trade certificated master mariner or a naval officer; and yet, so far as Acts of Parliament at present go, an owner may place his gardener on board his yacht as captain, and if such gardener has told his master that he knows how to command the craft, it would be difficult to satisfy a court that the owner was actually in fault by such appointment for a subsequent collision at sea.

The present certificate as master issued by the Board of Trade confers no benefit or exemption upon a yacht owner, and undoubtedly if an owner holds such certificate of competency he, being on deck before and at the collision, could not obtain the limitation of liability in any event.

Initial Stability.—The resistance a vessel at the first moment offers to being heeled from the upright position, as distinct from the resistance she may offer to being further heeled when inclined to considerable angles. Thus beamy boats are said to have great initial stability, because they resist powerfully, being heeled to small angles; narrow vessels, on the other hand, are readily heeled at first, but may offer greater resistance, as they are farther heeled, whereas a beamy boat's resistance may rapidly decrease as she gets over to large angles of say 30°.

Inlet.—A creek. A pipe to admit water to the hold.

Inshore.—Close to the shore.

In the Wind.—When sailing close hauled, if a vessel comes to nearly head to wind she is said to be "all in the wind."

In wale.—The clamp or strake of timber inside the top strake of a small boat, generally termed the gunwale.

Irish Pennants.—Loose ends of ropes, &c., hanging about a vessel's rigging or sails.

Iron Moulds.—Diluted oxalic acid will remove iron moulds from sails; but the instant the iron mould is removed the part should be well rinsed or soaked in fresh water, or it will be rendered rotten.

J.

Jack.—The Union Jack. The typical British flag that has "braved a thousand years, the battle and the breeze." It originally only had the red St. George's cross on a white field. Upon the accession of the Scotch King James to the English throne, St. Andrew's cross on a blue ground was added, and the flag was thereupon termed the "Union Jack" and National Flag, "For the Protestant religion and liberty." The red cross of St. Patrick was added (over the white St. Andrew's cross)

upon the union with Ireland 1801. (See "Union Jack" and "St. George's Jack.")

Jack in the Basket.—A boom or pole with a cage on the top used to mark a shoal or bank.

Jack, Hydraulic.—A mechanical contrivance used for the same purpose as a screw jack.

Jack Screw or Screw Jack.—A powerful screw used for moving heavy weights.

Jack Stay.—A rod of iron, or rope, usually wire rope, for sails or yards to travel on. Also the wire rope stay on the boom of laced sails, round which the lacing is passed.

Jack Yard. — The small yard on the foot of balloon topsails to extend them beyond the gaff. Termed also jenny yards and foot yards.

Jack Yard Topsail.—(See "Balloon Topsail.")

Jam.—In belaying or making fast a rope to close up or jam the turns together. To clinch the hitch of a rope by passing the end through a bight. (See "Wind Jamming.")

Jaws of a Gaff.—The horns at the end of the gaff which half encircle the mast. A rope called a "jaw rope," or jaw parrel, is fitted to the ends of the horns, and, passing round the mast, keeps the gaff in its place. Wood beads are rove on the rope to make it slide easily on the mast.

Jenny Yard.—(See "Jack Yard.")

Jetson.—Goods thrown overboard in heavy weather to lighten the ship. (See "Flotsam.")

Jib.—The outer triangular sail set on the bowsprit. A cutter usually carries six jibs—balloon jib, No. 1, 2, 3, 4, and 5 jib, the latter being the storm or spitfire jib.

Jibb or Jibe.—(See "Gybe.")

Jib-boom. — The spar beyond the bowsprit in schooners upon which the outer jib is set.

Jib Foresail. — In schooners the stay-foresail. (See "Fore-staysail.")

Jib Stay.—In schooners the stay to which jibs are hanked.

Jib Topsail.—A triangular sail made of duck set upon the topmast stay.

Jib Traveller.—The iron hoop, with hook and shackle, on the bowsprit to which the jib tack cringle is hooked.

Jigger Mast.—The mizen mast of yawl or dandy.

Joggle.—In the shipwright's craft, carpentry, and masonry, a notch or notches forming a box scarph to enable two pieces of wood, &c., to fit together. The heels of timbers are sometimes joggled to the keel in this manner. (Fig. 279.) This is also a "box scarph."

Joggles.—Notches cut in a boat's timbers for the plank to fit into.

Join Ship.—To come on board a vessel, or to enter as a seaman on board.

Jolly Boat.—A yacht's boat larger than a dinghy, and not so large as a cutter. Used by a merchant ship much the same as a dinghy by yacht.

Jolly Roger.—A pirate's flag. A white skull on a black field.

Jumpers.—A short frock made of duck worn by sailors.

The main stays of schooners when they lead forward to the fore deck.

Junk.—A Chinese ship. Also old rope. Also old salt beef as tough and hard as old rope or oak.

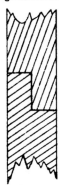

FIG. 279.

Jury.—A makeshift or temporary contrivance, as jurymast, jury rudder, jury bowsprit, &c., which may be fitted when either has been lost or carried away.

K.

Kamsin.—A south-westerly wind which is said to blow on the Nile for fifty days during March and April. The simoom.

Kedge. — The smallest anchor a yacht carries, used for anchoring temporarily by a hawser or warp. To kedge is to anchor by the kedge, or to carry the kedge anchor out in a boat and warp ahead by it.

Keg.—A small cask, or breaker.

Keel. — The fore-and-aft timber in a vessel to which the frames and garboard strake are fastened.

Keel.—An awkward-looking north-country boat with one lugsail forward.

Keel Haul.—A mode of punishment formerly in use in the Royal Navy. A rope, passed from yard-arm to yard-arm underneath the bottom of the ship, A man with a weight attached to his feet was made fast to one part of the rope and hauled from one yard-arm to the other, passing underneath the bottom of ship. Keel hauling is never practised now, but in punning language is sometimes referred to as "undergoing a great hardship" of some kind.

Keelson or *Kelson.*—An inside keel fitted over the throats of the floors.

Keep her Full.—When close hauled, an admonition not to keep too close to the wind.

Keep her Off.—An order to sail more off the wind ; to put the helm up. To keep off is to keep away from the wind.

Keep your Luff.—An admonition to keep close to the wind. In match sailing, an order given when a vessel is being overtaken by one coming up from astern not to give way and allow the vessel to pass to windward. It is an old maxim in close-hauled sailing, "keep your luff and never look astern," meaning that if you sail as close to the wind as possible the overtaking vessel must take her passage to leeward or risk a collision by trying to force a passage to windward.

Kentledge.—Rough pig iron used as ballast.

Ketch.—A two-masted vessel, something like a yawl, but with the mizen stepped ahead of the stern post, and not abaft it as a yawl has it. Ketches were formerly common in the Royal Navy for yachts and bomb boats. A rig now seldom used except by coasters ; it has all the disadvantages of the schooner or yawl rig, and none of the advantages. The Y.R.A. rules enjoin that the distance between the masts shall be half the length of water line, and the smaller sail of the two gaff sails must be aft.

Kevel or *Cavel.*—Large pieces of timber used for belaying ropes to, such as the horizontal piece which is bolted to the stanchions aft to belay the main sheet to.

Key Model.—A model made by horizontal layers or vertical blocks, showing either the water lines or vertical sections of a vessel.

Kit.—A sailor's belongings in the way of clothes, &c., which he carries in his bag or keeps in his locker.

Kittiwake.—A kind of seagull.

Knees.—Pieces of timber or iron shaped thus ∟ used to strengthen particular parts of a ship. A hanging knee is the one fitted under the beams ; a lodging knee is a knee fitted horizontally to the beams and shelf, or to the mast partners or deck beams. Floor knees are ∨-shaped, like breast-hooks.

Knight Heads.—Strong pieces of timber fitted inside and close to the stem to bear the strain of the bowsprit. Called also "bollard timbers." The name is said to be derived from the windlass bitts, the heads of which formerly were carved to represent the heads of knights.

Knot.—A geographical mile, or sixtieth part of a degree, termed also a sea mile or nautical mile. The Admiralty knot or mile is 6080ft., a statute mile is 5280ft. A sea mile = 1·1515 statute mile ; a statute mile = ·86842 sea mile.

KNOTS PER HOUR CONVERTED INTO FEET PER SECOND.

Knots per hour.	Feet per second.	Knots per hour.	Feet per second.	Knots per hour.	Feet per second.
1	1·688	11	18·57	21	35·45
2	3·376	12	20·26	22	37·14
3	5·064	13	21·94	23	38·82
4	6·752	14	23·63	24	40·51
5	8·44	15	25·32	25	42·20
6	10·13	16	27·01	26	43·89
7	11·82	17	29·70	27	45·58
8	13·50	18	30·38	28	47·26
9	15·19	19	32·07	29	48·95
10	16·88	20	33·76	30	50·64

Knots, Hitches, Bends, and Splices. — A Short Splice : Unlay the strands to an equal distance from each end of the rope. Intertwine the ends as shown in Fig. 280, and draw all close up together. Take one end of the rope in the left hand close up to the unlaid strands, and with it the unlaid strands of the other end of

FIG. 280.

the rope ; grasp these firmly, or, if more convenient, stop them with a piece of yarn. Take one of the strands (which are free), pass it over the strand (belonging to the other end of the rope) next to it, under the next strand and out, and haul taut. Pass each of the three strands in the same way, and then the three other strands, and the splice will be made as shown in Fig. 281. The operation can be repeated, or the ends can be seized with spun yarn round the rope. If the ends are stuck again, it is usual to taper each strand so as to make a neater job of it.

An Eye Splice : Unlay the strands of the rope and bring a part of the rope between the strands so as to form an eye (see Fig. 282.) Put one end through the unlaid strand of the rope next to it ; the succeeding end passes in an opposite direction over the strand and through under the next strand. The remaining end goes under the strand on the other side. Taper the ends and work them through the strands again, and serve.

FIG. 281.

FIG. 282.

FIG. 283.

Single Wall Knot (Fig. 283) : Unlay the end of a rope, hold it in the left hand, take a strand A, and form into a bight, holding it tight in the left hand to the standing part of the rope. Pass B round A, C round B, and up through the bight of A ; haul taut. To crown, lay one end over the top of the knot, lay the second over that, the third over the second, and then under the bight of the first.

Sheet Bend, or Common Bend (see Fig. 284) : Useful for bending two ropes together, or bending a rope to a cringle.

Bend for Hawser (Fig. 285).

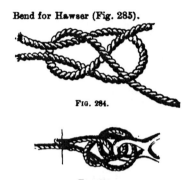

FIG. 284.

FIG. 285.

Midshipman's Hitch (Fig. 286).—Is made by taking half a hitch with the end of a rope A round the standing part B, C ; then taking another turn through the same bight ; when jammed together, another turn may be taken

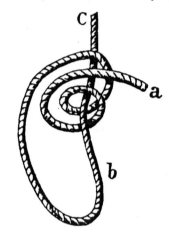

FIG. 286.

round C or stopped to it. Used for putting a tail block on to the fall of a tackle, shroud, &c., for a " Rolling Hitch," used for the same purpose.

Magnus Hitch (see Fig. 287).—Useful for bending ropes to spars, &c.

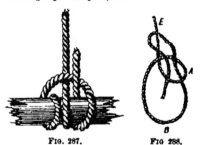

FIG. 287.

FIG 288.

Bowline Knot (Fig. 288): Take a convenient part of the end of a rope and form the bight A, then the large bight B ; pass the end through the bight A, then round the standing part E, and down through the bight A, and haul taut.

Running Bowline Knot (Fig. 289): After the bight A is made, take the bight B round E (which is the standing part), then up through

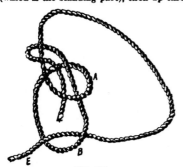

FIG. 289.

A, round the standing part, and down through A as before (see also "Clove Hitch," "Fisherman's Bend," "Timber Hitch," and "Blackwall Hitch").

L.

Labour.—A ship is said to labour when she pitches and rolls heavily, causing her frame to work.

Lace.—To pass a rope in and out.

Laid.—The make of a rope, as cable laid, hawser laid, single laid, laid with the sun, &c.

Land.—To go from a vessel to the shore; also to place anything. The outer edge of the plank of a clincher-built boat. The term "land" is used to mean the coast.

Land Boats—Carriages propelled by sails on land. The following account of land boats appeared in the *Scientific American*: "'The force of wind in the motion of sails may be applied also to the driving of the chariot, by which a man may sail on the land, as well as by a ship on the water,' remarks Bishop Wilkins, in the second book of his 'Mathematical Magick,' printed in London in 1648. Such chariots, he goes on to explain, have been used from time immemorial on the plains of China and also in Spain, but their most remarkable success has, says the learned author, been achieved in Holland, where 'it did far exceed the speed of any ship, though we should suppose it to be carried in the open sea with never so prosperous wind: and that in some few hours space it would convey six or ten persons twenty or thirty German miles, and all this with very little labour of him that sitteth at the stern, who may easily guide the course of it as he pleaseth.'

"The astonishment of the good bishop and his contemporaries at the speed attained may well be realised when it appears that Dutch sailing carriages, constructed as shown in Fig. 290, accomplished a distance of forty-two miles in two hours. This was an unheard of speed in those days for any means of locomotion. 'Men ran before it seeming

to go backwards, things which seem at a great distance being presently overtaken and left behind.' Until railroads were invented, without doubt the wind carriage outstripped

FIG. 290.—SAILING CHARIOT.

all other means of travelling; and it is perhaps a little anomalous that more efforts were not made towards its improvement. Bishop Wilkins himself made an effort in

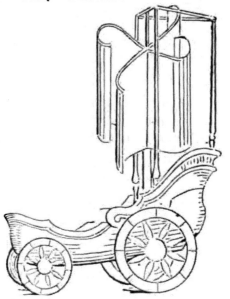

FIG. 291.—BISHOP WILKINS' CHARIOT.

that direction by rigging a windmill in the vehicle, whereby 'the sails are so contrived, that the wind from any course will have a force upon them to turn them about,' and he

Land Boats—continued.

proposed to gear this contrivance with his wheels, and 'consequently carry on the chariot itself to any place (though fully against the wind) whither it shall be directed.' This same thing was reinvented a couple of years ago in this country, as we noted at the time, and perhaps it might be uncharitably inferred that if, after the labour of two and a quarter centuries, our inventors could do no better than reproduce the venerable bishop's notion, the *Ultima Thule* of originality in wind carriages must be close at hand. Yet in reality the ice boat is probably the offspring

to average a speed of thirty miles per hour, and, with a strong breeze, to travel at the rate of forty miles in the same period. This last speed was reached with the wind right abeam. A distance of eighty-four miles has been passed over in four hours, the car sailing part of this time close hauled and over a disadvantageously curved track.

"The vehicle has four wheels, each 30in. in diameter, is 6ft. in length, and weighs 600lb. The sail has two booms, respectively 14ft. and 15ft. in length, and an area of about 81 square feet. The mast is 11ft. high, tapering from 4in. square at the heel to 2in. at the

FIG. 292.—PACIFIC RAILWAY SAILING CAR.

of the wind-impelled land vehicle; and the little carriages to be drawn along by huge kites, such as many an ingenious school boy has constructed, are allied to it. (Fig. 291.)

"It is curious to note, however, that while to the railroad is owing the abandonment of the wind carriage, to the same agency it now seems likely that its rejuvenation will be due. Wind vehicles are already in use on the long stretches of tracks which extend over the Western prairies, and the speed attained is said to rival that of the fast express train.

The engraving (Fig. 292) of a sailing car was devised by Mr. C. J. Bascom, of the Kansas Pacific Railroad. The vehicle is said

truck. It will be obvious that many of the laws applying to the ice boat apply equally well to the sailing car. A little consideration will show that when the latter is sailing at forty miles per hour it is travelling faster than the wind that impels it, and this is constantly the case in ice boat sailing. On the other hand, ice boats always sail best close hauled, in fact the sheet is almost constantly kept flat aft; the sailing car, as stated above, goes fastest with the wind directly on the beam or side. Of course the difference is due to the greater resistance offered by the larger and more elevated surfaces of the car body and its occupants, and to the friction of the axle journals, which probably, under ordinary condition, is sufficient to prevent the sailing car ever attaining the ice boat's speed.

"Mr. Bascom states that his car has been in active operation on the Kansas Pacific Railway for three years, being employed to convey repairing parties to pumps, telegraph lines, &c., along the route. It is of course exceedingly cheap to construct and maintain, and saves the labour involved in running a hand car."

Land Boats were to be met with on the flat sands of the Lancashire coasts, and were thus described by Mr. B. W. Hancock, of Leeds, in the *Mechanics' Magazine:* "A A, Fig. 293, is the deck, B B B B B are seats with cushions, C C are boards for the feet, D D is an iron rail round the seats, E is the steering wheel, F a seat for the man who attends to the sheet, &c., G the hole where the mast is

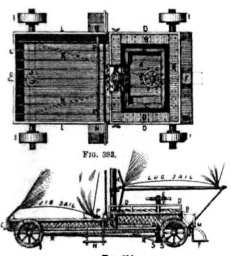

FIG. 393.

FIG. 294.

stepped, H H are steps with handrail, I I I I are the wheels, J is the nut which secures the pivot of front wheels. The dotted lines K on deck show the course of the steering gear and axle of front wheels, L L L is a rail about 1ft. high, just to keep anything from shaking off, M M M M are belaying pins, also M M at back of carriage; N in the centre of middle seat is made of wrought iron, to give the mast a good hold, O at front of carriage a hook to secure jib sail, P P is an iron bar for the ring of jib sail to slide on.

"In Fig. 294, A A is the edge of deck, B B sides of seats, D D the iron rail round the seats, E steering wheel, F the seat for man. In its position as a step, it works on hinges; the man can thus get up and pull the step up after him, forming a seat. H is the side step with hand-rail, I I are the wheels, L L is the rail round deck, Q is a belaying pin, also M at back of carriage. O at front is the hook for jib sail, P is the end of iron bar for ring

on jib sail to slip. R R are the ropes for steering, S S are supports for the axle of steering wheel, on which there is a great strain, T T is perforated zinc, U is iron ring to support boom.

"The deck, &c., should be made of light but strong wood, well put together, as it has to stand a deal of shaking and jerking. The wheels are also made of wood, they should be about 3ft. diameter, 1ft. wide tyres. Narrow wheels would sink in the sand and impede the progress of the carriage. The axles are wood cased with iron on the bearing parts; it is also advisable to put iron round the wheels. The steering gear will be best understood by referring to Fig. 340, where the dotted lines show the course of the rope or chain from one end of the axle to the steering wheel, where it is wrapped two or three times round the axle shown at S, and then back to the other end of front axle, in this way you have complete control over the carriage. The mast shown at X should be carried through the deck and secured underneath in a step, otherwise the deck will probably be torn up in a strong wind. The height of sails should be about twice the length of carriage, but space will not permit of their being shown here. The ordinary lug and jib sail, as shown, are by far the most manageable. As the wind changes they can be turned from side to side without difficulty."

Railway sail cars were in use some years ago on Herne Bay Pier and Southend Pier.

Land Fall.—The point or part of a coast a vessel first sights after being at sea. To make a good land-fall is to sight the land at the point calculated, "under the bowsprit end," as it is termed.

Land Lubber.—A person living on land and unacquainted with the duties of a seaman; also an awkward loutish cockney sort of person who on board ship cannot get into the ways of a seaman.

Landsman.—Men who have just joined a ship to train as seamen.

Lane.—A lane of wind is a current of air that travels in a narrow space and does not spread. Also ocean tracks for steamships.

On board ship the order to "Make a lane there," when a lot of men are standing together in passages or gangways, is an order for them to stand on one side so that others can pass.

Lanyards or *Laniards.*—Ropes rove through dead eyes, &c., by which shrouds and stays are set up.

Larboard.—The left side. In consequence of frequent blunders occurring through "larboard" being misunderstood for "starboard" or *vice versâ*, "port," as a distinctive sound, was introduced instead of larboard.

Larbolins.—The men composing the port watch. (See "Starbolins.")

Large.—With the wind abeam or abaft the beam. "She is sailing along large" means that the ship has the wind abeam or between the beam and the quarter.

Lash.—To lace, to bind together with a rope.

Lashing.—A lacing or rope to bind two spars together, or sails to a spar, &c.

Lateen Sail.—A large triangular sail, with the luff bent to a yard. It has no gaff.

Lateral Resistance. — The resistance a vessel offers to being pressed broadside on through the water. This resistance is assumed to be governed by the area of the plane bounded by the water-line, stem, keel, and rudder.

Launch.—The largest boat carried by a ship. To launch is to move an object, as "launch a spar forward," to launch a ship.

Launching a Boat Across a Flat Shore.—In making a truck to launch or beach a boat on a sandy or loose gravelly shore, the truck should run on rollers in preference to wheels, as the latter will sink into the sand or gravel, and render the transit very laboursome.

Laveer.—An obsolete sea term used to denote beating to windward.

Lay.—Used by sailors instead of the neuter verb "to lie:" as "lay to" for lie to, "lay her course" for lie her course, "lay up" for lie up, &c., or "she lays S.W." for lies S.W. This use of the active verb is sometimes justified by an appeal to the well-known naval song—

'Twas in Trafalgar's Bay
We saw the Frenchmen lay.

But, whether right or wrong, a sailor will never be brought to say, "there she lies" for "there she lays, or "she's going to lie up" for "she's going to lay up."

Lay of a Rope.—Right or left laid ; close laid, &c.

Lay along the Land.—When a vessel can just keep along a weather shore close-hauled, or when she lays along a lee shore.

Lay her Course.—A vessel is said to lay her course when sailing close-hauled, if her head points nothing to leeward of it.

Lay in Oars.—An order given to a boat's crew to toss their oars and lay them in board; generally curtly spoken "Oars." To "lay on your oars" is an order for the men to cease rowing, but not to toss their oars up ; to rest on their oars.

Lay of a Rope.—The way the strands of a rope are laid.

Lay Off.—To transfer the design of a vessel to the mould loft full size. This is never written or spoken "lie off."

Lay Out.—To move, as to lay out on a yard-arm, also to make a good forward and backward reach in rowing.

Laying Up.—Dismantling a yacht after a cruise has been brought to a termination. It is always much the best plan to have a mud dock dug for the yacht to lie in, as then the bottom will not foul, and if the vessel be coppered, she will haul out quite clean ; on the other hand, if she lies afloat, weeds and barnacles will accumulate on the bottom. It is much the practice now to haul vessels up high and dry during the winter months ; this is an excellent plan, and greatly assists in preserving the hull. The ballast is removed,

and the inside of the hull below the platform coated with red lead, black varnish, or a mixture of two-thirds Stockholm tar to one-third of coal tar ; black varnish or red lead is, however, to be preferred. The mast should be taken out before the vessel is hauled up, and with the other spars housed. In case the mast be not removed, all the rigging should be lifted over the mast, and the yoke taken off as well, so that no accumulation of damp may rot the masthead. The copper should be scrubbed and coated with a mineral oil such as paraffin. (See "Limber Boards.")

Lazy Guy.—The guy used to prevent the main boom falling aboard when a vessel is rolling, witl the wind astern.

Lazy Tack.—A running bight put on the tack cringle of a topsail, and round a stay to keep the sail from blowing away whilst it is hoisted.

Leach.—The up and down edge of a sail.

Lead.—A long weight or "sinker," of 7lb., 14lb., or 28lb. The line is "marked" thus :

Fathoms.		
2	a piece of	leather in two strips.
3	,,	leather three strips.
5	,,	white calico.
7	,,	red bunting.
10	,,	leather with a hole in it.
13	,,	blue serge.
15	,,	white calico.
17	,	red bunting.
20	,,	two knots.

There are usually 5 fathoms beyond this unmarked. In heaving the lead, if the vessel has headway, the lead must be cast ahead, so that when it touches the bottom the vessel is directly over it. If the first white mark is just awash when the lead is on the bottom, the leadsman sings out, " By the mark five." If it is less than five, say 4½, he sings out "Quarter less five," And not 4¾. If ¼ or ½ more than five, he sings out "and a quarter five," &c. There are no marks for 1, 4, 6, 8, 9, 11, 12, 14, 16, 18, and 19 fathoms, and these numbers are called "deeps ;" in sounding, the leadsman has to estimate the depth, as, for instance, between 5 and 7 marks, and will sing out, "By the deep 6." The deep-sea lead, pronounced "dipsey lead," weighs from 28lb. to 35lb., and has a much longer line. Up to 20 fathoms it is marked the same as the hand lead—at 30 fathoms 3 knots, at 40 fathoms 4 knots, and so on : the intermediate "fives" being marked by a piece of leather or a small strand with a knot in it ; 100 fathoms is marked by a piece of bunting, and then commence the knots again —1 knot 10 fathoms, and so on. In sounding with the deep-sea lead the vessel is usually hove to.

Lead Ballast.—Bricks of lead cast from moulds to fit inside the frames of a vessel without resting on the plank. Sometimes lead has been run into a yacht in a molten condition. When this has been done, the frame and plank have been first smeared with wet clay in order that the wood might not be injured. The vessel should be well caulked before the lead is run in. If molten lead is run into an iron or steel plated vessel, fires should be lighted underneath the keel to heat the plates, or otherwise the plates may be injured. The objection to running lead into a vessel is the extreme difficulty of getting it out again.

In casting a lead or iron keel, ⅛in. per foot is allowed each way for shrinking.

Lee.—The opposite side to that from which the wind blows.

Lee Board.—A very old-fashioned contrivance to check leeway. The board is usually trapeziform, and hung from the gunwale on either side. When sailing to windward it is dropped on the lee side to prevent lee way, hence the term "lee board." The board in

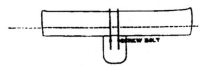

FIG. 295.

length should be about one-fifth the length of the boat, and at its broadest part two-thirds its own length in breadth, and its narrowest one-third its own length. If the board is fixed to an open boat, the gunwale should be strengthened at the point of attachment by a piece of timber worked inside at the back of the boat's timbers. For a boat 17ft. long this strengthening piece should be at least 5ft. in length by 6in. in depth, and be of 1½in. thickness. The board will be pivoted at its narrow end by an inch bolt; the neck of the bolt which passes through the board should be square, and a square iron plate should be fitted each side of the board, through which plates the bolt

FIG. 296.

will pass. The round part of the bolt will pass through the gunwale and strengthening piece; the bolt will be tightened up by a thumb nut, and, to prevent the latter working into the strengthening piece, it will be best to have an iron plate inside over the hole in the gunwale. The board should be made of inch stuff, with two through bolts of ⅜in. galvanised iron rod.

A good lee board (see Figs. 342 and 343) can be made of a board about 16in. by 2ft., suspended over the side of the boat (the top of the board being level with the keel) by two irons, which reach up the side over the gunwale, and are turned up along the midship thwart, to which they are fastened by means of two thumb screws; at the lower end two screw bolts connect the irons with the board; if necessary, one might be fitted on each side of the boat.

The advantages over the ordinary lee-board are that it is not unsightly, is always held parallel to the keel without straining the side, and two turns of the thumb screws will disconnect it in a moment from the boat. If these irons be fixed to different thwarts, a long board might be fitted in the same way; but a deep board is to be preferred.

Lee, By the.—In running nearly before the wind, when a vessel runs off her helm so much as to bring the wind on the opposite quarter to which the boom is ; a very dangerous proceeding, as if there be no boom guy a sudden gybe, or a gybe "all standing," may be the result. For safety, the helm should be put down the instant a vessel begins to run off. In match sailing, in running for a mark, yachts are often brought by the lee through a shift of wind, and frequently they are kept so, if a spinnaker or squaresail be set, and if near the mark, to save a gybe, every precaution being of course taken to prevent the main boom coming over, by hauling on the guy or pressing against the boom; this risk, however, should only be hazarded in very light winds.

Lee-going Tide.—The tide that is running to leeward in the direction of the wind. The opposite to weather-going tide, which see.

Lee Helm.—The helm put to leeward to luff, or to keep a vessel to or by the wind. Also synonymous with slack helm. If the centre of effort of the sails is much forward of the centre of lateral resistance, the vessel will have a tendency to fall off, and will require the helm to be put to leeward to keep her close to wind. The tendency can be checked by reducing the head sail, or by hardening in the sheets of the after sail and easing the sheets of the head sail. A vessel that requires lee helm will be an awkward one, and in a heavy sea a dangerous one to work to windward. The contrary to "weather helm," which see.

Lee Scuppers.—Inside the lee bulwarks by the scupper holes. To be always in the lee scuppers is to be always in disgrace.

Lend a Hand Here.—An order to a person to assist.

Let fall.—In rowing an order for a boat's crew to drop oars (after they have been on end) into the rowlocks, tholes, or crutches.

Let go and Haul.—In tacking a square rigged vessel the order given to let go the lee braces and haul in on the others.

Let Her Feel the Weight of It.—An order to keep a vessel more off the wind, and not allow her sails to shake. (See "Give Her the Weight.")

Lewis.—See "Mooring Rings."

Life Belts.—Appliances for support in the water. The cork life belts of the National Lifeboat Institution (6s. each), John-street, Adelphi, are the most highly recommended.

Life Buoy.—Usually a painted canvas ring stuffed with solid cork. When in the water, by placing the hands on the buoy it turns up over the head. The arms are then put through it.

and it forms a fine support under the armpits and, of course, encircling the body. This is a great improvement on the old-fashioned ball buoy, with rope bights on it. A life buoy should have an outside diameter of 30in., and contain from 12lb. to 15lb. of solid cork, and float for twenty-four hours whilst suspending 32lb. of iron. Cork shavings, granulated cork, &c., should not be used.

Light eye.—A bright white look in the sky above the horizon, sometimes betokening that a breeze may be expected from such a quarter.

Lights.—The lights which all vessels must exhibit between sundown and sunrise. (See " Side Light.")

Limber Boards.—Plank covering the floors of a vessel near the keelson. In yachts built with iron knee floors it is a common practice to fill up all cavities along the keel or hogging piece, fore dead-wood and apron, and dead-wood aft, with cement, after coating the wood with Stockholm tar.

Limber Clearer.—A small chain which is kept rove through the limber holes in the floors at the side of the keelson, to allow the bilge water to flow freely to the pumps; occasionally the chain is worked backwards and forwards to clear the holes. This contrivance is seldom met with in yachts.

Line.—A general name for a rope, or cordage.

Liner.—An old line-of-battle ship. An old name for ships of the first and second rate, as three deckers and two deckers.

Lines.—A general term applied to the drawing or design of a vessel as depicted by fore-and-aft lines. A vessel is said to have "fine lines" when she is very sharp fore-and-aft.

List.—A vessel is said to list when from some cause—shifting of ballast or cargo or weights—she heels over.

Listing.—A narrow strip of plank, usually 4in. in width, cut out of the plank in ship throughout her whole length, in order that the condition of her frames or timbers may be examined.

Lizard.—A piece of rope with a thimble eye spliced in one end, used in setting squaresails; sometimes the lizard is of two or more parts with a thimble in each, the whole being spliced into one tail.

Lloyd's Register.—The committee appointed in 1824 by "Lloyd's Society of Underwriters for the insurance of ships," to classify and regulate the building of, and keep a registry of all ships. (See "Underwriter.")

Lloyd's Yacht Register.—A register of yachts founded by Lloyd's, 1878, in which the build, age, condition, &c., of each yacht is set forth. There is published separately a book which contains rules and tables of scantling for the building of yachts. The offices are White Lion Court, Cornhill. (See "Yacht Register.")

Load-water-line.—The line of flotation when a vessel is properly laden or ballasted.

Load-water section.—The horizontal plane at the line of flotation.

Lob Sided.—Larger or heavier on one side than on the other.

Locker.—A small cabin, or cupboard, or cavity to stow articles in.

Log Board or Log Slate.—The slate on which the hourly occurrences in navigating a ship—her speed, canvas, courses, the strength of wind, direction of wind, and general condition of weather—are set down.

Log Line and Ship.—An ancient contrivance for testing the speed of a ship. The line is attached to a board (termed the ship), and is marked for knots every 50ft. (the proper distance would be 50·64ft., but an allowance is made for the following wake). According as the number of knots which run out in 30sec. by the sand glass, so is the speed of the vessel. There is a drift of some feet between the log ship and the first knot, the glass being turned as the first knot takes the water. The number of knots run out in the 30sec. marks the speed of the vessel. Massey's or Walker's log are now constantly towed, but the log line and ship are regularly used on board large steamers. (See "Harpoon Log.")

Log Official.—See "Official Log."

Long Boat.—A ship's launch; usually carvel built.

Long Leg and a Short One.—In beating to wind-

Fig. 297.

ward, when a vessel can sail nearer her intended course on one tack than another. Thus, say her course is E. and the wind S. E. by E. she would lie E. by N. one tack, which would be the long leg, and S. by E. on the other, which would be the short leg. (Fig. 297.)

Long Shore.—A contraction of along shore.

Long Tackle Blocks.—A double block with one sheave above the other, as a fiddle block, which see. Used for the runner tackle, &c.

Look.—The direction a vessel points when sailing by the wind. As, she "looks high," "looks up well," "looks a high course," &c.

Look-out, The.—The men stationed on the bow, &c., to watch the approach of other ships or to seek the land, &c.

Loose.—Adrift; to unloose to unfurl: to loose tyers of a sail, &c.

Lose her Way.—Said of a vessel when she loses motion or gradually comes to a stop.

Lose His Number at Mess.—(See Number.)

Lower.—To cause a thing to descend—as to "lower the topsail," &c. An order given to ease up halyards, as "lower," "lower away!"

Lower Masts.—The masts that are next the deck.

Lubber's Hole.—The opening in a masthead cap, by which seamen get into the top instead of by the futtock shrouds.

Lubber's Point.—The black line or stroke in the front part of a compass basin, by which the direction of a vessel's head is told. The lubber's point is always in a direct line with the vessel's keel, or stem and sternpost.

Lucky Puff.—A puff that "frees" a vessel in close hauled sailing.

Luff.—To come nearer the wind. To "spring your luff" is to luff all the ship is capable of, without making her sails shake.

Luff and Touch Her.—To bring the vessel so near the wind that the head sails begin to shake a little.

Luff of a Sail.—The weather cloth in a sail. (See "Weather Cloth.")

Luff Tackle.—A tackle composed of a single and double block, the standing part of the rope being fast to the single block.

Luff upon Luff.—One luff tackle hitched to the fall of another so as to make a double purchase.

Lugger.—A vessel rigged with lug sails like the fishing boats of this country and France.

Lug-Sail Boat.—A boat with a lug sail set on a yard. (See "Dipping Lug.")

Lurch.—When a vessel is left unsupported at the bow, stern, or amidships, so that she makes a sudden dive forward, or by the stern, or a heavy weather or lee roll.

Lutings.—Stoppings of white lead, putty, tar, varnish, &c., for seams and joins in planks, &c.; sometimes used with a strip of canvas as a kind of caulking.

Lying To.—The condition of a ship when hove to. (See "Trying" and "Lay.")

M.

Mackerel Sky.—A sky streaked with fine clouds, something in the manner of the stripes on the back of a mackerel.

Mackerel Tailed.—A boat with a very sharp or fine after body. "Cod's head and mackerel's tail" or "full forward and fine aft," once supposed to represent the form of least resistance.

Made.—Built, as built mast, &c., meaning that the mast is not made of one piece of timber, but by several pieces bound together like a cask.

Main.—The open ocean. The principal, as mainmast, main boom, main stay, main sail, &c.

Main Breadth.—The extreme breadth of a vessel.

Main Course.—The main sail of a square rigged ship.

Main Keel.—The keel proper, and not the keelson or false keel.

Mainsheet.—The rope or tackle which holds the aft clew of the mainsail, or main boom. A good arrangement of mainsheet for a small boat with boom to the sail is to make fast one end of the sheet to one end of the after thwart, or near thereto (so that the sheet is clear of the helmsman) take the other end through a thimble eye in a strop round the boom and down through another thimble eye strop at the other end of the thwart; the hauling part can be made fast by a turn and bight above the latter thimble. This arrangement would do for a 10ft. or 12ft. boat, but in one of larger size a block should be stropped to the boom and thwart instead of the thimbles. (See "Belay.")

Mainsheet Horse.—A mainsheet horse is frequently used in small boats, and in America in large yachts as well. Less mainsheet is required on a wind when the lower block travels on a horse, and therefore the boom cannot lift so much and assist in throwing the sail in a bag. In a seaway, however, there is some advantage in having more drift between the blocks than would be very likely given if a horse were used. For small boats to obviate the shifting of the mainsheet from side to side in tacking the horse is of advantage. The foresheet can travel on a horse if the boat be decked or half decked.

Mainsheet Slip.—The navy mainsheet slip is usually fitted to the gunwale, with a lanyard on the ring which holds the tongue to slip the sheet if necessary. This slip can also be fitted to a mainsheet horse, but practically

FIG. 298.

the hitch at *a* answers all the purpose, as the lanyard has to be manipulated by the hand just the same as any ordinary tongue and ring attachment has. (Fig. 298.)

Maintopman.—The mainmast headman of a schooner to pass the lacing of a topsail, keep the topsail yard clear, &c.

Make Fast.—To securely belay a rope or join two ropes.

Make Ready There.—An order sometimes given to prepare to tack or lower a sail, as "Make ready for going about there," the "there" referring to the crew.

Make Sail.—To set sails. To add to sails already set. To shake out reefs to commence sailing after laying to.

Make Stern Way.—To drive astern as a vessel sometimes will in tacking by getting in irons or through the head sails being thrown aback.

Making the Land.—After losing sight of the land to approach and sight it.

Making Water.—Leaking. A vessel is said to make no water if she is so tight that none ever gets through her seams, &c., into the hold.

Man.—To apply manual power to anything, as "Man the capstan," "Man the boat," &c.

Man Overboard.—A shout of alarm made on board ship when a man gets overboard by accident. In such cases it is not usual to wait for orders, but everyone joins in if he sees he can be of service in throwing a life-buoy, helping to launch a boat, jumping overboard, &c.

Mansard.—An architectural term, but used in America for a booby hatch or raised deck. A mansard roof to a house is a light structure above the masonry. It took its name from Mansard, a French architect of the 17th century.

Man Ship.—An old-fashioned custom in the Navy of mustering the crew along the bulwarks to cheer upon parting company or meeting another ship. Losing yachts generally man the bulwarks and cheer a victorious yacht, a custom probably derived from the practice in "fighting days" of one war ship cheering another which was an enemy. (See "Cheering.")

Marine Glue.—This composition is said to be composed of 1 part india-rubber, 12 mineral naphtha or coal tar heated gently, and 20 parts of shellac, mixed with it. The composition is now usually employed to stop the seams of decks after they are caulked. The old fashioned plan was to use white lead putty for the stopping and indeed it is at this present time occasionally used ; the objection to it is that it dries as hard as a cement and cracks, the result being that water gets into the caulking, rots it, and then leaky decks are the consequence. Moreover, hard putty is very difficult to get out of the seams without damaging the edges of the plank, and then in re-stopping ragged ugly seams are the result. Marine glue, on the other hand, can easily be renewed, and the edges of the plank remain uninjured.

In using marine glue the following practice should be observed : In driving the oakum or cotton thread (the latter is sometimes preferred as it can be laid in finer strands, a matter of consideration if the plank is closely laid) into the seams, the caulking iron should be dipped in naphtha, and not in oil, as, if the sides of the plank are touched with the latter the glue will not adhere ; naphtha on the other hand dissolves the glue and assists in closely cementing the seams. The plank should be quite dry when the glue is applied, or it will not adhere to the sides of the seams. The glue should be dissolved in a pot, and applied by lip ladles used for paying, two being kept going ; or the glue can be melted in the lip ladles. Great care must be taken that the glue is melted slowly, as if it be melted over too fierce a fire it will be spoilt. A little of the liquid glue can be usefully mixed with the other as it assists in keeping it dissolved. The glue that runs over the sides of the seams should be cleaned off with a broad sharp chisel and remelted. It is not advisable to scrape the surplus glue off the seams, as it cannot be so removed without leaving a ragged unsightly surface. The manufacturer of this marine glue is Mr. Jeffry, Limehouse.

A cheaper marine glue, not easily spoilt in melting, is made by the Waterproof Glue Company, Landport, Hants.

Mariner.—A sailor. Two hundred years ago it was spelt "maryner," and appears to have only been applied to men who were perfect as seamen. Thus, from a muster roll made in the seventeenth century, we find so many men set down as "maryners" and so many as "seafaring men."

Marks.—The pieces of leather, &c., on a lead-line (see "Lead.") In sounding it is usual to say, "By the mark," &c., if the depth of water accords to a mark ; if there be no "mark," as between three and five fathoms, the leadsman says, "By the deep four," &c. (See "Lead.")

Marle.—To hitch spun yarn round a rope to secure its parts, or round a hank of yarn to secure it. (See "Selvagee.")

Marline Spike.—An iron implement tapering to a sharp point, used to open the strands of rope for splicing, to turn eyebolts, &c.

Martingale.—A stay spread by a "dolphin striker" to help secure the jibboom, the same as a bobstay does the bowsprit.

Mast Carlines or Carlings.—Pieces of timber fitted fore and aft between the beams to support the mast, &c.

Master.—The chief officer of a ship. (See "Seaman.")

Master Mariner.—A master of a vessel who has a master's certificate of competency. An old-fashioned term. A "master mariner" is popularly known as a "captain" among yacht sailors ; but a master is only a self-dubbed captain. Master is the correct term, and the only recognised one in law. Yacht masters are not required to hold the Board of Trade certificate of competency.

Master Mate.—A mate certificated as master. This was originally written "master's mate," and meant a person appointed to assist the master of a man of war in carrying out his duties.

Masthead.—The part of a mast above the hounds. To masthead is to hoist anything up to the truck, &c.

Masthead Light.—The white light which steam vessels are required to exhibit at the masthead when under way. (See " Side Lights.")

Masthead Man.—In yacht parlance, the man who goes aloft to lace a topsail, &c.

Masthead Pendants.—The pendants and runners which help support the mast.

Mast Hoops.—The hoops to which the luff of fore and aft sails are seized to keep the sail to the mast.

Mast Rope.—The heel rope by which a topmast is sent up and lowered ; not, however, termed heel rope.

Match.—In competition as yachts in a race. Formerly all contests between yachts were termed matches. Of late years the term race has been more generally applied to such encounters.

Mate.—An officer next in command to a master.

Maul.—A heavy hammer used by shipwrights.

Meaking Iron.—An implement used to extract old caulking from seams.

Measurement.—Generally written admeasurement. The computation of a vessel's tonnage by certain rules. (See " Tonnage.")

Meet Her.—When a vessel begins to fly to or run off the wind, to stop her doing so by the helm. Generally to check a vessel's tendency to yaw by using the helm.

Meet, To.—To meet a vessel with the helm is after the helm has been put one way to alter her course to put it the other way to stop the course being altered any further. This is also called " checking with the helm."

Mess.—The number of officers or men who eat together. Disorder ; entanglement.

Middle Body.—The middle third of a vessel's length.

Middle Watch.—The watch between midnight and 4 a.m.

Mildew.—Sails if rolled up when they are damp frequently almost impossible to get the stains out entirely. New sails suffer most in this respect, as the " dressing " not being entirely washed or worked out of them will ferment and cause the mildew. The stains can be partly removed by scrubbing the sail with fresh water and soap ; then rub the sail with soap and sprinkle or rub whiting over it ; leave the sail to dry and bleach in the sun, and repeat the process more than once if necessary. Both sides of the sail should be scrubbed. Chloride of lime and other caustics and acids would remove mildew, but would almost certainly make the canvas rotten. If chloride of lime be used only the clear liquor should be allowed to touch the sail, and the latter should be well rinsed in fresh water afterwards (see " Bleaching "). If sails are stowed whilst damp or wet, they should be hoisted again as soon as possible for drying or airing.

Mile.—See " Knot."

Missing Stays.—To fail in an attempt to tack, or to go from one tack to the other.

Mizen Bumpkin.—A short spar that extends from the taffrail aft for the lower block of the mizen sheet to be hooked to. East country yachts have this bumpkin generally crooked downwards, the reason given being that the downward crook shows up the sheer of the yacht. A more practical reason, however, can be given, and that is, if a bobstay is used, a more effective purchase is obtained for it.

Mizenmast.—In a ship the after mast. So also in a yawl or ketch.

Mizen Staysail.—A sail set " flying " from a yawl's mizenmast head to an eye bolt on deck forward of the mizenmast. Generally set with a quarterly wind.

Moment.—A weight or force multiplied by the length of the lever upon which it acts. Sail moment generally means the area of sails and the pressure of wind upon them multiplied by the distance the centre of effort is above the centre of lateral resistance, which represents the length of lever.

Momentum.—A force represented by a weight and the velocity with which it is moved.

Moon.—Sailors say there will be a moon at such and such a date, meaning that there will be a new moon or full moon, from which the time of high water is calculated.

Moor.—To anchor by two cables.

Mooring Rings.—The rings by which the chain is attached to large stones used for moorings. Sometimes the bolts that hold these rings pass clean through the stone, and are secured underneath, but a more secure plan than this is that known as a " Lewis." In the engraving *a* is the ring or shackle, *b* a bolt with a

Fig. 299.

screw nut and linch pin ; *c c* movable parts of the bolt ; *d* the key or wedge. When the key is in its place the cavities, if any, can be filled with lead or sulphur.

Morning Watch.—The watch from 4 a.m. to 8 a.m.

Mosquito Fleet.—A term applied to small racing yachts at some ports. In 1894 the American Corinthian Mosquito Fleet claimed to have originated the term, and was referred to as follows : "The application of that insectism to yachts or boats was first made by an association in Barnegat Bay, U.S.A. It has not yet been adopted in England, and is one of those crazy Americanisms which are permitted because we love novelty above good taste." Dr. Grant, of New York, then correctly pointed out that the term has been used in England for many years, and traces the origin of the word to *musca* fly and *quito* diminutive or little, hence mosquito or little fly." As a matter of fact, a " mosquito fleet " has been in existence for many years on the Devonshire coast, the great port for them being Dartmouth. In the regatta programme of the Royal Western Yacht Club for 1866, the third event is scheduled as follows : " Prize of 6*l.* for the Mosquito Fleet of Pleasure Boats." There were nine entries, and Mr. R. Martin's Swallow was the winner, with Mr. Lander's Bantam second, Mr. Hudson's Butterfly third, and Mr. C. Hamilton's Boomerang fourth. It is not certain when the term Mosquito Fleet first came into use in this country ; but in 1859 "Vanderdecken," in an article published in *Hunt's Yachting Magazine* said, " The Mosquito Fleet may be justly esteemed the nursery for our yachtsmen ; the little yacht leads on to the handy 25, the flying 50, and the stately schooner of 200 tons."

Moulded.—The depth a timber is made between its curved surfaces as distinct from its siding, which is the thickness between its flat surfaces.

Moulded Breadth.—The greatest breadth of a vessel *without* the plank.

Moulded Depth.—(See " Depth.")

Moulds.—Curves used by draughtsmen. The skeleton frames made by shipwrights to cut the frames by.

Mourning Ribband.—A blue ribbon or stripe run round a yacht's side, instead of a gold or white one, to denote mourning. Mourning is also denoted by flying an ensign or burgee half-mast.

Mousings.—Yarns wound round the jaws of hooks to prevent them becoming detached.

'Mudian Rig.—A contraction of " Bermudian rig.'·

Muslin.—A slang term given to the sails : generally applied to balloon sails.

Mussle.—To seise an unruly sail and press the wind out of it in lowering.

Mussler.—A strong wind which blows directly down a vessel's intended course. Synonymous with " nose-ender."

N.

Nail-sick Clench-built Boat.—This is when the nail fastenings have become loose in a boat so that she leaks. Mr. J. C. Wilcocks recommends that the boat should have the whole of her ballast taken out ; let her then be thoroughly cleaned out and laid on her sides, with sufficient weight to keep her so until the water begins to come over the gun-

wale. A man should be inside with some chalk or white paint, and mark every leak which becomes visible, first on one side, then on the other ; or the boat can be hauled up and filled with water and marked outside. If the boat be decked, any recesses behind bulkheads or in the counter must be carefully examined, and marked in the same manner. After all the leaks have been discovered, let her be dried, and every nail examined ; the lands or joinings of the planks should also be tried with the blade of a very thin knife. Any rivets which have worked very loose must be cut out, and replaced with nails and rooves of a larger size, and through the chief parts of the bottom it will probably be necessary to put an additional nail between every two originally driven. Many of the old nails which are only a little slack should again be hardened by a few taps on the inside, a boy holding on against the head of the nail on the outside. After this work has been thus gone through, melt a pound of pitch in a gallon of boiling Stockholm tar, and give her a good coat inside up to the level of the inside of the lockers—that is to say, as high as it can be done not to interfere with the paint. The garboard strake fastenings, and also those of the hood ends, must also be examined, and will be certain to require careful caulking. In tarring the boat inside, the ledges or lands should be quite filled up with the boiling stuff.

Narrowing.—The wind is said to " narrow " when it blows at a smaller angle from ahead, or " shorten," which term refer to.

Neaped.—The situation of a vessel that gets ashore during high water at spring tides, and as the tides get shorter every day towards the neap tides she cannot be floated off till the next spring tides. Generally termed be-neaped.

Neap Tides.—The tides which occur between new and full moon ; spring tides being at or near the new and full moon.

Near.—Very close to the wind, so that the sails shake or lift.

Near the Wind.—Close to wind ; generally used in a sense to convey the meaning that the vessel is too near the wind, as " She's near forward," meaning that the head sails are shaking or lifting. (See " Nip.")

Nettles.—Small lines or ropes used to support hammocks when they are slung under the beams. Also reef points are sometimes termed nettles.

News.—The intimation conveyed sternly to the watch below to turn up when they do not obey the first summons, as " Do you hear the news there, sleepers ?"

Niggling.—Sailing close to the wind or too close·

Nip.—A short bight in a rope, such as the part that goes round a sheave, &c. To nip a vessel is to sail her very close, or too close, to the wind.

Nippering.—Joining a rope by cross turns.

Nock.—The weather corner of a gaff sail. The throat.

No Nearer.—An order given to a steersman not to luff any more, or not to bring the vessel any closer to wind. When sailing free a course is frequently given to the steersman thus, W.S.W. and no nearer; or S.E. and no nearer, which may be varied " Nothing to windward of W.S.W.," &c.

Nosebag.—A name given to a jib, generally meaning a jib that is too big for the after sail; or a jib that bellies out into a bag.

Nor'-wester.—A stiff glass of grog, usually rum.

Nose-ender.—Dead on end. A wind which blows directly down a vessel's intended course, involving a dead beat. (See " Muzzler.")

Noose.—A slip knot or running bight in a rope.

Number.—The number of a ship in the registry kept by the Registrar-General of Shipping; hence when a ship " makes her number " she hoists the signal flag denoting her number so that her name may be read. Also the number of a seaman on a ship's book. " To lose the number of the mess " is to fail to appear at mess through desertion, drowning, or sudden death.

O.

Oars !—An order given to cease rowing and toss up the oars. (See " Lay in Oars.")

Off.—The opposite to near (which see), as " Off the wind." " Nothing off " is an order given to a helmsman to steer nothing to leeward of a particular course, or to sail nothing off the wind, but to keep the vessel full and bye. (See " No Nearer.")

Off and On.—Beating along a shore by a board off and then a board on.

Official Log.—The record of a voyage containing all matters relating to the crew, &c., which the law requires to be kept.

Offing.—Away from the land, seaward. To make an offing is to sail away clear of the land.

" Off She Goes !"—The shout raised when a vessel begins to move down the ways at launching.

Oilskins.—The waterproof clothing worn by sailors, &c. The following is said to be a good dressing for them : Dissolve in one and a quarter pint rain water 6oz. common yellow soap over a slow fire; when dissolved, boil and stir in five pints of boiled linseed oil, in which 8oz. of patent driers have previously been mixed. Let the mixture simmer for a quarter of an hour, and then apply it hot, rubbing well in with a hard brush. Two coats at first and one every season. If the oilskins become sticky the paint must be got off by a mixture of soap and soda and soaking and hard scrubbing. Liquid ammonia one part to twenty of water and soap, all applied hot, form, it is said, a good mixture for removing the paint. The oilskins must be well dried before coating them again. (See also " Waterproofing.")

Oil on Troubled Waters.—There is no doubt that the use of oil for smoothing down broken water or preventing wave crests breaking was known to the ancients. Aristotle supposed that the thin film of oil prevented wave formation, by reducing the friction of the wind on the water surface. There is no doubt that this friction is the primary cause of wave formation, and if the whole water surface were covered with oil, possibly the wave formation would be reduced ; but this in no way accounts for the fact that the spreading of oil on a small portion of a disturbed water surface will suddenly arrest the breaking of waves. (See the article " Waves.") The fact is, what the oil does is to prevent the waves rising into cusps and then falling to pieces. Also, when these cusps are formed, waves rise to great—or, as it may be termed, unnatural heights. If the height of the waves much exceeds a certain proportion to the length, the wave crest becomes deformed, and finally breaks. It is the broken water— the broken water has actual motion—and not the undulations, which does the harm, and the oil, we suppose owing to its greater viscousness, prevents waves rising into the deformed conditions which bring about their disruption. It should be clearly understood that broken water—whether it is a wave tumbling to pieces in mid-ocean, or on the shore in the form of surf—has actual motion relative to the earth, and represents a great force. In the case of unbroken waves, the undulations only move ; that is to say, the wave motion travels, but not the water. An unbroken wave will pass under a boat and leave her in exactly the same position relative to the earth ; but if she be struck by a broken wave, she may be hurled a considerable distance, or, if she resists the force, she may be greatly damaged.

On account of the importance to navigators of a knowledge of the use of oil to prevent heavy seas from breaking on board, the Hamburg Nautical School offered a prize last year for the best essay on the subject, and it was won by Capt. E. Karlowa, of the Hamburg - American Steamship Company, whose paper is here condensed.

In the diagrams, the arrows denote the direction of the wind and sea; the flowing lines indicate the spreading oil.

Scudding before a gale (Fig. 300), distribute oil from the bow by means of oil-bags or through waste-pipes ; it will thus spread aft and give protection both from quartering and following seas. If only distributed astern (Fig. 301) there will be no protection from the quartering sea.

Running before a gale, yawing badly and threatening to broach-to (Figs. 302 and 303), oil should be distributed from the bow and from both sides, abaft the beam. In Fig. 302, for instance, where it is only distributed at the bow, the weather quarter is left unprotected

Oil on Troubled Waters—continued.

when the ship yaws. In Fig. 304, however, with oil-bags abaft the beam as well as forward, the quarter is protected.

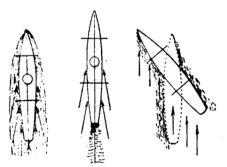

FIG. 300.   FIG. 301.   FIG. 302.

Lying-to (Fig. 304), a vessel can be brought closer to the wind by using one or two oil-bags forward, to windward. With a high

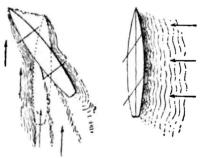

FIG. 303.   FIG. 304.

beam sea, use oil-bags along the weather side at intervals of 40 or 50 feet.

In a heavy cross-sea (Fig. 305) as in the centre of a hurricane, or after the centre has

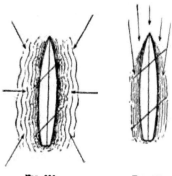

FIG. 305.   FIG. 306.

passed, oil-bags should be hung out at regular intervals along both sides.

Steaming into a heavy head-sea (Fig. 306),

use oil through forward closet-pipes. Oil-bags would be tossed back on deck.

Drifting in the trough of a heavy sea (Figs. 307 and 308), use oil from waste-pipes forward and bags on weather side, as in Fig. 308. These answer the purpose very much better than one bag at weather bow and one at lee quarter, although this has been tried with some success (Fig. 307).

Lying-to, to tack or wear (Fig. 309), use oil from weather bow.

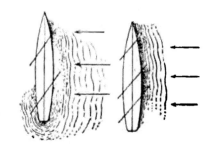

FIG. 307.   FIG. 308.

Cracking on, with high wind abeam and heavy sea (Fig. 310), use oil from waste-pipes, weather bow.

Towing another vessel in a heavy sea, oil is of the greatest service, and may prevent the hawser from breaking. Distribute oil from the towing vessel, forward and on both sides. If only used aft, the tow alone gets the benefit (Fig. 311.)

At anchor in an open roadstead, use oil in bags from jib-boom, or haul them out ahead

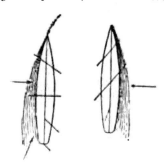

FIG. 309.   FIG. 310.

of the vessel by means of an endless rope rove through a tail-block secured to the anchor-chain (Fig. 312).

A vessel hove-to for a pilot (Fig. 313), should distribute oil from the weather side and lee quarter. The pilot-boat runs up to windward and lowers a boat, which pulls down to leeward and around the vessel's stern. The pilot-boat runs down to leeward, gets out oil-bags to windward and on her lee quarter, and the boat pulls back around her stern, protected by the oil. The vessels drift to leeward and leave an oil-slick to windward, between the two.

There are many other cases where oil may be used to advantage—such as lowering and hoisting boats, riding to a sea-anchor, crossing rollers or surf on a bar, and from life-boats and stranded vessels. Thick and heavy oils are the best. Mineral oils are not so effective as animal or vegetable oils. Raw petroleum

FIG. 311.

FIG. 312.

has given favourable results, but not so good when it is refined. Certain oils, like cocoa-nut oil and some kinds of fish oil, congeal in cold weather, and are therefore useless, but may be mixed with mineral oils to advantage. The simplest and best method of distributing oil is by means of canvas bags about one foot long, filled with oakum and oil, pierced with holes by means of a coarse sail-needle, and held by a lanyard. The waste-pipes forward are also very useful for this purpose.

FIG. 313.

It should be noted that oil has little or no effect on the broken water due to surf breaking on a shore; and the experiments made on the broken water, on bars of harbour entrances, show that the condition of the water cannot be much modified by oil; the wave breaking is, in such cases, mostly governed by the depth of the water. The deeper the water, the greater the effect of the oil, in modifying the wave breaking.

If a bar harbour has to be entered on a flood tide a boat could discharge oil so that it would run in ahead of her. On an ebb tide, the oil could be distributed by some apparatus in connection with the shore.

"A wave-smoother," made by The Storm Anchor Co., Campbell-road, Bow, is shown by Fig. 314 as intended for life-boats. It is a sail made of stout canvas, with a buoyant wooden yard on top, and a tube made of strong galvanized steel at bottom, large enough to contain from one to two gallons of oil. This tube acts at once as a sinker and yard; it is a self-distributor when in the sea, and a safe and strong receptacle for oil. The central figure shows it hanging in beckets, under the boat's thwart, whence it may be thrown overboard, and will then commence acting instantly, as storm-anchor and wave-smoother. Its four guys should be made fast to about 60 feet of the boat's painter, and veered ahead. It will not fail to keep the boat's head to the sea; and the oil, rising to the surface, will most effectually calm down the breaking and high-topping waves before they burst on the boat. By this system the boat will require little, if any, personal management, as the anchor and

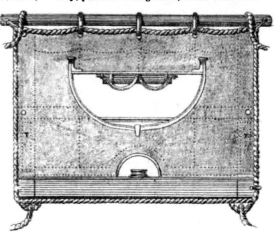

FIG. 314.

the oil acting together will render the terrible disaster of capsizing very remote.

If used for scudding, it should be tightly furled and towed astern by the four guys; but when the seas rise high, boats should be hove to.

If kept suspended under a thwart it can never be trodden on and burst, as it would be in any other place by a body of people hurriedly springing into a boat. When overboard it

Oil on Troubled Waters—continued.

will discharge oil at a uniform rate, and make one gallon go as far as five applied in any other way.

Vegetable oil mixed with one half fish oil and one-tenth weight of tow or oakum, is recommended.

Another wave smoother is made by the "Mermaid" Wave Subduer Company, 19, Castle-street, Liverpool.

Attempts made to still the waves for ships to have a comparatively smooth passage with a head sea have not been very successful. In 1888, trials were made on board the North German Lloyd liners with rockets containing oil fired ahead of the ships in the teeth of a gale. It was said that five rockets—we presume in instantaneous succession—were fired 900ft. ahead of the ship dead to windward in a gale, and that from 1500 sq. ft. to 2000 sq. ft. were covered with the oil liberated from the rockets. If the oil from these five rockets covered an area of, say 2000 sq. ft., the area would be more or less circular in form, with a diameter, say, of 50ft. Thus we assume that the oil spread out 25ft. in all directions whilst the ship was travelling 900ft.; we further assume that the speed of the ship would be, in a gale about 15 knots an hour, or 1516ft. per minute; thus the oil, whilst the ship traversed 900ft., would only have thirty-six seconds to spread in; or, in other words, a rocket would have to be fired every seven seconds to make an oily path for a ship travelling at the rate of 15 knots an hour. It should be noted that the oily path would be no broader than the ship, and that keeping in it would be like walking a chalk line under the influence of very exuberant spirits. We do not think such a streak as this would be of much value to a ship, even if she could keep actually in it, or just to leeward of it.

To make a continuous oily path for a ship travelling at the rate of 15 knots an hour, five rockets would have to be fired every seven seconds. Thus, forty-three rockets would have to be fired per minute, 2580 per hour, and 61,920 per twenty-four hours. If the ship travelled at the rate given, she would be about eight days on a voyage; and if rockets were required the whole time, 495,360, or practically half a million, would have to be fired. These could not possibly be manufactured and fired a distance of 900ft. under a cost of 6d. each, or a total cost of 12,384l. —a sum probably more than double the average amount of passage money per voyage. We do not, therefore, think that the luxury of having an oily track across the Atlantic is yet within range of things practicable.

O.M.—(See "B.M.")

On.—In the direction of, as "on the bow," "on the beam," "on the quarter," "on for that buoy," &c.

On a Bowline.—Close-hauled. Generally applied to the square rig when a ship has her bowlines hauled taut to keep the leeches of the sails from shaking when she is close-hauled.

On End.—A mast is said to be on end when in its place; literally, standing on its end. Generally applied to topmasts.

On a Wind.—Close-hauled; not off the wind.

On an Easy Bowline.—Not quite close-hauled: a good full.

One, Two, Three, Haul!—A cry raised by the foremost hand in hauling on a tackle. All hands throw their whole weight and strength on the rope or fall at the word "Haul!"

Open.—Upon sailing round a point or headland when an object comes into view.

Opposite Tacks.—When of two vessels one is on the port tack and the other on starboard tack. Cross tacks.

Ordinary Seaman.—On board a man-of-war a young sailor not yet efficient in his duties so as to entitle him to the rank of A.B.

Outer and Inner Turns.—In bending a sail to a yard, the outer turns haul the sail out taut along the yard, the inner turns secure the sail.

Outhaul.—A rope or tackle by which a sail is hauled out on a spar, as distinct from an inhaul by which it is hauled inboard.

Outrigger. — A contrivance of some sort for extending a sail or stay outboard. A name for a kind of row-boat which has the rowlocks extended beyond the boat's side by iron rod brackets.

Over-canvassed.—Too much canvas.

Overfalls. — The rough water caused by the tide pouring over a rough or precipitous bottom.

Overhang.—The "knee of the head" or the curved piece of wood fitted to the stem to form a graceful or ornamental curve. Also the inclination the stem has outwards from the end of the water-line forward; also the overhanging part of the counter aft. Anything that projects beyond the base.

Overhaul.—To overtake another vessel; to loosen the parts of a tackle; to ease up, to slacken, or free the fall of a tackle; to slacken or "lighten up" a rope.

Overlap.—When *any part*, spars and sails included, of one vessel covers or overlaps *any part* of another vessel. Generally when anything partly covers another thing.

Over-masted.—Masts that are too large or long for a vessel.

Over-rigged.—Generally more rigging, spars, and canvas than a vessel will properly bear.

Over-set.—To cause a capsize.

Overshoot a Mark.—To go up to a mark with too much way on so that the vessel shoots past it.

Over-reach or Overstand.—To stand so long on a reach that upon tacking the vessel can fetch much farther to windward of a mark than was necessary or desirable.

Overtake.—To approach a vessel that is sailing ahead. The "rule of the road" is that an overtaking vessel must keep clear of the vessel she overtakes; the vessel so overtaken must, however, keep her course steadily. In competitive yacht sailing this rule is somewhat different, as it allows the vessel that is overtaken to alter her course to windward to prevent the other passing her to windward; she must not, however, alter her course to leeward to prevent the overtaking vessel passing on her lee side.

P.

Paint.—(See "Black Paint.")

Painter.—A rope spliced to a ring bolt in the bow of a boat to make fast by at wharves, steps, or other landing places. "To let go the painter" is figuratively to depart.

Palm.—The guard and thimble used by sail makers. Also the fluke of an anchor.

Paltry.—A wind is said to be paltry which is light and intermittent, or varying a great deal in direction and force; baffling.

Parbuckle.—To roll a spar, cask, &c., by placing it in the bight of a rope, one end of which is fast, the other hauled upon.

Parcel.—To cover a rope with strips of canvas painted or otherwise. The canvas is wound round the rope and stitched or "served" with spun yarn.

Parrel or Parral.—Ropes or irons used to secure yards at the slings to the mast; rope parrels are commonly rove through balls of wood, so that they hoist easily on the mast. Parrels are used on the jaws of a gaff. An eye is usually spliced in either end of a parrel.

Part.—To break, to burst asunder, as the "fore stay parted about half way up to the collar."

Partners.—A strong frame of timber fixed between the deck beams to receive and support the mast, termed mast partners, but sometimes termed carlines.

Pass.—To reeve, as pass a lacing or earing. Also to hand a thing one from another.

Passage.—A voyage. To carry a person from one place to another is to give a passage.

Passengers.—A vessel of any description cannot, according to statute, have on board more than twelve passengers without taking out a licence. However, the opinion of the judges was expressed on the point in the Court of Queen's Bench in April, 1889. It appears that the owners of the steam tug Era were summoned before the Ipswich magistrates for carrying a party of friends, twenty-one in number, on a pleasure excursion on the river Orwell, she not having a passenger certificate in accordance with the 318th section of the Merchant Shipping Act, 1854. For the defence it was contended that the steamer was not plying within the meaning of the statute, and the magistrates declined to convict. The Board of Trade then took the case to the Court of Queen's Bench. The court without hesitation decided

that the magistrates were right not to convict, and the Lord Chief Justice, in the course of his judgment, said: "If the owner of a yacht took a party up and down a river for amusement, surely it is too clear for argument that such a case would not be within the Act. The case was not really within the meaning of the Act, and it would be straining the meaning of the Act to say that the steamer was in any reasonable sense plying." Mr. Justice Hawkins concurred, and stated it was not shown that the Era was plying at the time she took the party for an excursion on the Orwell. In spite of this judgment the Board of Trade in 1892 sanctioned a vexatious prosecution of the owner of the yacht Myrtle. But if the statute does not apply to an ordinary steamship like the Era when she is not plying, it cannot apply to a yacht. Judgment was given against the owner of the yacht, who was too late with his appeal.

Paul or Pawl.—An iron bar used to prevent the back recoil of the barrel of a windlass, &c.

Pawl Bitt.—A long timber from the deck to the keelson forming one of the bowsprit bitts.

Pay.—To run hot pitch and tar, or marine glue, &c., into seams after they are caulked.

Paying off Pennant.—A long streamer flown when a man-of-war is being paid out of commission.

Pay Off.—When a vessel's head goes off to leeward by virtue of the head sails being put aback or the helm being put up.

Pay Out.—To veer or slack out chain or rope.

Peak.—The upper after corner of gaff sails, gaff topsails, lugsails, &c. A sail is said to have a great deal of peak when the gaff or yard makes a small angle with a vertical. A low peak means a flat-headed sail. (See "Fore Peak.")

Peak Downhaul.—A rope rove through a single block at the gaff end to haul upon when lowering the mainsail.

Peak Halyards.—The halyards by which the peak of a sail is hoisted.

Peak Purchase.—A tackle attached to one end of the peak halyards.

Pendant.—A stout rope to which tackles are attached.

Pennant or Pendant.—A long white streamer with a St. George's cross at the hoist, used only by ships of the Royal Navy. It is said to owe its origin to the following incident: a Dutch Admiral hoisted a broom at his masthead as a symbol that he would sweep the English from the sea; the English Admiral retorted by hoisting a long streamer to denote that he would whip the Dutch off the sea; the English Admiral more nearly succeeded in his object than the Dutchman did. A Commodore has a broad pennant or swallow tail flag. (See "Burgee," "Hoisting Pennant," and "Irish Pennants," "Paying off Pennant.")

Peter.—(See "Blue Peter.")

Peter Boat.—A small fishing boat, sharp at both ends, common at the mouth of the Thames and Medway.

Petticoat Trousers.—An ancient garment worn by sailors, now only used by fishermen ; a kind of kilt often made out of a blanket.

Pig.—A heavy mass of iron or lead.

Pile Driving.—Pitching heavily and frequently in a short steep sea.

Pilot.—A person who takes charge of a ship in narrow or dangerous channels, and, who from his local knowledge of the same can, or ought to avoid the dangers of stranding.

Pintles.—The metal hooks by which rudders are attached to the gudgeon sockets.

Pipe.—To summon men to duty by a whistle from the boatswain's call.

Pipe up.—The wind is said to pipe up when it increases in strength suddenly.

Pitching.—The plunging motion of a vessel when she dives by the head ; the opposite motion to 'scending, which is rising by the head and sinking by the stern.

Planking.—The outside skin of a vessel ; plank laid on the frames or beams of a vessel whether inside or outside.

Plank Sheer.—The outside plank at the deck edge which reaches the timber heads, and shows the sheer of the vessel. Also the same as covering board.

Platform.—The floor of a cabin. (See " Deck.")

Ply to Windward. — Plying to windward is synonymous with beating to windward.

Point the yards.—To brace them up sharp when at anchor, so that they shall not feel the full force of the wind.

Point, to.—A vessel is said to point well when she lies very close to the wind. A term more used in America than in this country. Out point, to point higher, &c.

Points.—(See " Reef Points.")

Pole.—The part of a topmast about the shoulders.

Pole Mast.—A long mast without a topmast, but with a long " pole " or piece above the hounds.

Poop.—The raised part of a vessel at her extreme after end. To be pooped is when running before the wind a sea breaks in over the stern.

Poor John.—Dried hake, which is a coarse fish caught on the west coast.

Port.—The left hand side, the opposite to starboard. Formerly also termed larboard ; but Falconer says, in his dictionary (1789), that larboard should never be used in conning the helm, owing to the possibility of its being mistaken for starboard. To port the helm is to put the tiller to port so that the vessel's head goes to starboard. The term " port " is of uncertain origin, but it occurs in Arthur Pitt's Voyage, 1580. It was authoritatively adopted in the Royal Navy at the beginning of the present century.

Portable Dinghies.—Numerous plans have been suggested for the construction of portable dinghies for small yachts, the best known perhaps being one adopted by Biffen, the well-known boat builder, in 1858. The boat was divided longitudinally into halves, each half being a complete boat, the longitudinal bulk heads coming as high as the thwarts ; three iron clamps were fitted to one half of the keel, into which the other half of the keel was fitted. The top part of the bulkheads were kept together by thumb-screws inserted above the water line. The boat was 9ft. long, and 4ft. broad ; in shape she did not differ from an ordinary dinghy when put together. She was used in a 6 tonner, and when not in use one half was stowed on either side of the cabin below. It was said that this boat could be put together in half a minute. In 1862 Biffen built a similar boat which was not so well recommended, on account of the multiplicity of fastenings. The obvious objection to such contrivances is of course the trouble of putting the parts together when the boat has to be used. (See " Berthon's Collapsible Boats " and " Stowing a Punt.")

Port Lights.—Circular or square glass lights in the sides of a vessel. (See " Dead Lights.")

Ports and Portholes.—Square holes in the side of a ship for the guns, &c.

Port Sills.—The bottom framing of a port hole to which the lower half-port or shutter is hinged, also the frame to which the upper half-port is attached.

Pram or Praam.—A lighter with a shovel bow, used in Holland and the Baltic. Most modern yachts have now pram bows.

Preserving a Boat.—All small boats, if possible, should be hauled out of water or beached when not in use. Varnish preserves the wood from water absorption better than paint. Whenever the varnish becomes worn, the boat should be re-coated.

Press of Sail.—All the sail a vessel dare carry.

Preventers.—Additional ropes, stays, tackles, &c., used to prevent spars being carried away if their proper stays give out, as preventer backstays for the topmast, preventer bobstay, &c. A preventer is also any rope or lashing used to prevent something giving way.

Preventive Man.—An old fashioned name for a coastguard man, whose duty it is to prevent or detect the landing of smuggled goods. A " Double Dutch " story, current at Ryde, Isle of Wight, to illustrate the confused way of speaking by a native collierman, Tony Ford, was as follows : " I jumped out of window and put my hand out of bed to see if it was light, then I went down to the collier to have some breakfast for broth, and when I got on board I found she was gone. I said, ' I say, Mr. Spyman, lend me your Preventive Glass to look at that ship just gone out of sight round the point,' and he told me he had knocked about for six weeks in the month of March in a ship after she sunk in the Bay of Biscuits."

Privateer's Flag.—The Union Jack with a red border.

Protest.—A declaration that a yacht has not conformed to sailing rules ; also a term used by the Commissioner of Wrecks in case of a wreck being reported.

Puddening.—A sort of fender made of old rope, for a boat's stem, &c.

Puff.—A gust of wind. A free puff is when it enables a vessel to luff; a foul puff when it breaks her off.

Puncheons.—A part of the frame work of a deck-house. It is a kind of pilaster mortised into the coaming, and is the principal support of the deck-house roof. The panelled part of the framework is rabetted into the puncheons.

Punt.—A small boat or dinghy. (See "Stowing a Punt.")

Punt Building.—The following are directions for building a fishing punt as shown by Fig. 315:—Take for the sides two 1in. planks

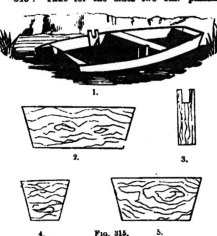

1.

2.   3.

4.   FIG. 315.   5.

16in. wide and 14ft. long; for the ends use 2in. plank. Cut the stern-piece 30in. long at bottom, and 40in. at top; cut the bow piece 12in. long at bottom, and 20in. at top; then cut a centre-piece 12in. wide, 40in. long at bottom, and 50in. long at top; put these pieces in position, and securely nail the sides to them; this can be readily done by bringing the planks into place by means of a rope, twisted by a short lever. After the sides are thus secured true up the bottom edges, and plank crosswise with three-quarter inch plank one-eighth of an inch apart; caulk these seams with oakum or cotton, and pitch the whole bottom, and 2in. or 3in. up the sides. A keel 1in., 2in., or 3in. deep can then be nailed on, depending on the depth of the water where the boat is to be used. For seats nail a plank across each end, and one for the rower over the middle piece; two row-locks, about 6in. above the sides of the boat, complete the job. These can be made of

plank, set up on end, and fastened to the inside of the boat. A common carpenter can make such a boat in about two days, and, if planed and painted, it looks well. The ends ought to incline outwards about 3in. to the foot. No. 1 shows the skiff completed, but with a stern piece adapted for steering with an oar; No. 5 is a diagram of the stern piece; No. 4 the bow piece; No. 2 the middle piece, and No. 3 the rowlock. By putting in two pieces in the middle the required distance apart, and perforating the cross planking between them, a well would be readily formed.

Mr. A. V. FitzHerbert thus describes his plan of building a punt (Fig. 316): For the stern.—Take a piece of red pine 3in. by 4in., and 2ft. long. Groove it out to receive the side boards, which should be white pine 1in. Each side of boat made of 1ft. wide plank next bottom, and a 6in. plank above it, making total depth when planed down about 17in., or a trifle less. The centreboard of 2in. plank, 1ft. wide, should be cut 44in. wide on top, and 40½in. along the bottom. The stern, also of 2in. plank, must be 30in. at top, and 24in. at bottom, by 17in. high, or half an inch higher. Fix the centreboard firmly upright on a bench, then nail the lower side planks on to it, at 6ft. 6in. from the stern. Next put in the stem, first of all fitting it to take the curve of the planks, and give it a slight slope aft. The planks had better be fastened with screws to it. Next fit in the stem, with a fair slope forward. The sides can be brought close together to meet the stem by tying a rope round them. Care must be taken to keep stem in line with centre of stern and centreboard. Having fastened in stem, centre, and stern boards,

Section of Stem with Inch Boards let in.

Section of Boat with outriggers.

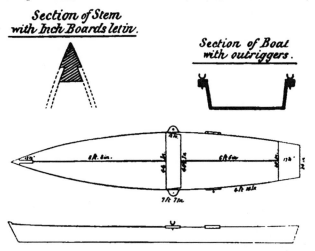

FIG. 316.

turn the boat upside down, and place the sides, stern, and centreboards level, to receive the bottom, which must be now laid on across the boat, of inch boards nailed on like

Punt Building—continued.

the top of a box, fitting well together at their inside edges, but slightly open at the outside to admit of caulking. After putting on the bottom, turn the boat right-side up, fit in ribs, of strips of boards, 1in. by 2in., and 17in. long. Nail them upright to the sides, with one end resting on the bottom of the boat, about 2ft. apart ; then put on the top board, and the hull is made. Along the bottom put two parallel keels about 3in. deep by 1in. to 1½in., and 15in. apart. Their use is, first, to keep the bottom boards together ; and secondly, to act as runners when dragging the boat from one place to another.

Put one wide seat in the stern, a seat to lift in and out 6ft. from the bow, and a movable seat for rowing or sliding, commencing at 5ft. 4in. from stern, and moveable for one yard forward ; this can be done by fastening a piece of 3in. pine to each side level with top of lower plank, and 1in. above this, and parallel with it, another lighter piece to keep the seat down.

There are two sets of outriggers, the after set for rowing when alone, the forward set for use when there are two in the boat. The after outrigger is made of 3in. by 4½in. red pine, grooved to a depth of 2in. to let in the side of the boat to which it is screwed ; it is 20in. long, and has three holes for the rowlocks, the centre one 4ft. 10in. from the stern of boat.

The forward outrigger is 7in. by 3in., red pine, also grooved, but has an iron bracket underneath to support it, and two holes for the rowlock, one further from the centre of boat than the other ; the centre of outrigger is 7ft. 7in. from the stern.

Purchase.—A tackle ; any contrivance for increasing mechanical power.

Put About.—To tack. To put about another vessel is to cause her to tack.

Put In.—To call at a port or harbour.

Put Off.—To leave, as to leave a ship's side or the shore.

Pykar.—An ancient English boat used for fishing.

Q.

Quarter Deck—The deck abaft the main mast where the crew are never seen unless duty calls them there.

Quarter Fast.—A warp or rope made fast to the quarter ; a quarter spring.

Quarter Master.—An officer who sees that the orders of the mate or master are properly executed, &c.

Quarter Timbers.—Large pieces of timber secured to the transom frame, to help form the counter.

Quarter Watch.—When the two watches are subdivided into four watches, so that only one quarter of the crew is on deck at one time ; sometimes observed in light weather.

Quarter Wind—The wind that blows on the quarter, or four or more points abaft the beam, but not dead aft. (See " Compass.")

Quarters.—That part of a yacht or ship nearest the stern.

R.

Rabbet or *Rebate.*—An angular channel or groove cut in the keel, stem, or sternpost, &c., to receive the edges or ends of the plank.

Race.—A competition between yachts. A strong current or tide running over a pit-like bottom producing overfalls. (See " Overfalls.")

Racing Flags.—The size of racing flags will be found under the head of " Flags."

Racking.—A rope or seizing used to lash the parts of a tackle together, by taking several turns, so as to keep them from running through the blocks, whilst the fall is cast off for some purpose, or whilst one hand belays the fall made fast to some fixture by one end and then passed round and round a rope to hold the latter by.

Raffee.—The square topsail set flying on the foretopmast of schooners, and formerly often set on cutters and ketches above the squaresail. Sometimes this topsail is triangular in shape, like a scraper.

Rail.—The timber fitted on to the heads of the bulwark stanchions. Called also " top rail."

Rainbow Fashion.—A ship dressed with flags from the jib boom end over the trucks to the taffrail.

Raising Iron.—A sort of chisel for removing the paying and caulking from seams.

Raising Tacks and Sheets.—To lift the clews of lower square sails before tacking or wearing.

Rake.—To lean forward or aft from the vertical, as raking masts, raking sternposts, raking stem, &c.

Rakish.—A vessel that has a look of speed about her, probably originating from the fast schooners of former days that had raking masts.

Ramp.—In close-hauled sailing, to sail a vessel along a heavy full without easing up the sheets.

Ramping Full. — Every sail bellying, full of wind—barely close-hauled.

Range.—Scope. To range is to arrange : to range the cable, to place a lot on deck in fakes ready for veering out.—To give a range of cable is to veer out enough in letting go the anchor to bring the vessel up without causing much strain to come on the bitts.—To sail near to, as to range up to windward, to range up alongside, to range along the coast, &c.

Rap Full.—The same as ramping full.

Rate of a Chronometer.—The daily loss or gain of a chronometer in relation to mean time.

Ratlines or *Ratlins.*—The small lines which cross the shrouds horizontally, and form the rungs of a ladder. Not generally used in yachts of 40 tons and under.

Rattle Down.—To fix ratlines to the shrouds.

Reaching.—Sailing by or along the wind. A "reach" is the distance sailed between tacks, and means the same as board. To "reach" another vessel is to pass her. In reaching a schooner of 150 tons, say, will pass a cutter of 100 tons; that is, will "fore-reach" her, but the cutter holding a better wind will generally keep the weather gauge. A "reach" is a distance a yacht can sail from point to point without tacking, and may be sailed with sheets eased up. Broad reach is with the boom well off the quarter. A reach is also the distance from bend to bend in a river or channel. Sailors mostly pronounce the word "retching." (See "Head Reach," and "Fore Reach.")

Ready About!—The order given to prepare for tacking.

Ready, All.—Everybody make ready.

Rear Commodore.—The third flag officer of a yacht club, who has no duties in the presence of the Commodore or Vice-Commodore. He has two white balls in the upper corner of his pennant.

Rear Guard.—See "After Guard."

Receiver of Wrecks.—An officer to whom in case of damage or wreck the facts must be reported.

Recognised Yacht Club.—A term very frequently used in yacht rules; formerly it was a general condition that "a member of a Royal yacht club shall be on board" each yacht competing in a match, who is responsible for the due observance of the sailing rules. Often the rule required that a member of the particular club under whose auspices the match was being sailed should be on board. All clubs, however, have not the right to be styled "royal," and the word "recognised" yacht club became introduced as an equivalent for "royal." Since the establishment of the Yacht Racing Association the term "recognised" is alone contained in the rule. No one seems to have known exactly what "recognised" meant; strictly it should mean a club with an Admiralty warrant, but any "yacht club" is considered "recognised" which is organised by yacht owners for the promotion of properly conducted yacht matches, and which do not enrol mechanics or labourers as members. The Admiralty will not now grant warrants to yacht clubs which cannot show a gross yacht tonnage of 2000 tons; but this is an imperfect test, as one yacht might be of that tonnage. (See "Admiralty Warrant," "Royal Yacht Club," "Burgee," and "Ensign.")

In 1895 the Y.R.A. having been appealed to for information as to what is a recognised yacht club, passed the following rule: "A yacht club shall not be considered a recognised yacht club within the meaning of the rule unless it shall have been proposed and accepted as such by the Council of the Yacht Racing Association, who shall have the power of cancelling such recognition should they deem it expedient so to do." All yacht clubs holding Admiralty warrants are considered recognised without application to the Y.R.A.

Reef.—To shorten sail by reefing. Also to shorten a spar, as to take a reef in the bowsprit. The topmasts of some yachts are made with one reef in them. In such cases a thimble eye is seized to the backstays for the blocks of the falls to be hooked to when the reef is taken in. The depth of such a reef is usually about one-sixth the length of topmast from first fid to sheave hole. When the topmast is lowered to second fid it is called reefing, not housing, housing only applying to lowering below the fids.

Reef Band.—A strip of canvas sewn across the sail in which the eyelet holes are worked to receive the reef points. Not always met with in yacht sails.

Reef Cringles.—The large cringles in the leeches of sails through which the reef pendants are rove and tacks or sheets hooked.

Reef Earing.—See "Reef Pendant."

Reef Knot.—See "Seamanship," farther back.

Reef Pendant (called also "reef earing").—A short and strong rope (with a Matthew Walker knot in one end). One end of the pendant is passed up through a hole in the cleat on one side of the boom and stopped by the knot in the end. The other end is then passed through the reef cringle in the sail and down through the sheave hole on the other side of the boom. Reef pendants are rove on opposite sides.

Reef Points.—Short pieces of rope attached to sails to secure the folds rolled up when reefing.

Reef Tackle.—The tackle hooked to the reef pendants.

Register.—A certificate of a vessel's register granted by the Board of Trade and registered by the Registrar-General of Shipping. It is not a document of title of ownership.

Registry.—A register of all British ships kept by the Registrar-General of Shipping. When a ship is registered, the following documents must be produced: (1) Certificate of Board of Trade measuring officer. (2) Certificate of Board of Trade Surveyor; in the case of yachts this certificate is not required. (3) Builder's certificate, or if the builder's certificate cannot be obtained, a document setting forth all that is known of the vessel. (4) Declaration of ownership. All vessels, yachts, or otherwise of 15 tons N.M. and over must be registered. Yachts, however, of less than 15 tons can be registered, and it is advisable to have them so registered for the sake of holding the certificate of register, obtaining the Admiralty warrant, and being able to prove nationality when visiting foreign ports. The name of a vessel once registered cannot be altered except with the sanction of the Board of Trade. A certificate of registry is a mere copy of the register kept at the port of registry, and of itself is not a document of title. A quantity of useful information on the registry of ships will be found in a little book by Mr. Miles Stapylton, published by Oliver, St. Dunstan's Hill, E.C., and called the "Imperial Guide to Registry of British

Shipping." (See also " Yachts " at the end
of the Appendix.)

Render.—To slacken or ease up. A rope is
said to render when it slackens up or slips
from a belaying pin or cavel.

Reeve.—To put a rope through a hole of any
kind.

Resistance. — According to Beaufoy, a plane
moved normally at a rate of 10ft. per second
meets with a resistance of 112·5lb. per square
foot. The resistance varies as the square of
the velocity. Generally understood to mean
the resistance a vessel meets with from the
friction of the water on her copper and from
the waves she makes. (See " Salt and Fresh
Water.")

Ribbands.—Long pieces of plank or timber,
usually three-sided, and sometimes called
harpings, secured to the frames of a vessel
in a fore-and-aft direction, when she is building, and representing the dividing lines or
geodetic lines.

Ribs.—The frames or timbers of a ship or boat.

Ride.—To rest at anchor, or to be held by an
anchor.

Ridge Ropes.—The ropes rove through the eyes
of metal stanchions fitted in the top rail.

Riding Down.—When men go aloft and hang on
the halyards and assist by their weight in
hoisting sails.

Riding Light.—The white globular lantern hung
on the forestay of vessels when riding at
anchor.

Rig.—The arrangement of a vessel's spars,
rigging, and sails, as schooner rig, cutter rig,
lugger rig, &c. To rig is to fit the spars with
rigging, &c. To rig out is to fit out.

Right Away.—In the direction of. An American term for quickly out of hand, or move
ahead.

Right Hand Rope.—Rope laid up or twisted with
the sun.

Right, to.—To bring a vessel back to the upright
position after she has been heeled.

Ring Bolt.—A bolt with an eye and a ring through
the eye.

Ring Tail.—The studding sail of a gaff sail.

Rings.—Rooves for bolt or nail clinching.

Rising Floor.—Distinct from flat floored, or flat
bottomed ; Sharp bottomed. (See " Dead
Rise.")

Risings.—Stringers fitted inside small boats to
strengthen them and support the thwarts.

Roach.—The curved part of the foot of a sail :
formerly the allowance made for the bellying
of a sail."

Roadstead.—An open anchorage.

Roaring Calm,—An equatorial calm.

Roaring Forties.—This term is sometimes applied
(but erroneously) to the calms which prevail
in the region lat. 40° N. long. 40° W. The
term, however, originated with the tearing
winds which blow in the South Atlantic
between lat. 30° and 50° S.

Rockered Keel.—A keel whose ends curve upwards
thus ⌣. (See " Cambered.")

Rogue's Yarn.—The coloured worsted yarns laid
in the strands of Government rope for identi-
fication. Each dockyard or Government
rope walk has a different colour.

Rolling.—The transverse motions of a ship when
amongst waves.

Rolling Hitch.—A way of fastening a rope to a
spar, &c. (See " Strop.")

Room and Space.—The distance from the centre
of one frame to the centre of another.

Roove.—(See " Ruff.")

Rope.—Ropes are of three kinds ; three-strand,
four-strand, and cable-laid. A number of
yarns twisted together forms a strand.
Three-strand rope (see Fig. 317) is laid right-
handed, or with the sun (sometimes termed
hawser-laid). Four-strand rope (see Fig. 318)
is also laid with the sun (sometimes termed
strand-laid). Four-strand rope is usually

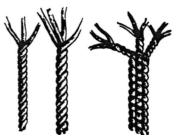

FIG. 317.   FIG. 318.   FIG. 319.

used for sheets and shrouds, pennants, and
generally for standing rigging. All rope
comes under the general term of cordage.
Cable-laid rope (see Fig. 319) consists of three
" three-strand " right-hand laid ropes laid
up together into one ; these ropes are laid
left-handed against the sun. Right-hand laid
rope must be coiled with the sun ; cable-laid
rope is coiled against the sun.

Rough-tree Rail.—The top rail fitted to the
stanchions above the bulwarks.

Round In.—To haul in on a rope.

Round To.—To bring by the wind. To come up
head to wind. A vessel is said to " go round "
when she goes about.

Round Turn.—To pass a rope twice round
a pin or cleat so as to make a complete
circle.

Rove.—The condition of a rope that has been
passed through a sheave hole or through any
aperture.

Rowlocks.—The fittings on the gunwale to receive
the tholes or crutches for the oars.

Royal. — The sail next above the topgallant
sail.

Royal Standard.—The flag of the Sovereign and
Royal family. It is always flown at the main.
When the Sovereign is on board, the standard
is flown at the main, and the Admiralty flag

(a red ground with fouled anchor) at the fore, and Union Jack at the mizen.

Royal Yacht Club.—A club which has obtained permission from the Home Office to use the prefix "royal." An Admiralty warrant obtained from the Admiralty does not confer the title; but a royal yacht club that has not also the Admiralty warrant can only fly the red ensign, and this can have no device. A club with an Admiralty warrant takes precedence of a club which has only a Royal warrant. (See "Recognised Club.")

Rudder Board, A.—Capt. Lowther, R.N., introduced the plan shown by Fig. 320 for increasing the area of rudders of shallow boats. Mr. W. Baden Powell uses a form of this rudder for the Nautilus canoes. This idea is not a new one.

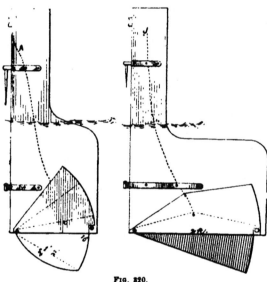

Fig. 320.

In 1780 Capt. Schank proposed a similar contrivance, and the plan is illustrated in Channock's "History of Marine Architecture," vol. iii., p. 409.

Rudder Trunk.—The trunk fitted in the counter to receive the rudder post into which the tiller is fitted.

Ruff or Roove.—A small ring or square plate placed over copper nails before clinching in boat building.

Rules of the Road.—Certain rules framed under the provisions of the Merchant Shipping Act.

In July, 1897, the following Steering and Sailing Rules (by Order in Council) came into force:

SCHEDULE I.

Rules concerning Lights, &c.

The word "visible" in these rules, when applied to lights, shall mean visible on a dark night with a clear atmosphere.

Art. 1. The rules concerning lights shall be complied with in all weathers from sunset to sunrise, and during such time no other lights which may be mistaken for the prescribed lights shall be exhibited.

Art. 2. A steam vessel when under way shall carry:

(a.) On or in front of the foremast, or if a vessel without a foremast, then in the fore part of the vessel, at a height above the hull of not less than 20ft., and if the breadth of the vessel exceeds 20ft., then at a height above the hull not less than such breadth, so, however, that the light need not be carried at a greater height above the hull than 40ft., a bright white light, so constructed as to show an unbroken light over an arc of the horizon of 20 points of the compass, so fixed as to throw the light 10 points on each side of the vessel, viz., from right ahead to 2 points abaft the beam on either side, and of such a character as to be visible at a distance of at least five miles.

(b.) On the starboard side a green light so constructed as to show an unbroken light over an arc of the horizon of 10 points of the compass, so fixed as to throw the light from right ahead to 2 points abaft the beam on either side, and of such a character as to be visible at a distance of at least two miles.

(c.) On the port side a red light so constructed as to show an unbroken light over an arc of the horizon of 10 points of the compass, so fixed as to throw the light from right ahead to 2 points abaft the beam on the port side, and of such a character as to be visible at a distance of at least two miles.

(d.) The said green and red side lights shall be fitted with inboard screens projecting at least 3ft. forward from the light, so as to prevent these lights from being seen across the bow.

(e.) A steam vessel when under way may carry an additional white light similar in construction to the light mentioned in subdivision (a). These two lights shall be so placed in line with the keel that one shall be at least 15ft. higher than the other, and in such a position with reference to each other that the lower light shall be forward of the upper one. The vertical distance between these lights shall be less than the horizontal distance.

Art. 3. A steam vessel when towing another vessel shall, in addition to her side lights, carry two bright white lights in a vertical line one over the other, not less than 6ft.

Rules of the Road—continued.

apart, and when towing more than one vessel shall carry an additional bright white light 6ft. above or below such lights, if the length of the tow, measuring from the stern of the towing vessel to the stern of the last vessel towed, exceeds 600ft. Each of these lights shall be of the same construction and character, and shall be carried in the same position as the white light mentioned in Article 2 (a), except the additional light, which may be carried at a height of not less than 14ft. above the hull.

Such steam vessel may carry a small white light abaft the funnel or aftermast for the vessel towed to steer by, but such light shall not be visible forward of the beam.

Art. 4. (a.) A vessel which from any accident is not under command, shall carry at the same height as the white light mentioned in Article 2 (a), where they can best be seen, and, if a steam vessel, in lieu of that light, two red lights, in a vertical line one over the other, not less than 6ft. apart, and of such a character as to be visible all round the horizon at a distance of at least two miles ; and shall by day carry in a vertical line one over the other, not less than 6ft. apart, where they can best be seen, two black balls or shapes, each 2ft. in diameter.

(b.) A vessel employed in laying or in picking up a telegraph cable shall carry in the same position as the white light mentioned in Article 2 (a), and, if a steam vessel, in lieu of that light, three lights in a vertical line one over the other, not less than 6ft. apart. The highest and lowest of these lights shall be red, and the middle light shall be white, and they shall be of such a character as to be visible all round the horizon, at a distance of at least two miles. By day she shall carry in a vertical line one over the other, not less than 6ft. apart, where they can best be seen, three shapes not less than 2ft. in diameter, of which the highest and lowest shall be globular in shape and red in colour, and the middle one diamond in shape and white.

(c.) The vessels referred to in this Article, when not making way through the water, shall not carry the side lights, but when making way shall carry them.

(d.) The lights and shapes required to be shown by this Article are to be taken by other vessels as signals that the vessel showing them is not under command and cannot therefore get out of the way.

These signals are not signals of vessels in distress and requiring assistance. Such signals are contained in Article 31.

Art. 5. A sailing vessel under way, and any vessel being towed, shall carry the same lights as are prescribed by Article 2 for a steam vessel under way, with the exception of the white lights mentioned therein, which they shall never carry.

Art. 6. Whenever, as in the case of small vessels under way during bad weather, the green and red side lights cannot be fixed, these lights shall be kept at hand lighted and ready for use ; and shall, on the approach of or to other vessels, be exhibited on their respective sides in sufficient time to prevent collision, in such manner as to make them visible, and so that the green light shall not be seen on the port side nor the red light on the starboard side, nor, if practicable, more than 2 points abaft the beam on their respective sides.

To make the use of these portable lights more certain and easy, the lanterns containing them shall each be painted outside with the colour of the light they respectively contain, and shall be provided with proper screens.

Art. 7. Steam vessels of less than 40, and vessels under oars or sails of less than 20, tons gross tonnage, respectively, and rowing boats, when under way, shall not be obliged to carry the lights mentioned in Article 2 (a) (b) and (c), but if they do not carry them they shall be provided with the following lights .

1. Steam vessels of less than 40 tons shall carry :

(a) In the fore part of the vessel, or on or in front of the funnel, where it can best be seen, and at a height above the gunwale of not less than 9ft., a bright white light constructed and fixed as prescribed in Article 2 (a), and of such a character as to be visible at a distance of at least two miles.

(b) Green and red side-lights constructed and fixed as prescribed in Article 2 (b) and (c), and of such a character as to be visible at a distance of at least one mile, or a combined lantern showing a green light and a red light from right ahead to 2 points abaft the beam on their respective sides. Such lantern shall be carried not less than 3ft. below the white light.

2. Small steamboats, such as are carried by sea-going vessels, may carry the white light at a less height than 9ft. above the gunwale, but it shall be carried above the combined lantern, mentioned in sub-division 1 (b.)

3. Vessels under oars or sails, of less than 20 tons, shall have ready at hand a lantern with a green glass on one side and a red glass on the other, which, on the approach of or to other vessels, shall be exhibited in sufficient time to prevent collision, so that the green light shall not be seen on the port side nor the red light on the starboard side.

4. Rowing boats, whether under oars or sail, shall have ready at hand a lantern showing a white light, which shall be temporarily exhibited in sufficient time to prevent collision.

The vessels referred to in this Article shall not be obliged to carry the lights prescribed by Article 4 (*a*), and Article 11, last paragraph.

Art. 8. Pilot vessels, when engaged on their station on pilotage duty, shall not show the lights required for other vessels, but shall carry a white light at the masthead, visible all round the horizon, and shall also exhibit a flare-up light or flare-up lights at short intervals, which shall never exceed fifteen minutes.

On the near approach of or to other vessels they shall have their side-lights lighted, ready for use, and shall flash or show them at short intervals, to indicate the direction in which they are heading, but the green light shall not be shown on the port side, nor the red light on the starboard side.

A pilot vessel of such a class as to be obliged to go alongside of a vessel to put a pilot on board, may show the white light instead of carrying it at the masthead, and may, instead of the coloured lights above mentioned, have at hand ready for use a lantern with a green glass on the one side and a red glass on the other, to be used as prescribed above.

Pilot vessels when not engaged on their station on pilotage duty, shall carry lights similar to those of other vessels of their tonnage.

Art. 9.*

Art. 10. A vessel which is being overtaken by another shall show from her stern to such last-mentioned vessel a white light or a flare-up light.

The white light required to be shown by this Article may be fixed and carried in a lantern, but in such case the lantern shall be so constructed, fitted, and screened that it shall throw an unbroken light over an arc of the horizon of 12 points of the compass, viz., for 6 points from right aft on each side of the vessel, so as to be carried as nearly as practicable on the same level as the side lights.

Art. 11. A vessel under 150ft. in length, when at anchor, shall carry forward, where it can best be seen, but at a height not exceeding 20ft. above the hull, a white light in a lantern so constructed as to show a clear, uniform, and unbroken light visible all round the horizon at a distance of at least one mile.

A vessel of 150ft. or upwards in length, when at anchor, shall carry in the forward part of the vessel, at a height of not less than 20, and not exceeding 40, feet above the hull, one such light, and at or near the stern of the vessel, and at such a height that it shall be not less than 15ft. lower than the forward light, another such light.

The length of a vessel shall be deemed to be the length appearing in her certificate of registry.

A vessel aground in or near a fairway shall carry the above light or lights and the two red lights prescribed by Article 4 (*a*).

Art. 12. Every vessel may, if necessary in order to attract attention, in addition to the lights which she is by these rules required to carry, show a flare-up light or use any detonating signal that cannot be mistaken for a distress signal.

Art. 13. Nothing in these rules shall interfere with the operation of any special rules made by the Government of any nation with respect to additional station and signal lights for two or more ships of war or for vessels sailing under convoy, or with the exhibition of recognition signals adopted by shipowners, which have been authorised by their respective Governments and duly registered and published.

Art. 14. A steam vessel proceeding under sail only, but having her funnel up, shall carry in daytime, forward, where it can best be seen, one black ball or shape 2ft. in diameter.

Sound-Signals for Fog, &c.

Art. 15. All signals prescribed by this Article for vessels under way shall be given :

1. By "steam vessels" on the whistle or siren.

2. By "sailing vessels and vessels towed" on the fog-horn.

The words "prolonged blast" used in this Article shall mean a blast of from four to six seconds duration.

A steam vessel shall be provided with an efficient whistle or siren, sounded by steam or some substitute for steam, so placed that the sound may not be intercepted by any obstruction, and with an efficient fog-horn, to be sounded by mechanical means, and also with an efficient bell.* A sailing vessel of 20 tons gross tonnage or upwards shall be provided with a similar fog-horn and bell.

In fog, mist, falling snow, or heavy rain storms, whether by day or night, the signals described in this Article shall be used as follows, viz. :

(*a*.) A steam vessel having way upon her, shall sound, at intervals of not more than two minutes, a prolonged blast.

---

* This Article will deal with regulations affecting fishing boats, and will be the subject of another Order, which will be submitted to Her Majesty for approval at a later date.

* In all cases where the rules require a bell to be used a drum may be substituted on board Turkish vessels, or a gong where such articles are used on board small sea-going vessels.

Rules of the Road—continued.

(b.) A steam vessel under way, but stopped and having no way upon her, shall sound, at intervals of not more than two minutes, two prolonged blasts, with an interval of about one second between them.

(c.) A sailing vessel under way shall sound, at intervals of not more than one minute, when on the starboard tack one blast, when on the port tack two blasts in succession, and when with the wind abaft the beam three blasts in succession.

(d.) A vessel, when at anchor, shall, at intervals of not more than one minute, ring the bell rapidly for about five seconds.

(e.) A vessel, when towing, a vessel employed in laying or in picking up a telegraph cable, and a vessel under way, which is unable to get out of the way of an approaching vessel through being not under command, or unable to manœuvre as required by these rules shall, instead of the signals prescribed in sub-divisions (a) and (c) of this Article, at intervals of not more than two minutes, sound three blasts in succession, viz., one prolonged blast followed by two short blasts. A vessel towed may give this signal, and she shall not give any other.

Sailing vessels and boats of less than 20 tons gross tonnage shall not be obliged to give the above-mentioned signals, but if they do not, they shall make some other efficient sound signal at intervals of not more than one minute.

Speed of Ships to be Moderate in Fog, &c.

Art. 16. Every vessel shall, in a fog, mist, falling snow, or heavy rain storms, go at a moderate speed, having careful regard to the existing circumstances and conditions.

A steam vessel hearing, apparently forward of her beam, the fog signal of a vessel, the exact position of which is not ascertained, shall, so far as the circumstances of the case admit, stop her engines, and then navigate with caution until danger of collision is over.

STEERING AND SAILING RULES.

Preliminary—Risk of Collision.

Risk of collision can, when circumstances permit, be ascertained by carefully watching the compass bearing of an approaching vessel. If the bearing does not appreciably change, such risk should be deemed to exist.

Art. 17. When two sailing vessels are approaching one another, so as to involve risk of collision, one of them shall keep out of the way of the other, as follows, viz.:

(a.) A vessel which is running free shall keep out of the way of a vessel which is close-hauled.

(b.) A vessel which is close-hauled on the port tack shall keep out of the way of a vessel which is close-hauled on the starboard tack.

(c.) When both are running free, with the wind on different sides, the vessel which has the wind on the port side shall keep out of the way of the other.

(d.) When both are running free, with the wind on the same side, the vessel which is to windward shall keep out of the way of the vessel which is to leeward.

(e.) A vessel which has the wind aft shall keep out of the way of the other vessel.

Art. 18. When two steam vessels are meeting end on, or nearly end on, so as to involve risk of collision, each shall alter her course to starboard, so that each may pass on the port side of the other.

This article only applies to cases where vessels are meeting end on, or nearly end on, in such a manner as to involve risk of collision, and does not apply to two vessels which must, if both keep on their respective courses, pass clear of each other.

The only cases to which it does apply are, when each of the two vessels is end on, or nearly end on, to the other; in other words, to cases in which, by day, each vessel sees the masts of the other in a line, with her own; and by night, to cases in which each vessel is in such a position as to see both the side lights of the other.

It does not apply, by day, to cases in which a vessel sees another ahead crossing her own course; or by night, to cases where the red light of one vessel is opposed to the red light of the other, or where the green light of one vessel is opposed to the green light of the other, or where a red light without a green light, or a green light without a red light, is seen ahead, or where both green and red lights are seen anywhere but ahead.

Art. 19. When two steam vessels are crossing, so as to involve risk of collision, the vessel which has the other on her own starboard side shall keep out of the way of the other.

Art. 20. When a steam vessel and a sailing vessel are proceeding in such directions as to involve risk of collision, the steam vessel shall keep out of the way of the sailing vessel.

Art. 21. Where by any of these rules one of two vessels is to keep out of the way, the other shall keep her course and speed.

Note.—When, in consequence of thick weather or other causes, such vessel finds herself so close that collision cannot be avoided by the action of the giving-way vessel alone, she also shall take such action as will best aid to avert collision. (See Articles 27 and 29.)

Art. 22. Every vessel which is directed by these rules to keep out of the way of another vessel, shall, if circumstances of the case admit, avoid crossing ahead of the other.

Art. 23. Every steam vessel which is directed by these rules to keep out of the way of another vessel shall, on approaching her, if necessary, slacken her speed or stop or reverse.

Art. 24. Notwithstanding anything contained in these rules, every vessel, overtaking any other shall keep out of the way of the overtaken vessel.

    Every vessel coming up with another vessel from any direction more than 2 points abaft her beam, *i.e.*, in such a position, with reference to the vessel which she is overtaking that at night she would be unable to see either of that vessel's side lights, shall be deemed to be an overtaking vessel; and no subsequent alteration of the bearing between the two vessels shall make the overtaking vessel a crossing vessel within the meaning of these rules, or relieve her of the duty of keeping clear of the overtaken vessel until she is finally past and clear.

    As by day the overtaking vessel cannot always know with certainty whether she is forward of or abaft this direction from the other vessel, she should, if in doubt, assume that she is an overtaking vessel and keep out of the way.

Art. 25. In narrow channels every steam vessel shall, when it is safe and practicable, keep to that side of the fair-way or mid-channel which lies on the starboard side of such vessel.

Art. 26. Sailing vessels under way shall keep out of the way of sailing vessels or boats fishing with nets, or lines, or trawls. This rule shall not give to any vessel or boat engaged in fishing the right of obstructing a fairway used by vessels other than fishing vessels or boats.

Art. 27. In obeying and construing these rules, due regard shall be had to all dangers of navigation and collision, and to any special circumstances which may render a departure from the above rules necessary in order to avoid immediate danger.

Sound Signals for Vessels in Sight of one Another.

Art. 28. The words "short blast" used in this Article shall mean a blast of about one second's duration.

When vessels are in sight of one another, a steam vessel under way, in taking any course authorised or required by these rules, shall indicate that course by the following signals on her whistle or siren, viz.:

One short blast to mean, "I am directing my course to starboard."

Two short blasts to mean, "I am directing my course to port."

Three short blasts to mean, "My engines are going full speed astern."

No Vessel under any Circumstances to Neglect Proper Precautions.

Art. 29. Nothing in these rules shall exonerate any vessel, or the owner, or master, or crew thereof, from the consequences of any neglect to carry lights or signals, or of any neglect to keep a proper look-out, or of the neglect of any precaution which may be required by the ordinary practice of seamen, or by the special circumstances of the case.

Open Boats and Fishing Vessels.

Art. 10. Open boats and fishing vessels of less than 20 tons net registered tonnage, when under way and when not having their nets, trawls, dredges, or lines in the water, shall not be obliged to carry the coloured side lights; but every such boat and vessel shall in lieu thereof have ready at hand a lantern with a green glass on the one side and a red glass on the other side, and on approaching to or being approached by another vessel such lantern shall be exhibited in sufficient time to prevent collision, so that the green light shall not be seen on the port side nor the red light on the starboard side.

The following portion of this Article applies only to fishing vessels and boats when in the sea off the coast of Europe lying north of Cape Finisterre:

(a.) All fishing vessels and fishing boats of 20 tons net registered tonnage, or upwards, when under way and when not required by the following regulations in this Article to carry and show the lights therein named, shall carry and show the same lights as other vessels under way.

(b.) All vessels when engaged in fishing with drift nets shall exhibit two white lights from any part of the vessel where they can be best seen. Such lights shall be placed so that the vertical distance between them shall be not less than 6ft. and not more than 10ft.; and so that the horizontal distance between them measured in a line with the keel of the vessel shall be not less than 5ft. and not more than 10ft. The lower of

Rules of the Road—continued.

these two lights shall be the more forward, and both of them shall be of such a character, and contained in lanterns of such construction as to show all round the horizon, on a dark night with a clear atmosphere, for a distance of not less than three miles.

(c.) A vessel employed in line fishing with her lines out shall carry the same lights as a vessel when engaged in fishing with drift nets.

(d.) If a vessel when fishing becomes stationary in consequence of her gear getting fast to a rock or other obstruction, she shall show the light and make the fog signal for a vessel at anchor.

(e.) Fishing vessels and open boats may at any time use a flare-up in addition to the lights which they are by this Article required to carry and show. All flare-up lights exhibited by a vessel when trawling, dredging, or fishing with any kind of drag net shall be shown at the after part of the vessel, excepting that, if the vessel is hanging by the stern to her trawl, dredge, or drag net, they shall be exhibited from the bow.

(f.) Every fishing vessel and every open boat when at anchor between sunset and sunrise shall exhibit a white light visible all round the horizon at a distance of at least one mile.

(g.) In fog, mist, or falling snow, a drift net vessel attached to her nets, and a vessel when trawling, dredging, or fishing with any kind of drag net, and a vessel employed in line fishing with her lines out, shall at intervals of not more than two minutes make a blast with her fog horn and ring her bell alternately.

Run.—The under part of a vessel aft defined by the buttock lines and water lines.

Run.—To sail before the wind. To come down by the run is to lower or overhaul without warning, or suddenly. To run away with a rope is to take hold of a fall and haul on it by running along the deck. Among sailors an agreement to work a single passage for so much money, independent of the time occupied.

Run Down.—To foul a vessel or other object wrongfully or by accident.

Run Foul Of.—To get into collision with a vessel or other object.

Run Out.—To veer out a warp or cable.

Run Over.—The same as run down. Generally denoting carelessness in bringing about a collision.

Runners.—A rope passed through a single block on a pendant with a purchase at one end. Also seamen who sail by the run.

Running Bowsprit.—A bowsprit that is fitted to run in and out and "reef" like a cutter's. Since 1856, most schooners have their bowsprits fitted in this way.

Running by the Lee.—To run with the boom on one quarter when the wind is blowing on the other quarter. A dangerous proceeding. (See "By the Lee.")

Running Off her Helm.—Said of a vessel if, when sailing, her stern flies up to windward (her head apparently going off to leeward) and giving her lee helm does not readily bring her to.

Running Rigging.—The parts of the rigging made to overhaul or run through blocks, as distinct from that set up by lanyards, shackles, &c.

S.

Saddle.—A projection on a spar to support another spar, as the saddle on the mast for the jaws of the boom to rest upon.

Safety Cleats.—See "Cruickshank's Cleats."

Sagging.—Bending or curved downwards; the opposite of hogging. Sagging to leeward is to make a great deal of leeway.

Sail.—Often applied to a ship, or an assemblage of ships, as "We saw ten sail off Ushant." (See "Sails.")

Sail Coats.—Covers for sails, usually made of painted canvas. A yacht master named Carey introduced the following plan, but it has not been adopted: The sail covers fit tight.

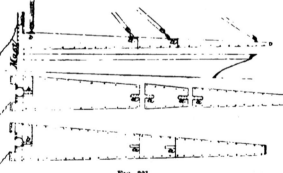

FIG. 321.

round the blocks, and by the parts overlapping one another at *a a* (Fig. 321) it is quite impossible that any wet should ever touch the sail; *b* shows the opening for the throat halyard block overlapped and laced. (See "Waterproofing.")

Sail Her Along.—In close-hauled sailing, an order given to the helmsman when he is keeping the vessel too close to wind, meaning that he is to keep her a little off; sail her fuller or harder or "give her the whole weight of it," meaning the wind, and keep her passing through the water as fast as possible.

Sail Her.—When lying to if way has to be got on again, the order is to "Sail her;" or, "Let the head sheets draw and sail her!" Also "Sail her" is a general admonition to a helmsman to be very careful in his steering. (See "Fill.")

Sailing Directions.—Books of pilotage which accompany charts.

Sailing on Skates.—In 1879 a gentleman, under the signature of "Glacianaut," published in *The Field* a description of a sail he had contrived for sailing on skates on ice. The sail is made of a piece of unbleached calico, with slightly rounded ends (Fig. 322); each end is attached (either by a lacing or by a wide hem, such as is common in window blinds) to a light stick or yard, of sufficient length

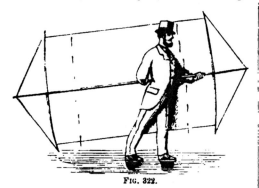

FIG. 322.

to stretch the sail. The sail is spread by a central mainyard, long enough to project 9in. beyond the sail at each end; this must be strong, stiff, and light, and must be fitted at each extremity with two stout eyes. A piece of stout line as a "lanyard" is made fast to the centre of each of the small yards, and rove through the eyes at the ends of the mainyard, then round the small yard, and through the eye again, finishing up with a "figure of eight seizing" round the main and small yards at the points where they cross one another. One lanyard is first rove and made fast, the other is then used as a purchase to strain the sail taut. The use of the rounded ends to the sail is now seen, as the small yards buckle when the strain of the purchase comes on them. To prevent the leaches of the sail from flapping, and to relieve the small yards, a light stay is led from each end of them to the extremity of the mainyard, and made fast to the second pair of eyes already mentioned. The size of sail for a gale is 6ft. by 3ft., 9ft. by 6ft. for light

wind; 7ft. 6in. by 5ft. is a good size for one skater to handle in ordinary wind. Two people can manage a sail together with great comfort. The 9ft. by 6ft. sail is none too large, and tall men could manage a larger one. Two rows of reef points would be a great addition, and might very easily be arranged. The sail must stand perfectly flat, and the yards and gear must be stout enough to bear the strain of setting everything up taut. In sailing alone, the skater should keep the greater part of his sail behind him; otherwise he will infallibly be taken aback if the wind is before the beam. Running before the wind needs no comment, but to work to windward satisfactorily and tack smoothly requires some practice.

When two go together, the front skater steers, and the other trims the canvas.

Tacking may be accomplished in two different ways:—When close hauled, say, on the starboard tack, the sail being on the leeside of the man, the right or weather foot will be in front, the other in a line behind it, the left hand will be forward, and the right (which answers to main sheet) holding the yard behind his back. When it becomes necessary to go about, by a slight inclination of his skates the skater luffs sharply, the sail shakes, the feet are changed, the hands remaining in the same position as before; the sail rapidly fills on the other side, and the skater shoots away smoothly on the port tack with his sail to windward of him. In moderate weather, the more smartly this is done the better. When blowing hard, it is necessary to take a wide sweep and shoot farther to windward in stays, running a little off the wind for a moment after filling away on the fresh tack. When tacking in this manner the yard will be alternately to windward and to leeward of the sail. In the former of these positions, the strain on it becomes very great; and for this, as well as other reasons, it may be desirable to tack in the other way, as follows:

When close hauled with the sail to windward of the man, and desiring to go about without bringing the wind on the other side of the sail, the skater, instead of luffing, turns his skates to leeward, keeping the sail spread behind his back, and running for a moment right before the wind. While in this position he rapidly shifts his hands along the yard until he reaches the point at which the balance of his head and after canvas becomes correct (this is a most important consideration). What was the after hand on the other tack becomes the fore hand now, and what was the leach now becomes the luff of the sail. With a slight turning of his skates to windward, and trimming his canvas accordingly, the skater hauls his wind in a moment, and shoots away on the fresh tack. This plan is recommended for sailing single-handed, and the former for two people.

Changing feet is perfectly easy; one foot can be slid in front of the other at any time.

Sailing on Skates—continued.

Any skates that are sure not to come off (as Acme often do) will answer equally well.

When close hauled, the skater keeps by far the greater portion of the sail behind him; when reaching, he pushes it more forward. This answers to setting a big jib; and when running, he stands right in the middle.

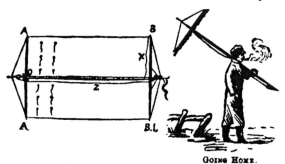

GOING HOME.

FIG. 323.

A Boom fixed. B Gaff. BB.1. Stay fixed. x End of stay which is made fast to gaff when under full sail. z Rope to pull up sail, made fast at O. (Fig. 323.)

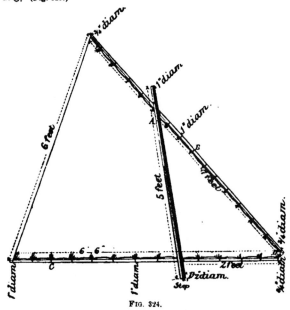

FIG. 324.

The following appeared in the *Field*, Dec. 4, 1880, as an improvement on the foregoing: (Fig. 324.)

"The mast is made 10ft. long, of deal, as thick as 'the long cue' (billiards) a little above the handle, tapering towards each end. At 1ft. distance from one end is fixed a yard, called the 'boom,' with a figure of 8 seizing, of stout whipcord and stays. To this is lashed a sail 8½ft. long, and 5ft. broad; my

other yard, the gaff, runs up and down the mast, having an iron hoop driven into it, the yard being bound with fine wire to prevent it splitting. In the sail is a double set of reefs at the distance of 1ft., and 2ft. from the boom. The yard is run up by means of a double block at the head of the mast, through one sheave of which runs the rope for pulling up, and through the other the stays. The advantage of having the sail this way is that in a stiff breeze one can go under 6½ft. of canvas, while in a light wind one can have 8½ft. Also lastly, and by no means the least advantage, when going home the whole sail can be reefed up to the boom, and put the mast over the shoulder like a shrimp net. To one end of the gaff the stay is fixed for good, so that in altering the reef, taking in or letting out, one has only one fixing of the stay, and when packing up the stay drawn through the block serves as a cord to tie up the whole sail to the boom."

The following description of a hand sail for sailing on ice appeared in the New York *Spirit of the Times*, Feb. 21, 1880:

"The first thing to be done after obtaining the sail, spars, &c., is to procure a strap about 1½in. wide, with a loop to act as a step for the mast; secure it round the ankle of the left foot, then step the mast, after which pass the left arm around the mast at A (Fig. 324) and hold it firmly to the body, then hold the yard with the right hand at B. This is done for the purpose of handling the sail, instead of sheet ropes at C, which could not be used. The boom and yard do not need to be connected at D, but merely held together by means of the stops on the sail. The boom and yard may be secured to the mast with small pieces of cord, or any other way the operator may think fit, for conveniently stowing his miniature sail while in transit. The spars should be of pine, thus making them much lighter to carry. The sail may be made of strong factory or twill cotton, and can be bent on the spars in the ordinary manner, with stops. It is not necessary to change the sail from one side of the body to the other when sailing on the port or starboard tacks, as the operator can more easily handle the yard with the right hand.

"It is usual when sailing to put one foot in front of the other, but the rule is not absolutely necessary. The strap around the ankle should be placed about one foot above the ice, or wherever the operator finds it more convenient for his height."

Sails.—Sails in this country are usually made of flax in the form of canvas, but several racing yachts since 1886 have had cotton sails. In America nothing but cotton canvas was formerly used; but since 1881 several suits of flax canvas have been sent to America by Messrs. Lapthorn and Ratsey. In 1851 the yacht America came here, and the superiority of the cut, make, and sit of her cotton canvas revolutionised sail making in England. In 1881 the cutter Madge visited America, and her flax sails were considered so superior to those of American yachts, that her success was partly ascribed to her English suit of Lapthorn sails. Cotton stretches slightly less than flax; but the objection to it is that in case of rain it takes up so much water and is not so durable as flax, and old cotton sails are fit for little else than the rag merchant. Information on the cutting out and making of yacht and boat sails will be found in Kipping's treatise on "Sail Making," 2s. 6d., Weale's Series.

St. Andrew's Flag.—A blue flag with white diagonal cross, thus ✕.

St. George's Jack.—A white square flag with red St. George's cross (right angled, thus ✚), used by admirals in the Royal Navy. A vice-admiral's flag has one red ball, and rear-admiral's two (horizontally). An admiral flies his flag from the main, vice from the fore, rear from mizen. St. George's Jack was the English flag before the union with Scotland and Ireland. (See "Admiral" and "Jack.")

St. Patrick's Cross.—A red diagonal cross, ✕.

Salt and Fresh Water.—A cubic foot of salt water weighs 64lb.; a ton contains 35 cubic feet. A cubic foot of fresh water weighs 62·5lb.; a ton contains 36 cubic feet: hence salt water bulk for bulk will sustain a greater weight. When a vessel goes from salt water to fresh she is sometimes lightened in ballast, in order that she may present the same surface for friction. There will be a loss of stability, and on the whole the practice is of doubtful utility. Regarding the case inversely, if a vessel be loaded down in salt water to the same depth that she has been floating in fresh water, and driven at the same speed, the resistance will increase in ratio to the superior density of salt water. No exact experiments have been made to ascertain whether a vessel, by floating somewhat lighter in salt than in fresh water, meets with a decrease of resistance. The comparison would be always attended with difficulty, as, if there were a difference in the resistance, it would be a very complicated matter unravelling it, as it would be necessary to know how much of the resistance depended on skin friction, and how much on wave making. We are inclined to think that the resistance (taking weight for weight) is a trifle less in salt water than in fresh. By removing weight, so as to float at the same load line as in salt water, the resistance in fresh water would be less, but the question of diminished stability, which removing weight involves, is such a serious

matter that removing weight for river sailing cannot be advised. (See "Yacht Architecture,' page 384.)

Salute.—A salvo of cannon fired as a mark of respect and honour to a royal personage, commodore, vice or rear commodore, flag, &c. A Royal Salute is twenty-one guns; admiral of the fleet, seventeen; admiral, fifteen; vice-admiral, thirteen; rear-admiral, eleven; commodore (no senior captain being present. See "Burgee."), nine; captains or other officers are not saluted. A captain or other officers' salute is returned with seven guns.

Among yacht clubs it is usual to salute a flag officer on his first hoisting his flag (swallow-tail burgee) on a club station at the beginning of a season, on his shifting his flag or on his promotion, and when he hauls it down at the end of a season, by eleven guns for a commodore, nine for a vice-commodore, and seven for a rear-commodore respectively. The club ensign is hoisted on the club flag-staff during the salute. It is unusual to salute a vice or rear commodore in the presence of a commodore, and if the commodore and vice or rear arrive together, neither of the latter is saluted. The Royal Cork Yacht Club has, however, a rule that a vice or rear can be saluted after a commodore has returned his salute. A commodore replies to a club salute, or to a salute by a squadron, with one salute of the number of guns he is entitled to. He returns a vice or rear commodore's salute with the guns each is entitled to, unless he receives a salute from both, then he returns with the number of guns he himself is entitled to. Strictly, however, the rear should not salute the commodore in the presence of the vice unless he obtains permission from the vice to do so. The regulation of the Royal Navy is that no salute is to be fired without permission of the senior officer present, except salutes to the senior officer himself; and further, if a salute has to be fired, only the senior officer of two or more yachts in company is to fire the salute. It is etiquette for a flag-officer of a club to return a salute, but a royal personage does not do so. The practice used to be for a yacht to "salute the flag" on arriving at a station; this practice is still in vogue in America, a junior always saluting first. If a winning yacht is saluted, it should be with five guns. A duke is saluted with fifteen guns, and any other nobleman thirteen.

The rule in the "Queen's Regulations" for a funeral salute is to fire the number of guns the officer would have been entitled to if alive.

Merchant ships are supposed to salute H.M.S. by striking topsails or any upper sail, such as a royal or top-gallant sail; but the practice is now little observed except by old-fashioned seamen, the dipping of an ensign being all that is done. In the old Queen's regulations for salutes we find the following obsolete instructions:

"If any of Her Majesty's subjects shall so far forget their duty as to attempt to pass

Salute—continued.

any of Her Majesty's ships without striking their topsails, the names of the ship and the master, the port to which they belong, the place from which they came, and that to which they are bound, together with affidavits of the fact, are to be sent to the secretary of the Admiralty, in order to their being proceeded against in the Admiralty Court."

If a merchant ship salutes a naval officer with the guns he is entitled to, the naval officer responds with five guns ; or seven if there are several merchant ships. A merchant ship now usually salutes a man-of-war by dipping the ensign ; the ensign is dipped (almost hauled down) and kept down until the man-of-war responds. This is repeated three times ; but some merchant ships only trouble to dip once, and then of course the man-of-war only responds once. (See " Dipping the Ensign ; " see also the " Queen's Regulations for the Royal Navy," to be obtained of Messrs. Harrison and Sons, St. Martin's-lane.)

Save All.—A water sail ; a sail set underneath booms in light weather.

Scandalize a Mainsail.—The peak is dropped down between the topping lifts until square to the mast and the main tack triced up. Sometimes the throat is lowered also.

Scant.—When the wind is very bare ; when the wind comes so that a vessel will barely lie her course.

Scantlings.—The dimensions of all kinds of timber used in the construction of a vessel.

Scarph or Scarf, or Scarve.—A method of joining pieces of wood by tapering their ends. A box scarph is when the ends are not tapered, but a half thickness cut out of each part so that when put together the parts form only one thickness.

Schooner.—A fore-and-aft rigged vessel. A topsail schooner has yards on her foremast, and sometimes on her mainmast, but no courses. It is claimed that the Schooner originated in America in 1713 in this way :—One Andrew Robinson (probably a Scotchman), built a vessel at Gloucester, Massachusetts, and as she was launched into the water a bystander said "How she scoons." The sharp-eared Mr. Robinson, with ready wit responded " A scooner let her be !" Webster in his dictionary, says that this story is well authenticated, because Mr. Moses Prince, eight years later, referred to Mr. Robinson as the " first contriver of scooners," and Moses Prince then went on to say " how mankind is obliged to this gentleman for this knowledge ; " but it can be doubted if mankind had felt any considerable benefit from schooners, recollecting the Baltimore clippers. Webster says the man exclaimed, " How she scoons " because the Scotch word " scon " is to skim as a flat stone will when thrown upon the water. Webster says this word "scon" might have been an Icelandic word " skunda," to make haste.

[The German "schäumen," to skim, and French, " écumer," to skim, are also relevant. The term " eskomer," often applied to fast sailers, was probably an old buccaneer term for their vessels ; hence the French Ecumeur, a corsair or sea rover. The word " eskomer " may have been derived from the Latin "scomber," a mackerel.] The probability is that schooner was derived from the Dutch " schoon," or rather the feminine " schoone," the final " e " being pronounced with a sound of " a " and as a syllable, meaning elegant, fair, beautiful, a belle, &c. ; " schoor," a forestay ; " schoornen," rowers), &c. Webster, without giving any authority, says that the Danish " skooner," German " schoner," and the Spanish " escuna," were all derived from the English, that is from the Englishman or Scotchman who built the " scooner " in Massachusetts. The Swedish for schooner is " skonare ; " but whether that was also derived from the term invented by Mr. Robinson is not recorded by Webster, and altogether the assertion about the derivation is open to very grave doubt. There is no question that this is a very cut-and-dried story about the bystander and Mr. Robinson, and most people will incline to the belief, in spite of the evidence of Mr. Moses Prince, that the word schooner is of Dutch origin. In the seventeenth century, according to Charnock, they had a number of two-masted vessels called " schoots ; " and in old English chronicles of the fifteenth and sixteenth century we find ships called " schippes," and shipmasters " schippers," now skippers ; and most likely there were schooters from schoots, and schooners from schoon. The mere fact of Mr. Robinson exclaiming " a schooner let her be," does not prove that the term did not exist before his exclamation was made, but rather shows that the term was a familiar one, and, as previously said, most people will believe that it is of Dutch origin.

Mr. Robinson's claim to be the inventor of the rig can also be very well disputed, as there is no doubt that the rig was an adaptation of the brigantine which had its origin as follows. In the Cotton MSS. is a note of the ships Henry VIII. possessed, and, in reference to the " Great Henry Grace à Dieu," as she is therein called, which was built at Erith, is the following : " being in good reparation, caulking except, so that she may be laid in dock at all times when the same shall be ready, and Brigandyn, the clerk of the ship, doth say, that before the said ship shall be laid in the dock, it is necessary that her mast be taken down and bestowed in the great store house at Erith." Now this Brigandyn was the inventor of the brigantyne rig : and in the Harl. MSS. in a passage relating to the state of Edward VI.'s navy is the following : " Item, the two gallies and the brigandyn must be yearly repaired." This brigandyn was as a matter of certainty named after " Brigandyn, the clerk of the ship ; " and in Charles II. reign there were five of them in the Royal Navy, named Discovery,

Dispatch, Diligence, Shark, and Spy, of about 80 tons. The rig, as depicted in old prints, represents them with a fore-and-aft main, and fore sail and square topsails, much the same as the topsail schooners of a later date.

In the Navy List of 1800 we find no brigantines, but the names of about seventy brigs and the names of about fifty schooners. The oldest of these schooners appear to have been built at New York in 1764, and between that year and 1777 (the year of hostilities with the American Colonies), the British Government bought eighteen schooners, and most likely all in America, where also many of the brigs came from, though most were built in England. There is not the smallest doubt that the English settlers in America had done much to improve both the rig and build of the brigantines, and in reference to this matter Charnock (1800 edition) says:

"On account of the constructors' attention being directed almost solely to one point, and owing to a certain portion of skill which they possessed, and had derived from a long experience in the art of building, with regard to swiftness only, the heavy sailing vessels employed in the purposes of British commerce fell before them an easy prey. . . . The American marine, however, soared not, but with very few exceptions, in its private capacity beyond the classes of brigs and schooners, those of the former denomination proving particularly destructive. Their dimensions were enlarged far beyond those limits which it had been customary to give vessels in that class, and their force on many occasions exceeded the greater part of the British sloops of war, nearly equalling some of the minor frigates. In defiance of the common prejudice then entertained against long and narrow vessels, the American builders ventured their opposition; and the success which attended the principles they introduced, materially differing from the practice of any country at that time, proved their superior skill in the construction of corsairs."

In the early days of English yachting, many gentlemen attempted to emulate the famous American brigs and schooners, the latter almost invariably being rigged with square topsails, until about 1840. The one point of sailing, however, which Americans had studied, "sailing close by the wind," seems to have been much neglected, and when the America, schooner, built in 1850, arrived in England in 1851, we had not a schooner which was fit to compete with her. The America was designed by Mr. G. Steers (the son of a Devonshire shipwright, who learned his trade at Dartmouth, Plymouth, and Guernsey) on principles expounded by the late Mr. Scott Russell from about the year 1834, and exemplified in a few English yachts, notably in the Mosquito, built in 1847. The fault of Mr. Scott Russell's designs, as exemplified in the Titania, was the short hollow entrance he attempted to demonstrate his theory by, although he kept the midship section well aft. This was not apparent in

the America. But the genius of George Steers, the Devonshire naval architect, appears to have died with him in 1856, as certainly there are no American yachts built since which can claim any improvement on that famous vessel, whether they be centre-boarders or otherwise.

Sciatic Stay.—According to old authorities this is synonymous with Triatic stay, which see.

Scope.—Length or drift of rope or cable.

Score.—A groove to receive a rope or strop, &c.

Scowing an Anchor.—When small boats have to anchor on ground known or suspected to be foul, it will always be prudent to scow the anchor (Fig. 325). Unbend the cable from the ring, and make the end fast round the crown, shank, and flukes with a clove hitch, and bring the end *a* back to *s*, and stop it round the cable with spun yarn or hitches; take the cable back to the shackle and stop it as at *b*; when the cable is hauled upon by the part *o* the stop at *b* will break, and the fluke of the anchor can be readily lifted out of its bed. Sometimes,

Fig. 325.

instead of scowing the anchor a trip line is bent to the crown and buoyed. (See "Anchor.")

Screens.—The wood shelves and screens painted red for port side, and green for starboard, in which a vessel's side lights are carried. (See "Side lights.")

Scroll Head.—The outward curved part of the knee at the upper fore part of the stem, called volute.

Scud.—To run before a gale of wind with very little canvas set, or "under bare poles."

Scull.—An oar. To scull is to propel a boat by working an oar over the centre of the transom on the principle of the screw.

Scuppers.—Apertures cut in the bulwarks or waterways to clear the deck of water.

Sea, A.—A wave. A heavy sea is when the waves are large and steep. When a quantity of water falls aboard a vessel it is said that "she shipped a sea."

Sea Boat.—A vessel fit to go to sea. A good sea boat is a relative term, and means a vessel that does not pitch badly or labour in a sea, or does not ship much water, and is, above all things, handy in a sea.

Sea, Depth of.—The soundings taken during the voyage of the "Challenger" added greatly to our knowledge of the sea depth. The following conclusions are stated in Moseley's Notes by a Naturalist on the "Challenger":

We are apt to form an erroneous impression as to the actual shapes and distributions of the elevations and depressions on the earth's surface, because only the very tops of the elevation stand above water. The outlines of the various continents and islands with which we are familiar on maps are merely lines marking the height to which the water reaches up. A very small proportion of the elevated masses projects above water, hence from an ordinary map we gain no truer impression of the form of the sculpturing of the surface of the earth itself than we should of a range of mountains if we viewed it when all but its summits were hidden by a flood.

So small a proportion does the mass of dry land elevated above the sea level bear to the hollows on the earth's surface beneath this level, that the cavities now occupied by the sea would contain three times the volume of the earth existing above the sea surface.

If the surface of the land and the sea bottom were brought to a complete level, the waters of the sea covering its even face would still have a depth of 1700 fathoms, being reduced in depth by the process only about 800 fathoms.

Although the depth of the ocean is so small in proportion to the vastness of its expanse, the depth is, nevertheless, so great as to be difficult of adequate realisation. The greatest depth as yet ascertained by sounding occurs in the North-west Pacific Ocean; it amounts to about five miles and a quarter.

The average depth of the ocean between 60° N. and 60° S. is about three miles, or 2500 fathoms. The great depth of five miles occurs only exceptionally over very small areas.

No sunlight penetrates the deep sea; probably all is dark below 200 fathoms, at least excepting in so far as light is given out by phosphorescent animals.

At depths of 2000 fathoms and upward the temperature of the water is never many degrees above the freezing point. The conditions under which life exists in the deep sea are very remarkable. The pressure exerted by the water at great depths is enormous, amounting roughly to a ton weight on the square inch for every 1500 fathoms of depth. Sir C. Wyville Thompson ("Voyage of the Challenger," vol. ii., p. 352, London, 1877) gives, among the conclusions arrived at, after the first general survey of the deep sea collections of the expedition, that animal life is present on the bottom of the ocean at all depths, but is not nearly so abundant at extreme as at more moderate depths. Moseley mentions the dredging of a fish from 2500 fathoms, which had a deep-sea shrimp in its stomach.

Seam.—The line formed by the meeting of two planks; overlapping parts of canvas in a sail.

Seaman.—A man trained in the art of sailing, rigging, and general management of a ship.

To make a good seaman a man must have practised the multitudinous details of his art with great diligence, and is then described as an "able seaman" or A.B. To say a man is a "seaman" means that he is thoroughly conversant with every duty of a sailor's life, and can not only "hand, reef, and steer," but can do every kind of work upon rigging, and even use the needle and palm.

The statutes relating to seamen are very numerous, and many of them affect, or can be made to affect, yacht sailors: however, many of the provisions of the Merchant Shipping Acts are rendered inoperative so far as yacht sailors go, because the signing of articles is not imperative.

SAILING MASTERS.

The master, mate, or engineer of a yacht need not possess a Board of Trade certificate, as sect. 136 of the Act of 1854 and sect. 5 of the Act of 1862, which, in effect, provides that no home-trade passenger ship or foreign-going ship, shall proceed to sea without having certificated master and mates, does not in any way apply to pleasure yachts. The Board of Trade have, however, instituted voluntary examinations for persons who command their own pleasure yachts, not, be it observed, for those who are not yacht owners but who may be desirous of taking charge of a yacht. A yacht owner, passing a satisfactory examination in navigation and seamanship, will be presented by the Board of Trade with a certificate entitling him to command his own yacht, which is a useless privilege, as he can take command of his yacht with or without the examination or certificate. The practical value set upon these very useless certificates by the Board of Trade may be gathered from one of the conditions: "The certificate will not entitle the holder to command any vessel except the pleasure yacht of which he may be, at the time, owner."

In connection with this matter, it may interest supporters of women's rights to know that a large yacht sailed in 1891 and 1894 for the Mediterranean whose master, as appears by the articles, is a lady. Of course, in vessels of any size, the owner, when master, has a sailing master under him; and for all legal purposes the master, and not the sailing master, is the recognised authority.

In 1891 a case arose at Cowes in which the question was raised whether or not seamen were bound to obey orders given by the owner as master in opposition to the advice and wishes of the skipper of the yacht, who was entered on the articles as sailing master. In this case it could not be contended that the owner was competent to handle the vessel, and the question was put by the magistrates before whom the case was heard, whether or not the seamen would be bound to obey if the owner had given an order which was utterly absurd, and would place the vessel and themselves in jeopardy? In this case the men were convicted, but it is a point which may probably be raised again, and it appears there might be circumstances in which serious complications might arise. It is not legally necessary for yachting seamen to sign articles. In many cases it is done, but in still more it is not, and in consequence endless disputes arise as to what the terms of the hiring are. One of the most fruitful sources of discord is the ownership of the clothes supplied by the owner, and under what circumstances he has the right to detain them; and, in default of a provision in the articles, no one at the present moment appears to know whether they are the property of the owner or the men. Cases have frequently arisen with regard to the right to detain clothes where the men have misbehaved themselves. A claim came before a county court (a not very satisfactory tribunal in these matters) a few years back, in which the judge decided that the men were justified in disobeying orders because two or three men had deserted, and it would have been imprudent, with about twelve hands on board, to sail a schooner of 160 tons from Portsmouth Harbour to Cowes!

Then the existing law as to punishment for desertion is most inapplicable to yachting seamen. If a man deserts, the master has power to have him brought on board again, and he can forfeit any wages due to him, and his clothes and effects. This may work very well in the case of merchant seamen, but as regards yachtsmen the enactment is a farce. A merchant seaman usually has a considerable arrear of wages due to him after he has been any time upon his voyage, and the forfeiture may be a severe punishment; but the yachtsman is paid weekly, and the clothes are supplied by the owner, so the punishment does not amount to much. Moreover, what owner wishes to retain a man at all who is brought on board in the custody of the police? If he deserts, the owner will be a wise man, as matters are at present, to let him go and make some other owner uncomfortable, rather than have the trouble, risk, and annoyance of retaining him against his will.

If no articles are signed, the rights, remedies, and duties of the owner of a yacht, his sailing master, and crew, are governed by ordinary master and servant law. When a man has once engaged to serve on board a yacht, as sailing master or in any other capacity, he will render himself liable to an action for breach of contract if, without a sufficient reason, he should refuse to enter upon his duty. Thus, a person agreed with a firm of shipowners to go in their ship as surgeon, but subsequently refused to go, the shipowners succeeded in an action against him, recovering as damages the difference between the sum they would have paid the defendant and the sum they had to pay another surgeon: ("Richards v. Hayward," 2 Manning & Granger, 574.) So, too, should the owner of a yacht refuse to receive a man into his service after having promised to do so, the owner will be liable to an action at the suit of the man: ("Clarke v. Allatt," 4 C.B. 335.)

So long as anyone employed on board a yacht retains his situation, he is bound to obey the lawful commands of his employer, and to act in accordance with the terms of the contract of hiring; but circumstances may often arise which may render a discharge necessary, although nothing may have been done which would warrant a summary dismissal. Under such circumstances the question arises, what notice must be given? The answer must depend upon the position held by the persons to be dismissed, for the same rule would not necessarily hold good in the cases of the sailing master and a seaman. The law nowhere says what notice is to be given or required to put an end to a contract of hiring and service, for it assumes, as in all other contracts, that both parties will fulfil the terms of the contract into which they have entered, and that the service will endure for the time agreed upon; or, if no time has been specified, then the hiring is general and in contemplation of law one for a year, which can only be terminated by reasonable notice expiring at the end of some completed year's service: ("Forgan v. Burke," 4 Ir. C. & R. 495.) It is the duty of a jury to decide what is reasonable notice in each particular case. As a matter of fact, however, the custom of different callings so far controls the strict law, that there are now but few trades or professions in which a contract cannot be terminated by giving that notice which from continual adoption has grown to be the "custom of the trade." It is well that it should be so, for, as Chief Justice Erle has said ("Nicoll v. Graves," 33 L. J., C. P. 259), "Where the duties of the servant are such that he is required to be frequently near his employer, if any ill-feeling should arise between them, the presence of that servant would be a constant source of irritation to the employer; and, on the other hand, it may happen that a well-intentioned servant may have a dissatisfied employer constantly finding fault with him, and the sooner he is free from such service the greater will be his happiness." With regard to domestic or menial servants, it is a well-established custom that their contract of service may be determined *at any time* by giving a month's warning or paying a month's wages; and there have been several cases in which the courts have taken judicial notice of customs held to be proved in different callings, and subject to which the parties are taken to have contracted. So far as is known, it has never yet been decided in a superior court what is the customary notice in the yachting world in the case of a master of a yacht; but, as he is generally a yearly servant, it is probable that the courts would hold a three months' notice sufficient in any case. But something might turn upon the time of year at which the notice expired; for if the three months ended in the middle of the yachting season, it might be difficult for a master to obtain another berth before the commencement of the next season. But this remark only holds good in the absence of any

Seaman—continued.

express stipulation or usage. If either side can bring evidence of a custom—which must be proved to be generally known and acted upon—the decision would be in accordance with that custom.

All yacht servants, from the master to the boy, may be dismissed without wages for:

1. *Wilful disobedience* of any lawful command of the owner—"an offence," said Sir William Scott, "of the grossest kind: The Court would be particularly attentive to preserve that subordination and discipline on board of ship which is so indispensably necessary for the preservation of the whole service, and of every person in it. It would not, therefore, be a peremptory or harsh tone. . . that will ever be held by the Court to justify resistance." In "Spain *v.* Arnott" (2 Starkie, 256), a farm servant was dismissed because he refused to go to a place a mile off before dinner, dinner being then ready. Lord Ellenborough said: "If the servant persisted in refusing to obey his employer's orders, I think he was warranted in turning him away. . . It would be exceedingly inconvenient if the servant were to be permitted to set himself up to control his employer in his domestic regulations. . . After a refusal on the part of the servant to perform his work, the employer is not bound to keep him on as a burdensome and useless servant." So, too, a regimental messman, having once refused to serve up dinner until threatened with arrest, was held to have been rightly dismissed, although he offered an apology next morning: ("Churchward *v.* Chambers," 2 F. & F. 229.) Again, where a man agreed (under 5 & 6 Will. 4, c. 19) to serve as carpenter's mate of a vessel during a South Sea voyage, but refused to work except to an English port, the court held him to have been rightly discharged: ("Renno *v.* Bennett," 3 Q. B. 768.) And, lastly, it has been decided that an employer was warranted in dismissing a servant who persisted, contrary to the employer's orders, in going to visit a relation believed by her to be in a dying state: ("Turner *v.* Mason," 14 M. & W. 112.) In the case of a master of a yacht, it may be doubted whether the refusal to obey an order involving unnecessary danger would be a good ground of discharge; nor, it is apprehended, would the failure to comply strictly with a command warrant a summary course of procedure; as, for instance, if an owner ordered the master to make fast to one buoy, and he, perhaps for what he considered a good reason, made fast to another near at hand.

2. *Gross moral misconduct*, such as robbery, violence, continued insolence, or drunkenness: ("Cunningham *v.* Fonblanque," 6 C & P. 49; "Speck *v.* Phillips," 5 M. & W. 279; "Wire *v.* Wilson," 1 C. & R. 662.) On these matters Sir W. Scott said: "Drunkenness, neglect of duty, and disobedience are offences of a high nature, fully sufficient to justify discharge without notice. Drunkenness is an offence particularly obnoxious on board

ship, where the sober vigilant attention of every man is required. At the same time the Court cannot entirely forget that in a mode of life peculiarly exposed to severe peril and exertion, and therefore admitting in seasons of repose something of indulgence and refreshment, that indulgence and refreshment are naturally enough sought for by such persons in grosser pleasures of that kind: and therefore proof of a single act of intemperance, committed in port, is no conclusive proof of disability for general maritime employment:" ("The Exeter," 2 C. Robinson, 263.)

3. *Incompetence.*—When a man ships on board a yacht, there is on his part an implied warranty that he possesses sufficient skill for the work he undertakes. No express promise that he has the requisite skill is necessary, and should he be found incompetent he may be discharged without notice: ("Harmer *v.* Cornelius," 28 L. J., C. P. 85.) But the incompetence must be closely connected with the work he undertakes; for example, a master employed to take charge of a sailing yacht could not be summarily discharged because he happened to be unacquainted with the management of a steam yacht, or *vice versâ*; or because he did not know how to manage a trawl, &c.

4. *Permanent illness* is, according to the best authority, a ground of dismissal, "for there is no difference between a servant who will not, and a servant who cannot, perform the duty for which he was hired" ("Harmer *v.* Cornelius," *ante*; "Cuckson *v.* Stones," 28 L.J., Q.B. 25), but mere temporary indisposition will not justify discharge. If a master receives injury in the performance of his duties, he, like the crew, can claim medical attendance until he is cured or dies, and no deduction can be made from wages.

Should the master be *rightfully* discharged for misconduct while the yacht is away cruising, the owner is under no liability to pay his passage either to his home or to the place at which he was engaged; for the dismissal was brought about by the man's own misconduct, which is not to be a tax on the employer: ("Turner *v.* Robinson," 5 B. & Adolphus, 789.) Should the offender refuse to leave the vessel, he may be removed by force, but the services of a policeman should be sought for, as, if unnecessary violence be employed, it will amount to an assault on the man.

On the subject of clothes the law is that the property in them is in the yacht owner; when, therefore, the servant is dismissed for misconduct, he cannot claim to take his clothes. If, however, he be hired expressly for the season, or for a year, at stated wages and his clothes, he then becomes entitled to them at the expiration of the season, or of the year, as the case may be: ("Crocker *v.* Molyneux," 3 C. & P. 470.) Should a servant be guilty of returning the clothes supplied to him to the tailor or draper in exchange for money or private clothes, a yacht owner is only liable to pay for the garments actually supplied, and not for those given in exchange, and is entitled to set off against a subsequent account for clothes, the price of those supplied and paid for, but subsequently taken back by the tradesman : (" Hunter v. Berkeley," 7 C. & P. 413.) See cases tried in County Courts—Dublin, August, 1874 ; Torquay, Nov. 17, 1877 ; Newport, Isle of Wight, Aug. 6, 1878 ; Southampton, Dec. 10, 1878.

The strictly legal side of the question only has been dealt with ; the questions of expediency and bounty are left to individual taste.

Agreement.—A form of agreement suitable for an owner and master to enter into is herewith appended.

𝔐emorandum of 𝔄greement entered into this   day of   , one thousand   hundred   , between   , of   , and hereinafter termed the owner, on the one part, and   , mariner of   , and hereinafter termed the master, on the other part.

The owner agrees to engage the master to serve in that capacity on board the yacht   , and to pay him as wages the sum of   per   , the said wages to be paid [here insert " weekly," " monthly," " quarterly," as the case may be] ; and the owner agrees to supply the master each year the yacht is in commission during this agreement with   suits of clothes complete, as usually found for the master of a yacht ; and the owner agrees that the said clothes shall be the property of the master, unless the master is discharged for misconduct, or discharges himself during any period that the owner's yacht is in commission ; [and the owner agrees to find the sailing master in food and a reasonable quantity of beer or other drink, or the equivalent in money of such food and drink, for the period the owner's yacht is in commission during this agreement ;] and the said sailing master, on his part, agrees to enter and abide in the service of the owner for the wages and other considerations aforesaid, and to the best of his ability to maintain discipline, strict sobriety, cleanliness, and general good conduct in the crew on board the owner's yacht, and to keep the owner's yacht in a smart, tidy, clean, and yacht-like condition, and to incur no expense for the maintenance of the hull or equipment of the owner's yacht further than lawfully authorised by the owner, and to willingly, carefully, and skilfully take the owner's yacht to such places as the owner may desire her to be taken, either on the coasts of the British Isles or the coasts of   , between   and   ; and when the yacht is put out of commission during this agreement the master, assisted by the crew, agrees to dismantle her and carefully store all her equipment as directed and to frequently visit the owner's yacht for the purpose of ventilating, pumping, and generally preserving and taking care of her and her equipment in the period she is out of

commission during this agreement ; and it is further jointly agreed between the owner and master that the wages shall commence to be earned and continue to be paid as aforesaid, on and after the   day of   , one thousand   hundred and   ; and it is further jointly agreed between the owner and master that this agreement shall terminate upon either the owner or master giving   notice thereof, but the owner may summarily cancel the agreement and dismiss the master should the master wilfully disregard any of the owner's reasonable commands, or be guilty of any misconduct, such as drunkenness, quarrelsomeness, violence of conduct, smuggling, continued absence, or neglect of duty, breaches of this agreement, gross carelessness, extravagance, or incompetence.

(Signed)   Owner.

        Sailing Master.

Witness,   .

COOKS AND STEWARDS.

A curious point might arise with regard to cooks and stewards. On shore, both these functionaries would most certainly fall within the category of domestic servants, and would, therefore, be entitled to a month's warning, or payment of a month's wages ; but where the duration of the contract can only be inferred from the fact that the wages are paid weekly, it would be taken to be a weekly hiring, in which case a week's notice would suffice ; or, again, owing to the fact that they cannot obtain situations as readily as shore servants, it is just possible that they might be held entitled to the same notice as the master, if they were hired on the same terms by the year and paid at the same intervals.

What has been said only applies when there has been no special stipulation at the commencement of the service, or no proof of custom. If an agreement has been made, the parties are bound by it ; as there are no reported cases deciding what the custom is, the question is still in abeyance. Every yacht owner knows what he believes to be the custom, but until his idea has been supported in a court of law it is only a surmise.

CREWS UNDER THE MERCHANT SHIPPING ACTS.

Mercantile marine offices (formerly known as shipping offices), under the care of superintendents and deputy-superintendents, have been established for the purpose of affording facilities for engaging seamen by keeping registries of their names and characters, and for securing the presence on board at the proper time of the seamen engaged (sect. 124 of Act 1854). These offices are established at every seaport in the United Kingdom in which there is a local marine board, and the Board of Trade secures premises and

Seaman—continued.

arranges for the carrying on of the general business. In the absence of other premises, the business of the offices may be transacted at Custom Houses (sect. 128), and mercantile marine offices may be established in London at sailors' homes (sect. 129). As these sections are not among the excepted ones, they apply to pleasure yachts; but obviously they are more adapted to the requirements of merchant shipping than to yachting.

By sect. 272 of the Act of 1854 the Registrar-General of shipping and seamen is to keep a register of all persons who serve in ships "subject to the provisions of this Act." That section applies to yachts, and therefore every yacht owner should comply with the terms of sect. 273, and make out and sign a list in a form sanctioned by the Board of Trade, stating, amongst other information, (1) the number and date of the yacht's register, and her registered tonnage; (2) the length and general nature of the voyage; (3) the names, ages, and places of birth of the crew, including the master, and their occupation on board; (4) the names of any members of the crew who have died or otherwise ceased to belong to the ship, with the times, places, causes, and circumstances thereof; (5) the names of any members of the crew who have been maimed or hurt, with the times, places, causes, and circumstances thereof, and some other matters shown in the form, but with which yachtsmen will not often be concerned.

By the Merchant Shipping Act, 1867 (30 & 31 Vict. c. 124), sect. 4, the owner of every ship—in which, it must be remembered, pleasure yachts are included—navigating between the United Kingdom and any place out of the same shall, unless exempted by the Board of Trade, provide, and keep on the ship, a supply of medicines and medical stores, in accordance with the scale appropriate to the ship. Lime or lemon juice, obtained from a bonded warehouse, and containing 15 per cent. proof spirit, is also to be kept on board. The lime or lemon juice is to be served out to the crew, as soon as they have been at sea ten days (except during the time the ship is in harbour and the crew supplied with fresh provisions), at the rate of an ounce per man per day. By the 4th sub-section lime juice need not be carried on ships bound to European ports, or to ports in the Mediterranean Sea, or to ports on the Eastern coast of America north of the 35th degree of north latitude, and to islands or places in the Atlantic north of the same limit.

With regard to the expenses attendant on illness and death, sect. 228 of the Act of 1854, which is one of the sections of the third part of the Act to which pleasure yachts are made subject by the Act of 1862, provides (1) that the expense of providing the necessary surgical and medical advice, with attendance and medicine, for any member of the crew, including the master, receiving any hurt or injury in the service of

the ship, and the expense of his burial, shall be borne by the owner of the ship, without any deduction from the man's wages. (2) If a man is, on account of any illness, temporarily removed from the ship to prevent infection, or otherwise for the convenience of the ship, and subsequently returns to the ship, the expenses shall be defrayed by the owner of the vessel. (3) The owner of the vessel is to pay for all medicines and advice. (4) In all other cases any reasonable expense incurred by the owner for any seaman in respect of illness shall, if duly proved, be deducted from the seaman's wages. By sect. 8 of the Merchant Shipping Act, 1867, where a seaman is by reason of illness incapable of performing his duty, and it is proved that his illness, and consequent incapacity to work, arises through his own fault, then he is not entitled to his wages for the time during which he is incapacitated.

Having noticed how far what may be called the general provisions of the Merchant Shipping Acts affect yachtsmen, we must now direct attention to such of the provisions of those Acts as bear more particularly on the relationship between the yacht owner and his crew, and the maintenance of discipline on board; and for that reason are of importance in every case where a yacht is fitted out, for however short a time.

II. *Maintenance of discipline where no written articles or agreement is signed.*—The common and statute law, having regard to the innumerable difficulties that might arise on board a ship unless the government were, so to say, despotic, has clothed the master of a ship with a very wide authority; and even if his conduct should, in exceptional cases, have been harsher than circumstances absolutely required, courts of law having jurisdiction in the matter will require very strong proof that the master has abused his authority, before they will allow that his conduct is any justification for a seaman's misconduct. As we have already stated, sect. 13 of the Merchant Shipping Act of 1862 extends the operation of the third part of the Act of 1854 to yachts, so far as the provisions are applicable, and with the exception of certain sections. Amongst the enactments so rendered applicable to yachts are those contained in the third part of the Merchant Shipping Act, 1854, for the maintenance of discipline, although no agreement has been signed. In speaking of a master's authority over the crew, the author of Boyd's "Merchant Shipping Laws" says: "The rule of law is that a captain's authority over the crew . . . . is, in the strict sense of the word, undefined; or, as it has been termed, despotic. He may, in short, inflict any punishment which is reasonable; that is, any punishment which is necessary to insure obedience to his command in all lawful matters relating to the navigation of the ship, and the preservation of good order . . . . The question must be one of fact, viz., whether the captain has used his power immoderately. The law is very favourable for captains, their power is most extensive, and they are only liable to punishment if they exercise it wrongly."

The following are some of the more important provisions of the Act of 1854 for maintaining discipline: Any master, seaman, or apprentice—which, by virtue of the interpretation clause of the Act of 1854, and sect. 13 of the Act of 1862, includes every person (except masters, pilots, or duly indentured apprentices employed in any capacity on board any sea-going pleasure yacht)—who "by wilful breach of duty, or by neglect of duty, or by reason of drunkenness," does any act tending to the immediate loss, destruction, or serious damage of such ship, or tending immediately to endanger the life or limb of any person on board, or, by neglect of duty or drunkenness, refuses or omits to do any lawful act proper or requisite to be done by him for preserving the ship from immediate loss, destruction, or damage, shall be guilty of a misdemeanor, and is in consequence liable to be proceeded against in a criminal court (sect. 239 of the Act of 1854). In the words of Lord Stowell, drunkenness is "an offence peculiarly noxious on board ship, where the sober and vigilant attention of every man, and particularly of officers, is required. At the same time the Court cannot entirely forget that, in a mode of life particularly exposed to severe peril and exertion, and therefore admitting, in seasons of repose, something of indulgence and refreshment; that indulgence and refreshment is naturally enough sought by such persons in grosser pleasures of that kind, and therefore that the proof of a single act of intemperance, committed in port, is no conclusive proof of disability for general maritime employment:" (The Exeter, 2 Robinson's Rep., p. 264.) So, too, in another case (wherein it was proved that a steward had been drunk once or twice during a nine months' voyage), the same judge said that the court would not "countenance any criminal excess of that kind; yet it cannot so far blind itself to the ordinary habits of men, living for such a length of time in a frequent condition of extreme peril and fatigue, as to feel much surprise that a seaman . . . should have been betrayed into two acts of indulgence of that nature; nor can it consider them as sinking him below the common average of a seaman's morality:" (The Lady Campbell, 2 Hagg. 5.) These two extracts, if not over-complimentary to seamen, show at any rate that they will not be judged too hardly. Thus it has been held that occasional drunkenness, in cases where no damage has ensued to the shipowner, is no cause of forfeiture of wages. But in the case of the Macleod (L. R. 5 Probate Division, p. 254), Sir Robert Phillimore, after quoting with approval the above extracts, held that the master of a ship, who had been habitually drunk during his employment, could not maintain an action for wages.

When a yacht owner takes or sends his yacht into foreign waters, one of the inconveniences he is open to is the desertion of one or more members of his crew; and this and other offences are dealt with in sect. 243 of the Merchant Shipping Act, 1854, which, not being one of the excepted sections, applies to seagoing pleasure yachts, whether articles are signed or not. The Act of 1854 authorised imprisonment for desertion and kindred offences, but by the Merchant Seaman Act of 1880 (43 & 44 Vict. c. 16) imprisonment has been abolished for desertion, for neglect or refusal to join ship after, and absence without, leave; and the worst that can now befall a yacht sailor deserting, in addition to the liability to forfeit his clothes, effects, and wages, is that, subject to any proceedings which may be taken against him to recover damages at common law, or under the Employers and Workmen Act, 1875 —which indeed would probably have no effective result—he may be conveyed on board again; while, if a yacht sailor gives forty-eight hours' notice of his intention to leave his ship, or to absent himself from duty, any court before whom he may be taken will not be justified in treating him as a deserter or absent without leave. In order to be guilty of desertion, a man must quit his ship with the intention of not returning. As, for instance, when a man leaves a yacht, and ships on board some other vessel other than a Queen's ship, or where, having obtained permission to go ashore, he refuses to return. Where a man goes on shore, gets drunk, and is left behind through being drunk, or through being locked up, he will not be held to have been guilty of desertion. If a *bonâ fide* deserter can be caught, and is brought before "any court," the court may, if the master requires, cause him to be conveyed on board, and any costs and expenses incurred by the owner or master of the yacht by reason of the desertion are to be paid by the offender, and, if necessary, deducted from any wages due or to become due to him.

For neglecting or refusing without reasonable cause to join his ship, or to proceed to sea in his ship, or for absence without leave at any time within twenty-four hours of the ship sailing from any port, either at the commencement or during the progress of any voyage, or for absence without leave at any time not amounting to desertion, and not treated as such by the master, a seaman (which term, as we have seen above, includes every person other than a master, pilot, or indentured apprentice employed in any capacity on board any sea-going yacht) is, if he has been lawfully engaged, liable to forfeit out of his wages a sum not exceeding the amount of two days' pay, and, in addition, for every twenty hours of absence either a sum not exceeding six days' pay, or any expenses which have been properly incurred in hiring a substitute.

A seaman who leaves any sea-going yacht on which he is employed, for the purpose of entering on board a Queen's ship, does not commit any offence.

For wilful disobedience to any lawful

Seaman—continued.

command, a seaman shall be liable to imprisonment for any term not exceeding four weeks, with or without hard labour, and also, at the discretion of the court, to forfeit out of his wages a sum not exceeding two days' pay.

For continued wilful disobedience to lawful commands, or continued wilful neglect of duty, he shall be liable to imprisonment for any period not exceeding twelve weeks, with or without hard labour; and also, at the discretion of the court to forfeit for every twenty-four hours' continuance of such disobedience or neglect, either a sum not exceeding six days' pay, or any expenses properly incurred in hiring a substitute.

The powers of a master of a ship are so great, that any roughness in giving an order, or the giving of an unnecessary order, will not justify a seaman, whether he is one of the crew of a yacht or of a trading vessel, in refusing to execute it. So too, in alloting work amongst the crew, although matters requiring the neatest work are in ordinary course given to the most experienced hands, yet no seaman may refuse to do even boys' work, if it should seem fit to the master so to order.

It is a general rule that any member of the crew of a ship is obliged to obey the order of the master or his superior officer, asking no questions, and making no objection, whether the duty to which he is ordered be that which properly belongs to an able seaman or not: (see Dana's Manual, 14th ed., pp. 153-158.) But, of course, a master ought not to order a man to exercise skill in some line in which he professed no skill at the time of shipping. For example, if a carpenter does not ship as seaman as well as carpenter, no nautical skill can be required of him; although he would have, when all hands are called, or if ordered by the master, to do any ordinary work, such as tailing on to a halyard (Dana's Manual, p. 149), or any one shipping as a seaman he need not be expected to understand the repairing of fishing nets. "Disobedience to lawful command," said Lord Stowell (The Exeter, 2 Robinson, p. 264), "is an offence of the grossest kind; the court would be particularly attentive to preserve that subordination and discipline on board of ship, which is so indispensably necessary for the preservation of the whole service, and of every person concerned in it. It would not, therefore, be a peremptory or harsh tone, or an overcharged manner in the exercise of authority, that will ever be held by this court to justify resistance. . . . . . The nature of the service requires that those persons who engage in it should accommodate themselves to the circumstances attending it; and those circumstances are not unfrequently urgent, and create strong sensations, which naturally find their way in strong expressions and violent demeanour. The persons subject to this species of authority are not to be captious, or to take exception to the want of a formal and ceremonious observance of behaviour."

It is further provided by the 243rd section of the Merchant Shipping Act, 1854, that for assaulting any master or mate, a "seaman" shall be liable to imprisonment for any period not exceeding twelve weeks, with or without hard labour. The same section provides that for combining with any other or others of the crew to disobey lawful commands, or to neglect duty, or to impede the navigation of the ship, or progress of the voyage, a "seaman" shall be liable to imprisonment for any period not exceeding twelve weeks, with or without hard labour.

For wilfully damaging the ship, or embezzling or wilfully damaging any of her stores or cargo, he shall be liable to forfeit out of his wages a sum equal in amount to the loss sustained, and also, at the direction of the court, to imprisonment for any period not exceeding twelve weeks, with or without hard labour.

For any act of smuggling, of which he is convicted, and whereby loss or damage is occasioned to the master or owner, the seaman shall be liable to pay to such master or owner such a sum as is sufficient to reimburse them for such loss or damage; and the whole, or a proportionate part of the man's wages, may be retained in satisfaction or on account of such liability, without prejudice to any further remedy. It will thus be seen that, irrespective of any contract or agreement with the seaman, the statute law of this country has entrusted the owner and master of a sea-going yacht with important powers for the preservation of discipline amongst the crew on board.

Inasmuch as the "master" is the person by whom the provisions of the above sections are usually put in force; and as, moreover, the common law has vested, as we have already noticed, in him such extensive powers over all on board his ship, it is important that yacht owners should not, as a general rule, enter into any arrangement whereby the legal status of the master is conferred on any person other than themselves. The word "master" is defined in the Merchant Shipping Act, 1854, as including every person (except a pilot) having command or charge of any ship; whilst, in yachting parlance, the master is understood to be the person engaged to navigate and manage the yacht under the orders and as required by the yacht owner.

It may be a question of doubt in some cases whether, notwithstanding that a sailing master may be employed, the owner of any unregistered yacht may not, when he is on board his yacht, be her "master" within the above definition in the Merchant Shipping Act, 1854, more especially if, as is generally the case, he takes any part in the working of the yacht; but with respect to British registered yachts no such question of doubt can arise, for the 44th section of the Merchant Shipping Act, 1854, requires that there shall be inserted in the ship's certificate of registry, amongst other details, the name of her "master," under the provisions of the

46th section of the same Act referred to on a previous occasion. Whenever the master of a British registered vessel is changed, the name of the new master must be indorsed on the ship's certificate of registry; and all officers of customs within the Queen's dominions may refuse to recognise any person as "master" whose name is not so inserted in or indorsed on the certificate of registry. Having regard to the provisions of these two last-mentioned sections, the owner of a British registered yacht should have his own name inserted in or indorsed on the yacht's certificate of registry as "master," not that of his captain or sailing master.

To say nothing of the legal proof thus afforded for all official purposes as to the person entitled to the status of "master" on board, or the express provisions of the 46th section of the Act of 1854 with reference to matters arising with the Customs, or questions affecting the revenue or quarantine, in all cases where the owner's name appears on the certificate of registry as master, the crew are, of course, precluded from denying his authority as "master," whilst at the same time they cannot refuse to obey the orders of the sailing master, who has the same power under the control of the master as the officers of a trading vessel.

Whenever any of the offences enumerated above are committed, an entry should be made in the form of log book approved by the Board of Trade, which on board foreign cruising yachts should always be carefully kept, and the entry should be signed by the master and also by the sailing master, the mate, or one of the crew; and the offender, if still in the yacht, should, before the yacht arrives at the next port, either have a copy of the entry or have it read over to him; and, in any subsequent legal proceeding the entries shall, if practicable, be produced or proved, and, in default of such production or proof, the court may, at its discretion, refuse to receive evidence of the offence. (Sect. 244 of the Act, 1854.)

The crew being servants paid weekly, can be discharged as any ordinary servant upon giving a week's notice, and can claim their discharge upon giving similar notice. When a member of a crew is discharged for no definite offence, he can claim his passage money to the port of shipment, but not if he discharges himself.

By the Merchant Seamen Act, 1880, additional facility is given for the settlement of disputes as to wages, &c., by extending the operation of the Employers and Workmen Act, 1875, so as to include seamen. Under the last-named Act, in any proceeding before a County Court in relation to any dispute between an employer and a seaman, arising out of or incidental to their relation as such, the County Court may (1) adjust and set off one against the other all claims found by the court to be subsisting between the parties; (2) may rescind any contract between the employer and seaman; (3) take security from a defendant for the due performance of a contract, instead of awarding damages for a breach thereof.

SIGNING ARTICLES.

We now come to the third part of our subject, namely, the position of master and crew and the maintenance of discipline when articles under the Merchant Shipping Acts are signed; or, in other words, when master and crew sign an agreement drawn up in a form sanctioned by the Board of Trade.

Sect. 149 of the Merchant Shipping Act of 1854, taken by itself, provides in effect that the master of every ship (except coasting vessels of less than 80 tons) shall enter into an agreement with every one of the crew in the form sanctioned by the Board of Trade, and the agreement must be signed by the master and all hands—whence the phrase signing articles. This section is one of the excepted sections of the third part of the Merchant Shipping Act, 1854, which does not apply to pleasure yachts, and therefore a yacht owner is not bound to enter into such an agreement with his crew. But if he likes to insist on a Board of Trade agreement, he can do so, although of course he must be prepared to find some yacht sailors refusing to ship with him on those terms. So long as a yacht only cruises in the home waters, Board of Trade agreements are not of much use, and it is only when she becomes a "foreign-going ship" that they are of such importance. By the interpretation clause of the Merchant Shipping Act, 1854, a foreign-going ship is interpreted as including anyone that proceeds between some place or places in the United Kingdom, and some place or places situate beyond the coasts of the United Kingdom, the Channel Islands, and the continent of Europe, between the river Elbe and Brest, inclusive. When, therefore, a yacht's voyage exceeds the above limits, the agreement should, with any necessary alterations, follow the form sanctioned by the Board of Trade for foreign-going ships. If a Board of Trade agreement is agreed to and adopted without alteration, it must contain the following particulars as to terms:

1. The nature, and as far as practicable, the duration of the intended voyage. Or, by a later statute (36 & 37 Vict. c. 85, s. 7), it may state the maximum period of the voyage or engagement and the places (if any) to which the voyage or engagement is not to extend. The statement under this head must be sufficiently plain to enable a man to understand the nature of the work for which he contemplates an engagement.

2. The number and description of the crew, specifying how many are engaged as sailors.

3. The time at which each seaman is to be on board or to begin work.

4. The capacity in which each seaman is to serve.

5. The amount of wages which each seaman is to receive.

Seaman—continued.

6. A scale of the provisions which are to be furnished to each seaman.

7. Any regulations as to conduct on board, and as to fines, short allowance of provisions, or other lawful punishments for misconduct, which have been sanctioned by the Board of Trade as regulations proper to be adopted, and which the parties agree to adopt; and the agreement shall be so framed as to admit of stipulations on the part of the employer and the employed which are not contrary to law.

These agreement forms can be obtained at the Mercantile Marine offices, and from the Board of Trade; they are printed, and spaces are left for filling in the signatures of the different stipulations.

Of course yacht owners may make any special written agreements which their crews will sign; but the Board of Trade form, having official sanction given to it, should be adhered to as much as possible. In the interpretation clause of the Merchant Shipping Act, 1854, the word "seaman," is to include "every person (except masters, pilots, and apprentices duly indentured and registered) employed or engaged in any capacity on board any ship." In steam yachts, therefore, the engineers and firemen would be seamen; as also would be on every yacht the cook and steward. It may be observed that a yacht owner, though he should adopt the forms of agreement signed by the Board of Trade, or a modification of them, is not compelled to require that all the persons engaged on board his yacht should sign them. He may, for instance, engage his cook and steward on the same terms as would be the case if their service would be performed on shore. Still, it will be found advisable that the authority of the master should be secured over all on board alike, by the medium of a written agreement.

The agreement is to be signed by all parties to it, the master signing first; and the document dates from the time of his signature.

In order to avoid any technical difficulties that may arise, the yacht owner should sign as master, and the regular sailing master as mate. The master to whom the men sign has sole control of everybody on board, and even in the movements of the vessel, and there is a story that a master of a yacht up the Mediterranean once threatened to put an owner in irons. Such gross misbehaviour, however, could not go long unrewarded.

In order to enable the crew to refer to the agreement, the master should at the commencement of the voyage have a legible copy (omitting the signatures) placed in some part of the vessel to which the men have access.

In the agreement to be signed, the crew contract as follows:

"The several persons whose names are hereto subscribed, and whose descriptions are contained below, and of whom [here insert number] are engaged as sailors, hereby agree to serve on board the said yacht in the several capacities expressed against their names until the said yacht shall be paid off [here insert the voyage or cruise to be made], and to conduct themselves in an orderly, faithful, honest, and sober manner, and to be at all times diligent in their respective duties, and to be obedient to the lawful commands of the said master or of any person who shall lawfully succeed him, and of their superior officers in everything relating to the said yacht whether on board, in boats, or on shore. In consideration of which services to be duly performed, the said master hereby agrees to pay the said crew as wages the sums set against their names respectively expressed. And it is hereby agreed that any embezzlement or wilful or negligent destruction of any part of the yacht's stores shall be made good to the owner out of the wages of the person guilty of the same. And if any person enters himself as qualified for a duty which he proves incompetent to perform, his wages shall be reduced in proportion to his incompetency. And it is also agreed that the regulations authorised by the Board of Trade, which in the paper hereto annexed are numbered [here insert the numbers of the regulations], are adopted by the parties hereto, and shall be considered as embodied in this agreement. And it is also agreed that if any member of the crew considers himself to be aggrieved by any breach of the agreement or otherwise, he shall represent the same to the master or officer in charge of the ship in a quiet and orderly manner, who shall thereupon take such steps as the case may require. And it is also agreed that any man guilty of misconduct shall be liable to be discharged by the master at any port in Great Britain or Ireland. That the voyage shall be considered as terminated when the yacht is paid off. Every A.B. who conducts himself to the satisfaction of the master shall receive	shillings per week conduct money when discharged. [Here insert any other stipulations which may be agreed upon, and which are not contrary to law.] In witness whereof the said parties have subscribed their names, &c. Signed		master, and		the		day of		18 ."

This passage gives a very fair idea of a seaman's duty, and the only difficulty is in deciding when a man ceases to be honest, orderly, faithful, or sober. The due performance of duty entitles the man to proper accommodation, food, treatment, &c.

The following regulations for the preservation of discipline are distinct from and in addition to the statutable offences previously set out:

1. Not being on board at the time fixed by the agreement—two days' pay.

2. Not returning on board at the expiration of leave—one day's pay.

3. Insolence or contemptuous language or behaviour towards the master or any mate . . .—one day's pay.

4. Striking or assaulting any person on board or belonging to the ship—two days' pay.

5. Quarrelling or provoking to quarrel—one day's pay.

6. Swearing or using improper language—one day's pay.

7. Bringing or having on board spirituous liquors—three days' pay.

8. Carrying a sheath knife—one day's pay.

9. Drunkenness, first offence—two and a half days' provisions; second offence—two days' pay.

10. Neglect on part of officer of watch to place the look-out properly—two days' pay.

11. Sleeping or gross negligence while on the look out—two days' pay.

12. Not extinguishing lights at the times ordered—one day's pay.

13. Smoking below—one day's pay.

14. Neglecting to bring up, open out, and air bedding, when ordered—half day's pay.

15. (For the cook.) Not having any meal of the crew ready at appointed time—one day's pay.

16. Not attending Divine service on Sunday, unless prevented by sickness or duty—one day's pay.

17. Interrupting Divine service by indecorous conduct—one day's pay.

18. Not being cleaned, shaved, and washed on Sundays—one day's pay.

19. Washing clothes on Sundays—one day's pay.

20. Secreting contraband goods on board with intent to smuggle—one month's pay.

21. Destroying or defacing the copy of the agreement which is made accessible to the crew—one day's pay.

22. Officers guilty of above offences shall be liable to fine of twice the number of days', pay which would be exacted from a seaman for like offence.

It does not, however, follow that the above table is to be adopted *in toto.* There is a blank space left in the agreement form, wherein is to be inserted the numbers of the above regulations which are mutually agreed upon. For example, smoking below is 13th on the list, and if the yacht owner wished to make smoking below a breach of discipline he would put 13 in the blank space in the agreement form, and so on.

For the purpose of legally enforcing any of the foregoing fines, the same course must be adopted as in the enforcement of the statutable penalties; that is to say, as soon as the offence is committed a memorandum of it should be inserted in the official log-book which should always be kept when the yacht is on a foreign cruise. The entry in the log-book must be signed by the master, mate, or one of the crew, and a copy of the entry must be read over to the offender before the ship reaches port, or departs from port, and if the offender is discharged before a mercantile marine superintendent the entry should be shown, and the fine, if any, should be deducted from the wages and paid over to the superintendent.

The following are the Queen's Regulations for the Royal Navy as to smoking:

"The hours when smoking is to be permitted, providing it does not interfere with the carrying on of duty, are as follows:

I. During the meal hours of the ship's company, and after quarters to 8 p.m. at sea and 9 p.m. in harbour.

II. On Sundays, and also on Thursdays, when it does not interfere with the duties of the ship, in the afternoons until the pipe "clear up decks."

III. The captain may also permit (if he sees fit) smoking during the night watches for a short period, not exceeding one hour in each watch.

IV. Smoking in the boats is prohibited when on duty, unless the boats are detached for any length of time on service, in which case smoking may be allowed within the hours prescribed on board ship."

WAGES.

A seaman's right to wages and provisions begins either at the time at which he commences work, or at the time specified in the agreement for his arrival on board, whichever first happens, so that if a seaman goes on board and works sooner than he need have done, his right to wages does not necessarily date from the time he went on board.

When a seaman is desirous of having not more than half his wages paid to his wife and family or placed in a savings bank, the stipulation may be inserted in the agreement signed by the master and crew; but it will in that case be necessary for the yacht owner to make provision for the amounts allowed being regularly paid on shore. In the case of merchant shipping, this is done by the owners or owners' agents. As advance notes are now illegal, the payments to the seaman's relations, under an allotment note, will not begin until the expiration of one month, or, if the money is to be placed in a savings bank, at the expiration of three months from the date of the agreement, because the payments are only to be made out of wages already earned.

Speaking generally, so long as a seaman only does his duty, although he may throw into the performance of it an extraordinary amount of zeal, he cannot maintain any claim for extra remuneration; and any promise by the master to pay something additional under ordinary circumstances is void; just as in hiring cabs licensed by the commissioners of police in London, a cabman can only claim his legal fare, although the hirer may have promised a larger sum for the journey. But if the circumstances are such that the men would be justified in refusing to proceed to sea—as for instance, if the vessel were unseaworthy, or dangerously short-handed—then, in the words of Lord Campbell, the sailors would be in the condition of freemen, and free to make a new contract and in that case they would be entitled to claim whatever extra sum the master might agree to give.

As regards the payment of wages, the seaman is entitled, at the time of leaving the ship, to 2*l.*, or quarter of the sum due to him,

Seaman—continued.

which ever is the least, and the balance must be paid by the master within two clear days (exclusive of Sunday and Bank Holidays) after the seaman leave the ship ; but this provision is scarcely in practice applicable to seamen on board yachts.

As we have already stated, the Employers and Workmen Act, 1875, now applies to seamen, and gives County Courts an extended jurisdiction in proceedings between a yacht owner and a member of the crew. The Act provides also that a dispute may be heard and determined before justices, but they may exercise jurisdiction where the amount claimed exceeds 10*l.*; nor can they make an order for the payment of any sum exceeding 10*l.*, exclusive of costs ; nor can they require security for more than 10*l.* from a defendant or his sureties. Should a yacht sailor find it necessary to sue for his wages, he will do either before justices in a County Court having Admiralty jurisdiction, or under the Employers and Workmen Act.

Sea Mile.—See " Knot."

Sea Pie.—A dish made up of all sorts in layers.

Sea Way.—Generally used in the sense of waves in an open sea, meaning a disturbed sea.

Seaworthy.—In every respect fit to go to sea. In chartering a ship it is insisted that she must be " tight, staunch and strong, and well equipped, manned with an adequate crew, provisions," &c.

Second Topsail.—A gaff topsail between the largest (the latter not being a large ballooner) and the jib-headed topsail.

Seizing.—A way of securing a bight of a rope by a lashing so as to form an eye, or of securing any parts of ropes together.

Selvagee Strop.—A strop made of spun yarn laid up in coils and marled. (See " Strop.")

Serve.—To cover a rope with spun yarn called " service."

Serving Mallet.—The mallet which riggers use to wind service round ropes and bind it up tightly together.

Set.—To hoist or make sail. This word is sometimes improperly confused with " sit " in reference to the way a sail stands.

Set Flying.—Not set on a stay or bent by a lacing ; a jib in a cutter is set flying.

Set of the Tide.—Direction of the current.

Setting Up.—Purchasing up rigging taut.

Sewed or Sued.—The condition of a vessel that grounds and on the return of the tide is not floated. If the tide does not lift her by 2ft. she is said to be " sewed " 2ft. If the tide on falling does not leave her quite dry, she is said to " sew " 1ft., 2ft., 3ft., or more, as the case may be.

Shackle.—A U-shaped crook with an eye in each end, through which a screw bolt is passed. Variously used, and are often preferred to hooks. (Fig. 326.) There is a shackle at every fifteen fathoms of cable, so that by unshackling it

the cable can be divided into many parts. Useful if the cable has to be slipped.

FIG. 326.

Shadow Sail.—This was a contrivance patented by Messrs. Harvey and Pryer, of Wivenhoe,

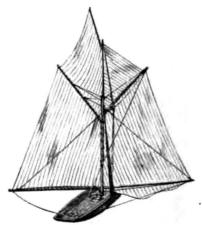

FIG. 327.

in 1874, as an improvement on the spinnaker. It consisted of a gaff, goose-necked to the fore

FIG. 328.

side of the masthead, and a boom to the fore side of the mast at deck. When the spars were in their places (the gaff being set up by halyards similar to the peak halyards of the mainsail), the sail was hoisted by its peak earing and throat, and hauled out by its clew to the boom end. Above the gaff a jib-headed topsail was hoisted. There were an after-brace for the gaff, an aft and a fore guy and topping lift for the boom. The sails were nearly of the dimensions of the main sails. (See Fig. 327.) Practically it was found that there was too much gear for the sail to be got out in a hurry, and in a strong wind the spars and gear would not have borne the strain of such large sails; and so the spinnaker remains in use. We believe Messrs. Harvey and Pryer's patent was fitted to the Seabelle, and she only tried it once in a match.

The plan appears to have been invented by Mr. N. M. Cummins, as that gentleman had a "shadow" fitted to his yacht Electra in 1869. Fig. 328 is a sketch of the Electra under the shadow or "cloud," as Mr. Cummins termed it. (See "Spinnaker.")

Shake, To.—To sail a vessel so close to wind that the weather cloths of the sails shake; the head sails generally are the first to shake, and if the helmsman does not notice it someone who does sings out, "All shaking forward;" or "Near forward."

Shake Out a Reef.—To untie the reef points and unroll a reef and hoist away.

Shallow Bodied.—With a very limited depth of hold.

Shape a Course.—To steer a particular course.

Sharp Bottomed or Sharp Floored.—A vessel with V-shaped sections.

Sharp Bowed.—With a very fine entrance or a bow whose two sides form a very acute angle.

Sharp Sterned.—A stern shaped something like the fore end or bow, thus <.

Sheathing.—The copper sheets put on the bottom of a vessel. 16oz. and 20oz. copper is generally used for yachts. Sometimes 20oz. copper at the load line, and 16oz. below. The sizes and weight of sheathing are usually as follows:—48in. by 20in., and more commonly for yachts 48in. by 14in. The weight per sheet of the 48in. by 20in. is 7·5lb., there being 18oz. to the square foot. The weight per sheet of the 48in. by 14in. is as under:

| 16oz. | 4·67lb. | 28oz. | 11·67lb. |
| 20 ,, | 5·83 ,, | 32 ,, | 12·33 ,, |

160 nails to a sheet, or 1cwt. nails to every 100 sheets. The allowance made for old copper is generally one-eighth less the price paid for new. That is, if the price of new copper be 80l. per ton, the price of old will be 70l. per ton. This price is subject to another deduction of 5lb. per cwt. for dross, &c. Copper is usually put on so that the edges overlap, but in the case of a few yachts the edges of the copper have been butted: that is, the edges were laid edge to edge and the nails were counter sunk and scoured down. Of course this plan entails enormous trouble, but the

superior surface it presents can be considered as a compensation. Many yacht builders obtain the copper sheathing of Messrs. Neville, Druce, and Co., 13, Sherborne-lane, E.C., and Messrs. Vivian and Son, Bond-court House, Walbrook.

Sheave.—The wheel within a block or in the sheave hole of a spar over which ropes pass.

Sheepshank.—A plan of shortening a rope by taking up a part and folding it into two loops

Fig. 329.

or bights, and then putting a half hitch of each standing part over a bight (Fig. 329).

Sheer.—The fore-and-aft vertical curve of a vessel's deck or rail of bulwarks.

To sheer is to put the rudder over when a vessel is at anchor, so as to cause her to move laterally and ride clear of her anchor. A vessel is said to break her sheer when she departs from the sheer that has been given her.

Sheer Hulk.—An old vessel fitted with sheers, whereby masts are lifted into other vessels.

Sometimes used in the sense that nothing but the hulk remains.

Sheer Masts.—Two masts fitted with guys for lifting masts or other things.

Sheer Plan or Sheer Draught.—A drawing showing a longitudinal vertical section or profile of a vessel.

Shelf.—A strong piece of timber running the whole length of the vessel inside the timber heads, binding the timbers together; the deck beams rest on and are fastened to the shelf.

Sheet.—A rope or chain by which the lower after corners of sails are secured.

Sheet Bends.—Fig. 330 is a single sheet bend, and Fig. 331 a double sheet bend.

FIG. 330.   FIG. 331.

Sheet Home.—To strain or haul on a sheet until the foot of a sail is as straight or taut as it can be got. When the clew of a gaff topsail is hauled close out to the cheek block on the gaff. In practice, a gaff topsail sheet, however, is seldom sheeted home, as when once home no further strain could be brought on it; a few inches drift is therefore usually allowed.

In square-rigged vessels a sail is said to be sheeted home when the after clews are hauled close out to the sheet blocks or sheave holes in the yard. This no doubt is the origin of the term.

Shifting Backstays. — The topmast backstays which are only temporarily set up and shifted every time a vessel is put about or gybed. (See " Preventer.")

Shifting Ballast. — Ballast carried for shifting to windward to add to stiffness. A practice forbidden in yacht racing.

Shifting her Berth. — When a vessel removes from an anchorage, &c.

Shift of Plank. — The distance one plank overlaps another.

Shift Ports, To. — To proceed from one port to another.

Shift Tacks, To. — To go from one tack to the other.

Shift the Helm. — To move the tiller from one side to the other ; thus, if it is put to port, an order to shift the helm means put it to starboard.

Shift of Wind. — A change of wind.

Shin Up. — To climb up the shrouds by the hands and shins, when they are not rattled down.

Ship, To. — To put anything in position. To engage as one of the crew of a vessel. To ship a sea, to ship a crutch, to ship a seaman, &c.

Ship Shape. — Done in a proper and unimpeachable manner.

Ship Shape and Bristol Fashion. — An expression probably originating in days gone by when Bristol shipbuilders and seamen were in great repute.

Ships' Papers. — These include builders' certificate, register (in case of not being an original owner, bill of sale as well), bill of lading, bill of health, &c. Also in the case of a yacht her Admiralty warrant.

Shiver. — To luff up and cause the sails to shiver or lift.

Shiver the Mizen. — To luff up until the mizen lifts or shivers.

Shoe or Shod. — Iron plates rivetted to the ends of wire rigging to receive shackle bolts.

Shore. — A beach. A support of wood or iron, a prop.

Short Tacks or Short Boards. — Beating or working to windward by frequent tacking.

Shorten. — The wind is said to shorten when it comes more ahead. To shorten sail, to take in sail.

Shoot. — To move through the water after the means of propulsion is withdrawn.

Shy. — The wind is said to shy when it comes from ahead or breaks a vessel off.

Side Kelsons. — Stout pieces of timber fitted fore and aft on either side of the keel.

Side Lights. — The red (port) and green (starboard) lights carried by vessels when under way. Small yachts during bad weather are not required to have their side lights fixed,

but must always have them ready on deck on their proper sides ready to show. Open boats must carry lights, and if the usual side lights are not used they must have lanterns fitted with green and red slides, to show when required. Steam yachts and steam launches, in addition to the *usual* side lights, must carry a white light at the masthead. Steam vessels when towing must carry two white lights (vertically) at the masthead. All vessels when at anchor are required to exhibit after sundown a white light at a height not exceeding 20ft. above the hull. This light must be visible one mile, and show all round the horizon. It is usual to put this light on the forestay. Pilot vessels carry a white masthead light, and exhibit a " flare up " every fifteen minutes. Fishing vessels and open boats, when riding to nets, carry a white light and show a flare up occasionally. If drift netting, a fishing boat must carry two red lights vertically. A ship which is being overtaken by another ship must show a white light or flare up over her stern. Previous to 1847 there had been no regulation as to the carrying of lights ; the custom being for ships to exhibit a light over their sides when approaching each other at night ; but in 1847 the Admiralty were empowered to make regulations respecting lights, and steamers were ordered to exhibit a white light at the masthead, a green light to starboard, and a red light to port, and vessels at anchor a bright light. And sailing ships were ordered to show, when required, a green light on the starboard side and a red to port. As between steamships and sailing vessels, the latter were required to present a light to the former where there was any danger of collision. The Admiralty Court acted upon the Admiralty Rules. The Order in Council issued in pursuance of the Act, and dated June 29, 1848, and the Act 1852, re-affirmed the former regulations as to steamers, and recommended all sailing vessels to be provided with red and green shaded lanterns, and lights to be shown on the port or starboard bow, according to the side a vessel might be approaching. Section 295 of the Merchant Shipping Act, 1854, confirmed the powers of the Admiralty to the same extent as before. The Merchant Shipping Act, 1862, did not alter the law with respect to steamers, but made it compulsory on sailing ships to keep their side lights fixed instead of displaying red or green lights by hand lamps. (See " Lights.")

Siding or Sided. — The size of a timber, &c., between its two planes and parallel sides. (See " Moulding.")

Sight the Anchor. — To heave up the anchor.

Signal of Distress. — An ensign hoisted jack downwards.

Sister Block. — A double block with two sheaves of the same size one above the other, and seized to the topmast shrouds of square rigged ships to receive the lifts and reef tackle pendants.

Sit.—Sails are said to " sit " well when they do not girt, pucker, belly, or shake. This word is sometimes wrongly written " set."

Skeet.—An instrument (usually a horn on a stick) for wetting sails. In old yacht club rules skeeting to windward only was allowed, as it was thought the skeet might be used as a means of propulsion. " Fire engines " were occasionally used for skeeting, but the practice has gone out of fashion.

Skids.—Pieces of timber put under a boat for resting her on deck, or when launching off.

Skiff.—A small boat used by coast watermen for the conveyance of passengers.

Skin.—The outside or inside planking of a vessel.

Skinning.—In stowing a mainsail lifting the outside part up time after time, the bunt forming a kind of bag.

Skin Resistance.—The resistance a vessel meets with owing to the friction of the water on her plank or sheathing. (See " Resistance.")

Skipper.—A slang term for the master of a yacht or other vessel. Ancient, " Schipper."

Skysail.—A square sail set above the royals.

Sky Scraper.—A triangular sail set above the skysail. Sometimes the sail next above the skysail is a square sail and termed a moonsail; the sail above that a stargazer.

Sky Pilot.—A term applied by sailors to chaplains. (See " Fire Escape.")

Slab Line.—A rope used to brail up the foot of courses.

Slab Reef.—A kind of half-reef in a mainsail below the first reef, it takes up the foot or slab of the sail.

Slack.—Not taut. To slack up a rope or fall of a tackle is to ease it.

Slack Helm.—When a vessel carries very little, if any, weather helm.

Slack Tide.—The tide between the two streams when it runs neither one way nor the other. There are high-water slack, and low-water slack.

Slack in Stays.—Slow in coming head to wind, and still slower in paying off.

Slant of Wind.—A favouring wind. A wind that frees a vessel when close-hauled.

Sleep, or All Asleep—When the sails are full and do not flap or shiver.

Sliding Gunter.—A gentleman under the signature of " Far West " says he has used a form of sliding gunter as shown by Fig. 332. It is fitted as shown, the sail goes up and down as a cutter's sail, but with one halyard. On letting go the halyard, the sail falls into the boat in a moment; it is made up on the boom, and covered in the usual way. If the traveller is made as shown it never jams, running up and down easily. The traveller does not come into play under full sail, but when reefed down the yard is sent up to its proper place, and the downhaul, which is spliced to the traveller, hauled taut; this holds the yard to the mast, setting the sail well. The masthead, or pole, should be as long as the distance between the tack and the upper reef cringle; the sail may be further

reefed by lashing the halyard a foot or more above where it is fast to the yard.

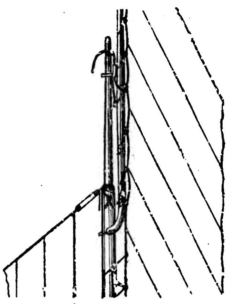

FIG. 332.

Sliding Keel.—An old term for a keel which was lifted at the ends in contradistinction a pivoted board. (See the chapter on " Centre-Boards.")

Slings.—Ropes or strops used to support or sling yards, &c.

Slip.—To let go, as to slip the cable.

Sloop.—A fore-and-aft rigged vessel something like a cutter, but usually has a standing bowsprit. Small sloops have only one head sail set on a stay. (See the " Trial.")

Slot.—An aperture generally for a pin or bolt to travel in.

Smack.—A small trading vessel usually cutter rigged. A fishing cutter.

Small Helm.—Said of a vessel when she carries weather helm.

Small Stuff.—A term applied in the dockyards to denote planking of 4in. thickness and under.

Snatch Block.—A block with an opening in the

FIG. 333.

shell so that a rope can be put over the sheave without reeving it. (See Fig. 333.)

Sneak Boat.—A shallow and beamy boat in use on the Ohio and Mississippi.

Snotter.—A double-eyed strop used to support the heel of a sprit on the mast. (See "Sprit Sail.")

Snow.—A two-masted vessel with a stay, termed a horse, from the mainmast head to the poop on which a trysail was set. Sometimes a spar was fitted instead of the stay.

Snub.—To bring a vessel up suddenly when she has way on and only a short range of cable to veer out. Sometimes necessary if the vessel must be stopped at all costs, but a practice likely to break the fluke of an anchor if it is a good and quick holder.

Snug.—Comfortably canvassed to suit the weather. Anything made neat, or stowed compactly.

So !—An order to cease, often given instead of "belay" when men are hauling on a rope.

Soldiers' Wind.—A wind so that a vessel can lie her course all through to her destination without tacking or any display of seamanship.

Sooji Mooji.—A caustic composition sold by yacht fitters for cleaning off old paint, varnish, &c. It can be obtained of any ship chandler, or of G. Wilson, Sherwood-street, Piccadilly.

Sound.—Not decayed or rotten; free of shakes, splits, crushings, &c.

Sounding.—See "Lead."

Soundings.—To be near enough to land for the deep sea lead to find a bottom.

Spales.—Cross shores used to keep the frame of a vessel in position whilst building.

Span.—A rope made fast by either end to a spar or stay, usually for the purpose of hooking a tackle to. Very long spans are now commonly fitted to gaffs to hook the peak halyards to.

Spanish Burton.—A purchase composed of three single blocks. A double Spanish Burton consists of one double and two single blocks.

Spanish Reef.—A knot tied in the head of a jib-headed sail to shorten the hoist or reduce the area of the sail.

Spanker.—The fore-and-aft sail set with boom and gaff on the mizen of a square-rigged ship; termed also the driver.

Span Shackle.—A bolt with a triangular shackle. The gammon iron that encircles the bowsprit at the stem. When it is directly over the stem the forestay is shackled to it.

Spars.—The masts, booms, gaffs, yards, bowsprit, &c., of a vessel.

Spars, Mensuration of.—Cubical contents of a spar can thus be found. Find the area of each end (see "Area of Circles);" add the areas of the circles together and halve the sum. Multiply the half by the length of the spar. If the spar tapers towards each end, the area of each end and the middle area should be taken, added together and divided by 3. And the plan is as follows: take the girth (see circumference "Areas of Circles") of the spar at each end and halve it. Find the square of the half, and multiply it by the length of the spar. If the spar tapers at both ends, find the girths at three places, halve and divide by 3; find the square of the quotient, and multiply it by the length of the

spar. The weight of spars can be found by multiplying their solid contents by the weight in pounds of a cubic foot of the wood the spar is made of. Thus a cubic foot of red pine will weigh from 32 to 40lb., and a cubic foot of oak from 53 to 60lb. (See "Weight and Bulk of Substances.")

Spectacle Strop.—A short strop with an eye at each end. (See Plate V.)

Speed Indicators.—The log-line, log-ship (see "Log Line"), and sand-glass have done service in testing speed for more than two hundred years; but they make at the best a clumsy contrivance, and it is not surprising that many attempts have been made to supersede it. Of these perhaps Massey's and Walker's logs are the best known, and, with certain limitations, the most reliable; but one objection to these has been that they do not show at a glance the rate of sailing, and, if anything fouls the log, the record of the distance sailed through the water is imperfect. Another disadvantage—although, it must be confessed, it is a small one—is that, before the distance run can be ascertained, the log has to be hauled in. In 1871 we recollect witnessing some experiments in America with a fantail log attached to a small wire, which necessarily turned with the log. The wire was attached to some clock-like machinery on the poop, and a dial recorded the number of miles sailed. This instrument was said to have kept a true record of distances in a voyage to the West Indies and back; but, as it does not appear to have come into general use, it may be presumed that it was subject to mishaps. Reynolds's "pendant log" is similar to the American contrivance, inasmuch as it registers on board the miles run.

The speed indicators which most resemble the line and log-ship in its results are those which only show the rate of sailing per hour, and do not record the distance traversed. Of these perhaps Berthon's log, or adaptation of it, is the most in favour, and if properly adjusted, marks very accurately the speed per hour at any moment. Berthon's log consists of a tube, which passes through the keel, or any immersed part of the hull, and, as the water will rise in this tube in accordance with the speed through the water, it was not a difficult matter to adjust a speed indicator in connection with the tube.

Another kind of log, on the dynamic principle, is one invented by the late Mr. Joseph Maudslay. This was a very simple contrivance, and consisted of an ordinary Salter's spring balance, a line, and small weight. The line was 25 fathoms long, and 1 inch in circumference. The lead weight was 6 inches long, $1\frac{1}{2}$ inches in diameter, and weighed about $2\frac{1}{4}$lb. The ends of the lead were rounded off. A hole was made through the lead from end to end, through which the line was passed and secured by a knot. With 12 fathoms of this line and lead immersed the resistance at two knots per hour was found to be 1lb., and for other speeds the resistance increased nearly as the square of the speed; thus at two knots the resistance is 1lb.; at ten knots, or five times greater speed, the resistance is 25lb., as 5×5=25. We some years ago tested this log with Berthon's, and on different occasions on the measured mile, and found the speed pretty accurately indicated so long as the water was smooth; but when it came to rough water, the lead jumped about so that it was impossible to arrive at the exact speed.

If lead weight is dispensed with the line will not jump out of the water so badly, and a steadier pull can be obtained. In 1877 we tried an experiment by towing a rope astern of a steam launch, and found the resistance to vary nearly as the square of the speed as set forth in the middle column. The rope forming the "log" was 13 fathoms long, the *whole* of which was permanently immersed. The rope was four stranded, "water-laid," and one inch and a quarter (1¼ inch) in circumference. A smaller line was spliced to the other as a tow line, as much of this being payed out as was sufficient to keep the larger rope immersed, or to prevent any part of the thirteen fathoms being towed out of water. At the splice, and on the larger piece of rope, was a piece of lead pipe about a foot long (with an inside diameter equal to the diameter of the rope). This served the double purpose of showing at a glance if the whole of the larger rope was not immersed, and helped to maintain the immersion. The after end of the larger rope should be whipped.

The log patented by Mr. Clark Russell is similar to this arrangement; but the spring balance had a compensating wheel gearing to prevent the index hand jumping. In 1888 a yacht captain brought out a similar contrivance, and it can be obtained of Messrs. Fay and Son, Southampton.

On the face of the spring balance the numbers of the knots should be engraved opposite the resistance in pounds as set forth in the table.

In all cases speed indicators or logs only show the speed through the water; and to calculate the distance made to the good over the ground the tide must be eliminated.

Knots.	Resistance of Proposed Log in lb.	Resistance of Maudslay's Log in lb.
2	1¼	1
3	2¾	2¼
4	4¾	4
5	7½	6¼
6	11	9
7	15	12¼
8	19¼	16-2oz.
9	24¼	20¼
10	30½	25
11	37	30¼
12	44	36
13	51¼	42¼
14	60	49
15	69	56¼

Speed of Yachts.—No doubt very exaggerated opinions prevail as to the speed an English yacht is capable of. Very frequently there is a mistake made about the distance sailed in a certain time; no allowance has been made for tide, or the speed has been inaccurately judged. So far as our experience goes, the following table gives the extreme speed sailing yachts of certain length and tonnage have attained:

Length.	Knots per hour.	Time per mile.
ft.		Min. sec.
9	3·75	16 0
16	5·00	12 0
25	6·25	9 36
36	7·50	8 0
41	8·	7 30
49	8·75	6 51
64	10·	6 0
81	11·25	5 20
100	12·50	4 48
121	13·75	4 21
144	15·00	4 0

These observed speeds correspond with the theory that speed varies as the square roots of the length on load water-line in vessels of similar form and proportions. Of course, the speeds could be exceeded if the boats could carry sufficient sail.

There are some apparently well-authenticated reports that yachts of 121ft. on the

LOG OF THE SAPPHO.

	Lat. N. D.	Lat. N. M.	Lat. N. S.	Long. W. D.	Long. W. M.	Long. W. S.	Miles.	Course.	Wind.	Remarks.
July 28	40	29	32	73	21	00	27	E. ¾ S.	S.W.	Fine breeze.
,, 29	40	32	38	67	27	0	279	E. ¾ S.	S.	Fresh breeze, making 9 to 14 knots thick fog; *ran 47 miles in 3 hours.*
,, 30	41	28	38	61	32	0	273	E. ½ S.	S. by W.	*Making* 16 *knots*, wind died out to calm, foggy.
,, 31	43	32	00	56	55	0	229	E.	W.S.W.	Light breeze and fog; got a glimpse of sun for latitude.
Aug. 1	44	41	39	54	26	15	112	E. by S. ½ S.	W.N.W.	Light breeze; dense fog 8 p.m., nearly calm.
,, 2	45	20	23	51	25	15	134	E. by S.	W. by S.	Nearly calm, only going 1 knot sometimes; dense fog.
,, 3	46	25	17	47	10	15	192	E. by S.	W.S.W.	Dense fog; moderate breeze; fog lifted 6 p.m.
,, 4	47	36	49	41	52	45	238	E. by S.	S.	Fine breeze, clear weather.
,, 5	49	31	18	35	21	15	315*	E. by S.	S.S.W.	Fresh breeze; *very smooth, sea like a lake.*
,, 6	50	58	56	29	33	15	244	E.S.E.	S.W.	Fog and rain; moderate breeze.
,, 7	50	56	49	24	14	30	192	S.E. by E.	W.S.W.	Fresh breeze, with swell.
,, 8	51	07	30	17	06	00	271	S.E. by E. ¾ E.	N.W. by N.	Fine breeze.
,, 9	50	42	25	10	12	15	255	S,E. by E. ½ E.	N.W. by N.	Overcast; fresh breeze, increasing to fresh gale; sighted land 4.15 p.m.
							96	E. by N. ¾ N.	N. by E.	
Total miles							2857			

* The run of 315 miles on Aug. 5 was an average of 13·1 knots an hour.

load-line have reached a speed of 16 knots per hour. The American yacht, Sappho is, said to have made such a speed; and as doubts have at various times been thrown upon the statement, an extract from her log book in crossing the Atlantic in 1869 is given on page 621. The Sappho left Sandy Hook Lightship 7 a.m. July 28, and arrived Queenstown Harbour 9 p.m. Aug. 9, Queenstown time, making the run in 12 days 9 hours 36 min. (two hours less to the Old Head of Kinsale).

It will be seen that the strong wind was on the quarter the whole way, and as the sea was exceptionally smooth, more favourable conditions for attaining high speed could not have been had. As a rule, with a strong wind, there is a great deal of sea, and this, of course, is an unfavourable condition for the attainment of high speeds.

In the Atlantic race of 1886, between the American yachts Dauntless and Coronet, the Dauntless logged 328 miles in 24 hours, whilst the biggest run of the Coronet was 291 miles.

It is equally well authenticated that the American yacht Meteor (which was lost in the Mediterranean), in a passage from Cowes to Lisbon in 1869, logged 319 miles in 24 hours, with a strong quarterly double-reef wind. During some portion of the 24 hours the Meteor logged 16 knots. The Cambria, in the Atlantic yacht race 1870 only attained a maximum speed of 11¼ knots, but there was a heavy quarter sea whenever she had a strong fair wind. The greatest sustained speed that we have ever been witnesses to in a match was in a race between the Livonia (106ft. on the water-line) and Columbia (98ft.) in America. The Livonia sailed the distance between the S.W. Spit buoy and Sandy Hook Lightship, 8¾ nautical miles, in 40 minutes, or at the rate of 13 knots an hour; and no doubt that some part of the time she was going 13¾ knots. The tide was not strong, and abeam. In a match of the Royal Victoria Yacht Club, Ryde, on Aug. 12, 1885, the Irex (cutter, 83·5ft. on the water-line) in a strong reaching wind went round a course of 50 miles in four hours eight minutes. The tide was equally with and against her, so the average speed through the water was 12·1 knots. We do not think this speed has been much exceeded by English yachts of the lengths given, but the late Mr. Thellusson stated that the Guinevere (121ft. L.W.L.) logged 14 knots. It is recorded that the American clipper ship Sovereign of the Seas in 1852 averaged 300 miles a day for eleven consecutive days, and 333 miles for four consecutive days. Her greatest distance any day, noon to noon, was 362 miles ; but in 1853, on a voyage from Oaten to New York she ran 396 miles on March 16, and on the 18th 411. The ship Red Jacket, New York to England, January, 1853, logged 417 knots, and in the Southern Ocean, July, 1852, she made the following remarkable record :

Date.	Knots.	Date.	Knots.	Date.	Knots
July 3	312	July 7	299	July 11	245
„ 4	300	„ 8	350	„ 12	300
„ 5	288	„ 9	357		
„ 6	400	„ 10	334	Total...	3185

On July 8 the latitude was 46° 38′ S., longitude 119° 44′ E. The foregoing particulars were published by her commander, Mr. Samuel Reid, in the *Field* of April 16, 1887. The James Baines, in the Southern Ocean, June 17, 1856, did 418 miles in the 24 hours, latitude 43° 31′ S., longitude 106° 15′ E. On the 18th she logged for a time 21 knots per hour. The Lightning is said to have averaged 18 knots for 24 hours —that is, 432 miles in the 24 hours, and the James Baines, on a voyage to Australia, in 1855, is credited with 430 knots in the 24 hours. In all cases nautical miles or knots are meant, and not statute miles.

The Melbourne in a passage to Australia in 1876 averaged 300 miles for 17 consecutive days. Her greatest runs were 374, 365, and 352 miles per 24 hours. (See " Time Allowance by Length.")

Spell.—The term of work allotted to any of the men in a watch. Thus there is the spell at the helm termed "trick ;" spell at the masthead to look out, spell at the pump, &c. When a man's time comes to be relieved and the one who has to take his place lags, the former sings out " Spell O ! " (See " Trick.")

Spencer.—A fore-and-aft sail set with gaffs in square-rigged ships, as trysails on the fore and main mast.

Spider Hoop or Spider Band.—An iron band round the mast with iron belaying pins in it.

Spiling.—Marking on a bar of wood the distances that a curved line (say that of a frame) is from a straight line.

Spilling Lines.— Ropes attached to sails for spilling them of wind in reefing or furling.

Spindle Jib.—A jib topsail.

Spinnaker.—A jib-headed sail reaching from the topmast head to the deck, first introduced in yacht racing in a Royal London match, June 5 1865, by Mr. William Gordon in the Niobe, and hence for some time termed a " Ni-obe." The term " spinnaker " appears to have been applied to it as a kind of nickname, without "rhyme or reason." In 1866 Mr. Herbert Maudslay had a similar sail made for his yacht Sphinx, and it was first used in a match of the Royal Victoria Yacht Club at Ryde. The men called the yacht "Spinks," and hence the Itchen Ferry men nicknamed the sail a "spinker," as the year before they called it a Ni-obe. From spinker came spinniker, or, as now written, " spinnaker." The word, as heard spoken by the crew of the Sphinx, was introduced into our nautical vocabulary by the author of this work in describing a yacht match he sailed at Ryde on board the Sphinx, Aug. 15, 1866, and reported in the *Field* of Aug. 18. The word next appeared in print in Hunt's " Yachting Magazine " for September, 1866, in reference to the same match, the word having apparently been taken from the *Field*. The author first spelt the word " spinniker," and the " spinnaker " form was not introduced until 1869.

Prior to the introduction of the spinnaker a square sail and square topsail or raffee were used. The accompanying wood-cut (Fig. 334) was made in 1854, and represents the Phantom (cutter, 27 tons) in a match on the Thames. Sometimes a large jib was hoisted by a block lashed half way up the topmast, and boomed out by the tack' (if allowed by the rules) when before the wind. These large head sails were, however, generally prohibited, and the following is a copy of the rule of the Royal Thames Yacht Club prior to 1865: "That all yachts cutter rigged, and not

Fig. 334.

carrying more than four fore and aft sails, be eligible to sail; but no jib to exceed 2ft. in the head nor to be hoisted above the main-mast head, neither shall it be boomed out." It was the rescinding of this rule in 1865 that brought into existence the "Ni-obe" or "spinniker." Mr. MacMullen, in his "Down Channel" (published in 1869), says that he had a similar sail in 1852; but booming out a big balloon or jib by the tack was always a common practice both on board yachts and fishing smacks.

Spindle Model.—A name given to a cylindrical model tapering at the ends.

Spindrift.—See "Spoon Drift."

Spirketting.—Timber worked inside a vessel under the shelf in a fore-and-aft direction.

Spitfire.—The smallest storm jib.

Splice.—To join the ends of rope together by interweaving the untwisted strands. An eye splice is formed by interweaving the untwisted end of a rope in the lay of the strands.

Split Lug.—A lugsail in two parts (Fig. 335);

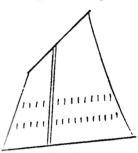

Fig. 335.

the fore part is sheeted like a foresail, and in going about the tack is never cast off, nor is the tack of the after part of the sail. The up and down lines on the sail show where it is divided and where the mast comes. To heave to, the clew (after cringle) of the fore part of the lug would be hauled up to the mast or to windward of it, easing the mainsheet as required. The split lug is not in much favour. The standing lug (or even balance lug) and foresail rig has all the advantages of the split lug without so much yard forward of the mast and without the disadvantage of not being able to lower the fore part or foresail. The most that can be said in favour of the split lug is that it points out the advantages of a main and fore-sail in preference to one sail.

Spoken.—Said when one ship has spoken to another by signal.

Spokes.—The bars of the steering wheel of a ship radiating from the boss. "To give her a spoke" is to move the wheel to the extent of the distance between spoke and spoke.

Sponson.—The platform ahead and abaft paddle wheels, usually outside the bulwarks, but sometimes inclosed.

Spoon Drift.—Spray blown from the crests of waves.

Spring.—A warp or hawser or rope.

Spring a Mast.—To crack or splinter a mast.

Spring her Luff.—To ease the weather tiller lines so that a vessel will luff to a free puff.

Sprit Sail.—A four-sided sail stretched by a pole termed a sprit (Fig. 336). This is a time-honoured contrivance for setting a sail

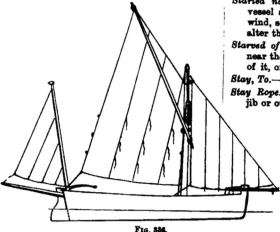

FIG. 336.

that has no boom, but a gaff is preferred if the sail has a boom.

Sprung.—Damaged by a cross way cracking or splintering. (See " Spring a Mast.")

Spun Yarn.—Small rope or cord used for serving, &c.

Square.—Said of sails when they are trimmed at right angles to the keel. A ship is said to have square yards when there is little difference between the lengths of upper and lower yards, or when her yards are very long.

Square the Yards.—To brace them across at right angles to the keel. Square the boom is to haul it out at right angles to the keel.

Squeeze.—A vessel is said to be squeezed when she is sailed very close to the wind in order that she may weather some point or object.

Stains on Deck.—Iron moulds, &c., can be removed from a deck by a solution of one part muriatic acid, three parts water.

Stand.—A term variously employed ; as to stand towards the shore, to stand E.S.E., and so on ; to stand on without tacking. A sail is said to stand when it does not lift or shake.

Standard.—(See " Royal Standard.")

Stand By.—The order to make ready ; as " Stand by to lower the topsail." " Let go the anchor," &c.

Standing Part.—The part permanently made fast to something, and not hauled upon.

Standing Rigging.—The rigging that is kept permanently in its place.

Stand Up.—A vessel is said to stand up well that carries her canvas without heeling much.

Starboard.—The right hand side. The opposite to port.

Starbolins.—The men and " Watches " who compose the starboard watch. (See " Larbolins.")

Start, To.—To move, as to slacken a sheet or tack. To start a butt is to cause a plank to start from its fastenings at its butt or end.

Started neither Tack nor Sheet.—Said when a vessel sails a long course without a shift of wind, so that there is no occasion for her to alter the trim of her sails.

Starved of Wind.—When a vessel is sailed so near the wind that she does not have enough of it, or feel the weight of it.

Stay, To.—To tack.

Stay Rope.—The luff or weather bolt rope of a jib or other sail.

Stays.—Ropes for supporting masts and other spars.

A vessel is said to be in stays when she is going through the operation of tacking. To stay is to tack. Strictly, when a ship is head to wind. Probably derived from the fact that a square rigged ship " stays " a long time before her head pays off, and she is then " in stays." (See " Missing Stays.")

Steady !—An order to put the helm amidships, or not to move it about.

Steerage.—In a yacht the space between the after athwartship bulkhead of the main cabin and the athwartship bulkhead of the after cabin. (The latter is generally known as the ladies' cabin.) Usually the term steerage is limited to the fore and aft passage and berths therein.

Steerage Way.—When a vessel moves through the water so that she can be steered. In simply drifting or moving with the tide a vessel has no steerage way on, and cannot be steered ; therefore steerage way means that a vessel relatively to the water moves ahead and passes the water.

Steersman.—A helmsman.

Steeve.—The upward inclination or rake which a bowsprit has, or which the plank sheer has forward. The running bowsprit has usually a steeve corresponding with the sheer forward ; a standing bowsprit has generally considerably more.

Stem.—The timber at the fore end of a vessel into which the ends of the plank are butted. To stem is to make headway, as against a current.

Stemson.—A piece of timber worked inside the stem.

Step.—A piece of timber or metal to receive a vessel's mast, &c. To step is to put a thing into its step.

Stern-board.—The name given to the three-cornered board aft in an open boat. (See " Stern Sheets.")

Stern Board.—A movement of a vessel sternwards.

Stern Way.—Moving astern : to make a stern-board.

Stern Post.—The strong timber to which the rudder is hung.

Stern Sheets.—The seat in the aft end of a boat.

Sometimes the three-cornered bottom board aft in a boat is termed the stern sheet. This board in a yacht's gig, in the bow or aft, is usually a wood grating. In small fishing boats the stern sheet is the platform on which the fisherman coils away his nets, lines, &c.

Stiff.—Not easily heeled; having great stability.

Stock of an Anchor.—The crossbar near the shackle.

Stocks.—The framework upon which a vessel rests whilst she is being built.

Stopper.—A rope or lashing used to prevent a rope or chain surging or slipping, as cable stopper, rigging stoppers, &c. The latter is usually a short piece of rope put on as a kind of racking to prevent the rigging or its tackles rendering. A stopper is sometimes put on with a hitch, as shown by Fig. 340. (See "Racking.")

Stooping.—To dive into a wave hollow. Generally an easy sort of pitching, caused by the undulation of waves or "swell."

Stops.—Yarns or short pieces of rope by which sails are secured when rolled up or stowed. Also the short lines by which sails are tied to yards when they are not laced.

Storm Anchor.—See "Floating Anchor" and "Oil on Troubled Waters."

Storm Sails.—The storm trysail and storm jib set in bad weather.

Stove in.—Broken in.

Stow.—To roll up. To furl a sail. To pack away any kind of article. A slang term telling a man to cease talking, as "stow that."

Stowing a Punt.—Mr. A. D. Ashford thus describes his plan for stowing a punt on board a small craft instead of towing her or carrying her on deck: "I had a craft built 20ft. keel, 24ft. over all, 6ft. 6in. beam, good rise of floor, and only small cockpit. The punt was stowed in the cabin, and there was good room to go round her and get anything required. When sailing, you do not want cabin in a small craft, and with ease I could get punt out or in single-handed; she was 8ft. long, and I have landed five men in her at one time. Fig. 337 is fore end of cockpit, closed up; Fig. 338 shows punt on floor of cabin. The slides, No. 1 of companion, fit into grooves in sides of Nos. 2 and 3; Nos. 2 and 3 also fit into grooves, and come out."

Mr. J. C. Wilcocks says: "Lieut.-Col.

Tupper had a schooner-rigged yacht of 9 tons built by Mr. Ogier, of St. Sampson's Harbour. The arrangement for stowing the punt was as described, but with the exception that the movable bulkhead at cabin entrance consisted of boards 9in. wide, connected with brass hinges in pairs. When removed from the grooves at top and bottom, they closed like a book, and were more handy for stowage than a panelled bulkhead. The lower groove was at platform level within

FIG. 337.

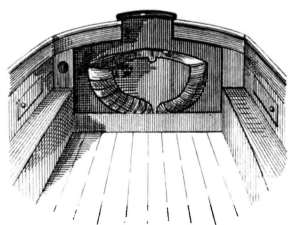

FIG. 338.

an inch. All small yachts should be thus fitted." (See also "Collapsible Boats.")

Straight of Breadth.—The distance where the breadth of a ship is equal or nearly equal amidships; now generally termed parallel length of middle body, because the two sides of a ship may be for some distance parallel to each other. A straight of breadth is seldom found in a yacht excepting in some long steam yachts; these frequently are of the same breadth for some distance amidships. (See "Body" and "Dead Flat.")

Strake or Streak.—A length of plank of any breadth.

Strand.—Yarns twisted together and they then make the parts or strands of a rope.

Stranded.—Said of a rope when one or more of its strands have burst. Cast ashore.

Strands.—Yarns when unlaid and used as "stops" are sometimes called strands.

Strap.—See "Strop."

Stream.—The direction of the flood tide and ebb tide. The tides in the Channel are usually referred to as the eastern stream for the flood and western stream for the ebb.

Stretch.—A course sailed. Also the elasticity of canvas or rope.

Strike.—To lower, as to strike the topmast, &c. Also to strike the ground when sailing.

Striking Topsails.—See "Saluting."

Stringers.—Strengthening strakes of plank steel or iron inside or outside a vessel's frame.

Strop or Strap.—A sort of hoop made of rope yarn, wire, or iron, used to put round spars, rigging, &c., to hook tackles to.

Fig. 339 shows a selvagee strop. (See also "Selvagee.")

A selvagee strop is put on to a rope to hook a block or tackle to, as shown in Fig. 340, the whole of the strop being used up in the cross turns.

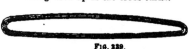

FIG. 339.

FIG. 340.

Another way of putting a strop on a block is shown in Fig. 341. The bights are passed through and through, round the rope until used up; the tackle is then hooked to the

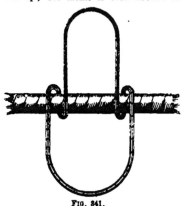

FIG. 341.

bights as in Fig. 340. A strop is usually put on a wire rope in this way, as it is less likely to slip.

Studding Sails.—Sails set outside the courses, topsail, &c., in square-rigged ships; called by sailors "stu'n's'ls."

Stuff.—Slang for sails, as, "Give her the stuff," meaning more sail. Also small rope, and picked hemp or cotton waste, and timber.

Surge.—When a rope renders round a belaying pin, &c.

Swansea Pilot Boats.—A very snugly rigged kind of schooner met with in the Bristol Channel. The rig comprises mainmast, foremast, and running bowsprit; the mainmast is stepped exactly in the middle of the boat, and has a great rake aft, so that the head of the mast plumbs over the after part of the cockpit, two sheaves are cut in it, through which the halyards are rove. The foremast is upright, with sheaves like the mainmast, and a block on the fore part under the sheave holes for the jib halyards. These masts require no rigging or stays, and are pole masted without any topmasts. The gaffs are short, being for a boat of 25 to 30 tons only about 6ft. long, and only require one halyard. One end of the halyard is spliced to a single block; the other end being passed over the first sheave in the mast, then through a single block, which is hooked on to the gaff, and finally through the upper sheave in the mast. This end is belayed. A purchase is formed by a rope passed through

the block on the halyard and through a block on deck. The fore halyards are rigged the same way, and the jib halyards are of the ordinary kind. The sails consist of mainsail, foresail, and jib; the two former being laced to the mast. These sails can be taken in in about one minute and a half, and set in about two and a half. The outhaul of the jib is passed under a sheave on the stem, and acts as a bobstay; there are no shrouds to bowsprit. The advantages of this rig are said to be that one man can handle a boat of 25 tons himself, and the boats are equally as handy with the foresail as without it, likewise the mainsail. They will stay or do anything either way, and with only the foresail and jib a boat can be sailed on a wind. (Fig. 342.)

Swell.—Long waves with unbroken crests, usually met with after heavy winds have subsided.

Sweep.—A long bend. To sweep is to impel by sweeps or large oars; formerly, vessels as large as 300 tons used sweeps, and by hard work could make three knots an hour. Sweeps are not permitted in yacht racing.

Sweeps.—Large oars.

Swig, To.—The fall of a tackle is put under a cleat or pin, and is held firmly by one or more of the crew; another man (or men) then takes hold of the part of the fall between the cleat and the block and throws his whole weight on it; as he comes up the other hand takes in the slack. By swigging on a tackle a couple of hands can often get in all that is required, where by steady hauling they might not have moved the blocks an inch. To drink.

Swimming.—If a person who cannot swim falls overboard, he should turn his face upwards towards the sky, and press his chest forward; he cannot then sink. He should keep the legs down as much as possible, and the mouth firmly shut. He should keep composed, and strike out slowly with the hands. A person could soon learn to swim by walking into the water breast high, and then striking out, holding the face well up towards the sky. It should be always borne in mind that the human body is somewhat lighter bulk for bulk than water; consequently a piece will appear above water until some of the fluid is swallowed. The proper thing to do is, therefore, to see that the piece of the body which floats out of the water is the face part, so that breathing can take place.

Swivel Hook.—A hook that revolves by a pivot inserted in a socket and clinched.

T.

Tabernacle.—A strong upright trunk used in barges to step the mast in on deck so that the mast can be lowered for going under bridges. It is in fact a lengthening of the mast, the trunk being the housed part with a hinge or joint on deck. In small boats that have no deck the mast is generally stepped at the bottom of the tabernacle, and not on the top. Used also in steam yachts.

Tabling.—The strengthening pieces of canvas sewn to the edges of sails where the roping goes on.

Tack.—The lower fore-corner of a sail. To tack is to go about or shift from one tack to another.

The side on which the wind blows on the sails, as starboard tack or port tack. This term probably originated with the square rig, as "port tacks" aboard means that the lower port corners of the sail are now hauled in-board, whereas when the wind was on the other side these corners had been hauled outboard by the sheets.

Tackle.—An arrangement of ropes and pulleys for increasing power; a purchase. (Pronounced "tay-kel" by sailors.)

Tackle-fall.—The hauling part of the rope of a tackle.

Tack Tackles.—The tackles employed to set down the tacks of sails.

Taffrail.—The continuation of the top rail round the aft side of the counter.

Tail Block.—A block with a tail or piece of rope stropped to it for making fast the block instead of a hook.

A tail block is put on to a rope by a rolling hitch, as shown in Fig. 343. The hitches are jammed up close together. The end of the tail can be seized back to the rope if required. Often when in a hurry only one hitch is taken

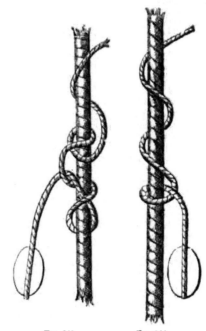

FIG. 343.   FIG. 344.

(Fig. 344), the tail being gripped round the rope with the hand. A tail tackle is put on to a rope in the same manner as a tail block.

Tail on.—An order to take hold of a rope and help haul.

Tail Tackle.—A watch tackle; that is, a double and single block. The single block has a hook; the double block a rope tail, which can be hitched to ropes or parts of rigging, &c.

Take In or Take Off.—To hand or furl a sail.

Take, To.—A jib is said to take when a vessel has been head to wind and the jib fills on one side or the other.

Take Up.—To shrink; to tighten up.

Tanning a Sail.—No tanning will entirely prevent mildew, if the canvas is left unopened and unaired an unlimited time. For a 20ft. boat boil in a furnace of 15 gallons 28lb. of catechu, until thoroughly dissolved; put in such sails as convenient, and let them soak a night; then spread and mop them over both sides with the mixture. If required very dark indeed, double the amount of catechu. Sails too large for a furnace or vat are mopped only on a floor of asphalte, or cement, with the mixture. Sails are sometimes "tanned" in a tan yard with oak bark and ochre.

The yarn of the Bembridge Redwings is dyed before it is woven.

Taunt.—Tall, high, towering. (See "A-taunto.")

Taut.—Tight; stretched as tightly as possible.

Taut Bowline.—A ship is said to be on a taut bowline when the bowlines on the leeches of the sail are hauled as taut as possible for sailing near the wind. With everything stretched as flat as possible for close-hauled sailing.

Tend.—To attend to a sheet and watch it to see if it requires hauling in or slacking out; generally to attend to any work on board ship.

Tenon.—A sort of tongue cut at the end of a piece of timber to fit into a mortise.

Thick Stuff.—Timber or plank over 4in. thick.

Thimble.—A ring, pear-shaped or circular, with a groove outside for ropes to fit in. When the thimble is pear-shaped it is usually termed a "heart thimble or thimble heart." These thimbles are used for the eye splices in ropes, whilst circular thimbles are mostly used for the cringles of sails, &c. For steel wire or iron rope the thimble is usually solid.

Thimble Eyes.—Eyes spliced in rigging round a thimble. A thimble seized in a strop.

Tholes.—Pins fitted into the holes in rowlocks for oars to work in.

Thread.—A vessel is said to thread her way when she weaves in and out among other vessels, or through a narrow channel. Thread of oakum or cotton for caulking small boats.

Three Sheets in the Wind.—Half drunk. "Three cloths shaking," said sometimes of a mainsail when a vessel is sailed too near the wind.

Throat.—The deepest part of the hollow of the jaws of a gaff, or the hollow of a V shaped knee, or the hollow of a floor. The throat halyards are those which are attached to the throat of a gaff. The upper weather corner of a gaff-sail is often called the throat, or nook, because it is attached to the throat of the gaff.

Through Bolt, or Through Fastening.—A bolt that passes through timber and plank, and clinched.

Thumb Cleat.—Pieces of wood put on spars, &c., to prevent ropes or strops from slipping.

Thwarts.—The transverse seats in a boat. (*See* "Athwartships.")

Tidal Harbour.—A harbour that can only be entered on certain stages of the tide.

Tides.—Usually the rise and fall or flow and ebb of the sea around the coast. The highest tides occur at the new moon and full moon. Tides estuaries, harbours, and bays vary a great deal.

Tight.—Impervious to water; well caulked; not leaky. Never applied to the tension of ropes, &c., which are always "taut." (See "Taut.")

Tiller.—The piece of timber inserted in the rudder head for steering; usually termed the helm.

Tiller Lines.—The lines attached to the tiller to move it by. (See "Tiller Ropes," which are a different thing.) Generally in yachts of 40 tons and over, a tackle is used. In large yachts

a second tackle is sometimes used, if the yacht carries much weather helm or is hard to steer: these second tackles are usually termed relieving tackles.

Tiller Ropes.—The ropes attached to the short tiller when a wheel is used for steering. The ropes pass round the drum on the same axis as the wheel. In large vessels the tiller ropes are frequently made of raw hide.

Timber-heads.—The heads or upper ends of the frames.

Timber Hitch.—A quick way of bending a rope to a spar. A loop or bight is formed by twisting the end of a rope round its standing part, thus (Fig. 345):

FIG. 345.

The end of the rope is shown on the right, and the standing part passing through the bight on the left.

Timbers.—The frames or ribs of a vessel.

Time Allowance. — The allowance made by one yacht to another in competitive sailing, proportional to the size of the yachts and the distance sailed.

In small boat sailing, an allowance of 1sec. per inch for every excess inch of length for every mile sailed, is a good allowance. Where length and breadth are multiplied together, 1sec. per square foot for every mile makes a good allowance. Where length and breadth are added together, the allowance might be 1¼ second per inch per mile. These allowances are only adapted for boats that do not differ much in length. Where the difference in length much exceeds a foot, the boats should be classed as a 21ft. class, 25ft. class, &c., unless the Y.R.A. graduated table of allowance for length be used.

In preparing the present time scale, which came into operation with the linear rating rule in 1896, the following equivalents between the ratings for the classes under the length and sail area rule, and the linear rating rule, were, on the recommendation of the yacht designers, adopted :—

Ratings under length and sail area rule.	Equivalents under linear rating rule.
0·5	18ft.
1·0	24ft.
2·5	30ft.
5	36ft.
10	42ft.
20	52ft.
40	65ft.

85 rating, under the length and sail area rule, has also been taken as equivalent to 80ft. rating under the linear rating rule.

The time allowances from 24ft. to 80ft. rating correspond nearly with those of the previous scale, but small alterations have been introduced to make the figures accord with a true curve, plotted with the vertical scale of seconds double the horizontal scale of feet.

Above 80ft. rating the time allowances accord with a tangent to the time scale curve from that point, increasing by 1·3 seconds per foot of rating. This principle has been followed with the object of increasing the time allowances to be given by yachts of the larger ratings.

In like manner, the time allowances for ratings under 24ft. accord with a tangent to the curve from that point.

The allowance a yacht has to make to any smaller yacht is obtained by multiplying the difference between the times set against their respective ratings in the time tables by the length of the course in knots. For example, the time a yacht of 70ft. rating has to allow a yacht of 65ft. rating over a 50-knot course is as follows:—

70ft. ... 199·20
65ft. ... 190·45

8·75
50

60)437·50

7·17·5 seconds.

When a fraction of a second equals or exceeds ·5 it is to be counted as a second, but fractions less than ·5 are to be disregarded. In the case illustrated above the time allowance is, therefore, 7 minutes and 18 seconds.

If one of the yachts is above and the other below 24ft. rating, the time allowances in the two tables found, from their respective ratings, added together, and multiplied by the length of the course, will give the time the larger allows the smaller yacht.

At a general meeting of the Y.R.A. held on the 12th November, 1896, the time scale above 90 rating was altered as follows:— The tangential or constant difference of 1·3 seconds per foot previously mentioned was increased by a cumulative addition of 10 per cent., or 0.13 for each foot, and the table has been altered accordingly.

SCALE OF ALLOWANCES FOR DIFFERENCES OF FEET AND 10THS OF FEET RATING.

Rating.	Time Allowance in seconds per knot.	Rating.	Time Allowance in seconds per knot.
24	0·00	26	23·10
·1	1·20	·1	24·13
·2	2·40	·2	25·16
·3	3·60	·3	26·19
·4	4·80	·4	27·22
·5	6·00	·5	28·25
·6	7·20	·6	29·28
·7	8·40	·7	30·31
·8	9·60	·8	31·34
·9	10·80	·9	32·37
25	12·00	27	33·40
·1	13·20	·1	34·36
·2	14·20	·2	35·32
·3	15·40	·3	36·28
·4	16·50	·4	37·24
·5	17·80	·5	38·20
·6	18·70	·6	39·16
·7	19·80	·7	40·12
·8	20·90	·8	41·08
·9	22·00	·9	42·04

Time Allowance—continued.

Rating.	Time Allowance in seconds per knot.	Rating.	Time Allowance in seconds per knot.
28	43·00	36	100·00
·1	43·90	·1	100·52
·2	44·80	·2	101·04
·3	45·70	·3	101·56
·4	46·60	·4	102·08
·5	47·50	·5	102·60
·6	48·40	·6	103·12
·7	49·30	·7	103·64
·8	50·20	·8	104·16
·9	51·10	·9	104·68
29	52·00	37	105·20
·1	52·84	·1	105·69
·2	53·68	·2	106·18
·3	54·52	·3	106·67
·4	55·36	·4	107·16
·5	56·20	·5	107·65
·6	57·04	·6	108·14
·7	57·88	·7	108·63
·8	58·72	·8	109·12
·9	59·56	·9	109·61
30	60·40	38	110·10
·1	61·18	·1	110·56
·2	61·96	·2	111·02
·3	62·74	·3	111·48
·4	63·52	·4	111·94
·5	64·30	·5	112·40
·6	65·08	·6	112·86
·7	65·86	·7	113·32
·8	66·64	·8	113·78
·9	67·42	·9	114·24
31	68·20	39	114·70
·1	68·93	·1	115·14
·2	69·66	·2	115·58
·3	70·39	·3	116·02
·4	71·12	·4	116·46
·5	71·85	·5	116·90
·6	72·58	·6	117·34
·7	73·31	·7	117·78
·8	74·04	·8	118·22
·9	74·77	·9	118·66
32	75·50	40	119·10
·1	76·18	·1	119·52
·2	76·86	·2	119·94
·3	77·54	·3	120·36
·4	78·22	·4	120·78
·5	78·90	·5	121·20
·6	79·58	·6	121·62
·7	80·26	·7	122·04
·8	80·94	·8	122·46
·9	81·62	·9	122·88
33	82·30	41	123·30
·1	82·93	·1	123·70
·2	83·56	·2	124·10
·3	84·19	·3	124·50
·4	84·82	·4	124·90
·5	85·45	·5	125·30
·6	86·08	·6	125·70
·7	86·71	·7	126·10
·8	87·34	·8	126·50
·9	87·97	·9	126·90
34	88·60	42	127·30
·1	89·19	·1	127·68
·2	89·78	·2	128·06
·3	90·37	·3	128·44
·4	90·96	·4	128·82
·5	91·55	·5	129·20
·6	92·14	·6	129·58
·7	92·73	·7	129·96
·8	93·32	·8	130·34
·9	93·91	·9	130·72
35	94·50	43	131·10
·1	95·05	·1	131·47
·2	95·60	·2	131·84
·3	96·15	·3	132·21
·4	96·70	·4	132·58
·5	97·25	·5	132·95
·6	97·80	·6	133·32
·7	98·35	·7	133·69
·8	98·90	·8	134·06
·9	99·45	·9	134·43

Time Allowance—continued.   *Time Allowance*—continued.

Rating.	Time Allowance in seconds per knot.	Rating.	Time Allowance in seconds per knot.	Rating.	Time Allowance in seconds per knot.	Rating.	Time Allowance in seconds per knot.
44	134·80	52	160·80	60	180·45	68	195·85
·1	135·16	·1	161·08	·1	180·66	·1	196·02
·2	135·52	·2	161·36	·2	180·87	·2	196·19
·3	135·88	·3	161·64	·3	181·08	·3	196·36
·4	136·24	·4	161·92	·4	181·29	·4	196·53
·5	136·60	·5	162·20	·5	181·50	·5	196·70
·6	136·96	·6	162·48	·6	181·71	·6	196·87
·7	137·32	·7	162·76	·7	181·92	·7	197·04
·8	137·68	·8	163·04	·8	182·13	·8	197·21
·9	138·04	·9	163·32	·9	182·34	·9	197·38
45	138·40	53	163·60	61	182·55	69	197·55
·1	138·75	·1	163·87	·1	182·76	·1	197·72
·2	139·10	·2	164·14	·2	182·96	·2	197·88
·3	139·45	·3	164·41	·3	183·17	·3	198·05
·4	139·80	·4	164·68	·4	183·37	·4	198·21
·5	140·15	·5	164·95	·5	183·58	·5	198·38
·6	140·50	·6	165·22	·6	183·78	·6	198·54
·7	140·85	·7	165·49	·7	183·99	·7	198·71
·8	141·20	·8	165·76	·8	184·19	·8	198·87
·9	141·55	·9	166·03	·9	184·40	·9	199·04
46	141·90	54	166·30	62	184·60	70	199·20
·1	142·24	·1	166·56	·1	184·80	·1	199·36
·2	142·58	·2	166·82	·2	185·00	·2	199·52
·3	142·92	·3	167·08	·3	185·20	·3	199·68
·4	143·26	·4	167·34	·4	185·40	·4	199·84
·5	143·60	·5	167·60	·5	185·60	·5	200·00
·6	143·94	·6	167·86	·6	185·80	·6	200·16
·7	144·28	·7	168·12	·7	186·00	·7	200·32
·8	144·62	·8	168·38	·8	186·20	·8	200·48
·9	144·96	·9	168·64	·9	186·40	·9	200·64
47	145·30	55	168·90	63	186·60	71	200·80
·1	145·63	·1	169·15	·1	186·80	·1	200·96
·2	145·96	·2	169·40	·2	186·99	·2	201·11
·3	146·29	·3	169·65	·3	187·19	·3	201·27
·4	146·62	·4	169·90	·4	187·38	·4	201·42
·5	146·95	·5	170·15	·5	187·58	·5	201·58
·6	147·28	·6	170·40	·6	187·77	·6	201·73
·7	147·61	·7	170·65	·7	187·97	·7	201·89
·8	147·94	·8	170·90	·8	188·16	·8	202·04
·9	148·27	·9	171·15	·9	188·36	·9	202·20
48	148·60	56	171·40	64	188·55	72	202·35
·1	148·92	·1	171·64	·1	188·74	·1	202·50
·2	149·24	·2	171·88	·2	188·93	·2	202·65
·3	149·56	·3	172·12	·3	189·12	·3	202·80
·4	149·88	·4	172·36	·4	189·31	·4	202·95
·5	150·20	·5	172·60	·5	189·50	·5	203·10
·6	150·52	·6	172·84	·6	189·69	·6	203·25
·7	150·84	·7	173·08	·7	189·88	·7	203·40
·8	151·16	·8	173·32	·8	190·07	·8	203·55
·9	151·48	·9	173·56	·9	190·26	·9	203·70
49	151·80	57	173·80	65	190·45	73	203·85
·1	152·11	·1	174·03	·1	190·64	·1	204·00
·2	152·42	·2	174·26	·2	190·82	·2	204·14
·3	152·73	·3	174·49	·3	191·01	·3	204·29
·4	153·04	·4	174·72	·4	191·19	·4	204·44
·5	153·35	·5	174·95	·5	191·38	·5	204·59
·6	153·66	·6	175·18	·6	191·56	·6	204·73
·7	153·97	·7	175·41	·7	191·75	·7	204·88
·8	154·28	·8	175·64	·8	191·93	·8	205·03
·9	154·59	·9	175·87	·9	192·12	·9	205·17
50	154·90	58	176·10	66	192·30	74	205·32
·1	155·20	·1	176·32	·1	192·48	·1	205·46
·2	155·50	·2	176·54	·2	192·66	·2	205·61
·3	155·80	·3	176·76	·3	192·84	·3	205·75
·4	156·10	·4	176·96	·4	193·02	·4	205·90
·5	156·40	·5	177·20	·5	193·20	·5	206·04
·6	156·70	·6	177·42	·6	193·38	·6	206·18
·7	157·00	·7	177·64	·7	193·56	·7	206·33
·8	157·30	·8	177·86	·8	193·74	·8	206·47
·9	157·60	·9	178·08	·9	193·92	·9	206·62
51	157·90	59	178·30	67	194·10	75	206·76
·1	158·19	·1	178·52	·1	194·28	·1	206·90
·2	158·48	·2	178·73	·2	194·45	·2	207·04
·3	158·77	·3	178·95	·3	194·63	·3	207·18
·4	159·06	·4	179·16	·4	194·80	·4	207·32
·5	159·35	·5	179·38	·5	194·98	·5	207·47
·6	159·64	·6	179·59	·6	195·15	·6	207·61
·7	159·93	·7	179·81	·7	195·33	·7	207·75
·8	160·22	·8	180·02	·8	195·50	·8	207·89
·9	160·51	·9	180·24	·9	195·68	·9	208·03

Time Allowance—continued.

Rating.	Time Allowance in seconds per knot.	Rating.	Time Allowance in seconds per knot.
76	206·17	84	218·72
·1	206·31	·1	218·85
·2	208·45	·2	218·98
·3	208·58	·3	219·11
·4	208·72	·4	219·24
·5	208·86	·5	219·37
·6	209·00	·6	219·50
·7	209·14	·7	219·63
·8	209·27	·8	219·76
·9	209·41	·9	219·89
77	209·55	85	220·02
·1	209·69	·1	220·15
·2	209·82	·2	220·28
·3	209·96	·3	220·41
·4	210·09	·4	220·54
·5	210·23	·5	220·67
·6	210·36	·6	220·80
·7	210·50	·7	220·93
·8	210·63	·8	221·06
·9	210·77	·9	221·19
78	210·90	86	221·32
·1	211·03	·1	221·45
·2	211·16	·2	221·58
·3	211·30	·3	221·71
·4	211·43	·4	221·84
·5	211·56	·5	221·97
·6	211·69	·6	222·10
·7	211·82	·7	222·23
·8	211·96	·8	222·36
·9	212·09	·9	222·49
79	212·22	87	222·62
·1	212·35	·1	222·75
·2	212·48	·2	222·88
·3	212·61	·3	223·01
·4	212·74	·4	223·14
·5	212·87	·5	223·27
·6	213·00	·6	223·40
·7	213·13	·7	223·53
·8	213·26	·8	223·66
·9	213·39	·9	223·79
80	213·52	88	223·92
·1	213·65	·1	224·05
·2	213·78	·2	224·18
·3	213·91	·3	224·31
·4	214·04	·4	224·44
·5	214·17	·5	224·57
·6	214·30	·6	224·70
·7	214·43	·7	224·83
·8	214·56	·8	224·96
·9	214·69	·9	225·09
·81	214·82	89	225·22
·1	214·95	·1	225·35
·2	215·08	·2	225·48
·3	215·21	·3	225·61
·4	215·34	·4	225·74
·5	215·47	·5	225·87
·6	215·60	·6	226·00
·7	215·73	·7	226·13
·8	215·86	·8	226·26
·9	215·99	·9	226·39
·82	216·12	90	226·52
·1	216·25	·1	226·66
·2	216·38	·2	226·81
·3	216·51	·3	226·95
·4	216·64	·4	227·09
·5	216·77	·5	227·23
·6	216·90	·6	227·37
·7	217·03	·7	227·52
·8	217·16	·8	227·66
·9	217·29	·9	227·80
·83	217·42	91	227·95
·1	217·55	·1	228·11
·2	217·68	·2	228·26
·3	217·81	·3	228·42
·4	217·94	·4	228·57
·5	218·07	·5	228·73
·6	218·20	·6	228·88
·7	218·33	·7	229·04
·8	218·45	·8	229·19
·9	218·58	·9	229·35

Time Allowance—continued.

Rating.	Time Allowance in seconds per knot.	Rating.	Time Allowance in seconds per knot.
92	229·51	100	246·67
·1	229·67	·1	246·94
·2	229·84	·2	247·21
·3	230·01	·3	247·49
·4	230·18	·4	247·76
·5	230·35	·5	248·03
·6	230·52	·6	248·30
·7	230·69	·7	248·58
·8	230·86	·8	248·85
·9	231·03	·9	249·12
93	231·20	101	249·40
·1	231·38	·1	249·69
·2	231·56	·2	249·97
·3	231·74	·3	250·26
·4	231·92	·4	250·55
·5	232·11	·5	250·83
·6	232·29	·6	251·12
·7	232·47	·7	251·40
·8	232·65	·8	251·69
·9	232·83	·9	251·97
94	233·02	102	252·26
·1	233·21	·1	252·56
·2	233·41	·2	252·86
·3	233·60	·3	253·16
·4	233·80	·4	253·46
·5	233·99	·5	253·75
·6	234·19	·6	254·05
·7	234·38	·7	254·35
·8	234·58	·8	254·65
·9	234·77	·9	254·95
95	234·97	103	255·25
·1	235·17	·1	255·56
·2	235·38	·2	255·87
·3	235·59	·3	256·18
·4	235·80	·4	256·50
·5	236·00	·5	256·81
·6	236·21	·6	257·12
·7	236·42	·7	257·43
·8	236·63	·8	257·75
·9	236·84	·9	258·06
96	237·05	104	258·37
·1	237·27	·1	258·69
·2	237·49	·2	259·02
·3	237·71	·3	259·34
·4	237·93	·4	259·67
·5	238·16	·5	259·99
·6	238·38	·6	260·32
·7	238·60	·7	260·64
·8	238·82	·8	260·97
·9	239·04	·9	261·29
97	239·26	105	261·62
·1	239·49	·1	261·95
·2	239·73	·2	262·29
·3	239·96	·3	262·63
·4	240·20	·4	262·97
·5	240·43	·5	263·31
·6	240·67	·6	263·65
·7	240·90	·7	263·98
·8	241·13	·8	264·32
·9	241·37	·9	264·66
98	241·60	106	265·00
·1	241·84	·1	265·35
·2	242·09	·2	265·70
·3	242·33	·3	266·05
·4	242·58	·4	266·40
·5	242·82	·5	266·76
·6	243·07	·6	267·11
·7	243·32	·7	267·46
·8	243·57	·8	267·81
·9	243·82	·9	268·16
99	244·07	107	268·51
·1	244·33	·1	268·87
·2	244·59	·2	269·24
·3	244·85	·3	269·60
·4	245·11	·4	269·97
·5	245·37	·5	270·34
·6	245·63	·6	270·70
·7	245·89	·7	271·06
·8	246·15	·8	271·42
·9	246·41	·9	271·79

Time Allowance—continued.

Rating.	Allowance in seconds per knot.	Rating.	Allowance in seconds per knot.
108	272·15	109	275·92
·1	272·52	·1	276·31
·2	272·90	·2	276·70
·3	273·28	·3	277·09
·4	273·66	·4	277·48
·5	274·03	·5	277·87
·6	274·41	·6	278·26
·7	274·79	·7	278·65
·8	275·17	·8	279·04
·9	275·54	·9	279·43
		110	279·82

TIME SCALE FOR RATINGS BELOW 24.

Rating	Seconds	Rating	Seconds
24·0	0·0		
23·9	1·2	16·9	85·2
·8	2·4	·8	86·4
·7	3·6	·7	87·6
·6	4·8	·6	88·8
·5	6·0	·5	90·0
·4	7·2	·4	91·2
·3	8·4	·3	92·4
·2	9·6	·2	93·6
·1	10·8	·1	94·8
·0	12·0	·0	96·0
22·9	13·2	15·9	97·2
·8	14·4	·8	98·4
·7	15·6	·7	99·6
·6	16·8	·6	100·8
·5	18·0	·5	102·0
·4	19·2	·4	103·2
·3	20·4	·3	104·4
·2	21·6	·2	105·6
·1	22·8	·1	106·8
·0	24·0	·0	108·0
21·9	25·2	14·9	109·2
·8	26·4	·8	110·4
·7	27·6	·7	111·6
·6	28·8	·6	112·8
·5	30·0	·5	114·0
·4	31·2	·4	115·2
·3	32·4	·3	116·4
·2	33·6	·2	117·6
·1	34·8	·1	118·8
·0	36·0	·0	120·0
20·9	37·2	13·9	121·2
·8	38·4	·8	122·4
·7	39·6	·7	123·6
·6	40·8	·6	124·8
·5	42·0	·5	126·0
·4	43·2	·4	127·2
·3	44·4	·3	128·4
·2	45·6	·2	129·6
·1	46·8	·1	130·8
·0	48·0	·0	132·0
19·9	49·2	12·9	133·2
·8	50·4	·8	134·4
·7	51·6	·7	135·6
·6	52·8	·6	136·8
·5	54·0	·5	138·0
·4	55·2	·4	139·2
·3	56·4	·3	140·4
·2	57·6	·2	141·6
·1	58·8	·1	142·8
·0	60·0	·0	144·0
18·9	61·2	11·9	145·2
·8	62·4	·8	146·4
·7	63·6	·7	147·6
·6	64·8	·6	148·8
·5	66·0	·5	150·0
·4	67·2	·4	151·2
·3	68·4	·3	152·4
·2	69·6	·2	153·6
·1	70·8	·1	154·8
·0	72·0	·0	156·0
17·9	73·2	10·9	157·2
·8	74·4	·8	158·4
·7	75·6	·7	159·6
·6	76·8	·6	160·8
·5	78·0	·5	162·0
·4	79·2	·4	163·2
·3	80·4	·3	164·4
·2	81·6	·2	165·6
·1	82·8	·1	166·8
0	84·0	·0	168·0

TIME ALLOWANCE BY LENGTH.

Rating yachts by length, in competitive sailing, has been practised since the early days of yacht racing, so far at least as small yachts are concerned; but the practice has not become general, for the principal reason that one yacht, say of 40ft. length, owing to greater beam, might be capable of carrying a larger quantity of sail than another yacht of 40ft. length, and so have greater speed. If sails were not the means of propulsion this would be of little consequence, as, length for length, vessels of varied proportions of beam might, if well modelled, be of equal speed; and the speed of vessels of different lengths will be found to vary nearly as the square roots of their lengths, unless there be some extraordinary variance in their general form. It is not, therefore, surprising to find that the roots of the linear dimensions of yachts have been many times suggested as a proper basis for a time allowance.

So far as our experience goes, the speed of yachts of different sizes accords with those set out in the table below; and these speeds also agree with the assumption that the speed varies as the square root of the length. When the configurations of the yachts are the same, the quality of immersed surface varies considerably.

Length.	Equivalent Tonnage.	Knots per hour.	Time per mile.	
ft.			Min.	Sec.
9	0¼	3·75	16	0
16	1½	5·00	12	0
25	4½	6·25	9	36
36	6	7·50	8	0
41	10	8·	7	30
49	20	8·75	6	51
64	40	10·	6	0
81	100	11·25	5	20
100	190	12·15	4	48
121	320	13·75	4	21
144	400	15·00	4	0

Thus, in the table it has been assumed that a yacht 64ft. long can sail one mile in six minutes; and that the time of other yachts per mile will vary as the square root of their respective lengths. Therefore, on this assumption, a yacht 9ft. long will sail a mile in sixteen minutes (or 960 seconds), and the time between a yacht 9ft. long and any other larger yacht will therefore be found by the equation

$$960 - \left(\frac{960 \times \sqrt{9}}{\sqrt{L}} \right)$$

The letter L in the equation is any other yacht.

This allowance assumes that the full speed of the yachts would be maintained; but in yacht racing we know that full speed is seldom kept up; and practice teaches us that an allowance based on the assumption that full speed would be maintained from start to finish, would be nearly always double what the larger yacht is capable of giving the smaller. Consequently, in the table which follows, only half the full-speed allowance has been given.

LENGTH CLASSES.

Time scale for boats sailing in Length Classes calculated in seconds and decimals for one nautical mile or knot.

Length L.W.L. in feet.	Time allowance in seconds per knot.	Length L.W.L. in feet.	Time allowance in seconds per knot.
9·0	0·0	25·5	190·56
9·5	12·02	26·0	193·26
10·0	24·00	26·5	195·80
10·5	34·80	27·0	198·35
11·0	44·80	27·5	200·90
11·5	54·15	28·0	203·29
12·0	62·89	28·5	205·64
12·5	71·12	29·0	207·92
13·0	78·80	29·5	210·16
13·5	86·13	30·0	212·32
14·0	93·05	30·5	214·45
14·5	99·59	31·0	216·56
15·0	105·81	31·5	218·53
15·5	111·73	32·0	220·49
16·0	117·37	32·5	222·42
16·5	122·73	33·0	224·29
17·0	127·88	33·5	226·13
17·5	132·79	34·0	227·92
18·0	137·49	34·5	229·68
18·5	142·02	35·0	231·40
19·0	146·35	35·5	233·09
19·5	150·52	36·0	234·73
20·0	154·58	36·5	236·35
20·5	158·40	37·0	237·92
21·0	162·12	37·5	239·48
21·5	165·72	38·0	240·94
22·0	169·19	38·5	242·48
22·5	172·55	39·0	243·94
23·0	175·79	39·5	245·37
23·5	178·93	40·0	246·77
24·0	181·97	40·5	248·20
24·5	184·93	41·0	249·50
25·0	187·78	50·0	287·30

RATING BY SAIL AREA AND LENGTH.

In 1880 Mr. Dixon Kemp devised a rule based on sail area and length of water-line as follows:

$$\frac{L \times S}{6000} = \text{Rating.}$$

In 1882 the rule was adopted by the Seawanhaka Yacht Club in America, and was so much approved of that the New York Yacht Club in 1883 took the matter up, mainly because they desired to try the effect of a rule on American yacht building, which would have a tendency to produce a longer and deeper type of model.

This rule was adopted for a period of seven years by the Y.R.A., from the year 1887 to 1895 inclusive.

In formulating the rule, Mr. Dixon Kemp had pointed out that the sail area in yachts of similar types is equal to their length squared; and, inverting this, the New York Yacht Club treated the length as equal to the square root of the sail area, and took the sum of the length and square root added together as the basis for a time allowance; but in order, it can be presumed, to discourage excessive length in relation to breadth, the actual formula adopted was $\dfrac{\sqrt{S} + L2}{3}$, and the Seawanhaka Yacht Club, $\dfrac{\sqrt{S} + L}{2}$. The latter in effect is practically the same as the English formula, but the formula of the New York Yacht Club has a varying effect.

By comparison the old Y.R.A. rule was very much easier on length than either the Seawanhaka Yacht Club rule or the New York Yacht Club rule. Take a given length and rating, and then add to the length the extent the sail area would have to be reduced to maintain the given rating as follows:

Y.R.A. RULE, 1887 TO 1895.

Length on L.W.L.	Area of sail possible.	Rating $= \dfrac{L \times S}{6000}$
30ft.	2000 sq. ft.	10 rating.
35ft.	1714 sq. ft.	10 rating.
40ft.	1500 sq. ft.	10 rating.

SEAWANHAKA RULE.

Length on L.W.L.	Area of sail possible.	$\dfrac{L + \sqrt{S}}{2} =$ Sailing length or rating.
30ft.	2000 sq. ft.	37·36ft.
35ft.	1578 sq. ft.	37·36ft.
40ft.	1206 sq. ft.	37·36ft.

NEW YORK YACHT CLUB RULE.

Length on L.W.L.	Area of sail possible.	$\dfrac{L2 + \sqrt{S}}{3} =$ Sailing length or rating.
30ft.	2000 sq. ft.	35ft.
35ft.	1225 sq. ft.	35ft.
40ft.	625 sq. ft.	35ft.

Thus for 33 per cent. difference of length the Seawanhaka rule reduces the sail 15 per cent. more than the old Y.R.A. rule; and the New York rule for 33 per cent. reduction in length reduces sail 44 per cent. more than the L × S rule. It can, therefore, be seen that the L × S rule gives a long vessel an exceedingly good chance, compared with either the Seawanhaka or New York rule; and that, in fact, it is much the best rule of the three for discouraging attempts to build boats of an extremely beamy type.

These statements as to the operation of the rules do not, however, apply to all ratings and lengths; thus, if applied to a vessel say of 80ft. water line and 9000 sq. ft. of canvas, if 33 per cent. be added to her length, her sail will be reduced 34 per cent., keeping, of course, the rating constant. This will best be seen by tabulation, as in the former case.

LENGTH AND SAIL AREA RULE.

Length on L.W.L.	Area of sail possible.	Rating $= \dfrac{L \times S}{6000}$
80ft.	9000 sq. ft.	120 rating.
106·4ft.	6767 sq. ft.	120 rating.

Length on L.W.L.	Area of sail possible.	$\dfrac{L\,2 + \sqrt{S}}{3}$ = Sailing length or rating.
80ft.	9000 sq. ft.	85ft.
106·4ft.	1781 sq. ft.	85ft.

Thus, when the length is 80ft. and the rating 120, the $\dfrac{L \times S}{6000}$ rule for 33 per cent. increase in length reduces sail 34 per cent., and the New York Yacht Club rule reduces sail 80 per cent.; so in this particular case it is 46 per cent. harder on length than the $L \times S$ rule.

The foregoing examples are very broad illustrations, and it would be unusual that for any given rating there should be a difference of 33 per cent. in length; and if we take a smaller difference in length the percentages are very much reduced. Thus, when the rating is 60, and the length on the water line 60ft., an increase of 7 per cent. (making 64ft. in the water line, reduces sail 6·2 per cent. under the $L \times S$ rule, and 19·6 per cent. under the New York Yacht Club rule, or 13·4 per cent. more than the Y.R.A.

In general terms it is perfectly correct to make a statement that the $L \times S$ rule is very much harder on sail than the New York rule.

In 1887 the New York Yacht Club adopted the Seawanhaka rule.

A length rating rule exactly equivalent to the $\dfrac{L \times S}{6000}$ rule would be

$$\sqrt[3]{L \times S}.$$

For particulars of the "Linear Rating" rule now in use, see farther on under Y.R.A. Rule 51.

GERMAN RATING RULE, 1899.

$$\text{Rating} = \dfrac{L + B + \tfrac{1}{4} G + \tfrac{1}{2}\sqrt{S}}{2}$$

Cruisers are measured according to the following formula:

$$R = \dfrac{L + B + \tfrac{1}{4} G + \tfrac{1}{2}\sqrt{S A} + d - F}{2}$$

R signifies the rating value; L, length of the yacht (in mètres); B, greatest beam; G, skin girth; F, freeboard; S A, sail area in square mètres; d, difference between the skin girth and chain girth in mètres.

For chain girth the greatest girth, wherever found, is taken from the top of the deck planking round the keel. In the case of foreign yachts, where their home certificate does not show the skin girth, these dimensions, in exceptional cases, may be taken from the designer's plans. The skin girth is taken from the top of the planking, at the same spot where the greatest chain girth has been found.

G is found by deducting from the skin girth twice the freeboard.

Ballasted plates are calculated in the same way as fixed fins, and must not be taken up

during a race. Freeboard is taken at that part of the yacht where the greatest breadth is found. The factor d is determined by deducting the chain girth from the skin girth.

FRENCH RATING RULE, 1899.

$$T = \dfrac{\left(L - \dfrac{P}{4}\right) P \sqrt{S} \times \dfrac{\sqrt{S}}{\sqrt{M}}}{1000}$$

In this formula T is tonnage; L, length on load water line; P, girth; S, area of sail, M, area of mid-section. Of course M is introduced as a divisor, with the idea of inducing moderately large under-water body.

Timing.—In timing vessels *passing* marks to finish a race or otherwise, the fairest plan is to take the time as each vessel's bowsprit end reaches the mark. In timing yachts that have to gybe or tack *round* marks, time must be taken when in the opinion of the timekeeper the yacht is fairly at or round the mark; this especially in the case of gybing.

Toggle.—A short rope with an eye at one end and a small piece of wood at the other, to insert in the eye and form a kind of strop or becket.

Ton.—A weight of 2240lb. avoirdupois. In hydraulics 35 cubic feet of sea water, represent a ton or 36 cubic feet of fresh water.

Tonnage.—The nominal size or capacity of a ship, variously estimated.

Since the early days when "tons burden" meant the actual tons weight of coal a vessel such as the north country keels would carry, the word "tonnage" has conveyed no fixed idea of bulk or weight. The nominal tonnage has been variously computed and the earliest record (See *Archæologia*, Vol. XI.) is that the "tons burden" of the ships of the Royal Navy in the 17th century was calculated by $\dfrac{L \times B \times D}{96}$. L length on keel, B extreme breadth, and D depth of hold. It was probably found that a ship was capable of filling up with coal to just half her cubical capacity, taking 48 cubic feet to the ton, hence came the divisor 96. Say a vessel was $\dfrac{80 \times 24 \times 12}{96} = 240$ tons, which would be about the amount of coal or other dead weight she would carry.

Owing probably to the inconvenience of arriving at the depth of laden vessels entering ports, the rule was altered to $\dfrac{L \times B \times \tfrac{1}{2}B}{94}$ and finally, in 1719, an Act was passed enjoining that the rule just stated should be law, but to allow for rake of stem $\tfrac{3}{5}$ of the breadth was ordered to be subtracted from the length.

In this rule it will be seen there were two assumptions. First, that the vessel was a rectangular figure, and, second, that her depth was equal to her breadth. The result was that ships were built under it as much like boxes as possible, and deep in proportion to breadth, because depth was untaxed and beam heavily taxed. However, in spite of learned arguments and much abuse (the rule of measurement was commonly referred to as the "iniquitous tonnage laws"), the rule remained in force as the law of the land until the passing of the Merchant Shipping Act in 1854. Under that Act the tonnage became one of cubic capacity (100 cubic feet to the ton), and for roughly estimating the tons of a laden ship the following rule was allowed to be used under the Act:

$$\left(\frac{\text{Girth} + \text{Breadth}}{2}\right)^2 \times \text{Length} \times \frac{17}{10000}$$

In the case of iron ships 18 was substituted for 17 in the fractional factor. This rule has now fallen into disuse, as, practically, all nations adopted the British rule, and the certificate of registry of course contains the tonnage. This rule has been several times put forward as one adapted for yacht measurement for racing purposes.

The builders' rough rule for estimating registered tonnage was for ships

$$\frac{L \times B \times D \times \cdot7}{100}$$

for yachts

$$\frac{L \times B \times D \times \cdot5}{100}$$

The latter rule was used by the New Thames and Corinthian Yacht Club (see "Corinthian") in the following form:

$$\frac{L \times B \times D}{200} = \frac{L \times B \times D \times \cdot5}{100}$$

The official tonnage rule of 1719 was as follows:

$$\frac{(L - \frac{1}{4}\,5) \times B \times \frac{1}{2}\,B}{94}$$

It is still in use among builders for estimating the size of ships or yachts, and is termed Builders' Measurement (B.M.), or Old Measurement (O.M.).

According to builders' measurement, length is taken along the keel from the sternpost to a perpendicular or plumb line dropped from the stem-head on deck.

When this rule was used for yacht rating it was found that by raking the sternpost the length of keel was shortened, and in order to prevent evasions in this way, the Royal Mersey and Royal London Yacht Clubs in 1854 passed a rule that the length should be taken on deck instead of along the keel. The tonnage of the vessels with very raking sternposts was, of course, much increased, and in order to let them off a little more easily, the whole beam was ordered to be subtracted from the length instead of ⅔ths of the beam. The rule then read

$$\frac{(L - B) \times (B \times \frac{1}{2}\,B)}{94}$$

(Multiplying by beam, then by half beam, is the same as multiplying by the half square of the beam.)

This is the rule known as the "Thames Rule," adopted by the Y.R.A. in 1875.

In 1879 the Y.R.A. altered the rule to length on load line.

In 1881 the Y.R.A. adopted a new rule, which came into operation in the following year (1882). The rule is $\frac{(L + B)^2 \times B}{1730}$; that is, add the breadth to the length, and multiply the sum thus obtained by itself, and then by the breadth. The product is divided by 1730.

This rule was abandoned after the season of 1886 for the length and sail area rule, which in turn gave place to the present Y.R.A. Linear Rating Rule in 1896. (See Y.R.A. Racing Rule No. 51, farther on.)

Top.—In square-rigged ships, the stage at the lower mast heads to give additional spread to the topmast rigging, and to form a kind of gallery for riflemen in war ships. There are fore top, main top, and mizen top. To top is to raise one end of a boom or yard by the topping lifts. (See Plate I.) The "top" of a vessel is the part above water.

Topgallant Bulwarks.—Bulwarks fitted above the rail to afford additional shelter on deck.

Topgallant Mast.—The mast next above the topmast in square-rigged ships.

Top Hamper.—Any real or supposed unnecessary weight carried on deck or masts.

Topmast Hoops.—Hoops were formerly used for jib-headed topsails, the same as they used to be for the original "gaff topsails." The hoops when not in use rest on the masthead. In hoisting the topsail the lacing is passed through an eyelet hole in the luff of the sail and through a hoop, and so on. When the sail is hoisted chock-a-block the lacing is hauled taut; in lowering the lacing is slackened. Hoops facilitate the hoisting and lowering of the sail, and admit of its being lowered and hoisted without a man going aloft.

Topping Lifts.—Ropes or tackles used to raise or support booms or yards.

Top Rail.—The rail fitted on the stanchions as a finish to the bulwarks.

Topsails.—Racing yachts usually are supplied with various topsails, viz., large jackyard topsail, a smaller one, jib-headed topsail, and jib topsail. Formerly a square topsail was carried as well, but spinnakers have superseded squaresails. A cruising yacht usually carries one square-headed topsail and one jib-headed topsail. American yachts usually carry one balloon topsail (called a club topsail) and one jib-headed topsail, called a working topsail, and a jib topsail. Schooners, both British and American, carry as well a main topmast staysail.

Topsail Schooner. — See "Square Topsail Schooner."

Topsides.—That part of a vessel above the wales; now in yachts sometimes understood as the part between the water-line and deck, or the freeboard.

Top Timbers.—The upper parts of the framing of a vessel.

Top Your Boom and Sail Large.—To leave in a hurry and sail off the wind.

Toss the Oars.—To throw them out of the row-locks and rest them perpendicularly, blades uppermost, on reaching a destination.

Toss up the Boom.—To raise the boom by the lifts.

Touching the Wind.—Luffing into the wind till the sails shake. (See "Luff and Touch Her.")

Tow Rope or Tow Line.—The rope or hawser used in towing.

Track.—The course or wake of a ship.

Trade Wind.—Winds that blow in one direction a considerable time, admitting of traders making expeditions voyages.

Trail Boards.—Carved boards fitted on the bow and stem of schooners.

Transom.—The frame at the sternpost of a vessel. In boats the transverse board at the stern, which gives shape to the quarters and forms the stern end of the boat.

Transverse.—Athwartships. At right-angles to the line of the keel.

Trapezium.—A four-sided figure with two sides or foot and head parallel, as a ship's square sail.

Trapezoid.—A four-sided figure whose sides do not form parallel lines, such as a cutter's mainsail.

Traveller.—An iron ring, thimble, or strop which travels on a spar, bar, or rope.

Traveller, Jointed.—The fishermen on the S.W. coast use a jointed mast traveller. The iron hoop is in two half moons, each end has an eye turned in (see Fig. 346); the two halves are connected by these eyes. The object in having a jointed traveller is to facilitate lowering. (See "Penzance Luggers.")

Fig. 346.

Treenails.—Bolts or plugs of wood used to fasten plank to the timbers of vessels. Pronounced "trennel."

Trestle Trees.—In ships long pieces of timber fitted at the masthead in a fore-and-aft direction to support the cross trees.

Triatic Stay.—A stay from foremast head to mainmast head in a schooner, and termed sciatic stay in old works.

Trick.—The time a man is stationed at the helm. (See "Spell.")

Trim.—The position of a ship in the water in a fore-and-aft direction. To trim a vessel is to set her in a particular position, by the head or stern. The term is sometimes erroneously used to represent the shifting of ballast transversely. To trim the sails is to sheet and tack them so that they are disposed in the best manner possible, in relation to the force and direction of the wind.

A passage. Sometimes used in Scotland to denote a board made in beating to windward. To trip a spar is to cant it. To trip an anchor is to break it out of the ground;

an anchor is a-trip when one of its flukes is on, but not in, the ground. (See "Anchor" and "Scowing")

Trip or Tripping Line.—A rope used to cant a spar, as trip halyards for a topsail, or the line bent to the crown of an anchor to trip it or break it out of the ground.

Trough of the Sea.—The hollow between wave-crest and wave-crest.

Trucks.—The wooden caps fitted on the upper mastheads to reeve the signal halyards through.

True Wind.—A wind that does not vary; the prevailing wind in contradistinction to eddies or baffling puffs.

Trying.—To "try" is when a vessel is hove to, to so trim her sails that she may gather head-way and make something to the good.

Trysail.—A small sort of gaff sail or sharp-headed sail set in heavy weather. The sail set on the fore and main mast of square-rigged ships similar to the spanker on the mizen. The origin of the term trysail was probably that in heavy weather it was the sail set to enable a vessel to "try," or to make some headway.

Tuck.—The form of the hollow in the quarter near the transom or stern-post.

Tug.—A towing boat. To tug is to tow.

Tumble In or Tumble Home.—When the sides of a ship near the deck incline inwards; the opposite to flaring.

Tumbler.—A piece of wood pivoted in the jaws of a gaff which is always in the plane of the mast.

Tumbler-fid.—A self-acting fid for a topmast.

Turk's-head.—A knot made to finish off the end of a rope.

Turn.—A circle made by a rope round a pin, &c. "Turn O!" is an order to belay. To catch a turn is to put the fall of a tackle or part of any rope round a belaying pin, stanchion, &c.

Turn in.—To secure the end of a rope by seizing.

Turning to Windward.—Working or beating for a point or object by short boards. Generally beating to windward. To turn is to tack.

Turn of the Tide.—When the tide changes from flood to ebb, or the contrary.

Twice Laid Rope.—Rope re-made from old rope. A term of reproach for articles of inferior quality.

Twiddler.—Small broom used in scrubbing the decks of yachts, to clean out corners, &c.

Twiddling Stick.—The tiller, hence "twiddling lines" are the tiller lines.

Two-blocks.—Said when a tackle has been used so that its two blocks come close together. (See "Chock-a-block.")

Tye.—A runner to which a tackle is hooked, used for hoisting lug-sails and squaresails.

Tyers.—Ropes or gaskets used to secure the mainsail of a fore-and-aft vessel when furled or stowed to the boom. The tyer that takes up the middle of the sail is termed the bunt tyer. (See "Gasket and Buntline.")

U.

Una Boat.—This is a centre-board boat with one sail introduced from America, where they are known as " cat boats." The mast is stepped close to the stem (sometimes with a rake aft), and the sail is laced to a boom and gaff. The name Una was given them because the first boat introduced at Cowes, from America, was

FIG. 347.

so named. These boats vary from twice to three times their beam in length, and are very shallow. If handled with care, they are safe enough, very fast, and in smooth water very weatherly and handy. In squalls they should always be luffed up in good time, or they might be blown over. (See Fig. 347.)

The term " Una rig " is now commonly used in England to denote a one sail boat. Undoubtedly the word " Una " refers to one sail, and not to the type of boat; hence we hear of all sorts of boats being " Una rigged," and in America the corresponding rig (termed " cat rig ") is applied to both deep-bodied and shallow craft. Whether or not any single sail could be properly classed under the term Una can only be decided arbitrarily. The one sail boat brought over here in 1853 and named " Una " had a gaff sail, and no other sail. The Royal Windermere Yacht Club Una class boats use gaff sails, and no spinnaker or head sail is allowed.

Unbend.—To cast loose a sail from its gaff, yard, &c. The opposite of bend.

Under Bowing the Sea.—When a vessel is close-hauled sailing in a cross sea, and gets the worst of it on the lee bow.

Under Canvas.—Proceeding by means of sail. With sail set.

Under Deck.—Below.

Under Hatches.—Below deck.

Under Run.—To follow up a rope, chain hawser, or cable, by hauling it in from a boat which moves in the direction that the cable, &c., is laid out.

Under Sail.—See " Under Canvas."

Under the Lee.—Sheltered from the wind by the sails of another vessel. Under the lee of the land, sheltered from the full force of the wind by the land.

Under-way.—Moving through the water under the influence of the wind, steam, or oars. Sometimes wrongly written under-weigh. It is said a vessel may be under-weigh when she is getting her anchor; but even then it would be the anchor, and not the vessel, that would be under-weigh.

In Admiral Smyth's " Sailor's Word Book," (edition revised by Admiral Sir E. Belcher, 1867), is the following :—" UNDERWAY.—A ship beginning to move under canvas after her anchor is started; some have written this *underweigh*, but improperly. A ship is under-weigh when she has weighed her anchor; she may be with or without canvas, or hove to. As soon as she gathers way she is *underway*. This is a moot point with old seamen."

The obvious objections to using *underweigh* in this limited sense is that a man might find himself saying. " We got *underweigh* at noon, but were not *underway* until two hours later." The fact is, underweigh is never written by seamen except through carelessness; but the odd thing is that greenhorns take to the word more kindly than they do to *underway*, probably because they have enough knowledge to know that to get underway the anchor must be weighed. The best naval writers never describe the operation of heaving up the anchor as getting *underweigh*; but always write " she weighed," or " she weighed anchor," or " we weighed," &c. To " get underway " is by them used in the sense of making preparation to get way on; and when the anchor is aweigh the ship may have way on or not. Dana (who may be taken as an unimpeachable authority) does not admit the word *underweigh* at all in his Seaman's Manual (revised edition by the Registrar-General of British Shipping); but in the instructions for making sail, &c., *underway* is always used thus : " Getting underway from a single anchor," " getting underway, riding head to wind," &c. So also underway is the term used in the Merchant Shipping Act.

In William Falconer's Marine Dictionary (the edition published 1779) *underweigh* is not to be found, but we come upon the following sections :

" UNDERWAY.—If it be in a tide way and with a leading wind, so that the ship can stem the tide, let it be a rule when the tide serves to get underway and sail against the flood, which gives time to clear a ship of her moorings, and affords a more powerful effect to the helm to clear of other ships, &c.

" WAY.—The course or progress a ship makes in the water under sail. Thus, when she begins her motion she is said to be under-way, &c."

" RIDING AT ANCHOR.—When a fleet of many ships is moored in a port or road care must be taken to preserve a considerable distance between the vessels, not only for the purpose of keeping them clear of each other, but to prevent them from running foul when getting underway."

"WEIGH.—To heave up the anchor of a ship in order to prepare her for sailing."

William Falconer, besides being a distinguished author, was a thorough seaman, and after long service in H.M.'s Navy, was lost in the wreck of the Aurora, 1769, aged 39.

Hutchinson (master mariner), in his "Practical Seamanship," published in 1795, uses the term "underway," and *underweigh* is not to be found in his book. R. H. Gower, in his "Seamanship," published 1808, also uses underway. Admiral Sir George Nares, in his "Seamanship" (6th edition, published 1882), always uses underway, and so does Admiral De Horsey in his writings.

Underwriter.—A person who attaches his name to a policy of insurance by the side of the amount he will share of the risk. The under part of some policies may have two or three hundred names attached, as the principle of underwriting is to have very little at stake on any one ship. To become an underwriter at Lloyd's a deposit of 5000*l.* cash is required, for which interest is paid. The entrance fee is 100*l.*, and the subscription is 12*l.* 12*s.* per year, together with 5*l.* 5*s.* for a seat in the rooms.

Union.—The national flag denoting the union of England, Scotland, and Ireland. The Jack is a small flag—a diminutive of the Union—only flown from the jack staff on bowsprit end or forepart of a ship. In the merchant service it must have a white border. When flown from the mast with a white border it is the signal for a pilot, and is called the Pilot Jack. To no other union flag is the term Jack applied. The "Union" is flown on forts, Government works, &c. The flag of England is the St. George's cross (+) red on a white ground. The national flag of Scotland is St. Andrew's, a white cross (×) or saltire on a blue ground, and on the union with England these two were combined. The Scottish flag remained unchanged; the English cross was merely placed over it, the white ground of the English flag giving place to the blue ground of that of Scotland. This was the first Union flag. On the union with Ireland the Irish saltire (St. Patrick's cross (×), red on white) was added, being placed side by side with that of Scotland; but for a requirement of heraldry, to be presently noticed, the flag would consist of a blue ground with one band of white representing the Scottish cross, and one of red of the same breadth beside it, representing the first cross, with a red cross over both—nothing more. But it is a law of heraldry that colour cannot be placed next colour, nor metal next metal, and so, to meet this, the red Irish cross has a narrow hem or border of silver (white) to separate it from the blue ground of the flag, and for the same purpose the red cross of St. George has, or rather should have, a similar narrow border of white of the same breadth as the border of St. Patrick's cross. In arranging the two saltires they are "counterchanged," that is, Scotland has precedence in the first and third quarters by its white cross being placed above the Irish one, while in the second and fourth quarters the precedence is ceded to Ireland by the red cross being placed over the white. The words of the heraldic blazon contained in the Order of the King in Council of Nov. 5, 1800, and announced to the nation by the Proclamation of Jan. 1, 1801, prescribes the form in which the national flag is to be constructed in these words : "The Union flag shall be azure, the crosses saltires of Saint Andrew and Saint Patrick, quarterly per saltire, counterchanged, argent and gules; the latter fimbriated of the second, surmounted by the cross of St. George of the third, fimbriated as the saltire." To these distinct words of the verbal blazon in the Proclamation all questions as to the form and proportions of the flag must be referred. The Order in Council refers to a "draft" or drawing of the flag, and of this drawing, the one which accompanies the Admiralty Memorandum professes to be a copy, both the drawing and the Admiralty measurement are obviously disconform to the blazon prescribed in the Proclamation. That blazon expressly directs that the cross of St. George "shall be fimbriated as the saltire," that is, it must have a border the same as that of the Irish saltire; but, so far is this from being the case, that, while in the drawing the hem or border of the cross of Ireland is less than one-sixtieth the width of the flag (which is quite as broad as it should be), the measurement given in the Admiralty Memorandum for the breadth of the border of the St. George's cross is one-fifteenth, and it is nearly the same in the drawing said to be a copy of that in the Council Records. This palpable error has been followed in almost all our flags. It will be seen in the diagram made from the Admiralty regulations given further on, but a border so broad is not a fimbriation at all. It really represents two crosses—a white one with a red one over. Mr. Laughton, the accomplished lecturer on naval history at the Royal Naval College, thus speaks of it : "A fimbriation," he says, "is a narrow border to separate colour from colour. It should be as narrow as possible to mark the contrast; but the white border of our St. George's cross is not, strictly speaking, a fimbriation at all. It is a white cross of one-third the width of the flag surmounted of a red cross." There is another error equally calling for correction, and for which the Admiralty Memorandum is responsible. When two saltires are directed to be represented on the same shield or flag, they must be of the same breadth. The crosses of Scotland and Ireland therefore, which on our flag are side by side, ought to be of precisely the same breadth. In the official drawing of 1800 they look nearly the same, and they were perhaps intended to be so; but the Admiralty Memorandum, disregarding the drawing and the verbal blazon alike, directs that the Scottish saltire shall be one-tenth the breadth of the flag, and that the Irish saltire shall be only one-fifteenth. If the diagram of the Admiralty were altered, so as to make the Irish saltire as broad as that of

Scotland; if the border of the Irish cross were made narrower; and if the border of the St. George's cross were reduced so as to make it of the same breadth as that of the Irish cross, it would more correctly show what the flag ought to be according to the heraldic blazon. Flags in the Royal Navy are measured by the number of breadths they contain in their widths, a breadth being equal to 9in. An eight breadth Jack will therefore be 6ft. wide and 12ft. long, being in length double its width. (See Fig. 348.)

ADMIRALTY SCALE FOR MAKING "UNION, JACKS."

St. George's Cross.—Red cross to be one-fifth the width of flag, borders to be one-fifteenth the width of flag, or one-third the width of red cross.

St. Andrew's Cross to be one-fifteenth the width of the flag, or one-fifth the width of St. George's Cross, or equal to the border of St. George's Cross.

8 BREADTH.

SCALE ⅛IN. = 1FT.

Blue, light shade (horizontal lines); red, dark shade (vertical lines).

FIG. 348.

St. Patrick's Cross.—Narrow white to be one-thirtieth the width of the flag, or one-sixth the width of St. George's Cross, or one-half of St. Andrew's Cross. Broad white to be one-tenth of the width of the flag, or one-half of the red of St. George's Cross, or equal to red of St. Andrew's Cross and narrow white together.

Breadth.	St. George's Cross.		St. Andrew's Cross.	St. Patrick's Cross.	
	Red.	White.	Red.	Narrow White.	Broad White.
	in.	in.	in.	in.	in.
18	32⅖	10⅘	10⅘	5⅖	16⅕
16	28⅘	9⅗	9⅗	4⅘	14⅖
14	25⅕	8⅖	8⅖	4⅕	12⅗
12	21⅗	7⅕	7⅕	3⅗	11⅘
10	18	6	6	3	8
8	14⅖	4⅘	4⅘	2⅖	7⅕
6	10⅘	3⅗	3⅗	1⅘	5⅖
5	9	3	3	1½	4½
4	7⅕	2⅖	2⅖	1⅕	3⅗
3	5⅖	1⅘	1⅘	1	2⅘
2	3⅗	1⅕	1⅕	⅗	1⅘
1¾	3⅛	1	1	½	1½
1½	2¾	⅞	⅞	½	1⅜

Union Down.—An ensign with the jack downwards, hoisted as a signal of distress.

Unmoored.—With anchors a-weigh. A vessel is also said to be "unmoored" when she is riding to a single anchor, as to be moored two anchors must be down.

Unreeve.—To haul out a rope from a hole, &c.

Unrig.—To dismantle a ship or any part of her, as to unrig a topmast or bowsprit.

Unship.—To remove a thing from its lodgment. The opposite of "to ship."

Up and down.—Vertically. The wind is sometimes said to be up and down the mast, when there is none at all, like Paddy's hurricane.

Upper Mast. — *Upper Stick.* — A topmast, a topgallant mast, &c.

Upper Strake.—The top strake running round a vessel at the deck edge under the covering board, usually stouter than the general planking, and almost always of hard wood to better hold fastenings.

Usages of the Sea.—Customs of the sea in relation to commercial pursuits, which are held in law to be binding.

Use of Oil at Sea.—(See "Oil.")

V.

Van.—The advanced part of a fleet.

Vane.—(*See* "Dog Vane.")

Vang.—A rope used to keep in the gaff of a schooner's foresail. A block is lashed to the mainmast head, through which the vang is rove and made fast to the fore gaff end; the fall of the rope leads to the deck. In square-rigged ships vangs are generally used on the spanker gaff. Sprit sail barges also use vangs.

Variation of the Compass.—The departure the compass needle shows from true North at certain parts of the globe. The difference between magnetic and true North usually expressed in degrees on charts. The variation widely differs, thus: in the English Channel it is about 23°, at New York only 5°. The deviation of the compass is due to local attraction. A chart called a "Variation Chart," shows by curved lines the changing variations of the compass needle for different parts of the globe. Variation must not be confused with the deviation due to local attraction in iron and composite ships.

Varmint. — Having good reliable qualities in a breeze to windward.

Varnish.—Black Japan: 1oz. lamp black, 2oz. bitumen, ½oz. acetate lead, ½oz. Turkey umber, ½oz. Venice turpentine, 12oz. boiled oil. Dissolve the oil in turpentine; powder the other ingredients, and stir in gradually. Simmer on slow fire ten minutes.

Copal Varnish: Copal 30oz., drying linseed oil 18oz., spirits of turpentine 50oz. Briskly

fuse the copal; heat the oil to close on boiling point, and pour it hot on the copal; mix
thoroughly; allow the mixture to cool a little
and add the turpentine, mix thoroughly.
When cool strain for use.

A Quick-drying Varnish: 7lb. copal (fused),
hot linseed ½gall., hot turpentine 1½gall. Carefully stir and boil together.

Oak Varnish: 7lb. pale resin dissolved in
2gall. oil of turpentine.

Varnish for Metals: Powder 1lb. of copal
and dissolve in 2lb. of strongest alcohol. A
very quick-drying varnish.

Varnish for Iron: Mastic (clear grains)
10lb., camphor 5lb., sandarach 15lb., elemi
5lb. Dissolve in sufficient alcohol.

Black Varnish or Polish for Iron: Resin
4oz., lamp black 2oz., beeswax 3oz., shellac
2oz., linseed oil 1qt. Boil together one hour,
and then stir in ½pt. turpentine.

Tar Varnish for Iron: Coal tar 1pt., lamp
black 1oz., heel ball ½oz., spirits turpentine
½pt, beeswax 1oz. Dissolve the heel ball and
beeswax in the turpentine, add the lamp
black and tar, warm and mix it thoroughly.
This mixture should be applied hot.

Tar Varnish for Wood or Iron: 1 gall.
coal tar, 2oz. oil of vitriol; mix thoroughly,
and add ½pt. of turpentine; mix, and apply
immediately. This dries quickly, and only
quantities sufficient for use should be made.

Varnishing a bright Boat.—Oil the planks, &c.,
and when the oil is dried in put on two coats
of copal varnish. If size is used instead of oil,
the varnish will peel off. To clean off
varnish: take a mixture of soda (2lb.), soap
(1lb.), boiled together, it will remove varnish
from spars, &c. It should be applied hot.
(See also "Caustic Soda.")

Veer.—To pay out chain. Veer is also used in the
sense of wearing or gybing. The wind is said
to veer when it changes in direction with the
sun; to back when it changes against the
sun, the wind is said to veer when it draws
more aft. To haul when it comes more
ahead.

Veer and Haul.—To slacken up a rope, and then
haul on it suddenly, in order that those who
are hauling on it may acquire a momentum.
Pulling by jerks.

Veer away the Cable.—The order to pay out or
slack away cable.

Veering a Buoy in a Vessel's Wake.—Throwing
overboard a buoy in the wake of a ship when
a man has fallen overboard, in the hope that
he may get to it, and pick it up.

Vertical.—At right angles to the horizon, or
perpendicular to the horizon.

Vessel.—A name for all kinds of craft, from a
canoe to a three-decker.

Victual. — To supply with provisions for a
voyage, &c.

Voyage.—The passage of a vessel by sea. A
short voyage is called a trip or a cast.

W.

Waist.—The middle fore and aft part of a vessel's
decks.

Waisters.—Green hands, or old decrepid seamen,
who are stationed about in the waist of a
vessel to haul upon ropes, &c.

Wake.—The peculiar eddying water that appears
after a ship has passed. Vessels are said to
leave a clean wake that do not cause waves
to form astern.

Wales.—Thick strakes of plank.

Walk Away with It.—(*See* "Run Away.")

Wall Knot.—A knot formed at the end of a
rope by unlaying and inter-weaving the
strands.

Wall Sided.—Up and down sides of a vessel
that neither tumble home nor flare out.

Wallow.—To lie in the trough of a sea and roll
heavily; to roll under the sea.

Warrants.—See "Admiralty Warrants."

Wash Strake.—A strake, fixed or movable, of
plank fitted to the gunwale of an open boat
to increase her height out of water.

Watch and Watch.—The arrangement whereby
one half of the crew is on deck for four hours,
then the other half for four hours.

Watch.—An anchor buoy or mooring buoy is said
to watch when it keeps above water.

Watches.—The divisions of time for work on
board a vessel. The crew of a ship is divided
for this work into two watches, port and
starboard, each watch being alternately on
deck, excepting in emergencies, when both
watches may be called on deck. Watches are
thus divided: From 8 p.m. to midnight is the
"First Watch." From midnight to 4 a.m. is
the "Middle Watch." From 4 a.m. to 8 a.m.
is the "Morning Watch." From 8 a.m. to
noon is the "Fore-noon Watch." From noon
to 4 p.m. the "Afternoon Watch." From
4 p.m. to 8 p.m. the two "Dog Watches."

Watching for a Smooth.—In a sea way looking
out for a time when the waves are smaller to
tack in, &c.

Watch Tackle.—A tackle consisting of single and
double block; the single block has a hook,
the double a tail.

Water.—One cubic foot fresh water ·0279 ton
or 62·39lb.; one gallon ·00447 ton. A ton
fresh water equal to 223·76 gallons. One
cubic foot salt water ·0286 ton or 64·05lb.;
one gallon ·0046 ton; ton 217·95 gallons.
One gallon fresh water weighs 10·01lb.; one
pint 20oz. A ton of fresh water is usually
taken as 36 cubic feet; a ton of salt water
as 35 cubic feet. (See "Cubic Measure of
Water.")

Water Ballast.—Water carried in tanks or
breakers as ballast. The tanks or breakers
should be either full or empty.

Water Borne.—Not resting on the ground, but
being in the condition of floating.

Watering.—Taking water into the tanks by the
hose or by means of breakers. Steam yachts

often " water " by filling their dinghy or their cutter, and then pump it into the tanks with the donkey pumps, if the water has to be fetched from shore.

Water Line.—A horizontal plane passing through a vessel longitudinally. Length on load water-line means the length in a straight line from the fore side of the stem to the aft side of the stern-post at the water level.

Water Logged.—The condition of a vessel, that, although her hold is full of water, she does not sink, owing to the buoyant nature of her cargo, or from other causes.

Waterproofing.—Boil 12oz. of beeswax in 1gall. of linseed oil for two hours; paint the cloth with this mixture twice or thrice. Colour as required.

Waterproofing Sail Cloth.—The recipe used by Mr. Berthon to render the canvas of his collapsing boats waterproof, and similar to that used in H.M. dockyards for hammock cloths, is as follows: To 6oz. of hard yellow soap add 1½ pints of water, and when boiling, add 5lb. (more or less according to the required consistency) of ground spruce ochre, ¼lb. patent driers, and 5lb. of boiled linseed oil. For waterproofing sheets, the ochre should be omitted, as it adds to the weight, lessens the flexibility, and is unnecessary. Existing coverings are made waterproof by preparations of india-rubber, oil, paint, &c. Fabrics coated with indiarubber are not proof against the effects of climate or rough usage, are not easily repaired, and, compared with those coated with the Chinese and other preparations, are very heavy, and, if the same dimensions, expensive. The recipe for " waterproofing " calico used by the Chinese, is said to be efficient, alike in the hottest and coldest climates, is believed to be composed of boiled oil one quart, soft soap 1oz., and beeswax 1oz.; the whole boiled until reduced to three-quarters of its previous quantity; but experiments are required to test the above proportions.

To waterproof cotton drilling boil a mixture of 6oz. hard yellow soap, 1½ pint water, ½lb. patent driers, 5lb. boiled linseed oil.

Mr. Arthur Hill Coates, a well-known amateur yachtsman, of Bangor, co. Down, gave the following instructions for water-proofing sail covers: To make a sail cover so that it is not stiff, but as soft as kid, use strong good calico; when the cover is made, wash out with boiling water all the finish or dressing, dry thoroughly, saturate with petroleum oil, ring out, and allow to dry in air. When quite dry, paint with whitelead, coloured to taste, mixed with raw linseed oil and turpentine, three thin coats. I have a cover five years old as good as the first day, and as soft as could be desired, and that never sticks. Waterproof coats and leggings for boating made the same way are a luxury.

Waves.—The formation of waves is a subject which has received much attention, but no completely satisfactory theory as to their genesis has yet been evolved. The general theory is, that the smooth sea is acted upon by the impact and friction of the moving air or wind, and that the waves increase in size and speed, until the wind force is incapable of further developing them. Deep sea waves vary much in length, even under similar influences of wind pressure, and its continuation. Captain Motter of the French Navy, measured a wave in the North Atlantic, 2720ft., or half a mile from crest to crest, and Sir James Ross, one 1920ft. long. Such waves however, are seldom met with, and Dr. Scoresby observed that Atlantic storm waves had lengths of from 500ft. to 600ft. Measuring the heights of waves is a more difficult matter than measuring their lengths, and there has been much exaggeration under this head. The late Sir E. Belcher, at the Institute of Naval Architects in 1862, mentioned a wave he had observed rise to 100ft. Professor Rankine, in his work on Naval Architecture, speaks of waves on rocky coasts rising to 150ft., and waves have been known to fly over the Eddystone Lighthouse. However, the greatest heights of deep sea waves as measured by Dr. Scoresby, and other accurate observers, have been 48ft., but it is rare to meet with waves exceeding 30ft. in height. Ordinary storm waves such as met with in the Atlantic of about 200ft. in length, have a height of about one-twentieth of their length, but the ratio becomes lower as the length of the waves increase, and waves of 1000ft. in length have been observed with but a height of 10ft. On the other hand, waves of 600ft. in length have been observed of unusual steepness, and with heights one-eighth of their lengths. A long series of observations made by M. Bertin on the heights and lengths of waves, would seem to prove that the average height of deep sea waves is as 1 to 25 of their length. This of course is applied to single waves only. In what is termed a " confused sea," where a long wave may overtake and pass through a short one, the general height becomes increased, almost to the extent of the combined heights of both waves, and the wave form under such circumstances, is more or less " confused." In the English Channel, superposed waves are common, and the waves generally being short and steep, heights are met with of about one eighth the length of the waves. (A wave length is the length from crest to crest, and wave height, the height from hollow to crest.)

The speed of waves is generally proportional to their length. Thus a wave 20ft. long will travel 6 miles an hour, and one 50ft. long, 9 miles; 120ft., 15 miles; 200ft., 19 miles; 400ft., 27 miles; 600ft., 32 miles; 1000ft., 42 miles. It must be understood that it is only the *wave motion*, or form, and not the water which travels, and no substance resting on the water is carried forward by the advance of waves further than the force of gravity may give a substance an alternate forward and backward motion, as it became differently situated on the sides of waves. Thus a ship

T T

will simply rise and fall with the waves and not be carried forward by them, and an unbroken wave would do a ship no harm in the sense of an impact due to the wave striking her. The danger from waves arises when they break over a ship, or when a ship by intercepting a wave causes it to break. (The best article in a popular form on Waves, and oscillations of ships among them, is in Sir W. H. White's "Manual of Naval Architecture.")

Waves, to Still.—(See "Oil on Troubled Water.")

Way.—Motion through the water, as underway, head way, stern way, steerage way, lee way, &c. (See "Under way.")

Ways.—Balks of timber arranged in a kind of shute to haul vessels upon or to launch them off.

Wear.—To bring the wind on the other side of a vessel by putting the helm up so that the vessel's head goes round away from the wind instead of towards the wind as in tacking. (See "Gybe.")

Weather.—The windward or "breezy" side of an object. The side on which the "weather" is felt; not to leeward. To weather is to pass on the windward side of an object. In cross tacking the vessel "weathers" another that crosses ahead of her. To weather on another vessel is to gain on her in a windward direction by holding a better wind than she does—to eat her out of the wind.

Weather Board.—On the weather side of a vessel. Sometimes in working to windward by a long board and a short one the short one is called "weather board."

Weather Boards.—Pieces of boards fitted over open ports to turn water or rain off.

Weather Cloth.—The cloth in a sail next the luff. The "weather" leach of a sail is the luff.

Weather Cloths.—Pieces of canvas fitted on ridge ropes and stanchions of yachts above the bulwarks; also the tarpaulins used to cover the hammocks when stowed in the nettings.

Weather Gauge.—The condition of a vessel that is to windward of another one. In slang, to possess an advantage.

Weather Helm.—The helm or tiller hauled to windward when a vessel owing to too much after sail has an inclination to fly up in the wind. If the centre of effort of the sails is much abaft the centre of lateral resistance, a vessel will require weather helm to keep her out of the wind. The tendency to fly up in the wind can be remedied by reducing the after sail, or setting more head sail, or by easing the main sheet. However, all vessels should carry a little weather helm. (The

contrary to "Lee Helm," which see.) It has been frequently argued that the effect of the water pressure on the rudder when the helm is to windward (that is the rudder to leeward), is to press the vessel bodily to windward, and no doubt there is some truth in this, although the influence of the rudder in this respect could be only small.

Weathering.—A relative term used in sailing to define the action of one vessel which is eating to windward of another, thus, if a vessel is said to be weathering on another she is eating her out of the wind, or closing up to her from the leeward, or departing from her in a windward direction. Weathering an object is passing on its windward side.

Weatherliness.—(See "Weatherly.")

Weatherly.—The quality of hanging to windward well or holding a good wind. This term is often improperly used to denote good behaviour in a sea way or in bad weather.

Weather Lurch.—A weather roll or a roll to windward. In running with the main boom well off, the boom should be always secured with a guy, or it may fall to the opposite side during a weather roll, and cause some damage.

Weather Tide, or Weather-going Tide.—The tide which makes to windward or against the wind. (See "Lee-going tide.")

Wedges of Immersion and Emersion.—(See "Immersed.")

Wedging Up.—Lifting a vessel by driving wedges under her keel to take her weight off the building blocks before launching.

Weepings.—The exudations of damp or water through the seams or cracks of planks, &c.

Weigh.—To raise a thing, as weighing the anchor. (See "Under way.")

Weight of Metal Plates in Pounds per Square Foot.

Thickness.	Iron.	Steel.	Brass.	Copper.	Lead.	Zinc.
in.	lb.	lb.	lb.	lb.	lb.	lb.
	2·5	2·6	2·7	2·9	3·7	2·3
	5	5·2	5·8	5·8	7·4	4·7
	7·5	7·8	8·2	8·7	11·1	7·0
	10	10·4	11·0	11·6	14·6	9·4
	12·5	13	13·7	14·5	18·5	11·7
	15	15·6	16·4	17·2	22·2	14·0
	17·5	18·2	19·2	20·0	25·9	16·4
	20	20·8	21·9	22·9	29·5	18·7
	22·5	23·4	24·6	23·8	33·2	21·1
	25	26	27·4	28·6	36·9	23·4
	27·5	28·6	30·1	31·4	40·6	25·7
	30	31·2	32·9	34·3	44·3	28·1
	32·5	33·8	35·6	37·2	48·0	30·4
	35	36·4	39·3	40·0	51·7	32·8
	37·5	39	41·2	42·9	55·4	35·1
1	40	41·6	43·9	45·8	59·1	37·5

Weight of Chains.

Chains.		Chain Cables.	
Diameter in inches.	Weight per Fathom in lb.	Diameter in inches.	Weight per Fathom in lb.
5/16	5½	½	13¾
⅜	8	⅝	22
½	14	¾	30
⅝	22	⅞	42
¾	32	1	55
⅞	43	1⅛	68
1	56	1¼	84
1⅛	71	1⅜	102
1¼	87	1½	120
1⅜	106	1¾	148
		2	180

Weight and Bulk of Substances.

Names of Substances.	Weight of Cubic foot in pounds.	Cubic feet in ton.
Cast iron	450·5	4·97
Wrought iron	486·6	4·60
Steel	489·8	4·57
Copper	555	4·03
Lead	707·7	3·16
Brass	537·7	4·16
Tin	456	4·91
Gold (22 carat)	1090	2·06
Gold (pure)	1210	1·85
Silver	551	4·07
Coal	53	42
Pine, white	29·56	75·6
„ yellow	33·81	66·2
„ Dantzic	40	55
„ red	38	60
English elm	35	64
American „	45	50
Teak	50	44
Mahogany	66·4	33·8
Oak, live (American)	70	32·0
„ white „	45·2	49·5
„ „ (English)	53	42
Cork	15	150
Marble, common	141·0	15·9
Millstone	130	17·2
Clay	101·3	22·1
Sand	94·5	23·7
Granite	165	13·5
Earth, loose	78·6	28·5
Water, salt (sea)	64·3	34·8
„ fresh	62·5	35·9
Ice	58·08	38·56

Will.—A sunken part of the deck aft, termed cockpit sometimes. In small vessels there is usually a well aft in which the steersman sits; the cabin of a small boat is usually entered from the well. The cabin of most American yachts, large or small, is usually entered from the cockpit aft.

Well That! Well There!—An order to cease hauling and belay.

Wexford Flat Bottom Boats.—These boats are built for the herring fishery, and are generally termed "cots." The fishing season lasts from about the middle of October to Christmas, and very often the boats are not put into the water for the rest of the year.

They are suitable to any coast without quays or shelter, and where there is often a heavy surf, making it necessary to haul boats above high-water mark every time they are used.

The beam of the boat, which is of the larger sort, is about one fourth of its length, say 6ft. beam to 24ft. in length, built of the undermentioned woods, viz.: the bottom and the beams of either white or yellow pine, the strakes of yellow pine, and the stem and stern posts, and the timbers of elm grown in the country.

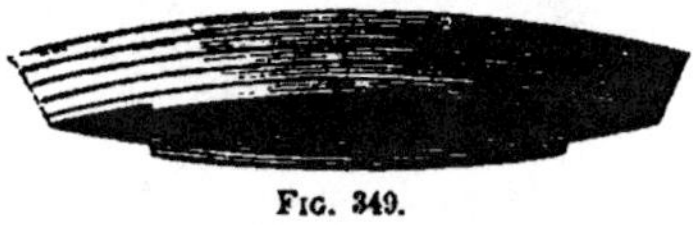

Fig. 349.

The accompanying sketch (Fig. 349) shows a boat turned over on its side exhibiting the bottom.

The bottom boards are of wood, not less than an inch and a half thick; they are laid down on heavy pieces of squared wood, and the elm timbers, which are sawn out of wood having the necessary bend, so as to reach from a few inches beyond the centre of the bottom to the top of the gunwale, are about two inches square—they cross one another, the bottom boards are then pegged to these timbers by driving pegs three-quarters of an inch thick and some 8in. in length through the timbers and boards; the ends are left to be cut off after the boat has been finished and turned over. These pegs are secured by cutting out a wedge from the lower end with a chisel, and then driving a wedge into the place from which it has been cut, thus filling the peg in the hole more tightly. No nails are used for the bottom except to attach the short piece of keel at the stern, say four feet; and the heads of those nails are sunk in the keel. The wooden pegs never move, and wear evenly with the bottom; breadth at bottom, 4½ft. The stem and stern are alike, no transom being required. The end of a short keel extends some two inches beyond the bottom of the sternpost to protect the rudder. The stem and stern posts are morticed for the ends of the bottom boards, and, as it is well to have them strong, there is a good lot of dead wood.

The first strake is three-quarters of an inch thick, and often an inch; but before fastening this on the beam of wood under the centre of the boat is either removed or sunk in the ground, say, three inches, and heavy weights of stones usually are placed on the bottom, near the centre, to bend the bottom boards, as it is considered that they do not row or sail so well on quite an even bottom.

The rest of the strakes are half an inch thick, and fastened on both to the timbers and themselves with iron nails, galvanised if procurable. Twelve-penny nails are used to fix to the bottom boards and timbers, and six-penny nails to the strakes. Of course these boats are all clincher built, and are rather heavy, weighing three and a half or four hundredweight. They require four men generally to run them down and haul them up upon rollers. These are some 6in. in diameter if the sand is heavy. Long boards are placed under the rollers. The sails are usually two or three sprit sails (see Fig. 350),

Fig. 350.

and sometimes a foresail. No keel boats are ever used, owing to the great advantage of a flat bottom for grounding.

Accidents seldom take place with these boats, but, like all shallow boats, they require very skilful handling.

The centre-board now remains to be described. It runs in a frame or sheath formed for it in the centre of the boat. These, when let down, draw about 3ft. below the bottom of the boat, and are about 2ft. broad. The board is about 1in. thick; no iron is used for them. When they near the shore they are hauled up. They are not required when the sails are not used. The depth of these boats is about 2ft. to the top of the gunwale, and they generally pull four oars. They are too broad for one man to scull. Of course they will not carry so much sail as a keel boat, nor will they sail so near the wind.

The ballast used consists of large stones. The fishermen at Wexford are a bold and hardy race, and they need be, for herring fishing on a December night is desperately cold work; but it is their harvest of the sea, and when four men can take from twelve to twenty mace of herrings in the night (the mace is 500, and worth from 15s. to 20s.), it pays them well. It is a pretty sight to see forty or fifty boats out of a night; but it is very cold work, and none but those brought up to it could stand it.

Wheel.—Used to give motion to the rudder by chains which pass over a barrel and lead through blocks to the tiller. When the tiller points *forward* the chain is put *over* the barrel first; when the tiller points *aft* the chain is put *under* the barrel first.

Where Away?—When an object is sighted, a question as to its bearing.

Wherry.—A small boat for rowing and sailing, usual rig a spritsail, main, and mizen, and foresail. (French "Houari.")

Whip.—A purchase consisting of one single block. A pennant vane.

Whip, To.—To bind the ends of rope with twine to prevent their fraying.

Whiskers.—Used to spread bowsprit shrouds.

Whistling for Wind.—In calms or light winds sailors sometimes amuse themselves by whistling in the hope that it will bring a breeze. They also scratch the boom for a breeze, or to make the vessel go faster. During heavy weather the superstition is all the other way, and no whistling or boom scratching is permitted.

Whole Sail Strength.—A wind of such strength that a yacht can just carry all her canvas, including her "best" (not ballooner) gaff topsail, to windward.

Wicked-looking.—Said of a craft which has a smart, raking appearance.

Winch.—A drum with crank handles, pawl, &c., fitted to the mast to get in the topsail sheet, &c.

Winch Roller Reefing Gear.—Rolling the foot of a sail round the boom is an old invention, the same as reefing square sails round the yards is, and pretty good proof of the value of the boom roller in short handed vessels is the fact that it is generally used by the pilots about the Isle of Wight, &c. They revolve the boom by the means of an endless chain on sheaves, and it answers very well; but various other plans are in use, and that invented by Mr. F. D. Marshall is highly recommended by yachtsmen who have seen it in use.

Mr. F. D. Marshall says: "After having tried the roller reefing arrangement, as depicted on the accompanying scale drawing (quarter full size), for three years it can be confidently recommended to fellow yachtsmen as suitable for yachts ranging from ½ to 10-rating. The facility with which any number of reefs may be taken in or shaken out is astonishing, and there is the further recommendation that the sail is not pulled out of shape by the reef earrings, but rolled smoothly and compactly round the boom. It has been urged that the mainsheet ring will chafe the sail when reefed, as the friction will be great, but on carefully examining the Lady Nancy's mainsail after three years of wear no sign of chafing is to be noticed. The mainsheet ring at the extremities must, of course, be well padded with soft canvas, and, if this is carefully done, the chafing is reduced to a minimum.

"It is not within the writer's knowledge who first invented this arrangement, but the Lady Nancy's, in the first instance, was made by Herr Heidtmann, of Hamburgh, but was improved and perfected by the writer. Previously he had seen a similar arrangement on some Hamburgh boats, and it was the facility with which these boats reefed that induced the writer to give the system a trial.

"The drawing is sufficiently clear, and little explanation is necessary. The apparatus, however, must be very conscientiously and strongly made of the toughest (preferably Swedish) iron.

Winch Roller Reefing Gear—continued.

"The mainboom must be quite *parallel* from end to end.

"The eyebolt, for fastening the tack of the sail to the boom, must be almost flush with the boom, otherwise the eye will cause an indentation in the sail when rolled. A split and hinged eyebolt is the best to adopt.

"The mainboom has a groove along its upper side, to take the foot rope of mainsail. This is necessary, to cause the foot to roll evenly around the boom.

"The sail must be laced to the boom.

"The topping lift is attached to a loose swivel plate, to prevent the lift rolling round the boom as the latter is revolved.

"The mainsheet ring is made of a grooved piece of iron (the grooving is for strength), to which is rivetted the outside bar of round iron. The ring must be of such strength that *it cannot spring open* in heavy weather and allow the mainboom to get adrift.

"The extremities of the ring are padded with soft canvas. Do not pad with leather, as this will stain the mainsail.

"*Modus Operandi.*—It is always advisable to *hoist* the mainsail before reefing, if at moorings, as the sail rolls around the boom tighter and snugger, although the reefing may be accomplished with the sail on deck, if care be taken to stretch the sail along the boom as latter is revolved. Having sail properly hoisted and peak well set up proceed to reef as follows: Slack throat halliard until hook (D) is free from traveller band (E). Untoggle as many mast hoops according to the quantity of sail to be rolled up. Have a piece of gas, or steam tube handy to ship on handle of ratchet, this lengthening of handle gives more leverage and power. Work the ratchet, and roll the sail around boom, so that boom travels *up the mast as high as you can reach, and work the ratchet* (assuming the sail is to be so much shortened). While the sail is being rolled up, slack mainsheet as necessary, remembering to keep sheet as taut as possible. Overhaul topping lift as mainboom goes skywards. Lower away on throat and peak halliards until boom is down in place. If sail is to be further shortened, proceed as before. When sufficient has been rolled up lower away until hook (D) can grip the band (E). Set up on throat and peek, over haul topping lift, and all is finished.

"NOTE.—Instead of reefing the sail *up* the mast as described the sail may be *rolled down* by simply slacking the main and peak halliards as the sail is taken up by the revolving boom. The topping lift will take the weight of the boom. Experience, however, has shown that a snugger job is made by rolling the sail up the mast and lowering boom afterwards."

Wind Bound.—(See "Bound.")

Windfall.—An unexpected advantage or acquisition of treasure.

Wind jamming.—A new-fashioned slang term for sailing by the wind. Wind jammers, a German brass band.

Windlass.—A horizontal barrel revolved by cranks or handspikes, for getting the anchor. In yachts a small neat capstan is now generally used.

Wind marks.—The marks or assumed marks on sheets to which they are hauled in for sailing by the wind.

Winds.—The following arrangement and description of winds has been generally adopted:

Velocity of wind in knots.	Pressure in lb. per sq. ft.	No. of force 0 to 12	Description of wind.	Sail Carried.
1.	·067			
2.	·027	1.	Light air	All balloon canvas.
3.	·060			
4.	·107	2.	Light wind	„
5.	·167			
6.	·240	3.	Light breeze	„
7.	·327			
8.	·427	4.	Moderate breeze.	Whole sail, including first topsail.
9.	·540			
10.	·667			
11.	·807			
12.	·960	5.	Fresh breeze	Jib headed topsail.
13.	1·13			
14.	1·31			
15.	1·50			Lower sail.
16.	1·71			
17.	1·93	6.	Strong breeze	One reef.
18.	2·16			
19.	2·41			
20.	2·67			Two reefs.
22.	3·23	7.	Moderate gale	Three reefs, or close reefs.
24.	3·84			
26.	4·51			
28.	5·23	8.	Fresh gale	Trysail.
30.	6·00			
32.	6·83			
34.	7·71	9.	Strong gale	Reefed trysail.
36.	8·64			
38.	9·63	10.	Heavy gale	Storm trysail.
40.	10·7			
50.	16·7	11.	Storm	Whatever small sail could be got to hold together.
60.	24·0			
70.	32·7			
80.	42·7			
90.	54·0	12.	Hurricane	No canvas made strong enough to stand such a force.
100.	66·7			

Windsail.—A canvas shaft or tube for conveying air to or from below deck.

Wing and Wing.—A schooner before the wind with the main sail off the lee quarter, and the foresail boomed out to windward. Sometimes termed goose winged. (See "Goose Wing.")

Wings of a Ship.—That part of a ship below water near the load line.

Wink.—A west country term for a kind of winch used in the bow of a boat by fishermen to raise the anchor. (See "Anchor.")

Winning Flag or Crowing Flag.—The racing flag which is hoisted after a race to denote that a yacht has won a prize. It is hoisted immediately below and on the same halyards as the burgee. When a regatta is concluded a yacht hoists under her burgee as many racing flags as she has won prizes at the regatta.

On arriving at a port, fresh from a regatta where she has been successful, she, in a like manner, hoists as many racing flags as she has won prizes; and if she calls at her own port she hoists as many flags as she has won prizes up to date. When she has sailed her last match she hoists as many racing flags as she has won prizes during the season. These are also hoisted when she returns to her own port. If a yacht has won more prizes than she has racing flags, it is usual to make up the deficiency with code signal flags or burgees.

Wire Rope, Weight of.—The weight, elasticity, and strength of iron and steel wire rope and hemp rope vary very considerably, according to the quality of the iron, steel, or hemp used in its manufacture. The following table of the weight of different sizes of rope, iron, hemp, &c., was compiled by the well-known civil engineer Mr. G. L. Molesworth:

Hemp.		Iron Wire.		Steel Wire.		Equivalent Strength.	
Circumference.	Pounds weight per Fathom.	Circumference.	Pounds weight per Fathom.	Circumference.	Pounds weight per Fathom.	Working Load in Cwts.	Breaking strain in Tons.
2¾	2	1	1	...	...	6	2
..	...	1⅛	1½	1	1	9	3
3¾	4	1¼	2	...	...	12	4
..	...	1⅜	2½	1¼	1½	15	5
4½	5	1⅞	3	...	...	18	6
..	...	2	3½	1⅝	2	21	7
5½	7	2⅛	4	1¾	2½	24	8
...	...	2¼	4½	...	...	27	9
6	9	2⅜	5	1⅞	3	30	10
...	...	2½	5½	...	...	33	11
6½	10	2⅝	6	2	3½	36	12
..	...	2¾	6½	2⅛	4	39	13
7	12	2⅞	7	2¼	4½	42	14
...	...	3	7½	...	...	45	15
7½	14	3⅛	8	2⅜	5	48	16
...	...	3¼	8½	...	...	51	17
8	16	3⅜	9	2½	5½	54	18
...	...	3½	10	2⅝	6	60	20
8½	18	3⅝	11	2¾	6½	66	22
...	...	3¾	12	...	...	72	24
9½	22	3⅞	13	3¼	8	78	26
10	25	4	14	...	...	84	28
...	...	4⅛	15	3⅜	9	90	30
11	30	4¼	16	...	...	96	32
...	...	4⅜	18	3½	10	108	36
12	36	4½	20	3¾	12	120	40

Manilla rope, if not dried up and chafed, is slightly stronger size for size than hemp.

Wiring.—A stringer or ledge running fore and aft in a boat to support the thwarts. (See "Clyde Sailing Boats.") Called also "Risings."

Wisby Laws.—A code of maritime laws which, with the rules of Oleron, for many centuries formed the basis of all regulations relating to seamen and ships. Wisby is a seaport of Gothland in the Baltic, and a port famous so long back as the 13th century.

Woof.—The threads or texture of any kind of cloth or canvas, &c.

Work.—A vessel is said to work when the different parts of her frame, planking, &c., are not securely bound together so that the various parts relative to each other alter their positions.

Working to Windward.—Proceeding by short tacks. Beating to windward. To work up to a vessel is to get nearer to her or catch her whilst beating to windward.

Wrinkle.—Something worth knowing; a piece of valuable experience.

Wrinkles in copper are generally a sign of severe strains in vessels, or that the vessel "works," or that her frame and plank shifts when she is underway in a sea. Sometimes wrinkles will show when a vessel is hauled up to dry and disappear when she is put in the water as the plank swells.

Y.

Yacht.—Generally any kind of vessel which is permanently fitted out and used by her owner for pleasure. The word is of Dutch origin. In the time of Elizabeth a "yacht" was kept for the use of the Sovereign, and since that date every succeeding monarch has had more than one yacht.

Schooners (see "Schooner") are supposed to have been evolved out of the old pinks, which were referred to by Spenser in his "Faerie Queen." They were certainly common among the many different vessels in the British navy during the reign of the Stuarts, and were chiefly remarkable for their sharp sterns. (In the "Navy List" for 1644 are the names of the "Paramour" pink and "Talbot" pink.) They were of Dutch origin; but they were certainly used by the Spaniards in the Mediterranean, and differed from the Xebecs by having flat instead of sharp floors. However, according to the researches of Admiral Smythe, a yacht existed in England in the time of the Plantagenets under the name of "esneoca." This name, esneoca, appears to have been dropped by the English in the reign of Charles II., when that Monarch was presented by the Dutch with a "yacht" named Mary, in the year 1660. Charles II. became very fond of yachting; and besides many yachts which were designed for him by Sir Phineas Pett, he is credited with having designed one for himself, named Jamaie, which was built at Lambeth.

The Jamaie was matched against a small Dutch yacht named Bezan in 1662 from Greenwich to Gravesend and back, and the King was gratified to find his vessel leading by three miles at the finish, although the little Dutch craft led by half a mile beating down, "the wind being contrary, but saved his stakes in returning, his majesty sometimes steering himself," according to Mr. Pepys. This is probably the first account of a yacht match, and the first record of an amateur helmsman. These yachts were, no doubt, sloop rigged, but yachts did not owe their origin to Charles II.; for, as before said, the Plantagenets had their royal yachts, and one later on, often referred to, the "Rat of White," was built by Queen Elizabeth at Cowes. It is scarcely possible, therefore, that the Dutch can claim a greater antiquity for yachts than the English ; and, indeed, so far as "yachting," as now understood, goes, there appears to be no doubt that it originated with Charles II., whose frequent yacht matches with his brother, the Duke of York, and his constant changing of his vessels, are duly recorded, by Pepys.

The following is a list of the yachts built by Charles II. :

reached 500, and the pastime of cruising and racing had taken a firm hold of all branches of the community. From this time forward the growth in the number of yachts became very rapid, as will be gleaned from the table which follows. The rigs are separated, and it will be seen that yawls have only become an important class since 1864. This has not been at the expense of cutters, as the numbers in that rig have increased in a steady ratio. The schooners have been the sufferers ; and, as the labour of racing a schooner is so very much greater and so much more expensive

Name.	Where built.	Date.	Length.	Breadth.	Draught Water.	Tons.
Charlotte	Woolwich (Pett)	1677	61·0	21·0	7·10	143
Cleaveland	Portsmouth (Deane)	1671	53·4	19·4	7· 6	107
Fubbs	Greenwich (Pett)	1682	63·0	21·0	7·10	148
Henrietta	Woolwich (Shish)	1679	65·0	21·8	8· 9	162
Jamaie	Lambeth (Charles II.)	1662	31·0	12·6	3· 6	25
Isabella	Greenwich (Pett)	1683	60·0	18·11	7· 9	114
Isle of Wight	Portsmouth (Fuzer)	1673	31·0	12·6	6· 0	25
Katherine	Chatham (Pett)	1674	56·0	21·4	7· 9	135
Kitchen	Rotherhithe (Castle)	1674	56·0	21·4	7· 9	135
Mary	Chatham (Pett)	1677	66·6	21·6	7· 6	166
Merlin	Rotherhithe (Shish)	1666	53·0	19·6	7· 4	109
Monmouth	Rotherhithe (Castle)	1666	52·0	19·6	7· 3	103
Navy	Portsmouth (Deane)	1673	48·0	17·6	7· 1	74
Queenborough	Chatham (Pett)	1671	31·6	13·4	5· 9	29

American yachting dates no farther back than the commencement of the present century. Mr. J. C. Stevens, when he resigned the commodoreship of the New York Yacht Club in 1855, wrote a letter to the members, in which he left one to infer that American yachting originated with him ; and he went on to say, " I have been a yacht owner for more than half a century, commencing in 1802 as builder, cabin boy, cook, and all the hands of the celebrated yacht Diver, 9ft. long, 3ft. wide, and 3ft. deep, ending as commodore of a squadron whose flagship, the Maria, carries her pennant one hundred and fifty feet above the surface of the sea ; " and her bottom, he might have added, four feet under the surface of the sea, as truly she was four feet in the water and one hundred and fifty in the air. The first American yacht club was the " New York Yacht Club," organised in 1844.

Various yachts were built at Cowes during the eighteenth century, but to Cork apparently belongs the honour of originating yachting as a national pastime. In 1720 the "Cork Harbour Water Club" was established ; but the yachts were small ; and not until about 1783 did any private person build a yacht of any considerable size. This yacht was built at Itchen for the Duke of Richmond, and between that date and 1812 various yachts were built at Cowes, Fishbourne, and Southampton.

In 1810 a club was started at Cowes (the club seal of the Royal Yacht Squadron bears date 1812), and thenceforward yachting made very rapid strides. In 1812 there were probably fifty yachts afloat, and these belonged exclusively to noblemen or to country gentlemen. In 1850 the number of yachts

than racing a cutter or yawl, there is small hope of the schooners coming into favour again.

NUMBER OF YACHTS.

			1850.	1864.	1878.
	Under	5 tons	4	52	160
5 tons, and not exceeding		9 tons	50	137	300
10	„	„	19	127	403
20	„	„	29	85	180
30	„	„	39	59	96
40	„	,	50	41	89
50	„	„	60	27	50
60	„	„	80	40	88
80	„	„	100	15	60
100	„	„	150	23	87
150	„	„	200	9	48
Above		200	10	30	40
		„		15	
Steam Yachts			3	33	282
Total			503	895	1883

RIGS.

	1850.	1864.	1878.
Cutters	372	574	754
Schooners	76	207	328
Yawls	45	54	328
Other Rigs	7	27	25
Steamers	3	33	282

TONNAGE.

	1850.	1864.	1878.
Gross Tonnage	22,141	39,485	89,420

Between 1878 and 1882 the number of steam yachts largely increased, as the following table will show :

	1882.	
	No.	Tonnage.
Under 100 tons	275	7,800
Under 200 tons	40	5,200
Under 300 tons	22	5,200
Under 400 tons	23	7,300
Under 500 tons	12	5,000
Exceeding 500 tons	12	7,000
Total	384	37,000

Yacht—continued.

In 1891, 1895, and 1899 the yacht fleet, according to "Lloyd's Yacht Register," was made up as follows :

YACHTS BUILT IN VARIOUS COUNTRIES.

1891.	Number.	Tonnage.
Steam yachts built in the United Kingdom	959	103,081
Sailing yachts ditto	2624	67,515
Total	3583	170,596
Steam yachts built in other countries	215	19,034
Sailing yachts ditto	1217	16,554
Total	1432	35,588
1895.		
Steam yachts built in the United Kingdom	1105	128,886
Sailing yachts ditto	3105	60,840
Total	4210	197,726
Steam yachts built in other countries	316	28,586
Sailing yachts ditto	1421	20,342
Total	1737	48,928
1899.		
Steam yachts built in the United Kingdom	1123	150,505
Sailing yachts ditto	3368	69,269
Total	4491	219,774
Steam yachts built in other countries	297	30,231
Sailing yachts ditto	1552	21,865
Total	1849	52,096

YACHTS OWNED IN VARIOUS COUNTRIES.

1891.	Number.	Tonnage.
Steam yachts owned in the United Kingdom	788	78,090
Sailing yachts ditto	2428	59,795
Total	3216	137,885
Steam yachts owned in other countries	386	44,025
Sailing yachts ditto	1413	24,274
Total	1799	68,299

YACHTS OWNED IN VARIOUS COUNTRIES.

1895.	Number.	Tonnage.
Steam yachts owned in the United Kingdom	876	93,684
Sailing yachts ditto	2865	59,899
Total	3741	153,583
Steam yachts owned in other countries	545	64,788
Sailing yachts ditto	1920	29,283
Total	2465	94,071
1899.		
Steam yachts owned in the United Kingdom	897	95,903
Sailing yachts ditto	3110	60,465
Total	4007	156,368
Steam yachts owned in other countries	573	84,843
Sailing yachts ditto	2051	30,669
Total	2574	115,512

It must be noticed that in the Acts of Parliament relating to maritime affairs, yachts are not generally referred to as a special class. The enactments refer to "every ship," "every British ship," "every seaman," as the case may be, and only occasionally to "pleasure yachts," and where these expressions are used yachts and yacht sailors are included, unless they are excepted in express terms. Moreover, it will be found in some cases that the Legislature has, by an express proviso, rendered pleasure yachts subject to the liabilities, and entitled to the privileges of trading vessels.

In 1854, the Merchant Shipping Act of that year (17 & 18 Vict. c. 104) repealed and consolidated into one Act, with amendments, very many previous enactments relating to the subject of British shipping. This Act came into force in 1855, and has in succeeding years been amended by later Acts which have repealed or modified certain sections of the principal Act; and these new provisions, which, in the case of nearly every Act, are to be read with the Act of 1854, will be noticed in their proper place.

The Merchant Shipping Act, 1854, consists of 548 sections, and is divided in eleven parts. The first treats of the Board of Trade and its general functions; the second of British ships, their ownership, measurement, and registry; the third of masters and seamen; the fifth part to pilotage; the ninth to the liability of shipowners; the tenth to the procedure under the Act, and the remaining parts to matters beyond the scope of these remarks.

1. With respect to the first and second parts of the Merchant Shipping Act, 1854, the provisions in them, speaking generally, apply to pleasure yachts, except where such vessels are expressly excepted by the terms of each particular section. By sect. 19 of the Act of 1854 every British owner of a yacht, whether used for pleasure (as yachts belonging to yacht clubs) or otherwise (as the yachts belonging to the Trinity House and the lighthouse boards), must register his yacht, unless she was registered before the provisions of the Act of 1854 came into operation; or unless she be of less burden than 15 tons register, and be used solely for navigation on the rivers or coasts of the United Kingdom. If a yacht belonging to a British owner is under 15 tons register, and is substantially used for cruising or racing in foreign waters, she comes within the enactment, and must be registered; but if she never ventures beyond coasting voyages, registration under the Act is, in her case, optional. It seems that, on the question whether a coasting pleasure yacht under 15 tons could be refused registration, there was no uniformity of practice at the Custom House at the outports; and accordingly, by a general order issued by the Board of Customs in 1880 to the registrars of British ships, it was directed in effect that any yacht was to be admitted to registration on the application of the owner, without requiring any statement that the vessel was to be employed for cruising in foreign waters. The yacht, if the owner resides in the United Kingdom, should be registered at the Custom House in London, or at one of the outports, and the owner's name should be indorsed as master on the certificate of registry, for the reasons given later on. If a yacht required to be registered under the Act is not registered, she will not be recognised as a British ship, and will not be entitled to any benefits, privileges, advantages, or protection usually enjoyed by British ships, nor to use the British flag; but, so far as regards the payment of dues, the liability to pains and penalties, and the punishment of offences committed on board the ship, or by any persons belonging to her, she will be dealt with as though she were a recognised British ship. In other words, an unregistered yacht of more than 15 tons has none of the advantages, and all the liabilities, of a registered ship (sect. 106). Further, by sect. 84 of the Act of 1854, whenever any registered ship is so altered as not to correspond with the particulars relating to her tonnage or description contained in the register book, then, if the alteration is made at a port where there is a registrar, the registrar of that port, but, if made elsewhere, the registrar of the first port having a registrar at which the ship arrives after her alteration, shall, on application made to him, and on the receipt of a certificate from the proper surveyor specifying the nature of the alteration, either retain the old certificate of registry, and grant a new one containing a description of the ship as altered, or indorse on the existing

certificate a memorandum of the alteration, and put his name to the indorsement.

By the Merchant Shipping Act, 1873 (36 & 37 Vict. c. 85, s. 3), the Board of Trade may exempt any class of ships from being marked in the manner provided by the Act on the stem, stern, and main beam; and accordingly the Board of Trade have issued the following instructions: " Pleasure yachts, barges other than sailing barges, pilot vessels, and vessels employed solely in river navigation, are to be exempted from the requirements of having the name marked on each of the bows, and of having a scale of feet marked on the stem and sternpost; but in these vessels the other requirements of the law are to be observed, viz.: those that require the name and port of registry to be marked on the stern and the official number and the number denoting the tonnage to be marked on the main beam, except in the case of yachts used for pleasure only, which, on special application in each case from the owner to the board, may be exempted from the observance of the regulations which require the name and port of registry to be marked on the stern, upon proof to the board's satisfaction that the owner is entitled to the privilege asked for. Yachts of the following clubs and pilot vessels have been exempted from the provisions of having the name and port of registry marked on the stern, namely." Then follows a list of Royal Yacht Clubs.

A provision is contained in the second part of the Merchant Shipping Act, 1854, which is most material with reference to the flags which British yachts may lawfully carry on the high seas. The 105th section of the Act provides in effect that anyone within the jurisdiction of the Admiralty, i.e., on the high seas, flying any colours representing those worn by the Queen's ships, or any distinctive national colours (except the red ensign, or the union jack with a white border,) without a warrant from Her Majesty or the Admiralty, shall be liable to a penalty not exceeding the amount of 500l. It should here be mentioned that the Admiralty Court has from ancient times exercised a jurisdiction *in rem* in cases where illegal colours have been carried. This jurisdiction the Admiralty Division of the High Court of Justice still preserves, independently of the provision of sect. 105 just referred to. As it is not the practice to issue Admiralty warrants to unregistered yachts, the white or blue ensign cannot be used on an unregistered yacht, nor can any yacht fly colours other than those allowed by the club or clubs to which the owner belongs. (See " Ensign."

The above provisions with respect to the registration of British yachts and the colours to be carried by them, are contained in the first and second parts of the Act of 1854; but part 3 of that Act is the most important to the yachtsman, as it deals, *inter alia,* with the maintenance of discipline amongst the crew, and with other regulations material to their engagement, conduct during the voyage,

Yacht—continued.

and discharge. By the Merchant Shipping Act, 1862 (25 & 26 Vict. c. 63, s. 13) it is enacted that "sea-going ships, being pleasure yachts," shall be subject to the whole of the third part of the Act of 1854, except twenty-nine sections, relating for the most part to things in which yachtsmen are not concerned, except sect. 149, which is specially noticed when considering the effect of signing articles under the head of *Seaman.* (See "Passengers.")

Yacht Club.—A club formed with the ostensible object of associating yacht owners, and promoting a fondness for the sea. (See "Recognised Yacht Club.")

Yachting Etiquette.—British yacht owners follow the regulations of the Royal Navy as far as possible in saluting, &c. (See "Saluting;" see also the "Queen's Regulations for the Royal Navy," which can be obtained from Messrs. Harrison and Sons, price 2s. 6d.) The New York Yacht Club in 1882 drew up the following code (revised 1898) for the guidance of young yachtsmen :

Section I.—Colours, &c.

1. *Rank.*—In making "colours," salutes, &c., the yacht always represents the rank of the owner, whether he is aboard or not.

2. *In Commission.*—Yachts in commission should make colours at 8 o'clock a.m. and haul down at sunset, taking time from the senior officer present.

3. *In Company with a U.S. vessel, &c.*—When in company with a United States naval vessel, or at anchor off a United States naval station, the senior officer should give the time for "colours" with such vessel or station.

4. *Entering Port before or after Colours.*—Before "colours" in the morning and after "colours" at sunset, the ensign and distinguishing flags should be shown when entering and leaving port, and should be hauled down immediately on coming to anchor.

5. *Night Pennants.*—At all other times yachts should fly a night pennant at the main, from "colours" at sunset until "colours" the next morning.

6. *Guns.*—No guns should be fired for colours except by the yacht giving the time; nor from "colours" at sunset until "colours" the next morning, nor on Sunday.

7. *Exceptions.*—Absent flags and meal pennants are not considered colours.

8. *Half Masting Colours.*—On Decoration Day and occasions of national mourning, the ensign only should be half-masted. On the death of the owner of the yacht, both the club flag and his private signal should be half-masted, but not the ensign. When mourning is ordered for the death of a member of the club, the club flag only should be half-masted. This rule should apply to yachts both at anchor and underway.

9. *Colours, how Half-masted.*—Flags should always be mastheaded before half-masting them and should be mastheaded before hauling them down. Saluting with the ensign at half-mast should be done by mastheading it first.

Section II.—Officers in Command of Anchorage.

1. *Duties.*—The senior officer present should be in command of the anchorage, should give the time for "colours," and make and return salutes, visits, &c.

2. *Station Vessel.*—His yacht should remain the station vessel until a senior to him in rank arrives and assumes the command of the anchorage.

Section III.—Pennants, Private Signals, &c.

1. *Flag Officers.*—Flag officers should always fly their pennants while in commission.

2. *Absence Flag.*—Yachts, when the owner is not on board, should fly at the starboard main spreader during daylight, a blue flag, rectangular in shape. The flying of the absent flag does not exempt the yacht from this routine.

3. *Single-masted Vessels.* — Single-masted vessels should fly the private signal of the owner when entering a home port of this club, or when approaching other yachts at sea; at other times the club flag except when with the squadron, when No. 5, Sect. VI., should apply.

4. *Owner's Meal Pennant.*—A white flag, rectangular in shape, should be displayed by day and a white light by night at the starboard main spreader on schooners, and at the starboard spreader on single-masted vessels, during the meal hours of the owner.

5. *Crew's Meal Pennant.*—A red pennant should be flown at the port fore spreader on schooners, at the port spreader on single-masted vessels during the meal hours of the crew.

6. Meal pennants should not be displayed while underway.

Section IV.—Lights.

1. *Commodore.*—From colours at sunset until sunrise, the Commodore should show when on board two blue lights perpendicularly at the stern; when absent, one blue light should be shown.

2. *Vice-Commodore.*—The Vice-Commodore should show lights, as provided for the Commodore, substituting red lights in place of blue.

3. *Rear-Commodore.*—The Rear-Commodore should show lights, as provided for Commodore, substituting white lights in place of blue.

4. *Captains.*—Captains, when on board, should show a white light under the main boom.

Section V.—Salutes.

All salutes should be returned in kind.

1. *Exceptions.* — The following rules should not apply to yachts leaving for or returning from a day's sail.

2. *To Vessels of the U.S. Navy.*—Yachts should always salute vessels of the United States Navy by dipping the ensign once.

3. *Entering Port.*—The Commodore, on entering port to join the squadron, should be saluted on coming to anchor by the yachts present. On all other occasions the Commodore should be saluted, on coming to anchor, by the officer in command.

Junior flag officers should be saluted, on coming to anchor, by the officers in command, unless the latter be a senior in rank, in which case they should salute him.

Captains should, on all occasions, salute the officer in command.

4. *Leaving Port.*—The senior officer, when leaving the anchorage, except temporarily, should indicate the transfer in command to the next in rank, by firing a gun on getting under way. All other yachts should salute the officer in command.

5. *Visits.*—All visits should be made according to rank.

6. *Passing.*—Yachts passing one another should always exchange salutes by dipping the ensign once, juniors saluting first.

Steam whistles should never be used to make salutes.

7. *From Yachts Entering Port.*—The salute from yachts entering port should be made by dipping the ensign once or by firing a gun, on letting go anchor.

8. *To Yachts Entering Port Entitled to a Salute.*—The salute to yachts entering port, entitled to a salute, should be made by dipping the ensign once, or by firing a gun, when they let go anchor.

9. *Official Salutes to Foreign Clubs.*—An official salute to a foreign club should be made by firing a gun with the flag of the foreign club at the fore on schooners and steamers, and at the main on single-masted vessels, or, in the absence of such flag, by half-masting the club flag and firing a gun. When the salute has been returned, or a reasonable time for its return allowed, the flag should be hauled down and the club flag hoisted again.

10. *After Sunset, &c.*—The salute from or to yachts arriving after sunset, or on Sunday, should be made immediately after "colours" on the following morning.

11. *Personal Salutes to Flag Officers.*—When a flag officer makes an official visit, a gun should be fired.

12. *Judge's Boat.*—A yacht acting as judge's boat should not be saluted during a race.

13. *Quarter deck.*—The quarter-deck should always be saluted by lifting the cap on coming on board or from below.

SECTION VI.—WITH THE SQUADRON.

1. *Joining or Parting Company.* — Yachts should report to the commanding officer on joining the squadron and should obtain his permission before leaving it.

2. *Guns and Signals.*—When under way, with the squadron, firing guns and signalling should be avoided except when joining or parting company, or when repeating signals.

3. *Squadrons passing at Sea.*—When squadrons of different clubs meet at sea, salutes should be exchanged only by the commanding officers.

4. *Salutes from Single Yachts.*—Salutes from single yachts at sea should only be answered by the flagship.

5. *Single-Masted Vessels.* — Single-masted vessels should fly the private signal of the owner when under way; when at anchor, the club flag.

SECTION VII.—FOREIGN YACHTS.

When a foreign yacht arrives, the senior officer present should send on board, without regard to rank, a tender of the civilities of the Club.

SECTION VIII.—VISITING A FOREIGN PORT.

1. *Salutes and Visits on Entering Port.*—Yachts should salute on entering port in the home waters of a foreign club, where any of its fleet are lying. After the tender of civilities has been made, owners of the entering yachts should visit the officer in command of the anchorage. All other visits should be made according to rank, visits to their equals in rank being made by the owners of the entering yachts.

2. *Both Squadrons in Port.*—If the squadron of this Club be at anchor also, the salute should be made to its commanding officer, unless it be a senior flag officer of this Club entering; when he should be saluted by the officer in command, and should in his turn salute the foreign squadron.

3. *Colours.*—The time for "colours" in the home waters of a foreign club should be given with its senior flag officer present.

4. *Meaning of Term "Foreign."*—The term "foreign" should be understood as applying to all clubs outside of the waters of New York and Newport harbours, and Long Island Sound.

SECTION IX.—BOAT SERVICE.

1. *Precedence.*—The order of entering and leaving boats is—juniors enter first and leave last.

2. *Boat Flags.*—Flag officers and the fleet captain should fly their pennants and captains their private signals, when in their boats; members, the club flag. After sunset a white light should be shown at the bow.

3. *Salutes.*—Passing one another, juniors should salute seniors by raising the cap.

4. *Hailing.*—Every boat approaching a yacht at night should be hailed.

5. *Answers to Boat Hails.*—The answer of the Commodore, when intending to board, should be "Commodore;" for junior flag officers and the fleet captains, "Flag;" for captains and members, "Aye, aye;" for captains returning on board, the name of their yacht; for visitors, "Visitors;" for sailing-masters, &c., "No, no," using the port side; for passing boats, "Passing."

Yacht Racing Association.—An association of yachtsmen originated in 1875 by Prince Batthyany-Strattman (at that time known as Count Edmund Batthyany), Capt. J. W. Hughes, one time owner of the Vanguard cutter, R.Y.S., and Mr. Dixon Kemp. The object was to provide one code of sailing rules for use in all matches, and to decide such disputes as might be referred to the Council of the Association. The Association and Council are constituted similarly to the Jockey Club. The following are the Y.R.A. general and racing rules, as sanctioned for 1900 :—

GENERAL RULES.
(Published by Permission.)

1. *Objects.*—The objects of the Yacht Racing Association shall be the promotion of the interests of yacht racing.

2. *Constitution.* — The Association shall consist of former and present owners of racing yachts, and such other persons interested in yacht racing as the Council may elect; and of representative members appointed by Royal or recognised yacht clubs, in accordance with the provisions of Rule 3.

3. *Club Representatives.*—Every Royal or recognised yacht club of the United Kingdom shall have the power to appoint representative members of the Association in the following proportion to the number of members on the club's books, viz.:—not exceeding 300 members one representative, above 300 members two representatives; each representative shall be a member of the club making the appointment, and shall not be selected from the elected members of the Association. Every club exercising the right of appointment shall pay a subscription of two guineas for each representative member it is entitled to appoint. The representative members shall have the full privileges of elected members. Each club desiring to exercise the right of appointment, shall, during the month of January in each year, communicate to the Secretary of the Yacht Racing Association the name or names of its representative or representatives.

4. *Lady Members.*—A lady, *bonâ fide* owner or part owner of a yacht, shall be eligible as a candidate for membership, but shall not be entitled to attend any of the Association's meetings or take any part in its management.

5. *Subscriptions.*—The subscription to the Association shall be two guineas for a member and one guinea for a lady member, annually, due on the 1st of January in each year. The subscription of a member elected after September 30th in any year shall cover that for the following year. A member of the Yacht Racing Association who has not paid his subscription for the current year, shall not be entitled to vote or take part in the proceedings at general meetings. A member whose subscription is two years in arrear shall be named with the amount in arrear in the annual statement of accounts. The Council shall have power, after due notice has been given, to remove from the list of members the name of any member whose subscription is more than one year in arrear. This rule shall also apply to representative members.

6. *Absent Members.*— Any member intending to be absent from the United Kingdom

Yacht Racing Association—continued.

during the whole period for which the annual subscription is due (1st January to 31st December), may, on his giving prior notice in writing to the secretary, be exempted from payment of his annual subscription, and in lieu thereof shall pay 10s. 6d. per annum until his return.

7. *Honorary Members.*—The council is empowered to elect honorary members, but such members shall not be entitled to attend any meetings or take part in the management of the Association.

8. *Council and Management.*—The affairs of the Association shall be managed by a president, two vice-presidents, and an honorary treasurer, to be elected annually by the Association, and a Council of twenty-four members. The president and vice-presidents and the honorary treasurer to be *ex-officio* members of the Council. One-sixth of the Council shall retire annually, but shall be eligible for re-election. Vacancies on the Council occurring between the annual meetings may be filled by the Council.

9. *Election of Council, &c.*—The election of members to fill the annual vacancies in the Council shall be conducted by balloting papers to be sent to each member at least fourteen days before the annual general meeting, when the members of the Council thus elected shall be declared. Candidates to fill the annual vacancies shall be proposed and seconded on or before the 14th of January in each year by members of the Association, and their names, together with their proposer and seconder, shall be stated in the balloting papers. A vice-president, the hon. treasurer, or any member of the council who has failed to attend a meeting of the Council for a period of one year, reckoned from January 1st to December 31st, shall cease to hold his office or be a member of the Council, and shall not be eligible to serve during the next year unless the Council recommend his re-election, and in the case of a member of the Council so recommended, his name shall be inserted in the list of candidates, and he shall be balloted for in the usual manner.

10. *General Meetings.*—There shall be a general meeting of the Association in London in February in each year on such day as the Council may appoint; fourteen days' notice of the meeting to be given to each member.

11. *Special General Meetings.*—The Council may call general meetings of the Association whenever they consider such a course necessary. They shall also call a general meeting upon the requisition in writing of ten members of the Association to consider such matters as shall be stated in the requisition.

12. *Duties of Council.*—It shall be the duty of the Council to elect members of the Association; to appoint the secretary and other officers, to frame rules, and to determine and settle all questions and disputes relating to yacht racing which may be referred to them for decision, which decision shall be final. And further, the Council shall take such other steps as they may consider necessary or expedient to carry into effect the objects of the Association, including the recognition of yacht clubs under Rule 2 of the Racing Rules.

13. *New Rules, Amendments, and Alterations.*—The Council shall consider all proposed alterations or additions to the rules, and provided they are approved by a majority of two-thirds of the members of the Council present at the meeting at which the same are considered, they shall be submitted for adoption to a general meeting, and shall be carried by a majority of two-thirds of those present at such general meeting. Nevertheless, at the request of any ten members of the Association the votes of all its members shall be taken by voting papers upon such proposed alterations or additions, which shall be carried by a majority of two-thirds of those voting. Any proposed alteration or addition not approved by a majority of two-thirds of the Council shall, if so desired by the member proposing the same, be submitted to a general meeting, but it shall not be adopted unless carried by three-fourths of the members present at such general meeting, or of three-fourths of those voting if any ten members request that the sense of all the members of the Association be taken by voting papers. Notice of any alteration or addition to the rules, intended to be proposed by a member of the Association, shall be given to the secretary in writing at least one month before the general meeting at which the same is to be brought forward; and notice of any proposed alteration or addition to the rules intended to be proposed at the annual general meeting must, on or before January 14th in each year, be sent in writing to the secretary, who shall, in due course, send an agenda paper for the meeting to each member.

Any member at a general meeting may move an amendment to any proposed alteration or addition to the rules, and such amendment, if not already considered by the Council, shall be carried by a majority of two-thirds of those present at the meeting, subject to subsequent ratification by a majority of two-thirds of the Council. Failing such ratification, the amendment shall be remitted to the decision of all the members of the Association by voting papers, and carried by a majority of three-fourths of those voting.

RACING RULES, 1900.

PART I.—MANAGEMENT.

1. *General Authority of Sailing Committee.*—All races, and yachts sailing therein, shall be under the direction of the flag officers, sailing committee, or officers of the day of the club under whose auspices the races are being sailed, hereinafter referred

to, together or separately, as the sailing committee. All matters shall be subject to their approval and control; and all doubts, questions, and disputes which may arise shall be subject to their decision. Their decisions shall be based upon these rules so far as they will apply, but as no rules can be devised capable of meeting every incident and accident of sailing, the sailing committee should keep in view the ordinary customs of the sea, and discourage all attempts to win a race by other means than fair sailing and superior speed and skill.

2. *Recognised Yacht Clubs.*—The term, a recognised yacht club, shall include every British yacht club holding an Admiralty warrant; and also such other yacht and sailing clubs giving races under these rules as may be accepted as recognised yacht clubs by the Council.

The Council shall have the power of cancelling recognition of any club should they deem it expedient to do so.

3. *Ownership of Yachts.* — Every yacht entered for a race must be the *bonâ fide* property of the person or persons in whose name or names she is entered, who must be a member or members of a recognised yacht club.

A yacht let on hire may be raced provided—

(a) That she is let for a period in excess of one month;

(b) That she is entered in the name of the owner, who is to be responsible in all contingencies, for all entries, racing expenses, and damages;

(c) That the crew are to be considered the servants of the owner;

(d) That the hirer (who must be a member of a recognised yacht club) shall, as representative of the owner, comply with all the rules and regulations of the Y.R.A.

4. *Every Yacht to have a Certificate.*—A valid Y.R.A. certificate shall be held by every yacht starting in a race under Y.R.A. rating, unless the owner or his representative signs and lodges with the sailing committee before the start a statement in the following form, viz.:

Undertaking to produce certificate.

The Yacht competes in the race of the on the condition that a valid certificate is to be produced within a fortnight, and dated not more than one week after the race, that she is not to be altered between the race and the date of certificate, and that she competes in the race on the rating of that certificate.

Signed _____

Date _____

5. *Time Allowance.* — In all races under Y.R.A. rating, the time to be allowed on arrival for differences in rating shall be according to the annexed scales, in proportion to the length of the course as notified on the programme or instructions.

6. *Entries.* — Entries shall be made with the secretary of the club in the following form at least forty-eight hours previous to noon of the day appointed for starting each race. In case of a Sunday intervening, twenty-four hours shall be added. Entries may be made by telegram, and it shall be deemed sufficient that the same shall have been dispatched before noon of the day on which the entries close, subject to the provision as to Sundays, but such entries by telegram must be confirmed in the proper form in course of post:

Form of entry to be signed by the owner, or his representative—

Please enter the yacht , owner , for the race at , on the . Her distinguishing flag is ; her rig is and her Y.R.A. rating* is . And I agree to be bound by the Racing Rules of the Y.R.A.

Signed this day of

* The rating may be omitted for races not under Y.R.A. rating.

In case the rating has from any reason been incorrectly stated in the form of entry; if the fact is notified to the sailing committee in writing before the entries close, the sailing committee shall regard only the yacht's correct rating at the time of starting; but otherwise the yacht cannot sail at a lower rating than that entered.

7.—*Refusal of Entry.* — A sailing committee may, if they consider it expedient, refuse any entry.

8. *Owner to Enter One Yacht Only.*—An owner may not enter more than one yacht in a race, nor the same yacht for two or more races advertised to be sailed on the same day and under the same club.

9. *Postponement of Races.* — The sailing committee shall have power to postpone any race should unfavourable weather render such a course desirable. Letter N of the commercial code hoisted over the flag denoting the race shall be the signal that a race has been postponed.

No new entry shall be received under any circumstances whatever for a postponed race.

10. *Sailing Over.*—A yacht duly entered for a race shall be entitled to sail over the course (subject, however, to Rule 9), for not less than half the value of the first prize.

11. *Re-sailed Races.*—A yacht which did not start or which has, in the opinion of the sailing committee, committed a breach of the rules in the original race, shall not be allowed to compete in a re-sailed race.

12. *Shortening Course.*—The sailing committee may shorten the course during a race, and the flag denoting the race, hoisted under the white peter, or in case of fog or darkness two guns fired, shall be the signal that the

Yacht Racing Association—continued.

race is to finish with the round about to be completed, or at such mark as the sailing committee may appoint, and the time allowance shall be reduced in proportion.

13. *Removal of Flag Vessel or Mark.*— Should any flag vessel or other mark be removed from its proper position, either by accident or design, the race shall be re-sailed, or not, at the discretion of the sailing committee.

14. *Declaration of Observance of Rules.* —The sailing committee shall award the prizes, subject to these rules, but before they do so, the owner, or his representative, shall sign a declaration that the yacht has strictly conformed to all the sailing regulations, as follows :—

Form of Declaration.

"I,   a member of the   Yacht Club, do hereby declare that I was on board and in charge of the yacht   while sailing in the race this day, and that all rules and regulations were obeyed during that race."

(Signed) _____

Date _____

15. *If a Yacht be Disqualified.*—If any yacht be disqualified, the next in order shall be awarded the prize.

PART II.—SAILING.

16. *Distinguishing Flag.* — Every yacht must carry, at her main topmast head, a rectangular distinguishing flag of a suitable size, which must not be hauled down unless she gives up the race. If the topmast be lowered on deck or carried away, the flag must be rehoisted in a conspicuous place as soon as possible.

17. *Fittings and Ballast.* — All yachts exceeding 36ft. rating must be fitted below deck with the ordinary fittings of a yacht, including the following :—

In Yachts not exceeding 42ft. Rating—

Two complete transverse bulkheads of wood, of average thickness at least ¾in., the spaces between to be fitted to form a forecastle and also one or more cabins.

The cabin or cabins shall contain not less than two sofas upholstered, and two sideboards or sideboard lockers and a table.

Water tanks of not less than 15 gallons' capacity.

In Yachts exceeding 42ft., and not exceeding 52ft. Rating—

Three complete transverse bulkheads of wood of average thickness, at least ½in., the spaces between to be fitted to form a forecastle and also one or more cabins.

The cabin or cabins shall contain not less than two sofas upholstered, or two standing cabin bunks fitted complete, two sideboards or sideboard lockers, one swing table, one fixed lavatory.

Water-tanks of not less than 20 gallons' capacity.

One fixed under-water w.c. fitted complete with all pipes and connections.

In Yachts exceeding 52ft. and not exceeding 65ft. Rating—

Four bulkheads as described above, the spaces between to be fitted to form a forecastle, saloon, and one or more other cabins.

The saloon to contain not less than two sofas upholstered, one swing table, two sideboards or sideboard lockers.

The cabins to contain not less than three standing cabin bunks fixed complete and two fixed lavatories.

Water-tanks of not less than 40 gallons' capacity.

Two w.c.'s as described above.

In Yachts exceeding 65ft. Rating—

Four bulkheads as described above, the spaces between as described for 65ft. rating.

Saloon and cabins as described for 65ft. rating, but cabins to contain not less than four standing cabin bunks.

Water-tanks of not less than 60 gallons' capacity.

Two w.c.'s as described above.

All yachts exceeding 42ft. rating shall have a fixed companion or ladder, and the forecastle furniture shall comprise cots or hammocks equal to the number of crew, and the usual lockers, seats, cooking apparatus, &c.

The following shall apply to all yachts starting in a race :—

During a race the platforms shall be kept down and bulkheads standing, and all the other fittings above specified retained on board except cots, cushions, and bedding ; no water may be started from or taken into the tanks ; no more than the usual anchors and chains may be carried ; no bags of shot may be on board ; all ballast must be properly stowed under the platforms or in lockers ; and no ballast or other dead weights may be used as shifting ballast or for altering the trim of a yacht.

No ballast shall be shipped, unshipped, or shifted after 9 p.m. of the day previous to that on which the race is sailed.

18. *Boats and Lifebuoys.*—Every yacht exceeding a rating of 50ft., and under a rating of 80ft., shall carry a boat on deck not less than ten feet in length and four feet three inches beam, and every yacht rating at 80ft. and over, one of not less than twelve feet in length, and four feet three inches beam, ready for immediate use, with oars lashed therein.

Every yacht shall carry at least one lifebuoy on deck ready for use.

19. *Lights.*—All yachts sailing in a race at night shall observe the Board of Trade rules as to the carrying of lights.

20. *Cruising Trim.* — When yachts are ordered to sail in cruising trim, the following

rules are to be strictly observed throughout the race :—

1. No doors, tables, cabin skylights, or other cabin or deck fittings (davits excepted) shall be removed from their places before or during the race.
2. No sails or other gear shall be put into the main cabin in yachts exceeding a rating of 73ft.
3. Anchors and chains suitable to the size of the yacht shall be carried, and yachts over 42ft. shall carry one at least on deck, with chain rove and shackled on ready for use.
4. Every yacht exceeding a rating of 50ft., and under a rating of 80ft., shall carry a boat on deck not less than ten feet in length and four feet three inches beam ; a yacht rated at 80ft. and over, her usual cutter and dinghy.
5. No extra paid hands, except a pilot, beyond the regular crew of the yacht, shall be allowed.

21. *Manual Power only to be Used.*—There shall be no restrictions as to sails, or the manner of setting and working them ; but manual power only may be used for hoisting and working them, or for working a centre-board or plate.

22. *Member on Board.*—Every yacht sailing in a race shall have on board a member of a recognised yacht club, to be in charge of the yacht as owner or owner's representative.

23. *Owner Steering.*—An owner shall not steer any other yacht than his own in a race wherein his own yacht competes.

24. *Crew and Friends in Yachts of 42ft. and under.*—In yachts of 42ft. rating and under, the total number of persons on board during a race under Y.R.A. rating shall not exceed the number set forth in the following table :—

	Persons.
Not exceeding 18ft. rating	2
Exceeding 18ft. and not exceeding 24ft. rating...	3
Exceeding 24ft. and not exceeding 30ft. rating...	5
Exceeding 30ft. and not exceeding 36ft. rating...	7
Exceeding 36ft. and not exceeding 42ft. rating...	9

Should an owner of a yacht elect to have such yacht measured for rating length with a smaller number of persons on board than set forth in the foregoing table, such number shall be stated on the certificate of rating, and shall not be exceeded in any race sailed under that certificate.

25. *Crew and Friends in Yachts above 42ft.*—In yachts above 42ft. rating there shall be no limit as to the number of paid hands, and no restrictions as to the number of friends or their working.

26. *Instructions for the Race.*—Every yacht entered for a race shall, at the time of entry, or as soon after as possible, be supplied with written or printed instructions as to the course to be sailed, marks, &c. Nothing shall be considered as a mark in the course unless specially named as such in these instructions.

Each yacht shall be given a number with the sailing instructions for purposes of recall, as specified in the succeeding rule.

27. *The Start.*—Fifteen minutes before the time of starting one of the following flags of the Commercial Code shall be hoisted as a preparatory flag for the yachts of each successive race to approach the starting line, viz :—

B of Commercial Code for the Yachts of the	1st Race.	
C	2nd	,,
D	3rd	,,
F	4th	,,

and so on.

Five minutes before the start the preparatory flag shall be lowered, a blue peter hoisted, and a gun fired ; after which, the yachts in the race shall be amenable to the rules. At the expiration of five minutes *exactly* the blue peter shall be hauled down and a second gun fired as a signal to start. Should the guns miss fire, the blue peter shall be the signal.

If any yacht, or any part of her hull, spars, or other equipment be on or across the starting line when the signal to start is made, her recall number shall be displayed as soon as possible, and a suitable sound signal also given to call the attention of the competitors to the fact that a recall number is being displayed. The yacht recalled must return and recross the line to the satisfaction of the committee, and the number must be kept displayed until she has done so ; and a yacht so returning, or one working into position from the wrong side of the line after the signal to start has been made, must keep clear of all competing yachts.

The numbers should be in white on a black ground, and the figures not less than 2ft. 6in. in height.

28. *Yachts Meeting.*—When two yachts are approaching one another, so as to involve risk of collision, one of them shall keep out of the way of the other as follows, viz :—

A yacht which is running free shall keep out of the way of a yacht which is close-hauled.

A yacht which is close-hauled on the port tack shall keep out of the way of a yacht which is close-hauled on the starboard tack.

When both are running free with the wind on different sides, the yacht which has the wind on the port side shall keep out of the way of the other.

When both are running free with the wind on the same side, the yacht which is to windward shall keep out of the way of the yacht which is to leeward.

A yacht which has the wind aft shall keep out of the way of the other yacht.

29. *Overtaking, Luffing, and Bearing Away.*—A yacht overtaking any other shall

keep out of the way of the overtaken yacht; and a yacht may luff as she pleases to prevent another yacht passing to windward, but must never bear away out of her course to hinder the other passing to leeward—the lee side to be considered that on which the leading yacht of the two carries her main boom. The overtaking vessel, if to leeward, must not luff until she has drawn clear ahead of the yacht she has overtaken.

30. *Rounding Marks.*—When rounding any buoy or vessel used to mark out the course, if two yachts are not clear of each other at the time the leading yacht is close to, and actually rounding the mark, the outside yacht must give the other room to pass clear of it whether it be the lee or weather yacht which is in danger of fouling the mark. No yacht shall be considered clear of another yacht unless so much ahead as to give a free choice to the other on which side she will pass. An overtaking yacht shall not, however, be justified in attempting to establish an overlap, and thus force a passage between the leading yacht and the mark after the latter yacht has altered her helm for the purpose of rounding.

31. *Obstructions to Sea Room.* — When passing a pier, shoal, rock, vessel, or other obstruction to sea room, should yachts not be clear of each other, the outside yacht or yachts must give room to the yacht in danger of fouling such obstruction, whether she be the weather or the leeward yacht; provided always that an overlap has been established before an obstruction is actually reached.

32. *Close-hauled Approaching a Shore.*—If two yachts are standing towards a shore or shoal, or towards any buoy, boat, or vessel, and the yacht to leeward is likely to run aground, or foul of such buoy, boat, or vessel (a mark vessel excepted), and is not able to tack without coming into collision with the yacht to windward, the latter shall at once tack on being hailed to do so by the owner of the leeward yacht, or the person acting as the owner's representative, who shall be bound to see that the leeward yacht tacks at the same time.

33. *Fouling or Improperly Rounding Marks.* —A yacht must go fairly round the course, rounding the series of marks as specified in the instructions; and, in order to round each mark, the yacht's track from the preceding to the following mark must enclose it on the required side. A yacht which, in rounding a mark, fouls it, or causes the mark vessel to shift her position to avoid a foul, shall be disqualified, unless on her protest it is established that she was wrongfully compelled to do so by another yacht, in which case such other yacht shall be disqualified. The yacht which fouled the mark must immediately either abandon the race or hoist a protest flag.

34. *Fouling Competing Yachts.* — If a yacht, in consequence of her neglect of any

of these rules, shall foul another yacht, or compel other yachts to foul, she shall be disqualified, and shall pay all damages as provided by Rule 41.

35. *Running Ashore.* — A yacht running on shore, or foul of a buoy, vessel, or other obstruction, may use her own anchors, boats, warps, &c., to get off, but may not receive any assistance except from the crew of the vessel fouled. Any anchor, boat, or warp used must be taken on board again before she continues the race.

36. *Anchoring During a Race.*—A yacht may anchor during a race, but must weigh her anchor again, and not slip. No yacht shall during a race make fast to any buoy, stage, pier, or other object, or send an anchor out in a boat, except for the purpose of Rule 35.

37. *Means of Propulsion.* — No towing, sweeping, poling, pushing, or any mode of propulsion except sails, shall be allowed, except for the purpose set forth in Rule 35.

38. *Sounding.*—No other means of sounding than the lead and line shall be allowed.

39. *Man Overboard.*—In case of a man falling overboard from any yacht, all other yachts in a position to do so shall use their utmost endeavours to render assistance; and if it should appear that any yacht so assisting was thereby prevented from winning a prize, the committee shall have power to order the race to be resailed between any yacht or yachts so prevented and the actual winners. A yacht shall be disqualified from winning a prize in a race or a resailed race if, when in a position to render assistance, she shall have neglected to do so.

40. *Finishing a Race.*—A yacht shall be timed for completing a race as soon as any part of the hull or spars be on or across the finishing line, but continues amenable to the rules so long as any part of the hull or spars remains on the line.

PART III.—PROTESTS, &c.

41. *Penalties for Infringing Rules.*—Any yacht disobeying or infringing any of these rules, which shall apply to all yachts whether sailing in the same or different races, shall be disqualified from receiving any prize she would otherwise have won, and her owner shall be liable for all damages arising therefrom, not exceeding in amount and subject to the same limitations as provided by the Merchant Shipping Act of 1894. A breach of these rules shall be considered "improper navigation" within the meaning and for the purposes of that Act.

42. *Protests.*—A protest on the score of a breach of the rules occurring during a race must be signified by showing a flag conspicuously in the main rigging of the protesting yacht on first passing the sailing committee.

All protests must be made in writing, and signed by the owner or his representative, and lodged with the sailing committee with such fee, if any, as may have been prescribed, within two hours of the arrival of the protesting yacht, unless such arrival shall be after nine o'clock p.m. and before eight o'clock a.m. of the following day, in which case the time shall be extended to noon on that day.

A protest made in writing shall not be withdrawn.

43. *Sailing Committee's Decision.*—Before deciding a protest a sailing committee shall give notice to the party protested against, and shall hear such evidence and make such other inquiries as they may consider necessary.

44. *Appeals to Council.*—A protest which has been decided by a sailing committee shall be referred to the council of the Y.R.A.

(a) If the sailing committee, at their own instance, should think proper to so refer it.

(b) If either of the parties interested make application for such reference, on a question of interpretation of these rules, within one week of the sailing committee's decision.

In the latter case (b) such reference must be accompanied by a deposit of 5l. in the case of yachts exceeding 36ft. rating, and of 3l. for yachts not exceeding 36ft. rating, payable by the party appealing, to be forfeited to the funds of the Yacht Racing Association in the event of the appeal not being sustained.

45. *Particulars to be Furnished by Sailing Committee.*—The reference to the council must be accompanied by the following particulars, as far as the same are applicable :—

1. A copy of the protest and all other written statements that may have been put in by the parties.

2. A plan showing—
   (a) The course ;
   (b) The direction and force of the wind ;
   (c) The set of the tide ;
   (d) The positions and tracks of the competing yachts involved in the protest.

3. A copy of the advertised conditions of the race and the sailing instructions furnished to the yachts.

4. The observations of the sailing committee thereon, with their decision.

46. *Expenses of Re-measurement incurred by Protest.*—In the event of a protest involving the re-measurement of a yacht the fees and expenses of such re-measurement shall be paid by the unsuccessful party to the protest.

47. *Persons interested not to take part in Decisions.*—No member of the sailing committee or council shall take part in the discussion or decision upon any disputed question in which he is an interested party.

48. *Disqualification without Protest.*—Should it come to the knowledge of a sailing committee, or should they have reasonable grounds for supposing, that a competitor in a race has in any way infringed these rules they shall act on their own initiative, as if a protest had been made.

49. *Penalties for Flagrant Breach of Rules.*—Should a flagrant breach or infringement of any of these rules be proved against the owner of a yacht, or against the owner's representative, or amateur helmsman, such owner, his representative, or amateur helmsman may be disqualified by the council, for any time the council may think fit, from steering or sailing in charge of a yacht in any race held under the rules of the Yacht Racing Association ; and should a flagrant breach of these rules be proved against any sailing master, he may be disqualified by the council, for such time as the council may think fit, from steering or acting as sailing master of a yacht in any race held under the rules of the Yacht Racing Association.

PART IV.—MEASUREMENT.

50. *Introductory.*—The measurements of hull and spars shall be taken by the Official Measurer of the Y.R.A. in accordance with the following rules. The sail area may be computed from measurements supplied by the sailmaker, checked by the aforesaid spar measurements, but if sailmaker's measurements cannot be obtained, or in case of dispute, the sail area shall be ascertained by the Official Measurer in the manner hereinafter directed.

51. *Rating Rule.*—The Y.R.A. rating shall be ascertained by the following formula :—

$$\frac{L + B + 0.75\,G + 0.5\,\sqrt{SA}}{2} = \text{Rating.}$$

Where L = Length in feet,
B = Beam in feet,
G = Girth in feet, and
SA = Sail area in square feet,

measured as hereinafter specified. In the rating, figures in the second place of decimals below 0·05 shall be disregarded, and those of 0·05 and upwards shall count as 0·1.

In the rating measurements and calculations, figures beyond the second place of decimals shall be disregarded.

Example of working :

L.W.L. = 45·6ft.   Beam = 13·0.
Girth = 23·4.   Sail area = 2600.

Three-quarter the girth is 17·55, as follows :

$$\begin{array}{r} 23·4 \\ 0·75 \\ \hline 1170 \\ 1638 \\ \hline 17·55 \end{array}$$

The square root of the sail area is 51 ($\sqrt{2600} = 51$). Half 51 is 25·5. Then the sum will be :

$$\begin{array}{r} 45·60 \\ 18·00 \\ 17·55 \\ 25·50 \\ \hline 2)101·65 \\ \hline 50·87 = \text{linear rating.} \end{array}$$

This will be about the linear rating of one of the present 20-raters.

U U

Yacht Racing Association—continued.

The classes under the new rule are as follows :

Old Class Rating.	New Class Rating.	Old Class Rating.	New Class Rating.
0·5	18ft.	10	42ft.
1·0	24ft.	20	52ft.
2·5	30ft.	40	65ft.
5·0	36ft.		

A new time scale was adopted (*see* page 629), but the allowances remain the

may be in the profile of stem, stern-post, or ridge of counter, within six inches of the water level.

53. *Beam.*—The beam shall be taken from outside to outside of the planking, at the broadest place, including wales, doubling planks and mouldings of any kind.

54. *Girth.*—The girth shall be measured along the actual outline of the vertical cross section from L.W.L. to L.W.L. under the keel, at a station 0·6 of the distance between the outer edges of the length marks from the fore-end (*see* Figs. 1 to 4). To this must be

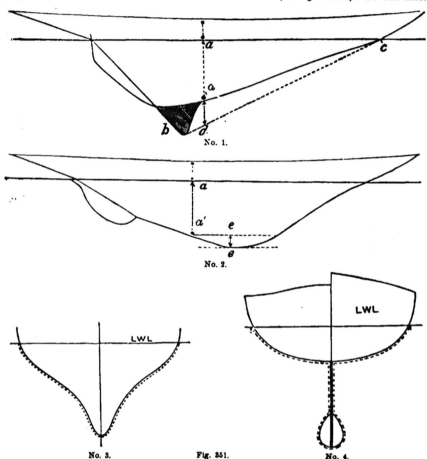

No. 1.

No. 2.

No. 3.　　　　**Fig. 351.**　　　　No. 4.

same in ratings from 80 downwards, though they are largely increased above.

52. *Length.*—The length shall be the fore and aft distance between the outer edges of the official length marks (*see* Rule 56). To this must be added the fore and aft distance of any projection beyond the plumb of these marks, of any part of the hull below them; also the fore and aft distances, beyond the actual water-line endings, to the fair lines, bridging any notches or hollows that there

added twice the excess of draught at any point forward of that station, over the draught at that station (*see* e e, Fig 2). For the purposes of these measurements any hollow in the fore and aft under-water profile must be treated as if filled up straight (as, *e.g.*, by the line c d in Fig. 1).

55. *Centre-Boards.*—Movable keels of any kind are to be treated as fixed keels and measured in the position which will give the maximum measurement.

56. *Owners to Mark Length and Girth.*—Owners must affix the official length marks at the bow and stern, on both sides of the yacht, in such manner as the council may direct, so that when lying in smooth water in her usual racing trim, with crew on board, at or about the mid overall length, she shall not be immersed beyond the plumb of the outer edges of the marks. Owners must affix the official girth marks on both sides as follows, viz: One under the rail or covering board, one not less than 2 inches or more than 6 inches above the water-line, and another on the side of the keel; these three marks to be in the same transverse plane, which must be perpendicular to the water-line, and at the distance 0·6 from the fore edges of the bow marks (*see* Figs. 1 and 2).

The distances between the water-line and the middle marks are to be measured on both sides when the yacht is lying in smooth water, trimmed as above specified, and deducted from the girth as obtained from mark to mark.

57. *Sail Area—Measurement of Sails.*—The secretary shall supply sailmakers, upon request, with diagrams in accordance with the subjoined sketch, and the measurements shall be taken as follows:

MAINSAIL.

A.—Measured from the top of the boom (under the pin for outhaul shackle on traveller, or clew slide, when hauled chock out) to the gaff under the pin of the sheave of the topsail sheet, provided the peak cringle of the mainsail does not extend beyond the pin; in the case of the yacht having no topsail, or of the peak cringle extending beyond the pin of the topsail sheet sheave, then the measurement to be taken to the peak lacing hole.

B.—Perpendicular to A, measured to underside of gaff close in to the mast.

C.—Measured from top of boom over the pin of the sheave or outhaul or end of clew slide to underside of gaff close in to the mast.

D.—Perpendicular to C, measured in to the mast, in a line with the top of the boom, or to tack cringle of mainsail, if below top of boom.

YARD TOPSAIL.

E.—Measured from upper side of gaff close in to the mast to pin of sheave for topsail sheet, or to lacing hole in jackyard.

F.—Perpendicular to E, measured to lacing hole in yard.

G.—From lacing hole to lacing hole in yard.

H.—Perpendicular to G, measured to pin of sheave for topsail sheet in gaff; or to lacing hole in jackyard.

JIB HEADER.

K.—Measured from top of gaff close in to mast to pin of halyard-sheave in topmast.

L.—Perpendicular to K, measured to pin of topsail sheet sheave in gaff; or to lacing hole in jackyard.

LUGSAIL.

To be measured as mainsail except as follows:

A.—Upper end measured to peak lacing hole in yard.

B and C.—Forward end measured to lower lacing hole in yard.

D.—Lower end measured to tack cringle of mainsail, if below top of boom, or forward of mast.

HEAD SAILS.

I.—The perpendicular I to be measured from the deck at the foreside of the mast to where the line of the luff of the foremost head sail or of the spinnaker halyard, as the case may be, when extended, cuts such perpendicular. In the case of a schooner the perpendicular I shall be measured upon the foremast unless she has a main spinnaker the height of which exceeds the perpendicular upon the foremast, in which case the excess shall be added to the perpendicular I.

J.—The base J to be measured from the foreside of the mast to where the line of the luff of the foremost head sail when extended cuts the bowsprit, other spar hull, &c., as the case may be. In all cases if the distance from the centre fore and aft line of the mast to the outer end of the spinnaker boom exceeds the distance from the foreside of the mast to the bowsprit end (where cut by the line of the luff of the foremost head sail), the excess shall be added to the base of the fore triangle. In the case of a schooner, the base J shall be measured from the foremast, but if the main or longest spinnaker boom exceeds the before-mentioned distance, the excess shall be added to the base J.

In the case of a yacht having no head sail, but carrying a spinnaker, the area for head sail shall be computed from the length of spinnaker boom, and the height from deck to where the line of the halyard of the spinnaker when extended cuts the mast.

A spinnaker may have a head-stick or board not longer than one-twentieth the length of the spinnaker boom, but not a foot yard, or more than one sheet, or any other contrivance for extending the sail to other than a triangular shape.

In the case of a yacht carrying a square sail, or square topsail, or raffee (together or separately) the actual area of the same shall be computed; and if such area exceed the area of the fore triangle, the excess shall be used in the total area for determining the rating.

FORESAIL OF SCHOONERS.

To be measured as mainsail, except that the lower end of A is to be taken at foreside

Yacht Racing Association—continued.

of mainmast, in a line with main boom goose-neck.

58. *Directions for Measuring Sails.*—The measurer shall himself take measurements I and J for fore triangle, G and E for yard topsail, and the length of spinnaker boom. If the other measurements are supplied by the sailmaker, the measurer shall check them himself by measuring the following:—

Boom : From lower end of A to lower end of D.

Gaff, or lug yard : From upper end of A to forward end of B.

Jackyard topsail : Sheet to outer lacing hole.

In cases where it is necessary for the official measurer to measure the sails, he shall do so in the following manner:—Take the

59. *Calculation of Sail Areas.*

MAINSAIL.

Multiply A by B and C by D, and add the two products together and divide by 2.

YARD TOPSAIL.

Multiply E by F and G by H, and add the two products together and divide by 2.

JIB HEADER.

Multiply K by L and divide the product by 2.

HEAD SAILS.

Multiply I by J and divide by 2.

LUG SAILS AND HEAD SAILS.

No deduction is to be made from head sail area on the score of any portion of the lug sail area ahead of the mast.

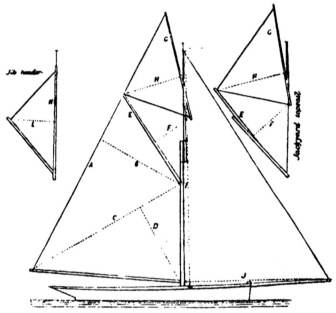

FIG. 352.

length of boom from mast to pin of sheave for outhaul, and length of gaff from mast to pin of topsail sheet sheave or lacing hole, as the case may require; then hoist the sail with the tack fast and set the peak and luff up taut, and let go the topping lifts so that the weight of the boom comes on the leach of the sail. With a line and tape, measure the leach and luff and the diagonal C. For the head sail measure the height I, and the distance J, as provided for in the section dealing with head sail. For topsail the sail should be hoisted and marked in a line with the gaff; then lowered and the other dimensions taken. From the measurements so taken a sail plan should be made and the other above-specified measurements obtained therefrom.

SAILS BOUNDED BY CURVED EDGES.

Any increase in the area of sails due to curved edges, extended by battens or otherwise beyond the line between the points for measurement, shall be computed as follows : Multiply the base E by two-thirds of the perpendicular P. *See* Fig. 353.

60. *Certificate of Rating.*—As soon as a yacht has been measured, the Official Measurer shall forward the measurements, with the sailmaker's diagram, to the secretary of the Yacht Racing Association, who shall thereupon issue a certificate of rating, which shall be in force from the date of the completion of the measurement. If from any peculiarity in the build of the yacht, or other

cause, the measurer shall be of opinion that the rule will not rate the yacht fairly, or that in any respect she does not comply with the requirements of these rules, he shall report the circumstances to the council, who, after due inquiry, shall award such certificate of rating as they may consider equitable, and the measurement shall be deemed incomplete until this has been done.

61. *Errors in Certificate.* — Should the certificate under which a yacht has sailed in any race or races be proved to have been incorrect for any reason, the Council may, after inquiry, correct such certificate as they may deem proper, and may revise the claim of the yacht to the prizes which she may have been awarded in such race or races.

62. *Certificate not to be granted to Yachts under 15cwt. in weight.* — No certificate of

(c) If any alteration is made so as to increase the beam or girth, or the length of any spar or spars, or the sail area, as respectively measured for rating.
(d) If any length or girth mark is moved from its position.
(e) If the weight is reduced to less than 15cwt., without crew.
(f) At the expiration of two years from the date of the latest certificate for which all the measurements were taken.

In such case the owner or his representative shall forthwith notify in writing the invalidity of the certificate to the secretary of the Y.R.A. A fresh certificate will after-

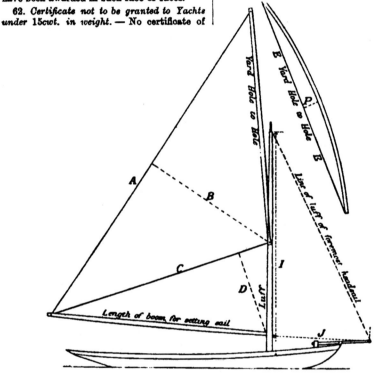

Fig. 353.

rating shall be granted to any yacht weighing less than 15cwt. in racing trim without crew.

63. *Obligations of Owner respecting Certificate.*—The certificate of rating shall cease to be valid under any of the following contingencies :—

(a) If any dimension measured for rating is found to exceed the measurement stated on the certificate.
(b) If one or both of the length marks fall within the length immersed when the yacht is lying in smooth water in measurement trim.

wards be issued, to date from the completion of such re-measurement as may be requisite.

It is especially incumbent on the owner, or his representative, to ascertain from time to time, by inspection of the length marks, whether the immersion of the yacht has from any cause whatever become such as to render the certificate invalid.

64. *Penalty for Infringement of Provisions relating to Certificate.*—If an infringement of any of the foregoing provisions in respect of the validity of the certificate of a yacht, should in the opinion of the council be proved against any yacht, such yacht shall be liable

Yacht Racing Association—continued.

to be disqualified by the council from starting in any race sailed under Y.R.A. Rules for the remainder of the current year, or such period as the council may direct, reckoning from the date at which her certificate is proved to have become invalid.

65. *Inspection to be Permitted by Owner.*—Every owner sailing under Y.R.A. Rules shall permit all reasonable inspection by or on behalf of the council, and shall afford all reasonable facility to carry out such inspection in regard to measurements, marks, and such other matters as fall within the scope of an official measurer's duty.

66. *Fees for Measurement.*—The owner of a yacht shall pay all fees and expenses for measuring such yacht to the measurer previous to the yacht being measured. A yacht shall not be measured until all arrears of subscriptions and fees, due from the owner to the Yacht Racing Association, have been paid.

67. *Re-measurement by order of Council.*—Where a re-measurement is made by the authority of the council, the expenses and fees of such re-measurement shall be paid by the Y.R.A. if the certificate is upheld.

68. *Publication of Certificates.* — The principal particulars of measurements, with the dates of the certificates, shall be periodically published.

69. *Partial Measurement.*—For the information of handicappers, or for other purposes, an owner, on payment of the specified fees, may have his yacht measured for length and sail area only, and receive a certified statement of such measurements from the secretary of the Y.R.A.

APPENDIX.

The Yacht Racing Association further recommend for the consideration of sailing committees :—

1. *Mixed Rig Races.* — That yachts of different rigs should, whenever practicable, be kept separate.

Allowance to Schooners and Yawls. — The rating of schooners and yawls to be reckoned for time allowance as follows, viz., schooners at 0·85, and yawls at 0·92 of their actual rating; provided that in case of a yawl, her mainsail does not exceed 0·37 of her total sail area, and that her mizen is not less than 0·06 of her total sail area. In the case of a pole-masted yawl, her mainsail shall not exceed 0·46 of her total sail area, and her mizen shall not be less than 0·075 of her total sail area. In schooners the fore-side of the mainmast at the deck shall be not farther forward than the middle of the rating length.

Ketches and Luggers.—Ketches and luggers shall be reckoned for time allowance at 0·85 of their rating : provided that in a ketch the distance between the masts does not

exceed half the rating length of the yacht, and that the smaller sail is carried aft. In the case of a lugger, to be entitled to the rig allowance, the yacht must have two or more masts, and the after, or the middle mast, at the deck must not be forward of the middle of the rating length, and in the case of a two-masted lugger if the area of the after lug be less than half the area of the main lug, she will be rated as a yawl.

Fractions to be used in Reducing the Rating.—In calculating the deduction for difference of rig, the rating by certificate to the exact fraction must be used. The time allowances to be calculated from each yacht's reduced rating; but schooners, ketches, luggers and yawls shall not be allowed to qualify to enter by their reduced rating in a class race.

2. *Time to be calculated on Reduced Rating all through.*—In races for mixed rigs, the time allowances between yachts of the same rig must be calculated on each yacht's reduced rating.

3. *Flying Starts.*—That flying starts should be adopted when practicable, but no time should be allowed for delay in starting.

4. *Moored Starts.*—That if the start is to be made from anchors or moorings, lots shall be drawn for stations, and springs shall be allowed on the same bridle or anchor chain or warp as the bowfasts, but are not to be carried to a buoy, pier, other vessel, or fixed object. If any yacht lets go or parts her bridle before the signal to start, or if she drags any moorings or anchor to which she is made fast for the purpose of starting, she shall be liable to be disqualified, unless such parting or dragging be explained to the satisfaction of the committee, or unless she has returned, after the signal to start, within the line of starting buoys so as not to obtain any advantage by the accident.

In a race starting from moorings, no paid hand may join or leave the yacht after the first gun.

5. That, as weatherliness is a quality which it is especially desirable to test in yacht racing, the courses should wherever possible be so laid out as to include a large proportion of windward work.

6. *No Limit to Race.*—That any limit to the time for concluding a race should be avoided as far as possible.

7. *Classification by Rating.* — That the classification of yachts should, when practicable, be as follows :—

For yachts whose rating, by
    Rule 51, does not exceed ... 18ft.
Above 18ft. and not exceeding 24ft.
  ,,   24ft.   ,,   ,,   30ft.
  ,,   30ft.   ,,   ,,   36ft.
  ,,   36ft.   ,,   ,   42ft.
  ,,   42ft.   ,,   ,   52ft.
  ,,   52ft.   ,,   ,,   65ft.
  ,,   79ft.

8. That whenever practicable a clause should be inserted in the programme pro-

viding that there shall be no time allowance in races for the classes not exceeding 65ft.

9. Yachts which have been raced previously to 1896, and which are over the new classes of linear rating (corresponding with the classes they competed in under the old rating rule) shall be allowed to compete in such new classes by allowing time on the excess rating, providing no alteration has been made in their hulls and no increase made in their load water-line length as defined by the Y.R.A. marks, and no increase made in their sail area since 1895.

10. *Length of Courses should be Exact.*—That as distance is an important element in the calculation of time allowance, the marks and flag boats should be placed so as to mark as accurately as possible the length of the course, for which time is allowed.

11. *Rounding Marks in Heavy Weather.*—That in heavy weather it should be arranged, if practicable, for yachts to stay instead of gybe round marks.

12. *Room at Starting.*—That sailing committees should be particularly careful to provide ample room between the points marking the starting line.

13. *Time to Elapse between Races.*—That when in the opinion of the sailing committee it is not desirable to observe the period of fifteen minutes provided for in Rule 27, the time may be shortened to ten or five minutes as may be desirable, but the time to elapse shall always be distinctly stated on the instructions for the race.

Yacht Register.—A book compiled by the well known committee of Lloyd's Society, at the request of yacht owners. Hitherto difficulty was experienced in arriving at the age and condition of a yacht, but the Register contains all the particulars an intending purchaser need know. Owners will derive benefit from having their yachts surveyed and classed at Lloyd's, and special facilities now exist for making such surveys and assigning characters. The Register contains the following particulars : Names of yachts ; official number, number in the Register ; signal letters ; rig ; sailmaker's name ; registered tonnage, N.M. ; Thames tonnage ; dimensions (length, breadth, and depth) ; repairs to yacht, and date thereof ; nature of repairs ; class ; materials used in her construction ; builder's name ; date of building ; port ; port of survey ; fastenings ; sheathing ; description of engines ; builders of engines, &c. The first part of the Register contains the rules and regulations for building for classification. These rules and regulations relate to wood, iron, and composite yachts ; and tables of scantlings, fastenings, &c., are given for each, together with a table for anchors, chains, &c., for sailing yachts and steam yachts. This part of the book is most valuable, and will be a large help to builders who have little experience of the particular work required in a yacht, and will as well be found of great use to the more experienced builders. A yacht can be built of any material and fastened in almost any way an owner or builder may desire, and still she can be admitted with a grade into the book. Existing yachts can be surveyed, and, if approved, assigned the A 1 class for fourteen years, or any other grade, according to their construction, condition, and age. The Register also contains full information as to the manner of having a survey effected ; list of surveyors and their addresses ; list of owners and their addresses ; list of subscribers and their addresses. The offices are Lloyd's Register of British and Foreign Shipping, White Lion Court, Cornhill, E.C. (See Lloyd's.)

Mr. John Harvey, the Wivenhoe yacht builder, was the originator of the Register, in this way. In November, 1876, he addressed a letter to Mr. Dixon Kemp on yacht construction, in which occurred the following passage :

"Lloyd's Registry of British and foreign built ships bears now, and has enjoyed for many years past, such world-wide reputation for integrity, that one feels as safe in the purchase of a vessel, or in the insurance or underwriting her, according to her standing on the list, as if every timber and fastening were open to inspection. Seeing that the general public are thus guardianed, we ask ourselves the question why any gentleman who is about to purchase or build a yacht should not have similar protection? Some agree that it would be better to build yachts in accordance with the directions given in Lloyd's book ; but there are reasonable objections to this, as an unnecessarily heavy and costly structure would be produced; and thus seeing and admitting that the unsatisfactory system of building yachts under no special survey continues, I submit that the state of things points to the necessity of framing a set of rules to be observed in the building of yachts such as Lloyd's have framed for the construction of merchant vessels."

From the knowledge Mr. Dixon Kemp had of yacht construction, he could not but agree that Mr. Harvey's scheme was an excellent one. He took it up warmly, and was fortunate in obtaining the co-operation of the following well-known yacht owners and yacht builders as a committee :

Marquis of Exeter.	Marquis of Ailsa.
Mr. Frank Willan.	Mr. W. Cuthbert Quilter.
Sir G. C. Lampson, Bart.	Sir Gamble, Bart.
Mr. Clement Millward, Q.C.	Mr. A. D. Macleay.
Capt. J. W. Hughes.	Mr. Benjamin Nicholson
Prince Batthyany.	(*Messrs. Camper and Nicholson*).
Capt. Garrett, R.A	
Col. Angus Hall.	Mr. John Harvey (*John Harvey, Ship and Yacht-building Company*).
Mr. W. Baden-Powell.	
Col. Dugmore.	
Sir Richard Sutton.	Mr. Dixon Kemp.
Sir W. B. Forwood.	Mr. J. A. Welch.

When the scheme was made public, Lloyd's society, divining exactly what was required, came forward and offered to undertake the whole of the work that had been sketched out at the preliminary meetings. This was at

Yacht Register—continued.

once recognised as a great advantage, as Lloyd's society had the machinery ready to hand for making surveys, and it was already foreseen that the proposed new society would experience some difficulty in obtaining and supporting duly qualified surveyors. Lloyd's adopted the scheme in its entirety; formed special rules for the building, equipment, and classing of wood, composite, and iron yachts; issued a special book containing these rules, which book contains a list of yachts and such particulars as it is necessary should be known concerning them.

Yard.—A spar used to extend a sail.

Yard Arm.—The extremities of yards.

Yarn.—A yarn is generally understood to mean one of the parts of a strand of a rope. The strands of old rope are separated and used as stops for temporarily securing sails when rolled up, &c. A narrative, a tale, a long story, or discourse. (*See* "Strands.")

Yaw.—When a vessel's head flies from one direction to another; generally when a vessel does not steer a straight or steady course.

Yawl.—A cutter-rigged vessel with a mizen mast stepped in her counter.

Yellow Flag or *Yellow Jack.*—The quarantine or fever flag.

Yoke.—The lower cap on the masthead. It is cut out of solid wood, and either strengthened by an iron plate over the whole of its top, or an iron band round its entire edge. The cross trees are fitted on the yoke. A yoke is also the crossbar put on the rudder-head of small boats, to which lines, termed yoke lines, are attached for steering.

Z.

Zig-Zag Work.—Working to windward by short boards.

INDEX.

"No outfit for Scotland could possibly be considered complete without one
of Scott Adie's Scotch Capes."—*The World.*

WORKS PUBLISHED BY HORACE COX.

NAVIGATION FOR YACHTSMEN: A Concise Treatise on Navigation
and Nautical Astronomy, Illustrating the most Modern Methods, and Specially Designed for the Use of
Yachtsmen. Compiled by VINCENT JOHN ENGLISH, Retired Lieutenant R.N. Demy 8vo., price
15s. net, with Illustrations and Charts.

DOWN CHANNEL. By R. T. McMULLEN. With Introduction by
Dixon Kemp, A.I.N.A. Revised Edition. Crown 8vo., Illustrated with Maps and Plates, price 7s. 6d.,
by post 7s. 10d.

THE COASTS OF DEVON AND LUNDY ISLAND: Their Towns,
Villages, Scenery, Antiquities, and Legends. By JOHN LLOYD WARDEN PAGE. Post 8vo., cloth,
with Map and Illustrations, price 7s. 6d., by post 7s. 10d. Large paper copies, 250 only, Roxburghe,
12s. 6d., by post, 13s.

PHEASANTS: Their Natural History and Practical Management. By
W. B. TEGETMEIER, F.Z.S. Illustrated by T. W. Wood. Third Edition. Price 7s. 6d., by post 7s. 10d.

MODERN DOGS OF GREAT BRITAIN AND IRELAND. By RAW-
DON B. LEE (Kennel Editor of the *Field* and Author of a Description and Reminiscences of the Collie,
the Fox Terrier, &c.). The work is admirably printed in large type, on good paper, and fully bears out
the eulogiums bestowed upon the earlier editions. This is the Standard Work on Dogs, and contains a
vast amount of information not to be found elsewhere.

> THE SPORTING DIVISION, containing Thirty-three Full-page Illustrations in Collotype, from
> drawings by ARTHUR WARDLE. New and Revised Edition. In Two Volumes. Price 21s. net.
> THE NON-SPORTING DOGS. Price 10s. 6d. net. (A New Edition now Ready.)
> TERRIER DIVISION. Price 10s. 6d. net. New and Enlarged Edition.
> THE FOX TERRIER: Its History and Reminiscences of. Third Edition. Fully Illustrated with
> Portraits and Tailpieces by ARTHUR WARDLE. By RAWDON B. LEE. Price 5s. net, by post 4d. extra.
> THE COLLIE AND SHEEP DOG: History and Reminiscences of. Illustrated with Portraits
> and Tailpieces by ARTHUR WARDLE. Price 3s. 6d. net, by post 4d. extra.

PRACTICAL LETTERS TO YOUNG SEA FISHERS. Important New
Work on Sea Fishing. By JOHN BICKERDYKE. The contents of the book comprise the following
subjects: The Art of Boat Sailing and Choice of Boats—Weather, Tides, Life Saving at Sea—Baits,
and How to Find Them—The Best Methods of Sea Fishing from the Shore, Boats, and Ocean Steamers—
Shrimping and Prawning—Lobster and Crab Catching—The Sportsmen's Sea Fish (Illustrated)—Modern
Improvements in Rods, Reels, Leads, and other Tackle used in Sea Fishing. Demy 8vo., price 7s. 6d.

MAKING A FISHERY. By FREDERIC M. HALFORD. Contents:
Selection. Tenure. Management. Weeds. Poachers. Netting. Wiring. Stocking. The Stew.
Grayling. Distribution. Demy 8vo., bound in cloth, price 7s. 6d., by post 7s. 10d.

HINTS ON THE MANAGEMENT OF HAWKS. Second Edition.
With numerous Additions and Illustrations. To which is added PRACTICAL FALCONRY. Chapters
Historical and Descriptive. By J. E. HARTING. Price 10s. 6d. net, by post, 10s. 10d.

HORSES, ASSES, ZEBRAS, MULES, AND MULE BREEDING. By
W. B. TEGETMEIER, F.Z.S., and C. L. SUTHERLAND. Price 5s. net, by post 5s. 4d.

POULTRY for the TABLE and MARKET *versus* FANCY FOWLS,
with an Exposition on the Fallacies of Poultry Farming. By W. B. TEGETMEIER, F.Z.S. Third
Edition. Demy 8vo., with Illustrations, price 2s. 6d., by post 2s. 9d.

LONDON: "FIELD" OFFICE, WINDSOR HOUSE, BREAM'S BUILDINGS, E.C.

Third Edition. Super-royal 8vo., in One Vol., price £2 2s. net, by post £2 3s.
In Two Vols., £2 7s. 6d. net, by post £2 9s.

YACHT ARCHITECTURE,

By DIXON KEMP,

Associate of the Institution of Naval Architects and Member of the Council.

THIS WORK enters into the whole subject of the laws which govern the resistance of bodies moving in water. It also deals comprehensively with the subject of STEAM PROPULSION as applied to yachts.

An easy SYSTEM for DESIGNING is provided, and every necessary calculation is explained in detail.

The latter part of the work is devoted to YACHT BUILDING, and engravings are given of every detail of construction and fitting, including laying off, taking bevels, &c. A section is also allotted to BOAT BUILDING.

The Plates (exclusively of those devoted to the elucidation of the text, and two hundred and thirty-two woodcuts) exceed seventy, and comprise the LINES of some of the most CELEBRATED YACHTS AFLOAT by the most successful builders and designers, including many of the most successful Yachts of 64ft. linear rating downwards built under the new rating rule

SUMMARY OF CHAPTERS.

CHAP.
I.—Displacement, Buoyancy, and Centre of Buoyancy explained.

II.—Proportions of Yachts and Tonnage Rules; Rules for Freeboard, Depth, &c.

III.—Stability as influenced by the Proportions, Form, Weight, and Ballasting of Yachts; their Centres of Gravity and Buoyancy. Profusely Illustrated.

IV.—The Motions of Yachts among Waves as influenced by their Forms and Proportions.

V.—Lateral Resistance, and the adjustment of its centre in relation to the centre of Effort of the Sails. This chapter also deals with Centreboards and their effect.

VI.—Power to carry Sail; the Impulse of the Wind as a Propelling Force; Apportioning Sail for Speed. Speed Formulæ, &c.

VII.—The Action of the Rudder and Steering Efficiency; Proportions of Rudders, &c.

VIII.—Resistance of Vessels moving in Water. The Wave Line Theory; the Stream Line Theory; the Wave Form Theory. Mr Froude's Admiralty Experiments, clearly defining the exact Influence of Form on Speed.
This Chapter will throw much light on what has hitherto been but obscurely understood.

IX.—Resistance Experiments with Models.

X.—Theory and Practice. The forms of many celebrated Yachts analysed.

XI.—Steam Yachting. The Boiler, Engine, Indicator, &c., practically explained at great length.

CHAP.
XII.—Propulsion by Steam. The action of the screw propeller and all the conditions which influence propulsion by steam explained, with numerous practical examples.

XIII.—Rules and Formulæ in use for determining the Displacement, Stability, and other qualities of a yacht fully explained.

XIV.—Working Examples for making all the necessary Calculations concerning a Yacht, every sum being given in detail.

XV.—Yacht Designing: being a complete System for putting into effect the Art of Designing Yachts by Scientific Methods.

XVI.—Laying Off, Making Moulds, Taking Bevels, &c. Taking Off a Yacht's Lines, &c.

XVII.—Yacht Building: Giving detailed examples for constructing yachts, with numerous plates and engravings of the various parts of the vessel, including large coloured lithographs on a half inch scale giving sectional views of a 40-tonner, 64ft. rater, and 52ft. rater.
This Chapter also deals with all the ironwork fittings of a yacht, including that for spars, a table of "sizes" for iron fittings for yachts of different tonnages being provided.

XVIII.—Spars and Blocks. Rules for fixing upon their lengths, girths, &c. Sizes of block, cordage, &c.

XIX.—Ballasting.

APPENDIX.—The Appendix contains a number of Tables useful in making calculations.

OPINIONS OF THE PRESS OF THE THIRD EDITION.

"With the third edition of 'Yacht Architecture,' the series of standard works for which yachtsmen the world over are indebted to Mr Dixon Kemp, may be said to have reached its majority; this book, just issued, marking the twenty-first year since the publication of the introductory volume. The first book, the large quarto, 'Yacht Designing,' came at an important time, when the professional yacht designer was just making a place for himself in England and assuming the work previously delegated to the yacht builder. Mr Kemp's clear and thorough presentation of the principles of designing, illustrated by the designs, then a comparative rarity, of successful yachts, did much to interest and to instruct yachtsmen, and to foster the study of designing both by builders and amateurs. Two years later, in 1878, he launched another book, 'Yacht and Boat Sailing,' an octavo volume of moderate thickness, but treating most comprehensively the subjects of practical seamanship and yacht racing, and describing in detail small craft of all kinds from the the canoe to the 10-tonner. From that date onward the larger size was abandoned, the successive editions of 'Yacht and Boat Sailing' down to the current one (eighth) have been of the same nominal size, though greatly increased in thickness. The care and thoroughness which made the second edition of 'Yacht Architecture' so valuable have left but little room for improvement of designing. . . . Whether dealing with the more abstruse theories of design or the everyday methods of the shipyard and boat shop, Mr Kemp's treatment of the subject is always direct and practical, and the book is quite as well adapted to the amateur and the working builder as to those of greater experience and education."—Forest and Stream, New York, Oct. 2, 1897.

"We had the pleasure of hearing an accomplished minister, Dr Charles Watson, lecturing on 'Invention.' In the course of his remarks we were surprised as well as delighted to hear him saying that in his estimation there was no more wonderful invention than a modern racing cutter. . . . The pith as well as the point of the scholarly divine's words were brought home to us on going over the pages of the new edition of Mr Dixon Kemp's great book on 'Yacht Architecture,' and we should fancy he must be a dull-souled individual indeed who could peruse its clearly written text without agreeing with Dr Watson that a modern racing cutter is a very wonderful thing indeed. When turning over the pregnant pages of this wholly admirable book one is constantly reminded that even into our very pastimes the spirit of science has been infused, and the same is well, for when a thing is to be done it is best that it should be done in the best way. . . . Let us interject here that the best worn copy of one of the books on Naval Architecture by Mr Dixon Kemp we ever saw was in the office of the Messrs Fife at Fairlie. . . . Mr Kemp has always been noted for the lucidity of his literary style, and it is a pleasure to go to this book for instruction, so clearly is it set forth. A draughtsman himself, Mr Kemp knows well the value of pictures as a teaching agent, and he has enriched his text with nearly forty plates, while designs of sailing yachts, steam yachts, and sailing boats number no fewer than seventy-one. The opening chapters of the book deal with the scientific aspect of the subject. . . . Scientific they are undoubtedly, but so clearly and lucidly are they written that one is enticed on, and on, and on as he reads, and it is ten to one if he reads them once he will go back to them again and again."—North British Daily Mail, Aug. 7, 1897.

London: HORACE COX, "Field" Office, Bream's Buildings, London, E.C.

230517LV00004B/2/P